HARRY HOPKINS

HARRY HOPKINS

A Biography by

HENRY H. ADAMS

Foreword by W. Averell Harriman

G. P. Putnam's Sons, New York

SBN: 399-11833-0

Library of Congress Cataloging in Publication Data

Adams, Henry H
Harry Hopkins.

Bibliography
Includes index.
1. Hopkins, Harry Lloyd, 1890-1946. 2. Statesmen—
United States—Biography.
E748.H67A63   1977   973.917′092′4 [B]   76-48985

PRINTED IN THE UNITED STATES OF AMERICA

Acknowledgment and thanks are made by Henry H. Adams and G. P. Putnam's Sons for permission to reprint excerpts from the following books:

Special Envoy to Churchill and Stalin, 1941-1946, by W. Averell Harriman and Elie Abel. Random House, Inc., 1975. Coypright © 1975 by W. Averell Harriman and Elie Abel. Reprinted by permission of Random House, Inc.

The Secret Diary of Harold L. Ickes, by Harold L. Ickes. Vol. I, *The First Thousand Days, 1933-1936,* Simon & Schuster, Inc., 1953. Copyright © 1953 by Simon & Schuster, Inc. Reprinted by permission of Simon & Schuster, Inc. Vol. II, *The Inside Struggle, 1936-1939* and Vol. III, *The Lowering Clouds, 1939-1941,* Simon & Schuster, 1954. Copyright © 1954 by Simon & Schuster, Inc. Reprinted by permission of Simon & Schuster, Inc.

Roosevelt and Hopkins: An Intimate History, Rev. Ed. by Robert E. Sherwood. Harper and Row, Publishers, Inc., 1950. Copyright © 1948 by Robert E. Sherwood. Reprinted by permission of Harper and Row, Publishers, Inc.

To *Catherine*
   Robin
   Sandy
   Jim
   Jo
   Eric
   Diane
   Nancy

Contents

Preface 11

Foreword 15

Prologue 21

Book One FRIEND OF THE POOR,
FRIEND OF THE RICH

1. Go East, Young Man 29
2. Money Flies 49
3. Works Progress Administrator 67
4. WPA—Floods, Drought, and Politics 89
5. The Valley of the Shadow 110
6. White House Janizary 127
7. Secretary of Commerce 148
8. Chicago-Go-Round 171

Book Two LORD ROOT OF THE MATTER

9. The Right-Hand Guest 183
10. Personal Representative 198
11. Lend-Lease 213
12. London, Moscow, and Argentia 230

13. The Last Days of Peace   249
14. The Past Is Prologue   262
15. No Raft at Tilsit   288
16. Conferences, Conferences   305
17. Where Mr. Roosevelt Leaves Off   326
18. From Nadir to Summit Again   352
19. Yalta   370
20. Last Days   384
    Glossary of Abbreviations   407
    Notes   408
    Bibliography   427

Preface

On March 4, 1933, Franklin D. Roosevelt took office as the thirty-second President of the United States. He brought with him a willingness to try any new ideas that might help to bring the nation out of the great depression.

The men he gathered around him, known collectively as the Brain Trust, had many ideas and were responsible for transforming a nation.

But one man, who was not a Brain Truster, had a greater effect on the country than any of them. He was a man of action rather than of ideas, a mixture of cynicism and idealism, of pragmatism and sentiment. His name was Harry Lloyd Hopkins.

From the unlikely background of a social worker, he went on to become one of the two or three most powerful men in the nation, serving first to fight the depression and then to fight the forces of tyranny.

When Hopkins arrived in Washington in May, 1933, he did not know Roosevelt well, but it was not long before they became close friends, as far as it was possible for anyone to be a friend of Roosevelt's. FDR called many people friends, and his relaxed manner of calling everyone from kings to laborers by their first names deceived many people into believing in an intimacy which did not exist. Roosevelt had many companions but his real friends can be counted on one hand. There were two women and three men: Lucy Mercer Rutherford and Marguerite "Missy" LeHand; Louis McHenry Howe, Edwin "Pa" Watson, and Harry Hopkins.

Among these, Roosevelt entrusted responsibility only to Hopkins. And those responsibilities grew with the years as the friendship deepened. As head of the Federal Emergency Relief Administration, of the short-lived

Civil Works Administration, and of the Works Projects Administration, Hopkins commanded the battle to bring immediate relief to the jobless. He was not the only one, for there were Harold L. Ickes, Secretary of the Interior, who ran the Public Works Administration, and Henry A. Wallace, Secretary of Agriculture, who headed the Agricultural Adjustment Administration. But it was Hopkins who ran the largest programs and spent the largest sums of money, first for direct relief through FERA and then for work relief through CWA and WPA.

He became, to Roosevelt's enemies, the symbol of all that was wrong with the New Deal. A free spender, with no sense of fiscal responsibility, a living example of squandermania. His answer was simple: "Hunger is not debatable." Because he rejected politics in relief, politicians denounced him and accused him of doing the things they wanted to do themselves.

But Roosevelt never lost faith in him, grooming him as a possible successor in 1940. His appointment as Secretary of Commerce was a step in that direction. It came to nothing, however, for Hopkins' body denied his will. A series of illnesses and operations seemed to bring his career to a close just at the moment he had hoped to hear himself nominated as the Democratic candidate for President.

The coming of World War II not only brought Roosevelt an unprecedented third term in the White House. It gave Hopkins the opportunity to render his greatest services. As Lend-Lease administrator, he was social worker to the free world. As Roosevelt's personal representative to Churchill and Stalin, he performed missions combining diplomacy and strategy which were too delicate and too important for the State Department and the military authorities. As Roosevelt's Administrative Assistant, he, more than anyone else, kept production running and the war agencies functioning. As Roosevelt's personal friend, he gave the President the loyal companionship he needed, and in the course of all these duties, he became the friend of most of the war leaders from Churchill down. When Roosevelt died, he made it possible for President Truman to make the transition quickly and surely.

In his last service, a trip to Moscow, he probably saved the United Nations, and however short that institution has fallen of the dreams of its founders, it then seemed the last best hope of man.

It seems fair to say that without Hopkins the war would not have been won as soon as it was and that Roosevelt would not have been the President he was.

No book of this sort can possibly be written alone. To those who have helped me, my thanks are due, especially to the staff of the Franklin D. Roosevelt Library in Hyde Park. The archivists know the material of this vast treasure house and cheerfully helped me with many questions and problems.

I am grateful to Robert Hopkins, younger of the surviving sons of Harry Hopkins, for reading and criticizing the manuscript. Also my thanks go to Governor W. Averell Harriman for criticism and corrections as well as for providing his keen insight on matters the records did not always make clear.

Finally I give the real credit to my wife, who has supported the project from the beginning. She has made it possible for me to work and has offered many valuable suggestions. *Forsan et haec olim meminisse juvabit.*

Foreword

If Sir Winston Churchill had been asked which two Americans, other than President Roosevelt, had done the most to defeat Hitler, he would have unhesitatingly replied: "Among the military, General Marshall, and among the civilians, Harry Hopkins." Churchill's relationship with Harry Hopkins started in early January 1941, the year that Britain was standing alone against the full force of the Nazi military might. President Roosevelt sent Hopkins to London to report on the British needs imperative to their survival. Now that the air battle for Britain had been won by a narrow margin, Britain faced the critical sea battle against the German submarine and surface vessels which were taking a devastating toll of ships carrying imports of vital food and industrial materials.

Churchill was somewhat puzzled when he learned that Harry Hopkins was coming over, as he had heard of Hopkins as a social worker involved in Roosevelt's work relief programs. However, Brendan Bracken, long-time intimate friend of Churchill and then in charge of war information, knew of Hopkins' close relations with Roosevelt. Bracken met Hopkins when he landed in England, took him by train to London, and introduced him to Churchill. Churchill immediately invited him for the weekend at Ditchley, an estate owned by Ronald Tree, M.P., which was used instead of Chequers during the full-moon weekends to avoid possible enemy air attack.

After dinner on the first evening at Ditchley, when the ladies had withdrawn, Churchill began talking about his postwar plans and the better life he hoped to bring to the "cottagers." He was startled by Hopkins' vigorous interruption: "I don't give a damn about your cottagers, I came here to see how we can beat that fellow Hitler." After a moment's silence, Churchill jumped up and asked Hopkins to accompany him to the library. Closeted alone together, they talked until four o'clock in the morning, discussing how to wage the war against Hitler's Third Reich. (This account of the evening was given to me by David Margesson, then Secretary of State for War, who was present at the dinner. It varies somewhat from other accounts, but I believe it vividly describes Churchill's attitude toward Hopkins when he arrived.)

That long talk started an intimate relationship which lasted throughout the war. Hopkins believed it essential that Roosevelt and Churchill develop mutual confidence to permit the closest working agreements. In spite of the differences in temperament and outlook of President and Prime Minister, Harry Hopkins catalyzed their relationship and helped achieve this objective of Allied cooperation. These differences often developed into irritations which Hopkins was able to smooth out. With his inimitable humor, Hopkins had an extraordinary faculty of saying blunt things to Churchill without giving offense.

I particularly recall Harry's toast to Churchill at the latter's 69th birthday dinner, attended by Roosevelt and Stalin at Teheran on November 30, 1943. Of the many toasts it was certainly the wittiest. Unfortunately, it was not recorded in full. He undertook the formidable task of questioning Churchill's references to the limitations of the British constitution on his powers as Prime Minister. When Churchill wanted to stall on a decision, Harry contended, he would assert that the constitution required him to consult the war cabinet or even Parliament. Hopkins said that after careful research he had made an important discovery about the British constitution—that it was exactly what the Prime Minister wanted it to be at any given moment. Churchill joined in the laughter.

Hopkins' long intimacy with Roosevelt made it possible for him to be candid on the most sensitive subjects. Roosevelt also had complete confidence that Hopkins was utterly loyal to him and his policies without the slightest consideration of any personal objectives.

When I needed the President's decision on some of my activities, I would first obtain Hopkins' support and then state my case on a single sheet of paper. I knew the President demanded this brevity; and, in fact, I had been with him when he had refused to turn to the second page of memoranda others had submitted. With my brief memorandum, we would both go to the President to get his approval. The President would usually reach for his pen to initial the memorandum, but Hopkins would stop him, saying: "Mr. President, before approving this you should call up Mr. Stimson, Mr. Hull, or perhaps General Marshall." The President would usually resist; but

Hopkins would insist, pointing out that if he did not call the individual in advance there might well be difficulties. The President, grumbling, would then call the individual in question, obtain his agreement, and all was well. The wisdom of this course was impressed on me when I learned that members of the Cabinet could obtain the President's initials on their memoranda but subsequently find that the President had reversed his position after talking to one of his other advisers. The President, quite correctly, always reserved the right to change his mind until a final decision was necessary.

Hopkins came to London again in mid-July 1941, only a few weeks after Hitler's invasion of Russia. The Red Army was in chaotic retreat and most military advisers believed Moscow was doomed. In talks with Churchill, the idea developed that Harry should go to Moscow to size up the situation there and determine whether aid to the Russians would be worthwhile. They telephoned Roosevelt, who immediately approved.

When Harry left London by train for Scotland, the first leg of his long journey, I felt he was embarking on as remote a trip as going to the moon today. He had a twenty-seven-hour flight ahead, from Scotland to Archangel, and then another lengthy flight south to Moscow.

Harry was much impressed with Stalin in their several long talks and became convinced that with Stalin's aggressive leadership the Soviets could hold out against the German advance. Stalin, on his part, gained a great respect for Harry's courage. Hopkins' obvious frailty and ill health, accentuated by his forgetting to bring his medicine, did not interfere with his determination. On the basis of Harry's reports, Roosevelt and Churchill set in motion the aid program that led to vast shipments of war matériel and food for the Red Army and the Russian people.

Two years later at Teheran, Stalin demonstrated unusual respect for Harry, which I never saw him show to anyone else. When Stalin entered a room, he always waited for others to approach him, but in Teheran, when he saw Harry, Stalin walked halfway across the room to greet him.

I had first met Harry Hopkins in May 1933 on the train to Washington. I later encountered him from time to time during the early New Deal days and on Long Island when he stayed with the Herbert Swopes (former editor of the New York *World*). We became good friends, but I didn't become close to him until it was proposed that the President appoint him as Secretary of Commerce. Though many businessmen and newspaper editors were appalled by the prospect, I thought it was a great idea. I was then Chairman of the Business Advisory Council to the Department of Commerce. I knew that Harry was fair-minded and would listen to us. If we sold him on our recommendations, his intimacy with the President would go a long way in gaining Roosevelt's approval. We had had little help from his amiable predecessor, Daniel Roper, who lacked the influence with Roosevelt.

Knowing that Harry would have trouble getting his nomination approved by the Senate Commerce Committee, I talked with each member of the Business Advisory Council and persuaded them to vote for a resolution of the Council supporting Hopkins' appointment. Senator Josiah Bailey, Chairman of the Committee, particularly opposed Hopkins, as they had experienced a personal difference. When I was called to testify and submitted this resolution, I have never been on and off the stand so rapidly. Later, I received several letters of recommendation from other prominent businessmen and brought them privately to Senator Bailey. I asked him whether I should put them in the public record or would he rather keep them himself. Much to my gratification he said he would keep them privately. Hopkins was furious; but I knew the Senator would never keep them secret unless he was prepared to approve the appointment. This, of course, the Committee eventually did.

During this period Hopkins developed political ambitions. He moved his residence to Iowa and there was talk of his running for the Senate. I was sure that his objective was eventually the Presidency, though unhappily, his subsequent illness made this impossible. I considered Harry Hopkins and Bill Douglas the two politically outstanding men of the New Deal. Hopkins might well have become President if his health had permitted, and I fully believe he had all the qualifications for greatness, had he attained that position.

Throughout the war Harry accompanied Roosevelt on all his bilateral meetings with Churchill and his trilateral meetings with Stalin and Churchill. He frequently functioned as Secretary of State at the discussions with British Foreign Secretary Eden and Soviet Foreign Commissar Molotov. After Yalta, Harry's health compelled him to go back to the Mayo Clinic, where he had to stay during the last weeks of President Roosevelt's life.

In early May, 1945, still a weak and saddened man, Harry returned to Washington to a little house which he and his wife, Louise, had rented in Georgetown, at 2924 N Street. On the doctor's orders he spent most of his time in bed.

Chip Bohlen and I were then in San Francisco attending the organizational meeting of the United Nations. Shortly after VE Day, Chip and I returned to Washington on the same plane. We discussed the worsening US/Soviet relations and how things could be improved. Chip came up with the suggestion that Harry might go to Moscow for talks with Stalin. I jumped at the idea. Stalin had great respect for Harry and knew him as

Roosevelt's closest adviser. The only problem was whether Harry was strong enough to stand the journey.

I vividly remember visiting Harry at his Georgetown house. He was in bed and obviously depressed. Much to my relief, when I suggested the possibility of his going to Moscow his spirits rose at the thought. After consulting his doctor, he told me that he would go if President Truman approved.

Harry had not been very intimate with President Truman, and I found that when I proposed the visit Truman resisted it. However, after I had pointed out all the advantages, he agreed. With this news, Harry's energy and enthusiasm seemed to revive.

We arranged to meet in Paris. Harry was accompanied by his wife, to take care of him, and by Chip Bohlen to advise and interpret. I went first to London to talk with Churchill, whom I had not seen since President Roosevelt's death. In Paris, Harry and I had a long talk with General Eisenhower about the problems of Germany and other matters affecting our relations with the Soviet Union. Ike particularly wanted Stalin to appoint promptly his representative on the Allied Control Commission for Germany. We then proceeded to Moscow, arriving on May 25th. Harry and Louise stayed with my daughter, Kathleen, and myself at Spaso House.

During the next two weeks, six long and extraordinarily intimate talks with Stalin took place. Stalin received Harry with great cordiality, and the talks were frank, blunt, and achieved some constructive results. Stalin appointed Marshal Zhukov as General Eisenhower's counterpart. Harry was instrumental in resolving one of the most controversial subjects holding up agreement in San Francisco on the United Nations Charter—it related to voting procedures of the Security Council. Stalin agreed to drop the Soviet demand for a veto on Security Council consideration of disputes brought by a member country.

After endless argument, Stalin also finally agreed to a limited compromise on Poland, providing for the inclusion in the Polish government of several independent Poles, including the Peasant Party leader, Mikolajczyk, who was to be the Deputy Prime Minister. This newly formed Polish Provisional Government of National Unity was then recognized by the British and the United States. This agreement might have worked, had it not been for the communist perfidy in preventing a free election. It was a long chance, and I was never optimistic that it would avoid an eventual communist takeover.

In the aura of goodwill that lasted after Harry departed, I was able to settle with Stalin the final differences between us on the United Nations Charter relating to the right of the assembly to discuss any subject its members wished. Molotov had been insisting that the discussions in the assembly be limited to an agenda agreed upon by the Security Council, in which the Soviets had a veto. On a number of other subjects Harry was able to reassure Stalin that President Truman was continuing the Roosevelt policies.

The final farewell banquet was unique in my experience because for the first time ladies were permitted. Louise Hopkins and my daughter, Kathleen, attended; but Stalin declined to include his daughter, Svetlana, on the excuse that she was occupied with her studies. Stalin was in a most cordial and friendly humor.

Harry left Moscow with a feeling of achievement on this, the last of his government missions. He certainly set the record straight with Stalin and set the stage for the Potsdam Conference, which Stalin agreed should take place in mid-July.

Harry was full of hope when Kathleen and I bade Louise and him good-bye at the airport in Moscow. He moved to New York shortly after his return to undertake his new duties as impartial chairman in the ladies' garment industry and to begin writing his book. He was forced to go to Memorial Hospital in New York after only four months, where he died on January 29, 1946. It was a sad day for me. I had lost one of my closest and most valued friends.

Harry Hopkins was one of the truly great men of my generation.

—W. AVERELL HARRIMAN

Prologue

It was a hot evening in Chicago as a frail, physically ravaged man sat in his hotel room preparing to write a letter to his closest friend. The friend happened to be the President of the United States.

The letter would be a farewell to all that the writer had lived for. Really it would mark the end of their association and intimacy, for a President has no time for those who cannot serve him, and the author of the letter was preparing to leave the government in order to regain his shattered health.

Harry Hopkins had done all he could and it was time to quit. Of all the hundreds who had flocked to Washington in the spring of 1933 to help Franklin Delano Roosevelt bring a New Deal to the American people, he alone had risen to the top. Others had higher titles, but he had the friendship and trust of the President.

He pulled a sheet of paper to him and began to write. When he got back to Washington in a couple of days he would dictate his official letter of resignation. This one, which would be in his own hand, was for Franklin Roosevelt only and would not become part of the public record. The pen moved across the paper.

August 17, 1940

My dear Mr. President:—
     A public letter of resignation is almost a vulgar institution. Why don't you abolish it? At any rate I have told you little that is in my mind and heart as I leave the government's service.

That service had lasted only seven years, but it had brought Hopkins more praise and blame, more affection and hatred, than fall to the lot of most men.

When he had come to Washington in May of 1933, in the depths of the great depression, his job was to spend money, and he had spent more than any man ever had in the history of the world, over nine billion dollars. In charge of various relief agencies, especially the Works Progress Administration, he had seen the men and women who worked for him build schools and airports, create thousands of miles of roads, produce plays, write books, paint murals, fight floods, and teach multitudes of adults to read and write.

He had won the friendship of Franklin Roosevelt, a man who had thousands of acquaintances but only five real friends in his life. He had worked at the President's right hand, and he had played with him and joked with him. They had cruised together, fished together, played poker together, and dreamed of making the United States a better place for its people. Hopkins' mind ran back over these things as he wrote.

> I think of the things that have made my years with you the happiest time of my life. The first exciting days—the exaltation of being part of government—our first formal dinner at the White House when I met [Supreme Court Justice Benjamin] Cardozo and another when [Assistant Attorney General] Bob Jackson tried to sell me some old underwear—and Cocos Island—did you ever see anything so green? Then there were those cigarettes in my pocket—it seems to me in all decency you should forget that one.

Almost from the first, Hopkins had been a member of the "Inner Cabinet," the small number of men around Roosevelt who made the real decisions. These men changed as time went on, but Hopkins remained. He had visited Cocos Island on a cruise with Roosevelt in the fall of 1935. The cigarette story refers to a time Hopkins inadvertently put a package belonging to FDR in his own pocket.

The years as relief administrator had been good and fruitful times. His programs had given men and women jobs and allowed them to recover their pride during the agonizing years of the depression. He knew he was doing a good job, and a necessary job, and he let the criticism of press and conservatives alike roll off him. If any man drew as much criticism as Franklin Roosevelt, Hopkins had that distinction. The kindest remarks made charged him with profligacy with other people's money, paying hard cash to men who spent their time leaning on shovels. Others accused him of using WPA funds to create a political machine for his own ambitions. Some called him an evil influence on Roosevelt, inveigling him to spend and spend and spend.

But the times were not always happy. Besides the suffering in the country, tragedy came to his own life. In October, 1937, Roosevelt attended the funeral of Barbara Hopkins, the mother of Harry's daughter Diana.

> And one day you went to church with me when the going wasn't so good—and life seemed ever so dark.

But there were other things to remember, more cheerful days, fighting days and working days. There was the time that the Supreme Court, the "nine old men," seemed ready to throw out the entire New Deal program and Roosevelt proposed to enlarge it to assure a sympathetic majority.

> Those nine old men—a better fight none of us ever took part in—
>
> And there was always New Years Eve—and the warm glow of Auld Lang Syne—with champagne. That's about the only time we get champagne around your house. Or am I wrong?
>
> I've always been getting on and off trains—and I saw America and learned to know its people. I like them. Whenever I was with you there were the everlasting Secret Service men—they seemed to be always at a dog trot—how many miles do you suppose they have dog trotted beside your car?
>
> You remember the day we got you up a blind road in Nevada and Mc [Marvin McIntyre, Roosevelt's Appointments Secretary] wanted to give up his life if the car rolled over the hill? And people at trains with nice faces that smiled. All of them work hard for a living and are devoted to you.

One time when Roosevelt and Hopkins were inspecting a WPA project in Nevada they took a wrong turn and the car nearly went over the edge of the cliff. McIntyre, who was as cadaverous as Hopkins himself, dashed to hold it back at the peril of being crushed as it teetered on the brink.

There was a lot for Hopkins to think about as his pen moved over the paper. There were people and places and events, and the memory of them shared by friends. However bitter the fighting in Washington, life for the "Inner Circle" went on smoothly in a spirit of comradeship and relaxation.

Once when the two men shared a moment alone, Roosevelt told Hopkins he would back him for President in 1940, but a few months later, those hopes faded when Hopkins underwent an operation for cancer of the stomach. Apparently recovered, he returned to Washington and went back to work. Roosevelt gave a boost to his ambitions to be President by appointing him Secretary of Commerce. The critics howled.

Hopkins hoped to make good as Secretary of Commerce, but he failed. Most of his time in office, he was so sick that he could not function. He could not absorb food, and he nearly starved to death. His doctors gave up on him, and Roosevelt set Navy medical specialists to work to find something to keep him alive. They succeeded, but only just. Hopkins, however, was thinking of other things as he continued his letter. The people he had met seemed important to him. The King and Queen of Great Britain, Marguerite (Missy) LeHand, Roosevelt's personal secretary and confidante, McIntyre, Secretary of the Treasury Henry Morgenthau, Ben Cohen, Rexford Tugwell, Felix Frankfurter, Sam Rosenman—all but Their Majesties luminaries in the White House—along with Eleanor Roosevelt, and her secretary Tommy, more formally Malvina Thompson Scheider, but neither FDR nor Harry Hopkins was much on formality.

He called these people to mind as he wrote:

> And one day two nice people came to visit you—he was a king—and I hope will be for a long time and she was a Scotch girl who got to be a Queen. And after dinner that night you and Missy and I talked it all over till 2 A.M.
>
> Then there were picnics! I suppose the Roosevelts have always had picnics—cold weather and nothing to drink.
>
> I never knew there were so many mayors and governors and congress-men and senators and county auditors and school boards and irrigation districts in the world. I have met them all. One of them had me arrested and you thought it was funny and promised to visit me in jail.

Hopkins must have smiled as he wrote those lines, but it had not seemed funny at the time. In March, 1935, Governor Martin Davey of Ohio, trying to control relief funds for political purposes, had a warrant issued for Hopkins' arrest, charging him with libel in writing an official letter. The President never got over joking about it. The real joke was that FDR had helped in writing the letter.

Then Hopkins thought about the times in the White House itself. He had been living there for four months as the President's guest. On May 10, 1940, Hopkins, feeling miserable, came to dinner. Roosevelt suggested he spend the night, and Hopkins agreed, and, like the man in the play, just stayed on. In the crisis of the collapse of France and of America's feverish rush to rearm, he made a few phone calls for the President, and then more and more. He began to speak with the voice of the President, and he got things done.

In his mind, the most important thing for America at that moment was the reelection of Franklin Roosevelt for a third term. On his own say-so, he went to Chicago to see to it that Roosevelt was renominated at the Democratic National Convention. This was his way. He knew what the Boss wanted and set about achieving it without bothering him with details.

That job successfully done, he returned to Washington and tried another month at work, but it was too much. On a final trip to Chicago on some Presidential chore, he felt he had reached the end of his rope.

The pen continued racing across the paper. The thoughts were coming faster now. There were the poker games in the White House and good conversations:

> I presume Henry Morgenthau and "Dollar" Watson ["Pa" Watson, Roosevelt's military aide] will talk about Powder River.
> The cheese store on 42nd St—and fresh fish in Iowa—and maps and rivers and forests and Admirals and dams and power plants—funny things that no President ever talked about before.

The "cheese store" wasn't a cheese store, and it wasn't in New York City. It was another Roosevelt joke. Judge Samuel Rosenman, who lived in Manhattan, came frequently to Washington to help write Roosevelt's speeches and join in the poker and conversation. Invariably he stopped in a delicatessen he patronized in Washington and brought some delicacy to augment the austere diet the housekeeper, Mrs. Henrietta Nesbitt, imposed on White House residents. When this happened, FDR would invariably say, "I suppose this came from that cheese store on 42nd Street."

The letter was coming to an end now.

> All these things I think of—and Mc [Intyre] and Steve [Early, Roosevelt's Press Secretary] and Tommy and Ben and Rex and Felix and Sam and Missy—I know they are important because I remember them—and they are good.
> This letter is simply to say that I have had an awfully good time—and to thank you very much. And by the way—my weather bureau tells me it will be fair tomorrow.
>
> Harry[1]

The last sentence is a reference to the favorable political climate Hopkins was finding in the Middle West.

Roosevelt's reply to this and to the official letter of resignation came on August 24:

> Dear Harry:
> I have your letter of August twenty-second and I fully understand all that you say and much that you have left unsaid.
> In giving me this letter of resignation it is possible only for you to break the official ties that exist between us—not the ties of friendship that have endured so happily through the years. I am accepting your resignation, therefore, to take effect at a date to be determined later, and I repeat that this resignation is accepted only in its official sense.

In other words, you may resign the office—only the office—and nothing else. Our friendship will and must go on as always.

> Affectionately,
> Franklin D. Roosevelt[2]

All was finished, but it was not finished. The end would not come for another five years, years of such service that Winston Churchill, who formed ties of friendship with Hopkins in war-ravaged Britain, felt moved to write after his death:

> A strong, bright, fierce flame has burned out a frail body.
>
> Few know better than I the services he rendered to the world cause. President Roosevelt had the gift of choosing generous and noble spirits to help him in peace and war.
>
> In Harry Hopkins he found a man not only of wide ranging vision but of piercing eye. He always went to the root of the matter. . . .
>
> He was a true leader of men, and alike in ardor and in wisdom in time of crisis, he has rarely been excelled.
>
> His love for the causes of the weak and the poor was matched by his passion against tyranny, especially when tyranny was for the time triumphant.
>
> To dynamic, compulsive and persuasive force he added humor and charm in an exceptional degree.
>
> We do well to salute his memory. We shall not see his like again.[3]

BOOK ONE

Friend of the Poor,
Friend of the Rich

CHAPTER ONE

Go East, Young Man

Harry Hopkins never ceased wondering over the marvel that he, the son of a harness maker, became the trusted confidant of three of the most powerful men in the world: Franklin D. Roosevelt, Winston Churchill, and Joseph Stalin.

In the late nineteenth century, Sioux City, Iowa, seemed as remote from Hyde Park, New York, where the youthful Franklin Roosevelt was growing up, as it did from London and Moscow. It was a railway town and a center of agriculture, situated in the extreme western part of the State, right on the Nebraska border. Here on August 17, 1890, the fifth child of David Aldona and Anna Pickett Hopkins was born. Christened Harry Lloyd, he was a blend of his serious-minded, devout mother and his easy-going, gregarious father.

His father believed himself descended from the family which had produced Stephen Hopkins, a signer for Rhode Island of the Declaration of Independence, and his brother, Ezek, who was commander-in-chief of the Continental navy early in the Revolutionary War. Ezek was later dismissed from his command for too much independence of spirit and failure to obey orders of the Continental Congress, and if the genealogy was correct, that same independence of spirit loomed large in Ezek's remote descendant, Harry.

Better documented is the story of Hopkins' maternal grandfather, Marcellus Emery, who was a graduate of Bowdoin College in the class of 1853. Moving to Bangor, Maine, he practiced law for a number of years and served as an alderman for a year. Apparently his legal work palled, for

29

in 1857 he became editor of two newspapers and crusaded against the approaching Civil War. When it came, he wrote:

> The loudest advocates of the existing deplorable war, in which the country has become involved, by the Abolition Republican party, are the political demagogues, the partisan priests, and the infamous speculators, who are coining fortunes out of the calamities of their country. The first want offices; the priests are for setting the niggers free; and the speculators are for the accumulating of pelf. The poor unfortunate people—the farmers, mechanics, and workingmen—are to be first taxed to death, and then enslaved, as a consequence of all this infamous business.[1]

Having lived in the South as a boy, Emery was naturally sympathetic to the Confederacy. That fact, and his membership in the Democratic Party in the Republican stronghold of Bangor, aroused a good bit of hatred among the fire-eating Republicans. The day the editorial just noted appeared, a mob ransacked the newspaper office and smashed the presses. Marcellus Emery barely escaped with his life, but, undaunted, brought out a small edition of the paper eight days later on a friend's press and in a vigorous editorial deplored the loss of free speech.

When he died in 1879, the successor to one of his newspapers commented: "He was the most positive of men. There was no negation in his character or method of thought. He planted himself on what he regarded as the rock of eternal truth, and no tempest of tongue, nor artillery of words could move him from his chosen citadel."[2]

His grandson, Harry, although less stylistically literary, was also one with "no negation in his character or method of thought."

David Aldona Hopkins was born in Bangor on June 26, 1856. Soon after the Civil War, his family moved to the West in search of gold. When he grew up, David struck out on his own, prospecting in the Black Hills. He found no gold, but in Vermilion, South Dakota, he found Anna Pickett, a schoolteacher. One of her pupils, a future United States Senator, wrote: "I have never forgotten her diligent effort to teach us something,—her patience with our faults and her always pleasant manner."[3]

She was born on February 23, 1860, in Lowville, near Hamilton, Ontario, but her family had moved as homesteaders to South Dakota when she was a girl. After a suitable courtship, Anna Pickett and David Hopkins were married and moved to North Bend, Nebraska, where he opened a wholesale harness business. They were an ill-assorted pair. Al Hopkins, as he preferred to be called, was easy-going, always popular wherever he went, and a wizard on the bowling alleys. Harry Hopkins recalled later:

One night Dad came home after a big match against someone who thought himself a champion. Dad took me down to the cellar on some pretext, like fixing the furnace, then reached in his pocket and pulled out $500 for me to look at. He had won it all that evening, but of course I wasn't supposed to tell my mother there was that amount of money in the house, she would have made Dad give it away to church missions.[4]

An intensely religious woman, Anna Hopkins gathered her family daily around a pump organ for singing of hymns, and she saw to it that they went to church daily and twice on Sundays. A devoted worker in the Methodist Church, she raised her children in stern rectitude, imbuing them with a sense of social responsibility and of service to fellow human beings. It may be noted that three of her sons went into service professions—two into social work and one into medicine.

Their first child, Adah May Hopkins, was born in North Bend on September 19, 1882. Then came Lewis Andrew on December 31, 1884, and Rome Miller Hopkins on January 12, 1887. Rome was named for a great friend of Al's early days in the West, who shortly after his namesake's birth, loaned Al $10,000 to open a store in Norfolk, Nebraska, a progressive city at the terminus of the North Western Railroad. "I have no recollection," wrote Rome Miller to Hopkins years later, "of your father ever taking a drink, smoking or swearing. Neither do I recall his ever tending strictly to business."[5]

While the family was in Norfolk, a girl, Etta, was born on April 19, 1889. She did not survive infancy. Then, after his parents had moved to Sioux City, Iowa, Harry Lloyd was born on August 17, 1890. His father opened yet another harness shop, this time retail, but he fared no better than before. After a year, "Dad" Hopkins, as he was now known, took a job as a traveling salesman in leather goods and moved the family to Kearney, Nebraska, where their last child, John Emery, was born on June 24, 1894.[6]

The Hopkins family endured a peripatetic existence for the next few years, residing variously in Kearney, Council Bluffs, and Hastings, Nebraska, and then for two years in Chicago. There an accident led to a change in the family's fortunes for a time. A horse-drawn dray ran over Dad Hopkins and broke his leg. He collected $10,000 out of court, of which half went to his lawyer. Staked with the remaining $5,000, he took the family to Grinnell, Iowa, where he bought yet another harness store. Anna Hopkins was influential in selecting Grinnell, for it was a college town, and she was looking forward to the education of her children. Grinnell College at that time was a leading Congregational institution. There was enough money for Dad Hopkins to acquire a white frame house on the corner of Elm Street and Sixth Avenue, across from Cooper School.

Harry was eleven when the family moved to Grinnell. His mother recalled that he had been delicate as a baby and that they had a hard time finding food that would agree with him. In Chicago, he had contracted a severe case of typhoid fever and consequently was a scrawny boy. His physical appearance brought him the nicknames of "Skinny," "Hi," and "High Pockets," but the one that stuck was "Hoppy," a name later endured by his three sons.

The limited demand for harnesses in Grinnell could not provide for the large Hopkins family, so Dad Hopkins diversified, supplying candy, newspapers, magazines, and, under the counter, cigarettes for the Grinnell College students. He claimed to know nearly every student in the college by his first name, and he was so popular that the shop prospered. So did the Hopkins family. Rome starred on the high school football team, and Adah began a career in social work which lasted until her marriage.

Naturally athletic, Harry Hopkins in high school played both baseball and basketball. He was only fair in the former, but in basketball he excelled. His high school team one year had the proud distinction of winning the Missouri Valley Championship.

He also played football, although he did not come up to the skill of his brother Rome. On one occasion on the football field he broke some bones in a leg and a classmate, Newton Olson, carried him on his back to school until the leg healed. While he was in high school, Harry did his first bit in politics. In elections for class officers, the teachers always rigged things so the best students were elected. Hopkins, no great student at that time, took exception to this process and arranged a campaign for a popular boy named Sam O'Brien, who was by no means an academic star. Sam won by a large majority. The faculty voided the election, and three more were held, Sam winning each. In the last "we again elected Sam with the same number of votes cast that there were voters present."[7]

Hopkins also enjoyed membership in several high school clubs, "The Stars" for boys only and a mixed one by the curious name of "3 x 3." One of the members of this second club was Hallie Ferguson, who years later, as Hallie Flanagan, would run the Federal Theater Project division of WPA for Hopkins. Her younger sister, Gladys, later recalled a meeting of the 3 x 3 Club at which she was serving a course in a progressive dinner. "Never will I forget my chagrin when the nice juicy stuffed tomato salad rolled down on your lap leaving a nice railroad track of whipped cream dressing over your coat. You were nice, but I bet there was murder in your heart, for the suit was new blue serge."[8]

In 1908, Hopkins entered Grinnell College, where he did nothing either to raise or lower the academic standards. As expected of a lively young man of his day, he set out to become a big man on campus, ran for class offices, and was elected in his senior year as permanent president of his class. During the summers, he earned money for his college expenses by playing semiprofessional baseball. His batting average and throwing arm had improved greatly since his high school days.

On one occasion during his senior year, he was approached by leaders of the sophomore class for advice on how to win the forthcoming annual frosh-soph battle. He gave his advice freely, and the sophomores accepted it. A bit later he was approached, quite independently, by the freshmen leaders and asked the same question. It appealed to his sardonic sense of humor to tell them how to counter the "possible" sophomore strategy.

When the great day came, both sides adopted Hopkins' strategy. The sophomores holed up in a barn where they would be safe from attack, and the freshmen climbed up on the roof and dropped "stink bombs" through a hole. The college authorities considered the whole thing unsporting, and everyone involved, except Hopkins, was penalized. His part was not revealed until years later.

While he was at Grinnell he made several lifelong friends, among them Robert and Florence Kerr and Harry C. Dodge. He was also influenced by three members of the faculty, who helped to shape his life's work. He served as assistant to the noted Harvard historian, Albert Bushnell Hart, who was at Grinnell for a year on an exchange professorship, and Hopkins continued to read history for the rest of his days.

Even more important was Professor Jesse Macy, who taught one of the first courses in political science in the country. A great believer in the Socratic method, Macy gave his students a thorough understanding of the political organizations of the United States and of the British parliamentary system. One of his principal beliefs was in the responsibility of the state to its citizens, for their welfare and well-being, as a right and not a privilege.

The third teacher with a great influence on Hopkins was Professor Edward A. Steiner, who taught a course called "Applied Christianity." Like all great teachers, Steiner gave his students more than the mere subject matter of his courses. He was a Jew, born in Czechoslovakia, with a doctorate from Heidelberg. Emigrating to the United States, he became a Congregational minister. The humanitarian in him led him to the writings of Tolstoy, and in 1903, he visited Russia to see the great novelist for materials for a book he proposed to write, *Tolstoy the Man.* The combination of Tolstoy's humanity, the Jewish sense of man's responsibility to his God, and the Christian ethic of love of neighbor had been worked by Steiner into a synthesis which influenced Hopkins permanently.

Hopkins had no very definite plans for his life's work when he graduated from Grinnell. As a temporary measure, he planned to open a newspaper in Bozeman, Montana, with a partner. He stopped in to say good-bye to Dr.

Steiner before leaving the campus. Steiner showed Hopkins a telegram he had just received from a friend who worked for Christadora House, a settlement institution on Avenue B in the lower East Side New York slums. Christadora House was looking for a young man to serve as counselor at its summer camp near Bound Brook, New Jersey, where poor city children could get the benefits of outdoor living and healthful exercise. Hopkins took the job, not because he felt any strong pull toward social work, but because it offered him an opportunity to see the East. Telling his prospective partner not to count on him, he took the train to Chicago.

Since he had a few spare days, Hopkins decided to take in the 1912 Republican National Convention which was being held in Chicago. He crashed the gate at the convention hall by brazenly telling a guard that he was Elihu Root's secretary. This was the convention in which Theodore Roosevelt tried to make his comeback for the Presidency after four years of William Howard Taft. Hopkins heard Teddy Roosevelt castigate the lords of "special privilege" and call Taft's renomination "naked theft." This was Hopkins' first experience with a Roosevelt, but he was to find his niche in the service of one of the Dutchess County branch of the family and not in the ranks of the man from Oyster Bay.

Hopkins also stopped off in Baltimore to see Woodrow Wilson win the Democratic nomination on the forty-sixth ballot, but whose "secretary" he was is unrecorded.

Enthralled by the hurly-burly of the two conventions—by rubbing elbows with the great and near great—Hopkins hoped someday to be a part of the political scene. He would be, but he had a long apprenticeship to serve first.

When he arrived at Bound Brook to take up his duties, he was appalled. Although he had seen poverty during his boyhood and, indeed, had experienced it when Dad Hopkins' fortunes were at an ebb, he had never known anything like the abject misery from which the boys at Bound Brook had come. He confessed that he had never before seen a Jewish boy, nor, it seems likely, an Italian, Polish, Greek, or Spanish boy. His classmates in high school and college were almost without exception of English, Irish, or Scandinavian extraction, well adjusted to a farming or business background. But Hopkins' charges from the slums knew nothing of the woods and the fields, nor of elementary hygiene and organized games. Yet they were eager to learn and Hopkins was eager to teach them. After the camp was over, Hopkins had been converted to his mother's missionary zeal.

Hopkins continued with Christadora House, as a worker with its boys' clubs. Flop houses, tenements, sweat shops, all kinds of human misery, existed side by side with the extravagance of the very rich. Hopkins was paid no regular salary; he worked for room and board and a few dollars a month pocket money.

The time he spent at Christadora House was an education to Hopkins. He worked hard, regularly attending meetings of the boys' clubs and learning from the members the attitudes peculiar to their own groups and gangs. He was a bit naive, perhaps, to give them lectures on civic betterment, but he had to talk about something, and his presence was endured by the boys in return for the shelter of the club and perhaps a few refreshments.

New York in 1912 compressed into the few square miles of Manhattan all the vices and virtues of the rest of the country. Here were the gangsters next to the philanthropists, the anarchists beside the better-government advocates, the sweat shops and the rich stores of Fifth Avenue. Here came the wide-eyed dreamers to make a fortune in the big city and the immigrants from Europe to find the streets paved with gold.

It was the New York of the Tenderloin, of Tammany Hall, of Diamond Jim Brady, of Millionaires' Row on Fifth Avenue, where thirty-five lavish houses between 42nd and 92nd Streets vied for elegance. From the vantage of Avenue B, Millionaires' Row looked incredibly distant, but Hopkins would bridge the gap in years to come, having friends not only among the social workers but also among the incredibly rich as well.

That summer, the trial, conviction, and execution of four gunmen who had murdered the proprietor of a gambling establishment drove home to Hopkins that the enemies of society could be heroes to the youth of the slums. When the four, known as Gyp the Blood, Dago Frank, Lefty Louie, and Whitey Lewis, were executed, Hopkins was attending a meeting at a boys' club. He was severely shaken when one of the boys rose and said, "I move that the whole club stand up for two minutes in honor of the four gunmen who died today." The motion carried without opposition. Hopkins later wondered, "What is responsible for the fact that thirty-five boys, all under sixteen, should wish to rise to their feet to pay homage to four men whose crimes their keen sense of right and wrong would naturally condemn under normal circumstances?"[9]

Finding the few dollars a month spending money grossly inadequate, in the spring of 1913 Hopkins called upon John A. Kingsbury, general director of the Association for Improving the Condition of the Poor, one of the strongest charitable organizations in the city. Kingsbury had no position to offer him, but put him on the payroll for $45 per month for training. He continued to live at Christadora House and worked there during the day, and in the evening he did assignments for AICP, largely in the tough waterfront districts. A few months later, Hopkins again approached Kingsbury, this time for a raise. Kingsbury laughed at him. Hopkins sheepishly admitted that he wanted to get married to a fellow worker at Christadora House, Miss Ethel Gross. Amused, Kingsbury agreed to put him on the payroll at an annual salary of $1,260 a year, and the wedding duly took place in late 1913. Three sons were born of this marriage, David, named after Dad Hopkins, on October 11, 1914, Robert, named for Robert Kerr, on May 17, 1921, and Stephen, named for the remote ancestor, signer of the Declaration of Independence, born July 16, 1925. There was also a daughter, Barbara, who died in 1920.[10]

During that fall, Hopkins campaigned for reform candidate John Purroy Mitchel. When Mitchel took office as Mayor in January, 1914, he named Kingsbury Commissioner of Public Charities, and Hopkins became executive secretary of the Board of Child Welfare. The salary of $3,000 per year was more wealth than Hopkins had ever seen, and it enabled him to take advantage of some of the opportunities of New York. He frequented the opera, the museums, the art galleries, and the more popular night spots. He began to make friends among the people with money, in show business, and the racing set.

In August, 1914, Mayor Mitchel introduced several experiments in the city government. Some of them appeared later as a part of the New Deal under Franklin Roosevelt. One provided work relief or "made" work in the parks. Hopkins was involved in this program and soon read reports in the unfriendly press of municipal workers "leaning on their shovels."

He had no future, however, in New York City government. Mitchel, for all his virtues, had the uncanny knack of antagonizing everyone he worked with, supporters and foes alike. Not only was he tactless, but he was also seen too much in high society, and there were charges that he was "too much Fifth Avenue, too little First Avenue." Although a decade later, New York would take to its heart a mayor, Jimmy Walker, who spent all his time in high society, in 1917 the accusation was enough to enable Tammany Hall to defeat Mitchel in the Democratic primary with one of their own, John F. ("Red Mike") Hylan.

When the United States entered the war in April, 1917, Hopkins tried to get into the Army, the Navy, and the Marine Corps, but was rejected by all of them for defective vision. (By coincidence, Hopkins had a son in each of those services in World War II.) His job with the city having ended, he joined the staff of the Red Cross and went to New Orleans. He welcomed the change in climate, for in 1916 he had been laid up for two months with an attack of pneumonia, another in the long series of illnesses which plagued his life and career. In New Orleans he was directed to report for physical examination for the draft. The director general of the Red Cross, choosing not to trust the draft board medicos to turn Hopkins down a fourth time, requested his exemption, pointing out that "his work in charge of the welfare of soldiers' and sailors' families in the Gulf Division [comprising Alabama, Louisiana, and Mississippi] is highly important, and plays a direct part in winning the war."[11] Hopkins was not drafted, and remained for a considerable time in New Orleans. In 1920, the League of Red Cross Societies in Geneva, Switzerland, offered him a high position, but the American Red Cross refused to let him go. Soon thereafter, he moved to Atlanta, in charge of the Red Cross activities in all of the Southeastern States. He remained there until October, 1922, when he resigned because his duties allowed him little home life.

> During the past five years with the Red Cross [he wrote] I have been forced by the very nature of my position to be on the road at least half and perhaps two-thirds of the time and the responsibilities of a growing family would at this time seem to necessitate my accepting a position wherein I can find it possible to establish a real home.[12]

Hopkins returned to New York and took charge for AICP of a project to study health conditions in the New York City area. This program, funded by a special grant from Albert G. Milbank, chairman of the board of the Borden Company, gave Hopkins a salary of $8,000 a year, which afforded comparative luxury in those days. Hopkins joined the commuter crowd, living for a time in Yonkers and then moving up to Scarborough because the Kingsburys lived there.

Kingsbury had a large library, and Hopkins borrowed books at every opportunity, at the same time buying as many as he could for his own library. He developed a great love for the English Lake and Romantic poets, especially John Keats, whose works he read over and over again, along with every biography of him he could lay his hands on. He even tried his hand at poetry of his own.

On weekends, he often tramped the woods with Kingsbury, who was fascinated by mushrooms. They put specimens in two baskets, one for the edible and one for the poisonous. It is fortunate that Kingsbury was an expert and never made a mistake. Hopkins also learned to play bridge, at which he became fairly expert, and a reasonable game of tennis. His golf, however, remained poor.

Hopkins also liked to entertain his friends at speakeasies, such as Leon and Eddie's or the Côte d'Or in New York. The noble experiment of Prohibition bothered him no more than it did most professional men of his time. He liked to be a lavish host, tipping extravagantly and ordering the best in the house.

This, one of the happiest times in Hopkins' life, was not entirely without its drawbacks. He had trouble with the director of AICP, Bailey B. Burritt. Hopkins believed he should be independent of Burritt's supervision and authority because his funding was independent. Burritt felt that if he had the responsibility for the health study, he should have the authority. Hopkins chafed under these strictures, because he was always impatient of orderly administration, finding later a ready home in the somewhat ramshackle administrative methods of Franklin Roosevelt. The difficulties finally led to Hopkins' departure from AICP in 1924 to accept the position of executive director of the New York Tuberculosis Association, a move engineered and approved by both Burritt and Kingsbury.

The Tuberculosis Association, under the careful stewardship of its president, Dr. James Alexander Miller, had built up a surplus of $90,000. To Hopkins, this meant only one thing, that the association was not spending enough money for the afflicted. With typical energy he set about expanding the programs, and at the same time he greatly increased the income of the association. One of the ways was the Christmas Seal program. Instead of asking people to write in for them, Hopkins devised the method of sending a sheet of a hundred stamps to everyone on a mailing list and asking recipients to send back a dollar or more. The dollar bills flooded into the office.

Neither Dr. Miller nor his successor, Dr. Linsley R. Williams, was able to give much time to the day-to-day operation of the association, and this suited Hopkins perfectly. For almost anyone else, the problem of tuberculosis would have been enough to handle, but Hopkins was constantly looking around for new opportunities. During his seven years with the association, he arranged for it to take over the New York Heart Association, the Associated Out-Patient Clinic, the Allied Dental Clinic, and the Children's Welfare Clinic. As a result of these new activities, the name was changed to the New York Tuberculosis and Health Association. Of course, it quickly ran through the surplus Dr. Miller had built up and was constantly in debt.

> Harry [Dr. Miller commented ruefully] never had the faintest concep-
> tion of the value of money. But then, that is true of most social workers I
> have known. Although in no sense personally dishonest, they can become
> unscrupulous in the handling of funds. They can convince themselves that
> the worthy end justified the means.[13]

In the summer of 1925, Hopkins took one of his rare vacations and traveled to visit his family, all of whom had left Grinnell by this time. (His sister Adah had married Frank Aimé, a New York electrical engineer.) Lewis had become a doctor, and after a stint in the Grinnell Clinic, had set up practice in Tacoma. Rome and Emery were both there also, and both at loose ends. In one of his uninhibited letters to Ethel (who remained home, pregnant with Stephen), Hopkins painted a vivid picture:

If Sinclair Lewis ever gets the complete history of the Hopkins family, he will make "Main Street" look like ten cents. I wouldn't have missed it for the world—Rome engaged to a Follies girl who happens to be Catholic and divorced—the hero selling alcohol a shade or two inside the law—Lewis flat on his back practising the "humbug act" and thoroughly disillusioned—and Emery, the 100% American selling baggage in a department store at $35 per. Rome smiles—plans matrimony and looks for bigger things—Lew smiles a little pathetically—changes the babies' diapers and looks for a better practice from now on—Emery reads of heroes in the American magazine—begets a healthy child—and plans to make some money soon. All are broke—complain but little—have no alibis—are securely nailed to females who think they could have made a respectable living had they been wearing the trousers.[14]

On the way back, he stopped at Spokane, where his parents were now living. Dad Hopkins had indulged his life's hobby by purchasing some bowling alleys, paying "much more . . . than they were worth." Fortunately both his parents were well, but his mother had retired from her intensive religious activity, being "contented to stay quietly at home. She of course longs for the time when she can be at home near some of the children, preferably Adah."[15]

Hopkins never hesitated to rush in, even when he did not understand a problem. He would seek out someone who could tell him about it and quickly absorb the essential details. One day early in 1928, Dr. Haven Emerson, who had been Health Commissioner of New York City, told Hopkins that it was outrageous that the men working on the subway tunnels under 42nd Street were not protected from silicosis and urged him to do something about it. Hopkins, who did not know silicosis from syllabub, promised that he would and promptly sought out Dr. Jacob Goldberg, secretary of the association. "Say, Jack—what *is* silicosis?" After Dr. Goldberg explained, Hopkins set up a committee to find a solution, and their report in 1929 resulted in the development of a vacuum apparatus to suck the silica dust from the air. The apparatus was subsequently used in all major excavation in the New York area, including the construction of Rockefeller Center and the Hudson and East River tunnels.

When Hopkins had to deal with things he knew nothing about, his method was always the same: find the expert who could brief him, and then set up a team to do what had to be done. Throughout his career, he worked intensely, at whatever cost to himself. Dr. Goldberg described Hopkins during his time with the association:

You could mark him down as an ulcerous type. He was intense, seeming to be in a perpetual nervous ferment—a chain smoker and black coffee drinker. He was always careless in his appearance. Most of the time he would show up in the office looking as though he had spent the previous night sleeping in a hayloft. He would wear the same shirt three or four days at a time. He managed to shave almost every day—usually at the office.[16]

The office brought Hopkins into daily contact with Barbara Duncan, who had been a nurse at Bellevue Hospital in New York. She had contracted symptoms of tuberculosis and took employment as a secretary for the association. She and Hopkins were attracted to each other, so much so that Hopkins went to a psychiatrist in an attempt to get over his infatuation. Simultaneously he began to psychoanalyze himself, reading extensively in the works of Freud, Jung, and Adler. He tried to talk the problem out with his sister Adah and with John Kingsbury. For a year or more this went on. Finally he and Barbara Duncan agreed that they must stop seeing one another, and at the suggestion of the psychiatrist, Kingsbury, who was going to Europe in 1928 to study social conditions, proposed that Hopkins go along. The Milbank Fund paid for Hopkins so that he could make a study of health care methods and organizations in France and England. His letters to Ethel suggest a determination to restore his marriage.

To save money, he booked passage third class on the steamer, but the second day out "the food and general lack of elbow room completely upset my plebeian ideas," and he transferred to first class, writing Ethel that he had never spent money better. He spent the days reading, loafing, looking at the sea, and in conversation with John Kingsbury and his wife, Jean. Thoroughly entranced with the sea voyage, he fairly bubbled in the letter to his wife until a small accident took place:

> As to my plans—I had bought a ticket for Paris, and planned to get off at Boulogne, but John spilled a pitcher of hot water on his foot and is laid up completely. No one seems able to stay with him so I am elected. I want to do it tho. So John, Jean and I are going to Rotterdam arriving July 3—and stay there until John is better or can go on to Paris. This I trust will be Thursday or Friday. I want to stick by John but if I am going to be reasonably truthful I must admit that vacationing as nurse for John and guardian for Jean is not exactly my idea of a happy holiday.[17]

When Hopkins finally arrived in Paris, he felt liberated. With a show of virtue he wrote that he went to see the Folies-Bergère but walked out at the end of the first act. He concluded, "I can understand why you raved over Paris. It is all true. It pleases me immensely to know that I am not blase and still capable of enthusiasm."[18]

In London, Hopkins settled down to real work. He visited the slums of the East End, which he was to see again thirteen years later during the Blitz. He admired the English school health program.

> . . . under the direction of skilled and devoted doctors and nurses. It was thrilling. We are amateurs indeed! . . . Next week the t.b. service and then the district health service—it would take six months instead of weeks to do this adequately. I am being royally received and the whole works is open.[19]

That last sentence could well apply to his visits to Britain in 1941.

The high point of his visit to London he described in an enthusiastic letter to his wife written from the Royal Palace Hotel in the Kensington district of London:

> I have just had the most exalting experience. Having had a real English dinner with a delightful physician in his very English home, he took me for a tramp over Hampstead Heath—a great park on the outskirts of London—we were discussing the Mental Deficiency Act of England or some equally uplifting subject when we suddenly came on a lovely path upon which was a very impersonal sign called "Keats Walk!" Upon enquiry it developed that here Keats walked with Fanny Brawne and over this very Hampstead Heath—Keats had roamed for hours and it is just the same now as then. Imagine my feeling! The doctor not knowing Keats could not share my enthusiasm but that didn't restrain mine for at last I was in Keats country and every memory of the years I have known him (—how long has it been—I think it dates from the time I was ill in N.Y. Hospital about eight years ago—) swelled my imagination and I saw his red head and proud step sauntering thru the green—it was [as] tho I could reach out and touch him—quite like a dream. But it was not—for not two blocks away was his home where he lived for three years and where the Ode to the Nightingale was written and other heavenly music. I saw his very house—and his garden that he sat in for hours on end. . . .[20]

Hopkins returned to quite a different enthusiasm that fall, for he met for the first time the man who would become his closest friend—Franklin D. Roosevelt. While Alfred E. Smith opposed Herbert Hoover for the Presidency, Roosevelt was running for Governor of New York. Hopkins campaigned ardently for both of them, and when Roosevelt came to New York City to give a speech, Hopkins met him.

To Roosevelt, Hopkins was just another face to be greeted and another hand to be shaken, but Hopkins never forgot the meeting. And soon other meetings followed, as his paths crossed those of Eleanor Roosevelt in her self-imposed role of social worker without portfolio.

In the ensuing election, Hoover won handily, even carrying Smith's own

New York by 100,000 votes, but Roosevelt pulled off a miracle and won the Governorship by the slim majority of 25,000 votes. Roosevelt had the backing of the party machinery, of course, but that had not put Al Smith over in the State. But Roosevelt's cheerful manner, and his promise to continue Smith's programs, brought him victory. While the New York voters approved of Smith's policies, they did not want to see him in the White House.

The election of Herbert Hoover seemed to promise a continuation of boom times. During the campaign, Hoover had proclaimed: "We in America today are nearer to the final triumph over poverty than ever before in the history of any land. The poorhouse is vanishing from among us. . . . We shall soon with the help of God be in sight of the day when poverty will be banished from this nation."[21]

For everyone expectation was in the air. The way to riches was in business, for business production had brought unprecedented prosperity, and if you did not have yours yet, just wait, for it would come. You shared in business by speculating in stocks. Herbert Hoover had proclaimed the future in his campaign slogan, "A Chicken in Every Pot and Two Cars in Every Garage."

During the spring and summer of 1929, Hopkins refused to follow the "smart money" in the stock market. He liked to use money, but he had no desire to make a lot. He enjoyed his rich friends, but he would never be one of them. His work and his failing marriage occupied him fully. That summer, Dad Hopkins died in Spokane. His will left all his property to his widow except for the sum of $1.00 to each of his children.[22] He was buried in Grinnell, where Anna was to be laid beside him in 1932.

Dad Hopkins went to his grave still the friendly, easy-going man he always had been, never having much money, and never wanting much. He was spared the suffering of the great depression which would make his third son a friend of Presidents and the greatest spender the world had ever seen.

When the stock market finally broke on Black Thursday, October 24, 1929, it dramatized the panic caused by the first signs of the great depression. During the previous year manufacturers had built up vast surpluses. When their products piled up in warehouses, they stopped production and laid off workers. This had the effect of decreasing demands for all sorts of goods, and more workers were laid off. And so the vicious spiral accelerated. A chicken in every pot was replaced with a pink dismissal notice in one pay envelope after another.

Herbert Hoover believed that the federal government had no direct role to play in alleviating the suffering caused by massive unemployment. He set up the President's Committee for Unemployment Relief, an organization of three thousand local groups to see to it that no one starved. But the PCUR was merely a coordinating group. It spent no federal funds, and it depended on local charities to supply the bread and soup for the bread lines.

Hoover's main approach was through the top. Since business had brought prosperity to America, properly aided, business could bring it back. He started the Reconstruction Finance Corporation to provide businesses with low cost loans for expansion. But expansion did no good when businessmen could not sell the goods they had nor use their existing plants to full capacity. The Federal Farm Loan Banks provided a billion dollars to building and loan associations to help farmers fight off foreclosure, but those faced with foreclosure had too little credit left to win approval of new loans despite such backing. Hoover also moved to expand private credit through the Federal Reserve System. He cut government expenditures to the bone, but nothing seemed to do any good.

Hoover felt the crisis was at least in part psychological. He made optimistic statements that "prosperity is just around the corner," and "business conditions are fundamentally sound," in order to inspire business confidence.

Certainly Hoover never developed any idea of using the federal government to finance or administer any kind of relief measures. Ideas of relief had not changed since the Poor Laws of England, which provided for the dole administered by local communities and charities. In those days, when stories of Horatio Alger were still read, there was a feeling that if a man lost his job, it was because of some weakness in himself, and when he had to go on the dole, it was a personal and family disgrace. The economic experts of the time believed that by hard work and moral living a man could make good, that is, if he didn't spend his money foolishly on drink and luxuries. (It is ironic that the heroes of the Alger novels never achieved fame and fortune by carefully saving their hard-earned dollars. They always got their hands on capital by marrying the boss's daughter, by saving a rich man from a runaway horse, etc. This capital was then carefully invested in speculative stocks or in business, and fame and fortune ensued.)

Hopkins moved into fighting the crisis in New York through the AICP. He still put in a full day at the office of the New York Tuberculosis and Health Association, and then in the evening would work until late at night in AICP headquarters. Hopkins' friend, William Mathews of AICP, had obtained a grant of $75,000 from the American Red Cross, and he and Hopkins and Dr. Goldberg devised a scheme of putting needy men to work in the parks of New York City, the Park Commission to assign the labor and the AICP to provide the funds to pay the men.

As usual, Hopkins parted company with the traditional social worker. When Hopkins saw a need, he acted quickly, got the money out, and worried about orderly procedures later. Organized welfare agencies accused Hopkins of unprofessional conduct for his speed in action instead of making the usual investigation which would have probed into an applicant's financial resources, those of his family unto the third and fourth generation, his age, health, and even his religious convictions. "Harry told the agencies to go to hell," Goldberg reported.[23] If a man asked for a job he got one.

Of course the $75,000 went fast, but Mathews succeeded in keeping dribs and drabs of money coming in until Roosevelt proclaimed that unemployment relief was a responsibility of the State.

In August, 1931, Governor Roosevelt established in New York State the Temporary Emergency Relief Administration. In asking the legislature for authority and for funding for TERA, he stated:

> Our Government is not the master but the creature of the people. The duty of the State toward the citizens is the duty of the servant to its master. The people have created it; the people, by common consent, permit its continual existence. . . .
>
> To these unfortunate [impoverished] citizens aid must be extended by Government, not as a matter of charity, but as a matter of social duty.[24]

The legislature appropriated $20 million for TERA, and Roosevelt began to look around for someone to run it. As chairman he named an old friend, Jesse Isador Straus, president of the R. H. Macy & Co. department store and known for his philanthropies. Straus hesitated, but yielded to Roosevelt's promise that he could have a good man as deputy in charge. After consulting friends, including John Kingsbury, Straus decided on William Hudson of the Russell Sage Foundation as his deputy. But Hudson's friends all urged him not to take the job. Roosevelt's crazy experiment in social work would fail. Hudson would get the blame, they argued. He had nothing to gain by risking the solid reputation he had built up with the Sage Foundation.

Hudson suggested to Straus that Harry Hopkins would be just the man for the job. "I would love it," said Hopkins promptly when asked if he would take it. And so Hopkins entered upon government service, which would lead him into fields of activity no one could dream of. It would also bring him into frequent contact with Franklin Roosevelt.

By this time Hopkins was alone. His efforts to salvage his marriage had failed, and his wife had divorced him in 1930, winning custody of the three boys and a settlement of half of whatever his salary was. (His son Robert later said that he rarely paid it, forcing Ethel to work to support the boys.) Hopkins, however, kept up close associations with the boys, and their mother never attempted to influence them against him. The divorce caused a nearly complete estrangement with Adah for a period of time and also a break with John Kingsbury, both of whom felt Hopkins had acted in a shabby fashion toward Ethel.

In 1931, he and Barbara Duncan were married. Their union was happy but short, for Barbara died of cancer in 1937. On November 15, 1932, their only child, Diana, was born. She was a joy to both of them, and she was to win the heart of Eleanor Roosevelt as well.

No one knew how long the TERA job would last, for the predictions of a swift return to prosperity on the lips of Republican spokesmen were echoed by people everywhere. Even the name, Temporary Emergency Relief Administration, suggested impermanence. Therefore, Hopkins kept his connection with the Tuberculosis and Health Association and worked on both jobs at once. As time passed, he grew more and more certain that the depression was not going to be conquered easily or swiftly.

TERA cooperated with other agencies of the State to provide employment, and so Hopkins came to know some of the people he would later work with in Washington, particularly Frances Perkins and Henry Morgenthau, Jr. After a year, Straus resigned as administrator and Hopkins assumed the post. He had the knack of finding out what Roosevelt wanted and then proceeding to do it. When Roosevelt said in a dinner conversation that young men from the city slums should be brought out to work in the fresh air on preserving the forests of New York State, Hopkins did not delay. He and Morgenthau, Roosevelt's Dutchess County neighbor and his Conservation Commissioner, put some 10,000 men and boys to work in a reforestation program which became the archetype for both the Civilian Conservation Corps and the National Youth Administration a few years later.

> We took the gas house gang [Morgenthau recalled], the bad boys who were loafing on the streets and getting into trouble, and we put them on the 4 a.m. train that ran up to the Bear Mountain area where they worked all day. Then because there was no housing for them, we took them back at night. F.D.R. was much interested in this conservation of human resources, as in all conservation work.[25]

As always, politics entered into the picture. Despite Hopkins' efforts to be impartial, the Republicans screamed that Democrats were getting all the jobs and the moneys under TERA, and the Democrats grumbled that all the plums were going to the Republicans. Since the volume of complaint from each side just about balanced, it seems clear that Hopkins was doing his job fairly.

Very soon Hopkins joined in supporting Roosevelt in his bid for the White House. James Farley and Louis McHenry Howe had worked on Roosevelt's campaign for over a year, and as a matter of fact, Farley had proclaimed the day after Roosevelt's reelection as Governor of New York in 1930, "I do not see how Mr. Roosevelt can escape becoming the next presidential nominee of his party, even if no one should raise a finger to bring it about."[26]

Plenty of fingers were raised against Roosevelt in the spring of 1932, including many in his own State. Normally one of the great advantages that the Governor of New York had in the convention was control of his own State's delegation, at that time the largest in the nation. But Roosevelt was at odds with Tammany Hall, whose strong leadership had been replaced by men whose greed outran their prudence. A series of scandals ensued, a sorry tale of graft and corruption, which led to the offices of the Tammany district attorney and of the New York City mayor, playboy Jimmy Walker. Roosevelt had no choice as Governor but to act, and he appointed the incorruptible Samuel Seabury to investigate. As a result, Tammany denied Roosevelt control of the New York delegation, for they supported Alfred E. Smith, who wanted a chance to avenge his defeat by Hoover in 1928.

Scenting victory for their party as the depression dragged its dreary way along, other Democrats threw their hats into the ring to join Roosevelt's battered fedora and Smith's brown derby. John Nance Garner, Speaker of the House, had no more ideas than anyone else on how to cure the depression, but he had the solid backing of his own Texas delegation and a goodly portion of the California one as well. Other candidates included Governor Albert Ritchie of Maryland and Newton D. Baker, once Secretary of War under Wilson.

When the convention assembled, Roosevelt lacked the necessary strength to win the required two-thirds vote for the nomination. It seemed anybody's ball game. After three ballots, Roosevelt still fell short by about eighty votes, so Farley struck a deal with Garner, whereby "Cactus Jack" would get the Vice Presidential slot. On the fourth ballot, the party named Roosevelt and Garner, but disgruntled Smith forces refused the customary appeal to make the nominations unanimous.

Roosevelt shattered tradition the next day. Instead of waiting at home for the customary delegation to call on him weeks later, he decided to fly at once to Chicago and make his acceptance speech while the convention was still in session. The trip from Albany to Chicago in a creaky Ford Trimotor plane was rough and took all day, but the imperturbable Roosevelt worked on his acceptance speech, while his wife, Missy LeHand, and Judge Sam Rosenman wrapped themselves in blankets, and John Roosevelt was airsick in the rear of the unheated cabin.

In Chicago, Roosevelt delivered a long and rambling speech, but his peroration contained two words that would ever after be associated with him.

"I pledge you, I pledge myself, to a new deal for the American people." So the New Deal was born. Not that Roosevelt had any idea of how it was to come about, for at that stage, he had no program worthy of the name. He set about trying to find one. Basically what he wanted was action. He took time to listen to anyone who had an idea and who could help in winning the election. His advisers ranged from cynical professional politicians at one extreme to college professors from Columbia University at the other. These last, including Raymond G. Moley, Rexford Tugwell, and Adolf A. Berle, constituted the Brains Trust, a term soon shortened to Brain Trust by the newsmen.

These men had ideas, but they were sometimes astonished at the cavalier way Roosevelt treated them. Once, for example, Moley presented him with two completely different drafts of a speech on tariffs, one advocating protectionism and the other approaching free trade. "Weave the two together," Roosevelt said airily.[27]

As expected, the Republicans renominated Herbert Hoover, who looked upon the campaign as an opportunity to vindicate himself before the American people and in the eyes of history. He failed utterly, for his austere manner and his stiff speaking manner contrasted badly with the flamboyant Roosevelt. The ensuing campaign saddled Hoover with responsibility for the depression, with failing to overcome it, and with insensitivity to the sufferings caused by it. The term "Hoover depression" endured, and the clusters of shacks built of packing cases, tin sheets, and tar paper became known as "Hoovervilles." Grimly Hoover fought back. To the end of his life, he believed that his measures would have led to recovery sooner than the New Deal did. He claimed that the depression was substantially over in Europe in 1935 or 1936, but that it hung on in America until the rearmament program for World War II brought it to an end.

If identifying Hoover with the depression was bitter politics, the Republicans tried equally merciless tricks. Hoover, of course would not condone them, but at the grass roots there were rumor and whispering campaigns. Alleged weaknesses and shortcomings in Roosevelt's performance as Governor of New York lacked national appeal, so stories circulated that Roosevelt's illness was not polio but syphilis, that passersby could hear maniacal laughter as his guards struggled to get him into a straitjacket in the State House in Albany.

Such tales had little impact except among those who were ready to believe the worst in any case. Certainly they had no effect on the outcome of the election.

Hopkins campaigned hard for Roosevelt when he could spare the time, for his two jobs kept him on the go. He wrote his brother Lewis:

> I very naturally am earnestly hoping that Roosevelt will be elected. I think he would make a far better president than Hoover—chiefly because he is not afraid of a new idea, and furthermore, is not identified with big business after the fashion of "the great engineer." I am convinced that Roosevelt is not only fearless, but a very able executive. All this business about his health is utter nonsense. I have seen a great deal of him within the past few months, and the amount of work that he can carry out is perfectly amazing. To be sure, I don't believe that the election of either of them is going to increase our respective salaries a bit.[28]

Roosevelt's smashing victory on November 8, 1932, filled Hopkins with hope, for he had gone about as far as he could with AICP and his experience with TERA made him want ardently to carry out a similar scheme on a national scale. He waited anxiously for a call from Roosevelt, but it did not come. Roosevelt was too busy organizing the main features of his administration to plan special agencies for Hopkins to head. A month after the election, Hopkins once again wrote Lewis:

> I look to see some pretty drastic changes made in Washington after the fourth of March [the inauguration day]. Certainly the unemployment situation is no better, and I can see no earthly reason for an upturn of business. It is going to be quite impossible, in my judgment, to get these ten or twelve million men back to work unless we have a universal five-day week, and I am not too sure about it even then. I have no sympathy with the "share the work" move that the big boys are advocating. Nor do I approve of the sales tax or other methods of taxation which have a horizontal base because that means that the people pay the taxes who can least afford it. I would shove the income taxes, inheritance, gift taxes, etc., higher than they now are. Certainly that should be done before we begin to tax every working man for each pair of shoes that he buys.[29]

So Hopkins remained running TERA as his former boss moved from Albany to Washington and the "Hundred Days" began. His call finally came after over seventy of them had gone by.

CHAPTER TWO

Money Flies

On May 22, 1933, seventy-nine days after Franklin D. Roosevelt's inauguration as President of the United States, Harry Hopkins became Federal Emergency Relief Administrator. Within minutes he was dashing off telegrams. He set to work without even waiting for the workmen to move his desk from the hall into his office. By nightfall he had made emergency grants to the Governors of Colorado, Illinois, Iowa, Michigan, Mississippi, and Texas. Roosevelt had given him simple instructions: to get relief to the millions of people who were out of work and did not know where to turn for food, clothing, and shelter.

"I'm not going to last six months here, so I'll do as I please," said Hopkins as he set to work.[1] The day after Hopkins started, the *Washington Post,* under the headline "Money Flies," reported in awe, "The half-billion dollars for direct relief of States won't last a month if Harry L. Hopkins, new relief administrator, maintains the pace he set yesterday in disbursing more than $5,000,000 during his first two hours in office."[2]

Along with millions of others, Hopkins had listened to Roosevelt's first inaugural address as the radio carried his words over what the networks then called a nationwide hookup. The firm, clear, confident voice rang out. "This great Nation will endure as it has endured, will revive and will prosper. So, first of all, let me assert my firm belief that the only thing we have to fear is fear itself—nameless, unreasoning, unjustified terror which paralyzes needed efforts to convert retreat into advance." Hopkins later declared, after he had helped write many of them, that Roosevelt's first inaugural was the finest speech he ever made.[3]

As Roosevelt spoke those words, America faced collapse. Banks closed their doors all over the country as desperate depositors lined up to withdraw their funds before the banks ran out of money. The national income had dwindled in four years from $81 billion to 39, and there seemed no way to stop the downward plunge. Relief funds of the towns, cities, counties, and States were exhausted. Normally law-abiding people joined in mobs to sack and loot food stores.

Oddly enough, in the midst of privation was plenty. Grain rotted in the fields because farmers could not afford the labor to harvest it. Millions wore threadbare rags while untold numbers of bales of cotton sat in warehouses unwanted by manufacturers who could not sell their finished products. In the West, sheepherders and cattle ranchers could not afford to drive their animals to market to have them sold for less than the cost of raising them. It was cheaper to slaughter them where they were and tumble the carcases into lime-coated pits.

In fact the capitalist system faced collapse. Money had nearly ceased to circulate, and the cycle of production, transportation, and consumption was totally out of kilter. The time offered a great opportunity for an imaginative leader—at that moment, the people would have followed almost anyone who seemed to have a solution. What manner of a man would he be?

In one of the great ironies of history two very different men came to power at almost the same time and in almost the same conditions. On January 30, 1933, Roosevelt's 51st birthday, Adolf Hitler became Chancellor of Germany. He used the truncheon and the gun to fight the depression in the Reich.

Franklin Roosevelt might well have become a dictator too, but it never occurred to him to do so. Certainly America was ripe for the strong man on a charger. But all of Roosevelt's moves were directed at saving the democratic process and the capitalist system. The bank holiday proclaimed after the inauguration and the banking reform measure saved the whole system of credit and monetary exchange. Other measures of the Hundred Days had the purpose of strengthening American institutions. These measures included the Agricultural Adjustment Act, the abandonment of the gold standard, the National Industrial Recovery Act, the creation of the Home Owners' Loan Corporation, and the Securities Exchange Act.

Obviously relief would have to become a major activity of the new national administration, but the press of more immediate demands of the Hundred Days came first. With the first emergency measures out of the way, the time had come to do something about the unemployed.

Roosevelt faced not a paucity of ideas but too many. Every mail brought to the White House plans for dealing with unemployment and relief. One drafted by Hopkins and William Hodson, Director of the Welfare Council of New York City, got lost in the pile of papers. Nor could would-be visitors get past the watchful guardians of Presidential time, secretaries Marvin McIntyre, Missy LeHand, and Grace Tully. Thousands of politicians, old friends, job seekers, Congressmen, crackpots, well-wishers, and people with ideas clamored for "just a few minutes with the Boss." Many of the claimants had credentials as good as or better than those of Hopkins.

Frances Perkins broke the logjam. She and Hopkins knew each other from their work in New York, when she had served as State Industrial Commissioner. Now, as Secretary of Labor, she could get Hopkins past the watchdogs if he could convince her he had a good plan.

Soon after the inauguration, Hopkins and Hodson came to Washington for a meeting with Miss Perkins. They gathered at the Women's University Club, which was so jammed that the only place they could find any privacy was, as Miss Perkins put it, "a hole under the stairs, and there in cramped, unlovely quarters, they laid out their plan. It was a plan for the immediate appropriation by the Federal Government of grants-in-aid to the states for unemployment relief. I was impressed by the exactness of their knowledge and the practicability of their plan."[4]

At her urging Roosevelt agreed to see Hopkins and Hodson. He took a good bit of convincing, because he wanted to balance the federal budget rather than spend more. He had not yet accepted the Keynesian ideas of deficit spending as a stimulus to the economy. Indeed one of his earliest measures was to reduce federal spending by cutting back veterans' benefits and reducing government salaries.

Hopkins' arguments, the very real sufferings of the unemployed, and the inability of the States to continue their own relief programs made the President change his mind. He enlisted the aid of Senators Robert Wagner of New York, Robert LaFollette of Wisconsin, and Edward Costigan of Colorado in drafting a bill to establish the Federal Emergency Relief Administration. After consultations with Hopkins and Miss Perkins on the New York experience with TERA, the three Senators drafted the bill that the President accepted.

In Congress, the bill produced some rather violent reactions. "It is socialism," Robert Luce of Massachusetts argued, but he added judiciously, "Whether it is communism or not I do not know." "I can hardly find parliamentary language," sputtered Simeon D. Fess of Ohio, "to describe the statement that the States and cities cannot take care of conditions in which they find themselves but must come to the Federal Government for aid."[5]

Other views prevailed, however, and the bill was finally approved on May 12. Ten days later Hopkins went to work to spend $500 million.

Hopkins found an office on the top floor of the delapidated Walker-

Johnson building on New York Avenue, a block and a half from the White
House. He refused to have the place redecorated; water pipes ran down the
faded and streaked walls. No carpet graced the bare floor. Hopkins had a
standard wooden desk of the type seen by the thousands in federal offices,
but seldom in the private sanctums of high officials. Outside his office, his
secretaries fended off hopefuls who would waste his time.

> When you got in to him [wrote Marquis Childs] he had a sort of trapped
> look. That was his manner with the press. He barricaded himself behind
> his shabby desk, his feet up, inhaling deeply on a cigarette, snarling back
> at his persecutors. The press liked it, they liked him. He was rarely tactful
> or tactical. Only half trying, you could get out of him a fine, angry
> contempt for all that was contented and Republican. It was an act, but on
> the whole it was a good act. He was sensitive, impressionable, and he
> looked as though he belonged on the other side of the desk with his
> tormentors.[6]

In addition to tormentors, Hopkins had a loyal and devoted staff. Willing
himself to work eighteen hours a day, Hopkins never explicitly demanded
that his assistants work as hard. He took it for granted that they would, and
they did. Even secretaries and clerks put in overtime with never a thought
for extra pay. Hopkins' driving spirit and enthusiasm infected everyone.
Nearly every person who came to work for him admired him almost to the
point of idolatry.

Chief of Hopkins' assistants was the 43-year-old, soft-spoken Aubrey
Williams. In addition to his responsibilities as assistant administrator,
Williams served as legman, maintaining liaison with Congress, Governors,
State relief officials, and other government offices. He had broad experience
in rural relief work, which did much to supplement Harry Hopkins'
background in the cities.

Corrington Gill, the youngest of Hopkins' principal aides, served as chief
statistician and kept up the myriads of records and reports demanded in the
operation of FERA. He came to Hopkins from the Federal Employment
Stabilization Board and welcomed the broader challenge Hopkins offered.

Jacob Baker and Colonel Lawrence Westbrook completed the upper
echelon of FERA. Baker ran the planning for work relief, including checks
on engineering soundness. Westbrook had charge of the rural rehabilitation
program, but he became more and more an idea man in the months ahead.

For the purpose of administering FERA, Hopkins divided the United
States into several districts, each with a manager. Districts contained
regional and local offices to work closely with local authorities. To maintain
connnections with the Washington headquarters, field representatives

traveled constantly, reporting problems by telephone and letter. Each field representative usually came to Washington about once a month.

Under the law, each State had to set up an agency to work with FERA. Thus the States established priorities according to local needs and submitted proposals for approval to national FERA headquarters. Hopkins personally examined each of these proposals with a wary eye for loopholes and subordinate clauses which would allow grafters and politicians to enrich themselves at the expense of the needy.

In Hopkins' view, the largest sums should go to work relief, which provided a man with something useful to do, put money in his pocket, and kept his self-respect. He well knew, as many of his critics did not, that the vast majority of his clients were not lazy, indolent, wastrels, or irresponsibles.

Unfortunately, particularly in the early stages, a good many administrators and social workers believed that because people had fallen on evil times they were incompetent to handle their own affairs. According to this view, they needed tending. Such social workers wanted to give vouchers good only for food and clothing at commissaries. If the persons on relief got money, they might spend it on something foolish.

Hopkins, on the other hand, insisted on payment, in cash, for labor expended on FERA projects. If a laborer wanted to stop in at a bar on the way home for a glass of beer, that was his business. Hopkins had no sympathy for those who deplored a working man having a glass of beer as they sipped a predinner cocktail.

During his first days in Washington, Hopkins was as busy as any man could be, and his family would have seen little of him in any case. He had come prepared for hard work, leaving Barbara and Diana in New York until he could find a place to live, if his job ever gave him the leisure to look. He stayed at the Cosmos Club, which its secretary described to him as having "good library and newspaper facilities, comfortable beds, very reasonable and very good food, and not very good bathroom accommodations."[7] The club, however, did take care of his physical needs while he set about the business of making FERA work.

One of Hopkins' most difficult tasks was to see to it that the States paid their fair share of relief expenditures. Ohio, for example, during the summer refused to put up additional funds, and he bluntly warned that he would make no more federal money available until the legislators came to their senses. "One of the reasons," he told the press, "the Legislature did nothing was that they thought I was bluffing. . . . If the Ohio Legislature decided the unemployed of Ohio are not important to them, I do not see why we should lose any sleep about it here."[8]

A similar fight occurred in Illinois, which was ruled by a Democratic legislature and Governor. Hopkins withheld funds and was backed by President Roosevelt. Governor Henry Horner at length persuaded the legislature to pass a sales tax to raise the money. "We accuse Harry L. Hopkins," the *Chicago News* charged indignantly, "of an attempt to coerce Illinois into doing his will, by provoking hunger and perhaps even violence in this state. . . . We accuse him of a deliberate effort to usurp the constitutional prerogatives of the Illinois legislature in the matter of state taxes."[9]

The *News* did have a point. Certainly Hopkins' actions challenged the concept of States' rights. Through his power of the purse, he did force State action. On the other hand, States' rights have a corollary of States' responsibilities. And the Illinois legislature was neglecting its duties to its own citizens.

If Hopkins spent freely for relief, he was stringent in the costs of operation of FERA. His own staff and FERA officials throughout the nation could purchase no cars or office equipment through relief funds. Any such allowance had to be approved in national headquarters, and approvals were few and far between. Hopkins' own salary was $8,000, down from the $15,000 he had earned before going to work for the government, and a good bit of that was supposed to go to the support of his first wife and his three sons.

Hopkins spent a large amount of time on the road. He and Roosevelt saw this as an essential part of his job. Roosevelt liked to send out trusted observers on the road, since his own job and his handicap prevented him from traveling as much as he would have liked. He taught people like Hopkins how to look at a town or neighborhood: what were the people doing? did they seem sullen or despondent? what was the state of the washing hung out to dry on the clotheslines? were the buildings cared for or neglected?

In August Hopkins visited all the States of the South, observing not only relief activities, but everything else. A few excerpts from his report are noteworthy:

> I have just visited all the States in the South and have talked to the Governor of each State, the N.R.A. Board, Public Works Board, the State Relief Administration, newspaper owners, bankers, planters, farmers, and labor leaders.
> My general observations are as follows:
> 1. The leaders in the South have a profound and abiding confidence in you.
> 2. They believe the Recovery program is going to work.
> 3. The crux of the Recovery program in the South will be found in the price which cotton brings during the next ninety days.

[Hopkins then went on to report in detail on the relief situation.] Relief in the South has been woefully inadequate and it is going to be necessary to almost double it to even give a minimum livelihood. . . . If those Federal projects which are to be authorized could be done so at once, such as the Naval Station at Pensacola—a city in which 35 percent of the entire population is on relief, it would be of inestimable value. . . . There is a tendency which is growing, to discharge Negroes and replace them with white labor.[10]

The South continued to present special problems. For some blacks, relief payments represented more money than they had ever earned in their lives, despite the fact that relief wages ran lower there than anywhere else in the country. A certain Phil Stone grumbled that relief funds "are not needed now and their use are [sic] even harmful. It is impossible to get lots of these people to work at all because plenty of able-bodied people are living off of the relief funds and doing nothing. These relief funds may even prevent the farmers from getting sufficient labor to gather their crops."[11] Hopkins reported to the President:

We sent a questionnaire [which] showed that the planters are having no difficulty whatever in getting workers. . . .

The plain fact of the matter is that a great many of the planters in the South are opposed to the Government's program of increasing wages and are fighting every move to raise the standards of the workers, which have been pitifully low.

As a matter of policy throughout the South, our Relief Administration refuses relief to anyone who is offered a job, even though the wage scale is very low, and refuses it.[12]

Despite Hopkins' efforts, an excessively large proportion of the money available went to direct relief. With winter coming on, the government had to provide the necessities of life, even if the money ran out. If the government bought farm surpluses, they could feed the hungry and help the farmers at the same time.

"We have got to do something about the price of wheat," Roosevelt said on October 16 to Henry Morgenthau, Jr., governor of the Farm Credit Administration. "Can't you buy 25,000,000 bushels for Harry Hopkins and see if you can't put the price up?"[13] Morgenthau for the next few days bought all the wheat offered at the rate of over $1 million a day. A few days later Ickes, Wallace, and Hopkins arranged to buy about $10 million worth of butter.

These commodities and others went to the needy through the Federal

Surplus Relief Corporation, a subsidiary of FERA. These measures relieved
suffering to some extent, but they were never enough.

Hopkins' job brought him into frequent contact with the President.
Roosevelt had a way of getting to know his principal assistants more closely
by inviting them to accompany him on trips to Warm Springs or Hyde Park
or outings on the Presidential yacht. On October 18, Hopkins received an
invitation for a cruise on Chesapeake Bay.

> The White House operator called about one [he recorded] saying that
> the President wanted Mrs. Hopkins and me to spend the week end on the
> "Sequoia" with him and Mrs. Roosevelt. Barbara could not be found on
> the telephone—but fortunately she called in—and we both appeared before
> the new "major domo" at 4:45. The President was ready at 5:30—Mrs.
> Roosevelt took the ladies in the closed car and Vernon [D. Spicer?], Gus
> [Generich, Secret Service men] and I were in the back seat of the
> President's car—moving swiftly thru to Annapolis—Admiral [Thomas] Hart
> on the boat—a slight little man and I fancy ever so dull. The Russian story
> had just "broke" [U.S. recognition of the Soviet Union] and the newspaper
> boys had come along hoping for a follow up but the President having
> already swallowed the "canary" was in a gregarious mood which meant no
> news tho you felt he was busting to tell them the whole story.
>   He had just finished a press conference and had read the correspon-
> dence between himself and Talinin [sic—Mikhail Kalinin, President of the
> U.S.S.R.]—dramatic as ever, he had the doors locked so that none of the
> boys could beat the "gun." He was obviously pleased—the conference had
> gone well—it was real news—how would the press handle it—he read
> everything—it might mean $400,000,000 trade a year which . . .[14] [The
> document, which is written in Hopkins' hand, breaks off at this point. He
> had a way of writing memoranda to himself to recall important occasions
> in his life. Unlike many other members of the Roosevelt administration, he
> did not keep a diary for very long. He began one on January 1, 1935, when
> he was home ill, kept it faithfully for a few days, and then began to neglect
> it. The entries become scattered for a few months and cease altogether in
> the middle of the year.]

As winter approached, it became increasingly clear to Hopkins that
FERA was inadequate. Something more needed to be done if real suffering
on a widespread scale was to be averted. What was needed, he felt, was a
vast work program on projects directed, managed, and paid for by the
federal government, but Hopkins feared it had no chance with Roosevelt,
who was under increasing pressure from conservatives to balance the
budget. Besides, organized labor was strongly against any program of
governmental "made jobs" as offering competition with union workers.

About this time, Hopkins made a swing through the Midwest. Stopping off in Chicago on October 28 to attend a football game with Robert M. Hutchins, president of the University of Chicago, he was waylaid by Frank Bane and Louis Brownlow, director of the Public Administration Clearing House, who had the facts and figures on the proposed program. Hopkins went along, but he still did not see how he could get Roosevelt to agree in face of labor opposition. FDR, Hopkins felt, would put off balancing the budget to avert real suffering, but to buck labor leaders would be political dynamite.

A day or so later, Hopkins was in Kansas City to confer on relief matters with, among others, the Federal Unemployment Director for Missouri, Judge Harry S. Truman. There Williams reached him by telephone to state in great excitement that they had found a precedent for the program, and, better still, it had been devised by the great labor leader, Samuel Gompers, who called it the "day labor plan." Knowing Roosevelt's love of history and his respect for precedent, Hopkins now felt he had the way to convince the President. He immediately telephoned the White House and got a luncheon appointment for the day of his return to Washington.

When Hopkins lunched with FDR, the President asked how many jobs would be needed.

"About four million."

"Let's see. Four million people—that means roughly four hundred million dollars."[15] Roosevelt was thinking of getting through the winter.

And so the Civil Works Administration was born.

Where was the money to come from? There was no chance that Congress would appropriate it in time to do any good. It would have to be found elsewhere. Then Roosevelt had an idea. Secretary of the Interior Harold L. Ickes held unexpended funds of the Public Works Administration.

The Public Works Administration was one of the New Deal measures intended to absorb large numbers of skilled workers in huge projects such as dams, bridges, and buildings, Such projects, naturally, had a long start-up time before any construction could begin, since it was first necessary to plan, make engineering studies, acquire land, frequently by condemnation, and bid and let contracts.

Hopkins and Ickes were eventually to squabble in an unseemly manner over whose agency was to do what, but these squabbles lay in the future. In the beginning Ickes cooperated completely.

> At twelve o'clock [Ickes noted in his diary for November 6, 1933] Secretaries Wallace and Perkins and Harry Hopkins, Emergency Relief Administrator, came in for a conversation by direction of the President. . . . We discussed a plan of Hopkins to put anywhere from two to four million

men back to work for standard wages on a thirty-hour-week basis. He
would continue to pay on account of these wages what he is now
contributing toward relief, and the balance would be made up out of
public works funds. This would amount to a maximum of $400 million for
the next sixty days. This would put a serious crimp in the balance of our
public works fund, but we all thought it ought to be done.[16]

Ickes clearly regarded this raid on PWA funds as a temporary expedient.
CWA was never intended to be a permanent agency of the government,
and on that basis Ickes was willing to cooperate. He was mistaken, however,
for many more times FDR reached into PWA funds to support Hopkins'
programs.

Ickes and Hopkins were an oddly assorted pair. Scrupulously honest in
administration of public money, they had totally different ideas of spending
it. Ickes was meticulous, some even said a fault-finder. It took a long time
for a project to clear his desk, and he wanted everything PWA built to be a
credit to his administration. In the long run, Ickes knew his projects would
pay off. Coulee Dam and the Triborough Bridge in New York City are
prime examples of the accomplishments of PWA.

Hopkins, sardonic and sometimes slapdash in his administration, had no
time for such measured steps. The projects undertaken by CWA were
supposed to be useful, and largely they were, but they had to be planned
and undertaken in a hurry. At the time of the meeting with Ickes, he had set
himself the goal of getting two million persons to work in about ten days
and an equal number more in another two weeks. One day a staff member
came in with an elaborate plan which would have taken a long time to start
up. He made the mistake of saying that the plan would "work out in the
long run."

"People don't eat in the long run," snapped Hopkins. "They eat every
day."[17]

CWA officially came into being on November 9, 1933, by Executive
Order. Originally the plan specified that half the workers come from relief
rolls and half from the labor market. This ratio went by the board in the
rush to get projects started. Some required more skilled labor than others,
and these naturally depended less on the manpower furnished by the relief
office. Others, such as road grading and ditch digging, required large
numbers of unskilled workers and few technicians.

Hopkins failed to meet his quota of hiring two million in ten days. But
his achievement was remarkable. At the end of the first two weeks, over
800,000 workers drew pay checks. A fortnight later, 1,976,625 people were
actually at work, and on January 18, 1934, the high point of CWA,
4,263,644 men and women were on the job.

All in all, Hopkins took pride in the CWA program. It provided jobs and paychecks, but, more important, it returned self-respect to the people who worked for it. As he put it in his only book, *Spending to Save:*

> I should like to clarify here the difference between work relief and a job on a work program such as CWA and WPA. To the man on relief the difference is very real. On work relief, although he gets the disciplinary rewards of keeping fit, and of making a return for what he gets, his need is still determined by a social worker, and he feels himself to be something of a public ward, with small freedom of choice. When he gets a job on a work program, it is very different. He is paid wages and the social worker drops out of the picture. His wages may not cover much more ground than his former relief budget but they are his to spend as he likes. . . . The wife of the WPA worker tossed her head and said. "We aren't on relief any more, my husband is working for the Government."[18]

"Working for the government" occupied millions of citizens as the dreadful winter of 1933-34 set in. It dropped below zero in Washington and Congressmen, muffled up to the eyes as they dashed from cars or taxis or streetcars to their offices, were constantly reminded of the sufferings of those without jobs and questionable shelter. In the mountain states the temperature dropped into the minus fifties.

In face of the desperate emergency, CWA approved projects right and left. Roosevelt's enemies seized on a few ill-conceived ones as examples of waste, corruption, the spoils system at work, and downright inefficiency. These charges and others started a lively debate over CWA and FERA and relief in general. Hopkins stood firm.

"Hunger is not debatable," he insisted.[19]

The President, obviously, had to have an impartial observer to let him know how CWA was working in the country. Although he trusted Hopkins, he did not as yet know him well enough to be sure he would not go wild and produce an impossible political situation. The outcries of CWA critics were bad enough. Were they justified?

Roosevelt found such an observer in Frank Walker, a friend of long standing. He was president of the National Emergency Council, a watchdog organization which kept an eye on all the emergency New Deal agencies. One of Walker's greatest assets was that everyone liked and trusted him. In addition, he understood and sympathized with the objectives of the administration's program. He was to become an essential link between the regular Democratic politicians and the New Dealers, for he had friends in both camps. He would later succeed Big Jim Farley as Postmaster General when Farley "took a walk" in 1940.

Walker's position in the middle was crucial. If Roosevelt's program was to work, and if he was to have any hope of reelection in 1936, he needed the cooperation of the regular Democratic leaders, many of whom were highly suspicious of the Brain Trusters and New Dealers who had flocked into Washington. He also needed the ideas, energy, and innovativeness of those same Brain Trusters and New Dealers, many of whom cared little for politics and politicians. Farley, for example, tended to judge all of Roosevelt's programs in terms of their political impact, and he had grave reservations about FERA and CWA. Hopkins, on the other hand, was a political ignoramus at that time and subordinated everything to doing his job. In Walker, Roosevelt had a man who could understand both considerations.

Walker took a long trip across the country and talked to politicians and to FERA and CWA officials. He went out to the job projects and talked to the workers. In Montana, he reported:

> I saw old friends of mine, men I had been to school with—digging ditches and laying sewer pipe. They were wearing their regular business suits as they worked because they couldn't afford overalls and rubber boots. If ever I thought, "There, but for the Grace of God—" it was right then. [But his shock went away when he heard these men. One of them pulled a few coins out of his pocket and said] "Do you know, Frank, this is the first money I've had in my pockets in a year and a half? Up to now, I've had nothing but tickets that you could exchange for groceries."

When Walker returned to Washington, he reported to FDR:

> I'd pay little attention to those who criticize the creation of C.W.A. or its administration. Hopkins and his associates are doing their work well. They've done a magnificent job. It is amazing when you consider that within the short time since C.W.A. was established four million idle have been put to work. During Christmas week many of them were standing in a payroll line for the first time in eighteen months. You have every reason to be proud of C.W.A. and its administration. It is my considered opinion that this has averted one of the most serious crises in our history. Revolution is an ugly word to use, but I think we were dangerously close at least to the threat of it.[20]

Walker's report could not have failed to strengthen Hopkins in Roosevelt's esteem. From then on the two men grew ever closer in respect and in friendship. At first Hopkins had been more the friend of Mrs. Roosevelt than of the President. Their common concern for suffering, their interest and activity in social problems had drawn them together. Early invitations to the White House usually came from Eleanor Roosevelt. But as the New

Year arrived Hopkins' relationship to Franklin Roosevelt began to change from government official to friend.

Despite its temporary nature, CWA achieved such a success that Hopkins hoped it might evolve into a regular program. But by late 1933 FDR had reverted to one of his budget-balancing phases and was listening to the arguments of his ultraconservative Director of the Budget, Lewis Douglas. "Douglas' job," said Roosevelt at a press conference in December, "is to prevent the Government from spending just as hard as he possibly can. That is his job. Somewhere between his efforts to spend nothing . . . and the point of view of the people who want to spend ten billions additional on public works, we will get somewhere, and we are trying to work out a program."[21]

Although disappointed, Hopkins set about winding down the CWA program. But first, he had to get more money from the Congress in order to get through the winter. The initial $400 million went fast, and he requested $950 million more, approximately half to be spent to taper off the CWA projects and the other half for direct relief. At a meeting of the CWA/FERA staff on December 6, he announced, "It is humanly impossible for anybody to inject any chance of permanence in this thing. If we get action from Congress right away, it will be on a basis of an emergency proposition which will see us through this Winter."[22]

Hopkins, while loyally following the President, felt in his heart that the program should continue. Where others, such as Ickes, who was known as "the great resigner," would have threatened to walk out, Hopkins doggedly went on carrying out the duties according to his understanding of the President's desires. He would not listen to suggestions from his staff that he refuse to cooperate. He sometimes had to be harsh, but he did what he had to do.

By this time, others had taken up the cry for some kind of a work program as opposed to direct relief. Even *Fortune,* spokesman for business, noted, "Direct relief is—purely and simply—the Dole. Almost as purely and simply, work relief is the Dole, too, except that it does provide a little more self respect for its recipients: at least it creates for them the fiction that they are still useful citizens and that there is work for them to do."[23]

This was scarcely an unmixed approbation of CWA, yet in the same issue, *Fortune* carried a story of how CWA took 250,000 bales of surplus cotton and set women to work making mattresses to be distributed to the poor who had none. Naturally the mattress manufacturers thundered about unfair competition, but they subsided when it was pointed out to them that there was small profit in selling items at zero dollars and cents.

Despite its real accomplishments, CWA expired, and FERA took up the burden once again. One CWA program continued: the Federal Arts

Program, which gave employment to writers, artists, sculptors, musicians, and scholars. This phase of the relief activity drew more howls and invective than almost anything else. It seemed that the critics feared ideas, that they wanted to compel artists to work on house painting, sculptors on street paving, and the rest on anything physical that would prevent their ideas from coming to light. Their work was "Un-American," "subversive," "decadent." These charges would be heard again when the Federal Arts Program was expanded under the Works Progress Administration.

It was good journalistic fun to dig through the list of Federal Arts Program projects for the esoteric, the odd, and the farcical. One such project discovered in New York City was a study of ancient safety pins. At a press conference, Hopkins was challenged to justify that one:

> Why should I? There is nothing the matter with that. They are damn good projects—excellent projects. That goes for all the projects up there. You know some people make fun of people who speak a foreign language, and dumb people criticize something they do not understand, and that is what is going on up there—God damn it! Here are a lot of people broke and we are putting them to work making researches of one kind or another, running big recreational projects where the whole material costs 3%, and practically all the money goes for relief. As soon as you begin doing anything for white collar people, there is a certain group of people who begin to throw bricks. I have no apologies to make. As a matter of fact, we have not done enough. . . . You may be interested in washing machines—somebody else in safety pins. Every one of those is under the direction of competent research people. You can make fun of anything; that is easy to do.[24]

The staccato sentences, the informality, the stout defense of his program and his people are all characteristic. Another man confronted with the "safety pins" might have told the press that the program was being investigated, that it had been terminated, that its instigators were being admonished, or any of the other smooth phrases common to Washington bureaucrats. Not Hopkins. That project and others like it were "damn good projects."

Such frankness and openness made Hopkins generally popular with the working reporters (as contrasted with their publishers who struck at him in order to hit the President). But on this occasion, there was a reporter less scrupulous than the others, and for the sake of a good story he wrote that Hopkins had said, "The people are too damned dumb." The phrase caught on as part of folklore of Hopkinsiana, and was hurled in his face innumerable times by editorial writers and radio commentators. It would not be the last time that Hopkins' enemies saddled him with something he had not said.

They struck at Hopkins' arrogance because they could not hit his financial administration. Every time CWA and later WPA was accused of financial peculation it would be traced to local fast footwork on the part of political appointees selected by someone on the State, county, or city level. An example is given in a report of one of his field representatives, Lorena Hickok, a woman whose outspoken bluntness matched Hopkins' own. Writing from Houston in April, 1934, on FERA matters, where federal assistance depended on matching what the States raised, she reported:

> Texas is a Godawful mess. As you know, they're having a big political fight in Austin. . . . And in the meantime—God help the unemployed. . . . I lunched with the committee, composed of businessmen, today. . . . According to their story, there's been nothing but delay, confusion, and politics—politics first, last, and always—in Austin for months. . . . Oh, everything is all messed up.[25]

Since time immemorial, political patronage has been a way of life, and Hopkins was doing his best to buck that system. As a result he had to be ridiculed, and if possible, destroyed.

The task of running FERA and CWA simultaneously and facing an unfriendly press began to get Hopkins down. Roosevelt noticed his strain and tried to help out. One Sunday in May, Hopkins accompanied FDR and others for a day-long cruise on the Potomac aboard the *Sequoia,* but such brief intervals were not enough. He was bone-tired, and the problems were multiplying.

Roosevelt, who believed to his life's end that a sea voyage would cure anything, decided to send Hopkins to Europe on an investigative job which would justify using government funds for his passage but which would be simple enough to give him a rest. FDR reckoned without his man, for Hopkins took his assignment seriously and got little rest for most of the trip. As he remarked in a letter to the President: "I have spent the past two or three weeks taking a look at housing and social insurance in England, Germany, Austria, and Rome. It hardly comes under the head of a vacation, and so Barbara and I are going to Sorrento this afternoon for two weeks' holiday."[26]

With few exceptions, Hopkins wrote very poor personal letters. Many of them read like form letters, and some undoubtedly were. On one occasion, he even signed a letter to his brother Lewis, "Very sincerely yours," but that may have been the fault of his secretary. One revealing letter to Lewis was written just before Hopkins' departure:

> I am planning to sail for Europe on Wednesday the 4th [of July] unless something interferes at the last moment. This, of course, is always possible around here. I can scarcely realize that I have been with the Government now for a year. I had no intention of remaining longer than that but I seem to be well on my way to stay through next winter anyway. I think you know, one of the great difficulties about this place is what to use for money. . . .
>
> The other side of the picture is that this has been a fascinating experience. It is worth any amount of money to have a ringside seat at this show. I have learned enough about it to know that one should not bank too heavily on anything here for more than a few months at a time. While the work is fascinating and the President is a grand person to work for I have no desire to stay here indefinitely.
>
> My immediate plans take me to England first and later to Germany, Austria and Italy to take a look at their housing programs and social insurance. By scraping bottom I can take Barbara with me and life is far too short to leave her behind. The baby is going to New Hampshire to be with some good friends of ours.[27]

Hopkins sailed on the SS *Washington* on July 4, 1934, armed with a letter of authorization from the President and letters of introduction from the Department of State to various officials, including Hitler and Mussolini. Additionally, FDR told him to have a look at the American embassies in the various capitals, for he suspected that some of the foreign service officers were less than sympathetic to the aims of the administration. So Hopkins began the first of his many confidential missions for Roosevelt.

In Britain Hopkins received a warm welcome. He noted that in such matters as social security and public housing, even the Conservative Party was well ahead of the New Deal.

While Hopkins was abroad, a drought which had been plaguing farmers in the United States intensified and the relief rolls swelled. He offered to return to help meet the emergency, for he could not bear to be left out of things. In Vienna, however, he received a message sent through diplomatic channels:

> From McIntyre. After consulting Steve[,] Perkins et al, see no reason you should interrupt vacation. Will keep you advised any emergency. William[s] doing fine job. Regards you and Mrs.[28]

Aubrey Williams was, it seems, judging from the frequent cables he sent

Hopkins, doing a fine or at least active job. Strikes added to the difficulties of the drought and the spreading relief rolls. McIntyre told Cordell Hull, the Secretary of State, "Williams acts in situations just like Harry Hopkins."[29]

Indeed, Williams did seem like Hopkins in action. He bought 9 million pounds of cheese and asked Harry for authorization to purchase 50 million pounds of rice. He moved FERA personnel around to meet emergencies. Hopkins may have been in Europe, but he was nearly as well informed as he would have been at his desk in the Walker-Johnson Building.

During the summer, Hitler made his moves for absolute power. Ernst Roehm and other possible Nazi rivals were murdered in the notorious "night of the long knives" in June, and while Hopkins was abroad Chancellor Engelbert Dollfuss of Austria was assassinated by Austrian Nazis. Mussolini moved troops to the Brenner Pass to discourage a possible German takeover of Austria.

A few days before the assassination of Dollfuss, and just after a belligerent speech by Hitler, Hopkins had an appointment with Mussolini. He wrote two accounts of his meeting, one apparently for possible publication or as an *aide-mémoire* for a report to Roosevelt. The second account, in his own hand, reveals his incisive ability to summarize a scene and a mood.

> My appointment to see Mussolini was for 7:15 at the Palazzo Venezia on Friday July 19. [Sic—the appointment was on Friday, July 20.] The letter from the secretary is presented at the gate—it is satisfactory—arms flash the Fascist salute—and a guard precedes me up the dark inner stairway of the old square palace of the Venetian ambassadors, which is the working office of "Il Duce." Your introduction is examined again and for the third time—and I am in a small reception room—green tile—walls dark & fine old pictures—a glass case in one corner filled with Venetian pottery.
>
> A widow in deep mourning was waiting—with a basket of flowers—nervously handling some letters—no sooner had I begun to wonder what she might desire from Mussolini than the guard—this time in civilian clothes came for me. He preceded me thru three rooms the last with a great horseshoe table where the Fascist Grand Council sits and opened the door into the great office.
>
> The Duce's desk is directly ahead—miles away—very small—but he came striding forward half way across the great room before I was scarcely in the door. A gray—rather flashy suit, light blue tie—soft shirt—and a broad smile, a firm handshake and he strides back with you to the long desk. He sits facing the great room—and motioned me to one of the two chairs on the opposite side of the desk.
>
> Mussolini talks with his eyes and his hands—his gray eyes grow enormously big—like monkeys—they flash—roll in the most amazing

fashion. His hands and arms move constantly but when deeply interested or asking an important question—he places his elbows on the table—head in his hands—and darts questions and answers like sharp knives. His smile changes like a flash—every thot seems to be expressed in his features. He is an actor—and controls his emotions like styles in an opera—I fancy he could pretend great anger or pleasure with great effect. But he has the jaw of a strong man and a personality of great fervor.

I had come to see him about public works and housing but when he learned that I had just been to Berlin—it was perfectly clear that he wished to talk of Germany—and one important element is Mussolini's relationship to Hitler. I had heard previously that he did not like Hitler and had taken the measure of the man at Venice 2 months ago but I was not prepared for the contempt which he expressed of Hitler's murders and his stupidity. He wanted to know how long I thot the gov't would stand—what the next move would be—the attitude of the people—how many were killed—the Austrian reaction—what did I think of Hitler's speech—how was it received by the foreign colony—Berlin.[30]

Hopkins and his wife Barbara sailed from Le Havre, again on the SS *Washington,* on August 16, arriving in New York August 23 and in Washington the next day. Roosevelt, himself, had just returned to Washington from a 10,000-mile cruise on the USS *Houston* through the Caribbean, the Panama Canal, to Cocos Island and Hawaii and back to Portland, Oregon. The two men lunched together at the White House on Saturday, August 25, but who talked more about his travels is unclear.

The following weekend, Harry and Barbara Hopkins drove to Hyde Park, accompanied by Rex and Florence Tugwell. Barbara Hopkins kept notes on sheets of Hyde Park stationery. They enjoyed cocktails with "President in his den office before dinner—movies (news reel & British Agent) at 10."[31] The visit included a clambake at the Morgenthau homestead and a great deal of good conversation. It was just the kind of relaxed home life the President enjoyed, surrounded by friends, and it marked the first time the Hopkins family had been included.

But there was small chance for such relaxation. It was a Congressional election year, and at the same time, Hopkins was determined to make a move to end the FERA approach to relief and turn to one based on the CWA experience of federal work projects. The time was ripe, he felt, and the President more sympathetic than ever before. It would all depend on whether the voters approved or repudiated the New Deal at the polls on November 6.

CHAPTER THREE

Works Progress Administrator

Harry Hopkins knew he was playing with political dynamite in proposing a permanent work relief program. In a few months voters would go to the polls in the first plebiscite on the New Deal.

Roosevelt could no longer command automatic support from Democratic members of Congress. The sense of national emergency had passed. The national income had risen twenty percent since he had taken office, and the politicians who had clung to his coattails and approved his programs began to assert themselves. Conservatives in the party had never liked Roosevelt and would have been happy to see him repudiated at the polls. And, of course, most Republicans looked upon him as inspired by the devil.

> It is difficult today [Frank Kent grumbled] to name any outstanding Democratic leader of the pre-New Deal period who is in sympathy with the Roosevelt policy. ... Except in the most perfunctory manner, none of them have been consulted by the President. Most of them have been completely ignored. Yet until two years ago, they were the most conspicuous and respected leaders of the party.[1]

The American Liberty League, an organization formed to fight New Deal measures, and made up of conservatives in both parties, led the pack against Roosevelt. While they found most New Deal ideas offensive, most of all they hated the very thought of relief spending. That meant they hated Harry Hopkins who persuaded Roosevelt to waste and waste and waste.

Under such programs—it mattered not whether FERA or CWA—

Americans paid huge taxes which were stripped from those who had "undergone self-sacrifice to attain" their hard-earned dollars "and bestowed upon those who have never developed the qualities to possess themselves of rewards."[2] This, of course, reflected the old Puritan ethic that only the incompetent or lazy could not find work. Even as manufacturers laid off workers they saw no connection between their actions and the rising numbers of unemployed.

One member of the Du Pont family complained that

> ... five negroes on my place in South Carolina refused work this spring, after I had taken care of them and given them a house rent free and work for three years during bad times, saying they had easy jobs with the Government. ... A cook on my houseboat at Fort Myer quit because the Government was paying him a dollar an hour as a painter.[3]

It did not seem to occur to this gentleman that he could have retained the services of the five Negroes and the cook if only he had been willing to pay adequate wages.

Since Hopkins and his henchmen were responsible for such behavior on the part of working men, he had to go.

One attack, typical of many, took place in the summer of 1934. Ray Branion, head of CWA in California, called from Los Angeles on June 21 to report that he and his assistant, Pierce Williams, had been indicted for "conspiracy to defraud the Government in allowing certain projects to have people put on the payroll without materials and equipment with which to work."[4] Apparently Branion had put the wrong people on the payroll. The California organization wanted to make sure that the people hired were good Democrats. Branion had carried out Hopkins' standing orders to hire workers without regard for political affiliation.

Never one to abandon his men, Hopkins wrote Attorney General Cummings:

> He [Branion] has been one of the best workers we have had in the whole field, and he and our own group feel that we are letting him down badly in the face of the jam which he is in. ...
> The President, at the same time, indicated that he wished that the indictments would be quashed in the immediate future. ... I think you should also know that the pendency of these indictments is creating a feeling of disturbing uneasiness on the part of relief workers throughout the United States that is becoming distinctly embarrassing to me. ...[5]

A few days after the election, when the case had served its political purpose, the Assistant Attorney General of California dropped all charges.

A telegram from Pierce Williams concluded, "Please convey our appreciation to Hopkins and those others close to you who have so chivalrously supported us."[6]

The strident voices of big business and of conservatives did their cause a disservice. The administration was vulnerable on many things. Excessive bureaucracy, hasty action, and inefficiency spring to mind at once. But the New Deal did offer action. To most people, FDR and his associates seemed to be trying. "I don't expect to make a hit every time I go to bat,"[7] remarked Roosevelt, but he did expect to be right about three-quarters of the time.

Despite favorable signs on the forthcoming election, New Dealers suffered pre-November jitters and urged FDR to take the campaign trail. He refused, preferring to give the nation the picture of a busy President who spent his time in running the country rather than in politicking. While Hopkins was at Hyde Park over the Labor Day weekend, FDR asked him to help write one or two radio speeches. Roosevelt wanted, as Hopkins recorded, "to clear up some misconceptions about his program which he believes are deliberately spread by the Tory Press and secondly to get what amounts to a mandate from the people to move the legislation which he is planning to introduce in the next Congress."[8]

On Friday evening, September 23, Hopkins went to the White House to help prepare the speech FDR was to deliver Sunday night. It was Hopkins' first experience in speech writing, a job he was to do from then on. On arrival he found that Henry Morgenthau, now Secretary of the Treasury, was there as well as Brain Truster Raymond Moley.

> Although I knew Moley was still close to the President, I was a bit surprised [wrote Hopkins] to learn of his presence at this time. Later I learned from Moley that he had helped the President in all his speeches and had his finger in the Green Bay speech this summer which upset the Wall St. boys no end. I remembered too that Moley had told me a few weeks ago that he thot the President's next speech should move to the "right." I imagine that he had told this to the President so that my invitation may be in order to bring out the appropriate "leftist" approach with which I was identified.
>
> The President asked us to dine which we did—Louis Howe was there— also the President's secretaries Miss LeHand and Miss Tully. As ever the conversation was light—gay but the thrusts tho kindly enough were pretty direct and spared no one.
>
> After dinner I noticed Louis Howe was not asked to join us. It may have been because he is not well—tho I rather think the President does not depend on him as much as formerly.[9]

Louis Howe, of course, was Roosevelt's trusted friend and confidant, having been with him since he started in politics. He was a little gnome of a man, utterly devoted to FDR. His only ambition had been to see that Roosevelt became President. He was the one man FDR could talk to openly because Howe had absolutely no ambitions of his own. He was one of the few outside the family who continued to address the President as Franklin. Even Hopkins in the intimacy of later years never failed to speak to him as Mr. President. The principal difference between the two men in their closeness of friendship with FDR was that Howe believed in Roosevelt the person and had little interest in policies or programs. Hopkins believed passionately in solving the problem at hand, whether in depression or war. He believed that Roosevelt was the one man who might get these things done. Howe was a political pragmatist; Hopkins a pragmatist of action. Both men were utterly devoted to FDR and both wore themselves out in his service.

> The four of us went to the oval room upstairs—the President with his face to the door—the ever present scissors on a table at his right with which he carefully cuts the stamps from the mail sent by the State Department. All of their envelopes are sent to him.
>
> It was perfectly clear that the President did not know what he was going to talk about and was greatly amused at my telling him of a New York business man who had told me that he had seen the manuscript. He asked Moley if had [sic]—and Moley promptly pulled a manuscript from his pocket—and the conversation indicated that he had earlier asked Moley to prepare something or knew that he was doing so. I think the latter was the case.
>
> The President then read it aloud—Missy was curled up on the couch— and said "the first five pages are spinach," with which sentiment Morgenthau and I agreed. This started the conversation as to what the speech should be about anyway and everyone agreed with the President that he couldn't cover too many subjects and that it better be confined to a talk on industry. . . .
>
> I suggested two ideas—one to take a final shot at price fixing and the other to get over the idea of the importance of a weekly or monthly income for labor rather than the fictitious hourly rate. I pressed as hard as I could for an economy of abundance in America rather than one of scarcity which has characterized the New Deal up to the present. [Hugh] Johnson had sold the President the notion that high prices in themselves will bring recovery.[10]

By this time, Hopkins had accepted the idea that government spending for work projects would stimulate the economy; and that as the workers spent their earnings, manufacturers and farmers would have to produce more to meet their demands, thus giving rise to employment. The idea was not original with Hopkins; "priming the pump" was a New Deal slogan. Still ambivalent, Roosevelt listened alternately to the balancers and the spenders.

Meanwhile the campaign went on. Businessmen and bankers kept on asking Roosevelt to say something encouraging to business. Roosevelt, however, preferred to build the confidence of the people as a whole. He asked the bankers and industrialists for specific suggestions, but they had none, other than reducing government spending and relaxation of controls. "One of my principal tasks," Roosevelt wrote wryly, "is to prevent bankers and businessmen from committing suicide!"[11]

Just before the election on November 6, Jim Farley forecast a Democratic victory in terms FDR thought wildly optimistic. But when the returns were counted, Roosevelt had his mandate. In the Senate such die-hard Republicans as David A. Reed of Pennsylvania, Arthur R. Robinson of Indiana, Simeon D. Fess of Ohio, and Roscoe C. Patterson of Missouri went down to defeat. A Pendergast man, Judge Harry S. Truman, ousted Patterson. In the House, the Democrats gained nine seats for a total of 322. Roosevelt, remarked William Allen White, "has all but been crowned by the people."[12]

A few days after the election, while driving with Aubrey Williams and others to the racetrack at Laurel, Maryland, Hopkins suddenly said: "Boys—this is our hour. We've got to get everything we want—a works program, social security, wages and hours, everything—now or never. Get your minds to work on developing a complete ticket to provide security for all the folks of this country up and down and across the board."[13]

In a few days he had a plan. He took it to Harold Ickes for suggestions, then two days before Thanksgiving, set off for the South with the program in his briefcase. He stopped off in South Carolina to show it to Senator James F. Byrnes and then continued to Warm Springs, where Roosevelt was "recharging his batteries."

There he found several friends, including Rex Tugwell and Donald Richberg, who had taken Frank Walker's place as executive director of the National Emergency Council. They worked, but they enjoyed themselves, too, spending a good bit of time in the swimming pool, tossing a ball back and forth and inspiring a reporter watching from a nearby hill to remark, "They seem to be practicing passing the buck."[14]

It might be fair to say that Hopkins planned "to pass the buck," but not in the sense the reporter meant. Tentatively entitled a Plan to End Poverty in America, his proposal called for large government spending on various projects to put people to work and so "pass the bucks" around.

The next day the *New York Times* commented:

> The fire-eating Administrator of Federal Emergency Relief, Harry L. Hopkins, may safely be credited with spoiling the Thanksgiving Day dinners of many conservatives who had been led to believe that President Roosevelt's recent zig to the right would not be followed by a zag to the left.
>
> Not that Mr. Hopkins had any idea that his EPIA (End Proverty in America) plan would leak out unauthorized, but now that it has leaked out it will bear examination.
>
> From the fragmentary advices in Washington, what Mr. Hopkins proposes to the President is about as follows:
>
> An expansion of the subsistence homesteads and rural rehabilitation programs to include as many families as need such accommodations or are in a position to accept them.
>
> A large-scale removal of families from submarginal (unprofitable) land to home sites where they can live on a more civilized scale.
>
> Federal advances of funds to both categories to equip their homesteads with tools, live stock, etc.
>
> An expansion of the program already in progress on an experimental scale to give factory work to the idle, through what the FERA softly calls "canning centres," "needlecraft centres," or the like.
>
> A large-scale, low-cost housing program to shelter those unable for one reason or another to move to subsistence homesteads, since it appears there is no purpose entirely to depopulate the large cities.
>
> A social insurance program to give security in the future.[15]

On January 4, 1935, FDR delivered his annual State of the Union Message to the Congress. A good bit of it presented the new relief plan. Hopkins, who was home sick with the flu, listened intently. "I thot it was a good speech," he noted in his diary, "and particularly because I had worked on it with him. . . . It was the first time any Pres. has ever put any body into a program for the people. Fortunately he means all that he says and more."[16]

The President's proposal was to return responsibility for relief of the unemployable—the ill, the elderly, the widows with children, the crippled, the handicapped—to the States, and to establish a vast federal program of work relief, somewhat along the lines of the CWA, but to operate on a continuing basis.

> The Federal Government must and shall quit this business of relief. . . .
> Work must be found for able-bodied but destitute workers. . . .
> I am not willing that the vitality of our people be further sapped by the

giving of cash, of market baskets, of a few hours of weekly work cutting grass, raking leaves or picking up papers in the public parks. We must preserve not only the bodies of the unemployed from destruction but also their self-respect, their self-reliance and courage and determination. This decision brings me to the problem of what the Government should do about approximately five million unemployed now on relief rolls.

It is my thought that with the exception of certain of the normal public building operations of the Government, all emergency public works shall be united in a single new and greatly enlarged plan.

With the establishment of this new system we can supersede the Federal Emergency Relief Administration with a coordinated authority which will be charged with the orderly liquidation of our present relief activities and the substitution of a national chart for the giving of work.

Ickes, apparently unaware that Hopkins had helped write the speech, recorded his pleasure that Harry had been distinctly unhappy at the slur toward CWA in the reference to "cutting grass, raking leaves or picking up papers." Even as the President spoke, Ickes began planning how he could get control of the proposed organization. Hopkins, well satisfied, kept his own counsel.

As guidelines, Roosevelt laid down six basic requirements for public work relief.

(1) The projects should be useful.

(2) Projects shall be of a nature that a considerable proportion of the money spent will go into wages for labor.

(3) Projects which promise ultimate return to the Federal Treasury of a considerable proportion of the costs will be sought.

(4) Funds allotted for each project should be actually and promptly spent and not held over until later years.

(5) In all cases projects must be of a character to give employment to those on the relief rolls.

(6) Projects will be allocated to localities or relief areas in relation to the number of workers on relief rolls in those areas.

To fund the new program, the President requested $4 billion dollars plus $880 million to continue existing relief programs during the changeover. This was promptly dubbed by the newspapers the "four point eight" program, and so it was known not only in the press but also in government circles.

Roosevelt kept one thing strictly to himself: who was to administer the program. The two obvious candidates were Ickes and Hopkins. But Hopkins offended the old guard in the Senate, while Ickes, with his stern rectitude and his slowness to act, found little favor in the House. If FDR had named either of them as his choice, the legislation might well have died in one house or the other. He therefore said nothing.

The Work Relief Bill passed the House easily enough in a few days, but the Senate was another story. The "four point eight" bill struck at the heart of the politician. Why should Congress vote such a vast sum of money to the President with no strings attached when the same sum offered such a magnificent opportunity for pork barrel and patronage?

While debate continued in the Senate, both Hopkins and Ickes began maneuvering for the post of director. On January 7, Hopkins' diary notes, "Raining—too miserable to go to office."[17] That afternoon, Ickes called in the guise of visiting the sick, but really to put his two schemes up to Hopkins. The first proposed a new Cabinet position with Hopkins as Secretary of Relief, a kind of forerunner of the Department of Health, Education and Welfare. Ickes cannot have been serious about this proposal. Congress would have had to create the new post and then confirm Hopkins as Secretary. Neither would stand a chance on Capitol Hill.

Ickes' second suggestion put Hopkins under him as deputy administrator of public works with the responsibility for everything that Ickes did not care to handle—that is, grubby relief matters and petty projects, and not the splendid monuments like dams and bridges that gave Ickes so much cause for pride. Ickes concluded his notes on the meeting: "It seemed clear to me that Hopkins took very much to the first suggestion and I think he would not be averse to the second one."[18]

Hopkins' diary gives a different impression.

> Ickes came out at two—worried about who was going to run the new works program—he has heard all kinds of rumors and came to suggest that I be his deputy—said new cabinet position should be created for me—that he would resign if President asked any one else to administer the job. He thinks Pres. has treated him badly on one or two things—feels sure Mrs. Roosevelt is after him—I told him that administration was up to Pres & I was making no suggestions.[19]

Hopkins and Ickes both testified before the Senate Appropriations Committee. Hopkins noted:

> The hearing was dull enough but for Senator Glass—the poor old fellow is of course opposed to the whole business. Why should this delightful gentleman who hasn't had a liberal thot in his life have anything to say as to what America is to be in the future. But the Senate is full of them tho much dumber.[20]

Meanwhile, the work of FERA had to go on. Some of the Governors who had come into office in the elections of 1934 had a try at getting control of relief in their States, including federal funds supplied by FERA. The most famous attempt was that of Governor Martin L. Davey of Ohio, who had squeaked into office on the Democratic ticket even though he was opposed by the party regulars.

Perhaps feeling the investigators closing in, Davey wrote Hopkins on March 4, 1935, proposing that the federal government take over all relief activities in Ohio. Blaming the relief administration in that State as "very wasteful and inefficient," he went on to say that he could "not in good conscience ask the Legislature to force upon the people of Ohio an additional tax burden as long as they know that there is so much waste in the present relief program. . . ."[21] In other words, Davey refused to come up with the matching funds the law required for FERA participation. Let the federal government do the whole thing. This was outright defiance, and Hopkins replied sternly:

> I have noted your statement that you do not intend to ask the Legislature for additional funds to meet Ohio's fair share of the relief problem in your State. I cannot believe that this represents the desires of the people of Ohio, and I am sure they wish to contribute their reasonable part toward the cost of the needs of the unemployed.
>
> I want to repeat that federal relief funds will be forthcoming only upon the condition that Ohio meets its reasonable proportion of the cost of relief.[22]

A few days later Hopkins had evidence that Ohio politicians had extorted contributions from suppliers of relief goods to make up the deficit of Davey's campaign.

> The evidence is complete in Ohio, [he noted in his diary] the political boys went too far this trip and I shall take great delight in giving them the "works." Took the evidence to the President this morning—he wanted to get into the scrap and asked me to prepare a letter for him to sign to me—instructing me to take over the state. He later signed it and approved one of my own [to Governor Davey] which was pretty hot. The President doesn't take a week to decide things like this nor does he need the advice of politicians—in fact no one was consulted about an action which will throw into the ash can a Democratic Governor and his political machine. In fact I think the boss liked the idea of their being Democrats.[23]

Roosevelt toned down the "pretty hot" letter to Governor Davey slightly, deleting such phrases as "do the dirty work" and "slush fund," but the result was dramatic and unexpected. Davey filed charges of criminal libel, quoting the entire letter in his affidavit. He threatened to have Hopkins arrested if he set foot in Ohio. Highly amused, FDR kept asking Hopkins if he wanted a Presidential pardon.

Meanwhile the relief bill was still being hotly debated in the Senate. Conservatives of both parties were struggling for a dole, with the delighted Republicans doing their bit to keep open the split in the Democratic ranks. Senator Vandenberg of Michigan stated that he agreed with a columnist who had written that the Congress should strike out all after the preamble to the bill and substitute two brief sections:

Section 1. Congress hereby appropriates $4,880,000,000 to the President of the United States to use as he pleases.

Section 2. Anybody who does not like it is fined $1,000.[24]

Since it was obvious that some kind of works program would get through the Congress, the question of who would run it increased in importance. The rivalry between Hopkins and Ickes intensified into a considerable feud, although both sides observed the amenities. Ickes made the serious mistake of believing he could outmaneuver Hopkins. He lobbied with his friends in the Senate, noting happily that Vice President Garner was

> ...very bitter against Hopkins and he said it would be absolutely suicidal if Hopkins should have the administration of this bill.... He spoke very cordially about my administration of Public Works.... Contrasted with this, he said that Hopkins' administration of FERA was almost an open scandal and that if there should be an investigation, they would hardly find a sound apple in the barrel.[25]

That morning of March 27 the newspapers had carried a story to the effect that Hopkins would be the administrator of the "four point eight." Roosevelt had just sailed from Jacksonville for a cruise on the *Nourmahal* but had not talked to reporters. Hopkins went as far as Georgia on the Presidential train, and that fact probably gave rise to the story. According to Marvin McIntyre, who was with the President, it originated, with a Washington dateline, in the Jacksonville newspapers. In Washington, Steve Early knew nothing about the matter and was ill prepared to face a grim and angry Secretary Ickes who stormed into his office demanding an explanation. Since Early had none, he could give Ickes little satisfaction. He did, however, announce to the press "that the President himself will pass personally on allotments and will act as chairman of the allotment board."[26]

While Ickes lobbied in the Senate, Hopkins made his efforts where they counted—with the President. Some ten days earlier he had recorded a meeting with FDR in his diary: "We went over the organization of the work program. More charts in pencil—he loves charts—no two of them are ever the same which is a bit baffling at times. He wants to see me Monday."[27]

Hopkins never made the mistake of underestimating his enemies, and he took some care to see to it that they underestimated him.

> "There are two kinds of administrators [he is reported as having once said to Charles E. Merriam]—gentlemen and go-getters. When a gentleman learns that his appropriation is being cut by the Bureau of the Budget, he accepts it. But I'm no gentleman. If my appropriation is ever cut, I simply call up the White House and ask the President to issue a stop order, saying that I will go over in a few days and explain why. Then I never go over. That is how a go-getter always beats a gentleman."
>
> "What happens," asked Merriam, "when two go-getters compete against each other?"
>
> "Then," said Hopkins, "I pretend to be a gentleman, and, when the other fellow finds out, it is too late."[28]

At length, on April 8, President Roosevelt signed the emergency relief measure. It had survived the various amendments tacked on in committee and on the floor with its basic elements unchanged. Two very significant riders, however, persisted in the joint House-Senate committee draft. One, inserted largely at the insistence of Senator William E. Borah of Idaho, stated, "No part of the appropriations. . . . shall be used for munitions, warships, or military or naval material."[29] The isolationist bloc, of which Borah was a prominent leader, had the illusion that if America cut her armed forces to the bone, she could avoid war. Unhappily Senator Borah, who died in 1940, did not live to see the tide of war in the Pacific turned in June, 1942, at the Battle of Midway. Then the *Enterprise* and *Yorktown,* which had been built with PWA funds, combined with the *Hornet* to sink four Japanese carriers. Japan never again could assume the offensive, and her defeat became inevitable.

The other amendment brought more immediate concern to Hopkins. It provided that "any Administrator receiving a salary of $5,000 or more per annum in this Program shall be appointed by the President by and with the advice and consent of the Senate."[30] This innocuous sounding provision was a Congressional declaration of war. It meant, simply, patronage. Formerly Hopkins had been able to cope with the anguished wails of Governors, mayors, and county officers for a voice in appointments to FERA staffs. Sometimes he listened and acceded to their wishes if their nominees were well qualified; sometimes he simply told them to mind their own business; sometimes, irritated beyond restraint by importuning, he simply told them to go to hell.

Under the new arrangement, every major appointment would have to be cleared with Big Jim Farley and with the appropriate Senators for each State. Of course, Hopkins could get around the provision by appointing some people at a salary of $4,999, but that was well below what his principal assistants were paid and so was not much of a loophole. The current staff of FERA, however, was safe, for FERA would simply be absorbed by the new organization, whatever it was, as was authorized in the new bill.

Upset by the patronage provision in the new law, Hopkins seriously considered resigning from government service. But he had no money saved, no job prospects, and nowhere to turn. Still, it required considerable persuasion on the part of FDR to keep him in Washington. He simply had to learn, as Roosevelt knew so well, how to live and survive in the two-party system. Up to this point, Hopkins had been tested only as an administrator, a job which he had mastered in his own saturnine, rough-and-tumble way. Now he would have to master the rough-and-tumble ways of two-party politics if he was to go further, or if he was to survive at all on the Washington scene.

> I thought at first [he said on a later occasion] I could be completely non-political. Then they told me I had to be part non-political and part political. I found that was impossible, at least for me. I finally realized there was nothing for it but to be all-political.[31]

If he had to be a political man, then he would devote to politics all the energy he had used in administration of relief. It might lead to much higher things, perhaps to the White House itself.

Probably Hopkins had not yet considered the idea that he might make a bid for the Presidency in 1940, but had it not been for the patronage amendment of the relief act of 1935, he would not have had the political know-how to consider it.

An example of what he faced under the new law came to him in a letter from Lewis, who wrote to protest that the appointment of a new Washington State relief director was "not approved by our governor but is being brought about by our new Sen. Schwallenbach [sic] who is working closely with his old friend *Jno C. Stevenson* of Seattle—a *clever, unscrupulous crook.*"[32]

Perhaps as a lesson in the art of politics to Harry Hopkins and the others concerned, the Old Master established his relief administration with himself in charge. Obviously no President could run such an organization, and it would take fast political footwork for one man to come out on top in real charge.

Both Hopkins and Ickes had to have a role in it, and early in April FDR asked each to submit an organizational proposal. Hopkins showed his to Ickes, who found it too complicated. But Ickes' real objection was that Hopkins would emerge "as cock of the walk," as he put it. Ickes' proposal was more streamlined, with each agency acting in a quasi-independent way and the agency heads forming a board presided over by the President. Ickes felt this would keep Hopkins from running away with the show. "I cut him down very sharply in my draft," Ickes noted with satisfaction in his diary.[33]

In the end, Roosevelt took neither proposal, although what he did accept came closer to Hopkins' draft than to Ickes'. He obviously wanted Hopkins in charge because Hopkins had demonstrated that he could act with decision and get things done in a hurry. "Honest Harold," however, could not be set aside. His reputation for probity and his record of producing monumental and useful public works forbade his exclusion. FDR had to face the realities of politics; the appointment of either Hopkins or Ickes to the top position would have been politically disastrous.

Characteristically Roosevelt found a way out. He kept the top job for himself and appointed a troika to run it for him. From New York he recalled amiable, moderate, faithful Frank Walker, former chairman of the National Emergency Council, everybody's friend. He and Hopkins and Ickes were to run the complex relief organization headed in name by the President.

The arrangement of the relief administration was so complicated that it took Roosevelt four news conferences to explain it to the press. On the charts FDR loved, soon fifty or more circles were connected with lines going in all directions. Near the top three large circles contained the names of Walker, Ickes, and Hopkins.

Walker's circle, entitled the Division of Applications and Information, would receive proposals for government spending from all sources, whether federal, State, or local. Then, after referring them to some of the small circles, each of which represented a government agency, Rural Resettlement, for example, DAI would get the proposals back and refer them to the second circle.

This was the Advisory Committee on Allotments, headed by Harold Ickes, which had the responsibility of recommending projects to the President for approval. It was directed "to meet in round table conference at least once a week." The round table must have been considerably larger than King Arthur's, for the committee included the secretaries of Interior, Agriculture, and Labor; the directors of the National Emergency Council and of the Works Progress Division and of the bureaus of the Budget,

Procurement, Soil Erosion, Emergency Conservation Work, Rural Resettle-
ment, Relief, and Rural Electrification; the Chief of Engineers, U.S. Army;
the Commissioner of Reclamation; and chiefs of the Forest Service, Bureau
of Public Roads, Division of Grade Crossing Elimination, and the Urban
Housing Division. Also there were representatives of the Business Advisory
Council, of organized labor, farm organizations, the American Bankers'
Association, the National Resources Board, and the U.S. Conference of
Mayors. Also both Walker and Hopkins were members ex officio of Ickes'
Advisory Committee, but he had no place in the divisions they headed.

The sheer size of this committee insured that it could never get anything
done. It could only approve or disapprove the proposals presented to it by
Walker's division. The astute Roosevelt obviously planned it that way. The
real power lay in the organization represented by the third big circle, the
Works Progress Division, headed by Harry Hopkins. That is, it would lie
there, if Hopkins had the wit to grasp it.

On first reading, it seemed that the Works Progress Division had little
function and that Hopkins had been shunted aside. Its task was to
coordinate, recommend, regulate, investigate. Most of these functions
seemed to duplicate what had already been assigned to Walker's division. It
was also to keep tabs on the progress (hence its name) of the various work
projects undertaken. Roosevelt referred to it as largely a "bookkeeping"
operation.

The section establishing the Works Progress Division contained two
little-noticed clauses. The first required Hopkins to certify that the needed
numbers of skilled and unskilled workers were available in an area where a
project was being considered. They had to be either unemployed or on
relief, for the work of these government-sponsored projects could not
compete with the private sector in demands for labor. The second
provision, which seemed almost an afterthought, gave Hopkins the
authority to "recommend and carry on small useful projects designed to
assure a maximum of employment in all localities."[34] This afterthought
gave Hopkins his opportunity, and under its authority he and his successors
in the job went on to spend over $10 billion on WPA projects.

If President Roosevelt put these two loopholes in his Executive Order
deliberately to see if Hopkins would discover and exploit them, it would
have been in keeping with his devious organizational methods and with his
pawky sense of humor. It would not have been the first nor the last time
that Roosevelt gave a job to several men at once and then sat back to see
who would come out on top.

Soon Ickes began complaining to his diary about Hopkins and his sly
ways. One of the first things Hopkins did was change the name of his

division to the Works Progress Administration (WPA), thereby infuriating Ickes who believed that Hopkins' sole aim was to confuse everyone with the similarity of initials of PWA and WPA.

Hopkins' diary for the early part of May shows his preoccupation with the new program. He was several times at the White House, once to find the President had been "knicked by the boys in a poker game over the weekend—he really shouldn't play poker—his game is terrible but he likes it." Later that same day, May 13, he noted: "All day planning the work program—which would be a great deal easier if Ickes would play ball—but he is stubborn and righteous which is a hard combination—he is also the 'great resigner'—anything doesn't go his way, threatens to quit. He bores me."[35]

The following day he paid a call on Louis Howe, who was dying of heart failure and emphysema. Howe had some strong but, according to Hopkins,

> ... very poor ideas about the work program—but I like him. To Frances Perkins' for conference with Bill Green about wage rates. These labor fellows are pretty dumb and Frances talks too much. —A tough day in all. Senators—Congressmen and busybodies doing their best to keep me from working. Dinner with Frank Walker and Jim Farley—Frank is bewildered.[36]

If Frank Walker was bewildered, he had a right to be, caught as he was in the crossfire of such prima donnas as Ickes and Hopkins. In a speech prepared for May 7, Hopkins had attempted to inject a little humor into the situation but had apparently thought better of it, for the passage is crossed out and marked "not used." It is worth noting, though, as an example of the objective kind of wit Hopkins could sometimes achieve:

> Now you are a long way from Washington, and you see these stories in the newspapers about rows. I know if you thought there was a fight here, that your sympathies would all be with me. You know Harold Ickes is always in the newspapers, always in a fight; while I am a mild sort of person and wouldn't think of getting in a fight. But I want to tell you the low-down is that the fellow who is making all the trouble around here is Walker. He is the one that really stirs up all the trouble; if you want to blame anyone, blame Walker. That is one of the things he is here for, to be blamed for everything that goes around. I certainly intend to do my share of it. I want to have a fine summer here.[37]

Despite the complexities of the organization, a great many projects won approval with the idea of getting money circulating as soon as possible.

Ickes got a quarter of a billion dollars for slum clearance and low-cost housing. Another $500 million went for highways, roads, streets, and eliminating grade crossings during the first allocation conference. Over the unfavorable report of the Army Corps of Engineers, President Roosevelt asked for and got $10 million for beginning the work on harnessing the twenty-foot tides in the Bay of Fundy at Passamaquoddy, Maine.

As summer came, Ickes got more and more disgusted with the complexity of the red tape required by the Advisory Committee on Allotments. All PWA projects had to be approved by this committee, a process Ickes described as "being cleared by a debating society." It was all the more irritating because Hopkins' projects did not have to be cleared by the committee. There were too many for the committee possibly to examine them. At one meeting, Ickes complained that Hopkins asked for blanket approval of some five hundred projects and received a lump sum of money for them to be spent just as he pleased. Many of them, Ickes suspected darkly and with some justification, should have belonged to his PWA, but no one could tell.

To make things even more galling to Ickes, Hopkins exercised a kind of veto over PWA projects with his power to certify or not that there was an adequate supply of labor to justify the project. After being turned down on this basis more than once, Ickes noted, "It was something more than mere coincidence that there were always workers available for one of Harry's projects, even if there were not for mine."[38] The real reason was that PWA projects required a high percentage of skilled labor, while WPA got along very well with mostly unskilled workers.

Despite all his grumbling, Ickes could never bring himself to hate Hopkins properly. Despite what he considered Hopkins' underhanded tricks, despite his jealousy over Hopkins' growing influence with Roosevelt, Ickes had to confess a continued liking for him, "the liking," he said, "of a man who had grown up under Scotch-Presbyterian restraint for the happy-go-lucky type who can bet his last cent, even if it be a borrowed one, on a horse race."[39] Often he would go into a meeting with Hopkins, nursing his wrath to keep it warm, only to find later "that I, too, was succumbing to the blandishments of Harry's personality."[40]

Hopkins had one pleasant interlude away from the fighting, for early in June his old alma mater, Grinnell College, conferred on him the honorary degree of Doctor of Laws. The occasion marked the renewal of Hopkins' association with Grinnell College, which continued until his death. He served for a number of years as a trustee.

Once more back into the fray in Washington, Hopkins sustained a temporary setback in his maneuverings against Ickes, who had complained to the President that Hopkins was getting a lot of jobs that properly belonged to PWA. On June 27, the two rivals met at the White House with the President.

> It was plain to see [noted Ickes with satisfaction] that Harry Hopkins was growing more and more unhappy as the discussion proceeded. Apparently he wants no rules that will prevent his organization from grabbing everything in sight. . . . He said that the only thing to do was for the whole program to be turned over to me and leave him free to go back to New York and find a job.[41]

Hopkins' depression, if it was real and not fancied by Ickes, did not last long, for early in August, Ickes again complains to his diary of Hopkins' high-handed ways. They had a spirited argument over a sewer system for Atlanta, which WPA was undertaking and which Ickes had good reason to believe ought to belong to his PWA. This time it was Ickes who talked of walking out on the whole relief setup. "I can see all kinds of possible scandals ahead and I don't care to become involved."[42]

All of this grumbling was going on despite a basic agreement reached by Walker, Hopkins, and Ickes that WPA projects would in general be limited to those which would cost $25,000 or less, while all those with an estimated cost above that sum would be handled by PWA. Hopkins, however, frequently got around this rule. He would blithely divide up a project estimated at, say, $300,000 into 12 parts and undertake them together. This approach had the advantage of getting the job done a lot faster than it would have been through PWA, but it was hard on Ickes' blood pressure.

Another thing which infuriated Ickes and disturbed Secretary of the Treasury Morgenthau was Hopkins' uncanny ability to get his hands on any loose money lying around unspent in the Treasury. He had a way of overspending his allocations and then approaching Morgenthau, who could never resist the appeal that men, women, and children would go hungry. Hopkins always got his money, leaving Morgenthau the job of explaining things to the President. FDR, however, invariably went along. To Ickes, these actions of Morgenthau meant that he had joined Hopkins in attempts "to undermine me and aggrandize themselves. The President certainly has a blind side so far as Morgenthau is concerned, and Hopkins seems to sing a siren song for him."[43]

While Hopkins won these victories over Ickes, he began to pay the cost in another way. On July 13, 1935, a visit to his doctor revealed a duodenal ulcer, "—nothing to drink and a rigid diet."[44] So began the series of illnesses which would change him from a robust, if slightly built man, to a fragile skeleton which only an indomitable will and heavy medication would keep alive.

Hopkins characteristically refused to let his health stand in the way of what he wanted to do. Immediately after leaving the doctor's office, he departed on a trip with the President and sat up all night playing poker. On this occasion he changed his mind regarding FDR's game. The President won $49. "I have decided the Pres. plays pretty well after all—at any rate—he beats me."[45]

The Jefferson Island Club, to which the party was bound, was located in Chesapeake Bay, about 20 miles southeast of Annapolis. It had been founded by several wealthy Democrats, including Owen D. Young, John W. Davis, and John J. Raskob. It featured a long colonial building with a low veranda overlooking a row of trees on the broad lawn sloping down to the water. Although he had received many invitations to use the club facilities, Roosevelt had never been there before this trip. As always, he made the outing a mixture of fun and politics.

After embarking at Annapolis in the *Sequoia,* the party spent the afternoon fishing in the bay. Accompanying Roosevelt, in addition to Hopkins, were Garner, Farley, Speaker of the House Joseph W. Byrns, Representative Sam Rayburn, Senator Joe Robinson, and others. On Sunday, July 14, a huge number of others came, "—all the political big wigs of the Democratic party with the usual gate crashers," Hopkins noted. "Much liquor—loud talk—the President seemed to have a good time—why I don't know."[46]

Despite his ulcer and his vigorous weekend, Hopkins showed no sign of letting up in his activities. His diary entry for Monday reveals a morning appointment with the President about relief in Puerto Rico and the cryptic note, "bought the surplus potatoe [sic] crop of Va. & Md. on the way out of the White House." He went on to a working lunch with Aubrey Williams, and appointments all afternoon with people who wanted something. "A Congressman wants an airport—another wants a river dredged."[47]

Soon came a showdown with Ickes. The Secretary of the Interior, whose wife had been killed in an automobile accident, returned to Washington from the funeral with grave misgivings about everything. His mood grew blacker when he learned that Hopkins had gone to Hyde Park with the President for the week. "I am thoroughly convinced," he wrote, "that he [Hopkins] is a lawless individual bent on building up a reputation for himself as a great builder, even at the expense of the President and the country. I think he is the greatest threat today to the President's reelection."[48]

His mood improved a little when FDR called him up and asked him to come to Hyde Park on September 11 for a conference on allocation of money for the rest of the year. He arrived late in the afternoon in time to help celebrate Missy LeHand's birthday. He noted a pleasant evening with movies, a good dinner, and good talk.

The next morning, Roosevelt confirmed his worst fears. He began by announcing cuts in all work and relief programs so that he could reallocate the money saved where need was greatest. Since, he said, PWA projects took a long time to get started, and since winter was coming, he had to take money from Ickes and give it to Hopkins. He cut Ickes' housing projects from $249 million to $100 million and lesser sums from other PWA activities. Ickes ended up with less money than when he had left Washington. All he got in exchange was the promise that Hopkins could no longer veto PWA projects. He would tell Ickes what the unemployment situation in a given area was, and then Ickes could make up his own mind.

The Secretary of the Interior left Hyde Park seething. He toyed with the idea of refusing the President's invitation to cross the country with him and return from the West Coast by sea through the Panama Canal.

FDR planned the long trip as a combination political junket and a rest. He hoped to persuade Hopkins and Ickes to bury the hatchet. Some cynics suggested that he ordered them to accompany him because he did not dare leave them in Washington unchaperoned, as it were, while he was away.

The train made various stops to give the President a chance to wave to crowds, shake hands, and flash his famous grin to his admirers. The Secret Service, however, found the trip a nightmare, for just the previous month Senator Huey Long had been assassinated in Baton Rouge, and only God knew how many crackpots might be tempted to have a go at the much loved but also much hated Roosevelt. At one stop, the President dedicated Boulder Dam, which had been begun under President Hoover but completed with PWA funding. Ickes felt justly proud of the work of his agency as he gazed up at the vast structure. However, the pride turned to ashes when FDR spoke, seeming to equate WPA projects with this vast undertaking:

> But can we say that a five-foot brushwood dam across the head waters of an arroyo, and costing only a millionth part of Boulder Dam, is an undesirable project or a waste of money? Can we say that the great brick high school, costing $2,000,000 is a useful expenditure but that a little wooden school house project, costing $10,000 is a wasteful extravagance?[49]

On arrival in Los Angeles, the President made a speech at the Coliseum and then his train moved down the coast to San Diego, where the heavy cruiser *Houston* awaited them. The ship sailed at 3:15 the afternoon of October 2. After exercises, the *Houston*, in company with the heavy cruiser *Portland*, set course for Cerros and Cocos islands. In the comfortable quarters on the *Houston* FDR intended to relax and enjoy himself thoroughly. The Presidential mess consisted of FDR, Harry Hopkins, Harold Ickes, Ross McIntire (Roosevelt's personal physician and a captain in the Navy Medical Corps), Lieutenant Colonel E. M. "Pa" Watson (his military aide), and Captain Wilson Brown (his naval aide). It was a congenial crowd, and, away from Washington, Hopkins and Ickes found that they could get along together and even enjoy one another's company.

The first few days were spent coasting along the shore of Lower California, stopping to fish at various times along the way. The trip almost ended early because of the Italian invasion of Ethiopia, and several members of the party thought the President ought to return to Washington. FDR, however, would have none of it. Hopkins prepared a statement for the papers that Roosevelt was keeping in touch with the situation, and the cruise went on.

Bad weather sent many of the party, including Hopkins, to their bunks. Before long, however, they gained their sea legs and set to fishing with enthusiasm. Everyone caught something, the record being a sailfish weighing 150 pounds landed by Gus Gennerich of the Secret Service. That same day the President caught one weighing 134 pounds. On that occasion, Hopkins, who was in the ship's boat with the President, lost his lunch while the fish was being landed. He had to take a lot of kidding about it from the rest of the party.

On arrival at the Canal, Hopkins and Ickes went ashore to do some shopping and then joined the rest for a motorcade across the isthmus, stopping along the way to review troops at Fort Clayton and to lunch at the officers' club there. The party, accompanied by the President of Panama and his wife, went back aboard the *Houston* while it was in the Pedro Miguel Locks.

That evening, after the official guests had left the ship, Hopkins presented the company with a special issue of the ship's paper, *The Blue Bonnet*. It contained quips directed at everyone in the party, not excepting the President. Here is Hopkins' account of what happened when he was seasick as FDR was hauling in his sailfish:

> Hopkins, the moment the catch was caught, stripped for action, moved from one side of the boat to the other, then like a cat moved back again— he looked sternly fore and aft and finally saw a school of sharks about to attack the sailfish. He leaned over the boat—looked intently into the blue

sea—was too busy to even give the President a cigarette—observers say Hopkins was pale and his fine features sharply drawn as he went manfully about his work. "I had a job to do," said Hopkins, "and I gave everything. . . ." All of the President's party were quick to congratulate Hopkins except Colonel Watson, who (against Navy Regulations—the Army apparently has none) spread the malicious rumor that Hopkins far from taking part in the piscatorial engagement was, in fact, limp, and instead of fighting the sharks was feeding them.[50]

Another passage from the special issue of *The Blue Bonnet* reported the burial at sea of the Hopkins-Ickes feud.

> The feud between Hopkins and Ickes was given a decent burial today. With flags at half mast—the bands trumpets muted—Pa freshly shaved—the Officers half dressed—the President officiated at the solemn ceremony which we trust will take these two babies off the front page for all time. Hopkins, as usual, was dressed in his immaculate blues, browns and whites, his fine figure making a pretty sight with the moondriffed sea in the foreground. Ickes wore his faded grays, Mona Lisa smile, and carried his stamp collection.
>
> The ceremony, tho brief, was impressive. Hopkins expressed regret at the unkind things Ickes had said about him and Ickes on his part promised to make it stronger—only more so—as soon as he could get a stenographer who could take it hot. . . . It was soon over. The President gave them a hearty slap on the back—pushing them both into the sea. "Full Steam Ahead," ordered the President.[51]

The high point of the trip appears to have been the call the ships made at the San Blas Islands, where the Indians still live in a primitive condition, pretty much cut off from the world. Ickes was upset that he could not buy any of the gold earrings or nose rings worn by the women, but everyone seems to have purchased *molas,* the brilliantly colored pieces of clothwork displaying primitive figures of birds and fish and abstract designs done in a kind of reverse appliqué. *Molas*—no one seems to have known the name— were made into the San Blas women's blouses.

While in the San Blas Islands, Hopkins and Ickes went off to one of the deserted islets to fish and enjoy a picnic. The heavens opened and both of them got thoroughly drenched. Neither of them really minded, and they had a good time together.

After leaving San Blas, the *Houston* ran straight for Charleston, South Carolina, because of reports of a hurricane brewing in the Caribbean. Roosevelt hoped to get in a little more fishing, but the *Houston's* captain refused to take any chances. On the evening of October 23, the ship reached Charleston, where the Presidential train waited for them.

Despite his early reluctance to go, Ickes was pleased that he had made the trip. He even had kind things to say about his rival: "Harry Hopkins fitted in well with his easy manners and keen wit."[52]

Hopkins, too, was pleased. "I had a perfectly grand time," he wrote his brother Lewis, "saw a part of the country that I had never visited before, and am really rested. ... For my own part, however, I have no desire to remain in government service forever. Don't be surprised if you hear of my getting out sometime before another year is out."[53]

If Hopkins had any intention of leaving government service, the whirl of activity that marked his return gave no evidence of it. Although the feud with Ickes had been buried at sea, the sea would give up its dead, and before long the rivalry became as intense as ever, but this time it rested on a paradoxical basis of friendship. And it was clear to everyone that both PWA and WPA would be around for a good long time to come.

CHAPTER FOUR

WPA—Floods, Drought, and Politics

Hopkins' administrative methods could well be described as helter-skelter. Much of his day he spent on the telephone, barking orders to a subordinate in Carson City or Ocala. He might be wheedling a Governor or cajoling a Senator. His telephone manner, depending on who was on the other end of the wire, was short and incisive or logical and persuasive. But he got things done, and his staff worked endless successions of sixteen-hour days helping him.

By this time, WPA had overflowed the Walker-Johnson Building, where Hopkins still maintained his self-consciously spartan office. The building, one observer noted, had a perpetual odor of a barnyard that has been sprayed with disinfectant.[1] Slouched in his favorite position, with the small of his back nearly on the seat of his chair, Hopkins kept in touch with the widespread organization by letter, memorandum, personal conversation, and above all the telephone.

Letters poured in, and those that survived the screening of the secretarial staff underwent a rapid and critical reading, with a scribbled note on the margin, such as "No," or even "Hell, no!" directing his long suffering but devoted secretary, Kathryn Godwin, to frame a proper and diplomatic reply for his signature. Even letters from his friends received the same treatment, although Hopkins would soften the tone by writing on the paper, "Tell him no," or "Say yes."

Of course, reports from the field, records, minutes demanded a lot of time. Most were required by law. It was, as he wrote Lewis, "a tough job loaded down with government red tape of an almost unbelievable variety. They have tied pink ribbons on everything but the telephone poles and may have to do that yet!"[2] Curiously enough, one of the criticisms leveled at WPA concerned the amount of red tape and the number of clerical employees it took to keep up with the paperwork required by the very persons who now criticized.

Hopkins had no time to let such criticism bother him. He saw himself, as always, in the forefront of a battle in a war against poverty, privation, and even real physical hunger:

> When this thing is all over [he told an audience in Chicago] and I am out of the Government the things I am going to regret are the things I have failed to do for the unemployed. I don't know whether you would have liked the job. Every night when you went home and after you got home and remembered there was a telegram you didn't answer, the fact that you failed to answer the telephone and the telephone call may have resulted in somebody not eating.[3]

Hopkins brought most of his FERA staff with him to the national WPA headquarters, including his principal assistants, Williams and Gill. He also needed good people on the State and lower levels of operation. "Ninety percent of this depends," said Hopkins at a staff meeting in June, 1935, "on the people we have to run it. Seventy-five percent of my job is over and finished when I have a good State Administrator in a particular state, and if the State Administrator isn't any good, then my troubles are doubled."[4]

Most WPA projects required little engineering skill. Indeed, for a time, Hopkins and his principal staff had a kind of blind spot toward technical experts and engineers. Prevailing civil service wages made it difficult to hire competent civilian engineers, and Hopkins resisted suggestions that he call upon the Army Corps of Engineers to supply WPA with experts. At this stage in his life, Hopkins, in accord with most of his liberal friends, tended toward suspicion of everything military.

At length, however, as a result of some publicity over WPA failures caused by bad engineering, he told his assistant Lawrence Westbrook, an Army reserve colonel, to find someone to be the chief engineer for WPA. Over considerable reluctance on the part of the Army, Westbrook obtained the services of Colonel Francis C. Harrington. Harrington, who had the nickname "Pink"—for his florid face and not, let it be emphasized, for his political views—remained with WPA until his death in 1940 and succeeded Hopkins as administrator in December, 1938.

An example of Hopkins' prejudices and his ability to overcome them shows in a note written by Westbrook:

> For the first two months after Harrington reported, Hopkins saw very little of him. He was not even invited to some of the most important staff meetings. Harrington pitched into his work, however, with great zeal and began to get real results. I took every opportunity to bring Hopkins and Harrington together, and finally Hopkins began to realize the latter's great worth and potentialities. The rest of the story is well known. Within six months after Harrington reported for duty, he had Army engineers in every region and many assigned to important specific projects. Their work was excellent and Hopkins gave them full credit.
>
> There is no doubt that the experience gained by engineer officers in WPA played a large part in qualifying them for the outstanding parts that so many of them played in World War II. Furthermore, the experience of Hopkins with these officers gave him a knowledge of the Army that he could not have otherwise possessed, and, I think, prepared the way for the close cooperation that was so effective during World War II.[5]

A requirement that most workers come from the relief rolls had many drawbacks. It forced some desperate persons to swallow their pride and "go on relief" when everything in their nature and background cried out against it. Some reported leaving home and walking past the local relief office for days on end before they could force themselves to go in. Not a few critics considered it morally wrong to force a man or woman to go on relief in order to qualify for a WPA job. They should, however, have directed their criticism at Congress and not at Hopkins.

Then, too, WPA had to contend with the drifters and the lazy who had never made any very serious effort to find jobs in industry, with the incompetent who could never hold a job, with the misfits and the incorrigibles who believed the world, or at least the government, owed them a living. All these crowded the relief offices, and many got on WPA payrolls, enjoying a security they had never known. Even when the opportunity to transfer to a job in the private sector came along, many of them refused, finding WPA more to their liking. It taxed the local administrators to keep up with these people, to drop those who refused reasonable private employment and rehire those laid off by employers. Such rehiring was official WPA policy, in order to encourage workers to accept temporary jobs.

Still, most workers did take other jobs when they were offered, and they took advantage of the opportunities to improve their skills while working on WPA projects so that they would have better prospects for a job outside

WPA. Hopkins resented criticism leveled against WPA workers as a bunch of no-good lazy bums who spent their time leaning on shovels. Once Farley sent Hopkins a clipping from a newspaper reporting how a WPA worker "fell while resting on his shovel and fractured a wrist." Farley suggested a "non-skid shovel handle."[6]

This type of joke Hopkins had to bear with as good grace as he could. More to his liking was the poem entitled *WPA Workers Answer Their Critics:*

> We've made a lot of lovely things,
> Just "leaning" on a shovel;
> Parks with flowers and sparkling springs,
> Just "leaning" on a shovel.
> The winding roads and the highways straight,
> The wonderful buildings that house the great,
> We built them all at our "lazy" gait,
> Just "leaning" on a shovel.[7]

If the scansion of the poem is a little inadequate, its meaning is clear.

But Hopkins had other things to occupy his mind in the fall of 1935, following his return from the cruise on the *Houston*. In addition to catching up on all the work that had piled up in his office while he was away, he worried about the health of his wife. Unfortunately, his worries were well founded. In December Barbara had her right breast removed in New York by Dr. Kenneth Johnson,[8] who found that the growth had spread. Hopkins told Ickes that he had tried to deceive "Barbara that it was a beneficient growth, but he rather suspects that she knows it was cancerous."[9]

Desperate to raise money for his wife's care, Hopkins retained a New York agency to arrange bookings for speaking engagements. Apparently the speeches were not a success, if Ickes can be regarded as a faithful reporter. On one occasion, he said, Hopkins stood up in Highland Park, Illinois, and remarked that he had no idea what he was going to talk about.[10]

The story, which came to Ickes second or third hand, is probably exaggerated, but it may contain an element of truth. The period marked a low point in Hopkins' life.

The severe winter of 1935-1936 kept Hopkins busy trying to put as many workers as possible on WPA payrolls. When he could get away from the office, he rushed home to be with his wife during her convalescence.

In March, 1936, WPA met its greatest challenge to date. Disastrous floods hit most of the Northeast. Unusually heavy spring rains fell on the still hard-frozen ground from Ohio east to Maryland and Virginia and north to

New England, swelling streams into rivers and rivers into rampaging torrents. Railroad bridges and highways washed out, and passes were flooded. Transportation came almost to a halt. The airlines did their best to rush in supplies, using their finest equipment, the dependable Douglas DC-3, which could carry some twenty-eight passengers or up to three tons of cargo. But some airports were flooded, and fallen power lines knocked out electric power and lights at others. One TWA flight to the flood areas carried a ton of rubber boots for the use of workers. Another flew in over 5,000 telegrams to areas cut off from the outside world.

Inconvenience was one thing, but to the residents of towns and cities located in the river valleys, the floods meant disaster. In Johnstown, Pennsylvania, a coal and steel city on the Conemaugh River, history almost repeated itself. At their peak the waters stood fourteen feet deep in the main streets, forcing thousands to flee for the hills. In all, twenty-two persons were drowned or battered to death by the debris tossed about by the flood waters.

The Golden Triangle of Pittsburgh stood deep under water, with all electric power knocked out. In Maryland, Cumberland was submerged. In threatened Washington the Army vacated Bolling Field, and for safety, the Navy sent its aircraft away from Anacostia to Hampton Roads. In New England, the Gloucester fishing fleet worked for days, rescuing people from upper floors of buildings that were normally miles inland.

To cope with the emergency, Roosevelt called upon citizens to contribute $3 million to the Red Cross for immediate use, and he appointed Hopkins to a Flood Emergency Committee, because only he had the organization to mobilize the vast numbers needed to repair dikes, drains, sewers, and embankments, to clear rubble, and to feed and shelter the homeless. Even before the rains ceased, thousands of WPA workers were working around the clock to fight the flood. Hopkins told the press:

> At a rough estimate we have 50,000 men on emergency flood work throughout the affected states. The number is probably rising all the time, however, because flood crests have still to be reached in many localities. And in addition to actual rescue work, our men are doing the clean-up which naturally follows such a catastrophe as this.[11]

Thousands of women sewed clothing and helped to distribute it, along with blankets, food, and safe drinking water. Nurses paid by WPA funds assisted with medical care. Men and women in WPA field kitchens prepared and distributed several hundred thousand pounds of food furnished by the Federal Surplus Relief Corporation.

All through the ravaged areas Hopkins gave his State administrators full authority to act as they saw fit in the emergency. All agencies of the government worked together, but it was the WPA that had the ability to put men and women to work quickly. When the waters abated, there still remained the massive task of cleaning up the thick layers of mud that clung to the streets and the sides of buildings.

Such a demonstration ought to have silenced the critics of WPA, at least for a time, but such was not the case. Side by side in the papers appeared stories of the flood and stories of the "inefficiency and waste" of WPA. Even as men filled sand bags and dug diversion ditches, wrangling began in Congress over FDR's request for an additional $1,500,000,000 to run WPA for another year.

"It's too much money," snarled Republican Senator Charles McNary. Old guard Democrat Bennett Champ Clark of Missouri said in disgust, "I'm sick of voting blank checks."[12] When the bill finally passed the House, WPA got almost the whole sum asked. As a petulant token of Congressional displeasure with "shovel leaners," $75 million was transferred to the CCC.

By this time Hopkins was clearly top man in relief. The Division of Applications and Information had been eliminated, and Frank Walker had thankfully gone back to New York. Ickes concluded that his PWA had little future. On May 5 he noted that the President

> ... made it perfectly clear that he was prepared to help Harry Hopkins carry out the desire that he has had at heart for the last two years to scuttle PWA and salvage from it whatever he can for the benefit of his own administration. The President said that such PWA projects as might qualify under the program could be carried on by WPA.[13]

On May 14, Ickes determined to have a showdown with the President over Hopkins, WPA, and PWA. That afternoon in the regular weekly Cabinet meeting, Ickes, who was in no good mood to begin with, wrathfully listened to Roosevelt caution Cabinet members against running down WPA when they were called on to testify before the Senate Appropriations Committee on the relief bill which had already passed the House. "It was as clear as day," Ickes fumed in his diary, "that the President was spanking me hard before the full Cabinet.... All the other members appeared to be embarrassed, but I could see Henry Morgenthau stealing a covert glance at me from time to time. Doubtless he enjoyed the spanking very much."[14]

Returning to his office, Ickes lovingly drafted and redrafted a letter of resignation as head of PWA and as Secretary of the Interior on the ground that FDR had repudiated him and his programs. By the end of the day, a special messenger had delivered the letter to the White House.

The next day Ickes remembered that he had a luncheon appointment with the President. In view of his letter, would he still be a welcome guest? He called Missy LeHand to find out. Had the President seen his letter, he asked. Yes. In that case, was he still expected for luncheon? Missy did not know, but she would find out. In a few minutes she called back. Yes, the President still wanted him to come.

When Ickes entered the President's office, Roosevelt said nothing, but looked at him with an expression of mock reproach and handed him a letter written in his own hand:

> The White House
> Washington
>
> Dear Harold:—
> 1. P.W.A. IS NOT "repudiated."
> 2. P.W.A. IS NOT "ended."
> 3. I did not "make it impossible for you to go before the committee."
> 4. I have not indicated lack of confidence.
> 5. I have *full* confidence in you.
> 6. You and I have the same big objectives.
> 7. You are needed, to carry on a big common task.
> 8. Resignation *not* accepted!
>
> Your affectionate friend,
> Franklin D. Roosevelt

After ruefully quoting this letter in his diary, Ickes noted, "What could a man do with a President like that?"[15]

Despite these reassurances, Ickes continued to feel that the President was selling PWA down the river, all in favor of Hopkins. Ickes resented Hopkins' growing intimacy with FDR and considered the relationship a real danger to Roosevelt's chances for reelection. It is perhaps just as well that Ickes did not know that shortly after the luncheon concluded, the President left for a weekend cruise on the Chesapeake, taking as his guests Barbara and Harry Hopkins, Florence and Rex Tugwell, and Missy LeHand. "Lots of fun—" Barbara Hopkins recorded; "Rex brought champagne. The President gave us cocktails and we played Missy's famous card game both Friday & Sat—nights."[16] What Missy's famous card game was, history does not reveal.

Ickes felt greatly disturbed that the House version of the appropriation bill gave the money for relief directly to Hopkins instead of to the President as before. He saw Hopkins using this money as an inexhaustible campaign chest in his bid for the Presidency.

Notwithstanding any Presidential ambitions Ickes might have had for himself—and he had them—he was appalled at the notion of Hopkins as

Chief Executive. He had no experience in elective office, his ideas were visionary, and he was a profligate and reckless spender. Also, Ickes believed he was the most unpopular man in Washington. This was going pretty far. There were two other candidates for that distinction, the President and Ickes himself.

According to some of his friends, Hopkins first began to believe in 1935 that he might become a candidate for President. In 1936, of course, the renomination of Roosevelt was certain, barring his death or disability. But in 1940, Roosevelt would surely retire, and who was better suited to carry on his ideas and program? The fact that Hopkins could pose such questions to himself shows how he always looked ahead to the next challenge. For the moment, WPA occupied his full attention, but in a few years, when the depression was over, he would need another demanding job to satisfy his ego. He felt, and with good reason, FDR would support him.

Hopkins' name appeared almost daily in the press, not always favorably, to be sure. WPA activities had an influence all across the country, and the people who benefited from them represented a wellspring of strength not only for the Democratic Party, but also for Hopkins. FDR was constantly reminded of the benefits of Hopkins' work by the indefatigable Eleanor Roosevelt. As she returned from each of her many trips about the country, she would report to the President on what WPA was doing for the people. Relief activities interested her more than almost anything else in her husband's programs, and she proved an effective advocate for Hopkins and his work. She had been instrumental, for example, in winning FDR's approval for establishing the NYA under WPA, when Hopkins hesitated about asking him because he did not "think he should be put in a position where he has to say officially 'yes' or 'no' now."[17]

Roosevelt also admired the tough-mindedness in Hopkins' character. He never shirked a fight, and he had taken on various State officials in a battle of probity versus politics. In addition to Governor Davey of Ohio, he had locked horns with William Langer of North Dakota, Eugene Talmadge of Georgia, and even the "Kingfish," Senator Huey Long, dictator of Louisiana. Whether his opponent was high or low, Hopkins always fought for his program.

Another great asset of Hopkins, at least from Roosevelt's point of view, was that he knew when to shut up. He could listen; he could be in Roosevelt's presence without perpetually bothering him for some favor for himself or for WPA. He knew how to endure FDR's oft-repeated stories of Hyde Park and Dutchess County, of politics and personalities. He could crack jokes with Roosevelt and could disagree without fear and agree without hypocrisy. And, best of all, he could be trusted. He never revealed a confidence.

He kept gaining friends in high places, friends who could help him in the years ahead. Despite Ickes' assiduous courting of Missy LeHand as a voice in court, Hopkins developed the close friendship with her. He was also friendly with Grace Tully, FDR's other personal secretary, and the White House guardians, Marvin McIntyre and Steve Early. He had friends in Congress and in the statehouses, including Governor Richard Leche of Louisiana and the LaFollette brothers, of Wisconsin, Governor Philip and Senator Robert.

More formal recognition came when he received an invitation to join the Jefferson Island Club that summer.[18] And always, he had a firm friend in Eleanor Roosevelt, who shared his zeal for helping the unfortunate and who took a motherly interest in both him and Barbara as well as in their daughter Diana.

In April, in the pages of his diary Ickes bitterly accused Hopkins of playing politics with WPA funds to woo Mayor Edward Kelly of Chicago.[19] Certainly Hopkins was cultivating him, as he was other city bosses, including Frank Hague of Jersey City, but there is no evidence to suggest anything improper. Neither Roosevelt nor Hopkins objected to any political benefits accruing to the Democratic Party from the WPA program, but each was adamant that it should not be manipulated for the purpose of winning votes. It was fine if people voted for Democrats because WPA existed; it was distinctly not all right if anyone used WPA jobs as a weapon, either to promise a job or to threaten its loss, in return for votes.

By this time, most of the original New Dealers had disappeared from the Washington scene, or would soon depart. General Hugh Johnson, who had headed NRA, had a brief tour as WPA administrator for New York City. Breaking with the administration, he began a newspaper column to castigate the New Deal. Former Brain Truster Raymond Moley, writing for *Newsweek,* soon became one of the harshest critics of FDR's economic policies. Tugwell's influence declined after 1935, for, as a theorist, he was appalled by the freewheeling pragmatism of Roosevelt and, incidentally, of Hopkins.

The new men Roosevelt gathered around him had no dreams of making over the country in accordance with some model of social perfection. The difference between the group of advisers who created the First New Deal in 1933 and the group who brought about the Second New Deal in 1935 and 1936 was more than the difference between the Columbia University Department of Economics, from which Moley and Tugwell had come, and the Harvard Law School, which produced Felix Frankfurter—later to be a Supreme Court Justice—and the indefatigable team, Benjamin Cohen and Thomas Corcoran. The new men had little patience with the central planning schemes. They wanted to establish in precise terms the roles of business, agriculture, transportation, industry, and government so that each could function under the free enterprise system.

Roosevelt, Hopkins, Ickes, and some others, as pragmatists could operate happily with either group, for their approach was to tackle a job until it was done. Hopkins saw no reason why such a state of affairs could not continue if he became President. Pragmatists of his sort were the only people who survived long around Roosevelt, for he became impatient with doctrinaires, and those who tried to force him to adopt their theories got short shrift.

Franklin Roosevelt and Harry Hopkins could no more have become communists than they could have walked across the Atlantic Ocean. Neither had the discipline of mind to embrace its rigid dialectic, and neither had any use for its monolithic state and its disregard for human values. Nor could they have been socialists. The Liberty League accused Roosevelt of campaigning against the Socialist Party and then carrying out all its proposals in the New Deal. Emphatically not, said Norman Thomas, the Socialist Party's perennial candidate for President. The New Deal embraced only a few measures sponsored by the socialists. While the Socialist Party would nationalize industry, Franklin Roosevelt wanted industrialists to behave themselves. If it took the power of the government to get them to do so, then he would use that power. Hopkins agreed. The proper role of business, he argued, was not to make huge profits for a privileged few; it was to make reasonable profits after paying such wages as would enable a worker to

> . . . buy back his full share of the goods he helped to put through the mill of national business. . . . There is reason to think that the present system is capable of giving to all its workers those things which are now the expectations of a comparative few: a warm, decent place to live in; a liberal diet; suitable clothes; travel, vacations, automobiles, radios, and college educations for those who want them.[20]

Given their similarities of views, it is not surprising that Roosevelt and Hopkins got on well together. Under the tutelage of the master, Hopkins learned politics, the practical kind which would change the Democratic Party into a coalition of conflicting and disparate interests that would hold political power for the next sixteen years. As might be expected, the second New Deal had no gospel. It was a practical approach, to keep all parts of the enterprises of the country balanced so that all might be free. It was in this sense that Roosevelt and Hopkins believed in free enterprise. And in this identity of views with the President, Hopkins laid claim to the role of heir apparent.

"For all his ability and selflessness, Hopkins did have an undeniable appetite for practical politics. He loved maneuvering, and he loved being in the know when the great plans were underway." So wrote Morgenthau in his diary that summer. "Moreover, he had supreme confidence in his own capacity for improvisation and would often embark cheerfully on huge programs without a full conception of the expense and of the difficulties involved."[21]

Hopkins seemed to receive something of a setback when the appropriation bill finally went through. A note of spite sounds in Ickes' diary entry for June 19:

> While PWA doesn't get a great deal of money, what we do get is ours without any interference by Hopkins. We ought to be able to put through a program of about $600 million, which isn't so bad. The important thing is that PWA is recognized as a going concern. The original bill started out to appropriate $1.5 billion to Hopkins, but in the law as finally passed Hopkins is not even mentioned. The money goes to the President.[22]

For Hopkins, who cared less for the show than the substance, the fact that the money was appropriated to the President was unimportant. He knew that he could get what he needed from that appropriation, and if that was not enough, then Henry Morgenthau would always be able to find more. Without wondering where his next billion was coming from, Hopkins rented a summer house on Long Island, where he installed his wife and daughter, planning to join them on weekends. "I hope to get away for at least six full weeks later this summer."[23]

By this time, everyone concerned knew that Barbara Hopkins' operation had not been successful and that her days were limited. Friends conspired to make them as pleasant and memorable as possible. Eleanor Roosevelt invited them to spend part of the summer at Campobello. She and the President would join them part of the time.

> I can probably [she wrote] get a woman to cook and look after you if you just want to bring a nurse for your little girl. The house is large but simple and easy to live in as you can close off any rooms you do not want. I am not putting the sail boat in commission, but you can get a boat by the day if you want to go off fishing or for a picnic on the water for a day.[24]

Although the Hopkins family did not go up at that time, they went a month later. Hopkins and FDR sailed, fished, and inspected the Passamaquoddy area for a proposed dam and tidal power electrical project.

Hopkins acquired the taste of the combination of work, politics, rest, and family life that marked a Roosevelt holiday. He liked it.[25]

The vacation gave him some time to think about his projected book telling the story of relief. "My purpose," he told his publisher, W.W. Norton, "would be to dramatize poverty in America and draw the implications of that thing. . . . I would not use it as a book in which I would say what a great job we have done." Norton approved, saying, "If you wrote most of it yourself, it would be forthright and people would know where you stood."[26] Unfortunately, most of the book was ghostwritten, but in certain places it bears Hopkins' own imprint. Its title, *Spending to Save,* was suggested by Roosevelt himself.[27]

As the time for nominations for the 1936 campaign approached, the voices of both the Republicans and the dissident old guard Democrats grew more strident. If anything, the latter group was louder. These men represented the former leaders of the Democratic Party, men like Al Smith, the standard bearer in 1928, and John W. Davis, the candidate in 1924. Conservative Senators and Congressmen and leaders of the Democratic National Committee were of like mind. They had gone along with Roosevelt in 1932, to their everlasting regret. They understood little of the New Deal and hated it whether they understood it or not. They had seen Roosevelt take power from their hands and place it elsewhere. Yet they had small hope of blocking his renomination in 1936 and running one of their own.

Viewed from the perspective of four decades, it is clear that nothing could have stopped Roosevelt's reelection in 1936, but the Republican Party did not have such a perspective. Cheered by the Supreme Court decisions in defense of the Constitution, many leaders hoped to reverse the abominations of the last four years. William E. Borah warned his fellow Republicans not to embrace conservatism blindly. He warned:

> The driving power in politics in this country for years to come will come from labor, from the producer, from small business, and from millions who have, through no fault of their own, been stripped of their life's savings and life's opportunities. . . . They are offered the Constitution. But the people can't eat the Constitution.[28]

The principal candidates for the Republican nomination were Senator Borah, former President Herbert Hoover, Kansas Governor Alfred Landon, Frank Knox, a prominent newspaper publisher who had once been a Rough Rider with Teddy Roosevelt, and Michigan Senator Arthur Vandenberg. By the time the convention opened in Cleveland, preliminary maneuverings had made Landon the man to beat.

Hoover, however, had other ideas. Bitterly resentful of what he believed to be unfair propaganda, he felt doubly betrayed: by the events of worldwide depression which had ruined his otherwise successful Presidency, and by unscrupulous politicians who had used the universal despair to blacken his reputation. Everything in him cried out against the New Deal, all the way from AAA to WPA. The New Deal, he quipped once, had about run out of letters for its alphabetical agencies, but he noted that the Russian alphabet might come in handy as it has thirty-four letters.[29] He hoped to win the nomination himself as vindication.

He never had a chance. Landon was nominated on the first ballot, with Frank Knox the unanimous choice as his running mate.

By no means a die-hard reactionary, Landon favored many of the New Deal measures, arguing that the Republican Party could carry them out better. He boasted that he had balanced the Kansas budget.

> They have taken it [Hopkins retorted sardonically] out of the hides of the people. . . . The Governor of Kansas has never put up a thin dime for the unemployed in Kansas. . . . Of course some cities and counties in Kansas have done well, but the State has not done anything. The last thing I knew about the Governor he was trying to get money out of me to keep his schools open.[30]

Landon wanted to present himself as a contrast to Roosevelt, so during the campaign he showed himself as a no-nonsense, everyday American. The American people, he felt, were tired of the great man image presented by FDR, who, with his aristocratic background, was so clearly not of the people. What Landon and his advisers failed to realize was that the people felt that Roosevelt, while not *of* them, was *for* them. Most politicians were the reverse.

The Democratic National Convention was a tame affair, for the renominations of Roosevelt and Garner were unanimous on the first ballot. The only controversial item was a move to get rid of the two-thirds majority required for the nomination of a Presidential candidate. In the end, the change met only perfunctory opposition.

Hopkins helped in the preparation of Roosevelt's acceptance speech, but Tom Corcoran supplied the most memorable passage:

> There is a mysterious cycle in human events. To some generations much is given. Of other generations much is expected. This generation of Americans has a rendezvous with destiny.[31]

After the conventions were over, Hopkins had to turn full time to the suffering caused by unprecedented drought in the central States. It had been bad in 1934, but this was much worse. While floods soaked the East, the Midwest had been abnormally dry all spring. As summer set in, blazing sun accompanied by high winds dried up what little moisture there was in the soil and plants.

Hopkins spent a good deal of time visiting those States hardest hit, urging his local administrators to find jobs for the destitute farmers. WPA people built reservoirs, ditches, dams, and terraces to hold the water if the rains ever came. Admittedly these were only stopgap measures, for generations of poor farming had turned the soil into dust which blew away, leaving the barren subsoil. The only permanent solution, Hopkins declared, lay in turning the farm lands into pasture and resettling the farmers.[32] Roosevelt appointed him to a Great Plains Drought Area Committee

> ... to carry on a study looking towards the most efficient utilization of the natural resources of the Great Plains area, especially towards practicable measures for remedying the conditions which have brought widespread losses and distress to so many inhabitants of the Missouri, Platte and Arkansas valleys, the panhandles of Oklahoma and Texas, and contiguous areas.[33]

While the committee went to work, Henry Wallace acted independently through the Department of Agriculture to buy cattle before they died of thirst. Most of them were slaughtered and the meat distributed to the needy.

Travels on his own as WPA administrator and as a member of the special committee kept Hopkins on the road for a good part of the summer and fall of 1936. He combined his inspections and encouragement of his administrators with making political speeches in defense of the WPA program and for the reelection of President Roosevelt. A good bit of his time was spent rebutting attacks on WPA, which the Republicans fell on with glee as the most vulnerable New Deal measure.

Early in the WPA program, Hopkins established an investigation division under Dallas Dort, whose job was to investigate and bring evidence to the Justice Department of fraud, corruption, and other criminal activities by WPA personnel. Dort and his W-Men, as they were sometimes called, reported directly to Hopkins. Offices throughout the country handled routine matters, but when the charges were especially serious, Hopkins sent out a special team from Washington.

Sometimes Dort was condemned for making a perfunctory investigation. An example of the kind of case that made the headlines and gave the

Republicans ammunition occurred in West Virginia. Senator-elect Rush Holt had not been of constitutional age to take his seat when Congress convened in January, 1935, and while he waited for his thirtieth birthday to come around, his senior colleague, Senator Matthew Neely, won the best WPA jobs for his own constituents. Holt levied various charges at WPA, and Hopkins sent Alan Johnstone to West Virginia to find out what was going on. Johnstone reported that generally the State was in good shape, and that Hopkins could stop worrying about it. The essence of the difficulty, Johnstone said, was that Holt felt left out after Neely had grabbed all the plums.

Hopkins' letter to Holt charged that if there was any politics in WPA in West Virginia, it was largely the result of Holt's own activities. Administrative appointments had been made solely on merit, and sixty percent of them had been persons with no political endorsement of any kind. The only instance of soliciting WPA workers for political contributions which the investigators had discovered was a drive "to pay the expenses of broadcasting a speech delivered by Senator Holt . . . on February 7."[34]

> The investigation . . . was a sham, a fraud, and a farce [Holt was to storm on the floor of the Senate]. Sending any of Mr. Hopkins' force down to investigate in West Virginia was like sending Baby Face Nelson to investigate John Dillinger. . . . There are more lies per square inch in that particular report than in any other report in the history of the United States.[35]

Usually the troubles in WPA activities occurred because some politician of whatever party felt he saw an opportunity to win power or coerce votes. Senator Vandenberg brought Hopkins' attention to one case in Pennsylvania. Extensive newspaper publicity had been given to a charge that Harry W. Fee had demanded a twenty-seven dollar contribution from WPA worker Mary C. Shearer. Failure to contribute meant that "it will be necessary to place your name on the list of those who will not be given consideration for any other appointment after the termination of the emergency relief work." On investigation, Hopkins found that only a dollar and a quarter had been contributed. Fee apologized and posted a notice on the bulletin board that workers' jobs were safe whether they contributed or not. Hopkins reported to Senator Vandenberg:

> I am sure you know that I cannot be held responsible for the acts of dumb politicians who take it upon themselves to write letters to our employees. . . . The politician who asked for the contributions was told in words of one syllable that our staff was under no obligation to contribute

and that their jobs would be fully protected in case they did not contribute, and not one single person on this staff was removed from office because of his failure to contribute, nor will he be.[36]

In almost every case, improprieties could be traced back to local politicians. Senators and even Governors were involved, and both parties. The huge sums of WPA moneys simply provided too much temptation.

Another sort of scandal could usually be traced back to laxity on the part of local WPA officials. Occasionally it would be found that a person carried on WPA payrolls had been dead for a year or more. Someone had worked in his stead rather than let the job go begging. This practice was commonest in New York City until the newly appointed local administrator, Colonel Brehon B. Somervell, moved in. "I think this is swell publicity," he told the press, "and the more weaselers we can find the better pleased I'll be. If there are any dead men on the payrolls, we want to know it."[37]

With the approval of the President, Hopkins issued a proclamation included in the pay envelope of every WPA employee:

> No employee of the Works Progress Administration, either administrative or engaged on a project, is required to make any contribution to any political party.
>
> No Works Progress Administration employee's job will be in jeopardy because of the failure of said employee to make such contribution.
>
> No employee of the Works Progress Administration shall at any time solicit contributions for any political party and evidence of such solicitation will be cause for immediate discharge. The question of whether or not to contribute to any political party is a matter entirely for the voluntary decision of said employee.
>
> No person shall be employed or discharged by the Works Progress Administration on the ground of his support or nonsupport of any candidate of any political organization.[38]

Two months before the election, Hopkins issued another statement, advising the workers that they were free to vote just as other citizens were. This missive had an unexpected effect, for in many Southern states citizens too poor to pay the poll tax showed up at the election booths and demanded ballots. They claimed that Hopkins' statement gave them the right to vote, poll taxes or not. When they were turned away, they blamed not Hopkins, but the local voting officials. This was a plus for the Roosevelt administration.

The political sniping at him and his administrators developed a healthy cynicism in Hopkins. On one occasion, when Al Smith remarked that no one was going to shoot Santa Claus just before a hard Christmas, Hopkins snapped, "The hell they won't. Santa Claus really needs a bullet-proof vest."[39]

On a Western trip during the summer, Hopkins delivered several speeches in support of WPA and the President. These talks roused the ire of Farley, who tried to silence him for the duration of the campaign.

> In this period [wrote Farley] I called Harry Hopkins to complain about his making speeches on relief during his western trip. I told him that 75 percent of the complaints we were receiving were about WPA and that most of the dissatisfaction within the party had been caused by WPA. Evidently he found my frankness disturbing, because he phoned me August 24 to say we were real friends and that he did not want anything to come between our friendship. I told him that I might be wrong, but believed that the people had the impression he was a spend-thrift and that he was extravagant in his use of government funds.[40]

Farley was wrong about Hopkins' supposed surrender. An entry in Morgenthau's diary is revealing:

> Hopkins was terribly upset when he had lunch with me. It seems that Farley called him up Saturday, August 22, and told him he was the most unpopular man in the Administration; that he was the greatest handicap to the President, and that he did not want Hopkins to make any campaign speeches and wanted him to discontinue all press conferences. I gather before they got through they both lost their temper at each other.
>
> Hopkins is seeing the President this afternoon about it. He said he felt it was up to him to defend his work, and I agreed with him. I think Farley overstepped the bounds of his authority.[41]

Evidently Roosevelt also believed that Farley had exceeded his authority, for the next day, August 25, Hopkins left with FDR on the Presidential Special for a trip to view the drought areas. The President planned to hold a series of conferences with the governors of the afflicted States. And far from being muzzled, Hopkins made a great many speeches while he was on the trip.

In early August at a press conference, the President told the reporters that he planned to go to the Dakotas to confer with their Governors, then on to Wisconsin to discuss problems with the Governors of Wisconsin and Minnesota. Then his manner grew arch. He would move on to Iowa to confer with the Governors of—he smiled, shut his eyes, and leaned back in his chair—Iowa, Nebraska, Missouri, Oklahoma, and—he opened one eye and winked—Kansas.[42]

On arrival in Des Moines, "Applause was rather scattered, but the same apathy was noticeable when Governor Landon arrived about fifteen minutes later."[43]

Neither the President nor the Governor of Kansas made any effort to exploit political advantage from the meeting, except that FDR made a few joking remarks about things Landon should do when he was in the White House. "Harmony dripped so steadily from every rafter," one observer said later, "that I fully expected one of the candidates to withdraw."[44]

Hopkins sat in on this harmony session, as he did on all the conferences with the Governors and other important officials. At Springfield, Illinois, in early September, he broke off from the Presidential party to go to Chicago to work on his book with Howard Hunter, one of his State administrators, and two of his ghostwriters, Morton Milford and Mrs. Marion Merrell. For the rest of the trip until the book was completed, he worked with them at odd times in order to meet the deadline.

Hopkins did not rejoin the President's party but made his own journey of inspection of WPA projects, visiting ten States. On the trip he had another chance to meet his benefactor, John Kingsbury, who was now making a survey of all WPA projects. While in Tacoma, he spent a weekend with Lewis, and in Portland, Oregon, he had time to have dinner with his younger brother, Emery.

The report of Hopkins' trip gives a wide sample of the various kinds of projects WPA undertook at the time. He inspected a reservoir in Wyoming and an arsenal of some 130 buildings in Utah. He saw a public golf course built on reclaimed land in Washington and a recreational center at Timberline Lodge in Oregon. In Portland he approved the progress of a new airport, and in San Francisco that of a landfill near Yerba Buena Island, later to be known as Treasure Island, which would provide the site for the San Francisco World's Fair in 1939. In San Francisco, too, he attended a concert by the Symphony Orchestra Unit of the Federal Music Project, a subsidiary of WPA.

Governors and mayors rolled out the red carpet for him. Businessmen listened to his speeches, and, strangely enough, approved. His talks have not survived, but parts of one delivered in Los Angeles on September 19 were transcribed:

> I have never liked poverty. I have never believed that with our capitalistic system people have to be poor. I think it is an outrage that we should permit hundreds and hundreds of thousands of people to be ill

clad, to live in miserable homes, not to have enough to eat, not to be able to send their children to school for the only reason that they are poor. I don't believe ever again in America are we going to permit the things to happen that have happened in the past to people. We are never going back again, in my opinion, to the days of putting the old people in the alms houses, when a decent dignified pension at home will keep them there. . . . I think further than that, that this economic system of ours is an ideal instrument to increase this national income of ours, not back to 80 billion where it was, but up to 100 billion or 120 billion. The capitalistic system lends itself to providing a national income that will give real security for all.[45]

Of another occasion, Paul Shriver, State administrator for Colorado, wrote:

> I have not talked with anyone who attended the luncheon who did not come away thoroughly sold not only on Mr. Hopkins but upon the program. . . . One of the newspaper reporters told me that while he had been in the newspaper business for fourteen years he had never heard anyone who was more impressive and who did more to destroy any erroneous impressions than did Mr. Hopkins.[46]

When Hopkins returned to Washington, he wrote a nine-page summary of his impressions of the trip, obviously as source material for a speech. His conclusion, however, reveals his pride in the accomplishments of his program and his sensitivity, carefully concealed from the public, to the criticism of his enemies.

> In state after state, I found capable administrators and engineers . . . smiling with justified pride at the quality of the work that was emerging.
> Undisturbed by the taunts of those who make a business of fault-finding, with that protective covering everyone who tries to do a big job must acquire, administrative workers were plugging away at their jobs, confident that the results will speak for themselves in due time. It is a constant source of inspiration to work with people like that.
> From the workers themselves, however, came perhaps the deepest sense of satisfaction on this trip. There has been no greater slander in recent years than the false characterization of these men as a lot of lazy-shovel-leaners. Get out and meet them if you don't believe it. I have no patience with the judgment pronounced by those who rely on club lounge gossip to condemn the jobless who got their first break through this program. In man-to-man contact you find them pretty much the same as other

Americans. They are eager to work for what they get and proud of the
work they are doing.[47]

Viewed all in all, Hopkins' trip was a genuine inspection and evaluation
journey; but, considering his ambitions, if it was not a political junket as
well, it was a very good imitation of one.

Hopkins had little to do with the final stages of the 1936 campaign. By
the time he returned from the West, Roosevelt had begun his carefully
calculated series of major addresses. As FDR grew more Presidential,
Landon became more vehement, saying things toward the end that he
would later regret. He frequently attacked Hopkins and the WPA program,
and once Hopkins struck back. He made a savage attack, not on Landon,
but on his charges against the relief program. Already he had learned from
the master the trick of not mentioning an opponent's or critic's name. Why
give him free publicity?

In spite of every favorable political sign, many of the New Dealers grew
nervous. Their worries increased when the *Literary Digest* published its
forecast of the election results. Never had it been wrong. The *Digest*
predicted that Landon would sweep to an easy victory, carrying 32 states
with 370 electoral votes, while Roosevelt would win only 16 states for a total
of 161 electoral votes.

Roosevelt, more optimistic, predicted his own victory by 360 to 171
electoral votes. Big Jim Farley startled everyone by his wild forecast that
Landon would carry only Maine and Vermont, with their eight votes in the
Electoral College.

On Tuesday, November 3, Hopkins and his wife were in the Iridium
Room of the St. Regis Hotel in New York. With them were Dorothy
Thompson, her sister, Mrs. Howard Wilson, and Lawrence Westbrook.
Except for the Hopkinses and Colonel Westbrook, practically everyone in
the room wore a Landon sunflower button.

In a letter to Robert Sherwood, Miss Thompson described the scene. The
guests were dancing to the music of a Russian balalaika orchestra, surely a
curious choice for a hidebound Republican gathering. A screen had been
set up to flash the election returns. As they came in overwhelmingly for
FDR, the guests stopped looking. After Landon had conceded, Miss
Thompson suggested that Hopkins propose a toast to the President of the
United States.

"Here?" he asked. "Are you crazy? We'd probably be lynched." She
insisted that he do it, pointing out that Roosevelt was his candidate. She
was, she said, neutral in that election, even though she was wearing a
sunflower. Finally she got up and proposed the toast herself. No one
responded except for the four accompanying Miss Thompson.

We drank our toasts and Harry choked on his, he was so amused, and spurted champagne just past my nose. . . . Still, I thought Harry's own feeling a little hilariously vindictive. Whereas I was perturbed by the attitude of the crowd, he was delighted with imagining the further chagrins they would feel before the next administration was over.

I did not see Harry for a long time after that. I thought he became progressively more mellow and—tolerant.[48]

The man whom Farley had characterized as "the greatest handicap to the President" returned to Washington rejoicing. He saw a new role for himself, to make the New Deal a lasting thing. Henceforth his eyes would look beyond the realm of WPA and would embrace the whole program as FDR saw it. He would be in the forefront of the battle. If the Lord willed, he might lead it after 1940.

CHAPTER FIVE

The Valley of the Shadow

Harry Hopkins had been hurt more than he let anyone know when Farley charged that he was a liability to the President. Roosevelt ignored such talk, and their continued close relationship indicated that FDR valued his friendship more than any possible political handicap Hopkins might bring. But to have men whom he considered friends make such a charge and keep on making it after the 1936 election depressed him.

Rumors abounded of Hopkins leaving the government. "All I can say," Senator Robert LaFollette wrote, "is that this resignation talk is a hell of a Christmas present for your friends."[1] Hopkins, however, had no intention of leaving, for he was setting his goals higher. His unspoken reply was to bind himself closer and closer to Roosevelt.

During the previous summer Roosevelt's old friend and devoted slave, Louis Howe, had died, leaving a gaping hole in FDR's life. Now Roosevelt had no one he could talk to in complete confidence, no one to whom he could give his complete trust. Only two persons in Roosevelt's life ever filled that role, Louis Howe and Harry Hopkins, but Hopkins' time had not come yet. And it would come as a result of the friendship already existing between the two men and of the loyal help Harry Hopkins was able to perform in the weeks and months following Roosevelt's second inauguration.

Eleanor Roosevelt could never have filled such a role in Franklin Roosevelt's life. While she was raising their children, Louis Howe was already pursuing his goal of making Roosevelt President some day, and he was the coach, the mentor, and the confidant. Then her terrible discovery of

FDR's affair with Lucy Mercer estranged Eleanor as far as their personal relationships were concerned. She busied herself with establishing her own field of activities, living a parallel and separate life from her husband. Only FDR's lengthy recuperation from polio occupied her for a time, but once he took up an active life again, she returned to her many activities.

During Roosevelt's years in the White House, Eleanor was not privy to his counsels. She would often serve as his eyes, reporting what she had seen on her many trips around the country. She would often urge him to adopt one course of action or another. Occasionally this practice of hers irritated him, particularly when she intruded on the sacred cocktail hour to bring up some suggestion or request the President had no idea of accepting. She was his wife and the mother of his children, but she was not his friend. Except for official functions, even their social life tended to be separate. She would invite people to a meal at the White House, but the President usually avoided such encounters, unless the guest interested him. One guest they both liked was Harry Hopkins, and he was equally at home with both of them.[2]

Hopkins' circle of friends had widened considerably since he had come to Washington. At first, the people he knew were either associates in FERA, CWA, or WPA or friends from his New York days. He was so busy, spending long hours at his desk or in railroad sleeping cars and day coaches, that he had little time to develop the friends he needed to survive long in Washington circles and friends in other parts of the country.

Criticism and congressional interference forced him into politics. Learning how to play the political game took him more and more into the corridors and offices of political Washington. A list of his personal friends compiled about this time for the purpose of mailing Christmas cards contains 151 names. It included nine Senators, six members of the Cabinet, three Governors, including Murphy of Michigan, three Mayors, including LaGuardia of New York, and a great many others in and out of government whose names were commonplace in those days, such as Bernard Baruch, Felix Frankfurter, William O. Douglas, and Joseph Kennedy. Significantly it did not include Vice President John Nance Garner.[3]

Almost at the very beginning of Roosevelt's second term, Garner began to break with the administration. Never a New Dealer, he had gone along with Roosevelt during the first term since that was what was expected according to the unwritten code of politics. In his second term, the President, according to these rules, was expected to run the government quietly, while those who had supported him for four years engaged in the scramble for first place on the ticket in the next election. The two-term tradition in effect made every President a lame duck during his second term. Everyone knew that in four years someone else would occupy the Oval Office. The incumbent's main political power lay in his strong influence in naming his successor.

After the election in November, Roosevelt received a good many suggestions that he take it easy for the next four years. Why not spend a good bit of time in Warm Springs? The waters there would help his legs, and the climate would help clear up his chronic sinus complaint. And he had plans to make for his estate at Hyde Park. Surely he would want to get his papers in order so he could write his memoirs.

The New Deal had done its work, these advisers argued. If he muzzled his wild-eyed henchmen like Corcoran and Cohen, Ickes and Hopkins, business confidence would return and the country would prosper.

But Roosevelt had no intention of becoming a lame duck President. He intended to continue the New Deal, and he meant to use the power of the federal government to promote the general welfare against special privilege.

For all his advocacy of the New Deal, Roosevelt was basically an economic conservative, insofar as he had any theory. The great English economist, John Maynard Keynes, expressed disappointment at finding him so illiterate in economics. Worse, he had no desire to learn. His conservatism really represented a habit of mind rather than a well thought-out position. It bothered him that the only things that seemed to work required deficit spending. His programs have been labeled liberal in that they favored the rights of the individual against the rights of big business and even against the government. Since such programs threatened the structure of political give-and-take among officeholders, business, politicians, and industrialists and bankers, Congress saw Roosevelt's second term as an opportunity to get things back to normal by 1941, when one of their own would be in the White House. Democratic leaders in both the Senate and House misread the 1936 election as a mandate for the Democratic Party. Actually it was a vote of confidence in FDR, but congressional leaders thought the huge Democratic majorities gave them the strength to challenge the President.

Roosevelt, of course, saw his triumphant reelection as a mandate to continue the New Deal pragmatic responses to specific crises. And crises there still were. Even as he was preparing his second inaugural address—"I see one third of a nation ill-housed, ill-clad, ill-nourished"—marchers of the Workers' Alliance of America demonstrated in front of the White House chanting, "We don't want promises; we want jobs. . . . President Roosevelt, keep your promises. . . . President Roosevelt, we've just begun to fight. . . . Give the bankers home relief; we want jobs!"[4]

The Workers' Alliance, organized by David Lasser, was a union of WPA workers whose principal tactic was intimidation of legislative bodies by threats of riot. It never developed the power to have much influence, but Lasser sometimes became a thorn in Hopkins' side.

Roosevelt's well-known luck seemed to desert him as he raised his hand to take the oath of office for his second term. This was the first inauguration to be held under the Twentieth Amendment, which provided that the Presidential term should begin on January 20 rather than March 4. As though in protest at the shattering of a tradition, cold rains drenched the Capitol steps, soaking impartially the gay bunting and the dignitaries and spectators. The Roosevelt family Bible, brought down from Hyde Park for the occasion, was swathed in cellophane. Water dripped off Roosevelt's hair and off Chief Justice Charles E. Hughes's whiskers. Roosevelt's clear voice took on special emphasis as he swore "to support the Constitution of the United States." Roosevelt later said he wanted to cry out, "Yes, but it's the Constitution as I understand it, flexible enough to meet any new problem of democracy—not the kind of Constitution your Court has raised up as a barrier to progress and democracy."[5]

The rains that fell on Washington came from a huge winter storm which for two weeks poured down cascades of water, the worst of it deluging the Mississippi and Ohio river valleys from Memphis to Pittsburgh. Flood conditions surpassed those of 1936. In Cincinnati, where the normal flood stage was 52 feet, the waters rose to 73. In Louisville, they stood at 51 feet, 23 feet higher than normal flood stage.

Once again Hopkins' WPA organization rose to action. Once again he served on a national committee to deal with the emergency. In fact, on January 24, Hopkins became liaison officer between the President and all emergency agencies dealing with the flood disasters. Roosevelt told Hopkins to set up his headquarters in the Cabinet Room and to be available day or night.

In an article prepared for the *Saturday Evening Post* but never published, Hopkins describes the operation of the command headquarters of the Flood Committee:

> The President took an intimate and decisive part in this and subsequent conferences, acting calmly and speedily. He has an amazing memory, apparently never forgetting a significant detail. He knows the height of the gauges in all the important floods. He knows the levee system and all its danger spots. . . . Through these days of terrible devastation, he was interested not only in the fate of the big cities, but in the suffering of people in the smallest inundated towns.
>
> Once I saw him roused to indignation. The farmers in one of the river bottoms were going to be evacuated; and some shrewd fellows, of the sort to whom a public emergency is an opportunity for private gain, were going

about among the farmers, saying, "You can't take your pigs along, and they'll be a dead loss if you don't sell now—we'll take them off your hands at a dollar apiece."

This might seem to some people a small matter, but it did not seem so to the President. He was not satisfied until it had been arranged that the Federal Surplus Commodities Corporation would buy the livestock of such unfortunate farmers at the market price.[6]

After the crest of the floods had passed, Hopkins headed an inspection committee to visit the flood areas and report to the President. Members were the Chief of Army Engineers, the Surgeon General, Colonel Harrington of WPA, and the vice chairman of the Red Cross.

> We went on February 1st . . . a week's trip by railroad, boat and automobile through the destruction, misery, and organized human effort of the flood zone. In Arkansas, we motored over roads, already running board deep in water, which were closed to passage an hour or two later. There 35,000 people were housed in tents, temporary hospitals erected, commissaries established, and we heard the intimate stories of families dispossessed from their homes and land by a preventable flood. In Paducah we traveled in a coast guard boat nearly three miles up the main street of that submerged city, rows of automobiles beneath the water as a traffic hazard, and cats in the trees as almost the only sight of life.[7]

Such emergency action shows Hopkins at his best. He liked to respond with bold, dramatic measures in a given situation. Routine bored him, and for this reason, he began to tire of WPA. He had good men in the key positions and established policies to deal with almost every situation. Political interference and politically inspired attacks on the agency and on him personally could only hurt him in the long run.

As he prepared to move ahead in his second term, Roosevelt had several plans, and Hopkins hoped to help in any way he could. Although James Roosevelt had been installed in place of Louis Howe as his father's personal secretary and lived in the White House, Hopkins was never far away. Ickes' diary records a good many poker games held in the Executive Mansion, and sometimes Hopkins was a winner. He and Early presented a skit for the President's birthday on January 30, mocking a radio broadcast covering the flood areas. In the broadcast, Early played the three roles of the Announcer, a radio voice from Louisville, and Hopkins. Hopkins, even more versatile, played Marvin McIntyre, Secretary of the Army Woodring, James Roosevelt, a radio voice from Louisville, Missy LeHand, the Announcer, and Steve Early. The humor was, perhaps, sophomoric, but it did amuse FDR, who loved political satire. Typical scene: Early, speaking as Hopkins: "I am leaning heavily on my old friend, Governor Davey of Ohio, in handling this flood. He has just urged me to come to Ohio and promises me a trip down the river in a nice, leaky boat."[8]

The first major proposal that Roosevelt presented to Congress brought the war between the executive and legislative branches out into the open, and involved the judicial branch as well, for it was the celebrated Supreme Court "packing" plan.

On February 5, Roosevelt sprang it on Congressional leaders, just a few hours before it was to be delivered to the Hill. His proposal was entitled a "Plan for the Reorganization of the Judicial Branch of the Government." Instead of challenging the Court on the merits of its decisions, Roosevelt, characteristically, preferred the indirect approach. The bill spent much time analyzing judicial inefficiency and congestion, and proposed to solve those problems, at least as far as the Supreme Court was concerned, by permitting the President to make additional appointments to the Court when any Justice, having reached the age of seventy, did not retire within six months. Such additional appointments could total no more than six.[9]

The Supreme Court "packing" plan ran into immediate opposition. Chief Justice Hughes demonstrated the speciousness of Roosevelt's argument of inefficiency by testifying that the Court was substantially up to date in its work. FDR's enemies in Congress were in no mind to give him additional powers; even Vice President Garner joined the opposition.

Hopkins, out of Washington on the flood inspection trip when Roosevelt cooked up the Court scheme, soon pitched in to defend it. On March 1 he urged in a radio broadcast:

> It is a plain fact at the present time that unless the complexion of the Supreme Court can be changed, two or three elderly judges living in cloistered seclusion and thinking in terms of a bygone day can block nearly all the efforts of a popularly elected President and a popularly elected Congress to correct these ills. Those who oppose this plan are not afraid *for* democracy. They are afraid *of* democracy.[10]

Hopkins made his broadcast out of loyalty to FDR. The affair was basically none of his business other than as a citizen. The only discernible effect of his talk was to bring him more unfavorable comment in the press. Certainly it did not affect the opposition in Congress.

Hopkins had only a tiny part in the court fight, but its importance to him was great, for the conservatism of the Court threatened his programs as much as anyone else's. In the next two years, he had the satisfaction of seeing three of his friends elevated to the Supreme Bench: Felix Frankfurter, Frank Murphy, and William O. Douglas.

In the end Congress passed a mild bill that made a few minor reforms. Roosevelt reluctantly signed it into law. Old Willis Van Devanter resigned while the bill was before Congress, and Roosevelt named as his replacement Hugo Black, the first of his Supreme Court appointments, which led the President to remark that he had lost the battle but won the war. He nearly lost the war as well, for the blow to his prestige gravely endangered his control of the party and of his grand coalition. It took a greater war, one in which real bullets were used, for him to regain his former political strength.

While the fight went on in Congress, Hopkins and Ickes resumed their squabbling, and once again Roosevelt prescribed a fishing trip for them. He would not be with them, this time, but he intended to keep in touch.

Actually the feud between Ickes and Hopkins was more official than personal. The trip provided more of a rest for both of them than it did a burying of the hatchet. They left the hatchet in Washington.

In a mellow mood Ickes recorded in his diary for April 9, 1937:

> So yesterday I called up Harry Hopkins and this morning I got word from him that he would be glad to go with me to St. Petersburg, or rather join me there. I am delighted at this because Harry and I have always gotten along very well personally and he will make the best kind of a companion. The trip wouldn't have done me a great deal of good if I hadn't someone like him to go with me."[11]

Hopkins and Ickes sailed in the Coast Guard Cutter *Saranac,* visiting Key West and Fort Jefferson on the Dry Tortugas, where Dr. Samuel Mudd had been imprisoned for tending John Wilkes Booth after he had assassinated Lincoln. Both men had a proprietary interest in the old fort, for it had recently come under the Department of the Interior as a national monument, and WPA workers were cleaning it up.

On the trip, the vacationers exchanged facetious messages with the President, in which FDR had the last word, saying, "If you both stay away another week debtor nations will pay war debts and we can all head for Samoa."[12]

During the trip, Hopkins and Ickes revealed more of their personal lives than ever before. Hopkins told of his earlier marriage and his divorce. It surprised Ickes to learn that Hopkins had three sons by that marriage and that their support made him hard up for cash. Hopkins predicted that Ickes would be one of the first to be considered by the President for a Supreme Court appointment. However gratifying this might be to Ickes, not even Hopkins could read Roosevelt's mind.

The trip South did not do Hopkins as much good as it might, for he had personal worries. In addition to his concern for Barbara, his brother Rome, the family ne'er-do-well, had written him in December that he was in a jam and broke. Then Harry learned that his eldest son, David, was having difficulties making ends meet in college, and, to cap things off, wanted to get married. His father counseled patience, only to have the story break in the New Orleans papers that May. David's fiancée, Cherry Preisser, was a featured dancer who had appeared in Broadway shows, including a starring role in the *Follies*. While the show was on the road in New Orleans, she and David fell foul of a persistent reporter, who turned their denials into a story of their engagement. "In all the newspaper reports," David wrote his father, "we were inaccurately quoted and in some cases libelously so."[13]

No doubt Hopkins was somewhat mollified, for if anyone knew the wiles of persistent reporters, he did. In any case, the story mattered little, for the couple married secretly on June 22, in Gretna, Mississippi, across the river from New Orleans. A few days later, David wrote his father a letter explaining, or rather failing to explain, their reasons for the step. As things turned out, however, Hopkins accepted the marriage in good part and became devoted to his daughter-in-law.

Another wedding took place about this time, and this one tickled Hopkins' sense of humor. Roosevelt's youngest son, Franklin, Jr., married Ethel du Pont in Wilmington, Delaware, on June 30. An alliance of the Du Pont family, industrial tycoons par excellence, and the Roosevelts of the New Deal seemed like mixing oil and water. Ironically, in accordance with wedding custom, the Roosevelts occupied the right side of the church and Du Ponts the left.

Both families carried the proceedings off with an air. FDR had invited a good many of his liberal friends, including Morgenthau and Hopkins. After the ceremony, FDR held court at the reception for over a thousand guests.

Roosevelt was more welcome at the festivities than he might have been a few months earlier, for he had swung to the right in his thinking. His conservative friends had persuaded him that with recovery going well, deficit spending threatened the country with inflation. Announcing his goal of balancing the budget, Roosevelt used, not a paring knife, but a meat ax on government programs, particularly relief. He cut WPA rolls heavily and brought PWA projects almost to a halt.

Congress, meanwhile, savoring the victory over the President in the Court packing affair, proceeded to bottle up the "must" legislation Roosevelt proposed; wages and hours regulation; low-cost housing programs, reorganization of the executive branch, a comprehensive farm program, and the creation of seven additional agencies modeled after the

Tennessee Valley Authority. When Congress adjourned in August, only the Wagner Housing Act had been passed. All the rest failed, and the failure cost Roosevelt a great deal in political influence and power.

Even in essential legislation, Congressmen made things as difficult as possible for Roosevelt and his administrators. WPA needed a deficiency appropriation. Hopkins and Roosevelt agreed on $1,500,000,000, and duly recommended the sum to Congress. In the House, the rebels sprang into action at once. Part of their reaction came from Hopkins' lobbying for Roosevelt's "must" legislation. Some members of the House believed he had stepped out of line in urging support of his own requests for funds.

> Two weeks ago [Representative Joe Starnes of Alabama said of Hopkins on the floor of the House] he had the power to override one of the ablest members of the House of Representatives. . . . A week ago, according to the press, he came on the Hill and held a meeting in the office of the majority whip of the House, and yesterday he entered into the sanctum sanctorum, the office of the majority leader of this House, or the holy of holies. That is what the members of the House resent.[14]

Hopkins fought hard to preserve the appropriation from the ax which would have reduced it by one third to a billion dollars. Although this particular amendment lost, the House Appropriations Committee members had tasted blood. They proceeded to saddle the appropriation with one amendment after another, earmarking funds for many a pet pork barrel project. Under these provisions, WPA could not have functioned. They took particular glee in an amendment reducing the salary of the administrator of WPA from $12,000 per year to $10,000. No name was mentioned, but none was needed. The Committee was getting its revenge for the invasion of the sanctum sanctorum.

Some of the news commentators rejoiced. Franklyn Whitman wrote in the *Washington Post,* "Nothing that has happened around here in a long time has given us so much pleasure. . . . It was a pleasant sight to see someone slap the smartalecky Harry Hopkins down."[15]

In a more judicious tone, the *Baltimore Sun* commented:

> It was a remarkable outburst in the House yesterday that cut Harry Hopkins' salary from $12,000 to $10,000. This was pure spite, for what is a saving of $2,000 a year in a job like that?
>
> But while the business has no monetary significance, it is highly significant as revealing the emotional state of members. They must hate Hopkins with a frantic hatred when they are driven to do as childish a thing as cutting $2,000 off his salary to express their anger and resentment.
>
> No member voiced on the floor the real reason for this feeling toward

Hopkins, but there is no mystery about it. They hate Hopkins because they are afraid of him; and they are afraid of him because they think he is capable of building up an organization in their individual districts to fight them, if they do not vote according to his orders.[16]

Fortunately for the integrity of WPA and for the health of Hopkins' budget, all of the earmarking provisions and the salary-cut amendment were knocked out when the full House voted on the committee report.

Shortly after the Congress completed action on the appropriation, Hopkins enjoyed a stay at Jefferson Island. Soon thereafter, in early July he received a package and a letter from the Secretary of the Club:

> You have been charged with losing your head upon occasion, with losing public money upon occasions, have been tried and found not guilty of either charge, but when a man loses his pants and the *corpus delicti* comes into the possession of the public, there is no excuse.
>
> One may lose his head or his heart, his dog, or even his sweetheart, but losing his pants is a bit difficult to explain.
>
> But you are artful in that way, so I suppose you will come out of it with another acquittal.
>
> Cordially,
Harry B. Hawes
>
> P.S.—Some who visited the islands may have expected to lose their shirts but not their pants. Yours go with this letter.[17]

Unfortunately that summer brought few opportunities for pleasant relaxation, for Barbara Hopkins had little longer to live. Hopkins took her for a long and final holiday to Saratoga Springs, New York, where they enjoyed the company of friends, especially the Herbert Bayard Swopes. They were determinedly gay, but both of them knew the truth. Friends from Washington, such as Howard Hunter, came up for weekends to help them lose money at the races.

In the latter part of September, Hopkins returned to Washington. Never one to make a bid for sympathy, Hopkins concealed the nature of her illness from all but a few. On September 21, Jesse Jones wrote Barbara that he had played poker with her husband the previous night. "Harry tells me that you are quite miserable with pleurisy and I hope you will soon get relief. There is nothing much more painful."[18]

But Hopkins did not keep the situation from Lewis, who wrote,

> In your trouble we can only send to you and Barbara our sincerest sympathy. The inevitable result of her condition leaves you as it would me scarcely knowing where to turn for help. But this I've learned, Harry, from

the years of my own experience in meeting what we call death. That mystery, like the mystery of life, can only be approached by way of love and faith.[19]

Eleanor Roosevelt wrote from Seattle, expressing hope that the doctors might be wrong and offering to take Diana, who was five years old at the time, into the White House and Hopkins too, if it would help. "Remember always that your friends (& I hope you count me one) would give much to be of any use they can be to you."[20] FDR telegraphed his concern from his own Western trip. LET ME KNOW IF WE CAN DO ANYTHING ALL SEND LOVE.[21]

No amount of good wishes could help. The end came at 7:30 on the morning of Thursday, October 7, 1937, at Garfield Hospital in Washington. Hopkins, who had been at Barbara's bedside almost constantly for forty-eight hours, was with her when she died. Roosevelt, after delivering a major address in Chicago, announced that he was returning to Washington to attend the funeral.

On October 8, Ickes took Hopkins to his home for dinner and what comfort he could give. "He looked pretty much shaken," Ickes noted. "I let him talk about Barbara when he wanted to, but otherwise I tried to keep the subject on indifferent matters of mutual interest. I am afraid that he is going to feel her loss very heavily."

The two men sat up far into the night, discussing various things. Hopkins told of his impressions of Roosevelt, especially what he had learned of FDR's early days when, as he put it, Roosevelt "was the playboy of the Wilson Administration." Roosevelt, according to Hopkins, only became serious about public affairs after his attack of polio, when his enforced leisure turned him to reading books of history and biography. Hopkins gave much of the credit for his development to Eleanor Roosevelt and to Louis Howe, who "kept hammering at him that he could have a political future."[22]

Roosevelt led the mourners on Saturday as Barbara Hopkins' casket was borne into the Mount Pleasant Congregational Church, where the Reverend Russell J. Clinchy conducted the service. Pallbearers were Henry Morgenthau, Frank Walker, Aubrey Williams, Pa Watson, Marvin McIntyre, and Steve Early. Eleanor Roosevelt, Mayor Fiorello LaGuardia, the Kingsburys, the Langdon Posts, and many other friends witnessed the committal in Rock Creek Cemetery.

Business kept Hopkins so occupied for the next few months that he had little time to mourn. Eleanor Roosevelt took Diana under her sympathetic wing, and the little girl lived a good bit of time in the White House. For her father new problems rushed in in battalions. The recession of 1937 began, and across the seas war clouds began to gather.

At this time, Hopkins had little concern for foreign affairs, but as an interested citizen he watched dismayed the rising challenge to freedom in Europe and Asia. The Spanish Civil War raged, and Mussolini and Hitler openly aided the rebels under Franco, while the Russians supported the loyalists. Congress reacted by adopting a Neutrality Act which imposed an arms embargo on belligerents, forebade loans, and prohibited American citizens from taking passage on belligerent ships. By voluntarily abandoning the principle of freedom of the seas, for which the United States had fought in 1917 and 1918, Congress hoped to stave off another war. Roosevelt would later regret that he had signed the Neutrality Act.

Within a few months, other ominous signs appeared. A clash between Japanese and Chinese troops in July at the Marco Polo Bridge, just west of Peking, led to a Japanese invasion of China, with thousands killed in Shanghai. In Europe, Italy and Germany drew close to an alliance which boded ill for their neighbors.

These warning signals from abroad alarmed Secretary of State Cordell Hull, and he suggested that Roosevelt make some statement about them during his Western trip that fall. In Chicago, the heart of the isolationist Midwest, he chose to make his views known. The occasion was the dedication of a PWA bridge, but the subject was international. Referring to the increasing hostilities in Spain and in China, the President warned that if the current terror and international lawlessness got worse, there was no reason to believe that the United States would be immune. He went on to propose collective action by the peace-loving nations in the form of a quarantine of the aggressor:

> When an epidemic of physical disease starts to spread, the community approves and joins in a quarantine of the patients in order to protect the health of the community against the spread of the disease. . . . War is a contagion, whether it be declared or undeclared. . . . We are determined to keep out of war, yet we cannot insure ourselves against the disastrous effects of war and the dangers of involvement.[23]

The roar of the crowd marked approval, but the delayed reaction was almost uniformly critical. Roosevelt's friends and advisers were mostly shocked into silence, while the isolationists roared. Some Congressmen even talked of impeachment. The former NRA administrator, Hugh Johnson, wrote in the *New York World-Telegram* warning against alliances or associations that might lead America into foreign war, "at least without taking this people into much more confidence than is displayed in this collection of warlike hints."[24]

"It is a terrible thing," Roosevelt later remarked, "to look over your shoulder when you are trying to lead—and to find no one there."[25]

At this stage in his life, Hopkins tended to agree with the isolationists, if only because his attention had been so totally occupied by domestic matters. As his association with Roosevelt deepened, he would be drawn into international affairs more and more until he was FDR's right hand man in them as in everything else.

The economic crisis facing the United States caused more immediate concern. Roosevelt's new fiscal conservatism has been named as the cause of "Roosevelt's recession," but the story is more complex than that. In late summer stocks entered a steep decline, one which was written off as a normal seasonal drop. The usual explanations appeared—readjustment, profit taking, corrective realignment. But the drop steepened as panicky investors, remembering 1929, tried to get out.

Although Roosevelt believed things were fundamentally sound, he dared not say so in public. It sounded too much like Hoover.

The recession of 1937 resulted from several factors, of which cutbacks in government spending played a part. During the winter and spring, business had built up large inventories, and when the summer slack season came along had laid off a good many workers. This, coinciding with reductions in federal relief payments, dried up purchasing power and started the downward cycle. And once started, the decline got worse. A wave of sit-down strikes that summer also contributed to the decrease in buying power. Once a few warning signs appeared, customers tended to become more cautious in their spending.

On October 19, known as "Black Tuesday," the market broke completely as seventeen million shares were dumped. It was the worst drop since 1929, and it shook Roosevelt's faith in budget balancing. Yet he was not ready to go along with the spenders, such as Hopkins and economist Leon Henderson, now with WPA, who that spring had predicted the plunge. Others urging spending to offset the loss of public buying power included the "Gold Dust twins," Corcoran and Cohen, Lauchlin Currie, and James Roosevelt, still working as personal secretary to his father. Still FDR hesitated.

He summoned Congress into special session and once again urged on it wages and hours legislation, a permanent national farm act, administrative reorganization, and regional planning to cope with economic problems. The special session was a disaster, and when Congress adjourned for Christmas it had passed not one of the measures Roosevelt had asked.

Roosevelt believed that the recession arose out of a strike of capital; businessmen, in his view, were refusing to invest in expansion or new enterprises in order to force repeal of the controls imposed during the last four years. Therefore, he would do nothing to help them. Of course, he would do what he could to prevent suffering among the unemployed. Doggedly, Hopkins took up that burden.

The pressure of work brought no relief to Hopkins. He moved out of the Kennedy-Warren, where he had been living with his wife, to a house on N Street in Georgetown. He looked bad, and when Ickes saw him at a White House luncheon early in November he was shocked. "Missy LeHand," he noted, "says that he speaks of Barbara as if she were still alive, and there is some fear about his health. He hasn't been well, anyhow, for some time."[26]

Roosevelt prescribed another of his favorite cures, a sea voyage. Since Roosevelt felt a bit under the weather himself, he decided on a short cruise in the Caribbean aboard the *Potomac*. Besides Hopkins, his guests included his son James, Ickes, and Assistant Attorney General Robert Jackson, as well as his usual coterie of "Pa" Watson and Ross McIntire.

The party left by train from Union Station on November 27 just before midnight and arrived in Miami at 8:45 on the morning of November 29. Aboard the *Potomac*, Hopkins and Ickes shared a large stateroom.

They had a rather miserable cruise. Heavy weather afflicted both Ickes and Hopkins with seasickness, and they thankfully sought their bunks when the evening poker games broke up. They did have a few days of pleasant fishing, and on one of them FDR took Pa Watson in the boat with him so that he "might act as Referee in Chicanery between these two enthusiastic competitors."[27] The competitors had no need for his services, for neither of them caught anything.

Before leaving on the trip, Roosevelt had undergone treatment for an infected jaw. It got no better, so he cut the cruise short. Ickes noted:

> I was a good deal worried about the President on this trip. . . . He looked bad and he seemed listless. During the first two or three days I wondered whether or not his trouble was spiritual or physical. . . . I talked to Harry Hopkins about it and also to Bob Jackson. They didn't seem to feel much reassurance themselves. At any rate, they could not give me any. The result was that I felt pretty low in my mind.[28]

On his return to Washington, Hopkins found an invitation to spend Christmas at the White House, but he had to go to the Mayo Clinic in Rochester, Minnesota, instead. His doctor feared he had cancer of the stomach.

The Mayo Clinic doctors recommended immediate surgery. Lewis wrote that he was coming to Rochester, and friends did what they could. Florence Kerr came to Washington to take care of Diana, who had left the White House and was living in the Georgetown house. Mrs. Kerr wrote Hopkins of Diana's reaction to a telephone call from him. "O, Daddy often calls me. He just likes to talk to me, I guess." The letter went on, "My own reaction to your call was something else again. You don't fool me one little bit, my dear, and I felt as tho I'd had a good stiff clout on the side of the head." Another passage in the letter reveals how difficult it was for Hopkins to accept help. "People are going to want to do things for you, Harry, in moderation I hope, but something nevertheless. Don't stiff arm them. It takes a lot of grace to receive graciously. But you do others good that way."[29]

On December 20 Dr. Wolford Walters removed approximately two thirds of Hopkins' stomach to cut away the cancerous growth. In view of Hopkins' lingering hope that he might yet win the nomination for the Presidency, reporters were told he had undergone surgery for ulcers.

His doctors warned him that he had only a two-to-one chance against recurrence. He had a great many visitors, including Rome and Rome's wife, Helen. Bombarded with letters, Hopkins felt thankful to have his secretary with him. Two of the letters which pleased him especially came from a businessman and a Negro. The businessman praised his work and "the exceedingly great service you have rendered the country," and the Negro said, "You have done more to help our Great President to help the poor people of my race than any other man in America, and I pray God that you will be spared to live many years to come."[30]

In his last act of 1937, Hopkins presented the Seton Guild Girls of Rochester with seven sample boxes of toys produced by WPA workers and sent to him by the Kansas City District office.

The new year found Hopkins convalescent. He wrote Marvin McIntyre that he had no bad postoperative effects and that the operation should give him a complete cure. He wrote Missy LeHand that he expected to go to New Orleans for a time and then on to Florida. "It may be that the President will be going fishing in February and perhaps you can come down to Florida. We will find someone for a chaperone. Perhaps Steve will do."[31]

Joseph Kennedy invited Hopkins to stay at his Palm Beach house as long as he liked. Hopkins' doctors firmly prescribed complete rest and forbade him to return to work before the beginning of April. Roosevelt reinforced the order. He had received daily bulletins from Dr. Walters, and sent frequent notes of encouragement. Eleanor Roosevelt continued to look after Diana, who spent part of the time in the White House and part with James and Betsey Roosevelt on their farm in Massachusetts.

After leaving the Mayo Clinic, Hopkins went to New Orleans. He visited John Hertz, founder of the Yellow Cab Company and of the Hertz U-Drive rental car system. Then he moved to Palm Beach. By that time, in early February, Florence Kerr had resumed caring for Diana and kept Hopkins up to date with chatty letters. David Hopkins, who was working for an advertising agency in New York, wrote regularly. So did David's wife, Cherry, who had gone to Chicago on a dancing engagement. This gave the opportunity for a gossip columnist to hit at Hopkins by starting the rumor that Cherry and David Hopkins had split up. Hopkins promptly denied the story, but it was another irritation to impede his recovery.

In March, Diana went back to the White House for another stay, and Mrs. Roosevelt's secretary, Malvina Thompson, wrote: "Mrs. Roosevelt is delighted to have her here. This morning when I went in to ask her a question, I found her cutting out paper dolls for Diana and having a grand time! Don't tell the newshawks!"[32]

Toward the end of his stay in Florida, Hopkins spent some time at the race tracks. Steve Early joined him there. "Harry Hopkins with me and Pa Watson. Golfing and racing at Tropical Park the chief form of recreation."[33]

While Hopkins was in Florida, a reorganization bill was nearing a vote in Congress. Originally proposed in January, 1937, the bill had been bottled up in one committee after another, while a coalition of enemies rose in revolt against the President. Actually, Roosevelt's proposals were scarcely more radical than Hoover's. They were an effort to do what businessmen and other critics had long called for to bring more efficiency to the executive branch of the government. The bill, the work of a group of political scientists and public administration experts, however, had fatal political weaknesses. It called for an expansion of the White House staff, strengthening management agencies, putting independent agencies under regular departments, and strengthening auditing methods by creation of the post of Auditor General.

The two proposals which doomed the bill were one to extend the merit system in government "upward, outward, and downward to cover practically all non-policy-determining posts,"[34] and another to create two new Cabinet departments, Social Welfare and Public Works.

The first proposal would have had the effect of removing too much patronage from political leaders, and the second, his enemies feared, would have meant a Cabinet post for Hopkins as the first Secretary of Social Welfare.

The bill never had a chance. Senator Walsh of Massachusetts called it a matter of "plunging a dagger into the very heart of democracy."[35] Town meetings were held in condemnation, and paid advertisements appeared in principal newspapers. Commentators warned of Hitlerism and of one-man rule.

Stung by the absurdity of the accusations, Roosevelt summoned reporters to his house at Warm Springs to receive a Presidential announcement:

A: I have no inclination to be a dictator.

B: I have none of the qualifications which would make me a successful dictator.

C: I have too much historical background and too much knowledge of existing dictatorships to make me desire any form of dictatorship for a democracy like the United States of America.[36]

The pronouncement did no good. On April 8, the House of Representatives voted 204 to 196 to recommit the bill to committee, effectively killing it. Ickes blamed the defeat of the measure on the proposed Department of Social Welfare. "The opposition was headed up," he wrote, "by the Catholic Church which fears Harry and some of his principal assistants because they have been social workers and are in favor of birth control and that sort of thing—or at least supposed to be."[37]

Hopkins, however, took a more philosophical view. Shortly after his return to Washington, he wrote Herbert Swope, "I have no idea whether the Reorganization Bill will pass or not and, if it does, what my fate will be. It really isn't very important. The last few months have made me revamp my point of view about what is important in this life, and I find that warm and understanding friends are at the top."[38]

CHAPTER SIX

White House Janizary

Enforced idleness during early 1938 gave Hopkins a lot of time to think. Whatever the fate of his own Presidential ambitions, the New Deal must survive and prosper. Somehow the President must return to the paths he had abandoned when he took the advice of the budget balancers and cut spending sharply.

Relief spending had dominated Hopkins' life in one form or another ever since he had left college, but as he worked it out in the sunshine of Florida, the opportunity now at hand called for a complete program of financial security for everyone, and he determined to devote himself to that goal.

No President other than Roosevelt, or perhaps Hopkins, if he had realized his Presidential ambitions, could have carried out such a program, but at the moment there was no hope for it even under Roosevelt. As the recession deepened that winter, FDR clung to his fiscal conservatism. Perhaps he felt that the pressures of an unfriendly Congress left him no choice. But at that juncture, nothing Roosevelt could have done, except perhaps resign, would have pleased the coalition that had seized control of both Houses.

While in Florida, Hopkins had worked out a plan which would make it possible for some sort of financial security to become a reality. If he were to become President, he would work for it; if not, the best man to do so would be Roosevelt. Thus during the next year, Hopkins simultaneously pursued his own Presidential ambitions and let fall the hint that he favored a third term for Roosevelt.

His strategy involved restoring some kind of party discipline around the national leader. Even before he went to Rochester for his operation he had discussed with friends such as Corcoran, Ickes, and Jimmy Roosevelt the idea of purging the party of the conservatives as they came up for reelection. It was an idea which would recur.

The first task, as Hopkins saw it, was to turn the President from his conservative aberration, which won him no friends in Congress nor among the businessmen it was calculated to appease. Certainly his conservative policies drew him no votes from the men and women who lost their jobs during the recession.

On March 25, the stock market cracked sharply again, and Hopkins was ready. From south and north, he and Aubrey Williams descended on Warm Springs, armed with masses of figures and recommendations prepared by Leon Henderson. The arguments convinced FDR, and by the time he returned to Washington, the President had decided to spend his way into recovery.

Vacationing Treasury Secretary Morgenthau returned to Washington to find the spenders in charge. Armed with cautious recommendations from his staff, he went promptly to the White House for a meeting to have it out. It went the other way. Flanked by his son Jimmy and by Harry Hopkins, FDR opened the meeting by saying:

"We have been traveling fast this last week and have covered a lot of ground, and you will have to hurry to catch up."

"Mr. President," Morgenthau replied, "maybe I never can catch up."

"Oh, yes, you can—in a couple of hours."[1]

As the President outlined the program, Morgenthau's face got grimmer and grimmer. The next morning he remarked to his staff that the spenders had carried the day. "They have just stampeded him during the week I was away. He was completely stampeded. They stampeded him like cattle."[2]

The following evening, April 12, there was another meeting at the White House, attended by most of those connected with the government's spending programs, including Marriner Eccles, Chairman of the Federal Reserve Board, Hull, Ickes, Morgenthau, Wallace, RFC head Jesse Jones, Jimmy Roosevelt, and Hopkins. Morgenthau had a memorandum outlining his views, but it was scarcely heeded. Hopkins described a program of heavy public works, combining loans and grants, increased spending for highways, flood control, NYA, CCC, WPA, and a host of other projects all calculated to give the economy a shove and rekindle prosperity. After he was through, Roosevelt read a rough draft of the message he was sending Congress to implement the Hopkins plan. Morgenthau, in despair, contemplated resignation, but Ickes thought the "message was certainly mild enough. As I observed when he asked me for my opinion, it would not offend the most captious."[3]

On April 14, Roosevelt took the plan to the people in his first fireside chat in five months. He acknowledged the recession and seized the initiative. He called upon Congress to pass the wages and hours bill which had been stalled for nearly a year, and then he spelled out his program. He proposed that Congress appropriate $1,250,000,000 for WPA, FSA, NYA, and CCC. PWA would get a billion, the U.S. Housing Authority $300,000,000 for slum clearance and low-cost housing. New highways would be given $100,000,000, and there would be $37,000,000 for flood control and $25,000,000 for new federal buildings. An additional $2,150,000,000 would be made available for the credit market by reducing the reserve requirements in the U.S. Treasury and in banks. The total package amounted to $4,862,000,000. Without much dissent to a President who was willing to spend in an election year, Congress passed the program pretty much as submitted.

A few days after the fireside chat, Ickes and Hopkins met with the President to coordinate the successful strategy in guiding the relief bill through Congress. Ickes noted:

> I have heard from two or three sources lately that Harry Hopkins has been speaking of me in very friendly and complimentary terms. . . . Harry is pretty disgusted with the way some supposed New Dealers have been acting. Harry himself is a man who sticks to his guns and isn't afraid either of a fight or a licking.[4]

The apparent change came about because Hopkins no longer considered Ickes a rival. He now had his sights set on higher goals. He knew that his days as WPA administrator were numbered, and the proposal the President had adopted included WPA, PWA, and all the other activities. Hopkins viewpoint was now on the higher level of overall planner. He could let Aubrey Williams fight Ickes while he kept his eye on the whole program.

Hopkins in his new role as chief of the "Inner Cabinet" appeared more and more in public with the President, as he attended almost every meeting Roosevelt had with his advisers. And, in an unprecedented move, Roosevelt directed him to attend meetings of the Cabinet.[5]

On April 29, Hopkins received a telephone call from Missy LeHand, instructing him to be in her office that afternoon at 2:00. When he appeared, she informed him that the President wanted to take him into the Cabinet meeting. Hopkins protested that he had no business being there and demurred again when the President came through her office on his way to the meeting. FDR smiled enigmatically and remarked that there was more than one way of skinning a cat. Hopkins guessed that this was a reference to the fact that Congress had not gone along with the Cabinet position of Welfare Secretary, which would have been his. Since everyone knew that the Vice President had done everything he could to insure the defeat of the reorganization bill, Hopkins guessed that FDR wanted to flout Garner with his presence.

> He said [Ickes wrote of his conversation with Hopkins] that he was glad to be there because he had had an opportunity to see the Vice President giving himself away. He noted that on a couple of occasions when the President was talking, the Vice President, in an audible voice, addressed remarks to someone at his end of the table. He is fully persuaded, after watching the Vice President in action, that he has stimulated the opposition to the President within the Democratic organization. I have been convinced of this for many months.[6]

Over Hopkins' objections, FDR directed him to continue to attend the meetings. No precedent existed for the presence of outsiders. Even Garner's attendance was questionable, according to usage, but FDR had invited him from the first, on the ground that should anything happen to him the Vice President would be informed of policy. But there was no reason for an outsider to be there, unless one of three conditions existed. First, the President might wish his chosen heir apparent to be up to date in all matters pertaining to operations of the government. Second, the President might wish the outsider to function in the manner of a chief of staff, the personal assistant who exerted authority in the President's name to carry out his decisions. Or, third, the outsider might be a potential member of the Cabinet. As far as Hopkins was concerned, all three conditions were valid.

Roosevelt at this time took Hopkins' possible Presidential candidacy very seriously. He had made up his mind to retire when his term ended, although he did not close the door to any possibility. As his successor he wanted someone whose judgment he could trust, who was loyal, who could get things done, and who would carry on the New Deal. Hopkins, to his way of thinking, fit all these criteria, and no one else did.

About this time, Roosevelt summoned Hopkins. After a discussion of the rudeness of members of the Supreme Court in ignoring the traditional visit to the White House, Roosevelt turned the conversation to a successor should Justice Louis D. Brandeis retire. The obvious selection was Felix Frankfurter, a friend of both Roosevelt and Hopkins. Although he was suitable for the "Jewish" seat on the Supreme Bench, Roosevelt felt the appointee should come from west of the Mississippi, since all the rest of the Court was from the East.

Dropping that subject, Roosevelt turned to the possible successors to the Presidency. He did not finally rule out a third term for himself, but he wanted to return to his home and take care of the management of his estate.

The Presidency was costing him too much, and his mother was dipping into capital to pay the expenses on the Dutchess County estates, including Val Kill and the Hyde Park home.

According to Hopkins' notes, Roosevelt considered and dismissed as Presidential material Secretary of State Cordell Hull as too old, Secretary of Agriculture Henry Wallace, with no reason given, and Secretary of the Interior Harold L. Ickes as too "combative." Also eliminated were Paul McNutt of Indiana, Michigan Governor Frank Murphy, and Pennsylvania Governor George Earle. His comment on Senator Robert M. LaFollette, Jr., "fine—later—Secretary of State soon," according to Hopkins' notes, is revealing in view of LaFollette's isolationist stand two years later.

Farley was dismissed after lengthy discussion. He had no knowledge of and no interest in foreign affairs, and he had never supported the New Deal. Yet Roosevelt considered him "clearly the most dangerous" of the possible candidates because of his wide popularity among party leaders. If Farley ran for Governor of New York, which he was considering, his probable election would make him a leading candidate for the nomination in 1940.

Roosevelt then turned to a consideration of Hopkins as his possible successor. As the conversation progressed, Hopkins became convinced that he was the chosen one. First Roosevelt considered the liabilities. Hopkins' first marriage had ended in divorce, but his second marriage had been a happy one. Others had been divorced, and Cleveland had survived a major scandal before becoming President.

FDR then considered the handicap of Hopkins' health. The doctors at the Mayo Clinic has assured Roosevelt that the chances were two to one against a recurrence. Nevertheless the job of President was a strenuous one, a man killer, and Roosevelt went on to say that he believed he could have walked with no brace on his left leg if he had not run for the Governorship of New York in 1928.

Having dealt with the liabilities as he saw them, FDR turned to the positive side. He felt Hopkins could be nominated and elected and that he was best fitted of all the candidates to carry on the work of the New Deal and the liberal program begun in 1933. He promised to do everything he could to help and said he would appoint Hopkins as Secretary of Commerce by the end of the year. This would broaden his experience and remove him from the fire of those who hated relief expenditures and relief administrators. He went on to discuss strategy, that Hopkins should not make his move too soon so that his enemies and rivals would have no chance to join forces against him. He ended the conversation with, according to Hopkins' notes, "assurances and hopes."[7]

Roosevelt kept his promise and appointed Hopkins Secretary of Commerce just before Christmas at the end of the year. And at every available opportunity during the rest of 1938, Hopkins was photographed with his chief, so that his name, face, and position would be impressed on the public. No one appears in a photograph with a President unless the President desires it—at least not often. Of course, casual group and crowd scenes are another matter, but the newspapers and newsreels had many pictures that year of Roosevelt, Garner, and Hopkins; Roosevelt, Farley, and Hopkins; Roosevelt, Hull, and Hopkins; Roosevelt, This-or-That-Public-Figure, and Hopkins. On April 13, for example, he attended the opening of the baseball season with FDR. The President threw out the first ball, and the Senators beat Philadelphia 12 to 8.

Certainly Hopkins believed. He told several friends in strict confidence that he had "the green light." And he began to move to establish a base. He inquired into voting residency requirements in New York and in his native Iowa and considered buying a farm in Iowa.

That Eleanor Roosevelt approved Hopkins as her husband's successor was strongly hinted in a column she wrote in her syndicated "My Day." "It was good to see Mr. Harry Hopkins yesterday and to have him spend the night with us. . . . He seems to work because he has an inner conviction that his job needs to be done and that he must do it. I think he would be that way about any job he undertook."[8]

Eleanor Roosevelt had been Hopkins' first friend in the White House. Yet soon after he had recovered from his operation and began to be ever closer to the President, he began to drop in her esteem. She saw the more human side of him, and that side was a disappointment to her idealistic absolutism. The change, she felt, began after Barbara Hopkins' death.

> It is a natural development [she wrote] to seek entertainment and diversion when your life is lonely. What surprised some of us was the fact that Harry seemed to get so much genuine pleasure out of contact with gay but more or less artificial society. People who could give him luxuries and the kind of party in which he probably never before had had the slightest interest became important to him. I did not like this side of Harry as much as the side I first knew, but deep down he was a fine person who had the courage to bear pain and who loved his country enough to risk the curtailment of his life in order to be of service, after all chance of fulfilling any personal ambition was over.[9]

Eleanor Roosevelt, however, always remained a good friend to Hopkins. Later that summer, she inquired what arrangements he had made for Diana in case anything happened to him. She offered to serve as Diana's guardian; much moved, Hopkins drafted a new will including this provision. For the rest of his life, she never failed to worry about his health.[9]

It did not take long for Hopkins to size up the Cabinet. One day at an especially dull meeting, he scribbled a note and passed it over to Morgenthau:

> My dear Mr. Secretary:—
> News Bulletin No. 1.
> A.   Wallace is unhappy—cause wheat & other trouble.
> B.   Dan [Roper] is just the same thank you.
> C.   Fanny [Frances Perkins] is on both sides still.
> D.   The Sect'y of State would like to see the Sect'y of War in Canada and why not?
> E.   The Sect'y of War wants to stay & so does Helwig.
> F.   Farley is *still* away.
> G.   And how are you?
>
> Harry[10]

Hopkins had thus been the major force behind Roosevelt's return to the New Deal. The other great decision he helped to inspire turned out to be a disaster, the so-called "purge" of 1938. Even before his operation, Hopkins had assembled a group of liberals, including Corcoran, Ickes, and James Roosevelt, to consider ways of purging the party of conservatives and obstructionists. Someone named the group the Elimination Committee, and it had the aim not only of party discipline but control of the 1940 convention in favor of a liberal.

The first move of the Elimination Committee took place in Florida. Senator Claude Pepper faced an uphill fight for renomination by the Democrats, and during his convalescence, Hopkins worked with him to plan strategy. James Roosevelt announced administration support for Pepper in February, and in the ensuing primary, Pepper was the winner, which insured his victory in November.

Soon after his return to Washington, Hopkins summoned a meeting of the Elimination Committee to his home in Georgetown. This time it was enlarged to include also Assistant to the Attorney General Robert Jackson, Joseph Keenan, David Niles, and Benjamin Cohen. Hugh Johnson soon dubbed the group the "White House Janizaries," and it was clear from the first that Hopkins was Number One Janizary. Farley, who ought to have been leading the fight, according to the view of the Janizaries, was halfhearted, and spent most of his time working with the regular Democratic organizations in various localities.

Roosevelt hesitated to intervene in local elections, for he had spent too many years cultivating the delicate political relationships on which political careers are based. Despite their differences in viewpoint and background, Roosevelt genuinely liked a number of the men who opposed his programs. Still, he felt he had no choice. Political discipline had to be reestablished in the Democratic Party, and the recalcitrants had to be taught the lesson that double-crossing a President led to disaster.

In addition, Roosevelt had a dream that he could be the one to found a genuine Liberal Party, in which the liberal Democrats and liberal Republicans could find a home. He would gladly trade off the old guard Southern Democrats for northern Republican liberals. This was an idea he was to explore later with Wendell L. Willkie.

The opening gun in the war against the Democratic rebels was fired by Hopkins. In Iowa, anti-New Deal Senator Guy Gillette intended to run for reelection. Opposing him in the Democratic primary was a former Representative, Otha D. Wearin, who had, after a conservative start, swung around to the liberal side as a follower of Maury Maverick. Wearin called a press conference in late May to announce that he had administration backing and referred reporters to Hopkins. At first Hopkins said nothing, but he finally issued the statement: "If I were voting in Iowa, I would vote for Wearin on his record."

Of course, the statement, mild as it was, created a furore in Congress. Bert Wheeler told the Senate:

> Mr. Hopkins, for whom I have always had a high regard, is supposedly carrying out a Governmental relief program on a non-partisan and non-political basis. Yet his statement says in effect to the relief workers in Iowa: "You people ought to vote for Mr. Wearin and vote against Senator Gillette. . . ." Congress in appropriating for the relief of the underprivileged never intended that those funds should be utilized to slaughter a member of this body.[11]

In a press conference, FDR was asked if he approved of Hopkins' statement. He replied, off the record:

> That's just another of those things. When some candidate announces that he has White House endorsement, if I say he has not, that gives support to his opposition. If I say he has, of course the opposition won't like it, and so I can't say anything, but in this case I will tell you off the record, and I want you to make it absolutely off the record, no; I did not approve of this statement.[12]

Morgenthau, however, believed that he approved, if not the statement, at least the move to support Wearin in Iowa. Wearin, however, lost in the primary.

On June 24, in a fireside chat Roosevelt broke with tradition and assailed the "copperheads" in the party, saying, "As President of the United States,

I am not asking the voters of the country to vote for Democrats next November as opposed to Republicans or members of any other party."

And so the celebrated "purge" was on. It was a disaster for Roosevelt. Some incumbents he knew he could not beat, so he stayed clear of Pat McCarran in Nevada and Alva Adams in Colorado. But in Georgia he declared war on Senator Walter George, who won despite Presidential disfavor. The same thing happened with Cotton Ed Smith in South Carolina and Millard Tydings in Maryland. Only in New York City, where John O'Connor, the ultraconservative chairman of the House Rules Committee was beaten, did the purge win. Roosevelt insisted that this triumph made the whole effort worthwhile.

Hopkins played little or no part in the purge, after he had his fellow Janizaries help launch it. They felt they had accomplished a great deal in getting Roosevelt to move at all.

Hopkins' influence in getting Roosevelt to return to deficit spending and attempt the purge is hard to assess properly. By no stretch of the imagination can it be said that Hopkins forced FDR to take those steps. No one could move Roosevelt in any way he did not wish to go. When he "got his Dutch up," as he put it, nothing in the world could make him change his mind. When Hopkins had arrived in Warm Springs that March, he found Roosevelt in a frame of mind to try something, almost anything, to get the initiative back from Congress and to pull the country out of the recession. It seems clear that Hopkins caught him at the right moment, that he had a carefully thought-out program that gave promise of working. Hopkins, most important, had the knowledge of how to present a proposal to FDR, for he knew how to talk to him. Roosevelt disliked reading lengthy reports, voluminous manifestos, and the jargon of political and social scientists; they bored him. He would call in the author, and, tapping the mass of paper before him, would say, "Tell me what it's all about." If the author could not tell in few words the essence of the plan, the arguments for and against, the probable cost, and perhaps, even the political consequences, then he would get short shrift. Roosevelt would begin to look vague. He might launch into a long, pointless story of his boyhood in Hyde Park. The plan would never be heard of again.

Hopkins made none of these mistakes. He had an enormous capacity for absorbing huge masses of information. He could go unerringly to the heart of a problem so that the issues had to be faced. Thus, he made it possible for the President to decide. Since FDR and Hopkins usually agreed on goals, his problem was to sell the President on his methods. It did not always work, for Roosevelt had his own ideas and prejudices. He was sometimes accused of believing whatever he had been told by the last person to talk to him. This was usually a mistaken idea, for FDR was often merely being agreeable when his visitor thought he was agreeing. Hopkins, however, often convinced him, but it was always to make a choice of alternatives he was already considering. No one, not even Hopkins, could sell a completely foreign or uncongenial idea to Franklin Roosevelt.

Another asset Hopkins enjoyed in his relationship with FDR was that he never confused work time with fun time. He could relax and tell stories; he could listen, and he knew the importance of the two of them being silent together. He shared this talent with Missy LeHand, with whom he developed a warm friendship, but its core was in their relationship to Roosevelt, not in any romantic attraction between the two of them. Missy's love was for FDR, but she was fond of Hopkins and joined the President in worrying about his health.

By this time, Hopkins was equally at home as the Number One Janizary, leading the fight for New Deal programs, and as one of the congenial social crowd, along with Dr. Ross McIntire, Colonel Pa Watson, Jimmy and Betsey Roosevelt, Missy LeHand, Marvin McIntyre, and Steve Early. But he was the only one who was in both worlds and who also ran one of the largest activities of the government.

When Hopkins returned to his office in the Walker-Johnson Building, he largely left the day-to-day operations to Aubrey Williams, jumping in only to deal with such emergencies as took place in Cleveland, where the work relief rolls jumped from 20,000 to 70,000. Funds ran out, and workers were paid with food baskets from the Federal Surplus Commodities Corporation. The shortage of funds resulted from the failure of the Ohio legislature to appropriate its share of relief money. The same thing happened in Chicago, where the relief rolls had risen 240 percent from 50,000 to 120,000.

Coping with this kind of crisis had become routine to Hopkins. During his illness, he had been thinking about a plan to prevent such crises from recurring. Previous economic crises in the nation's history, he felt, had been met by the availability of the frontier. Ever westward lay the opportunity, and government land grants had spread the population to new areas where new riches could be created. But the geographical frontiers no longer existed to offer new opportunities. Hopkins said:

> The new frontier is idle men, money and machines, and all the resourcefulness, ingenuity and courage that reside in twelve or thirteen million unemployed men is helpless to take up this new frontier without tremendous organization of productive forces such as only Government can supply when business is in the doldrums.... This program must be such that American citizens accept it as a matter of right—with no feeling of social inferiority.[13]

His new frontier program had six main parts:

1. Take care of unemployed young people in the CCC and NYA.
2. Find jobs through the United States Employment Service for those who could work.
3. Assist persons laid off from industry with a program of unemployment insurance.
4. When unemployment insurance benefits run out, find a place for the unemployed on WPA rolls until private industry can absorb them.
5. Extend Social Security benefits to all the aged.
6. Provide direct support of other persons who cannot work, such as widowed, unmarried, and deserted mothers, those physically or mentally handicapped, and children too young to work.

"I believe our economic life based on a profit motive," said Hopkins, "is the most effective economy known to assure the well-being of all."[14]

His critics, of course, labeled his plan as everything from socialism to communism, and it was never permitted to come to a vote. Yet it was, if nothing else, a plank in Hopkins' platform for 1940.

During that spring and summer of 1938, Hopkins heeded his doctors' advice to take things easier and get more relaxation. He packed Diana off to camp and spent a good many weekends with his friends on Long Island, at Saratoga Springs, and in New York City. He went out for cruises with Roosevelt, and he played poker with Jesse Jones and Ickes. He made a speech at Chautauqua, New York, to explain his new frontier program, and he received honorary degrees from the University of South Carolina and the University of Arkansas. His name was connected in a romantic way with Mrs. Dorothy Donovan Thomas Hale, a wealthy widow of the smart set, who maintained homes in New York City, Southampton on Long Island, and Paris. He said that it was nobody's Goddamned business whether he was engaged to her or not. Nothing ever came of the affair, if it was one, and that fall Mrs. Hale committed suicide by leaping out of her sixteenth-floor apartment window.

Congress struck back at the politically active Hopkins. Considerable stir was roused when Hopkins was quoted as predicting that nine out of ten WPA workers would vote for Roosevelt if he were running for election at that moment. A Senate committee exonerated him, however, on the ground that what he had said was in reply to a reporter's question and not a coercion of WPA workers.

More fruitful were investigations into politics in WPA State administrations. In Kentucky, where Hopkins had ordered an inquiry, he was accused of a whitewash. Nothing to Hopkins' discredit was discovered. It was the same story in other States, and although Hopkins was kept busy for a time answering Congressional queries, the matter quietly faded away. As Robert Sherwood put it, many of the investigators "secretly thanked heaven that this investigation had been conducted in Kentucky and not in their own states."[15] In any case, the Congressmen were afraid to push him too hard, for he knew where too many bodies were buried.

He had a brief spell of illness in late May, when he was confined to a hospital on Long Island. It was not serious, and Pa Watson, Ross McIntire, and Steve Early mocked him in a telegram: WE THREE RESPECTFULLY SUGGEST THAT ONE WAY TO AVOID THROAT INFECTION IS TO KEEP YOUR MOUTH SHUT STOP YOU WILL BE SURPRISED TO LEARN HOW WELL THIS WORKS.[16]

While Hopkins was in New York, he had several conversations with Tugwell on his political prospects. Tugwell urged him to run for Governor of New York, which was still his official residence despite his long years in Washington. On June 16, Tugwell wrote him:

> I have been talking with one or two people here whose judgment I value, and they agree with me in what I told you the other day about the importance of the New York governorship. The logical and usual approach to the Presidency is through state governorship, and the weight of the governorship of the greatest state is always a tremendous advantage.[17]

In the same letter, Tugwell noted that the way into New York politics was through Farley. That ended the matter, so far as Hopkins was concerned, for he knew that Farley would never support him for Governor. Farley was busy at that time dropping suggestions that Hopkins would not do.[18]

Although he gave up the idea of running for Governor of New York, Hopkins remained very much in the picture as a Presidential candidate. Assistant Secretary of State Adolf Berle considered Hopkins impossible and felt that Ickes would be the best candidate of the progressives, but thought that "the President will—or—can—" do very little "to control howling Harold."[19] Ickes confided to his diary on September 4: "There seems to be a growing feeling that the President is interested now in building up Harry Hopkins. Certainly Harry is closer to the President than he has ever been and as close or closer than anyone else at the time being."[20]

The following day, he went into Hopkins' candidacy in more detail, almost fretting at what he saw ahead:

> I told Tom Corcoran that if Harry were the candidate I could support him, something that I could not say about everyone. I was frank to say, however, that I doubted whether Harry would be a strong candidate, even

admitting that the men and women on his WPA rolls constitute a very powerful political machine. I do not think that Harry as a candidate would appeal to the sober sense and business judgment of the average American. . . . Apparently the operation he underwent at the Mayos' for ulcers of the stomach was successful, but I know that there is a very general impression among the newspaper correspondents in Washington that he is in bad health. He looks frail although he does not appear to be ill.[21]

Hopkins, however, did not consider himself to be in bad shape. On August 17, he wrote Lewis that he was going to spend the weekend with Diana at her camp in New York State. "I have been feeling grand in spite of really putting in a tough summer."[22]

The summer had been tough on James Roosevelt, too. The strain of acting as his father's assistant brought on gastric ulcers. A stint at the Mayo Clinic and a rest at Campobello failed to improve his health, and in September he went back to the clinic for an operation. Roosevelt took Hopkins with him as he hurried to Rochester on word that James's condition was critical. On September 12, Roosevelt was sitting in his private railroad car in the yards at Rochester listening with Hopkins to Hitler's Nuremberg speech. Roosevelt knew enough German to understand and translate Hitler's shouts that Germany was about to move against Czechoslovakia.

When Czechoslovakia was created out of lands belonging to the Austro-Hungarian empire at the end of World War I, a large number of German citizens in the northwestern part of the new country suddenly found themselves Czech nationals. This area, known as the Sudetenland, was a thorn in the side of nationalistic Germans, and Hitler seized upon the cause. He was ready for another challenge to the West.

Roosevelt felt that the danger to peace was real, and that if war came in Europe, it would be difficult to avoid American involvement. He knew, too, as Commander-in-Chief, that the United States armed forces were in a state of weakness verging on anemia. Roosevelt had backed away from internationalism following the reaction to his "quarantine" speech in the fall of 1937 and had taken no action following the Nazi Anschluss with Austria in the spring of 1938, but he was keenly concerned. The sinking of the U.S. Navy gunboat *Panay* in China by arrogant Japanese airmen in December, 1937, had revealed the low esteem in which the United States was held by the Japanese warlords. Although Japan had apologized and paid an indemnity, Roosevelt was upset at the failure of Congress and the American people to respond to a blatant challenge to American rights.

Roosevelt and Hopkins, in face of the unwillingness of Congress to provide funds for American defenses, came up with the idea that WPA work could be done as well for military as for civilian purposes. Airfields could be built, barracks erected, machine tools produced, and stand-by factories prepared.

After hearing Hitler's threatening speech, Roosevelt told Hopkins to go out to the West Coast and make a secret survey of the capacity of the aircraft manufacturing industry there with a view of how it could be expanded for war production. As a result of Hopkins' findings, Roosevelt called for an increase in the number of military aircraft for the Army and Navy to 8,000. Hopkins had discovered that the existing capacity of the aircraft industry was about 2,600 planes a year.

Influenced by his report, a committee consisting of the Assistant Secretary of the Navy, the Assistant Secretary of War, and Aubrey Williams recommended that the capacity be increased to 15,000 within two years and that an additional three plants which could turn out 16,000 more aircraft be built with WPA funds and labor.

This Western trip marks Hopkins' first major move into the role of confidential investigator for Roosevelt. The President knew that from no one else could he get an objective answer to the questions he had, and from no one else would he get some kind of plan of action. Hopkins had many times shown that he was ready to move fast in response to an emergency and that he could view a situation without rose-colored glasses. He would make many more such trips for the President.

The trip also marked Hopkins' first involvement in problems of national defense and in procurement of armaments. It was not connected solely with his WPA duties. It had the express purpose of bringing a trustworthy report to the President. It could be undertaken only by a man on whose judgment the President relied and in whom he had complete confidence as a man. Roosevelt sent Hopkins when he could not go himself.

Shortly, after Hopkins' return to Washington, the Munich crisis threatened the world with war. Roosevelt could do little to avert catastrophe, for the more war threatened in Europe, the louder the isolationists shouted their warnings. On September 26, 1938, he sent cables to all leaders in the dispute warning of the consequences of a rupture, reminding them of the opportunities for peaceful settlement through the Kellogg-Briand Pact and other international agreements, and expressing his hopes for a peaceful and fair settlement of their differences. Hitler's response was immediate: a long-winded justification of German claims.

Roosevelt appealed to Mussolini to urge a continuation of negotiations. In a Cabinet meeting that day, September 27, there was some discussion of a further message to Hitler. Hopkins was opposed to sending one, arguing that it would do no good and possibly might worsen the situation, but the President decided to make one further appeal. Arguing that the situation in Europe might lead to a general war, "as unnecessary as it is unjustifiable," he urged another meeting in some neutral European city where the four nations could work out their differences and which "would offer the opportunity for this and correlated questions to be solved in a spirit of justice, of fair dealing, and, in all human probability, with greater permanence." To ward off any political consequences at home, Roosevelt added to his message, "The Government of the United States has no political involvements in Europe, and will assume no obligations in the conduct of the present negotiations. Yet in our own right we recognize our responsibilities as a part of a world of neighbors."[23]

Whether Roosevelt's message to Hitler had any effect cannot be known, but Mussolini did respond and urged caution on the Führer. This, coupled with the advice of his own moderates, led Hitler to agree to meet with Prime Minister Neville Chamberlain, Premier Edouard Daladier, and Mussolini at Munich on September 29. At the Munich Conference, Czechoslovakia was divided while the Czech representatives waited outside the meeting room to learn what was to happen to their country. Hitler agreed to respect the integrity of the rest of the unfortunate nation and expressed his intention never to go to war with France or Great Britain. These terms were inscribed on a piece of paper which Chamberlain waved for the newsreel cameras as he stepped from his plane in London and proclaimed that he had achieved "peace for our time."

In the universal thankfulness that war had been averted, one voice of dissent could be ignored.

> Do not suppose [Winston Churchill warned in the House of Commons a few days later] that this is the end. This is only the beginning of the reckoning. This is only the first sip, the first foretaste of a bitter cup which will be proffered to us year by year unless, by a supreme recovery of moral health and martial vigour, we arise again and take our stand for freedom as in the olden time.[24]

On November 14, Roosevelt convened a momentous meeting at the White House to get things moving on defense, especially the expansion of American air power. The Munich Pact had shocked many Americans, revealing as it did the moral and military weakness of France and Great Britain. In mid-October, Ambassador William C. Bullitt returned from Paris to report on the state of Europe. The picture he gave in private talks with Roosevelt was a frightening one of huge German military buildup, especially in combat aircraft. The French, Bullitt reported, knew that the rapid expansion of their own air fleets could come only from American production. The British also were interested in buying American aircraft, and Roosevelt was sympathetic.

Although he approved of the idea of assisting France and Britain with the output of American aircraft factories, Roosevelt was unable to act. The isolationists were already assailing the sale of American-made munitions abroad, mostly small arms ammunition, and any attempt to deliver aircraft would only increase the clamor. The isolationists, not all of whom thought alike, had three main if contradictory arguments: American sale of armaments abroad would involve the United States, thereby increasing the risk of war. Americans should not be building armaments, for that could be viewed as an aggressive move by her potential enemies, while if America remained weak, her enemies would ignore her. Finally, sale of American armaments to foreign countries would weaken American defenses.

At the November 14 meeting, Roosevelt assembled only those persons whom he believed he could trust with his plans. Left out were Secretary of War Henry Woodring and Secretary of the Navy Claude Swanson. The latter was in uncertain health, and the former an avowed isolationist. Roosevelt enjoyed serving as his own Secretary of the Navy, so Swanson was little missed. Assistant Secretary Louis Johnson took Woodring's place. Morgenthau was there and Robert Jackson. Morgenthau brought his Solicitor of the Treasury Herman Oliphant. Completing the civilian group was Harry Hopkins.

On the military side were Army Chief of Staff General Malin Craig, his deputy, Brigadier General George C. Marshall, and Major General Henry H. Arnold, newly appointed Chief of the Army Air Corps. Roosevelt also had his military and naval aides, Pa Watson, and Captain Daniel J. Callaghan.

The lengthy meeting ranged over projected military appropriations, plans, and weaknesses. It became clear that the President wanted an enormous expansion of the air strength of the United States. What he really wanted was an Army Air Corps of 20,000 planes, with an annual capacity of the industry to produce 24,000 aircraft. Since he realized that Congress would give him no more than half of what he asked, he told the Army officers to plan on the basis of 10,000 aircraft over a two-year period. Of these 8,000 could be produced by existing commercial plants and 2,000 from plants to be built with government funds. In addition, Hopkins would have the responsibility of building aircraft factories capable of turning out 10,000 planes a year, but these were to be kept in a standby status until need for them arose.

Although the President talked with enthusiasm about large numbers of planes, he showed little interest in the procurement of the men for the Army to fly and maintain them. General Marshall disagreed with the overemphasis on aircraft and the undersupply of men, and when asked told Roosevelt exactly what he thought.

I remember [he noted] that ended the conference. The President gave me a . . . startled look and when I went out they all bade me good-bye and said that my tour in Washington was over. But I want to say in compliment to the President that that didn't antagonize him at all. Maybe he thought I would tell him the truth so far as I personally was concerned, which I certainly tried to do in all our conversations.[25]

This meeting brought Hopkins and Marshall together for the first time. At the moment it was of little consequence, but it ripened into an association which caused Marshall to write a few days after the German surrender in 1945, when Hopkins informed him that he was leaving the government:

As a matter of fact I was not at all surprised to get your news. Political repercussions seemed to indicate such action and your state of health would make it advisable, because you have literally given of your physical strength during the past three years to a degree that has been, in my opinion, heroic and will never be appreciated except by your intimates.

For myself, I wish to tell you this, that you personally have been of invaluable service to me in the discharge of my duties in this war. Time after time you have done for me things I was finding exceedingly difficult to do for myself and always in matters of the gravest import. You have been utterly selfless as well as courageous and purely objective in your contribution to the war effort.[26]

A few days after Hopkins' designation in December as Secretary of Commerce, he asked Marshall for an appointment. Marshall quickly went to Hopkins in his new offices in the Commerce Building and outlined a picture of such grave deficiencies in Army preparedness that Hopkins urged him to see the President at once. Since he was not yet Chief of Staff, Marshall refused, but he had gained Hopkins' interest and support.

More important, for the rest of his life, Marshall believed that he owed his subsequent appointment in 1939 as Chief of Staff to the influence of Hopkins. Marshall also believed that Roosevelt did not develop real confidence in him until after Pearl Harbor, and so for all that time, Hopkins was Marshall's chief contact with the Commander-in-Chief and his friend in court.

In the closing days of 1938, Hopkins as principal adviser and executive officer to the President paid little attention to WPA except as a resource in defense preparations. The rest of its activities he left to Aubrey Williams and to Francis "Pink" Harrington. He was up to his ears in the election campaign. While supporting the President's purge, he was building his own base for 1940. He visited Chicago to keep in touch with Mayor Kelly, ostensibly about a WPA project to build an airport to serve Chicago. Ickes had already declined the project for PWA, and Kelly was trying the other side. This brought Ickes to a fury, but it died away when Hopkins dropped the plan. Ickes then needled Hopkins by allowing him to believe he would run for Mayor of Chicago, which of course would have cut into Hopkins' Illinois strength if Ickes had been elected. It was all good fun, however, for Ickes had no intention of running, although he was urged to do so by friends.[27]

The Hopkins boom for President was gathering enough strength to cause Farley some concern. He called a meeting in Chicago of several state party chairmen which Howard Hunter wrote Hopkins "was pretty adroitly planned to build defenses against you or any other liberal candidate. The play was all aimed at continuing some of the worst reactionary state and county groups."[28]

Roosevelt had come to the conclusion that it was time to relieve Hopkins as WPA administrator. On December 16, FDR told Ickes:

> Harry had been kicked around a lot and he thought that he would make a good Secretary of Commerce because he gets along well with the big businessmen with whom he comes in contact. As a matter of fact, Harry does get along well with the economic royalists. There is something debonair and easygoing about him that makes him personally attractive; he seems to like to accept invitations to expensive homes; he loves horse racing and poker and women, and, except for his social-service and relief records, he would be highly acceptable to this class.[29]

Hopkins could look back on his days in Federal relief with some degree of satisfaction. His organizations had given employment to between two and three and a half million persons at any given time. They had constructed over 11,000 buildings, including schools, gymnasiums, hospitals, courthouses, firehouses, hangars, and recreational facilities and had made major improvements to some 30,000 others. They had constructed over 40,000 miles of new road and improved 150,000 miles of existing road. They had completed over a hundred airports, some 1,400 athletic fields, nearly 800 parks, 1,800 swimming pools, and 155 miles of levees and embankments for flood control. They had reforested over 20,000 acres and planted some 20 million trees and shrubs. They had established libraries, art classes, music classes, had staged theatrical productions, and had given employment to many artists and writers.

WPA bought talking-book machines for the blind. It taught nearly 200,000 illiterates to read and gave another 150,000 useful skills to enable them to earn a living. No member of the Washington office or top regional and State administrator was ever found guilty of misappropriation of public funds, although plenty of accusations were made. Where peculations, mostly the result of local political pressure or maneuvering, were discovered, they were prosecuted. Most projects had originated in the communities which they served, and the expenditure of funds was supposed to relieve suffering and to build something worthwhile, although in Hopkins' mind, the first motive was always the stronger. In contrast to countries where the suffering of the great depression was causing many people to turn to other ideologies, the American people in general retained their faith in the capitalist system and in native institutions, because they felt that the government under the New Deal was trying to do something for them. Of course every liberal, from Roosevelt on down the line, and especially Hopkins, Ickes, and Frances Perkins, was called a socialist or worse, but even the indefatigable Martin Dies, Chairman of the House Un-American Activities Committee, could find nothing against them.

Shortly before Christmas, reporters asked Hopkins about the rumors that he was to be named Commerce Secretary. "Don't kid me, boys," he replied. "This is the Christmas season and I'm accepting anything."

One of the things he accepted was an invitation to Ickes' home for dinner and a poker game. The guest of honor was Roosevelt, and the usual crowd of McIntyre and McIntire, Pa Watson, and Steve Early was there, plus Frank Walter. It was a happy time and a good prelude to the announcement made two days later, December 23, that Hopkins was to be the new Secretary of Commerce.

On Christmas Eve, Hopkins was sworn in at the White House where he and Diana had gone to spend the holidays with the Roosevelt family. At the ceremony were several of Hopkins' friends, including Ickes, Aubrey Williams, David Niles, Corrington Gill, and "Pink" Harrington, whom Roosevelt had named to take Hopkins' place as WPA administrator. Aubrey Williams, who had hoped to get the job, was trying not to look disappointed, but he knew that some injudicious statements made during the campaign had cost him any chance he might have had. Actually Roosevelt was trying to de-emphasize WPA, and in selecting Harrington, an Army officer, he was removing the organization as much as possible from politics and from the limelight.

At the ceremony, Roosevelt read Hopkins' commission with considerable feeling, and Attorney General Homer Cummings administered the oath. Ickes noted that Hopkins' clothes were in good order and "I suspect that Harry had really sloughed off his slouchy habits preparatory to living up to his new job."[30]

There was, however, a shadow on the ceremony. Ickes thought Hopkins looked pale and thin. And in a note written to Lewis three days earlier,

Hopkins had remarked of his visit to the White House that "I fear it will be a bit strenuous for me."[31] But no one took any heed of such warning signs. It was Christmas and time for rejoicing and goodwill toward men.

Early Christmas morning, Hopkins wrote a long letter to his daughter. Perhaps it was not so much to her then as to remind her later of Christmas in the White House, with the only family she had, for the Roosevelts had made her one of their own. Hopkins seldom let anyone know his feelings, and this letter is the more interesting in revealing a side he never showed the public.

> It is ever so early Christmas morning my dear one—and you are still fast asleep dreaming I hope of Santa Claus and the happy day to come. My own heart is heavy because of mother and last night when Mrs. Roosevelt and I came to kiss you good night and the hot tears came rolling out while I smiled at you.
>
> We have been here since Friday afternoon the twenty third—Sarah and Kate are here with their father and mother—and little Franklin who is hardly six months old with his parents—and dear Grandmamma whom you love so much and Aunt Betty and Harry Hooker and Hall, Mrs. Roosevelt's brother.
>
> You have played and romped all over the house—and we celebrated Jimmy's birthday on Friday night—and Missy left to go to Boston for Christmas, and that was too bad for we both like her so much.
>
> And yesterday morning all my friends came to the oval room where I was sworn in as Sect'y of Commerce—and Mrs. Roosevelt gave me one of her Bibles and the name of everyone who was there is written in it. How good the President is! And I do so want to do a good job for his sake.
>
> And on Christmas Eve we went with the President to the lighting of the great Christmas tree across the way—and then he read Dickens Christmas Carol—and the cold, heartless Scrooge was unhappier than ever and his reformation the pleasanter. The President reads aloud better than anyone I know—he takes infinite pains with each word and phrase—placing the emphasis just right—and withal reading with such obvious pleasure to himself. And you laughed when he said "humbug" in a loud voice and "good afternoon" even louder. But Tiny Tim is still happy and ever he will be—for as the President said after the reading, "This is the only good Christmas story in a hundred years." The President had read this story to his children every Christmas Eve for many years—and the little book is one of his priceless possessions.
>
> I filled your red stocking and hung it in the President's bedroom alongside of three others and there you will find it soon my dear—for there is a Santa Claus who has filled [it] to the very top for the dearest girl in the world.
>
> Daddy[32]

The admission of Harry and Diana Hopkins into the Roosevelt family Christmas was more than act of kindness. For Franklin Roosevelt, Christmas meant family. Political friends had no part of the Christmas festivities. Roosevelt gathered around him his children and grandchildren, those closest to him, for a frankly sentimental, traditional Christmas, and for Hopkins to be included meant that he was counted as one of the Roosevelt family. This intimate relationship was to continue until Roosevelt's death. It was interrupted three times by Hopkins' serious illnesses, but it never came to an end until an April afternoon in 1945 when Roosevelt complained of a terrible headache and never spoke again.

CHAPTER SEVEN

Secretary of Commerce

In the plush office in the Commerce Building, in January, 1939, Harry Hopkins tried to bid farewell to the easygoing informality that he had known in WPA headquarters. No more did he receive visitors in shirtsleeves, sitting far down on his spine and his desk piled high with untidy heaps of papers. Now he sat erect, wearing tie, coat, and vest, to live up to his huge office with rich paneling. His secretary kept his desk clean. Papers were put away and half-drunk cups of coffee were no longer in evidence.

This was the new Hopkins. Like an actor changing roles, he put aside his costume for *Tobacco Road* and put on that for *The Late George Apley.* In truth, neither role suited him very well, but he was more comfortable in the easy clothes of the social worker than in the stuffed shirt of the ultra-respectable.

The news of his appointment to the post of Secretary of Commerce, although rumored for weeks, stunned many newspapers and businessmen. "Surely," the *Chicago Daily News* opined, "this is the most incomprehensible, as well as one of the least defensible, appointments the President has made in his six and one-half years in the White House." [1] On the other hand, Kiplinger's Washington Letter took a more balanced view:

> *He's now the Roosevelt first choice* as the Roosevelt successor. Thus it isn't just an ordinary cabinet shift.
> *And Hopkins himself is positively anxious to be President.* This is definite. It means he will use the Secretaryship as a buildup. He is sick of WPA, and the bad smell about it, the social worker reputation. He wants to show he is

a big man, a broad man, can administer business. So he'll whoop it up in Commerce, try to make a new name for himself.

To politicize business will be one of his major objectives. This means he will try hard to draw business into the New Deal orbit. He will organize business elements which want to "go along with gov't." [2]

Harry Hopkins also possessed friends who believed he could do anything. Florence Kerr wrote him during the confirmation hearings:

All I could think of at the session yesterday was—Don't you fellows know, can't you sense that he is one of the greatest men alive. Do any of you softies on the committee think you could take what he has or do what he has done! You are not worthy to unlatch his shoes—and never will be. [3]

In between the extremes, most people adopted an attitude of watchfulness. But the appointment was not as unpopular as the perfervid editorial writers and the loudest politicians and businessmen made out. In Hopkins' personal letters, over 2,000 notes, telegrams, and letters of congratulation are preserved, some of them formal, but most reflecting genuine enthusiasm on the part of the writer.

Nor was he the stranger to business that the unfriendly press made him out to be. In his work as WPA administrator, he had negotiated with thousands of businessmen, had signed countless contracts for supplies, equipment, and materials. And he had powerful friends in the business world, including John Hertz, Bernard Baruch, and Averell Harriman, of the Union Pacific Railroad. Harriman, in particular, supported his selection. He wrote:

The business community was somewhat surprised and shocked by Harry Hopkins' selection for the Department of Commerce, as he was considered to be more interested in social work than in business, and thought to be "a bit" more liberal than the average businessman liked. As I recall it, I was then Chairman of the Business Advisory Council. We had a meeting in St. Louis. I talked individually to each member of the Council on the way out on the train and to others that we met who came from different directions. I took the point of view that Hopkins was extremely intelligent and had an open mind and would listen to our advice. He was close to Roosevelt; and if we could persuade him as to the soundness of our positions, it would go a long way toward getting the President's support. We had had cordial relations with Secretary Roper, but he had little or no influence with the President. My arguments prevailed, perhaps because they had confidence in my judgment. In any event, the Council unanimously endorsed Harry's nomination and I was authorized to submit this endorsement to the Commerce Committee. [4]

Despite Harriman's endorsement, the Commerce Committee hearings threatened to become a Roman circus. Insulting questions were thrown at him by Senator Hiram Johnson of California for the better part of a day. This spectacle elicited from the *New York Times* an editorial entitled "Fair Treatment for Harry Hopkins."[5]

Before the hearings began, the committee chairman, Senator Josiah Bailey of North Carolina, made a vitriolic speech on the floor of the Senate attacking Hopkins' administration of relief. The two men met in the lobby of a downtown hotel and had to be restrained from coming to blows. "Bailey and Harry Hopkins had a personal encounter," reported a witness, Under Secretary of the Treasury John Hanes. "It is one of the few cases on record, I guess, where a member of the Executive Department was going to sock a Senator, and almost did, and vice versa." [6]

Hanes went to see Bailey, who was "as mad as a hornet," but was a fine gentleman. He finally agreed to ask some questions and make a few personal remarks on the floor of the Senate, and then abstain from voting.

True to his promise, Bailey was reasonable in his questions. Hopkins, who had recovered his composure, admitted freely that he had been indiscreet in some of the speeches he had made while he was WPA administrator. "I do not want to imply I withdraw the contents of those speeches, but if I had the road to go over again I would not have made them as Relief Administrator." [7]

Senator Vandenberg of Michigan gave him a thorough grilling, but the exchange was marked by unfailing courtesy on both sides. One of Hopkins' most uncomfortable moments came when Vandenberg asked him if he had ever registered as a Socialist. After some evasion, Hopkins admitted that he had done so in a New York City election, being "profoundly moved by desire to see reforms in New York City and to see the United States keep out of war." [8]

The biggest furor during the hearings rose over a statement attributed to Hopkins: "We will spend and spend, tax and tax, elect and elect." These words had appeared in a column by Arthur Krock in the *New York Times* and were immediately denied by Hopkins in a letter to the editor.[9] Nevertheless, the saying caught on, much in the same way as "the people are too damned dumb."

At the Senate hearing, Krock refused to reveal his source, stating, "It was a most logical statement, it seemed to me, of what Mr. Hopkins might have said." [10] Since the evidence that Hopkins had made the statement was only hearsay, the Commerce Committee properly decided to disregard it.

Actually the remark originated in a casual conversation with Max Gordon, Heywood Broun, and Daniel Arnstein at the Empire City Race Track the previous summer. Neither of the latter two remembered anything like the famous statement, or, indeed, anything worthy of quotation. Even Max Gordon, a well-known theatrical producer, admitted that Hopkins had not actually said those words, but "that's what he meant!" [11]

Viewed dispassionately, the words do not seem to be Hopkins' style. They bear all the marks of a well-rounded punch line in a Broadway comedy or revue. Hopkins' style was bluff, abrupt, and impromptu. The famous quotation has too much of the literary polish to be convincing for an offhand remark.

On January 23, 1939, the Senate confirmed Hopkins after a week's debate, 58 to 27. It was almost a straight party vote, two Republicans voting to confirm, and five Democrats voting against him. Most of the five had been on the purge list or had had bitter political fights over WPA with him.

When Hopkins took office, he hoped to establish better relations between business leaders and the administration. Some businessmen were cautiously optimistic because of Hopkins' friendship with Roosevelt. At least their ideas and beliefs would get a hearing as never before, for Hopkins' predecessor, Daniel Roper, had had almost no influence with FDR and scarcely saw him except at Cabinet meetings.

Hopkins depended on the Business Advisory Council, set up by Roosevelt in 1933, to help him foster cooperation between business and government. In no formal sense a public or government institution, it was composed of businessmen, picked its own members, and offered advice only to the Secretary of Commerce. Nor did its members draw any compensation from the government. Its chairman at this time was Harriman, a friend of Roosevelt since boyhood. Other members included Edward R. Stettinius, Jr., who would succeed Cordell Hull as Secretary of State, Robert F. Wood of Sears Roebuck, Juan Trippe of Pan American Airways, and M. B. Folsom of Eastman Kodak.

Among Hopkins' many other businessmen friends were Nelson Rockefeller, William Batt of S.K.F., Jesse Jones, and Bernard Baruch.

Although the press kept badgering him for policy statements or offhand opinions that might turn into headlines, Hopkins held his tongue until he was ready for a major pronouncement. He decided to make his first speech in Des Moines, Iowa, to emphasize his Midwestern background.

In one of the shabbier moves of his life he attempted to appear as an Iowa farm boy who had made good in the wide world but whose heart remained in the cornfields. The speech was largely staff written, and sounded that way. Hopkins did not have Roosevelt's knack of taking the work of his speech writers and changing it into something uniquely his own. Accompanied by Averell Harriman as guarantor of his respectability, Hopkins rose on February 24 to address a meeting of the Des Moines Economic Club and the nation as a whole via radio. "I was born and raised

in Iowa," he proclaimed; "my father and mother spent their lives here."
Averell Harriman introduced him. It was a black-tie affair, but Harriman
had not brought a dinner jacket, having been on a railroad inspection trip.

> As an apology [he wrote] for not having one on, I said that I had tried to
> rent one in town but the shopkeeper told me he rented his last one to a
> fellow named Harry Hopkins. Obviously it was a joke and everyone knew
> it was a joke. Harry of course did not rent a jacket; he had his own. I guess
> I thought kidding Harry was a good way of showing I was on good friendly
> terms with him. My speech was a strong commendation of Harry, whom I
> admired greatly and was personally very fond of.[12]

The *Time* reporter missed the joke and reported Hopkins had worn a rented
dinner jacket. Perhaps he thought it made a good story to depict the new
Secretary of Commerce as a bumpkin who was playing at being a
gentleman.

The speech had something for everyone: businessmen, farmers, labor,
small businessmen. "With the emphasis shifted," he assured his listeners,
"from reform to recovery, this Administration is now determined to
promote that recovery with all the vigor and power at its command." It
seemed strange to men who believed nothing but the worst of New Dealers
to hear him say "that a minimum volume is necessary to break even on
fixed expenses," or "Labor must fully realize that under our economic
system, businessmen have to make money to hire workers."[13]

Near the end, he took some notice of the rising menace to peace. It is
significant that the press did not generally report this passage, for most were
too bemused with painting the picture of the reformed social worker urging
"ideas which the Republican Party has been urging for six years as essential
to recovery." [14]

> We find ourselves in a world which seems to have gone almost crazy in a
> welter of hates and fears, and in which a new and competitive philosophy
> has suddenly emerged. A world in which dictatorships—both red and
> black—have swept aside with ruthless decision almost all of the liberties
> and freedoms that have made life beautiful and wholesome. It is said that
> in respect to some of the harsh brutalities of life, these dictatorships are
> vastly more efficient than the democratic government with which we are
> familiar. I suppose that it is true that they can raise armies and
> manufacture guns and mobilize military power more quickly and more
> destructively than a democratic nation.[15]

But Hopkins left the idea at that. He had no proposal to offer other than
the obvious one of keeping America strong.

The speech was so laden with political overtones that Farley called it "Hopkins' Acceptance Speech," while his liberal friends worried that Hopkins had sold out to conservatism, "another lost liberal," as Ickes put it.[16]

While he was in Iowa, Hopkins visited the Kerrs at Grinnell, and asked Robert to look into how he might reestablish his voting residency in Iowa. He told Kerr that he was anxious to buy a farm to back up that claim and to give substance to his image of a man of the soil. Consciously or unconsciously, he was probably imitating Roosevelt, who always stated his occupation as tree farmer when asked at the voting booth in Hyde Park. Roosevelt, however, was partly sincere, for he did keep an eye on the timbering operation of the Hyde Park estate and derived a small income from it.

Shortly after his return to Washington, a reporter asked Hopkins about the administration's new policy of business appeasement. He grew quite indignant at the term, pointing out the social programs which still remained in effect, and regretted that a desire to cooperate with business appeared to the cynical press as a retreat.

Hopkins fortunately obtained the services of Edward J. Noble as under secretary, for he was fated to spend little time in the Commerce office. Noble, who was chairman of the board of the candy company which manufactured Life Savers, had taken leave to serve with the Civil Aeronautics Board, and Hopkins wooed him to Commerce. He had a respectable record as a sensible businessman, and his appointment was regarded as further assurance to business.

Soon Noble had to take over most of the functions of his chief, for Hopkins was a sick man. In addition to the worry of doing well in his new post, Hopkins was upset by his brother Rome, who had lost his job in Minnesota and was being supported by Harry while he looked for something to turn up in Florida. Hopkins wrote him stiffly, "I am sending you another fifty dollars but I am frank to say that I am doing it with some reluctance for I fear this is going on indefinitely, and I feel very strongly that I am supporting you at the expense of my children for whom I have nothing."[17]

There was one happy note, however, for just at that time, David and Cherry Hopkins presented him with his first grandchild, a girl named Cherry for her mother.

Hopkins had been ill before he went to Iowa with what he described as a touch of the flu, and felt miserable all the time he was there. At the urging of Lewis, he consulted a specialist in New York, who found no trace of recurrence of the cancer. Dr. Hopkins, however, was so disturbed by the report of his New York colleague that he wrote the President urging him to "add the real weight of your request that he follow Dr. Johnson's advice. Dr. Johnson also recommended more rest, which I feel sure Harry will not take without your orders." [18] FDR cooperated and replied that he had had a "long talk with Harry on the necessity for his doing as the Doctor advised. He was grand about it and left the following night for South Carolina." [19]

His host was Bernard Baruch, who invited Hopkins to spend some time at Hobcaw Barony, his estate near the junction of the Waccamaw and Pee Dee Rivers. It was a storybook place, with rolling lawns, a manor house, wild areas given over to game and fish, and trees dripping with Spanish moss. And Baruch, as elder statesman par excellence, could give Hopkins advice on his political future.

Baruch, however, was preoccupied with the growing threat of war. Hopkins had no special competence in foreign affairs. Like any other intelligent man of the period, he had read the papers when he had the time and he had talked with Roosevelt, but his professional life had been almost entirely directed to domestic problems.

While Hopkins was at Hobcaw, Hitler, on March 14, contemptuously tore up the Munich pact and took over the rest of Czechoslovakia. This act gave Baruch his opportunity, and he pounded away at the theme that the United States was inextricably interwoven with European affairs, whether the people liked it or not. He told him of the one man in England who knew the truth and who was kept sidelined for telling it. This man, Winston Churchill, had warned Baruch the previous year, "War is coming very soon. We will be in it and you will be in it. You will be running the show over there, but I will be on the sidelines over here." [20] Hopkins, who knew of Churchill only as a name, may have taken little note of that statement, but he should have. Churchill was to become one of his closest friends, and Hopkins, rather than Baruch, would be to a great extent "running the show" in the United States.

Hopkins' education in foreign affairs continued when he went for a vacation with Roosevelt to Warm Springs. Before departing, he wrote Lewis about how poorly he had been feeling after a "very bad case of intestinal flu." He sounded depressed and tired as he went on to tell of his hopes to get a house in Grinnell, in which to "spend my declining years." He went on:

> Rome seems to have gone from bad to worse. I have supported him since last April and took a further flier on him on a venture in Florida which did not turn out very well. I have told him I can't continue it any longer but at any moment I expect to hear of him in financial trouble some way or other.[21]

Hopkins wrote a description of his stay with FDR at Warm Springs, and it shows an informative picture of the President on vacation, and of Hopkins' ability to fit in with his habits.

> We left Washington early in the afternoon of Wednesday March 29—Mrs. Roosevelt had invited Diana to stay at the White House while I was in Warm Springs—so promising real live ducks for Easter—I kissed my adorable one good bye and for the first time in two weeks stepped out of doors on my all too wobbly legs. I had a room in the President's car and slept the afternoon through—and now more than a week has passed and I am feeling ever so much better.
>
> There is no one here but Missy—the President and me—so life is simple—ever so informal and altogether pleasant. And why not—I like Missy—the President is the grandest of companions—I read for hours—and sleep ever so well—the food as ever around the W. H. menage is medium to downright bad.
>
> The President wakes up about eight thirty—breakfasts in bed—reads the morning paper and if left alone will spend a half hour or so reading a detective story. I would go in about nine thirty—usually much talk of European affairs—[Joseph] Kennedy and Bullitt our ambassadors in London and Paris would telephone—Hull and [Sumner] Welles from the State Department so we had the latest news of Hitler's moves on the international checkerboard. His secretaries and aides would come in at ten thirty with mail, schedule of appointments—gossip of the Foundation—light chit-chat for half an hour when the President dressed before going to the pool for his daily treatment at eleven. He may keep an appointment before eleven—gets in his little car—drives by the press cottage for an interview—this takes about twenty minutes—after the pool he will drive by the golf links—home for lunch at one.
>
> Lunch usually has been F.D.R. with Missy and me—these are the pleasantest because he is under no restraint and personal and public business is discussed with the utmost frankness. The service incidentally is as bad as the food. There are thousands of men in America who get infinitely better care than the President—this in spite of the fact that he is crippled. I would fire them all.
>
> He will sleep a bit after lunch—and at three drive over the countryside with a guest—visit his farm—look at the new tree plantings—back around four thirty for an hour's dictation. Then relax till dinner at seven. The ceremonial cocktail with the President doing the honors—gin and grapefruit juice is his current favorite—and a vile drink it is! He makes a first rate "old fashioned"—and a fair martini—which he should stick to—but his low and uncultivated taste in liquor leads him woefully astray. Missy and I will not be bullied into drinking his concoction which leads him to take three instead of his usual quota of two.

Dinner therefore is gay—as it should be—and the President reminisces long over the personal experiences of his life—he tells incidents well—tho he has a bad habit of repeating them every year or so. I fancy Missy has heard them all many times but she never flickers an eyebrow.

After dinner the President retreats to his stamps—magazines and the evening paper. Missy and I will play Chinese checkers—occasionally the three of us played but more often we read—a little conversation—important or not—depending on the mood. George Fox comes in to give him a rub down and the President is in bed by ten.[22]

The rest in Warm Springs did Hopkins considerable good, and he was able to resume his activities on his return to Washington. Robert Kerr replied discouragingly about the matter of Hopkins' Iowa residency for voting purposes. Two lawyer friends had pointed out that the mere owning of property would not carry weight with the authorities. He would have to move his household possessions to Iowa, establish Diana in residence, and visit her frequently. Despite this discouragement, Hopkins wrote back that he was thinking of buying a house to give Diana

> . . . security and confidence that comes with a place that is really home. All of the friends I made up to the time I was twenty-one years of age are in Grinnell, and the town is full of families who were intimately associated with my father and mother. The College will ever afford me many satisfactions. At any rate I am anxious to settle there permanently, and I wish you would look around for a place for me to see when I come out in the next few weeks.[23]

As a further bit of evidence of his interest in Iowa, it is noteworthy that in April he was appointed a member of the Board of trustees of Grinnell College as its "foremost citizen." [24]

A cartoon in the *Washington Post* by Herblock gave the political interpretation of the time. It shows Hopkins in a real estate agency in Grinnell, with a salesman holding up a book of pictures of houses and saying, "Yes sir, a typical mid-western home? Nice, big front porch? Perhaps something in the way of a log cabin? Something with a lot of farm land and near the railroad tracks? Lease till 1941?" [25]

In the end, Hopkins did lease a farm outside of Grinnell for two years. He paid $1,800 per year and left the management to a tenant farmer. It brought him a small profit, but he never lived there and visited the place only once.[26]

During the latter part of April, Hopkins had another bout with illness, which caused Lewis some concern. Harry spent the time in Kentucky and attended the race track with his friend John Hertz, but Lewis was suspicious that more than the flu was involved. "Stomach flu may cover a multitude of undiagnosed ills but your trouble is lasting too long for your physical and my mental comfort." [27]

While he was in Kentucky, he met some relatives of Mary Todd, the wife of Abraham Lincoln. Lincoln had been an interest of Hopkins for many years, and he was fascinated by a scurrilous story reflecting on the virtue of Lincoln's mother and on Lincoln's paternity; the story, Hopkins said, was still widely believed in Kentucky. He sent the story to Carl Sandburg, Lincoln's noted biographer, with whom he had some acquaintance.[28]

During the spring, the Treasury Department, with Hopkins' help, had been working on a repeal of the undistributed profits tax, which business looked on as a barrier to expansion. Hopkins thought he had Roosevelt's concurrence, but in June, the President shied away. The bad news came when Hopkins hosted a dinner in the White House for eight members of the Business Advisory Council. Originally Roosevelt had intended to be host, but at the last moment, he sent word he was not up to attending the dinner but would see the guests afterwards. At his press conference the next day, Hopkins reported "a very frank and altogether friendly discussion of the problems we are discussing at the moment." When he tried to minimize the status of the Business Advisory Council, it was widely interpreted in the press as the end of Hopkins' and the administration's efforts to "appease" business. It was also one of Hopkins' last important official actions for a long time to come.[29]

In June, Hopkins visited the New York World's Fair, but, as he wrote in a letter, "I did the Fair in a limousine and saw none of the nude women." Of more immediate interest, however, was the forthcoming visit to Washington of King George VI and Queen Elizabeth of Great Britain. In the same letter, Hopkins went on to say:

> "All my energy now is being directed toward meeting Their Britannic Majesties, King George the Sixth and Queen Elizabeth. I bought the correct uniform though I have a sneaking suspicion that it isn't going to quite fit. Under any circumstances I know I am going to look a little ridiculous and feel more so, but I promise not to disgrace you.[30]

The visit of Their Majesties went off well. Hopkins attended the festivities in Washington, looking, as he predicted, ridiculous in his cutaway, but it was Diana who had the most impressive experience. Mrs. Roosevelt told the Queen that Diana had said the only kind of queen she knew anything about was a fairy queen. Queen Elizabeth suggested that Diana be in the hall as she and the King left to attend a formal dinner at the British embassy.

The king was resplendent in his uniform [Mrs. Roosevelt wrote], but Diana had eyes only for the queen, who wore a white, spangled dress and a jeweled crown. She looked like a fairy queen and the illusion was so perfect that when I presented Diana she curtsied to the queen and ignored the king. Both of them said a few kind words to her and then went down in the elevator. A few minutes later Diana and I went down to the usher's office and I turned over to Harry Hopkins a starry-eyed little girl who will never forget, I hope, what a fairy queen really looks like. She said: Oh, Daddy, I have seen the Fairy Queen.[31]

Just over eighteen months later, Hopkins and Their Majesties were to meet again, this time in London, as the bombs were falling. She was not wearing a crown, and Hopkins had no cutaway. But the second meeting was of more importance than the first.

Hopkins had taken a house at Delabrooke, near Mechanicsville, Maryland. It was about fifty miles south of Washington, so that he could get to the office if he felt like it. He seldom felt like it.

When his sons Robert and Stephen visited him at the house that summer, they were amazed to see how ill he was, for his letters had never revealed anything but optimism. He spent a great deal of time in bed, sometimes forcing himself to go fishing with the boys. Roosevelt dropped in to see him one afternoon, having come up the Patuxent River on the *Potomac,* and Hopkins was furious because the housekeeper had dressed Diana up in a starched white dress. He insisted she be changed into a playsuit.

At this point, Hopkins decided that he could never be President. On June 17 he issued a statement to the press that Roosevelt was his choice in 1940. The end of his personal ambition was unimportant to him by now, for Hopkins was fighting to stay alive. His condition steadily worsened, and on July 4, he quit work completely. He began to make plans for something to do when he had left the government service, and again his thoughts turned to Iowa. He considered opening a motion picture theater in Grinnell. "I am really serious," he wrote a friend, "about exploring this theater question because I have a feeling a going theater in Grinnell would make a modest sum of money regularly." [32] The project never materialized and is noteworthy only as evidence of Hopkins' state of mind. According to Ickes, Hopkins was worried because he felt he had not made good as Commerce Secretary. "As a matter of fact, he is hardly even pretending to be working at his job. He is never at his office and can't be reached by long distance, as I found on Saturday when I tried to reach him." [33]

Hopkins did come into a little money that summer as the result of the settlement of his mother's estate. Lewis Hopkins was executor, and forwarded his share of the sale of the family house along with a breezy letter full of good advice on his health and aspersions on their brother Rome, whom he called a "pathological liar."

"I'm not concerned about Rome & Helen but I am about you and I want an honest statement as to your health—weight, appetite, discomfort, strength ect. [sic]. I want to make my plans accordingly. Adah's two reports have been very disquieting." [34]

Dr. Hopkins' fears were justified and on August 22, Hopkins left to enter the Mayo Clinic. Dr. Ross McIntire told Ickes that he was sure Hopkins had cancer.[35]

Actually it was not cancer. It took a good while to discover what Hopkins did have, and the examinations were extensive and wearing. His friends tried to keep him cheered. Roosevelt wrote him soon after his admission to the clinic, inviting him to come to Hyde Park on his way back, "if I am there—which means if there is no war in Europe." [36] Hopkins, who had no idea of the seriousness of his condition, wrote Missy LeHand that he expected to be out soon after Labor Day.

On September 8 the doctors told Hopkins their verdict, and he wrote Lewis to report.

> I am sorry I haven't written you before but I have been undergoing some pretty heroic treatments here and have no conclusive news to give you. On the positive side, I think this can be said—I am not absorbing proteins and fats in any adequate manner. My protein count, or whatever you call it, is one-third of normal. This is in spite of a very well-regulated diet. In other words, nothing that I can take by mouth seems to make any difference so they are pushing a variety of things intravenously and intramuscularly, including some material which they are using experimentally here.
>
> I have had a very serious edema in my feet which is fairly well cleared up. My eye sight is going back on me, and I have lost about thirty pounds from my top weight a year ago. I weigh about 130 pounds now. Of course, if they can find the technique to assure the absorption of proteins and fats, my weight naturally will go back up.
>
> They have found no evidence of a recurrence of my old difficulty although there are one or two suspicious signs but in the main the doctors tell me that they believe a recurrence is not in the picture. They simply haven't ruled it out as yet.[37]

This letter was more optimistic than the Mayo physicians, who had despaired of his life. Roosevelt intervened and had Hopkins brought to Washington, where he could have Navy specialists work on his case. As Secretary of Commerce, Hopkins was by law entitled to treatment in a government hospital, and the saving of money was of no small importance to him.

On September 13, he wrote Lewis that he was leaving Rochester the next day:

> While they are unwilling and unable to rule out the possibility of a recurrence of my old difficulty, it seems more and more clear that it is better than a fifty-fifty chance that my difficulty is centered entirely on a nutritional problem. There is no question but that I have improved here under treatment, in spite of the fact that my weight is still very low, but I feel much better.[38]

The letter continues with medical detail, which brought Lewis on the first train from Tacoma.

It took time and the combined efforts of Hopkins' private doctor and the naval doctors, including Ross McIntire, to find a treatment that would work. Despite a setback in November, he kept his sense of humor and was able to write one of the doctors at the Mayo Clinic a sardonic letter complaining about the inability of the medical men to put a name to his disease.

> I still have a "deficiency disease, cause unknown," and that, I may say, is a pretty thin diagnosis for a bright young man who has spent five months in bed. . . .
>
> I weigh 140 pounds, my appetite is excellent, my spirits are "good to very bad." My strength is not so hot but [Dr.] Yater assures me that I am "fine" in spite of being lashed to the bed and doused with interminable drugs—which I now take every fifteen minutes and am buying by the bushel instead of by the box. I would hate to think of the condition of a patient that Yater would say was doing only "fairly well"! [39]

Although Hopkins was unable to return to the office, he was able to leave the house a little to soak up some sunshine and get fresh air. Friends came to see him, and he received hundreds of letters. Carl Sandburg's contained an offer to come by the house and sing some quaint old songs of America:

> One by Joseph Warren in 1775 has a wild air to the words [wrote Sandburg]:
>> Lift up your hands, ye heroes,
>> And swear with proud disdain,
>> The wretch that would ensnare you
>> Shall lay his snares in vain.
>> Should Europe empty all her force

We'll meet her in array
And fight and shout and fight
for free Amerikay.

Hopkins sent the poem to Roosevelt with the note, "According to Carl Sandburg, the pronunciation 'Amerikay' was customary with both Lincoln and Jeff Davis. . . . It is certainly vigorous English." [40]

While Hopkins was fighting for his life at the Mayo Clinic and then in Washington, the days of peace had ended. On September 1, 1939, the Wehrmacht smashed across the Polish border. The poorly armed but heroic Poles put up a futile resistance. Two days later, France and Britain issued ultimatums to Germany, and when the deadline expired at 11:00 a.m. British time, Prime Minister Chamberlain mournfully told the House of Commons and the world that Britain was at war.

Sidelined as he was, Hopkins played no part in the events of that fall as Poland was crushed, by the Germans from the west and the Russians from the east. The "Phony War" then began, with neither side making any move against the other, except on the seas. On November 30, Russia attacked Finland, but the Finns put up a resistance that won the admiration of the Western world.

Bedridden most of the time, Hopkins kept up with the news by the radio broadcasts. "Having listened to the radio for the past three months at all hours of the day and night over every station in the United States, I now look upon myself as a full blown authority," he wrote his friend Harry Butcher, who was vice-president of the Columbia Broadcasting System and who would be an aide to Eisenhower in Africa and Europe. He went on to say that he liked the broadcasts of William L. Shirer in Germany and Edward R. Murrow in London and Elmer Davis. "I am frank to say your French boys pall, though they mean well. They have mush in their mouth and have read too much Flaubert to suit me. I am fed up with the sunshine and flowers in Paris!" [41]

Throughout the country debate raged on how to help England and France while keeping out of the war. Loudest of all roared the voices of the isolationists, whose fears of involvement sometimes overrode reason. Some opposed any strengthening of the armed forces of the United States, lest the move provoke Germany and Russia, but most Americans looked at their Army and Navy and disliked the weakness they saw. Years of Congressional starvation had made the United States not a second- but a fifth-rate military power. If the war should spread, America had better look to her defenses.

The Navy was, perhaps, the better off, for the Vinson-Trammell Act of 1934 had provided for an eight-year replacement of the obsolescent ships used in World War I. Most of the aircraft carriers, battleships, and cruisers which were to fight in World War II were designed and many of them laid down under provisions of this act. A buildup in air production had begun, but slowly. The Army was pitifully weak. In September, General George C. Marshall, who had become Chief of Staff, reported that the Army was fast nearing its authorized peacetime strength of 280,000 men, which made it seventeenth in size among the nations of the world.

Roosevelt moved cautiously, although he knew better than most the perils from overseas. His long interest in the Navy, his reading of naval history, and his experience as Assistant Secretary of the Navy in World War I had taught him a fundamental truth which is not apparent to landsmen: that the oceans of the world are broad highways and not barriers. But he would have to educate Congress and the people who tended to look upon the Atlantic and Pacific as moats which could keep them safe from danger.

Proclaiming, as required to by law, that the United States would be neutral, Roosevelt further proclaimed a limited national emergency. One of his first goals was the repeal of the Neutrality Acts, which actually favored Germany, for Britain and France were cut off from European resources and needed to obtain food and war matériel from overseas. Germany was pretty much impervious to naval blockade, for in the heartland of Europe were most of the materials she needed. The effect of the embargo was equivalent to the blockade of American ports to British and French ships.

Roosevelt, therefore, convened a special session of Congress to win repeal of the embargo provisions and allow cash-and-carry by belligerents. The bill had stormy going in the Senate. Even its supporters were determined to weaken it. Roosevelt, mindful of hostility he had encountered when he had recently attempted to push legislation in Congress, wisely kept his hands off. Despite organized opposition by isolationist pressure groups, the bill passed the Senate on October 27 by a vote of 63 to 30. The House acted on November 2, and the following day the President signed the measure into law. Voting, however, was almost entirely by party lines. The Republicans, mindful of the elections to come and the chance to label the administration as warmongers, largely voted against the repeal.

Another major administration measure that fall was to help sponsor a Pan-American conference in Panama in order to underwrite hemispheric solidarity in keeping the war from the New World. The chief results of the conference were agreements on neutral rights and responsibilities, the reaffirmation of the Monroe Doctrine insofar as transfer of possessions of belligerents was concerned, and the formation of a neutrality zone extending 300 miles out from the entire hemisphere, excluding Canada, which was already in the war. Belligerent warships were forbidden to engage in hostilities in those waters.

Throughout the fall of 1939 and into the winter, Hopkins spent most of his time at home, much of it in bed. He offered his resignation as Secretary of Commerce, but Roosevelt refused it, saying, "Why you'll be back in your office in a couple of weeks and going great guns!" [42] But it was nearly a year before Hopkins went back to the Commerce Department and then it was to clean out his desk before leaving for good.

John Hertz tried to persuade him to go to Florida, offering to take a doctor and a couple of nurses along, but Hopkins refused on the ground that he ought to stay where he could be treated at the Naval Hospital if necessary. Hertz did install a motion picture projector in Hopkins' house and kept him supplied with films so that the time might not hang so heavy.[43] Hopkins hoped to spend Christmas again at the White House, but in the end, he and Diana stayed in Georgetown.

By early January, 1940, he was able to get out for walks when the weather permitted, and he had been to the White House for dinner. On January 26, he attended a Cabinet meeting for the first time since June, but he was far from well. That same day he wrote Lewis:

> I had dinner with the President Wednesday night [January 24] and seemed to manage with reasonable ease. I am still having difficulty finding enough proteins to go around. . . . They tell me I am getting a great deal more than I was a few months ago but it is still about forty per cent below normal.[4]

The few signs of reviving activity caused his enemies to renew their attacks on him in unfriendly news stories. The regular decennial census was due that year, and since it is a responsibility of the Commerce Department, Hopkins was condemned by some on the alleged ground that politically inspired questions which invaded privacy had been included. Hopkins snapped back that Senator Charles W. Tobey of New Hampshire, who had led the criticism, was making false charges for "purely partisan political reasons." [45] As a matter of fact, Hopkins had not even seen the questions before they were announced; they had been prepared by an advisory group not connected with the Federal Government.

For a time Hopkins toyed with the idea of acquiring property near Beaufort, South Carolina, "to spend the end of my days in," but the idea never seems to have progressed beyond the inquiry stage.[46] In view of what he had been through, he cannot be blamed for thinking along the lines of "declining years" and "the end of my days."

Still, there were other sides to Hopkins' recovery. Both Ickes and Missy LeHand reported that he was toying again with the idea of running for President, perhaps not in 1940 but in 1944, when his health would be completely restored. His state of mind seems to have been up and down. He was properly appreciative when Bernard Baruch presented him with a life membership in the Jefferson Island Club, which indicated he wanted to keep in contact with the prominent Democrats who frequented it, but when a chance to get out of the lease on the Iowa farm came along, he jumped at it, thus abandoning his "Presidential" base. No clear picture emerges of his activities that spring, except that he did try to do a little work from his home, but as he wrote a friend, "I am only able to be up four or five hours a day." [47]

Meanwhile, the war had exploded into new violence. On April 9, 1940, German forces, in simultaneous operations, invaded Denmark and every important seaport in Norway from Narvik in the far north, down and around to Oslo. The operations were accomplished in spite of the Royal Navy, just a few days after Prime Minister Chamberlain had made the fatuous remark, "Hitler has missed the bus."

The following month, on May 10, German forces swarmed across the borders of Holland and Belgium. Breaking through the Ardennes Forest, Panzer divisions cut the forces in Belgium and Holland off from the rest of the Allied armies and forced the retreat to Dunkirk and eventual evacuation of the British and French troops trapped there. Then, after a short space for regrouping, the Germans were able to drive directly for Paris and all of France.

On that same May 10, Hopkins was a guest for dinner at the White House. He was feeling miserable, and Roosevelt persuaded him to spend the night. He stayed not only for the night, but for the next three and a half years, off and on. He occupied a suite on the southeast corner of the second floor, near the Oval Study, and down the hall from the President's quarters. The bedroom had served Lincoln as a study. Directly across the hall from Hopkins' rooms were the guest quarters which would be occupied by Winston Churchill when he visited the White House.

May 10 was also the day that Chamberlain resigned as Prime Minister to be succeeded by Churchill, who promised nothing but "blood and toil, tears and sweat." In these words he inspired a nation and silenced those who still wished to appease and seek a negotiated peace.

Soon after he moved into the White House, Hopkins was up to his neck in politics and in the rearmament program. Activity seemed to accomplish for him what ten months of rest had not been able to do.

The continuing Nazi victories in the west shook everyone in Washington and in the country at large. Gone was the isolationist opposition to strengthening the defenses of the United States. Republicans and isolationist Democrats alike stridently blamed the administration for allowing the Army and Navy to fall into such a sorry state. Hopkins consulted trade experts, businessmen, and others on the problem of stockpiling critical materials which might be cut off in the event of war. Congress was willing to appropriate the money if only to forestall criticism that its inaction had endangered the security of the country.

Gradually some sort of an organization around the President emerged. Hopkins' genius for quick action and for grasping the essence of a problem proved invaluable to Roosevelt. It became increasingly clear that Roosevelt intended to keep the reins in his own hands, and this required an assistant he could trust and whose agile mind could keep up with what was going on. While Hopkins had been ill, Thomas Corcoran had filled this role, but he had never developed a close relationship with FDR.

When Hopkins began to take up an active part again, it was clear that there would be a showdown between him and Corcoran; the White House simply was not big enough for both of them as first advisers to the President.

Hopkins has been accused of ruthlessly destroying his rival. The truth more probably is that he did nothing to save him. Hopkins never exceeded the authority the President gave him, and he never backed the President into a corner. Corcoran did both. This was the mistake that Colonel House had made with Wilson and that Sherman Adams was to make with Eisenhower, and the results were the same.

With Corcoran gone, Hopkins more and more became the man to see. FDR would scribble on a piece of mail from a Senator—"Harry, do something. FDR." Or on a recommendation of an agency, "Look into this, Harry, and let me know. FDR."

Witnesses have described Hopkins at work in the White House at this time. He would be in the big bed, still in pajamas, the counterpane piled high with papers, a telephone to his ear, and a cigarette hanging from his lips. He would bark into the telephone, hang up abruptly, and grin impishly at his visitor.

He turned to his many friends in business and industry as men who could get things done. Hopkins would hector them, coax them, implore them to do what they had believed to be impossible.

Hopkins also had imagination, and he knew that the Allies were not going to win the war with 1918 weapons. Modernization was essential, and Hopkins fostered it as much as possible. He gave his blessing to an agency to evaluate inventions which might be useful. When Vannevar Bush asked for a hearing, Hopkins knew that a man of his reputation in science must have something and agreed to see him in the White House.

Bush came as spokesman for an informal group of scientists, including Presidents James B. Conant of Harvard and Karl T. Compton of the Massachusetts Institute of Technology. Bush was president of the Carnegie

Institution. These men and some others had met to consider ways in which scientific knowledge could be applied to counter and outstrip the Nazi advances in technology, which were winning them the victories in France. They well knew that if they approached the armed forces, they were likely to get short shrift from cautious bureaucrats who tended to be suspicious of new ideas.

Like Hopkins, Bush was a no-nonsense man and was able to state his idea for a National Defense Research Council in vigorous language. He presented Hopkins with a succinct outline, which Hopkins read with approval. He then picked up his telephone and arranged for Bush to see the President.

Bush prepared answers to all kinds of objections. When he arrived in the Oval Office, he found that Hopkins had already sold Roosevelt on the proposal. The President shook hands, made a pleasant remark or so, and scribbled on Bush's memorandum, "O.K.–F.D.R."

This seemingly cavalier treatment of Bush was a fair sample of how Hopkins eased the President's way, conserving his time for issues on which he had to be fully informed before reaching a decision. In the instance of Bush, Hopkins was convinced of the soundness of the proposal and of the man who presented it. Roosevelt accepted his judgment, so no lengthy discussion was necessary.

Bush and Hopkins together drafted a letter from the President to Bush formally establishing the National Defense Research Council and giving it the power to coordinate scientific work and to operate in close cooperation with the military and naval authorities. It included the following:

> Recently I appointed a special committee . . . to study into the possible relationship to national defense of recent discoveries in the field of atomistics, notably the fission of uranium. I will now request that this committee report directly to you, as the function of your Committee includes this special matter, and your Committee may consider it advisable to support special studies on this subject. . . .[48]

Thus was Hopkins, indirectly, in from the beginning on the development of the atomic bomb.

The President signed the letter to Bush on June 15, the day following the fall of Paris, when the fortunes of the Allies seemed at a low ebb.

The story of how the Nazi forces, having driven the British and part of the French armies into the sea at Dunkirk, turned and drove south into France has been told many times. In vain Premier Paul Reynaud pleaded for American aid; Roosevelt could offer only sympathy and words of encouragement. Reynaud resigned to be succeeded by elderly Marshal

Henri Philippe Pétain, who soon sought an armistice. It was signed June 21, 1940, in the same place, the forest of Compiègne, and in the same railway car in which the German surrender had taken place in 1918.

The question remained: could Britain hold out? Reports from Ambassador Joseph Kennedy, whose friends in London belonged to the so-called "Cliveden set"—the fashionable conservatives who had been the voice of appeasement—sent increasingly gloomy reports.

At the outbreak of the war, Churchill, then serving as First Lord of the Admiralty, a position corresponding to the Secretary of the Navy in the United States, had initiated correspondence with Roosevelt. Signing himself "Naval Person," Churchill kept Roosevelt informed of Cabinet decisions and of naval matters of mutual concern. When he became Prime Minister, Churchill continued the correspondence, now signing his missives "Former Naval Person." Armed forces communications facilities were used, thus bypassing both the State Department in Washington and the Foreign Office in London.

On the basis of Churchill's cables, Roosevelt discounted the pessimistic reports of his own ambassador. He refused to believe that Britain would fall and made the basic decision to render all the aid in his power.

Many things had to be done before America could be of much help to Britain or even be ready to defend itself. Industrial mobilization was one of the most important requirements, but so were food production, manpower training, and resource allocation. Hopkins was instrumental in helping Roosevelt form the National Defense Advisory Commission, whence all later war boards and agencies would spring. The NDAC comprised:

William S. Knudsen for industrial production
Edward R. Stettinius, Jr., for industrial materials
Sidney Hillman for labor and employment
Chester C. Davis for farm production
Ralph Budd for transportation
Leon Henderson for price stabilization
Dr. Harriet Elliott for consumer protection

There was no chairman. When Knudsen asked who was boss, Roosevelt replied with a laugh, "Well, I guess I am." [49]

Roosevelt's reasons can be readily deduced. He had little faith in the regular departments of the government to perform other than routine functions. Ever since the earliest New Deal days, his total program for dealing with the emergency of the depression had operated through special agencies accountable primarily to him and only secondarily to Congress. Examples such as WPA, AAA, NRA, and PWA are obvious. Even though

PWA was administered by Harold Ickes, it was not part of the Interior Department.

Roosevelt preferred to keep the programs he was most interested in close to him, depending on persons he felt could get the job done, rather than on those named to their posts for political reasons, as most Cabinet officers were. Similarly, he preferred to rely on special envoys to report on conditions in other lands rather than depend on the routine channels of embassies and the State Department. Thus he was to use Hopkins for quick trips to London and Moscow and Averell Harriman for extended stays in those capitals.

Roosevelt was the one man who understood the importance of what was going on in Europe and Asia and the implications for America. He was fast teaching Hopkins. While the newspapers, the business leaders, and Congressmen were still thinking that there was ample time, that a rearmament program could be accomplished without affecting production of new cars, new washing machines, and new sewing machines for peacetime use, Roosevelt knew that the hour was late and the moment of danger was at hand. He needed men who could get things done.

Hopkins' conversion from isolationism was complete. A newsman asked him whether the program of the United States meant getting into the war.

> Hell, [replied Hopkins] I mean the tough implications! Suppose that Germany wins the war in the next two months and does on the economic fronts what they have done on the military fronts. What will they do in South America presuming they win, and then, what are we going to do about it? Or—suppose this war lasts two or three years. What effect is that going to have on the economy of this country? This is not a matter of sitting down at the dinner table and talking about it. . . . I belong to the school that does not talk about things—you *do* them.[50]

Getting things done in Washington that June was not so easy. Politics and politicking occupied everyone. Would the President run again? If he did, would he be reelected? The entire House of Representatives and a third of the Senate cast their anxious votes with their minds on the people back home. Would the voters repudiate them for spending huge sums on defense, or would they repudiate them for failing to do so?

Roosevelt had no doubts, for he realized that certain things had to be done whether he ran or not. He asked for and received the resignations of Secretary of War Woodring and Secretary of the Navy Charles Edison. Woodring opposed aid to Britain, and Edison, in the President's view, was too much dominated by his subordinates. Neither man, he felt, was the person to be in charge of the Army and Navy while America rearmed.

Roosevelt had decided to emphasize the bipartisan nature of the rearmament program by appointing Republicans to the vacated positions. On the eve of the Republican Convention in Philadelphia, he named Henry L. Stimson as Secretary of War and Frank Knox as Secretary of the Navy. Stimson had been Secretary of State under Hoover and had advocated collective resistance when Japan moved on Manchuria in 1931. Knox had been the Republican nominee for Vice-President in 1936. He was a stern critic of the New Deal, but he was a patriot. Both men were prepared to enlist for the duration.

The appointments of Stimson and Knox just before the Republican Convention brought howls of protest from GOP leaders. Some even demanded that the two men "be read out of the party." It was all a dirty political trick, they said, designed to throw the Republicans into confusion as they met to nominate their standard bearers.

The Republicans did not need any outside contributions to confusion when they assembled in Philadelphia. They had plenty of their own. The Old Guard was being challenged by an upstart, an apostate Democrat by the name of Wendell Willkie.

In some respects, the Republicans seemed to have a golden opportunity. Disasters in Europe—the surrender of Denmark, Norway, Holland, Belgium, and France—seemed made to order to show administration incompetence. In the closing days of hostilities between Germany and France, Italy had fallen on the French rear in order to win a seat at the victors' table. On that day, June 10, Roosevelt was scheduled to deliver the graduation address at the University of Virginia, where Franklin, Jr. was graduating from the law school. On the way to Charlottesville, Roosevelt was burning with indignation over Italy's action. Suddenly he pulled out the copy of his speech and restored a passage the State Department had cut out: "On this tenth day of June, 1940, the hand that held the dagger has struck it into the back of its neighbor."

That night, with the President out of town, Hopkins called up Adolf Berle, whom he had been bedeviling all day to get more aid to France by means of any pressure the State Department could exert. He suggested that Berle have dinner with him at the White House. Berle reported the evening in his diary.

> We had a priceless evening, discussing every kind of thing that one could think of; dining in his bedroom. The President was in Charlottesville making a speech. I think Harry had done a good deal of work on the speech, but the President in the main had done it himself.... Sumner Welles apparently had been at the White House in the afternoon, trying to argue the President out of putting in the phrase that Italy's declaration of war was a dagger thrust into the heart of a friend.
>
> Harry felt that the war now definitely threatened the United States. So,

he thought, did the President. The problem therefore was to get some help
to people now and build up new defenses. As he said, none of us will be
here a few months from now unless we actually get things done.[51]

The Republicans, gathered by the thousands in their convention hall,
were determined to see that none of the men in the White House that
evening would be there much longer. Harold Stassen, Governor of
Minnesota, in the keynote address charged, "We are tragically unprepared.
We are too woefully weak to give the Allies that material assistance this
nation wants to give them. We are sadly wanting in the state of our defenses
of this hemisphere." [52] It made no difference that the Republicans had for
years helped to vote down appropriation after appropriation to strengthen
the national defense. It was an election year, and all shortcomings could be
charged to the Democrats and particularly to "that man in the White
House."

The leading contenders were New York's "boy wonder," District
Attorney Thomas E. Dewey, and Senator Robert A. Taft of Ohio. There
was an outside chance for Senator Arthur Vandenberg of Michigan. A
bunch of enthusiastic amateurs were calling for the nomination of Wendell
L. Willkie of Indiana, but the party regulars were not worried. Willkie
supporters had enthusiasm, but no organization. They had the crowds, but
the regulars had the delegates.

The result was a shock. On the sixth ballot, Willkie was nominated. To
make peace with the regular organization, he agreed to take party faithful
Charles L. McNary of Oregon as his running mate. He stated that he hoped
the Democrats would nominate Franklin Roosevelt for a third term. "I
want to take on the Champ!"

The Champ was keeping his own counsel. He was still keeping it when
Hopkins set out for Chicago to take control of the convention away from
Jim Farley and the others like him who were determined to replace
Franklin Roosevelt with one of their own.

CHAPTER EIGHT

Chicago Go-Round

Harry Hopkins bore no formal credentials with him as his train pounded over the rails from Washington to Chicago. He was going on his own, and yet with Roosevelt's approval. He was to be FDR's representative *at* the convention but not his representative *to* the convention.

No one knew whether Roosevelt would run for a third term in defiance of tradition. After he had been nominated, many of his associates picked out the moment he had decided to run, and their guesses ranged from the opening of the war in Europe in September, 1939, to the time of the collapse of France in June, 1940.

Even Eleanor Roosevelt did not know what his decision would be; she hated the idea, but she feared he would run. His son Elliott was so sure he would not that he was supporting Garner, a sure sign that not all Roosevelts thought alike, for, by this time, Cactus Jack was *persona non grata* to FDR. Elliott later thought that May 10 was the date his father made up his mind to run, yet Elliott was in Texas that spring, and therefore no better informed than anyone else.

The one man in a position to know Roosevelt's plans and strategy was Harry Hopkins. Living in the White House, in daily, even hourly, contact with FDR, he knew better than anyone else what was going through that complex mind. He told Paul Appleby, who was to serve as his lieutenant in Chicago, that Roosevelt did not finally make up his mind until the day after he was nominated.[1] That would mean after he had won the battle for the nomination of Henry Wallace for Vice-President.

Hopkins' statement is the only one that explains Roosevelt's actions in connection with the convention. His plan was simple: he would submit to a draft. If the nomination came to him with no strings attached, he would accept. If not, he would retire to Hyde Park.

As the war in Europe went from serious to grim to desperate to disastrous, Roosevelt and Hopkins believed that the United States faced the gravest crisis since the Civil War. The country was by no means united, and many sincere, loyal Americans honestly saw no threat in events in Europe. Businessmen were preparing to do business with Hitler, for Nazism might be the wave of the future. Because of the temporary alliance between Germany and Russia marked by the Russo-German nonaggression pact of August, 1939, American Communists were joined by many left-wingers in wishing the Germans well.

Isolationists saw no peril in a German victory, but they saw much in American intervention. Even furnishing arms to Britain was risky. At best, should Britain be defeated, they would simply be added to the German arsenal; at worst, supplying Britain might lead America into the war.

At home, the conservatives thought that their time had come to gain power once more. Conservatism in the Republican Party, Roosevelt felt, had received some degree of setback by the nomination of Wendell Willkie, but since Willkie was showing evidence of supporting Roosevelt's views on foreign policy, his campaign would have to be made against the New Deal. This would force him to the conservative side, from which he had not strayed far anyway. He was, as Ickes put it, "a simple, bare-foot Wall Street lawyer."

Conservatives on the Democratic side were no better, and they would seize control of the party and install one of their own in the White House if they were not stopped. Since many of them were also isolationists, the election of one of them would imperil the cause of freedom which Britain was now upholding alone.

Roosevelt reluctantly came to the conclusion that it was his duty to the party and to the country to run if they called on him. It would have to be a genuine call. He would accept the nomination on his own terms or not at all. If he announced himself as a candidate for the nomination, he would have to make deals with the party conservatives. There would be no deals. The conservatives could surrender completely or they could name one of their own.

He gave Hopkins a statement to be presented to the convention. In it, Roosevelt released his own delegates, leaving them free to vote for anyone. That would, of course, include Roosevelt.

Shortly before he left for Chicago, Hopkins had a lengthy discussion with David Lilienthal, who knew the Republican nominee better than anyone else in the Government. Lilienthal was director of the Tennessee Valley

Authority which had had many contacts and conflicts with Willkie's own firm, the Commonwealth and Southern, until TVA bought out its interests in the region. Lilienthal had come to urge that the material details of Willkie's fight with TVA in the files not be made part of the campaign, for he felt it would be improper to use government documents in a political manner. He was prepared for a difficult argument, but to his surprise, Hopkins agreed with him completely. FDR's plan was to campaign, if he ran, on the basis of principles, and Hopkins saw no reason to operate any differently.

The most important thing in the world now, Hopkins told Lilienthal, was national unity, to protect the country from the perils overseas. He spelled it out with considerable feeling:

> We now have only one objective, and that is total national defense, not partial defense or defense a piece at a time, but total defense. That conception includes a great many things in addition to munitions. It sets up as a goal that every man in the country able to work shall have a job, because a man who is out of a job and down on his luck and disheartened is a danger to our defense and a weakening of it. . . .
>
> Now we have called in to take charge of that job a considerable group of men who have had no use for the New Deal but who are competent fellows and are in accord on that objective of total defense. . . .
>
> If these men get the impression that those in the Government are merely using the defense program and using their services as a cover for other kinds of objectives, it will bring the whole program into collapse and discredit. This requires complete candor and a dismissal of prejudices, that were justified most of the time but are now out of the window.[2]

At this hour, the preparations for defense were more important than anything else, even the New Deal. If New Dealers could not understand, they would have to go. And during the war years, most of them went.

Arriving in Chicago well before the July 15th opening of the Democratic National Convention, Harry Hopkins set up operations in suites in three separate hotels. One was in the Stevens, where Jim Farley's official Democratic headquarters was located. Hopkins rarely used this suite but kept it staffed in order to keep an eye on Farley and his comings and goings.

Across the street in the Blackstone was Hopkins' main headquarters, where his son David acted as aide-de-camp. By coincidence, he was in Suite 308-309, where, in 1920, Republican bosses had gathered in the "smoke-filled room" to give the nomination for President to Warren G. Harding. A telephone bypassing the hotel switchboard had been installed in the bathroom, so that Harry could call the White House direct. The bathroom was the only place he could be sure of privacy.

His third suite was a few blocks away, in the Ambassador East. Here he slept, and here he could confer privately, away from the hubbub of the conventioneers. This suite also had a telephone which did not go through the hotel exchange.

When Hopkins arrived in Chicago, he found that Farley, Garner, and Senator Millard Tydings of Maryland had joined forces to deny Roosevelt the nomination by acclamation. If they could, they would deny him the nomination itself. Hopkins' job was to stop them.

He was brutal about it. He wasted no time in subtlety. The only thing that mattered was the renomination of Roosevelt, and it must be a genuine draft, or the party would find itself without a leader who would win in November. It was not enough for FDR to win a majority of the delegates. If he were not nominated by acclamation or something close to it, he would refuse to run.

Brooding in his headquarters in the Stevens, Farley glumly watched the procession of leaders and delegates swarming into the Blackstone.

> All the leaders in the country [he wrote later] began trekking to the unofficial Roosevelt headquarters Harry Hopkins and Jimmy Byrnes had in a Blackstone Hotel suite. . . . Many never came in to see me at all. A few came in to pay their respects to me, and some of those were timidly ill at ease. Others were swinging aboard the Roosevelt band wagon. . . .
>
> From the outset the temper of the delegates was bad. While many feared to come near me they were incensed over the way I had been treated. Their resentment was heightened by anger over the treatment they had received at the hands of Hopkins. His manner was arrogant rather than ingratiating. He offered nothing and demanded blind obedience. Murmurings of mutiny grew until the delegates were downright ugly, but the President's maneuvering over the years saved the day. Delegates lacked a rallying point for revolt and were forced to surrender, grumblingly and glumly, on the never genuine threat that Roosevelt might not run and thus leave the party without its greatest vote getter.[3]

If Hopkins was winning control of the delegates, Farley controlled the organization of the convention. The story began going around that Farley intended to pack the galleries with partisans to stampede the delegates into naming someone other than Roosevelt. In answer to that, Hopkins dropped the word that FDR would refuse if more than 150 votes were cast against him.

In the end, Farley's strategy collapsed. The opposition could not rally around a single candidate, and no stampede took place. Several of the rebels, including Farley, had their names placed in nomination, but on the first ballot Roosevelt won 946 out of 1,100 votes. Four more votes than Hopkins' magic 150 were cast against him, but that was close enough.

The more difficult fight was over the Vice Presidential nomination. Out of the many candidates, Roosevelt picked Henry A. Wallace, an incomprehensible choice to many of his loyal followers. Wallace was a committed New Dealer, but he was something of a mystic and not noted for practicality. Yet Roosevelt admired him.

> He is the kind of a man I like to have around [he told Secretary of Labor Frances Perkins]. He is good to work with and he knows a lot, you can trust his information. He digs to the bottom of things and gets the facts. He is honest as the day is long. He thinks right. He has the general ideas we have. He is the kind of man who can do something in politics. He can help the people with their political thinking.[4]

When Hopkins telephoned to confirm the choice of Wallace, he talked to Judge Rosenman.

"There's going to be a hell of a lot of opposition," Hopkins said. "So far there must be at least ten candidates who have more votes than Wallace. It'll be a cat-and-dog fight, but I think that the Boss has enough friends to put it over."

Whether the Boss had friends enough remained to be seen. He certainly had enough enemies to make it difficult. When Rosenman reported the conversation with Hopkins, FDR did not seem surprised.

> Well, I suppose all the conservatives in America are going to bring pressure on the convention to beat Henry. The fellow they want is either Jesse Jones or William Bankhead. I'm going to tell them that I won't run with either of those men or with any other reactionary—I've told them that before and I'll tell them again.

While Hopkins was selling the delegates on Wallace, the telephone kept ringing at the White House. Most of the callers objected to Wallace, some vehemently. A telegram arrived from Secretary of the Interior Harold L. Ickes, suggesting that he might be a suitable compromise candidate.

"Dear old Harold," said Roosevelt. "He'd get fewer votes even than Wallace in that convention." [5]

Part of the opposition to Wallace came from a last struggle of the old guard. If they could beat Wallace, then Roosevelt might well refuse the nomination, and this would give them a chance for one of their own, Farley, Garner, Tydings, or Burton Wheeler. It was a good strategy and it came close to working.

When the convention met that night, Hopkins had done all that he could. He had laid down the law to his last delegate. He had issued his last warning. "Do you want a Vice Presidential candidate or a Presidential candidate? Beat Wallace and the President won't run." He left his suite in the Blackstone and went over to the Ambassador East, where he could be alone with David to listen to the convention over the radio. He was too tired to go to the convention hall, nor was there any need.

He heard Eleanor Roosevelt address the rebellious delegates. She never mentioned Wallace, and she tried to lift the convention out of the mire of partisan politics into which it had slipped. Whoever became President, she told her attentive audience, faced

> ... a heavier responsibility, perhaps, than any man has ever faced before in this country.... You cannot treat it as you would an ordinary nomination in an ordinary time. . . . You will have to rise above considerations which are narrow and partisan. This is a time when it is the United States we fight for.[6]

After her speech, the roll call of States began in a fairly dignified manner, but it didn't stay that way. Still, many delegates laid Wallace's final victory to her speech. It was very close.

In the Oval Study, the President sat at a card table playing solitaire and listening to the radio. Around him were some of his close associates, including Pa Watson, Missy, and Sam Rosenman. As the bickering on the convention floor increased, Roosevelt's face grew grim. At length, hearing nomination after nomination in defiance of his known preference for Wallace, FDR asked Missy to give him a pencil and pad of paper. He wrote five full pages, while the others watched curiously. Finally he passed the sheets to Judge Rosenman, saying, "Sam, take this inside and go to work on it; smooth it out and get it ready for delivery. I may have to deliver it very quickly, so please hurry it up." [7]

It was a statement refusing the nomination. It would be delivered if the convention did not name Wallace.

When FDR had adjusted Rosenman's editing to his own satisfaction, he laid aside his cards and listened to the vote. When the roll call ended, Wallace had only a little over 500 votes. He needed 551. Then Michigan and Massachusetts, which had passed at their turn, gave him enough to put him over. Others fell into line, but when the final result was officially announced, Wallace had only 627.7 votes.

Roosevelt had won, but at what cost in bitterness? The tone of the delegates was so ugly that Hopkins had to get hold of Wallace and prevent him from reading an acceptance speech.

After things had quieted down, Roosevelt's familiar voice rang through the hall, carried by radio from the White House.

> Lying awake, as I have on many nights, I have asked myself whether I have the right, as Commander-in-Chief of the Army and Navy, to call on men and women to serve their country, or to train themselves to serve and, at the same time, decline to serve my country in my own personal capacity, if I am called upon to do so by the people of my country. . . .

He made it abundantly clear that appeasement and isolation would be no part of his program. He would continue to aid Britain and to resist Hitler and all that he stood for.

> I would not undo, if I could, the efforts I made to prevent war. . . . I do not recant the sentiments of sympathy with all free peoples resisting such aggression, or begrudge the material aid that we have given to them. I do not regret my consistent endeavor to awaken this country to the menace for us and for all we hold dear. . . . So long as I am President, I will do all I can to insure that that foreign policy remains our foreign policy.

He would not have time, he continued, to campaign in the usual sense of the word, for his duties as chief of state forbade it. He added a note of warning.

> I shall never be loath to call the attention of the nation to deliberate or unwitting falsifications of fact, which are sometimes made by political candidates.

And so the convention ended. Roosevelt had captured the control of the party machinery, but now he had to turn to the professionals to run the campaign against Wendell Willkie. He knew that the New Deal amateurs could never swing the votes he needed to win.

Jim Farley, angered and frustrated at the way the convention had gone, took a walk, as he expressed it. He resigned as party chairman and was replaced by Edward J. Flynn, who accepted the job only on the condition that New Dealers, especially Hopkins, were kept out of the campaign.

Hopkins was already feeling himself a drag on the President. To the criticisms that he was drawing the salary of Secretary of Commerce and doing nothing in return were added the charges that he was getting free room and board in the White House.

Both statements were unfair, but they made good political ammunition. Roosevelt had several times refused to accept Hopkins' resignation from the Commerce post. And Hopkins paid his own share of the White House expenses. The formidable Mrs. Nesbitt, who ran the White House staff, saw to that. (Later, after Hopkins had remarried and his wife had moved into the White House with him, she was assessed fifty cents a day for food for her little dog, Susie.)

> Hopkins was not at Cabinet [reported Ickes spitefully in his diary for August 4]. I suppose that he is visiting some of his rich friends on Long Island or elsewhere. [A few days later he noted] I had Henry Morgenthau in for lunch on Tuesday. In him I discovered another man who distrusts Harry Hopkins. I suspect that he always has. Of course, more than some of us, Henry would feel jealous of anyone who was particularly close personally to the President.[8]

Dr. Ross McIntire told Ickes that something had gone wrong in the relationship between Hopkins and Roosevelt, but Ickes had his doubts. A letter Hopkins wrote about that time to his former wife, Ethel, tells another story:

> I am resigning here within the next ten days—the going is too tough and if I am to ever get really well again I must take it easy for a year or two. As yet I am not sure what I am going to do but I am on the track of something that will pay $5000 a year and be not too exacting. This much I feel pretty sure can be counted on but no more. So all of our plans will have to be adjusted accordingly. . . .
> The going will be a little difficult for everybody for a while but I feel sure I am going to get better.
> No matter what you may hear—be sure that everything is well between the President and me.[9]

The position he referred to in the letter was director of the newly established Franklin D. Roosevelt Library in Hyde Park, where FDR planned to leave his personal and official papers for the use of the public. Roosevelt also intended to ask Henry N. MacCracken, president of Vassar, to make Hopkins a professor.[10]

Hopkins did resign as Secretary of Commerce later that August and left Washington to take a suite in the Essex House Hotel on Central Park South in New York. He was determined to relieve the President of the embarrassment of his presence during the campaign. Roosevelt, however, continued to do as he pleased and took Hopkins up to Hyde Park for a visit early in September so he could think things over. Hopkins must have inspected the gray fieldstone building that would house the library, but he still had not made up his mind what he was going to do.

Inactivity suited him ill. He restlessly made a few trips to Washington and did occasional chores for the President, but in the whirl of activity of the campaign and the frenetic race to prepare for possible war, he felt out of it. He wandered back and forth, seeing friends, and later in September he was at the deathbed of Francis C. Harrington.

All of this aimless activity was Hopkins' reaction to his farewell to public life. His burning energy required some kind of outlet. But as Wendell Willkie crisscrossed the country attacking FDR, there was little he could do to help his friend. He was not impressed when Robert Jackson suggested, "From your position you may be able to do a great service in coordinating otherwise scattered if not conflicting effort." [11] He was realistic enough to know that he could render no such service from New York. And he saw little prospect of a return to Washington. That fall, his career seemed finished and his future dismal.

At that moment no one could know that his greatest service to his President and to his country lay just ahead. He would be doing just what Jackson had written, "coordinating otherwise scattered if not conflicting effort." He would be facing problems and exercising responsibility on a global scale. While others were sometimes called by the press "assistant president," Hopkins actually would be. Among Americans, only Roosevelt himself would have a greater part to play in the years ahead.

BOOK TWO

*Lord Root
of the Matter*

CHAPTER NINE

The Right-Hand Guest

During his exile in New York, Hopkins made many trips to Washington and frequently dropped in at the White House. Once he got there Roosevelt would revert to habit and say, "Harry, would you mind tending to this?" And, tend to it he would, although he had no authority whatever. No authority, that is, except for his friendship with the President of the United States.

Early in September, 1940, FDR asked him to get Sam Rosenman back to Washington. There was a speech to be made, and Roosevelt had no speech writers. The old ones like Tugwell and Corcoran were gone. Only Rosenman and Hopkins had that experience.

The indefatigable Louise Hachmeister, chief telephone operator at the White House, tracked Rosenman down in Portland, Oregon.

"I thought the President wasn't going to campaign this fall," protested Rosenman.

"Never mind about that. You better get on back," Hopkins told him. "The President has to make a speech to Dan Tobin's [Carpenters'] union convention on the eleventh." [1]

Thus ended Sam Rosenman's vacation. He was not to have another until long after the war had ended.

Ineluctably Hopkins was drawn back into the center of things. He kept his rooms at the Essex House, which was not far from Rosenman's apartment on Central Park West, and a good bit of preliminary speech writing for Roosevelt was done there. One day in October, the playwright Robert Sherwood called on Hopkins in his suite. Harry told him that the

President had to give a speech for Columbus Day, that it was supposed to be a routine talk on hemispheric solidarity. "But," Hopkins added, "the President wants to talk to the American people about Hitler. So far as he is concerned, there is absolutely nothing important in the world today but to beat Hitler." He paused and glared at Sherwood. "What do you think the President ought to say?" [2]

The surprised Sherwood quickly found himself being dragged along to Sam Rosenman's apartment and put to work revising the tepid draft that had come from the State Department.

Thus was formed the speech-writing team that would serve Roosevelt for the rest of his life. The team worked shorthanded if one of the members was ill or out of the country, but at least one was always on hand. Hopkins seldom created speeches. He had a special knack for tearing apart the drafts the others had written. Knowing Roosevelt better than they did, he could spot phrases that did not ring true, that did not square with FDR's thinking. From his long experience on the firing line of the Roosevelt administration, he could detect passages which would have exposed the President to needless political risks. He also knew what FDR was likely to say on most subjects, so he could give direction to the successive drafts until they were ready to be presented to the President.

Then the work would start over. Roosevelt took great pains with his speeches. He well knew that his words, especially in those critical days, carried immense weight, not only at home but also abroad. Accordingly, he worked over what Hopkins, Rosenman, and Sherwood prepared for him to make it uniquely his. They were expected to stay on the job until the speech was just right.

On October 18, Roosevelt announced that he would break his silence in the race against Willkie to make five campaign speeches. Then the work of the team got really hectic. When it was over, Hopkins was once more living in the White House, performing as though he had never been away.

"Everything," noted Ickes sourly early in November, "has to seep through Harry Hopkins into the White House." [3]

During the months since the conventions, Wendell Willkie had crossed and recrossed the country, speaking, speaking, speaking, until his abused voice became a croak. He challenged the Champ to come out and fight.

Roosevelt refused to take the bait. He had told the convention in his acceptance speech that his duties in Washington would not permit him to campaign in the usual sense. Professional politicians in the party objected, but FDR's political instinct was sure. The view of a President too busy for political junkets had vast impact on the people asked to make sacrifices for the common good.

But Roosevelt's stand was not only a political gambit. It was the solid truth. As Hopkins had told Sherwood, Roosevelt believed that there was nothing as important as beating Hitler. That included his own reelection as President. In his firm belief that he had to gird the nation for possible war, he took some highly unpopular steps which he felt were essential for the country's safety, but which might have risked the election. Yet he could not move too fast. He well remembered that no one had followed when he called in 1937 to quarantine the aggressors.

The issue of compulsory military service posed the greatest threat to his reelection, but Roosevelt never flinched. The safety of the nation demanded it. The conscription bill, sponsored by Republican Representative James W. Wadsworth and Democratic Senator Edward R. Burke, drew fire from isolationists in both parties. Roosevelt did not actively support it until he announced in a press conference on August 2 that he favored some form of "selective service." The screams redoubled. Pacifists, religious leaders, educators, and isolationists orchestrated a fugue of dictatorship, militarism, warmongering, and intervention. Said Senator Burton Wheeler in a radio address:

> Enact peacetime conscription and no longer will this be a free land—no longer will a citizen be able to say that he disagrees with a government edict. Hushed whispers will replace free speech—secret meetings in dark places will supplant free assemblage—labor and industry, men and women will be shackled by the chains they have themselves forged.[4]

Senator Wheeler did not make it clear in just what way the passage of the Burke-Wadsworth bill would automatically repeal the Bill of Rights. But then, that was not his way. His speeches tended to be longer on emotion than on logic.

Another important decision Roosevelt had to make that summer was whether to let the British have fifty destroyers of World War I vintage. Britain needed them desperately, for her destroyer fleet had suffered enormous losses in the Norwegian campaign and in the Dunkirk evacuation. Ships were being lost almost every day, until it was doubtful whether the British could keep their convoys operating unless they got replacements—and quickly.

Eventually Roosevelt and Churchill worked out the famous destroyers-for-bases deal, Britain getting the old destroyers and other equipment in return for long-term leases of bases ranging from Argentia in Newfoundland to the Caribbean and Bermuda in between. Wendell Willkie supported the selective service act and the destroyers deal, although he regretted that the President did not seek Congressional approval of the latter.

Hopkins had little or nothing to do with either measure; rearmament and the campaign against Willkie took up his time. At first, Willkie seemed to be making little headway. He stumped the country, trying to rouse the people. He drew cheers from the rich and well-to-do, but often jeers, catcalls, tomatoes, and eggs when he tried to speak to factory workers and residents of poorer sections.

In fact, he had no real issues he could honestly put forward. He hated Hitler as fiercely as Roosevelt did. He supported most of the New Deal measures. He argued that a Republican administration would rearm the country and conduct social reform better than the Democrats. Many people found that hard to believe. This approach got him precisely nowhere.

A decent man and a loyal American, Willkie never felt at home with the leaders of his own party. He and Roosevelt thought alike on most issues, but the necessity of role playing as opposing Presidential candidates led them both to say things they would later regret. "I can't guarantee either of you to the other," wrote William Allen White to Roosevelt during the destroyers debate, "which is funny, for I admire and respect you both." [5]

As the campaign began to get dirty in public, a peculiar episode involving his Vice-Presidential running mate Henry Wallace threatened Roosevelt's campaign. Wallace, a man of many interests, became involved in spiritualism and theosophy. He attended seances and he corresponded with a certain Madame Zelda on theosophy. The letters were in code, with Roosevelt referred to as "the Flaming One." A considerable mass of these "Guru Letters" had accumulated, and the lady had sold them to a newspaper unfriendly to the administration. Copies had been made, and one set reached the Republican National Committee. By some method, never revealed, FDR got hold of another set.

At first he seemed to think it funny. Knowing Wallace's reputation for stern morality and strict rectitude, he inquired if there were any evidence that Wallace and Madame Zelda had ever registered together at a hotel. Told that the relationship was strictly theosophical, he shook his head. "Too bad," he said. "The American people understand romance and would forgive Henry for it. They do not understand theosophy and I fear they would never forgive him for that."

A little later, Supreme Court Justice William O. Douglas and Hopkins were drawn in on the matter.

"How does one get rid of his Vice-Presidential running mate?" asked Roosevelt.

Douglas thought it over and then replied that if Wallace would resign, the National Committee could name another.

"Suppose he won't resign?"

"Then you'll have to have another Democratic Convention."

"My God!" said FDR.

"This may kill the Old Man," said Hopkins as he and Douglas left the room.

As it turned out, the matter never came to light. Wendell Willkie had seen a great deal of a woman in New York. The Democrats agreed not to use the girl friend if the Republicans would not use the Guru Letters. Hopkins got hold of the originals and kept them in his locked files in the White House.[6]

Willkie's campaign entered on a new note of stridency. Instead of calling Roosevelt an appeaser, he now assailed him as a warmonger. "If," he charged, "his promise to keep our boys out of foreign wars is no better than his promise to balance the budget, they're already almost on the transports."

Willkie's new extremes were on the front pages of most newspapers, for he was supported by a majority of the owners and editors. Most working reporters, on the other hand, favored Roosevelt. While it is hard to keep the President of the United States off the front pages, particularly in times of national crisis, it is remarkable how stories favorable to FDR were buried inside.

If Willkie commanded the attention of much of the nation's press, Roosevelt was supreme on the radio. No American politician has ever been his equal in speaking to an audience, whether in an auditorium or over the air. Willkie, on the other hand, made a poor radio speaker. He slurred his words and tended to sound petulant rather than sincere.

Willkie's new tactic of extremism began to catch on with large sections of the American people. He depicted the President as a reckless meddler in the affairs of Europe who threatened to drag America into the war. He charged that if Roosevelt were reelected, the United States would be in the war by April. His ratings rose in the Gallup poll, and Democrats feared that his momentum would carry him past Roosevelt on November 5.

The defection of John L. Lewis, president of the United Mine Workers of America and of the Congress of Industrial Organizations, brought another worry to the Democrats. Burly John Lewis had supported Roosevelt in his first two campaigns, but had fallen out with him during the industrial unrest of 1937 and 1938. He predicted that labor en masse would desert FDR in 1940, and he ordered his CIO members to vote for Willkie. He promised that if Roosevelt were reelected, he would resign as president of the CIO.

Although Roosevelt and Hopkins were reported to be tremendously upset by his defection, Roosevelt had little to worry about. Other labor leaders, such as Sidney Hillman, William Green, and David Dubinsky, supported him and predicted he would win the labor vote. As it turned out, they were right. Lewis could not even deliver his own CIO to Willkie. He promptly resigned and devoted himself solely to his United Mine Workers.

Although his advisers urged him to wait until after the election, FDR set October 16 as the date for young men to register for the draft under the Selective Service Act. He even refused to postpone the drawing of registration numbers to see which men would be called first for military training. The drawing was set for October 29, exactly one week before the voters would go to the polls.

Instead of shirking this challenge, Roosevelt took part in the drawing ceremony. Blindfolded Secretary of War Stimson reached into the huge jar, pulled out a capsule, and handed it to the President. He opened it, and the familiar voice announced, "The first number which has been handed me is serial number one five eight." Before the drawing, Roosevelt spoke briefly. He made no reference to the draft or conscription. Instead he talked of a "muster," which conjured up visions of Minutemen grabbing muskets from over the fireplace or the door and going off to join Washington at Valley Forge.

On October 23, Roosevelt made his first campaign speech. In keeping with the theme of patriotism in the air, he selected Philadelphia as the place to fire his opening salvo. Hopkins, Rosenman, and Sherwood had produced the text for Roosevelt to finish off in his own way. Not all members of the administration approved of this writing team. Adolf Berle was caustic in his diary:

> The crew working on the President's speeches this year are: Harry Hopkins, Sam Rosenman, and Robert Sherwood of New York, and a good playwright. The influences chiefly playing on the situation, however, are Frankfurter and Justice Douglas. This means a highly intelligent crew—and, except for Sam Rosenman, as unscrupulous a crew as ever put together. Rosenman is square. Harry Hopkins is nice and likeable, but would commit murder for the ·President. The rest of the bunch would commit murder on general principles, either for the President or for themselves.[7]

In Philadelphia, Roosevelt proclaimed, "I consider it a public duty to answer falsifications with facts. I will not pretend that I find this an unpleasant duty. I am an old campaigner, and I love a good fight."

In New York on October 28, he succeeded in hanging the isolationist label on Willkie. After citing the Republican voting record in Congress of opposing defense appropriations, he came with relish to a euphonious grouping of the names of three archconservative Republicans, Joe Martin, Hamilton Fish (who represented Roosevelt's own Dutchess County district), and Bruce Barton. When he intoned "Martin, Barton, and Fish," the crowd caught on at once. A little later in the same speech, the phrase occurred again, and this time the audience chanted it with him. Two days later in Boston, when he mentioned Martin, someone in the audience yelled, "What about Barton and Fish?"

The fear-of-war hysteria came to a climax just before Roosevelt's Boston speech. The draft numbers, drawn only the day before, let approximately 800,000 young men know they were about to exchange civilian clothes for khakis. As the President's train made its way from Washington to Boston, Hopkins, Rosenman, Sherwood, Missy LeHand, and Grace Tully were all busy on the speech. Roosevelt worked with them when he could, but every time the train stopped, he had to snap his braces into place, rise, put on his coat, and go out on the rear platform to make a brief speech to the crowds gathered to see the President go by.

In going over the speech, the writers came to a passage in which Roosevelt was assuring parents that their sons would be well cared for in the Army. Hopkins handed him the latest telegram from Ed Flynn, urging him to say again that American boys would not be sent into foreign wars.

"But how often do they expect me to say that?" asked Roosevelt. "It's in the Democratic platform and I've repeated it a hundred times."

"I know it, Mr. President," replied Sherwood, "but they don't seem to have heard you the first time. Evidently you've got to say it again—and again—and again."

And so this passage was inserted in the speech.

> And while I am talking to you mothers and fathers, I give you one more assurance.
> I have said this before, but I shall say it again and again and again.
> Your boys are not going to be sent into any foreign wars.

Sam Rosenman suggested that he follow the Democratic platform and add the words "except in case of attack," but Roosevelt was tired of the whole sorry argument.

"Of course we'll fight if we're attacked," he snapped. "If somebody attacks us, then it isn't a foreign war, is it? Or do they want me to guarantee that our troops will be sent into battle only in the event of another Civil War? "[8]

Following the Boston speech, Roosevelt spoke in Brooklyn on November 1. This was a talk on special privilege in the Republican Party and the fact that it had been drawing the radicals of the right and left to it.

> Something evil is happening in this country [he stated] when a full page

advertisement against this Administration, paid for by Republican supporters, appears—where, of all places?—in the *Daily Worker,* the newspaper of the Communist Party.

Something evil is happening in this country when vast quantities of
Republican campaign literature are distributed by organizations that make
no secret of their admiration for the dictatorship form of government.

When the President's train left New York that night, no work had been
done on the speech he was to deliver the next evening in Cleveland. This
was in some ways the most important of the campaign, for it would be the
last, summing up what he had said earlier and putting the issues into focus.
Sustained by sandwiches and coffee brought in from the dining car, the
speech team went through the file that had been brought along from the
White House. In it were clippings, suggestions from citizens high and low,
paragraphs dictated by Roosevelt at odd moments, and drafts written by
various government agencies. Wrestling with this recalcitrant material, the
three writers began to see some shape emerging. At about 2:00 in the
morning, Hopkins felt too ill to continue and went to bed, leaving
Rosenman and Sherwood to work throughout the night. They napped for
an hour as the sun was coming up.

After breakfast, while the President made his short speeches at train
stops, the trio was hard at work again. Successive drafts were typed by the
secretaries, while Hopkins tore them apart.

When the President sat down to lunch with them, they were struck with
how weary he looked. His face was drawn and gray. He rambled on, telling
pointless stories about Maine lobstermen and about sailing along the New
England coast. But, as the lunch progressed, his powers of recuperation
asserted themselves. His face took on a healthy color, and his usual high
spirits returned.

"Now!" he exclaimed brightly. "What have you three cutthroats been
doing to my speech?"

For six hours the President worked with them, and that evening, before
40,000 men and women in Cleveland, Roosevelt delivered what Sam
Rosenman believed was the second-best campaign speech he ever made.
(The best would be in 1944.) Hopkins was too tired to listen. He went to
bed.

During the campaign, Hopkins had done more than help write speeches.
He continued to harry businessmen, industrialists, and producers to speed
production. He generally had a telephone at his ear, even when talking to
visitors. Sometimes he might have two phones going at once, one connected
to an office in an aircraft factory in California and the other to a Navy
procurement office in Boston.

Because of his wide contacts throughout the country, he was often to assume the troubleshooter role insofar as the campaign was concerned. Upon learning that Negro voters were growing cool toward Roosevelt, he summoned Dr. Will Alexander, who had been head of the Resettlement Division and was much interested in racial matters.

> Will [said Hopkins, sitting up in bed in the White House], this fellow Willkie is about to beat the Boss, and we damn well better do something about it. . . . The President has done more for the Negroes in this country than anybody ever did since Abraham Lincoln, and you can't get a word out of any of them. It looks as though they are all going to go against him. . . . If you can, tell me what to do.[9]

The Negroes wanted many things, Alexander explained, but as symbols they wanted two of their distinguished men appointed to posts worthy of their abilities: Benjamin O. Davis, who had been passed over, promoted to brigadier general, and Judge William Hastie named as civilian aide to Secretary Stimson. Both appointments would be symbols that the Negroes had a place in the Army on a higher level than that of cannon fodder. Hopkins made a couple of telephone calls, and the appointments were made.

The Negroes did not desert Roosevelt. Analysis of the voting showed that he had won more Negro votes in 1940 than in either of the two earlier campaigns.

After the Cleveland speech, the writing team broke up temporarily. They had already prepared the remarks Roosevelt would make the night before election, a nonpolitical statement urging people to vote. Roosevelt wanted to incorporate into these remarks a passage from his Cleveland speech, "freedom of speech is of no use to the man who has nothing to say and freedom of religion is of no use to the man who has lost his God." To this he wanted to add, "A free election is of no use to the man who is too indifferent or too lazy to vote."

Hopkins bristled at the last bit. "I don't think," he said, "you ought to insult the people in this speech." He objected to the words "or too lazy." He was still sensitive to the slurs cast on WPA workers. After reflection, FDR agreed with him, and the offending words were cut.[10]

While Rosenman and Sherwood departed for Washington, Hopkins and Roosevelt rode the campaign train to Hyde Park to await the outcome. On the morning of November 5, FDR voted as usual in Hyde Park. Hopkins did not, for though he had long since lost his Iowa residency he had not been long enough in New York to register. After luncheon in the Big House, as the Roosevelt home was known, the President, Pa Watson, Ross

McIntire, and Harry Hopkins whiled away the afternoon with a poker game. When dusk fell, everyone except for the President and his mother went to Val-Kill for a buffet supper of creamed chicken and rice, cake, ice cream, and coffee. Talk was light as promising early returns from Connecticut arrived.

Soon the supper party returned to the Big House and found FDR ensconced in the dining room, his coat off and his tie loosened. The littered table bore tally charts, pencils, news-ticker tearsheets and telephones that led to the White House and to Ed Flynn's headquarters at the Biltmore Hotel in New York City. Hopkins went in and out of the room, but soon he decided to go to his bedroom so that he could rest while he listened to the returns. Sherwood, who had come up from Washington with his wife, joined him there. The returns by then were running heavily to Willkie, and Hopkins began to look worried. He kept his ear turned toward the little portable radio he had set up and once in a while entered some figures on a tally sheet. But, too nervous to be systematic, he covered most of the sheet with doodles. Then by 10:00 the results were running so heavily for Roosevelt that he relaxed, and at 11:00 Flynn proclaimed victory. Hopkins rose and went downstairs to partake of the traditional victory feast of scrambled eggs.

A delegation of Hyde Park neighbors came along, one of whom carried a sign reading SAFE ON THIRD. Roosevelt and his family went out on the portico to greet the neighbors, and Eleanor Roosevelt noticed Harry Hopkins standing by himself off to one side. He suddenly did a little jig of triumph, and smashed his right fist into the palm of his left hand. He could not have said, "We made it" any louder if he had shouted.[11]

Roosevelt did not retire until about 2:30 when he was sure that late returns would not upset the results. Hopkins was long since in bed.

On returning to Washington with the President, Hopkins set up his headquarters once more in the White House suite of rooms. He accompanied FDR on a cruise on the *Potomac,* and both of them had a chance to catch up on sleep. The only other guests were Bob Jackson and Frank Walker. The weather was miserable, but that did not bother FDR. It always bothered Hopkins who did not share his friend's enthusiasm for sea life.

A routine now established itself in the White House. About 8:30 the President would ring for breakfast, which he ate in bed with a cape thrown around his shoulders. Amid the toast crumbs he would read the dispatches brought in by the usher on duty and the morning newspapers: the Washington papers, the *Chicago Tribune,* the *New York Times* and *New York Herald Tribune,* and the *Baltimore Sun.* He read rapidly and remembered what he read. Then his personal staff would come in: Steve Early, Marvin McIntyre, Pa Watson, and confidential secretary William

Anna Pickett Hopkins, Harry Hopkins'
mother. *(Franklin D. Roosevelt Library.)*

Harry Hopkins, about 1927 *(Courtesy of
Robert Hopkins.)*

Montage of Hopkins as Works Progress Administrator, 1935. *(WPA Photo in the National Archives.)*

Hopkins and "Pa" Watson aboard USS *Houston*, October, 1935. *(Franklin D. Roosevelt Library.)*

Leaving the White House after a Conference with FDR, May 8, 1935. Left to right: Harry L. Hopkins, Harold Ickes, and Frank Walker. *(UPI photograph.)*

Roosevelt and friends aboard USS *Houston*, October, 1935. Back row, left to right: Secret Service man, Gus Gennerich, Ross McIntire, Secret Service man; front row: "Pa" Watson, Harold Ickes, FDR, Hopkins, and Wilson Brown. *(Franklin D. Roosevelt Library.)*

Hopkins speaks at a luncheon at the Mayflower Hotel, Washington, for the Women's and Professional Division of WPA, January, 1936. Left to right: Florence Kerr, Hopkins, Eleanor Roosevelt, and Ellen Woodward. *(WPA photograph in the National Archives.)*

Harry and Barbara Hopkins attend WPA Artists' Index Exhibit at National Gallery Museum, December 17, 1936. *(Franklin D. Roosevelt Library.)*

Cartoon appearing in the Columbus *Evening Dispatch*, August 6, 1936. *(Courtesy of the Columbus, Ohio, Dispatch.)*

Hopkins, about 1937. *(WPA Photograph in the National Archives.)*

Harry Hopkins and Diana with FDR in Washington, about 1937. *(Franklin D. Roosevelt Library.)*

Hopkins attends a baseball game at Griffiths Stadium, 1938. Seated, left to right: FDR, James Roosevelt, Hopkins, unidentified, Marvin McIntyre. *(WPA Photograph in the National Archives.)*

Hopkins takes oath of office as Secretary of Commerce from Supreme Court Justice Stanley Reed as FDR looks on. *(Photograph by Underwood and Underwood.)*

Christmas, 1938, at the White House. Left to right, rear: Mrs. James Roosevelt, Eleanor Roosevelt, Mrs. Sarah Roosevelt, FDR, James Roosevelt, Betsey Roosevelt, Franklin D. Roosevelt, Jr., and Harry Hopkins. Front row: Sarah Roosevelt and Diana Hopkins. *(Franklin D. Roosevelt Library.)*

(Franklin D. Roosevelt Library)

THE WHITE HOUSE
WASHINGTON

August 24, 1940.

Dear Harry:

      I have your letter of August twenty-second and I fully understand all that you say and much that you have left unsaid.

      In giving me this letter of resignation it is possible only for you to break the official ties that exist between us -- not the ties of friendship that have endured so happily through the years. I am accepting your resignation, therefore, to take effect at a date to be determined later and, I repeat, that this resignation is accepted only in its official sense.

      In other words, you may resign the office -- only the office -- and nothing else. Our friendship will and must go on as always.

      Affectionately,

Franklin D. Roosevelt

Honorable Harry L. Hopkins,
Secretary of Commerce,
Washington, D. C.

Letter from Roosevelt accepting Hopkins' resignation as Secretary of Commerce. *(Franklin D. Roosevelt Library)*

Hopkins and son David at the Blackstone Hotel during the Democratic National Convention, July, 1940. *(Franklin D. Roosevelt Library.)*

Hopkins in his room in the White House, which never looked this neat except for a formal photograph. (Life *photograph by Thomas D. McAvoy.)*

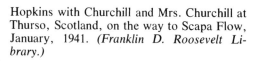

Hopkins with Churchill and Mrs. Churchill at Thurso, Scotland, on the way to Scapa Flow, January, 1941. *(Franklin D. Roosevelt Library.)*

Churchill and Hopkins en route to Scapa Flow, January, 1941. *(Franklin D. Roosevelt Library.)*

Strolling the deck of HMS *Prince of Wales* en route to Argentia, August, 1941. Left to right: General Sir John Dill, Churchill, Hopkins, Admiral of the Fleet Sir Dudley Pound, and Air Marshal Sir Wilfred Freeman. *(Franklin D. Roosevelt Library.)*

(Courtesy of Vice Admiral W. R. Smedberg III, USN, Retired, and the U. S. Naval Academy Museum.)

☆ ☆ DINNER ☆ ☆

IN HONOR OF

THE RIGHT HONORABLE WINSTON CHURCHILL
PRIME MINISTER OF GREAT BRITAIN
AND HIS STAFF

⚓

GIVEN BY

THE PRESIDENT OF THE UNITED STATES
FRANKLIN D. ROOSEVELT

⚓

ON BOARD THE

UNITED STATES FLAGSHIP AUGUSTA
SHIP HARBOR, NEWFOUNDLAND
SATURDAY . . . . . . AUGUST 9, 1941

☆ ☆ PRESENT

FRANKLIN D. ROOSEVELT,
PRESIDENT OF THE UNITED STATES.

HONORABLE
SUMNER WELLES,
UNDER SECRETARY OF STATE.

ADMIRAL
HAROLD R. STARK, U.S.N.,
CHIEF OF NAVAL OPERATIONS.

GENERAL
GEORGE C. MARSHALL, U.S.A.,
CHIEF OF STAFF.

ADMIRAL
ERNEST J. KING, U.S.N.,
COMMANDER-IN-CHIEF,
ATLANTIC FLEET.

MAJOR GENERAL
HENRY H. ARNOLD, U.S.A.,
CHIEF OF AIR CORPS.

HONORABLE
HARRY L. HOPKINS

HONORABLE
AVERILL HARRIMAN

RIGHT HONORABLE WINSTON CHURCHILL,
PRIME MINISTER OF GREAT BRITAIN.

HONORABLE
SIR ALEXANDER G. M. CADOGAN,
G.C.M.G.,
PERMANENT UNDER SECRETARY OF
STATE FOR FOREIGN AFFAIRS.

ADMIRAL OF THE FLEET
SIR ALFRED D.P.R. POUND,
G.C.B., G.C.V.O.,
CHIEF OF THE NAVAL STAFF.

GENERAL
SIR JOHN G. DILL, K.C.B.,
C.M.G., D.S.O.,
CHIEF OF THE IMPERIAL
GENERAL STAFF.

AIR CHIEF MARSHAL
SIR WILFRID R. FREEMAN, K.C.B.,
D.S.O., M.C.,
VICE CHIEF OF THE AIR STAFF.

LORD CHERWELL

Roosevelt comes aboard HMS *Prince of Wales* for Divine Service, Sunday, August 10, 1941. Hopkins is the figure in the overcoat, with his hands in his pockets, standing in the left of the picture, behind Under Secretary of State Sumner Welles, Army Chief of Staff General George Marshall, and Chief of Naval Operations Admiral Harold R. Stark. Roosevelt is to the right, on the arm of his son Elliott. Churchill can be seen standing in front of the Royal Marine Honor Guard. *(Franklin D. Roosevelt Library.)*

Churchill demonstrates his "Zip Suit" in front of the White House to Hopkins; his Naval Aide, Commander C.R. Thompson; Diana; and Fala, January 3, 1942. *(Franklin D. Roosevelt.)*

American leaders at the Casablanca Conference, January 20, 1943. Back row, left to right: Hopkins, Lieutenant General Henry H. Arnold, Lieutenant General Brehon Somervell, and Averell Harriman; front row: General George C. Marshall, FDR, and Admiral Ernest J. King. *(Franklin D. Roosevelt Library.)*

Hopkins with his son Robert at the Casablanca Conference, January, 1943. *(Navy Department photograph in the National Archives.)*

Lunch in the field, north of Rabat, January 21, 1943. Left to right: Hopkins, Lieutenant General Mark Clark, FDR, and Major General George Patton, Jr. *(Franklin D. Roosevelt Library.)*

FDR celebrates his 61st birthday in the air, en route from Trinidad to Miami, January 30, 1943, while returning from Casablanca. Left to right: Admiral William D. Leahy, FDR, Hopkins, and Lieutenant Howard M. Cone, in command of the Boeing Clipper. *(Franklin D. Roosevelt Library.)*

Louise, Harry, and Diana Hopkins working at a victory garden in the White House grounds, 1943. *(U. S. Office of War Information photo in the National Archives.)*

Churchill, Brendan Bracken, and Hopkins at the Quebec Conference, August, 1943. *(Franklin D. Roosevelt Library.)*

Leaders at the Quebec Conference, August, 1943. Left to right, rear row, seated on the wall: Anthony Eden, Brendan Bracken, and Hopkins. Front row, seated: FDR, Mackenzie King, and Churchill. *(Franklin D. Roosevelt Library.)*

Hopkins and Robert Hopkins at the pyramids during the Cairo Conference, November, 1943. *(Franklin D. Roosevelt Library.)*

A break at the Teheran Conference, November–December, 1943. Left to right: General Marshall; Sir Archibald Clark-Kerr, British Ambassador to USSR; Hopkins; interpreter; Stalin; Foreign Minister V. Molotov; and General Voroshilov. *(Franklin D. Roosevelt Library.)*

Watching the USS *Quincy* arrive at Malta, February 2, 1945. Standing at the rail, left to right: Secretary of State Edward R. Stettinius, Foreign Minister Anthony Eden, and Hopkins. *(Franklin D. Roosevelt Library.)*

Hopkins, in *The Sacred Cow*, en route to Yalta, February, 1945. *(Franklin D. Roosevelt Library.)*

Ambassador John G. Winant, Anna Roosevelt Boettiger, and Hopkins on USS *Quincy* in Alexandria Harbor, Egypt, February 15, 1945, returning from the Yalta Conference. *(Franklin D. Roosevelt Library.)*

Aboard USS *Quincy* at Alexandria, February 15, 1945, returning from Yalta Conference. Left to right: Ambassador John G. Winant, FDR, Secretary of State Edward R. Stettinius, and Hopkins. *(Franklin D. Roosevelt Library).*

(2) *The German Situation in Western Europe Becomes Critically Weakened.*

Although Roosevelt favored Gymnast, a plan to invade North Africa, he agreed to the proposal of Bolero-Roundup under the persuasion of Stimson, Marshall, and Hopkins. He directed the latter two to fly at once to London to present the idea to Churchill and the British Chiefs of Staff.

Hopkins cabled Churchill: "See you soon. Please start the fire." [25] Hopkins referred to the notoriously poor heating system of Chequers. He hoped not to have to wear his overcoat indoors there this time.

Hopkins had a better trip across the Atlantic than the two previous ones. On the first, he had merely bought a ticket on the regular Clipper to Lisbon and on the second he had bummed a ride on an Army bomber. This time the party had an entire Clipper requisitioned by the government for the trip. They departed from Baltimore early on the morning of April 4. Marshall took two officers with him as aides, and Roosevelt sent along a Navy doctor, Commander James R. Fulter, to take care of Hopkins, since he could not be trusted to look after himself.

It was a very pleasant flight, with the luxurious Clipper uncrowded by the five men. On the way to Bermuda, the plane had an engine failure, and the party was delayed for two restful days over Easter Sunday. General Marshall was asked to read the second lesson in the service at the Pembroke Parish church. He prepared well, but at the church he was given a slip of paper listing several additional verses. The one that gave him trouble was Revelation 1:11: "Saying, I am Alpha and Omega, the first and the last: and, What thou seest, write in a book, and send it unto the seven churches which are in Asia; unto Ephesus, and unto Smyrna, and unto Pergamos, and unto Thyatira, and unto Sardis, and unto Philadelphia, and unto Laodicea."

"More unpronounceable words than I have ever seen collected in one chapter," he later wrote a friend.[26] When he came to the familiar Philadelphia, he intoned it with impressive force which brought considerable amusement to the party.

On April 8, the faulty engine having been replaced, the Clipper flew to Lough Erne in Northern Ireland. From there they went on in a land plane to Hendon Airport, north of London.

Hopkins, of course, was well acquainted with the wreckage produced by bombing. Marshall experienced it for the first time and mentioned the contrast with the safety of American cities. The contrast showed even stronger in spirit, for the British put up stoically with privation, while Americans whined over shortages of gasoline, automobile tires, golf and tennis balls, and household appliances.

"This war," Hopkins told the British reporters, "is not going to be won by

production alone. It is going to be won by tough fighting. You can be sure
that our contribution is not going to be confined to the production of
guns." [27]

That afternoon, Hopkins and Marshall met with Churchill at 10
Downing Street, and the general laid out the broad outline of the American
plan. Hopkins cabled the next morning:

> THE PRIME MINISTER'S RESPONSE WAS GOOD AND I WOULD SAY INDICATES
> THAT THE PROPOSAL WILL BE EXPLORED HERE SYMPATHETICALLY AND I
> BELIEVE SUCCESSFULLY. WE DINED LAST NIGHT WITH CHURCHILL, ATTLEE,
> GENERAL BROOKE AND EDEN. SOME FURTHER PROGRESS WAS MADE. MARSHALL
> MEETING CHIEFS OF STAFF ALL DAY TODAY. . . . ALL WELL. HARRY.[28]

At dinner that evening, Churchill displayed his talent as a military
historian by discussing the American Civil War and World War I. General
Sir Alan Brooke, the new Chief of the Imperial General Staff, however,
turned the conversation back to the present by expressing grave reservations toward the American plan.

Hopkins and Marshall had never met Brooke before. Neither Marshall
nor Brooke formed a good first impression of the other. Marshall later told
Hopkins that Brooke might be a good fighting man but that he lacked Dill's
brains. Equally unimpressed, Brooke wrote, "I liked what I saw of
Marshall, a pleasant and easy man to get on with, rather over-filled with his
own importance. But I should not put him down as a great man." [29]

Both men later had reason to revise their opinions upward.

After many arguments, the British accepted the American proposals in
principle. Marshall thought that meant that only the details needed to be
worked out. What the British meant was that the American scheme was
good only if more specific study led to a promise of success. They agreed to
undertake that study, but did not promise to mount the invasion of Europe
the next spring.

Roosevelt somehow learned that Hopkins had been sitting up with
Churchill and promptly wired General Marshall: "Please put Hopkins to
bed and keep him there under 24-hour guard by Army or Marine Corps.
Ask the King for additional assistance if required on this job." [30]

Marshall had a hard time carrying out these instructions, for Hopkins
would invariably slip out after he had been sent to bed. He had only a short
stroll to the embassy from Claridge's, and there he could talk to Harriman
or Winant. He might, if he could find transportation, go on to Downing
Street to see the late-working Churchill. If he did none of those things, he
found someone to take on in a game of gin rummy.

On April 15, Churchill invited Hopkins to address British war leaders in
private. Harold Nicolson recorded:

> We are addressed by Harry Hopkins in the large Committee Room. He is very astute and makes a good impression. The implication of what he said was that we should be mad to get rid of Winston, since he is the only man who really understands Roosevelt. It was cleverly done. He talks of Anglo-American relations and says that there are many people in the U.S.A. who say that we are yellow and can't fight. It is true that we have been beaten in everything we do. Somebody asks him whether America can advise us on the sort of propaganda we ought to conduct. He gets out of it well. He says, "Well, we are the worst propagandists in the world and you are the next worst. Why not consult someone better?" [31]

After many more discussions, Hopkins and Marshall started for home on April 18. First they flew to Northern Ireland to inspect American troops. Word came to them there that Premier Henri Philippe Pétain of France had resigned and the Nazi collaborator Pierre Laval had succeeded him. Hopkins wrote Clementine Churchill about an incredible night outside of Londonderry:

> Our Army decided they knew better than the British Government where we should stay and we wound up in a most interesting and outlandish household and that night at dinner I surely learned what rationing means! I will tell you all about it next time I see you but it is enough to say that I wouldn't have missed it for the world.[32]

Hopkins cabled the President: TALKED TO FORMER NAVAL PERSON WHO THINKS MARSHALL AND I SHOULD RETURN LONDON. DO YOU THINK SITUATION REQUIRES OUR REMAINING IN ENGLAND UNTIL THIS MATTER CLEARED UP? [33]

In order to speak to the President directly, Marshall and Hopkins flew back to Scotland and from a small hotel in Port Patrick tried to put in a transatlantic call. The British telephone system was ill-suited to such wild demands, and although an accompanying British officer vouched for them, the canny Scots muttered about the two daft foreigners who wanted to talk to the President of the United States. Since they were traveling incognito, they could not demand any special priority. At one point they found themselves talking to Churchill's aide at 10 Downing Street, and he promptly got things straightened out. Roosevelt told the travelers to come on home, and they took off from nearby Stranraer just ahead of the police coming in to investigate. They arrived without incident in New York for lunch the next day.

On the way across the Atlantic they learned of the Doolittle raid on Tokyo by Army planes flown off the *Hornet*. They had enjoyed the thought of the discomfiture of the Japanese war lords, but it was not in such raids that the war would be won.

When Hopkins returned to Washington, he found relations with Russia getting more difficult. The Soviets accused the British and Americans of failing to deliver promised supplies. With the coming of spring, the lengthening hours of daylight in the Arctic made every convoy going through to Murmansk a major fleet operation for the Royal Navy. Ships waiting for escorts were piling up in Reykjavik and Loch Ewe. During the months of April, May, and June, 84 merchant ships loaded with various supplies for Russia had set sail. Only 44 of them got through. Later the losses got worse.

Even more than he wanted supplies, Stalin wanted a firm promise of a second front in Europe. He sent Molotov to Washington to fight for both. Molotov arrived on the afternoon of May 29. The talks ranged over many matters but always returned to the refrain: second front now. At length, after several days, Molotov left Washington with a statement of hope that some sort of second front would be undertaken in 1942 if it proved feasible. In Britain, on the way back Molotov received an aide mémoire expressing the Anglo-American position:

> We are making preparations for a landing on the Continent in August or September 1942.... Clearly, however, it would not further either the Russian cause or that of the Allies as a whole if, for the sake of action at any price, we embarked on some operation which ended in disaster and gave the enemy an opportunity for glorification at our discomfiture.... We can therefore give no promise in the matter, but, provided that it appears sound and sensible, we shall not hesitate to put our plans into effect.

Molotov and Stalin interpreted the statement as a firm commitment.

Hopkins also attempted to get more aid to China, as his heavy correspondence with T. V. Soong attests, but China was fourth in line, after the United States, Britain, and Russia.

Hopkins did enjoy some relaxation that spring. He was seen escorting the movie actress Paulette Goddard around town and once she was his guest at Hyde Park. But he was seeing a great deal more of Louise Macy. She too was a guest at Hyde Park, but occasionally had to fend for herself when FDR summoned her escort to discuss a message from Churchill or Hull.

The war news was brighter, just a little. Although Corregidor in the Philippines had fallen, the Japanese had been turned back from Port Moresby, New Guinea, in the Battle of the Coral Sea in May. And in the early part of June, the Battle of Midway, which cost Japan four aircraft carriers, finally stopped its expansion. Even the battle of production was going better, and Hopkins got a chuckle out of a settlement between two big contractors in Hawaii who had been battling over everything. The

formal terms were simple: "We mutually and jointly duly agree to cooperate and work with those sons-of-bitches if they will do likewise." [34]
On May 30 Hopkins noted:

> The Prime Minister called me at 7:00 p.m. today, obviously from Chequers where he was entertaining Winant, Harriman, Arnold, Somervell and Eisenhower for the weekend.
>
> The Prime Minister was obviously in good spirits and told me he was sending twice as many bombers that night over Germany as had ever gone before. He indicated the weather was good and he was very hopeful of the outcome. They were apparently planning to stay up all night to learn the results.
>
> He also indicated that the battle in Africa was going well and said to me, "I may see you very soon." [35]

That night in the first 1,000-plane raid over Germany, the British devastated Cologne. Many of the bombers were made in America. Regular ferry flights of American-built B-17s and B-24s crossed the Atlantic, a sharp contrast to the pitiful twenty that had accompanied Hopkins on his flight to England the previous June.

Churchill's statement, "I may see you very soon," referred to his plan for another meeting to determine once and for all the strategy for 1942 and 1943. The British Chiefs of Staff were less and less enchanted with the plan Hopkins and Marshall had carried to London in April, and they wanted some answers. On the other hand, American military planners suspected that the British wanted to run the war to suit themselves, relegating the Americans to the background. The British opposed Arnold's idea of daylight precision bombing by Americans. If the British had their way, all planes the Americans could send over would be flown by RAF pilots in night saturation bombing.

Churchill and his Chiefs of Staff by this time strongly opposed the Sledgehammer-Roundup concept and had been struck by a sentence in one of Roosevelt's messages, "Do not lose sight of GYMNAST," [36] a proposed invasion of northwest Africa. With Churchill's love for peripheral operations, this apparent weakening in the President's position seemed providential. Churchill himself favored a landing in northern Norway in order to join hands with the Russians.

At any rate, Churchill decided that the time had come for another conference. Roosevelt agreed, and the British party left by seaplane from Scotland shortly before midnight on June 17 and landed in Washington after a nonstop flight of twenty-seven hours. Roosevelt and Hopkins were in Hyde Park at that time, so the next day Churchill flew up to join them, while Brooke and the other military figures began conversations with the American Joint Chiefs.

As usual, Churchill had prepared his position well. He was particularly opposed to Sledgehammer, which in the months since Hopkins' and Marshall's visit to London had changed from an emergency sacrificial operation to a plan for a limited landing in September, 1942, on the Cherbourg peninsula of France to establish a beachhead. The following spring, the beachhead was intended to serve as base for a drive into Germany. Churchill's paper noted:

> We are bound to persevere in the preparation for "Bolero," [an obvious error for Roundup] if possible in 1942, but certainly in 1943. The whole of this business is now going on. Arrangements are being made for a landing of six or eight divisions on the coast of Northern France early in September. However, the British Government do not favour an operation that was certain to lead to disaster, for this would not help the Russians whatever their plight, would compromise and expose to Nazi vengeance the French population involved, and would gravely delay the main operation in 1943. We hold strongly to the view that there should be no substantial landing in France this year unless we are going to stay.
>
> No responsible British military authority has so far been able to make a plan for September, 1942, which had any chance of success unless the Germans become utterly demoralised, of which there is no likelihood. Have the American Staffs a plan? At what points would they strike? . . . If a plan can be found which offers a reasonable prospect of success, His Majesty's Government will cordially welcome it, and will share to the full with their American comrades the risks and sacrifices. This remains our settled and agreed policy.
>
> But in case no plan can be made in which any responsible authority has good confidence, . . . what else are we going to do? Can we afford to stand idle in the Atlantic theatre during the whole of 1942? Ought we not to be preparing . . . some other operation by which we may gain positions of advantage, and also directly or indirectly to take some of the weight off Russia? It is in this setting and on this background that the French Northwest Africa operation should be studied.[37]

Having known firsthand the horrible slaughter of trench warfare in World War I, Churchill resisted placing massive forces on the continent of Europe. He would have no "river of blood," as had occurred at Passchendaele and the Somme. Ever since the brilliant strategic planning of the elder Pitt in the Seven Years War, peripheral strategy had been British policy. Brooke shared these views. He wanted to hit all around the perimeter of German positions until they were so weakened that the operation in Western Europe would be little more than mopping up.

Back in Washington, the talks continued. The old informality re-established, with Churchill once more installed in the rooms across the hall from Hopkins. As before, they strolled back and forth between each others' rooms, their paths this time unencumbered by Christmas gifts.

Word of the fall of Tobruk to the Germans came the first day back in Washington. This major bastion in Libya had previously withstood an eleven-month siege. Rommel now threatened the entire British position in the Middle East. Alexandria might fall at any time, and with it would go the Suez Canal and the oil resources of the Arab states.

The high officials gathered in Roosevelt's office to consider what could be done agreed to strip the American Army of 300 Sherman tanks and send them by fast convoy to Egypt. Afterwards, Hopkins filled Brooke in on the President's remarks and attitudes. Brooke later wrote:

> As I was walking out of the President's room, Hopkins said, "Would you care to come round to my room for a few moments' talk? I could give you some of the background which influenced the President in the statements he has just made and the opinions he has expressed." I went with him, expecting to be taken to his office. Instead, we went to his bedroom where we sat on the edge of his bed looking at his shaving-brush and toothbrush, whilst he let me into some of the President's inner thoughts.
>
> I mention this meeting as it was so typical of this strange man with no official position, not even an office in the White House, and yet one of the most influential of men. A man who played a great and nebulous part in the war as the President's right-hand man. A great part that did him all the more credit when his miserable health is taken into account.[38]

It seemed futile to discuss possible offensives when the British might at any moment have to yield the entire Middle East. In addition, word came from London that Churchill's opponents in Parliament were calling for a vote of censure which might force him to resign. Churchill had no choice but to return to face his critics. He left with the agreement that the planners would continue to work on Roundup. Significantly, they would also work on Gymnast.

Hopkins accompanied Churchill to Baltimore, where his seaplane was waiting. He had some news for his friend, for he planned to be married to Mrs. Louise Macy at the end of July. It was, Churchill felt, one bright spot in a disastrous conference.

Following these inconclusive meetings, the Americans seriously considered diverting their major effort to the Pacific. The German summer offensive began in Russia. Sevastopol fell and the Wehrmacht rushed eastward across the Don to Voronezh and Rostov. The Battle of the Atlantic was going badly, and in early July the Luftwaffe and U-boats hit a north Russian convoy so hard that the Royal Navy declared they could send no more convoys so long as the endless hours of daylight continued.

The American plan to turn to the Pacific may have been bluff to force the British into some kind of action, but it was no bluff in the mind of Admiral King, Commander-in-Chief, U.S. Fleet and Chief of Naval Operations, in succession to Admiral Stark.

In Hyde Park and in Washington, Hopkins and Roosevelt considered their problems endlessly. They were delighted to receive word from London that Churchill had defeated his opponents in the Parliamentary crisis by a vote of 475 to 25. But that did not solve the problem of what form Anglo-American strategy should take.

On July 15, Roosevelt and Hopkins returned to Washington from Hyde Park, where Louise Macy had also been a guest, this time as bride-to-be. They met with Marshall and King, who urged the President to reach accord with the British. Otherwise, the United States should turn its full strength to the Pacific. Roosevelt firmly opposed the Pacific alternative, so he decided to send Hopkins, Marshall, and King to London to get a firm commitment for some kind of activity in the Atlantic theater during 1942. He favored the cross-Channel operation, but if the British were intractable, then they should settle upon Gymnast.

For once Hopkins hated to go. He normally enjoyed the secrecy, the VIP treatment, and the excitement, but this time was different. His wedding had been set for July 30 and was to be performed in the White House. He wanted nothing to delay it.

That evening over dinner, Hopkins and Roosevelt discussed the forthcoming trip. Hopkins' notes quote the President directly:

> I cannot agree that if it be impossible to develop BOLERO in 1942 that we should turn our faces away from Germany and toward Japan.
> In the first place I am not content with the British Cabinet position. I want to know what our men on the ground—Eisenhower, Spaatz, Clark and Stark—think. Do they agree with the British Cabinet? Can you get a confidential report to them?
> Even though we must reluctantly agree to no SLEDGEHAMMER in 1942, I still think we should press forward vigorously for the 1943 enterprise. I see nothing in the message from England to indicate any luke-warmness on their part for the 1943 enterprise. I am somewhat disturbed about this readiness to give up 1942. Will they also give up 1943?
> But my main point is that I do not believe that we can wait until 1943 to strike at Germany. If we cannot strike at SLEDGEHAMMER, then we must take the second best—and that is not the Pacific. There we are conducting a successful holding war. Troops and air alone will not be decisive at once—it requires the increasing strength of our Navy—which takes time.
> If SLEDGEHAMMER cannot be launched then I wish a determination

made while you are in London as to a specific and definite theatre where our ground and sea forces can operate against the German ground forces in 1942.

The theatres to be considered are North Africa and the Middle East. . . .

Under any circumstances I wish BOLERO and ROUNDUP to remain an essential objective even though it must be interrupted.

I am prepared to consider in event SLEDGEHAMMER is not mounted—an appropriate transfer of air and landing craft to the Southwest Pacific.[39]

In essence Roosevelt demanded that American ground forces engage German ground forces somewhere in 1942.

By this time American forces began arriving in the United Kingdom in significant numbers. Eisenhower commanded Bolero and met frequently with British planners. Ira Eaker kept busy organizing the U.S. Eighth Air Force, to fly American bombers out of British bases.

Hopkins and his party left from Washington on July 16. Arriving at Prestwick, Scotland, the following afternoon, Hopkins was delighted to see his old friend Harry Butcher, formerly with CBS, but now with the Army in England and an aide to Eisenhower. Dirty weather grounded the VIP plane awaiting them but, in expectation of such a contingency, Churchill had sent his private train. "We boarded the train at the town of Prestwick at 6 o'clock," wrote Butcher. "The train trip gave opportunity for extended visiting. Harry Hopkins, Steve [Early], and I were apparently the last to bed. Harry and Steve played gin rummy. I bet on Steve, unfortunately." [40]

The Prime Minister directed the train to stop at Chequers, but Marshall and King demanded a talk with Eisenhower before they let themselves in for the wiles of Winston Churchill.

Soon after they arrived at Claridge's, Churchill telephoned in a fury demanding to know why his express orders had been disobeyed. Hopkins later reported, "The Prime Minister threw the British Constitution at me with some vehemence. As you know, it is an unwritten document so no serious damage was done. Winston is his old self and full of battle." [41] To placate him, Hopkins left the warriors to their own devices and went to Chequers alone. Peace was soon restored. Roosevelt wired, "Give Winston my best and tell him not even he can stop that wedding." [42]

The talks started badly, for each side repeated the basic positions it had taken all spring and summer. At one point Hopkins scribbled a note and passed it to Marshall: "I feel damn depressed."

Gradually Marshall came around to the force of Brooke's arguments that Sledgehammer was impossible in 1942. The Allies simply did not have enough strength to face the sixty-odd divisions the Germans kept in France in spite of their heavy commitments in Russia.

The talk swung around to North Africa. Finally they agreed to launch Gymnast, but Hopkins cabled Roosevelt that the planners wanted to postpone the final decision until September 15. He urged him to force a decision at once by setting a target date not later than October 30 for the landings. Roosevelt promptly complied.

Once they had reached a basic agreement, the Combined Chiefs of Staff quickly approved a directive, subject only to an OK from Churchill and Roosevelt. Since he was on the scene, Churchill gave his at once, but the text had to be sent across the Atlantic for FDR's approval.

Meanwhile the American party prepared to go home. They gathered in their rooms at Claridge's packing and relaxing. Quite a crowd gathered in Hopkins' suite for lunch. Harry Butcher joined Steve Early, Averell and Kathleen Harriman, and Pamela Churchill, daughter-in-law of the Prime Minister. Eisenhower came in from Marshall's suite.

> Found Kathleen [Butcher noted] had forgotten her "short-snorter" bill, so she was penalized five shillings for each short-snorter present. We discovered Harry hadn't been made a short-snorter, and he joined with pleasure and cash. [Persons flying an ocean during World War II would have all other passengers sign a dollar bill. On subsequent flights, or in service clubs, if a passenger could not produce his short-snorter bill, he had to pay a dollar fine to each short-snorter present. Some frequent travellers pasted their short-snorter bills together to make a ribbon several feet in length.] He was happy to be going home, as his wedding with Louise Macy is set for the 30th at the White House. The Prime Minister and Mrs. Churchill and the Harrimans sent lovely silver gifts to be carried home.[43]

The afternoon dragged on. Hopkins talked to the President by telephone but learned that the text of the agreement had not yet reached Washington.

At length the President called back to say that the text had arrived and he was calling a meeting of his advisers. These had to be Stimson, Knox, and Arnold, since Hopkins, Marshall, and King were all in London. Butcher's account continues.

> If he, the President, had disagreed, the party could not have left London as planned. Finally another call came from Washington, and about 6 o'clock, Harry, who had been receiving numerous callers, and had been ducking in and out of parlor and bedroom doors, and trying to be host while conducting an international negotiation via trans-oceanic telephone, poked his head out of a bedroom door and said:
> "O.K., boys, we're going home." [44]

Before leaving London, Marshall told Eisenhower to begin planning the

North African operation, now named Torch. If his and King's recommendation meant anything, Ike would also command it.

The Americans left for Prestwick that evening and flew to Iceland, where Marshall inspected troops. Harriman cabled Captain John McCrea, Roosevelt's Naval Aide: PLEASE INFORM THE PRESIDENT I SAW THE VISITING FIREMEN TAKE OFF, ALL WELL AND IN GOOD SPIRITS. ONE OF THEM ASKS YOU TO ARRANGE "TO KEEP LOUISE CURRENTLY INFORMED." [45]

The following day, Roosevelt cabled Churchill:

> THE THREE MUSKETEERS ARRIVED SAFELY THIS AFTERNOON AND THE WEDDING IS STILL SCHEDULED.
>
> I AM, OF COURSE, VERY HAPPY IN THE RESULT AND ESPECIALLY IN THE SUCCESSFUL MEETING OF MINDS.
>
> I CANNOT HELP FEELING THAT THE PAST WEEK REPRESENTED A TURNING POINT IN THE WHOLE WAR AND THAT NOW WE ARE ON OUR WAY SHOULDER TO SHOULDER.[46]

Hopkins and Louise Macy were married at noon, July 30, in the Oval Study, with David Hopkins acting as his father's best man. The President gave the bride away, and the Reverend Russell Clinchy conducted the service. Witnesses included Hopkins' other two sons, Diana, Mrs. Roosevelt, Sam Rosenman, Robert Sherwood, Marshall, King, and members of Mrs. Macy's family. A simple luncheon of cold salmon, hot chicken, vegetables, and wedding cake followed, while an orchestra played appropriate music. At 3:00 the couple departed for a brief honeymoon on a small farm in Connecticut, a few days away from celebrities, from Washington, and from the war.

CHAPTER FIFTEEN

No Raft at Tilsit

The hatred that lies near the surface of the minds of little men spewed forth over Harry Hopkins' wedding in the White House and the alleged extravagance of his honeymoon. Such people planted rumors that grew with each retelling and survived denials for years.

While Harry and Louise Hopkins enjoyed the little farm in Connecticut, the story had them living in luxury on the yacht *My Kay IV* at government expense and waited on by servants paid for by the Navy—or Coast Guard—or someone. The yacht had belonged to Roy Fruehauf, manufacturer of truck-trailers, and had been purchased by the Coast Guard for conversion to antisubmarine work. When the sale went through, Fruehauf had the boat out on a cruise on the Great Lakes. The Coast Guard told him to take his time about returning to Detroit.

According to one version of the story, the Coast Guard delayed working on the craft so the Hopkinses could enjoy their honeymoon. According to another, the Coast Guard boarded it off New London and forcibly evicted the Fruehaufs to make way for Harry and Louise Hopkins. No one explained why anyone would want to engage in a pleasure cruise in the Atlantic with German U-boats on the prowl.

Although White House spokesmen and Fruehauf denied all the versions of the story, the rumors persisted for years. In fact, Hopkins three months later asked how he could sue his accusers.

Then his enemies accused Hopkins of accepting an emerald necklace worth half a million dollars given by Lord Beaverbrook on behalf of the British government in appreciation of Hopkins' work in Lend-Lease. There was nothing to this story, either, although Beaverbrook did send a wedding present. Some Congressmen even threatened an investigation of the doings of Harry Hopkins, but it never came to anything. The Hopkins-haters did not dare.

The picture of Hopkins as profligate spender which was left over from New Deal days persisted through the war years. (It still persists. In connection with a welfare bill before Congress in the 1970s, a newspaper cartoon showed a man with a shovel digging up a grave labeled WPA. The wielder of the shovel bore a strong resemblance to Harry Hopkins.) Since nearly everything that he did in the war years was top secret, he could not refute the poison pens and poison tongues by giving out the true story. It probably made no difference, for Hopkins' enemies were not of the kind that any refutation could have convinced.

Eleanor Roosevelt had grown increasingly disenchanted with Harry Hopkins. She felt he had "lost some of his values"[1] and was too much addicted to the company of his rich and powerful friends. This was rationalization. She resented most the fact that Harry Hopkins gave her husband a kind of companionship she could not. FDR almost never relaxed with her, for she could not be relaxed with him. Having assumed her attitude toward Hopkins, she began to resent little things, such as the requirements of Harry's diet and his desire for avocado salads or his practice of dropping ashes on the carpets or burning cigarette holes in her table cloths.

When she heard the news of his engagement, she was relieved, for it would mean that the couple would surely want a place of their own and she would be rid of the interloper except during the working day. She was dumbfounded when he told her that FDR wanted him and Louise to live in the White House and asked how she felt about it. Temporizing, she said she would discuss the matter with her husband. She did her best to talk FDR out of the idea. She asked if he had considered what it would mean to the couple and to Diana, how hard it would be to start married life in someone else's house.

"Franklin said finally that the most important thing in the world at that time was the conduct of the war and that it was absolutely necessary that Harry be in the house. That settled that. . . ."[2]

While the newlyweds were away, the suite Hopkins occupied got a fresh coat of paint. On August 10, 1942, Hopkins was back at work. Mrs. Hopkins, known to her friends as "Louie," slipped out of the house early in the morning to be at her job as a nurse's aide in Columbia Hospital at 9:00. This left Harry Hopkins free to go the President's room so that the two of them could talk over the war news and map out the activities of the day.

The main change in routine took place when Louie got back from the hospital. She and Harry would sit in their room, having a cocktail or two and entertaining friends, including the President's daughter Anna, who had moved back to Washington while her husband, John Boettiger, was serving in the Army. This activity would continue until it was time to join FDR for his ritual cocktail hour and the "little sippy" prepared by the Presidential hands. Eleanor Roosevelt complained, "They really are quite *high* sometimes before they sit down to dinner." [3]

A few weeks after the marriage, Eleanor Roosevelt was glad of the opportunity to make a trip to England and get away from the frustrating scene in Washington. Before she left, Hopkins told her not to depend on Ambassador Winant but to consult Harriman on everything. Since Harry had suggested one course of action, she determined to take the opposite. She wrote:

> I was sure that Averell Harriman would not have agreed with Harry, because he was in London and knew what a wonderful reputation Mr. Winant enjoyed with the British officials. However, Harry always tended to lean primarily on his own friends and he knew Averell better; I think he never really knew or understood Mr. Winant. [4]

Hopkins was quite right in his advice to Eleanor Roosevelt. Winant had slight influence with British officials, for he usually knew little that was going on. As an afterthought, Harriman and Churchill sometimes handed him copies of correspondence between them and Hopkins and the President, but Winant's files were far from complete.

On August 13, Hopkins had departed with FDR for a few days in Hyde Park. Louie remained behind to talk to Eleanor Roosevelt on arrangements for living in the White House. It must have been an uncomfortable time for both of them. Two days later Louie joined Harry in the Roosevelt mansion. On Monday, August 17, Mrs. Roosevelt rose to the occasion of Hopkins' 52nd birthday by having a dinner for him at Val-Kill Cottage, where she always lived when the President was in Hyde Park.

Other weekends Hopkins spent at Roosevelt's new retreat in the Catoctin Mountains of Maryland, about two hours by automobile from Washington. The President could no longer use the *Potomac,* by then in naval service. In any case, he could not venture out to cruise in the face of U-boat threats.

Roosevelt named the camp Shangri-La, for the Asian monastery in James Hilton's novel *Lost Horizon.* He had jokingly given this name to the supposed base of the planes which had bombed Tokyo in April. Actually they flew from the carrier *Hornet.* (Roosevelt probably had in mind both the notions of an idyllic retreat and a place where the unexpected could be planned for the discomfiture of the enemy. President Eisenhower renamed Shangri-La Camp David.)

The camp, a former Marine training station, included several rustic pine cabins furnished with cast-off Navy furniture. FDR appropriated the biggest house; he loved to sit on its screened porch looking out over the beautiful valley. The house had a bedroom with its own bathroom for the President. There were three guest bedrooms, each equipped with two metal cots and a threadbare rug on the floor, also Navy surplus. The guests shared one bathroom, the door of which did not close properly. FDR took pleasure at their embarrassment and never had the door repaired. On the walls of the living room hung favorite pictures and the original of his favorite cartoon. It depicted a little girl running to tell her mother, who was standing in the doorway of a fashionable house, "Look, mama, Wilfred wrote a bad word!" The bad word which Wilfred had written on the sidewalk was "Roosevelt."

Several other cabins, all as sparsely furnished as the main house, dotted the property; they were for use of staff members and other guests. There were also quarters for the Marine guards and a cabin for the Secret Service men.

Regulars at the camp developed their own names for some of the trappings of Shangri-La. The main gate was called Tell it to the Marines, the President's lodge, the Bear's Den, and his swimming pool, Bear Wallow, with its adjacent bathhouse, Hickory Limb. The telephone exchange, which had direct lines to Washington, was called One Moment Please.

Hopkins and the President used to spend hours together at Shangri-La, in the living room if it rained and on the screened porch when the sun shone. Sometimes they would send for Grace Tully, FDR's head personal secretary since Missy LeHand's stroke, to take dictation. But mostly they worked alone, drafting papers in their own hands. A message to Churchill, for example, might be written by Hopkins in consultation with FDR. Then the President would mark it with his interlineations and inserts. Then Hopkins edited Roosevelt's changes, and finally the note "O.K.—FDR" would appear somewhere on the draft, and Miss Tully or her assistant, Dorothy Brady, would type the official copy to be taken to the Map Room for transmittal to London.

Other times, the two men talked or played cards together. Periods spent at Shangri-La were primarily for relaxing. Guests were chosen for their ability to be congenial companions, who knew how to use their time with the President. This meant no shop talk unless he brought it up, or unless Hopkins approved. If a guest abused the President's hospitality and sneaked in a remark to the effect that it would be better if FDR did such and so in connection with Congress or with a governmental department, or if he pleaded for one of his own pet projects, he never got another invitation.

Louise Hopkins made a good many of the trips to Shangri-La with her husband. She knew that the President had first call on Harry's time. Opportunities did come for the couple to be together. FDR liked to be alone occasionally, to work on his stamps, to play solitaire, or to read. Then he was not to be disturbed except for an emergency.

That summer of 1942 the United States had made its first offensive moves in the Pacific, with landings on the Solomon Islands of Guadalcanal and Tulagi on August 7. Then followed six months of some of the hardest and dirtiest fighting of the war. Simultaneously, MacArthur drove forward in New Guinea on Buna and Gona.

These moves in the Pacific added another dimension to the war, but they were at the far end of the line, with priority given to Torch, the forthcoming invasion of North Africa.

Churchill had the difficult task of explaining to Stalin why there would be no second front in Europe in 1942. He decided to go to Moscow. Harriman thought it vital that Churchill be accompanied by an American. "Hopkins would be best," he told Eden, "but if he is not available I am ready to go." [5] Harriman was assigned and caught up with Churchill in Egypt. They had a hard time with the Soviet leader, but Stalin's interest quickened when he learned of the plans for Torch. Roosevelt was kept informed through Hopkins.

While primarily concerned with such major matters, Hopkins, as the chief of staff, could not avoid trivial concerns. Before her trip to England, Eleanor Roosevelt had planned an international youth conference in Washington. One of her speakers was to be Harold Laski, a Fabian socialist Laborite, whom Churchill found offensive. From Moscow Churchill telegraphed to Hopkins:

> HAROLD LASKI IS ASKING APPROVAL FOR HIS GOING TO THE UNITED STATES, QUOTING ESPECIALLY FROM MRS ROOSEVELTS INVITATION TO ATTEND SOME YOUTH CONGRESS. LASKI HAS BEEN A CONSIDERABLE NUISANCE OVER HERE AND WILL I DOUBT NOT TALK EXTREME LEFT WING STUFF IN THE UNITED STATES. ALTHOUGH I LIKED HIS FATHER AND HAVE MAINTAINED FRIENDLY RELATIONS WITH THE SON HE HAS ATTACKED ME CONTINUALLY AND TRIED TO FORCE MY HAND BOTH IN HOME AND WAR POLITICS. UNLESS THEREFORE MRS ROOSEVELT MAKES A PERSONAL POINT OF IT I SHOULD BE GLAD IF THE INVITATION WERE NOT PRESSED.[6]

Laski did not come, and Mrs. Roosevelt's opinion of the worth of Harry Hopkins dropped further.

The domestic political scene by this time distracted Roosevelt from his activities as war leader. The spirit of national unity brought about by Pearl Harbor had long since given way to partisan politics brought about by the Congressional elections to be held that November. The confusion in

Washington, the inevitable result of rapid expansion, drew attacks from Roosevelt's political opponents. Policies evolved slowly, and when they did come they were not as clear as they should have been. Government agencies and the regular offices bickered and vied for power in the unseemly Battle of Pennsylvania Avenue. Congress steadfastly ignored the threat of inflation in spite of repeated Presidential requests for action. In an election year, they did not dare impose new taxes or controls on prices and wages. They put floors on farm prices but no ceilings, so that food costs promised to go out of sight. The Office of Price Administration, under the genial Leon Henderson, had too much responsibility and too little authority. For a time Henderson rivaled Hopkins in unfavorable stories in the press.

Some of his advisers urged Roosevelt to make full use of his war powers to issue Executive Orders to control prices and wages, but Hopkins and Henderson persuaded him that he could not let Congress evade its responsibilities simply because it was an election year. Accepting this view, on September 7 he sent a Labor Day message to Congress and also addressed the nation in a fireside chat. The lengthy message to Congress called for ceilings on prices and wages and higher taxes on everyone except "persons with very low incomes." He proposed an individual income ceiling of $25,000, with the excess to be taxed one hundred percent. He reminded Congress that while he had the authority to take action himself, "I can only say that I have approached this problem from every angle, and that I have decided that the course of conduct which I am following in this case is consistent with my sense of responsibility as President in time of war, and with my deep and unalterable devotion to the processes of democracy." Unless Congress took action by October 1, he would exercise his executive powers.

In the fireside chat FDR dwelt less on fiscal details than on what Americans had accomplished fighting the enemy on Guadalcanal and in the naval actions nearby. In a pointed thrust at Congress, he said, "Battles are not won by soldiers or sailors who think first of their own personal safety. And wars are not won by people who are concerned primarily with their own comfort, their own convenience, their own pocketbooks."

Shortly afterwards, Roosevelt left on a trip through the country. He inspected Army training camps, Naval stations, and airfields and industrial plants, including the new Ford facility at Willow Run, Michigan, which was turning out B-24 Liberators, the Higgins boatyards in New Orleans, and the Boeing factory in Seattle, where B-17s were made. It was all supposed to be highly secret, but so many people saw the President that secrecy became a joke.

Hopkins stayed behind "to act as a messenger," as he put it in a letter to

Max Beaverbrook. "We are in the throes of a fight with Congress," he continued, "over stabilization of the cost of living. They seem to be determined to do everything that is wrong but I fancy the President will come out on top." [7] He constantly sent Roosevelt top secret messages in code dealing with the pending legislation, with strategy and the war situation, with correspondence with Churchill, and with the political gossip in Washington. He suggested changes in telegrams drafted by Marshall and others.

On October 1, Roosevelt returned to Washington. The next day the Economic Stabilization Act cleared Congress and was on his desk for signature. The $25,000 income maximum proposal was not adopted. One of FDR's first actions under the new legislation was to accept James F. Byrnes's resignation from the Supreme Court to serve as Director of Economic Stabilization. The press immediately began referring to Byrnes as "assistant president," and some went so far as to state that he had taken over from Hopkins, whose star was supposed to be setting.

Those rumors were far from the truth. Byrnes's job had nothing to do with the strategy of the war. His appointment simply reduced the huge piles of papers on Hopkins' desk, bed, and bureau.

"Shortly after Jimmy Byrnes moved in," Hopkins told Sherwood, "I went to talk to him about something and he told me, 'There's just one suggestion I want to make to you, Harry, and that is to keep the hell out of my business.' He smiled very pleasantly when he said it, but by God he meant it and I'm going to keep the hell out." [8] Hopkins being Hopkins, it seems unlikely that his efforts to stay out were one hundred percent successful. His areas of responsibility in production often overlapped Byrnes's problems, and the two men had to confer frequently.

On October 13, Hopkins cabled Churchill to decline a suggestion that he visit London:

> I HAVE BEEN GIVING CAREFUL CONSIDERATION TO GOING TO ENGLAND AT THIS TIME AND IT SEEMS TO ME THAT THERE IS NO AWFULLY GOOD REASON WHY I SHOULD MAKE THE TRIP NOW. THE MOST SERIOUS PROBLEMS WITH WHICH WE HAVE TO DEAL IMMEDIATELY ARE IN THE FIELD OF PRODUCTION AND I AM SURE THOSE CAN BE IRONED OUT BETWEEN LYTTELTON AND NELSON. NELSON CAN NOT GET AWAY FOR AWHILE AND WE ARE EXPECTING LYTTELTON SOON AND I AM SURE HE SHOULD COME ALONG WHENEVER IT IS CONVENIENT, THE SOONER THE BETTER. . . .
>
> THERE MAY BE REASONS IN YOUR MIND FOR MY COMING TO ENGLAND AT ONCE WITH WHICH I AM NOT FULLY ACQUAINTED BUT THERE IS SO MUCH TO DO HERE THAT I DO NOT WISH TO COME UNLESS IT IS IMPORTANT TO YOU AND THE PRESIDENT.
>
> MY SON ROBERT IS IN ENGLAND.[9]

Although Hopkins did not get abroad at that time, Wendell Willkie undertook a round-the-world mission to show American solidarity with the Allies; among others, he visited Churchill and Stalin. On his return, he wrote the book *One World,* a statement of the need for international postwar cooperation to avert another war.

Hopkins resented Willkie for privately circulating reports critical of the British. One of them concerned a banquet given in Willkie's honor in the Kremlin, where Stalin had accused the British of stealing over a hundred Lend-Lease fighters consigned to Russia. Willkie seems to have swallowed the story whole and repeated it widely on his return.

This was a matter Hopkins knew a great deal about, for he had been in on it from the beginning. When it became impossible to get convoys through to Murmansk and Archangel during the summer, the hundred fighter planes sat in crates aboard freighters swinging uselessly at anchor in Scotland. To free the desperately needed ships, Harriman recommended and Hopkins approved a plan to have the planes unloaded until convoys to north Russia resumed. Stalin was informed, yet his suspicious nature kept him from believing the account, and he told Willkie that Churchill had stolen the fighters. An observer had noted: "Stalin recognized that shipping difficulties made it impossible for us to deliver everything that we had promised but added that even though no ships had been lost, we still would have failed to meet our protocol commitments by a large amount." [10]

Correspondence on shipments to Russia bulks large in the files of the Map Room. Many bitter Russian messages left Roosevelt, Hopkins, and Churchill in no doubt of Stalin's mood over the failure of the western Allies to land in Europe in 1942. Among ideas that were suggested to placate Stalin was stationing a joint Anglo-American air force in the Caucasus area. While Roosevelt was still on his tour, Hopkins telegraphed him on this matter:

> I REALIZE THAT ANY AIR FORCE IN THE CAUCASUS WOULD BE ALMOST A TOKEN FORCE BETWEEN NOW AND CHRISTMAS BUT IT SURELY COULD BE BUILT UP WITH BRITISH COOPERATION TO AN EFFECTIVE FIGHTING UNIT BY NEXT SPRING. IT SEEMS TO ME WE MUST ASSUME THAT GERMANY CAN NOT BREAK THROUGH THE CAUCASUS THIS WINTER AND TO MAKE OUR PLANS ACCORDINGLY. . . .
>
> IF WE MUST NOW TELL STALIN THAT THE CONVOYS ON THE NORTHERN ROUTE MUST BE DISCONTINUED, THEN IT SEEMS TO ME THAT IT IS ALMOST IMPERATIVE THAT WE MAKE A DIRECT AND FIRM OFFER TO PLACE OUR ARMED FORCES AT HIS SIDE IN RUSSIA AGAINST GERMANY.[11]

Relations between Russia and the Western Allies remained less than satisfactory that fall until it became apparent that the Germans had been stopped at Stalingrad. Russian needs then became less desperate, and cables from Stalin took on a slightly less surly tone.

The tide began to turn in other areas as well. In the Solomons, the Americans were wearing the Japanese down in a series of desperate land and sea battles. In the North African desert, Rommel was stopped cold, and by late October the process of driving him from Egypt and eventually from Africa commenced.

In the United States and Britain, everyone was working full speed on Torch. In midsummer, Admiral William D. Leahy, a former Chief of Naval Operations, was recalled from his post as ambassador to Vichy France to serve as Chief of Staff to the President and as Chairman of the Joint Chiefs. His job relieved Hopkins of various chores, including many strategic problems. It is not too much to say that Leahy, like Byrnes, acted as a kind of assistant to Hopkins, although neither would have admitted such a relationship.

In recognition of Hopkins' important work, on November 13 FDR formally notified him of a pay raise to $15,000, the same paid to a Cabinet member:

> November 13, 1942
>
> My dear Mr. Hopkins:
>
>   On March 27, 1941 I designated you to advise and assist me in carrying out the responsibilities placed upon me by the act of March 11, 1941 entitled "An Act to Promote the Defense of the United States." Almost from the beginning of your service in this connection, I have utilized you for many other special duties. Your services have evolved to the point where you have become an integral part of the staff of the Commander-in-Chief and I now depend upon you to a very large extent for the coordination of the requirements of the United Nations.
>
>   Because of your increased responsibilities I am fixing your compensation at the annual rate of $15,000 effective November 15, 1942.
>
>   Very sincerely yours,
>   Franklin D. Roosevelt.[12]

Thus Harry Hopkins had finally worked his way back to what he had earned as Secretary of Commerce two years earlier.

One of the first problems Hopkins had to cope with in earning his new salary concerned a visit of Madame Chiang Kai-shek to the United States. T. V. Soong cabled Hopkins from China that Madame was seriously ill and wished to go to the United States for treatment. At Hopkins' request, General Marshall on November 5 arranged for a plane to fly to Chengtu to pick her up and bring her to New York. Hopkins drew the job of escorting her to Washington.

Such a distraction interrupted Hopkins' work on the final preparations for Torch. Several times it seemed that the operation might collapse of its own weight. From the first, Roosevelt had wanted it to be an all-American show because of the hatred he believed the French in North Africa felt for the British following fighting between them after the collapse of France.* American planners feared that forces landed on the Mediterranean shore would be trapped if Hitler countered by driving through Spain to take Gibraltar; therefore, they insisted on Casablanca as one of the targets. The other could be Oran. The British, on the other hand, failed to see how the Americans could do the job all alone, especially since the Royal Navy would have to furnish part of the support. In addition, they felt landings as far west as Casablanca and Oran would have no chance of trapping the Afrika Korps in Tunis between the Torch troops and those of General Sir Bernard Montgomery's British Eighth Army coming west from El Alamein in Egypt. They insisted on adding Algiers to the objective.

In the end they compromised. An American force would take Casablanca, an Anglo-American one Oran, and a British one Algiers. They planned to try to make Torch appear to be an American operation. As it turned out, it mattered little, for the French fought the Americans as fiercely as they fought the British.

The landing was originally scheduled for October 30, but Eisenhower, who had been named Supreme Commander, asked for a few days additional time to get things lined up properly. Roosevelt agreed without a murmur, even though it was most inopportune for him and the Democratic Party. A successful landing in Africa would have helped the administration in the November 3 election. But the date set for Operation Torch was November 8, and it was, said FDR, a decision for the responsible commander and not for the Democratic National Committee.

The election was nearly a disaster for the Democrats. The Republicans gained 47 seats in the House and 10 in the Senate, resulting in the lowest majority Roosevelt had ever had in his entire time as President.

Hoping to avoid shedding French blood, the Allies had arranged to smuggle General Henri Giraud out of France and have him at Eisenhower's side as the troops landed. Unfortunately, the French North African commanders would not obey Giraud's orders. Then it developed that Admiral François Darlan, Pétain's deputy, was in Africa at the bedside of his seriously ill son. When the admiral saw that the landings had succeeded, he gave orders for resistance to cease. The French obeyed him, but Eisenhower came in for an avalanche of adverse criticism by the liberal press in Great Britain and the United States. Except for the generally hated

* See the author's *Years of Deadly Peril: The Coming of the War* (New York: David McKay & Co., Inc., 1969.)

Laval, Darlan had done most to cooperate with the Nazis in France. His recognition by Eisenhower dulled the crusade image the British, the Americans, and the selected French leaders in North Africa had hoped to maintain.

On November 14, Roosevelt discussed with Hopkins a long cable from Eisenhower in which he set forth his reasons for dealing with Darlan:

> CAN WELL UNDERSTAND SOME BEWILDERMENT IN LONDON AND WASH-
> INGTON WITH THE TURN THAT NEGOTIATIONS WITH FRENCH NORTH
> AFRICANS HAVE TAKEN. THE ACTUAL STATE OF EXISTING SENTIMENT HERE
> DOES NOT REPEAT NOT AGREE EVEN REMOTELY WITH SOME OF PRIOR
> CALCULATIONS. THE FOLLOWING SALIENT FACTS ARE PERTINENT AND IT IS
> EXTREMELY IMPORTANT THAT NO REPEAT NO PRECIPITATE ACTION UPSET
> SUCH EQUILIBRIUM AS WE HAVE BEEN ABLE TO ESTABLISH.
>
> FOREMOST IS THE FACT THAT THE NAME OF MARSHAL PETAIN IS SOME-
> THING TO CONJURE WITH HERE. EVERYONE FROM HIGHEST TO LOWEST
> ATTEMPTS TO CREATE THE IMPRESSION THAT HE LIVES AND ACTS UNDER THE
> SHADOW OF THE MARSHAL'S FIGURE. THE CIVIL GOVERNORS, MILITARY
> LEADERS AND NAVAL COMMANDERS WILL AGREE ON ONLY ONE MAN AS
> HAVING AN OBVIOUS RIGHT TO ASSUME THE MARSHAL'S MANTLE IN NORTH
> AFRICA. THAT MAN IS DARLAN. . . .
>
> IT MUST BE REMEMBERED THAT HOSTILITIES IN MOROCCO CEASED BY
> ORDER OF DARLAN AND NOT REPEAT NOT BY FULL MILITARY CONQUEST.
> FRENCH MILITARY POSITION IN THAT AREA IS STILL SUCH AS TO BE CAPABLE
> OF CAUSING ADDITIONAL TROUBLE. . . .[13]

Roosevelt accepted Eisenhower's arrangements as a temporary expedient to save life and to speed the victory in North Africa. He did not like the situation, but he liked the uninformed criticism of the press and even of some of his own liberal advisers even less. Hopkins drafted a reply to Eisenhower for Roosevelt's signature:

> I WANT YOU TO KNOW THAT I APPRECIATE FULLY THE DIFFICULTIES OF
> YOUR MILITARY SITUATION. I AM THEREFORE NOT DISPOSED TO IN ANY WAY
> QUESTION THE ACTION YOU HAVE TAKEN. INDEED YOU MAY BE SURE OF MY
> COMPLETE SUPPORT OF THIS AND ANY OTHER ACTION YOU ARE REQUIRED TO
> TAKE IN CARRYING OUT YOUR DUTIES. YOU ARE ON THE GROUND AND WE
> HERE INTEND TO SUPPORT YOU FULLY IN YOUR DIFFICULT PROBLEMS.
>
> HOWEVER I THINK YOU SHOULD KNOW AND HAVE IN MIND THE FOL-
> LOWING POLICIES OF THIS GOVERNMENT:
>
> 1. THAT WE DO NOT TRUST DARLAN.
>
> 2. THAT IT IS IMPOSSIBLE TO KEEP A COLLABORATOR OF HITLER AND ONE
> WHOM WE BELIEVE TO BE A FASCIST IN CIVIL POWER ANY LONGER THAN IS
> ABSOLUTELY NECESSARY.
>
> 3. HIS MOVEMENTS SHOULD BE WATCHED CAREFULLY AND HIS COMMU-
> NICATIONS SUPERVISED.[14]

At the same time, urged by Hopkins and others, FDR gave a statement to the press emphasizing the temporary nature of the arrangement with Darlan and that the French people themselves would in time establish their own form of government.

Privately Roosevelt was furious that the State Department with its representatives in North Africa had not understood the situation better so that the whole mess might have been avoided. As it turned out, the Allies did not long have to live with the Darlan organization in North Africa, for on Christmas Eve Darlan was assassinated by a half-mad French Gaullist-royalist.

When Eisenhower's explanatory cable was received, Hopkins and his wife were in Hyde Park with Roosevelt. With them was Diana and a girl friend of hers who had come along to help Diana celebrate her tenth birthday on November 15. But, as always, there was little rest for her father, for the work went on. Couriers carried papers back and forth from Washington.

With the success of the North African operation assured, Roosevelt in a speech suggested that possibly the turning point of the war had been reached. More cautiously, Churchill said, "Now, this is not the end. It is not even the beginning of the end. But it is, perhaps, the end of the beginning."

Already minds in Washington and London grappled with the problem of what next. Montgomery had Rommel in full retreat, and if Eisenhower's forces could move east with equal speed into Tunisia, they might well trap most of the Afrika Korps between them. But Eisenhower's drive failed, the Germans poured troops into Tunisia to block him, and by the end of the year it was evident that hard fighting lay ahead before the Germans would be driven out of Africa.

Still, the German defeat in Tunisia was certain, and it was high time to make plans. Churchill wanted Hopkins, Marshall, and King to come to England once more to decide what to do. The Americans still wanted Roundup to make a landing in northern France in 1943, but Churchill began to talk of further softening up in the "soft underbelly" of Europe before moving across the Channel.

Such backsliding by the British was precisely what Marshall had feared when Operation Torch got the go-ahead. He wanted to wind up the African episode and get on with the main business of an operation aimed at the heart of Germany.

Roosevelt and Churchill concluded that a joint conference with Stalin was necessary. Hopkins strongly urged such a meeting. As he well knew from his experience in Moscow, the only Russian who could give definite answers on anything was Stalin himself. Nothing would happen if the Combined Chiefs of Staff tried to coordinate strategy with the Russian military leaders. Every minor shift in position or argument would have to be referred back to the Kremlin anyway. Once again Hopkins wanted to play the "marriage broker." He had brought Roosevelt and Churchill together at Argentia. Now he hoped to bring them both face to face with Stalin.

On December 2, Hopkins drafted a cable to Churchill for Roosevelt.

> I HAVE BEEN GIVING A GOOD DEAL OF THOUGHT TO OUR PROPOSED CONFERENCE WITH THE RUSSIANS AND I AGREE WITH YOU THAT THE ONLY SATISFACTORY WAY OF COMING TO THE VITAL STRATEGIC CONCLUSIONS THE MILITARY SITUATION REQUIRES, IS FOR YOU AND ME TO MEET PERSONALLY WITH STALIN. MY THOUGHT WOULD BE THAT EACH OF US WOULD BE ACCOMPANIED BY A VERY SMALL STAFF MADE UP OF OUR TOP ARMY, AIR AND NAVAL CHIEFS OF STAFF. I SHOULD BRING HARRY AND AVERELL BUT NO STATE DEPARTMENT REPRESENTATIVE ALTHO I BELIEVE WE SHOULD ARRIVE AT TENTATIVE PROCEDURES TO BE ADOPTED IN EVENT OF A GERMAN COLLAPSE. I SHOULD LIKE TO SEE THE CONFERENCE HELD ABOUT JAN FIFTEENTH OR SOON THEREAFTER. TUNIS AND BIZERTE SHOULD HAVE BEEN CLEARED UP AND ROMMEL'S ARMY LIQUIDATED BEFORE THE CONFERENCE. AS TO THE PLACE. ICELAND OR ALASKA ARE IMPOSSIBLE FOR ME AT THIS TIME OF YEAR AND I BELIEVE EQUALLY SO FOR STALIN. I SHOULD PREFER A SECURE PLACE SOUTH OF ALGIERS OR IN OR NEAR KHARTOUM. I DON'T LIKE MOSQUITOES. I THINK THE CONFERENCE SHOULD BE VERY SECRET AND THAT THE PRESS SHOULD BE EXCLUDED. I WOULD QUESTION THE ADVISABILITY OF MARSHALL AND THE OTHERS GOING TO ENGLAND PRIOR TO THE CON-FERENCE BECAUSE I DO NOT WANT TO GIVE STALIN THE IMPRESSION THAT WE ARE SETTLING EVERYTHING BETWEEN OURSELVES BEFORE WE MEET HIM. *On the other hand I realize the importance of you and me going into that conference only after the fullest exchange of views and a complete understanding. I will try to suggest a method in the next few days and would welcome any other suggestions from you.*

[The italicized words were deleted by Roosevelt and the following correction made in his own hand:] I THINK THAT YOU AND I UNDERSTAND EACH OTHER SO WELL THAT PRIOR CONFERENCES BETWEEN US ARE UNNECESSARY AND WHEN THE TIME COMES WE CAN WORK THINGS OUT FROM DAY TO DAY. OUR MILITARY PEOPLE WILL ALSO BE IN CLOSE COOPERATION AT ALL TIMES FROM NOW ON.

[Hopkins' draft continues:] I THINK THAT THIS CONFERENCE MAY WELL RESULT IN KNOCKING OUT GERMANY SOONER THAN WE ANTICIPATED. AS YOU KNOW STALIN HAS ALREADY AGREED TO A PURELY MILITARY CON-FERENCE TO BE HELD IN MOSCOW AND I HAVE TODAY SENT HIM A MESSAGE URGING HIM TO MEET YOU AND ME. I BELIEVE HE WILL ACCEPT.

[Roosevelt then added a conclusion in his own hand:] I PREFER A COMFORTABLE OASIS TO THE RAFT AT TILSIT.[15] [On July 7-9, 1807, Napoleon Bonaparte met with Czar Alexander I of Russia and King Frederick William III of Prussia on a raft at Tilsit in the Neman River to settle two treaties. Prussia gave Napoleon all the lands between the Rhine and the Elbe, and, in a secret pact, Alexander agreed to join France against

England if the British refused to accept the proffered French terms for peace.]

During a luncheon on November 30, Roosevelt told Harriman that he wanted no "ringers" at the conference, by which he meant any State Department personnel, especially Cordell Hull. During these times, Roosevelt and Harry Hopkins acted as a two-man State Department in relations with Churchill, Stalin, and nearly anything else pertaining to the war. Roosevelt's statement that he wanted no ringers meant that Harriman would have to persuade Churchill, who liked to include everyone, to leave Eden behind.

On his return to England, Harriman reported to Hopkins that he had been "thoroughly beaten up" by the Prime Minister at the suggestion that he leave Eden behind, but that Churchill had finally agreed out of deference to the President's wishes. No one seems to have suggested to Stalin just whom he might bring.

As it turned out, it didn't matter, for Stalin refused to come to the meeting, stating that he could not get away even for a day in view of the military situation. Roosevelt offered to postpone the conference from January to March, but again Stalin refused. The truth of the matter was that Stalin saw no value in talk until the British and Americans agreed to a second front.

So the proposed Big Three conference became the fourth Churchill-Roosevelt meeting. In retrospect it was perhaps just as well, for the decisions made there concerned Russia only in matters of supply. The British and Americans had to decide what they were going to do next. The North African operations and the lack of progress in taking Tunisia doomed Roundup for 1943, although the British continued to pay lip service to the idea.

Casablanca became the site of the conference. The Anfa Hotel complex, five miles south of the city, included a group of villas suitable for housing Roosevelt, Churchill, and their parties. Plenary sessions could meet in the hotel. The detached area could be easily guarded by troops and the Secret Service. An airfield nearby afforded easy transportation for the important people involved. Roosevelt thought the arrangements "grand" and was anxious to be off. But first, there were things to be done at home.

On November 26, Thanksgiving Day, Roosevelt had a special service in the White House attended by about two hundred people, including some of "the same old chiselers so well known to the Social Bureau." [16] After dinner, Roosevelt boarded his train for Hyde Park, taking Diana Hopkins and a friend with him. Diana's father had to go to New York to escort Madame Chiang Kai-shek to the Harkness Pavilion of Presbyterian Hospital, where she had engaged the entire twelfth floor.

Madame Chiang had invited Hopkins because she wanted him to change the entire strategy of the war. She felt, quite rightly, that China was getting the little end of the stick, and she wanted the war against Germany to be deferred so that Japan could be defeated first. Yet she had little interest in American operations in the Solomons and New Guinea. The only thing that counted was what was going on in and for China. Hopkins was relieved to drop her off. Afterwards he drove up to Hyde Park with Mike Reilly, head of the Presidential protection division of the Secret Service. Louise Hopkins arrived on Saturday after she had completed her work at the hospital.

On Sunday evening, Churchill made a speech on the progress of the war. Hopkins cabled: DEAR WINSTON. YOUR FRIEND, HIS WIFE AND MINE HAVE LISTENED TO YOUR SPEECH. MUSSOLINI DID NOT LIKE IT. WE DID. HARRY.[17]

Back in Washington, Hopkins went about his routine, driving himself harder than he should. Just before Christmas occurred an unfortunate episode that had his old enemies and a lot of new ones in full cry against him. The *American* magazine published an article under his name entitled "You Will Be Mobilized." Although it was mostly ghostwritten, it reflected Hopkins' impatience with the business-as-usual approach of many Americans even after a year of war. It depicted harsher rationing and more rigid regimentation than actually did come about during the war. A sample:

> Through forced savings and taxes our spending will be limited. Rationing and priorities far more widespread than at present will determine the kinds of food, clothing, housing and businesses which we will have, and will affect every detail of our daily lives. We should not be permitted to ride on a train, make a long distance telephone call, or send a telegram without evidence that these are necessary.[18]

The article inspired a spate of letters directed to Hopkins, some of hate, but mostly from people who were overage, lame, halt, or blind wanting to know how they could serve. Hopkins responded to many of those letters individually and often made telephone calls to line up jobs. The general public never learned of these services as Hopkins reverted temporarily to the long dormant role of the social worker.

The public heard about something totally different: Bernard Baruch's wedding present.

Although Baruch believed that Hopkins blocked his employment in government service during the war, he still remained friendly, and his wedding gift was a dinner dance at the Carlton Hotel for sixty of the most important people in Washington, from Donald Nelson and James F. Byrnes to Steve Early and Robert Sherwood. The President did not attend.

The lavish menu was a reminder of the good life, but ill-considered for wartime Washington:

Bowl of Caviar with Trimmings
Pâté de Foie Gras
Cheese Croquettes
Baked Oysters Bonne Femme
Celery, Radishes, Olives, Pecans
Tortue Clair (en terrine)
Crème au Champignons Frais
Profiteroles
Mousse of Chicken
Gallantine of Capon
Cold Tongue
Beef à la Mode
Corned Beef in Jelly
Turkey   Chicken   Virginia Ham
Calves Head Vinaigrette
Truite en Gêlée
Homard en Aspic
Terrapin (Baltimore style)
Chicken à la King
Steamed Rice
Sliced Tomatoes   Crisp Lettuce
Mayonnaise   French Dressing
Russian Dressing
Mixed Green Salad
Assorted Cheese and Crackers
Socle of Raspberry Ice
Petit Fours
Demi Tasse

The guests found gifts at their places and drank vintage champagne, poured liberally by attentive waiters. Normally such an occasion would have received favorable notice from admiring society reporters, and the ordinary citizen would have not given it a second thought.[19]

Now it became a first-rate scandal. And oddly enough, Hopkins got more blame than Baruch. To hear some of the comments, it would seem to have been the worst orgy since Belshazzar's feast, lacking only "mene, mene, tekel, upharsin" on the walls.

But Hopkins weathered that attack as he had so many others. This would not be the last.

Christmas in the White House was subdued that year. Families were too scattered for the old-fashioned rituals the President loved. On New Year's

Eve, there was the traditional gathering in the White House. At the moment of midnight, FDR lifted a glass of champagne for his annual toast "To the United States of America." Then he added another one, "To the United Nations."

Earlier the guests had enjoyed a movie. Roosevelt and Hopkins had a hard time keeping their faces straight when the title flashed on the screen. The movie starred Humphrey Bogart and was entitled *Casablanca*.

CHAPTER SIXTEEN

Conferences, Conferences

The year 1943 might well be known as the Year of the Conferences. Roosevelt and Churchill met on four separate occasions, in Casablanca in January, in Washington in May, in Quebec in August, and in Cairo, Teheran, and Cairo in November and December. In Teheran they met with Stalin as well.

Hopkins missed no session of any importance in these conferences, advising, placating ruffled egos, and smoothing things behind the scenes.

By this time, his duties were less executive and more in the nature of alter ego of the President, especially in foreign policy and military strategy. He bridged the gap between the military aspects of war planning, as represented by the Joint and Combined Chiefs, and the political application of strategy as the responsibility of the President and the Prime Minister. As chairman of the Munitions Assignment Board, he still had to keep himself informed on matters of production and allocation of war matériel.

Two days after the State of the Union address on January 7, 1943, Roosevelt and Hopkins with others left the White House late in the evening to board a train for Miami, on the first leg of a journey that would take them to Casablanca to meet with Churchill and, later in the conference, with Charles de Gaulle. This would be the first time that a President had left the United States in wartime and the first time a President had flown. (In 1932, Roosevelt had gone by plane to Chicago to accept the nomination at the Democratic National Convention, but he was not yet elected President.)

While newspapers and magazines ran stories about how men such as Jimmie Byrnes were taking over in the government from the reviled Hopkins, that gentleman was speeding along the rails southward in the new private railway car, the *Ferdinand Magellan,* which had been provided for the President by the Association of American Railroads. Nearly twice the weight of the normal Pullman car, it had bullet-proof glass on all the windows. Its greater weight gave it a smoother ride than a standard car. As always, the train moved slowly in accordance with Roosevelt's orders, for his infirmity meant that he could not use his legs to counter the bumps and lurches of high-speed travel. Thus it took some forty-eight hours to reach Miami.

Hopkins kept full notes on his trip to Casablanca, and some of them are revealing:

> Monday Evening Jan 11—'43
> Trinidad
>
> We left Miami at 6:05 this morning and landed here at 4:45. P.M. All this after two nights and a day on the train from Washington. Eleanor and Louise said good night at the rear door and I must say that I didn't like the idea of leaving a little bit. Only because Louise had been very unhappy all evening because of the political attacks on us. [These attacks were, of course, inspired by Bernard Baruch's "Lucullan feast" and by the "Beaverbrook emeralds," which had now grown in value, according to some of the press, to anywhere between three and five million dollars.]
>
> Admiral Leahy—Admiral McIntyre [sic—Hopkins consistently misspelled Dr. McIntire's name to make it like that of Marvin McIntyre—the error will be silently corrected henceforth] the President's doctor, Capt. McCrae, his naval Aide and half dozen secret service men, Arthur [Prettyman] his butler—two or three army officers made up the party. Grace [Tully] was going along as far as Jacksonville.
>
> To bed early and up late with a long, sleepy Sunday thru the Carolinas and Georgia to Miami. We were called at 4:30 Monday morning. Knowing my airplane capacity, I ate nothing—found the President alone in his car and we laughed over the fact that this unbelievable trip was about to begin. [FDR was always excited about making a trip, and the fact that he was going so far and to such out-of-the-way places added to his excitement. In a sense, he was playing hooky from Washington.] I shall always feel that the reason the President wanted to meet Churchill in Africa was because he wanted to make a trip! He was tired of having other people—particularly myself, speak for him around the world. He wanted no more of Churchill in Washington, for political reasons he could not go to England, he wanted to see our troops, he was sick of people telling him that it was dangerous to ride in airplanes. He liked the drama of it. But above all, he wanted to make a trip!

It is not at all clear why FDR felt he could not go to England for political reasons. It was nearly two years to another national election, and at that time he had no idea of running for a fourth term. Since both King George and Winston Churchill had visited the United States, there seems no adequate reason why he could not have returned their calls. Probably he preferred the glamor of Africa to England in January, as did Harry Hopkins, who, Eisenhower noted, hated Chequers more than the devil hates holy water.[1]

> The genesis of it was this [Hopkins' memo to himself continues.] Last July Marshall, King and I went to London. I had told the President that there seemed to be no determination on the part of the Chiefs of Staff of either the U.S. or England to fight in 1942. This in spite of the fact that Marshall and I had gone to England in April '42 when the plan to cross the Channel was agreed upon. But it dragged—in spite of Marshall, and it was obvious that nothing was going to happen. The result of that trip was the landing in N. Africa in Nov. 1942. On the assumption that we are going to drive the Germans out of Africa, it became clear to me that there was no agreed upon plan as to what to do next. We had to strike somewhere— across the channel, at Sardinia, Sicily or thru Turkey. But where? [Hopkins' strategic sense was now global, as is evident from the fact that the objectives he mentioned were all discussed by the military experts at Casablanca.]
>
> Furthermore I told the President that the next major strategic move should not be made without consultation with Stalin. Twice Stalin refused the urgent invitation of the President to meet with himself and Churchill. The Russian front was too urgent. The next best thing was a meeting between Churchill, Roosevelt and their respective staffs. And the President wanted to meet in Africa! Churchill agreed. The army have found a safe place outside of Casablanca. And we are off to decide where we shall fight next. King, Marshall and their aides are ahead of us by two days to iron out all possible difficulties in advance. [The idea that King and Marshall could iron out difficulties in advance with their British opposite numbers was a large measure of wishful thinking. The British and Americans were far apart still in strategic concepts.]
>
> The President was carried on to the plane this morning in the dark—it taxied out of the harbor and long before sunrise took off with few people knowing the President was on his way to Africa. I sat with him, strapped in, as the plane rose from the water—and he acted like a sixteen year old, for he has done no flying since he was President. The trip was smooth, the President happy and interested. Dr. McIntire was worried about the President's bad heart—but nothing happened—he slept for two hours after lunch. He asked the pilot to go over the Citadel in Haiti. We saw no ships and made a perfect landing at the Naval Base in Trinidad. The Admiral and General met us—took us for cocktails and dinner at a hotel run by the Navy. And at nine to bed for we are to be called at 4.15 A.M.[2]

Before turning in, Hopkins sent a somewhat cryptic telegram to his wife:
ALL WELL. NO TOOTH PASTE. BEST LOVE. HARRY.[3]

The journal continues, recounting how Hopkins was awakened the next morning after a good night's sleep. Admiral Leahy became too ill to continue the journey and remained in Trinidad. The party drove down to the seaplane in the dark after Roosevelt had finished a leisurely breakfast, his dilatoriness bothering no one, "tho the Secret Service were having fits."

> The ship took to the air beautifully and the ride all the way to Belem—we landed at 3.15 P.M.—was as smooth as glass. We flew tho at about 9000 feet and McIntire was quite disturbed about the President,—who appeared to be very pale at times. We flew over the Citadel in Haiti—the wild waste lands of Honduras—hit the S. American coast in Dutch Guinea [sic—Guiana]. We flew over literally millions of acres of desolate jungle. Why any one should want to explore them is beyond me. The Amazon delta is a great sight with river mouth widening out to a width of a hundred miles—the equator cutting it in two.

Hopkins obviously confused his geography. They had flown over the Citadel in Haiti the previous day. And their flight could not possibly have taken them to Honduras, which lies as far southwest of Haiti as Trinidad is southeast. He must have meant Hispaniola, which is shared by Haiti and the Dominican Republic.

The references to Roosevelt's weak heart reveal a secret which was carefully kept from the public. Dr. McIntire tried to minimize the fact, even in his own mind, but it gave him concern in such conditions as high-altitude flying in nonpressurized aircraft. By the next fall he felt that conditions had deteriorated enough to bring in a Navy cardiac specialist, Dr. Howard Bruenn, and assign him nearly full time to care for the President.

Hopkins' notes describe their arrival at Belem, where the party was taken to the officers' quarters for drinks and a rest. "I wangled two bottles and a cold turkey to take to Africa." At 6:00 that evening they left for the journey across the South Atlantic, which took over eighteen hours. "Everyone was dog tired so we turned in early." The next day, Hopkins relieved the boredom of the trip by teaching Ross McIntire gin rummy and by reading a detective story.

> We landed in this big harbor at the mouth of the Gambia river—an old slave port. The cruiser Memphis and one of our destroyers are in port. Capt. [Henry Y.] McCown met us—we took a trip around the harbor in a motor whale boat. The President was hoisted to the deck and one of the men carrying him slipped as he stepped onto the cruiser and the President landed on his rear. We had dinner with the Captain. This is built for a

flagship—the President has the Admiral's quarters and I have the Captain's next door.

McIntire heard that we had to fly over mountains 13,000 feet to get to our rendezvous with Churchill. Something will have to be done about that in the morning for the President can't stand that height.

The next morning, after a rather poor night on the *Memphis,* the party left the cruiser and drove to an airfield where a Douglas C-54 awaited them. Hopkins noted that "the mountains seem to have shrunk during the night."

> We went 7 hours over the desert—that is hardly worth fighting for—we saw an American air field used to move fighter planes into the battle areas—it is supplied entirely by air. We crossed the Atlas mountains—great snow capped peaks seemed incongruous after the desert. Then we suddenly came on the fertile fields of N. Africa—looking like the Garden of Eden should look and probably doesnt. Camels—olive groves—oranges—wheat fields—no cows—rain—miles of black earth. The President missed nothing. We landed at the airport about 15 miles from Casablanca. The President's son Elliott was there to meet him. Much "hush, hush"—and the President, Elliott and I were hustled into a car blacked out with mud to drive to our Villa. It is a lovely, modern, California bungalow—part of a hotel—taken over by the Army. The President, Elliott and I are staying here.

The Hotel Anfa and its villas sit on a hill overlooking the Atlantic. In January, the weather tends to be crisp and cool at night and pleasantly warm by day. A military guard surrounding the entire complex made it easy for the participants to visit back and forth informally.

> Churchill has a house about fifty yards away. I went over to bring him back for a drink before dinner. He was in fine form but looks older. We walked back—and the three of us had a long talk over the military situation. The British 8th Army is attacking tonight. [Montgomery's Eighth Army had been held up by the German defenses at Buerat for some weeks, but Monty had accumulated enough supplies and ammunition so he felt justified in making a drive on Tripoli, which was captured January 23.]
>
> The two staffs are in the big hotel across the street and just before dinner I found them all having a cocktail. The President invited the British and American chiefs to dine with him—and Churchill—and Averell. Much good talk of war—and families—and the French. I went to bed at twelve but I understand that the Pres. and Churchill sat up till two.[4]

One of the more pleasant features of the Casablanca Conference was the family reunions. In addition to Elliott Roosevelt, Lieutenant Franklin, Jr., had leave from his ship to serve as an aide to the President. Churchill's son Randolph attended as well, and to Harry Hopkins' delight, his son Robert, a sergeant in an Army photographic unit, came back from a foxhole at the front. Eisenhower arranged the necessary orders on his own. Many critics of Roosevelt protested that other fathers were not reunited with their sons, but FDR ignored such criticism. Most of the sons worked hard. "I was not an idle guest," wrote Robert Hopkins. "I worked hard recording the conference on film for the official records." [5]

Decisions made at Casablanca included a plan to invade Sicily no later than that July. Churchill hoped that the invasion, Operation Husky, would drive Italy out of the war. The Americans agreed to the Sicilian operation only because they finally realized that the Allies lacked the strength to stage the cross-Channel invasion in 1943. Troops currently in the Mediterranean had to do something; they could not spend a year in idleness. Many officers on both sides felt that Sardinia would have made a better target than Sicily to knock Italy out of the war. Aircraft based in Sardinia could have covered landings in the north of Italy, while from Sicily planes could reach only as far north as Naples. As the opponents predicted, Sicily and then the mainland sentenced the Allies to a long, costly march up the Italian peninsula.

The most ticklish problem at Casablanca was dealing with the French. Obviously it was undesirable for the Americans and British to govern French North Africa as occupied enemy territory. While the assassination of Darlan had relieved the British and Americans of a major embarrassment, the problem of which Frenchmen could be trusted remained. Hull blocked Hopkins' suggestion that his old friend Jean Monnet be brought in as a major adviser for the French Commissioner. But Monnet got to North Africa after all, for Hopkins persuaded the President after they had returned to Washington to send him to Algiers to help handle the Lend-Lease supplies and equipment which were being sent to equip the French army being formed there. It was not the first time nor the last that Hopkins managed to get around the prejudices of Cordell Hull.

The more important problem with the French arose from the factions bitterly jealous of each other. In North Africa, French soldiers, sailors, and civil officials grudgingly accepted the authority of General Giraud, but in England brooded the vain and austere figure of General Charles de Gaulle, who sulked because Churchill and Roosevelt had not informed him in advance of the landings in North Africa in November. De Gaulle refused to have any part in North African affairs, and the Free French, whose forces he commanded, were idle in the United Kingdom. He had been invited to Casablanca, but had haughtily refused.

On January 19, Hopkins dictated a lengthy memorandum of the events of the day. Some of it is too detailed in political and diplomatic matters to quote, but other passages are of interest:

> I arranged to have dinner with Harriman and Churchill tonight because the President and Elliott are dining with General [George S.] Patton. The Prime Minister was anxious that the President not tell Giraud that DeGaulle had refused to show up, because he was hoping to get a message from DeGaulle any minute. He said he wanted to come to see the President around five or six o'clock tonight. I went back to the house and told the President that the Prime Minister did not want Giraud told.
>
> I attended the conference between the President, Giraud, [Robert] Murphy [State Department political adviser on French North Africa], Captain McCrea, Elliott, and Giraud's Military Aide, Captain Beaufre. The President laid out to Giraud in a masterful fashion, his concept of French resistance, emphasizing the fighting. . . . I gained a very favorable impression of Giraud. I know he is a Royalist and is probably a right-winger in all his economic views, but I have a feeling that he is willing to fight. He is about six feet, two inches and a man of about 63 or 64. He has the appearance of health and vigor. He spoke with a good deal of modesty, but with confidence. Had a feeling that he had made up his mind that he was going to do whatever the President wanted in Africa. Apart from fighting in the war, it is impossible to tell whether or not he has political ambitions. He did not give me that impression except when he stressed later, with great vigor, his determination to head the civil as well as the military areas in Africa.
>
> Giraud speaks no English, but the President's French seemed to me to be better than usual, and Murphy, who did the interpreting, didn't have much to do. It was only when the President wanted to be perfectly sure that Giraud knew what he was saying on an important matter, that he had Murphy interpret. Giraud laid out his problems, which his aide had previously told me, and the President settled them all to Giraud's complete satisfaction but on the sovereignty point he was adamant, and insisted that Giraud, at the moment, act only as a representative in North Africa, and that he not in any sense speak for France, and that the understanding about all other French possessions should be worked out only when DeGaulle arrived. . . .
>
> We had lunch with the President, Averell, Robert and Elliott. I took a nap after lunch and then General Patton arrived to take Elliott and me downtown to do a little shopping. We went by the docks and saw the beaches on which our men landed at Casablanca and saw how the Navy knocked the hell out of the Jean Bart [a nearly completed French battleship which moved to Casablanca when France surrendered and whose guns opposing the Americans on November 8 were silenced by shells from the American battleship *Massachusetts*]. A great convoy of ours was just steaming into sight. We saw the steel landing fields for airports

being loaded on the trains and American soldiers and sailors everywhere in the city. Shopping was pretty fruitless except for some rugs. I got back to the house about six o'clock and found the Prime Minister and his son, Randolph, talking to the President about this and that. I am going off to dinner with the Prime Minister, Averell, Randolph and Robert in a few minutes.[6]

On January 21, Hopkins, Harriman, Murphy, and Ross McIntire accompanied Roosevelt on a drive with Patton to Rabat, 85 miles northeast of Casablanca to visit U.S. General Mark Clark's Fifth Army. The party journeyed in jeeps, an experience that FDR later remarked was enough to last a lifetime. They lunched in the field on troop rations, which included boiled ham, sweet potatoes, green beans, fruit salad, bread, butter, jam, and coffee. FDR kept the mess kit from which he had eaten as a souvenir of the occasion. A band entertained the guests with "Chattanooga Choo Choo," "Naughty Marietta Waltz," "The Missouri Waltz," "Deep in the Heart of Texas," and "Alexander's Ragtime Band."

The following day, Hopkins dictated further notes. De Gaulle had finally arrived, brought only by the threat that if he persisted in his sulks, the British and Americans would no longer recognize him as leader of the Free French. Hopkins breakfasted with Robert and then spent a good bit of the day talking to Churchill and Roosevelt.

> I found Churchill in bed in his customary pink robe, and having, of all things, a bottle of wine for breakfast. I asked him what he meant by that and he told me that he had a profound distaste on the one hand for skimmed milk, and no deep rooted prejudice about wine, and that he had reconciled the conflict in favor of the latter. He commended it to me and said he had lived to be 68 years old and was in the best of health, and had found that the advice of doctors, throughout his life, was usually wrong. At any rate, he had no intention of giving up alcoholic drink, mild or strong, now or later. . . . We discussed the state of the conference for some time and he seemed satisfied with the outcome. I told him it seemed to me like a pretty feeble effort for two great countries in 1943. I told him, however, that I had watched this war develop for a long time now, and realized that the Chiefs of Staff may agree to do nothing today, but tomorrow, when the President puts the heat on, they will suddenly decide they can do a little more than they think they can at this conference. . . .
>
> The President had been lunching with Marshall and I came in on the tail end of that. Marshall was talking about the difficulties of not having Eisenhower a full General. He said it was difficult to do in view of the fact that Eisenhower's army is mired in the mud, and the President told General Marshall that he would not promote Eisenhower until there was some damn good reason for doing it, that he was going to make it a rule

that promotions should go to people who had done some fighting, that while Eisenhower has done a good job, he hasn't knocked the Germans out of Tunisia.

Roosevelt later changed his mind and promoted Eisenhower soon after the Casablanca Conference because of the uncomfortable situation created by the fact that a good many of Eisenhower's British subordinates outranked him.

That evening the President entertained at dinner the Sultan of Morocco, which caused Churchill to pull a long face because the dinner would be dry in deference to the guest of honor's Muslim religion.

The Sultan arrived at 7:40, which caused me to put on my black tie for the first time on this trip. He had expressed a desire to see the President alone prior to Churchill's arrival at eight, and he came loaded with presents—a gold dagger for the President, and some gold bracelets for Mrs. Roosevelt and a gold tiara which looked to me like the kind the gals wear in the circus, riding on white horses. I can just see Mrs. Roosevelt when she takes a look at this. The Sultan proved to be a undersized, inconsequential looking man, in white silk robes, age 32. He said little or nothing before dinner, during dinner or after dinner. He put on a pretty sickly smile and occasionally agreed with the Grand Protocol Officer, who was an old gent with white whiskers and bad teeth, who talked incessantly and said nothing. The old man spent his life agreeing with the Sultan. There was a tough-looking old bastard who was known as the Grand Vizier, who didn't say a word, and who, I learned later from General Patton, runs the show. Apparently the etiquette prevents the drinking of liquor publicly, so we had nothing alcoholic either before, during or after dinner. I fortified myself an hour earlier, however. Also, no part of a pig could be eaten, and the Sultan didn't smoke. He had a young son there with a red fez on, which he kept on while eating. He was a kid about thirteen and seemed quite bright. At dinner I sat next to General [Auguste] Nogues, the Governor, who is the bird that DeGaulle wants pitched out of here. He has been the Resident Governor here for many years. He obviously likes it, because he lives in a big palace and is the big shot in this part of the world. I wouldn't trust him as far as I could spit. He didn't seem to me to be in a very easy frame of mind, because I imagine that he knows perfectly well that we may throw him out at any minute. Churchill was glum at dinner and seemed to be real bored. A smart British Marine walked in about the middle of dinner with a despatch, but I have a feeling Churchill cooked that up beforehand, because I saw the despatch later and it certainly wasn't one that required the Prime Minister's attention at the dinner. Took some pictures after dinner. The President gave the Sultan his picture in a handsome silver frame, and a good time seemed to be had by all, except the Prime Minister.[7]

The next morning Roosevelt, Churchill, and Hopkins met with Marshall, King, Arnold, Somervell, Pound, Dill, Brooke, Portal, Mountbatten, and Ismay. The military leaders presented an eleven-page position paper outlining plans for 1943. The first point stressed increased efforts to defeat the U-boat in the Battle of the Atlantic and the second "assistance to Russia in relation to other commitments."

The third point set the invasion of Sicily, with the target date a favorable July moon. Eisenhower remained Supreme Commander, with British General Sir Harold Alexander as his deputy, and Admiral Sir Andrew B. Cunningham and Air Marshal Tedder in command of naval and air forces respectively. The buildup of troops in the United Kingdom (Operation Bolero) would continue, but Churchill carefully avoided any commitment to an invasion of France in 1944.

In the Pacific, Churchill and Roosevelt approved plans for further limited advances by Nimitz's and MacArthur's forces and for the recapture of Burma. This in fact really gave the Americans pretty much a free hand in the Pacific so long as they kept within the idea of Germany-first.

The following day the famous "shotgun marriage" between Giraud and De Gaulle took place. Hopkins had a good bit to do with arranging it, so again he might well be called the marriage broker. As Hopkins heard their stories, Giraud was quite willing to cooperate with De Gaulle, who had only to name which subordinate position he wanted. De Gaulle was equally ready to accept Giraud as his subordinate.

Hopkins' notes continue:

> I left them in my room and went to see the President to tell him the news. He was none too happy about it but I urged him not to disavow de Gaulle even tho he was acting badly. Believing as I did and still do that Giraud and de Gaulle want to work together I urged the President to be conciliatory and not beat De Gaulle too hard. If there is any beating to be done let Churchill do it because the whole Free French movement is financed by them. I told the Pres. I thot we could get an agreement on a joint statement issued by De Gaulle and Giraud—and a picture of the two of them.

Hopkins was too optimistic. Each general stubbornly insisted on top position in the French administration. Churchill worked on Giraud and the President on De Gaulle. Finally Churchill walked out on Giraud in disgust. Then Hopkins had an idea.

> Churchill walked in [to Roosevelt's villa] and I went after Giraud believing that if the four of them could get into a room together we could get an agreement. This was nearly twelve o'clock and the press conference

was to be at that hour. The President was surprised at seeing Giraud but took it in his stride. De Gaulle was a little bewildered. Churchill grunted. But the President went to work on them with Churchill backing him up vigorously. De Gaulle finally agreed to a joint statement and before he could catch his breath, the President suggested a photograph. By this time the garden was full of camera men and war correspondents who had been flown down the day before.

I don't know who was the most surprised—the photographers or de Gaulle when the four of them walked out—or rather the three of them because the President was carried to his chair. I confess they were a pretty solemn group—the cameras ground out the pictures. The President suggested de Gaulle and Giraud shake hands. They stood up and obliged—some of the camera men missed it and they did it again. The two Frenchmen and their staffs left and Churchill and the President were left sitting together in the warm African sun—thousands of miles from home to talk to the correspondents of war and the waging of war.

At this news conference Roosevelt made his famous statement that the Allies would demand unconditional surrender from Germany, Italy, and Japan. There are many versions of how this statement originated. Roosevelt always maintained that it just popped into his mind during the news conference. Churchill backed him up but was irritated that he had not been consulted first and that there had been no preliminary discussions on a matter of such importance.

Actually there had been discussions, and everyone agreed it was a good idea to insist on unconditional surrender, but Churchill had no idea FDR would make it public, but he had to go along with it in the cause of Allied unity. Hopkins' notes offer no enlightenment, for they simply record the bald statement that Roosevelt announced the policy.

That same afternoon several of the party, including Hopkins, Robert, Harriman, Churchill, Randolph, and the President, drove to Marrakesh. Along the way they enjoyed a picnic lunch. "As the British fixed up the lunch we had plenty of wine and scotch." They stayed in a very pleasant villa. Hopkins wrote:

> Our host was a young archaeologist named Pendar (Louie rented his flat in Paris)—he was one of our secret agents in N. Africa prior to the Landing. . . .
> Averell, Randolph, Robert and I went to visit a big fair—story tellers—dancers—snake charmers—and 15,000 natives. Very colorful. The great trading market was near—but nothing much to sell—tho thousands were milling thru.
> Dinner was good—army style—the company aglow—much banter—Churchill at his best. The President tired.

The party went on late, marred only by the necessity of drafting a telegram to Stalin on the results of the conference. It broke up about two in the morning, and Hopkins shared a room with his son that night. Robert was leaving to go back to Algiers with Harriman as the President and his party began the journey home.

Hopkins' last notes for the African journey were written in Bathurst, Gambia, on January 25 and 26 and describe the departure from Marrakesh.

> Up early for breakfast—very cold—said good bye—Churchill was up and we talked a bit. Drove to the field with Robert and saw him fly off to the front again. The big ramp was rolled up again and the Pres. pushed up on his wheeled chair. Churchill walked up in his ever flaming bathrobe and the inevitable cigar. Churchill and I took one last walk together—he pleased by the conference—expressed great confidence of victory—but warned of the hard row ahead.
>
> We had an uneventful trip of eight hours to Bathurst—we skirted the Atlas mountains because McIntire did not want the President to fly so high. Incidentally Churchill has his paints and palette with him and promises to paint the mountains from the tower in the villa. He told me he was going to send it to the President as a remembrance of the conference. The President has a bad cough and looked very worn. When we got to the Memphis he had a little fever. Everybody went to bed by nine. I went to sleep reading a history of the Gambia River. The British can have it.
>
> *   *   *
>
> Thursday Jan 26
aboard the Memphis
>
> Slept well and long. The President is still running a little fever—but it seems to be nothing very serious. I think the fishing we had planned is off. Ross says he won't let the President go to Liberia unless the fever clears up but I don't believe anyone can stop the President from going. Loafed all morning—all lunched together. Lord Swinton the Br. High Commissioner is coming aboard at four and doctor or no doctor—the President is going to get on a tug and go up the Gambia.[8]

Hopkins was quite right. Roosevelt did insist on going aboard the British seagoing tug to see the river, and the following day he flew to Liberia for lunch with President Edwin Barclay. Then, at 11:30 the night of January 28, the Presidential party embarked in the PanAm Clipper for the flight across the Atlantic to Brazil. In Natal he met with Brazilian President Getulio Vargas. A week later Brazil entered the war against Germany.

After a stop at Trinidad to pick up Admiral Leahy, the plane continued to Miami. While on the last leg, Roosevelt celebrated his 61st birthday. At a table for four, FDR, dressed in slacks and a pullover sweater, sat next to the window. Across the table was Hopkins. The other companions were Admiral Leahy and Lieutenant Howard M. Cone, USN, in command of the aircraft. The naval station at Trinidad had supplied a large birthday cake and champagne for everyone.

On his return to Washington Hopkins found, as usual, a large accumulation of mail, both official and personal. He was pleased by a letter from Barbara Hopkins' brother, Captain Donald Duncan, in command of the large new aircraft carrier *Essex,* the first of a class of 27,000-ton carriers which would do most of the sea fighting in the Pacific. Duncan wrote:

> I was surprised and delighted yesterday to have David report on board the Essex, baggage and orders in hand. I have not had an opportunity to talk to him yet but I presume he is getting settled aboard ship and I will have a visit with him before long. I am glad to have him and will do my best to keep him from getting his feet wet.[9]

Other letters pleased him less. There seemed no end to the flood of hate resulting from the stories about the "Beaverbrook emeralds" and the Baruch dinner. Roosevelt talked him out of suing the Patterson, McCormick, and Hearst newspapers for repeating and enlarging upon those stories.

The strain of the trip to Africa told on both Roosevelt and Hopkins, and when the President went up to Hyde Park the following weekend, Hopkins was too ill to make the journey.

A nasty problem facing Roosevelt on his return from Casablanca was more squabbling among the businessmen who had come to Washington. Donald Nelson, head of the War Production Board, who was frequently criticized in the press and in Congress as not strong enough, had quarreled with two others high in WPB, Charles E. Wilson and Ferdinand Eberstadt. When Senator Claude Pepper of Florida introduced a bill to replace the strife-torn WPB, Roosevelt knew that he had to make a change. He agreed with James Byrnes' urging that Baruch be appointed to the top production post and directed Byrnes to prepare a letter to Baruch.

Without delay, Byrnes took the letter in person to Roosevelt, "fearing that if the President told Hopkins that night of the proposed change, he might be dissuaded by Hopkins, who Baruch thought was unfriendly to him." [10] FDR signed the letter, and Byrnes delivered it to Baruch, who asked to be allowed to think the matter over for a day. The next day, however, Baruch became sick, and by the time he had recovered and gone to see Roosevelt to accept, the President had changed his mind and never mentioned the letter or the job. To the end of his days, Baruch believed Hopkins had blocked the appointment. There is no evidence in the Hopkins papers, but it seems likely that he persuaded FDR to give Nelson another chance. Eberstadt left, and peace was restored to WPB—for a time, at least.

The development of the atomic bomb occupied a good deal of Hopkins' attention that spring. In the early stages, the British and American scientists had shared their scientific knowledge, but as development moved from the theoretical to the engineering phase, which was concentrated in the United States, the British felt left out. At Casablanca Churchill had asked Hopkins to look into the situation when he got home. On February 24, he cabled Churchill:

> I HAVE BEEN MAKING INQUIRIES AS A RESULT OF YOUR REQUEST TO ME IN REGARD TO TUBE ALLOYS. [The British code expression for the atomic bomb.] IT WOULD BE OF HELP TO ME TO HAVE ANDERSON SEND ME A FULL MEMORANDUM BY POUCH OF WHAT HE CONSIDERS IS THE BASIS OF THE PRESENT MISUNDERSTANDING. SINCE I GATHER THE IMPRESSION THAT OUR PEOPLE HERE FEEL THAT NO AGREEMENT HAS BEEN BREACHED, I SHOULD LIKE PARTICULARLY TO HAVE COPIES OF ANY RECORDED CONVERSATIONS OR REFERENCES OR MEMORANDA WHICH WOULD REVEAL THE NATURE OF THE MISUNDERSTANDING.[11]

Churchill replied with two lengthy cables, but since few British people were working on production, Britain continued to be left out on a "need-to-know" basis.

(In 1949, a preposterous story appeared in gossip columns that Hopkins had given the secret of the atomic bomb to the Russians. If the record of his loyalty is not enough to discredit the story, there is other evidence. As a member of the Munitions Assignment Board, Hopkins took part with the British on political discussions on production allocations. He knew nothing of the theoretical or practical sides of producing operational weapons. The most he could have told the Russians was that the Americans were working on such a bomb, and Stalin undoubtedly knew that just as the Americans and British knew of German experiments on heavy water to produce an atomic bomb.)

In spite of the bright hopes engendered by the Casablanca Conference, things went badly for the Allies that spring of 1943. The only bright spot was the defeat of the German Sixth Army at Stalingrad. March was the worst month of the entire war in the North Atlantic, with 120 ships, a total of nearly 700,000 tons, sunk. Montgomery was stalled near Mareth, and in Tunisia, the Americans received a bad setback at the Faid and Kasserine passes and had to back off from ground they had already taken. The fortunate result of the setback was to bring General George Patton from the sybaritic life he was leading in Morocco to take command of II Corps.

The Russian offensive inspired by the victory at Stalingrad ran down on

February 15, and the Russians braced for the inevitable German counter-offensive later in the spring. They called louder than ever for a second front.

Already strained relations between Russia and the Western Allies were not improved when U.S. Ambassador Standley held a press conference in Moscow on March 8 to charge that the Russian government did not tell its people of the extent and kinds of American and British aid under Lend-Lease. Many people considered his statement a major indiscretion, but Harriman cabled Hopkins from London:

> I FIND MY BRITISH AND AMERICAN FRIENDS, SENIORS AND JUNIORS, SECRETLY PLEASED THAT ADMIRAL STANDLEY SPOKE OUT IN MOSCOW EVEN IF IT WAS INDISCREET.
>
> THERE IS GROWING FEELING HERE THAT WE ARE BUILDING UP TROUBLE FOR THE FUTURE BY ALLOWING THE RUSSIANS TO KICK US AROUND, AS EVIDENCED FOR EXAMPLE BY MAISKY'S SERIES OF PUBLIC SECOND FRONT TALKS AND PRIVATE DISCUSSIONS WITH AMERICAN NEWSPAPERMEN REGARDING INADEQUACY OF AMERICAN MILITARY AND SUPPLY AID.[12]

Demands from Russia were bad enough, but Hopkins also had to help explain to Madame Chiang Kai-shek why China got so little. Recovered from her illness, she visited the White House in February. She urged Hopkins to visit China, evidently feeling that such a trip would be as productive as his trips to Russia.

A month later, Anthony Eden came to the United States. He and Hopkins and Roosevelt had many lengthy talks, particularly emphasizing planning for the postwar world. Hopkins was also in on most of Eden's discussions with other officials on the problems of shipping and armaments. Eden's stay enabled him, Roosevelt, and Hopkins to discuss matters fruitfully without the intervention of the State Department. Of course, Eden also made the proper obligatory calls on Hull.

Sometimes Hopkins' could not achieve his ends. Fiorello LaGuardia from the first had been begging to get into the war in some way. Hopkins conceived the idea that LaGuardia's knowledge of Italian and of municipal government would make him a great help to Eisenhower in the occupation of Sicily. Hopkins proposed that LaGuardia be given a commission and sent to join Eisenhower's staff. Roosevelt seemed to go along with the idea, and after a conference with him, LaGuardia wrote an excited letter to Hopkins on March 17:

> Dear Harry:—I saw the Chief yesterday—and I am so happy that I can be of service to my country—besides cleaning the streets of N.Y.C.—I expect

to get my medical exam—next week—The Chief indicated I could be commissioned right after I finish the Executive Budget in early April.

I am to be assigned to Genl Eisenhower's staff & am confident that I will be able to do a good job & be really useful.

After I am finished with the medicos—I will want to have a talk with you—to bring me up to date in certain matters with which you are familiar.

Will be seeing you soon.

Sincerely
Fiorello

Mch 17/43

Writing this by hand as I do not want office to know until last minute.[13]

But LaGuardia never got the job. Stimson firmly opposed his appointment, and unless FDR had wished to force a showdown which might have resulted in Stimson's resignation, there was nothing to be done. The Little Flower remained a civilian throughout the war and the appointment went to former Lieutenant Governor Charles Poletti of New York. He proved to be an excellent choice, but Hopkins always felt LaGuardia had been the victim of prejudice on the part of people who should have known better.

Harriman kept Hopkins particularly well informed of the situation in Britain and of the Prime Minister's moods and state of health. After returning from Casablanca, Churchill had been seriously ill with pneumonia. He was a difficult patient, especially as he took a more serious view of his sickness than his doctors did. He was alternately demanding his forbidden cigars and worrying about the implications of his fever. To Hopkins he wrote that he "had had a bad time and might easily have been worse." [14] But a month later, Harriman was able to write, "Last night Prime Minister was in better form and spirits than I have seen him in months." [15]

In March Churchill cabled Hopkins that Prime Minister John Curtin of Australia wished to have the Order of Knight Grand Cross of the Bath conferred on MacArthur. Churchill did not think that Marshall or King would object, but he feared that Admiral Nimitz, whose command in the Pacific was on the same level as MacArthur's, would be offended. Churchill did not know Nimitz, or he would not have worried, for decorations and honors meant as little to the admiral from Texas as they meant much to MacArthur. Hopkins replied:

> THERE IS A FEELING HERE THAT HONORS SHOULD NOT BE GIVEN TO HIGH RANKING OFFICERS AT THIS TIME. MOST PEOPLE BELIEVE THAT DECORATIONS FOR VALOR IN THE FIELD OF ACTION ARE ALL RIGHT BUT THAT IT SHOULD STOP THERE. HOWEVER IF YOUR LOUD SPEAKING FRIEND IN THE SOUTHWEST [Curtin] CAN BE MUZZLED FOR A WHILE BY GIVING MACARTHUR A DECORATION NEITHER THE WORLD NOR THE WAR WILL COME TO AN END

ANY SOONER AND I DON'T THINK THAT NIMITZ, MARSHALL OR KING WILL LOSE ANY SLEEP.[16]

After Eden had left Washington, Churchill cabled that he was delighted to learn that Roosevelt had agreed for Hopkins and Marshall to meet with him, Ike, and Brooke in "Torch Land." They would decide where they would go after Sicily. Hopkins replied that Eden must have misunderstood and that he saw no reason for a meeting until the situation in Tunisia was cleaned up. Roosevelt amplified this in a cable to Churchill on April 11:

OUR STAFFS NOW URGENTLY AT WORK ON WHAT TO DO AFTER HUSKY. I THINK THERE ARE TWO OR THREE GOOD ALTERNATIVES BUT UNTIL OUR RESPECTIVE STAFFS GIVE US THEIR VIEWS I SEE NO ADVANTAGE OF IMMEDIATE CONFERENCES WITH MARSHALL AND HARRY. IT IS QUITE POSSIBLE AND, I HOPE PROBABLE, THAT WE CAN REACH AGREEMENT QUICKLY ABOUT OUR POST-HUSKY OPERATIONS. AT THE MOMENT WE HAVE THE TUNISIAN BUSINESS TO CLEAN UP AND THAT MAY TAKE LONGER THAN WE THINK. SHOULD THAT BE UNDULY DELAYED THAT, IN ITSELF, MIGHT WELL UNFAVORABLY AFFECT HUSKY AND IF ROMMEL'S ARMY SHOULD ESCAPE IN ANY SUBSTANTIAL FORCE TO HUSKY LAND THAT WOULD MAKE IT DOUBLY DIFFICULT. . . .

I AM PLANNING TO LEAVE EARLY IN THE WEEK FOR A TWO WEEKS TRIP OF ARMY AND NAVAL BASES. THIS TRIP WILL BE OFF THE RECORD. HENCE I DO NOT WISH IT KNOWN IN ENGLAND. I HAVE GOOD COMMUNICATIONS, HOWEVER, AND YOU CAN GET IN TOUCH WITH ME QUICKLY. HARRY WILL REMAIN HERE.[17]

So once more Harry Hopkins stayed behind to mind the store. It would be futile to try to cover all the topics he had to deal with, for cables came in daily from Chungking, Moscow, London, and North Africa. Hopkins had to decide which should be sent on to Roosevelt and which he could handle himself. He had little time for relaxation. It was pleasant in the midst of the brickbats to read, in the *Atlantic Monthly,* a compliment for a change in the impressions of J. S. Knowlson, a former dollar-a-year man with the WPB:

I lost ten pounds and a lot of personal prejudices. I find to my rather shocked surprise that I once made a memorandum like this: "I have been talking with Hopkins and I can't escape the conviction that he has the clearest, coolest mind of anyone I have ever seen here. He factors complicated problems into simple terms, and he has given direction to my thought." I don't know anything about Mr. Hopkins's social planning or his other ideas, but my one regret is that I did not see more of him in Washington.[18]

The more Churchill thought over Roosevelt's cable of April 11, the more he worried that there would be no plan for anything after Tunisia and Sicily. On April 29 he cabled to suggest a meeting to thrash out these and other problems, saying that he could be in Washington by May 11. The President agreed to the meeting by return cable.

Then on May 2, Churchill cabled again stating that he was fully aware of the problem of the coal crisis in the United States and suggested that it might be well, under the circumstances, for him to stay at the British embassy rather than at the White House.

Roosevelt replied:

> I AM REALLY DELIGHTED YOU ARE COMING. I AGREE MOST HEARTILY THAT
> WE HAVE SOME IMPORTANT BUSINESS TO SETTLE AT ONCE; THE SOONER THE
> BETTER. MARSHALL AND KING HAVE POSTPONED THEIR PACIFIC TRIP. I WANT
> YOU OF COURSE TO STAY HERE WITH ME.[19]

The coal crisis was the result of one of John L. Lewis' periodic interruptions of production which infuriated the public and the fighting man overseas alike. It did not bother the bushy-browed Lewis, who viewed the matter as a personal struggle between himself and the President. When Lewis would not yield, the President ordered the mines seized by the government. Hopkins' old rival, Harold Ickes, as Solid Fuels Administrator for War, was to run them under protection of the Army. Still the United Mine Workers chieftain was adamant and Roosevelt had a broadcast prepared urging the miners over the head of their leader to go back to work as a patriotic duty.

Just as Roosevelt was about to speak to the nation, word came that Lewis had reached an agreement with Ickes for the men to go back to work in two days. Furious at this attempt to steal the limelight from him, Roosevelt gave the speech anyway.

While Churchill was on the high seas, on May 7, U.S. troops under Patton captured Bizerte in Tunisia, and a few minutes later the British Eighth Army under Montgomery entered the capital city of Tunis. To all intents and purposes the African campaign was over.

On May 11, Hopkins went up to Staten Island in New York harbor to meet Churchill and his party of nearly a hundred who had crossed the Atlantic on the huge liner *Queen Mary,* which was serving as a troop transport. In peacetime she carried about 3,500 passengers in luxury. Now she transported some 15,000 troops to England in anything but luxury. For the Prime Minister, a whole deck had been set aside and securely shut off from the part of the ship where German and Italian prisoners of war were being taken to Canada.

The Prime Minister's party departed at once by special train for Washington, and that afternoon Churchill was back in his old familiar rooms in the White House. Hopkins was once again free to stroll across the hall to talk with him, but Churchill had to be more careful. It would hardly do for him to break in on Louise Hopkins in the deshabille he affected on the second floor of the White House.

Accompanying Churchill was Max Beaverbrook, still out of the government, but frequently consulted by Churchill. Although the two were friends, they clashed on almost every imaginable occasion. So, when Roosevelt invited Beaverbrook to spend the weekend of May 15 with Churchill and others at Shangri-La, the "Beaver" regretfully declined because of possible criticism in the British press.

Hopkins telephoned Beaverbrook in some indignation. "The President of the United States is not in the habit of selecting his guests in deference to the sentiment of the British press or any other press." [20] Max Beaverbrook went.

The journey to Shangri-La gave rise to another famous Churchill legend. As he, Roosevelt, and Hopkins were riding up together in a White House limousine through Frederick, Maryland, Churchill noticed signs advertising Barbara Fritchie candy. He asked who the lady might be, and Roosevelt replied that she was a semi-fictional character of the Civil War. John Greenleaf Whittier had written a poem about her. The President tried to quote the poem, but all he could remember was:

> "Shoot if you must, this old gray head,
> But spare your country's flag," she said.

Thereupon, Churchill proceeded to quote the whole poem, adding that he had not thought of it in thirty years. He then inquired if Gettysburg was nearby, and told that it was about forty miles away, he remarked that a road they had just crossed might be the very one by which Longstreet moved up. He went on to give a detailed summary of the battle.

After a rainy weekend at Shangri-La, Hopkins wrote Pamela Churchill, Randolph's wife:

Dear Pam:

Averell brought me your nice note from London.

You know you need not have told me what a terrible correspondent I am. I never write letters.

Winston is having the time of his life here and we just returned from the country. Max was along with us and we all had a grand time although the weather was terrible.

I never need an excuse to go to England. I just haven't had any business there, although I presume going to see you would be business enough. . . .[21]

Hopkins returned to Washington in a sardonic mood. All through the weekend, he had spent hours listening to Churchill use all his oratorical powers in favor of more operations in the Mediterranean. In the view of the Americans, the British wanted to squander in the Mediterranean material and men badly needed for the invasion of northern France.

Sir Charles Wilson, Churchill's personal physician, described how Hopkins mimicked Churchill:

> "The great prize when Sicily falls is to get Italy out of the war. Bulgaria's defeatism in 1918 brought about the collapse of Germany; might not Italy's surrender now have similar consequences? It will surely cause a chill of loneliness to settle on the German people and might very well be the beginning of the end." The words were the P.M.'s, but somehow they sounded less convincing when put by Harry like this.[22]

The strategic discussions at the Trident Conference, as the meeting was known, were long and sometimes acrimonious. The American Joint Chiefs firmly opposed anything which might delay the buildup in Britain for Roundup, although they conceded that limited moves to drive Italy from the war were worthwhile. Thus in the end, they accepted a campaign in Italy limited to the troops already in the theater, so long as those moves did not interfere with Bolero and Roundup for 1944.

The British refused to accept Roundup in 1944 definitively, but they agreed with it "in principle." Brooke argued that it could not be undertaken unless the Allies made a major commitment in Italy to pull German defenders away from France. In the end the Combined Chiefs agreed that British and American forces would invade the Italian mainland after the end of the Sicilian campaign and that Roundup would definitely be scheduled for the spring of 1944, with a target date of May 1. Germany would be softened up by intensive bombing by both the RAF and American Eighth Air Force.

The President and the Prime Minister accepted this compromise, but at the last minute, Churchill had second thoughts and tried to add a paragraph leaving open the question of further diversionary operations in the eastern Mediterranean at the expense of Bolero and Roundup. Brooke was furious and credits Hopkins with being able to talk Churchill out of his idea.

But Churchill did not give up entirely. When the conference was over, he asked Marshall to fly with him to North Africa to talk with Eisenhower. He believed that he could convince the two American generals of the soundness of his diversionary plans. As it turned out, he could not.

Other decisions taken at Trident involved the squabble between General Joseph Stilwell and General Claire Chennault in China. Both men attended the meetings, each trying to win control of the supplies coming to the theater. The matter of the invasion of Burma (Operation Anakim) was reconsidered and revised. The end was a compromise, with Stilwell and Chennault each given a portion of the meager supplies available.

Also approved were King's plans for a Central Pacific offensive to supplement those in the South Pacific under Admiral William F. Halsey, Jr., and in the Southwest Pacific under MacArthur. In winning this one, it was a case, as King put it, of King *contra mundum,* for both the British and the American Army and Air Force feared that such commitments would weaken the principle of Germany first. Everyone, however, realized that the American Navy, which was now building up to overwhelming strength in the Pacific, could not remain idle until Germany was defeated.

They also considered a plan to seize control of the Azores for use as bases in the war against the U-boats. Fortunately, however, this proved unnecessary, for the State Department persuaded the Portuguese to permit the Americans to establish bases there.

Churchill and Marshall with others left May 26 by plane for Algiers, and the following day Hopkins accompanied Roosevelt to Hyde Park. A guest for the occasion was Princess Martha of Norway. It was a good period of rest for Hopkins, especially as Louise and Diana were able to join him for the weekend.

In five months, Hopkins had participated in two major conferences with Churchill and Roosevelt, and in two minor ones, with Eden and with Madame Chiang Kai-shek. There were the never-ending pressures of the day-to-day routine, with the Munitions Assignment Board and with practically everyone else in Washington. He was tired, but there would be no letup. There were more decisions to be made and more conferences to come before the year ended.

CHAPTER SEVENTEEN

Where Mr. Roosevelt Leaves Off

In 1943 Harry Hopkins' power in Washington reached its peak. That June *The United States News* ran an article which stated that President Roosevelt was giving more time and thought toward grand strategy and problems of the postwar world than anything else. "Hopkins is taking over more and more where Mr. Roosevelt leaves off; is taking a more and more prominent part in shaping domestic policies, in making decisions on price, subsidy, roll-back, tax policy, in political maneuvering." [1]

The article went on to say that the new "inner cabinet" consisted of Hopkins at the head, Ben Cohen, Sam Rosenman, and Associate Supreme Court Justice Felix Frankfurter. Each of the "czars" in rubber, food, rationing, price control, found himself taking orders from this inner cabinet. Even James Byrnes did not always know what orders his office was issuing. Hopkins was the executive who carried out the policies determined by the inner cabinet. Hopkins was also credited with being the moving spirit behind electing Roosevelt for a fourth term and dumping Wallace as Vice-President.

This view of Hopkins is clearly overstated. He did have enormous power, but Roosevelt never gave unchecked authority to anyone. He, and he alone, was President of the United States, and Hopkins knew it. The secret of his survival with Roosevelt lay in his uncanny ability to know what the President wanted, and if he didn't know, find out. His frequent contacts with FDR ensured that when he acted it was in accordance with the Boss's wishes. Even at this time, he did not originate policy and try to justify his actions on that supposed policy to the President. He settled policy with him, reduced it to its essential terms, and then took action.

Many held the curious view that Roosevelt was a weak, malleable person, who could be sold on a policy by anyone who talked to him. Despite the fact that the political graveyards were littered with the careers of those who crossed FDR or tried to force him to accept one policy or another, the legend persisted. Attempts were made to convince him that the way to win the war was to attack Germany across the North Pole or to make rubber out of turnips. When the ideas got nowhere, their proponents blamed Hopkins, calling him a Svengali whose sinister influence misled Roosevelt.

But FDR was no Trilby, as those knew who had seen him "get his Dutch up." Hopkins knew it better than anyone. Though his enemies would not believe it, he had given up all personal ambition by this time. He only wanted to do the job he uniquely could to serve the President and win the war.

His enemies could not know how highly such men as Churchill, Beaverbrook, Eden, Stalin, Marshall, King, and many others esteemed Hopkins, and they wouldn't have believed it if they had known. To them Hopkins was someone to be destroyed, and they never stopped trying. They could not know that only he had that capacity, by abusing the President's trust or by driving his frail body beyond its limits. It was the latter that happened.

An example of the petty attacks made on him was a story in the *Chicago Daily Tribune* to the effect that the White House staff, particularly those in higher positions, lagged in the purchase of war savings bonds. Turning to Hopkins, the story alleged: "Government employees seeking to get him to contribute part of his substantial salary each month toward war bond purchases are put off, they said, with a tale about his wife buying them for him." The story also dragged up the Baruch dinner, but this time Hopkins appeared as the wasteful host.[2]

Harry Hopkins usually did not let unfriendly stories bother him, but this one seems to have got under his skin. His secretary worked out figures showing that in bond purchases for himself and for Diana, he was well over fifteen percent of his salary, half again as much as the norm of ten percent set by the paper.

Hopkins wrote a letter to the editor which was never published. It concluded:

> I realize that anyone in public life is subject to political attack by
> newspapers which are unfriendly to this administration. I do not object to
> that but I do object to your lying about me. I do not say that you do this

deliberately, but I do believe that the person who wrote the article, whom
you quote, and the paper which originally published the article did do it
deliberately.[3]

With such a background of unfriendly stories, it was a pleasure and a
surprise for Hopkins to read a friendly "Profile" in *The New Yorker* [4] which
went back to his Grinnell and New Deal days as well as giving recognition
to the job he was performing during the war. He remarked about the
article, "I seem to turn out a mixture of a Baptist preacher and a race track
tout." He went on to send a note of appreciation to the magazine, even
though it had described him as resembling "an animated piece of shredded
wheat."

There was little time for notes to editors, either of praise or blame, for too
many things had to be done. Just as the Trident Conference was ending,
Roosevelt announced a reorganization of the home front machinery, with
an Office of War Mobilization under James F. Byrnes. The new organization included Stimson, Knox, Hopkins, Fred M. Vinson, and Nelson as
heads of their various departments and boards. This technically made them
subordinate to Byrnes, but in practice Hopkins, Stimson, and Knox
continued to go their ways as before. They were members of OWM only
insofar as the War Department, the Navy Department, and the Munitions
Assignment Board affected the civilian economy. So far as Hopkins was
concerned, OWM represented just another meeting to go to periodically.

Harriman remained in Washington for a month after Churchill had left
and during that time held discussions with Roosevelt and Hopkins on the
need for replacing Ambassador Standley in Moscow. The admiral's
outburst in the spring, while truthful, had ruined his effectiveness in
Moscow. Roosevelt had a difficult time coming up with a replacement. He
tried to persuade former Ambassador Joseph E. Davies to go back, but
Davies' health would not permit it. Davies urged Roosevelt to name
Hopkins to the post, but Roosevelt turned that idea down flatly. Hopkins'
health would not permit it either, and FDR had no intention of losing his
services in Washington.

Averell Harriman was admirably suited for the job but could be ill-
spared from the Lend-Lease post in London. Besides, despite Roosevelt's
and Hopkins' urging, Harriman did not want to go:

> I had just seen what a hopelessly restricted life the foreign diplomats led
> in Moscow, the way they were fenced in. I was also thoroughly enjoying
> my relationships with Churchill and the British. I felt I was accomplishing
> a great deal there in connection with the war and I recognized that in
> Moscow I would be at the end of the line, probably losing such value as I
> had in London.[5]

Harriman returned to London without committing himself, but promised to think it over and send back word when he had made up his mind.

Roosevelt perforce turned much of his attention to domestic matters that summer, for the truce between Ickes and John L. Lewis broke down, and the miners walked out again. Congress passed the Smith-Connally anti-strike act, which Roosevelt vetoed, only to have it passed over his veto. Many Democrats joined the Republicans in the vote, inflicting on Roosevelt the worst defeat he had ever taken from Congress. Even in wartime members of his own party refused to follow his leadership on domestic matters.

Then broke out an unseemly public quarrel between Vice-President Henry Wallace and Secretary of Commerce Jesse Jones, which infuriated Roosevelt against both of them. He abolished Wallace's Bureau of Economic Warfare and transferred its functions and some of those of Jones's department to the OWM. All in all, it was a turbulent period which caused anxiety in Britain that the American leadership did not know where it was going.

Roosevelt was also anxious to meet privately both with Stalin and with Chiang Kai-shek. Privately meant without Churchill, but the Prime Minister took a strong objection to that idea, and nothing ever came of it.

Operation Husky, the invasion of Sicily, took place on July 10, and succeeded from the first, although the fighting soon led to an undignified rivalry between Montgomery and Patton and hence exacerbated Anglo-American rivalries and suspicions on all levels.

A few personal glimpses come through in Hopkins' correspondence that summer. To Missy LeHand, still trying to recuperate from her stroke, he wrote:

> Mme. Chiang has finally decided not to visit us any more and has returned home. She was a very beautiful gal and had I not been married and about 20 years younger, I would have surely taken a more personal interest in her. She had a couple of queer people with her whose sex I have not yet determined. . . .
>
> Diana, who outgrows her clothes every two months, has gone off to camp. I, never having been a very good parent, confess that I am not unhappy to have her in the mountains this summer. She has been extremely well, her work in school is very good, and she often asks about you.
>
> Robert is in Africa. David is on an aircraft carrier and Stephen is going into the Marines in the morning, so everybody is in the war but me. . . .
>
> Steve is more crabbed than ever. Mac is thinner and Pa is fatter. Grace plays Gin Rummy so badly that she has been pretty much keeping me in spending money for the past year.

> The President is in good health and spirits in spite of trouble on all
> sides.[6]

He also wrote Diana at camp, apologizing for not answering two or three
of her letters. He sent the addresses of her half brothers so she could write
to them. But, while the letter to Missy LeHand was easy and relaxed, that to
Diana is stiff. It was not lack of affection; it was just that generally he didn't
know how to write to children.

While the Sicilian campaign was going on, King Victor Emmanuel
ousted Mussolini and complicated, almost comic-opera negotiations began
for the surrender of Italy to the Allies. The Italian government under
Marshal Pietro Badoglio sent emissaries scurrying to all points of the
compass trying to arrange for Italian capitulation and Allied occupation
before the Germans could take over.

Hopkins had nothing to do with these negotiations. In fact, while they
were going on, he accompanied General "Hap" Arnold to Restigouche,
Canada, for some salmon fishing.

Almost as soon as the Trident Conference ended, its strategic agreements
began to come unstuck. In dispatch after dispatch, the British counseled
delay in mounting Roundup, now renamed Overlord. Although the British
planners working under the direction of General Sir Frederick Morgan
were strongly in favor of Overlord, the indefatigable Prime Minister
persisted in resurrecting plans for the eastern Mediterranean. On the way to
the new conference, he even dug up the long buried Operation Jupiter, for
the liberation of Norway.

Marshall appreciated the dread Churchill had for massive rivers of blood
(Churchill's term) that might follow an invasion of France, but he did not
believe the casualties would be anywhere nearly as serious as the Prime
Minister feared. What worried him more was that Churchill's strategy of
peripheral operations and blockade would lead to a drawn-out war which
the American people would not support. He earnestly warned the President
of his fears, and educated him as well as he could to be on his guard against
Churchill's wiles and skill in argument. Hopkins joined Marshall both in
the strategic view of the importance of sticking to the agreed plan for
Overlord and in warning against Churchill's seductive fluency.

Churchill once more crossed the Atlantic in the *Queen Mary,* bringing
with him this time his wife and his daughter, Mary, who was a lieutenant in
the army but serving as her father's aide-de-camp. From Halifax, Nova
Scotia, Churchill and his daughter made a lengthy detour to Niagara Falls
on the way to Hyde Park, where they arrived on the afternoon of
August 12.[7]

Hopkins and Roosevelt came to Hyde Park in even more leisurely fashion. Stealing time from work, they went fishing in the Lake Huron area, loafing as though they had no cares in the world. During the trip Hopkins certainly told Roosevelt that he planned to move out of the White House soon to try to establish a more normal home life. On July 19 he had signed a lease on a house at 3340 N Street in Georgetown. Roosevelt accepted the fact that his friend would leave the White House, but he couldn't understand why.

After the Hyde Park session, on August 14 Churchill went on to Quebec to get ready for the conference to be held in the Hotel Château Frontenac. Roosevelt and Hopkins returned to Washington to tidy up a few affairs before boarding the train for Quebec on the evening of August 16. The Joint Chiefs had gone ahead to talk with their British opposites. Churchill buttonholed Marshall to sell him on the joys of peripheral strategy. At Hyde Park he had failed to woo Roosevelt away from Overlord. He hoped for better success with Marshall.

Before Roosevelt and Churchill could really settle down to the business of the conference, they had to deal with the Italian situation and especially report to the suspicious Stalin. Hopkins probably drafted the cable which was sent to Moscow on August 19:

> ON AUGUST 15TH THE BRITISH AMBASSADOR AT MADRID REPORTED THAT GENERAL CASTELLANO HAD ARRIVED FROM BADOGLIO WITH A LETTER OF INTRODUCTION FROM THE BRITISH MINISTER TO THE VATICAN. THE GENERAL DECLARED THAT HE WAS AUTHORIZED BY BADOGLIO TO SAY THAT ITALY WAS WILLING TO SURRENDER UNCONDITIONALLY PROVIDED THAT SHE COULD JOIN THE ALLIES. . . .
>
> WE ARE NOT PREPARED TO ENTER INTO ANY BARGAIN WITH BADOGLIO'S GOVERNMENT TO INDUCE ITALY TO CHANGE SIDES; ON THE OTHER HAND THERE ARE MANY ADVANTAGES AND A GREAT SPEEDING UP OF THE CAMPAIGN WHICH MIGHT FOLLOW THEREFROM.[8]

The message goes on with further arguments for accepting the Italian surrender and a copy of the instructions sent to Eisenhower.

Stalin replied coldly three days later:

> I have received your message on the negotiations with the Italians and on the new armistice terms for Italy. Thank you for the information.
>
> Mr Eden informed Sobolev that Moscow had been kept fully informed of the negotiations with Italy. I must say, however, that Mr Eden's statement is at variance with the facts, for I received your message with large omissions and without the closing paragraphs. It should be said, therefore, that the Soviet Government has not been kept informed of the Anglo-American negotiations with the Italians.[9]

This was one of Stalin's milder messages of criticism. As Soviet fortunes improved, he was no longer the suppliant, and his demands and his accusations of Western bad faith grew blunter. Churchill and Roosevelt realized that unless the three of them got together in person to thrash things out, the alliance might collapse. Stalin agreed but it took until November to bring them face to face at Teheran.

The chief business of the Quadrant Conference at Quebec was to nail down a decision on Operation Overlord, for the British had not yet made a firm commitment. Despite surface differences, the British and American planners were closer together than they seemed.

They finally hammered out an agreement setting Overlord for May 1, 1944, unless the strategic situation later required a review of that decision. Churchill kept the pot boiling by trying to define terms under which the cross-Channel operation might be undertaken. First Germany had to be substantially weakened by air and by diversionary operations. In fact, Churchill's attitude could be summed up by saying that he always supported Overlord but he always objected to carrying it out. This attitude is illustrated by an entry in the diary of Churchill's physician, Sir Charles Wilson, later Lord Moran:

> Harry Hopkins was in a curious mood this morning. He told me that at yesterday's session Winston "came clean" about a Second Front, that he "threw in his hand." Hopkins said this in rather an aggressive way, as if I were in the P.M.'s camp.
>
> "Winston is no longer against Marshall's plan for landing on the coast of France. At least, so he says."
>
> Harry grinned.
>
> "But he might change his mind again, as he did last year. I don't believe he is really converted.
>
> "Why," Hopkins went on, "before he said he agreed we had the most solemn warning of what might happen. The old, old story of enormous casualties, and the terrific strength of the German fortifications."
>
> Why is this man so bitter? Harry is sure that Winston's obstinacy, his drawn-out struggle to postpone a second front in France, has, in fact, prolonged the war; that if he had been reasonable earlier we might now be in sight of peace. Is Hopkins right? That must remain the riddle of the war. . . .
>
> When Hopkins questioned whether the P.M. meant what he said, I wonder if he is speaking for anybody but himself. I must not, of course, make the mistake of taking him for a typical American, any more than I would argue that Max Beaverbrook is a fair sample of our countrymen. . . .
>
> It appears that the President and Hopkins are no longer prepared to acknowledge Winston as an infallible guide in military matters.[10]

The Quebec Conference ended with a victory for Marshall's strategy, which Hopkins supported all down the line. If it was a defeat for Brooke, it cost him in another way. Originally when Roundup had been planned, British and American forces were to have been about equal, and the Americans had agreed that it would be under British command to balance Eisenhower's command in North Africa. Churchill had promised the job to Brooke. But, at Quebec, Churchill realized that the command would have to go to an American since soon after the landings, American forces would far outnumber the British. Brooke bore the disappointment like a soldier, but it left him embittered, and he never missed an opportunity to criticize Eisenhower's generalship on the continent of Europe.

It became clear at Quebec that Americans would more and more call the tune in strategy, although Churchill would keep on fighting for British domination. Britain was becoming the junior partner as American production and armed forces grew in strength. For example, one of the decisions reached at Quebec, and which Churchill would oppose to the last, was for an invasion of the south of France to coincide with the Overlord landings. Under Operation Anvil, troops would land in the Toulon area and push up the Rhone River valley to join with those coming across from Normandy.

On August 25, Roosevelt and Hopkins returned to Washington after an overnight train ride from Quebec. Hopkins, utterly exhausted, had to go to the hospital for a complete rest. He was in bed when the Italian mainland campaign began with British landings in the Reggio di Calabria area in the toe of Italy on September 3 and when the Americans and British landed at Salerno on September 9. The Italian government surrendered a few hours before the Salerno landing. But the Germans quickly and brutally occupied Italy, and the fighting continued.

Churchill, after spending a week in Canada, arrived at the White House on September 1 for discussions with Roosevelt. On the tenth, the President went up to Hyde Park, leaving the Prime Minister "to use the White House not only as a residence but for any conference I might wish to hold." [11]

Availing himself of this permission, Churchill called a conference of British and American leaders to discuss the progress of the fighting in Italy. In Roosevelt's absence, Hopkins dragged himself out of bed to represent the President. The meeting reached no significant conclusions, but it certainly was a historic event to have the British Prime Minister treating the White House as an extension of Ten Downing Street.

In the hospital, Hopkins had time to take stock of himself and consider the future. During the Quebec meeting, he had taken a few hours to go fishing on Grand Lac de l'Epaule with Winston and Clementine Churchill and Averell Harriman. His conversation with Harriman gives some inkling of how his thoughts were running.

In the afternoon, while fishing on the lake, Harriman talked alone with Hopkins about their respective personal plans. Hopkins, who had considered running for the Senate from Iowa and had even thought about the presidency, told Harriman that he no longer had any political ambitions. He looked forward to a quiet life after the war with freedom to write. This would mean getting a job that offered him a reasonable income and the time he needed for his writing. They also talked about relations with Russia, weighing the pros and cons of Harriman's going to Moscow as ambassador. Hopkins had been impressed by the argument of the Joint Chiefs of Staff that Russia was bound to be the dominant power in Europe after the war. He believed that winning her friendship was vitally important for the United States, not only for its effect in Europe but even more urgently as a means of hastening the defeat of Japan by bringing the Soviet Union into the Pacific war as a fighting ally.[12]

Hopkins also had time to ponder responses to his attackers. Their number was increased by two previously friendly newsmen, Drew Pearson and Walter Trohan. Pearson's attack was rather trivial, that Hopkins had changed the place cards at a White House dinner, infuriating Eleanor Roosevelt, who insisted that the Hopkinses move out. Eleanor Roosevelt denied that there was a word of truth in the entire story. Hopkins was more mild:

> While you have said a good many things about me in the last six months that were inaccurate, I have never before thought they were malicious. Because our personal relationship over many years has been on a perfectly friendly basis, this sudden determination to attack me, personally, on grounds which are totally untrue, is quite incomprehensible to me.[13]

The attack by Trohan was more serious. It appeared in the *Chicago Sunday Tribune* of August 29, 1943, with a huge cartoon of a leering Hopkins and a leering Rasputin. Portions of the text went:

> One evening in 1907, a tall, broad-shouldered peasant strode across the highly polished floor of the salon of Count Alexander Pavlovich Ignatiev. . . . He bowed clumsily to an ill assorted circle of nobles, politicians, schemers, charlatans, adventurers, clergy, and dignitaries. . . . Rasputin went on to sway Russia by the power of his eye. Nicholas, the czar of all the Russias, fell on his knees before this curious mixture of penitent and debauchee and called him a "Christ." The czarina believed in him implicitly. For almost nine years this preacher of redemption thru sin virtually ruled Russia. . . .
> On a May day in 1933 a lean, gangly figure with thinning brown hair and dandruff made his way with his face twisted by a sardonic grin thru an

ill assorted group of representatives, crackpots, senators, bums, governors, job seekers, political leaders, and toadies . . . in the person of Harry Lloyd Hopkins, son of an Iowa harness maker, Santa Claus had come to town. He emptied his hands of other people's money. This strange and contradictory figure spent on and on to sway a nation and then the world. The President of the United States brought him into his official family and then into his private family and poured his innermost thoughts into the spender's prominent ears. The wife of the President adopted his small child in all but name.

[Trohan went on to quote approvingly the remarks of Representative Dewey Short of Missouri:] Would the followers of the Rasputin of the White House . . . and there are many in high and important places in our government today . . . use this war as a smoke screen to saddle upon America a type of government and a kind of economy entirely foreign and contrary to those we have ever known? [14]

When he left the hospital, Hopkins wrote Joe Davies, "Is this libelous? I never knew a lawyer in my life who said anything was libelous. Can't you dig up some bright young men in your office who will tell me that these bastards can be sued for libel?" [15]

Davies investigated and answered that still nothing was libelous—at least, the Trohan article was not, because Hopkins was a public figure and therefore subject to criticism. The opinion quoted the famous jurist Cockburn, "Those who fill a public position must not be too thin-skinned in reference to comments made upon them."

With that, Hopkins had to be content. Reflection must have told him that the esteem of Roosevelt, Churchill, Marshall, Harriman, and others was far more important than the malice of Drew Pearson, Walter Trohan, and the *Chicago Tribune.*

An unpleasantness which came up that fall concerned General Marshall. After the decision at Quebec that the commander of Overlord would be an American, everyone assumed that Marshall would get the job. In fact, Churchill suggested it to Roosevelt, and Roosevelt had discussed the possibility with Marshall. Soon after the conference, a furor broke loose with charges being hurled that Roosevelt was planning to kick Marshall out of his job as Chief of Staff and replace him with General Brehon Somervell.

That spring and summer, Somervell, who was Chief of the Army Services of Supply, had worked on a plan to reorganize the supply and administrative services as Marshall in 1942 had reorganized the ground services. Parts of the plan leaked to the press, and reorganization became confused with Roosevelt's plan to appoint Marshall to command of Overlord. Many called Somervell a power-mad opportunist, who sought to undermine his own chief. Worse, he became identified as a Hopkins man when someone dredged up the fact that he had been head of the New York City WPA. Soon the story went around that a sinister group in the White House, led by Rasputin Hopkins and including Justice Frankfurter, Sam Rosenman, David K. Niles, and others, was using its influence to replace Marshall with Somervell and send the former to Europe where he could no longer work his wiles on the President. Then the story went to wilder extremes, that the same group, all Jewish but Hopkins, was working to remove not only Marshall but other important Army officers and replace them with political appointees.

The raising of the Jewish issue was irrelevant except that it showed the anti-Semitic bias of the accusers, but the rest of the charges caused headlines: "Global WPA Seen Aim in Marshall Plot," "Hopkins' Slimy Hand."

Throughout the hullabaloo, Marshall said no word in public or in private, except possibly to his wife. Like Brooke, Marshall desperately wanted command of Overlord, but he refused to lift a finger to get it. His stern rectitude demanded that he serve where ordered. He would join no political games played by the politicians and by ambitious officers in the Pentagon. He also knew that the President, Stimson, and Hopkins all wanted to give him the command he longed for, and that he would get it unless Roosevelt decided otherwise. The only danger to his hopes lay in the fact that he was too good in his present job as Chief of Staff.

A light moment in the squabble came when a Nazi propaganda broadcast from Paris on October 5 announced, "General George C. Marshall, the U.S. Chief of Staff, has been dismissed. President Roosevelt has taken over his command. This occurred two days ago, but has not yet been commented upon in Washington."

Marshall sent Hopkins a note: "Dear Harry: Are you responsible for pulling this fast one on me? G.C.M." Hopkins turned the note over to Roosevelt, who scribbled at the bottom of the page, "Dear George:—Only true in part—I am now Chief of Staff *but* you are President. FDR." [16]

In view of all the uproar, Roosevelt tried to devise some plan which would permit Marshall to command Overlord but would not seem a demotion. Hopkins had an idea, which Roosevelt liked enough to put up to Churchill, to give Marshall command not only of the cross-Channel operation but of all Allied forces, other than Russian, fighting in Europe. The text of Hopkins' typewritten memorandum—which was "secret" until its declassification on February 1, 1973, by the Deputy Archivist of the U.S.—reads:

THE WHITE HOUSE
WASHINGTON

October 4, 1943

MEMORANDUM FOR

THE PRESIDENT

My dear Mr. President:

I feel very strongly that, from the point of view of organization, Marshall should have command of all the Allied forces, other than the Russian, attacking the Fortress of Germany.

It is essential that there be one strategic air force and that our bombers not be frozen either in England, Italy or Africa. It is only human nature for a theatre commander to want to hang on to his airplanes. By the same token, the disposition of the ground forces, the use of ships and landing craft should be under a single commander.

I have talked to General Wedemeyer about this—who had previously been consulted by General Marshall. Wedemeyer feels that, from a military point of view, it is sound organization.

While we might have to give someone like Montgomery command of Overlord in order to satisfy the British, I think it would be wise for us to agree to that in order to get our main objective of Marshall's command over the whole business.

It seems to me that, above everything else, we want liquidity in our offensive in Europe against Germany and, whether we want it or not, the march of events, it seems to me, will undoubtedly require it.

It is simply impossible for anybody to know at what point or points we may need to change our emphasis and the force of our attack.

If Churchill would agree to such an organization, then I can see no difficulty about the early announcement of the change in commanders. Indeed, there would be every reason for doing it.

I believe there is a good chance of getting Churchill to agree to this.

/Signed/Harry
/Typed/H.L.H.[17]

Churchill, however, point-blank refused the notion of an overall command, for he wanted strategic control of the Mediterranean in his own hands. So Roosevelt had to keep on trying to come up with some idea of how to give Marshall the command of Overlord without creating a political and military disaster.

The State Department joined the War Department in giving FDR headaches that fall. Although he was gratified by Averell Harriman's eventual decision to accept the position of ambassador to the Soviet Union, other news overshadowed the good. On September 25, Cordell Hull finally forced the resignation of the able and brilliant Sumner Welles as Under Secretary of State. Roosevelt much preferred Welles to Hull, but Hull had more political backing, and when the showdown came, Welles had to go. Roosevelt felt especially irritated, for he had planned to send Welles to Moscow for the Foreign Ministers Conference scheduled for the latter part of October. As it was, Hull met with Eden and Molotov in a highly successful conference. Hopkins salvaged something from the wreckage by getting Roosevelt to give the job to Edward R. Stettinius.

About this time, a rumor appeared that Hopkins would be sent to London as ambassador to replace John G. Winant. The story, which broke on October 14, provoked a plaintive cable from Winant to Hopkins.

> A SITUATION HAS DEVELOPED HERE SINCE MY RETURN SIX MONTHS AGO THAT CUTS DOWN MY USEFULNESS. . . . NINE-TENTHS OF THE INFORMATION I GET IS FROM BRITISH SOURCES. MATTERS OF SERIOUS CONCERN IN RELATION TO FOREIGN POLICY ARE PASSED THROUGH OTHER CHANNELS WHETHER TO THE PRIME MINISTER OR TO MR. EDEN. BRITISH OFFICIALDOM HAS BEEN BOTH FRIENDLY AND FRANK WITH ME BUT THERE IS NO SERVICE QUICKER TO UNDERSTAND WHEN A MAN HAS BEEN STRIPPED OF AUTHORITY. . . .
>
> DURING THE LAST THREE OR FOUR MONTHS THERE HAS BEEN A WHISPER-ING CAMPAIGN THAT I WAS TO BE RELIEVED AND THAT AVERELL WAS TO SUCCEED ME. YESTERDAY THE LONDON PAPERS CARRIED A NEW STATEMENT THAT YOU WERE TO SUCCEED ME. THESE THINGS WOULD NOT BE DAMAGING IF IT WERE NOT KNOWN THAT YOU AND AVERELL HAVE DONE A CONSIDER-ABLE PART OF THE EXCHANGE THAT NORMALLY FALLS TO THE OFFICE I HOLD.[18]

Hopkins, who had been ill again, delayed answering until October 25. He tried to set the record straight.

> I had occasion the other day to talk to Stettinius about the importance of keeping two or three of their Ambassadors thoroughly informed on the state of affairs here and, more particularly, about the current affairs of importance.
>
> I know exactly how you feel about it and if I were in your shoes I would feel just the same.
>
> There is, of course, nothing to the story of my becoming Ambassador to Great Britain and never any notion that Harriman would become Ambassador there. The President has repeatedly stated to me and others that he wanted you to stay there throughout the war and has always refused to consider replacing you when they had other jobs in mind for you here in America. I know the President not only has absolute confidence in you, but feels you are doing the best job of any Ambassador to England. I am sure the country shares this view. I certainly do.[19]

Winant stayed on, but it cannot be said that he got much more information than in the past.

A good many messages went back and forth between London and Washington during that period. The campaign in Italy was going unexpectedly slowly. On October 1, the Allies entered Naples, but the Germans established a series of defensive lines across the peninsula a few miles north and held them grimly throughout the fall and winter. In the Greek islands, on his own hook, Churchill had British forces occupy Leros, Samos, and Cos and a beachhead on Rhodes. The Germans promptly threw them out of Rhodes and Cos, and Churchill frantically tried to have the entire Allied Mediterranean strategy recast to preserve Leros and Samos. The President refused to help out. The day of his acceptance of Churchill's opportunism was over. He was more concerned with trying to work things out with Russia.

Finally, in September, Stalin wrote that he might be able to get away for a conference with the President and the Prime Minister. He rejected such meeting places as Scapa Flow, Alaska, and North Africa, and suggested that Teheran might be suitable. Roosevelt countered with ideas of Cairo, Iraq, Asmara, Turkey, Beirut, or aboard ships in the eastern Mediterranean. Stalin turned them all down. It had to be Iran or nothing. Roosevelt explained to him the constitutional provision that he must sign bills within ten days or they would become law without his signature, but Stalin parried this with the statement that he had a war involving over five hundred divisions on both sides to run and could not get too far away from Moscow. Churchill and Roosevelt almost gave up the idea of meeting with Stalin, in favor of another session of the two of them in Cairo in December, but at the last moment, Roosevelt gave in, the Army having figured out how they could get papers to him in Teheran in the required time.

And so came about the final conferences of 1943. Churchill and Roosevelt would meet with Chiang Kai-shek in Cairo on November 22. Then, without Chiang, they would fly on to Teheran on November 27 to meet with Stalin. On the conclusion of those talks, Churchill and Roosevelt would return to Cairo for final discussions.

On Thursday evening, November 11, after dark, Roosevelt, Admiral Leahy, and Harry Hopkins left the White House and were driven to the Washington Navy Yard, where they boarded the *Potomac*, restored to Presidential service for this mission. At 9:00 the following morning they transferred to the great new battleship *Iowa* off Point Lookout, where the Potomac River empties into Chesapeake Bay. The battleship was under command of Captain John McCrea, until recently Roosevelt's naval aide, and a good friend of Harry Hopkins.

As soon as the President and his party were aboard, the *Iowa* got

underway and moved down to Hampton Roads to refuel for the voyage
across the Atlantic. They were ready for sea at 10:00 that evening, but like
all sailors, the President was superstitious about sailing on a Friday,
preferring to wait until the next day, even if it was the thirteenth!

Just as eight bells sounded midnight, Captain McCrea gave the order to
take in the lines, and six minutes later the *Iowa* was under way. The largely
uneventful voyage included an anxious incident the second day out.
Hopkins, consistently misspelling *torpedo,* recorded:

> This afternoon the Captain arranged for an anti-aircraft drill. Three
> balloons are released—tied together—and the batteries of forties and
> twenties let loose when the balloons reach a proper height and distance
> from the ship. The other method is for the five inch battery to fire one
> shell—it explodes at perhaps 20,000 feet—then the other five inch guns try
> to hit the ball of smoke left by the original explosion.
>
> The President was wheeled from the luncheon table to the deck just
> outside his mess—Wilson Brown [his Naval Aide], Ross McIntire, Pa
> Watson and I went along. The firing began—it seemed pretty good to me
> altho the five inch guns made a whale of a racket in spite of the cotton
> which all of us put in our ears.
>
> We had just moved to the port side to see the five inch guns fired the
> second time. Suddenly an officer from the bridge two decks above leaned
> over and yelled "It's the real thing! It's the real thing!" The President
> doesn't hear well anyway and with his ears stuffed with cotton he had a
> hard time getting the officer's words which I repeated to him several times
> before he understood. I asked him whether he wanted to go inside—he said
> "No—where is it?"
>
> Just as I got to the starboard side to find out—everything fired at once at
> the wake of a torpedoe about six hundred yards away—the firing lasted
> about thirty seconds—the wake went well astern.
>
> It was a torpedoe alright [sic]—but not from a German submarine. One
> of our destroyers had let loose a torpedoe directly at the Iowa. The first the
> Iowa heard about it was a flash from the destroyer that a torpedoe was
> running toward the Iowa and it was four or five minutes later that the
> message came that the torpedoe was fired by our own escort.
>
> The commander of the destroyer explained it as follows—the torpedoe
> was in place but with no primer attached—the torpedoe must have been
> unloosed because of the heavy seas in some unaccountable fashion. But
> Admiral King and Capt. McCrea thot this pretty thin. An investigation is
> afoot.
>
> Can you imagine our own escort torpedoing an American battleship—
> the newest and biggest—with the President of the United States aboard—
> along with the Chief of Staff of the Army and the Chief of Naval
> Operations?
>
> In view of the fact that there were twenty army officers aboard, I doubt
> if the Navy will ever hear the last of it.[20]

During the crossing the Chiefs of Staff met frequently with the President so that they would be ready to present a united front to the British. The *Iowa* arrived at Mers el Kebir, the naval port a few miles west of Oran, on the morning of November 20. There they were met by Eisenhower, Admiral Cunningham, Elliott and Franklin, Jr., and Robert Hopkins. The party then flew to Tunis in a C-54, irreverently named *The Sacred Cow,* outfitted for the President.

While Eisenhower showed FDR the battlefields, both those of the immediate war and those of the Punic Wars two millennia earlier, the President took occasion to explain to him the present idea for command of Overlord.

> Ike, [he said] you and I know who was the Chief of Staff during the last years of the Civil War [General Henry W. Halleck, who had earlier been commander of the Department of the West and of the Army of the Potomac], but practically no one else knows, although the names of the field generals—Grant, of course, and Lee, and Jackson, Sherman, Sheridan and the others—every schoolboy knows them. I hate to think that fifty years from now practically nobody will know who George Marshall was. That is one of the reasons why I want George to have the big command— he is entitled to establish his place in history as a great General.

Roosevelt went on to explain the latest plan for reorganization of American high commands. Marshall would go to London, either as commander in chief of Allied forces in Europe, other than Russian, or as commander of Overlord. Eisenhower would return to Washington as Acting Chief of Staff. Eisenhower was unenthusiastic but said he would go where he was sent. As it happened, King had a talk with Eisenhower which revealed that things were by no means settled, for King felt Marshall was indispensable as a member of the Joint Chiefs of Staff.

The Sacred Cow and three other planes took off early Sunday morning, November 22, for Cairo and arrived late that afternoon. In the shadow of the pyramids, the conferees got down to business. There were two main objectives of the Cairo Conference: first, to coordinate plans with Chiang Kai-shek for the defeat of Japan, and, second, for the British and Americans to reach a broad agreement on strategy and plans for the European war before confronting Stalin in Teheran.

As far as the Pacific war was concerned, Roosevelt pushed hard for the firm scheduling of Anakim, the recapture of Burma. Churchill, though less convinced of its necessity as a means of defeating Japan, enthusiastically supported it as a necessary step in restoring the British Empire. He believed, along with Admiral King, that Japan could be defeated by sea power, but Generals Chennault and Stilwell, agreeing for once in their lives, argued that Japanese forces would have to be defeated on the ground in Asia and that only China could provide the needed manpower.

Hopkins attended all conferences with Chiang, as did Madame Chiang, who acted as interpreter. On his departure from Cairo, the Generalissimo was well satisfied with the Anglo-American promise to launch Anakim early in 1944 and to reopen the Burma Road to China as soon as possible. In about ten days, both decisions would be reversed because of agreements reached at Teheran.

On November 25, Roosevelt hosted the celebration of Thanksgiving Day at his villa, the residence of Ambassador Alexander C. Kirk. Among those present were Churchill and his daughter Sarah, Hopkins and Robert, Winant, Pa Watson, and others to the number of twenty. Roosevelt carved the two huge turkeys with a skill which filled Churchill with admiration. "Speeches were made of warm and intimate friendship. For a couple of hours we cast care aside. I had never seen the President more gay." [21]

The Thanksgiving dinner provided a welcome respite from the tensions which had grown up between the British and American delegations. While Harriman was traveling to Cairo from Moscow he had worried about the forthcoming meeting with Stalin, and he warned the Allied military chiefs that it would be unfortunate if Stalin and the Soviet general staff representatives believed the British and Americans were ganging up on the Russians. He need not have worried.

The problem was the Prime Minister. Although he had left Quebec committed to Overlord, he kept drifting off in favor of something else. Sir Charles Wilson summed it up in his diary on November 25:

> Ran into Harry Hopkins, and found him full of sneers and jibes. He had just come from a meeting of the Combined Chiefs of Staff, who were framing a plan of campaign to put before Stalin at Teheran. According to Harry, Winston hardly stopped talking, and most of it was about "his bloody Italian war." Harry went on in his dry, aggressive way:
> "Winston said he was a hundred per cent for Overlord. But it was very important to capture Rome, and then we ought to take Rhodes."
> Harry made it clear that if the P.M. takes this line at Teheran and tries again to postpone Overlord the Americans will support the Russians.[22]

The British and Americans were still far apart when their planes took off early on the morning of November 27 to keep their rendezvous with Stalin in the Iranian capital. Harriman joined Hopkins in *The Sacred Cow* for the six-and-a-half-hour flight over the Suez Canal, Jerusalem, Baghdad, the Tigris and Euphrates Rivers, and the barren desert. On the way Hopkins discussed with Harriman the possibility of American postwar aid to Russia among other matters of interest.

Because of fears for the President's security, no official party greeted the plane at the airport a few miles from Teheran. Roosevelt and the others went by limousine directly to the American legation as guests of the minister, Louis G. Dreyfus. He had politely declined the hospitality of the young Shah, who offered one of the royal palaces.

The President's party spent only one night at the legation, for the Russians had uncovered evidence of a plot to assassinate one or more of the Big Three and did not want Roosevelt exposed to the risk of driving back and forth. Secret Service head Mike Reilly objected to moving the President to a residence in the Russian compound, but FDR overruled him. Churchill, staying at the British embassy, very near the Soviet headquarters, was not so exposed.

On the off chance that it might be needed, the Russians had completely rebuilt and redecorated the building into which Roosevelt, Hopkins, and Leahy moved. Thoughtfully they provided several new bathrooms which Mike Reilly appreciated. He appreciated less the eighty microphones they had installed throughout the structure.

American Secret Service men and American soldiers guarded the building inside and out. All the servants, except for the Filipino stewards who accompanied Roosevelt, were NKVD men. As they bent over to make beds, the outlines of Lugers showed clearly underneath their white coats.

A few minutes after Roosevelt was installed in his new quarters, Stalin came to call, much to Churchill's disgust. The Prime Minister had asked to see Roosevelt earlier that morning in order to settle ahead of time the military matters they would discuss with Stalin at the plenary session scheduled for 4:00 that afternoon. But Roosevelt, wishing to meet with Stalin alone first, refused. Churchill began to talk about going home.

Roosevelt and Stalin met alone, attended only by their two interpreters, Charles E. Bohlen and V. N. Pavlov. After suitable amenities, Stalin summed up the situation on the Russian front. They discussed the Far East, and Stalin expressed a low opinion of the quality of the Chinese armies, but laid the difficulty to the incompetence of their leaders. Since at this time, the Communist forces in China were beginning to move toward dominance, Stalin's remark seems the more significant.

The conversation turned to France. Stalin dismissed De Gaulle as a man who behaved as though he were head of a great country when in fact he had little power and was out of touch with "the real France," represented by Pétain.

After forty-five minutes of discussion, Roosevelt and Stalin broke off for the plenary session. Harriman noted that Stalin paid a special mark of respect to Hopkins:

At Teheran, Stalin and Hopkins met for the first time since 1941. Harriman watched with satisfaction as Stalin, upon entering the conference, spotted Hopkins across the room and walked over to greet him warmly. It was not Stalin's habit to take the initiative this way; as a rule he waited for people to approach him. "Stalin showed Hopkins a degree of personal consideration which I had never seen him show anyone else except Roosevelt and Churchill," Harriman recalled. "I believe that Stalin's feelings for Hopkins went back to July 1941. Hopkins was the first Western visitor to Moscow after the German attack, when things were going pretty badly. Stalin evidently saw in Hopkins a man who, in spite of ill health, has made that long, exhausting and hazardous journey to bring help. It was an example of courage and determination that impressed Stalin deeply. He had not forgotten.[23]

During the entire Teheran Conference, Hopkins performed the functions of Secretary of State, working with Eden and Molotov and attending the plenary sessions.

The first meeting largely concerned military strategy. The British and Americans were surprised that Stalin had not brought his military staff to the meeting. Only his old crony, Marshal Klementy Voroshilov, accompanied him. Western military leaders generally regarded Voroshilov as incompetent. Marshall and Arnold missed the opening session, as they had been misinformed of the time of the meeting and were in a car seeing the sights of Teheran. As it turned out, their absence did not matter much, for Churchill, Roosevelt, and Stalin did most of the talking.

Roosevelt, invited to take the chair, began with a summary of the war in the Pacific, largely for Stalin's benefit. He sketched the successful ten-month drive through the Central Solomons that had culminated with American seizure of bases on Bougainville. He covered MacArthur's New Guinea operations and the opening of the Central Pacific drive with the seizure of Makin and Tarawa in the Gilberts. He pointed out the immense distances in the Pacific and how American submarines were devastating the merchant marine which Japan depended on to exist. He went on to the proposed operations in Burma to bring support to the Chinese.

The conversation then turned to Europe and Overlord. FDR pointed out that operations in northern France would be impossible before May 1, 1944, because the English Channel was such "a disagreeable body of water." Churchill broke in to say that the British had "every reason to be thankful that the English Channel was such a disagreeable body of water."

Then Roosevelt came to the crux of the matter, saying that he did not favor any operations which might postpone Overlord, but that he and Churchill had been discussing possible future moves in the Aegean, the Adriatic, and in Italy. Stalin dismissed the Mediterranean plans. The only way to defeat Germany, he insisted, was through France. He did approve of Operation Anvil, the landing in southern France to support Overlord. He had no use for the campaign in Italy and said the capture of Rome did not matter. Churchill glowered.

The meeting ended with Stalin's casual remark that when the war against Germany had ended, Russia would join in the war against Japan.

At 8:30 that evening Roosevelt hosted a dinner for Stalin, Molotov, Churchill, Eden, British Ambassador to Russia Sir Archibald Clark Kerr, Harriman, Hopkins, and three interpreters. The Filipino stewards managed to produce an American style meal under severe difficulties, for the kitchen lacked most essentials, even a stove, until the Russians at the last moment supplied one.

Discussion topics included the future of Germany and France and how they were to be treated after the war.

Near the end of the dinner, Roosevelt turned green and began to perspire profusely. Hopkins got up at once and had the President wheeled to his bedroom. Admiral McIntire made a quick examination and reported that it was a mild attack of indigestion. (It is possible that Roosevelt's attack was something more serious than indigestion, for shortly after returning from Teheran he began to experience the marked weight loss that made him look so haggard for the rest of his life.) The President did not rejoin the diners, but went directly to bed. Churchill and Stalin discussed Poland with no agreement. Stalin criticized the policy of unconditional surrender as only serving to unite the Germans to fight harder.

The next morning Roosevelt seemed completely recovered. He and Stalin met again alone with their interpreters, and Roosevelt brought up his idea of an international organization of some thirty-five or forty member states devoted to peacekeeping in the postwar world. In addition to general membership, the proposed organization would have what he called the Four Policemen, Russia, the United States, Britain, and China, who would enforce the decisions of the organization and would respond immediately to any threat to peace. Stalin was doubtful. Smaller countries might resent such action by the great powers, and in any case he could not see China as a great power as she was then constituted. Roosevelt pointed out that China was a nation of 400 million people and it was better to think of them as friends rather than a potential area of trouble.

The plenary session that afternoon was devoted to a detailed presentation of the plans for Overlord. Before they got down to the discussion, Churchill made a presentation on behalf of King George of a bejeweled ceremonial "Sword of Stalingrad." Stalin received it with the first sign of emotion any Westerner had ever seen him display. He kissed the hilt, and Churchill believed his eyes were shining with tears.

After a review by Marshall, Brooke, and Voroshilov of the military discussions carried out that morning, Stalin asked bluntly: "Who will command Overlord?"

Roosevelt glanced at Churchill and then confessed that it was not yet decided. Stalin made an impatient gesture and replied, "Nothing will come out of the operation unless one man is made responsible."

Churchill then took the floor to say that everyone was of one mind on Overlord, but—— He then began to expound on opportunities on the northern shore of the Mediterranean and the eternal magnet, Rhodes. Stalin listened quietly. According to Hopkins' report to Sir Charles Wilson, he doodled, drawing wolves' heads and smoking one cigarette after another. Hopkins noted that they looked as though he had rolled them himself.

Stalin heard him out and then said, "If we are here to discuss military matters, Russia is interested only in Overlord." Wilson relates:

> Marshal Stalin then said he wished to ask Mr. Churchill an indiscreet question, namely, do the British really believe in Overlord or are they only saying so to reassure the Russians?
>
> The Prime Minister replied that if the conditions set forth at Moscow were present it was the duty of the British Government to hurl every scrap of strength across the Channel.[24]

Roosevelt summed up: "We are all agreed that Overlord is the culminating operation, and that any operation which might delay Overlord cannot be considered by us."[25]

That evening the Russians gave the dinner, as lavish as Russian energy could make it. They brought huge amounts of caviar, some to be consumed at the dinner and the rest to be taken home by the guests as a memento of the occasion. During the discussions, Stalin teased Churchill unmercifully. He charged that Churchill wanted a "soft peace," and went on to say that to make sure that Germany did not rise again in twenty or thirty years and plunge Europe into another disastrous war, 50,000 of their officers should be shot.

Churchill was horrified. "The British Parliament and people will never tolerate mass executions!" He elaborated at length. Roosevelt, in a clumsy attempt to make Churchill see the joke, suggested that the number be reduced to only 49,000. Churchill was not amused. He stomped out of the dining room. Stalin, realizing he had gone too far, went after him and assured him that it had all been a jest. For the rest of the evening, Stalin paid tribute to British valor and suggested ways British influence might be extended in the world.

The next morning, according to Charles Bohlen, Hopkins went on an errand that only he could have done. Bohlen describes it:

> After the Russian dinner—as I later heard—Hopkins went to see Churchill at the British Embassy and told him that he was fighting a losing battle in trying to delay the invasion of France. The view of the United States about the importance of an assault across the Channel had been firmly fixed for many months, Hopkins said, and the Soviet view was equally adamant. There was really little Churchill could do, Hopkins emphasized, in advising the Prime Minister to yield with grace. It is still not clear whether Hopkins acted under Roosevelt's instructions in going to Churchill. I was not privy to Roosevelt's talks with Hopkins or with Harriman. But at that time Roosevelt was relying more and more on Hopkins, virtually to the exclusion of others. At Teheran, Hopkins's influence was paramount.[26]

Apparently Hopkins' visit did the trick, because when the Big Three met for luncheon, Roosevelt read the decision of the Combined Chiefs: "We will launch Overlord during May, in conjunction with a supporting operation against the South of France on the largest scale that is permitted by the landing craft available at that time."

A gratified Stalin asked when the commander would be named. Roosevelt replied that he would need three or four days to consider the matter and to discuss it with his staff.

The luncheon and the plenary session that afternoon were marked by cordiality. Hopkins missed the luncheon to attend a meeting with Eden and Molotov to discuss the bases the United Nations would need for peacekeeping functions after the war. Hopkins stressed that the United States had no interest in strong points in Europe, but would seek to establish bases in the Far East, especially on Formosa and in the Philippines, even after the islands had become an independent nation.

That day was Churchill's sixty-ninth birthday, and he insisted on playing host at the British embassy. The occasion outstripped all the others in cordiality. According to Harriman, Hopkins was one of the stars of the evening:

> Hopkins made one of the wittiest after-dinner speeches I ever heard, in tribute to Churchill [Harriman recalled]. Unfortunately it has not been fully recorded. He undertook the formidable task of teasing Churchill without offending him. After long study, Harry said, he had made a great discovery—that "the provisions of the British Constitution and the powers of the War Cabinet are just whatever Winston Churchill wants them to be at any given moment." His toast might not have been so well received had

it come from someone Churchill valued less highly. In any event, the Prime Minister joined in the laughter with the rest of us. Hopkins' relationship with Churchill was so deeply rooted in mutual respect and warm affection that he could say pointed things, in his uniquely humorous way, without arousing the Prime Minister's resentment.[27]

The next day at luncheon, the military decisions having been reached, the Big Three and Hopkins turned to political questions. One of the topics which had come up several times during the conference was how to persuade Turkey to enter the war on the side of the Allies. Hopkins, living up to the title that Churchill had jocosely bestowed on him, "Lord Root of the Matter," wanted it to be absolutely clear just what form of military assistance the Allies would have to give Turkey if she entered the war. Hopkins wrote out his own comments for inclusion in the official record:

> Mr Hopkins again pointed out that the United States Chiefs of Staff had not given consideration to the detailed requirements of the Turkish operation. The whole of the Mediterranean was soon to come under the Combined Chiefs of Staff—hence the resources must be examined in the light of that fact.
> It should be clearly understood that the American side believe that there are no landing craft available for an attack on Rhodes—and more important still that even if the landing craft were available—no decision has been reached as to whether or not the landing craft could not be used to better advantage in some other operations.
> Under any circumstances it should be clearly understood that no mention can be made to [Turkish] President [Ismet] Inonu, implied or otherwise that an amphibious landing can be made on Rhodes.[28]

The discussions ranged over many topics. Near the end Hopkins slipped a paper to Roosevelt, which said, "Mr. President: What do you think of letting the Russians give dinner tonight—your last chance at Russian food. Harry."

Roosevelt scribbled on the bottom: "OK but I have to leave *early* as we sleep at the camp. FDR." [29]

The Big Three had planned to confer another day, but the weather reports indicated that conditions would deteriorate over the mountains and that the American party had better leave the next morning, December 2. It took a lot of effort to ready the communiqué and the Declaration of Iran, one of the better written documents of the war. Stalin signed the English version after Pavlov had translated it aloud. It read, in part:

> We recognize fully the supreme responsibility resting upon us and all the United Nations to make a peace which will command the good will of

the overwhelming mass of the peoples of the world, and banish the scourge and terror of war for many generations. . . . We shall seek the cooperation and the active participation of all nations, large and small, whose peoples in heart and mind are dedicated, as are our own peoples, to the elimination of tyranny and slavery, oppression and intolerance. We will welcome them, as they may choose to come, into a world family of democratic nations . . . Emerging from these cordial conferences, we look with confidence to the day when all peoples of the world may live free lives, untouched by tyranny, and according to their varying desires and their own consciences. We came here with hope and determination. We leave here, friends in fact, in spirit and in purpose.[30]

The years to come would reveal, tragically, that different men put different interpretations on the words "tyranny," "slavery," "democracy," and "oppression."

After taking his farewell of Stalin, Roosevelt, accompanied by Hopkins and his personal retinue, left the Russian compound and drove to Camp Amirabad, headquarters for the American Persian Gulf Command. That night they were guests of General Donald Connolly, who had been an engineer officer for Hopkins during WPA years. Early the next morning, the President took a jeep ride around the camp and talked to the GI's, who were bored stiff in this area of heat and desert where the war never came.

At 9:45 *The Sacred Cow* took off for Cairo and arrived that afternoon. There the President and his party were joined by the members of the Combined Chiefs of Staff, who had left a day earlier and stopped off in Jerusalem for a day of rest and sightseeing.

The meetings at Cairo with Inönü and the other Turks were pleasant, but they were conclusive: Turkey would not enter the war. That was that. Churchill argued with Inönü at length, but Roosevelt and Hopkins said little. Privately they hoped Turkey would not enter the war and further strain Allied resources.

The plans for military operations agreed on at Cairo earlier and at Teheran were already being revised. The British planners insisted that Anvil comprise at least two divisions. The landing craft would have to come from somewhere. The only possible source was the operation against Burma, the main promise Chiang Kai-shek had been able to win at the meeting ten days earlier. Two component parts of Anakim had to go: Buccaneer, amphibious landings on the Andaman Islands in the Bay of Bengal, and Tarzan, the land offensive in north Burma.

Roosevelt soon discovered that Churchill, having yielded on Overlord for 1944, was in no mood to yield further. Hopkins scribbled a note to Eden: "Anthony:—It looks like Buccaneer is out & our military plans hence will be agreed to tomorrow. Harry." Eden replied: "If so, you have been very generous, but our chances next year will surely benefit. President has been grand about it all." [31]

Hopkins got the job of drafting the message to Chiang that he would not get what he had been promised at Cairo. Hopkins said nothing of the possibility of Russia entering the war against Japan. He knew better. No one could keep a secret in Chungking. Chiang replied bitterly, but it did no good. The decision had been made.

On Saturday evening, December 4, Harry Hopkins had another nasty job. He went to call on Marshall at the request of the President. Marshall remembered his saying that Roosevelt was "in some concern of mind over my appointment as Supreme Commander." Marshall understood at once that the President had decided not to give him command of Overlord and had sent Hopkins to find out how he would take it. Hopkins was embarrassed, because he admired Marshall as he admired few other men and he wanted him to have the job. But he had his own instructions from Roosevelt. Marshall replied that he would "go along whole-heartedly with whatever decision the President made."

FDR obviously hoped to avoid the decision by having Marshall remove himself from the running, but Marshall took no action one way or the other. Near lunchtime the next day Roosevelt sent for Marshall. The General later recorded that the President

> ... asked me after a great deal of beating about the bush just what I wanted to do. Evidently it was left up to me. Well, having in mind all this business that had occurred in Washington and what Hopkins had told me, I just repeated again in as convincing language as I could that I wanted him to feel free to act in whatever way he felt was to the best interest of the country and to his satisfaction and not in any way to consider my feelings. I would cheerfully go whatever way he wanted me to go and I didn't express any desire one way or the other.... Then he evidently assumed that concluded the affair and that I would not command in Europe. Because he said, "Well, I didn't feel I could sleep at ease if you were out of Washington." [32]

Roosevelt thereupon picked Eisenhower to command Overlord. He sent for him and said, "Well, Ike—you'd better start packing." Eisenhower misunderstood at first and thought the President was telling him to get ready to go back to Washington to take over as Acting Chief of Staff. The misunderstanding was soon cleared up, and during the flight from Cairo to Malta and on to Sicily, Roosevelt held long talks with Eisenhower on the difficulties of his job and how to defend himself against the wiles of Churchill.

Hopkins and Roosevelt and most of his party flew on from Sicily to

Dakar, where they again boarded the *Iowa* for the passage across the Atlantic. They arrived in Chesapeake Bay on December 16, and as soon as they had transferred to the *Potomac,* Hopkins radioed his wife: "Arrived well and ever so anxious to see you, my darling.... Get out my heavy underwear and light the fire." [33]

Roosevelt, too, made use of the *Potomac's* radio facilities. After leaving Cairo, Churchill came down with pneumonia, and FDR sent through the Map Room:

> I HAVE JUST LEFT THE IOWA AND AM ON MY WAY UP THE POTOMAC. I AM DISTRESSED ABOUT THE PNEUMONIA AND BOTH HARRY AND I PLEAD WITH YOU TO BE GOOD AND THROW IT OFF QUICKLY. THE BIBLE SAYS YOU MUST DO JUST WHAT MORAN [Sir Charles Wilson, now Lord Moran] SAYS, ONLY I CANNOT AT THIS MOMENT PUT MY FINGER ON THE CHAPTER AND VERSE.[34]

Churchill recuperated in Marrakesh, brooding the while over operations in the Mediterranean. This time, he won his way, and Allied troops made the controversial landing at Anzio, which was expected to result in the capture of Rome in January. But the operation was better in concept than in execution, and Rome held out until June 4, 1944.

For the first time in years Hopkins did not spend Christmas with the Roosevelts. While FDR celebrated at Hyde Park, Hopkins and his wife and daughter stayed in their Georgetown house. A few days later he wrote Stephen:

> We have just fought the "Battle of Christmas" here and a very successful one it was. It is the first time I have had Christmas in my own house for years and Louie made it the pleasantest that I think I ever had in my life.[35]

He also wrote his other two sons and his ex-wife Ethel, bringing her up to date on Robert, who had returned to Algiers.

On New Year's Day Hopkins suddenly told friends who had dropped in to see the house that he was coming down with a cold and that he had better go upstairs to bed.

His illness was more than a cold and it kept him out of action for nearly seven months. But his body rallied once more, and some of his greatest and most controversial services lay ahead.

CHAPTER EIGHTEEN

From Nadir to Summit Again

On January 5, 1944, Roosevelt cabled Churchill, "Harry is temporarily on the sick list with the flu, but I think he will be in the Naval Hospital only a few days. This epidemic is very widespread but while it is not serious it makes you feel the way an Italian soldier looks." [1]

But Harry Hopkins' difficulty was more than the flu, and it dragged on. Churchill wired: "I should be grateful for more news of Harry." After consulting Dr. McIntire, Roosevelt replied: "Harry Hopkins is improving slowly following a severe attack of influenza. This was complicated by a digestive disturbance. He should be ready for full activity in a month's time." [2]

While Hopkins was in Bethesda Naval Hospital, one of the strangest episodes in his career took place. A certain C. Nelson Sparks, a rabid, old guard Republican, published a book entitled *One Man—Wendell Willkie,* a scurrilous attempt to block Willkie from winning the Republican nomination again in 1944. In it he published a letter purporting to come from Harry Hopkins. It read:

THE WHITE HOUSE
WASHINGTON

August 17, 1943

Dear Umphrey:
What has been done in the * * * matter? Will you write me,please. What developments in the other situation? Willkie is going to be the man,in my

opinion,and I can promise you good cooperation from that quarter if you think it would be helpful.

Sincerely yours,
(signed) Harry Hopkins

Dr.Umphrey Lee
Southern Methodist University
Dallas,Texas.

According to Sparks, this letter proved the complicity of the White House in trying to engineer the nomination of Willkie by the Republicans in 1944 and that Hopkins was up to his thinning hair in the scheme.

Hopkins promptly denied that he had written the letter, and Dr. Lee, President of Southern Methodist University, denied that he had received it. Anti-Willkie forces denounced both Hopkins and Dr. Lee, claiming that Lee planned to run against Senator Tom Connally in the forthcoming election. Hopkins asked the FBI to look into the matter. Isolationist Republican Senator William Langer of North Dakota thought the Senate ought to investigate, but if he had his way the investigation would not be as impartial as that conducted by the FBI.

In a speech which took up 57 pages of the Congressional Record, Langer assailed Hopkins, flourishing photostats of the letter which Sparks had provided. Sparks, who turned out to have been mayor of Akron, Ohio, and was later a supporter of publisher Frank Gannett, claimed that he had been given the letter by George N. Briggs, an assistant to Harold L. Ickes. Briggs, so the story went, had obtained the letter from Ickes, who had received it from oil man Frank Phillips, who had got it from Lee.

Hopkins dragged himself out of his sickbed on January 21 to testify before a federal grand jury looking into the case. He stayed only ten minutes, just long to testify that he had not originated, dictated, or written the letter and that the signature on it was not his. Robert Hopkins has stated that the Briggs affair bothered his father more than almost any other attack on him.[3]

Examination showed that the letter, while typed on genuine White House stationery, could not have originated in Hopkins' office. His stock of White House paper differed from the sample in size of type and in the fact that in his the word "Washington" was centered under "The White House." A supply of stationery matching the sample letter was found in Briggs's desk. The typewriter used to write the letter came to light in the office of Briggs's receptionist. It developed that Briggs must have written it himself, for other samples of his typing also revealed the idiosyncracy of failing to space following a comma, as occurred five times in the letter. The obliterated word indicated by asterisks was "Alamo," but no one could explain its significance. Handwriting experts testified that the signature was not that of Harry Hopkins.

When questioned by the FBI, Briggs told an involved story of how he had received the letter and had wanted to help Sparks stave off the nomination of Willkie.

As soon as he learned of Briggs's probable involvement, Ickes suspended him without pay, and the grand jury later returned an indictment charging him with forgery, mail fraud, and false pretenses. The 55-year-old Briggs, however, never came to trial, for he died of a stroke in October before his case was reached.[4]

While the Briggs matter was at its height, radio commentator Fulton Lewis, Jr., made a vitriolic attack on Hopkins, implying that he was using the Bethesda Naval Hospital illegally, thereby robbing the taxpayers and depriving servicemen of the medical care they needed. After the broadcast, Hopkins received several crank letters, ranging from the insulting to the obscene. Normally he ignored such letters, but, ill as he was, they got under his skin this time. Sam Rosenman, however, advised him to forget the whole thing and gave him a letter citing the authority under which he and certain other civilians employed by the federal government were entitled to use service hospitals.[5]

As soon as he could travel, Hopkins planned to go to Florida to escape the bitter Washington winter. John and Fanny Hertz invited him to stay at their house in Miami Beach. On February 2, he wrote Mrs. Hertz:

> I hope you will not be too disturbed with your impending visitor. In the first place, I will be up and around. I am not confined to bed. In fact I fully expect to do a little swimming, lie in the sun and give you some early lessons in Gin Rummy!
>
> The doctors are making out a complete diet for me but it is not very restricted and as soon as I get my hands on it I will send you a copy of it.
>
> The doctors insist that I take a nurse with me because I have to have about two injections a day, plus an ungodly amount of medication which must be taken on time and they are very anxious that the time I spend in the south I be kept under a careful routine of medication. Otherwise she won't have much to do. . . .
>
> Louise is anxious to come down during the latter part of my visit and bring me home. The three of us would not need more than two rooms.[6]

A few days later, he wrote Hertz that the White House would install a direct line to Hopkins' room in the Hertz residence. It would seem that Harry Hopkins was not completely out of the picture.

Hopkins and his nurse Adda Johnson left Washington on February 11, aboard the *Silver Meteor* of the Seaboard Railway, due to arrive in Miami the next afternoon.

Before he left Washington, Hopkins had thought a lot about the latest military operation in the Pacific, the invasion of the Marshall Islands, which took place on the last day of January. On February 2, he wrote Stephen, now a private first class in the Marines. His outfit was scheduled to make the landing on Kwajalein.

> You can imagine how much my thoughts have been with you during the last few days and I hope that all has gone well. I am sure it has. The Japs can never withstand the force we are throwing at them in the Marshalls.
>
> David is on an aircraft carrier somewhere in that show and it may be you have already seen him.
>
> I heard from Robert a day or two ago and he is being assigned to a new theatre which will get him in the big European push whenever it comes.
>
> Louise and Diana are both well and altogether enjoying the new house.[7]

The letter continues with an account of his illness and a brief summary of the Briggs affair.

Unhappily, the letter was never delivered.

Sometime during the morning of February 12, Hopkins' nurse received a message which had been put aboard at Jacksonville:

> PLEASE DELIVER THE FOLLOWING URGENT MESSAGE TO MISS ADDA JOHNSON PASSENGER SEABOARD SILVER METEOR EAST COAST TRAIN 43 CAR SA 25 COMPARTMENT G FOR DELIVERY TO THE HON HARRY L HOPKINS. "I AM TERRIBLY DISTRESSED TO HAVE TO TELL YOU THAT STEPHEN WAS KILLED IN ACTION AT KWAJALEIN. WE HAVE NO DETAILS AS YET OTHER THAN THAT HE WAS BURIED AT SEA. HIS MOTHER HAS BEEN NOTIFIED. I AM CONFIDENT THAT WHEN WE GET DETAILS WE WILL ALL BE EVEN PROUDER OF HIM THAN EVER. I AM THINKING OF YOU MUCH (SIGNED) F D R"
>
> THE WHITE HOUSE.[8]

It developed that Stephen had been working as an ammunition carrier under fire and as a flank security man and was trying to dig a foxhole in the front line when he was hit. Louise Hopkins told reporters that she and Harry had a hard time keeping him out of the Marines until he had finished at the Hill School.

Letters of sympathy from Churchill, Chiang Kai-shek, and Madame Chiang, among others, poured in from all over the Allied world. Eleanor Roosevelt wrote: "I know you decided long ago that the war had to be won at all costs & you have done so much yourself that I hoped you might be spared this sacrifice." [9] George Marshall offered, "If by any chance you would like to have your other boy who has flirted with danger in Tunisia, Sicily and Italy, pulled back, at least for a time, to safer ground I will see to it quietly and immediately." [10]

Hopkins replied to Marshall at once:

> The blow was hard and biting but I am overwhelmingly proud of Stephen. Then too I am sure he died as gallantly as he lived through a short but happy life. As for Robert, I hope you will not send for him. The last time I saw him in Tunis he told me he wanted to stay until we got to Berlin—in fact we have both agreed to meet there.[11]

A short time later Hopkins received a beautifully lettered parchment scroll:

Stephen Peter Hopkins
Age 18

> "Your son, my lord, has paid a soldier's debt:
> He only liv'd but till he was a man;
> The which no sooner had his prowess confirm'd
> In the unshrinking station where he fought,
> But like a man he died."
>
>
>
> Shakespeare.
> To Harry Hopkins from Winston S. Churchill
> 13 February, 1944.
>
>

The quotation is from the last scene of *Macbeth.*[12]

After a stay of about a month in Miami Beach, Hopkins went once more to the Mayo Clinic, and Roosevelt informed Churchill that "he stood the trip well, feels reasonably well but has not gained weight. He is to be fattened up for the next three or four weeks and then they will decide whether an operation is necessary." [13]

An operation did turn out to be necessary, and on March 29, Dr. John Waugh performed surgery for a fistula. There was no sign of cancer and none of an ulcer. By mid-April Hopkins was up walking on the porch of the hospital, and his weight loss from the operation had been only half that feared by the doctors.

Oscar Cox wrote on April 21:

> You certainly are missed in this town—and your not being here is missed in many spots of the World. This place certainly needs your sure knack of hitting the jugular. The last three returning from London that I have seen say that the top British feel pretty lost since you have been out of the

harness. The Russians, too, constantly ask about you—and it's more than politeness. Jean Monnet keeps moaning about how much you are needed here.

So for many good and sufficient reasons many of us hope you will be back in full operation again—and soon.[14]

While he was at the Mayo Clinic fattening up for the operation, Hopkins prepared an article for the *American* magazine. Unlike most articles bearing his name, he seems to have written this mostly himself. It was a plea for a fair and patriotic discussion of the issues in the forthcoming Presidential campaign. Someone, he said, had suggested that the election be postponed until the end of the war, but, he wrote, ". . . if America can't stand the strain of a war-time Presidential election, Democracy is a failure."

He most feared the kind of campaign that would tear the country apart. "I want to see a sane, determined debate of the real issues of the campaign, worthy of our dignity as a democracy. In this election we are not merely electing a President of the United States and a Commander-in-Chief of our armed forces. We are electing a leader of the world."

> At this point, [he continued] some talented analysts of political motives already have begun to dissect my statements. If they do not like the President, they probably are saying, "Oh, the administration through Harry Hopkins, is crying for quarter. Now that a show-down has come, they are asking the opposition to be good to them. They are trying to win a stronghold by guile. They are afraid of the fight ahead.
>
> I *am* afraid of the fight ahead, but only for two reasons. I want us here at home to keep our dignity among nations. I want us to maintain our national unity. And I want us to keep the faith of our fighting men. I am in the government, but I am a citizen. My sons are in this war. I want victory and a lasting peace. I do not want us to say anything here at home that will hurt the spirit of the boys abroad. . . .

The article expresses bitterness against some of the people at home who profiteer and use the black markets, as contrasted with the sacrifices the servicemen were making. Written a few weeks after Stephen's death, his words take on a special poignancy.

He proposed a national committee to oversee the election debate, to ensure that issues and not personalities were discussed. He outlined some of the issues that could be validly argued. The article concludes:

> I, for one, would like to see all the facts come out and the facts debated. I am entirely devoted to the Administration and its policies, but if the people of the United States, in the light of knowledge and reason want to

keep or change their leadership, I think they should, as you must. That is Democracy, the thing we would die for.[15]

The article was never published, for Roosevelt, after submitting it for comment by the State and War Departments, killed it. He stated that he did not want anyone in the administration writing at that moment on foreign affairs.

Around the middle of May, Hopkins traveled by Army plane from Rochester to White Sulphur Springs, where the Army had taken over the famous hotel as a convalescent center. On weekends, Louise visited him in his cottage. He had a hard convalescence—he developed jaundice and had to go into the nearby hospital for treatment.

Roosevelt tried to cheer up the invalid in a letter of May 18.

> It is grand to get the reports of how well you are getting on at White Sulphur Springs, and I have had a mighty nice letter from Rivers—couched mostly in medical terms—which, however, I have had translated!
>
> The main things I get from it are two. First, that it is a good thing to connect up the plumbing and put your sewerage system into operating condition. The second is (and this comes from others in authority) that you have got to lead not the life of an invalid but the life of common or garden sense.
>
> I, too, over one hundred years older than you are, have come to the same realization and I have cut my drinks down to one and a half cocktails per evening and nothing else—not one complimentary highball or night cap. Also, I have cut my cigarettes down from twenty or thirty a day to five or six a day. Luckily they still taste rotten but it can be done.
>
> The main gist of this is to plead with you to stay away until the middle of June at the earliest. I don't want you back until then. If you do come back before then you will be extremely unpopular in Washington, with the exception of Cissy Patterson who wants to kill you off as soon as possible—just as she does me. . . .
>
> Lots of love to you both. Tell Louise to use the old-fashioned hatpin if you don't behave.[16]

Hopkins was still at White Sulphur when Rome fell (June 4) and when the Allies crossed the Channel to land on the Normandy beaches (June 6). Two weeks later came the invasion of Saipan in the Marianas. He could think how the two massive operations, half a world apart, had come about as a result of American production and of the no small part he had played in getting things moving.

Marshall sent a plane to pick Hopkins up at White Sulphur, and on July 4, he returned to continue his convalescence at home in Georgetown. The next day he wrote letters of thanks for the many kindnesses he had received during his illness. He had some news of her half brothers to give Diana:

David is coming home from the Pacific for a two weeks' leave and a special course which I think he is going to take in Florida. I have had three or four letters from Robert and the last one broke the news to me that he is going to get married! It wouldn't hurt you any if you picked up your pencil and wrote him a note. If you don't know his address, send it down to me. If you don't know what to say to a brother when he is about to get married, it's high time you learned, so do try to do it.[17]

Robert's marriage to an English girl caused some stir. Sherwood, who was serving in England with the Office of War Information, wrote a rather disapproving letter, but Hopkins gave his approval, and later Beaverbrook described the girl in a letter as "absolutely first rate." [18]

That summer of 1944 the Republicans nominated Thomas E. Dewey of New York for the Presidency and John Bricker of Ohio for the Vice-Presidency. Willkie had withdrawn as a serious candidate earlier. Dewey's candidacy was one of the many things Roosevelt and Hopkins had to talk about when Hopkins occasionally went to the White House to try to get back into the swim of things. At other times they talked over a special telephone in the Georgetown house connected with the White House switchboard.

But Hopkins' return brought disappointment to both men. He had lost touch with the situation, for too much had happened, and Roosevelt had turned to other people for the help Harry used to provide. In addition, Hopkins could work only two or three hours a day, and that was in defiance of his doctors, who wanted him to do no work at all. To Dr. Waugh he wrote how well he was feeling and that it was "chiefly due to the fact that I am eating about 4,000 calories a day, which is outrageous but no doubt good for me." [19]

Churchill, however, tried to use Hopkins in his old role as intermediary with the President. He still opposed the Anvil plan for the invasion of southern France, and all during the spring tried to convince the Americans to divert the forces to the area of Trieste for a drive up the Ljubljana Gap so that American and British forces would be in central Europe before the Russians got there. The Combined Chiefs kept turning him down, but in the meantime, Anvil had been delayed until August because its landing craft had to be used in the Normandy invasion. On July 19, Churchill cabled Hopkins that he had given up on Anvil, but hoped "it will not ruin greater projects." [20] Less than three weeks later, he cabled again to propose that the Anvil forces be diverted to the Brittany peninsula west of Normandy. The old confident Hopkins shows in the reply:

WHILE I HAVE SEEN NO ANALYSIS OF LOGISTICS INVOLVED, I AM ABSOLUTELY CERTAIN YOU WILL FIND THE SUPPLY PROBLEM INSURMOUNT-ABLE. DIVISIONS ARE ALREADY AVAILABLE FOR EISENHOWER'S IMMEDIATE

BUILD-UP WHICH WILL TAX THE PORTS TO THE LIMIT. THEN TOO, NO ONE
KNOWS THE CONDITION OF THE BRITTANY PORTS.

IT SEEMS TO ME THAT OUR TACTICAL POSITION TODAY IN OVERLORD IS
PRECISELY AS PLANNED AND AS WE ANTICIPATED IT WOULD BE WHEN ANVIL
WAS LAID ON. TO CHANGE THE STRATEGY NOW WOULD BE A GREAT MISTAKE
AND I BELIEVE WOULD DELAY RATHER THAN AID IN OUR SURE CONQUEST OF
FRANCE.

I BELIEVE TOO THE MOVEMENT NORTH FROM ANVIL WILL BE MUCH MORE
RAPID THAN YOU ANTICIPATE. THEY HAVE NOTHING TO STOP US. THE
FRENCH WILL RISE AND ABYSSINIATE [sic] LARGE NUMBERS OF GERMANS,
INCLUDING, I TRUST, MONSIEUR LAVAL.

A TREMENDOUS VICTORY IS IN STORE FOR US.[21]

That finished the matter. The landings in southern France took place on
schedule on August 15, and the advance up the Rhone was swifter than
anyone had hoped. The code name had been changed to Dragoon because,
as Churchill put it, he was dragooned into it.

On July 11, Roosevelt had announced that he would run for a fourth
term if the Democratic National Convention saw fit to nominate him. Then
he set off cross-country to San Diego, California, where he would embark
in the heavy cruiser *Baltimore* to go to Pearl Harbor for a meeting with
Nimitz and MacArthur.

On July 20, the day Roosevelt was renominated, Hopkins cabled
Churchill, "I am not with the President but am going to remain here until
he returns even tho I am working but two or three hours a day." [22]

Hopkins had little energy to spare for politics and played no part in the
Democratic Convention that year, although Henry Wallace wrongly
believed that he led the moves to dump him as Vice-Presidential nominee
in favor of Senator Harry S. Truman of Missouri. Hopkins led a rather
restricted life during the next few months. He would rise at 7:30, and, after
breakfast, read the papers until about 10:00. Then he would work until
about 1:00, have lunch, and retire to his room to nap and read until 5:00,
with the telephone cut off. Then he might work some more until dinner,
and afterwards relax with his wife and friends.

Besides, a kind of coolness had developed in his relationship with
Roosevelt. There was little outward sign of it, but the President seldom
telephoned him. Their relationship might have regained its former intimacy
sooner had not Roosevelt embarked just then on his Western trip, which
extended into September.

During the next months, Hopkins did a great deal of routine work on
various government jobs but was seldom in a position to influence events.
He did advise Roosevelt not to agree to a meeting with Churchill in
Scotland; he felt that if they were to meet without Stalin, it ought not to
appear that the President was going to Churchill. Let Churchill come to

him. Roosevelt accepted this advice, and suggested Bermuda. As it turned out, the two leaders met in Quebec.

On August 28, Hopkins cabled Churchill to explain why he would not attend: "Although I am now feeling much better I still must take things easy and I therefore feel that I should not run the risk of a set-back in health by attempting to fight the battle of Quebec on the Plains of Abraham where better men than I have been killed." [23] Never before had Hopkins allowed a threat to his health to interfere with his doing what he believed he had to do. It seems probable either that Roosevelt did not invite Hopkins or invited him so half-heartedly that he realized that the President did not want him.

Roosevelt soon had reason to regret that he did not have his sharp-eyed adviser with him, for Hopkins would have saved him from a serious mistake.

At that time, Hopkins' mind was turning to what he might do when the war had ended. In mid-August he had been talking with Oscar Cox on problems of postwar Germany—how it would be governed, implementing surrender terms, security measures. Cox wrote:

> He had the feeling that probably one of the most important single factors in the picture was the man that the Americans picked to act in Germany after the peak point of military control is over. . . . His feeling was that there was a lot of loose talk and thinking about treating Germany on too soft a basis and that someone like Stimson who knows what the issues are, who is tough and could administer the problems on a tough and intelligent basis, was of first importance.[24]

It began to develop that the man Hopkins had in mind for the job in Germany was himself. At lunch with Morgenthau on September 4, he discussed the problem, and the Secretary of the Treasury confided to his diary:

> At lunch with Hopkins, we got on the German question, and he said he thought 70% of the question was to put a strong man under Eisenhower to really run German economy, and eventually put the man in charge and let him run the country. I said, "I understand from people in the War Dept. that you want to go yourself." He brushed that aside and said, "Well, what I wanted to do was sort of go on a roving mission as Ambassador." So I said, "Harry just what is your interest in this thing and do you want to go?" He said, "Stimson asked me that same question," and finally after several questions he said, "I will be completely frank with you and tell you what I have in mind. I have had several discussions with the President, and I have made up my mind that when the war is over there is nothing for me in Washington. I have devoted all of my time to the war. I have paid no

attention to trivial matters, and it would be a terrific anticlimax for me to stay around after the war in Germany is over." He said, "There are several very important jobs to be filled by the President; and one is Jimmy Byrnes' job and the other one is who is going to go to Germany." [25]

After his luncheon with Hopkins, Morgenthau went on to Quebec to present his own plan for dealing with Germany. The notorious Morgenthau Plan proposed to reduce Germany to an agricultural level so that she would never again have the industrial base to menace the world. As he read his proposals to Churchill and Roosevelt, Morgenthau was disturbed by the Prime Minister's "low mutters and baleful looks." Nevertheless, the next day Churchill dictated a version very close to what Morgenthau had proposed.

> The ease with which the metallurgical, chemical and electrical industries in Germany can be converted from peace to war has already been impressed upon us by bitter experience. It must also be remembered that the Germans have devastated a large portion of the industries of Russia and of other neighboring Allies, and it is only in accordance with justice that these injured countries should be entitled to remove the machinery they require in order to repair the losses they have suffered. The industries referred to in the Ruhr and in the Saar would therefore be necessarily put out of action and closed down. . . .
>
> The program for eliminating the war-making industries in the Ruhr and in the Saar is looking forward to converting Germany into a country primarily agricultural and pastoral in its character.[26]

Roosevelt and Churchill initialed this plan without much thought and turned to other matters. Then things began to happen. Stimson and Hull objected violently and so did Hopkins when he heard about it. Morgenthau had not stopped to consider how a country as populous as Germany could support itself with only an agricultural economy. His scheme had parallels to ancient Rome's vengefulness at the end of the Third Punic War in destroying all Carthaginian buildings and salting the fields to sterility. Eden told the Prime Minister bluntly, "You can't do this. You and I have said quite the opposite."

Stimson prepared a strong statement, which concluded, "The sum total of the drastic political and economic steps proposed by the Treasury is an open confession of the bankruptcy of hope for a reasonable economic and political settlement of the causes of war." [27]

The Morgenthau Plan was sent up to Hopkins, who by this time was with Roosevelt and Churchill at Hyde Park. Hopkins was still in the shadows, but he would soon emerge. Churchill describes the occasion:

I lunched there on September 19. Harry Hopkins was present. He was obviously invited to please me. He explained to me his altered position. He had declined in the favour of the President. There was a curious incident at luncheon, when he arrived a few minutes late and the President did not even greet him. It was remarkable how definitely my contacts with the President improved and our affairs moved quicker as Hopkins appeared to regain his influence. In two days it seemed to be like old times. He said to me, "You must know I am not what I was." He had tried too much at once. Even his fullness of spirit broke under his variegated activities.[28] [Churchill tells this same episode of a luncheon in identical words of the period before the Quebec Conference of 1943. He has obviously confused the occasions, but it is clear that the episode belongs here. The only problem is his reference to "In two days," for Churchill left Hyde Park that same evening and sailed for home the next day. The essence of the story, however, is true: Roosevelt and Churchill got along better when Hopkins was present.]

Faced by the united opposition of Stimson, Hull, and Hopkins, Roosevelt backed away from the Morgenthau Plan. At first he denied any such arrangement, but when confronted with his initials, along with those of Churchill on the document, he said that he had signed without thinking.

Roosevelt apparently initialed the agreement to please his old friend Morgenthau. If Hopkins had been at Quebec, he would have let no friendships interfere. What Cox had referred to as his "sure knack of hitting the jugular" almost certainly would have spotted the trap in the agreement, and he would have talked his two friends out of it.

It is a fair inference that as a result of the Morgenthau Plan episode, FDR decided that he could no longer keep Hopkins at arm's length. Hopkins' return to power and intimacy closely followed the conclusion of the Quebec Conference.

In early October Hopkins, by now back working full-time at the White House, saved the President from another blunder. The massive successes against Germany on both the western and eastern fronts raised so many political questions of postwar arrangements that it would take another meeting of the Big Three to settle them. In the west, all of France had been liberated, and Allied forces threatened Germany itself. In the east, the Russians' summer offensive had penetrated into Poland. They had taken most of the Baltic region, as well as Bulgaria and Rumania and were advancing into Yugoslavia and Hungary. They stood on the frontiers of Turkey and Greece, and Churchill worried about the spread of Soviet influence into the Balkans. He was especially anxious for a Big Three meeting so that these problems could be thrashed out.

Roosevelt, however, felt he could not leave the United States during the election campaign. Churchill forcefully asserted that events and the Russian armies would not wait for the election returns. But FDR remained adamant, so Churchill suggested that he and Eden go to Moscow at once to discuss with Stalin and Molotov proper spheres of influence in the Balkans and elsewhere.

On October 4, Hopkins, while making a routine check of the outgoing and incoming traffic in the Map Room, discovered separate but similar messages from Roosevelt to Churchill and Stalin being processed. Drafted by Admiral Leahy according to FDR's instructions, the messages gave approval of the Moscow meeting and wished the two leaders good luck. Realizing at once that the message in effect permitted Churchill to speak for Roosevelt in dealing with Stalin, Hopkins, on his own authority, ordered the message stopped. He went back to his office and called Charles Bohlen in the State Department. "Chip, get the hell over here in a hurry." [29]

Bohlen, as alarmed as Hopkins over the proposed message, worked out a new draft while Harry went off to find the President. He found him shaving in his bedroom. As soon as Roosevelt heard what Hopkins had to say, he realized he had made a mistake and asked him to stop the message. He was relieved to learn that it had already been stopped.

A little later Roosevelt approved the revised messages without change.

> I AM SURE YOU [i.e., Stalin] UNDERSTAND THAT IN THIS GLOBAL WAR THERE IS LITERALLY NO QUESTION, MILITARY OR POLITICAL, IN WHICH THE UNITED STATES IS NOT INTERESTED. I AM FIRMLY CONVINCED THAT THE THREE OF US, AND ONLY THE THREE OF US, CAN FIND THE SOLUTION OF THE QUESTIONS STILL UNRESOLVED. IN THIS SENSE, WHILE APPRECIATING MR. CHURCHILL'S DESIRE FOR THE MEETING, I PREFER TO REGARD YOUR FORTHCOMING TALKS WITH THE PRIME MINISTER AS PRELIMINARY TO A MEETING OF THE THREE OF US, WHICH CAN TAKE PLACE ANY TIME AFTER THE ELECTIONS HERE AS FAR AS I AM CONCERNED.
>
> I AM SUGGESTING UNDER THE CIRCUMSTANCES, IF YOU AND THE PRIME MINISTER APPROVE, THAT MY AMBASSADOR IN MOSCOW BE PRESENT AT YOUR COMING CONFERENCE AS AN OBSERVER FOR ME. MR. HARRIMAN NATURALLY WOULD NOT BE IN POSITION TO COMMIT THIS GOVERNMENT IN RESPECT TO THE IMPORTANT MATTERS WHICH VERY NATURALLY WILL BE DISCUSSED BY YOU AND MR. CHURCHILL.[30] [A similar message went to Churchill on the same date with appropriate changes in references to persons in the text.]

Harriman missed some of the meetings, but his presence served to keep Roosevelt informed and made it clear that Churchill spoke for himself and not for the United States.

Hopkins played no part in the election campaign that fall, for his wife was ill and later required surgery. He made none of the trips and had no part even in the preparation of speeches for the campaign. About all he contributed to the reelection of Roosevelt was to refute some of the Republican propaganda. One story said that after the war men would be kept in service to avoid throwing large numbers on the job market all at once. A voter wrote to ask Hopkins about it. He replied that a committee had considered the idea but rejected it. An answer came back by return mail: "I shall make known to you that which for me would have been a startling and utterly unthinkable thing to do some weeks ago:—I AM GOING TO CAST MY VOTE FOR MR. ROOSEVELT. . . ." [31]

A serious situation arose in connection with the problem of military security. Hopkins recorded the incident in a memorandum to himself:

> One morning late in Oct 1944 I was visiting with General Marshall in his office. He told me that he had received information that someone in the armed services had given Governor Dewey confidential and secret information relative to our breaking the Jap codes. He stated he believed that Dewey was given the factual information that we had broken the Jap codes. Furthermore it was his (Marshall's) belief that Dewey intended to state this fact publicly for political purposes. General Marshall told me that the information that Dewey might have been given did not disturb but the disclosure of the method of our acquiring the information would be fatal to our military interests.
>
> Therefore Marshall stated that he had undertaken on his own behalf and without consulting any one to write to Gov. Dewey. In this letter he asked Mr. Dewey in the first paragraph not to read further because he would be told highly secret military information—unless he was prepared to keep it in strict confidence.
>
> Later that day I repeated this conversation to the President. While he expressed no criticism of Marshall's action he said he felt confident Gov. Dewey would not for political purposes give valuable military information to the enemy. "My opponent must be pretty desperate if he is even thinking of using material like this."
>
> The President wondered what officer or government official had been so faithless to his country as to give Governor Dewey this information.[32]

Louise Hopkins' operation took place on November 1, so that the Hopkinses could not be with Roosevelt at Hyde Park for the election returns on November 7. By this time, everyone in Roosevelt's entourage was confident of the results, and Hopkins joined in a five-dollar White House pool on the electoral vote Roosevelt and Truman would win:

Sherwood	484
Early	449
Hopkins	440
Rosenman	431
Watson	400

The final result was Roosevelt 432 to Dewey 99, so Rosenman kept the stakes he was holding.

Hopkins had no doubts. On the day before the election, he wired Beaverbrook:

IT IS APPARENTLY GOING TO BE A CENSUS RATHER THAN AN ELECTION AND ROOSEVELT WILL WIN BY A LANDSLIDE. OTHERWISE I WILL UNDERWRITE THE BRITISH NATIONAL DEBT, JOIN THE PRESBYTERIAN CHURCH AND SUBSCRIBE TO THE CHICAGO TRIBUNE.[33]

On November 10, the Roosevelts returned to Washington, and Hopkins was among the first to talk to them.

> This morning, upon the President's return from Hyde Park, I spent an hour with him and Mrs. Roosevelt. . . .
> The President told me he meant it when he said, in Boston, that it was the meanest campaign he had ever been in in his life. He said he thought that they hit him below the belt several times and that it was done quite deliberately and very viciously and he feels quite strongly that he has scores to settle with some individuals about that. He was particularly resentful about the whispering campaign which he believes was a highly organized affair.

The memorandum continues on the same sheet of paper, but the remainder is written on a different typewriter, which suggests a later addition:

> Mrs. Roosevelt urged the President very strongly to keep in the forefront of his mind the domestic situation because she felt there was a real danger of his losing American public opinion in his foreign policy if he failed to follow through on the domestic implications of his campaign promises. She particularly hoped the President would not go to Great Britain and France and receive great demonstrations abroad for the present, believing that that would not set too well with the American people.
> She impressed on both of us that we must not be satisfied with merely making campaign pledges; the President being under moral obligation to see his domestic reforms through, particularly the organizing of our economic life in such a way as to give everybody a job. She emphasized that this was an overwhelming task and she hoped neither the President nor I thought it was settled in any way by making speeches.[34]

Neither Roosevelt nor Hopkins had an opportunity to follow her advice. Roosevelt spent the remaining months of his life almost entirely on relations among the Big Three, planning the postwar world, and trying to organize the United Nations. Hopkins worked closely with him on all these problems and had no energy to spare for anything else. After Roosevelt's death, when Hopkins assisted President Truman, he no longer had any real power.

One day, about the time that Hopkins intercepted Roosevelt's ill-considered messages on the Moscow meeting of Churchill and Stalin, Cordell Hull, who said he was very sick and could stand the strain no longer, told Roosevelt that he must resign. Hull was adamant, but finally FDR persuaded him not to announce his resignation until after the election.

Now that the election was past, Roosevelt accepted Hull's resignation. Newsmen and Washingtonians began to speculate on his successor.

Roosevelt would have liked to appoint Sumner Welles, but his nomination would have been a direct slap in the face to Hull, and the old Tennessean would have risen from his death bed to rally his friends in the Senate to defeat it.

Hopkins talked Roosevelt out of appointing Jimmy Byrnes, the most obvious choice. He knew Byrnes would insist on running foreign affairs and would not sit on the sidelines while Roosevelt and Hopkins dealt with Churchill, Stalin, and Chiang Kai-shek. Byrnes, remember, had once told Hopkins to "keep the hell out of my business." Hopkins persuaded FDR to appoint Under Secretary of State Edward R. Stettinius. Stettinius would be amenable to the President's ways, and Hopkins knew he could work with him.

Now that Hull had left, Stimson began to wonder whether at seventy-seven he might be a drag on the President. On December 12, Hopkins noted:

> Stimson asked me to have lunch with him today.
>
> At the end of our lunch it was clear that the reason he had asked me to see him was that he wanted to know whether the President wished him to resign. He stated that he realized that he was getting along in years and that he is not as strong as he used to be and that he had been seriously considering the wisdom of resigning.
>
> I told him that I doubted very much that the President wanted him to resign, in fact, was quite sure that he did not. I told him that, from my point of view, he was the most respected member of the Cabinet; that he had the confidence of the American people, the rank and file of the army and of General Marshall. I told him, further, that I was sure he had the President's complete confidence.[35]

Stimson took Hopkins' advice and remained on the job.

That same day, Hopkins recorded a strange episode which had taken place three days earlier. The Prime Minister called him about seven that evening. It was a bad connection, and "he sounded as tho he was very angry and stirred up about something and wanted me to do something about it. I got the words 'Greece' and 'Halifax.' Inasmuch as it was impossible to make him understand what I was saying, I told him I would find out about it in the morning." [36]

Hopkins learned that the trouble concerned Greece. As the defeated Germans left, Greek Communists tried to seize power. Churchill landed British troops to keep order and support the constitutional monarchy. No American ground forces were in Greece, but American naval units operated under British command in the Mediterranean. This was what the fuss was all about.

The next morning, December 10, Hopkins discovered that Admiral King had ordered that no American ships help supply the Greeks. It seemed to Hopkins that King was getting into political areas where he did not belong. Leahy agreed and persuaded King to withdraw the order. Hopkins then saw Halifax and talked him out of sending the stiff diplomatic protest he had prepared on orders from Churchill. He could tell the Prime Minister to simmer down, that everything had been settled.

Hopkins took action entirely on his own responsibility. Churchill accepted his judgment and refrained from sending any message, and Roosevelt never learned of it. Churchill ended the matter by flying to Athens on Christmas Day and acting as mediator between the quarreling forces. He established a regency under Archbishop Damaskinos, and the exiled King George agreed to stay out of the country until he was summoned by the Greek people.

A few days before Christmas, Hopkins sent Churchill a cable more expressive than most of the messages that passed between them:

> DEAR WINSTON: I WANT YOU TO KNOW, ON THIS FATEFUL CHRISTMAS, THAT I AM WELL AWARE OF THE HEAVY BURDENS YOU CARRY. SINCE OUR FIRST MEETING I HAVE TRIED TO SHARE THEM WITH YOU. I WOULD SHARE THEM NOW.
>
> THE RAGING BATTLE AND THE OVERHANGING CLOUDS ARE THE PRELUDE TO A SURE AND GLORIOUS VICTORY FOR US. WHAT A GALLANT ROLE YOU PLAY IN THE GREATEST DRAMA IN THE WORLD'S HISTORY, NO ONE KNOWS BETTER THAN I.
>
> THERE ARE SOME OF MY COUNTRYMEN WHO WOULD DESTROY ME BY THE ASSERTION THAT I AM YOUR GOOD FRIEND. ALL I CAN SAY IS THAT I AM EVER SO PROUD THAT IT IS SO.
>
> AND YOU WILL KNOW WITH WHAT AFFECTION LOUIE AND I SEND YOU AND CLEMMIE OUR WARMEST CHRISTMAS GREETINGS.[37]

As the year ended, the war drew rapidly to a close. The Germans had made their last grand effort in the Battle of the Bulge in December, 1944.

The Japanese fleet had been reduced to impotence in the Battle for Leyte Gulf in October, and the Philippines were being freed. The Russians were moving steadily forward. Mussolini was gone, and nearly all Italy was under Allied control.

In the new year would come the last conference of the Big Three of Roosevelt, Churchill, and Stalin, the most controversial of them all. And Hopkins would have his part to play.

CHAPTER NINETEEN

Yalta

The Roosevelt administration was dying. One by one, old friends departed, worn out in service like Cordell Hull, or gone to the grave, their jobs unfinished. Death had touched the inner circle. Louis McHenry Howe had been the first to go eight years earlier. Then, the previous summer, Missy LeHand, who had never recovered from her stroke, succumbed to a cerebral hemorrhage. And, shortly before Christmas, 1944, Marvin McIntyre, a man said to be without enemies, had gone.

As he prepared for his fourth inauguration, Roosevelt himself had but three months to live. His personal physician, Admiral McIntire, had known for over a year that FDR was a dying man. In March, 1944, he had arranged for Lieutenant Commander Howard Bruenn, a cardiac specialist, to examine the President. The results were ominous. Roosevelt might expire at any time from congestive heart failure. From that moment, Dr. Bruenn was never far from the President's side.

Roosevelt never inquired why he was being attended by a heart specialist. Perhaps he did not want to know. Perhaps he thought it was irrelevant. His thoughts dwelt mostly on the creation of the United Nations, and he felt that only he could work with Stalin and Churchill to that end. In this sense Roosevelt believed himself the indispensable man. Another President could finish the job of winning the war, but no other man could arrange the peace.

Others were tired or ill. Sam Rosenman wanted to quit. So did Frances Perkins. Roosevelt had to plead with both of them to stay on, at least until the war was won.

And then there was Hopkins. Apparently in good health—for him—he had no reserves of strength. Any serious exertion or strain could start the descent which might well prove irreversible. But he gave no thought to quitting so long as he could be of service.

On January 21, 1945, the day after Roosevelt's fourth inauguration, Hopkins set out for London in *The Sacred Cow*. Once again the tired warrior returned to the game he loved, spokesman for Roosevelt—to Churchill, De Gaulle, and the Pope.

During the autumn of 1945, Hopkins wrote of the origins of the Yalta Conference:

> As early as the middle of September, 1944, the President was contemplating a second conference with Stalin and Churchill. There were a variety of pressing problems which the President believed warranted such a conference and both Churchill and Stalin were agreeable to the conference. Churchill was, indeed, insistent on it. The reasons were obvious.

Hopkins went on to point out the various problems of the postwar world that needed settling, now that the military strategy was generally agreed upon. Especially important was the United Nations organization, to which preliminary shape had been given that fall by the Dumbarton Oaks Conference. Hopkins' statement continues:

> ...All of the President's close advisers were opposed to his going to Russia; most did not like or trust the Russians anyway and could not understand why the President of the United States should cart himself all over the world to meet Stalin. This argument carried no weight with me. The all-important thing was to get the meeting. There was not a chance of getting that meeting outside of the Crimea. The President's advisers gave me a lot of acid criticism when they found out that I was the one who had talked to [Andrei] Gromyko [then ambassador to the United States] about the possibility of going to the Crimea. When they descended on the President to urge him not to go the President wavered again and cooked up a lot of counter proposals, none of which made any sense. I was sure the President would wind up by going to the Crimea, the primary reason being that it was a part of the world he had never visited and his adventurous spirit was forever leading him to go to unusual places and, on his part, the election being over, he would no longer be disturbed about it for political reasons.[1]

On the trip to London, Hopkins took Charles E. Bohlen with him for companionship and as a State Department representative. A Russian expert, Bohlen later served as the American interpreter at Yalta.

It was on this trip to London, Paris, Rome, Naples, and Malta [Bohlen wrote later] that I came to admire Hopkins. We talked a great deal on the long plane rides, and I began to see that though Hopkins only faintly understood the importance of the ideological factor in Soviet thinking, he did possess hard common sense about foreign affairs. He was also objective about himself, a characteristic all too uncommon to those close to the throne.[2]

The plane stopped at Bermuda and the Azores en route to London. Hopkins was tired when he arrived, for he was suffering from chronic colitis, which got progressively worse during the rest of the trip. He found Churchill as "volcanic" as he expected. The trouble went back to December when Stettinius had publicly criticized British interference in Italian domestic politics. Hopkins succeeded in calming Churchill down, and by the time he left for Paris, they had regained their usual terms of amiability. Hopkins radioed the President, then at sea on the heavy cruiser *Quincy* on his way to the Yalta Conference:

Have had very satisfactory visit London. Leaving for Paris tomorrow. Churchill well. He says that if we had spent ten years on research, we could not have found a worse place in the world than Magneto [code name for Yalta] but that he feels that he can survive it by bringing an adequate supply of whiskey. He claims it is good for typhus and deadly on lice which thrive in those parts. Sorry to hear that Watson seasick as usual. Regards to all.[3]

On the same day, he cabled his wife, "Weather miserable. Conferences satisfactory. . . . Am feeling pretty well." [4]

Arriving in Paris, Hopkins and Bohlen visited Eisenhower, who was living in the outskirts in a building known as Brown House. Its owner had a passion for things Napoleonic, and Hopkins gazed with fascination at all sorts of memorabilia of the Emperor from books to pottery and weapons. But Hopkins' stop in Paris had a more serious purpose: to try to restore some degree of cordiality to Franco-American relations, then at a low ebb. He failed, for the egomania of Charles de Gaulle was not to be appeased.

Hopkins first met with Foreign Minister Georges Bidault, who warned that De Gaulle would not be easy. "He makes no effort to please."

Nor did he. The meeting began on a frosty note. De Gaulle listened impassively when Hopkins suggested that relations between the two countries could be improved. He retorted, "If you really mean that you believe that relations between the United States and France are not all that they should be, why don't you do something about it?" Resisting an impulse to say, "Why don't you?" Hopkins listened while De Gaulle complained that he had not been invited to attend the Crimea Conference. He admitted that the United States had been of great aid to France, "but vou always seem to do it grudgingly and under pressure." [5]

The meeting ended as chilly as it had begun. De Gaulle, of course, resented the fact that the Big Three did not count France as an equal partner in the war against Germany. France was not an equal partner, as anyone but the stubborn Frenchman knew. France's military strength was only token and she was an economic cripple from the long occupation and the fighting since the previous June.

The meeting with De Gaulle represented Hopkins' greatest failure as an intermediary; no one could have succeeded with De Gaulle at that time. Some have suggested that no one ever could at any time.

The next day at luncheon with Bidault, Hopkins said that the President hoped to meet with De Gaulle on the way back from Yalta, preferably on French territory in the Mediterranean. On his own authority, he even suggested that perhaps De Gaulle might attend the last part of the Yalta Conference when the Big Three had finished the military discussions and turned to European political affairs. Bidault agreed to let him know later what De Gaulle thought.

In Paris, Hopkins ran into his son Robert and into Elliott Roosevelt. He took Robert along to Yalta.

The next day the Hopkins men and Bohlen went on to Rome, where they stayed as guests of Ambassador Alexander C. Kirk. Hopkins, accompanied by Myron C. Taylor, Roosevelt's personal representative to the Vatican, had an audience with Pope Pius XII. Taylor reported that Hopkins showed a surprisingly deep religious feeling and was considerably exalted by the meeting.[6]

That afternoon, the party flew on to Caserta, near Naples, where they met Stettinius, who, Hopkins said, was still in Churchill's black books for the Italian dispute. He went on to say that he agreed that the question of Italy could not be left entirely in British hands.

On arriving at Malta on January 31, Hopkins was a very sick man, but he went about his business as though there were nothing wrong. He attended meetings of the Combined Chiefs of Staff which involved a serious dispute between the British and Americans for the final drive into Germany. Eisenhower planned one drive under Montgomery in the north and another under General Omar Bradley in the south. Montgomery, almost openly contemptuous of Eisenhower's generalship, demanded that everything be concentrated in the north under his own command, and Brooke concurred with the little field marshal. Brooke went too far when he asked to have Eisenhower summoned to Yalta to explain his strategy, a move which would have amounted to a "no confidence" vote in his leadership. Hopkins and Marshall indignantly rejected Brooke's request. In the end, Eisenhower stayed at his headquarters and compromised by beefing up Montgomery's armies at the expense of Bradley. As it turned out, the stronger Montgomery got bogged down in the Ruhr, while Patton's Third Army under Bradley raced across southern Germany in the closing days of the war.

The Combined Chiefs proposed to transfer all shipping in excess of military needs to the Pacific, but Hopkins reminded them that the populations of the liberated countries had to be fed with food brought by ship. The Chiefs agreed to leave allocation of shipping in his hands, but he never got a chance to exercise that authority.

Churchill, having developed a fever on the way down, also was ill when he reached Malta. His doctor, Lord Moran, noted:

> He has developed a bad habit of running a temperature on these journeys.
>
> It is not the flesh only that is weaker. [John] Martin [principal private secretary to Churchill] tells me that his work has deteriorated a lot in the last few months; and that he has become very wordy, irritating his colleagues in the Cabinet by his verbosity. One subject will get in his mind to the exclusion of all others—Greece, for example.[7]

When Roosevelt reached Malta on the morning of February 2, everyone was shocked at his appearance. Normally after a sea voyage he came ashore refreshed, tanned, and full of life. But this time it was different.

> His condition [Bohlen noted] had deteriorated markedly in the less than two weeks since I had seen him. He was not only frail and desperately tired, he looked ill. I never saw Roosevelt look as bad as he did then, despite a week's leisurely voyage at sea, where he could rest. . . . I was relieved somewhat, however, to note that his illness did not affect his speech.[8]

Thus the three key members of the Anglo-American contingent to Yalta were sick men. Worst off was Hopkins. Moran described him: "Physically he is only half in this world. He looked ghastly—his skin was a yellow-white membrane stretched tight over the bones." [9]

From Luqa Airfield on Malta, planes started taking off at ten-minute intervals at 11:30 the night of February 2 for the 1,250-mile flight to Yalta. Twenty American and five British transport planes were used, in addition to sixteen fighters to escort the planes assigned to the President, Churchill, General Marshall, and Admiral King.

A little past noon the next day, *The Sacred Cow*, with Roosevelt and Hopkins aboard, as well as Admiral Leahy, Anna Boettiger, General

Watson, Mike Reilly, Roosevelt's valet Arthur Prettyman, and the now ever-present Commander Bruenn, landed in the Crimea. The party set out on the eighty-mile drive over the mountains from Saki Airfield to Yalta. The trip took five hours. Every fifty yards a woman soldier in uniform was on guard and presented arms as the dignitaries passed. They stopped once for rest and refreshment, enjoying caviar and vodka, black bread, smoked sturgeon, champagne, butter, cheese, and boiled eggs.

Along the way the visitors gazed at evidence of the German withdrawal. They saw wrecked and rusting tanks, blasted trees, and gutted buildings. In Yalta, which they reached about 6:00 that evening, most of the buildings had been leveled. But the Nazis had spared three large former palaces, hoping to use them themselves when they had won the war. The Americans stayed in Livadia Palace, built in 1911 as a summer house by Czar Nicholas. Although the building contained fifty rooms, the Americans filled it to overflowing. The President, of course, had the czar's ground-floor suite of rooms, which had the only private bathroom in the building. The Secret Service had inspected and tried to debug (in both senses of the word) the building before the President arrived, but Mike Reilly warned FDR that he could not be sure all listening devices had been found. Apparently the fumigation was more successful, for Averell Harriman reported that the Russian staff had come from the best hotels in Moscow and things were "certainly clean when Roosevelt arrived." [10]

Harry Hopkins had a room to himself, as did Byrnes, Harriman, Bohlen, Pa Watson, Marshall, and Arnold. To the amusement of everyone, Admiral King was assigned the frilly, ornate bedroom of the Czarina, while Marshall was in the Czar's official sleeping quarters. Nicholas had seldom slept there for fear of assassination. Lesser officers fared worse. Five generals shared a bedroom, and in another, sixteen colonels could listen to each other snore. And the entire party of 215 had to share five bathrooms.

The British were quartered some miles away in the Vorontsov Palace. Between was the Soviet delegation in Koreiz, which was a country estate with guest houses rather than a palace.

The Army Signal Corps cooperated with the Navy in rigging a telephone line to the amphibious command ship *Catoctin* in Sevastopol, eighty miles away. The Russians recommended against bringing the ship to Yalta because of the many unswept German mines. The telephone line worked poorly, until Mike Reilly told the Russians that he proposed to station American service men every hundred yards along the entire eighty-mile length. Amazingly the trouble cleared up at once.

Dr. McIntire put Hopkins to bed as soon as they arrived at Livadia. He lived largely on paregoric, plasma, and liver extract, but even then McIntire said "there were times when I did not think we would bring him back alive." [11] Hopkins attended none of the formal dinners of the Conference nor any of the subordinate or staff meetings, but he did pull himself out of bed to participate in all plenary sessions but the first. When Harriman and others needed to consult him, they went to his bedroom.

For the plenary sessions, the representatives of the three nations sat around a large table in the Livadia grand ballroom. Stalin again invited Roosevelt to preside, and he sat at the head of the table. On his right was Harry Hopkins, and on his left Bohlen, who served as interpreter. On Hopkins' right was Stettinius, and next to him Leahy. On Leahy's right was the Russian group, with Stalin sitting between Maisky and Molotov, both of whom understood English. Across the table from Stalin was Churchill, with Eden on his right and his interpreter on his left.

Roosevelt came to Yalta with an illusion, one shared by Hopkins, that he could handle Stalin better than Churchill could. He had refused Churchill's pleas for preliminary talks so that Stalin would not believe that the Americans and British were ganging up on him. It was a bad decision, because the two Western countries had many common interests. In any case, Stalin never believed that they had not laid their strategy first. It was what he would have done in their position.

It is ironic that the two American pragmatists, Roosevelt and Hopkins, approached the Yalta Conference with such idealistic preconceptions. Churchill and Stalin did not.

Bred on European politics, they were prepared to discuss spheres of influence, *cordons sanitaires,* and all the other arrangements great powers have made for centuries. This does not imply that Churchill was not an idealist; he was, but he realized that idealistic goals could be achieved only through international politics. Roosevelt, the supreme domestic politician, went to Yalta as impractically idealistic as Woodrow Wilson at Versailles. And Hopkins shared the visions of his friend. Perhaps the fact that both men were dying made them impatient of the slow give-and-take of international politics.

Yet it must be said that neither Roosevelt nor Hopkins was naive at the meetings which they attended. They worked and struggled, arguing their cases well to achieve their goals. And they won agreement on most of them. Their naiveté lay in trusting Stalin, who yielded on various matters, but when the conference was over went right on doing as he pleased.

An example is Poland. Britain and France had gone to war in 1939 to preserve an independent Poland, and now it was becoming a vassal of Russia. Throughout the war the Western powers had backed the Polish government in exile, headquartered in London. Free Polish troops and Free Polish ships had fought the bitter fight. But in early 1945, Russian troops overran the country on the way to Germany, and Russian-backed Poles set up a Communist government in Lublin. They ignored the Free Polish government in London.

Roosevelt and Churchill argued that the Polish people should decide their own form of government. They urged that the Lublin and the London Poles work together to set up free elections.

Stalin countered that he needed a friendly Poland on his border, because Poland for centuries had been the invasion corridor to Russia from the west. It soon became obvious that Stalin regarded as friendly only a government he could dominate. That meant the Lublin government. Finally he agreed to add "some democratic leaders from Polish emigre circles." Bohlen might well have been suspicious of the word "democratic," for, as history has shown, it meant something very different to Stalin than it did to Roosevelt and Churchill. The Polish matter ended with a promise of invitations for some London Poles to meet with the Lublin Poles to arrange for free elections after the war. Harriman, Clark Kerr, and Molotov were named to a commission to spell out terms for reorganization of the Lublin government and for free elections. They got nowhere.

Other matters considered at the conference included reparations from Germany. Russia demanded that Germany repay the terrible damage that had been done to the Soviet countryside, towns, cities, villages, factories, farms, and homes. They wanted payment in kind, not in money. Roosevelt and Churchill objected, FDR remembering America had to lend money to Germany after World War I to pay reparations of only $3 billion. Stalin wanted $20 billion, half for Russia and half for the rest of the Allies. The British objected to the mention of any specific sums. Hopkins scribbled a note and passed it to FDR:

> Mr. President
> The Russians have given in so much at this conference that I don't think we should let them down. Let the British disagree if they want to—and continue their disagreement at Moscow. Simply say it is all referred to the Reparations Commission with the minutes to show the British disagree about any mention of the 10 billion.
>
> Harry [12]

Later the Russians argued that the minutes indicated that Roosevelt had agreed to the ten billion, but, at the moment, Hopkins' advice seemed sound and Roosevelt went along.

Voting in the United Nations presented another problem. All three agreed that in the Security Council, the permanent members, the United States, Great Britain, Russia, China and, later, France would have a veto on any substantive matter. They disagreed on whether the veto should apply to procedural matters. If it did, any of the great powers could block even discussion of a grievance against it. At length, they agreed that the veto should not apply in procedural matters. Later at the founding conference of the United Nations in San Francisco, Molotov tried to renege on that agreement.

The Russians also wanted the two constituent Soviet republics of Ukrainia and Byelorussia to be given seats in the General Assembly. Roosevelt had said before he left Washington that if the Russians insisted on two or three extra votes, he would demand forty-eight on the ground that each of the States was as sovereign as Ukrania and Byelorussia. In the end, Stalin offered two additional votes to the United States, and agreement was reached. For reasons best known to himself, Roosevelt decided to keep the extra American votes a secret unless he had to disclose it to win Congressional approval of the United Nations. When the news broke the following month, critics immediately wanted to know what other secret deals Roosevelt had made at Yalta.

The Big Three quickly agreed that each of their countries would have an occupation zone in Germany: Russia in the east, Britain in the northwest, and the United States in the southwest. Churchill proposed that France be given an occupation zone as well on the ground that French participation would be necessary to keep the peace once the war was won. Stalin objected that other countries would then demand their zones, but Churchill responded that France was a special case because of her long frontier with Germany. Stalin shrugged his shoulders and concurred, provided a French zone came out of the territory already assigned to the British and Americans.

Although Roosevelt accepted the idea of a French zone, he objected to giving France a seat on the Allied Control Council for Germany. But before the meeting of February 10, Hopkins and Harriman persuaded the President to change his mind. Hopkins pointed out that France, ever jealous of her prerogatives, would be easier to manage on the Council than off it. When Churchill and Roosevelt agreed, Stalin went along.

While they were still thinking about the French, Hopkins received a message from Bidault. De Gaulle would not come to Yalta but he would be delighted to meet Roosevelt on his way back to the United States at a time and place of the President's choosing. Roosevelt returned a cordial invitation for De Gaulle to meet him aboard the *Quincy* in Algiers.

Roosevelt and Hopkins believed that they had won a great victory when Stalin promised that Russia would enter the war against Japan two or three months after the Allies had finished off Germany. Marshall and most of the other generals agreed that Russian troops would be needed to deal with the large Japanese armies in China. Naval leaders, especially King, disagreed;

they believed that sea and air power by themselves could force Japan to surrender. Why give Russia a voice in Far Eastern affairs when Japan could be beaten without her?

Neither the Americans nor the British knew that no one could have prevented Russia from joining the war against Japan. Stalin intended to have his place at the victors' table.

The Yalta Conference ended February 11 after lunch, the morning having been occupied in tinkering with the wording of the communiqué and in other last-minute details. FDR, Averell Harriman, Pa Watson, who was ill, and several others drove by Balaklava to spend the night aboard the *Catoctin.* A little later, Harry and Robert Hopkins went through the passes of Krymskiye Gory to Simferopol, where a train waited for them. Stettinius and others stayed to have a few last words with Molotov. They would catch up to Hopkins at Simferopol.

The decor of the train, which had once belonged to the Romanovs, reflected the elaborate tastes of the Czar and his family. Unhappily it was locked. Hopkins and Robert stood for what seemed hours in the cold, bitter wind until Robert found someone with a key and with gestures persuaded him to open the door. Then there seemed to be no food except for black bread and tea, and Hopkins ruefully remembered a box of chocolates he had given away to the Soviet driver. He turned in to sleep in an ordinary berth.

Ironically, there was plenty of other food aboard the train, but the two Russian stewards expected a party of eight. They refused to have anything to do with a party of two. When Stettinius and the others who were to travel on the train showed up, the stewards served a lavish banquet and Hopkins was assigned the royal bedroom.[13] Hopkins said of the experience the previous night, "If I ever see a foreigner on a station platform in America again I'll show him the washroom and buy him a drink." [14]

During the night the train had moved from Simferopol to Saki, where the American planes stood ready for departure. As soon as Roosevelt and his party arrived, Hopkins went aboard *The Sacred Cow* for the flight to Egypt. At 10:55 in the morning it turned onto the head of the runway to begin its takeoff roll. That afternoon they landed near the Suez Canal and embarked in the *Quincy,* which swung at anchor in the Great Bitter Lake. Hopkins sent a message to his wife:

> Have finished conference and have arrived on second leg of journey where heavy underwear is not needed. Miss you terribly, and send you my dearest love. Call Avis up and tell her that Chip [Bohlen] is well but difficult to keep in nights.[15]

So the Yalta Conference ended. An optimistic Roosevelt felt that they had laid the basis for lasting peace. Hopkins shared these feelings, later telling Sherwood:

> We really believed in our hearts that this was the dawn of the new day we had all been praying for and talking about for so many years. We were absolutely certain that we had won the first great victory of the peace—and, by "we" I mean *all* of us, the whole civilized human race. The Russians had proved that they could be reasonable and farseeing and there wasn't any doubt in the minds of the President or any of us that we could live with them and get along with them peacefully for as far into the future as any of us could imagine. But I have to make one amendment to that—I think we all had in our minds the reservation that we could not foretell what the results would be if anything should happen to Stalin. We felt sure that we could count on him to be reasonable and sensible and understand-ing—but we never could be sure who or what might be in back of him there in the Kremlin.[16]

These bright hopes, of course, faded quickly.

The Soviet Union and Stalin himself began to interpret every agreement reached at Yalta to suit their own purposes. The Americans and the British had negotiated in good faith. They were prepared to make compromises, Churchill was even willing to pick up again the weary thread of European politics. They were prepared for difficulties. They were not prepared for outright duplicity.

Later Hopkins wrote a memorandum on a strange episode which took place following the Yalta Conference:

> The last night before the Yalta conference broke up the President flabbergasted Churchill by telling him for the first time that he was going to fly to Egypt and had arranged for the King of Egypt [Farouk I], Ibn Saud and Haile Selassie to hold conferences with him aboard the cruiser in Great Bitter Lake on three successive days. There were a number of people present when the President told Churchill about this and Churchill had no adequate opportunity to ask the President what these visits were all about. Later that night he, Churchill, sought me out, greatly disturbed and wanted to know what were the President's intentions in relation to these three sovereigns. Fortunately I could tell him I did not know because I had asked the President the same thing. I had already made up my mind that it was, in the main, a lot of horseplay and that the President was going to thoroughly enjoy the colorful panoply of the sovereigns of this part of the world who thought that President Roosevelt of the United States could probably cure all their troubles. I did know he intended to talk to Ibn Saud about the Palestine situation. Nothing I said, however, was comforting to

Churchill because he thought we had some deep laid plot to undermine the British Empire in these areas.

The next day the Prime Minister told the President that he was also going into Egypt after a brief visit to Greece and see each of these sovereigns himself, and had already sent the messages asking them to remain in Egypt for conferences with him immediately after the President had left.

The public aspects of these conferences have been widely written about and I, therefore, do not intend to repeat those here. The only really important thing was the discussion the President had with Ibn Saud about Palestine and this was short and to the point.

I am sure the President did not realize what kind of man he was going to be entertaining when he invited Ibn Saud to meet him—a man of austere dignity, great power and a born soldier and, above all, an Arabian first, last and all the time. He had spent his life fighting and enjoyed it and his subjects all enjoy fighting and they don't like the Jews. So, when the President asked Ibn Saud to admit some more Jews into Palestine, indicating that it was such a small percentage of the total population of the Arab world, he was greatly shocked when Ibn Saud, without a smile, said "no."

[Hopkins continued summarizing the discussions between the President and Ibn Saud. He concluded:]

There is no doubt that Ibn Saud made a great impression on the President that the Arabs meant business. . . . And I never could reconcile the President's statement at a press conference later that he had learned more from Ibn Saud about Palestine in five minutes than he had learned in a lifetime—because the only thing he learned which all people well acquainted with the Palestine cause know, is that the Arabs don't want any more Jews in Palestine. They have been threatening the British for years with civil war if the lid is opened any farther and Ibn Saud merely told the President what he had undoubtedly told the British, and anybody else who wanted to ask him, many times before.[17]

Ibn Saud indeed made a strange arrival when he came to the *Quincy.* He insisted on traveling according to Arab custom, even aboard the American destroyer sent to Jidda to pick him up. As the destroyer approached the *Quincy,* Hopkins and Reilly called the President to come and take a look. Wheeling himself around a gun mount, Roosevelt observed that rich oriental rugs covered the foredeck of the destroyer, a tent in the bow flapped in the breeze, and a dead goat hung from a davit on the fantail. Sitting in the superstructure above the scene was King Ibn Saud in a golden chair. His guards, in Arab robes and armed with rifles and scimitars, manned the rail.

After the kings had departed, on the afternoon of February 14, the

Quincy got under way for the passage of the rest of the Suez Canal and on around to Alexandria, where she arrived late the next morning. Churchill was there in the cruiser *Aurora*. As soon as the *Quincy* had tied up to her buoy, the Prime Minister sent a handwritten note to Hopkins:

> My dear Harry,
>   If convenient I will come on board at 12:30 as there are a few things I should like to talk over with the President. Randolph is with me and if you have room I should like to bring him to lunch. Otherwise he will come aboard and pay his respects afterwards.
>   I do hope you are well.
>
>   As ever,
>   W [18]

Hopkins was far from well, but he did attend the lunch. It was an historic occasion, for it was the last time that Roosevelt and Hopkins were to see Churchill.

At 4:00 that afternoon, Churchill clasped Roosevelt's hand in both of his and left the *Quincy*. Then the cruiser and her escort got under way for the three-day passage to Algiers.

En route Hopkins was confined to his stateroom, too ill to do anything but rest and sleep. But he had to step into action once more.

Among the mail and messages that had come aboard during the brief stop at Alexandria was a telegram from De Gaulle rudely rejecting the invitation to meet Roosevelt at Algiers. Infuriated, Roosevelt called in Steve Early and dictated a brief and insulting message to the vain Frenchman. Early thought it was pretty hot and consulted Hopkins before releasing it. Hopkins told Early to warn FDR that any such public statement would antagonize the French people. No one cared how De Gaulle felt, but there was no point in uniting the French people behind him.

Early came back to Hopkins' stateroom a few minutes later to report that the President "had his Dutch up" and insisted on the statement being released as he had dictated it. Hopkins then turned to Bohlen, who had dropped in, and said, "Chip, go and see what you can do with the President." Bohlen protested that if Hopkins and Early had not been able to change FDR's mind, there was little hope that he could. Hopkins insisted, and Bohlen went.

He found the President in his cabin putting stamps in albums, but still adamant. "What you don't seem to realize is that the United States has been insulted through its President and this requires an appropriate answer."

Bohlen, not yielding, finally said, "We can all admit that De Gaulle is one of the biggest sons of bitches who ever straddled a pot." FDR laughed and said, "Oh, go ahead, you and Harry try your hand at a draft."

The final version merely expressed regret that De Gaulle could not join the President. It avoided vituperation and kept the dignity of the United States.[19]

On the day after leaving Alexandria, Pa Watson suffered a cerebral hemorrhage. Gloom settled over the ship. Pa had been everyone's friend. Hopkins later wrote that he had been "with Pa during the time of his last illness and up until the day that he no longer knew anyone.... He was cheerful and his same old self right up to the last." [20]

Before they reached Algiers, Hopkins came on deck and sat with the President and his daughter Anna. At length Hopkins told FDR that he and Chip Bohlen wanted to get off in Algiers. He needed to rest and proposed to spend a few days in Marrakech and then fly home. Roosevelt could not understand it. Anyone could rest better in a ship than anywhere else. But Hopkins was firm. Anna tried to argue with him after he had left the President, but to no avail. Hopkins knew he would find little rest on the voyage home because Roosevelt wanted him to work on the speech he would have to deliver to Congress on the Yalta Conference. When Anna reported back to her father, he said wearily, "Let him go."

On February 18, the *Quincy* reached Algiers, and immediately after lunch, Hopkins stopped in to say goodbye to Roosevelt. The farewell was not very cordial. FDR was irritated to be left with all the work. He put out his hand and said "Goodbye" and turned away.

So the two great friends parted. They never saw each other again.

When the ship was on the way to Gibraltar, Pa Watson died. Roosevelt had no one except Sam Rosenman, who had been summoned from London, to help him. Roosevelt later said that he believed Harry Hopkins had left because he was bored.

Hopkins remained a few days in Marrakech at the Taylor villa. Then he flew home via the Azores and Bermuda and arrived in Washington on February 24. Three days later he left for the Mayo Clinic, "which," as he wrote John Hertz, "is very discouraging, but I am sure this time it is not too serious and I should not be there too long." [21]

He was still there six weeks later when death came to Franklin D. Roosevelt in Warm Springs.

CHAPTER TWENTY

Last Days

Disillusion set in over the Yalta agreements almost as soon as Roosevelt made his report to Congress on March 2, 1945. Critics assailed the U.N. veto as giving Russia an advantage and wondered what other sellouts had been made. In Moscow, British, American and Russian representatives made little progress in the face of Soviet intransigence. *Pravda* announced that Foreign Minister Molotov would not go to San Francisco for the meeting to draft the charter of the United Nations. Since Eden would represent Britain and Stettinius the United States, the substitution of Ambassador Andrei Gromyko for Molotov seemed a calculated affront to the United States and Great Britain.

Roosevelt planned the American delegation to San Francisco with great care. He intended to avoid the mistake of Woodrow Wilson, who had refused to take any Republicans to Versailles. Congressional members would be Senators Arthur Vandenberg and Tom Connally and Representatives Sol Bloom and Charles A. Eaton. On March 23, Roosevelt called these men to the White House for a briefing and confided to them the arrangement of three votes for Russia and three for the United States in the General Assembly if the Americans decided they needed them. They were never used. This information leaked to the newspapers.

At the Mayo Clinic, Hopkins saw the whole story of the extra votes as an opportunity for the isolationists to seize the reins again and as a chance for Roosevelt's enemies to reassert themselves. His fears seemed justified when the Senate rejected Roosevelt's nomination of Aubrey Williams to head the Rural Electrification Administration. Williams, of course, had been

Hopkins' main assistant back in WPA days. Vindictive old Senator Kenneth McKellar of Tennessee led the opposition. McKellar had no personal objections to Williams; it was what he represented. Aubrey Williams stood for everything hated by the old guard and the conservatives of the South. As the living embodiment of the worst of the New Deal, he had to be destroyed. Old canards about FERA and WPA were dragged out. McKellar, although not a member of the Senate Agriculture Committee, insisted on testifying as a witness and insulted Williams unmercifully. Voting to reject his confirmation were nineteen Democrats, most of them from the South. Williams' defeat served notice that Congress intended to bring Roosevelt to heel after he had been riding so high in his conduct of the war.

As he left for Warm Springs shortly after the Senate had turned Williams down, Roosevelt anticipated a fight on his hands in dealing with Congress in the years ahead. Was it to be 1937 all over again?

On the afternoon of April 12, the telephone rang in Hopkins' room in the Mayo Clinic. Chip Bohlen was on the line. Hopkins listened and then was silent for a long time. Finally he said, "I guess I better be going to Washington." [1]

His first coherent thought was to tell someone. It had to be Churchill:

APRIL 12, 1945

PRIME MINISTER WINSTON S. CHURCHILL
LONDON
LEAVING HERE TOMORROW TO ATTEND SERVICES IN WASHINGTON AND HYDE PARK. WILL CABLE YOU ALL THE DETAILS TOMORROW. I CANNOT TELL YOU WHAT GOES THROUGH MY MIND AND HEART. ALL I KNOW IS THAT WE HAVE LOST ONE OF OUR GREATEST FRIENDS AND THE WORLD ITS MOST OUTSTANDING CHAMPION OF HUMAN FREEDOM AND JUSTICE.

HARRY L. HOPKINS [2]

He called up Robert Sherwood to talk. He seemed, according to Sherwood, to be exalted, saying, "You and I have got something great that we can take with us all the rest of our lives. It's a great realization. Because it's *true* what so many people believed about him and what made them love him. The President never let them down." [3]

The next day, he flew to Washington. On Saturday Hopkins conferred with the new President of the United States, Harry S. Truman. Like most Presidents, Roosevelt had kept his Vice-President largely in the dark. Truman knew almost nothing of what had gone on at Yalta, what the Joint and Combined Chiefs were thinking, what sort of a person Churchill was. And Stalin.

The men talked on. At that moment, Hopkins was indispensable to the United States because only he could tell the new President the things he had to know. The war was not over. There could be no faltering of leadership.

Truman ordered lunch trays brought in, and the two Harrys continued their discussion. They ranged the world, and they covered the personalities of the world leaders. Churchill. Stalin. Eden. Molotov. Ismay. Brooke. Attlee. Eisenhower. Nimitz. MacArthur. Chiang Kai-shek. Soong. The list was endless.

Truman asked Hopkins to render him the same kind of service that he had given Roosevelt, but Hopkins refused. He was too ill and too weak. He would make all his papers available and he would help any time Truman really needed him, but he could not stand the strain of steady work. Truman accepted those terms.

At 4:00 that afternoon the service for the funeral of Franklin Delano Roosevelt began in the East Room of the White House. Half an hour earlier, mourners had begun to enter the room, including both friends and foes of the late President. Thomas E. Dewey was there and so was Big Jim Farley. Delegations from both houses of Congress and members of the Supreme Court joined the military and civilians who filled the room almost to overflowing. Louise Hopkins sat in one of the folding chairs, her husband standing behind her. The Right Reverend Angus Dun, Bishop of Washington, announced the hymn, "Eternal Father, Strong to Save." Hopkins broke into sobs as the singing began. Eleanor Roosevelt noted that he looked as though he were about to die himself.

When the services were over, Hopkins saw reporters briefly, but parried their questions. "I just came back to say goodbye to a very good friend of mine." Asked whether he would remain as a principal adviser to Truman, he answered, "Naturally, like every other citizen, I would want to do everything I could to help him make his administration a success. But there should be no implication in that general statement that should apply to me personally." 4

Robert Sherwood and his wife accompanied the Hopkinses to their house in Georgetown, and Harry went to bed immediately. But Sherwood was amazed to see the old fire in his eyes, and he talked of the job ahead.

> God damn it, now we've got to get to work on our own. This is where we've really got to begin. We've had it too easy all this time because we knew he was there, and we had the privilege of being able to get to him. Whatever we thought was the matter with the world, whatever we felt ought to be done about it, we could take our ideas to him, and if he thought there was any merit in them, or if anything that we said got him started on a train of thought of his own, then we'd see him go ahead and

do it, and no matter how tremendous it might be or how idealistic he wasn't scared of it. Well—he isn't there now, and we've got to find a way to do things by ourselves.

I'm pretty sure that Jimmy Byrnes and Henry Wallace and Harold Ickes are saying right now that they'd be President of the United States today if it weren't for me. But this time I didn't have anything to do with it. I'm certain that the President had made up his mind on Truman long before I got back to the White House last year. I think he would have preferred Bill Douglas, because he knew him better and he always liked Bill's toughness. But nobody really influential was pushing for Douglas. I think he'd gone off fishing out in Oregon or someplace. And Bob Hannegan [Chairman of the Democratic National Committee] was certainly pushing for Harry Truman and the President believed he could put him over at the Convention. So the President told him to go ahead and even put it in writing when Bob asked him to. People seemed to think that Truman was just suddenly pulled out of a hat—but that wasn't true. The President had had his eye on him for a long time. The Truman Committee record was good—he'd got himself known and liked around the country—and above all he was very popular in the Senate. That was the biggest consideration. The President wanted somebody that would help him when he went up there and asked them to ratify the peace.

[Then, somewhat inconsistently in view of the beginning of the conversation, Hopkins said that most of the members of the Roosevelt administration, except for Stimson and Forrestal, should resign. He intended to do so himself immediately.] Truman has got to have his own people around him, not Roosevelt's. If we were around, we'd always be looking at him and he'd know we were thinking, "The *President* wouldn't do it that way!" [5]

Although he had intended to go to Hyde Park for the burial, Hopkins felt too weak to stand the trip and the emotional strain of the service. So the Sherwoods left him in bed and went on to Union Station to board the funeral train.[6]

Truman wanted to keep Hopkins' services as long as possible. He wrote: "I, too, trusted him implicitly, and unless his health had been seriously impaired I hoped that he would continue with me in the same role he had played with my predecessor." [7] Hopkins, however, felt that he could not go on much longer and said that he planned to leave the government on May 12, a month after the death of President Roosevelt. That would be ample time to fill the new President in on what he knew.

When he was not briefing Truman, Hopkins spent most of the time in his home, reading, resting, and worrying about things he could no longer oversee. He dictated occasional memoranda setting the record straight on events as he knew them. Thus, after Roosevelt's death Stalin changed his mind and did send Molotov to San Francisco. According to the stories released to the papers, the initiative came from Truman, but Hopkins noted the full story that Harriman had arranged matters. The purpose of the incorrect account given the papers, Hopkins stated in a memo, "was, obviously, to give Truman an advantageous break with the American public which was quite understandable, but it was a political decision made by Justice Byrnes." [8] Hopkins wrote a similar memo denying a story by Drew Pearson that the Americans and British at Yalta had agreed to let the Russians capture Berlin.

He wrote such notes in order to have the facts clear after his retirement from government, when he planned to write several books. He still considered the idea of becoming Director of the Roosevelt Library at Hyde Park, and there he would have time to write. He corresponded with publishers and editors of magazines and finally engaged Brandt and Brandt as literary agents.

Almost all of his old friends visited him at his home when they could, and he kept pretty well up to date on the war, fast drawing to a close in Europe. On May 4, which marked the end of effective German resistance in the west, he received a telegram from Eden, Molotov, and Stettinius, then in San Francisco working on the United Nations Charter:

> AT A DINNER LAST NIGHT WE THREE DRANK A SPECIAL TOAST TO YOU IN SINCERE RECOGNITION OF THE OUTSTANDING PART YOU PERSONALLY HAVE PLAYED IN BRINGING OUR THREE COUNTRIES TOGETHER IN THE COMMON CAUSE. WE REGRET THAT YOU ARE NOT WITH US AT THIS MOMENT OF VICTORY.
>
> WITH OUR AFFECTIONATE PERSONAL REGARDS.[9]

In a special broadcast commemorating VE Day, NBC arranged for many prominent men who had played significant roles in winning the war to join in a roundup of statements. Hopkins was included:

> As the bells ring out, proclaiming the surrender and destruction of the Germany army, none of us can forget who has won the victory. It was won by the fighting men of our armed forces, and those of our gallant allies. To our soldiers, our sailors and airmen, to British Tommies, to the Red Army, to the underground fighters, belongs the everlasting glory. Millions have been wounded and killed that we might be free.
>
> But there can be no real elation in America until our cruel and bitter enemy in Japan is completely destroyed. Every soldier, sailor, and marine in that far Pacific must know that the whole might of our country will be thrown against that last stronghold of tyranny.
>
> One thing above all we owe to the Allied armies in Europe, and that is this: Had they not crushed the Nazi power in Germany, the San Francisco conference could never have taken place; for Hitler would have ordered us to Berlin and the whole world would have been the slaves of Germany.

But now we can go to whatever church we like. No one can choose our friends. We can say what we please. All because American, British, French and Russian boys fought, bled and died on the battlefield.

Surely if the soldiers of the United States, Great Britain, France and the Soviet Union can fight together and win a glorious military victory, then, indeed, in spite of every difficulty, the Allied statesmen in San Francisco will create the basis for a just and lasting peace.

I cannot but think today of that little garden in Hyde Park where Franklin Roosevelt lies in eternal peace. No man in the world contributed more to victory and freedom. And I believe that the free people of the earth will forever bless his name.[10]

But the fair promises of international cooperation which Hopkins and others mentioned in their VE Day broadcasts proved more illusion than fact. Already the Soviet Union had shown that it would interpret the Yalta agreements to suit itself in Eastern Europe. In San Francisco, Stettinius and Harriman battled Soviet intransigence, but the Lublin Poles remained in control in Warsaw. Molotov, flatly denying the agreement at Yalta, stalled the San Francisco meeting by insisting on big power veto in the Security Council of procedural as well as substantive matters. This disagreement threatened to end the United Nations even before it was begun.

In a meeting with the press, Harriman stated:

We must recognize that our objectives and the Kremlin's objectives are irreconcilable. The Kremlin wants to promote Communist dictatorships controlled from Moscow, whereas we want, as far as possible to see a world of governments responsive to the will of the people.[11]

Many commentators blamed Harriman for the deterioration of relations with Russia. In the euphoria of the times, newsmen could not understand how Harriman could have spent so much time in Russia and failed to discern her real nature. Of course, Harriman did understand; it was the idealistic reporters who clung to illusions.

Harriman had these matters very much in mind as he and Chip Bohlen flew back to Washington on May 9. They discussed the deterioration in Soviet-American relations since the Yalta Conference and the rigid Russian positions at San Francisco. They also talked about the case of the sixteen missing Polish leaders, lured from their homes with a promise of a meeting with Marshal Zhukov, Russian commander in the occupied areas. The Poles had disappeared, and only a few days before, Molotov had told Stettinius that they had been arrested on charges of "diversionist activities against the Red Army."

Bohlen suggested that it might be a good idea if Hopkins could go to Moscow to talk to Stalin face to face.

> I jumped at the idea [Harriman remembered later]. Stalin had told me of his respect for Hopkins' courage and determination. He had been particularly impressed that Hopkins should have made the long trip to Russia in July 1941 in spite of his ill health. Stalin also knew that Hopkins was Roosevelt's most intimate and loyal associate. I was concerned, however, whether Hopkins would be well enough to stand the rough trip. So, before proposing the mission to Truman, I went to see Hopkins. I found him ill and feeble in the little Georgetown house he was renting.[12]

Hopkins was equally enthusiastic, but feared President Truman would veto the plan. He was right. When Harriman went to the White House to make the suggestion, Truman said no. After Harriman had spent considerable time arguing, Truman said he would like to think it over, and Hopkins spent several anxious days worrying that it would all come to nothing.

While he was waiting, Hopkins decided that the trip to Moscow, if he made it, would be his last service for the government. He confided his decision to a few friends, including General Marshall, who replied promptly:

> I have just read your note of May 12 and appreciate your writing. I will treat the matter as most confidential.
>
> As a matter of fact I was not at all surprised to get your news. Political repercussions seemed to indicate such action and your state of health would make it advisable, because you have literally given of your physical strength during the past three years to a degree that has been, in my opinion, heroic and will never be appreciated except by your intimates.
>
> For myself, I wish to tell you this, that you personally have been of invaluable service to me in the discharge of my duties in this war. Time after time you have done for me things I was finding it exceedingly difficult to do for myself and always in matters of the gravest import. You have been utterly selfless as well as courageous and purely objective in your contribution to the war effort.
>
> I am very glad that you are actually to be released from further obligations except of your own personal choosing because I think you owe it to yourself and your family, and I might also say to your friends.[13]

Truman consulted the State Department and Jimmy Byrnes on whether he should send Hopkins to Moscow, and both were opposed, but Cordell Hull from his retirement thought it an excellent idea, and Truman decided to take his advice.

Hopkins had several sessions with Truman for briefing and left for Paris on May 23, accompanied by his wife. Harriman went on ahead to talk to Churchill and tell him of Hopkins' mission. On May 24, Harriman joined Hopkins in Paris and the two lunched with Eisenhower before going on to Moscow. Eisenhower was full of the difficulties of dealing with the Russians now that the war in Europe had ended and was particularly disturbed that the Russians had not yet named a representative to the Allied Control Council for Germany.

Flying to Moscow on the evening of May 25, Hopkins, Louise, Harriman, and Chip Bohlen viewed mile after mile of battered buildings and blasted trees. Passing over the ruins of Berlin, Hopkins remarked, "It's another Carthage."

Hopkins hoped for quick agreement with Stalin on the issues that divided Russia and the United States, but Harriman had his doubts. As ambassador, he had experienced all of the frustrations in dealing with the Russians.

The first meeting took place at 8:00 the next evening in Stalin's office in the Kremlin. Present were Hopkins, Harriman, and Bohlen on the American side, and Stalin, Molotov, and Pavlov, the interpreter, on the Russian side.

Stalin's greeting was cordial. As Bohlen later noted, Stalin "certainly went out of his way to be extremely courteous to Hopkins, not only because of his regard for the adviser to Roosevelt but also because he wanted to make a slight bow in the direction of the new President." [14]

The talks went on for ten days, and it seemed that Hopkins was getting everything he asked for. The matter of the veto on procedural matters cleared up quickly when Hopkins explained the issue to Stalin. Molotov grumpily tried to defend his action, but Stalin dismissed his argument and said the Soviet Union would accept the American and British view. The veto would not apply to procedural matters.

There were matters of misunderstandings on curtailment of Lend-Lease now that the war was over, and Stalin accepted Hopkins' statements and explanations. Truman had asked Hopkins to find out when Russia would enter the war against Japan, and Stalin told him unequivocally that Russian troops would be in place along the Manchurian border by August 8. Stalin agreed to meet with Truman and Churchill at Potsdam in Germany beginning July 15.

Then came the failures. Hopkins could not win the release of any of the sixteen missing Poles. The most Stalin would do was suggest some leniency for a few whose crimes were not as grave as those of the rest.

Hopkins pushed for implementation of the Yalta agreement to widen the Warsaw government to include representatives of the Free Poles in London. Stalin agreed that four or five places in the government might be held by the non-Lublin Poles. Encouraged, Hopkins went on to explain what free elections meant to Americans: freedom of speech, of assembly, secret votes, and all political parties, except Fascists, represented. Stalin admitted that such freedoms might be extended in peacetime, but even then under certain limitations. Russia would insist on a friendly government in Poland, and that clearly meant one subordinate to Russian control.

(After Hopkins had returned to Washington, Truman and Churchill had to give up trying to save Poland from becoming a Russian satellite. They recognized the Lublin government, and even though Stalin kept his promise and allowed a few Poles from London to join the government, they had no real power, despite the fact that one was named Deputy Prime Minister. Eventually they had to flee the country to avoid arrest.)

The Russians extended lavish hospitality to Hopkins and Louie during their stay in Moscow. At a dinner in the Kremlin on June 1, Hopkins had a private talk with Stalin, only the interpreter Pavlov being present. He tried again to win the freedom of the sixteen Poles, but Stalin refused to budge.

> I closed the conversation [Hopkins wrote later] by telling him that I thought the real solution lay in his releasing these men entirely so that we could clear the atmosphere not only for the immediate discussions about Poland but in preparation for the Berlin [Potsdam] Conference.
> He repeated that the men should be tried but that he would let me know.[15]

Hopkins never heard further from Stalin on the matter.

The Russians tried to present Louise Hopkins with some gift to take back to America. One day a truck arrived at the American embassy with a large variety of beautiful fur coats, white fox, blue fox, black fox, red fox, ermine, and mink. There were expensive brocades and precious and semiprecious stones. She was invited to make a selection. Hopkins, mindful of the furor over the "Beaverbrook emeralds," would let her accept only a small semiprecious Ural stone as a memento.

On the night of June 6, Hopkins bade Stalin farewell, and the next morning, the Hopkinses and Bohlen flew to Berlin. Marshal Zhukov acted as host there, arranging a tour of the ruined city and serving them lunch at a light buffet, which Bohlen described as "light on food, heavy on vodka." [16] During lunch they discussed arrangements for the forthcoming meeting of the Big Three in Potsdam.

Flying on to Frankfurt am Main, they stayed overnight with General Eisenhower. Hopkins later wrote a note describing some of the events of his stay in Frankfurt. It opens with a statement on negotiating on the Polish question, and then continues:

> When I reached Frankfurt there was an urgent telephone message from Churchill which I answered and in which he insisted on my going to London. I stalled about this, telling him my health was not too good and that I thought I ought to get right back but would let him know, and that under any circumstances I would not go without the approval of the President. I felt it unwise for me to go to England and see Churchill before

reporting to Truman, so I gave Churchill no encouragement. Churchill wired Truman and Truman replied in the negative to Churchill. I was not acquainted with this until I got to Paris when Churchill again called me and told me the answer had come from Truman and expressed great regret at the decision and acted a little petulant about it over the telephone. I told him, however, that there was nothing I could do about it and, under any circumstances, my health was such that I felt I should not do anything but go right home.[17]

The lengthy memorandum describes several conversations with Eisenhower on politics, and his troubles with the Russians and with De Gaulle. Eisenhower arranged for Harry and Louise to have the suite he maintained in the Raphael Hotel in Paris, and on Friday afternoon, June 8, they flew to the French capital, where they spent the weekend seeing friends and inspecting Louise's apartment and furnishings, which had survived the German occupation intact.

On the evening of June 11, Hopkins and Bohlen embarked on the flight to Washington. Louise remained in Paris at the request of the Army authorities to visit several hospitals and to arrange for the shipment of her personal belongings home.

On the way across the Atlantic, Bohlen and Hopkins talked over what they had accomplished in Russia. Bohlen, who knew the Russians far better than Hopkins, expressed alarm at the tendency of the Americans, both military and civilian, to believe that if they gave trust to the Soviets, they would win trust in return. When he heard General Lucius D. Clay in Frankfurt repeat this assertion, Bohlen told Clay that within a few months, he would become one of the American high officials most opposed to the Soviets. Bohlen's prediction proved true.

Despite his optimism, Hopkins had his reservations. He knew the serious limitations on individual freedom in the Soviet Union, and Stalin's remarks on the sixteen Poles confirmed that civil liberties as understood in the United States were unknown to the Soviet mind. He feared that there would be stormy times ahead. But he did not foresee the Cold War. He thought that a resurgent Germany presented a greater menace than Russia. To Winant he wrote on his return:

> The Germany I saw was a shambles, but I confess I am a little disquieted by suggestions I hear from some quarters that we do little or nothing to prevent the Germans from starting this business all over again. I have no confidence in them whatever but I have a good healthy respect for their ability to hit us again in another 25 years.[18]

On his return to Washington, Hopkins enjoyed the best press he had ever known. Commentators lauded his achievements in Moscow as ushering in a whole new era of understanding and cooperation with the Soviet Union. Certainly he tried, and he could not be blamed for the fact that no one could have diverted Russia from the course she was determined to follow in the wake of the war in Europe.

Hopkins' last mission cannot be called a success. But he did as much as anyone could have. No one could have wrung more concessions from Stalin, and most would have achieved less.

The day following his return to the United States, Hopkins had breakfast with Truman and gave him a full verbal account. Actually he amplified the reports he had filed from Moscow and also filled in the President on Stalin's manner and the personal details he would need in the forthcoming Potsdam Conference.

After the breakfast, Hopkins returned to his Georgetown house and went to bed to recover from a bug he had picked up in Europe. At least so he wrote his friends. It seems more likely that he needed to recover from the exhaustion of the trip.

More than one Washington correspondent predicted that as a result of the Moscow trip he would have a role in the new administration as personal adviser to Truman just as he had been to Roosevelt. But Hopkins knew better. He knew that he had been the essential transitional figure, the only one who could give Truman the information and background he needed in the early days. But those days were ending. When Hopkins returned to the United States from Moscow, Roosevelt had been dead for two months, and the Truman leadership was emerging. Even if he had been well, Hopkins realized that he would have no large part to play with President Truman.

On his arrival home he found in the mass of accumulated correspondence a letter from Judge Sam Rosenman that seemed to offer the solution to his problem. Rosenman had hoped to leave the government to accept a job in New York, but Truman persuaded him to stay on for another year. Rosenman immediately thought of Hopkins for the job and wrote:

> That turn of events made it impossible for me to act as impartial chairman in the Ladies Garment Industry. I called David Dubinsky [head of the International Ladies' Garment Workers Union] and told him of my decision and suggested that you be substituted for me.
>
> He has just phoned me and said that the employers are agreeable. David Dubinsky expects to be in Washington . . . and wants to talk with you. I think you should have a word with me before you see him.[19]

The upshot of all this was that Hopkins did get the post of Impartial Chairman Coat and Suit Industry, to give the official name from the letterhead. It paid a salary of $25,000 a year, ten thousand more than Hopkins had earned in the service of the country. As he wrote to

Beaverbrook: "My salary is paid half by the industry and half by the union and it only requires a day a week and no very arduous work at that." [20]

While negotiations for this job were going on, Hopkins was giving some time to the problems of the continuing war in the Pacific and to those of conversion of the economy to peacetime. Truman invited him to Potsdam, but Hopkins hoped that he would not have to go. When Truman replaced Stettinius as Secretary of State with James Byrnes, it settled the matter. Hopkins knew that his presence in Potsdam would tend to sideline Byrnes, for Stalin and Churchill would talk with him rather than with Byrnes or even, for that matter, Truman. Accordingly, on July 2 he wrote the President:

> Dear Mr. President:
> The time has come when I must take a rest. I have, therefore, reached the decision that I should now retire from the Government Service and, hence, not be able to accompany you to the Berlin area for your impending conference with Mr. Churchill and Mr. Stalin.
> I want you to know how, along with millions of other Americans, I applaud your courageous and liberal administration of this government's domestic and foreign policy. The fact that you have and are surrounding yourself with competent and able men but adds to the confidence this nation has in you.
> If I express my gratitude for your more than generous attitude toward me personally—it is that you may know that I leave the Government with a deep satisfaction in your confidence.

Truman replied the next day:

> Dear Harry:
> I am sorry that I cannot persuade you to remain in government any longer. I should have liked it not only because of the great service which you could continue to render to the nation, but also because it would have given me great pleasure to have you associated with my Administration.
> However, I understand fully the reasons which prompted your decision—and I do not feel that I can justifiably ignore them.
> There are few people in the United States who know more fully than I the substantial role which you have played in the prosecution of our war. I know how much President Roosevelt relied upon you as he started the nation on the hard task of preparation to meet aggression from abroad. . . .
> I am sure that you must feel much pride and a deep sense of accomplishment in all your great and patriotic service to our country during the last twelve years.
> I know that I shall have to call upon you in the future—and I hope that you will soon be fully and completely recovered so that you can give me the benefit of your counsel. [21]

Now that he had gone, even Hopkins' former enemies and critics had kind words to say about him. But he never cared about those. What he did value were the comments of his friends who knew what he had done. General Ismay wrote: "I shall always regard you as one of the few outstanding figures of these war years, and I shall remember your courage, your helpful kindness, and your warm friendship as long as I live." [22] Beaverbrook wired: I MUST SAY THAT YOU HAVE MADE THE LARGEST CONTRIBUTION OUTSIDE THAT OF YOUR DEAD FRIEND AND I SHALL EVER REMAIN YOUR ADMIRING DEVOTED AND AFFECTIONATE FRIEND.[23]

These typify the letters and telegrams Hopkins received from both the famous and the unknown. There was even a little poem sent from England, using the name Roosevelt had given him, Harry the Hop. One verse read:

> Let us recognise now, that in writing the roll
> Of those who have brought us so near to our goal,
> We must put in a place of his own at the top
> That courageous American, Harry the Hop.[24]

Oxford University invited him to come in October to accept the honorary degree of Doctor of Civil Laws "in recognition of your eminent services to the Allied cause." [25] Unhappily, Harry Hopkins was not fated to make the trip to England.

The next busy weeks involved the furious activity of moving out of the Georgetown house and finding a place to live in New York. The Hopkinses finally settled on 1046 Fifth Avenue. He wrote Diana:

> You are going to be delighted with the new house. Your room is overlooking Central Park, big enough for you to rattle around in, with a bathroom of your own. Mummy says you are going to have to make your own bed this year, so you better learn how. There is an entrance to the park just a block away and plenty of room to play in the house so you won't be knocking everybody down after this. It is right on the bus line to your school. I would not think it would take you more than 5 or 10 minutes at the most to get to school. If it pleases you any, there are movies all over the place.[26]

On August 4, Harry and Louise Hopkins left Washington to move to New York and then on to Maine for a ten-day vacation. Among other things, he wanted time to think over the various offers he had received from publishers. He finally settled on Harper & Brothers, who offered a huge advance and the services of Cass Canfield as editor.

Before he left Washington, Hopkins was shaken by the defeat of the Conservative Party in the British general election, which necessitated Churchill's resignation as Prime Minister. He congratulated the victorious

Clement Attlee and commiserated Churchill. To Hopkins it seemed that all the giants of the war were going down, one after another.

One of the minor occupations that helped to fill his time was the writing of letters of resignation. He had held so many government posts that he could not remember what they all were until he had his secretary compile a list. One such letter he addressed to Truman in Potsdam. Truman replied:

> Your July tenth letter resigning as Chairman of the President's Soviet Protocol Committee reached me in Babelsburg, just outside of Berlin and Potsdam, where I was billeted.
>
> The first time you are in Washington I wish you would come in and see me. There are several things I want to talk to you about.

Added in longhand to the typed letter was, "Take care of yourself! *Get well.*"27

On September 4, Hopkins went to Washington for the last time to receive the Distinguished Service Medal, which President Truman presented in the Rose Garden of the White House. Later Truman wrote him:

> ...for your information, I don't think I have ever performed a ceremony, since I have been President, which gave me as much satisfaction as the one when I pinned the Distinguished Service Medal on you.
>
> The only other one that at all rivals it was the Medal of Honor for General [Jonathan] Wainwright [who had been a prisoner of the Japanese from 1942 to 1945].28

On September 6 Hopkins was formally inducted as Impartial Chairman at the Astor Hotel. The war had finally ended four days earlier with the Japanese surrender aboard the battleship *Missouri* in Tokyo Bay, and the transition to peace was on the mind of everyone. Hopkins tried in his induction speech to face some of the problems, but more important, the address was a profession of faith. As his last formal public utterance, it is worth noting:

> America is now faced with two great tasks, both of which require immediate action. The one task relates to the transfer of a whole nation from a war time economy to the attainment of economic prosperity in the pursuit of peace. The other encompasses the part the United States is to play in securing a lasting peace.
>
> If I speak of our domestic problems first, it is because every nation that would exercise its influence abroad must have within itself the moral vitality and economic strength that will give its citizens confidence in their own security and well being.
>
> I believe most Americans interpret a good life in very simple terms. We desire an opportunity to earn a living and we desire the establishment of conditions in which that basic right can be fulfilled.

There are some who recoil from this expression, feeling that in some mysterious way, the opportunity to earn a living will lead to the destruction of our lives by bureaucratic government, and worse, that it will destroy the incentive for hard work which has been so characteristic of our American tradition.

I believe that neither of these fears have a solid base. I believe that full employment must and can be attained within the framework of our traditional democratic processes. Having waged a total and successful war against the most powerful enemies on earth, it is unthinkable that we cannot implement the energies of our private economic system to win the peace at home. It is a contradiction in terms to proclaim on the one hand that our economic system is the best one in the world and on the other to admit that that system may not be able and certainly should not attempt to assure every man able and willing to work a right to an opportunity to secure the reasonable necessities of life that make up what we know as the American standard of living.

While there are many and varied things to be done to achieve our objective, there is one sure way to destroy any hope of its attainment and that is to encourage the processes that will lead to inflation. And this can be prevented only if there is the most patient and understanding cooperation amongst all of the groups responsible for our economic welfare. . . .

The gateway to a secure and prosperous America is open. And I believe we shall, passing thru that gate, find a way of life that will assure, for all time, the economic freedom of every American citizen. . . .

I have often been asked what interest we have in Poland, Greece, Iran or Korea. Well I think we have the most important business in the world— and indeed, the only business worthy of our traditions. And that is this—to do everything within our diplomatic power to foster and encourage democratic government throughout the world. We should not be timid about blazoning to the world our desire for the right of all peoples to have genuine civil liberty. We believe our dynamic democracy is the best in the world. Well, why not say so in a language the world will understand? . . .

But the forces of democracy are on the march in England, France, China and a host of other nations. I believe that our country's interests throughout the world are jeopardized by the advent of any kind of totalitarian government whatever its name or label. . . .

We rejoice in the promise of a world free and at peace.

We have an abiding faith in our way of life. . . .[29]

As a matter of fact, Hopkins had little to do as Impartial Chairman. He had to deal with only one routine case. He spent most of his time working at home on his proposed books. He planned to write at least two, one on the war, and one on the Roosevelt he knew. He engaged an assistant, Sidney Hyman, to help him in the vast task of organizing his papers, and his secretary of many years' standing, Miss Dorothea Krauss, to take dictation and type.

Unfortunately, practically nothing was done. As in 1940, when he was temporarily out of the government, Hopkins found it impossible to settle down to the long discipline of organizing and writing a book. His mind raced like the engine of a car not in gear. He would dictate a note of some event which he remembered, such as the origin of the Yalta Conference and of his stay with Eisenhower in Frankfurt on the way back from Moscow. But he never looked at the notes after they had been typed. One day he would work on the introduction to the book, and the next his mind would be on the Yalta Conference, and he would spend the time going over the papers on Crimea. When a story of a wartime revelation broke in the newspapers, he would feel a compulsion to open the files on the episode so that he could correct the record. But he never did. He did insist, however, that none of the important papers, even those that bore on his private life, should be destroyed. He told Hyman:

> This is the sort of thing I would object to having destroyed in the Roosevelt papers. The whole story of Roosevelt—and my story is part of it—is going to come out anyway in the next fifty years. I feel we will both come out with credit. And I don't see any point in trying to edit my past by destroying papers which showed precisely what I did and how I did it. I want people to know that I played politics; I also want them to know *why* I played politics.[30]

Hopkins had a keen sense of the importance of history, but he was not the man to write it. At the time of his death, all that existed were the raw materials and a few scattered notes.

When he was not engaged in working on his papers, he wrote many letters to friends, as though their replies would indicate to him that he was not forgotten. He saw a great deal of Bernard Baruch, who lived nearby, and many friends dropped in for a drink and a chat.

During October, his health began to fail again, and on the fourth he wired Lord Halifax asking him to inform the Oxford University authorities that he would not be able to come to England to accept the honorary degree and inquiring if it could be postponed until the following June. By the middle of the month, he was confined to the house, mostly to his own bedroom. On November 9, he informed Edward Stettinius in a letter that he was going to Memorial Hospital in New York City. "It concerns nothing more than trying to find out how to keep well once I show signs of improvement. I am not disturbed about it altho it is an awful bore." [31]

He had no easy hospital stay. In the first place, he was worried about money. His medical bills and rent on the Fifth Avenue residence ate up his salary as Impartial Chairman and also the large advances he had received for his proposed books. He had to go into debt, but fortunately Bernard Baruch was ready to lend generously with no expectation of repayment.

Another worry was the Joint Congressional Committee to investigate the surprise attack on Pearl Harbor. He feared, and with good cause, that the Republicans and isolationists on the committee would use the occasion to fix the blame on Roosevelt, and that he would be dragged in and his conduct castigated. Although the revisionist historians tried hard to prove that Roosevelt enticed the Japanese into attacking Pearl Harbor to justify his own plans and to get the United States into the war, they ignored Hopkins. He read the reports of the hearings each day, and he wrote to Secretary Forrestal for information in case he had a chance to testify. But even though he tried hard to persuade his doctors to let him go, they refused.

All through the Christmas and New Year holidays, Hopkins stayed in his room in the hospital. In mid-January, 1946, Churchill made his first visit to the United States since he had stepped down as Prime Minister. Leaving the ship in New York, he embarked immediately for Florida, where he wired:

> I AM SO SORRY THAT MY CONTINUOUS PASSAGE THROUGH NEW YORK DID NOT ENABLE ME TO COME TO SEE YOU AS I HAD PLANNED IF WE HAD PAUSED AS ORIGINALLY ARRANGED. I AM LONGING TO SEE YOU EITHER IN WASHINGTON OR NEW YORK MY DEAR FRIEND. WITH EVERY GOOD WISH FROM,
>
> CLEMMIE AND WINSTON.[32]

Churchill ever after regretted that he did not pause in New York, for Hopkins was dead before the former Prime Minister left Florida.

On January 22, Hopkins wrote what seems to be the last letter of his life. Addressed to Churchill, it showed flashes of Hopkins' humor:

> My dear Winston:
>
> Only being laid up in the hospital prevented me from meeting you at the boat the other day and I do hope you will find it possible to get to New York because it appears altogether unlikely that I could possibly be in Florida during the next month.
>
> All I can say about myself at the moment is that I am getting excellent care, while the doctors are struggling over a very bad case of cirrhosis of the liver—not due, I regret to say, from taking too much alcohol. But I must say that I dislike having the effect of a long life of congenial and useful drinking and neither deserve the reputation nor enjoy its pleasures.
>
> The newspapers indicate you and Clemmie are having a quiet and delightful time and I hope you won't let any Congressional Committee of ours bore you.
>
> Do give my love to Clemmie and Sarah, all of whom I shall hope to see before you go back, but I want to have a good talk with you over the state of world affairs, to say nothing of our private lives.[33]

Sometime in January, Robert visited his father in Memorial Hospital to say goodbye before going out to the West Coast. "He always had these miraculous recoveries," Robert noted, "but this time he looked so dreadful that I decided the only thing that might pull him out would be if President Truman would send him on a mission." [34]

Robert called Truman, who said he would think it over. But the doctors put their feet down. It made no difference, for this time the miraculous recovery failed. The end came at 11:35 on the morning of January 29, 1946. His wife was at his bedside.

The funeral took place on Friday, February 1, in St. Bartholomew's Episcopal Church, at 2:00. Except for Robert, who wanted to remember his father as he was alive, all the surviving family members attended, including David and his wife Cherry, Hopkins' brother Lewis, his sister Adah, and notables without number.

The workers in the garment industry observed five minutes of silence as the services began.

The rites were conducted by the Reverend George Paull T. Sargent, Rector of St. Bartholomew's, assisted by the Reverend Russell J. Clinchy, who had performed the funeral service for Barbara Hopkins and the wedding rites for Harry and Louise. The hymns, with one or two exceptions, were the same as those Hopkins had heard nearly ten months earlier at the funeral of his friend and mentor, Franklin D. Roosevelt. Honorary pallbearers were Bernard Baruch, Howard Hunter, James Forrestal, David Dubinsky, Lord Halifax, Isadore Lubin, Felix Frankfurter, and David Niles.

Among the many editorials commenting on Hopkins' death, a small number by unregenerate Roosevelt haters took up the familiar surly refrain that Hopkins had never been elected to public office and that steps would have to be taken to prevent the phenomenon of a Harry Hopkins in the White House from ever occurring again.

It was a vain hope. During the Roosevelt years, the character of the American government, for better or worse, changed permanently and irrevocably. During those years, America changed from a major power to a superpower, and the old, lingering concept of sovereign States coordinated by the federal government became obsolete. In his first Inaugural, Roosevelt sounded the note of a strong federal government prepared to act in the emergency for the good of all the people. Where Hoover had believed that the problems of unemployment and relief belonged to the States, Roosevelt saw them as responsibilities of the nation. Only the power of the federal government could deal with them.

From the beginning, Presidents had relied on the Cabinet as advisers and executive officers. While Roosevelt respected the institution of the Cabinet, he did not feel that it could solve all problems. That was the reason for the

Brain Trust. FDR was ready to take ideas where he found them. If they came from Cabinet members, well and good, and if they came from Moley and Tugwell, equally good. Strong Cabinet members, such as Frances Perkins, Henry Morgenthau, and Harold Ickes, were as much Brain Trusters as the men drawn from academe. All of them found themselves performing many extra-Cabinet duties.

Roosevelt did not emasculate the Cabinet as a policy-making body. He deemphasized it. During the first Hundred Days he established the earliest of the many boards, commissions, agencies, administrations, and committees to deal with specific problems in fighting the depression. Unlike Cabinet officials, their heads were not subject to Senatorial approval; in fact the only restraints Congress had were the power to withhold funds and the power to investigate. But most went on and on, multiplied exponentially when the war came.

All of this new organization needed coordination. Theoretically each head of a major agency had the same right of access to the President enjoyed by a Cabinet member. There was no way that the President could see them all as often as they demanded audience. There had to be some man whose loyalty and judgment Roosevelt trusted to handle the problems, coordinate activities, and decide what should be done in most cases without bothering the President about it. In the beginning, Louis Howe had filled that role. But Howe was a consummate politician and not a man who really understood policy. He offered Roosevelt the friendship and companionship he required, but most of the difficult problems were beyond his ken and ended up on FDR's desk.

After Howe's death, Roosevelt tried his son James in the job, but James did not know the right people, he did not know the ways of the federal government, and the strain of the position led to ulcers which threatened his life and made it impossible for him to return to the work.

Hopkins, meanwhile, had grown ever closer to Roosevelt in friendship, and FDR came more and more to rely on his judgment. Before his illness at the end of 1937, Hopkins had a voice in matters far removed from WPA, and Roosevelt's decision to appoint him Secretary of Commerce was only in part to give him a buildup in his possible bid for the Presidency. It also meant that Hopkins, as a Cabinet member, would be in a position, officially, to set and help administer policy. His failing health, however, blocked the most effective use of his talents, and he went into obscurity for a time.

When he entered the White House on May 10, 1940, too ill to go home that night, no one could have foreseen the outcome. Probably neither he nor Roosevelt realized what he would do in the years ahead. The position of principal assistant to the President just evolved. At first, it was a case of Roosevelt sitting around in the evening in the Oval Study talking with a man who was a good listener and who would never betray his trust. Hopkins was not a "yes man," but he and FDR shared so many common attitudes that the social worker and the Hudson Valley patrician seldom disagreed, except on details—almost never on principles.

When Hopkins left the White House after the Democratic National Convention in 1940, the pleasant association seemed to end. But Roosevelt soon discovered that Hopkins had quietly done all kinds of little chores during that summer, and with him gone, they were coming right back to the President's desk. No one else could handle them. Pa Watson was great for poker and conversation, but he did not have the hard-headed knowledge of politics needed to get things done. Steve Early and Marvin McIntyre were secretaries and never ventured far outside that role.

When Hopkins came back to the White House during the 1940 campaign, he helped write Roosevelt's speeches, but that part of his job became minor as the months went on. He began to function as chief of staff. He had no pretense of authority other than the freedom to use the President's name. It seems unlikely that Roosevelt ever formally authorized such use, but when Hopkins called a manufacturer or a government official to say, "The President would like . . ." it took a bold man to say him nay.

In Hopkins Roosevelt found not only a companion who could laugh, joke, sympathize, and passionately discuss human suffering and the cause of freedom. He also found a coldly pragmatic mind able to cope with the jungle of Washington politics, a mind which could retain the details of production, material supply, and the tangle of organization of the Roosevelt administration.

Hopkins had a mind like a sponge. He could absorb, remember, and recall vast amounts of information. He also had a mind like a limpet, for once he had tackled a problem, he never let go until it was solved. He had no use for the fine arts of diplomacy when there was something to be done. Many a high-level ear in Washington and elsewhere in the United States burned red after a telephone conversation with Hopkins, which might begin, "Say, Joe, where the hell are those bearings for the B-17 engines . . . ?"

Yet he did learn diplomacy, not of what he called the "cookie pusher" kind, but of talking turkey to men such as Churchill and Stalin, Eden and Molotov. Behind his words lay the power based on a combination of his own integrity and the faith placed in him by Roosevelt. He no longer had any personal ambitions after his resignation as Secretary of Commerce but lived only to serve the country, which he could best do by serving the President of the United States, who happened to be his best friend.

But Hopkins had his weaknesses. He was jealous of his position and brooked no rival. He might have saved Thomas Corcoran's Washington career, but he did not lift a finger to do so. He blocked Byrnes's appointment as Secretary of State following the resignation of Cordell Hull because at that time he and Roosevelt were making the foreign policy of the United States. The appointment of the complaisant Edward Stettinius meant that happy arrangement could continue. As soon as he conveniently could after becoming President, Truman got rid of Stettinius and named Byrnes. That to Hopkins was probably the handwriting on the wall, for it was then he decided not to go to Potsdam with the new President and to resign from government service.

After Congress passed the Lend-Lease bill, Hopkins, as the first administrator, went at the job much as he had done when he first came to Washington, acting swiftly, decisively, cutting red tape, making the quick decisions to get things rolling. After a few months, however, he abandoned all pretense of being anything other than the principal assistant to the President. Except when interrupted by his illness, that was his job for the rest of the war. He was the only one who had the full broad vision of all aspects of the war—other than Roosevelt. Other men had a view of major portions, such as Marshall and King of strategy, Hull of foreign affairs, Nelson and Knudsen of production, Byrnes of the home front, Stimson and Knox of military affairs, and Morgenthau of economics. But only Hopkins and FDR shared the overall view and saw the interrelationships of war, politics, economic matters, diplomacy, and hard practicality. Only a man of such wide vision and understanding could have performed the job Hopkins did for Roosevelt. Only a person of iron integrity could have continued to keep Roosevelt's trust and could have won the trust and respect of such men as Marshall, Stimson, Knox, Forrestal, King, Churchill, Eden, Beaverbrook, Ismay, Stalin, Gromyko, Molotov, T. V. Soong, Chiang, and Eisenhower. Only a man of immense ability to handle detail could have kept the wartime machine in Washington from complete breakdown. Roosevelt had a habit of tossing a knotty problem to people with airy instructions to work something out. Hopkins was the man who followed up and saw that something worked out.

Other men have enriched themselves in government service, but Hopkins never took a dollar from the government other than his salary and expenses for official trips. In fact, from July to November of 1940, he worked for nothing at all, and he was $25,000 in debt when he died.[35]

Roosevelt is commonly credited with the beginning of the "imperial Presidency," and such a kind of administration requires a man to fill the role Hopkins played. Although Truman tried to reverse the trend toward concentration of power in the White House, even he had to have a chief of staff. His crony Harry Vaughn was useless in the job, but then he found Clark Clifford. Eisenhower had Sherman Adams, who exerted more power in less cause than Hopkins ever considered using, because Eisenhower could not be bothered with details. Roosevelt did not particularly want to know the details either, but he did want to know what was going on. Eisenhower cared only for results, and so long as all seemed to be going smoothly, he let Adams run the ship.

Kennedy was another President who wanted to be abreast of almost all matters, but he found that he needed administrative assistants to keep things going. Of course, his real chief of staff was his brother Robert, the Attorney General, but the "Irish Mafia" of Kenneth O'Donnell and Laurence O'Brien handled the day-to-day operations. Johnson held on to the "Mafiosi," but added cronyism in the person of Bobby Baker.

Nixon entered the White House with a promise that he would reduce the size of the President's personal staff, but under him it grew greatly. The great wielders of power were irreverently known as the Berlin Wall or All the King's Krauts. They were, of course, Henry Kissinger, John Ehrlichman, and H. R. Haldeman. Among them they were doing the job that Hopkins had handled alone. And under them the White House staff grew to over two hundred.

Democracy is founded on trust. The voters choose men and women to represent them, trusting in their integrity, judgment, and ability. That their trust is too often betrayed is a fundamental weakness of the system, for voters often do not vote rationally. They will elect and reelect a fool or knave because of his personality or what he can do for their own local interests. But in framing the Constitution, the Founding Fathers tried to provide for betrayal of trust by elected officials by forcing them to face the voters periodically. In the case of appointed officials, they provided for confirmation by the advice and consent of the Senate. And for both elected and appointed offices, they established the process of impeachment.

During the Roosevelt administration began the process which has no end in sight, the appointment of special agencies to do particular tasks outside the scope of the regular government departments represented in the Cabinet. There had been special agencies before, of course, but the real growth started in 1933 and has not ceased. These agencies have been authorized by acts of Congress, but the only effective restraint is the President's power to remove them, a power seldom exercised. Nor can the President himself control or supervise their activities. He must delegate his authority to the White House staff, and he must have a chief to coordinate the staff. The power of this chief is precisely what the President chooses to give him, and it derives from the inherent powers of the Presidency, which make the incumbent both Chief Executive and Commander-in-Chief of the armed forces, both in peace and war.

The pious hope of the editorial writers after Hopkins' death that there would never be another man in the White House performing as he did represented a yearning for a Jeffersonian simplicity in government impossible for a superpower.

The resignation of President Nixon shows that a President can be held accountable for his own actions and for those of his subordinates. Nixon basically did not trust the people nor the processes of democracy. Roosevelt trusted both. Almost instinctively, Roosevelt rejected as friends and associates those who were willing to subvert the democratic process, although the facts of political life meant that he had to deal with them. But Roosevelt's background and upbringing combined with his own sympathies to make him a champion of the underprivileged. It was a case of *noblesse oblige* on a national and later international scale. And in the unlikely person of an Iowa-born social worker named Harry Lloyd Hopkins, he found a kindred spirit. Both men took and used power for what it would do, not what it would do for them. In exercising that power, both men left an example of integrity and honor which their successors have sometimes failed to match.

Hopkins' contribution lay in serving Roosevelt, because he saw that as the way to serve the country. He guided the new President on the way to continuing what Roosevelt had started, trying to teach him the vision as well as the methods.

Those who hated Roosevelt hated Hopkins, and those who admired Roosevelt admired Hopkins. A man is known by his friends and enemies, and Hopkins, along with FDR, had plenty of both.

Glossary of Abbreviations

AAA   Agricultural Adjustment Administration
ABDA   American, British, Dutch, Australian Command (Southwest Pacific headquarters under General Archibald Wavell)
AICP   Association for Improving the Condition of the Poor
CCC   Civilian Conservation Corps
CWA   Civil Works Administration (headed by Hopkins)
DAI   Division of Applications and Information (of the Office of Emergency Management)
DDAR   Division of Defense Aid Reports (of the Office of Emergency Management)
FERA   Federal Emergency Relief Administration
FSA   Farm Security Administration
MAB   Munitions Assignment Board
NRA   National Recovery Administration
NYA   National Youth Administration
OEM   Office of Emergency Management
OPA   Office of Price Administration
OPM   Office of Production Management
OWM   Office of War Mobilization
PCUR   President's Committee for Unemployment Relief
RAF   Royal Air Force
RFC   Reconstruction Finance Corporation
PWA   Public Works Administration (headed by Ickes)
SPAB   Supply Priorities and Allocations Board
TERA   Temporary Emergency Relief Administration (of New York State)
TVA   Tennessee Valley Authority
WPA   Works Progress Administration (headed by Hopkins)
WPB   War Production Board

Notes

In order to avoid an excessively large number of notes, there are no citations for statements which appear in almost every book about the period of the Roosevelt administration, nor for excerpts from Roosevelt's speeches. The speeches have been edited and collected by Samuel I. Rosenman in *The Public Papers and Addresses of Franklin D. Roosevelt,* 13 volumes (New York: Harper & Brothers, 1938-1950).

To save space in the notes, only abbreviated references are given. Full descriptions are in the bibliography.

The following abbreviations are used throughout these notes:

FDRL   Franklin D. Roosevelt Library, Hyde Park, New York
HP   Hopkins Papers, located in FDRL
HPL   Hopkins Personal Letters and Papers (microfilm copies in the FDRL of personal papers now in possession of Robert Hopkins.)
Messages   The Messages between Franklin D. Roosevelt and Winston S. Churchill, 1939-1945, and Related Materials, published in microfilm, 6 reels, by FDRL
MR   Map Room File, located in FDRL
OF   Official File, located in FDRL
PPF   President's Personal File, located in FDRL
PSF   President's Secretary's File, located in FDRL
Sherwood   Robert E. Sherwood, *Roosevelt and Hopkins, an Intimate History.* Rev. ed. New York: Harper, 1950.

PROLOGUE

1. Letter, Hopkins to Roosevelt, Aug. 19, 1940, HP, Box 96, FDRL.
2. Letter, Roosevelt to Hopkins, Aug. 24, 1940, HP, Box 96, FDRL.
3. *New York Times,* Jan. 30, 1946.

CHAPTER ONE

1. *Bangor Democrat,* Aug. 12, 1861, included in letter of Kenneth C. McGills to Hopkins, Aug. 26, 1936, HPL, Reel 7, FDRL.
2. *Bangor Daily Commercial,* Feb. 24, 1879. In ibid.
3. Letter, Sen. Peter Norbeck to Hopkins, July 6, 1935, HPL, Reel 19, FDRL.
4. Sherwood, p. 15.
5. Letter, Rome Miller to Hopkins, Aug. 24, 1937, HPL, Reel 19, FDRL.
6. These birth data are taken from the front page of Anna Hopkins' Bible, entered in her own handwriting. There are certain inconsistencies to be noted. Adah's name is spelled Ada, and John Emery appears as Emery John. I have followed the usage

by which they were later known. Harry Hopkins compounded the confusion by spelling his younger brother's name Emory. He was generally known in the family as Em. The relevant page from the Bible is reproduced in HPL (microfilm) Reel 3, FDRL.

7. Letter, Newton Olson to Hopkins, Aug. 16, 1934, HPL, Reel 9, FDRL.

8. Letter, Gladys Ferguson Mossman to Hopkins, May 9, 1934, HP, Box 93, FDRL.

9. Sherwood, p. 23.

10. The Hopkins papers do not contain a record of this daughter's birth date nor her name. Her death is referred to in a letter from Alfred Fairbank, Manager of the Southwestern Division of the American Red Cross, to Hopkins, dated June 21, 1920. HP (microfilm), Reel 24-4, FDRL. Robert Hopkins informed me that her name was Barbara. Date on Ethel Gross Hopkins is from letter, Robert Hopkins to the author, October 14, 1976. She was the daughter of Benclon and Celia Gross. Born in Hungary on June 24, 1886, she died in Australia on August 16, 1976.

11. Letter, Leigh Carroll to Draft Board 135, New York City, July 11, 1918, HPL, Reel 24-4, FDRL.

12. Letter, Hopkins to James L. Feiser, Sept. 12, 1922, HPL, Reel 24-4, FDRL. This is a fair sample of Hopkins' "official prose style" which brought him deservedly poor grades in composition at Grinnell.

13. Sherwood, p. 29.

14. Letter, Hopkins to Ethel Hopkins, June 2, 1925, HPL, Reel 24-4, FDRL.

15. Letter, Hopkins to Ethel Hopkins, undated, HPL, Reel 24-4, FDRL.

16. Sherwood, p. 29.

17. Letter, Hopkins to Ethel Hopkins, undated, HPL, Reel 24-4, FDRL.

18. Letter, Hopkins to Ethel Hopkins, July 4, 1928, HPL, Reel 24-4, FDRL.

19. Letter, Hopkins to Ethel Hopkins, July 17, 1928, HPL, Reel 24-4, FDRL.

20. Letter, Hopkins to Ethel Hopkins, July 18, 1928, HPL, Reel 24-4, FDRL.

21. Smith, *The Shattered Dream,* p. 5.

22. Sherwood errs when he says that David Hopkins died in 1930. In a letter to Hopkins, his mother discusses provisions of the will, and the uncashed check for $1.00 to the account of David A. Hopkins (deceased) is in the Hopkins Papers. See Sherwood, p. 19; Letter, Anna Hopkins to Hopkins, HPL, Reel 19, FDRL; Check, Dec. 11, 1929, HP, Family Correspondence, FDRL.

23. Sherwood, p. 30.

24. Ibid., p. 31.

25. Blum, *Morgenthau Diaries: Years of Crisis,* pp. 26-27.

26. Burns, *Roosevelt: The Lion and the Fox,* p. 123.

27. The account of the nomination of Roosevelt is largely based on Burns, pp. 123-45; Lash, *Eleanor and Franklin,* pp. 461-71; and Elliott Roosevelt and James Brough, *An Untold Story,* pp. 277-308.

28. Letter, Hopkins to Lewis Hopkins, Sept. 8, 1932, HP, Family Correspondence, FDRL.

29. Letter, Hopkins to Lewis Hopkins, Dec. 8, 1932, HP, Family Correspondence, FDRL.

CHAPTER TWO

1. Sherwood, p. 45.
2. *Washington Post,* May 23, 1933. Quoted in Sherwood, pp. 44-45.
3. Zevin, p. ix.
4. Perkins, p. 184.
5. Schlesinger, *Coming of the New Deal,* pp. 264-65.
6. Childs, pp. 22-23.
7. Letter, William C. White to Hopkins, May 22, 1933, HPL, Reel 10, FDRL.
8. Charles, p. 38.
9. Ibid., p. 42.
10. Memorandum, Hopkins to Roosevelt, Aug. 29, 1933, HP, Box 95, FDRL.
11. Letter, Phil Stone to James Farley, Sept. 2, 1933, HPL, Reel 7, FDRL.
12. Letter, Hopkins to Roosevelt, Oct. 12, 1933, HPL, Reel 7, FDRL.
13. Blum, *Morgenthau Diaries: Years of Crisis,* p. 58.
14. HPL, Reel 9, FDRL.
15. Sherwood, p. 51.
16. Ickes, Vol. I, p. 116.
17. Sherwood, p. 52.
18. Hopkins, *Spending to Save,* p. 114.
19. Sherwood, p. 52.
20. Ibid., pp. 54–55.
21. Schlesinger, *Coming of the New Deal,* p. 290.
22. Minutes of Staff Meeting, Wednesday, Dec. 6, 1933, HP, Box 49, FDRL.
23. *Fortune,* October 1933. Quoted in Sherwood, p. 57.
24. Press Conference, April 4, 1935, HP, Press Conferences, FDRL.
25. Letter, Lorena Hickok to Hopkins, April 11, 1934, Morgenthau Papers, Box 123, FDRL.
26. Letter, Hopkins to Roosevelt, July 25, 1934, HPL, Reel 6, FDRL.
27. Letter, Hopkins to Lewis Hopkins, June 29, 1934, HPL, Reel 3, FDRL.
28. Cable, McIntyre to Hopkins, July 17, 1934, forwarded by letter from U.S. Embassy in Berlin, July 18, 1934, HPL, Reel 6, FDRL.
29. Cable, Aubrey Williams to Hopkins, July 24, 1934, HPL, Reel 6, FDRL.
30. Holograph memorandum, Hopkins to self, HPL, Reel 6, FDRL.
31. Barbara Hopkins; notes to self, holograph, HPL, Reel 19, FDRL.

CHAPTER THREE

1. Schlesinger, *Coming of the New Deal,* p. 472.
2. Ibid., p. 476.
3. Ibid., p. 485.
4. Memo of telephone conversation, Hopkins with Branion, June 21, 1934, HP, Box 85, FDRL.
5. Letter, Hopkins to Cummings, Oct. 12, 1934, HP, Box 49, FDRL.

6. Telegram, Pierce Williams to Lorena Hickok, Nov. 12, 1934, HP, Box 49, FDRL.

7. Burns, *Roosevelt: The Lion and the Fox,* p. 176.

8. Hopkins holograph memo to self, Sept. 25, 1934, HPL, Reel 9, FDRL.

9. Ibid.

10. Ibid.

11. Schlesinger, *Coming of the New Deal,* p. 503.

12. Ibid., p. 507.

13. Sherwood, pp. 64-65.

14. Ibid., p. 65.

15. *New York Times,* Nov. 15, 1934.

16. Hopkins Diary, Jan. 4, 1935, HP, Box 6, FDRL.

17. Hopkins Diary, HP, Box 6, FDRL.

18. Ickes, Vol. I, pp. 265-66.

19. HP, Box 6, FDRL.

20. Hopkins Diary, Jan. 31, 1935, HP, Box 6, FDRL.

21. Letter, Davey to Hopkins, March 4, 1935, HP, Box 95, FDRL.

22. Letter, Hopkins to Davey, March 8, 1935, HP, Box 95, FDRL.

23. Hopkins Diary, March 16, 1935, Box 6, FDRL.

24. Charles, p. 103.

25. Ickes, Vol. I, p. 330.

26. Stephen Early Diary, March 27, 1935, FDRL.

27. Hopkins Diary, March 16, 1935, HP, Box 6, FDRL.

28. Schlesinger, *Politics of Upheaval,* p. 352.

29. Sherwood, p. 67.

30. Ibid., p. 68.

31. Ibid., p. 68.

32. Letter, Lewis Hopkins to Hopkins, April 22, 1935, HP, Box 90, FDRL.

33. Ickes, Vol. I, p. 341.

34. Sherwood, p. 69.

35. Hopkins Diary, May 13, 1935, HP, Box 6, FDRL.

36. Hopkins Diary, May 14, 1935, HP, Box 6, FDRL.

37. HP, Box 170, FDRL.

38. Ickes, Vol. I, p. 380.

39. Schlesinger, *Politics of Upheaval,* p. 347.

40. Ibid.

41. Ickes, Vol. I, pp. 387-88.

42. Ibid., p. 410.

43. Ibid., p. 429.

44. Hopkins Diary, July 13, 1935, HP, Box 6, FDRL.

45. Ibid.

46. Hopkins Diary, July 14, 1935, HP, Box 6, FDRL.

47. Hopkins Diary, July 15, 1935, HP, Box 6, FDRL.

48. Ickes, Vol. I, p. 434.

49. *Time,* Oct. 7, 1935, p. 13.

50. *The Blue Bonnet,* Oct. 16, 1935, HP, Box 51, FDRL. Material for the *Houston*

trip has largely been taken from a souvenir log compiled by one of the officers of the ship; from Ickes, Vol. I, pp. 446-61; and from the diary Hopkins kept for Oct. 5, 6, and 7. *The Blue Bonnet* was the ship's newspaper. The souvenir log, copies of *The Blue Bonnet,* and Hopkins' diary are located in HP, Box 51, FDRL.

51. *The Blue Bonnet,* Oct. 16, 1935. Sherwood attributes the story of the burial of the feud to the President, and subsequent writers have followed him. However, both Ickes in his diary and the officer on the *Houston* who kept a souvenir log of the trip state that the author was Hopkins. Besides, the style is his, including the simplified spelling and the heavy use of dashes.

52. Ickes, Vol. I, p. 461.

53. Letter, Hopkins to Lewis Hopkins, Oct. 30, 1935, HPL, Reel 3, FDRL.

CHAPTER FOUR

1. "Harry Hopkins," *Fortune,* July, 1935, p. 63.
2. Letter, Hopkins to Lewis Hopkins, Oct. 30, 1935, HPL, Reel 3, FDRL.
3. Sherwood, p. 85.
4. Charles, p. 132.
5. Sherwood, pp. 75-76.
6. Letter, Farley to Hopkins, Sept. 6, 1938, HPL, Reel 18, FDRL.
7. Letter, Paul Anderson to Hopkins, Dec. 17, 1937, HPL, Reel 1, FDRL.
8. Letter, Hopkins to Dr. Johnson, Jan. 3, 1936, HPL, Reel 18, FDRL.
9. Ickes, Vol. I, p. 498.
10. Ickes, Vol. I, p. 479.
11. WPA Press Release, March 20, 1936, HP, Box 52, FDRL.
12. *Time,* March 30, 1936, p. 20.
13. Ickes, Vol. I, p. 575.
14. Ibid., p. 581.
15. Ibid., p. 582–83.
16. Notes by Barbara Hopkins, May 16, 1936, and Barbara Hopkins Diary entry, May 17, 1936, HPL, Reels 3 and 19, FDRL.
17. Eleanor Roosevelt, p. 162.
18. Letter, Joe T. Robinson to Hopkins, July 9, 1936, HPL, Reel 8, FDRL.
19. Ickes, Vol. I, p. 537.
20. Hopkins, *Spending to Save,* pp. 179-80.
21. Blum, *Morgenthau Diaries: Years of Crisis,* p. 257.
22. Ickes, Vol. I, p. 620.
23. Letter, Hopkins to Lewis Hopkins, May 29, 1936, HPL, Reel 3, FDRL.
24. Letter, Eleanor Roosevelt to Barbara Hopkins, June 13, 1936, HPL, Reel 3, FDRL.
25. Letter, Eleanor Roosevelt to Barbara Hopkins, July 12, 1936, HPL, Reel 3, FDRL; *Time,* Aug. 10, 1936, p. 15.
26. Transcript of telephone conversation between Hopkins and W. W. Norton [June 1936], HPL, Reel 17, FDRL.
27. Telegram, Hopkins to Kathryn Godwin, Sept. 15, 1936, HPL, Reel 6, FDRL.
28. Schlesinger, *Politics of Upheaval,* p. 526.

29. Ibid., p. 544.

30. Ibid., p. 532.

31. Rosenman, pp. 106-07.

32. *Time,* July 13, 1936, p. 13.

33. Letter, Roosevelt to Hopkins, July 18, 1936, HP, Box 96, FDRL.

34. *Time,* March 23, 1936, p. 21.

35. Congressional Record, 74th Cong., 2d Sess., Pt. IV, 80:3657.

36. Charles, p. 153.

37. *Time,* Aug. 31, 1936, p. 15.

38. Hopkins to State Administrators, March 13, 1936, HP, Box 37, FDRL.

39. Schlesinger, *Coming of the New Deal,* p. 277.

40. Farley, pp. 63-64.

41. Henry Morgenthau Diary, Aug. 24, 1936, Vol. 30, p. 25, FDRL.

42. Schlesinger, *Politics of Upheaval,* p. 609.

43. "Report on Mr. Hopkins' Western Trip, August 25 through September 29, 1936," p. 2, HP, Box 53, FDRL.

44. Schlesinger, *Politics of Upheaval,* p. 610.

45. Sherwood, p. 84.

46. Letter, Paul Shriver to Robert Hinckley, Sept. 29, 1936, HPL, Reel 8, FDRL.

47. Hopkins' notes on his Western trip, undated, HP, Box 54, FDRL.

48. Sherwood, pp. 86-87.

CHAPTER FIVE

1. Letter, Robert LaFollette to Hopkins, Dec. 15, 1936, HPL, Reel 15, FDRL.

2. See Elliott Roosevelt and Brough, *Untold Story* and *Rendezvous With Destiny;* see also Lash, *Eleanor and Franklin.*

3. HP, Box 6, FDRL.

4. Sherwood, p. 88.

5. Burns, *Roosevelt: The Lion and the Fox,* p. 291.

6. Untitled article with letter of Martin Sommers of the *Saturday Evening Post* to Hopkins, Feb. 24, 1937, HPL, Reel 17, FDRL.

7. Ibid.

8. Skit by Early and Hopkins at President's stag birthday party, Jan. 30, 1937, p. 7, HP, Box 92, FDRL.

9. Burns, *Roosevelt: The Lion and the Fox,* p. 296.

10. Sherwood, p. 89.

11. Ickes, Vol. II, p. 11.

12. HPL, Reel 8; Elliott Roosevelt, *F.D.R. Letters,* Vol. I, p. 675. Elliott Roosevelt is mistaken here and in his and Brough's *Rendezvous With Destiny* in saying Hopkins and Ickes were on the *Houston.* Ickes makes it clear in his diary with his description of how the small vessel rolled that they were not aboard a heavy cruiser. As he published it, the text is slightly emended.

13. Letter, David Hopkins to Hopkins, undated, HPL, Reel 21, FDRL.

14. *Time,* June 7, 1937, p. 12.

15. Sherwood, p. 91.

16. Ibid., pp. 90-91.

17. Letter, Hawes to Hopkins, July 8, 1937, HPL, Reel 8, FDRL.

18. Letter, Jesse Jones to Barbara Hopkins, Sept. 21, 1937, HP, Personal Correspondence, FDRL.

19. Letter, Lewis Hopkins to Hopkins, undated, HPL, Reel 16, FDRL.

20. Letter, Eleanor Roosevelt to Hopkins, Sept. 28, 1937, HPL, Reel 16, FDRL.

21. Telegram, Roosevelt to Hopkins, Oct. 1, 1937, HPL, Reel 16, FDRL.

22. Ickes, Vol. II, p. 225.

23. Langer and Gleason, *Challenge to Isolation,* p. 19.

24. *New York World-Telegram,* Oct. 6, 1937.

25. Burns, *Roosevelt: The Lion and the Fox,* pp. 318-19.

26. Ickes, Vol. II, p. 246.

27. "Log of the Cruise of President Franklin D. Roosevelt to Dry Tortuga and Florida, 29 November 1937-6 December 1937," HPL, Reel 21, FDRL.

28. Ickes, Vol. II, p. 260.

29. Letter, Florence Kerr to Hopkins, undated, but written Dec. 16, 1937, HPL, Reel 16, FDRL.

30. Letter, Ralph E. Flanders to Hopkins, Dec. 24, 1937; letter, Joseph E. Clayton to Hopkins, Dec. 29, 1937, HPL, Reel 1, FDRL.

31. Letter, Hopkins to McIntyre, Jan. 6, 1938, HPL, Reel 16, FDRL; letter, Hopkins to LeHand, Jan. 6, 1938, HPL, Reel 1, FDRL.

32. Letter, Malvina Thompson Scheider to Hopkins, March 5, 1938, HPL, Reel 1, FDRL.

33. Early Diary, Vol. 3, March 19-April 4, 1938, FDRL.

34. Burns, p. 344.

35. Ibid.

36. Ibid., pp. 345-46.

37. Ickes, Vol. II, pp. 56-57.

38. Letter, Hopkins to Swope, April 6, 1938, HPL, Reel 10, FDRL.

CHAPTER SIX

1. Blum, *Morgenthau Diaries: Years of Crisis,* p. 420.

2. Ibid., p. 421.

3. Ickes, Vol. II, p. 367.

4. Ibid., p. 382.

5. Early, Scrapbook for 1938, FDRL; Ickes, Vol. II, pp. 372, 378, 396.

6. Ickes, Vol. II, p. 387.

7. Hopkins Memo to self, undated, HP, Box 215, Sherwood Materials, FDRL; see also Sherwood, pp. 94-98.

8. Quoted in Sherwood, p. 99, and in Elliott Roosevelt and James Brough, *A Rendezvous with Destiny: The Roosevelts of the White House,* p. 195.

9. Eleanor Roosevelt, *This I Remember,* pp. 170-71.

10. Morgenthau Diary, Sept. 2, 1938, Vol. 138, FDRL.

11. *Time,* June 6, 1938, pp. 9-10.

12. Morgenthau Diary, June 1, 1938, Vol. 138, FDRL.

13. *Time,* July 18, 1938, p. 9.

14. Ibid.

15. Sherwood, p. 98.

16. Telegram, Watson, McIntire, and Early to Hopkins, May 31, 1938, PPF, Box 4096, FDRL.

17. Letter, Tugwell to Hopkins, June 16, 1938, HPL, Reel 18, FDRL.

18. See, for example, a conversation with Morgenthau on Sept. 14, Farley, p. 146.

19. Adolf A. Berle Diary, June 9, 1938, Box 210, FDRL.

20. Ickes, Vol. II, p. 459.

21. Ibid., pp. 462–63.

22. Letter, Hopkins to Lewis Hopkins, Aug. 17, 1938, HPL, Reel 21, FDRL.

23. Langer and Gleason, *Challenge to Isolation,* pp. 33–34. See also Ickes, Vol. II, p. 478.

24. Churchill, *The Gathering Storm,* p. 328.

25. Pogue, *Marshall: Education of a General,* p. 323.

26. Letter, Marshall to Hopkins, May 13, 1945, HPL, Reel 21, FDRL. Sherwood prints a somewhat edited version of this letter. See Sherwood, p. 101.

27. See Ickes, Vol. II, pp. 484-85, 505-06, 511, 512-13. Also, letter, Ickes to Hopkins, Nov. 21, HP, Box 91, FDRL.

28. Letter, Howard O. Hunter to Hopkins, Dec. 6, 1938, HP, Box 121, FDRL.

29. Ickes, Vol. II, p. 526.

30. Ibid., p. 535.

31. Letter, Hopkins to Lewis Hopkins, Dec. 21, 1938, HPL, Reel 15, FDRL.

32. Letter, Hopkins to Diana Hopkins, Dec. 25, 1938, HPL, Reel 19, FDRL.

CHAPTER SEVEN

1. Sherwood, p. 107.

2. Kiplinger Washington Letter, Friday, Dec. 23, 1938. In HPL, Reel 14, FDRL.

3. Letter, Florence Kerr to Hopkins, undated, HPL, Reel 14, FDRL.

4. Letter, W. Averell Harriman to the author, June 8, 1976.

5. *New York Times,* Jan. 12, 1939.

6. Morgenthau Diary, Jan. 6, 1939, Vol. 159, FDRL.

7. Sherwood, p. 108.

8. Ibid., p. 109.

9. Hopkins' letter to the editor, *New York Times,* Nov. 14, 1938, HPL, Reel 18, FDRL.

10. Sherwood, p. 103.

11. Ibid. See also Senate Committee Print, "Nomination of Harry L. Hopkins to be Secretary of Commerce: Individual Observations of Senator Josiah W. Bailey, Chairman of the Committee on Commerce, Relative to the Nomination of Harry L. Hopkins to be Secretary of Commerce," 76th Congress, 1st Session. The legend of the "tax and tax" remark persists. The phrase, attributed to Hopkins, appeared in a letter to the editor of *The Baltimore Sun* in September, 1976.

12. Letter, Harriman to the author, June 8, 1976.

13. *Time,* March 6, 1939, p. 12.

14. Remark of Representative Bruce Barton as carried on Associated Press news ticker, Feb. 27, 1939, HP, Box 117, FDRL.

15. Sherwood, p. 111.

16. Ickes, Vol. II, p. 585.

17. Letter, Hopkins to Rome Hopkins, Feb. 15, 1939, HPL, Reel 21, FDRL.

18. Letter, Lewis Hopkins to Roosevelt, March 6, 1939, PPF, Box 4096, FDRL.

19. Letter, Roosevelt to Lewis Hopkins, March 13, 1939, PPF, Box 4096, FDRL.

20. Sherwood, p. 113.

21. Letter, Hopkins to Lewis Hopkins, March 25, 1939, HPL, Reel 21, FDRL.

22. Hopkins memo to self, HPL, Reel 20, FDRL.

23. Letter, Robert Kerr to Hopkins, March 22, 1939, HPL, Reel 16; letter Hopkins to Robert Kerr, March 28, 1939, HPL, Reel 2, FDRL.

24. HPL, Reel 7, FDRL.

25. Ibid.

26. Lease from Aetna Life Insurance Company to Hopkins, June 14, 1939, HPL, Reel 16; letter, Robert Kerr to Hopkins, undated, HPL, Reel 21, FDRL.

27. Letter, Lewis Hopkins to Hopkins, April 24, 1939, HPL, Reel 21, FDRL.

28. Letter, Hopkins to Sandburg, April 28, 1939, HPL, Reel 18, FDRL.

29. Early Diary, June 1, 1939, Vol. 4, FDRL; Hopkins' Press Conference, June 2, 1939, HP, Box 118, FDRL; *Time,* June 12, 1939, p. 11.

30. Letter, Hopkins to Mrs. Leona Ettlinger, June 5, 1939, HPL, Reel 8, FDRL. Mrs. Ettlinger was John Hertz's daughter.

31. Eleanor Roosevelt, p. 195.

32. Letter, Hopkins to Edwin Weisl, July 5, 1939, HPL, Reel 19, FDRL.

33. Ickes, Vol. II, July 28, 1939, p. 687.

34. Letter, Lewis Hopkins to Hopkins, July 5, 1939; letter Lewis Hopkins to Hopkins, July 31, 1939, HPL, Reel 21, FDRL.

35. Ickes, Vol. II, p. 699; letter, Hopkins to David Hopkins, Aug. 22, 1939; letter, Hopkins to Lewis Hopkins, Aug. 22, 1939, HPL, Reel 21, FDRL.

36. Letter, Roosevelt to Hopkins, Aug. 25, 1939, HPL, Reel 3, FDRL.

37. Letter, Hopkins to Lewis Hopkins, Sept. 8, 1939, HPL, Reel 3, FDRL.

38. Letter, Hopkins to Lewis Hopkins, Sept. 13, 1939, HPL, Reel 21, FDRL.

39. Letter, Hopkins to Dr. Andrew Rivers, Nov. 25, 1939, HPL, Reel 16, FDRL. Dr. Wallace M. Yater was Hopkins' physician in Washington, professor of medicine at Georgetown University, and a former member of the staff at the Mayo Clinic.

40. Letter, Sandburg to Hopkins, Nov. 20, 1939; letter, Hopkins to Roosevelt, Dec. 16, 1939, HPL, Reel 10, FDRL. Sherwood's account of this episode is incorrect, for it was Hopkins who sent the poem to the President, not the other way around as Sherwood describes it. Sherwood, pp. 133-34.

41. Letter, Hopkins to Harry C. Butcher, Nov. 8, 1939, HPL, Reel 9, FDRL.

42. Sherwood, p. 122.

43. Letter, John Hertz to Hopkins, Oct. 3, 1939; letter Hopkins to John Hertz, Oct. 12, 1939; letter, John Hertz to Hopkins, Nov. 20, 1939, HPL, Reel 8, FDRL.

44. Letter, Hopkins to Lewis Hopkins, Jan. 26, 1940, HPL, Reel 21, FDRL.

45. *Newsweek,* Feb. 19, 1940, p. 19.

46. Letter, Hopkins to Edmund P. Grice, Jr., Feb. 9, 1940, HPL, Reel 7, FDRL.

47. Letter, Hopkins to F. F. Clendinin, May 7, 1940, HPL, Reel 16, FDRL.

48. Quoted in Sherwood, p. 155.

49. Burns, *Roosevelt: The Lion and the Fox,* p. 435.

50. Sherwood, p. 161.

51. Berle Diary, June 10, 1940, Box 212, FDRL.

52. *New York Times,* July 25, 1940.

CHAPTER EIGHT

1. Appleby, p. 755.

2. Lilienthal, p. 192. Although Lilienthal puts the passage in quotation marks, the manner is not in tune with Hopkins' abrupt, explosive style. The matter, on the other hand, is clearly his. There is a question of date also. Lilienthal's journal entry is marked July 11, 1940, but Farley says that Hopkins was in Chicago from July 10 until the end of the convention. See Farley, pp. 259-306.

3. Farley, pp. 260-61.

4. Perkins, p. 133.

5. Samuel I. Rosenman, pp. 213-14.

6. Joseph P. Lash, *Eleanor and Franklin,* p. 806.

7. Rosenman, p. 215.

8. Ickes, Vol. III, pp. 294, 295.

9. Letter, Hopkins to Ethel Hopkins, undated, HPL, Reel 24-4, FDRL.

10.Lash, *Roosevelt and Churchill, 1939–1941,* p. 114.

11. Letter, Robert Jackson to Hopkins, Sept. 23, 1940, HPL, Reel 8, FDRL.

CHAPTER NINE

1. Rosenman, p. 223.

2. Sherwood, p. 183.

3. Ickes, Vol. III, p. 361.

4. *New York Times,* Aug. 13, 1940.

5. Telegram, White to Roosevelt, Aug. 11, 1940, PSF, Box 67, FDRL.

6. The Guru Letters are now in the FDRL. See also Byrnes, pp. 127-28; Douglas, pp. 338-39.

7. Berle, Diary, Oct. 25, 1940, Berle Papers, Box 212, FDRL.

8. There are many versions of this episode. I have tried to put together the most reliable. See Sherwood, p. 191, and Burns, Roosevelt, *The Lion and the Fox,* pp. 448-49.

9. Will Alexander, Oral History Project, Columbia University.

10. Sherwood, pp. 197-98.

11. Details of election night at Hyde Park are taken largely from Sherwood, pp. 199-200, Lash, *Eleanor and Franklin,* pp. 815-18, Burns, pp. 451-55, and *Time,* Nov. 11, 1940.

12. Letter, Hopkins to F. F. Clendinin, Nov. 18, 1940, HP, Box 86, FDRL.

13. Ickes, III, pp. 371-72.

14. Sherwood, pp. 2-3.

15. Ibid., p. 224.

CHAPTER TEN

1. There are many versions of the story of Roosevelt's decision to send Hopkins to London. See Sherwood, pp. 230-33; Davis and Lindley, *How War Came,* pp. 173-74; Baker, p. 49; Harriman and Abel, *Special Envoy to Churchill and Stalin, 1941-1946,* p. 10; Beard, pp. 14-15.

2. Harriman and Abel, p. 110.

3. Baker, p. 50.

4. HPL, Reel 20, FDRL.

5. Sherwood, p. 235.

6. Ibid., p. 206.

7. HPL, Reel 19, FDRL. This was a holograph report written for FDR. It was returned to Hopkins on his arrival back in Washington.

8. Ibid.

9. Ibid.

10. Churchill, *Grand Alliance,* pp. 19-20.

11. *Daily Telegraph,* Jan. 11, 1941.

12. Clipping from Walter Winchell's column, "Coast to Coast," HPL, Reel 13, FDRL.

13. Cable, Churchill to Roosevelt, Messages, Reel 1, FDRL.

14. OF, 4117, Box 1, FDRL. Quoted in Sherwood, p. 243.

15. Ismay, p. 216.

16. Moran, p. 6. Sir Charles Wilson became Lord Moran when he was elevated to the Peerage.

17. Memorandum to Mr. Hopkins of Lady Astor's telephone call by J. Seymour of January 21, 1941, HPL, Reel 19, FDRL.

18. OF, 4117, Box 1. Quoted in Sherwood, p. 254.

19. Hopkins; memo to self, Jan. 25, 1941, HPL, Reel 19, FDRL. Quoted in Sherwood, p. 256.

20. Letter, Eleanor Roosevelt to Hopkins, Jan. 25, 1941, HPL, Reel 21, FDRL.

21. Hopkins' memo to self, Jan. 30, 1941, HPL, Reel 19, FDRL.

22. Sherwood, p. 259.

CHAPTER ELEVEN

1. *New York Times,* Jan. 12, 1941.

2. Ickes, Vol. III, p. 433.

3. Ibid., p. 459.

4. Harriman and Abel, p. 3.

5. Berle Diary, March 16, 1941, FDRL.

6. Letter, Roosevelt to Hopkins, March 27, 1941, HP, Box 214, FDRL.

7. Ickes, Vol. III, p. 471.

8. Oscar Cox Diary, April 5, 1941, Cox Papers, Box 145, FDRL.

9. Sherwood, p. 280.

10. Ibid., p. 284.

11. Letter, Hopkins to Elmer C. Dawkins, April 7, 1941, HPL, Reel 19, FDRL; letter Hopkins to Charles E. Payne, April 7, 1941, HPL, Reel 12, FDRL.

12. Messages, Reel 1, FDRL.

13. Morgenthau Diary, Vol. 397, p. 301A, FDRL.

14. Ickes, Vol. III, p. 511.

15. Sherwood, p. 295.

16. Berle, Diary, May 26, 1941, FDRL.

17. Sherwood, p. 297.

18. Ibid., p. 258.

19. Memo, Hopkins to Roosevelt, June 14, 1941, PPF, Box 4096, FDRL.

20. Letter, Dr. Andrew B. Rivers to Hopkins, June 15, 1941, HPL, Reel 19, FDRL.

21. Letter, Hopkins to Dr. Rivers, June 19, 1941, HPL, Reel 19, FDRL.

22. Sherwood, p. 303.

23. Memo, Oscar Cox to Hopkins, June 23, 1941, Cox Papers, Box 145, FDRL.

24. Memo, Stimson to Roosevelt, June 23, 1941, PSF, Box 74, FDRL.

25. Sherwood, p. 312.

CHAPTER TWELVE

1. Elliott Roosevelt, *As He Saw It,* p. 27.

2. Cable, Hopkins to Roosevelt, July 26, 1941, HP, Box 303, FDRL.

3. Kennedy, pp. 155-56.

4. Maisky, p. 177.

5. Ibid., p. 179.

6. HP, Box 303, FDRL.

7. Maisky, p. 183.

8. Messages, Reel 6, FDRL.

9. Sherwood, p. 320.

10. HPL, Reel 19, FDRL.

11. Maisky, p. 181.

12. Flight to Archangel with Mr. Harry Hopkins 27 July-2 August, 1941, Report by Flight Lieutenant D. C. McKinley, DFC, Commanding PBY Catalina W 6416 of RAF Coastal Command, HPL, Reel 19, FDRL.

13. HPL, Reel 19, FDRL; quoted in Sherwood, p. 326.

14. Hopkins, "Inside Story," pp. 14-15.

15. Memorandum by Hopkins of Conference with Mr. Stalin, July 31, 1941, State Department, *Foreign Relations of the United States, 1941,* pp. 880-82.

16. Sherwood, p. 330.

17. Memorandum by Hopkins, *Foreign Relations.*

18. Flight to Archangel.

19. Messages, Reel 6, FDRL.

20. Hopkins to Sir John Tovey, Aug. 7, 1941, HPL, Reel 19, FDRL.

21. Hopkins to Diana Hopkins, Aug. 8, 1941, HPL, Reel 21, FDRL.

22. HP, Box 303, FDRL.
23. *Knoxville Journal,* Aug. 2, 1941.
24. Roosevelt, *As He Saw It,* p. 22.
25. Letter, Hopkins to Churchill, Aug. 9, 1941, HPL, Reel 19, FDRL.
26. Letter, J. M. Martin to Hopkins, Aug. 9, 1941, HPL, Reel 19, FDRL.
27. *New York Times,* Aug. 15, 1941.

CHAPTER THIRTEEN

1. Sherwood, p. 376.
2. Ickes, III, p. 607.
3. Letter, Clementine Churchill to Hopkins, Aug. 24, 1941, HPL, Reel 6, FDRL.
4. Letter, F. G. Beaumont-Nesbitt to Hopkins, Sept. 2, 1941; Letter, Hopkins to Beaumont-Nesbitt, Sept. 3, 1941, HPL, Reel 20, FDRL.
5. Letter, Julius F. Stone to Hopkins, Oct. 28, 1941; letter, Stone to Hopkins, Nov. 5, 1941, HPL, Reel 20, FDRL, Sherwood, p. 379.
6. Beard, p. 278.
7. Letter, Hopkins to Mrs. Betsey Cushing Roosevelt, Nov. 10, 1941, HPL, Reel 16, FDRL.
8. Letter, Hopkins to Lewis Hopkins, Nov. 17, 1941, HPL, Reel 21, FDRL.
9. Letter, Hopkins to Marguerite LeHand, Nov. 12, 1941, HPL, Reel 12, FDRL.
10. *Time,* Nov. 17, 1941, p. 15.
11. Letter, Hopkins to Cox, Nov. 7, 1941, Cox Papers, Box 15, FDRL.
12. Memorandum, Hopkins to Roosevelt, Nov. 27, 1941, Stephen Early Papers, Box 23, FDRL.
13. Testimony of Commander Schultz, Pearl Harbor Attack, XI, p. 5555ff.
14. HPL, Reel 19, FDRL. Quoted with some inaccuracies in Sherwood, pp. 430-34.

CHAPTER FOURTEEN

1. Gunther, p. 86.
2. Churchill, *Grand Alliance,* p. 609. This cable does not appear in Messages, and the only available text is in Churchill.
3. Sherwood, p. 456.
4. Pogue, *Marshall: Ordeal and Hope,* p. 280.
5. Churchill, *Grand Alliance,* p. 673.
6. Letter, Hopkins to Clementine Churchill, Jan. 14, 1942, HPL, Reel 11, FDRL.
7. HP, Box 213, FDRL.
8. Timmons, p. 314.
9. HP, Box 213, FDRL.
10. Letter, Mrs. Laurence Lowman to Hopkins, undated, but answered by Hopkins, Jan. 22, 1941, HPL, Reel 19, FDRL.
11. Letter, Hopkins to Mrs. Laurence Lowman, Jan. 22, 1941, Reel 19, FDRL.
12. Letter, Steinhardt to Hopkins, Jan. 9, 1942, HPL, Reel 13, FDRL.
13. Letter, Hopkins to James I. Wendell, July 8, 1942, HPL, Reel 13, FDRL.

14. Sherwood, p. 495.

15. HP, Box 213, FDRL. Quoted in full in Sherwood, pp. 502-03.

16. Harriman and Abel, p. 123.

17. Cable, Harriman to Hopkins, Feb. 22, 1942, MR, Box 13, File 1942, FDRL.

18. Cable, Hopkins to Harriman, May 18, 1942, MR, Box 13, File 1942, FDRL.

19. Rigdon, p. 11.

20. Harriman and Abel, p. 128.

21. Hopkins, memo to self, March 11, 1942, HP, Box 154, FDRL.

22. Pogue, *Marshall: Ordeal and Hope,* p. 304.

23. HP, Box 207, FDRL.

24. *New York Herald-Tribune,* March 17, 1942.

25. Cable, Hopkins to Churchill, HP, Box 136, FDRL.

26. Pogue, *Marshall: Ordeal and Hope,* p. 307.

27. *Daily Telegraph,* April 9, 1942.

28. Cable, Hopkins to Roosevelt, April 9, 1942, Messages, Reel 1.

29. Bryant, Vol. I, p. 285.

30. Sherwood, p. 531.

31. Nicolson, p. 222.

32. Letter, Hopkins to Clementine Churchill, April 21, 1942, HPL, Reel 11, FDRL.

33. Cable, Hopkins to Roosevelt, April 18, 1942, Messages, Reel 1.

34. Letter, Ben Moreell to James Forrestal, May 21, 1942, HPL, Reel 11, FDRL.

35. Hopkins, memo to self, May 30, 1942, HP, Box 136, FDRL.

36. Letter, Admiral Lord Louis Mountbatten to Roosevelt, June 15, 1942, HP, Box 194, FDRL.

37. Churchill, *Hinge of Fate,* pp. 381-82.

38. Bryant, pp. 329-30.

39. HP, Box 213, FDRL.

40. Butcher, p. 24.

41. Sherwood, p. 607.

42. Cable, Roosevelt to Hopkins, undated, Messages, Reel 6. Draft in Roosevelt's handwriting, only copy found.

43. Butcher, p. 31.

44. Ibid., p. 32.

45. Cable, Harriman to McCrea, July 26, 1942, MR, Box 12, File 1A, FDRL.

46. Cable, Roosevelt to Churchill, July 27, 1942, Messages, Reel 1.

CHAPTER FIFTEEN

1. Elliott Roosevelt and Brough, *Rendezvous With Destiny,* p. 317.

2. Eleanor Roosevelt, p. 256.

3. Elliott Roosevelt and Brough, *Rendezvous With Destiny,* p. 318.

4. Eleanor Roosevelt, p. 263.

5. Harriman and Abel, pp. 146-47.

6. Telegram, Churchill to Hopkins, Aug. 14, 1942, HP, Box 136, FDRL.

7. Letter, Hopkins to Beaverbrook, Sept. 26, 1942, HPL, Reel 20, FDRL.

8. Sherwood, p. 634.

9. Telegram, Hopkins to Churchill, Oct. 13, 1942, MR, Box 13, File 1942, FDRL.

10. Memo, Isidor Lubin to Hopkins, Oct. 30, 1942, HP, Box 180, FDRL. See also Sherwood, p. 636.

11. Telegram, Hopkins to Roosevelt, Sept. 22, 1942, MR, Box 15, Inspection Trip File, FDRL.

12. Letter, Roosevelt to Hopkins, Nov. 13, 1942, HP, Box 214, FDRL.

13. Telegram, Eisenhower to Combined Chiefs of Staff, Nov. 14, 1942; Eisenhower, *Papers,* Vol. II, pp. 707-09.

14. Telegram, Roosevelt to Eisenhower, Nov. 15, 1942, HP, Book 8, Footnote Folder, FDRL.

15. Draft of message, Roosevelt to Churchill, [Dec. 2, 1942,] Messages, Reel 2, FDRL.

16. Hassett, p. 142.

17. Cable, Hopkins to Churchill, Nov. 29, 1942, HPL, Reel 20, FDRL.

18. Hopkins, "You and Your Family Will Be Mobilized," p. 14.

19. *Pittsburgh Sun Telegraph,* Dec. 21, 1942, Clipping in OF, 4117, Box 3, FDRL.

CHAPTER SIXTEEN

1. Butcher, p. 118.

2. Hopkins, memo to self, Jan. 11, 1943, HPL, Reel 20, FDRL. Sherwood quotes all the memoranda Hopkins wrote in connection with the Casablanca Conference, but the accuracy of his transcriptions leaves something to be desired.

3. Telegram, Hopkins to Louise Hopkins, Jan. 11, 1943, MR, Box 15, FDRL.

4. Hopkins, memos to self, Jan., 1943, Reel 20, FDRL.

5. Robert Hopkins' statement and memo to the author, May 15, 1976.

6. Hopkins, memo to self, Jan. 20, 1943, HPL, Reel 20, FDRL.

7. Notes dictated by Mr. Harry Hopkins to Chief Ship's Clerk Terry, Saturday morning, January 23, 1943, HPL, Reel 20, FDRL.

8. Hopkins, memo to self, Jan. 24, 25, 26, 1943, HPL, Reel 20, FDRL.

9. Letter, Capt. Donald B. Duncan to Hopkins, Jan. 16, 1943, HPL, Reel 3, FDRL.

10. Byrnes, p. 173.

11. Cable, Hopkins to Churchill, Feb. 24, 1943, HP, "Tube Alloys" folder, FDRL.

12. Harriman and Abel, p. 198.

13. Letter, LaGuardia to Hopkins, March 17, 1943, HP, Box 16, FDRL.

14. Moran, p. 95.

15. Cable, Harriman to Hopkins, March 20, 1943, MR, Box 13, File 1943, FDRL.

16. Cable, Hopkins to Churchill, March 29, 1943, HP, Box 299, FDRL.

17. Cable, Roosevelt to Churchill, April 11, 1943, Messages, Reel 2, FDRL.

18. Quoted in memo of Oscar Cox to Grace Tully, May 3, 1943, OF 4117, Box 4, FDRL.

19. Cable, Roosevelt to Churchill, May 2, 1943, Messages, Reel 2, FDRL.

20. Sherwood, pp. 728-29.

21. Letter, Hopkins to Pamela Churchill, May 17, 1943, HPL, Reel 11, FDRL.

22. Moran, p. 102.

CHAPTER SEVENTEEN

1. "Tomorrow," *The United States News,* June 14, 1943, p. 5.

2. *Chicago Daily Tribune,* May 28, 1943.

3. Hopkins, Letter to the Editor, June 26, 1943, HPL, Reel 11, FDRL.

4. *The New Yorker,* Aug. 7 and 14, 1943 (pp. 25-28, 30-31; and pp. 27-30, 32, 34-35).

5. Harriman and Abel, *Special Envoy,* p. 214.

6. Letter, Hopkins to Missy LeHand, June 29, 1943, HPL, Reel 18, FDRL.

7. Churchill, *Closing the Ring,* p. 82.

8. *Stalin's Correspondence,* Vol. I, p. 144.

9. Ibid., pp. 148-49.

10. Moran, pp. 117-18.

11. Churchill, *Closing the Ring,* p. 137.

12. Harriman and Abel, p. 224.

13. Letter, Hopkins to Drew Pearson, Aug. 16, 1943, HPL, Reel 18, FDRL.

14. *Chicago Daily Tribune,* Aug. 29, 1943.

15. Letter, Hopkins to Joseph E. Davies, Sept. 17, 1943, HP, Box 137, FDRL.

16. Sherwood, p. 763.

17. Memo, Hopkins to Roosevelt, Oct. 4, 1943, MR, Box 17, FDRL.

18. Cable, Winant to Hopkins, Oct. 16, 1943, HP, Box 257, FDRL.

19. Letter, Hopkins to Winant, Oct. 25, 1943, HP, Box 257, FDRL.

20. Hopkins memo to self, undated, HPL, Reel 20, FDRL.

21. Churchill, *Closing the Ring,* p. 341.

22. Moran, pp. 140-41.

23. Harriman and Abel, p. 268.

24. *Foreign Relations of the United States, Cairo and Teheran,* p. 539.

25. Moran, p. 147.

26. Bohlen, p. 148.

27. Harriman and Abel, p. 277.

28. HPL, Reel 21, FDRL.

29. Ibid. Sherwood reproduces facsimiles of both documents, p. 763.

30. Harriman and Abel, pp. 282-83.

31. HP, Box 139.

32. Marshall's story is given with minor differences in Sherwood, pp. 802-03, and in Pogue, *Organizer of Victory,* pp. 320-22.

33. Wireless, Hopkins to Louise Hopkins, Dec. 16, 1943, MR, Box 17, FDRL.

34. Telegram, Roosevelt to Churchill, Dec. 16, 1943, MR, Box 17, FDRL. A paraphrased version as actually transmitted appears in Messages, Reel 3, FDRL.

35. Letter, Hopkins to Stephen Hopkins, Dec. 28, 1943, HPL, Reel 16, FDRL.

CHAPTER EIGHTEEN

1. Cable, Roosevelt to Churchill, Jan. 5, 1944, Messages, Reel 3, FDRL.

2. Cable, Roosevelt to Churchill, Jan. 25, 1944, MR, Box 18, FDRL.

3. Author's interview with Robert Hopkins, May 15, 1976.

4. Letter, J. Edgar Hoover to Hopkins, Feb. 9, 1944, and Enclosure, a 38-page report on the investigation, HP, Box 134, FDRL; *Newsweek,* Jan. 24 and Jan. 31, 1944; *Time,* Jan. 24 and Jan. 31, 1944; *New York Times,* Oct. 6, 1944.

5. A transcription of the broadcast, the crank letters, and Judge Rosenman's letter are found in HPL, Reel 20, FDRL.

6. Letter, Hopkins to Mrs. John Hertz, Feb. 2, 1944, HPL, Reel 11, FDRL.

7. Letter, Hopkins to Stephen Hopkins, Feb. 2, 1944, HPL, Reel 20, FDRL.

8. Telegram, Roosevelt to Station Master, Jacksonville, Florida, Feb. 12, 1944, HPL, Reel 20, FDRL.

9. Letter, Eleanor Roosevelt to Hopkins, Feb. 12, [1944], HPL, Reel 21, FDRL.

10. Letter, Marshall to Hopkins, [Feb. 13, 1944], HPL, Reel 19, FDRL.

11. Pogue, *Organizer of Victory,* p. 102. Hopkins noted on Marshall's letter, "This has been answered by me—long hand HLH." Therefore no copy exists in the Hopkins Papers. The original is in the Marshall Research Library in Lexington, Va.

12. The original is in Robert Hopkins' possession. A copy is in OF, 4117, Box 4, FDRL.

13. Telegram, Roosevelt to Churchill, March 11, 1944, Messages, Reel 4, FDRL.

14. Letter, Oscar Cox to Hopkins, April 21, 1944, Cox Papers, Box 148, FDRL.

15. Untitled article by Hopkins, HPL, Reel 17, FDRL.

16. Letter, Roosevelt to Hopkins, May 18, 1944, HPL, Reel 20, FDRL.

17. Letter, Hopkins to Diana Hopkins, July 5, 1944, HPL, Reel 21, FDRL.

18. Letter, Sherwood to Hopkins, July 7, 1944, HPL, Reel 20, FDRL; letter Beaverbrook to Hopkins, Oct. 23, 1944, HPL, Reel 20, FDRL.

19. Letter, Hopkins to Dr. John Waugh, July 10, 1944, HPL, Reel 20, FDRL.

20. Cable, Churchill to Hopkins, July 19, 1944, MR, Box 13, File 1944 (Incoming), FDRL.

21. Cable, Hopkins to Churchill, Aug. 7, 1944, MR, Box 13, File 1944 (Outgoing), FDRL.

22. Cable, Hopkins to Churchill, July 20, 1944, MR, Box 13, File 1944 (Outgoing), FDRL.

23. Cable, Hopkins to Churchill, Aug. 28, 1944, MR, Box 13, File 1944 (Outgoing), FDRL.

24. Cox Diary, Aug. 15, 1944, Cox Papers, Box 149, FDRL.

25. Morgenthau Diary, Sept. 4, 1944, Vol. 768, FDRL.

26. Blum, *Roosevelt and Morgenthau,* pp. 596-97.

27. Stimson, p. 579.

28. Churchill, *Triumph and Tragedy,* p. 161. For earlier statement see Churchill, *Closing the Ring,* p. 82.

29. Bohlen, p. 162.

30. Cable, Roosevelt to Harriman for Stalin, Oct. 4, 1944, MR, Box 13, File 1944 (Outgoing), FDRL.

31. Letter, James J. Devlin to Hopkins, Oct. 25, 1944, HPL, Reel 15, FDRL.

32. Hopkins, memo to self, undated, HPL, Reel 20, FDRL.

33. Cable, Hopkins to Beaverbrook, Nov. 6, 1944, MR, Box 13, File 1944 (Outgoing), FDRL.

34. Hopkins, memo to self, Nov. 10, 1944, HPL, Reel 20, FDRL.

35. Hopkins, memo to self, Dec. 12, 1944, HP, Box 220, FDRL.

36. Sherwood, p. 840.

37. Cable, Hopkins to Churchill, Dec. 21, 1944, HPL, Reel 20, FDRL.

CHAPTER NINETEEN

1. HPL, Reel 20, FDRL. This particular item was written in Oct., 1945.

2. Bohlen, pp. 167-68.

3. Wireless, Hopkins to Roosevelt, Jan. 24, 1945, Messages, Reel 6, FDRL.

4. Cable, Hopkins to Louise Hopkins, Jan. 24, 1945, HPL, Reel 21, FDRL.

5. Sherwood, p. 847.

6. Ibid., p. 848. See also letter, Taylor to Hopkins, Jan. 31, 1945, HPL, Reel 13, FDRL.

7. Moran, p. 232.

8. Bohlen, pp. 171-72.

9. Moran, p. 243.

10. Letter, W. Averell Harriman to author, July 21, 1976.

11. McIntire, p. 95.

12. Facsimile in Sherwood, p. 860.

13. Author's interview with Robert Hopkins, May 15, 1976.

14. Stettinius, p. 285.

15. Wireless, Hopkins to Louise Hopkins, in memo from Ogden Kniffen to Dorothea Krauss, Feb. 13, 1945, MR, Box 131, FDRL.

16. Sherwood, p. 870.

17. Hopkins, memo to self, HPL, Reel 20, FDRL. Written in Oct., 1945.

18. Letter, Churchill to Hopkins, Feb. 15, 1945, HPL, Reel 20, FDRL.

19. Bohlen, pp. 204-05.

20. Letter, Hopkins to Rear Admiral John McCrea, April 21, 1945, HPL, Reel 12, FDRL.

21. Letter, Hopkins to John Hertz, Feb. 27, 1945, HPL, Reel 11, FDRL.

CHAPTER TWENTY

1. Bohlen, p. 209.

2. Cable, Hopkins to Churchill, April 12, 1945, HPL, Reel 20, FDRL.

3. Sherwood, p. 880.

4. AP Ticker clipping, April 14, 1945, HPL, Reel 20, FDRL.

5. Sherwood, pp. 881-82.

6. Truman, *Memoirs,* Vol. I, p. 257; Sherwood, p. 82; letter, William R. Emerson, Director of Franklin D. Roosevelt Library, March 29, 1976, to author. Sherwood notes that Hopkins did not go to Hyde Park, but in his *Memoirs* President Truman wrote that he conferred with Hopkins on the way up and back. I have examined the official list of the passengers on the funeral train, and Hopkins' name does not appear. William R. Emerson, Director of the Franklin D. Roosevelt Library, wrote me, "Neither these documents nor our research here at the Library give any indication that Hopkins made the trip to Hyde Park for the funeral." In view of the

immense pressures on him in the days immediately following Roosevelt's death, it is not surprising that President Truman confused the times of the conversations he had with Hopkins.

7. Truman, *Memoirs*, Vol. I, p. 30.

8. Hopkins' memo to self, April 23, 1945, HPL, Reel 20, FDRL.

9. Telegram, Eden, Molotov, and Stettinius to Hopkins, May 4, 1945, HPL, Reel 20, FDRL.

10. Hopkins' VE-Day Broadcast over NBC, May 8, 1945, HPL, Reel 20, FDRL.

11. Harriman and Abel, p. 457.

12. Ibid., p. 459.

13. Letter, Marshall to Hopkins, May 13, 1945, HPL, Reel 21, FDRL.

14. Bohlen, p. 218.

15. Hopkins' memo to self, June 1, 1945, HPL, Reel 20, FDRL.

16. Bohlen, p. 222.

17. Hopkins' memo to self, July 13, 1945, HPL, Reel 20, FDRL.

18. Letter, Hopkins to Winant, July 4, 1945, HPL, Reel 19, FDRL.

19. Letter, Rosenman to Hopkins, June 5, 1945, Reel 19, FDRL.

20. Letter, Hopkins to Beaverbrook, July 6, 1945, HPL, Reel 18, FDRL.

21. Hopkins' letter to Truman and Truman's reply dated respectively July 2 and July 3, 1945, are in HP, Box 214, FDRL.

22. Letter, Ismay to Hopkins, July 4, 1945, HPL, Reel 11, FDRL.

23. Cable, Beaverbrook to Hopkins, July 5, 1945, HPL, Reel 18, FDRL.

24. Letter, Major Lockhart to Hopkins, July 6, 1945, HPL, Reel 21, FDRL.

25. Letter, Douglas Veale, Registrar of Oxford University, to Hopkins, June 19, 1945, HPL, Reel 21, FDRL.

26. Letter, Hopkins to Diana Hopkins, July 28, 1945, HPL, Reel 21, FDRL.

27. Letter, Truman to Hopkins, Aug. 18, 1945, HPL, Reel 21, FDRL.

28. Letter, Truman to Hopkins, Sept. 18, 1945, Reel 21, FDRL.

29. HPL, Reel 20, FDRL.

30. Sherwood, p. 921.

31. Letter, Hopkins to Stettinius, Nov. 9, 1945, HPL, Reel 16, FDRL.

32. Telegram, Churchill to Hopkins, Jan. 15, 1946, HPL, Reel 11, FDRL.

33. Letter, Hopkins to Churchill, Jan. 22, 1946, HPL, Reel 11, FDRL.

34. Author's interview with Robert Hopkins, May 15, 1976.

35. Ibid.

Bibliography

MANUSCRIPT SOURCES

The Hopkins Papers located in the Franklin D. Roosevelt Library constitute 117 linear feet of materials. They include personal letters, official letters, official files and reports of FERA, CWA, and WPA, confidential political files, papers in connection with his work as Secretary of Commerce, Lend-Lease administrator, and Special Assistant to the President. They also contain the notes and materials used by Robert Sherwood in compiling his *Roosevelt and Hopkins*.

The Hopkins Personal Letters and Papers were removed by the family from the Roosevelt Library after they had been microfilmed. The microfilms are in the library and constitute 24 reels. Materials include personal letters, a few official letters, many of Hopkins' memoranda to himself, thank-you and get-well notes and cards, drafts of speeches and articles, and family memorabilia.

The messages between Franklin Roosevelt and Winston Churchill between 1939 and 1945 have been published by the Roosevelt Library in microfilm on six reels. They contain messages from Hopkins to Churchill and some from Hopkins to Roosevelt. In addition, many of the drafts of Roosevelt's messages were written by Hopkins.

The following collections were examined, but most of them yielded little or nothing not duplicated in the two sets of Hopkins materials noted above:

Adolf A. Berle Papers
Wilson Brown Papers
Oscar Cox Papers
Wayne Coy Papers
Mary M. Dewson Papers
Stephen T. Early Papers
Franklin D. Roosevelt Library, Inc., Papers
William D. Hassett Papers
Lorena Hickok Papers (many of these are still not open for inspection)
Howard Hunt Papers
Emile Hurja Papers
Isador Lubin Papers
Map Room Files. Most of the material concerning Hopkins is duplicated in the Roosevelt–Churchill Messages.
Henry M. Morgenthau, Jr. Papers (these include his diary of 800 + volumes)
Frances Perkins Papers
Franklin D. Roosevelt Papers, Official File
Franklin D. Roosevelt Papers, Personal File
Franklin D. Roosevelt Papers, President's Secretary's File
Franklin D. Roosevelt Papers, Map Room File

Samuel I. Rosenman Papers
Henry A. Wallace Papers
Aubrey W. Williams Papers
Henry Stimson Diaries in Yale University Library

PRINTED SOURCES

Periodicals

Extensive use has been made of *Time, Newsweek, The New York Times, United States News, Fortune, The Times* (London), *The Daily Telegraph* (London), and *The Daily Express* (London). Hopkins' articles appear mostly in the *American* magazine and are cited in the notes. His "Profile" in *The New Yorker* is also cited in the notes.

Books

On Hopkins' death, the *New York Times* reported that he had nearly finished his memoirs. This story was erroneous, for he had done little or nothing. Robert E. Sherwood, the playwright, who had become a speech writer for Roosevelt and was a personal friend of Hopkins, was asked to put Hopkins' memoirs in order for publication. They were too incomplete, so Sherwood wrote *Roosevelt and Hopkins,* published in 1948, revised edition, 1950, a monumental work for its time, but which fresh material has outdated.

Appleby, Paul. "Roosevelt's Third Term Decision," *American Political Science Review,* 44 (Sept. 1952), pp. 754–65.

Asbell, Bernard. *The F.D.R. Memoirs.* Garden City, N.Y.: Doubleday, 1973.

Baker, Leonard. *Roosevelt and Pearl Harbor.* New York: Macmillan, 1970.

Baruch, Bernard. *The Public Years.* New York: Holt, Rinehart and Winston, 1960.

Beard, Charles A. *President Roosevelt and the Coming of the War, 1941.* New Haven: Yale Univ. Press, 1948.

Berle, Beatrice Bishop, and Travis Beal Jacobs, eds. *Navigating the Rapids 1918-1971: From the Papers of Adolf A. Berle.* New York: Harcourt Brace Jovanovich, 1973.

Bishop, Jim. *FDR's Last Year, April 1944-April 1945.* New York: Morrow, 1974.

Bloom, Sol. *The Autobiography of Sol Bloom.* New York: Putnam's, 1948.

Blum, John Morton. *From the Morgenthau Diaries,* Vol. I, *Years of Crisis, 1928-1938.* Boston: Houghton Mifflin, 1959. Vol. II, *Years of Urgency, 1938-1941.* Same: 1965.

———, ed. *The Price of Vision, The Diary of Henry A. Wallace, 1942-1946.* Boston: Houghton Mifflin, 1973.

———, ed. *Roosevelt and Morgenthau.* Boston: Houghton Mifflin, 1973.

Bohlen, Charles E. *Witness to History, 1929-1969.* New York: Norton, 1973.

Bryant, Arthur. *The Alanbrooke Diaries,* Vol. I, *The Turn of the Tide.* New York: Doubleday, Vol. II, *Triumph in the West, 1943-1946.* London: Collins, 1959.

Buchanan, A. Russell. *The United States and World War II.* 2 vols. New York: Harper & Row, 1964.

Bullitt, Orville H., ed. *For the President: Personal and Secret: Correspondence between Franklin D. Roosevelt and William C. Bullitt.* Boston: Houghton Mifflin, 1972.

Burns, James MacGregor. *Roosevelt: The Lion and the Fox.* New York: Harcourt Brace & World, 1956.

———. *Roosevelt: The Soldier of Freedom.* New York: Harcourt Brace Jovanovich, 1970.

Bush, Vannevar. *Pieces of the Action.* New York: Morrow, 1970.

Butcher, Harry C. *My Three Years with Eisenhower.* New York: Simon and Schuster, 1946.

Byrnes, James F. *All in One Lifetime.* New York: Harper, 1958.

Campbell, Thomas M., and George C. Herring, eds. *The Diaries of Edward R. Stettinius, Jr., 1943-1946.* New York: New Viewpoints, 1975.

Charles, Searle F. *Minister of Relief: Harry Hopkins and the Depression.* Syracuse: Syracuse Univ. Press, 1963.

Childs, Marquis W. *I Write from Washington.* New York: Harper, 1942.

Churchill, Winston S. *History of the Second World War,* Vol. I, *The Gathering Storm,* 1948. Vol. II, *Their Finest Hour,* 1949. Vol. III, *The Grand Alliance,* 1950. Vol. IV, *The Hinge of Fate,* 1950. Vol. V, *Closing the Ring,* 1951. Vol. VI, *Triumph and Tragedy,* 1953. All: Boston: Houghton Mifflin.

Connally, Senator Tom, as told to Alfred Steinberg. *My Name is Tom Connally.* New York: Crowell, 1954.

Cunningham, Admiral of the Fleet Viscount Cunningham of Hyndhope. *A Sailor's Odyssey.* London: Hutchinson, 1951.

Daniels, Jonathan. *The Time Between the Wars: Armistice to Pearl Harbor.* Garden City: Doubleday, 1966.

———. *Washington Quadrille: The Dance Beside the Documents.* Garden City: Doubleday, 1968.

———. *White House Witness, 1942-1945.* Garden City: Doubleday, 1975.

Davis, Forrest, and Ernest K. Lindley. *How War Came.* New York: Simon and Schuster, 1945.

Davis, Kenneth Sydney. *Experience of War: The United States in World War II.* Garden City: Doubleday, 1965.

Dawson, Raymond H. *The Decision to Aid Russia: Foreign Policy and Domestic Politics.* Chapel Hill: Univ. of North Carolina Press, 1959.

Donahoe, Bernard F. *Private Plans and Public Dangers.* Notre Dame: Univ. of Notre Dame Press, 1965.

Douglas, William O. *Go East, Young Man: The Early Years.* New York: Random House, 1974.

Dyer, Vice Admiral George C., USN, Ret. *The Amphibians Came to Conquer: The Story of Admiral Richmond Kelly Turner,* 2 vols. Washington: U.S. Government Printing Office, 1971.

Eccles, Marriner S. *Beckoning Frontiers: Public and Personal Recollections.* New York: Knopf, 1951.

Eisenhower, Dwight D. *Crusade in Europe.* Garden City: Doubleday, 1948.

———, *The Papers of Dwight David Eisenhower: The War Years,* Alfred D. Chandler, Jr., et al., eds. 5 Vols. Baltimore and London: Johns Hopkins Press, 1970.

Farley, James A. *Jim Farley's Story: The Roosevelt Years.* New York: McGraw-Hill, 1948.

Feis, Herbert. *Between War and Peace: The Potsdam Conference.* Princeton: Princeton Univ. Press, 1960.

———. *Churchill, Roosevelt, Stalin: The War they Waged and the Peace they Sought.* Princeton: Princeton Univ. Press, 1957.

———. *The Road to Pearl Harbor: The Coming of the War Between the United States and Japan.* Princeton: Princeton Univ. Press, 1950.

Fischer, Louis. *The Road to Yalta: Soviet Foreign Relations, 1941-1945.* New York: Harper & Row, 1972.

Flynn, Edward J. *You're the Boss.* New York: Viking, 1947.

Flynn, John T. *The Roosevelt Myth.* New York: Devin-Adair, 1948.

Freedman, Max, ed. *Roosevelt and Frankfurter: Their Correspondence, 1928-1945.* Boston: Little, Brown, 1967.

Greenfield, Kent R., ed. *Command Decisions.* Washington: Office of the Chief of Military History, 1960.

Grew, Joseph C. *Turbulent Era: A Diplomatic Record of Forty Years, 1904-1945.* 2 vols., ed. by Walter Johnson. Boston: Houghton Mifflin, 1952.

Gunther, John. *Roosevelt in Retrospect, A Profile in History.* New York: Harper, 1950.

Harriman, W. Averell, and Elie Abel. *Special Envoy to Churchill and Stalin, 1941-1946.* New York: Random House, 1975.

Hassett, William D. *Off the Record With F.D.R., 1942-1945.* London: Allen & Unwin, 1960.

High, Stanley. *Roosevelt—And Then?* New York: Harper, 1937.

Hollis, Sir Leslie. *War at the Top.* London: Michael Joseph, 1959.

Hopkins, Harry L. "The Inside Story of My Meeting With Stalin," *American Magazine,* Dec., 1941, pp. 14-15.

———. *Spending to Save: The Complete Story of Relief.* New York: Norton, 1936.

———. "You and Your Family Will Be Mobilized," *American Magazine,* Dec., 1944, pp. 18-19.

Hull, Cordell. *Memoirs.* 2 vols. New York: Macmillan, 1948.

Huthmacher, J. Joseph. *Senator Robert F. Wagner and the Rise of Urban Liberalism.* New York: Atheneum, 1968.

Ickes, Harold L. *The Secret Diary of Harold L. Ickes.* Vol. I, *The First Thousand Days, 1933-1936.* Vol. II, *The Inside Struggle, 1936-39,* 1954. Vol. III, *The Lowering Clouds, 1939-1941,* 1954. All: New York: Simon and Schuster.

Ismay, Lord Hastings. *The Memoirs of General Lord Hastings Ismay.* New York: Viking, 1960.

Israel, Fred L., ed. *The War Diary of Breckenridge Long: Selections from the Years 1939-1944.* Lincoln: Univ. of Nebraska Press, 1966.

Kennedy, Major General Sir John. *The Business of War.* London: Hutchinson, 1957.

Kenney, William. *The Crucial Years, 1940-1945.* New York: Macfadden Books, 1962.

King, Ernest J., and Walter Muir Whitehall. *Fleet Admiral King: A Naval Record.* New York: Norton, 1952.

Koenig, Louis W. *The Invisible Presidency.* New York: Rinehart, 1960.

Koskoff, David E. *Joseph P. Kennedy: A Life and Times.* Englewood Cliffs: Prentice-Hall, 1974.

Krock, Arthur. *Memoirs: Sixty Years on the Firing Line.* New York: Funk & Wagnalls, 1968.

Langer, William L. *Our Vichy Gamble.* New York: Knopf, 1947.

———, and S. Everett Gleason. *The Challenge to Isolation, 1937-1940.* New York: Harper, 1952.

———, and S. Everett Gleason. *The Undeclared War, 1940-1941.* New York: Harper, 1953.

Lash, Joseph P. *Eleanor and Franklin.* New York: New American Library, 1973.

———, *Roosevelt and Churchill, 1939-1941.* New York; Norton, 1976.

Lawson, Don. *The United States in World War II.* New York: Grosset & Dunlap, 1964.

Lilienthal, David E. *The Journals of David E. Lilienthal* Vol. I, *The War Years, 1939-1945.* New York: Harper, 1964.

Loewenheim, Francis L., Harold D. Langley, and Manfred Jonas, eds. *Roosevelt and Churchill: Their Secret Wartime Correspondence.* New York: Dutton, 1975.

McIntire, Vice Admiral Ross T. *White House Physician.* New York: Putnam's, 1946.

McNeill, William Hardy. *America, Britain & Russia: Their Co-Operation and Conflict, 1941-1946.* London: Oxford Univ. Press, 1953.

McSherry, James E. *Stalin, Hitler and Europe, 1933-1939.* Cleveland and New York: World, 1968.

Maisky, Ivan. *Memoirs of a Soviet Ambassador: The War: 1939-43,* Andrew Rothstein, tr. New York: Scribner's, 1968.

Matloff, Maurice, and Edwin M. Snell. *Strategic Planning for Coalition Warfare,* 2 vols. Washington: Office of the Chief of Military History, 1953, 1959.

Millis, Walter, ed. *The Forrestal Diaries.* New York: Viking, 1951.

———. *This is Pearl: The United States and Japan—1941.* New York: Morrow, 1947.

Moran, Lord. *Churchill: Taken from the Diaries of Lord Moran.* Boston: Houghton Mifflin, 1966.

Morgenthau, Diaries—See Blum, John Morton.

Nelson, Donald M. *Arsenal of Democracy: The Story of American War Production.* New York: Harcourt, Brace, 1946.

Nicolson, Harold. *The War Years, 1939-1945.* Nigel Nicolson, ed. New York: Atheneum, 1976.

Parmet, Herbert S., and Marie B. Hecht. *Never Again: A President Runs for a Third Term.* New York: Macmillan, 1968.

Perkins, Frances. *The Roosevelt I Knew.* New York: Viking, 1946.

Pogue, Forrest C. *George C. Marshall: Education of a General, 1880-1939.* New York: Viking, 1963.

———. *George C. Marshall: Ordeal and Hope, 1939-1942.* New York: Viking, 1966.

———. *George C. Marshall: Organizer of Victory.* New York: Viking, 1973.

———. *The Supreme Command.* Washington: Office of the Chief of Military History, 1954.

Rauch, Basil. *Roosevelt from Munich to Pearl Harbor.* New York: Creative Age Press, 1960.

Reilly, Michael F., as told to William J. Slocum. *Reilly of the White House.* New York: Simon and Schuster, 1947.

Richberg, Donald R. *My Hero: The Indiscreet Memoirs of an Eventful but Unknown Life.* New York: Putnam's, 1954.

Rigdon, William M., with James Derieux. *White House Sailor.* Garden City: Doubleday, 1962.

Rollins, Alfred B., Jr., ed. *Franklin D. Roosevelt and the Age of Action.* New York: Dell, 1960.

———. *Roosevelt and Howe.* New York: Knopf, 1962.

Roosevelt, Eleanor. *This I Remember.* New York: Harper & Row, 1949.

Roosevelt, Elliott. *As He Saw It.* New York: Duell, Sloan and Pearce, 1946.

———, ed. *F.D.R. His Personal Letters, 1928-1945,* 2 vols. New York: Duell, Sloan and Pearce, 1950.

———, and James Brough. *A Rendezvous With Destiny: The Roosevelts of the White House.* New York: Putnam's, 1975.

———, and James Brough. *An Untold Story: The Roosevelts of Hyde Park.* New York: Putnam's, 1973.

Roosevelt, Franklin D. *Nothing to Fear: Selected Addresses of Franklin D. Roosevelt.* Benjamin D. Zevin, ed. New York: World, 1946.

———. *The Public Papers and Addresses of Franklin D. Roosevelt,* ed. Samuel I. Rosenman, 4 vols. New York: Duell, Sloan and Pearce, 1945-1950.

Rosenman, Samuel I. *Working With Roosevelt.* New York: Harper, 1952.

Schlesinger, Arthur M., Jr. *The Coming of the New Deal.* Boston: Houghton Mifflin, 1959.

———. *The Crisis of the Old Order.* Boston: Houghton Mifflin, 1957.

———. *The Politics of Upheaval.* Boston: Houghton Mifflin, 1960.

Seligman, Lester G., and Elmer Cornwell, Jr. *New Deal Mosaic: Roosevelt Confers With His National Emergency Council, 1933-1936.* Eugene, Oregon: Univ. of Oregon Books, 1965.

Sherwood, Robert E. *Roosevelt and Hopkins, An Intimate History.* Rev. ed. New York: Harper, 1950.

Smith, Gene. *The Shattered Dream: Herbert Hoover and the Great Depression.* New York: Morrow, 1970.

Stalin's Correspondence with Churchill, Attlee, Roosevelt and Truman, 1941-1945. London: Lawrence & Wishart, 1958. Published originally by the Ministry of Foreign Affairs of the U.S.S.R. and the Foreign Languages Publishing House, 1957. The English edition binds the two Russian volumes in one, with separate pagination for each volume.

Stettinius, Edward R., Jr. *Roosevelt and the Russians: The Yalta Conference.* Ed. by Walter Johnson. Garden City: Doubleday, 1949.

Stimson, Henry L., and McGeorge Bundy. *On Active Service in Peace and War.* New York: Harper, 1948.

Taylor, A. J. P. *Beaverbrook.* New York: Simon and Schuster, 1972.

Thompson, Laurence. *1940.* New York: Morrow, 1966.

Thompson, Walter H. *Assignment: Churchill.* New York: Farrar, Straus & Cudahy, 1955.

Timmons, Bascom N. *Jesse H. Jones: The Man and the Statesman.* New York: Holt, 1956.

Truman, Harry S. *Memoirs by Harry S. Truman.* Vol. I, *Year of Decisions,* 1955. Vol. II, *Years of Trial and Hope, 1946-1952,* 1956. Both: Garden City: Doubleday.

Tugwell, Rexford G. *The Brains Trust.* New York: Viking, 1963.

———. *The Democratic Roosevelt: A Biography of Franklin D. Roosevelt.* Garden City: Doubleday, 1957.

———. *In Search of Roosevelt.* Cambridge: Harvard Univ. Press, 1972.

Tully, Grace. *F.D.R., My Boss.* New York: Scribner's, 1949.

Wallace, Henry A., Diary: See Blum, John Morton, ed., *The Price of Vision.*

Watson, Mark Skinner. *Chief of Staff: Plans and Preparations, United States Army in World War II.* Washington: Historical Division, Dept. of the Army, 1950.

Wechter, Donald. *The Age of the Great Depression, 1929-1941.* New York: Macmillan, 1948.

Welles, Sumner. *Whither Are We Heading?* New York: Harper, 1946.

Wheeler, Burton K., with Paul F. Healy. *Yankee from the West.* Garden City: Doubleday, 1962.

Whitehead, Don. *The FBI Story.* New York: Random House, 1956.

Wilmot, Chester. *The Struggle for Europe: World War II in Western Europe.* New York: Harper, 1952.

Wilson, Theodore A. *The First Summit: Roosevelt and Churchill at Placentia Bay 1941.* Boston: Houghton Mifflin, 1969.

Winant, John Gilbert. *Letter from Grosvenor Square: An Account of a Stewardship.* Boston: Houghton Mifflin, 1947.

Zevin, Ben D. See: Roosevelt, Franklin D., *Nothing to Fear.*

Index

Abbreviations, glossary of, 407
Adams, Alva, 135
Adams, Sherman, 165, 404
Advisory Committee on Allotments, 82
Afrika Corps, 297, 299
Agricultural Adjustment Act (1933), 50
Agricultural Adjustment
  Administration (AAA), 12
Aimé, Frank, 38
Aircraft industry, 140
Alexander, Sir Harold, 314
Alexander, Will, 191
Alexandria, Egypt, 283
Allied Control Commission for
  Germany, 19, 378, 391
Allied Dental Clinic, 38
American Liberty League, 67, 98
American magazine, 237, 302, 357
American Red Cross, 36-37, 93
Anakim operation, 325
Anvil operation, 333, 345, 359-60
Anzio, Italy, 351
Appleby, Paul, 171
Arauca, German vessel, 217
Archangel, Russia, 236, 240
Argentia, Newfoundland, 231, 243
Argentia conference, *see* Atlantic
  conference
Army, U. S., 161, 162, 164, 249-50, 358

Army Air Corps, U. S., 142
Army Corps of Engineers, 82, 90
Army Signal Corps, U. S., 375
Arnold, Henry H., 142, 231, 243, 265,
  275, 276, 281, 286, 314, 330, 344, 375
Arnstein, Daniel, 150, 219
Associated Outpatient Clinic, 38
Association for Improving the
  Condition of the Poor (AICP), 35,
  37-38, 43, 48
Association of American Railroads, 306
Astor, Lady, 208
Atlantic, Battle of the, 283
Atlantic Charter, 247, 265
Atlantic (Argentia) conference, (1941),
  243-47, 249, 250, 254, 264-65, 267-68
Atlantic Monthly, 321
Atomic bomb, 166, 318
Attlee, Clement, 397
Augusta, USS, 243, 244, 245, 246, 247
Aurora, USS, 382
Austin, Warren, 260
Austria, 139
Azores, 325, 372

Badoglio, Pietro, 330, 331
Bailey, Josiah, 18, 150
Baker, Bobby, 405
Baker, Jacob, 52

Baker, Newton D., 46
Baltimore Sun, 48, 192
Bane, Frank, 57
Bangor, Maine, 29, 30
Bankhead, William, 175
Barclay, Edwin, 316
Barkley, Alben, 260
Barton, Bruce, 189
Baruch, Bernard, 111, 149, 151, 154,
   164, 219, 302-03, 317, 399, 401
Bataan Peninsula, Philippines, 269
Bathurst, Gambia, 316
Batt, William L., 151, 194, 250
Beardall, John R., 243, 247
Beaufre, Captain, 311
Beaumont-Nesbitt, F. G., 251
Beaverbrook, Lord Max, 208, 250, 266,
   267, 275, 288-89, 294, 323, 327, 359,
   366, 395, 396, 404
Belgium, 164
Benson, USS, 217
Berle, Adolf A., 47, 169-70, 188, 216,
   225
Berlin, Irving, 226
Bermuda, 361, 372
Bernhard, Prince, 227
Bethesda Naval Hospital, 352, 354
Bidault, General, 373, 378
Biggers, John, 194
Bismarck, German battleship, 224, 225
Bismarck Islands, 269
Black, Hugo, 116
"Black Tuesday," 122
Bloom, Sol, 259, 260, 384
Blue Bonnet, The, 86-87
Boettiger, Anna Roosevelt, 290, 324,
   383
Boettiger, John, 290
Bogart, Humphrey, 304
Bohlen, Charles E., 18, 19, 343, 347,
   364, 371, 372, 374, 375, 376, 377, 379,
   382, 383, 385, 389-90, 391, 392, 393
Bolero operation, 275, 276, 277, 282,
   284, 324
Booth, John Wilkes, 116
Borah, William E., 77, 100
Bougainville, 344
Boulder Dam, 85
Bound Brook, New Jersey, 34
Bracken, Brendan, 15, 200, 203
Bradley, Omar Nelson, 374

Brady, Diamond Jim, 35
Brady, Dorothy, 291
Brain Trust, 11, 47, 402
Brandeis, Louis D., 130
Brandt and Brandt, 388
Branion, Ray, 68
Bricker, John, 359
Briggs, George N., 353-54
Britain, *see* Great Britain
British Joint Staff Mission, 220
Brooke, Sir Alan, 278, 281, 282, 283,
   285, 314, 321, 324, 333, 346, 373-74
Broun, Heywood, 150
Brown, Wilson, 86
Brownlow, Louis, 57
Bruenn, Howard, 308, 370, 375
Budd, Ralph, 167
Bulgaria, 363
Bullitt, William C., 141
Buna, 292
Burke, Edward R., 185
Burke-Wadsworth Bill, 185
Burma, 269, 314, 325, 344, 349
Burma Road, 342
Burns, James H., 214, 216, 256
Burns, John, 271
Burritt, Bailey B., 38-39
Bush, Vannevar, 165-66
Business Advisory Council, 151, 157
Butcher, Harry, 161, 286
Byrnes, James F., 71, 84, 174, 294, 302,
   306, 326, 328, 367, 375, 388, 390, 395,
   403-04

Cadogan, Sir Alexander, 231
Cairo conference (1943), 305, 339, 341-
   42, 349
Callaghan, Daniel J., 142, 195
Camp David, Maryland, 290
Campobello, New Brunswick, 99, 139
Canfield, Cass, 396
Cardozo, Benjamin, 22
Casablanca, 297, 301, 305, 309
Casablanca conference (1943), 305,
   309-16, 318
Caserta, Italy, 373
Casey, Richard G., 200
Censorship, 259
Cerros Island, 86
Chamberlain, Neville, 141, 164
Chennault, Claire, 325, 341

Chiang, Madame, 296, 301-02, 319, 325, 342, 355
Chiang Kai-shek, 240, 254, 272, 329, 339, 342, 349, 350, 355, 404
Chicago, Illinois, 32, 34, 121, 136, 171
Chicago News, 54, 148
Chicago Tribune, 192, 327, 334
Children's Welfare Clinic, 38
Childs, Marquis, 52
China and the Chinese, 121, 240, 301-02, 319, 325, 342, 343
China Incident, 257
Christadora House, New York City, 34-35
Churchill, Clementine, 231, 232, 234, 251, 268, 279, 333, 400
Churchill, Pamela, 286, 323
Churchill, Randolph, 310, 312, 315, 382
Churchill, Sarah, 342, 400
Churchill, Winston S., 12, 15-16, 17, 19, 26, 29, 141, 154, 164, 167, 185, 196, 199-200, 201, 202, 203-11, 212, 216, 220, 221, 222, 228, 229, 230, 233, 234, 237, 240, 241, 242, 254, 263-68, 275, 278-81, 282, 283, 284, 285-86, 290, 294, 295, 299, 300, 302, 305, 307, 310, 318, 320, 321, 322, 323, 324-25, 327, 333, 337, 339, 351, 352, 355, 356, 359, 362, 367-68, 372, 374, 382, 385, 392-93, 396-97, 400, 403, 404; Atlantic conference, 244-47; Cairo conference, 341-42; Casablanca conference, 309-16, Quebec conference, 331, 332-33, 361-63; Roosevelt and, 167, 185, 196, 244-48, 250, 263, 268, 305, 323, 331, 342, 343-49, 375-81, 382; Stalin and, 292, 343-49, 367, 370, 375-81; Teheran conference, 343-49; Trident conference, 323-25; Yalta conference, 375-81
Civilian Conservation Corps (CCC), 45, 128, 129
Civil War, 30
Civil Works Administration (CWA), 12, 57, 58-63, 67, 73
Clark, Bennett Champ, 94
Clark, Mark, 312
Clay, Lucius D., 393
Clendinin, F. F., 193
Cleveland, Ohio, 190

Clifford, Clark, 404
Clinchy, Russell J., 120, 287, 401
Coast Guard, U. S., 288
Cocos Island, 22, 86
Cohen, Ben, 24, 97, 112, 122, 133, 326
Cold War, 393
Combined Chiefs of Staff, 265, 266-67, 273, 286, 299, 305, 324, 342, 347, 348, 349, 359, 373-74
Commerce Committee hearings, 150-51
Commerce Department, U. S., 148, 163
Compton, Karl T., 165
Compulsory military service, 185
Conant, James B., 165
Cone, Howard M., 317
Congress, U. S., 51, 57, 112, 116, 117-18, 121, 122, 125, 129, 134, 137, 139, 142, 162, 165, 212, 261, 262, 264, 293, 294, 329, 385
Congressional Record, 353
Connally, Tom, 260, 353, 384
Connolly, Donald, 349
Cooper, Jere, 260
Coral Sea, Battle of the, 280
Corcoran, Thomas, 97, 101, 112, 122, 128, 133, 138, 165, 183, 403
Corregidor, Philippine Islands, 280
Costigan, Edward, 51
Cox, Oscar, 216, 218, 228, 356-57, 361, 363
Craig, Malin, 142
Cripps, Sir Stafford, 274, 275
Cumberland, Maryland, 93
Cummings, Homer, 68, 145
Cunningham, Sir Andrew B., 314, 341
Currie, Lauchlin, 122
Curtin, John, 320
Czechoslovakia, 139, 141, 154

Dago Frank, 35
Daily Worker, 190
Daladier, Edouard, 141
Damaskinos, Archbishop, 368
Darlan, François, 297-99
Davey, Martin L., 24, 75-76, 96
Davies, Joseph E., 328, 335
Davis, Benjamin O., 191
Davis, Chester C., 167
Davis, Elmer, 161
Davis, Jefferson, 161
Davis, John W., 86, 100

Dawkins, Elmer, 218
Declaration of Panama (1939), 222
Defense Cabinet Committee, 216
De Gaulle, Charles, 305, 310, 311, 312,
    313, 314-15, 343, 372-73, 378, 382-83,
    393
Delabrooke, Maryland, 158
Democratic National Convention
    (1912), 34; (1932), 46-47, 305; (1936),
    101; (1940), 171-77; (1944), 360
Denmark, 164, 222, 223
Depression of the 1930s, 47, 50
Des Moines, Iowa, 151
Destroyers-for-bases deal, 185
Dewey, Thomas E., 170, 359, 386
Dies, Martin, 145
Dill, Sir John, 231, 265, 314
Diviison of Defense Aid Reports
    (DDAR), 216
Dodge, Harry C., 33
Dollfuss, Engelbert, 65
Doolittle, James, 279
Dort, Dallas, 102
Douglas, Lewis, 61
Douglas, William O., 18, 111, 115, 186-
    87, 188, 268, 269
Dreyfus, Louis G., 343
Drought, 102
Dubinsky, David, 188, 394, 401
Duke of York, HMS, 264
Dumbarton Oaks conference, 371
Dun, Bishop Angus, 386
Duncan, Donald, 317

Eaker, Ira, 285
Earle, George, 131
Early, Stephen, 25, 76, 97, 114, 120,
    124, 125, 136, 138, 145, 198-99, 223,
    224, 247, 258, 259, 285, 286, 302, 365,
    382, 403
Eaton, Charles A., 260, 384
Eberstadt, Ferdinand, 317, 318
Eccles, Marriner, 128
Economic Stabilization Act (1943), 294
Eden, Anthony, 18, 202, 292, 301, 319,
    321, 325, 327, 331, 338, 344, 345, 347,
    349-50, 384, 388, 403, 404
Edison, Charles, 168
Edward, Duke of Windsor, 195
Ehrlichman, John, 405

Eighth Air Force, U. S., 285, 324
Eighth Army, British, 297, 309
Eisenhower, Dwight David, 19, 165,
    266, 275, 281, 285, 286, 290, 297, 298,
    299, 307, 310, 312-13, 314, 319, 321,
    324, 331, 333, 341, 350, 372, 373, 374,
    390-91, 393, 399, 404, 405
Elimination Committee, 133
Elizabeth, Queen, 157-58, 210-11
Elliott, Harriet, 167
Emerson, Haven, 39
Emery, Marcellus (Harry's
    grandfather), 29-30
End Poverty in America program
    (EPIA), 71-72
England, *see* Great Britain
Enterprise, USS, 77
Equitable Life Assurance Society, 221
Essex, USS, 317
Ethiopia, 86

Farley, James, 59, 60, 71, 78, 81, 84, 92,
    105, 110, 131, 132, 133, 138, 170, 173,
    174, 175, 177
Faymanville, Philip R., 250
Federal Bureau of Investigation, 353,
    354
Federal Emergency Relief
    Administration (FERA), 11, 51-66,
    67, 73, 75, 78, 90
Federal Farm Loan Banks, 43
Federal Reserve System, 43
Federal Surplus Commodities
    Corporation, 136
Federal Surplus Relief Corporation, 55-
    56, 93
Fee, Harry W., 103
Ferguson, Gladys, 32
Ferguson, Hallie, 32
Fess, Simeon D., 51, 71
Fifth Army, British, 322
Fifth Army, U. S., 312
Finland, 161
Fish, Hamilton, 188-89, 259
Flood control, 128
Flood Emergency Committee, 93, 113-
    14
Floods, 92-94, 113-14
Flynn, Edward J., 177, 189, 192
Folsom, M. B., 151

Foreign Ministers Conference (1943), 338
Formosa, 347
Fort Clayton, Panama, 86
Fort Jefferson, Dry Tortugas, 116
Forrestal, James, 276, 387, 400, 401, 404
Fortune magazine, 61
Fox, George, 156
France and the French, 141, 161, 162, 164, 254, 297, 310, 343, 345, 360, 363, 372-73, 376, 378, 382
Franco, Francisco, 121
Frankfurt am Main, Germany, 392
Frankfurter, Felix, 24, 97, 111, 115, 130, 188, 199-200, 326, 336, 401
Frederick, Maryland, 323
Free French, 310, 312, 314
Freeman, Wilfred, 231
Fruehauf, Roy, 288
Fulter, James R., 277

Garner, John Nance, 46, 76, 84, 111, 115, 132, 171, 174, 175, 213
Generich, Gus, 56, 86
George, King, of Greece, 368
George, Walter, 135
George VI, King, 157-58, 196, 205, 210-11, 307
German reparations, 377
Germany and the Germans, 121, 139, 161, 162, 164, 172, 239, 270, 276, 277, 283, 295, 299, 315, 319, 325, 332, 333, 345, 361, 362, 363, 374, 378, 393
Gilbert Islands, 269
Gill, Corrington, 52, 90, 145
Gillette, Guy, 134
Giraud, Henri, 297, 310, 311, 314-15
Glass, Carter, 74
Goddard, Paulette, 280
Godwin, Kathryn, 89
Goldberg, Jacob, 39-40, 43, 44
Gompers, Samuel, 57
Gona, 292
Gordon, Max, 150, 151
Grand Alliance, The (Churchill), 244
Great Britain and the British, 141, 161, 162, 164, 167, 172, 177, 185, 196, 198, 210, 212, 214, 220-21, 228, 231, 262,

267, 269, 278, 281, 284, 297, 299, 318, 324, 330, 342, 376, 396
Great Plains Drought Area Committee, 102
Greece, 363, 368
Green, William, 81, 188
Greenland, 222, 223
Greer incident, 252-53
Grew, Joseph, 255
Grinnell, Iowa, 31, 32, 42, 153, 156, 158
Grinnell College, 31, 32-33, 82, 156
Gromyko, Andrei, 384, 404
Guadalcanal, 292
Guam, 269
Guru Letters, 186-87
Gymnast operation, 267, 277, 281, 283, 284, 286
Gyp the Blood, 35

Haakon VII, King, 211
Hachmeister, Louise, 183
Hague, Frank, 97
Haldeman, H. R., 405
Hale, Dorothy Donovan Thomas, 137
Halifax, Lord, 202-03, 207, 220, 229, 399, 401
Halsey, William F., Jr., 325
Hanes, John, 150
Hannegan, Robert, 387
Harding, Warren G., 173
Harper & Brothers, 396
Harriman, W. Averell, 13, 149, 151, 152, 168, 194, 199, 211, 215-16, 219, 234, 243, 246, 250, 264, 271, 273, 274, 278, 281, 287, 290, 292, 295, 301, 311, 312, 315, 316, 328-29, 333-34, 337, 342, 344, 345, 347, 364, 375, 376, 377, 378, 379, 388, 389, 391; foreword by, 15-20
Harriman, Kathleen, 19, 20, 234, 286
Harrington, Francis C., 90-91, 114, 143, 145, 179
Hart, Albert Bushnell, 33
Hart, Thomas, 56
Hassett, William, 193
Hastie, William, 191
Hawes, Harry B., 119
Hemingway, Ernest, 195
Henderson, Leon, 122, 128, 167, 251, 271, 293

Hertz, Fanny, 354
Hertz, John, 124, 149, 156, 163, 219, 354, 383
Highland Park, Illinois, 92
Highway program, 128, 129
Hillman, Sidney, 167, 188, 214, 251
Hilton, James, 290
Hirohito, Emperor, 257
Hitler, Adolf, 17, 50, 65, 121, 139, 140, 141, 154, 172, 177, 184, 186, 214, 221, 228, 297
Hodson, William, 44, 50, 51
Holland, 164
Holt, Rush, 103
Home Owners' Loan Corporation, 50
Hong Kong, China, 269
Hood, HMS, 224
Hoover, Herbert H., 41, 42-43, 47, 85, 100, 101
Hopkins, Adah May (Harry's sister), 31, 32, 38, 40, 45, 401
Hopkins, Anna Pickett (Harry's mother), 29, 30-31, 39, 42
Hopkins, Barbara (Harry's daughter), 36
Hopkins, Barbara Duncan (Harry's wife), 23, 40, 53, 56, 66, 92, 95, 97, 99, 117, 119-20, 401
Hopkins, Cherry Preisser, 117, 125, 153, 401
Hopkins, David (Harry's son), 117, 125, 153, 173, 272, 287, 317, 329, 401
Hopkins, David Aldona (Harry's father), 29, 30-31, 39, 42
Hopkins, Diana (Harry's daughter), 23, 45, 53, 120, 123-24, 125, 137, 145, 147, 156, 157-58, 163, 242, 275, 287, 289, 299, 301, 325, 329, 330, 351, 358, 396
Hopkins, Ethel Gross (Harry's wife), 35, 38, 44-45, 178, 351
Hopkins, Etta (Harry's sister), 31
Hopkins, Ezek, 29
Hopkins, Harry Lloyd, ancestry of, 29-30; Argentia conference, 243-47; birth of, 29; boyhood of, 32-33; Cairo conference, 341-42; career, estimate of, 403-04; children of, 36, 45; Churchill and, 15-16, 17, 26, 203-11, 230-34, 241-42, 244-48, 264, 278-81, 285-86, 294, 367-68, 382, 385;
confidential investigator, 140; CWA administrator, 12; death of, 20, 401; Distinguished Service Medal award, 397; divorce, 44-45; early employment, 34-48; education of, 32-33; End Poverty in America program, 71-72; executive officer for FDR, 193-94; Federal Emergency Relief administrator, 11, 49-66; foreign missions, 40-41, 63-66, 198-211, 230-48, 262, 284-287, 277-79, 371-74, 390-94; honorary degrees, 82, 137, 396, 399; Ickes feud, 74-88, 94-97, 99, 116; illnesses of, 12, 18-19, 20, 23-24, 32, 36-37, 72, 83-84, 123-25, 138, 153-54, 156-57, 158-61, 163, 224, 240, 253, 255-56, 317, 338, 351, 352, 356-58, 373, 399; Impartial Chairman Coat and Suit Industry, 394-95, 397, 398, 399; "Inner Cabinet" chief, 129-45, 262-87, 292, 326; intimacy with FDR, 11-12, 15, 16, 17, 22, 25-26, 29, 41, 56, 98, 99-100, 110-11, 147, 155-56, 183, 193, 195, 252, 289, 360, 402-03, 406; Lease-Lend program administrator, 12, 214-29, 230-47, 251, 404; letter of resignation, 21-26, 397; marriages, 35-36, 45, 287; Munitions Assignment Board chairman, 266-67, 305, 318, 325, 328; new frontier program, 136-37; opposition to, 67-68, 118-19, 276, 288-89, 302-03, 317, 327-28, 334-35, 353-54; parents of, 29, 30-31, 42; Pius XII and, 373; political interest of, 34, 36, 41-42, 47-48, 138; post-war plans of, 361-62, 386-87, 391-97, 398-99; Potsdam conference, 20; presidential ambition of, 96, 109, 124, 127, 130-32, 138, 144, 158, 163; presidential representative, 198-212; Quebec conference, 331, 332-33; Roosevelt Library director, 178, 193; Secretary of Commerce, 17-18, 23, 131-32, 143-47, 148-70, 177, 178; siblings of, 31, 32, 38, 39, 45, 48; social worker, 34-48; Special Assistant to the President, 250-51, 262, 271; speech writer, 69, 72-73, 101, 183-84, 188-91, 197, 250, 253, 268, 403; Stalin and, 12, 17, 18-20,

237-40, 391-92; Teheran conference, 343-49; Trident conference, 323-25; Truman and, 385-86, 387; WPA administrator, 12, 22-23, 74-88, 89-109, 113, 114, 117, 118, 119, 139-40, 143, 144-45; Yalta conference, 375-81
Hopkins, Helen, 197
Hopkins, John Emery (Harry's brother), 31, 38, 39, 106
Hopkins, Lewis Andrew (Harry's brother), 31, 39, 48, 63-64, 78, 88, 90, 106, 119-20, 123, 139, 145, 153, 154, 156, 160, 163, 401
Hopkins, Louise Macy (Harry's wife), 18, 19, 20, 270, 280, 283, 284, 287, 288-90, 291, 302, 306, 323, 325, 351, 355, 358, 364, 365, 386, 392, 393, 396
Hopkins, Robert (Harry's son), 13, 36, 44, 158, 272, 310, 311, 315, 316, 329, 341, 351, 359, 373, 379, 401
Hopkins, Rome Miller (Harry's brother), 31, 32, 38, 117, 124, 153, 154, 197
Hopkins, Stephen (Harry's son), 29, 36, 38, 158, 256, 271, 272, 329, 351, 355-56
Horner, Henry, 54
Hornet, USS, 77, 279
House, Edward, 165
House Appropriations Committee, 118
Housing Authority, U. S., 129
Houston, USS, 66, 86, 87
Howe, Louis McHenry, 11, 46, 69-70, 81, 110, 120, 370, 402
Hughes, Charles Evans, 113, 115
Hull, Cordell, 65, 121, 128, 131, 151, 213, 215, 225, 231, 239, 253, 255, 257, 258, 261, 263, 274, 276, 301, 319, 338, 363, 367, 370, 390, 404
Hundred Days, the, 48, 50, 402
Hungary, 363
Hunter, Howard, 106, 119, 401
Husky operation, 310, 329
Hutchins, Robert M., 57
Hylan, John F., 36
Hyman, Sidney, 398, 399

Iceland, 222-23, 287
Ickes, Harold L., 12, 55, 57-58, 71, 73, 74, 76, 79, 80, 81, 82-83, 84-85, 86, 87, 88, 92, 94-95, 98, 99, 112, 114, 116, 120, 123, 126, 128, 129, 130, 131, 133, 137, 138-39, 144, 145, 158, 168, 172, 175, 178, 184, 194, 215, 217, 224, 251, 322, 329, 353, 354, 402
Indochina, 254, 257
Inflation, 293
Inner Cabinet, 263
Inönü, Ismet, 348, 349
Iowa, 339-40, 351
Ismay, Sir Hastings, 206, 207, 314, 391, 404
Italy and the Italians, 86, 121, 169, 310, 315, 324, 330, 331, 333, 339, 373

Jackson, Robert, 22, 123, 133, 142, 179, 192
James, Reuben, USS, 254
Japan and the Japanese, 121, 139, 169, 239, 254, 255, 257, 258, 260, 269, 272, 280, 315, 342, 344, 378-79, 391, 397
Jefferson Island Club, 84, 97, 119, 164
Johnson, Adda, 354, 355
Johnson, Hershel V., 201-02
Johnson, Hiram, 150, 259, 260
Johnson, Hugh, 97, 121, 133
Johnson, Kenneth, 92
Johnson, Louis, 142
Johnston, Tom, 207
Johnstone, Alan, 103
Johnstown, Pennsylvania, 93
Joint Chiefs of Staff, 305, 331, 341
Joint Declaration of Principles, 265
Jones, Jesse, 119, 128, 137, 151, 175, 269, 329
Juliana, Princess, 227
Jupiter operation, 330
Justice Department, U. S., 259

Kalinin, Mikhail, 56
Kearney, Nebraska, 31
Kearney, USS, 254
Keenan, Joseph, 133
Kellogg-Briand Pact (1938), 140
Kelly, Edward, 97, 144
Kennedy, Sir John, 231
Kennedy, John F., 405
Kennedy, Joseph, 111, 124, 167, 201, 203, 208
Kennedy, Robert F., 405
Kent, Frank, 67
Kerr, Sir Archibald Clark, 345
Kerr, Clark, 377

Kerr, Florence, 33, 123-24, 149, 153
Kerr, Robert, 33, 153, 156
Keynes, John Maynard, 112
King, Ernest J., 243, 246, 265, 275, 276,
    284, 285, 286, 287, 299, 314, 320, 325,
    327, 340, 341, 368, 374, 378, 404
King, MacKenzie, 251
King George V, HMS, 207, 220
Kingsbury, Jean, 40
Kingsbury, John A., 35-36, 38, 39, 40,
    44, 106, 120
Kiplinger's Washington Letter, 148-49
Kirk, Alexander C., 342, 373
Kissinger, Henry, 405
Knowlson, J. S., 321
Knox, Frank, 100, 101, 169, 213, 214,
    215, 221, 239, 251, 253, 258, 259, 263,
    276, 286, 328, 404
Knoxville Journal, 242
Knudsen, William S., 167, 194, 214,
    251, 269, 271, 404
Krauss, Dorothy, 298
Krock, Arthur, 150
Kurusu, Saburo, 257, 258

LaFollette, Philip, 97
LaFollette, Robert, 51, 97, 110
LaFollette, Robert, Jr., 131
La Guardia, Fiorello, 111, 120, 227,
    319-20
Landon, Alfred, 100, 101, 106
Langer, William, 96, 353
Lascelles, Sir Alan, 210
Laski, Harold, 292
Lasser, David, 112
Laval, Pierre, 279, 298
League of Red Cross Societies, 37
Leahy, William D., 296, 308, 316, 317,
    339, 364, 374, 376
Leche, Richard, 97
Lee, Umphrey, 353
Lefty Louie, 35
LeHand, Marguerite "Missy," 11, 24,
    46, 51, 69, 70, 85, 95, 97, 114, 123,
    124, 129, 136, 156, 159, 176, 189, 193,
    224, 256, 291, 329, 370
Lend-Lease Administration, 216-29
Lend-Lease Bill, 198, 208, 211, 212,
    213-15
Lend-Lease program, 197, 214-29, 230-
    47, 251, 256

Lewis, Fulton, Jr., 354
Lewis, John L., 187-88, 322, 329
Lewis, Whitney, 35
Lilienthal, David, 172-73
Lincoln, Abraham, 116, 157, 161, 164,
    260
Lincoln, Mary Todd, 157
Lindemann, Frederick, 234
Literary Digest, 108
Litvinov, Maxim, 239, 265
London, England, 41, 201, 207, 230
London Sunday Times, 201
Long, Huey, 85, 96
Lothian, Lord Philip, 196
Lovett, Robert, 273
Lowman, Mrs. Laurence, 270
Lowville, Ontario, 30
Lubin, Isadore, 401
Luce, Robert, 51
Lyttleton, Oliver, 267

MacArthur, Douglas, 259, 266, 267,
    269, 292, 314, 320-21, 325, 344, 360
McCracken, Henry N., 178
Macy, Jesse, 33
Maisky, Ivan, 232, 235, 319, 376
Malaya, 257
Malay Straits, 259
Malta, 373
Manchuria, 169
Matgesson, David, 16
Marshall, George C., 15, 142-43, 162,
    219, 221, 231, 243, 249-50, 255, 257,
    258, 263, 265, 266-67, 270, 275, 276,
    277, 278, 279, 284, 285, 286, 287, 294,
    296, 299, 312, 314, 320, 324, 325, 327,
    330, 331, 332, 335-37, 341, 344, 346,
    350, 355-56, 358, 365, 374, 375, 378,
    390, 404
Marshall Islands, 355
Martha, Princess, of Norway, 325
Martin, Joseph, 188, 189, 259, 260
Martinique, 222, 224
Massachusetts, USS, 311
Mathews, William, 43, 44
Maverick, Maury, 134
Mayo Clinic, 123, 131, 139, 159, 161,
    356-57, 383, 384
Mayrant, USS, 243
McCarran, Pat, 135
McCormack, John, 259

McCown, Henry Y., 308
McCrea, John, 287, 306, 311, 339, 340
McDougal, USS, 246
McIntire, Ross, 86, 123, 136, 138, 145,
    159, 160, 178, 191-92, 193, 194, 195,
    243, 247, 306, 307, 308, 312, 316, 345,
    352, 370, 375
McIntyre, Marvin, 24, 25, 51, 64, 65,
    76, 97, 120, 124, 145, 224, 370, 403
McKellar, Kenneth, 385
McKinley, D. C., 235-36, 240
McNary, Charles L., 94, 170, 260
McNutt, Paul, 131
Memphis, USS, 309
Mercer, Lucy, 111
Merrell, Marion, 106
Merriam, Charles E., 77
Miami Beach, Florida, 356
Middle East, 283
Midway, Battle of, 280
Mikolajczyk, Deputy Prime Minister of
    Poland, 19
Milbank, Albert G., 37
Milbank Fund, 40
Miller, James Alexander, 38
Missenden, Sir Eustace, 201
Missouri, USS, 397
Mitchell, John Purroy, 36
Moley, Raymond G., 47, 69, 97, 402
Molotov, Vyacheslav M., 18, 19, 239,
    280, 338, 344, 345, 347, 376, 377, 378,
    379, 387, 388, 389, 384, 391, 403, 404
Monnet, Jean, 199, 310, 357
Monroe Doctrine, 162, 222
Montgomery, Bernard, 299, 309, 318,
    322, 329, 373
Moran, Lord, 374
Morgan, Sir Frederick, 330
Morgenthau, Henry, Jr., 24, 25, 45, 55,
    69, 70, 83, 94, 99, 105, 117, 120, 128,
    133, 134, 142, 178, 213, 215, 223, 252,
    269, 361-63, 402
Morgenthau Plan, 362-63
Moscow, Russia, 237
Mountbatten, Lord, 314
Mudd, Samuel, 116
Munich conference (1938), 140-41
Munich Pact, 154
Munitions Assignment Board, 266-67,
    305, 318, 325, 328
Murphy, Frank, 111, 115, 131

Murphy, Robert, 311, 312
Murrow, Edward R., 161
Mussolini, Benito, 65-66, 121, 140, 141,
    221, 330

Natal, 316
National Defense Advisory
    Commission (NDAC), 167
National Defense Research Council,
    161
National Emergency Council, 59, 71
National Geographic magazine, 229
National Guard, 250
National Industrial Recovery Act
    (1933), 50
National Youth Administration (NYA),
    45, 128, 129
Navy, U. S., 161-62, 164, 214, 221, 315,
    325
Navy Department, U. S., 328
Neely, Matthew, 103
Nelson, Donald, 251, 268, 302, 318,
    328, 404
Nelson, HMS, 207
Nesbitt, Henrietta, 25, 178
Netherlands East Indies, 270
Neutrality Acts, 121, 162, 225, 226, 253
New Deal, 12, 21, 23, 47, 57, 66, 67, 69,
    71, 97-98, 101, 109, 112, 127, 130,
    133, 172, 218, 385
New Guinea, 292, 344
New Orleans, Louisiana, 36-37
Newsweek, 97
New Yorker, The, 328
New York Heart Association, 38
New York *Herald Tribune,* 192
New York, New York, 35, 38
New York Times, The, 72, 150, 192,
    247, 256
New York Tuberculosis Association, 38
New York Tuberculosis and Heart
    Association, 38, 43, 45
New York World's Fair, 158
New York *World-Telegram,* 121
Nicolson, Harold, 278
Niles, David, 133, 145, 401
Nimitz, Chester W., 266, 314, 320, 360
Nixon, Richard M., 405, 406
Noble, Edward J., 153
Nogues, Auguste, 313
Nomura, Kichisaburo, 257, 258

Norfolk, Nebraska, 31
North Africa, 286, 296, 297, 299, 301, 310, 322, 324
North Bend, Nebraska, 30
Norton, W. W., 100
Norway, 164, 330
Nourmahal, USS, 76

O'Brien, Laurence, 405
O'Brien, Sam, 32
O'Connor, John, 135
O'Connor, Richard, 221
O'Donnell, Kenneth, 405
Office of Price Administration (OPA), 293
Office of Production Management (OPM), 214, 251, 263
Office of War Mobilization (OWM), 328, 329
Oliphant, Herman, 142
Olson, Newton, 32
One Man—Wendell Willkie (Sparks), 352
One World (Willkie), 295
Overlord operation, 330, 331, 332, 335, 336, 337, 341, 342, 344, 345, 346, 347, 350, 358-60
Oxford University, England, 396, 399

Pacific War Council, 275-76
Panama Canal, 86
Pan-American conference (1939), 162
Panay, USS, 139
Park Commission, NYC, 43
Paris, France, 40, 372-73, 393
Patterson, Robert, 269, 271, 276
Patterson, Roscoe C., 71
Patton, George S., 311, 313, 318, 329, 374
Pavlov, V. N., 343, 348, 391, 392
Payne, Charles E., 218
Pearl Harbor, attack on, 254-55, 258-61, 400
Pearson, Drew, 334, 335, 388
Pepper, Claude, 133, 317
Perkins, Frances, 45, 51, 57, 81, 145, 175, 370, 402
Pétain, Henri Philippe, 167, 279, 298, 343
Philippine Islands, 267, 269, 280, 347, 369

Phillips, Frank, 353
"Phoney War," 161
Pittsburgh, Pennsylvania, 93
Pius XII, Pope, 373
"Plus Four," 215, 216
Poland, 19, 161, 345, 363, 376-77, 389, 391-92
Poletti, Charles, 320
Port Patrick, Scotland, 279
Post, Langdon, 120
Potomac, Presidential yacht, 123, 158, 192, 217, 243, 247, 290, 339, 351
Potsdam conference, 20, 391, 392, 394, 395
Pound, Sir Dudley, 231, 264, 314
Pravda, 384
President's Committee for Unemployment Relief (PCUR), 42-43
Prestwick, Scotland, 230
Prettyman, Arthur, 193, 306, 375
Prince of Wales, HMS, 224, 231, 241, 242, 243-44, 246, 247
Public Works Administration (PWA), 57-58, 81, 82, 83, 85, 88, 94-95, 99, 117, 144

Quadrant conference, *see* Quebec conference
Quebec, Canada, 331, 361
Quebec conference (1943), 305, 331, 332-33, 363
Queen Mary, RMS, 322, 330
Quincey, USS, 372, 378, 379, 381, 382, 383

Rascob, John J., 84
Rayburn, Sam, 84, 259, 260
Rearmament program, 169, 186
Recession of 1937, 120, 122-23, 127, 129, 135
Reconstruction Finance Corporation (RFC), 43
Red Army, 17
Reed, David A., 71
Reilly, Mike, 302, 343, 375, 381
Relief Act (1935), 78
Reorganization Bill (1937), 125-26, 129, 130
Reparations Commission, 377
Republican National Convention

(1912), 34; (1932), 47; (1936), 100-01; (1940), 170; (1944), 359
Reynaud, Paul, 166
Reynolds, Quentin, 234
Richberg, Donald, 71
Ritchie, Albert, 46
Rivers, Andrew B., 227
Robin Moor, SS, 226-27
Robinson, Arthur R., 71
Robinson, Joseph, 84
Rockefeller, Nelson A., 151
Rockland, Maine, 247
Roehm, Ernst, 65
Rome, Italy, 358, 373
Rommel, Erwin, 221, 270, 283, 296, 299
Roosevelt, Betsey, 124, 136, 255
Roosevelt, Eleanor, 24, 41, 45, 56, 96, 97, 99, 110-11, 120, 124, 125, 132, 157, 171, 176, 192, 194, 287, 289, 290, 292, 306, 334, 366, 386
Roosevelt, Elliot, 171, 230, 243, 244, 309, 311, 341, 373
Roosevelt, Ethel du Pont, 117
Roosevelt, Franklin D., Argentia conference, 243-47; Cairo conference, 341-42; Casablanca conference, 309-16; Churchill and, 167, 185, 196, 244-48, 250, 263-68, 305, 323, 331, 342, 375-81, 382; death of, 383, 385, 386; declaration of war, 261; defense measures, 140-43, 162, 167-68, 173; governor of New York State, 42, 44, 45-46; Hawaii meeting with MacArthur and Nimitz, 360; illness, 374; presidency of, 11, 15, 21, 24, 49-51, 67-68, 101, 108-09, 112-13, 128-29, 133-34, 135-36, 176-77, 184-85, 223-27, 250, 262-63, 292-94, 326-27, 365-66, 370, 401-03, 405-06; presidential candidate, 46-48; Quebec conference, 331, 332-33, 361-63; Stalin and, 343-49; Supreme Court "packing" plan, 23, 115-16; Teheran conference, 16, 343-49; Trident conference, 305, 323-25, 328, 330; United Nations and, 384; Yalta conference, 375-81
Roosevelt, Franklin D., Jr., 117, 169, 243, 309-10, 341
Roosevelt, James, 114, 122, 123, 124, 128, 133, 136, 139, 260, 402
Roosevelt, John, 46
Roosevelt, Theodore, 34
Roosevelt Library, Hyde Park, 178
Root, Elihu, 34
Roper, Daniel, 18, 133, 149, 151
Rosenman, Samuel, 24, 25, 46, 175, 176, 183, 184, 188, 189, 190, 191, 193, 200, 224, 225, 253, 268, 287, 326, 336, 354, 365, 366, 370, 383, 394
Roundup operation, 275, 277, 282, 301, 324, 330, 333
Royal Navy, 283, 297
Rumania, 363
Russia and the Russians, 17, 161, 172, 228, 231, 233, 236-37, 238-40, 270, 276, 280, 283, 295-96, 318-19, 342, 363, 369, 375, 376, 377, 380, 389, 391-92, 393
Russo-German nonaggression pact (1939), 172
Rutherford, Lucy Mercer, 11

Sage Foundation, Russell, 44
Saipan, 358
Salerno, Italy, 333
Sandburg, Carl, 157, 160-61
San Francisco, California, 106
Saranac, U.S. Coast Guard cutter, 116
Saratoga Springs, New York, 119, 137
Sardinia, 310
Sargent, George Paull T., 401
Saturday Evening Post, 113
Saud, King Ibn, 381
Scarsborough, New York, 38
Scheider, Malvina Thompson, 24
Schultz, Lester R., 257
Schwallenbach, Senator, 78
Scott, Hugh, 255
Seabury, Samuel, 46
Secret Service, U. S., 217, 243, 291, 308, 343, 375
Securities Exchange Act (1933), 50
Selective Service Act (1940), 185, 188
Senate Appropriations Committee, 94
Senate Foreign Relations Committee, 213, 214
Sequoia, yacht, 56, 63, 84
Shangri-La, Maryland, 290-92, 323
Shearer, Mary C., 103
Sherwood, Robert, 108, 138, 183-84,

185, 188, 189, 190, 191, 192, 200, 224, 225, 228, 268, 287, 294, 302, 359, 365, 385, 386
Shirer, William L., 161
Shriver, Paul, 107
Sicily, 310, 314, 319, 329
Singapore, 257, 268, 269, 272
Sioux City, Iowa, 29, 31
Sixth Army, German, 318
Sledgehammer operation, 276, 282, 284-85
Smith, Alfred E., 41, 42, 100, 104-05
Smith, Cotton Ed, 135
Smith-Connally anti-strike act (1943), 329
Socialist Party, 98
Social Welfare Department, 126
Solomon Islands, 269, 292
Somervell, Brehon B., 104, 271, 281, 335-36
Soong, T. V., 254, 280, 296, 404
Southeast Asia, 257
Spanish Civil War, 121
Sparks, C. Nelson, 352-54
Spending to Save (Hopkins), 59, 100
Spicer, Vernon D., 56
Springfield, Illinois, 106
Stalin, Joseph, 12, 16, 17, 18-20, 29, 231-32, 237-40, 250, 280, 292, 295, 299, 305, 316, 318, 329, 339, 342, 364, 387, 390, 391-92, 403, 404; Churchill and, 367, 375-81, 370, 375-81; Roosevelt and, 343-49, 375-81; Yalta conference, 375-81
Stalin, Svetlana, 20
Standley, William H., 250, 271, 319, 328
Stark, Harold R., 221, 243, 255, 257, 258, 260, 263, 265, 270, 284
Starnes, Joseph, 118
Stassen, Harold, 170
State Department, U. S., 168, 169, 184, 199, 223, 253, 299, 301, 325, 337, 358, 390
Steiner, Edward A., 33, 34
Steinhardt, Laurence A., 237, 238, 239, 271
Stettinius, Edward R., Jr., 151, 167, 251, 256, 338, 373, 376, 379, 389, 395, 399, 404

Stevenson J. C., 78
Stilwell, Joseph, 325, 341
Stimson, Henry L., 169, 188, 191, 213, 214, 215, 219, 221, 225, 228-29, 239, 251, 252, 253, 255, 258, 259, 263, 268, 275, 276, 277, 286, 320, 328, 336, 362, 363, 367, 387, 404
Stock market crash of 1939, 42
Stone, Julius F., 252
Stone, Phil, 55
Straus, Jesse Isador, 44
Sudetenland, 139
Suez Canal, 283, 382
Supply Priorities and Allocation Board, 251
Supreme Commander, 265-66, 297, 314, 350
Supreme Court, U. S., 23, 115-16, 130, 294
Swanson, Claude, 142
Swope, Herbert Bayard, 11, 119, 126

Taber, John W., 276
Taft, Robert A., 170
Taft, William Howard, 34
Talmadge, Eugene, 96
Tammany Hall, 46
Tedder, Arthur William, 314
Teheran conference (1943), 16, 17, 305, 332, 343-49
Temporary Energency Relief Administration, NYS (TERA), 44, 45-46, 48
Tennessee Valley Authority (TVA), 172-73
Third Army, U.S., 374
Thomas, Norman, 98
Thompson, Dorothy, 108-09, 234
Thompson, Malvina, 125
Thors, Thor, 223
Tilsit, 300
Time magazine, 256
Tinkham, George H., 213
Tobey, Charles W., 163
Tobin, Daniel, 183
Tobruk, fall of, 283
Tojo, Hadeki, 255
Torch operation, 287, 296, 297, 299
Tovey, Sir John, 207, 241, 242
Treasury Department, U. S., 157

Tree, Ronald, 15

Trident conference (1943), 305, 323-325, 328, 330

Trinidad, 316, 317

Trippe, Juan, 151, 199, 273

Trohan, Walter, 334-35

Truman, Harry S., 12, 19, 20, 57, 71, 360, 365, 367, 385-86, 387, 388, 390, 391, 394, 395, 397, 401, 404

Truman Committee, 387

Tugwell, Florence, 66, 95

Tugwell, Rexford, 24, 47, 66, 71, 95, 97, 138, 183, 402

Tulagi, 292

Tully, Grace, 51, 69, 97, 189, 260, 291, 306

Tunisia, 299, 301, 321, 322

Turkey, 349, 363

Tuscaloosa, USS, 195, 196, 243

Tydings, Millard, 135, 174, 175

United Mine Workers, 322

United Nations, 12, 18, 19, 265, 366, 370, 371, 377-78, 384, 389

United Nations Charter, 19

United States News, The, 326

Vandenberg, Arthur, 76, 100, 103, 150, 170, 384

Van Devanter, Willis, 116

Vargas, Getulio, 316

Vaughn, Harry, 404

Vermilion, South Dakota, 30

Victor Emmanuel, King, 330

Vinson, Fred M., 328

Vinson-Trammell Act (1934), 161

Voroshilov, Klementy, 344, 346

Wadsworth, James W., 185

Wagner, Robert, 51

Wagner Housing Act, 118

Wainwright, Jonathan, 397

Wake Island, 269

Walker, Frank, 59-60, 79, 80, 81, 83, 94, 120, 192

Walker, James, 36, 46

Wallace, Henry A., 12, 55, 57, 102, 128, 131, 133, 171, 175, 176, 186-87, 251, 259, 260, 269, 326, 329, 360

Walter, Frank, 145

Walters, Wolford, 124

War Department, U. S., 259, 328, 337, 358

Warm Springs, Georgia, 71, 125, 128, 135, 154, 155, 156, 383

War Production Board, 269, 317

Washington, SS, 64

Washington Post, 49, 118, 156

Watson, Edwin M. "Pa," 11, 25, 86, 87, 123, 125, 136, 138, 142, 145, 176, 191, 192, 193, 194, 195, 243, 247, 273, 342, 365, 375, 379, 383, 403

Waugh, John, 356, 359

Wavell, Archibald, 209, 266

Wearin, Otha D., 134

Wedemeyer, General, 337

Welles, Sumner, 169, 223, 225, 231, 243, 246, 261, 338, 367

Wendell, James I., 271

Westbrook, Lawrence, 52, 90, 91, 108

Wheeler, Burton K., 134, 175, 185, 213

White, William Allen, 71, 186

White Sulphur Springs, West Virginia, 358

Whitman, Franklyn, 118

Whitman, Walt, 209

Whittier, John Greenleaf, 323

Williams, Aubrey, 52, 64-65, 71, 84, 90, 120, 128, 129, 136, 140, 143, 145, 384-85

Williams, Linsley R., 38

Williams, Pierce, 68, 69

Willkie, Wendell L., 134, 169, 170, 172, 177, 179, 184, 185, 186-87, 188, 192, 195, 208, 212, 214, 215, 268, 295

Wilson, Sir Charles, 207, 264, 324, 332, 342, 347

Wilson, Charles E., 317

Wilson, Mrs. Howard, 108

Wilson, Woodrow, 34, 165, 376, 384

Winant, John Gilbert, 211, 215, 216, 232, 233, 235, 241, 274-75, 278, 290, 338, 339, 342, 393

Wood, Robert F., 151

Woodring, Henry, 142, 168

Workers' Alliance, 112

Work Relief Bill, 73-78

Works Progress Administration (WPA),
    12, 22-23, 67-88, 89-109, 113, 114,
    117, 118, 119, 128, 129, 139-40, 143,
    144-45
WPA Workers Answer Their Critics
    (poem), 92
World War I, 36, 282
World War II, 12, 77, 91, 161, 164, 165-
    67, 172, 201, 220-21, 249, 258-59, 261,
    269-70, 272-73, 275-80, 283-85, 292,
    295-96, 299, 318, 322, 339, 341-42,
    355, 358-60, 395, 397

Yalta Conference, 371, 375-81, 388, 399
Yonkers, New York, 38
Yorktown, USS, 77
Young, Owen D., 84
Young, Philip, 216
Yugoslavia, 363

Zelda, Madame, 186
Zhukov, Georgi K., 19, 389, 392
Zones of Occupation in Germany, 378

PERSONAL FINANCE

SEVENTH EDITION

Robert S. Rosefsky

John Wiley & Sons, Inc.
New York   Chichester   Weinheim   Brisbane   Singapore   Toronto

ACQUISITIONS EDITOR   Marissa Ryan
MARKETING MANAGER   Rebecca Hope
PRODUCTION EDITOR   Edward Winkleman
DESIGNER   Laura Boucher
PHOTO EDITORS   Hilary Newman and Lisa Gee
ILLUSTRATION EDITOR   Anna Melhorn

Cover and chapter openings photo: Adam Cohen/Photonica

This book was set in Palatino by Digitype and printed and bound by R. R. Donnelley
Crawfordsville.   The cover was printed by Lehigh Press.

This book is printed on acid-free paper. ∞

Library of Congress Cataloging-in-Publication Data
Rosefsky, Robert S.
    Personal finance / Robert S. Rosefsky.—7th ed.
        p.   cm.
    Includes bibliographical references and index.
    ISBN 0-471-23822-8(alk. paper)
    1. Finance, Personal.   I. Title.
    HG179.R67   1998
    332.024—dc21   98-5649
                                              CIP

Printed in the United States of America

10 9 8 7 6 5 4 3 2

To my wife and beloved companion, Linda Sue, and to our children: Debbie and Mark, and their Max and Samantha, Michelle and Paul, Adam and Linda, Joshua and Lindsay. And to the little ones on the way. Greater blessings or riches no person could ever have. And yes, I count them regularly.

About the Author

Dr. Robert Rosefsky's credentials—as author, educator, and professional financial consultant—uniquely suit him for the task of creating the definitive text on personal financial matters.

After receiving his B.A. degree from Yale University and his Juris Doctor degree from Syracuse University College of Law, Dr. Rosefsky practiced law and served as vice president and director of a commercial bank for several years, in which capacity he dealt with the public as a professional "problem solver," primarily in financial matters. He then directed his efforts toward the mass media, hoping to educate a broader audience in a field that had been long ignored: personal financial planning.

Dr. Rosefsky has written ten books on various financial subjects, and his advice has been widely syndicated through newspapers, radio, and television. Most recently he has served as Money Advisor for ABC's radio and television affiliates in Los Angeles.

His experience as an educator is both innovative and extensive. In affiliation with the Consortium for Community College Television, he has created, and presents, two college credit television courses: "Personal Finance" and "You and the Law." The "Personal Finance" telecourse has won an Emmy Award as best instructional series. Tens of thousands of students from all parts of the nation have received credits at their local colleges for completing these courses.

Dr. Rosefsky has taught Business and Economic Reporting at the university of Southern California School of Journalism, as well as financial planning programs for the UCLA Extension Program, for the University of Southern California College of Continuing Education, and for Coastline Community College.

Preface

You can run, but you can't hide.

The world is full of people who want to help you handle your money. For better or for worse. Such as,

Hello my friend, I'm J. Fairly Nicely of Intergalactic Capital Management and I'd like to tell you how to get RICH! If you will just let me be your Retirement Adviser/ 401(k) Guru/IRA Specialist/Insurance Counselor/Stock Portfolio Manager/Real Estate Tutor/Automotive Maven/Banking Guide/Financial Planner/Overall Money Management Mentor, I can solve all of life's problems for you.

Sound familiar? If it doesn't, it soon will.

The J. Fairly Nicely's will come at you over the phone, through the mail, across the Internet, and from every form of advertising now or ever to be invented. They will be convincing. Alluring. Intriguing. Hard to understand, yet hard to resist.

Many will have excellent ideas and well-proven techniques that can indeed help you with your financial concerns.

Some will be crackpots, scam artists, and poorly trained or overly greedy salespersons who want to make a fast buck from you.

So how do you cope? How do you sort it all out?

First you learn. You learn the basic concepts of managing your money. You learn how to identify and prioritize your personal goals and then construct plans that will help you reach those goals. You learn how to crunch the numbers that will help you make the right financial decisions. You learn the jargon of J. Fairly Nicely so that you can decipher the sales pitches and proposals that J. will heap on you. You learn what you can do on your own—thank you very much—and on what you will need professional help. And when you've learned all of that, you will be able to confidently choose which J. Fairly Nicely can be of help to you, and which of them you can dismiss.

That's what this book and this course are all about. To give you knowledge. To give you confidence. To give you the ability to control your own financial destiny.

We have all the tools you'll need:

- In addition to your instructor's caring guidance and this book, there is a Study Guide filled with exercises to help you sharpen your skills, plus carefully selected video supplements to expose you to an array of outside experts.

- There is the Internet, which has become one of the most dynamic and productive ways of acquiring financial information. We have invested heavily—in time, money, and expertise—to develop Internet activities that will enhance your learning. From the springboard of our Web-site—**http://www.wiley.com/college/rosefsky**—you will be able to access the following:

1. Exercises that will teach you how to use the Internet as a research and problem-solving tool for most of the subjects in the book. These were developed by Walt Woerheide of The Rochester Institute of Technology, with guidance from the Wiley staff and myself. Topics that have Internet exercises will be indicated by a WWW icon like the one you see in the margin.

2. Personal Finance Updates will be posted on the web site regularly to keep you on top of any developing trends that can impact on your financial well-being. There is also a tie-in with *The Wall St. Journal* that will help you understand the economics of everyday life.

3. The Decision Maker software will help you crunch the numbers needed to make wise judgments in common areas of financial concern. The software can be downloaded from the site.

Within the book itself you'll find some new elements that have been added since the last edition. The first part of the book has been restructured to put greater emphasis on the importance of planning and prioritizing. It's entitled "Family Economics," and it will help you understand and deal with the relationship between the economy and your career, your spending habits, and your goals.

Each chapter has a new feature, "For Better or For Worse," which will help you anticipate outside influences that can affect your financial well-being. The more you can anticipate the unexpected, the better you'll be able to dodge the bullets or take advantage of the good breaks.

And finally, there is, in every sentence in every chapter, my best effort to make these subjects easy to understand, all the better to help you achieve what you want for yourself. It's all there for the taking. Use it wisely, today for learning, and in the future as a continuing reference source. Good fortune to you.

Robert S. Rosefsky, J. D.

Words in the text that are underlined in color are more fully defined in the Glossary at the end of the text. The Internet icon refers you to our Website, from which you can choose the resources that you need. This site can be located at **http://www.wiley.com/college/rosefsky**

Contents

Preface   **vii**

PART ONE   FAMILY ECONOMICS

■ **Chapter 1**   **The Economy—How it Works, and What it Means to You**   **1**

Forces That Shape Our Lives   2
A Serious Game   3
Fish, Berries, and Logs: Where It All Began   6
Here and Now   19
The Results   25

■ **Chapter 2**   **Working, Planning & Budgeting**   **32**

The Role of Work in Your Life   33
Factors in Choosing Your Work   33
Economic Trends   38
The Job Quest   44
Changing Careers   45
Your Work and Income: Protection and Regulation   47
Success Is What You Make It   54
The Master Plan   54
A Goal Worksheet: Here and Now   58
Shaping Future Goals   65
The Sources from Which Future Goals Can Be Accomplished   68
The Financial Statement: A Planning Tool   69
Some Thoughts on Spending Habits   73

■ **Chapter 3**   **Sensible Shopping and Spending**   **79**

The Bad Habits   80
The Good Habits: Groceries and Toiletries   80

The Good Habits: Clothing and Accessories   85
The Good Habits: Major Home Furnishings   88
Recreation   93
Vacation and Travel   94
Recreation at Home   106

■   **Chapter 4**   **Frauds and Swindles and How to Avoid Them**   **117**

Barnum was Right   118
Bait and Switch   120
Mail-Order Madness   121
Frauds on The Street   125
Frauds in The Home   126
Home Improvements   128
Investment Schemes   132
Leisure and Luxuries   135
Snake Oil Sam's Miscellanea   136
What to Do About It   138
Your Best Defense   140

■   **Chapter 5**   **Transportation: Buying, Financing, and Insuring Your Cars**   **146**

The Cost of Getting From Point A to Point B   147
Buying A Car   149
Financing: Direct Versus Through the Dealer   157
Warranties   159
Automobile Insurance   161
Car Pooling   165
Car Rental   166

PART TWO   A ROOF OVER YOUR HEAD

■   **Chapter 6**   **Buying a Home**   **171**

The Dilemma   172
Types of Housing   175
How to Buy a Dwelling at the Right Price   178
Making the Purchase   186

■   **Chapter 7**   **Financing a Home**   **198**

How Home Financing Works   198
Shopping for Financing: Where to Go, What to Look For   208
Applying for Home Financing   214
Creative Financing   215
Tax Complications   217
Timing, Timing, Timing   218

■ **Chapter 8**   **Housing Costs and Regulations**   **224**

Property Insurance   225
The Types of Policies and Coverage   226
Property Taxes   232
Utilities   234
Maintenance and Repairs   234
Laws Regulating Housing   235

■ **Chapter 9**   **Renting**   **243**

Pros and Cons of Renting   244
To Buy or to Rent: A Case History   248
Shopping for Rentals   249
The Lease and Its Key Clauses   250
Month-to-month Tenancy   255
Combinations of Leasing and Buying   255
Rent Laws   256
Terminating a Lease   258

■ **Chapter 10**   **Selling Your Home**   **264**

What's Your Home Worth?   265
Using a Real Estate Agent   268
Tax Implications When You Sell Your Home   274
Moving Expenses   275
Tax Deduction of Moving Expenses   276

PART THREE   WHERE THE MONEY IS

■ **Chapter 11**   **Financial Institutions**   **282**

Your Choices   282
The Middlemen   283
The Institutions   284
Services Available at Financial Institutions   288
Laws That Govern Financial Institutions and Their Transactions   301

■ **Chapter 12**   **Credit and Borrowing**   **316**

Buy Now, Pay Later   317
What Is Credit?   318
How the Cost of Credit Is Figured   322
Shopping for Loans   331
Dos and Don'ts When You Apply for a Loan   335
Credit Abuses   337
Cures for Overindebtedness   341
Discipline   344

PART FOUR   MAKING YOUR MONEY GROW

■ **Chapter 13**   **Making Your Money Grow: An Overview**   **350**

Today Dollars and Tomorrow Dollars   351
Investment Criteria   353
Investigation   360
Sources of Investable Funds   363
Who Can Help You?   365

■ **Chapter 14**   **Making Your Money Grow: The Money Market**   **372**

What Is the Money Market?   373
Types of Money Market Investments   376
Investing in the Bond Market   381
Miscellaneous Money Market Investments   394

■ **Chapter 15**   **Making Your Money Grow: The Stock Market**   **407**

A Perspective   408
Stock Ownership as a Form of Investing   408
How the Stock Markets Operate   413
Who Invests in the Stock Market, and What Are They Seeking?   417
Basic Stock Market Information   424
Price And Value: What Can Affect the Worth of a Stock?   441
Mutual Funds in the Stock Market   443
Choosing Your Broker: A Guide Through the Investment Jungle   446

■ **Chapter 16**   **Making Your Money Grow: Real Estate and Other Opportunities**   **455**

Myths and Facts about Real Estate Investing   456
Income-Producing Real Estate   458
Investing in Vacant Land   468
"Turnover" Investing   471
Investing In Mortgages   473
Group Investing   477
Investing In Small Businesses   478
Gambling In Commodities   479
Foreign Exchange and Deposits   481
Precious Metals   482
Strategic Metals   484
Gemstones   485
Collectibles   486
Television "Investment Opportunities"   487
Private Lending   487
Knowledge   488

PART FIVE PROTECTING WHAT YOU WORK FOR

■ **Chapter 17** **Life, Health, and Income Insurance** **496**

Coping With Risk 497
Why Life Insurance? 498
The Basic Elements of Life Insurance 499
Buying Life Insurance: Who Needs It, and How Much? 512
Insurance When the Risk Might Not Occur 520
Health Insurance 521
Health Care Checklists 528
Income Insurance 533
Long-Term Care Insurance 537

■ **Chapter 18** **Financial Planning For Later Years** **547**

If Not for Yourself, Then for Your Parents 548
Reaching Financial Maturity 548
Financial Arrangements For The Later Years 557
Tax and Pension Laws: How They Affect the Rights of Workers and Retirees 564
Do-it-yourself Pensions: IRAs, Keoghs, and 401(k)s 569
Pensions and Taxes 577
One Final Caution 578

■ **Chapter 19** **Estate Planning** **586**

If Not for You, Then for Your Parents 587
Unexpected Problems 587
What Is an Estate? 589
What Is Estate Planning? 589
The Rights Involved in Estate Planning 590
The Language of Estate Planning 591
The WILL 593
Other Devices for Passing on Accumulated Wealth 599
How to Proceed 602
What Should Your Estate Plan Accomplish? 603
How Estate Taxes Work 609

■ **Chapter 20** **Income Taxes** **617**

Be Prepared 618
The Importance of Knowing about Income Taxes 618
The Basic Concept of Income Taxes 620
Tax-Cutting Strategies 638
Filing Your Return 642
What Happens to Your Return? Examinations and Audits 642

■   **Chapter 21**   **Working for Yourself**   **656**

When Is a Good Time to Start a New Venture?   657
Taking The Leap   662
The Start-up Form of Your Venture   666
Where Will the Money Come From?   672
Nit-picked to Death by Regulations?   677
Where to Get Help: The F.A.I.L.-Safe Team and the M & Ms   679

Glossary   **687**

Index   **700**

avoid taking home unsold watermelons, and you could end up a big loser. If the harvest is just right but the weather is cold, people might not be interested in buying the melons at all, and again you end up a loser. In the first case, the supply exceeded the usual demand. In the second case, the supply was customary, but the demand was low. On the other hand, if your harvest is just right and the demand is high because the weather is hot and dry, you could reap a tremendous profit.

- **Luck**   This is, to be sure, a very unscientific aspect of economics. But it is present in every one of the other influences. Whether good or bad, it's unpredictable. The ability to take advantage of good luck and avoid the ravages of bad luck can make a distinct difference between success and failure in an economic endeavor.

In many cases these influences overlap, intertwine, and influence each other. But whether taken individually, in combination, or as an aggregate, they do shape and give direction to the human forces that constitute an economic population.

Effects and Results

The forces go to work and are influenced one way or another by the various factors just mentioned. Here's a brief rundown of some of the potential effects we'll explore in the course of this chapter:

Exercise 1.1

- Inflation or deflation (rising or falling prices and wages)
- Employment or unemployment (good jobs or lack thereof)
- Growth of an economy or recession
- Survival of an economic entity or termination of the entity
- An attractive investment climate or an unattractive one
- Surpluses or deficits (having money in the bank or being excessively in debt)

Many of these effects and results can become influences in their own right. The football team suffers a loss, and the score against them is so lopsided that the players are humiliated. This effect—humiliation—lowers their morale to such a point that they lose their next game, which they had been heavily favored to win. The effect has become a cause in its own right. Or a company develops a highly touted product, only to have the public ignore it because of a poor advertising campaign. Not only does the company thus lose money, but also some of the top managers quit over the marketing program, and the company suffers even further as a result. The effect—poor sales—has become an influence in its own right on the future of the company.

FISH, BERRIES, AND LOGS: WHERE IT ALL BEGAN

To get a better idea of how these forces and influences interact, let's examine the history of three fictional primitive tribes: The Fish People, the Berry People, and the Log People. Any similarities between the economic concerns of these ancient folk and those of your own family, your employer, or your nation are not coincidental.

The Fish People lived at the water's edge, and they harvested a bounty from the sea. Their work was not physically demanding, but it required patience, cunning, and long hours. As long as they were willing to work, there were fish to be caught. An endless supply of fish seemed assured, and their leader, Mug, told them that they could become rich through hard work and through the expansion of their fishing grounds. The fish they didn't need for their own purposes they would trade with the Berry People for berries and with the Log People for logs. Men, women, and children all worked. They saw no limit to the amount of fish they could catch and thereby no limit to the amount of berries and logs they could acquire from their neighbors. Their energies and their expectations were high. They desired to expand and to become ever wealthier.

A few miles inland, on a plateau blessed by constant sunshine lived the Berry People. The plateau was covered with thousands of wild berry bushes of all kinds—black, huckle, rasp, straw, and goose. These delicious berries were always in demand by the Log People and the Fish People. Nature blessed the Berry People: The berries grew in abundance with little need for care. The only work that the Berry People had to do was to pick their crop. What they didn't keep for themselves they packaged to deliver to the neighboring tribes in return for their products. With the sun, the rain, and the soil doing most of their work for them, the Berry People tended to be lazy and greedy. Their leader, Wump, assured them that everything was going their way and they should take advantage of it and live the good life. Wump saw no need to plan for the future. The future, it appeared, would take care of itself.

Beyond the plateau the land rose into wooded hills. This was the domain of the Log People. They had devised tools to cut down the plentiful trees that surrounded them, and they traded the logs to their neighbors for fish and berries. The neighbors found the logs necessary for building fires, creating shelters, and fashioning additional tools for their own uses. Work for the Log People was physically demanding. Cutting down the trees and chopping them into pieces with their primitive tools was bone-wearying. It had become custom among the Log People for only the men to work at cutting the trees since their physical prowess was greater than that of the women. The women tended to the home and to the needs of their men, who returned exhausted from their work at day's end. The Log People were content with their modest lot and aspired to neither wealth nor power. Their

leader, Theodore, had told them, "This is the way it has always been with us, and this is the way it probably always will be."

The three tribes had agreed that for trading purposes one fish equal in length to Mug's forearm would be equal to one basket of berries the size of Wump's head, which in turn would be equal to one log the length of Theodore's leg. Thus, if the Fish People wanted to acquire 10 logs, they would have to deliver 10 appropriately sized fish to the Log People. And so on.

The three tribes lived in harmony, trading among themselves as their needs and desires dictated. The following, in no particular order of importance, are some of the occurrences that shaped the lives of these tribes. As you read, bear in mind the economic influences that were outlined earlier.

The Empty Forest

For as long as the Log People could remember, the big trees had always been there. Many years before, when all the tribes were much smaller, all their needs had been filled by chopping down just two or three trees a year. But in recent years all the tribes had expanded considerably and were demanding much more wood than they had formerly needed. The Berry People were building more elaborate log huts, the Fish People needed logs to make rafts, and all three tribes were making more furniture, tools, fences, and fires for heat and cooking.

Whereas the big trees used to be just a few minutes' walk from the Log People's village, the choppers now had to walk much farther to get to the available trees.

Theodore had done too little calculating, and he had done it too late. Never before faced with the problem of not having trees close at hand, the thought of planting new trees had never dawned on him. And when he finally did realize that new plantings were needed, he was dismayed to discover that it took many years for the seedlings to grow into mature trees. Meanwhile, it was now taking the choppers three hours to get to the mature trees and six hours to drag the logs back to the village. The time needed to create a single log had multiplied many times, and thus it was costing the Log People dearly to acquire one fish or one basket of berries. Humankind was suffering its first energy crisis.

Though blessed with a natural resource that could be renewed, the Log People had failed to renew it, and they were suffering accordingly. Furthermore, by failing to anticipate the ever-increasing cost of acquiring the natural resource, their problems were compounded. Eventually Theodore would invent the wheel, which would make possible the creation of a wagon. This would sharply cut down the time and energy needed to get the logs. But in the meantime, waiting for their new plantings to mature, the Log People settled into an era of economic distress.

All Dried Up

As long as the Berry People could remember, there had always been enough rain. How shocking it was then when one year it did not rain. The drought was devastating. Many of the berry bushes produced no fruit at all; some bushes withered and died; and the berries that did grow were puny and tasteless. The Log People and the Fish People would no longer accept one basket of berries in equal trade for a fish or a log because the berries were of such poor quality. They insisted on two baskets for one fish or one log, and the Berry People found themselves with no choice. Until they could remedy the problems caused by the drought, they would have to do with fewer fish and fewer logs. The unpredictable forces of nature had seriously undercut the life of the Berry People, and Wump, their leader, vowed to do something about it.

Wump searched the surrounding countryside and discovered a solution to their problem: an underground spring. He told his people that their only salvation would be to carry buckets to the spring and bring water back for the bushes. But the Berry People had grown so lazy throughout the fat years that they were unwilling to work hard carrying water to save themselves. Many of them refused to accept Wump's warnings about the ultimate consequences of their failure to work hard, believing that the rains would come the next day, or the next, or the next. But the rains didn't come, and the Berry People were on the edge of extinction.

Fearing the worst, Wump retired to his private quarters to concentrate on how to save his people. It came to him in a flash! The head of the underground spring was at a point of land higher than the Berry People's plateau. Why not, Wump reasoned, fashion a trench leading from the spring to the plateau. "We could then direct the water to flow through the trench and onto our parched berry bushes."

He announced his plan to the people, telling them that it would take a lot of hard work to dig the trench, but that once it was completed, abundant water would flow to their bushes. Faced with the ultimate crisis, the Berry People did the necessary work. Within a few weeks, the trench had been dug and the water began to flow. Soon the bushes would be blooming again, and they'd be back to one basket of berries for each fish or each log. Prosperity was just around the corner.

Wump had researched the problem and had developed a means of coping with it. Wump's technology—the first irrigation canal—had overcome the adverse forces of nature as well as the weak spirit of his people. Wump also knew that they should never again take for granted that the rains would fall. Planning for the future was something that *had* to be done, for, Wump admitted to himself in his private moments, it *was* possible for the spring to dry up someday.

The Disappearing Fish

The fish always swam close to the shore settlement of the Fish People—until one strange day when the fish disappeared. Disbelief quickly spread throughout the village. In panic, they ran up and down the shore and put rafts out to sea. Far from their village the fish still swam, but why did they no longer swim near the village, where it was so convenient to catch them? Mug stood knee-deep in the water in front of the village and tried to reason the answer. It came through his nose. There was a strange and offensive odor to the water. Mug sniffed until the odor could be identified. It was the odor of human waste.

Mug realized immediately why the fish had disappeared. For as long as he could remember, the Fish People had disposed of their waste in the water near the village, relying on the tides to carry it out to sea. But over the years the pollution had become so dense that the tides could no longer wash the water clean. Simply enough, the fish were repelled by the polluted water and sought other grounds.

Mug told the village council that unless drastic action was taken immediately, their hopes and dreams would quickly fade. It would be necessary, he suggested, for the waste to be carried to some distant inland point and buried. He realized that this would drain the work power of the people, but only by doing so would the water eventually cleanse itself and allow the fish to return. The Fish People were motivated to realize their expectations. So they commenced an energetic program of waste disposal.

In just a few months the water had cleansed itself and the fish had returned. Even though it was more costly to the Fish People to remove the waste from the village, they were willing to do the necessary work.

They had realized that their well-being could be harmed by polluting their environment, and they were willing to pay the price to correct the problem. Had the price been much higher, Mug worried, the people might have objected to paying it and the village could have been split into factions moving up and down the coast, thus destroying the entity of the Fish People.

The First Price Wars

It had taken many years for the Log People to recover from their first energy crisis. To ensure that it would not happen again, they worked hard to plant as many trees as they could as close to their village as space allowed. But during the time it took for these new plantings to become mature trees, the Fish People and the Berry People had taken their own steps to avoid being caught in a shortage of logs from the Log People. The Fish People had started to collect driftwood and found that it was suitable for repairing

their huts. The Berry People found that dead bushes made excellent fuel for their fires—better, in fact, than the Log People's logs. The Fish People and the Berry People began an active trade between each other in driftwood and dead berry bushes. That was the situation when the Log People's new trees came to maturity. Not only did they have more logs available than the other tribes needed, but there was now an added factor: competition. Berry bushes burned better and driftwood was more decorative. The supply of logs was too great and the demand too little. The Log People were again facing poverty. They literally had logs to burn.

Faced with stiff competition from their neighbors and being on the losing side of the law of supply and demand, the Log People had no choice but to cut the price of their logs if they were to survive. Instead of trading one log for one fish or one basket of berries, they traded two logs. In effect, the cost to the Log People had doubled. With the supply of logs so high the Log People saw no end to their dilemma. This dilemma—otherwise referred to as "too much money chasing too few goods"—has come to be known as the basic cause of a phenomenon called inflation. Another historical first for the Log People!

The Value of Good, Hard Work

The horror of the drought stayed in the minds of the Berry People for many years. Adding to this his constant fear that the underground spring could someday dry up, Wump succeeded in creating a force of energetic workers out of what had been lazy playboys and playgirls.

Wump organized the workers into efficient squadrons. One tended the underground spring and continually looked for new sources of water. Another tended to the irrigation canal to make sure it had no leaks. Another dug catch-basins to store excess water, and yet another tended to the pruning and fertilizing of the berry bushes. The Berry People knew that their crop would grow only on that particular plateau. They had no desire to plant in other areas, but they realized that by improving the yield on the plateau bushes, they could become wealthier.

Wump urged the workers to exert themselves, and he congratulated them for jobs well done. The workers appreciated Wump's concern for their welfare, and they cooperated with his plans to the best of their ability.

The fruits of their labors were soon evident: some of the bushes grew twice as many good berries as they had in the past; still others grew fewer berries, but they were much larger, much sweeter, and much more desirable. Because of this cooperation between Wump, the manager, and the workers, the Berry People had become more efficient. They were turning out more goods and better goods for a given amount of labor. Building on his earlier technological advance (the irrigation canal), Wump had succeeded in increasing the productivity of the population.

Smoking a Fish

After the Fish People implemented their waste disposal program, they found more fish than ever in the waters off their village. Now they faced a curious dilemma: they could catch more fish than they could trade to the other tribes. Still motivated by their desire for wealth and expansion, they deliberated on what to do with this excess of natural resource. The problem was that there was no way to keep a fish after it had been caught. It simply rotted and had to be thrown away.

If only there were some way that fish could be kept for an indefinite period. The village council met in Mug's hut to deliberate. They threw some fish on the fire for that evening's meal and commenced their discussions. Someone suggested inventing a freezer, but Mug noted that they did not yet have a place to plug it into. Other ideas flowed freely, with discussion and debate ensuing. The proceedings became so intense that the council forgot about the fish that were on the dying fire. Many hours later, still not having reached a conclusion, hunger got the best of them. They were dismayed to find that the fish had been too thoroughly cooked. The juices were dried out and the meat smelled of wood smoke.

Thus, they all went to bed without any supper that evening. But, on a hunch, Mug did not throw away the overcooked fish. He put them into a box to see what might happen to them.

Three days later, Mug sniffed at the overcooked fish. To his amazement, they did not smell rotten. He picked off a piece of flesh and tasted it. It was dry and smoky tasting, but curiously appealing. Mug said nothing of his discovery and three days later tried it again. It still tasted good. Then Mug announced the great breakthrough to the Fish People.

Purely by accident, technology had created a new product: smoked fish. Experiments began with different kinds of fish and woods to find the combination that would extend the life of smoked fish for the longest time. In the ensuing weeks the techniques were refined and perfected.

The Log People and the Berry People were at first skeptical of this new edible item, but on tasting it they found it satisfying. The popularity of the smoked fish spread rapidly among the tribes. In addition to providing a new taste sensation, it also solved two other important problems. One was that the people could never travel more than one day from their village, because they couldn't carry a supply of fish that would last that long. If they could carry a supply of fish that would last many days, they could explore realms far beyond their villages and expand their universe accordingly.

The other problem was that there were occasional shortfalls in the amount of fish needed to satisfy their daily appetites. By laying in a supply of smoked fish, they could get through those brief shortages comfortably. Needless to say, all these factors meant more sales for the Fish People. Here, technology (albeit accidental), as applied to the natural resources of the Fish People, allowed them to gain some control over the law of supply and

demand. No matter how high or unexpected the demand, they could meet it with either fresh or smoked fish. And if demand should drop, they could either smoke the fish or leave it in the water until needed. And by ensuring themselves of a market for one form of fish or another during all seasons, the Fish People were able to keep their village budget on an even keel.

Bad News, Good News

Meanwhile, back in the Log People's village, Theodore and his advisors were trying to figure out a way to avoid the problem of an oversupply of logs. They reviewed what had caused the problem in the first place. Their major mistake was that they had relied on incomplete information in deciding how many new trees to plant. They couldn't remember precisely, but they thought they had either been told, or had let themselves believe, that there was a market for as many trees as they could produce. Thus, the overplanting. Now they realized how detrimental that information had been.

Theodore explained that they must seek correct information on which to base their planting decisions. "Let's determine just how many logs we can really sell at a fair price, and we'll plant accordingly." This was no easy task, for they all knew that it took many years between the planting and the cutting of the trees. Theodore assigned people to get the facts: How large will the populations of the tribes be when today's plantings mature? What kind of demand will they have for logs at that time? What kind of competition can be expected from driftwood and dead bushes? Are there other kinds of trees that can be planted that will be more salable? Can farming techniques be developed to make the trees grow taller and faster while still retaining the quality of the wood, if not improving it?

Theodore's people worked hard at their tasks and returned a year later with their recommendations. Theodore felt much more confident in guiding his people with this researched information than he had with the suppositions, guesses, and impulsive thinking that had guided them in the past. He took the conclusions to each of the clusters in the village who tended their own groves. He gave them lessons in how to plant, how much to plant, and how to tend the growing trees properly.

It took a full generation for all of this effort to pay off, but the rewards were worth the wait. The Log People had utilized education, market research, and the proper dissemination of information to stabilize and strengthen their economic well-being.

A Crushing Blow

Many years had passed since Wump had stirred the Berry People to new heights of productivity. Things were going perhaps a bit too well for the Berry People, and the old ways of laziness and greed had begun to recur.

Wump was much older now, and his influence was not as strong. His successor, Terwilliger, was intrigued by tales of the good old days when the Berry People had to do little work and were richly rewarded by nature.

In his zeal, Terwilliger cast about for ways that the Berry People could do less work and still earn more fish and logs. His idea was greeted with unanimous approval by his followers. They would double the size of the berry baskets. Despite the time involved in making the larger baskets, they were confident that the investment would be well worth it. By using the double-size baskets, they would save considerably on their packing costs and on overall handling. In short: less work, less expense, and more net income.

Terwilliger was delirious with the prospects, and his enthusiasm spread rapidly. So confident was everyone about Terwilliger's idea that nobody bothered to question it. Terwilliger sent messengers to the Log People and the Fish People to inform them of the forthcoming event: "New, bigger, better berry baskets for all!" He posted signs to extol the virtues of the new baskets and promised discounts for advance orders.

Mug and Theodore responded politely, saying that it sounded very interesting and that they'd certainly be willing to give the new baskets a try. Terwilliger interpreted their remarks as an enthusiastic endorsement of the new baskets. He was so sure that the demand would be great that he risked putting the entire crop on the market all at once.

The pickers picked their fingers to the bone to fulfill Terwilliger's orders. Thousands of double-size baskets were laid out on the delivery wagons. Terwilliger escorted the first wagon to the Fish People's village and presented the first basket to Mug. Mug was flattered by the gift and poured the double basket of berries into a large bowel for his family to taste. Then, to everyone's shock, they discovered that the berries on the bottom of the basket had been crushed by the weight of the berries on the top of the basket. Fully one-third of all the berries in the basket were damaged, and Mug responded angrily. "You told me I'd be getting two baskets' worth of berries in one, and in fact I only have a little more than one basket's worth of usable berries! You led me to believe that I was getting fair value for my two fish! I've been cheated!"

Stunned and embarrassed, Terwilliger apologized. He admitted that they had never tested to see whether the double-size baskets would create any crushing problems. They had just assumed that if a single-size basket did not result in crushing, neither would a double-size basket.

But it was too late for Terwilliger and the Berry People. Word of mouth spread quickly. Terwilliger had put the entire crop on the line and now found it difficult even to give it away. The bulk of the crop rotted in the double baskets, and the Berry People were flung instantly into poverty. Their underlying force—greed—had been thrown back in their faces by dreadful marketing procedures. Despite the quality of the product, the lack of research, poor packaging, and misleading advertising had resulted in a disaster for the people in the Berry village.

Help Wanted

One aspect of the smoked fish development brought unexpectedly good results: with several days' supply of fish, all the tribes were able to venture into previously unexplored areas. They found numerous other tribes specializing in their own products. To the north there were tribes that produced wheat, chickens, and apples. To the south there were tribes that produced barley, bananas, and a strange bubbling beverage that the natives called *beer.* None of these tribes had ever seen a fish—either fresh or smoked. The Fish People were eager to tap this vast new market. But they had some serious problems. All the available population was already working overtime to supply fish to the Berry and Log tribes. And the leader of the Fish People had long ago determine that only the Fish People should work the teeming waters by the village. How then could they catch more fish to sell to these outlying tribes?

First the leaders agreed that outsiders should be allowed to work in their village. Then they had to create a reason for outsiders to *want* to work in the fishing village. They decided to allow any outsiders a share of profits in addition to a basic wage for their labor. The women of the Log People found this an attractive proposition. By this time, cutting the logs and caring for the trees had become easier as a result of improved tools, and the women were freer to explore other opportunities for themselves. They welcomed the chance to receive payment for their work and were further satisfied that their village would benefit from the added wealth that they would bring home. Even some of the more energetic Berry People found the offer intriguing, and thus the first export business was created: selling to the outlying tribes.

Governmental policy, coupled with the creation of an incentive to invest (in this case time rather than money), was responsible for bringing a new era of prosperity to the three tribes.

Making Munny

The discovery of the outlying tribes and the opportunity to trade with them brought great changes to the Fish, Berry, and Log People. As the populations of the three tribes had grown, it was becoming ever more cumbersome to handle fish, berries, and logs each time a transaction occurred. The leaders agreed to create small tokens, made of stones, that would represent either a fish, a basket of berries, or a log. Thus, instead of trading the goods themselves, they could trade the tokens that represented the goods. Each token was referred to, in their primitive language, as a *Munny.* Now, if a Fish Person sold a large quantity of fish, he could take Munnies in exchange, rather than load himself up with berries and logs that he might not need at that time. Later, if that Fish Person wanted to acquire a basket of berries, he

could trade a Munny for it rather than having to carry a fish clear across town.

Before long, the more enterprising members of the tribes began to accumulate large quantities of Munnies, and to protect themselves against thieves, they asked the leaders of the tribes to oversee the creation of a bank that would hold their Munnies for them.

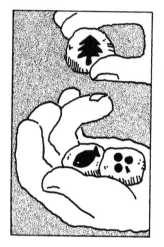

In addition to the Munny tokens, the three tribes had many other things in common. They were physically close to one another; they had many similar traditions and beliefs from centuries of living near, and trading with, one another; and they felt a need to help defend one another against any outside attacks. Eventually, they decided to formalize their common interests by creating a pact that would bind them together as an entity called the United Tribes. Meanwhile, and in similar fashion, the tribes in the north had joined together as the Wheat/Apples/Chicken Alliance. And the southerly producers of barley, bananas, and beer had joined together as the 3-B Federation. Each of these two other groups had created their own tokens representing their products, and the Alliance tokens, the 3-B tokens, and the Munny tokens were freely interchanged as the groups traded actively among one another. For many years all the peoples of these nations regarded one Alliance token as being equal to one Munny token, which was equal to one 3-B token. And for all those years the amount of trade among the nations was equal. Each bought and sold the same amount from one another, year in and year out.

The Building Binge (Fiscal Policy)

Then an unusual thing began to happen in the United Tribes. Their government decided to build a series of magnificent roads connecting the three villages. Many citizens objected, saying that the roads weren't needed and that no Munnies were available to pay for the building of the roads.

The United Tribes government responded, "We will surely need these roads in the future as our population grows. And having these roads will make us the envy of the Alliance and the 3-B Federation. Our national pride is at stake. And there's no problem about the Munnies—we'll borrow all we need from investors. If they lend us ten Munnies for one year we'll pay them back eleven Munnies at the end of the year. We'll get all the Munnies we'll need!"

Then the critics asked: "But where will you get the Munnies to pay back the investors?"

"No problem," said the government. "Since all of our citizens will benefit from these magnificent new roads, we'll have all of them pay us a certain number of Munnies every year. We'll call that a *tax*, and we'll use it to pay off the investors."

The road-building program got under way, and the government liked it

so much that it then embarked on building parks and gardens and rest stops along the way. Some of the people in the government received favors from the builders. The more they built, the more Munnies they taxed the citizens. There seemed to be no end in sight to the government's spending. The more it spent, the deeper in debt it went, and the higher the taxes went for the citizens. Some citizens finally rebelled and said, "Stop! We're paying too many Munnies in taxes, and we're not getting benefits accordingly."

But some other citizens replied, "Keep spending. We make a very good living as road builders, and we want that to continue."

This incident describes what is known as fiscal policy, which has to do with how a government decides to spend money and how it will raise the money it spends—normally through taxation and borrowing. If a government's income and expenses are equal, it is said that the government, like a family or a business, has a balanced budget. If a government takes in more money than it spends, it has a surplus. If it spends more than it takes in, it has a deficit. The fiscal policy of a government can have many influences—for better or for worse—on the well-being of its people.

The Beer Bust (Monetary Policy)

Another unusual development in the United Tribes was the insatiable craving for beer, which was available only through the 3-B Federation. Despite warnings from the government, they consumed an ever-growing quantity.

The rulers of the 3-B Federation saw a unique opportunity: "Right now the United Tribes can get beer only from us. So let's raise the price as high as traffic will allow. Someday they'll figure out how to make their own beer, or they'll be able to get it from someone else, so we'll stash away a lot of what we earn today to protect us against that competition in the future."

The citizens of the United Tribes were shocked when the price of their beer doubled, from one Munny to two Munnies per flask. But the drinking continued without letup. Very soon the flow of Munnies from the United Tribes to the 3-B Federation became a flood. The United Tribes found themselves so short of Munnies that they could barely afford to buy berries and fish and logs, which they needed far more than beer.

"We will not be denied our beer!" shouted angry United Tribes protesters. "Carve more Munny tokens if you have to!"

"That would be wrong," replied the government. "Each Munny should be backed by something of value—either a log or a basket of berries or a fish, or by our credible promise that any of those items can be purchased in the future at a reasonable price."

The government's dilemma relates to monetary policy, which deals with how much money a government will allow to float through the economy. If there's not enough, the economy will shrink, and jobs and incomes will disappear accordingly. If there's too much, the value of the money becomes

questionable, and sellers will raise prices to protect themselves against the possibly declining value of the money they receive.

Governments attempt to control economic health through monetary policy—in effect, controlling the amount of money available. There is no one formula that is guaranteed to work, but the wrong formula can be quite disruptive. In the United States major tensions have arisen over monetary policy with respect to buying oil, automobiles, and electronic goods from abroad. Our thirst for those items has been comparable to that of the United Tribes beer drinkers, and our money has flowed out accordingly.

The Banking Bombshell (Regulatory Policy)

The Building Binge and the Beer Bust caused serious problems for the United Tribes. One group, the bankers, came forward with a proposal to cure the ills. They said, "Our government is too strict with us. We take in depositors' Munnies, and the government guarantees that those Munnies will be safe in our hands. But in order to keep that guarantee intact, we are very limited as to how we can put that money to work. If the government will relax its regulations on us, and allow us to lend money more aggressively to builders and developers, we can help create jobs and incomes, and we can thus restore the health of our economy."

The government listened to these persuasions and was convinced of their value. Some people in government received favors from banks for helping to change the laws. Some people in banking received favors from builders and developers for helping to make loans to them. Some people who processed the loans received favors for saying that the properties being built were worth a lot more than they really were.

After a few years of this lending activity—during which, indeed, many construction and related jobs were created—the borrowers began to default on paying their loans. Many of them had built buildings that no one wanted to occupy. So the builders did not receive enough income from the buildings to allow them to pay their loans. But the people who had deposited their Munnies with the banks did not have to worry, for the government guaranteed that their Munnies were safe.

But if the banks had lost the Munnies on bad loans, where would the Munnies come from to pay off the depositors? From the taxpayers—and in huge amounts. Thus did the economic fortunes of the United Tribes suffer further from a failure of regulatory policy. This scenario was all too real in the United States during the late 1980s and early 1990s. It was referred to as the savings and loan bailout. Savings and loan companies (S&Ls) had been very strictly regulated: almost all of their lending was restricted to single-family homes. Then Congress gave in to demands from the savings and loan industry and allowed them very

broad lending powers, while at the same time insuring the safety of depositors' money.

Hundreds of S&Ls went haywire, lending huge amounts of money on very high-risk projects. Unsavory promoters involved in these loans pocketed tens of millions of dollars in illicit fees. When the high-risk projects couldn't pay back their loans, the S&Ls collapsed. But the government—that is, the taxpayers—still had to pay off the depositors in the failed companies. Cost to U.S. taxpayers: hundreds of billions of dollars, and a severe drag on the economy for years.

This is but one example of flawed regulatory policy. The ripple effects can exert a harsh influence on the economic well-being of everyone directly or indirectly involved.

Tit for Tat (Trade Policy)

The Wheat/Apples/Chicken Alliance had been trading happily with the United Tribes for many years. Apples and berries went across their borders in great abundance. Two ripe apples for one basket of berries was the going rate of exchange. Many members of the United Tribes began to prefer the Alliance's apples to their own home-grown berries. So great was the appetite for apples that the jobs of many berry growers were in jeopardy.

"We must protect our workers' jobs," said the leaders of the United Tribes. "To do so, we must make apples more expensive: three apples for one basket of berries will be the price from now on. If the apple growers don't like that, then let them go sell their apples elsewhere."

This amounted to a tax on the import of apples. In trading terms, such a tax is called a tariff. When the apple growers heard about it they vowed to get even. "We can't stop another nation from putting a tariff on the apples they buy from us. But we can certainly retaliate. From now on we will allow a quota of only 1,000 baskets of berries into our country each week!"

Trade between the two groups quickly dwindled to a trickle, and both were hurt by the obstacles to free trade that each had imposed on the other. The trade policies of both groups had been counterproductive. Workers suffered instead of being helped. In addition to tariffs and quotas, a government's trade policy can include offering low-cost loans and tax incentives to producers of certain goods; these financial benefits can make the targeted products cheaper to foreign purchasers. But cries of "unfair" and "let's get even" are sure to follow.

Nations also may encourage or cease trading with other nations as a result of political, religious, or philosophical differences. Trading partners with the United States—the world's richest single market—cherish the designation of Most Favored Nation (M.F.N.) status, as that gives them the best terms for dealing with Uncle Sam.

Nations are continually negotiating with each other, and with blocs of

nations, to seek fairness and advantage in their trading activities. Trade policies can thus affect the economic well-being of countless citizens.

Here Today, Gone Tomorrow (Industrial Policy)

The leaders of the United Tribes had an excellent idea: "Let us encourage the building of proper homes for our people. No more living in tents and caves. We shall have split-level condos and clustered housing on golf courses and spiffy single-family bungalows with jacuzzis and garage door openers." And so an industrial policy favoring home building was put into effect. Those who built homes received favorable tax treatment. Those who sold carpeting and appliances and furniture and paint and tile prospered handsomely. Investors in all of these companies reaped bonanzas. The leaders of the United Tribes awarded themselves generously for having satisfied so many people. Everyone connected with the home building industry boom was ecstatic!

But after a few years many people in the United Tribes became disgruntled. "Some people are getting rich at the expense of others. Home builders get fabulous tax breaks, but all the rest of us have to pay more taxes to pick up the slack. This is unfair. We should throw out our existing leaders and get new ones!"

So the leaders of the United Tribes replaced their industrial policy favoring home building with one favoring scientific research. This sent the home-building industry, and all its workers, suppliers, and investors, into a deep depression. But the research scientists loved it. Until the next industrial policy came along.

Although some might deny that the United States—epitome of the free market—espouses industrial policies, the fact is that we have had a succession of them for many decades. In the 1950s it was the building of the interstate freeway system. In the 1960s the space race began in earnest. Real estate development was favored in the 1970s and early 1980s, until the rug was pulled out from under it—with disastrous effects—by the 1986 Tax Reform Law. Sometimes industrial policy will disfavor a given segment of the economy, as tobacco makers and health-care deliverers found out in the 1990s. When the government bestows, or removes, its blessings by way of industrial policy, the results in jobs and incomes will be considerable. What effects have you felt, or might you feel from a change in industrial policy?

HERE AND NOW

The adventures and midadventures of these primitive peoples illustrate some of the most basic economic influences that we live with day to day. All these influences intertwine, overlap, and interact. Let's put these phenomena into a modern perspective.

Productivity

Productivity is a measure of efficiency: How much output can be generated by a given individual or group, considering the cost of raw materials, labor, capital, and overhead? Here are some examples of how conditions can affect productivity.

- You work in a factory that makes farnolas. At your average pace, you can turn out ten farnolas an hour. But your foreman is a mean person, and every time he makes the rounds, you get so aggravated that your efficiency drops, and for the next four hours you can turn out only nine farnolas an hour. The same goes for all your co-workers.
- The owner of the factory learns of the morale problem that's being caused by the foreman. The foreman is replaced with a much friendlier person, and you find yourself able to turn out eleven farnolas an hour. Your productivity has improved through a change in management, at no extra cost to the factory owner. This can mean greater profits for the owners of the company. And if you are paid on an incentive basis, it can also mean an increase in your pay.
- The owner of the factory installs an improved lighting system and better air conditioning. The added visibility and comfort factors for the workers enable them to become more efficient. The productivity of the factory has been increased as a result of capital investment.

Examine the various aspects of productivity in your home, your workplace, and your school. Where and how can matters be improved? Is the cost of making those improvements justifiable? Be your own efficiency expert. It could mean extra money in your pocket.

Government

The stories of the primitive tribes have already illustrated how government policies can affect the economic status of individuals and entire nations. Other activities of our government further illustrate these phenomena in very real terms.

For example, throughout the 1990s spending by our government resulted in annual federal budget deficits in excess of $200 and $300 *billion*. Where did the money that was spent come from? Most of it was borrowed and will eventually have to be repaid. Some of it was borrowed from U.S. individuals and institutions, but ever-increasing amounts of it were borrowed from foreigners. When a government owes money to its own citizens, it's relatively easy to establish a repayment schedule that everyone can agree to. But when a government owes money to foreign individuals and institutions, repayment plans are not as flexible.

The government spending did provide jobs and benefits for millions of Americans. But the repayment of the borrowed money that provided those jobs could mean higher future taxes.

How have specific government actions affected your individual economic well-being, for better or for worse? How can you anticipate future government actions that could affect you, and what defensive actions can you take to protect yourself?

International Matters

For the foreseeable future our involvement in the global marketplace will have the most indelible influence on our economic well-being. The previous discussion on trade policy illustrates some of the concerns, and the Consumer Alert section at the end of this chapter discusses other aspects. The best career and investment advantages will flow to those who are the most knowledgeable in international matters.

Technology

The irrigation canal the Berry People built and the fish-smoking technique that the Fish People developed were examples of technological development that improved conditions for the population. Advancing technology plays an extraordinary role in our economy. It relates directly to productivity in most cases, and lack of it can mean stagnation.

The most stunning example of technological advancement has been in the area of electronics. Improvements in computer chips have reduced the cost of doing calculations to a tiny fraction of what it was just a few years ago. Superconductors and fiber optics represent other areas of continuing technological advance. Major breakthroughs hold the promise of new materials that will permit electricity to flow with virtually no resistance. In time, this could result in computers that are vastly more efficient than the most powerful ones now in existence, medical diagnostic equipment that will make X-rays and scanning look primitive by comparison, electrical generating facilities that will be much more efficient than those we have today, and similar wonders that scientists once only dreamed about.

New developments in bio-technology and genetics hold the promise of better health and longer productive lives for all. What technological advances have affected you in your home and work life in recent years? Are they for better or for worse? How might advancing technology affect your job in the future?

Information

Information in the general sense is gathered from life experience, from education, and from what we learn through the media. To the extent that we take advantage of the information available to us, we can improve our lot considerably.

The creation and flow of information will have a major impact on the U.S. economy as the undeveloped nations of the world learn, grow, and become consumers of products that we will manufacture for sale to them. Roughly three-quarters of the earth's population is still considered undeveloped. In those nations, 60 to 90 percent of the people still work at agriculture to create enough food to feed the population. (In the United States, only about 2 percent of the population feeds the other 98 percent with a lot left over to be exported.) As the citizens of these undeveloped nations learn more about agriculture and health, they will become more self-sufficient and secure. As they learn basic trades and skills, they will become better able to support themselves and their families. As they continue to improve their lot—largely through education and training—they will have money to spend on such things as tools, medicines, books, and teachers. This, in turn, will beget more information, sharper skills, and more income. Sooner than later, these billions of people will be buying things that we've long since become accustomed to: running shoes and blue jeans, tape recorders and tennis rackets, furniture and television sets, movie tickets, and so on. For many years to come, these billions of people will look to the existing industrial nations to provide most of these goods—and our economies will boom. Eventually, those nations will be self-sufficient in most of those goods, and whole new patterns of international economy will emerge. But for the next twenty to fifty years, information will be the seeds planted abroad that will bear fruit back home.

STRATEGIES FOR SUCCESS

Keeping Up-to-Date Can Pay Off

It's difficult indeed to predict accurately the long-term fluctuations in our nation's economy. But, by keeping up-to-date on certain key statistics, you can gain a good sense of short-term trends, and you can plan your investments and other economic activities accordingly. Each month the government publishes the Index of Leading Economic Indicators. This tends to be the most reliable gauge of expected growth or shrinkage in the economy in the months ahead. Also, major borrowings by the U.S. Treasury tend to set trends for interest rates throughout the nation. The "Credit Markets" section of *The Wall Street Journal* carries news and analyses about these borrowings on a regular basis. Keep up with these matters, and see if your awareness doesn't help you manage your own personal finances.

Capital Investment

Even with all the skills, enthusiasm, and technology that an individual or business can muster, money is still needed to make things happen. Every large business—even a General Motors, an IBM, or an Exxon—started as a small business. And small businesses grow when they are able to attract money: capital investors. A company whose management, product, and profitability are attractive to investors will be able to raise more capital to improve and grow. Simply put, working for such a company can mean career advancement for you.

Not all capital investment comes from outsiders. Specific businesses must also have reason to believe that they can invest their own money internally and reap rewards accordingly. Here again we see the intertwining of various economic influences: the government can create incentives for a business to invest in its own future through tax credits and similar devices.

Forecasting

All economic entities must do some accurate forecasting if they are to survive. If the Log and Berry and Fish people had looked ahead, they might have avoided their troubles.

Likewise, in today's world we must be alert to future changes in the value of money, the cost of labor, the price of raw materials, the costs of shipping, building, communicating, traveling, litigating, medicating, everything else that goes into life and business.

Over the long run, with very few and short-lived exceptions, inflation will be a force to contend with. Costs rise. Workers expect pay raises. A drought in the Midwest makes the price of bread go up. A war between oil-producing nations makes the price of gasoline go up.

A government wants to ward off inflation, so it raises the cost of money by boosting the interest rates that banks have to pay when they borrow money from the government. "How can *that* work?" you ask. In recent years, governments have followed the theory that by boosting the cost of money, it will be more expensive to borrow. By making borrowing more expensive, you deter people and businesses from buying things. With the demand for things thus dampened, prices will stabilize. This has worked more often than not when properly implemented.

Since money is an ingredient of everything that is built, bought, stored, delivered and stashed away, sensing the future value of money becomes a basic part of economic management. The most common concern regarding the future value of money is: How much will the purchasing power of your work be eroded by inflation? In other words: If you have to work one hour today to earn enough to buy a six-pack, and the price of a six-pack increases by 10 percent a year, then next year you'll either have to work one hour and

six minutes to buy a six-pack. Or you'll have to get a raise to offset the extra cost. If you don't do either, then your purchasing power will have been eroded by inflation: the future value of your money will be less—in terms of what it can buy—than it is today.

Long-term planning—retirement for individuals, new factories for businesses—must take this phenomenon into account. If, for example, you spend $100 a week on food, and inflation runs at an average of, say, 3 percent a year, then in thirty years the bill for the same food will be $190! (That's an increase of 3 percent each year for thirty years, or 90 percent. Compounding hasn't been considered to keep this concept simpler to understand.) If you plan to retire in thirty years, how much will you have to put away each year until then to be able to afford your current lifestyle?

The calculations can be tricky indeed, and they must take into account many unknowns. For example: your needs in thirty years may be less than they are now, such as needing only one car for a family instead of two. Your ability to put away money might get easier as your income increases—which it should. Say that you now need to save 8 percent of your annual income in order to reach your desired goals. If your income increases in the future, you may find that you'll only have to save, say, 5 percent of your annual income to reach your goals. And if inflation increases from its current level, the amount you can earn on your savings can also increase proportionately. Page 357 has further details on how to realistically evaluate this dilemma for your own personal purposes.

Marketing

Everybody is selling something. When you apply for a job, you are selling yourself. The "package" you present to the employer can determine whether you get the job. In addition to looking at your résumé and application, the employer observes how you dress, how you speak, and how you carry yourself. She takes account of your level of enthusiasm, your knowledge of the company and the industry, and your overall personality. In short, applying for a job is a marketing effort that you make on your own behalf. The better you market yourself, the better your chance for success.

Similarly, employers must make efforts to market their own products. Those efforts include knowing the marketplace, learning what the competition is doing and planning, designing a package that will appeal to the public, informing the public of the benefits of the product (advertising), and establishing a price structure for the product that the public will accept.

Nature and Natural Resources

Until we discover or invent some new kind of energy source to power our vehicles, our factories, and our homes, we will be living in the age of petroleum. Petroleum is a natural resource found in some of the most unreachable places on the planet: miles beneath the ocean, in the frozen wastelands of the polar icecaps, and in the middle of hostile deserts. Nature has given us the gift of petroleum as a fuel. But nature has also seen to it that access to this gift can be costly and challenging.

Just as the Log People found it necessary to go farther and farther afield to chop down their trees, we may soon find it necessary to go to ever-increasing expense to acquire our basic fuel commodities, as well as other important natural resources. Sometimes ingenuity will replace one natural resource with another resource that is more readily available. For example, nuclear power might someday replace petroleum as our primary source of energy. But what about clean water and clean air? As those natural resources—which we take for granted—become more scarce, what can replace them? The economic and social well-being of everyone on earth will be affected by our ultimate need to modify our habits or to replace some of these resources.

THE RESULTS

It has not been the intent here to give you textbook definitions of such things as inflation, recession, deficits, surpluses, and other economic phenomena. Rather, it is hoped that the foregoing discussion will help you understand the influences at work in the world, in our nation, and in your individual environment. At the end of each chapter in this book you'll find a section titled Ups & Downs: The Economics of Everyday Life. These sections will help you focus on the specific causes of economic activity as they affect your day-to-day personal financial affairs. Your better understanding of these forces and influences will enable you to become a better manager of your personal economy, and will help you to take advantage of opportunities that you might not have previously recognized.

PERSONAL ACTION WORKSHEET

How Do You React?

As this chapter has illustrated, a great many matters—both close at hand and remote—can affect your financial well-being. An awareness of these matters should alert you to defensive or corrective actions that you can take to protect yourself. Consider the following list of incidents that might have had a bearing on you in the past year. Think deeply about the not-so-obvious effects. What reactions did you have, or could you have had, either to fend off harmful effects or take advantage of good effects?

Incident	Effects on You, Direct or Indirect	Your Reactions, Actual or Possible
❐ Strikes (local, regional, or national)	_____	_____
❐ Weather conditions	_____	_____
❐ Business conditions for your employer	_____	_____
❐ Business conditions in your city, in the nation	_____	_____
❐ Your own health	_____	_____
❐ Health of your family	_____	_____
❐ Changes in tax laws	_____	_____
❐ Changes in working conditions	_____	_____
❐ International incidents	_____	_____
❐ Your acquiring more education	_____	_____

CONSUMER ALERT ——————————————————————————

The Global Marketplace

Exercise 1.2

You work at the XYZ Company—minding your own business, taking care of yourself as best you can, and saying, "I couldn't care less about international trade. It doesn't affect me now. And it won't affect me in the future. So why worry?"

Bad call.

Historic changes are taking place around the world, and new patterns of competition and opportunity in international trade will affect *virtually everyone.* Your company might find new markets in other countries; that could benefit your career. Or your company might be harmed by international competition; that could be bad for you. Your pension fund might be invested—for better or for worse—in companies involved in world trade; that could impact on your retirement income. There's really no place to hide. But an awareness of what's going on now, and what might happen in the future, can alert you to make the right moves.

These are the major trends that will be shaping world economic events in the years ahead.

North America   Trade pacts with Canada, Mexico, and the nations of the Caribbean can create a unified market of some 400 million people. Good news: easier trading with our neighbors, and more customers for U.S. made goods. Bad news: U.S. workers will have to compete with lower wage earners in those other nations.

Western Europe   A unified trading bloc in Western Europe can match North America in size and wealth. Money and labor and goods will move freely across borders, just as they now move across state borders in the United States. This will encourage giant multinational European companies, which will be stiff competition for Americans and Asians.

Eastern Europe   The former Soviet Union and its former allies are decades behind the West in basic infrastructure. They need incalculable billions of dollars to build new highways, factories, and power plants to get them into the twenty-first century on a par with the West. U.S. companies have a great opportunity to help Eastern Europe rebuild. In the long term, Eastern Europeans may become good customers for U.S. products and services. But competition for that trade with Western Europe and Asia will be ferocious.

Asia   Japan will be the hub of a giant industrial wheel encompassing more than 2 billion people from China to India and all points between. Low-cost labor coupled with huge amounts of money will result in an industrial juggernaut. But their infrastructural needs are equally gigantic, which the United States can help provide.

UPS & DOWNS   *The Economics of Everyday Life*

The Ingredients

The Ups & Downs sections in each chapter have been created to help you understand the ingredients in the economics of everyday life, to help you successfully ride the ups and downs of prices, interest rates, job opportunities, investments, tax laws, and even the whims of nature.

Following are the basic ingredients that go into the cost of almost everything. As they go up and down, so can your own financial well-being. Keep these basic ingredients in mind as you read the rest of this book, and particularly the Ups & Downs sections.

Capital   Every product or service you acquire has a capital ingredient: money, either cash-in-hand or borrowed. The farmer needs money to buy seed and fertilizer and equipment. The doctor needs money to pay for rent and staff and technology and continuing education. The bank needs money (from depositors and investors) to lend to borrowers.

Labor   The creation of every product or service involves some human efforts. Labor costs can vary widely, depending on the skills being used and the bargaining ability of the workers.

Social Costs   Capital and labor used to be considered the core elements of cost. But today much of the cost of any product or service also helps pay for—via taxes—social welfare programs, education, and a wide range of governmental activities.

Marketing   A lot of money goes into the design, packaging, and advertising of any product. You pay for it when you buy the product.

Governmental Regulations   Add up the costs of tax law compliance, payroll recordkeeping, pension plan administration, health and safety precautions, union relations, discrimination policing—it's a bundle.

"Postage and Handling"   A few decades ago the cost of delivering goods was relatively minimal. But now the costs and complexities are far more significant, involving fuel, equipment, insurance, and storage.

After-service   The age of consumerism has added its costs to an item after it has been purchased: namely, warranties, consumer hotlines, product recalls, defense of lawsuits, and supply of replacement parts.

These ingredients are examined more closely in later Ups & Downs sections.

?   WHAT IF . . . ?

How would you deal with these real-life possibilities?

As the world changes, any of the following could cause you to make adjustments in your own economic life. Consider each phenomenon, and evaluate how you might react. What adjustments might you make in your work, your budgeting, your style of living, your future plans?

1. The company that you (or your spouse) work(s) for announces that it's starting an export division. (Or your company provides goods or services to another company that is starting an export division.) There is every reason to believe that the venture will be a success. The initial target for foreign sales will be Central America. New opportunities at home and overseas will be available to those with skills in language, marketing, and customer service.

2. Your employer is being clobbered by foreign competition. Attempts to keep up are futile. It's only a matter of time—perhaps six months to a year—before the company folds.

3. The government announces a job retraining program offering instruction in high-tech applications, computer sciences and engineering. There's no cost, but you'll have to devote fifteen hours a week for a year to get the training, which holds promise but no guarantees of better jobs.

4. The government opens the door wide to new immigrants. Many foreigners, with skills like yours and willing to work for less money, are on their way here.

NUMBER CRUNCHERS

Do the calculations to make decisions in these real-life possibilities.

Exercise 1.3

1. Ask a bank what interest rate you'd have to pay today for a 36-month new-car loan of $10,000, and what the monthly payments would be. If you waited six months to buy the car (at the same price as today), and interest rates then had moved up by one percentage point, what would your monthly payments be then? What if rates had dropped by one point?

Exercise 1.4

2. What is the interest rate today and the monthly payments on a 30-year fixed-rate home loan of $120,000? What would your payments be if you took out the loan six months from now, after rates had moved up one percentage point? Down one point?

Exercise 1.5

3. Determine the current rate of inflation (the Consumer Price Index, or CPI). Using that as a rough gauge, what would happen to the price of a car, a home, or a year's worth of college tuition if the CPI was two percentage points higher each year for the next two years?

4. You invest $5,000 in a mutual fund that is pegged to move up and down in sync with the Dow Jones Industrial Average. What will your investment be worth if that average moves as follows over the next three years: (a) +5%, −8%, +12%? (b) −7%, +16%, −2%? (c) +12%, +9%, −8%. (Don't count taxes or dividends.)

STRATEGIES FOR SUCCESS

Biblical Wisdom Helps You Manage Your Money

Remember the biblical story about the seven fat years followed by the seven lean years (Genesis 41)? Simply put, the message is: When times are good, put away something for the lean years. Any economy—your nation's or your family's—will go through times of relative prosperity alternating with relative austerity. When times are good, when income is high, it can be tempting to spend everything you're earning. But better to heed the ancient wisdom: Put some aside when the putting is good. You'll be happy you did when times aren't so rosy. A dollar put away during the fat years can grow to be $1.25 . . . $1.50 . . . or more to have on hand during the lean years.

FOR BETTER OR FOR WORSE

Things beyond our control often impact our personal and financial well-being, for better or for worse. Some are more predictable than others. How could you be affected if the following real-life phenomena happened? Could you have seen it coming? What steps could you have taken to minimize damage or maximize advantage? The better able you are to anticipate and recognize these forces, the better equipped you are to deal with them.

1. The Federal Reserve announces that interest rates will be increased by 0.5 percent, effective immediately.

2. Severe floods in the Midwest devastate the current grain crops. More than 30 percent of the expected harvest will be lost, and 20 percent of the next crop is threatened by expected weather conditions over the next six months.

3. Your state government announces that a maximum-security prison costing $80 million will be built ten miles from where you live.

Exercise 1.6

2

Working, Planning & Budgeting

Without work all life goes rotten. But when work is soulless, life stifles and dies.
Albert Camus

Shun idleness. It is a rust that attaches itself to the most brilliant metals.
Voltaire

You may call it *the rat race* or *the daily grind*. Someday you'll look back on it and wonder, "Where did all the time go?" This is the essence of family economics: (1) earning the money; (2) setting goals as to how you'll spend it, and (3) developing disciplined budget plans that will enable you to reach those goals. All of these matters are going on simultaneously, and they are subject to change at any given time. It's quite an exercise to coordinate them properly and to make wise adjustments when the need arises. This chapter will help you focus on all three of these "moving targets" so that you can plan, prioritize, and achieve what you want for yourself. Specific decision-making tools in this chapter include:

- How to accurately determine what a given job is worth: putting a dollar sign on the basic wage, the fringe benefits, and the longer term potential
- How to protect your legal and financial rights as an employee
- How to clarify your financial goals: setting them, putting the necessary priorities on them, and developing a workable plan to meet your goals
- How to use a financial statement as a planning and goal-meeting device

THE ROLE OF WORK IN YOUR LIFE

Work is perhaps the single most powerful force shaping your life. Your work creates the bulk of your income. It is that income, put to proper use, that allows you to be self-sufficient. It provides you with the necessities of life, as well as whatever luxuries may be within your reach. Income that isn't needed now can be invested for your future welfare.

Work can be a training ground. The job you do today gives you experience. That experience should enable you to accept future assignments that will be more challenging and rewarding and will promise greater benefits.

And work—for better or worse—can play an important role in many of the nonfinancial aspects of your life. The type of work you do can clearly shape a great deal of your social life, leading you into friendships and activities generated by the working environment.

As a well-planned working career progresses, it should create more leisure time, along with more dollars to spend in that leisure time. If you are to make the most of this powerful force that shapes so much of your life, it's necessary to look at work in a broad perspective. Your job is not simply a means of filling the hours from nine to five. You must look at not only what you might be doing today, tomorrow, or next week, but also where your aspirations and abilities can lead you. You must examine the ways you can maximize the rewards and pleasures available to you through work. Finally, you must consider how you can most efficiently use the fruits of your labor—your income—to satisfy current and future needs and desires.

FACTORS IN CHOOSING YOUR WORK

You have an extraordinary range of opportunity available to you in choosing your work. In every part of the country, there are community colleges and state universities, which offer relatively low-cost education that can lead to virtually any type of career. When the economy of our nation is dynamic and expanding, it offers new types of work opportunities and increasing chances for advancement within chosen fields of endeavor.

We are at the forefront of many new technologies, which will create challenging new opportunities in genetic engineering, laser technology, satellite communications, space exploration, weapons and defense systems, and much more. Even our leisure activities generate tens of billions of dollars a year in jobs for our citizens, ranging from neighborhood health clubs to professional sports teams to our worldwide exporting of movies and television programs.

Your ability to achieve your fullest work potential has few limitations. Achieving full potential is often interpreted as making a lot of money. That's not necessarily an accurate description of achieving full potential. Indeed, many people work so hard to make a lot of money that they never

find themselves with the *time* to enjoy the *money* they've made. They may consider themselves failures.

There are important criteria other than money. Consider such rewards as a sense of self-satisfaction; the pride and pleasure you can feel from being creative, from being innovative, from being part of a winning team; a sense of personal growth that enhances your social, family, and community life. You can't spend these rewards, but they are invaluable.

You must determine your own balance of the rewarding aspects of work: money, leisure time, advancement, comaraderie, and pride in your achievements. That sense of balance is not easily achieved. Many people work years or decades before sensing that they have achieved it. Many people never find it, and many give up prematurely because they feel it's beyond their grasp. Others never strive to achieve it at all. There is no easy formula that can guide you toward the balance that is right for you. It's an ongoing quest, subject to change as your own needs and desires change. Your ability to achieve the right sense of balance will depend on your *desire* to do so and on a number of other factors, which we'll now examine.

Attitudes and Aspirations

Your choice of work, and your pursuit of success, will be shaped not only by your own attitudes and aspirations but also by those of others. Evaluate how each of the following influences might affect your work and career:

- Your ideas of what you want to achieve. For example: "I would like to have my own business."
- The degree to which you mold your own ideas of success based on other people. For example: "My friend Pat has everything going just right. If I could achieve what Pat has, I'd be very satisfied."
- The degree to which you are influenced by others. For example: A teacher may sense that you have certain aptitudes and, without your being aware of it, may motivate you to seek a career that you might not otherwise have considered. Or relatives may gently nudge, or emphatically push, you in one career direction or another, perhaps more for their own sense of self-satisfaction than for yours.
- The extent to which you are influenced by traditional social values. Will you be satisfied with the type of life that society has typically extolled: a good job, a nice family, living in a pleasant neighborhood, and becoming part of the community? Do you aspire to more than that? Or do you rebel against those values?
- The extent to which a change in your family circumstances can reshape your attitudes. For example: "I had great dreams for myself, but now I must make them secondary to the demands of my family."

Or, "I had great dreams for myself and, now, with the help and encouragement of my family, I can begin to achieve those goals."

- The extent to which you are supported by your employer. Can you profit from the support you receive from your employer? Can you overcome lack of support from your employer?
- The extent to which you view your current work as merely a job or as one step on the ladder of a long-range career. Are you just putting in your forty hours, or do you have ideas that will benefit the company and lead to your advancement?

How do you really feel about all these elements? Can you distinguish between the positive and negative influences as they affect your own attitude? Can you take advantage of the good influences? And can you walk away from the bad influences?

Education

Education is the major foundation on which a successful career is built. As Table 2–1 illustrates, on average, the more education people receive, the greater the income they'll receive.

If you project these figures out to a full working career, you can readily see that the college graduate in Table 2–1 will earn roughly double what the high school graduate earns. However, as attractive as the college graduate's lifetime earnings seem to be relative to the high school graduate's, the cost of obtaining that education creates a serious dilemma for many people. Table 2–2 illustrates the rising cost of obtaining a college education.

The debate over the value of *college* may never be resolved, but there can be very little argument that *education*—college, on-the-job training, or self-education—plays an integral role in career advancement and the achievement of one's fullest potential.

Bear in mind that educational facilities *alone* do not necessarily equip you for a more rewarding career. It's *what you do* with them that will make all the difference.

TABLE 2–1   **Income and Education**

Education of Householder	Average Annual Income, 1998 Dollars, Est.
Elementary school	$34,900
High school (4 years)	47,000
College (4 or more years)	91,500

Source: U.S. Census Bureau.

TABLE 2–2 **Rising College Costs**

If You Were to Start a Four-Year College Career in	Your Cost for the Four Years (room, board, tuition, books, transportation, and other expenses)* Would Be About:	
	Public (State) Colleges	**Private Colleges**
2000	$53,300	$112,500
2001	56,500	119,200
2002	59,900	126,400
2003	63,500	134,000
2004	67,300	142,000
•	•	•
•	•	•
•	•	•
2016	135,400	285,700

Exercise 2.1

*Costs are based on a 6 percent per year inflation factor.
Source: U.S. Department of Health and Human Services, 1996.

Aptitudes

In the career sense, aptitude generally means what you're best suited for. But what you're best suited for might not necessarily be the thing you enjoy most or from which you can generate the best level of income. For example, a young man worked in his father's clothing store during vacations. His father convinced him to take over the clothing store when he graduated. Because of the extensive on-the-job training, he had an *aptitude* for retailing; security and income seemed assured by following that course. But he never like retailing. Although the income and security were comfortable enough, he soon felt stifled, unproductive, discontented. By common methods of measurement, his aptitude was for retailing. But for him it was the wrong career.

What, then, is aptitude? It's a very precarious balance of many personal elements, some of which can be measured and some of which defy measurement. In the absence of a clear sense of direction, guidance counseling can be of some help in sorting out these various elements:

- What do you enjoy doing?
- What do you do well? (This is not the same as what you enjoy. Many of us do things well but don't necessarily enjoy doing them. And many of us enjoy doing certain things that, regrettably, we don't do that well. The difference should be noted.)
- What can you do to generate a desirable level of income and security?
- To what extent, if any, are you seeking to satisfy the expectations of others? Many people, such as the young retailer just noted, embark on careers because others expect it of them.

Personal Experience

Your personal experiences, both at work and in your private life, can affect your career choice and the success you may achieve. Any prior job can help you determine whether you like a particular type of work and whether you are good at it. Prior jobs can also lead to references that you can use later in seeking employment.

Other personal experiences—in or out of the workplace—can help you evaluate your comfort level in various situations:

- Do you enjoy being among other people, or are you more of a loner?
- Do you tend to be a leader or a follower?
- Are you content to be confined in a specific location for extended periods of time, or do you feel a strong need to move around in different locations?
- Is your span of concentration long or short on menial tasks? On more difficult tasks?
- Do you accept criticism constructively, or do you rebel against it?
- Are you a fast learner or a slow learner?
- Are you assertive or shy with other people?
- Are your ambitions greater or less than those of your peers?
- Can your energy be sustained for long periods of time, or does it come and go in spurts?
- Are you basically a patient or an impatient person?

Consider what kind of work opportunities and environments will most happily blend with your own traits to provide you with maximum satisfaction without forcing you into painful compromises.

The Changing Composition of the Work Force

Patterns of work life in the United States are changing. In the years to come, few individuals will be left untouched by the changes. To be aware of emerging trends that can affect your career is to be prepared to cope and to adjust. Let's briefly examine some of these trends.

The percentage of males participating in the work force is diminishing, while the percentage of females is sharply increasing.

Men are entering the work force later in life because of longer schooling, and they are leaving the work force sooner because of earlier retirement programs. Improvements in disability and health care benefits have also enabled men to leave the labor market when health problems have arisen.

A drastic drop in the birth rate has resulted in more women being able to work uninterrupted by childbearing. The availability of day-care facilities and tax benefits for child-care expenses have also aided many women wanting to enter the work force.

These factors, together with rapid gains by women in education and job opportunities, are resulting in dramatic shifts in the roles of men and women. Role separation is being replaced by role sharing for vast numbers of married couples. More than half of all married couples have two incomes, providing some protection to a married couple in the event of a layoff, compared to the once-typical family unit that depended predominantly on the man's income.

In the years ahead, the struggle will intensify between men and women for comparable jobs, comparably paid. What traditionally had been "male jobs" and "female jobs" are intermixing. With rare exceptions, sexual distinctions in the work force will all but disappear. How will these shifting demographic trends work to your advantage? To your disadvantage?

ECONOMIC TRENDS

The pendulum never stops swinging. As the primitive tribes in chapter 1 learned, many economic trends can create or threaten job opportunities. Awareness of these trends is essential if you want to take advantage of the good swings and avoid the troubles of the bad swings. Here is a summary of the most common trends; they can affect not only your career but your investment efforts as well.

- **Business Cycles**   On a national or regional level we refer to these cycles as *growth periods* and *recession periods.* One typical pattern: the economy is booming thanks to policies that make it easy to borrow money. Companies build new factories, buy new equipment, and hire new workers. When workers are in demand they can ask for, and get, higher wages. The higher wages translate into higher prices for the things that these workers make. The rising prices—inflation—hit a point where some people say, "I can't afford that." So they stop buying that thing, and the workers who make it are out of a job. Workers without jobs can't buy things either, so the layoffs spread. Pretty soon the economy's pendulum has swung from a growth period to a recession period. After a time, the laid off workers begin to find jobs again, and the pendulum starts to swing back the other way.

  The U.S. economy was booming in the 1980s, then went into recession in the early 1990s. By the late 1990s the pendulum had swung back the other way. Until? When the early 1990s recession hit, the buzzword for laying off workers was *downsizing.* Why was there so much downsizing? Because there was too much *upsizing* in the 1980s. Riding on boom times then, too many businesses thought that growth and prosperity would never end, so they took on more employees than the future would find prudent. Another way of looking at this phenomenon is to take into account the law of gravity: what goes up

must come down. No one has yet been able to find a way around the law of gravity.

(It's amusing to note some of the econo-babble that companies use to make bad things seem not so bad. A sampling of other expressions used by major corporations to describe firing people: *Release of resources. Career-change opportunity. Rightsizing. Strengthening of global effectiveness. Normal payroll adjustment. Career transition program. Schedule adjustments.* Yeah, right.)

Business cycles also occur in industrial categories. The sudden popularity of sport utility vehicles was a boon to the automobile industry. The invention of the video cassette recorder was a boon to the movie industry and created the video sales/rental industry. The invention of the computer spawned countless new enterprises, from mouse pad makers to publishers who sell books explaining how to work the computers, and all points in between. Eventually, the causes of these phenomena fade, and the businesses and jobs fade as well. And the pendulum swings.

- **Geographical Shifts**   When air-conditioning became cost-effective (after World War II) there was a huge shift of population from the chilly Northeast and Midwest to the sunny South and Southwest. Many cities throughout the Snowbelt began to shrivel as people left, resulting in more closings and lost jobs. When the Cold War ended around 1990, hundreds of thousands of jobs in the defense industry were wiped out. A huge percentage of those jobs were in the Sunbelt, and migrations began back to the Snowbelt. In the 1970s Americans were buying imported cars in record numbers, and auto workers in the Midwest began losing their jobs as a result. By the 1980s many of the foreign auto companies were building factories in the United States, so jobs started coming back to U.S. workers. In the mid-1990s the North American Free Trade Agreement joined the United States, Mexico, and Canada in a pact that would make it easier for those nations to trade with each other. Mexican wages were much lower than those in the United States and Canada, so a lot of U.S. jobs went south of the border. But then the Mexican economy began to improve, so Mexicans became customers for goods and services made in the United States and Canada. The pendulum swings. Can you cite any other examples, particularly that might pertain to you personally?

- **Political Changes**   When the Democrats controlled Congress in the early 1990s they attempted a massive plan to revamp our health care industry (which represents about 14 percent of all the money spent each year in the United States). The health care industry shuddered with fear. In came the Republicans, and out went the health care overhaul. The health care industry breathed a sigh of relief, but in the

meantime they had begun their own forms of consolidation to hopefully stave off governmental intervention. (See chapter 17 for more details.) Anyone remotely connected to the health care industry—including anyone needing medical care—was impacted by this political change.

Since 1969 the U.S. government has been unable to balance its budget. Spending outpaced income year after year. This was largely due to differing philosophies between the Republicans and the Democrats. The taxpayers made up the difference. In 1997 the two parties stopped their bickering long enough to pass spending and taxing laws that would supposedly balance the budget by 2002. We'll see, but while we wait some taxpayers get a break, and some who had been the beneficiaries of government spending will get broken. The pendulum swings.

Job Retraining

International competition, emerging technology, and changes in our government's industrial policies can also create or threaten job opportunities. The possible need to retrain yourself for a new type of work cannot be ignored. Various programs have emerged to assist workers in getting effective retraining. Keep yourself up to date on what's available. You never know when you might need it.

Financial Rewards

Of all the factors that might affect your choice of work, perhaps none is as persuasive as money. But, as the vignette at the start of chapter 1 indicated, that can be a mistake. As you may recall, the choice there was between higher income today but little advancement opportunity in the future, or less pay today with much more rewarding potential. You must, of course, evaluate actual potential with great care.

Beyond the base earnings you must carefully evaluate the full range of fringe benefits that may be available, and that can be worth thousands of dollars to you. Here are the major fringe benefits you should know about. The Personal Action Worksheet at the end of this chapter will help you evaluate and compare fringe-benefit packages at various places of employment.

Pension Plans

In a pension plan, the employer puts money aside every year for the benefit of eligible employees. In accordance with what is known as the *vesting plan*, you must work for the company for a given number of years before those benefits are locked up on your behalf. Normally, you don't receive the

money in the pension plan until you retire. Pension plan benefits vary considerably from one company to another. (See chapter 18 for a more detailed discussion of pensions and vesting.)

Profit-Sharing Plans

These are similar to pension plans. A certain percentage of the company's annual profits are divided up among employees, and you're entitled to your share in accordance with the vesting plan. Commonly, your vested interest will not be paid out until you quit or retire. A particularly attractive aspect of pension and profit-sharing plans is that you don't have to pay income taxes on your employer's contributions during the years in which that money is credited to your pension or profit-sharing account. (See chapter 18 for more details.)

Investment Programs

A popular fringe benefit is known as the 401(k) plan. This is a form of investment program in which part of the employee's pay is placed in the plan, and that portion of pay escapes income taxes until the money is eventually withdrawn by the employee. The earnings of this plan are also tax-deferred. Employees generally have a choice of different types of investments, including a guaranteed income plan, similar to a savings program; a mutual-fund type of plan that invests in a variety of stocks; and a plan that invests in the stock of the company the employee works for. It's generally possible to mix and match among the different plans, and the mix can be changed at various intervals. It's also common for the company to chip in some money for each dollar the employee puts in. For example, for every dollar an employee puts in, the company might put in 25 cents. (See chapter 18 for more details.)

Health Insurance Plans

Health insurance plans are among the most common type of fringe benefits offered to employees. But not all employers offer this potentially valuable benefit. And plans that are offered can vary widely, from skimpy coverage to extensive coverage. As health care costs continue to rise, employees are being asked to bear part of the cost of the group insurance. See chapter 17 for more details.

Life Insurance

Life insurance is not as common a benefit as health insurance, but its inclusion in benefits packages is growing. As with group health insurance, the employer is able to purchase coverage for many employees at a lower cost

than you could obtain on your own. Group life insurance may be a flat fixed sum or may vary in relation to your earnings at the company.

Educational Programs

Many employers will pay all, or a part of, the cost of courses that the firm recommends or that you wish to take in the furtherance of your career. That education is an asset you can take with you wherever you go.

"Family-Friendly" Benefits

Some fringe benefits might be more important in terms of family convenience than money. The number of holidays and vacation days—paid, unpaid, or any combination thereof—should be established. Sick leave is of major importance: How many days of paid sick leave—full or partial—would you be entitled to? When sick-pay benefits run out, is there a disability-income program that would kick in to pay all or part of your income?

Where and when you work is negotiable with some employers. Flextime, if offered, would allow you to vary the hours of your working day to coordinate with your family needs. Telecommuting—working at home and connecting with work through phone, fax and e-mail—is a benefit that many can enjoy; indeed, some employers are realizing that productivity increases with some workers when they telecommute.

Miscellaneous Benefits

The list of additional benefits grows each year as employers compete for good workers. Some of these may be negotiable—you don't ask, you don't get. Here is a rundown of some of the more popular benefits being offered:

- **Cafeteria plans** This benefit lets workers choose between a number of various fringes, which might include insurance for life, health, and disability, investment plans, and vacation time. If you don't want one particular benefit you can dump it and get extra value on another benefit. These are also known as *flexible benefit plans.* If this is available, you must choose with great care and understand what options you have if you want to change the mix later on.
- **Flexible spending accounts** With these you can set aside some of your earnings and avoid paying income taxes on that amount, provided you set the money aside to be used for certain qualified expenses such as dependent care or unreimbursed medical costs. Be careful: In order to preserve the tax-free status of those earnings, the money must be spent during the year on those qualified expenses. If it isn't, the money is forfeited. Learn what expenses qualify, and estimate very carefully what your actual expenses in those areas will be before you embark on the plan.

- **Education**   This might include training that will aid you in improving your work skills, which, in turn, could lead to higher pay and job advancement. Free seminars on financial and retirement planning are also offered by some companies.
- **Stock options**   This would give you the right to buy shares of stock in the company at a lower-than-market price. In some plans you obtain *warrants,* which give you similar rights. If you do partake of such a fringe benefit, investigate its limits: Do the options or warrants expire after a certain time? If you buy the shares through these plans, do you have to wait for any period before you can sell them?
- **Housing-related perks**   Does the employer offer a relocation package that would pay all or part of your moving costs? Separate components of such a package can include paying for your closing costs on selling your former home and/or buying a new home; job hunting expenses for you or your spouse; and temporary living quarters while you wait for your permanent new home to be available. If your employer does not pay for any relocation costs, some of them might still be tax deductible to you. See the section on moving expenses in chapter 10.
- **Personal benefits**   Day care, counseling programs, employees' cafeteria, recreational facilities, and on-site infirmaries are commonplace in larger companies.

Where the Jobs Are

Your job skills have to coordinate with other factors: that there is a need for those skills; that the need exists in a place you want to live; and that you're willing to move to a new place to match your skills with the need. If you

STRATEGIES FOR SUCCESS

How to Leave a Job the Smart Way

When you want to quit a job, emotions can overcome common sense. That's when costly mistakes happen. Before you hand in your resignation, find out *specifically* what will happen to your fringe benefits if you quit now, or if you wait until later. Will you lose vesting rights on your retirement plan? How much will it cost you to take over your health insurance protection so that you don't go uninsured until the coverage from a new job kicks in? The same with any other group plans—life insurance, dental insurance, and so on. Worried about being laid off? Don't quit in anticipation: If you do so, you could lose your right to future unemployment insurance benefits.

TABLE 2–3   **Fastest Growing Occupations, 1992–2005**

Occupation	Rate of Growth
Home health aides	+138%
Human services workers	+136%
Personal and home care aides	+130%
Computer engineers and scientists	+112%
Systems analysts	+110%
Physical and corrective therapy assistants	+92%
Physical therapists	+87%
Paralegals	+85%
Occupational therapy assistants and aides	+78%

Source: U.S. Bureau of Labor Statistics, 1996. Statistical Abstract of the U.S.

live in Omaha and are interested in marine biology, or if you crave a career in forestry and you live in Miami, you'd best start packing your bags. Every few years the U.S. Bureau of Labor Statistics ranks occupations expected to grow the fastest in the decade ahead. Table 2–3 shows the most recent results.

THE JOB QUEST

Exercise 2.2

Seeking a job—one that will lead to a career—is a matter of selling.

Any successful salesperson knows that advance preparation is essential if a sale is to be made. In the selling process that we call seeking employment, your *sales kit* consists of a number of different elements.

- **Your résumé**   This is the history of your past experience in school and at work. It should succinctly inform your prospective employer of all the training you've had, as well as activities that would establish a broader profile of you as a person. The employer wants individuals who get along well with their fellow workers, who exhibit a constructive and productive attitude, and who are, in general, well-rounded members of the working team.

- **Your references**   Written references include full-time work situations, part-time and charitable work and involvement with civic, religious, or social organizations. The references help to establish your reputation for trustworthiness, integrity, and industry. An accumulation of references from responsible individuals can enhance your opportunities for current employment and future advancement.

- **Your presentation**   This is perhaps the most critical aspect of your *sales pitch:* What can you do for the employer that other applicants for the job might not be able to do? Applicants normally have an opportunity to make their presentation during the job interview.

Self-Employment: A Working Alternative

You can perform many types of work—particularly in consulting and creative fields—as an independent contractor or as a sole proprietor instead of as an employee. As a self-employed person you have to pay your own Social Security taxes (self-employment tax), and you'll have to provide your own health and unemployment protection. You might be entitled to some attractive tax deductions, and you can establish a retirement plan that can offer benefits not available to regular employees. Before embarking on this path, you should get advice from an accountant. (See chapter 21 for a full discussion on self-employment.)

CHANGING CAREERS

Nearly one-third of all U.S. workers change careers in any given five-year period—*careers,* not just jobs. A job change implies going from one employer to another, but doing the same work. A career change is much more drastic: altering virtually the total structure of one's work, whether with the same employer or with a new one or on one's own.

Although there are no valid statistics concerning the success quotient in career changes (did the change bring the money, happiness, challenge,

---

STRATEGIES FOR SUCCESS

Prepare Yourself Well for Job Interviews

The better prepared you are for a job interview, the better your chances of getting the position you want. Attend to all the details of good grooming. Learn as much as you can about the company: Talk to current employees for down-to-earth information. For major companies, check *Standard & Poor's* listing at your local library. Also, inquire at your local newspaper for recent items about the company. Be prepared to tell your interviewer how you think you can help the company, and supply convincing reasons why you want to work there. Don't nag about what kind of pay, hours, and benefits you'll have. Don't smoke or chew gum, and try not to fidget. Rehearse interviews with a close friend to help you get over the nervousness.

contentment you were seeking?), changing careers can be an infectious phenomenon. Self-employment is a particularly powerful lure.

Children are asked from their earliest days, "What do you want to be when you grow up?" They are seldom asked, "*How many* different things would you like to do when you grow up?" Many choose a career at an early age with the assumption that it will be their one and only career. Too little thought is ever given to the possibility that the chosen career may be limited in its overall satisfactions. Many people are poorly prepared for the day they find their first careers have reached a dead end. They have acquired neither the skills nor the outside interests nor the flexibility that could assist them in a career change. Many recognize the value in making a change but are reluctant to move for fear of giving up the security they have already achieved. They might thus resign themselves to continuing an unsatisfying career.

Many others, however, will have acquired other skills, other interests, and a sense of flexibility that can broaden their perspective and allow them to adapt easily to a new career situation.

You may never have any notion of changing your career until you encounter one of the factors that can motivate you to seek a change. Figure 2–1 illustrates the typical flow patterns of a career change. Look at the far left column, Motivating Factors. Any one of those factors, or others not included in this chart, may prompt you to begin exploration, which can include diagnosis and testing as well as counseling and referral. Many will

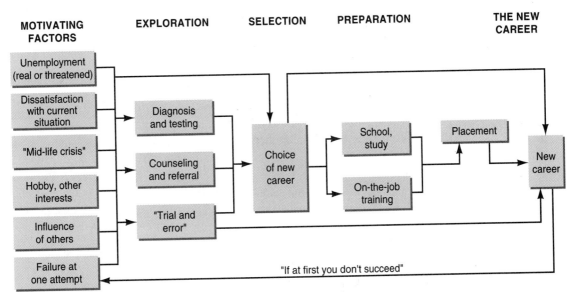

FIGURE 2–1 Typical flow patterns in a career change
Source: Adapted from a study by the Rand Corporation, "Mid-Life Career Redirections."

opt for the "trial-and-error" method of exploration, which can be costly, time-consuming, and frustrating.

Donald and Ellen

Let's briefly trace Donald and Ellen's career change patterns. Donald started as assistant manager in a shoe store. But when the owner's son expressed a desire to be the manager of Donald's store, Donald began to fear for his job. He had long enjoyed his hobby of assembling electronic kits, and he wondered if there might not be some better career opportunities for him in that field.

The motivating factors—suspected unemployment and an enjoyable hobby—led Donald to do some exploring. He had his aptitude in electronics tested and made careful inquiry in his community about job opportunities that would put his skills and interests to best use. After due exploration he made his selection. He would train himself to work on the development of video game cartridges. He took some appropriate courses in electronics at a local community college and did some apprentice work for a company that manufactured game cartridges. He was able to do this in the evening while maintaining his flow of income from the shoe store. In the months it took him to prepare for his new career, the game cartridge company hired Donald and he hit the ground running.

Ellen was not so successful. She had been happy as a musician, playing in a combo at local nightclubs. Her family was appalled. They nagged her about seeking a more respectable profession—working in a bank, selling insurance, becoming a stockbroker—a career *they* could be proud of.

The family's nagging was the main motivating force in Ellen's career change. She just wanted to get it over with and get them off her back. So she didn't bother with any diagnosis or counseling. She just looked through the want ads for the first opportunity in a white-collar position, and within a week she was in a training course for life insurance sales. Her first few weeks in the new career were disastrous. She neither liked the work, the people she dealt with, the hours, nor the need to sell life insurance. Ellen's failure at her first attempt finally motivated her to seek some professional counseling. The counselor told her that she'd do best as a musician and that her family would just have to learn to live with it. With new-found confidence in herself, Ellen went back to her old job with the combo and lived happily ever after.

YOUR WORK AND INCOME: PROTECTION AND REGULATION

Exercise 2.3

Your financial and legal rights as an employee are regulated and protected by a variety of federal and state laws. It's important that you be aware of how these laws can affect your work and income. Following is a brief summary of the most important such laws.

Your Paycheck

The Internal Revenue Service requires that your employer withhold some of your pay to be applied toward your income taxes, Social Security taxes, and other state and local income taxes. It's then the employer's responsibility to forward these amounts to the appropriate authorities.

The amount withheld should be as close as possible to your actual taxes for the year. More than 80 percent of all workers have more withheld than is necessary to pay their taxes. The result is that they get a refund for the amount that has been overpaid when they file their tax return the following year. The average refund check is about $1,400. These workers are, in effect, paying about $117 a month into an account with the government on which they earn no interest at all.

W-4 Form

The amount withheld from your pay is based on the number of *allowances* you claim on the W-4 form you filed with your employer when you began work. The more allowances you claim on your W-4 form, the less will be withheld from your pay, and thus the higher your take-home amount. You can claim allowances for yourself and for members of your family. You can also claim additional special allowances if, for example, you itemize your income tax deductions and if you are entitled to certain income tax credits. A worksheet accompanying the W-4 form explains in detail how these special allowances work. You can easily amend your W-4 form as needed to reflect the proper number of allowances so that your take-home pay will be adjusted accordingly.

W-2 Form

By the end of January of each year, you should receive a set of W-2 forms from your employer. These forms reflect the total amount you were paid for the prior year and the total amounts that were withheld for taxes and for Social Security. The information on the W-2 form will assist you in completing your returns. The W-2 form enables the Internal Revenue Service to verify your total pay and the amount that was withheld.

1040 ES Form

If you receive income that is not subject to withholding you may have to pay an estimated tax quarterly during the year. The federal form 1040 ES contains a worksheet that will assist you in estimating your total tax obligation from income not subject to withholding. Income that is not subject to withholding can include such items as money received from independent contract work, tips, and investment income.

Workers' Compensation

If you suffer injuries in conjunction with your employment, you are entitled to certain benefits under the workers' compensation law of your state. You may be entitled to benefits even if the injury was your own fault. But if you injured yourself deliberately, or if you were drunk or under the influence of drugs, you may not be entitled to benefits.

Workers' compensation benefits can include both medical expenses and reimbursement for lost income.

In general, if you accept workers' compensation benefits from your employer, you might not be able to bring a lawsuit against him or her for loss or damages you may have suffered. If workers' compensation benefits and other medical insurance will not adequately compensate you, consult an attorney at the earliest possible time. Each state has workers' compensation review boards that will evaluate claims and pass judgments accordingly. Check with your employer to determine the extent of possible coverage.

Unemployment Insurance

If you are discharged from a job that is covered by unemployment insurance, you are entitled to a limited number of weekly checks to tide you over until you find employment elsewhere. If you are discharged for cause—such as for violation of your employer's rules—you might *not* be entitled to unemployment benefits. The unemployment insurance program is administered separately by each state. Unemployment insurance funds are generally paid in by employers, with some additional subsidy from the federal government.

If you are discharged, you should immediately file a claim with your state unemployment office. You will have to appear in person each week to claim your check. You must be willing to accept any suitable full-time job that becomes available. If the employment office offers you such a job and you refuse it, you could lose your unemployment benefits.

If you are discharged from a full-time job, you can take on a part-time job and still receive *partial* unemployment benefits. If, after discharge, you receive workers' compensation income, severance pay, or a pension from the former employer, you may be ineligible for unemployment insurance benefits. If your claim for benefits is turned down, you are entitled to file an appeal with the unemployment insurance office.

If you leave a job voluntarily, you will not likely be eligible for any unemployment benefits. The following dilemma can occur: Michelle worked at a job that was covered by unemployment insurance. She feared that her job was in jeopardy. She quit in order to have time to seek a more secure job. One week later she learned that she would have been discharged because of a mass layoff. It took her two months to find another job. During

that time she did not receive any unemployment benefits because she had quit voluntarily. Had she remained on the job for one more week and been discharged, she could have been entitled to unemployment insurance for almost two months.

Many workers wrongly view unemployment insurance as a form of welfare. It is not: It is insurance. If you had a fire in your home, you certainly wouldn't refuse the payments from the insurance company. Unemployment insurance is the same type of thing: The benefits should not be turned down because of pride or lack of knowledge of the situation.

Employee Retirement Income Security Act (ERISA)

This complex law established a variety of protections for your rights under any pension or profit-sharing plan an employer might offer. One of the most important requirements of ERISA is that all employees covered by such plans be provided with a description of their benefits at least once a year. A great deal of your financial welfare—particularly for the future—may depend on your pension or profit-sharing plan. The description you receive should be read carefully, and if any part of it is not clear, seek clarification from your personnel office.

The Individual Retirement Account (IRA) was also created as part of ERISA. See Chapter 18 for further details on ERISA and IRA.

Your Right to Work and Discrimination

A number of federal and state laws protect workers from discriminatory workplace practices. If you are denied a job or fired from a job in violation of these laws, you can pursue your rights through the appropriate state or federal agencies.

Here's a rundown of these major federal laws. Most states have adopted parallel laws and have established agencies to administer them. If you have specific questions or problems, contact the nearest office of the U.S. Department of Labor or your state Department of Labor for assistance.

The Federal Fair Labor Standards Act

The Federal Fair Labor Standards Act protects minors from being employed in "oppressive" jobs. These can include jobs that are hazardous or detrimental to the health and well-being of minors. In most states, minors under age 14 are not allowed to take jobs, and work permits are required until they reach a prescribed age. These laws also limit the number of hours and times of day during which minors can work.

The Age Discrimination in Employment Act (1967)

The Age Discrimination in Employment Act applies to workers between the ages of 40 and 65. It is a violation of the law for covered employers to refuse to hire or wrongfully discharge individuals in that age bracket because of age alone.

The Fair Employment Practices Law

The Fair Employment Practices Law, also known as the Civil Rights Act of 1964, provides perhaps the broadest antidiscriminatory measures. Under this statute, "It is unlawful for an employer to fail or refuse to hire or to discharge any individual, or otherwise to discriminate against any individual, with respect to compensation, terms, conditions or privileges of employment because of such individual's race, color, religion, sex or national origin." Sections of the law apply such prohibitions to employment agencies and labor unions as well as to employers. A 1990 federal law extended these protections to disabled persons.

There are some exceptions under this law. For example, a Japanese restaurant has the right to hire a Japanese chef without fear of violating the law. An employer cannot be required to hire a worker of one sex when a job reasonably requires that a member of the other sex is more appropriate—such as a restroom attendant. Distinctions in pay and other employment matters can be allowed if the company has a good faith seniority or merit system or a system that distinguishes among employees who work in different locations.

The Equal Employment Opportunity Commission (EEOC) has power to begin actions in court to correct violations of the law. State agencies may also provide means of resolving a problem.

Wage and Hour Laws

The federal wage and hour laws apply to people whose work is in any way involved with interstate or foreign commerce. If your work doesn't fall into that category, you are probably protected under your state wage and hour law. These laws generally set a maximum number of hours you can be required to work each week and establish a minimum wage to which you are entitled. Check the current regulations associated with your job.

Plant Closings

A 1989 federal law requires that employees be given advance notice of plant closings or large-scale layoffs. This rule applies generally to companies with 100 or more employees.

Family Leave

A 1993 federal law, the Family and Medical Leave Act, gives employees the right to take twelve workweeks of leave during a twelve-month period to care for a newly born or adopted child, or to care for a spouse, child, parent, or oneself if that person has a serious health problem. The leave time is generally unpaid, but certain employment benefits are to continue during the leave time. The law pertains to employers with fifty or more workers; some states have overlapping laws. See your personnel office for more specific details.

Americans with Disabilities Law

The federal law bans employers from refusing employment to workers who might be mentally or physically disabled. Employers may not ask prospective workers about the existence, nature, or severity of a disability. However, employers do have the right to ask disabled persons—or any other prospective employees—about their abilities to perform specific tasks. The law also mandates that employers provide "reasonable accommodations" for the needs of disabled workers, including special equipment, working hours, and working conditions.

Employers with fifteen or more workers are required to comply with the law.

Health and Safety Regulations

State and local laws require building owners and employers to be responsible for safety conditions within work areas covered by the laws.

The federal Occupational Safety and Health Act (OSHA) sets standards to protect the health and safety of workers in their working environment. If an unsafe condition exists, an employee can complain to the Department of Labor, which can require the employer to correct the condition.

As a general rule, if you complain about an employer, under OSHA or the other federal employment laws, it is illegal for the employer to retaliate against you for having made a complaint.

Union Matters

Tens of millions of workers are members of labor unions. Labor unions negotiate wages and other benefits for members and can act on behalf of members if unfair employment practices occur.

The National Labor Relations Act of 1935 and the Labor-Management Relations Act of 1947 (also known as the Taft-Hartley Act) govern relations between management and labor with respect to unions. Under the National Labor Relations Act, *employers* are prohibited from:

- Unreasonably interfering with employees who are attempting to organize a union or bargain collectively
- Discriminate against workers by imposing hiring conditions that discourage union membership
- Interfering with a labor union in its formation or administration
- Refusing to bargain collectively with appropriately elected representatives of the employees
- Discrimination against any worker because he or she has complained against the employer under the law

The Labor-Management Relations Act generally prohibits *employees and unions* from:

- Forcing workers to join a union
- Refusing to bargain collectively with an employer once the employer has received proper certification of the union's status as the employee's bargaining agent
- Becoming involved in illegal work stoppages
- Requiring an employer to pay for work that was not performed
- Charging excessive initiation fees or union dues to employees belonging to the union

The federal National Labor Relations Board (NLRB) oversees laws relating to unions and management.

Garnishment

If you do not pay your legal debts, your creditors can sue you and obtain a judgment against you. That judgment may entitle them to garnishee your wages, which could require your employer to send a portion of your wages to the judgment creditors.

Under the Federal Consumer Credit Protection Act (1968), also known as the Truth in Lending Law, there are limits to how much of your pay can be garnisheed by a creditor. Most states have similar laws. Check to determine local regulations.

A garnishment can be extremely embarrassing to the employee. Federal Law prohibits an employer from discharging an employee just because his wages have been garnisheed. If, however, an employee's credit performance becomes so improper that the employer is overloaded with garnishment claims, the employer could make a good case for dismissing the employee.

Employment Policies and Contracts

The conditions of many workers' employment are covered by contracts between employer and employee or between employer and union. These

contracts should spell out all pertinent matters relating to employment, including pay, raises, fringe benefits, vacation privileges, sick-pay provisions, and causes for rightful termination. If your employment is covered by a contract, you must acquaint yourself with all the provisions. When the contract expires, either you or your union representative will have to renegotiate it. Renegotiation should commence many months before the termination date.

Most workers are not covered by contracts but by the ongoing employment policies of the employer. Except where state or federal law prevails, many of these policies can be changed at the sole discretion of the employer. Such changes could occur with respect to fringe-benefit programs, sick-pay benefits, hours and place of employment, and pay-raise schedules. Protect yourself by obtaining current policies and advance notice of any intended changes in writing.

SUCCESS IS WHAT YOU MAKE IT

Your success in your work will depend on more than just fulfilling your basic duties as an employee. Your initiative, your creativity, and your willingness to cooperate can all help you move up the ladder toward higher pay, greater recognition, and career advancement. Your current job might not be what you have in mind for a lifetime career, but every good experience can build your knowledge, and every good performance can result in a positive reference that will help you achieve the ultimate potential you are seeking for yourself.

Viewed positively and patiently, your work can provide you with an ongoing sense of challenge and achievement. Viewed negatively and impatiently, your work and your personal life can end up in a rut. The choice is yours.

THE MASTER PLAN

You can go through life on a hand-to-mouth basis, living as best you can from day to day, spending when the mood strikes you and hunkering down when the money runs out. This is known as "having too much month at the end of the money." It's not fun. It's frustrating, often painful, and frightening when you don't know what next week or next month might bring. Of course, everyone's life has its fair share of uncertainties. But you don't want to live that way; you can have The *Master Plan.*

A Master Plan consists of a number of phases. First is the goal-setting: What do you want to achieve for yourself in the near term and the longer term? Second is the prioritizing: Which of your clearly defined goals deserve the most attention and earning power? Third is the risk management

phase: How can you best protect your goal-path from the destructive risks that everyone faces? Fourth is the need to update: As your needs and desires change, as older goals get accomplished and newer ones appear, how do you adjust your overall financial patterns to remain in control of your own destiny?

Before we explore these matters in more detail, and consider tools you can use to build and maintain a master plan, here are some thoughts that will help you to tackle the challenge of creating The Master Plan.

Goal Setting

Exercise 2.4

First of all, understand that there is no single correct set of goals, budgets, or plans. Countless guidelines are suggested in consumer literature. There are statistics galore that will show you how much people spend and save. These can be helpful in giving you an overview, but when all is said and done, you must establish The Master Plan that suits *your own needs and desires.* Not your friends'. Not your parents'. Not your neighbors' or co-workers' or party-mates'. *Your own.*

The easy way might be to clip an article from a magazine that tells you how your household budget should work, and follow it to the letter. The hard way is to sit down with your family members, analyze what you want to achieve, crunch a lot of numbers, work out specific spending and saving patterns, and then embark on the rocky road. Have no doubts: the hard way is the better way.

Goals fall into many categories. The most obvious are the time-related goals: short term and longer term. Short-term goals mainly mean taking care of the here and now in comfortable fashion. Longer-term goals require a lot of advance planning: educating your children, going into business for yourself, retiring comfortably when you want to, and the like. We'll take a closer look at these issues later in this chapter.

One way to help you sort out the goals is to think of your money as Today Dollars and Tomorrow Dollars. Today Dollars are those you need for here and now. Tomorrow Dollars are those you put away today to be used in the future. Some Tomorrow Dollars have to be consciously put away: you have savings plans and investment programs that you contribute to regularly. Some Tomorrow Dollars will accumulate as a result of how you spend some of your Today Dollars. For example, some of your current earnings from work may be set aside in a pension plan and for Social Security. And part of your payments on your home loan go toward reducing how much you owe. Some of your life insurance payments may be building up a cash reserve that you can later tap into. In all of these cases, your Today Dollars are being turned into Tomorrow Dollars automatically. This book is designed to help you understand and keep track of it all.

Prioritizing

Some goals are more important than others. It's important to have the means to educate your children. It's not so important (for most people) to have a stash of money to take a gambling fling in Las Vegas every six months. Think in terms of *Must Goals* and *Maybe Goals*. Must Goals are those that you simply must accomplish: You must have a certain amount of money (or ability to borrow) at some fixed point in time. You don't want to have to say to your child, "Pat, I'm sorry we can't send you to college, but I spent and borrowed every penny on gambling flings in Las Vegas, and I lost it all."

Maybe Goals are those about which you can say, "Maybe, after we've embarked on a well-disciplined program to meet our Must Goals, we can start working toward some more fun goals. Failure to meet a Must Goal can be devastating: "I can't afford to retire," and so on. Failure to meet a Maybe Goal isn't that big a problem. "Okay, so we didn't go to Europe this year. Maybe, if we stick to our budget, we can do it next year, or the next." As you sort through your goals, use the Must and Maybe designations as your starting point in prioritizing.

Family Concerns

The changeover from single person to married person requires a complete new look at your goals, your priorities, your spending patterns, and your need to revise them all. The change from married person to parent takes you a giant step further in your need to re-examine everything.

Consider these important aspects of family financial planning. Some day you may have to deal with them all:

- **The costs in having children**   The thought of having to pay uninsured maternity expenses might be the single best form of birth control there is. Talk to your family doctor to learn what these expenses might be, and then examine your health insurance to learn the extent of your coverage for maternity.

- **Health care**   Family health care is quite a different matter from individual concerns. Will all family members be covered by an insurance plan? What deductibles and co-payments will apply? With children, a whole range of pediatric specialists can add to the mix of necessary care providers. How does your health plan cover this?

- **Educational costs**   The cost of higher education has grown faster than the normal rate of inflation (see Table 2–2). If you're going to have college-bound children, the time to start planning for their education is now, even if they are not born yet. Tax law changes in 1997 give some attractive tax breaks for the college-bound. See chapter 20.

- **Children's spending money**   Even this issue must be faced. Will they get allowances? How much? Who will determine the size of the allowances: you or peer group pressure? ("Gee, Mom, Fran gets twice that amount. Why can't I have that much?") Will they have to work (home chores and/or real jobs) to be entitled to a given allowance? The amount of an allowance, and the conditions under which a child gets it, can considerably affect a child's ability to establish a sense of self-sufficiency and self-worth.

- **Housing**   The roof over your head may need some enlarging as the family grows. To what extent might your family's well-being be affected by the size and facilities of your home? Considering gender and age of children, such matters as bedroom and bathroom sharing can impact on the family's comfort patterns. Buying a new home, or modifying an existing one, can be costly. You must evaluate the cost–benefit ratio and plan accordingly.

- **Role modeling**   As your children observe and are affected by your spending patterns, so will they adopt similar patterns, for better or for worse. If you know you spend too much money willy-nilly, and you know you're not being wise, it won't do much good to hope that your kids are smarter. They do as you do, not as you say.

"The good life" is something that we not only strive for; an avalanche of advertising tells us what we need in order to be happy. Common sense should prevent anyone from falling prey to this lure, but it doesn't always do the trick. Having The Master Plan and sticking to it is your best defense against the lures of instant gratification. Just as a guide to how your fellow Americans are chasing the good life, Table 2–4 illustrates some shifts in recent spending habits.

TABLE 2–4   Shifts in Spending Habits

We're Buying More Of	1989	1996 (increase as % of total consumer spending)	We're Buying Less Of	1989	1996 (decrease as % of total consumer spending)
TVs, VCRs	1.09%	2.74%	Food in restaurants	5.59%	5.42%
Computers	0.11	1.30	Doctors' service	3.73	3.61
Brokerage services	0.56	1.02	New cars	2.51	1.57
Toys	0.78	0.94	Furniture	1.04	0.94
Airline tickets	0.58	0.61	Tobacco	1.29	0.91

Source: U.S. Department of Commerce, Bureau of Economic Analysis, 1997.

The percentages in Table 2–4 may seem small, but remember that they represent percentages of *trillions* of dollars' worth of consumer spending.

Risk Management

Life, in a broad sense, is a series of risks. Success in life is navigating those risks safely. No one is immune to unforeseen catastrophes, such as illness, property destruction, premature death of family breadwinners, and loss of work. The Master Plan can succeed only if you establish sound risk-management techniques, the primary one of which is insurance: life, health, disability, property, public liability. These tools are discussed at length in the appropriate chapters of this book. The secondary form of risk management is self-insurance: "I can't afford, or don't want to spend, money for insurance policies, so I'll take my chances all the way." That's the easy way out. As with basic planning, discussed earlier, have no illusions: the hard way is the better way.

The Need to Update

As we mature, old goals are accomplished or abandoned, and new ones arise, perhaps unexpectedly. These shifts require a revision of our Master Plan. Moreover, as we achieve old goals and strive toward new ones, we may have to make certain tradeoffs—adjustments in priority to allow us to accomplish something that may not have been there yesterday.

In short, a workable Master Plan is only as valid as its revisions. In addition to developing the disciplines of saving wisely and spending prudently, we must develop the habit of periodically reviewing and revising the overall plan so that it will clearly satisfy the sought-after lifestyle. For the family, it may be a yearly meeting at which everyone sits down to evaluate and plan for the future. For the individual, it may be an annual meeting with a banker, accountant, lawyer, or other advisor to do the same. An important part of such a review is to go step by step through each item and ask ourselves: "Am I doing it right? Am I getting bogged down in unproductive spending habits? Will I arrive at my appointed destination on time with the right amount of dollars?"

A GOAL WORKSHEET: HERE AND NOW

Table 2–5 is a worksheet. It lists all the common expenses we have to meet and contains spaces for the amounts you are now spending (or setting aside), as well as projected amounts you will be spending one and two

TABLE 2–5   Goal Worksheet—Current and Ongoing Expenses

	Current Estimated Monthly Expenses	Estimated Monthly Expenses One Year from Now	Estimated Monthly Expenses Two Years from Now
Food and beverage			
Shelter			
Clothing and linens			
Protection against risk (insurance)			
Entertainment			
Education			
Health care costs			
Transportation			
Little rainy day fund			
Cost of credit			
Travel and recreation			
Personal business			
Children's allowances			
Miscellaneous personal expenses			
Luxuries			
Charity and religious expenses			
Income taxes			

Exercise 2.5

years from now. Filling out the worksheet serves several purposes: it will provide a clearer picture of your current financial situation; it will aid you in anticipating future goals as your needs change; and it can help you determine what expenses might be modified to supply more spendable dollars in another area.

Each of the items in the worksheet is discussed here in more detail.

As you calculate each expense, include any debt repayment that may be part of the total expense. In other words, any payments on an automobile loan would apply toward your overall transportation expense. Also, separate from debt payments that portion attributable to interest, and include those interest items under the category "cost of credit." It's important to get a clear-cut picture of what all your credit is actually costing you, and it may come as quite a surprise.

Table 2–6 sets forth average budgets for families of varying levels of income. Consider them only as broad guidelines, not as recommendations.

TABLE 2–6   Annual Budget for Four-Person Families

Item	Lower Budget (under $15,000), Percentage of Total	Intermediate Budget ($15,000–$30,000), Percentage of Total	Higher Budget (over $30,000), Percentage of Total
Food	31.2	24.7	21.1
Housing	19.0	22.2	22.9
Transportation	7.4	8.8	8.0
Clothing	6.9	6.9	6.1
Personal care	2.6	2.2	2.1
Medical care	9.7	6.1	4.3
Miscellaneous	4.2	4.8	5.7
Other items	4.1	4.3	4.9
Personal income taxes	8.0	14.7	20.6
Social Security and disability	6.3	6.3	5.1

Totals may not add up to 100% because of rounding.
Source: U.S. Department of Labor, latest data available.

Food and Beverage

This includes food and beverages consumed at home and at restaurants, alcoholic beverages, lunch money, snack money, and tips.

Shelter

Calculate each of the following components separately:

Basic Expense: Rent or Mortgage Payment

If you are an owner, remember that a portion of your mortgage payment applies to the reduction of your debt. This portion, referred to as principal, can be recovered when you sell or refinance the property. But because that future time is unknown, the total mortgage payment should be considered as a current expense.

Property Taxes

Owners are billed each year for property taxes. The bill may include separate allocations to the city, the county, the school district, and any other jurisdictions with the right to tax local properties.

Property Insurance

Property insurance for both owners and renters includes coverage for fire and other damage to your dwelling and its contents, public liability and medical payments coverage for costs incurred by people who may be injured on your premises, plus specially scheduled protection for loss or theft of valuable property.

Utilities and Communications

In an energy-conscious world, the cost of utilities (electricity, heat, water) cannot be taken for granted. Consider how those costs can be reduced by various energy-saving techniques. Ample literature is available from utility companies, home improvement dealers, and at your local library or bookstore.

The cost of communicating has multiplied in recent years. Once upon a time there were only telephones. Today cellular phones, fax machines, e-mails, pagers, and computers all talk to each other. In addition to the cost of the equipment, there are monthly service and usage charges to pay—to the telephone companies and the Internet providers. Just figuring out which local and long-distance telephone service is the most cost-effective takes some educated number-crunching. It's easy to spend more than $100 a month, just for the connections, let alone the usage charges. Calculate with care to determine if you're getting value for the money you're spending in this area; if not, you should have no problem getting along with less.

Maintenance and Repairs

A program of preventive maintenance can be decidely less costly than after-the-fact repair.

Renovation and Improvements

Whether you renovate your dwelling cosmetically (painting, landscaping, etc.) or functionally (adding new equipment, rooms, etc.), you must take into account how much of the expenses can be recaptured when the house is sold. Improvements that are too personal may not appeal to a buyer. Improvements that are too costly—that would cause the house to be priced much higher than other homes in the neighborhood—stand a poor chance of repaying the cost. See chapter 10 for more details on selling your home.

Appliances and Reserves for Replacements

Items in your home, such as the water heater, dishwasher, refrigerator, furnace, and other appliances, can be costly to replace. Rather than waiting for these items to die and then scrambling to find the money to replace them,

put aside a few dollars each month now so that you'll have a replacement fund to buy new items later.

Clothing and Linens

Clothing expenses are based on two main factors: need and style. Too many budgets are thrown into disarray because of excessive purchases of clothing and accessories. And although sheets, towels, and blankets may be relatively minor budget items, shopping with an eye to durability and washability can keep replacements to a minimum.

Protection Against Risk

This is the insurance package that protects you against illness, accident, disability, claims by others for damages you may have caused them, and the premature death of the breadwinners. The workings of the insurance plans (health, life, disability, and auto) are discussed in later chapters, but the costs, taking deductibles into account, should be included here.

Entertainment

Much of the money spent on entertainment tends to be spent impulsively. This is natural; when we get the urge to escape, we don't always stop to examine how the expenses might affect our normal budgetary program. The frequent result: a severe budget "leak."

Take the time to make a detailed listing of all entertainment expenses so that you can determine where excesses might occur.

Education

This should include tuition for college, private school, religious education, and adult education, and all textbooks and related reading materials and supplies. Include also tutors and expenses for school clubs, uniforms, and equipment.

Health Care Costs

Over and above any premiums you may pay for health insurance, include here any costs you incur that are not reimbursable by any insurance program. In addition to visits to doctors, include prescriptions, dental ex-

penses, eyeglasses, hearing aids, therapeutic equipment, and the costs of any other special treatments or devices needed.

Transportation

This should include the cost of both privately owned vehicles and public transit—and don't overlook the cost of motorcycles and bicycles, their maintenance, repairs, and parts. (Chapter 5 discusses transportation costs in greater detail.)

Little Rainy Day Fund

Distinguish "little rainy day" funds in your immediate budget program from "big rainy day" funds for your long-range budget. The little rainy day fund is a handy source of money—perhaps kept in a savings account—that can be used to equalize some of the inevitable fluctuations that occur in a month-to-month spending program. It should be added to regularly and tapped as little as possible. The more it can grow, the better off your big rainy day fund will be.

Cost of Credit

Apart from interest on a home mortgage, which is included in the shelter category, list all costs you are incurring for all your other credit uses. This would include all interest *and late charges* on all charge accounts, credit cards, personal loans from any source, loans against life insurance policies, and overdraft checking accounts. Not enough attention is paid to this cost, which can add roughly 10 to 30 percent *a year*, plus any late charges, to the goods and services you're purchasing.

Travel and Recreation

This is separate from your normal transportation and entertainment expenses. It refers primarily to vacations, travel to visit family and attend out-of-town weddings, and other functions. Expenses include transportation, lodging, meals, entertainment, tips, shopping (souvenirs, etc.) car rental fees, baby-sitting fees, special clothing and equipment, and any costs involved in maintaining your dwelling while you are away.

Personal Business

Include all expenses you incur in keeping your financial matters under control: legal fees, accounting fees, income tax preparation charges, investment and advisory expenses, safety deposit box rentals, checking account costs, and the purchase of necessary equipment and supplies related to these matters (a computer, stationery, filing equipment, etc.).

Miscellaneous Personal Expenses

When budgets fail to balance it's usually because too many dollars have dribbled away in unnoticed fashion. Big items—utility costs, rent, mortgage payments and the like—are easy to trace. But the variety of smaller "miscellaneous" expenses are too easily forgotten. This results in the *Miscellaneous Bulge*, and the *Dollar Diet* is the best remedy. The Dollar Diet costs nothing, and will help you solve the overspending problems. Here's how: In a separate notebook keep track of every nickel, dime, and dollar you spend for at least two months. You must write the item down before you spend the money. If you change your mind about buying the item, cross it off your list. At the end of the two months you'll not only be able to track your excess spending, you'll also have conditioned yourself to stop and question every expense before you make it. Here are the items to track:

tobacco	allowances	hygiene and toiletry
alcohol and tobacco	gum, candy, snacks	products
music (CDs, tapes)	gasoline and other car care	magazines, newspapers
beauty parlor/barber	videos, bought or rented	entertainment
minor clothing items	transit (buses, taxis, trains)	cosmetics
gifts, greeting cards	laundry, dry cleaning	dining and drinking out
school lunches		

Luxuries

This is an optional category for those who have a goal of acquiring certain luxuries as a part of their expense program. What are such luxuries? It all depends on the individual—obviously, what one might consider a luxury, another might view as an ordinary acquisition. Luxuries must be designated in terms of priority with regard to all your other expenses. What might you be willing to give up in order to acquire them?

Charity and Religious Expenses

This includes membership in religious organizations and contributions to them, as well as other charitable contributions, such as the United Way, Red Cross, medical-oriented charities (American Heart Association, American Cancer Society), and so on.

Income Taxes

List all amounts paid via withholding or otherwise for federal, state, local, and Social Security taxes.

SHAPING FUTURE GOALS

Table 2–7 lists people's most common major goals. These goals are not listed in any order of priority; that is for you to determine. Complete the columns accompanying the goals to get a better idea about what priorities you want to attach to them.

Sort out these goals using the *Must* Goals/*Maybe* Goals distinction that was discussed earlier. Some account must be given to inflation, but it is impossible to predict. Throughout most of the 1990s inflation was not of great concern, averaging about 2 percent to 3 percent a year. But there were periods during the 1970s and 1980s when inflation flared at double-digit rates, upwards of 10 percent to 12 percent a year! Our national policies have focused on avoiding dangerous inflation, but unpredictable economic forces can always bring it back.

TABLE 2–7   **Major Future Goals**

	How Much Will Be Needed?	When Will It Be Needed?	Amount per Year	Priority
Education	_____	_____	_____	_____
Housing (new shelter)	_____	_____	_____	_____
Retirement	_____	_____	_____	_____
Stake for your children	_____	_____	_____	_____
Stake for yourself	_____	_____	_____	_____
Care of elderly or disabled	_____	_____	_____	_____
One-shot expenses	_____	_____	_____	_____
Big rainy day fund	_____	_____	_____	_____

For purposes of this exercise you might want to do "best case" and "worst case" scenarios. As you project your future needs, build in a low inflation factor, say 2 percent a year, for the best case, and a high factor, say 8 percent, for the worst case. The Decision Maker software program that was designed as a companion to this book can help you with these calculations. The software is available on the Internet at http://www.wiley.com/college/rosefsky.

Also, in the study guide that accompanies the text there are chapter exercises titled, "What's It to You?" These are designed to help you prioritize concerns in the full spectrum of personal finance. The segment in chapter 2 will be of particular help.

Let's now take a closer look at each of the items in Table 2–6.

Education

This refers to higher education for children, and, in light of current trends, it can be a most challenging goal (see Table 2–2). College education traditionally must be funded at a fairly fixed point in time.

Preparations to meet this goal must begin as early as possible. These preparations can include a savings/investment program; awareness of loan, grant, and scholarship programs; and communications between parents and child regarding the child's own contribution to the financial needs, such as through work.

Housing (New Shelter)

Individuals and families owning a home have an advantage over those currently renting: they will be building equity that can be applied toward the purchase of a new house or some other goal. Current renters must accumulate a large enough down payment to enable them to obtain their first home. Later chapters on housing provide assistance in working out the arithmetic of buying versus renting and focus on how home ownership can be accomplished.

Retirement

With rare exceptions, this is the most predominant Must Goal for everyone. You don't have a chance to do it over if you reach a point when work ceases and there's not enough to live on. It's never too early to begin focusing on this important goal. (Chapter 18 contains more guidelines to help you achieve that focus.)

Stake for Your Children

Many parents want to provide their children with a stake to help them get started in life. The stake might be used to help them buy a home, to get them started in a career, or just to provide a cushion to assist them in coping with the world's vagaries. If this is one of your goals, you must give it priority in line with other goals.

Stake for Yourself

As discussed earlier, career changing is a prevalent phenomenon in our society. Many of these changes involve going into business for oneself, and often a substantial stake is needed. Put a priority on any such goal you may have, and keep it in mind each time you renew and revise this list. (See chapter 21 for a further discussion on self-employment.)

Care of Elderly or Disabled

This should be called a need rather than a goal, since we all hope that those near and dear to us will be able to maintain themselves throughout their lifetime. But it doesn't always work out that way. Parents and other close relatives might become dependent on us for a measure of support. If this is anticipated, it can be planned for and is easier to cope with.

One-shot Expenses

These might be must goals, or they could be maybe goals. They can include such items as a "once in a lifetime" trip, a large wedding for one's child, a major purchase of jewelry or luxury items, or a generous gift to a charity. These are voluntary goals, and their priority may be high or low. The higher the priority, the earlier the planning must be done.

Big Rainy Day Fund

We earlier mentioned the "little rainy day" fund. The big rainy day fund is directed more to major unanticipated expenses that anyone might confront—uninsured medical expenses; extended periods of layoff from work; emergency needs of other family members; uninsured losses; and so on. Generally, this item has a fairly high priority. Proper insurance can minimize much of the risk, and there's always the possibility that the fund will never be needed and can, at some point, be allocated to other goals.

THE SOURCES FROM WHICH FUTURE GOALS CAN BE ACHIEVED

In addition to keeping a careful watch on your goals and their shifting priorities, it's also important to be alert to the sources of money. They, too, are subject to change over the years, and it's important to be able to adjust goals and priorities in line with changes in the sources of income.

Income from Work

This is the primary source from which your current and continuing goals will be met. If you don't use all your current income in meeting your current goals, the excess can be put aside to meet future goals. Or it can be spent now on nonessentials. This extra money—what you earned minus what you spent—is called discretionary income. It's good to be in the position of having some. But the choice between spending it now or putting it away for the future can be quite perplexing.

Savings/Investments

Depending on the risks you take with your money, you may have a reliable or an unreliable source of dollars. Prudence can assure your future; speculation can demolish it. Be well aware of possible consequences before you make any decisions in this extremely important area.

Equities

Homeowners build a source of future funds as they reduce their mortgage debt and as the home (usually) increases in value. Owners of ordinary life insurance policies are also building a source of future funds. Both forms of equity—your share of ownership—can amount to substantial sums. If they are tapped too early, by refinancing your home or prematurely cashing in your life insurance policies, the ability to meet future goals may be seriously impaired. Know what these values are and what they can amount to in the future. Later chapters on housing and life insurance will assist you in determining those future values.

Borrowing

Borrowing is a convenient way of meeting goals. With regard to housing, transportation, and college tuition, borrowing allows you to accomplish what otherwise may take many years of accumulation. But beware: Bor-

rowing means that you're accelerating the use of future income, with an added cost of roughly ten to thirty percent a year for interest. And since funds borrowed now must be repaid in the future, that repayment can impinge on your future cash flow. Prudent borrowing can enhance your current lifestyle; imprudent borrowing can devastate your future lifestyle.

Enforced Savings: Pensions, Social Security, Profit-sharing Plans

These represent current income shifted to future accessibility. To many people, these enforced savings represent all, or a substantial part of, the sources for meeting retirement goals. But a danger exists: Many people will find that their reliance on these sources has been *in error*—there isn't as much as was expected. Even though need for this money may be many years off, it's vital that a close estimate of what will be available is maintained on a continuing basis.

Inheritances, Gifts, and Other Windfalls

For most of us, this category may be a complete imponderable. But if you have any reasonable assurance that inheritances or gifts will be coming your way, it would be wise to try to determine the after-tax amount involved; this can have a considerable effect on your other ongoing financial plans.

THE FINANCIAL STATEMENT: A PLANNING TOOL

Can you imagine buying an automobile with no dashboard indicators on it? No speedometer, no gas gauge, no mileage indicator, and no oil, brake, or battery warning lights? And to top it off, the hood is sealed shut, requiring two days in the shop every time you want to check your oil, battery, and other innards. It might be okay for an occasional spin to the supermarket, but to take it out on the highway would be risky, to say the least.

In much the same sense, any individual, family, or business needs a proper set of *financial indicators,* as well as easy access to the inner workings, so that periodic tune-ups can be done quickly and simply.

A thoughtfully prepared and *regularly updated* financial statement is an invaluable package of gauges, meters, and warning lights. It can tell you how fast you're going, how your fuel is holding out, how much fuel you'll need in the future, and how smooth your ride is.

Financial statements provide a picture of the exact financial condition of the person or business involved. But financial statements reflect the condition *only on the given day.* The value of a single statement is limited. The true value comes in comparing it with past statements, so that strong and weak points can be spotted and evaluated.

The Elements of the Financial Statement

Exercise 2.6

The financial statement consists of three major elements: assets, liabilities, and net worth. Figure 2–2 illustrates these and other features of a typical financial statement in simplified form.

PERSONAL FINANCIAL STATEMENT
As of_____ (date)_____

Purpose of Loan: _____   Source of Repayment:_____

Personal Information: Name, current address, previous address, length of time at addresses, Social Security number, telephone (home and work), marital status, current employer, previous employer, length of time with employer

*Assets**		*Liabilities**	
Cash	_____	Loans payable to banks	_____
Securities (stocks, bonds, savings)	_____	Other debts (credit cards, charge accounts, finance companies, etc.)	_____
Money owed to you (from friends, family, contracts, refunds)	_____	Taxes due (income, property, etc.)	_____
Life Insurance cash surrender value	_____		
Real estate (less loans against)	_____		
Personal property (autos, home furnishings, etc.)	_____		
Total Assets $	_____	Total Liabilities $	_____

NET WORTH: Assets minus Liabilities $_____

Annual Income: Itemize salary or wages, rental income (net), business income (net), dividends, interest, other
Total Income $_____

Annual Expenses: Itemize loan payments (home, car, credit accounts), taxes, insurance, living expenses, other
Total Expenses $_____

NET CASH FLOW: Income minus Expenses $_____

FIGURE 2–2   Simplified Sample of Personal Financial Statement
*All assets and liabilities should be itemized as of *current value.* All insurance coverage (life, health, property, public liability) should also be detailed.

Assets

Assets are the sum total of everything you own, plus everything owed to you. The value of assets is figured as of the date of the statement. Because the value of many assets does change, it's essential to evaluate them anew each time a statement is prepared.

Included among your assets are your house, cars, personal property, bank accounts, cash value of life insurance, stocks, and other securities. Also included are money or property due you as a result of a pending inheritance, personal debts owed to you, property settlements, and so on.

Liabilities

Liabilities are debts—everything you owe. As with assets, these are figured as of the date of the statement, and values must be updated accordingly.

Included among liabilities will be the mortgage on your home, amounts owed on loans, contracts, and other personal debts. A detailed financial statement will break down liabilities into long term and short term. This can aid an analysis of your condition by distinguishing which debts will fall due within, say, one year and which will fall due at some more distant time.

Net Worth

Your net worth is the difference between assets and liabilities. You arrive at net worth by subtracting liabilities from assets. A storekeeper might see it this way: If he wanted to close up shop altogether, he would sell off all assets and use the money to pay off all liabilities. What's left would be his net worth.

Here's a simple example of how net worth is calculated on one particular item. Kim has a car valued at $10,000. However, she still owes the bank $2,000. Therefore, her net worth in this asset is $8,000. The asset (car) minus the liabilities (debt to bank) equals net worth, $8,000.

Other Aspects

Financial statements will also include a brief summary of your annual earnings and living expenses, as well as schedules of your life insurance holdings, your investments, and your property, both real and personal.

From time to time, you may be required to provide personal financial information to obtain credit. In such instances, you'll sign a statement that says that the information you have given is accurate; that you have given the information so that the other party can act in reliance on it; that you

have not withheld any pertinent information; and that you agree to notify the other party of any adverse changes in your circumstances. In providing this information and then signing the statement, you are legally binding yourself to the accuracy of the information given. If you give false or incomplete information you may be putting yourself in jeopardy. An insurance policy can be voided, a loan can be declared in default, a debt can be refused discharge in bankruptcy proceedings. The way to avoid such concerns is to be certain that the information on any financial statement is *accurate*.

The Uses of the Financial Statement

As an Early Warning Signal

An ongoing program of updated financial statements can help you spot troubles before they get out of hand. A financial mess can be lurking beneath the surface for years before it begins to hurt. For example, you might be slipping into excessive debt. By tracing your debts over the years via your financial statements, the signals may become evident early enough to warn you to correct the situation. Or your nest egg might not be growing as rapidly as it should be, and this can be spotted by comparing a series of annual financial statements. It's all a matter of keeping track, and the financial statement program is a most important tool for this.

For Keeping the Reins on Your Credit

Good credit, wisely used, can be of immense value. Knowing well in advance your borrowing needs and your borrowing capabilities helps assure wise use of credit. Through your financial statements, you can maintain a close watch on your current debts, items that need replacement in the future, such as a car, and your anticipated future income (your ability to afford tomorrow's needs). You think that you'll need a new car two years from now. But considering what other things you might have to borrow for between now and then, how will that car loan fit into your overall plans at that time? The financial statement gives you the data that can help you cope with the future. See chapter 12 for more details.

In Helping to Protect You Against Loss

If you keep your financial statements up to date—at least yearly—you'll be forcing yourself to keep accurate current valuations on all your property. The value of any property is subject to change, and only by knowing true current values can you be sure of obtaining the necessary insurance to protect you against loss. See chapters 5 and 10 for more details.

In Maintaining a Sensible Life Insurance Program

Provision must be made to maintain comforts in the event of the premature death of a breadwinner. Life insurance is the most common means of ensuring this. A life insurance program should be planned in conjunction with the availability of other assets that can be cashed in to provide for needs. The financial statement is a reliable indicator of assets that can be converted into cash without undue sacrifice, should the necessity arise. This can help you tailor your life insurance program to your specific needs rather than guessing what that program should consist of. See chapter 17 for more details.

In Helping to Establish a Worry-Free Estate Plan

Your progressive financial statements provide the best possible at-a-glance gauge of what type of estate planning you need. Prudent estate planning requires a regular checkup of your net worth: which assets and liabilities are increasing and decreasing? At what rate? Until what time? Which assets have income potential, and to what extent? See chapter 19 for more details.

In Helping to Plan Your Long-Range Budget

The financial statement, regularly updated, is a simple device to keep your current and future goals in clear focus and to provide ongoing measurement of the sources from which those goals will be met.

As an Aid in Borrowing

On those occasions when a financial statement is required as a condition for getting a loan, you'll expedite matters considerably if you are prepared with a current statement, as well as statements from recent years. It will speed up application processing and serve as evidence of your financial good housekeeping.

SOME THOUGHTS ON SPENDING HABITS

One object of this chapter is to help you establish financial habits that will allow you to accomplish your goals. But all too often we are waylaid in the pursuit of those goals by commercials urging us to buy things that promise us happiness and satisfaction in almost every phase of life.

Spending habits born out of impulse, gullibility, or low sales resistance can be extremely counterproductive to one's financial welfare. We are all subject to impulsive spending, but we must control it.

Spending habits may have been unconsciously inherited from our parents, and we must evaluate their objective. Peer-group pressure—"keeping up with the Joneses"—can also influence spending habits, and succumbing to it can be costly and unsatisfying.

Spending habits are a powerful force in shaping your overall well-being. To the extent that spending habits control you, you'll have a much more difficult time achieving your own personal potential; when *you* control these habits, you will indeed be the master of your fate. Chapter 3 will help you develop wise spending habits.

 ## PERSONAL ACTION WORKSHEET

What Is Your Real Income?

Real income consists of both wages and fringe benefits. Wages are visible every time you get your paycheck, but fringe benefits are difficult to evaluate. Following is a list of common fringe benefits. Note the ones you now enjoy. If your employer didn't make them available to you, estimate how much it would cost you to obtain them on your own. Tally the total value of all your current fringe benefits. Compare the value of that package with what may be available from another employer you may be thinking of transferring to.

Benefit

Value, or Cost of Obtaining Benefit on Your Own (per Year)

- ☐ Health insurance $ _____
- ☐ Disability insurance _____
- ☐ Life insurance _____
- ☐ Pension contributions _____
- ☐ Profit-sharing contributions _____
- ☐ Investment-fund contributions _____
- ☐ Automobile _____
- ☐ Uniform allowance _____
- ☐ Educational programs, seminars _____
- ☐ Dental insurance _____
- ☐ Legal insurance _____
- ☐ Club membership _____
- ☐ Use of athletic, other facilities _____
- ☐ Retirement counseling _____
- ☐ Personal financial counseling _____
- ☐ Medical, psychological counseling _____
- ☐ Other _____ _____

CONSUMER ALERT ——————————————————————————

Goals Should Satisfy Yourself, Not Others

Linda and Gary faced a dilemma common to many young married couples.

"We both have good jobs with a lot of potential, and we're confident that we can afford to buy a home in the near future. We've found a funky old cottage about twenty miles out of town right on the lake. It's run down and would need a lot of work, but the price is right, and we love the location. Even with improvements, it would still be funky, but it's 'our thing.'

"That's where the problem arises. Our folks, and a lot of our friends, have been hounding us to buy a place in a neighborhood that's the 'in' place for up-and-coming career couples.

"To us that's phony, but we can't deny that it does offer good contacts and whatever advantages may come from living in the 'right' neighborhood. It would cost a lot more than our funky bungalow, and we'd really be strapped to make the monthly payments. But, then, our friends and family say, 'You'll reap a bigger profit when you sell the "right" place, compared with what you might gain when you sell the bungalow.'

"When we boil it all down, it's the two of us against a lot of them. We know we're young and naíve. We respect the experience of others. But we feel guilty—if we buy the bungalow, we're being self-indulgent and foolish. If we buy into the 'right' area, we're being sensible and mature—supposedly. Just who are we supposed to be trying to please anyway?"

The ending, at least for Linda and Gary, was a happy one. They bought the bungalow and fixed it up, and eventually their friends and family admitted that they had done the right thing.

As Linda later put it: "The final decision came down to this: Do we strive toward goals that we ourselves have set, or do we live our lives as others want us to? Well-meaning though the others may have been, we have to express our own independence and live our own lives. Fortunately, we made the right choice. Other couples in the same boat might have done better to listen to the others. To each his (or her) own—as long as you know what your own is."

UPS & DOWNS   *The Economics of Everyday Life*

Why Spending Habits Change

A lot of factors can influence how you spend your money. You're very conscious of some of them: You just got a raise, or you just got fired. There are also influences that sneak up on you, and some of them can be dangerous.

Inflated Expectations   This is human nature at work in one of its most devilish ways. "I'm *positive* I'm going to get a raise . . . a bonus . . . a winning lottery ticket . . . a big profit on the stock I just bought . . . So why wait? I'm going to start spending that money NOW!" And worse: "I'm going to go into debt now and I'll repay it just as soon as the money flows in." The dangers are obvious. Keep alert to signals that your own expectations may be inflated.

Expectations of Inflation   Yes, it sounds like the above, but it's quite different. From time to time the media will sound warnings that inflation is picking up—the cost of everything is rising. This often sends people on buying sprees: Buy now, before the prices go up. This buying activity prompts merchants to raise prices to take advantage of rising demand. And then you have a classic case of a self-fulfilling prophecy. The buying urge, in *expectation* of inflation, often causes people to buy things they don't need.

The Lure of Eee-zee Credit   We're all bombarded with offerings of credit cards, home equity loans, and the like. All too often the lure is overpowering, and a spending spree ensues. Bear in mind: The fact that someone is willing to lend you money doesn't necessarily mean that you should borrow it or that you're in good shape to repay it.

Self-indulgence   The cry of self-indulgence is "I MUST have that, and I MUST have it NOW!" Advertising, fads, trends, and just plain keeping up with the Joneses can open checkbooks by remote control. There's some self-indulgence in everyone. Beware.

Hunkering Down   Spending cuts can be prompted by a concern over your employment prospects. This may prompt you to get back to basics and salt away what you can to see you through tough times. But determine the realities of the job market; don't rely on rumors or suppositions. Also, you might be hit by the reality of how much you have to start putting aside today to meet future goals. When you fully realize the importance of the following sentence, you're on your way to good financial health: "What I don't spend today I can put away and spend in the future."

?

WHAT IF . . . ?

Test yourself: How would you deal with these real-life possibilities?

1. Your parents will be retiring soon. You worry that they will not have enough income to live in the style to which they've been accustomed. How much, if at all, can you help them financially? What are you willing to give up for their sake? On the other hand, if you don't care to or can't help them right now, how will you react if they run into serious financial problems a few years from now?

2. Economic conditions are harsh, and your boss tells you that you're going to have to take a pay cut of 10 percent if you want to keep your job. Where will you cut your spending to offset this cut in income?

3. A major national company is opening a branch in your city and is hiring people with your skills. You'd like to apply there. Make up a shopping list of all the things you'd need to know about working for the company to enable you to make a wise decision.

4. There have been rumors that your company may be acquired by another—one with a reputation for running a "lean and mean" shop. You fear that your job is in jeopardy. What can you do, now and when the merger occurs, to protect yourself? If the worst case does occur, what sources of income can you tap—your savings, your former employer, and/or the government—to tide you over until you find a new job?

NUMBER CRUNCHERS

Do the calculations to make decisions in these real-life possibilities.

1. Your place of work is a quick and easy bus ride from home. Dress is casual on the job, and there is a pleasant low-cost employees' cafeteria. You have a new job possibility that's in an upscale area ten miles from your home. There's no mass transit to that place, so you'd have to drive. The new job would require more fashionable clothing, and all of the lunch-hour restaurants are pricey: You'd have to pay two to three times as much for a lunch as you now pay in the employees' cafeteria. Considering the expenses involved in this new job (commuting, clothing, lunches, etc.), how much of a pay increase would you have to get in order to earn the same take-home pay you're now earning?

2. You've become hooked on a new leisure pursuit—golf? scuba diving? photography? skiing? You really want to get involved, but it's going to cost a lot of money. You estimate it will take $1,000 to get set up. Then, at a low level of involvement, it will cost an average of $100 per month; at a high level, $200 per month. How much of your desire can you fit into your existing budget if you go for the low level of activity? The high level?

FOR BETTER OR FOR WORSE

Things beyond our control often impact our personal and financial well-being, for better or for worse. Some are more predictable than others. How would you be affected if the following real-life phenomena happened? Could you have seen it coming? What steps could you have taken to minimize damage or maximize advantage? The better able you are to anticipate and recognize these forces, the better equipped you are to deal with them.

1. The company you or your spouse works for declares bankruptcy.
2. You have a child who is a senior in high school. You've sacrificed so that you could save almost $30,000 to send your child Pat to college. Pat decides not to go to college and claims the decision is final and non-negotiable.
3. You're living on a very tight budget, with little or nothing going into savings. Your employer announces a 401(k) plan (see chapter 18 for details) that will contribute 50 cents to your account for every dollar you put in.

Sensible Shopping and Spending

"Money may be the husk of many things, but not the kernel. It brings you food, but not appetite; medicine, but not health; acquaintances, but not friends; servants, but not faithfulness; days of joy, but not peace or happiness."

Henrik Ibsen

You can be better off by $1,000 or more per year! That's how much a Smart Shopper can save in routine shopping for food, pharmaceuticals, and the like. And for big-ticket items—appliances, home furnishings, electronic goods, and vacation travel—you can reap big savings by following the guidelines in this chapter, which will tell you, among many other things:

- How to recognize built-in bad shopping habits and replace them with good money-saving habits

- How to cut 10 percent, 20 percent, and even more from much of your food and drugstore spending

- How to find affordable and enjoyable vacation travel

- How to shop for the best values in at-home leisure electronic equipment

- How to find no-cost or low-cost personal enrichment activities that can enhance your leisure time and your life

THE BAD HABITS

Every day we are bombarded with hundreds, if not thousands, of advertising messages: on television, radio, the internet and billboards; in newspapers and magazines; and in our mail. Advertising shows us the choices we have for products and services. But advertising must also be approached with caution: in addition to those instances when advertising is misleading (see chapter 4), advertising can create costly buying habits. It can motivate us to buy on impulse, spending dollars we might have put to better use. It can prompt us to buy a product that promises certain benefits when comparable products offer the same benefits at a lower cost.

Advertising isn't entirely to blame. No ad ever reached out and twisted anyone's arm to buy a particular product. We must accept the blame for our own impulsiveness and unwillingness to take a few extra moments to pick the product that can satisfy our needs at the best possible price.

If you have any doubts about the tendency toward poor shopping habits by the average American, conduct a simple experiment *after* you've read this chapter: Be a supermarket spy. Push a cart so as not to raise suspicion, and follow other shoppers up and down the aisles of the supermarket. Notice how they succumb to impulse, brand favoritism, and lack of adequate comparisons. After doing this you'll at least feel confident that *you* know how to save as much as 20 percent on the bulk of your shopping—and, for a family that spends an average of $100 a week on such items, or more than $5,000 a year, that's a savings of about $1,000 per year.

Let's now examine some of the specific Smart Shopper techniques, particularly those that can be employed at the supermarket, where the majority of our day-to-day shopping budget is spent. (All price comparisons referred to in the following material are based on regular prices, not on specials or discounts.)

THE GOOD HABITS: GROCERIES AND TOILETRIES

Unit Pricing

Suppose a 14-ounce bottle of Heinz ketchup is $1.39 and a 64-ounce bottle is $3.76. Which is the better buy? The smaller bottle is cheaper, of course, but it's not the better buy. On a *per ounce* basis, the bigger bottle is the better buy. In the small bottle the ketchup is 10¢ per ounce. In the big bottle the ketchup is 5.9¢ per ounce. The exact same product is 4.1¢ per ounce cheaper—almost 60 percent per ounce cheaper—when bought in the larger container.

TABLE 3–1   **Unit Pricing Comparisons**

Product	Size	Cost per Package	Cost per Ounce	Savings per Ounce with Larger Package
Taster's Choice Coffee	7 oz.	$7.89	$1.13	
	2 oz.	3.59	1.80	37%
Mott's Applesauce	48 oz.	2.67	5.6¢	
	23 oz.	1.58	6.9¢	12½%
Del Monte Corn	15¾ oz.	.69	4.4¢	
	8¾ oz.	.56	6.2¢	26%
Treetop Apple Juice	128 oz.	3.89	3.3¢	
	46 oz.	2.29	4.9¢	33%
Best Foods Mayonnaise	32 oz.	2.78	8.7¢	
	8 oz.	.89	11.1¢	22%
Del Monte Peach Halves	29 oz.	1.56	5.4¢	
	8¼ oz.	.79	9.6¢	44%

This is what's known as unit pricing: calculating the price of a product by the unit—ounce, pound, and so on—rather than by the container it comes in.

Consider Crest toothpaste: a 2.5-ounce tube at $2.29 comes to 91.6¢ per ounce. An 8.2-ounce tube at $2.99 comes to 36.5¢ per ounce—a difference of almost 55¢ per ounce, or a savings of 60 percent per ounce if you buy the big tube. See Table 3-1 for other examples.

Brand Label versus Generic Label

A box of 100 Lipton teabags: $3.65. A box of 100 store-brand teabags: $2.89—a savings of 76¢, or 21 percent. The difference in taste may be

insignificant, but even if there is a distinguishable difference in taste, is it worth the sacrifice for the 21 percent savings?

Brand-name products are those regional or national items whose names are known to us through advertising and general familiarity. Generic products, in the broad sense, are those that are privately labeled for specific stores or chains of stores. In many cases, the quality of generic products is equal to their brand-name counterparts. Indeed, many are made by the same manufacturers and to the same specifications. Some generic products may not have the same quality as their brand-name counterparts, but the difference may be so slight as to justify buying them for the savings that can be realized. At the very least, a trial of the generic products is certainly warranted. If you're dissatisfied, you can always go back to the brand label. But if you're satisfied with the generic label, you can reap substantial savings.

Pharmaceuticals and Prescriptions

Generic products also offer considerable savings in the drugstore. Table 3–2 compares some common items that can be purchased without a prescription. (The survey was conducted at a major chain outlet, and the pharmacist gave assurance that the generic products were comparable to the brand-name products.) Many prescription items are also available in generic form, and at considerable savings. If your doctor gives you a brand-name pre-

TABLE 3–2   Brand Label versus Generic Label

Product	Size of Package	Cost of Package	Savings
Advil 200 mg	100 ct.	$8.69	37%
Generic equivalent	100 ct.	5.49	
Q-Tip cotton swabs	500 ct	3.99	20%
Generic equivalent	500 ct.	3.19	
Pampers Baby Fresh wipes	96 ct.	3.79	26%
Generic equivalent	96 ct.	2.79	
Heinz vinegar	32 oz.	1.35	12%
Generic equivalent	32 oz.	1.19	
Carnation Coffee-mate	22 oz.	2.99	38%
Generic equivalent	22 oz.	1.85	
Neosporin	1 oz.	6.99	43%
Generic equivalent	1 oz.	3.99	
Johnson's baby powder	15 oz.	3.49	32%
Generic equivalent	15 oz.	2.39	

scription, ask whether there is a generic equivalent. You can also ask the pharmacist to call the doctor and request approval to substitute a generic prescription for a brand-name prescription.

Bulk Buying

Many stores will offer substantial discounts—10 to 20 percent—if you buy by the case. Indeed many cities have "warehouse"-type supermarkets that specialize in by-the-case merchandising at much lower prices than at regular markets. In addition to the discounts you can obtain, buying in bulk quantity protects you against inflationary price increases on those products.

Most common nonfood products have a virtually infinite shelf life—you can keep them in storage almost indefinitely without any deterioration in their quality.

Convenience Foods

A simple experiment: we cooked a six piece box of Aunt Jemima Frozen French Toast. Then, using ingredients from scratch that cost the same as the box of the frozen "convenience" food, we made a platter of fresh French toast. Almost the same exact time was involved. (It did take a few extra minutes to wash out the bowls that used the fresh ingredients.) Results: From scratch we got twelve slices of toast that looked, smelled, and tasted delicious. The Aunt Jemima toast had no aroma, and looked and tasted a bit like cardboard. The winner by a big margin: do-it-yourself. The loser, in value for money and taste: the convenience food.

Convenience foods might save a little time, but they rarely will save money. And what you get for your money with convenience foods is a

STRATEGIES FOR SUCCESS

Impulsive Shopping Can Cost You Plenty

One study revealed that shoppers will pay two to three times more for a given type of item if a credit card sign is visible near the cash register. ("Oh, what the heck, let's buy the better version—we can use our plastic!") And a psychologist reports that certain symbols and visual cues, such as "Discount" and "Last Day of Sale," can prompt impulsive and unnecessary spending. Stores know this, and they use every trick they have to move merchandise. Don't let your impulses get the best of your common sense, lest you spend more than you can reasonably afford.

compromise. Here are a few more examples. Fresh versus frozen strawberries: in the summertime an equal batch of each is about the same price. Is there even a close call in taste? In the winter imported fresh berries will cost more than the frozen. You be the judge.

Buttered frozen vegetables cost only a few pennies more than plain ones. Go for it? That little pat of butter works out to about $5 a pound for the butter. Ditto for pre-sugared cereals and the like. You're paying a bundle to have someone else spoon a bit of sugar for you. And the worst of all: paying upwards of $4 for a gallon of water at the market! Not you, you say? Don't bet on it. Read the Consumer Alert section at the end of the chapter.

Coupons and Specials

Cents-off coupons are offered by both manufacturers and stores. If you don't use coupons on products that you *regularly* buy, you're throwing money away. Smart Shoppers will take perhaps an hour per week to scour the ads looking for coupons offering discounts on all products they commonly buy. The savings can be many dollars per week—an hour well spent. In addition, savings can be multiplied at stores that double the value of many coupons. By combining coupons with sales prices on items you would buy anyway, you can really stretch your grocery dollars.

Miscellaneous Money Savers

Don't Shop While Hungry

If you shop while you're hungry, you're more likely to load up your basket with nonessentials, snack foods, impulse items, and so on.

Shop with a List

Carefully plan your needs in advance, and write them down on a list. Stick to the list if you want to keep your budget in line.

Avoid Snack Foods

Snack foods tend to be costly, and the nutritional value you get for your money is questionable. The following case history best illustrates this warning:

"I came home from work early one afternoon and found my children sitting around our kitchen table eating DingDongs. As I watched an en-

tire box of DingDongs disappear, I realized that our household went through $10 worth of DingDongs and similar snack foods per week. That's more than $500 a year! I immediately ordered an end of all Ding-Dongs in our house. My children looked at me aghast. I didn't want to interfere with their after-school snacking, so I told them that rather than spend money on DingDongs, they could make cookies and cakes from scratch on their own. This delighted them, for three or four days. Then the task of cleaning up after themselves began to be too much for them. The baking tapered off and so did the snacking. Not only did our food budget go down noticeably, but I'm sure I detected a drop in our dental bills as well."

Bend a Little

In general, supermarkets stock their highest-profit-margin items at eye level. The better bargains for you—in terms of unit price and generic availability—tend to be on the lower shelves. A little bit of bending will save you a lot of money.

Look for Extra Bargains

Many markets will discount bread, pastries, and produce after they have been on display for a day or so. If the market doesn't advertise these items, ask your manager what is available. Many markets also have a "thrift" shelf, where slightly damaged nonfood items are placed. These can represent substantial savings.

Know Your Local Market

Habit often finds us shopping at the same market most of the time. It's also wise to get to know the other markets that are convenient to you. You might find that they offer a better price on most of the products you commonly buy. Also, get to know the individual managers at each of the markets. The managers are there to please the public, and the better they know you, the more likely they are to offer you that extra special little item: a better choice in the produce department or the meat department, a tip that a certain item you're buying will be going on sale the next day, an offer to sell you an overstocked item at a discount.

THE GOOD HABITS: CLOTHING AND ACCESSORIES

"That looks absolutely smashing on you. Wear it anywhere and you'll have them all drooling."

"Your taste is excellent. I can tell that you're a real fashion leader."

"That's what absolutely everybody is wearing today. If you want to be with it, you'll buy it now before we run out of stock."

"As long as you're buying the slacks, you ought to get some nice things to go with it. Here's a nice matching sweater."

Vanity, thy name is clothing shopper. Young or old, male or female, few of us are immune to the flattering persuasions of the clothing salesperson. But Smart Shoppers keep a firm grip on their common sense, never letting it succumb to moods, to ego, to fads, or to impulse. Smart Shoppers have carefully studied their practical needs for clothing and accessories and are willing to take the time to shop for those items that offer the best value (appearance considered) for the money.

Only you can decide how you want to look or how you should look. There's little argument that the well-dressed, well-groomed person can enjoy certain advantages over the poorly dressed or slovenly person. To that extent, appropriately attractive clothing and accessories can be considered an investment in one's social and business well-being.

On the other hand, excessive spending on clothing will not necessarily produce commensurate results. You must find the balance that's right for you. And that balance must include both the desired appearance *and* the cost of creating that appearance. The following material can help you with the budget-balancing tricks of affording the look you want.

Ego and Impulse

The salespeople's flattering remarks at the beginning of this section are samples of just a few of the tricks of the clothing trade. But long before we enter the clothing stores, our brains and our egos have been preconditioned. Few products are more lavishly and glamorously advertised than clothing. The advertising lets us believe that we can look like models in *Vogue* or *Gentleman's Quarterly,* and the salesperson confirms it.

Nothing can cripple a budget more devastatingly than vanity and impulse. You can't fit designer jeans on a nondesigner body. But we spend ourselves silly trying. True, a few salespeople will be honest enough to tell you that a particular outfit makes you look like a hippopotamus. But they are there to sell clothing, and they know well that nothing sells clothing more rapidly than flattery. Arm yourself accordingly: Don't act on <u>impulse</u>. And shop around before you make a decision.

Embellish the Simple

You can stretch your clothing dollars farther by sticking to basically simple outfits and embellishing them with attractive accessories. For example, a common men's outfit—navy blue blazer and gray slacks—can take on a va-

riety of appearances, depending on the accessories, all of which give the basic unit a different look. Similar combinations are possible with basic women's outfits. A variety of simple accessories can offer much more diversity for the money than a variety of outfits can.

Miscellaneous Money Savers

A Sense of Timing

Use the calendar to your advantage. Buying clothing and accessories off season can represent substantial savings. You won't have as abundant a choice of fashions or styles, but you can pick up bargains that will be well worth your shopping trip.

For a better selection of merchandise, check out the seasonal sales at most large clothing and department stores. Major sales usually take place after Christmas and after Easter. Shop early for the best selection.

Consider Seconds

Seconds (or irregulars) are items of clothing with minor flaws in them. The price of a second can be well below the price of an otherwise identical item. And the flaw itself may be so minor that no one will really notice it. Factory outlets and discount stores are good sources of seconds.

Cleanability and Durability

How readily will a particular garment soil, and what will be required to clean it? Is it hand-washable or must it be dry-cleaned? The care labels on the garments indicate the recommended cleaning techniques. The durability and cleanability—or lack thereof—represent an important element in your overall clothing investment.

Beware of Counterfeits

People will pay a good deal extra for items that display the name or initials of a leading designer or manufacturer. Thus, manufacturers happily create counterfeit versions of designer items that might be woefully inferior to the genuine articles. So, beware: If you find yourself obsessed with an opportunity to buy a "genuine" Armani at a price that seems too good to be true, don't be disappointed if it falls into shreds after the first or second wearing. You're most likely to get stung buying such articles at swap meets, from street vendors, or from stores that seem to open one week and close the next.

Know Store Policies

If you buy a garment, will you be able to return it if it doesn't suit you? Will the store refund your cash, or will it simply allow you a credit against other purchases? Or will the store refuse to take it back altogether? If the store does allow return privileges, how long does that privilege last? Many items offered on sale are sold on an as-is basis, preventing you from getting any kind of refund or exchange privilege. Almost always, if you want to return any items, you must bring in your sales receipt in order to get credit or a refund.

Buying for Children

Young children outgrow most clothing before it has had a chance to wear out. Except for one or two dressy outfits, or items that might be handed down to younger children, it is false economy to buy top-of-the-line clothing for children. Look to factory outlets, discount stores, and special sales for the best bargains on children's clothing.

Rummaging

Have an annual rummage through your closets and dressers to get rid of unneeded clothing and other personal items. If you don't know a hand-me-down recipient, donate your used clothing to thrift shops. If you itemize your income tax deductions, you can claim a deduction for the donated clothing.

THE GOOD HABITS: MAJOR HOME FURNISHINGS

Your overall budget can be drastically affected by your need for major home furnishings: furniture, carpeting, and appliances. In weighing your housing/furnishings considerations, you must take into account the following:

- How long will you be living in the dwelling? If you're settling in for a long stay, a bigger investment in furnishings is more easily justified. If you'll be living there for only a year or so, it might not make sense to burden yourself with major expenses for furnishings. Determine whether your job, your marital status, or the growth of your family is likely to dictate a move in the near future.
- Are there youngsters (or pets) on the scene? Children (and dogs and cats) can wreak havoc on furnishings. A jelly spot on a sofa, a urine stain on a carpet, plus assorted other blemishes have to be expected when little ones are about. The family with young children and active pets must evaluate how the furnishings will withstand the onslaught. If you buy expensive furnishings while the children are very young, you may be faced with expensive cleaning and repair costs, or the furnishings could look a shambles by the time the children are grown

and more responsible. It makes more sense to buy more modest furnishings while the children are young.

- Will your tastes change? Will your selections today still please you one year, five years, ten years from now?

  For example: Today you might be very excited about strong pastel colors in your upholstery and carpeting, accented by chrome and glass tables and accessories. It might indeed look beautiful. But say you weary of it within a few years. Or you move to a new location where the furniture absolutely clashes with your new surroundings. You may then look back on your original choice as money wasted, money that could tally many hundreds, if not thousands, of dollars.

  You might be better off choosing a more conservative design and color range for the major items and accenting those pieces with relatively inexpensive accessories, such as throw pillows, lamp shades, and area rugs. Those can be changed easily and inexpensively and can give your premises a very different look at a much lower cost than a whole truckload of new furnishings.

- What is the focal point of your social life? Will you be doing a lot of entertaining at home? Or do you prefer to go out a lot for your social life? It may not be possible to afford both fine home furnishings and a lavish outside entertainment budget. Many people don't realize this until after they've invested heavily in furnishings and then find themselves in a budgetary crisis. If you'll be spending a major portion of your social life at home, you can justify more expense for the furnishings. On the other hand, if you're not a homebody, you should structure your budget more to suit your "going out" needs and less to satisfy your at-home needs.

Furniture

- With wood furniture, how are the parts joined together? Is the piece all wood or does it utilize less expensive fiberboard in unseen places? Does it stand firm and solid? Do doors, drawers fit and operate properly? What is the quality of the hardware? What is the quality of the finish and any decorative elements? Bear in mind that for tables, a synthetic surface (such as Formica) can wear more durably than wood.

- With upholstered furniture, pay attention to the construction elements as with the wood furniture just noted. How is the fabric anchored to the piece? Do the patterns and colors match properly? How durable is the fabric? What are the sun- and soil-resistance factors of the fabric? What is the stuffing made of, and how long will it hold its shape? How does it sit? Test it for firmness, comfort, clothing against fabric. The more carefully you shop, the more readily you'll see that better quality costs more. Only you can decide whether the better quality is affordable and worth the price for you.

- If you're handy with a paintbrush, you might find that unfinished wood furniture offers you better value for your money. Secondhand furniture in good condition and "seconds" (new furniture with minor flaws) can also be feasible alternatives.

- What guarantees do you have if something goes wrong with furniture: a leg comes unglued, fabric detaches from the frame, cabinet doors fall off? Better furniture dealers will usually guarantee to fix or replace defects that are not due to normal wear and tear. Determine how long such a guarantee will last. "Cash and carry" stores may offer little or no guarantee. To erase any doubts, ask about the guarantee before you decide on your purchase, and then have it put in writing.

- Some furniture dealers will deliver and set up your furniture at no additional charge. Other dealers charge for delivery. Still other dealers, such as warehouse and factory outlets, may not offer delivery service at all. Depending on where you live and how easy the access is to the rooms in which the furniture will be placed, delivery and setup charges can add considerably to your cost. Shop these charges as carefully as you do the furnishings themselves. Naturally, if you have access to a truck and some strong helpers, you can save considerably by doing your own delivery and setup.

- Don't guess on color or size of furniture. If you guess wrong, you could end up with an expensive purchase that doesn't suit you. Take color samples of any carpet, wallpaper, paint, and/or drapes with you to furniture stores, or ask the furniture dealer to give you color swatches of the pieces to match against the existing room. Take careful measurements before you shop. Draw your room to scale on graph paper and test out different furniture arrangements. Most large stationery stores sell plastic cut-out templates showing various sizes and types of furniture. This can be a handy tool to help you determine what pieces of what size can go in any given room. If you are considering buying convertible sofas, reclining chairs or expanding tables make sure you measure properly for both the basic and expanded versions of each piece.

- Acting on impulse can be dangerous. Visit many stores, looking for those whose reputation and inventory suit your budget. Scour the ads for sales: home furnishings are very sale-prone, and the best buys are available to those who are patient and willing to hunt.

Bedding (Springs, Mattresses)

The consensus of consumer testers is that quality pays in bedding. A well-constructed box spring and mattress can last twenty years, perhaps even

Consider Renting Instead of Buying

In many circumstances, it may be wiser to rent rather than buy costly household items, particularly furniture. For example: if it's likely that you'll be doing a lot of moving within the next few years, moving your own furniture can become a costly proposition. Most cities have furniture rental businesses that can furnish an apartment or a house, top to bottom, in a few hours, in a wide variety of styles and colors. Also, look into rental plans that give you an option to purchase the items.

longer. An off-brand product may cost 20 to 30 percent less than a major brand, but it may last only half as long. Evaluate the choice accordingly. Dealers offer frequent sales on bedspring and mattress items that are similarly constructed but do not have matching covers. Since you see the mismatched covers only when you take off the sheets, there's no reason not to take advantage of these special buys.

Carpeting and Other Flooring

The possibilities—and the price ranges—are limitless. Area rugs, bare polished wood, linoleum, vinyl tile, brick, fake brick, stone, fake stone, ceramic tile, adobe tile, and carpeting ranging from synthetic grass to luxurious wood represent but a sampling of the types of flooring available.

Personal taste, budget, durability, and cleanability must all be taken into account when you choose flooring. Of particular concern in making a decision on flooring is the length of time you'll be in the home. Most flooring, once installed, can't be taken with you. The obvious exception is area rugs. Carpeting can be removed, but it's difficult to install it in a new dwelling. The cost of lifting, moving, recutting, and reinstalling old carpeting in a new dwelling can come close to the cost of brand-new carpeting.

All carpeting and other flooring materials should be shopped for as carefully as furniture. Note that medium shades tend to show soil and dirt least, that patterned and multicolored carpeting tends not to show wear patterns as readily as solid-color carpeting, and that different types of carpet fabric have distinctly different levels of soil resistance and cleanability. In addition to pricing the carpeting, determine the cost of padding and installation. And check the reputation of the dealer with the Better Business Bureau for reliability and willingness to adjust complaints.

Appliances

What you *need*, what you would *like*, and what you can *afford* are all up to you. Before you make buying decisions, bear in mind the following:

Installation

Will such appliances as dishwashers, disposals, and trash compactors fit into your existing space? Or will extensive work have to be done to accommodate them? If so, how much will that added work cost? Will any special installation be necessary for any given appliance? An electric clothes dryer may require special wiring. A gas clothes dryer will require a gas line. Both will require a venting outlet. Is your existing wiring suitable for air-conditioning? A refrigerator with a built-in ice cube maker will require a water line to the site. A gas water heater must be properly vented, as must a kitchen exhaust fan. Determine these special requirements and get cost estimates for them before you make your buying decision.

Service and Warranties

On major items (clothes washers and dryers, dishwashers, freezers, refrigerators, and room air conditioners), a one-year warranty for parts and labor is common. In addition, the sealed systems in such units might have warranties for as long as five years. Don't be content with the salesperson's promises: Examine the written warranty before you make a buying decision. Find out whether warranty service is performed by the dealer or must be obtained from another source. Determine the reliability of the service source. A check with the local Better Business Bureau is advisable.

With smaller units (television sets, food processors, CD players, and video recorders) much shorter warranties are common. With most television sets, the warranty for labor is ninety days, but some may be as long as one year. The warranty on the picture tube and other parts will commonly be one to two years. The source of service is again very important. Will the dealer or a nearby service center be able to correct problems under warranty? Or will servicing involve time, money, and inconvenience for you?

For example, a comparison of two similar brand-name food processors revealed the following: Although the warranties were identical, one brand had to be sent away for warranty servicing, whereas the other could be repaired locally. In the case of a breakdown in the first unit, the cost of packing and shipping it, plus the return postage required under the warranty, represented more than 10 percent of the original purchase price of the unit. The latter unit could be serviced simply by delivering it to the original dealer.

With most appliances you can obtain a service contract to take care of problems after the original warranty has expired. Refrigerators and freezers are constructed to last decades, and any major defects will usually show up during the initial warranty period. For such products, extended service contracts might not be worth the money. The cost of an extended service contract

for an automatic clothes washer, dishwasher, or room air conditioner might be less than the cost of one service call. If you have a knack for maintaining appliances, you might find a service contract an unnecessary expense.

Periodic servicing of some major appliances is a must. Furnaces and central air-conditioning units should be checked and lubricated periodically, filters should be changed, and the entire systems should be checked for leaks. An annual check-up prior to the heating and cooling seasons, respectively, can be far less expensive than repairing a major breakdown.

Paying for It

If you haven't yet established credit or if you've had credit problems, you'll probably be attracted to stores that offer "easy credit terms, no down payments—past credit history no problem." What appears in the advertising to be "easy credit" may indeed be costly. If a merchant or a lender is taking a risk with you, you will be charged accordingly.

Home furnishings represent major budget items, and credit is commonly used to obtain them. Follow the guidelines set forth in chapter 12. Consider what financing terms a dealer offers and compare those terms with banks in your area. For buyers with no credit or with credit problems, it might be far cheaper to obtain a cosigner for credit purchases rather than get involved with high-interest-rate lenders that ply their wares at the "easy credit" emporiums.

Information Sources

Exercise 3.1

Consumer Reports magazine, available at your local library, is the best single source for learning about and comparing home furnishing items. To locate information on the product you plan to buy, check the index in the back of the latest issue. *Consumer Reports Buying Guide* indexes all subjects covered for the previous year. Kiplinger's *Personal Finance* magazine can be another helpful source.

With most appliances you can obtain specification sheets from the manufacturer or dealer. These give you abundant information about each product; you should read and compare different brands before you make your decision. The more time you take to compare, study, and shop, the better equipped you'll be to make the right buying decision.

RECREATION

How much of your disposable income should you devote to recreation and leisure? That's a very personal decision that each individual and family must make for themselves. Some people will go overboard on their leisure expenses, leaving them in a budgetary bind. Some people will consciously choose to curtail other types of expenses—living in a more modest

dwelling, driving a more modest car—in order to enjoy their leisure freely. Others will forgo leisure activities so that they can live in a more elaborate dwelling and drive a more elaborate car. These are personal choices. If you're overspending on leisure, however, you can either make adjustments or suffer the consequences. The same holds true if you are not partaking of any meaningful leisure activities. The rest of this chapter will help you think about the balance you'd like to achieve, and it might motivate you to take action. We will explore two broad areas of leisure and the important financial considerations relating to them. Those areas are vacation and travel, and recreation at home.

VACATION AND TRAVEL

Exercise 3.2

From the weekend camping trip to the elaborate cruise or European junket, you want to be certain that everything goes right. It's a shame to waste money, but it's even more disappointing to have wasted time. You can always go out and make more money, but you can never go out and make more time. Careful planning is therefore essential.

Using a Travel Agent

The proper professional to assist you with your vacation and travel plans is a travel agent. Well-trained and experienced travel agents have many tools to help you get the most out of your vacation dollars. Among these tools are:

Exercise 3.3

- The *Official Airline Guide (OAG)*, which gives complete information on virtually every commercial flight in the United States, as well as many international flights
- Directories of hotels, resorts, car rental agencies, and cruises, providing detailed information on costs, facilities, reservation requirements, and often the quality of the various services and facilities
- Publications by airlines, resorts, states, nations, and tour-packaging companies, providing an excellent means for familiarizing yourself with various opportunities, price ranges, available dates, and other useful information
- Personal experience, since agents travel extensively to examine locations of concern to their clientele
- Computer on-line services that can instantly show the agent the availability and times of flights, data on hotel rooms, rental car prices, and even weather reports in most cities of destination

A travel agent can give you advice and guidelines on choosing a vacation that will satisfy your interests and budget. Furthermore, the agent can make

all necessary reservations for travel and accommodations. The more advance time you give the agent to work on your plans, the wider choice you'll have of flights, hotel rooms, rental cars, and the like. Visiting a travel agent at the last minute will probably prove frustrating, but even in such cases the agent can probably do more for you than you could on your own.

Travel agents earn their money in commissions they receive from airlines, hotels, cruise companies, and tour operators that they book for you. Agents normally charge their clients only for out-of-pocket expenses made on the clients' behalf, such as long-distance telephone calls. Some travel agents impose service charges for issuing and amending some airline tickets. Inquire in advance how much, if anything, a given agent would charge for given services.

In some cases, a travel agent can save you money by knowing of a group tour whose itinerary matches the travel you are planning. Making arrangements for you to take part in the group tour could cut your costs considerably. If agents don't volunteer such information, ask them if they know of any such possibilities.

Choosing a travel agent is like choosing any other kind of professional advisor. Personal recommendations are always worth seeking out. Also, the neatness and efficiency of the travel agent's office can often be a giveaway to the quality and efficiency of service, or lack of it. The agent should be a member of the American Society of Travel Agents (ASTA) and should have credentials from the International Air Transport Association (IATA).

The Internet also offers a wide array of travel information and booking capabilities, but with the Internet you don't get the benefit of a travel agent's personal experience and knowledge of various destinations, carriers, hotels and so on. Further, with the Internet, you might have to give your credit card number to a stranger at the other end of the Web. Do so at your own risk. (Why do you think they call it a Web?)

A Wealth of Information

In addition to the printed material a travel agent can offer you, there is an abundance of literature on travel that you should take advantage of at the earliest possible planning stages. Whether you're traveling on your own or with a group, the more you can learn about your destination, the more choice you'll have as to what you'll want to see and do. Visit your local bookstore and library and choose from among the following worthwhile publications.

Exercise 3.4

- The choice of good travel guidebooks grows every year. The Fodor and Dorling-Kindersley guides are directed toward the more affluent traveler. The Birnbaum guides seem more appropriate to the younger (thirties and forties) traveler who does not have to pinch pennies. The *Let's Go* and *Under $25 a Day* series will appeal to all those who must mind their travel budgets carefully.

- The Mobil *Travel Guides* cover the United States and are very detailed with respect to hotels, motels, and sightseeing facilities.
- Michelin guides provide excellent information on many major European cities and countries.
- Travel magazines abound. Also, you can write to the Chamber of Commerce of the cities you plan to visit and ask them for any tourist information they have available.

Air Fares

The pricing of airline tickets is an incredible jumble. If you want to fly from point A to point B, the price of your ticket will depend on how far in advance you make your reservations, the day of the week you're traveling, how long you're staying at your destination, and the class of service you choose. And, depending on the type of plan you choose, you might or might not receive a refund of all or part of your ticket if you have to change your travel plans. The best guide through this maze is a travel agent, who has access to all these fare structures. Each airline will quote you only its prices for a given trip. The travel agent can quickly determine all possible choices between points A and B. Table 3–3 illustrates the spectrum of fares

TABLE 3–3   Airline Fare Comparison

These fares were quoted on one specific date for flights on the same future date. All fares are round trip.

Phoenix/Los Angeles	
Lowest	
Special excursion, must stay over a Saturday night, must book seven days in advance, no refunds	$68
Middle range	
No restrictions, but limited seats per flight; coach	$174
Highest	
First class, no restrictions	$390
Los Angeles/New York	
Lowest	
Special excursion, same restrictions as above	$462
Middle range	
Seven-day advance booking, 50% penalty for cancellation	$518
Highest	
Coach, no restrictions	$1,340
First class, no restrictions	$1,980

available between Los Angeles and Phoenix as a short-flight example and between Los Angeles and New York as a cross-country flight example.

Frequent Flyer Plans

Most major airlines offer frequent flyer plans, which enable travelers to accumulate points for distance traveled on a given airline. Once you've accumulated the necessary points, you are entitled either to free travel on the airline or upgrades. Many airlines also cooperate with hotels and car rental agencies, which in turn provide lodging and car rentals at discounts. The more you use the designated companies, the more points you'll accumulate. Be sure you know what restrictions the plan has. How long do you have to use the points you've accumulated? Are there exclusions as to days you cannot travel with your bonus points?

Most frequent flyer awards cannot be sold or given away to anyone else, but there may be exceptions; check with your airline for specifics.

Almost all airlines now have credit cards tied in with their frequent flyer plans, which allow you to earn miles by charging on the card. This is in addition to earning miles by using car rental, hotel, and other services tied in with the airline's frequent flyer program. If you're a frequent credit card user, this can be an excellent way to accumulate more miles toward your free travel. But please follow the advice in chapter 12 on credit and borrowing, and pay your credit card bills in full every month. That way you don't have to pay any interest on the credit card. If you find yourself paying interest on charges you incurred to earn miles, you're offsetting the value of the miles by what you're spending in interest.

Airlines impose blackout restrictions, which are days you can't use your frequent flyer miles to travel. Most of these days are around holiday seasons. Furthermore, airlines strictly ration the number of frequent flyer reward seats on all flights, which can make it very difficult for you to get flights on the days you want, unless you book many months in advance. For example, travel between Europe and the United States during the summer months is so heavy that frequent flyer awards have to be booked late in the previous year if you want to have a decent choice of flights from which to choose.

Some frequent flyer plans—British Airways is one example—offer a number of hotels that will give you rooms in exchange for frequent flyer mileage. This can be a good way to get around the heavily booked seasons. If you can't use your mileage to get a free flight, pay for the flight and use your mileage to get a free hotel room instead. That way you get extra mileage for the flight, and you can have a better choice of times to travel.

Frequent flyer mileage expires after a fixed time. Use 'em or lose 'em. Each airline will announce its own expiration schedule. If you're faced with losing points here's a tactic that can gain you an extra year. Before the points expire, get your award ticket, even if it doesn't have a specific flight on it. Once you have the award ticket, you have an extra year to use it.

Wholesalers (Consolidators)

You can achieve substantial savings on international travel by using wholesalers, who make available sharp price reductions. They advertise in the Sunday travel sections of major newspapers, particularly *The Los Angeles Times, The New York Times,* and the *Chicago Tribune.* If you can't find those papers at your local newsstand, check at your local library.

Wholesalers commit themselves to a number of discounted seats on given transoceanic flights, and they pass part of the savings on to their customers. Many also offer discounts on hotels in destination cities. Before you book with these companies, check how long they have been in business and the manner in which they conduct their business. These discounted tickets are usually nonrefundable if you alter or cancel your travel plans. Wholesalers, as a rule, offer a wide selection of regularly scheduled flights to different destinations on different airlines.

Seasonal Bargains

One good way to stretch your travel dollar is to take advantage of the seasonal bargains in many major resort areas. You might not have the best weather, but the low prices might more than make up for the climate. Off-season hotel prices in many tourist areas can be as little as one-half to one-third of the high-season price. Samples include resorts in Las Vegas, Arizona, and Florida, where summertime prices are a fraction of wintertime rates. Similarly, England and Europe can be much cheaper in the winter than during the hot and crowded summer months. If the weather is of secondary concern to you and you primarily want to see the sights and partake of the tourist opportunities, ask your travel agent for the off-season fare alternatives available. You can see more of the world for less money than you might think.

Near-home Vacations

If air, bus, or train fares threaten to use up too much of your vacation budget, consider the travel opportunities within an easy day's drive of your own home. How many New Yorkers have never been to Boston or Washington, or vice versa? How many San Franciscans have never been to Los Angeles, and vice versa? And so it goes throughout the nation. Close-to-home opportunities for fun, adventure, and enrichment are abundant, no matter where you live. Not to take advantage of these opportunities is to deny yourself recreation.

Good weekend getaway values can be found in hotels that cater to business travelers during the week. Packages can include sharply discounted room prices, meals, cocktails, and bargain tickets to local attractions.

Package Tours and Resorts

If you're not inclined to hassle over travel details, thousands of package tours are available to you. These offer an almost all-inclusive price for your vacation, which includes travel, accommodations, sightseeing, a guide where appropriate, and some meals and extras. Package tours are available through resorts, airlines, travel tour companies, and major travel agencies. Package tours can often save you money. It's wise to compare what the same travel would cost if you bought each component (air, hotel, rental car, etc.) separately. Experienced travelers probably prefer to create their own packages. The novice might appreciate the convenience and possible cost savings of the package.

If you are considering a package tour, study the brochure that details what you get for your money. Pay attention to the following:

- Most packages are advertised as costing from a certain amount of dollars. That little word *from* is vitally important. It describes the *lowest* possible price for the package. If you want a better choice of rooms, dates, or amenities the price can escalate rapidly.

- Many of the advertised "extras" do not represent a true travel bargain, though on the surface they seem appealing. A "free welcoming cocktail" or a "free bottle of champagne" in your room may sound alluring, but it's worth only a few dollars at most. The more important things to evaluate, in terms of cost, are the basic room accommodations and meals, if any.

- If meals are included as a part of the package, find out what kind of menu and what kind of choices will be available to you. The basic package price might include minimal food service, with anything extra at an added cost. You can avoid disappointment by finding this out in advance.

- If recreational facilities, such as tennis or golf, are included in the package, determine if those facilities are available any time you want them, or only at certain times, which might be inconvenient.
- If the package includes transportation, when will the flights leave? Night flights can knock your body clock awry and render you incapable of enjoying yourself at your destination.
- How much free time will you have, particularly on a multicity guided tour? There are horror stories of tour groups being herded around like sheep. After a few days of that, you might not know whether you're in Athens, Greece, or Athens, Georgia. To protect yourself, make sure you examine the day-to-day itinerary, which should be included in the travel brochure. Too little free time can leave you exhausted; too much free time can mean that you'll be out spending money on your own, and that can leave you broke. Look for the happy balance with your travel agent as your guide.

Do-It-Yourself Tours and Vacations

More-experienced travelers often prefer to make their own arrangements. This means more time spent in the planning stages but more free time during the trip rather than following the tour guide's timetable. Careful research is the key to a successful do-it-yourself trip.

For intercity travel, particularly on a foreign trip, rail, bus, and air travel passes may be available. These passes can represent a considerable saving over individual bookings from city to city. Some of these passes for European travel must be purchased in the United States.

When booking do-it-yourself travel, it's essential that you get all your reservations confirmed in writing from the hotels, car rental agencies, and any other facilities you'll be using. Make certain that those confirmations spell out exactly what you're getting for your money: the type and price of the room, the arrival and departure dates, and the type and price of the car you are reserving. Take these written confirmations with you. If you pay any deposit in advance, be certain to get a receipt for that deposit; and make sure when you make final payment for your stay that you are given the proper credit for that deposit.

Cruises

Cruises have often been thought of as an indulgence only for the wealthy. But when you consider that for one all-inclusive price you receive your room, meals, entertainment, all facilities of the ship, and transportation from port to port, the price of a cruise might not be much different than a stay of comparable length at a resort or a budgetwise trip abroad.

Cruises, like tour packages, are advertised on a *from* basis. The price in the advertising is for the lowest-priced stateroom on the ship. It will proba-

bly be on the lowest deck, inside (as opposed to an outside room with a porthole), and at the far end of the ship (either fore or aft) where the motion of the boat will be more noticeable than in the center. But aside from the stateroom, all passengers have equal use of all facilities on the ship at all times. The food is the same, the entertainment is the same, the access to all facilities is the same. If a minimum stateroom isn't available, the price of better staterooms escalates rapidly. Since life on a cruise ship is spent predominantly in the public rooms, and on shore, and the stateroom is used for little else than sleeping and changing clothes, the booking of a minimum stateroom should not prove a hardship to most travelers.

The all-inclusive price means just that: elaborate meals, snacks, and midnight buffet; nightly professional entertainment and dancing to live bands; daily movies; plus lectures and lessons on a wide variety of subjects. Not included are alcoholic beverages, laundry, tips, and on-shore expenses.

With respect to on-shore expenses, travelers should avoid buying things (jewelry, perfume, watches, and the like) they can obtain at home for a similar price. When shopping in foreign ports, it's always important to ask: "If I'm not satisfied with this when I get it home, how can I get the matter corrected?" It's one thing to visit a local jewelry store where you bought a watch that stopped working. It can be quite something else to try to get a watch fixed if you bought it in a tiny shop in some exotic Caribbean island.

Your travel agent can provide you with schedules of all ships leaving from accessible ports. Many cruises also offer substantial air fare discounts to get you from your hometown to the port city. The travel agent can provide you with deck plans of ships. Study the deck plans carefully. Notice where the minimum-rate rooms are and where higher rate rooms are. Choose a stateroom that will give you adequate comfort, cost considered.

Most cruise lines offer discounts if you book or pay for your passage in advance. If you're sure you're going to take a specific cruise, it can make good sense to take advantage of these discounts. Not only can you reduce your ticket price by hundreds of dollars, but also the savings you realize are not taxable.

Another way to cut the cost of a cruise—if you have a flexible schedule—is to take advantage of late booking discounts offered by most lines. If a ship sails with empty rooms, the revenue those rooms could have generated is lost forever. So cruise lines will often offer steep discounts on unsold rooms shortly (perhaps a few weeks) before sailing to generate what revenue they can before it's lost. Check with your travel agent for details.

Trip Insurance

Whether you're going on a cruise, a package trip, or a do-it-yourself trip, you can buy insurance that will provide a refund if you or a member of your family becomes ill and is thus unable to travel. Such insurance may also provide that if a close member of your family who was not taking the trip becomes ill or dies you can get a refund. Ask your travel agent for details on this trip insurance.

STRATEGIES FOR SUCCESS

Condo Rentals Can Mean Big Vacation Savings

Staying in a motel or a resort can be expensive. And the bigger your family and the longer you stay, the more expensive it gets. In most resort areas, it's possible to rent condominiums for a lot less than you'd pay for a hotel room. (Owners who use the condo for their own vacations during part of the year put them up for rent when they're not using them.) Condos usually come fully equipped (kitchen, linens, towels, etc.) and many have nice amenities, such as tennis courts, swimming pool, and the like. If you don't need the services of a hotel (room service, telephone operator, etc.), a condo can give you a lot more vacation for a lot less money. Check with the Chamber of Commerce or Visitors Bureau in the city you plan to visit for references on condo rentals.

Travel Scams

The travel industry is not without its fair share of con artists. The problem has become more severe in recent years, as telephone solicitations have blanketed the country offering all sorts of supposed free travel to innocent and gullible victims (See chapter 4.)

Home-exchange Programs

If you're the trusting type, a home-exchange program can offer you the best of both worlds: the chance to live in a distant city at very little expense. The idea behind a home exchange is that you swap residences with a family in another city—either in the United States or abroad. In addition to eliminating hotel bills, you also have kitchen facilities at your disposal so that you can save considerably on food costs. You might even swap the use of each other's automobile.

Ask your travel agent for the names and addresses of various home-exchange programs. Sponsors of these programs charge a modest fee for providing you with a subscription to a swapping listing. When you've found a good match you should correspond in detail with them to make certain that you both know enough about the home and facilities to satisfy each other. To the extent possible, get personal references on the other individuals so that you can feel a sense of trust, since they will be living in your home. But the fact that you are living in each other's homes does help keep the level of trust high. You needn't own a house to get involved in an exchange; apartments and condominiums can be just as acceptable as a single-family home.

Pocket Money

Traveler's checks are the best way to carry money with you on vacation. Personal checks are rarely accepted, but most tourist areas do accept common credit cards. Cash is convenient, but if lost, it's gone forever. If traveler's checks are lost, the issuing company can arrange for an immediate refund.

Traveler's checks are available at most major banks and through some travel agencies. They are issued by such companies as American Express, Bank of America, Citicorp, Visa, and Mastercard. The cost of traveler's checks is about $1 per $100 worth of checks. Many banks make traveler's checks available to their customers at no charge.

Foreign Money

If you are traveling to another country, you'll have to convert at least some dollars into the currency of that country. You'll probably be able to charge hotel bills and restaurant bills on most major credit cards, but you'll need local currency for such things as taxis, minor purchases, and tips. Unless you've established a bank account in the foreign country, it will be extremely difficult for you to cash a personal check. Traveler's checks, again, are the best way to carry money. Cash your traveler's checks at local banks. You'll obtain a much better rate of exchange than you will at hotels, shops, or restaurants.

ATM machines in major tourist cities allow you to withdraw the local currency from your checking account at home. You can also use your credit cards to borrow local currency. Mind the cost of doing the latter.

Precautions Before You Leave Home

Secure your peace of mind by taking a few simple precautions. If you don't have a trustworthy person to stay at your home while you're away, make certain that all valuables are out of harm's way. Either put them in a safety deposit box at your bank or leave them with someone you trust. Be certain to stop all mail and newspaper deliveries by contacting the Post Office and newspaper circulation office. For less than ten dollars you can buy timers that turn your lights on and off at various times of the day and night to make it appear that someone is at home. Ask neighbors to keep an eye out for any strange persons around your home. If you leave your car in the driveway, it will accumulate dust and tip off a would-be burglar that the home is empty. Leave a car key with a neighbor or friend and ask him or her to move the car around every few days and to keep it dusted off. Check with your property insurance agent to determine what

coverage, if any, you have for valuables you plan to take with you. What additional coverage might be advisable? Alert your local police that you will be away; very often they will keep an extra eye on the property for you. Consider hiring a private patrol service to provide surveillance on your home while you're away. Check with your telephone company to see whether they have a call-forwarding service that will inform callers how you can be reached if you do, in fact, wish to be reached.

Make arrangements for all payments falling due during your absence. If that's not feasible, explain to your creditors that you will be gone for a while and ask them if they can waive any late charges or make other accommodations. If you neglect to take care of such matters, you risk having late payments show on various accounts, which could be detrimental to your credit rating. If you have investments with a stockbroker, determine what action, if any, you might want the broker to take in your absence. If that's not practical, leave word with the broker as to how you can be reached if the need arises. If you have any savings certificates or other securities maturing during the time you'll be absent, make arrangements with the bank or broker accordingly. The better you take care of such details before you leave, the better time you'll be able to have.

Know Your Rights

If you are traveling on a common carrier—particularly an airplane—make certain you know in advance what your rights are in the event you get bumped from your flight or your luggage is lost or damaged. Bumping means that there's no room for you on the plane. The Federal Aviation Administration (FAA) requires that airlines make payments to passengers who are bumped. There are limitations on how much an airline is responsible for in the event of lost or damaged luggage. Never pack valuables or needed prescriptions in luggage that is to be checked. Rather than risk the anguish of even a temporary loss, carry those items with you on the plane.

Buying Big-ticket Vacation Items

It's a curious facet of human nature: Most people are not in their "right minds" when they are planning a vacation or are actually on the vacation. During the planning stages, there's an aura of excited anticipation. That's when one might say, with a burst of wild enthusiasm, "Let's go for broke and *buy* that boat we've always wanted!" Or, while on the vacation itself, a similar loss of reality can occur, in response to which one might say, "It's foolish to spend money *renting* a place here—let's *buy* a place!"

Then, in the rosy glow of a vacation mentality, you find that you've plunked down a few thousand dollars and signed a whopping contract for the balance of payments on the new motor home, boat, or vacation home.

Before you write that check or sign that contract, consider the following:

- On a minimal purchase of any of those items—say $20,000—the interest alone that you will pay on your debt will be in the neighborhood of $2,000 to $3,000 per year. That amount, in itself, can pay for one or more very nice vacations every year. Is it worth it?

- For the first year or so you'll get great enjoyment out of your purchase. But human nature being what it is, we tend to want to change the scene for our vacations every few years. Three years from now, will you still want to go boating in your boat, or spend your vacation in a place that by now may have become boring to you? Your thoughts at the time you made the purchase may have been, "We'll love it forever!" But, a few years later, you may wish you'd never taken the plunge. The time to think of that is *before* you take the plunge.

If you're contemplating a big-ticket vacation expenditure, the best precaution is to proceed on a test basis. Rent for a year or two, and see if it's really your style. The rental will probably cost you less than the interest alone on a purchase, and if you don't like it, you can walk away. Contrary to what many salespersons may tell you, it's *not* always that easy to unload an unwanted camper, boat, or home in a distant resort area.

Time Sharing: Easy Solution?

Time sharing is a recent phenomenon. Simply stated, time sharing means that you buy the right to use a specific facility for one or two weeks during the year. Part of the time-sharing concept is that you can exchange your location for one of many others each year. If you weary of your condo in Waikiki after a few years, you can swap it for a villa in Switzerland or a resort in Miami or a castle in Spain.

Exercise 3.5

It all sounds very attractive, and some people have found great satisfaction in it. But the time-sharing phenomenon is also rife with misrepresentation and fraud. Many people have purchased time-sharing interests in resorts that were never built. Many find that the facilities are inferior to the way the salesperson represented them. Others discover that the so-called guaranteed cost is not guaranteed at all—that increasing assessments boost the cost much higher than was anticipated. And, to make matters worse, many find that the exchange privileges are not as represented.

Time-sharing sales pitches are very high-pressure. The most prudent approach to a time-share sales offering is to visit the place in person to be certain that it is as represented to you. Study your contract carefully to determine what your exchange privileges, if any, might be and what added costs you might have to incur in the future. All due caution is advised before you sign any contract.

RECREATION AT HOME

Major vacation travel may occur only once every few years, and only a few weekends may be devoted to camping, traveling, or sightseeing. But every day there are hours of leisure time to fill at home or in your community. Following are some considerations—financial and otherwise—on some of those ways of filling your leisure time at home.

Electronics

The electronics boom offers increasing sophistication at decreasing costs. As a new century dawns, virtually every home in the United States will have one or more of the following: cable television offering dozens of channels; dish antennas capable of receiving scores, if not hundreds, of television channels from satellites; video player/recorders; wide-screen television sets—five feet or more across; and computers capable of interacting with television for educational, work, and game-playing purposes.

And sooner than later there will be video/computerized facilities that will print newspapers and magazines on recyclable plastic right in our living rooms and that will permit us access to virtually everything that's ever been filmed or printed via giant computers reached through satellite connections.

In short, we're in an electronics revolution, and the emergence of new techniques and equipment will shape our leisure lives to a great extent.

With so many marvels due in the future, it is frustrating to deliberate today what investments should be made in electronic leisure equipment. "Should I buy something today only to have it become obsolete next month because of a more advanced model?" The point is well taken. But whatever you do invest in today, you can still enjoy for many years while planning the next investment in more advanced equipment. Let's examine some of the specific items that tempt you currently.

Video Cassette Recorders

Video cassette recorders can be used to record anything that is broadcast through your television set—including incoming cable and pay TV signals.

When VCRs were first introduced in the early 1970s, they were priced at about $2,000, and they had very little flexibility. Currently, you can obtain top-quality equipment for well under $500, and the machines are equipped with internal computers that allow you to set them to turn on, record, and turn off many days in advance. Other common features include fast-forward, slow-motion, and freeze-frame capabilities.

Prerecorded tapes, including movies, sporting events, and instructional material, can be purchased or rented. Rental rates for cassette tapes can be as low as a dollar. Compare that with the cost of taking the family to a

movie theater. Blank recording tapes with a capacity of upwards of six hours can be purchased for well under $5.

In shopping for a VCR, bear in mind the following criteria: Will you benefit from the costly optional extras included in many sets, or will you be better off with a lower cost, no-frills set? What type of warranty comes with the set? If service is needed, can it be done locally, or must the set be sent away to a service bureau? Competition is very keen with these products, so it will pay to shop around and seek discounts at local dealers.

In addition to stores that sell and rent prerecorded material, many public libraries are now offering prerecorded cassettes to their local communities.

Video Cameras

One of the most popular items in the home electronics market is the video camera, which has replaced the old-fashioned home movie film camera. There is a wide selection of cameras priced under $500, and models with new features are always being introduced. This year's best deal might be obsolete before you get it home. But if you let yourself worry about that, you'll never enjoy using it. So, after doing the necessary homework, make your best purchase, and don't look back to see what you might have bought had you only waited another month or two.

Personal Computers

Technology is advancing so rapidly with these devices that it's difficult to predict what will be available to the public next month, let alone next year. The basic component is the home computer, which can be attached to a printer and/or to your telephone. The cost of these units ranges from a few hundred dollars to thousands of dollars, depending on their capabilities.

Popular uses of the home computer include accessing the internet, financial planning, word processing, instructional programming, and a wide variety of games. Many more sophisticated uses are available to the small businessperson and the professional person, including billing, inventory control, and a host of other bookkeeping and calculating functions

Shopping for a home computer, programs, and games will take a lot of careful homework. How much use will you make of the equipment? Can you justify the cost of doing your projected work on the computer, or can you get it done more inexpensively using more traditional methods? Rapid change is expected in the home computer market, so you must decide whether you will be buying something that will too quickly become obsolete or that will serve justifiable purposes for at least three to five years. And as with the video player/recorders, you must determine the extent of warranty as well as the availability and cost of service. Finally, beware of what has befallen many home computer buyers: After the novelty wears off, it is relegated to the expensive toy status, gathering dust in a forgotten corner.

The Internet

An interesting historical note: The previous edition of this textbook, published in 1996, made scant notice of the Internet. It was in its infancy, and who could have known what it might have grown into. Today the Internet is still little more than a baby, but it has become a rapid growth phenomenon of science-fiction caliber. Its ultimate future shape is still years away from clear definition.

Surfers beware: to the gullible, the Internet can be a dangerously costly place. For much of what is on the Internet there is no gatekeeper, no editor, no arbiter of taste or truth who controls what can be put there. Unlike a magazine, a book, a newspaper or a broadcast, no one with any authority has necessarily approved what is distributed. This opens the doors wide for fraudsters, tipsters, and just plain sloppy writers whose purported facts might be nothing more than rumors, disguised sales pitches, or just plain falsities. Further, anything that is put on the Internet can be altered by hackers, and this can go unnoticed by the original authors. Hackers have broken into the CIA and State Department computers. Very little is beyond their reach.

Scam artists go to great lengths on the Internet to get your credit card number or personal identification numbers for your ATM cards. Advice from a CompuServe customer service rep, who deals with such problems on a daily, if not hourly, basis: "Don't give your credit card number to *anyone* on the Internet. If the deal is valid, you can do it by mail." Someday there will be totally secure ways of doing electronic commerce via the Internet. Until then, follow the CompuServe advice. Shop on the Internet if you will, but pay for what you buy through the mail. (That way you also have added protection: If you're caught in a scam, the mail fraud laws may protect you. There is as yet no comparable protection on the Internet.)

Fax Machines

Fax machines are becoming as common as the toaster in the typical American home. The ultimate homeowner's version (already available in costly business models) will be the combined fax/answering machine/telephone/copier/scanner/computer. And it will be about the same size as your toaster.

Large-screen Television and Home Theater Equipment

Large-screen television sets range between $1,000 and $4,000, but technological advancement is expected to bring the price down over the coming years. Eventually, by utilizing fiber optics, large-screen television sets may be hung on a wall like a picture. In the meantime, the existing large-screen sets are strictly a luxury purchase. They definitely can enhance the pleasure you get from watching television; if you can justify the added cost of that extra pleasure, you may want to begin shopping around for a large-screen TV.

In development is a new concept of television, known as High Definition Television (HDTV). It promises movie-screen clarity on the home TV set, as well as a vast array of industrial and scientific uses. It may be well into the twenty-first century before HDTV becomes an *affordable* reality. When it does, it could replace existing TV sets and transmission modes.

Personal Enrichment

A great deal of your leisure time can be put to rewarding and productive use without your having to spend a lot of money. Look into the activities that may be available at your local library, college, church or synagogue, or community center, often at no charge. You're likely to find an interesting assortment of concerts, art exhibits, theatrical presentations, and lectures.

Carefully examine the continuing education catalogs of your local community college or university. You'll find a variety of courses and seminars that can amuse, entertain, and stimulate as well as educate. These programs are generally offered on weekends and evenings so that you can take advantage of them without interfering with your work.

Volunteer work—through religious and civic organizations—can be a very rewarding use of your leisure time. Volunteers are eagerly sought, and by helping others, you can help yourself.

Sports, Hobbies, and Out-on-the-Town

Athletic activities, whether individual, such as jogging, or organized in teams, such as softball, are among the most popular modes of spending leisure time.

Health Spas and Athletic Clubs (Tennis, Golf, Racquetball, Etc.)

Membership in such facilities can be very expensive, and you must determine whether the cost will be justifiable. You may be subjected to a rigorous sales pitch to convince you that you'll spend every nonworking hour on the premises becoming a better person. You will be expected to sign a contract committing you to monthly payments for your membership. If possible, take a trial membership to see whether this particular facility is really right for you. Will you use it as much as the salesperson tells you? And will the benefits to you be as delightful as the sales brochure suggests? Determine how long the facility has been in business, and talk with current members to ascertain their level of satisfaction. Be aware that many such facilities run into financial problems. This can result in a sharp increase in cost to members or, in the worst (and not that uncommon) case, the facility simply closes down and disappears along with your money.

Individual Sports and Hobbies

Many of these activities—such as skiing, sailing, scuba diving, photography—can involve considerable investment on your part. If you are already committed to such activities, you know what it is costing you. If you are contemplating embarking on any such activities, calculate in advance the cost of getting set up. Then, as with the health spas and athletic clubs, give it a trial run first to see if it's really right for you.

Professional Sports

If you're a "sports nut" and you live in a major league city (for baseball, football, hockey, basketball, soccer), you know how expensive it can be to satisfy your cravings. If you're a frequent spectator at any of these sports, consider sharing season tickets with other fans. The total cost over the full season might be considerably less for the same number of admissions as if you were buying tickets for each event. Also, inquire at the ticket offices to determine when discounts and group plans may be available. Your employer or union may also offer discount packages to sporting events.

A Night on the Town

Dining out and attending movies or concerts are regular items on many people's leisure-time schedule. Since we often do such things on impulse and since the activity finds many of us under the influence of alcohol, it's all too easy to ignore what the activity is costing. When you say, "Sure, let's have another bottle of wine" enough times in a month, you could unwittingly be impairing your ability to buy necessities the following month. And since a very high percentage of dining-out activity is paid for by credit card instead of hard cash, it's easy to succumb to the temptation to spend more than what is reasonable. Furthermore, if the credit card bill isn't paid in full by the end of the month, you'll start building up interest costs, which can end up increasing the price of that meal or that bottle of wine by 20, 50, or even 100 percent if you wait long enough to pay the bill.

In many cities you can purchase discount books that offer savings at restaurants, movies, sporting events, and tourist attractions. These books are often available through charitable organizations, so your fee goes to a good cause and you get benefits as well. You can also take advantage of the discount coupons for restaurants that appear in local newspapers and mailings.

Out-on-the-town expenses should be budgeted in advance and, whenever possible, paid for in cash or by check. Nobody is telling you not to have a good time. You just must be careful of having too good a time now at the expense of not being able to have a good time later.

The Ultimate Leisure

The poet William Wordsworth wrote these lines:

> The world is too much with us.
> Late and soon, getting and spending,
> We lay waste our powers.
> Little we see in nature that is ours.
> We have given our hearts away, a sordid boon.

Wordsworth, a nature lover himself, was bemoaning the fact that we get so caught up in the day-to-day business of life that we neglect the beauties and pleasures that nature offers us. We have, as he says, given our hearts away—sold out to the daily tumult of our regular work routine. Although that may have its own rewards, we may be missing out on more valuable things. A modern (and anonymous) philosopher put it more succinctly on a popular poster: "Don't run so fast that you can't smell the flowers."

PERSONAL ACTION WORKSHEET ———————————————

Vacation Planner

No worksheet can help you determine how much pleasure you'll have on a vacation. But this planner can aid you in calculating and comparing the costs of various leisure holidays, Estimate each item carefully. A travel agent can be of great help, at no additional cost to you. Bon voyage!

	Estimated Cost		
Travel Expense Item	Vacation #1	Vacation #2	Vacation #3
Getting there			
❐ Airplane	_____	_____	_____
❐ Bus	_____	_____	_____
❐ Train	_____	_____	_____
❐ Car	_____	_____	_____
❐ Meals, lodging en route	_____	_____	
Getting about			
❐ Rental car	_____	_____	_____
❐ Buses, tours, excursions	_____	_____	_____
Room and board			
❐ Hotel, motel (are any meals included?)	_____	_____	_____
❐ Meals (not included in hotel price)	_____	_____	_____
❐ Snacks, drinks	_____	_____	_____
Activities			
❐ Equipment use and rental (boats, skis, lifts, horses, etc.)	_____	_____	_____
❐ Amusements (movies, amusement parks, concerts, plays, etc.)	_____	_____	_____
Miscellaneous	_____	_____	_____
Total estimated expense	_____	_____	_____
Cash available to pay for vacation	_____	_____	_____
Amount to be financed (loans, credit cards, etc.)	_____	_____	_____
Interest cost on amount financed (assuming you pay it off in 12 monthly installments)	_____	_____	_____

CONSUMER ALERT

Beating the High Price of Water

Would you pay $4.00 for a gallon of ordinary water?

Of course not, you say, but you may already have done so many times.

Example: The supermarket offers a six-pack of canned iced tea for $2.29. Six cans of 12 ounces each total 72 ounces. At $2.29, that's 3.18¢ per ounce. There are 128 ounces in a gallon, so at 3.18¢ per ounce you are paying $4.07 per gallon for canned iced tea. But all you are really getting is ordinary water, with a few cents worth of tea flavoring, added to it.

Likewise with juice products. How many quarts of Hawaiian Punch can you make from a can of the concentrated product? Compare the cost of doing so with buying regular canned Hawaiian Punch. What other products offer you the same choice? If you've been buying the canned instead of the concentrate, how much extra have you been paying to buy water and haul it home from the market?

Paying $4.00 per gallon for ordinary water is, obviously, absurd. It's bad enough to pay $1.30 or so for a gallon of gasoline—but at least that product is capable of propelling a 4,000-pound vehicle 20 to 30 miles at speeds in excess of 50 miles per hour. What will the water do by comparison?

You can't say that nobody is foolish enough to spend $4.00 for a gallon of water. The product wouldn't be on the shelves if nobody bought it.

Calculate how much money you might have paid in the last year to buy water at the supermarket. From now on, be a Smart Shopper. Buy the concentrates and use your own tap water. Think of what can be saved, in both money and energy.

UPS & DOWNS   *The Economics of Everyday Life*

Why Food Prices Fluctuate

Nature is the culprit with respect to produce, meats, fish, and dairy products. Seasons change regularly: you can buy strawberries in the summer for under a dollar a box, but the price zooms in winter when they are flown in from New Zealand. Floods, droughts, freezes, and hot spells also wreak havoc with prices.

Many other elements enter into the cost of food, some of which have nothing to do with the food itself.

New products   Each year about 12,000 new products are created for U.S. supermarkets. And about 80 percent of those new products fail. The makers pass some of the cost of these failed products onto the public by increasing the price of successful products.

Slotting allowances   Food manufacturers are in fierce competition to get the best display space in the best markets. Busy stores charge "slotting allowances" for the shelf space they offer to manufacturers. These extra fees can add to the cost of the product.

Failure fees   A retailer doesn't want to give up valuable shelf space to an unproven new product. Where competition is most intense, retailers ask for *failure fees*. If choice space is given to a manufacturer for a new product, and the new product fails to reach a given sales volume, the manufacturer will have to pay a penalty to the store.

Coupons and rebates   Each year the United States is flooded with some 270 *billion* cents-off coupons. We redeem about 7 billion of them, representing a "savings" to the redeemers of $3.1 billion. Add the cost of processing, printing, and distributing. There's no such thing as a free lunch. Someone is absorbing all that expense.

Technology   Scientific advances have been very much to the consumer's advantage. Genetic engineering provides bigger yields. New packaging allows for longer shelf life. At the checkout counter, the laser machine that reads the bar codes helps the market control costs, thus keeping prices down.

Human nature   As an experiment a supermarket set up two crates of identical bananas side by side, one unlabeled, the other with a popular brand label. The branded bananas were priced much higher than the unlabeled ones, but shoppers were loyal: They paid the higher price for the branded bananas, while the unlabeled ones went begging. This speaks for itself.

?
WHAT IF . . . ?

How would you deal with these real-life possibilities?

1. You're buying a new TV for $400, with a one-year warranty. The store offers an extended warranty for three years, at an extra cost of $150. You're no good at fixing electronic gizmos. Would you buy the warranty? If so, why? If not, why not?

2. Both your washing machine and dryer are on their last legs. Buying new machines will cost about $800, and you're strapped for cash, so you'd have to finance them. There's a nice laundromat nearby. What will you do to solve your dilemma?

3. Economic conditions are harsh, and you have to take a pay cut of 10 percent. How much can you reduce your food budget to offset that pay cut, without sacrificing good nutrition? What would you give up? What would you substitute? Now, look at the rosy side as well—a 10 percent pay raise. How much of that would go into your food budget? For what specifically?

NUMBER CRUNCHERS

Do the calculations to make decisions in these real-life possibilities.

1. You're moving into a new dwelling and you have no furniture. Develop a list of all the furniture you'll need to live comfortably. Go shopping. How much would it cost you to buy everything for cash? How much would it cost you to finance everything, given varying amounts of down payment? (See the loan calculation tables in chapter 10) Visit a furniture rental store: How much would it cost you to rent everything?

2. Make a list of the ten items you purchase most frequently at the food market. Every week for one month compare the prices on those items at your own market and two other markets. Take all factors into account: coupons, special discounts, cost of getting to and from market, other conveniences. Where do you get the best deal, all things considered?

3. Ask your pharmacist to help you on this one: What are the ten most frequently prescribed drugs, and how much do they cost in typical dosages? Compare these costs with the costs of identical generic products. If you regularly use any prescription item, is there a generic equal, and how much does it cost?

4. Examine ads for book, record, or video clubs, particularly those that offer "12 for only $.99 each, as long as you agree to buy 6 more at our regular price . . . ," or comparable deals. Calculate how much you'd actually end up spending including shipping costs. Compare that with buying the same items at local stores or borrowing them from your local library. Which is the best deal?

FOR BETTER OR FOR WORSE

Things beyond our control often impact our personal and financial well-being, for better or for worse. Some are more predictable than others. How would you be affected if the following real-life phenomena happened? Could you have seen it coming? What steps could you have taken to minimize damage or maximize advantage? The better able you are to anticipate and recognize these forces, the better equipped you are to deal with them.

1. You've long been saving up for a once-in-a-lifetime three-week trip abroad, and now you've finally booked it and paid for it. One of your parents gets seriously ill just weeks before you're scheduled to go.

2. A new manager takes over at the supermarket you regularly use. He's an ogre. The staff morale goes from chipper to mean, and the condition of the market goes from sparkling to dingy. But their prices become more attractive. The next nearest market is three miles farther away from you.

3. A local furniture store has a going-out-of-business sale, and you charge $3,000 on your credit card buying goods that normally would have cost twice that. But the store goes out of business—totally—before they deliver your furniture.

Frauds and Swindles and How to Avoid Them

There's a sucker born every minute.

P. T. Barnum

The statement is as true today as it was in Barnum's time. Despite all the consumer education material available today, an abundance of shady, misleading, and illegal business still goes on in every community every day. There are schemes that can relieve the unwary and the greedy of a few dollars or of many thousands of dollars. And more often than not, the swindlers get away with their schemes and skip from one city to the next, laughing at their victims all the way. Chances are good that someday you may be a victim of consumer fraud. But you'll have a strong defense against that possibility if you heed the techniques in this chapter:

- Spotting and avoiding the deals that sound too good to be true; that promise something for nothing; that promise instant wealth, health, or success

- Knowing whom to inform if you discover a fraudulent scheme in the works

- Knowing where you can get help if you find yourself the victim of a swindle

BARNUM WAS RIGHT

No one is immune to the wiles of the con artist or the shady business operator. Young and old, rich and poor, succumb to some scam at one time or another. Because most business activities are indeed legitimate, we tend to trust people. We believe what we're told. We believe what we read in advertisements. And despite the ever constant rule of *caveat emptor—buyer beware*—we are not wary enough. If we are led to believe that we are getting something that sounds too good to be true, or something for nothing, we tend to believe it. And we part with our money without even asking questions. Sometimes it's nothing more than our own greed that does us in. Sometimes we are simply gullible—believing preposterous statements. And sometimes a salesperson wins our confidence so totally that we act as if we're hypnotized when we write out our checks.

Consumer fraud will never go away. According to a presidential crime commission study, more than 90 percent of the victims of consumer fraud never do anything about it. The majority of the victims are not even *aware* that they've been defrauded until it's far too late to do anything about it. Those who are aware of having been defrauded are reluctant to report it to the police, either out of embarrassment or out of belief that the police won't do anything about it. Thus, with few exceptions, promoters and swindlers run free throughout our society, taking advantage of our weaknesses, our greed, our gullibility, and our basically trusting natures.

Exercise 4.1

This chapter will explore some of the more common types of consumer fraud. Every type of fraud has endless variations, so don't for a moment think that the schemes described here are the only ones. You must be aware of certain *basic patterns* that can alert you to possible fraud. These basic patterns appear in the following situations:

- You're led to believe that you're getting something for nothing or are offered a deal that sounds too good to be true. There is no such thing as something for nothing, and any deal that sounds too good to be true is usually neither good nor true.

- Someone tries to sell you something with such vigor that you find yourself on the verge of spending money for something you might otherwise have ignored. In such cases, you should immediately ask yourself, "If this thing is so good, then why is he willing to sell it to me? Could it be that he'll get more benefit by selling it to me than I can by buying it from him?"

- A salesperson or an ad offers you something that is not available through normal channels. This may be a miracle cure, a chance to get rich quick, or a chance to become famous. These offerings will do nothing but deplete your bank account.

Although most advertising media (newspapers, magazines, radio, television) attempt to police the advertising they present to the public, there are definitely flaws in the system. Some policing efforts are not adequate, and misleading advertising can slip past the censor's scrutiny. Moreover, misleading advertising that appears in an otherwise legitimate medium takes on an aura of legitimacy. "It must be so if it appeared in the daily paper. If it weren't legitimate, the newspaper wouldn't run it." Being constantly alert is no guarantee that you'll never get stung. But *lack* of constant alertness will almost guarantee that you *will* get stung.

One final warning before we embark on tales of the wild and woolly world of consumer fraud. Nothing could please Snake Oil Sam more than a brand new medium where he can offer his scams and ripoffs with virtually total impunity.

That medium is the Internet. For all the good things available on the Internet, we're just beginning to see the tip of the tip of what is going to be the biggest iceberg in history: consumer abuses beyond measurement.

Sam makes billions of dollars every year through the legitimate advertising media—print, broadcasting, mail, and so on. But at least with those media there is some policing; some ads do get censored or are refused. Those that do reach the public are susceptible to prosecution if they turn out to be scams. The advertisers can be found. State and federal agencies can step in. And if the mail is used as part of a scam, federal mail fraud laws can be used to nab the culprits. Still, Sam gets away with an incredible haul.

Now imagine the Internet, where nothing has to be edited by any responsible authority. And if something is responsibly edited, hackers can break into the system and change it, and you'll never know the difference. On the Internet virtually anything can and does get published. There are no regulators or official censors. The advertisers can hide themselves in cyberspace, far from the reach of any law enforcement. Snake Oil Sam is in absolute Cyber-Heaven!

All of the swindles outlined in this chapter can be initiated on the Internet and through e-mail with lightning-like suddenness. Snake Oil Sam lurks in chat rooms waiting for the gullible and the greedy. The investment arena is particularly dangerous on the Internet. If a salesperson from a legitimate firm sells you a deal over the phone, through the mail, or in person, you have at least some hope of getting some help from the firm, from the National Association of Security Dealers, from the Securities and Exchange Commission or from your state's Department of Securities. Dealing with an unknown entity on the Internet leaves you with absolutely no recourse. You'll be out there flapping your wings in cyberspace, and Snake Oil Sam will laugh all the way to the bank. (He knows better than to entrust his money to strangers on the Internet.) Surf accordingly.

BAIT AND SWITCH

This is probably the oldest game of all. The bait is an attractive enticement to lure you into a store in a buying frame of mind. The switch occurs when you are in the store and the salesperson diverts you from the bait item to another item that offers him a higher profit. The switch can happen in many ways.

For instance, you're watching late-night television, and here comes good old Gideon Gotcha "out here in automobile land ready to sell you folks some beautiful cars of all makes and models. Here's a 1998 Cadillac with only 1,600 miles on it, in perfect condition, with brand-new radial-ply-biased-steel-double-whitewall-hand-autographed tires, and a built-in Hammond organ in the back seat! And how much would you expect to pay for this beautiful car? About $25,000? Maybe at some other place, but not at Gideon Gotcha's! Would you believe only $8,995!"

You rush down to Gideon Gotcha's where you find that the lot is closed for the night. You camp on the doorstep and when Gideon comes in to open up, you hand him an envelope full of cash and tell him you want the $8,995 Cadillac you saw on television just a few hours ago.

"Oh, I'm really sorry," says Gideon, "but we sold it during the night. I got a call at my house from a customer who sent a courier at 4 A.M. with the cash. But now that you're here, maybe I can interest you in a brand-new Caddie whose classic beauty will withstand the years better than the Mona Lisa. And since you came down so early in the morning, I could make a special deal for you. . . ."

Or you see an ad in the newspaper offering an entire side of beef for only 79¢ a pound. A fantastic deal! You rush to the place, and the butcher is happy to show you the side of beef that was advertised.

"Of course," he points out, "It's got some funny green spots here and there, but maybe we can cut them out. Anyway, if you boil the meat for fifteen or twenty minutes, it should kill any contamination that may have gone deeper. Now, if you don't like that particular side, we've got some regular sides over here in the cooler for $3.99 a pound."

Bait and switch tactics are outlawed by the Federal Trade Commission, as well as by many state and local laws. Nonetheless, they still occur in abundance. Your best protection against getting involved is your own careful scrutiny of the advertising, your willingness to shop around for similar products, and your ability to resist the temptation in the first place.

A distinction should be made between bait and switch and "loss leaders." A loss leader is a product offered by a merchant at a lower-than-normal price to entice you into the store where, it's hoped, you'll buy other merchandise as well as the loss leader. Supermarkets and discount stores use loss leaders all the time, and there's nothing wrong with this practice if you are getting the goods as represented and not a cheap replacement.

Where loss-leader advertising is employed, legitimate merchants will note in their advertising any catches in their offering, such as a limited supply, or will make clear that the offer is good only at certain stores or at certain hours. The Federal Trade Commission says that if a loss leader or other kind of promotional product is offered, the merchant is expected to have a sufficient amount on hand to meet what he reasonably expects to be the demand. Many merchants, realizing the value of pleasing their customers, will offer rainchecks if they run out of the supply of a loss leader.

If you detect a bait and switch operation in action in your community, alert the newspaper (or radio or TV station) where the advertising was placed. You may also want to notify the local Better Business Bureau and the police department. Very likely, nothing much will be done to the merchant who employed these tactics, but he'll be warned, and he might even promise not to do it again. Until next time.

MAIL-ORDER MADNESS

In terms of both dollar volume and number of incidents, the U.S. Postal Service is probably the single biggest carrier of fraudulent activity. Although many billions of dollars' worth of perfectly satisfactory goods are sold through the mail each year, the level of abuse also runs very high. Mail-order swindlers owe their success not just to the greed and gullibility of victims but also to the fact that the fraud inspection division of the U.S. Postal Service is woefully understaffed. A false or misleading advertisement can cover the country for many months before postal inspectors are able to gather enough evidence to put a stop to it. In the meantime, the promoters will have made their fortune and disappeared, only to reappear shortly thereafter using a different name and selling a slightly different product. And the chase begins again, with the promoters usually the winners.

Mail order starts with an advertisement printed in a newspaper or magazine, broadcast on radio or television, sent through the mail or beamed on the Internet. You are dealing with people you don't know. If something goes wrong, you might not be able to get it corrected. If you're dealing with *legitimate* mail-order purveyors, most problems should be fairly easily corrected. But if you find yourself in the hands of a mail-order swindler, it is safe to assume that there's virtually no chance of your ever getting satisfaction or your money back.

Following is a brief sampling of mail-order swindles, based on actual experience: To determine how cleverly the promoters toy with the minds and bank accounts of potential victims, I became an intentional victim of a number of offerings. The results should speak for themselves.

Vanity Rackets

The price of an ego trip can be high indeed. Vanity rackets prey on the desire of so many people to be recognized. Ads offer to publish your book, your song, your poem, or even your baby's picture in a directory that is to be sent to television producers.

Anyone who has ever tried to have a song or a book published through normal channels knows how frustrating it can be: Rejection slips pour in, and it seems as though there's no way to achieve success. How wondrous it is, then, when you see an ad by a publisher soliciting your work. "Authors wanted." "Songwriters wanted."

In the legitimate publishing world, most books and songs are created by established artists—usually with the help of agents—under contract to the publisher. In the vanity publishing world, publishers print virtually anything, provided you pay them enough money. The veiled promises of fame and fortune will never materialize. You will have paid a high price to have your ego massaged.

Do vanity publishers really seek quality? Or will they publish anything that comes in attached to a big enough check? Seeking an answer to this question, I wrote an intentionally atrocious song and sent it off to three different vanity music publishers. If they were looking for any kind of quality, they would have rejected my lyrics instantly. Here are the words to my song:

Ethel Is My Only Love
(sing slowly)

Oh oh oh oh Ethel
Ethel Ethel will you be my blessing
Cuz when I look at you and sigh,
It makes me feel high. Oh me oh my.
It seems like only yesterday that we were in high school together.
I can't believe how old we are now, forever.
Oh oh oh oh Ethel
I feel just lousy without you
You are my only love—not Rita anymore.
Seriously, I mean it.
Oh oh Ethel. Yeah, yeah, yeah.

This drivel was accepted, not once, not twice, but all three times by the vanity publishers. Here is a sampling of some of the literature they sent me:

Dear Mr. Rosefsky:
We have good news for you! Your song has been rated #5 on our top 30 evaluation chart. We sincerely believe that your song poem, with the proper servicing, has the potential for a hit song. We have already contacted nearby publishers, and the response to it was positive. Publishers' acceptance seems assured. If you have as much faith in your song as we have, you will want to take advantage of our offer.

Each of the acceptances requested that I send in $80 to $90 for "servicing" of the song. The next step would be to pay them $200 to $300 for complete scoring or orchestration. Following that, the sky was the limit. I could pay for as many records to be pressed as I wished to, and they would distribute them and I would receive royalties. Legitimate music publishers assured me that a product from a vanity publisher stood no chance of being played on a radio station or distributed to music stores.

Tabloid newspapers and the Internet are the primary sources of potentially fraudulent advertising. I found an ad offering $300 for my baby's picture. If the baby picture was "acceptable," it would be published in a magazine that was distributed to movie and television producers looking for child talent. I sent in a picture of my 30-year-old cousin, Herbie, who at the time weighed in excess of 200 pounds. The photo was taken in the midst of an attack of indigestion. The magazine "accepted"the picture for publication, provided I send them $12.95. Responsible people in the motion picture and television industries assured me that they had never heard of the magazine, nor would they ever hire talent through such a publication. Yet it's likely that many thousands of checks for $12.95 each were sent by parents eager to have their children achieve fame and fortune.

Would-be inventors are also easy prey for swindlers who promise to patent and market products in exchange for big up-front fees.

Get-rich-quick Schemes

How far wrong can you go? You send away $30 for a book that promises to make you rich overnight. and if you don't like it, they promise to send you your money back. Such ads abound because it's difficult to prove them illegal. You will indeed receive a book. Judging from all those I've seen, it will be a cheaply produced paperback that will teach you how to become rich: Write a similar book on your own, take out ads in magazines, and let people send *you* money. You'll also get your name on dozens of other mailing lists, one of which is likely to hit you for big money in the future.

Other get-rich-quick schemes are nothing more than blatant chain letters instructing you to sent $30 to a name at the top of an enclosed list. You're then to duplicate this letter five times and put your name at the bottom of the list. Within weeks you are promised thousands of people all over the country will be sending you $30. Chain letters are illegal. Not only do such schemes never produce money for you, but they could involve you in a federal lawsuit.

Work-at-home Schemes

These promise ways to supplement your income by working at home. They appeal to people who can least afford to lose money—the elderly, the invalid, the poor.

- **Addressing envelopes.** You send $20 to the promoter and receive instructions on how to approach local businesses to sell them your services as an envelope addresser. But you are competing with professional mailing houses that can turn out thousands of envelopes in the time it would take you to do a few dozen.
- **Handicraft kits.** For your $20, you'll receive a kit of materials with instructions on how to turn them into baby booties, key chains, and the like. The promise is that the company will buy it back from you in finished form at a profit to you. You make the product and send it back to the company, only to be told that it's not up to their standards. They're very sorry, they'll say, but perhaps you'd like to try again by ordering another kit.

The postal fraud authorities and the Council of Better Business Bureaus agree: They have never seen a work-at-home scheme that worked, except for the promoters.

Quackery

Lose weight . . . cure baldness . . . look younger . . . live longer . . . improve your sex life. Shades of Snake Oil Sam, who sold caramel-flavored alcohol to the gullible from his traveling sideshow wagon.

Example: The ad told me that I could grow taller. Cost: $15 with a money-back guarantee if I wasn't satisfied. I received a single sheet of paper with a program of exercises titled "Erecto-Dynamics." I was to do these calisthenics for at least twenty minutes every day for a full year. But most important to the growing taller program was that I should stand up straighter. As for the money-back guarantee, it was contingent on my having my height verified by a doctor before the start of the year's program and at the end. The expense of having a doctor verify my height would be more than the money I'd get back from the promoter.

Quackery is of particular concern to the postal fraud authorities, for not only can you lose money but your health can be endangered if you fail to seek proper medical attention, relying instead on the pufferies of Snake Oil Sam. If your condition can't be helped by a professional, you certainly won't be helped by these mail-order offerings.

One aspect of the quackery phenomenon seems to grow without any end in sight, and it must be raking in billions of dollars from the gullible and the lonely: so-called psychics who clutter up the television airwaves

and other media. Do Number Cruncher exercise 2 at the end of this chapter if you have any doubts about the money being generated by this nonsense. And bear in mind: There's no such thing as a "free" psychic.

As with so many other fads and scams, they will run their course and disappear. But the people behind the scenes—the ones who create and administer new scams—will not disappear. They'll be out there drumming up new ways to separate you from your money as long as there's a you and as long as there's money.

FRAUDS ON THE STREET

When you respond to an advertisement, you have time to consider your response. But when you're confronted by a stranger on the street, the surprise element can be enough to embroil you in a money-losing proposition.

The Pigeon Drop

This classic old scheme, the pigeon drop, has dozens of variations. In a typical operation, a person is approached by a stranger who chats with the victim for a few minutes to win her friendship and confidence. Then the stranger announces that he has just found a wallet that contains a lot of money but no identification.

The stranger offers to split the find with the newfound friend, the victim. At this point, the victim, taken in by the con man's friendship and generosity, is willing to do almost anything the con man advises. The con man then quickly suggests that before they split the loot, they should double-check the legality with a lawyer and that the victim, in order to show good faith, should put up an equal amount of cash and let the lawyer hold it while a decision is made as to who is entitled to the money.

It seems crazy that the victims would put up the cash, but they do time and time again—and often thousands of dollars are involved. As soon as the victim delivers the cash, the whole package is left with the con man's "lawyer," who promptly disappears. The victim's money? Gone in a flash. Elderly people are traditional marks for this scam. They tend to be more easily won over by the confidence game, and they're less likely to give chase. But no one is excluded from the potential of the pigeon drop.

Phony Goods

This type of swindle occurs mostly during the Christmas season, but it can pop up at any time, in any place. The scheme is decisive in its swiftness and simplicity. You're approached by a stranger offering to sell you anything

from watches to jewelry to perfume to a color TV set "still in the carton." The price is too good to be true. It won't be until you get the item home that you find that the watch has no innards, the perfume is kerosene, the jewelry is cut glass, and the color TV set still in the carton is nothing more than a wooden box. Similar shenanigans can take place at flea markets and swap meets.

If you do fall prey to such a scheme, you can be certain that you will not be able to get your money back. If you are able to find the seller, he'll deny ever having seen you, and it's unlikely that the police will bother to assist you in what they would consider a relatively petty matter.

FRAUDS IN THE HOME

You don't always have to go out to encounter con artists. Sometimes they'll come to you, knocking on your door, calling, or sending e-mail. As with street schemes, the element of surprise works in favor of con artists. They are prepared to sell to you, and you're totally unprepared for a sales pitch. You have no way of finding the swindler if things go wrong.

"900" Scams

There are, it seems, 900 ways you can get taken if you are careless in making "900" calls on your telephone. The sales pitches are intriguing: You can talk to psychics, acquire credit cards, pour your heart out to the opposite sex, be lured into dangerous investment schemes, and much more. And the costs of doing so will be on your next month's telephone bill. Many people make the mistake of thinking that the deals must be legitimate because the telephone company is involved. Wrong! Abuses with "900" numbers, ranging from excessive charges to outright swindle, have been rampant. If you get trapped once, the telephone company might waive the charges for your first misadventure. But that's it. Beware also of seemingly toll-free numbers such as "800" and "888" which rack up the charges on your credit card. Know before you dial that those expenses can mount up and that if you fail to pay you can lose your telephone, your credit card, and your good credit standing.

Cellular Phones

How's this for a growth business? In 1991, when cellular phones were still in the novelty stage, Snake Oil Sam racked up $100 million in fraudulent activities with the phones. By 1995 his take had grown to $600 million, accord-

ing to the Cellular Telecommunications Industry Association. How did/ does he do it? Easier than you may think. He can sit by the side of the road and scan any phone in use. With the data he retrieves he can program a clone phone with your number. He sells that cloned phone to an eager buyer, who proceeds to use your number to make and receive calls, tallying up hundreds of dollars in costs in just a few hours.

How can that hurt you? If your phone is cloned and you don't check your monthly bill (or your employees' bills) you could be paying for someone else's calls. If you do discover improper use, your carrier might remove the invalid charges from your bill the first time. But $600 million of fraudulent calls were not reported to carriers' attention in 1995, the last year for which such statistics were available.

Fraud prevention programs are available on most cellular systems at little or no cost to you the user. But you have to use it regularly. You never can tell when that person by the side of the road has a scanner aimed at you.

Courier Services

Whether the scam involves investments, "free" vacations, or any other offering in which money has to be delivered to the con artists, victims are quickly won over when they are told, "We can send a Federal Express (or UPS) courier right over to pick up your check." The use of these well-known services adds legitimacy to the pitch and convinces many victims who might otherwise have avoided the scam. So when you hear that a courier service will fetch your check, don't let that sway your opinion of the offer's credibility.

Scholarship Scams

College students (perhaps such as yourself) face heavy costs for their schooling. The money pressure makes them easy targets for Snake Oil Sam. In recent years over 300,000 students and their families have been victimized by upwards of 200 scholarship scam artists. Their pitch is devilishly simple. Victims are told that they have qualified for a scholarship that can help them meet school expenses. All they need to do is send in, say, $279 or so for processing fees. Bye-bye money.

So many swindles are based on the eagerness of people to get their hands on needed money, and they're willing to pay good money in advance for the hope of getting the money they seek. Be well aware that legitimate scholarship donors do not ask for money up front. If you become aware of such a pitch, contact the Federal Trade Commission. They're on the lookout for these criminals.

HOME IMPROVEMENTS

Our homes are our castles. They're also among the favorite targets for swindlers. The stakes are large in home improvement frauds and the legal consequences can be devastating. Note the similar patterns that emerge in the following three case histories—stories that might almost be amusing if, in fact, they were not true.

The Squirrels

An elderly widow lived alone in a house surrounded by overhanging oak trees. Although she was financially secure, the loneliness of her days left her an easy mark for any unscrupulous person who could win her confidence.

The home improvement salesman was well trained to win her confidence. She soon told him of a grave concern of hers: she had antique furniture stored in her attic, and she was worried that squirrels that lived in the oak trees would gain access to her attic and gnaw the furniture into ruins. The salesman had a ready solution: he would install "squirrel deflectors" on her roof. These aluminum panels would reflect sunlight; when the squirrels tried to jump from the trees to the roof, they would be blinded by the reflected light and would fall to the ground.

The elderly widow couldn't sign the contract fast enough, and the deflectors were installed. The price: $1,500. The installation was defective; serious damage was done to the roof, and a legitimate roofer had to repair the damage at considerable cost.

The Furnace

An innocent homeowner was approached by a succession of rip-off artists as follows:

Day One: A young lad offers to clean out the homeowner's furnace for a very minimal sum of money. The homeowner agrees, the work is done, and the lad is paid.

Day Two: A "work inspector" asks the homeowner if he can see the furnace. He is supposedly checking up on the work that his furnace-cleaning crew has been doing in the neighborhood.

Day Three: A man representing himself as a "furnace inspector" asks to see the furnace. He tells the homeowner that the furnace has serious cracks in it and that he must "condemn" the furnace.

Day Four: The man from Day Two returns, telling the homeowner that he is sorry to hear that his furnace has been condemned. But he has a wonderful deal on the new furnace that can be installed immediately.

The homeowner buys the whole scam. He signs a contract for the new

furnace. The contract is immediately sold to a finance company. The installers leave the old furnace in the homeowner's yard, and the homeowner has it checked by another furnace company. It is then that he learns that there is nothing at all wrong with the original furnace, but by that time he has no energy to fight the matter any further.

The Model Home

The salesman told the gullible young couple that their house had been chosen as part of an advertising program. They would receive "free" aluminum siding on the house. All they had to do was tell their friends and neighbors who had done this magnificent work. Thereby, the home improvement company would receive many referrals and everybody would be happy. The young couple couldn't sign the contract fast enough.

The work was done and, a month later, to the couple's amazement, they received a bill from a finance company for the first installment on a very expensive contract. Then—too late—they read the contract in detail. It stated that they had to pay for the installation, but that they would receive a discount for every referral that resulted in another installation. If they made enough referrals that resulted in enough contracts, then presumably their own job would have cost them nothing.

Is this a fraud or not? The contract was explicit, but the young couple failed to read it or understand it. Then the siding began to peel, and their "model home" began to look a shambles. They called the improvement company to repair the shoddy work, but the company's phone had been disconnected. The finance company that had purchased their contract was demanding payment. The couple had to hire a lawyer at a considerable cost to void the contract, and had to repair the house at their own expense.

Warning Signals

In addition to the "too good to be true" and "something for nothing" appeals of the home improvement pitch, there are some other aspects of the sales presentation that should cause you to be wary.

The "Perfect" Guarantee

The materials and installation may be accompanied by an "unconditional lifetime money-back" guarantee. The guarantee is only as good as its written statements and only as good as the ability of the guarantor to perform. A guarantee should be spelled out in explicit detail, and you should understand exactly what is and is not guaranteed. A guarantee is meaningless if you can't locate the guarantor.

STRATEGIES FOR SUCCESS

Listen for the "Uh-oh" Music

Filmmakers use this gimmick to increase the audience's sense of anticipation: Just before the monster leaps out of the closet, or just before the bad guys ambush the good guys, you'll hear "uh-oh" music—music that signals that something bad, or frightening, is about to happen. Most of us, if we're reasonably cautious, have a sixth sense that plays "uh-oh" music in our minds before we find ourselves on the brink of being swindled. The melody may differ from time to time, but the lyrics are generally: "This sounds like something too good to be true," or "How far wrong can I go?" "Listen for the "uh-oh" music. It's telling you to beware. And most of the time it's exactly right.

Big Savings

You might be told that the work will save you hundreds of dollars over what it would cost through other contractors. You can never know this for sure unless you have properly drawn plans and specifications and obtained bids from reputable local contractors. Until you have done that, the salesperson's words are nothing more than puffery.

"Will Last Forever"

The salesman might say that materials, such as aluminum siding, are "maintenance-free forever." No substance yet discovered by science and affordable to the average homeowner is maintenance-free forever.

"Sign Up Now or Never"

Salespeople will be very anxious to get you to sign a contract right away. They know that if you don't, and if you have time to think about the deal, they may lose you. This is where the pressure begins. They may try to convince you that getting other prices will be a waste of your time; that their price is certainly the lowest; and that their low price won't be available later. This "now or never" kind of pressure can be convincing. Note well: When you're dealing with legitimate contractors, any contract can wait for a day or so. If you feel that by not signing right away you're losing out on something special, you had best begin preparing yourself for the worst.

Credentials

A reputable home improvement contractor's past history will speak for itself. You can visit his place of business, and you can talk to customers who

have used his services. The shady promoter will make a big fuss about his credentials. He may have become a member of the Chamber of Commerce and he may have established a bank account and lines of credit with local suppliers. But all these credentials don't mean that you're getting good value for your money. It can be difficult to spot the credential-laden con artist. It's necessary to look behind the credentials and try to spot the warning signals.

Brand Names

Home improvement swindlers use the names of national firms to convince customers that they themselves are legitimate. The impression given is that the promoters are in direct alliance with the manufacturers and that such national firms certainly wouldn't condone anything but the highest quality workmanship with regard to their products. Thus the salesperson must be of the highest caliber.

Anyone can buy most of these name-brand products. Many homeowners have been bilked, believing that the contractor will use such brand-name products, only to find that inferior materials were used.

How to Avoid Home Improvement Rackets

Unless you are absolutely certain of a contractor's integrity, follow these steps to avoid being swindled on a home improvement project:

1. Do not sign any home improvement contracts unless you have firm, clear, detailed plans and specifications.
2. Do not sign any contracts until you have comparable bids from other licensed contractors based on those plans and specifications.
3. Do not sign any contracts until you have had the documents checked by an attorney.
4. Do not sign any home improvement contracts until you have discussed with your banker the overall financing of the project.
5. Be aware of state and federal laws that give you the right to rescind (cancel) a contract, particularly if it involves your giving a mortgage on your property to the other party. See the truth-in-lending law in chapter 13.

If you want the job done right and you want to get the most for your money, there are no shortcuts around these steps. It is a lot of work, but when you are spending thousands of dollars and risking damage to your house if you hire unqualified people, it is worth the effort.

INVESTMENT SCHEMES

"Here's the deal, with a rock-solid guarantee: You give me your money—$1,000, $5,000, $10,000, whatever—and if at any time you're unsatisfied with what I'm doing with it, just let me know and I'll immediately return the unused portion thereof."

Who would fall for an offer like that? You'd be surprised. When it comes to the area of investments—making your money grow—greed and gullibility reach their peak, and the opportunities for fraudulent activities are infinite. The fast-buck artists promise instant fortunes and huge tax savings in stocks, commodities, gold, silver, gemstones, land, and virtually anything else that might capture a victim's attention. You might be solicited through the mail, through advertising, or through the Internet but one of the most common media used by investment promoters is the telephone.

The Boiler Room

In a boiler room operation, fast-talking, hard-driving salespersons telephone would-be victims across the country, offering their latest miracle for getting wealthy. How do they get your name? Probably from mailing lists: If you subscribe to any financial periodicals or if you have bought any money-related books through the mail or the internet, your name will be on those lists, sold by the list owner.

Following is a sample—with little exaggeration—of what you're likely to hear if you receive a telephone call from a boiler room operation:

"Good morning, Mr. Rosefsky, this is J. Fairly Nicely of Mammoth Investments on Wall Street. I'd like to tell you how you can double your money within six months. Would you be interested in hearing that? . . . Mammoth has been authorized to sell stock in Amalgamated International—you've heard of them, of course—they've just discovered one of the world's largest linoleum deposits, and mining of the linoleum is expected to start next week. I'm authorized to offer you 500 shares at $10 per share, but the offer is good only for the next hour. Now get this: We know for a fact that the big brokerage firm Merrill-Lynch-Shearson-Webber is going to the market with a public offering price of $20 per share. You'll double your money, but you've got to buy *now*. Could you hold on just a moment, my other phone is ringing . . . (You now hear him supposedly talking on another phone.) . . . Yes, Mr. Gates, we still have some shares left in the linoleum venture. How many would you like? . . . Yes, Mr. Gates . . . 10,000 shares at $10 apiece . . . you've got it. Now Mr. Rosefsky, as I was saying, I just sold 10,000 shares, so I can offer you only 300, but if you really want the 500, maybe I can arrange it. . . . You seem hesitant; is there any reason why you wouldn't want to double your money?"

Yes, people do run to their checkbooks and send money to J. Fairly Nicely and his ilk without hesitation or fear. And that's probably the last they'll ever see of their money. But that's not the last they'll hear of J. Fairly Nicely, for he'll sell their name to other boiler room operations and, some other day, in some other way, they'll be offered a partnership in a veal farm, a future interest in a grove of velcro trees, or syndication rights on a herd of prize-winning naugahydes.

The pitchman's spiel is so frenetic that it doesn't give the victims time to think about anything other than doubling their money. If the would-be victims did stop to think, the first thought might be: "If this deal is so good, how come you're selling it to me? Why don't you just keep it all yourself?" If that question is asked, the answer will be: "I've hocked my house, my wife, my kids, and my gold fillings to raise every penny I could to buy into this. I can't buy it all, but I'm buying all I can." He may even sound all choked up at this point.

Your best defense against the wiles of the boiler room operator is to take advantage of a technical device built into your telephone. It's called the hang-up button. It works like a charm.

Ponzis and Pyramids

Charles Ponzi was a hustler who plied his skills in Boston during the 1920s. He so popularized an ancient scheme that it has carried his name ever since—the Ponzi scheme. It was simple and straightforward, and it attracted victims like a magnet. It worked like this:

Ponzi told victims, "You give me $100 today, and in 30 days I'll give you back $120." Thirty days later he did just that. His initial investment of $20 paid off, since now his believers would do exactly what he said. "Want to try again for another 30 days?" The first wave of investors took the plunge again. Ponzi had no trouble soliciting a second wave, and he used their money to pay off the first wave. Then he would solicit a third wave, and use their money to pay off the second wave, and so on.

In a Ponzi scheme new investors are constantly solicited and their money is used to pay off older investors. Keeping the investors happy keeps the money pouring in, but at some point the promoter will skip.

Closely related to the Ponzi scheme is the pyramid scheme, which is the basis for chain letters and multilevel distributorships. The promoters who start these schemes can make money, but at the risk of jail sentences, for the schemes can be illegal. Here's how the concept works: You have to pay money to someone to get in on the action. You are then entitled to seek money from others below you in the pyramid. As new players pay you, they, in turn, solicit others. This might involve a simple exchange of money. Or it might involve a business venture in which participants receive territories or licensing rights.

Participants succeed depending on how well they enlist subparticipants. If you carry the concept to its logical conclusion, you can quickly see how foolish it is. For example: You buy into a scheme that requires you to enlist ten other people. Each of those ten other people must then enlist ten additional people, and so it goes. If you carry this out to the tenth level down, 10 billion people must be involved in the pyramid for everyone to be satisfied. That's double the population of the entire earth.

Pyramid schemes collapse because they run out of people who are willing to participate, and the victims find that their names never move high enough on the list to recoup their investment.

Who Can You Trust?

Across the nation, talk radio has become a vehicle for all sorts of brainwashing activities, political, psychological and, in frightening dimensions, financial. People hear advice given on the radio, and for some unfathomable reason they take it as gospel. I have personal experience in this field. For ten years I hosted a financial call-in show in Los Angeles, and it never ceased to amaze me how much personal information people would give to me—a stranger—on the air while tens of thousands of other strangers listened in, and how avidly they followed my advice. My wife is a psychotherapist, and she is equally amazed at how the instant-shrink given out over the airwaves is gobbled up by the public, and how dangerous that can be: What's good for Pat from Peoria in two minutes of chat can be catastrophic for others who follow the same advice.

One popular radio talk show host whose program was carried daily for fifteen years in almost 200 stations recently pleaded guilty to nine felony charges, including fraud and conspiracy, for misleading his listeners to the tune of more than $21 million. Among his dirty deeds on the air: Unbeknownst to his listeners, he was paid to tout investments that he knew were worthless. He claimed that he had investigated various ventures when in fact he had not. He became involved with telephone pitchmen to further urge his listeners to part with their money in various schemes. He urged listeners to invest in certain precious metals by claiming falsely that he had put his own money into those metals. And before all of these felony counts, he had pleaded guilty to perjury and tax evasion charges. This was not a nice person, but he had the attention and respect of millions of listeners, and countless others who got hot tips from those listeners.

Who can you trust? Never, never make an investment that you learned about through the media—print, broadcast, Internet, mail, e-mail, or whatever-else-is-yet-to-be-invented—without doing your own independent investigation and then getting at least two other opinions from reputable people in that business.

LEISURE AND LUXURIES

Land Frauds

Will Rogers once said, "Land is the best investment there is cuz they ain't going to print no more of it." Tens of thousands of people have taken that remark seriously and have lost uncounted hundreds of millions of dollars on land swindles. They may not have realized that Will Rogers was a comedian, and this statement was one of his biggest jokes.

Land fraud schemes flourished in the 1970s and then slowed down as the impact of a newly created federal agency—the Office of Interstate Land Sales Regulation—began to be felt. Unscrupulous salespeople sold unwitting victims worthless swampland in Florida and barren desert in Arizona under the guise of "future retirement communities," "vacation rancheros," and just plain double-your-money-in-a-hurry investment opportunities.

Time Sharing

The swindlers didn't stop just because of the creation of a new federal agency. Many of the land salespeople switched to a new concept that emerged in the 1970s and 1980s called "time sharing." Time sharing is legitimate. However, abuses have been considerable. In a typical time-sharing situation, you buy the right to use a vacation facility for one or two weeks per year. The sales pitches are very high-pressure affairs.

Abuses occur when the facilities are not built in accordance with the original promises, when the facilities are never built at all, when the facilities are so poorly managed that you can't enjoy them, and when you learn that six other families have been sold the same space for the same time that you thought you had exclusive use of it. Promoters lure buyers to the sales meetings by promising what seem to be expensive gifts, such as television sets, automobiles, and free travel opportunities. Often, however, after you've sat through a two-hour presentation, you find that the gift is a cheap, perhaps worthless, electronic gadget. (Chapter 3 contains more information on time sharing.)

Vacation Ripoffs

It's hard to say no to an offer of a "free" vacation in some exotic place: plane fare, hotel room, rent-a-car, meals all included, plus $1,000 cash to spend as you wish! All you have to do is pay a $250 registration fee up front. That secures your airline ticket and hotel room, and it's fully refundable when you

check in. What have you go to lose? $250 is what you've got to lose if you fall for this scam—and more, if you give the caller your credit card number. Your common sense may tell you to stay away from such a deal, but when they offer to send a Federal Express courier around to pick up your check, that may just convince you to take the plunge. After all, if Federal Express is involved . . . ?

All That Glitters . . .

Gold, silver, and precious gems have been the subject of fraudulent schemes that show no sign of abating. Examples include:

- **Counterfeit coins** Countless counterfeit gold coins have been circulated across the nation. Speculators have snapped them up without making any attempt to verify their legitimacy. When those speculators dig out the phony coins to sell, they're in for severe disappointment if buyers recognize that the coins are phony.
- **Gold-painted lead** Tens of millions of dollars were lost by eager gold investors who dealt with companies that promised future deliveries of gold bullion. The investors had to pay up front, but the future deliveries never took place. In many cases investors learned that the bars of supposed gold sitting in the promoters' vaults were nothing more than lead covered with gold paint.
- **Junk gems** Tons of worthless stones were passed off to gullible buyers as valuable rubies, sapphires, emeralds, and diamonds. Intriguing ads made it appear that phenomenal bargains could be had in these stones. To make matters worse, once the junk gem buyers had completed their mail order transactions, their names were sold to other sucker lists. The more sucker lists your name appears on, the sooner you'll fall for another scheme.

SNAKE OIL SAM'S MISCELLANEA

Advance Fee Loan Schemes

Snake Oil Sam is adept at filling his pockets through a pitch known as the advance fee loan scheme. Those who need money and who are having difficulty borrowing it from their bank are easy prey for this rip-off. The scheme promises that you'll receive the loan you need if you pay a sizable amount of money up front. Once the up-front money is paid, the swindler disappears with your money.

Credit Repair Clinics

Credit repair clinics appeal to people who have more debt than they can handle or bad credit histories. Unscrupulous credit repair clinics promise to relieve you of your debt problems, for a large sum of money, of course. As you can guess at this point, the up-front money you pay disappears without your getting any benefit from it.

Home Equity Loan Swindles

If borrowers give lenders mortgages on their homes in order to borrow money, the interest paid on these loans can be tax deductible. Such transactions are known as home equity loans. (See chapter 12 for more details.) Borrowers who don't think they can meet the lending criteria of banks may be lured into paying unconscionable fees and interest in order to obtain such loans from private, nonbank lenders. And if repayment is not made properly, unscrupulous lenders will be swift in starting foreclosure proceedings, which could cost the borrowers dearly.

Health Insurance Scams

Employers are frightened by increasing health care costs, yet they don't want to give up their plans for fear of losing valued employees. Enter the con artist selling phony health insurance plans that feature low costs and generous benefits. The employer pays the initial premiums, which quickly disappear into Snake Oil Sam's vast bank account. Doctors and hospitals end up holding the bag, having provided services in the honest belief they'd get paid. And employees end up uninsured, and perhaps uninsurable.

The Double Whammy

Pity the poor victims of the double whammy. They've already lost money in one swindle. Now they've been approached by the "Federal Consumer Protection Service" (or some other such phony but governmental sounding agency), which offers to recover the money they lost in the first swindle. That's right, they have to pay a hefty fee up front to get this service. If you don't know the outcome by now, please send me your name and address; I have a treasure map you might want to buy.

STRATEGIES FOR SUCCESS

Protect Yourself with Second and Third Opinions

If someone is trying to sell you something, no matter how convincing the sales pitch may sound, you must remember that the seller stands to benefit from making the sale. Maybe the seller will benefit more than you, the buyer. This can be especially so if what's being pitched is a fly-by-night investment scheme. Before you part with your money, or before you sign a contract, get a second opinion on the matter from someone who is not selling anything and who has no ax to grind. Protect yourself further by getting a third opinion. The more money at stake, the more this strategy will protect you.

WHAT TO DO ABOUT IT

Exercise 4.2

The sad fact is that if you do become a victim of a fraudulent scheme, there's little chance you'll get your money back unless you're willing to spend a lot of time and a lot more money on legal fees. And even if you are willing to spend money on legal fees, you can't sue someone you can't find: the con artist knows how to disappear quickly and totally.

Even though the chances of getting your money back may be slim, you still should take action if you believe you've been defrauded. If nothing else, your action may help put a stop to the fraud, thus benefiting your fellow citizens. And if they do the same, their actions will benefit you. Here are the main places to file complaints:

Federal Trade Commission

The Federal Trade Commission (FTC) is an agency that deals with deceptive business practices. FTC officials emphasize, however, that they do not represent individual consumers.

The FTC does not have the staff or the funds to investigate every complaint that comes to its attention. When there are enough complaints against a company, the investigative staff will look into it. If the FTC has reason to believe that a deceptive practice has occurred, the agency calls this to the attention of the alleged offender and attempts to work out a "consent order." A consent order is a document in which the alleged offender promises not to do what he has been accused of doing but does not admit that he was guilty of doing it. If he does violate the consent order, serious punishment can follow.

From the time that consumer complaints start trickling in until the time a consent order is obtained, many months can elapse. If an out-and-out

fraudulent activity has been underway, the perpetrator may long since have vanished by the time the consent order is issued.

The FTC can function only if it gets input from the public. Although the victim of fraud may derive little direct benefit from reporting the case to the FTC, doing so does help the agency in its attempts to bring such practices to an end.

The Postal Service

Contact the Mail Fraud Division of the U.S. Postal Service if you suspect that the U.S. mails have been used to perpetrate a fraud. As with the FTC, the postal service cannot track down every complaint. The more complaints there are on a given matter, the better chance the Postal Service has of obtaining a satisfactory conclusion.

State and Local Governmental Agencies

All fifty states have some form of consumer protection office. Frequently, it's associated with the attorney general's office. Many large cities also have consumer protection agencies. As with the aforementioned federal agencies, lack of money deters these agencies from direct aid to the victim of a fraud, but they should be contacted anyway, immediately, and with all pertinent details. If there is any hope at all of apprehending the promoters, your local police or sheriff's office should also be contacted.

Your Local Newspapers and Broadcast Services

Newspapers, radio stations, and television channels throughout the nation have increasingly reported on consumer fraud. These reports are provided at considerable expense by the media as a public service. Very often they're able to resolve matters right on the spot.

Better Business Bureaus

Better Business Bureaus can be helpful before the fact. A call to your local BBB prior to a transaction might disclose whether the firm you're dealing with has a record of complaints with the bureau. BBB personnel might give you general guidelines as to types of suspect business endeavors. The BBB might also provide arbitration services to help you iron out a dispute you have with a local business. If you're dealing with a business located in another city, you should contact the Better Business Bureau in that city to de-

termine whether the firm has a clean record. Understand that if a business has a clean record with the BBB, it does not necessarily mean that all is on the up and up. The clever con artists will know how to keep a BBB record clear and will also time activities cleverly enough so that he or she can be out of town before the complaints begin hitting the BBB office.

Financial Institutions

Banks, savings and loan associations, credit unions, and consumer finance companies are all actively involved on a day-to-day basis with the flow of IOUs generated from all kinds of business activities. If a deceptive practice is under way, an alert to these institutions could bring an end to the activity. Such institutions might be buying fraudulently induced IOUs, before anyone is aware that a fraud is in the works. The sooner the institutions know of it, the sooner they can stop buying the IOUs, and that can be the death knell for the fraudulent endeavor.

Your financial institution can also help you if you consult it before you sign any contracts. An astute loan officer might spot trouble that you missed.

Small Claims Court

Your local small claims court can assist in settling a claim of fraudulent or improper business practices *if* you can locate the party who has wronged you. Small claims courts differ from place to place, but, in general, you do not need a lawyer to represent you. If the amount of money involved in a claim exceeds the court's limit, it will not hear your case. Contact your local court to determine their rules and procedures.

YOUR BEST DEFENSE

No one is immune to the wiles of Snake Oil Sam. Your common sense is your best defense against losing money. To successfully manage your finances, heed the following cautions:

1. Analyze your needs and desires before you make a commitment to buy anything.
2. Obtain a basic knowledge of the product you're seeking to buy.
3. Compare the product you're interested in with that offered by other manufacturers and retailers.
4. Study carefully the guarantee behind the product, as well as the reputation of the manufacturer and retailer.

5. Realistically analyze your financial ability to buy the item, and shop carefully for financing arrangements.

6. Take prompt and appropriate action in the event the product or service does not live up to your expectations or to the representations made by the seller.

 PERSONAL ACTION WORKSHEET

Fraud-avoidance Techniques

This is a two-part exercise. First, answer the following questions—*before* you enter into any dealing with persons whose reputations are uncertain or unknown. Since you have read this chapter and answered the questions honestly, your choice should be clear.

Second, write down for future reference the telephone numbers of the indicated consumer protection sources.

1. If I'm not satisfied with the product or service I get from this person, what assurance do I have that I'll be able to get my money back?

   _____

2. Does this deal sound too good to be true or as though I'm going to be getting something for nothing? _____

3. Am I being pressured to sign up right away, or to buy right away, lest I lose the chance forever? _____

4. If the secret method (or investment technique, etc.) is so good, why is the salesperson selling it to me? Could it be that he or she will make more money by selling it to me than I can make by buying it?

   _____

5. Have I checked with the appropriate consumer protection sources to learn what I can about this company? _____

6. Do I really need the product or service that's being sold? And can I get it through other sources without any worry about satisfaction?

   _____

Consumer Protection Source	Telephone Number
☐ Better Business Bureau	_____
☐ City, state consumer protection agency	_____
☐ Small claims court	_____
☐ Consumer journalists (radio, TV, newspaper)	_____
☐ Federal Trade Commission (nearest office)	_____

CONSUMER ALERT

Learning to Say No Can Save $$$

Many good products are sold door-to-door, but there are also many flim-flams conducted in that mode. Your best protection is to learn how to say no. An old friend, best known as Sybil the Intrepid, had a way of saying no with such style and flair that anyone can benefit from her tactics. Here is how Sybil the Intrepid once handled a door-to-door vacuum cleaner sales-person:

> *Sybil:* Oh, I've heard about your product, and I understand it's simply mar-velous. I'd like you to give me a demonstration right now, but first I must see your identity card.
>
> *Salesperson* (enthusiastically): No problem. Here's my card from the com-pany.
>
> *Sybil:* No, that's not what I meant. I mean your *identity* card.
>
> *Salesperson* (now slightly flustered and confused): Well, here's my driver's li-cense . . . my voter registration card . . . my library card . . .
>
> *Sybil* (deceptively calm): No, no . . . those aren't what I mean. I mean your *identity* card. Your card that verifies that you aren't a member of the Commu-nist party.
>
> *Salesperson* (now almost apoplectic): But I've never heard of such a thing. I don't have such a card.
>
> *Sybil* (with a straight face that would make your hair curl): There, there now . . . that's all right. You just come back anytime with your proper identity card and I'd love to have you demonstrate your vacuum cleaner. We just can't let Communists in the house. You understand, I'm sure. 'Bye now. (The door closes ever so gently.)

UPS & DOWNS   *The Economics of Everyday Life*

Why Scams Come and Go

Home improvement scams predominate in the spring and summer months. Holiday shopping cons and counterfeit goods are most evident in November and December. But many other kinds of fraudulent activities ebb and flow with changes in economic trends.

High interest rates and other conditions that make borrowing difficult—such as lenders going through an overly cautious phase—stimulate the advance fee loan scheme and similar abuses. Lenders offering "eeezee credit" pop up out of nowhere. Some demand fees up front; some charge exorbitant interest; some demand more collateral than need be pledged; some do all of the above. Be prepared for tough dealings if you don't pay it back as agreed.

Low interest rates, and/or rising inflation will spawn a host of investment scams. This is what the victims hear: "Because of today's low interest rates, your hard-earned savings accounts aren't paying you what they should. . . . And/or, rising inflation is eating up too much of your investment earnings. . . . Follow me, and I will lead you to investments with higher earnings and/or less erosion by inflation. . . . Trust me, for I am only interested in your well-being." At the very least, following that siren lure will result in your money being exposed to higher risk. At the worst, the money could disappear. If you leave your money where it is, in a safe harbor, it might not earn as much as it could, but at least it will be there when you need it.

Fads and trends can include collectibles such as plates, dolls, figurines, sports cards, and memorabilia. The more knowledgeable get in early, knowing how to buy and sell wisely. The more naive and gullible get in late, when the good bargains have been had, and the shysters are creating items for sale that will prove worthless.

Legal loopholes and lax enforcement   The greatest financial debacle in American history—the savings and loan crisis—was largely the result of fraudulent appraisals and fraudulent accounting. It came about because of government laxity in regulating lenders' activities, and then its failure to stop the guilty parties quickly enough. The victims—American taxpayers—will foot the bill for a generation or two.

? WHAT IF . . . ?

How would you deal with these real life possibilities?

1. You learn that a friend is involved in a scam—not as a victim, but as a perpetrator. This person is naíve and without malice, but he or she can get into serious trouble if the authorities catch up with the con artists. Your friend is making good money in the endeavor and is unaware of the danger. How can you help your friend without exposing him or her to legal problems?

2. A stranger telephones you and very cleverly gets you to divulge your telephone credit card number or your bank credit card number. A few weeks later it dawn on you that you have blundered in giving out your number. What can/should you do to protect yourself against having unauthorized charges rung up on your account?

3. Your mail contains a packet announcing that you might have won $10 million in a Grand National Sweepstakes. You're encouraged to subscribe to magazines, but you need not make a purchase to win the prizes. However, you do subscribe to a few magazines, hoping that that will improve your changes of winning. When you do this, you alter your normal name slightly (spell out your middle name, for example, or misspell your last name) so you can trace how many other sucker lists your name will be sold to over the next year or two. Keep track. How many?

NUMBER CRUNCHERS

Do the calculations to make decisions in these real-life possibilities.

1. You receive a chain/pyramid letter instructing you to send $10 to the name at the top of the list of five names, then send copies of this letter to the other names, removing the name on top and putting yours at the bottom. Soon, the letter promises, as your name reaches the top of the list, you'll receive $10 from each of five other people—a total of $50 for your $10 investment. As each level of mailing multiplies the number of names by five, calculate how many levels there would be before every person living in your city would be on one of the lists. (Remember, this activity is illegal. Don't really do it. Just do the calculations.)

2. Identify a few "900" telephone pitches. (They abound on late-night cable TV stations and in tabloid newspapers.) Assume that each number receives 1,000 calls every day from all around the nation and that each call lasts 10 minutes. Based on their quoted rates, calculate how much revenue each "900" advertiser generates every day, week, month, and year.

FOR BETTER OR FOR WORSE

Things beyond our control often impact our personal and financial well-being, for better or for worse. Some are more predictable than others. How would you be affected if the following real-life phenomena happened? Could you have seen it coming? What steps could you have taken to minimize damage or maximize advantage? The better able you are to anticipate and recognize these forces, the better equipped you are to deal with them.

1. Hoping to reap a bonanza of thousands of dollars, you've put $300 into what turns out to be a pyramid scheme. The promoters promise to give you your money back, but before they do the police arrest them and bust the whole scam.

2. Interest rates have gone up, and banks are cutting back on their lending. You need to borrow $5,000 urgently. A stranger calls and tells you where you can get the money you need if you're willing to pay a small fee up front.

3. A site on the Web offers a hard-to-resist tip on the stock market. A friend of yours tells you she made a bundle on it.

Transportation: Buying, Financing, and Insuring Your Cars

You show me someone who's drowning in debt, and I'll show you someone who bought too much car, and whose payments for it are like concrete shoes.

Robert Rosefsky

Urban sprawl is a very accurate way of describing today's typical U.S. city, whether large or small. We have a lot of space to use, and we've used it. In the process, we've put a lot of distance between our homes, our places of work, our shopping centers, and our recreational facilities. The cost of moving about is a serious matter and must be taken into account in anyone's financial planning. This chapter will help you solve the common problems you face in trying to keep your transportation expenses in line:

- How to make the best choice when you buy a car
- How to deal with car dealers
- What kind of financing arrangement is best for you
- How much car insurance you should have, and how much it will cost
- What your car warranty is worth
- Leasing as an alternative to buying a car

THE COST OF GETTING FROM POINT A TO POINT B

The average cost of owning, financing, operating, and insuring an automobile is about 35¢ for each mile driven. This means:

- If you drive a mile or two to pick up a loaf of bread at the supermarket, the cost of getting to the market and back can be higher than the cost of the bread itself.
- That inexpensive treat of not so many years ago—the weekend drive in the country—can now cost you $20, $30, $40.
- If you drive a twenty-mile round-trip commute to work, it's costing you $35 per *week* to get to your job and back.

In short, driving from point A to point B is an expensive proposition. And new technology (air bags, anti-lock brakes, etc.) and new gadgets (cruise control, tilt steering wheels, etc.) continue to add to the cost.

Decades of conditioning have patterned much of our lives around the car: getting to work, shopping, school, recreation all depend largely on the availability of a car. In many cities, mass transit provides a less costly (and often less convenient) alternative. For the most daring, motorcycles and mopeds provide less costly (and less safe) transportation. For the energetic, bicycling, walking, and jogging may be the best alternatives of all.

For most people, driving is a major budget item, and an increase or decrease in driving can have a definite bearing on the budget. If you are choosing a dwelling or seeking a job, the cost of commuting must definitely be calculated.

As noted previously, a twenty-mile daily round-trip commute can cost $35 a week—$150 per month. That $150 per month in commuting costs is what you'd pay on $18,000 worth of mortgage at a 10 percent fixed annual interest rate. In other words, if you didn't have to drive to and from work, that $150 per month in commuting costs could be used to pay off an $18,000 higher mortgage on your home.

Your overall ability to make ends meet and manage your money prudently requires that you keep a tight control on all your transportation costs.

Figuring the Cost per Mile

The 35¢ per-mile figure noted earlier is, of course, an approximation. It's based on a small-sized car being driven 15,000 miles per year and kept for four years. It takes into account the following:

- The depreciation (difference between the purchase price and what it might be worth when you later sell it or trade it in)
- Operating and maintenance costs (including tune-ups, oil, tires, lubrication, and average necessary repairs)

- Operating and maintenance costs (including tune-ups, oil, tires, lubrication, and average necessary repairs)
- Interest (presuming that the car is financed for an average of three years)
- Taxes and fees (including sales tax, property taxes, registration, titling fee, license costs, necessary inspections)
- Insurance (public liability, collision, comprehensive)
- Gasoline (the amount can vary considerably, depending on your driving habits and the maintenance of your automobile)

The following factors will affect the cost per mile of driving your car:

Equipment

Cost, weight, and usage of optional equipment can have a distinct bearing on your overall operating costs. Example: An air-conditioning unit is one of the more expensive optional extras that can be installed in a car. The cost can exceed $700. In addition, the cost of registration, insurance, and interest will increase accordingly. The use of the air conditioning can also decrease your gas mileage by as much as 12 percent (see Table 5–1).

Maintenance

Proper, regular tuneups can improve your gas mileage by almost 13 percent (see Table 5–1). Proper tire inflation and rotation can also improve gas mileage as well as the overall ridability of the car. And a periodic troubleshooting checkup by a reliable garage can help prevent costly problems before they occur.

TABLE 5–1   How Speed, Air Conditioning, and Tuneups Can Affect Gas Mileage

Miles per Gallon	Speed				
	30 mph	40 mph	50 mph	60 mph	70 mph
With air conditioner on	18.14	17.51	16.42	15.00	13.17
With air conditioner off	20.05	19.71	18.29	16.23	14.18
MPG increase with air conditioner off	10.5%	12.6%	11.4%	8.33%	7.7%
Before tuneup	19.3	18.89	17.29	15.67	13.32
After tuneup	21.33	21.33	18.94	17.40	15.36
MPG increase after tuneup	10.5%	12.9%	9.54%	11.04%	15.3%

Source: U.S Department of Transportation, 1994.

Insurance

The number of cars on your auto policy, the number of drivers, and the safety record of the drivers can have a major effect on your car insurance costs. The section on car insurance later in this chapter explores these matters in greater detail.

Driving Habits

Hot-rodding, drag racing, speeding, and jackrabbit starting can diminish your gas mileage and also create more wear and tear on the basic mechanical aspects of the car. It may seem like fun, but it's going to cost you.

Knowledge

Knowing how to buy right, finance right, and insure right can definitely save you money. the more you know about the care and maintenance of your car, and the more of it that you can do yourself, the more money you'll save. A car care book or a short course in basic car maintenance can be an investment that pays for itself many times over each year.

BUYING A CAR

With individual tastes, habits, needs, and budgets as different as they are, there is no firm rule of thumb that describes the "best" buy for anyone's dollars. And with an almost infinite variety of cars to choose from—differing in age, condition, size, equipment, and cost—even general guidelines are difficult to set forth. The following considerations, however, weighed carefully as you shop, can help you find the vehicle that's right for your needs and for your budget.

Needs versus Desires

Exercise 5.1

You must clearly distinguish between your automotive *needs* and your automotive *desires*. The difference between the two can cost you thousands of dollars, with little to show for that money but some chrome, vinyl, and extra things that can go wrong in the car. For generations, American car buyers have been conditioned to believe that the automobile is a reflection of an individual's power, prestige, sex appeal, and success. If you can afford to succumb to that kind of hypnosis, feel free. The other side of the coin—never advertised by automotive manufacturers—is that when people find themselves in a financial jam, very often it's because they're paying far more for their car than their budget realistically can allow. If you're willing

to sacrifice in other areas (housing, clothing, food, future savings, recreation) for the sake of a more luxurious car, that's your choice. Just be aware of the potential consequences.

In examining your automotive needs, be honest with yourself and with your budget. Three factors can boost the price of an automobile, and you must be careful that the price of your automobile does not exceed your ability to pay. These three factors are size, *flair*, and optional extras.

Size

How big a car do you really need for the bulk of your driving purposes? Larger cars cost more than comparably equipped smaller cars and can consume considerably more fuel. Can you justify a larger car because of your use of it—such as extensive traveling for business purposes or frequent hauling or children or cargo? If you don't need a large vehicle much of the time, consider purchasing a smaller car and renting a large vehicle for those rare occasions when you might need one.

Flair

Flair refers to the sportiness, the "muscle," the luxurious aspects of driving that many people crave. Make no mistake—flair is very expensive, and it won't get you from point A to point B any more safely or quickly than a basic set of wheels will. Your choice. Your money.

Optional Extras

In fact, optional extras aren't really optional. They're already built into the car, and you can't have them taken out. Optional extras can add $3,000 and more to the basic cost of the car, and many of them may be of marginal value. Racing stripes, fancy wheel covers, vinyl roofs, luxurious upholstery,

and an assortment of electronic gadgets provide very little in the way of essential transportation. In many cases, they just provide something extra to break down and need repair, usually after the warranty has expired.

New versus Used

Exercise 5.2

A used car in good mechanical condition can provide you with decent transportation for many years and many tens of thousands of miles—at a much lower cost than a similar new model. Note the qualification "in good mechanical condition." A prerequisite to buying a used car is a thorough analysis by a responsible mechanic. The buyer of a used car has no way of knowing what accidents or operating problems the car had in the past. The seller may not divulge all that is known about the car's history. Indeed, if the car has had more than one prior owner, the current owner may not have any idea about the car's history. The cost of a thorough inspection can be a very inexpensive way of finding out whether you're getting a good or a bad deal, but the bad deal will end up costing you many times what the inspection will cost.

If you buy a used car from a private individual, you'll take it on an as-is basis, unless the seller agrees to some sort of private warranty, which should be in writing. See the discussion on warranties, later in this chapter, for details on used car warranties.

Shopping Criteria

Since this textbook is devoted to money handling and not car handling, we'll leave the details of road testing and comfort testing up to the individual reader. Here are some of the financial considerations to be borne in mind when shopping for a new car.

STRATEGIES FOR SUCCESS

Alternative Sources of Good Used-car Buys

Used-car dealers and private parties are the common places to buy used cars. The dealers can be expensive. The private parties might not reveal hidden defects. (Dealers might also hide hidden defects, but reputable ones frequently offer at least some minimum warranty, which can give you some protection.) You could do better on a used-car purchase at a car rental agency's disposal lot. Major agencies, such as Hertz and Avis, sell rental cars to the public after they've been driven for a certain distance and time. These cars may have been better maintained than privately owned cars, and they may have decent warranties. Check wholesalers, too: middlemen who take trade-ins from new-car dealers and sell them to used-car lots. Don't expect any warranties, but the price might be right.

Exercise 5.3

After you've decided what pleases you with respect to size, color, equipment, and handling, refer to the Personal Action Checklist at the end of this chapter for a guide to what you'll get for your money. In addition to the base price, list separately each optional extra and its cost. This will cause you to stop and think twice about the value of those extras and will also give you a better comparison of the total product you're getting for your money.

The dealer will quote you a price that's different from the sticker price, taking into account the value of any car you are trading in. Haggling over the price of a new car is still one of the great old American traditions. The dealers almost expect that you'll haggle, and, if you don't, you could be spending hundreds of dollars more than you have to.

Don't guess: Be precise with each dealer's offerings with respect to warranty, extended service contracts, insurance, and financing terms.

To the extent possible, check the dealer's reputation in the community for service and adjustment of complaints. With respect to service, determine whether he offers pick-up and drop-off when the car is taken in for work, and whether the dealer has loan cars available, and at what price, in case you have to leave your own car there for an extended period.

Games Dealers Play

The automobile business is extremely competitive. Competitiveness breeds anxiety, and that, in turn, may cause dealers to bend the ethics of good business practices in order to win a sale. Some of these practices are illustrated in the following tale. Try to spot the pitfalls as they occur.

You're planning to buy a car, and you've set your heart on a Rammer-Jammer XJKB. You've priced it at two dealerships, which are within a few dollars of each other, and about $4,000 in cash will be required over your old trade-in. You want to try one more dealership, which advertises heavily that they will "meet or beat any deal in town."

You and your spouse take a drive to that dealership one evening. A pleasant chap takes you for a test-drive of the model you've been admiring. You're very impressed with the seeming honesty of this nice fellow, and you're intrigued when he suggests that the trade-in value of your old car might be $1,000 more than what other dealers have quoted you! He explains that this dealer's inventory of used cars is very low and he's offering better deals on trade-ins to build up his inventory. What's more, he thinks the boss has been overcharging too many customers, and he doesn't like people to get a raw deal. Thus, he tells you, he's going to take it upon himself to see that you get the best possible deal available.

He takes you into his office to do some calculating. After a few moments, he looks up at you with a smile. "If I can get the boss to take $3,000 plus your trade-in, would you sign the contract tonight?"

Get Price Quotes in Writing

If you're quoted a price on an automobile, have the salesperson put it in writing. Make sure it's adequately detailed, including any extras, financing terms, down payment, and so on that may be part of the deal. And be certain to have the salesperson indicate—again, in writing—how long this price quote will last. If you go out comparison shopping and return to the original dealer two hours later, you don't want to be told, "Sorry, that price quote was good for only 10 minutes." If they won't put the quote in writing, you have nothing to go on later. And, if they won't put it in writing, maybe it's because they don't want to have to honor it. What does that tell you?

Three thousand! You were almost willing to pay $4,000 for exactly the same car at a different showroom. Of course you'd be willing to take a deal for $3,000. The salesman spots your enthusiasm and proceeds.

"Look," he says, " the boss doesn't like me to approach him unless he's sure the customer will take the deal. Let me fill out the contract showing a $3,000 trade difference, and you give me a good faith check for $50. That way, he knows he's got a firm deal *if* he signs the contract. If he doesn't go for the deal, I'll give you back the contract and your check and you can rip them both up. What have you go to lose?"

You've got nothing to lose, or so you think. You're sitting there planning how you can spend the $1,000 you've just saved and itching to get behind the wheel of the new car that's just a signature away.

"Okay," you say, "fill out the contract and I'll sign it."

He leaves the room with the signed contract and the check, and you and your spouse sit and snicker over the tremendous deal you're getting. "I was ready to pay $4,000, and we're stealing it for $3,000," you say. (There's a little bit of larceny in all of us.)

You sit and wait for 10, then 20, minutes. Just as you're about out of patience, the man sticks his head in the door and says, "I think everything is okay. I'm going to take the car to the service department and get it ready so you can take it home tonight if you want."

Another man enters the room. He is the assistant boss. He tells you that he appreciates how anxious you are to get into that new car. But, sadly, there seems to have been a snag. The pleasant man that you were so fond of has been doing a lousy job for the dealer. As a matter of fact, the assistant boss continues, it seems as though he was off by $1,000 on your deal. He vastly overestimated the value of your trade-in. "We'd love to have you in this car because I know you want to be in it," the assistant boss says, "but we've just got to talk about a $4,000 trade difference, not $3,000." The bubble has burst.

"In the first place," the assistant boss goes on, "we didn't even give your trade car a test-drive. Let me have the keys to it so our service manager can check it out and give you a fair trade-in price." Bewildered, you hand over your keys, and he disappears with them.

You and your spouse debate the matter in the closing room and agree that if you can strike a deal between $3,500 and $4,000, you'd still go for it since it would be better than any of the other quotes you'd been given.

The assistant boss reappears with your contract and you tear it up. "Where's my $50 check?" you ask. "Don't worry," he says, "I'll get it for you in a few minutes. Now, about your deal," he begins. "We've given your trade-in a good look, and it needs a lot of work and new tires. A good deal for us would be $4,300 plus your trade-in, but, since you've been here so long and have been so patient, we can bend some and let you have the new Rammer-Jammer for $4,100."

The grind is beginning to wear you down. You're starting to wonder when you're going to get back your $50 check and the keys to your old car. You're tense now, but you feel that you can get the deal for $3,900, which is still $100 better than the next best deal. You discuss it with your spouse and decide that since you've been here this long, you might as well hang around a little longer and hope the deal can be wrapped up for $3,900.

A few minutes later, salesman number three comes in. This is the boss, and he's high pressure all the way. The hour is getting later, and you're getting more and more tired. The boss now is pushing hard to close you at $4,050, which, as he says, "I'm losing money on."

Then comes the clincher. You again demand your check and your keys, and he informs you that the cashier has left for the night and the check has been locked up. The used-car appraiser has also left for the night and, thinking that your old car had been accepted as a trade-in, he parked it in the lot and locked up the keys in his office. "Don't worry," says the boss, "we can give you a ride home tonight and pick you up in the morning to get your old car and the check. I assure you, there's absolutely no problem. Now, about this deal. . . "

The final thrust: "Look folks, I know how late it's getting, and I want to get out of here as badly as you do. Let me ask you this—if I give you the deal for $4,000, will you take it? Then we'll all go out and have a drink." Resignation has set in, and you agree to the deal. After all, it's still as good as the best deal you had any other place. Wearily, you reach for your pen.

Interwoven throughout this intrigue are four types of sales tactics (Did you recognize them?), which have brought a poor reputation to a small segment of the automobile sales industry. These are:

The Highball

The salesman quotes a much higher trade-in value on your old car than is reasonable, which causes the first strong opening pull on your purse

strings. The opposite of the highball is the lowball, in which the salesman looks at the sticker price on the new car and suggests a too-good-to-be-true discount from that price. The tactic here is to lead you to believe that you're going to get a better deal than you thought possible, all the quicker to get you into the showroom where the heavy pressure can be applied.

The "T.O." or "Takeover" Operation

This is a ploy involving a succession of salespeople ranging from low pressure to high pressure. The first one's job is to soften you and win your confidence. Subsequent salespeople increase the pressure until the closer takes over. The process is designed to wear down your resistance gradually. The first salesman's job was accomplished when he got you to sit down in the closing office, not just in a mood to buy, but with a raging desire to buy, albeit at a price that would later turn out to be impossible. The success of the takeover operation depends on the next phenomenon.

The Bugged Closing Room

It doesn't occur to most people that a closing room might be bugged. This is a devious trick and is not employed by a legitimate dealer. By listening in on your conversations, salespeople know where your soft spots are and how far they can take you. If they determine that you have strong sales resistance, they can always fall back on the following.

The "Disappearing Check" Trick or the "Keys are Locked Up for the Night" Gambit

This is the last straw. By claiming to have "misplaced" something of value, such as a check or car keys, salespeople are, in effect, nailing you to the wall until your resistance breaks. The best way to avoid being trapped in this manner is not to write any checks and to stand by as they test your trade-in car so you can retain the keys until the deal is either made or not made.

If you fall prey to these tactics in your car shopping, you might sign a contract you otherwise wouldn't sign. Even though, in the above case, you thought you got the same deal you could have had elsewhere, that isn't necessarily so. Had you gone back to the other dealers for a follow-up bargaining session, you might have gotten a still better deal. Awareness of these tricks and a willingness to walk away from shady tactics are necessary weapons when shopping for a car. The dealer sells hundreds of cars each month. You buy only one every few years. He knows a lot more about the tricks of bargaining and striking a deal than you do. He's entitled to a fair profit, but that doesn't give him the right to take advantage of you—all of which leads back to the most important point: Know the person with whom you are dealing. There's no substitute for integrity.

Your Old Car: Selling It Yourself versus Trading It In

Exercise 5.4

It's difficult to determine whether you can do better by selling your own used car or by using it as a trade-in on a new purchase. First, check the used-car price directory and used-car lots to see what cars similar to yours are selling for (see Table 5–2). The directory is available at all dealerships and at most banks. Bear in mind that the prices on cars at lots are the asking prices, not necessarily the selling prices. If you can find a buyer who will pay your price, it may be wise to make a deal. But before do, you must go to various dealers to determine the different prices you'd be expected to pay with and without a trade-in.

If you can't find a buyer quickly, you might be in for more headaches than the project is worth. You'll have to advertise the car for sale, and you'll have to be available when interested buyers want to take it for a test-drive. Not only could that be inconvenient; you could feel uncomfortable having a stranger take your car for a good long test-spin.

The way in which sales taxes are calculated can make a big difference in whether you should sell your old car on your own or trade it in to a dealer. You must determine these matters for your locale. (1) If you sell to a private party, are local sales taxes payable? (2) If you trade the car to a dealer and buy a new one, is the sales tax figured on the total cost of the new car, or on the difference between the cost of the new car and the trade-in value of the old car? For example, say the price of a new car is $12,000, the trade-in value of your old car is $4,000, and the sales tax is 7 percent. If the sales tax is figured on the price of the new car, the tax will be $840. If it's figured on the difference ($8,000), the tax will be $560. Do your research accordingly.

How Much Haggling Room Do You Have?

There is no rule of thumb, but here are some broad guidelines. Your haggling room will depend on the value of your trade-in, whether you're fi-

TABLE 5–2   **Abbreviated Listing from Typical Used-Car Price Directory as of Summer 1997**

1995 Chevrolet Model	Trade-In	Market
Cavalier 6 cylinder 2-door convertible	$9,170	$11,185
Corsica 4 cylinder 4-DR sedan	6,000	7,225
Lumina V6 4-door sedan	8,565	10,320
Camaro V8 Z28 2-door convertible	11,815	14,065

Note: Optional extras, destination charges, preparation charges, taxes, and licensing fees not included. Average wholesale and retail prices are for clean, reconditioned cars ready for sale. See separate listings in directory for increase/decreases in price due to equipment, condition, and mileage.

nancing through the dealer (see the next section, "Financing"), and how anxious the dealer is to move his current inventory. Generally speaking, dealers work on a mark-up of about 20 percent. Thus, it might not be unreasonable to expect a discount of 5 to 10 percent off the sticker price. To get much more than 10 percent is going to take some hard bargaining, but if you don't ask for it, they're not going to volunteer it. *Consumer Reports* magazine publishes annual price listings of new model cars, which can serve as a more specific guideline to your bargaining powers. Consult these lists before you go shopping.

When Is the Best Time to Buy?

Late summer and early fall tend to be when dealers are clearing out their old inventory to make room for the new model cars shipped from the factories. There may be a smaller assortment of cars to choose from at this time of year, but there's a strong chance that you will get a better price than you might have earlier in the model year.

This is also a time when dealers tend to sell their demonstrator models—cars that have been driven by employees of the dealership. Demos can be very good bargains. They tend to be well equipped and well taken care of, and many dealerships offer them with full warranty, even though they have been driven for a few thousand miles or more.

FINANCING: DIRECT VERSUS THROUGH THE DEALER

Assuming you have the necessary trade-in or down payment and acceptable credit, most dealers can arrange financing for you right on the spot. You can also make your own financing arrangements through your bank (and in many instances, your car insurance company). Which is better?

It can be very convenient to have the dealer arrange for the financing. It saves you time, but it can cost you extra money. Determine the Annual Percentage Rate (APR) the dealer will charge you for the financing. (See chapter 12 for a more detailed discussion of interest rates and installment loans.) Compare the dealer's APR with that offered by other lenders. The APR is the apples versus apples way of comparing interest rates. Have any APR quote put in writing and signed by the salesperson. If the dealer is charging more for financing, then obviously it wouldn't pay to borrow through the dealership unless there are extenuating circumstances, such as a desire not to increase your borrowing any further at your regular bank.

Exercise 5.5

Dealers can receive benefits from lenders worth hundreds of dollars, depending on the amount of financing involved. Thus, dealers are anxious to arrange financing for you. If you play the game advantageously, you'll let the dealer believe that you're going to do the financing through him before you make a commitment to purchase the car. This is liable to result in a

lower price for the car, since the dealer will anticipate additional profit through the financing. He may, if he suspects your wise buymanship tactics, give you two prices for the car—one if you finance with them; one if you don't. Act accordingly.

Another important advantage in dealing with your own bank is that you are dealing with people who know you and who can help you, should problems arise. If the dealer arranges the financing for you, it may be with a bank or finance company you've never dealt with. In such a case, if you run into problems with lateness or other financial distress, the institution is liable to regard you as little more than a number in their computer, and any help may be hard to come by.

Interest Rate and Rebate Incentives

Exercise 5.6

Dealers often offer incentive plans involving either low interest rates for financing or cash rebates, which will reduce the price of the car. When such opportunities are available, it can be wise to examine their benefits. But the incentives do not necessarily get you the best all-around deal. The incentives might be available on only a limited number of models. And there may be little or no room for haggling over the price on such models. In short, you might end up spending more for a car then you otherwise would have in order to get the incentives.

Wherever you arrange your financing, it's essential that you do not allow the loan to last longer than you expect to own the car. If you expect to trade every three years, you shouldn't finance for more than three years. (See the section on "Credit Abuses" in chapter 12 on how this timing of your loans can be important to you.)

Leasing as an Alternative to Buying

Exercise 5.7

Leasing has become an extremely popular way to acquire a new car. As previously leased cars come back onto the market—when the leases expire and the roughly 75 percent of lessees choose to return the cars to the dealers rather than buy them—there is also a dynamic business in the leasing of used cars.

The main good and bad points of leasing new cars are well known:

- **Basic cost**   Leased cars generally involve a lower down payment and lower monthly payments than purchased cars. But the small print in the leasing ads and contracts can narrow the gap. Read it with care, and add up all the numbers. Note that leasing is subject to a more stringent credit review than normal financing.
- **Purchase option**   At the end of the lease, which may run from two to five years, you'll have an option to buy the car. In a "closed end" lease, which is the most common type, the purchase price will be spelled out in advance. In an "open end" lease the purchase price will

depend on market conditions. Make sure you have the option you want specified in writing. If you don't want to purchase the car you can just walk away from it, after paying any applicable costs noted in the next paragraph.

- **Unanticipated costs** If you want to end a lease before the term is up you might have to pay a hefty early termination fee. Also, whenever you do turn the car in, you have to absorb the cost of any repairs needed—including dings, dents, scrapes, stains, scratches—which can add many hundreds of dollars to your expense. In addition, if you drive the car more miles than the lease allows (usually about 15,000 miles a year) you have to pay an excess mileage fee, which might be 10 to 15 cents a mile.

- **Tax considerations** If you lease a car for personal use, the lease payments are not tax deductible. Neither is the interest on your car loan if the car is for personal use. (A possible exception: If you buy a car with the proceeds of a home equity loan the interest may be deductible. See chapter 12 for more details.) Cars used for business purposes may offer some deductibility for either lease or interest costs. See your tax advisor for the latest regulations.

One of the problems with leasing cars has been the complexities of the lease contracts and the way in which leasing is advertised. Too much misleading information and consumer abuse resulted in an outpouring of complaints from the public. To combat this problem, the Federal Trade Commission issued new regulations that went into effect in October 1997 designed to clarify the language in leasing contracts. All dealers' lease plans must conform to this simple one-page form. Items covered include the specific amounts of down payments and monthly payments, any other charges that are part of the deal, the value of any trade-in, and clear language warning of any early termination penalties that must be paid. The new form will not be required for leases totaling more than $25,000, so *buyer beware* is the order of the day for anyone signing up for the big-ticket items. Others should review this FTC-mandated contract carefully before it's signed.

WARRANTIES

Many manufacturers now offer *limited warranties* on new cars extending for as long as seven years. These limited warranties generally cover the basic drive train and transmission in the car. Many other items, such as power windows, windshield wipers, radio, and dashboard circuits, may still be restricted to a twelve months or 12,000-mile limitation, whichever comes first.

The matter is further confused by the availability of additional warranties that extend beyond the basic manufacturer's warranty. Some of these plans are offered by the manufacturers themselves, and others are offered by private insurance companies. These extra warranties can cost hundreds of

dollars, depending on how many miles and/or how many months they run. Often, the price of these warranties can be negotiated along with the price of the automobile. If you are mechanically inclined or know a good, trustworthy mechanic, the extended warranties may be of less value to you. If you're a novice when it comes to dealing with a broken-down car, the warranty might give you peace of mind. The best bet of all: Take an automotive repair course at your local community college, or buy one of the many good guidebooks on automotive repair. This might not enable you to do your own repairs, but at least you'll be able to determine whether an item can be fixed at minimal cost or whether the $700 estimate the garage gives you is an honest one.

Used car warranties from dealers have traditionally been limited to thirty days, which offers little protection to buyers. Some have no warranties at all: you take the car as-is.

But many manufacturers now have extended warranties for used cars, particularly for the growing number of formerly leased cars that are being returned to dealerships. Before these expanded warranties are offered, the cars are refurbished as needed, and thusly certified by the dealer. The cost of the refurbishment and the cost of the warranty will be passed along to the buyer. Also, in some cases, buyers must pay a certain portion—a deductible per repair—as part of the deal. The warranties are further limited to cars of a certain age or maximum mileage. In other words, if a car's age or mileage exceeds the set limit, it will not be eligible for the expanded warranty.

Table 5–3 illustrates a sampling of expanded warranties that may be available on certified used cars. Note that the length of the expanded warranties differs considerably from maker to maker. What does this program offer? By paying for the refurbishment and the warranty on an older car, you could get a lot more vehicle for the same money as you'd pay for a new car, and with a reasonably good warranty standing behind it. For example, you might get an older certified Lexus or Infiniti for the same price you'd pay for a new Chevrolet. The choice might not be easy to make, but at least there is a choice.

TABLE 5–3   Used Car Warranties from Selected Manufacturers in Late 1997

Make	Maximum Age/Mileage	Expanded Warranty	Deductible
Ford	3 yrs./50,000 mi.	1 yr./12,000 mi.	$100
G.M.*	3 yrs./60,000 mi	1 yr./12,000 from purchase or 4 yrs/50,000 mi. total	-0-
Toyota**	4 yrs./55,000 mi.	6 yrs./100,000 mi.	$ 50
Honda	3 yrs./60,000 mi.	6 yrs./72,000 mi.	-0-
Volvo	5 yrs./75,000 mi.	1 yr./12,000 mi.	$ 50
Acura	4 yrs./50,000 mi.	5 yrs./62,000 mi.	-0-

*Includes Buick, Chevrolet, Geo, GMC, Oldsmobile, and Pontiac.
**Warranty is on power train only. Broader coverage available at extra cost.

AUTOMOBILE INSURANCE

Automobile insurance protects you against the hazards inherent in owning and using an automobile—damage to the machine itself, and damage it may cause others for which you may be responsible. Each state requires motorists to maintain a minimum level of financial responsibility against their being involved in an automobile accident. Most commonly, this minimum responsibility is met by obtaining an automobile insurance policy that includes the all-important public liability protection.

Types of Coverage

Exercise 5.8

The typical automobile insurance policy packages many different types of insurance together. These types of coverage are as follows.

Public Liability for Bodily Injury

This is the single most important financial aspect of your automotive insurance policy, and possibly of your entire personal insurance program. Should your car injure or kill other people, this coverage will defend you against claims and will pay, up to the limits of coverage, any claims for which you're found to be legally responsible. Coverage is generally in two phases, one for injury to a single individual involved in an accident and a second phase for all individuals involved. The limits of coverage are usually expressed as follows: $10,000/$20,000. This coverage would protect you for up to $10,000 worth of claim from any single individual and for up to $20,000 for all parties injured in the accident. The amount of protection you choose is up to you. You may have to comply with a minimum required by your state, which may be as low as $10,000/$20,000 (more commonly expressed as 10/20). Or, if you are prudent and aware of the potential circumstances, you might choose much higher limits, perhaps as high as $100,000/$300,000, or even higher if it's available. The difference in cost between the minimal coverage and the more extensive coverage is only a few dollars per month—an investment that many would have a hard time turning down.

Public Liability for Property Damage

If your automobile causes damage to the property of others, this coverage will defend you against claims and will pay claims for which you are found to be legally responsible. The limit of coverage is usually expressed as a number following the limits for bodily injury liability. For example, public liability limits of 25/50/10 would mean that your property damage liability limits are $10,000 (following the bodily injury limits of $25,000 and $50,000).

In this case, if you caused injury to the property of others, you would be protected for up to $10,000 of such damage.

Property damage liability covers damage to the property of *others*—not to your own property. It can include damage to the automobiles of others or damage to buildings. Property damage coverage will usually not be less than $5,000, and a ceiling of $50,000 should be adequate in most situations, unless you crash into a new Rolls-Royce or careen through a commercial building.

Your public liability protection for bodily injury and property damage will cover you in your own car or if you're driving someone else's car, as well as covering other persons who drive your car with your permission. It also provides legal defense for claims made against you.

Medical Payments

If you, or members of your household or guests who are driving in your car, are injured while driving (or even struck while walking), the medical payments provision will reimburse all reasonable actual medical expenses arising out of the accident up to the limits of the policy. Generally, these payments will be made regardless of who was at fault. The minimum may be as low as $500, but much greater coverage than that can be obtained at a reasonable added annual cost. As with the public liability portions of the coverage, the prudent motorist does well to consider taking much higher than minimal limits on the medical payments provisions, for the added extra cost is small indeed compared with the immediate protection obtained.

Uninsured Motorists

Regrettably, not everyone who drives an automobile is properly insured. You might be caused serious harm by a motorist with little or no insurance protection. You could be out tens of thousands of dollars in medical expenses and lost income, and the party at fault may have little or no money with which to reimburse you for the damage. Although the courts may find the person legally responsible for making payments to you, you may never be able to recover. Uninsured motorist protection is designed to take care of this problem, providing you with reimbursement for your losses through your own insurance company.

Recent statistics from the National Association of Insurance Commissioners reveal that a shocking number of drivers are not insured. Table 5–4 illustrates the percentage of uninsured motorists in a sampling of states.

These figures may actually *understate* the number of uninsured drivers, since many drivers will obtain insurance in order to register their cars and then let the insurance lapse when payments are due on it. These lapsed policies may not show up in the count of "insured" drivers.

TABLE 5–4   Uninsured Drivers in Selected States

State	% of Drivers Uninsured
Alabama	24%
California	24%
Florida	31%
Illinois	19%
Maine	15%
Missouri	15%
Oklahoma	15%
Texas	18%

Unfortunately we don't have a choice as to who might cause us harm in an automobile. It could be an adequately insured individual, or it could be an uninsured individual, or a hit-and-run driver we will never see again. This form of protection is quite inexpensive, and the motorist is assuming an unnecessary risk by not having it.

Comprehensive Insurance

This is a broad form of protection for loss caused other than by collision. It includes loss due to theft and damage to your car due to fire, glass break-age, riots, windstorm, hail, and other causes. Limited protection on contents is also available. Deductibles are common in such policies. If the deductible is, for example, $50, the motorist will have to pay the first $50 worth of any such loss, and the insurance company will pay for damages over the de-ductible amount. Check your policy to determine whether you are pro-tected against theft if you leave your car unattended and/or unlocked. Some policies will not protect the motorist under these circumstances.

Collision Insurance

This coverage protects you against damage done to your own car, should you be in a collision with another car or an object such as a telephone pole or a building. Collision insurance usually carries a deductible. If car A and car B collide and the accident was the fault of the driver of car A, his or her property liability insurance will pay for the damage to the owner of car B, and the collision insurance covering car A will pay for the damage to car A. Collision protection tends to be fairly expensive. If you're driving a car more than five or six years old, the cost of collision protection might be so high that it discourages you from maintaining collision insurance in view of the limited recovery you can expect on an older car. Weigh the cost and the protection accordingly.

How Much Will It Cost?

Exercise 5.9

The cost of automobile insurance can vary considerably depending on the age, safety record, and occupation of the owner, and the purposes for which the car is used. Younger drivers have to pay a higher rate for their automotive insurance, primarily because those drivers have a generally bad statistical record for accidents and claims. Some companies will offer discounts for drivers with safe records and for younger persons who have taken driver education courses. Other discounts may be available where more than one car is insured and where compact cars are involved. In shopping for the best automobile insurance all available discounts should be inquired about from each agent.

The amount of the deductibles have a bearing on the total premium cost. As with deductibles in other forms of personal insurance, you are assuming a higher risk in exchange for paying a lower premium. The premium saved is an actual saving, whereas the higher risk may never occur.

If You Are in an Accident

If you are in an automobile accident, you should obtain the following information from the other party: the driver's name and license number, the plate number of the automobile, and the insurance policy number covering the other driver. The other driver will expect the same information from you. Depending on the extent of personal injury or property damage, a police report may or may not be taken. Also determine whether your state requires a detailed report to be filed with the state department of motor vehicles. Notify your insurance company at the earliest possible time. Your own insurance company can arrange for you to have your car repaired; they will later recover the amount for the repairs from the other driver's insurance company if the other driver was at fault.

If you were at fault and the other driver is paid for a claim against your insurance policy, that might result in an increase in your insurance rates. You might prefer to pay for the other party's costs directly rather than incur higher insurance premiums for the next few years. Discuss this possibility with your insurance agent before you proceed either way.

If injuries or damages are extensive, there may be a lawsuit by one driver against the other. Some states have no-fault laws, which allow a determination as to who can receive what payments, regardless of who might have been at fault in the accident. In other states, it might take a jury trial to determine who was at fault and what damages should be paid to the injured party. It could take years before such claims are heard by a jury. In reality, most such claims are settled out of court by the parties within a few months after the accident.

Personal injury lawyers who represent injured parties usually take 30 to 40 percent of recoveries as their fee, plus out-of-pocket expenses. Such fees

are based on the amount you receive over and above your own medical and repair expenses. In other words, if you retain a lawyer who is able to get you an award of $10,000 for your pain and suffering, you may end up netting $6,000. And it might take you many months before you can get that much. On the other hand, you might be able to negotiate on your own with the other insurance company for $3,000 to $5,000. That would be cash right on the spot, compared with an unknown amount that you might or might not receive many months later. In short, the personal injury lawyer can be helpful where circumstances indicate more severe injuries, lost work time, extensive suffering, and so on.

Automobile Clubs

Another form of worthwhile insurance can be obtained through automobile clubs. For a modest annual fee, these clubs provide towing insurance, which will get your car to a service station at no out-of-pocket cost to you should your car break down on the road. Auto club insurance can also provide you with bail in the event of arrest; travel services are an added plus included with the price of the annual premium.

CAR POOLING

It can definitely pay to become involved in a car pool. Whether you're carpooling to work, to pick up and deliver children at school, or even to shop at a supermarket, there can be considerable saving in the cost of operating your automobile. Table 5–5, based on a U.S. Department of Transportation study, gives some examples of the annual savings that can be realized by continuous participation in a car pool.

TABLE 5–5   Annual Car-Pool Savings

Round-trip Commute (Miles)	Type of Car	Cost of Driving Alone	Cost of Shared-driving Car pool	
			2 Persons	4 Persons
20	Subcompact	$944	$517	$282
20	Standard	1,380	756	410
40	Subcompact	1,640	933	517
40	Standard	2,414	1,369	756
80	Subcompact	2,852	1,625	933
80	Standard	4,226	2,397	1,369

Projected savings, based on $.35 per mile cost, as described earlier. Savings reflect the fact that all the parties in the car pool own and maintain a car.

CAR RENTAL

Aside from the commonplace airport and hotel car rental agencies used with business travel and tourism, car renting is increasingly popular with residents of cities where the ownership and parking of automobiles is costly and inconvenient. There are a number of major national rental firms with computerized reservation services and garage facilities well located in most major cities. These include Hertz, Avis, National, Dollar, Budget, and Thrifty. There are hundreds of smaller firms that, because they don't have the high advertising and rental overheads, can offer lower prices on rentals.

Rental Terms

Whatever your rental needs, it definitely pays to shop around for the best deal. Many rental firms regularly offer discounts at special times of the week, month, or year. Discounts are also available through auto clubs and through a corporate account that your company may have with one of the major rental firms.

Rental plans vary considerably. Most popular are those that charge a fixed amount per day which includes unlimited mileage or you may pay a fixed amount per day plus an added amount per mile. In both cases, the customer pays for gasoline used. If you can determine the number of miles you expect to drive you can figure which of these two plans would be cheaper.

The major rental firms allow you to pick up a car in one city and leave it in another. Depending on the cities involved, there may be a drop-off charge. Determine in advance what drop-off charges will be connected with intercity usage.

Rental Car Insurance

Car rental firms also offer you two different types of protection: collision and medical. The typical car rental contract states that you are responsible for the first $1,000 or $2,000, or more, of any damage to the car as a result of a collision, such as your running the car into a tree. The rental company will offer what's known as a collision damage waiver (CDW) for roughly $8 to $12 per day. If you pay for this collision damage waiver, that clears you of the responsibility of paying that initial amount in case of a collision. However, for the CDW to be effective, you must be using the car in accordance with the strict terms of the rental agreement. If the collision occurs when an unauthorized driver is at the wheel or when the use of the car is unauthorized, you may lose the advantage of the collision damage waiver. Your own personal auto insurance policy may cover you for some of these expenses. Check with your auto insurance agent to be sure. In addition, some

major credit card companies now cover these expenses if the rental is charged on their card.

Also, ask your agent the extent of your protection for medical expenses if you are injured while driving a rental car. If you are comfortable with the protection you already have, either on your auto policy or your own health insurance program, it may not be wise to spend the extra money for the car rental company's medical insurance protection.

✔ PERSONAL ACTION WORKSHEET

Car Shopping Comparison

Use this checklist to help you compare offerings from various dealers. Remember, the price of the car itself is not the only factor that determines how good the deal is.

	Dealer A	Dealer B	Dealer C
❑ Base price of car	_____	_____	_____
❑ Cost of operational extras (list items separately) _____	_____	_____	_____
_____			
_____			
❑ Dealer prep, delivery charges	_____	_____	_____
❑ Total sticker price	_____	_____	_____
❑ Trade allowance on your old car	_____	_____	_____
❑ Trade difference: new car cost less trade-in	_____	_____	_____
❑ Sales tax and license cost	_____	_____	_____
❑ How long will this offer be good?	_____	_____	_____
❑ Financing: What APR is offered?	_____	_____	_____
❑ Insurance: If offered, terms and cost	_____	_____	_____
❑ Reputation for fair dealing	_____	_____	_____
❑ Reputation for service and adjustment of complaints	_____	_____	_____
❑ Convenience in getting to and from when service is needed	_____	_____	_____
❑ If buying a used car:			
physical condition	_____	_____	_____
mechanical condition	_____	_____	_____
extent of warranty	_____	_____	_____
❑ Treatment by sales person	_____	_____	_____

⚠

CONSUMER ALERT

Service Station Sharpies Commit Highway Robbery

Most service station operators are honorable and reliable businesspeople. Sad, then, that a few sharpies smudge the reputation of an otherwise honest industry.

Long-distance travelers are particularly vulnerable to these tactics—far from home, in strange territory, they stop for gas and find themselves facing such money-gouging abuses as

- **Tire "Honking"** While you're not looking, a swift kick at your tire with a boot that has a sharp nail point embedded in the toe gives you a sudden flat and a sales pitch to buy a costly new tire.
- **Slashing** A few quick slices with a well-hidden razor blade can destroy a fan belt or a radiator hose in an instant.
- **The White Smoke Trick** The attendant sprays a few drops of a chemical on your hot engine, and a cloud of white smoke erupts. It's actually harmless, but you're then susceptible to a pitch for costly engine repairs—which, of course, aren't needed in the first place.
- **Bubbling Battery** Drop a few grains of Alka-Seltzer, or the like, into a battery and watch it bubble over. The unwary will find themselves paying for a new battery before they have time to say "plop, plop, fizz, fizz."
- **Shocking Shocks** A few dribbles of oil under the shock absorbers is enough to convince many drivers that the absorbers need replacement. The same can hold true for the transmission and so on.

The common ploy following any of these tactics is a statement by the attendant that "you ought not drive more than a few hundred feet with your car in this condition. . . ."

The best protection against such events is to have your car properly serviced before you set off on a long trip; never leave the car while it's being serviced; keep your eye on the attendant at all times. If you really do suspect a problem, take it to another station for a second opinion, or to a dealer who sells your make of car.

UPS & DOWNS *The Economics of Everyday Life*

Why Gasoline Prices Go Up and Down

Geopolitics   This includes wars and other disputes involving oil producing nations. When Iraq invaded Kuwait in 1990, oil prices soared. Refiners feared that a war would cut off a major supply of oil, and the law of supply and demand forced prices up. By the time Iraq was defeated, it was clear that supplies would be adequate, and thus the price came back down.

Monopoly   Most of the world's oil comes from the OPEC nations—the Organization of Petroleum Exporting Countries. When they agree on the quantity of oil they will produce and the price they will charge, that can have enormous impact on world oil prices.

Taxation   Federal and state taxes on gasoline have a direct effect on what you pay at the pump. California boosted state taxes a nickel per gallon to generate money for mass transit and environmental projects, and in 1993 new federal taxes added 4.3 cents per gallon.

The cost of money   Oil drillers, refiners, and distributors borrow money just like other businesses do. As interest rates move up and down, those borrowing costs are felt at the gas pump.

Competition   Oil companies and individual stations constantly battle to win your business. Price is their most common weapon.

Speculation   There are commodities exchanges where speculators can bet on the future price of oil. (See chapter 16). Heavy enough betting in one direction or the other can influence the price you pay.

? **WHAT IF . . . ?**

How would you deal with these real-life possibilities?

1.   You're involved in an auto accident in which the other party is clearly at fault. Your total costs will be about $4,000, plus another $1,000 in lost income. The other person's insurance company offers you $6,000 to settle the matter right away, leaving you with $1,000 cash-in-hand to pay for possible future medical costs. A lawyer who specializes in such matters tells you she can probably get $15,000 from the insurance company, of which $5,000 will cover your costs and losses and $5,000 will go to the lawyer, leaving you with $5,000 cash-in-hand. You are cautioned that this may take many months, possibly a few years, and that the amount of money is not guaranteed but is highly assured. What would be your course of action? Why?

2.   You lend your car to a friend for a few days. Later, you have second thoughts: What kind of insurance, if any, does your friend have that would protect you if she was in an accident and hurt someone else? How much protection does your own policy offer you in such a case? What can you do to adequately protect yourself?

NUMBER CRUNCHERS

Do the calculations to make decisions in these real-life possibilities.

1. Dealers are pushing hard to sell cars. They're offering incentives that include low interest rate financing, rebates on the purchase price, or discounts on "special options" packages. Get all these details from one or more dealers and crunch the numbers to determine which of the incentives will be the best for you. (Note that the low-interest financing may be limited to loans of certain length and that the "special options" packages might include items that you ordinarily wouldn't want or need.)

2. How would your overall budget be affected if you gave up your car? Calculate how much you'd save by doing so, and how much it would cost you to get around, including using mass transit, car pools, rental cars as needed, taxis as needed, and more efficient use of another car in your family. Don't forget to include the cash you could get by selling your car, and the down payment and interest you wouldn't have to spend by not buying another car.

3. How much can you lower your car insurance premiums by raising the deductibles? How much more risk will this create for you? Is it worth it? What about reducing your risk by decreasing the deductibles? Get actual figures from your agent; don't guess.

FOR BETTER OR FOR WORSE

Things beyond our control often impact our personal and financial well-being, for better or for worse. Some are more predictable than others. How could you be affected if the following real-life phenomena happened? Could you have seen it coming? What steps could you have taken to minimize damage or maximize advantage? The better able you are to anticipate and recognize these forces, the better equipped you are to deal with them.

1. As you are driving out of the city after work on Friday for a nice weekend getaway, you remember that you forgot to renew your auto insurance policy the day before, the last day of the grace period.

2. You were planning to buy a car when the new models come out in September. Planned price tag, about $20,000. An increase in local sales taxes of one percentage point is announced to take effect on August 1, long before the new models arrive, and when the selection of current models is fairly thin.

3. The deal you've been offered on a new car is mouth-watering. Then you hear rumors that the manufacturer plans to discontinue that line next year.

6

Buying a Home

"The eyes of other people are the eyes that ruin us. If all but myself were blind, I should want neither fine clothes, fine houses, nor fine furniture."

Benjamin Franklin

Where to live? House, apartment, condominium? Central city, suburb, or somewhere in between? How much of your available budget should be devoted to housing? Scrimp now for the sake of something better in the future? Or spend now and not worry about the future?

There are no easy answers to these questions. Individuals and families must decide what will best suit their specific needs and desires, taking into account applicable financial, geographical, architectural, and personal factors. This chapter will help you evaluate those important factors and will also help you resolve these other common problems:

- How to find a dwelling in the right price range
- How to make the best use of real estate agents
- How to handle the contracts and other documents involved in a housing transaction
- How to get ready for the closing when you buy a house or condominium
- How to know your legal rights as a home buyer

THE DILEMMA

Financial Factors

A house (or condominium) is the single largest purchase most people will ever make, and they generally have to live with it longer than most other purchases. A mortgage loan is the biggest debt most people will ever incur, and monthly payments (including utility costs and maintenance obligations) represent a major portion of most budgets.

If you have the down payment to allow you to purchase a home and if you can meet the monthly payments without crippling your budget, owning a home can offer very attractive financial benefits. Property taxes and interest paid on your mortgage are allowable income tax deductions (see chapter 20). The money saved on taxes can be applied toward your housing costs. Through these tax breaks, the government, in effect, subsidizes homeownership. (Tax aspects of homeownership are discussed in greater detail in chapters 9 and 22.)

Homeownership also offers the possibility of attractive profits. Home values have historically increased over the years and are likely to continue to do so, despite occasional regional downturns, as happened in the late 1980s and early 1990s. In general, considering the initial costs of acquiring a home, a profit is not likely if the home is owned for only one or two years. If ownership continues for three years or more, however, the likelihood (and amount) of potential profit increases. Not only are the profit potentials attractive, but also tax laws favor those who sell their homes at a profit. (Taxation on the sale of a home will be discussed in more detail in chapter 10.)

Geographical Factors

You cannot afford to overlook the cost involved in getting to and from work, shopping, schools, and other places, whether by private automobile or by mass transit.

Consider, for example, choosing between house A and house B, which are identical in all respects (including price) except one. House A is closer to work, schools, shopping, and entertainment facilities. You estimate that if you buy house A, your overall transportation costs will be, say, $100 per month less than if you bought house B. Furthermore, if you bought house B, you'd have to spend, on average, an extra twenty hours a month driving or on mass transit, as compared to house A. How will these factors affect your choice? See Figure 6–1, the Travel Time/Cost Worksheet.

You must also evaluate the condition of the neighborhood: whether stable, declining, or improving, not only can it affect your state of mind and comfort level but it can also be of great importance to the future resale

FIGURE 6–1   Travel time/cost worksheet

All other things being equal between house A and house B, the location of which house will involve more travel time and travel cost to get you and your family to common destinations? Use this worksheet to help calculate the differences. Calculate both minutes of driving time and miles driven per month.

Destination	Distance to and from (Minutes/Miles)	
	House A	House B
School(s)	_____ / _____	_____ / _____
Major shopping places	_____ / _____	_____ / _____
Church/synagogue	_____ / _____	_____ / _____
Major entertainment places	_____ / _____	_____ / _____
Work (husband)	_____ / _____	_____ / _____
Work (wife)	_____ / _____	_____ / _____
Carpooling	_____ / _____	_____ / _____
Other	_____ / _____	_____ / _____

Exercise 6.1

value of your house. Evaluate: Two houses are identical, except that one is less costly than the other. But the less costly one is in a declining neighborhood. Today it might seem to be the better buy, but what of the future?

Architectural Factors

When making a housing decision, consider the architectural aspects: design, layout, size, and physical condition. They all have a bearing on getting the best value for your money.

Design

The design that appeals to you is largely a matter of taste, but added or unusual features come at a price. To what extent can you justify what could be costly design elements? If you expect to do business entertaining in your home, the extra investment in appearance might pay off.

Layout and Size

Exercise 6.2

The arrangement and size of the rooms and the size of the house are practical considerations. The house should suit your household's needs as they exist today and as you expect them to be for many years to come. It's uncomfortable to live in tight quarters, and it can be very costly to expand later.

Physical Condition

Invest in a professional service that can inspect all the physical aspects of the house: roof, walls, foundation, heating system, plumbing, and so on. Any contract to purchase should be contingent on your approval of the building inspection.

Personal Factors

Sometimes we base major financial decisions not on what we prefer but on what we think others think best for us. (Reread the Consumer Alert section at the end of chapter 3.) That can be a sorry mistake. A house is the major element in your personal lifestyle. You have to live in it, deal with it, and enjoy it. To that end, consider the following:

Privacy

A house has a lot of privacy; condominiums and apartments have relatively less. On the other hand, if you prefer the closeness and camaraderie of others, you might find that in a condo or an apartment.

Leisure Activities

Assuming that a given house and a given condo are about equal in space, location, and quality, the house will cost more than the condo. If most of your leisure activities are home-based, it can make sense to spend the extra money and buy the house. On the other hand, if most of your leisure activities are outward-bound (skiing, fishing, hiking, and traveling), it might make more sense to buy the condo, so that you'll have more money available for those leisure activities.

Fix-it Chores

If you have a knack for patching, painting, fixing up, and taking care of things, you might feel more comfortable in your own home, whereas if you have ten thumbs, you're likely to feel put upon if faced with taking care of the myriad items that need attention in a home. An apartment or a condominium might be preferable, particularly if the landlord or condominium developer is responsible for most of the maintenance on the premises.

The Future

Spending less on housing now than you can afford will allow you to have still more money in the future. Evaluate this reality as it might apply to your situation.

The Personal Action Worksheet at the end of this chapter will help you evaluate all these factors.

TYPES OF HOUSING

Houses

Although it is possible to rent a house, outright ownership is the more common means of acquiring this type of dwelling. The typical purchase involves a cash down payment that may represent as little as 5 percent of the purchase price, up to the more common range of 20 to 30 percent. The balance of the purchase price is paid over an extended period of time, with payments projected for as long as 20 to 30 years. The buyer's promise to repay the remaining balance is secured by signing an IOU commonly preferred to as a mortgage. (In some states this is referred to as a *trust deed*.)

Table 6–1 illustrates common features in new houses, and cost factors, comparing recent numbers with those in earlier years.

TABLE 6–1   **Bigger, Better, and Not a Lot More $$$$$**

What do typical home buyers get for their money? Following are important characteristics of new single family homes in 1975, 1985, and 1995. Figures are national averages. The last line, Income to Cost Ratio, indicates how much new homes cost relative to current earnings. As you can see, a new home now costs only slightly more, relative to income, than it did in 1975. And you get a lot more for your money.

	1975	1985	1995
Central air conditioning	46%	70%	80%
2½ baths or more	20	29	48
4 bedrooms or more	21	18	30
1 fireplace or more	52	59	63
2-car garage or larger	53	55	76
1,200 square feet or less	25	20	10
2,400 square feet or more	11	17	28
Average square feet	1,645	1,785	2,095
Median selling price	$39,300	$84,300	$135,000
Per capita personal income	$6,053	$14,170	$22,560
Income to Cost Ratio	15.4%	16.7%	16.7%

Sources: U.S. Bureau of Economic Analysis; Bureau of Census, 1997.

Condominiums and Cooperatives

Condominiums and cooperatives are somewhat similar, and so are often confused, but their differences should be clearly understood. Both refer to multiple housing complexes, and, in each case, an individual resident has a form of ownership. In a *cooperative*, each resident owns an undivided percentage of the total building. In a condominium, the resident owns his or her own specific dwelling unit.

Here's how they work. Picture an apartment house, five stories high, with four apartments on each floor. All the apartments are of equal size and value. On a cooperative basis, each of the twenty residents would own an undivided one-twentieth of the total building. In effect, it's like twenty partners owning the whole project, each having an equal vote. The cooperative owners enter into an agreement that sets forth what type of vote is necessary to take various actions. For example, it may require a simple majority vote—eleven out of the twenty—to commit the group to improvements or repairs of a certain value. It may take a three-quarters vote to commit all the members to major expenses. And it may take a unanimous vote to reach an agreement to sell the project. Each cooperative group determines its own rules and regulations.

All the members of the cooperative have individual lease agreements with the cooperative for the premises they occupy. A master agreement among all the cooperative members will also spell out such matters as the right to sublease one's apartment to nonmembers; the right to sell one's interest to outsiders; and the right to bequeath their interest in the cooperative to members or nonmembers of their family. Usually, any members of the cooperative who wish to dispose of their interest are first required to offer it back to the other members of the cooperative, perhaps at a preagreed price or based on a preagreed formula for setting a price.

The business affairs of the cooperative may be run by a volunteer member of the group or by a hired professional, depending on the size and complexity of the building management. Cooperative members are responsible for their share of property taxes, property insurance, utilities, and maintenance. If the cooperative has borrowed money—a mortgage—each member will have to sign the mortgage to ensure payment.

In a *condominium*, each of the twenty occupants owns a separate and distinct unit. As in a cooperative, all the individual owners enter into agreement with all the others regarding basic management of the property, maintenance of the common areas, and rights of the individual owners to sublease and sell to parties of their own choosing. Each owner is responsible for individual property taxes and property insurance and, as with a cooperative, is additionally responsible for taxes and insurance applying to the common areas of the building.

Condominiums and cooperatives can come into being in one of two ways: An existing building can be converted into condominium or coopera-

Co-op owner owns undivided 1/20 of whole building, with right to live in one specific unit.

Condo owner owns one unit outright.

tive ownership, or a new structure can be developed and sold to occupants on a condominium or cooperative basis.

In the former situation—conversion—the contractual consent of the occupants is required in advance. Occupants who don't want to go along with the conversion may find themselves having to move.

In the latter case—new construction—there can be many potential pitfalls before the building is completed and all the units are sold. During the construction period, there is dual ownership: the developer owns all the unsold units and buyers own their separate units. A developer who is not able to sell all the units may rent the unsold units to tenants. This can cause serious friction between the tenants and those who have already purchased their units.

Other problems that can occur in new developments include:

* Developers may reserve ownership of recreational facilities, charging occupants a fee for their use. If developers are not contractually limited as to the amount they can charge for recreational facilities, the fees can grow to unsatisfactory levels.

* Developers may scrimp on construction, knowing that once each unit is sold, it's up to the individual owner to take care of its maintenance. This can cause costly maintenance and renovation headaches for individual owners.

* Developers may run into financial problems before the projects have been completed. This can put owners who have already bought units into financial jeopardy. The financial condition of the developer should be carefully checked before a purchase contract is signed.

In a house, owners can do as they please as long as they don't break any laws or create nuisances for their neighbors. They can sell when they like, to whom they like, at the price the market will bear. But in condominiums and cooperatives, many of the rights of the owners are subject to their contract with the association, and also possibly with the original developer. Although many people regard condominiums and co-ops as the best of both worlds—offering the convenience of apartment living with the advantages of homeownership—such contractual agreements often prove that this is not the case.

Mobile Homes

A mobile home customarily involves a combination of ownership and rental. The unit itself is purchased from a dealer and is often financed on a long-term installment loan basis. The unit is then shipped to the owner's destination, usually at the owner's expense, where it is moored on its pad and hooked up to the available water, gas, and electricity. The owner pays a rental for the pad to the park management and is responsible for individual

insurance and utility costs. In some instances mobile home purchasers may have the units installed on property that they already own, thus avoiding the rental fee.

Because mobile homes are not of the same permanent construction as regular houses, an owner should be alert to the possibility of depreciation in value compared with the customary increase in value that permanent homes enjoy. If you are shopping for a new mobile home, compare the prices of similar *used* mobile homes to get an idea of the likely future value of your current purchase. Before making a final decision, evaluate this depreciation carefully.

It's also important to consider the rental arrangements for the site on which a mobile home is placed. Commonly, such sites are rented on a month-to-month basis. If the owner of the park decides to sell the entire property, that could mean eviction on short notice for the site renters, requiring a costly move.

Multiple Units

Other forms of dwellings are represented by multiple-unit buildings and townhouses (or, as they're called in some parts of the country, rowhouses). A common form of multiple-unit housing is the *duplex*, in which two dwelling units occupy the same building, either side by side or one above the other. Similar structures may house three units (a *triplex*) or four units (a *fourplex*). Beyond four units, the buildings would normally be referred to as apartment houses. You might buy a duplex, triplex, or fourplex with the intention of living in one of the units and renting out the others. This can be attractive if the style of living suits you, for the rental income can offset your own dwelling costs and provide a tax shelter. (A detailed discussion of the tax-shelter benefits of rental real estate is provided in chapter 16.)

HOW TO BUY A DWELLING AT THE RIGHT PRICE

Exercise 6.3

Buying a dwelling—and whether it's a co-op, a condo, or a house, we'll use the all-encompassing term *house* for purposes of simplicity—may be the largest and most complicated transaction you'll ever enter into. It's worth doing it right, even if it means spending a lot of time and energy in the process.

The critical elements in buying a house are:

- Knowing your price range
- Using a real estate agent
- Timing
- Looking for the anxious seller
- Driving a hard bargain
- Knowing your needs
- Finding comparable values
- Evaluating the age of the dwelling

STRATEGIES FOR SUCCESS

Shop for Financing Before You Shop for a Home

If you're planning to buy a home, shop for the financing before you shop for the property itself. Most lenders can give you at least a tentative commitment as to how much of a loan you can get. Some lenders will even prequalify you for a loan, subject only to their appraisal of the property you select. Knowing in advance how much you can borrow allows you to zero in on the right price range from the start. More important: If you know in advance that you can get a loan, you are in a better bargaining position with sellers. You're talking from strength. The sellers know they won't have to wait to find out if you can get the financing you need.

- Understanding warranties
- Determing financing costs
- Estimating utility costs

- Estimating furnishing costs
- Determining property taxes
- Evaluating resale potential

Knowing Your Price Range

Exercise 6.4

Consider how large a down payment you can afford and what monthly payments you can handle. The higher your down payment, the lower your monthly payments, and vice versa. It is reasonable to assume that monthly housing costs for most families will exceed 40 percent of their after-tax income. For many families, two incomes are needed to buy a house. (For more details on financing, see chapter 7.)

Using a Real Estate Agent

Exercise 6.5

Many people think of using a real estate agent only when they sell a house. But there are many advantages to using a real estate agent when you are buying.

Most agents belong to an association of local real estate professionals called a multiple listing service. This service publishes a directory, usually weekly, of all houses in the area that are for sale through real estate agents. Listings contain extensive information on each house, including its physical features and costs. The listings provide considerably more information than you can glean from the classified ads. By using the listings, a real estate agent can help you locate the right house in the right neighborhood at a considerable saving to you of time and energy.

A good agent is a skilled negotiator and should be able to help you bar-

gain for the best possible price. And good agents are in constant touch with the financial markets so that they can help you obtain financing. Furthermore, the services of a real estate agent cost the buyer nothing; the agent's commission is paid by the seller.

It's not easy to find a good real estate agent to represent you as a buyer. Many agents are leery, and perhaps rightfully so, of would-be buyers who are really just "lookers." They can't afford to spend much of their time unless they know that a would-be buyer is really serious. If an agent thinks a buyer is serious and will, in fact, work with the agent all the way, the agent is more likely to work hard on the buyer's behalf. A contract between the real estate agent and the buyer is not customary; the agent acts on good faith between the parties.

When you do find an agent who will work with you to find the right place, be sure that he or she is willing to show you properties that are listed by agencies other than the listing broker. You want to be sure that you are getting a good look at all available properties in the community.

Timing

Timing can be critical in the purchase of a house. To the extent possible, make certain that your financing arrangements for your new home coincide with the expected closing date. Also, arrange as far in advance as possible for your departure from your current dwelling. If you're living in an apartment, be certain to give proper and timely notice of your departure to your landlord. If you're living in another house or condo, do as much as you can to assure that your dwelling will be sold as closely as possible to the time you take possession of the new dwelling. If you fail to coordinate these transactions, you could become an *anxious seller* of the dwelling you now occupy. As the next paragraphs indicate, the plight of the anxious seller is not a happy one.

Looking for the Anxious Seller

The *anxious seller* is the person from whom you are most likely to get a good buy and, accordingly, is worth seeking out. A real estate agent can be of considerable help in locating anxious sellers. The listings referred to earlier often contain information that can help identify anxious sellers.

Here are the situations in which you will most typically find anxious sellers:

- The house has been on the market for a particularly long time. The seller realizes that each month that goes by is costing an extra month's

worth of payments. The sooner the *anxious seller* can unload this house, the sooner the drain on his or her funds will cease.

- The house is vacant. The seller has moved into a new dwelling and is making payments on both. Nothing makes a seller more anxious to sell than making payments on two dwellings.
- There has been a major change in the family, such as divorce or death. In either instance, the owner is often more anxious than usual to wrap up the sale of the property, if only for relief from the legal complications that go with such situations.

Driving a Hard Bargain

It's traditional for a seller to ask one price and for the buyer to offer a lower price; buyer and seller will ultimately settle for something in between. Unless the demand for houses vastly exceeds the supply, this type of bargaining is almost taken for granted. It may seem distasteful to you to bargain over the price, but be forewarned that when *you* sell a house, buyers will haggle with *you* over the price. The real estate agents representing the buyer and the seller will generally convey the offers and counteroffers back and forth, so that you don't actually have to come face to face with the seller on this matter. This is all the more reason to consider a real estate agent when you buy: the agent is better able to handle this delicate phase of the purchase than you might be. Agents can show you the difference between asking prices and actual selling prices on recent sales in the area. This can help you determine your bargaining leeway.

STRATEGIES FOR SUCCESS

Exercise 6.6

Pros and Cons of Buying Foreclosures

No one likes to capitalize on someone else's misfortunes. But you might be able to buy a home that has been foreclosed for a much lower price than market value. Check with local lenders to find out what they have taken over in foreclosure. Better still: a friendly banker or real estate agent may know of properties about to go into foreclosure. You may be able to get first crack at it before the general public does. Beware, though, of the dangers in foreclosed property: the physical condition may be sorely neglected, and costly work may be needed. There may be other liens hiding. Don't buy without a thorough inspection, title search, and legal advice.

Knowing Your Needs

A good price on too small a house today may prove to be a regrettable decision if, in a few years, you have to enlarge the house or tolerate the inconvenience of inadequate space. Similarly, if a house later proves to be too large for your needs, you may look back at the original purchase as having been more costly than necessary. Although changes in household size aren't always predictable, the possibilities must be considered, particularly when you're putting out many thousands of dollars for a down payment and signing an IOU for a great deal more.

Finding Comparable Values

Once you've located an area in which you want to live and have taken into full account the costs of commuting to work and other facilities, you should determine if a specific house is priced comparably to others in the vicinity. Your real estate agent can help you by examining the records of recent sales in the area. All other things (size, quality, location) being equal, comparable houses should sell for comparable prices. You might be fortunate in finding a seller who is disposing of property on a distressed basis—that is, personal circumstances require a quick sale at less than might otherwise be obtained. Such circumstances could be a job transfer, a drastic change in family situation, or the need for cash. On the other hand, you might find someone who is asking the maximum he or she thinks the traffic will bear. Unless you do some checking, you might succumb to a high asking price when, in fact, you could have obtained a better buy if you had researched comparable sales in the neighborhood.

Evaluating the Age of the Dwelling

Be careful not to compare apples with oranges. This is particularly true concerning houses that are equal in size and quality but differ in age. The age of a house can have a distinct bearing on the value you get for your money. Aside from decor, you have to evaluate physical deterioration. In certain neighborhoods, the old saying, "They don't build them like they used to," may be perfectly true. Certain older homes have been built with better-quality materials and finer craftsmanship than more recent homes. However, an older house can mean expensive repairs. A detailed inspection by a qualified contractor will reveal the current condition and the need to spend money on such things as foundations, sidewalls, roof, heating system, plumbing, wiring, and appliances.

One advantage of older homes might be an assumable mortgage that carries a lower rate of interest. Another advantage can be that as you make payments on the older mortgage, you build up your equity at a faster rate.

TABLE 6–2   Rate of Debt Reduction on Mortgage ($60,000 Mortgage, 30-Year Term, 9% Fixed Interest Rate)

During	% of Debt Paid Off	Dollars Paid Off	Dollars Still Owed at End
1st 10 years	10.6%	$ 6,360	$53,640
2nd 10 years	25.9	15,540	38,100
3rd 10 years	63.5	38,100	–0–

Example: During the first 10 years of this loan, you will have paid off 10.6% of the debt, or $6,360. But during the second 10 years, you will have reduced the original debt by 25.9%, or $15,540. Thus, if you stepped into a seasoned mortgage as opposed to a brand-new mortgage and you stayed for 10 years, a much larger portion of the payments would come back to you when you sold.

The older a mortgage gets the greater portion of each monthly payment goes to principal. Table 6–2 illustrates an example. Offsetting this advantage, a larger down payment is probably needed with the older mortgage. Careful analysis is needed.

Understanding Warranties

Unless warranties are specifically spelled out in a contract and agreed to by the parties, they may not be enforceable. Customarily, brand-new homes are sold with a one-year warranty by the builder. Limited warranties on used homes can be purchased from companies that specialize in such matters. The buyer and seller must negotiate which of them will pay for such a plan, if it's to be included in the deal. New-home warranties generally cover the premises with respect to cracks, leaks, and breakdowns of mechanical equipment. In addition to such warranties, the buyer and seller might agree to other specific clauses. For example, if the roof leaks within the first twelve months, it will be repaired at the seller's expense. This agreement between the two parties, if properly drawn up and executed, binds the seller to make good on the promise if, in fact, the roof does leak. A seller might offer such warranties as an inducement to a buyer; or a buyer might request such warranties from the seller as part of the overall bargain. There is no legal requirement that a seller offer such warranties, and, lacking anything in writing, the buyer has little protection.

Another form of warranty is on specific mechanical equipment. For example, a water heater may be installed with a seven-year guarantee. During the seven-year period, the house changes hands. The remaining guarantee on the water heater could accrue to the benefit of the new buyer. The same might be true of any other mechanical equipment.

In the purchase of a new house, the buyer should determine what mechanical equipment warranties are included in the builder's overall warranty. For example, the warranty on a water heater may begin as of the date of installation. The unit may actually have been installed a year prior to the sale of the house to the ultimate buyer. Thus, one full year of the warranty may have already elapsed before the buyer even begins to use the appliance.

Any warranty—on a house, an appliance, or any other product or service—is only as good as its specific legal statements, and it's only as good as the ability of the warrantor to perform.

Determining Financing Costs

"How much down, and how much a month?" Those are the predominant questions asked when considering any kind of financing. It's not always as simple as that, however. You have to determine how much of a down payment you can make without interfering with your other predictable financial needs. Bear in mind that once money has been used for a down payment on a house, that money can't be retrieved unless you refinance or sell the house. Both transactions can be costly and time-consuming, if in fact they're feasible at all. Before you commit your down payment dollars, think about what else you might need that money for, such as emergency medical expenses or other personal matters.

The monthly payments must be in line with your overall budget. Examine the terms of the proposed mortgage to determine if the payments can change in future months or years. This can be the case if you have an adjustable rate mortgage or some other plan that allows the lender to alter the interest rate and thus the monthly payments. (These escalation possibilities are discussed in more detail in chapter 7.)

To your advantage will be the tax breaks given to homeowners: The interest you pay on your mortgage is tax-deductible (as are the property taxes you pay). This can result in a sharply lower income tax bill each year. You can realize those tax savings immediately, instead of having to wait until you get your tax refund, by amending your W-4 form at work to reflect your deductions and increasing your take-home pay accordingly. You can use that extra spendable money to meet your mortgage payments.

Estimating Utility Costs

If you're buying a used home, determine the utility costs the former owners incurred. Obviously, not all families will utilize the available energy in the same way, but that's at least a beginning guideline to help you determine the costs you'll be facing. If you're buying a new home, this task is more

difficult. But if the same builder has erected comparable homes in the immediate vicinity, talk to the owners of those homes and inquire about their utility expenditures. A visit to the local utility companies might also be helpful in getting these preliminary estimates. Also, a physical examination of the insulation in the house can be important. If insulation is inadequate, you should evaluate the cost of bringing it up to standard compared with the cost of additional fuel you'll use if you don't correct it. Your local utility company can assist you in these considerations.

Estimating Furnishing Costs

Beyond the cost of the house itself, your mortgage payments, and utilities, you must also consider furnishing the house to suit your tastes. If the decor is not satisfactory, how much will it cost to repaint, repaper, and otherwise change it? Other items that can run into considerable expense include carpeting, draperies, and cabinetry. You'll also want to determine how much of your existing furniture can be used and how much additional furniture you may need to complete the interior satisfactorily. Evaluating these elements is part of your initial buying decision. Where will the money come from to provide the necessary furnishings and changes in decor? Do you have the cash? Will you finance these purchases over the customary three- to five-year term of a home-improvement loan? Can you add these purchases to the overall cost of your home and include them in the mortgage? Whichever step you take, how will it affect the balance of your regular budget?

Determining Property Taxes

You should research not just what property taxes are on the home you're planning to buy, but also what they might become. People in the local tax assessor's office can be of some help, as can members of the City Council and the local news media. If economic conditions indicate that property tax increases are likely, you should attempt to budget accordingly. Property taxes can be deductible on your federal income tax returns.

Evaluating Resale Potential

When buying a house, it might seem foolish to guess what you might be able to sell it for in five, ten, or fifteen years. Granted, there's no reliable way to predict what any property in any community might bring even a year or two after purchase; but it is foolish to ignore the question altogether. Some neighborhoods show signs of slow and gradual deterioration,

whereas others seem to have a fairly certain future of increasing property values. There may be subtle changes underway in the neighborhood that can deflate the value of property. If you envision reselling the home within a relatively short period of time—say, four to seven years—your real estate agent can help you estimate the possibility of increase or decrease in value. If you'll be in the home longer than that, you'll do best to put your thoughts into the hunch category and hope for the best.

Once you've made all the necessary evaluations, you're ready to visit your attorney and discuss the terms of the sale.

MAKING THE PURCHASE

You've found a house that is desirable and affordable. You've made an offer and the seller has accepted. What happens next? Commonly, the seller's real estate agent prepares a brief memorandum of agreement setting forth the basic terms of the deal. Both parties sign this memorandum, and the buyer may be asked to pay some earnest money to bind the deal. The memorandum controls until a formal purchase contract is entered into.

The Purchase Contract

The purchase contract is a very important aspect of a real estate transaction. It sets forth the names of the parties involved, describes the property, dictates the terms and conditions of the sale, stipulates the kind of deed the seller will deliver to the buyer, and states where and when the closing is to take place. Generally, a purchase contract is prepared by the seller's representative, either a real estate agent or an attorney. Note well: If the other party's representative has prepared a contract for your signature, you must assume that the contract will favor the other party. Only by having your own representative review the document can you be assured of the fullest protection of your own interests.

The Parties to the Contract

The names and addresses of the parties are set forth in the contract. Customarily a married couple will acquire the house jointly. Laws differ from state to state as to the specific ways joint property can be held. Examples include: "Mr. and Mrs. X as joint tenants"; "Mr. and Mrs. X as tenants by the entirety"; "Mr. and Mrs. X as tenants in common." You must determine the different ramifications of each form in your state and have your title listed accordingly.

If there has been a change in the sellers' status since they purchased the property, such as through divorce or the death of one spouse, steps must be

taken to assure that the proper current legal status of the sellers is incorporated in the contract. This is for the buyers' protection.

If the contract gives the buyers a "right of assignment," then the buyers can transfer their rights to buy the property to other persons. This can be beneficial to the buyers if, for example, an expected job transfer is cancelled, thus eliminating the need to buy the house. In general, where a right of assignment is given, the sellers reserve the reasonable right to approve the new buyers.

Description of the Property

The purchase contract should contain the full legal description of the property—not just the street address. The proper legal description should be either a surveyor's description or a subdivision description. The surveyor's description indicates the boundaries and their length, all relating to a particular starting point. The subdivision description may refer to a specific parcel within a larger subdivision, whose map has been filed under local legal requirements by the original developer of the property. Such a description might refer to a lot as "lot #17 of the XYZ subdivision, which is registered in the County Recorder's book of maps #576, at page 148."

Title

Your title to a piece of property represents the rights you have regarding that property. There may be certain restrictions as to how you can use any given piece of property; and your use of the property may be subject to the rights of other people. The purchase contract will commonly state that you are receiving "title free and clear of all liens and encumbrances, except as otherwise noted." What does this mean? It means that you are receiving the property without any restrictions and subject to no other rights of other people, unless such other restrictions or rights are specifically spelled out. If your contract says that you are receiving the right to use the property "free and clear," when in fact you are not, you may have the right to get out of the contract. Your lawyer or your title insurance company will search the appropriate records to determine whether any other such rights or restrictions do exist. If you take title to property having restrictions you could find it difficult to finance or sell the property. It could also mean lawsuits to resolve whether the rights and restrictions are valid.

"BLOTS" ON THE TITLE   Restrictions on your use of the property and rights that others may have to use your property are referred to as *blots* on the title. The most common form of blots are easements, liens, and restrictive covenants.

- **Easements**   Many years ago, the owner of a piece of property might have given a neighbor the right to lead cattle across the property to a

watering hole. The neighbor may have paid for this right and, in return, received a document setting forth that right. Later, when the owner of the property sold to another buyer, the neighbor's right to cross the property was included as a part of the deal. Thus, the new buyer acquired the property subject to the neighbor's right to use it. Until the owners of the adjoining properties agree to terminate this right, it will continue through all subsequent transfers of the property.

This is a form of easement, and it exists today in many forms. It's not uncommon for a utility company to have easements across residential property for the purpose of installing utility lines and underground piping. These rights may have been reserved but not yet exercised by the utility company. That these rights have not yet been exercised does not mean that the easement has expired. Easements may have been created many years before, yet they will continue to run with the property until they are terminated by mutual agreement.

- **Liens** Laws on the subject of liens differ from state to state. A lien on the property comes into being when the owner of the property has a debt that has not been paid, and the creditor takes legal action to collect the debt. If the legal action is successful, the creditor may wind up with the right to force the owner to sell his or her property (real estate and personal) in order to satisfy the debt.

For example, John borrowed $10,000 from Mary and could not repay it when the debt became due. Mary began legal action, but John still refused to pay. Mary won a judgment against John that technically gave her the right to force a sale of John's house to satisfy the debt. Mary, in effect, had a lien on John's house. The lien was properly recorded according to state law. Anyone then buying John's house would own it subject to Mary's right to force a sale in order to satisfy John's debt to her.

Other liens can arise out of a property owner's failure to pay taxes, in which case the government will have a lien. Or, if a property owner has failed to pay contractors or workers who have performed work on the property, a so-called mechanic's lien can arise.

Note that a debt alone does not give rise to a lien. The creditor must pursue the legal requirements set forth in the state in order to "perfect" the lien. Not until the lien is legally perfected does the creditor have any claim on the property. Because many months often elapse between the signing of a purchase contract and the final closing of a real estate transaction, a lawsuit could occur in the meantime and result in a lien coming into being prior to the actual date of closing. Thus, it's common for a title search to occur both on the signing of the purchase contract and again just before the closing to make certain that no liens have arisen in the interim. A proper purchase contract should disclose the existence of any actual liens. If the contract does not disclose liens that do exist, the seller is promising to sell some-

thing that he or she cannot in fact deliver: a *free and clear* title. In such a case, the buyer should have the right to bow out of the contract, re-coup any monies paid in, and possibly collect damages suffered as a result of entering into the contract.

- **Restrictive covenants**   Such covenants prevent you from doing certain things on your property. For example, a restrictive covenant might state that you may not build a house of less than a certain value. Such a covenant, or promise, may have originated with the subdivider of the property, who wanted to ensure that the subdivision was developed with homes of at least a minimum quality, thus protecting the financial interests of all those buying lots. Buyers want to know that their investment would not be diminished by the construction of buildings of lesser value.

Exercise 6.7

TITLE INSURANCE   Even though the proper record books have been searched and no blots against your title have appeared, that doesn't prevent someone from making a claim against your property. Such claim might be invalid, but it can be a costly nuisance for you to prove that it's invalid.

To prevent such problems and losses, homeowners acquire an insurance policy known as title insurance. This insurance policy protects both the homeowner and the mortgage lender against such claims. A title insurance policy does not establish the *value* of your property. It sets forth the maximum amount of monetary damages you can expect to recover if a claim is made against your title.

The Deed

The deed is the legal document by which the title to the property passes from the seller to the buyer. It's the actual symbol of ownership. The purchase contract should spell out when you will get it.

The contract should also stipulate that the deed will be transferred at the time of closing. If the contract does not call for the deed to be delivered at the closing, you should receive an explanation before consenting to sign the contract.

There are different kinds of deeds, and they convey different interests in a piece of property. The highest and most complete form of deed is called a *full warranty deed.* In such a deed, the seller warrants that he or she has clear title to the property (subject to any stated exceptions), is conveying the title to you, and will protect you against any outside claims made against the property.

The lowest form of deed is called a *quit claim deed.* By this document the seller conveys to you whatever interest the seller has in the property, with no further assurance as to title. By virtue of a quit claim deed, the seller is saying, in effect, "I hereby quit, or give over to you, the buyer, any claim I may have to this property." If, in fact, the seller has full and complete title to

the property, this is what is conveyed to the buyer. If, in fact, a seller has no claim whatever to the property, that too is what is conveyed to the buyer. In other words, a seller could convey to a buyer via a quit claim deed "all of my right, title, and interest in the Grand Canyon." The seller has no interest whatsoever in the Grand Canyon, but it's still a valid deed. He or she is simply giving over any rights he or she may have, and it's up to the buyer to determine that those rights are worthless.

Once buyers take title to a property, they can convey only the title they have received. You can't convey more than you actually own. If you receive a quit claim deed to a piece of property and later want to sell it, you can't give anything more than a quit claim deed—unless it's been otherwise legally established that you do, in fact, have free and clear title.

The buyer should demand the highest form of deed the seller is capable of delivering. If your purchase contract calls for you to receive a certain type of deed and, at the closing, the seller does not deliver the type of deed promised, you technically might be able to void the deal or bargain for better terms.

In a type of property transaction known as a *land contract*, the right to use the property transfers to the buyer, but the buyer does not obtain a deed until certain contractual terms have been complied with. This might take many years. (This type of transaction is discussed in greater detail in chapter 7.)

Manner of Payment

The purchase contract sets forth the manner in which the buyer pays the seller for the property. (See chapter 7 for a more detailed discussion of where the buyer gets the money to pay the seller.)

Buyers planning to obtain their own financing for a purchase should make certain that a financing contingency clause is in the contract. This clause will state, in effect, that if the buyer is not able to obtain financing at an agreeable rate of interest by the date of the closing, the buyer can back out of the deal with little or no penalty.

Closing Date

The purchase contract should set forth the date and place of the closing. The closing is the official event at which the transfer of deeds, checks, and IOUs takes place. When a closing date is fixed, both parties must perform by that date or risk forfeiture. Of course, the parties can agree to amend the date of closing. This is done when financing arrangements have been delayed or where personal circumstances unavoidably alter the plans of either or both of the parties.

In some states, the signed contracts and other documents are held by a third party pending completion of all the buyer's and seller's obligations. This is known as *escrow* and is commonly performed by an attorney, an es-

crow company, or the escrow department of a bank. The party holding the papers in escrow (the escrow agent) will have been instructed by both buyer and seller not to release the papers for the closing until all the obligations of buyer and seller have been performed as agreed. In cases where an escrow agent is used, the *close of escrow* is the same as the closing date.

The parties will usually agree to have the closing date (close of escrow) from one to three months after the signing of the purchase contract, though any other agreement is possible if both parties are willing.

Seller's Obligations

As part of the negotiations, the seller may agree to perform certain services or work on the property. For example: The seller agrees to have the house painted for the buyer's benefit. If the seller fails to perform as agreed, what recourse does the buyer have? It all depends on how the seller's obligation was worded in the original purchase contract. If the buyer was careful enough, the seller's obligations would have been spelled out in detail, including the color and type of the paint to be used, the number of coats to be put on, and specific damages should the seller not perform in accordance with the contract.

Default and Recourse

What if either party fails to perform in accordance with the agreement? What are the rights of the other party? Much depends on the nature of the default and how serious it is in relation to the overall transaction.

For example, if the seller has agreed to paint the house at his or her own expense and has done so substantially but has omitted some minor touchup, this type of default would probably not destroy the entire transaction. In such a case, the parties could negotiate a quick and simple settlement. But more serious defaults—by either party—can create serious questions as to the rights of the parties. The broadest remedy to either party is to bring a lawsuit against the other for *specific performance.* A judgment of specific performance would require the defaulting party to perform in accordance with the specific terms of the original contract.

Perhaps a simpler way of resolving disputes and defaults is for the buyer and seller to agree to arbitration proceedings in the event that one of them does not perform as promised. Arbitration may provide a quicker and less expensive means of resolving disputes than lawsuits do.

The Closing

The closing may take place at the offices of the escrow company or the mortgage lender, at one of the attorney's offices, or at the offices where the

recording of the documents will take place. The signed deed, in accordance with the purchase contract, will be delivered to the buyer, and the appropriate monies or IOUs delivered to the seller. Also, the appropriate "adjustments" will be made, and payment passed accordingly.

Adjustments and Closing Costs

The adjustments are a prorating of any expenses that will have been incurred on the property by the seller. For example, property taxes on the house total $800 per year, payable in installments on January 1 and July 1. The closing takes place on April 1. The seller will have paid a $400 property tax installment on January 1. This covers the first six months of the year. Thus, the buyer will have to reimburse the seller for $200 worth of property taxes, representing April 1 to July 1, during which the buyer will have occupancy of the property.

By the time of the closing, the buyer should have also made arrangements with an insurance agent to have the property insurance in effect in the buyer's name. The buyer should also arrange with the local utility companies—gas, electricity, water—to have the name on the meters changed, effective the date of closing. The buyer is responsible for these costs from the time of closing onward.

Other sums of money can change hands at the closing. The closing is the time for the seller to pay any real estate commissions to the agent. The lawyers and the title insurance company will also receive payments due them. Perhaps the single biggest closing cost will be the fees that the borrower has to pay to the lender who made home financing arrangements. Under a federal law, the Real Estate Settlement Procedures Act (RESPA), a lender is required to give advance notice to a borrower of the closing costs, or a reasonable estimate thereof. This law will be discussed in more detail in chapter 7.

Recording

Individual state laws govern the recording requirements for the appropriate documents. The recording of the mortgage agreement is the responsibility of the lender, and the recording of the deed is the responsibility of the buyer. Recording these documents as required by state law puts the world on notice that the lender has a mortgage lien on the property and that the owner has ownership of the property. The buyer's attorney or title insurance company should have searched the title to the property up to the time of closing. But if the search was concluded days, or even hours, prior to the closing, it is possible for a lien to have sneaked in against the property. Although this happens rarely, it can cause tremendous problems. Thus, the ultimate precaution is to have a search conducted at the time of closing to be certain that no liens have attached themselves to the property prior to the actual moment of transfer and then to record the documents immediately.

PERSONAL ACTION WORKSHEET

Home-buyer's Guidelines

The following evaluations can be helpful in your quest to buy a home or condominium. Seek the aid of a real estate agent in doing this analysis.

Factors	Home #1	Home #2	Home #3
❏ Condition of neighborhood (present and future trend)			
❏ Approximate miles driven per month			
to work			
to schools			
to routine shopping			
to other			
❏ Transportation costs per month			
❏ Physical condition of building			
walls, foundation			
roof			
plumbing			
wiring			
heating, air conditioning			
landscaping			
appliances			
insulation			
❏ Estimated refurbishing costs			
❏ Asking price			
❏ Down payment			
❏ Terms offered by seller			
❏ Price seller will probably accept			
❏ Monthly mortgage payments			
❏ Property taxes and insurance			
❏ Estimated utility costs			
❏ General maintenance and upkeep			
❏ Closing costs			

Check, and Double-check, Statements by Sellers

A home seller, or her real estate agent, might be tempted to stretch the truth when discussing certain features of a house or condo. If you're a buyer, the following precautions might be helpful in clarifying matters that would otherwise not be spelled out in the contract.

If the Seller, or the Seller's Real Estate Agent, Says:	You Should:
"Our utility bills are amazingly low— this home is really energy efficient."	Ask to see the last year's actual bills. If the seller doesn't have them, check with the utility companies. Understand, however, that different families will consume different amounts of energy.
"That water stain on the ceiling is from an old leak. We had it patched up watertight years ago."	Get a garden hose and, with the owner's permission, simulate a heavy rain on the roof. You'll find out soon enough whether the leak is still there.
"The basement is dry as a bone, winter and summer."	Check for watermarks around the basement wall. Better still, hire a contractor, who'll know better what to look for.
"Oh, we're just a quick 5/10/20 minutes from the school/ freeway/airport . . . etc."	If traveling time is important to you, drive these routes yourself, at various times of day, to find out what is involved.
"You'll just love the neighbors."	Go knock on the doors. Find out for yourself. They won't be there forever, but they can make a difference.

If both parties agree that the seller is to correct certain conditions, make certain that such corrections are clearly spelled out in the contract. Then, make certain that the corrections are completed before the deal is consummated.

UPS & DOWNS *The Economics of Everyday Life*

Why Housing Costs Go Up and Down—Part I

Whether you're buying or selling a home, you can't ignore the ebbs and flows in housing prices. Hopefully, you'll buy low and sell high. Unfortunately, the ups and downs don't always coincide with your personal plans.

As the housing industry goes, so do many others. Makers of appliances, carpets, drapes, paint, wallpaper, furniture, gardening tools, furnaces, water heaters, and so on, all depend on a robust housing market for their own successes. So, a slow housing market hurts more than just the builders and building trades. Conversely, in a booming market the ripple effects are felt far and wide.

Many factors influence housing costs. Let's examine them here, and in the Ups & Downs section of chapter 10, which deals with the same concerns.

Timing   It can take years for a housing development to go from scratch to move-in date. A developer must acquire the land, obtain permits, and arrange for financing before construction begins. Once the developer projects the building of 5, or 50, or 500 homes in a targeted price range, it's very difficult to change course. But if a lot of conditions change in that time, it can make a shambles of sales and price projections. If he finds himself with too many homes for sale in a down market, he may have to drastically cut prices. If his completion date coincides with an up market, he may be able to command higher prices. These price fluctuations in new developments can spread to pricing on existing homes as well.

Jobs   Local employment is an extremely important influence on housing prices. In a growing area, where new jobs are being created, people's confidence in the future is strong and they are willing to make the financial commitment to buy a home. The law of supply and demand kicks in: More people wanting to buy will boost prices; more people wanting to sell will depress prices.

Interest rates   Home loans go hand-in-hand with home purchases. As interest rates come down, it becomes easier for people to buy homes: They can more easily qualify for a loan because their monthly payments will be lower. This can spark a rally in home buying, which will exert an upward pressure on prices. As interest rates move up, it's more difficult for buyers to qualify for the higher monthly payments. This can prompt home sellers to lower prices in order to attract the shrinking number of buyers. (See Ups & Downs, chapter 7, for a discussion on what causes the movement in long-term interest rates, and the Ups & Downs in chapter 10 for more on housing costs.)

? WHAT IF . . . ?

How would you deal with these real-life possibilities?

1. You've found the house of your dreams. The asking price is $150,000. Your "comfort zone"—the price range you can live with—is $120,000 to $130,000. You offer $125,000. The seller counteroffers $140,000. What are your options from this point?

2. You've found a house that's priced in the low end of your comfort zone. It's smaller than what you really want, but you can see ways to add on to it. The cost of the add-on, however, will boost the overall cost of the house above your current comfort zone level, and perhaps overprice it relative to other houses in the immediate neighborhood. All things considered, this house comes closest of all you've seen to meeting your criteria. How do you resolve the dilemma?

3. It's a buyer's market out there! Housing prices are low, and interest rates on home loans are as low as they're likely to be for years. You're anxious to buy, and you know you can qualify for a loan, but you're coming up short in the down payment department. What steps can you take to become a homeowner, before the market turns against you?

NUMBER CRUNCHERS

Do the calculations to make decisions in these real-life possibilities.

Exercise 6.8

1. Assume three housing prices: $120,000, $150,000, and $180,000. Further assume down payments of 5 percent, 15 percent, and 25 percent. With an interest rate of 10 percent and a mortgage term of 30 years, calculate the dollar amount of the down payment and the monthly payments required for each house at each down payment level. The mortgage tables in chapter 7 will enable you to crunch these numbers. The purpose of this exercise is to prompt you to become adept at working out these formulas; this skill will come in handy when you apply for a home loan.

2. You're considering buying a house that meets all your criteria except for one: the floor coverings. You'd want to replace 130 square yards of carpet and 300 square feet of vinyl tile. Get cost estimates, including installation, in various price ranges. What does this do to your budget?

3. Compare the cost of hiring a professional moving company to get you from your current abode to your new home, with the cost of a do-it-yourself move. Consider everything: packing, manpower, gasoline, wear and tear on yourself, the value of your time. What's the best deal, all things considered?

FOR BETTER OR FOR WORSE

Things beyond our control often impact our personal and financial well-being, for better or for worse. Some are more predictable than others. How would you be affected if the following real-life phenomena happened? Could you have seen it coming? What steps could you have taken to minimize damage or maximize advantage? The better able you are to anticipate and recognize these forces, the better equipped you are to deal with them.

1. You are negotiating to buy a new dwelling. The realtor tells you that some empty farmland a few blocks away may be rezoned from agricultural to industrial.

2. You've signed a contract to buy a new dwelling. The seller has moved out. Before the closing, and before you move in, a thunderstorm reveals some serious roof leaks that you hadn't been aware of.

3. You've just moved into your new home, and a neighbor informs you that she is converting her home into a halfway house for delinquent teenage girls.

Exercise 6.9

7

Financing a Home

It is impossible to win the great prizes of life without running risks. And the greatest of all prizes are those connected with the home . . . the intimate and homely things that count most.

Theodore Roosevelt

The great American dream has long been to own one's home. Is the dream beyond reach? Probably not. This chapter will acquaint you with methods of home financing and will equip you with the knowledge you'll need to pursue your own dreams of owning a home. Among the techniques you'll learn about are:

- How to evaluate different types of home financing plans
- Where you can shop for home financing
- Which home financing terms are negotiable
- How to structure a financing package that suits your housing budget

HOW HOME FINANCING WORKS

Not many years ago if you were shopping for a home loan you might have visited a dozen different lenders and found very little difference between their home financing plans. Most lenders would have quoted approximately the same interest rate, which would remain fixed for the entire term of the loan, usually thirty years.

But that's not so any longer. If you visited a dozen different lenders today, you'd find several dozen different plans based on fixed rates, adjustable rates, or some combination. Sorting them out can make your head spin.

A home loan is probably the largest IOU you will ever sign, and it will be with you for years, perhaps even decades. A difference of one-quarter of a percent in interest can mean a difference of thousands of dollars over an extended period of time. If you want to get the best arrangement for your money, it's essential to do the homework before you commit on any home loan.

Your First Step

If you're planning to finance a home purchase, you should, after reading this chapter, begin to shop for available financing plans *before* you start looking for houses. Talk to various lenders in your community and get an idea as to the kinds of financing that are available to you: how much down payment will be required, how much in monthly payments will be required, and what other terms and conditions the lender will impose. This exercise will give you general guidelines as to the type of housing you can afford and will make it easier for you to do your house shopping in the appropriate price range.

Furthermore, if you can get a tentative agreement from a lender as to a financing arrangement, you'll be more confident in your actual house hunting, knowing that you can probably conclude a deal that falls within your price range. Also, knowing in advance what kind of financing you can realistically obtain can enable you to bargain better with a seller. A seller who is convinced that you won't have to wait around for weeks to find out whether you can get the financing may be willing to drop the price in order to save that waiting time. You have a lot to gain and nothing to lose from such a tactic.

Say you're interested in buying a house that costs $150,000. You've saved up $20,000 of your own money, but that's all you have. How can you buy the house?

You can borrow the other $130,000. You can go to a bank or any other lender that offers home financing and make arrangements to borrow the needed amount. If your application is approved you will sign a document promising to repay the full amount to the lender over a period of time, plus an agreed-on amount of interest. This document is commonly called a mortgage. (In some states, the document is referred to as a trust deed. There are some minor technical differences between a mortgage and a trust deed, but the basic concept is the same.) This mortgage might be referred to as a *purchase money mortgage,* or a *first mortgage*. With a purchase money mortgage, as in this case, you borrow the money to purchase the property. The designation of the mortgage as *first* means that the lender stands first in line to take back your property in the event you default in your obligation to make the payments. Table 7–1 illustrates various relationships between income, down payment required, size of loan, and payments thereon.

Or there may already be a mortgage on the property that you might be able to assume. Say that there is a mortgage on the property for $130,000.

TABLE 7–1 **How Large a Home Loan Can You Get?**

Lender's limit, as a percentage of monthly income	If you have this much monthly income							
	$2,500	$3,000	$3,500	$4,000	$4,500	$5,000	$5,500	$6,000
	Here is what you can get, on a 30-year loan, at 9 percent fixed rate (upper figure is amount of loan, lower figure is monthly payment, in dollars).							
25 percent	77,600	93,800	108,700	124,200	139,800	155,700	170,800	186,300
	625	750	875	1,000	1,125	1,250	1,375	1,500
30 percent	93,800	111,800	130,400	149,100	167,700	186,300	205,000	223,600
	750	900	1,050	1,200	1,350	1,500	1,650	1,800
35 percent	108,700	130,400	152,200	174,000	195,700	217,400	239,100	260,900
	875	1,050	1,225	1,400	1,575	1,750	1,925	2,100

Example: If your monthly income is $3,500 and your lender will make a loan whereby your monthly payments will not be more than 30% of your monthly income, you could get a loan of $130,400, with monthly payments of $1,050. Income tax implications are not taken into account, but you should calculate your own.

You could become the owner of the property by paying the seller your $20,000 in cash and then stepping into the seller's shoes as the person responsible for making the payments on the existing mortgage. In effect, you assume the seller's debt. You take it over. What if the existing mortgage on the property is only $120,000? After paying the seller your $20,000 in cash, you'll still be shy of the total purchase price by $10,000. In such a case, the seller might be willing to take your IOU for the $10,000. Your IOU would be known as a *second mortgage*. The terms of payment would be whatever you and the seller agreed to, and the seller, holding your second mortgage, would stand second in line behind the holder of the first mortgage to get paid in the event that you defaulted on the debt.

A mortgage contains two very important legal considerations. First, you are legally committing yourself to make the payments to the lender as agreed. Second, you are giving the lender the right to take steps to take back the property from you if you fail to make the payments. In other words, you have given the lender a security interest in the property as collateral for the loan.

If a borrower fails to make payments as agreed, the lender can begin a legal action known as a *foreclosure proceeding*. Foreclosure proceedings differ somewhat from state to state, but basically they allow the lender to cause the property to be sold at public auction. The lender recovers whatever money is owed out of the proceeds of the auction sale. The first mortgage holder gets first crack at the auction proceeds. If there is any money left over after the first mortgage holder is paid off, that can go to a second mortgage holder, and so on. For example: William owes $60,000 on a first mortgage and $10,000 on a second mortgage. William defaults and the property

is foreclosed. The property is sold at auction, and, after foreclosure expenses are taken out, $66,000 remains. The first mortgage lender recovers the entire $60,000 owed. The remainder, $6,000, goes to the second mortgage holder. This means, obviously, that the second mortgage holder has suffered a $4,000 loss on the transaction.

The basic costs of a mortgage are the same whether the mortgage has a fixed interest rate or a variable interest rate:

- The interest, which is the *rent* you pay for the use of the lender's money
- The acquisition fees
- The insurance costs

How Interest Is Figured

Fixed Rate Loans

In the standard fixed interest rate mortgage, your interest cost is calculated on the unpaid amount of the debt at each given monthly point. Here's an example:

On a $70,000 mortgage, set to run for thirty years at a 12 percent interest rate, the monthly payments for interest and principal would total $720. During the first month of the mortgage loan, the debt the borrower owes is the full $70,000. Since 12 percent of $70,000 is $8,400, that would be the total interest for the full year if the debt did not change.

But we're interested now only in the first month, which is the first one-twelfth of the year. One-twelfth of the full year's interest is $700. (One-twelfth of $8,400 equals $700.) Therefore, $700 is the amount of interest due for the first full month of the mortgage. Thus, in that first month, the total payment of $720 is broken down as follows: $700 for interest and the remaining $20 applied toward the debt.

Going into the second month, the debt due has been reduced by $20, from the original $70,000 to $69,980. During the second month of the mortgage, the interest is calculated on this new debt of $69,980. One-twelfth of 12 percent of that amount equals $699.80. That's the amount of interest due during the second month. In the second month, therefore, your total payment of $720 is broken down as follows: $699.80 for interest and $20.20 to reduce the debt.

The debt has now been reduced by an additional $20.20, leaving a full balance owing of $69,959.80 going into the third month. In the third month, the interest due is one-twelfth of 12 percent of $69,959.80, or $699.60. The payment for the third month is broken down as follows: $699.60 for interest and $20.40 to reduce the debt. A breakdown of the first three payments would thus be as follows:

	Interest	Principal	Debt Remaining
First month	$700.00	$20.00	$69,980.00
Second month	699.80	20.20	69,959.80
Third month	699.60	20.40	69,939.40

That's the basic formula on which fixed mortgage interest is figured. As each month goes by and the amount of the debt shrinks, the amount of interest paid gets smaller and smaller. As the interest portion of your total monthly payment decreases, the principal portion increases. As you can see from this example, and from Table 7–5 (later in this chapter), the payments during the early years of a mortgage are mostly interest. It's not until many years into the mortgage that the interest and principal portions of each monthly payment equal each other. In the last few years of a mortgage, the principal portion is substantially greater than the interest portion.

Adjustable Rate Loans

An adjustable rate loan, most simply stated, means that your interest rate can be adjusted up or down over the months and years. By adjusting the interest rate, your monthly payments might also change. In the last twenty years, the standard interest rates for home loans have fluctuated wildly, ranging from under 7 percent to almost 20 percent. No one knows which way they will head in the future. But if you are concerned that interest rates might move higher than they are now, you might be uncomfortable with an adjustable rate loan.

In order to make an intelligent choice between a fixed rate loan and an adjustable rate loan, you have to understand the jargon of the adjustable loan and how it works. The following statements may not make any sense to you when you first read them, but they're not far from what you might be told when you apply for an adjustable rate loan:

"Your initial rate will be 8 percent. The base rate will be 9 percent, with semiannual adjustments. The index will be the floating Treasury Bill rate, which is now 6.8 percent, and there will be a margin of 3 points over that. You'll have an annual cap of 1 percentage point, a lifetime cap of 5 percentage points, and you can avoid negative amortization by making the full payment upon each adjustment."

Is that enough to make your head spin? Let's take it one small piece at a time.

- **Initial rate**   The initial interest rate might be attractively low, designed to lure you to a given lender. The initial rate will last only until the first interest adjustment occurs, which is usually after six months.

- **Base rate**   The base rate is the interest rate on which the lifetime cap is calculated. If you have a lifetime cap of 5 percent, that means that your interest rate over the life of the loan cannot be greater than 5 percentage points above the base rate. In the earlier example, the base rate is 9 percent and the lifetime cap is 5 percent. That means that your interest rate over the life of the loan cannot exceed 14 percent. Borrowers can be confused by thinking that the lifetime cap is calculated from the initial rate, which in this example is 8 percent. In that case, the maximum interest you could ever have to pay on the loan would be 13 percent. You must determine the exact terms and conditions of these items before you commit to the loan.

- **Index**   The index is an arbitrary number, beyond the control of the lender, which is used to determine interest adjustments. The common indices are the so-called *cost of funds* for certain savings institutions or an interest rate that the U.S. government pays when it borrows money. In the example above, the index is based on the interest rate the U.S. government pays on its very short-term borrowings (Treasury Bills). At the time you were quoted the terms of the loan, that index rate was 6.8 percent. All indices will move up and down as interest rate trends change.

- **Margin**   The index plus the margin equals the interest rate you'll be required to begin paying at the start of each adjustment period. For example, if, after the first six months of your loan, the index has increased from 6.8 to 7.2 percent, the interest rate you will have to pay on your loan from that time on will be 10.2 percent: the index of 7.2 percent plus the margin of 3 percentage points. Similarly, if the index rate goes down, so will the rate you pay.

- **Lifetime cap**   As explained earlier, this fixes the maximum interest rate you will pay during the life of the loan. The lifetime cap is added to the base rate to get the ultimate maximum. If you commit yourself to an adjustable rate loan that does not have a lifetime cap, and if there are no laws otherwise protecting you, then there will be no limit on how high your interest rates can go over the life of your loan. This situation is obviously not desirable.

- **Annual cap**   The annual cap puts a limit on how much your monthly payments can increase during the course of a year. (In some loans, this cap may be based on a shorter period of time, such as six months.) Let's look at a rather extreme example. Assume you have a loan of roughly $120,000 and your current interest rate is 10 percent. That would require monthly payments of approximately $1,050. Assume also that during a one-year period, interest rates soared to 13 percent. If you did not have an annual cap of 1 percent as stipulated in the example, your monthly payment at the 13 percent rate would jump to $1,330. But because you have the 1 percent annual cap, your monthly payment cannot exceed $1,140, which is the payment that

would be required for an interest rate of 11 percent. This brings up one of the most troubling dilemmas in the entire adjustable rate loan arena: the possibility of *negative amortization*.

- **Negative amortization** Following along with the preceding example, the 1 percentage point annual cap on your loan meant that your monthly payment could not increase by more than $90 during the one-year period—it couldn't go beyond $1,140. But, in reality, interest rates increased from 10 to 13 percent. Without the cap you would have had to take on a monthly payment of $1,330, which is $190 more than the $1,140 limit. What happens to that $190? Does the lender just forget about it? In most instances, the lender does not forget about it. The annual cap simply put a limit on your monthly payments during that set period of time. It did not stipulate that you would never have to pay extra interest over and above the limits set by the annual cap. Here we have a case of negative amortization: Technically, you would owe an extra $190 in interest each month. But since the annual cap prevents you from having to pay it each month, that amount is added to your overall debt. In other words, your debt would be growing by $190 each month if you fell into a negative amortization situation. Needless to say, if negative amortization continues for an extended period of time, it can leave you with a much bigger debt that you originally started with. You can avoid the negative amortization trap by increasing your monthly payments to cover all interest that may be due, regardless of the annual cap.

It should be quite obvious by now that all these terms have to be clearly understood and explained to you before you make a commitment to an adjustable rate mortgage.

Fixed versus Adjustable

Choosing between a fixed rate loan and an adjustable rate loan is a perplexing choice. With the fixed rate loan, you know exactly where you stand today, and where you'll stand any number of years from today. The fixed rate loan is easy to understand, and it holds no surprises for you. The adjustable rate loan may look more attractive because it will generally have a lower starting interest rate. And, of course, there's always the hope that interest rates may go down. Indeed, in recent years, they have gone down. But then they have gone back up again. And then they come back down again. You'll never know where you are on the roller coaster until you get to the end of the ride and look back.

One of the simplest rules of thumb in making the choice is to determine, as best you can, how long you expect to be living in the dwelling with the mortgage. If the base rate on the adjustable loan is 2 to 3 percentage points lower than the fixed rate that might otherwise be available to you, and if you are reasonably certain that you will be in the house no longer than

three to five years, then the adjustable rate loan will probably be better for you, assuming that you have reasonably good caps on the loan. On the other hand, if you expect to be in the house for five to seven years or longer, the fixed rate loan will probably be better for you. It won't necessarily be cheaper over the long run, but it will be more stable, and that stability is important in the overall management of your finances. Put another way, over the long pull, you may end up having paid somewhat more in interest, but you will have gained considerable peace of mind over that long term.

Another feature of the adjustable rate loan should be noted: Commonly, adjustable rate loans are assumable by a creditworthy buyer. In other words, having an assumable loan might make it easier for you to sell your home in the future, if the buyer wants to take on your existing assumable loan. But again, timing enters the picture. If you are not going to sell for, say, seven years, the value of the house may have increased enough so that the balance due on the assumable adjustable loan is relatively low. That would mean that the buyer at that time would have to come up with a much larger down payment in order to meet your price. Under such circumstances, the assumable loan might be less attractive to both buyer and seller. Furthermore, it could well be that at that time the buyer would prefer a fixed rate loan, in which case your assumable loan is of little or no value to either party.

Exercise 7.2

Many lenders offer added attractions to their adjustable rate plans, and new ones are occasionally introduced. There are special plans for first-time buyers. Some plans allow very low down payments, with outside parties (such as an employer) being permitted to contribute part of the down payment. Some plans start out as adjustable rate loans but carry an option to switch at some later time to a fixed rate loan. And some plans start off at a fixed rate but can be converted to an adjustable rate at some agreed upon future time. It can all become very confusing—yet another reason to start shopping for the financing before you shop for the house itself.

Acquisition Costs

Exercise 7.3

In addition to the interest you pay on your mortgage, you will probably also have to pay certain fees to lenders for putting the mortgage on their books. Lenders may expect you to reimburse them for the legal expenses involved in preparing the papers, for the credit bureau costs involved in checking your credit history, for expenses for appraisals on the property, and for the cost of the title search.

In addition to these fees, you may be asked to pay points to lenders. Points are a one-time added fee that lenders impose on you to improve the yield on their investments. Generally, a point equals 1 percent of the amount of the mortgage. Thus, two points on a $70,000 mortgage would total $1,400. All these added costs—the fees and the points, and the ways you

have of paying them—should be explained to you at the time you make application for the mortgage.

Insurance Costs

A lender may require you to obtain insurance to protect its interest primarily and your own interest secondarily. Title insurance, as discussed in chapter 6, is almost universally expected by the lender, the cost of which will be borne by the borrower. The lender will also expect the borrower to carry adequate fire insurance on the premises, so that the lender will be protected in the event of such catastrophe. The lender might also urge the borrower to obtain life insurance, so that the mortgage can be paid off by the insurance in the event the borrower dies. And default insurance may be involved: this insurance guarantees that payments will be made for a set period of time in the event the borrower defaults. FHA and VA loans include this kind of protection for the lender. In addition, many private firms offer default insurance, which, if required by the lender, will be at the borrower's expense.

Exercise 7.4

If you are required to carry default insurance, it can add approximately a quarter percent to your interest costs. That can mount up into a sizable sum over the years. After you have proved your good payment record to the lender, the lender may be willing to release you from the default insurance requirement. This release would reduce your monthly payment by the amount that was allocated for the insurance. This should be negotiated at the outset. If you have the right to be taken off the default insurance program, it should be spelled out in your initial agreement. The lender might not be willing to give you this right, but if you don't ask for it, you certainly won't be able to get it later on.

Escrow, or Reserve, Accounts

In some mortgage arrangements, the borrower may be required to pay an added monthly sum, which will be used to pay property insurance premiums and property taxes as they fall due. This is commonly known as an escrow account or a reserve account. Example: Your property taxes are $900 per year and your property insurance is $300 per year—a total of $1,200 per year. With an escrow account, you will pay an additional $100 per month over and above the basic monthly payment. The lender will pay your property taxes and insurance premiums out of that fund as those bills come due. Some lenders may require an escrow account; some may offer it as an option. In some states, lenders pay interest on the funds they hold for your benefit. Budget-conscious homeowners often find that an escrow account can be a simple way of leveling out their total annual budget program. It can be easier and more convenient to pay out a fixed monthly amount

rather than have to meet large insurance and property tax bills when they come due. The lender normally analyzes escrow accounts once a year to determine how much will be needed in the account for the following year. The lender will notify the borrower of any adjustments in the monthly payment.

Other Important Clauses

Mortgages can contain other important clauses that can affect your legal rights as well as your monthly payments.

Balloon Clauses

The balloon clause allows the lender to demand that the entire loan be paid off at a set time. If you're not aware that such a clause is in your mortgage, it could come as a shock if the lender exercised this privilege.

Due on Sale Clause

A due on sale clause states that if you sell the home, the existing loan must be paid off at the time of sale. A new buyer can negotiate with the lender to keep the loan in place, but at currently prevailing interest rates.

Assumption Clauses

An assumption clause means that the owner of a house can sell the house to another party and the new buyer can assume the existing debt. The new buyer, in other words, steps into the shoes of the former owner and becomes liable for the balance on the debt, as well as all other terms and conditions of the mortgage. Assumption privileges are subject to the lender's right of approval. The lender might, for example, refuse to allow a person with a bad credit history to assume an existing mortgage. If you are buying a house that has an assumable mortgage, you should determine in advance whether or not you will be permitted to assume the mortgage. If you are entering into a new mortgage, the existence or absence of an assumption clause can affect your ability to sell the house later.

Prepayment Clauses

You might come into a sum of money and wish to make advance payments on your mortgage, either wholly or partially. Do you have the right to do so and, if so, will it cost you anything? Some mortgages contain prepayment privilege clauses that allow you to make such advance payments on your debt without suffering any penalty. On the other hand, some mortgages have prepayment penalty clauses stating that you must pay a penalty if you do prepay.

SHOPPING FOR FINANCING: WHERE TO GO, WHAT TO LOOK FOR

If you buy a house with an existing mortgage that you plan to assume, you'll be locked into the terms of that mortgage. But you can still discuss revision of any of the terms with the lender. It might be worth your while to do so to help tailor a different payment program that would better suit your own financial circumstances.

If you seek your own original financing, the following shopping list, tables, and the Personal Action Worksheet at the end of this chapter can help you to work out a deal that's best suited to your circumstances.

Where to Shop

The major sources of home financing are savings associations and banks, plus some credit unions and insurance companies. There are also private mortgage brokers in most communities who act as middlemen in finding mortgage loans for home buyers. Mortgage brokers are usually paid by the lenders for their services.

FHA and VA Loans

The difference between fixed interest and adjustable interest loans has already been discussed. There's another broad distinction that should be considered, for it can affect the amount of down payment you'll be required to make. This distinction is between insured loans and noninsured loans.

Lenders don't really want to foreclose on properties if the borrower defaults. Foreclosure is a messy, costly, and aggravating proceeding. A lender would much rather have some form of guarantee that all or a portion of the payments will be made as agreed. Indeed, lenders *can* obtain insurance that will offer those guarantees. There are two main sources of this insurance: the U.S. government and private insurance companies.

The U.S. government offers two types of insurance plans. One is offered through the Federal Housing Administration (FHA), and the other, through the Veterans' Administration (VA). FHA will insure certain mortgage loans if both the buyer and the property meet governmental requirements. The VA will also guarantee loans made to eligible armed services veterans, again providing that all qualifications are met. Because the government is guaranteeing repayment of these loans—at least in part—the lenders are willing to take greater risks with such loans than they would if there were no guarantee. In short, the lenders are willing to make these loans to borrowers with smaller down payments. Check with local lenders for current requirements.

Lenders can also obtain insurance through private companies. As with the FHA and VA loans, the private insurance plan means a lower risk for lenders. Borrowers might have to pay a slightly higher monthly payment as a result of their loans being insured, but the cost can be well worth it if it allows them to purchase a house with a relatively small down payment.

One type of insured loan is the FHA-245, also known as the graduated payment plan. This loan is geared toward younger people who might not be able to meet the high monthly payments currently called for. In the graduated payment plan, the monthly payments for the first few years of the loan are lower than they would be under a regular plan. As the years go by, and as the borrower's income presumably increases, the payments increase accordingly.

Noninsured loans, whether at a fixed rate or adjustable interest rate, generally require a down payment of roughly 20 percent of the purchase price of the property.

Ginnie Mae, Fannie Mae, and Freddie Mac

In most cases, once you have signed your home loan IOU to the lender, the lender will turn around and sell that IOU. A number of entities are chartered by the government to buy loans from lenders. The most well known are the Government National Mortgage Association, the Federal National Mortgage Association, and the Federal Home Loan Mortgage Corporation. Their nicknames, derived from their initials, are, respectively, "Ginnie Mae," "Fannie Mae," and "Freddie Mac." Private entities (such as insurance companies, pension funds, and individual investors) might also buy home loans from lenders.

Here's an example of how this works: You sign a thirty-year home loan agreement (the IOU), payable to XYZ Bank, for $150,000 plus interest. As part of the deal, you pay XYZ Bank $3,000 in points, as well as other processing fees. XYZ turns around and sells your IOU to Ginnie Mae for the face amount of $150,000. XYZ Bank keeps the $3,000 in points as its earnings on the deal, and it now has its $150,000 back to lend to someone else. Ginnie Mae then turns around and pools your IOU along with others like it and sells the whole package to investors. (See chapter 6.) This concept creates a steady flow of money for home loan purposes, which in turn helps our economy grow.

You might never be told that your loan has been sold; it doesn't matter. You continue to make your payments to XYZ Bank, and the bank forwards them to whomever has bought your loan. **Warning:** If you are told to send your payments to anyone other than the original lender, check with all parties involved that this change is legitimate and get confirmation thereof in writing.

Conventional and "Jumbo" Loans

In order to sell loans to Ginnie, Fannie, or Freddie, the loans must meet strict requirements regarding your income, your credit, and the value of the property. The loan also must not exceed a fixed dollar amount, which recently was somewhat over $200,000. That ceiling is usually increased slightly every year for newly written loans.

Loans above the maximum amount are referred to as jumbo loans. Ginnie, Fannie, and Freddie may not buy jumbos, but other investors might. Because lenders can easily sell qualifying conventional loans to Ginnie, and so on, they may charge borrowers a lower interest rate than a jumbo borrower would have to pay. Thus, if the amount of loan you're seeking is at or near the current conventional limit, it could pay you well to structure your finances so that you can qualify for the lower interest rate that likely will come with the conventional loan.

RESPA

What points and other fees will you have to pay in order to get the financing you're seeking? Under the federal Real Estate Settlements Procedures Act (RESPA), lenders are required to give you a copy of a government booklet, *Settlement Costs*, no later than three days after you have made your loan application. The information in this booklet is very important. It describes your rights under the federal law and contains helpful advice on completing your property transaction. The law also requires that the lender give you a good faith estimate of all settlement costs (or closing costs, as they're often called). You should also determine whether the closing costs are to be paid at the closing or whether they can be added into the mortgage and spread out over the life of the mortgage.

Interest Rates

What will be the original interest rate, and what fluctuations might it be subject to in the future? Table 7–2 is a handy guide to help you find the monthly payment for any size mortgage at various interest rates and terms of repayment. Table 7–3 illustrates how different interest rates can affect your actual costs on a mortgage—and those cost differentials can be tremendous, as the table clearly shows.

How Much Down Payment Is Required?

The amount of the down payment required and the amount you have available for down payment may not jibe. If you have more than enough, you're

TABLE 7–2   Monthly Mortgage Payment Finder (Fixed Rate) (Per $1,000)

Annual Fixed Interest Rate	Length of Mortgage			
	15 years	20 years	25 years	30 years
7%	8.99	7.76	7.07	6.66
7½%	9.28	8.06	7.39	7.00
8%	9.56	8.37	7.72	7.34
8½%	9.85	8.68	8.06	7.68
9%	10.15	9.00	8.40	8.05
9½%	10.45	9.33	8.74	8.41
10%	10.75	9.66	9.09	8.78
10½%	11.06	9.99	9.45	9.15
11%	11.37	10.33	9.81	9.53
11½%	11.69	10.67	10.17	9.91
12%	12.01	11.02	10.54	10.29

Example: What would the monthly payment be (interest and principal) on a $90,000 mortgage for 30 years at 9% interest? Find the factor where the 9% line meets the 30-year column. That factor is 8.05. 8.05 times 90 = 724.50. The monthly payment, then, would be $724.50.

in good shape, but then you'll have to decide *how much* of your available funds you want to use as a down payment. If you have less than the required amount, how will you raise the difference? If one lender requires a higher down payment than another, the interest rate may be lower or the other terms may be more favorable. These must be compared.

TABLE 7–3   How Interest Rates Affect Your Out-of-Pocket Costs ($120,000 Mortgage for 30 Years)

Fixed Rate (%)	Monthly Payment	Total Amount Paid Out After			
		5 years	10 years	20 years	30 years*
7	$ 799	$47,940	$ 95,880	$191,760	$287,640
8	881	52,860	105,720	211,440	317,160
9	966	57,960	115,920	231,840	347,760
10	1,054	63,216	126,432	252,864	379,296
11	1,144	68,616	137,232	274,464	411,696
12	1,235	74,088	148,176	296,352	444,528

Example: What would be the difference in cost to you on a $120,000 loan between an interest rate of 8 percent and 9 percent? During the first five years the 8 percent loan would cost you $52,860 (monthly payment of $881 times 60 months) compared with $57,960 for the 9 percent loan—a difference of $5,100. Tax deductibility of interest will also affect your out-of-pocket costs. Calculate accordingly.

*To find the total *interest* paid over the full thirty-year life of the loan, subtract the original amount borrowed ($120,000) from each of the amounts in this column.

TABLE 7–4　How Down Payment Affects Your Costs (Purchase Price $160,000, 30-Year Mortgage, 9 Percent Fixed Rate)

Down Payment		Amount of Mortgage	Monthly Payment	Total Payments After		
Percent	Dollar Amount			10 years	20 years	30 years
5	$ 8,000	$152,000	$1,224	$146,800	$293,700	$440,640
10	16,000	144,000	1,159	139,700	278,200	419,100
15	24,000	136,000	1,095	131,400	262,800	394,200
20	32,000	128,000	1,031	123,720	247,440	371,160
25	40,000	120,000	966	115,920	231,890	347,760
30	48,000	112,000	902	108,290	216,480	324,870

Example: What would be the difference in cost to you if you make a 10 percent down payment versus a 20 percent down payment on a $160,000 purchase, with a fixed interest rate of 9 percent for a 30-year loan? With a 10 percent down payment, after 20 years you will have made total payments of $278,200 ($1,159 a month times 240 months.) With the 20 percent down payment, after 20 years you will have made total payments of $247,440. In other words, by making the larger down payment you will save almost $31,000 in payments over 20 years. However, if you did have the 20 percent available and only used half of it as down payment, you would have had $16,000 to spend or invest over the years.

Exercise 7.5

Table 7–4 illustrates how different-sized down payments can affect your total mortgage expense over a period of years. There is no easy solution to the dilemma of how much to pay down. It must be resolved based on your own personal circumstances as they are now and as you expect them to be.

How Long Should the Mortgage Run?

Exercise 7.6

The longer the mortgage, the lower the monthly payment. But that means a higher interest expense over the long term. However, it's unlikely that you'll stay with that mortgage for more than ten or twelve years, for the average American changes houses and moves on within that time. Table 7–5 shows the rate at which your debt is paid off over the years, and Table 7–6 illustrates the different cost factors involved for mortgages of varying terms.

Other Services from Lender

You should try to determine what other kinds of financial services are available to you from respective lenders. Some may offer nothing more than friendly and helpful advice. Don't underestimate the value of this service. Advice can come in handy and may be the deciding factor in your choice of a lender for your home financing.

TABLE 7–5   Mortgage Reduction Schedule, 30-Year Term, Any Amount

	Percent of Original Balance Still Unpaid	
Years Elapsed	At 9% Fixed Rate	At 12% Fixed Rate
5	95.9	97.7
10	89.4	93.4
15	79.3	85.7
20	63.5	71.7
25	38.8	46.2
30	-0-	-0-

Example: On a loan of $100,000 at a 9 percent fixed interest rate, after 10 years of making payments, 89.4 percent of the original balance, or $89,400, will still be unpaid. Ouch. On a loan of $120,000 at 12 percent fixed rate, after 20 years of making payments, 71.7 percent of the original debt, or $86,040, remains unpaid. Double ouch. It's not until the last five or so years that the debt is rapidly reduced. Review the earlier section in this chapter on how interest is figured.

TABLE 7–6   How the Length of a Mortgage Can Affect Your Costs ($120,000 Mortgage at 9 Percent Fixed Interest Rate)

Length of Loan	Monthly Payment		Amount Paid After				
			10 years	15 years	20 years	25 years	30 years
15 years	$1,218	Int.	$ 84,840	$ 99,240			
		Prin.	61,320	120,000			
		Total	$146,160	$219,240			
20 years	1,080	Int.	$ 94,800	$126,360	$139,200		
		Prin.	34,800	68,040	120,000		
		Total	$129,600	$194,400	$259,200		
25 years	1,008	Int.	$100,200	$140,880	$170,400	$182,400	
		Prin.	20,760	40,560	71,520	120,000	
		Total	$120,960	$181,440	$241,920	$302,400	
30 years	966	Int.	$103,200	$149,040	$188,040	$216,360	$227,760
		Prin.	12,720	24,840	43,800	73,440	120,000
		Total	$115,920	$173,880	$231,840	$289,800	$347,760

Example: On a 20-year loan of $120,000 at a 9 percent fixed interest rate, you will have paid a total of $129,600 in the first 10 years. Of that amount, $94,800 will have been interest and $34,800 will have been principal (reduction of the debt).

Notes Regarding Mortgage Calculation Tables:

- Using Tables 7–2 and 7–5, you can structure "what if" projections for a wide range of possible mortgage terms. These can help you prepare comparisons regarding how the interest rate (Table 7–3), amount of down payment (Table 7–4), and length of loan (Table 7–6) will affect your own specific loan needs.

- Income tax deductions for interest paid are not taken into account, since they will vary from person to person and from time to time. But you should estimate how those deductions will affect your cash flow.

Exercise 7.7

- The calculations do not cover adjustable rate mortgages, since the numbers on those loans can vary widely from year to year. You can, however, estimate an *average range* that an adjustable loan will likely cover, and do your "what if" projections accordingly.

- In the calculations, amounts are rounded off.

APPLYING FOR HOME FINANCING

Exercise 7.8

After you've done your shopping for rates, terms, and other clauses, you will decide which lender you want to make formal application to. Before you do, spend a few dollars to examine your credit file at your local credit bureau to make sure that everything is in order. Erroneous information can find its way into your credit file, and you have rights under the federal Fair Credit Reporting Act to have false information corrected. See chapter 11 for more details on your rights under this law. The lender will do a credit check

---

STRATEGIES FOR SUCCESS

A Shorter Home Loan Is Better, If You Can Afford It

The most common home loans run for a thirty-year term. But if you can afford to make higher monthly payments, you can be much better off taking a shorter term on your home loan. Example: On a fixed rate 8 percent loan of $100,000, the monthly payments on a thirty-year term will be $734. For a fifteen-year term at 7.75% (rates being lower for a shorter-term loan), the payments will be $941—a difference of $207 per month. If you can handle those higher payments, you'll be considerably happier after ten years. After ten years on the original fifteen-year loan, you'll owe about $50,000. But ten years into the thirty-year loan, you'll still owe more than $90,000. Why? On the longer loan, most of your payment goes toward interest, with very little toward actually reducing your debt. Discuss these alternatives with your lender before you make a commitment.

on you. If false information has not been corrected in your file, it will cause delays in processing your application.

In addition to obtaining detailed financial information on you—including your income and your debts—the lender will appraise the property you are buying. A title search will also be called for to assure that the lender can be properly secured if a loan is made. These processing steps can take from a few days to a few weeks and might entail some fees that you will be expected to pay, whether the loan is approved or denied. You should determine in advance just how long the processing will take and what cost, if any, you will have to assume.

If your application is approved, you should obtain a copy of the lender's commitment, in writing, so that there is no mistake about the terms of the arrangement. It's very likely that any commitment will extend for only a limited time at the given interest rate. If the purchase transaction is not completed within that specified time, the lender could back out of the commitment, at least at the quoted interest rate. If you suspect that the transaction will not be completed within the time of the lender's commitment, you should move quickly to attempt to get it extended.

It could happen that a lender will approve your application, but with the contingency that you provide a cosigner; or the loan may be approved for a lesser amount than you had requested. In the event a cosigner is required, the lender is asking you to find someone else who will sign the IOU with you. This shouldn't be taken as an insult. It may merely mean that the lender doesn't feel comfortable with your age, the amount of job experience you've had, or or your credit history. After payments on the loan have been made for a few years, you can request that the cosigner be removed from the obligation. Discuss this possibility in advance with the lender.

CREATIVE FINANCING

When interest rates go up, home loan financing becomes more difficult to obtain. When lenders evaluate a loan application, they compare your income with the amount of monthly payment that would be required to pay the size loan you're seeking. Higher interest rates could boost your monthly payment over the level the lender feels comfortable with, and the lender might decline your loan.

In times of higher interest rates, lenders, brokers, buyers, and sellers have put their heads together to come up with unique ways of accomplishing everyone's desires. These generally fall under the category of creative financing. Following are some examples of creative financing techniques. Before you commit yourself to any such technique, it is essential that you get adequate legal advice. These arrangements can be very complex and can create legal pitfalls that you might not be aware of. Protect yourself before you sign anything.

STRATEGIES FOR SUCCESS

Ask Lender for "Rate Lock"

If interest rates are moving upward at the time you're looking for a home loan, you could run into a serious problem. A lender might quote you a given interest rate on the day you apply for the loan. But the loan might carry a higher interest rate by the time the transaction is completed, which could be months later. And that higher interest rate could really put you into a bind. When you shop for a loan, ask if the lender will give you a rate lock—a guarantee that the interest rate on the loan will not go above a certain level, no matter when the transaction is completed. It might cost you something to get a rate lock, but it could be worth it if interest rates are on an upward spiral.

Land Contracts

A land contract can be anything that a willing buyer and a willing seller agree to. Example: Sam, the seller, and Bob, the buyer, are negotiating the terms of a potential deal. Sam is asking $180,000 for his house. Bob has no money for a down payment but is willing to pay $190,000—$10,000 more than Sam is asking. Both Sam and Bob know that a normal lender would not consider financing such an arrangement with no down payment. But if Sam is willing to accept Bob's terms, they can enter into a contract accordingly. It's customary in a land contract for the deed not to be delivered to the buyer until an agreed-upon amount of time has elapsed, during which time, presumably, the buyer will have proved his or her ability to make the payments in timely fashion.

The Sleeping Second

Selma, the seller, is asking $120,000 for her house. She wants $50,000 as down payment, and she's willing to carry the buyer's IOU in the form of a first mortgage for $70,000. Bernice, the buyer, has the $50,000 down payment, but she doesn't have enough income to make the monthly payments on a $70,000 first mortgage. She does, however, have enough to make the payments on a $50,000 first mortgage. They agree that Selma will carry a $20,000 sleeping second. Bernice will make the payments on the first mortgage. The second mortgage will have no payments for the first three years—or whatever other time the parties agree to. Interest will accrue on that sleeping second, probably at a higher rate than a normal second mortgage, since Selma is being very accommodating to Bernice. At the end of the agreed-upon time, either the second mortgage has to be paid off, which will

mean refinancing the entire deal, or payments must begin on the sleeping second, or whatever else the parties have agreed to.

Buying Down

One type of creative financing, buying down, is more commonly seen in new housing where developers are attempting to sell homes during times of high interest rates. Say, for example, that the current prevailing rate is 9 percent, but buyers cannot afford home loans of more than 7 percent interest. A hungry developer might contribute the 2 percent difference in order to sell the homes. As a rule, the developer would do this for only the first few years of the loan, at the end of which time it would be understood that the buyer would then take over the higher monthly payments. This enables buyers to get into homes at a lower monthly payment, banking on the expectation that after a few years their incomes will have increased enough to allow them to live comfortably with the higher payment.

Shared Appreciation Loans

If a buyer cannot afford either the amount of the down payment or the monthly payments, the seller, or any other third party, might enter into an agreement with the buyer to provide a portion of the down payment or the monthly payments. In return for doing that, the outside partner or seller would share in any future appreciation in the value of the house. This is a shared appreciation loan. This kind of arrangement offers very attractive potentials, but it is not without risks and it requires the assistance of a knowledgeable attorney from the very outset.

TAX COMPLICATIONS

The home financing arena is further muddled by major tax law changes created by Congress in 1986 and 1987. These changes relate to how much of your home loan interest expense can be deductible on your tax return. Limitations on deductibility will come into play, for the most part, if you *refinance* an existing home loan or if you borrow money using your home as collateral (so-called home equity borrowing, in which you give the lender a mortgage as security). The amount of your interest deductions can be affected by the *date* you do such borrowing, the *amount* you borrow, and the *purpose* for which you are borrowing. Professional tax counsel should be sought whenever you borrow using your home as security.

TIMING, TIMING, TIMING

A final word to those who embark on the stormy seas of home loan shopping: A great deal depends on your getting your loan paid out to you at the exact time you need it. Delays in processing loan applications can cause a domino effect with wide repercussions. If you learn that your loan processing is delayed for whatever reason, you might not be able to have your closing at the time you wanted it. Technically, that might give the seller the right to cancel the whole transaction, though most sellers will go along with moderate delays if they are approached properly at the earliest possible time. A delay in your closing means that you'll have to continue living where you are for another month or two. That means added cost and inconvenience. If you are in an apartment and you've already given notice to your landlord that you expect to leave on November 1 and you find that your home loan application won't be completed until December 15, you're in a pickle.

To the best of your ability, make certain that you establish a workable schedule with the lender from the outset. Complete the proper paperwork within the prescribed time frame. Delays may be caused by the lender as well as the borrower, and there's little you can do to prevent that. But the more open and thorough your communications with the lender, the better able you'll be to anticipate and deal with any possible delays.

PERSONAL ACTION WORKSHEET

Financing Comparisons

It's expected that most home financing plans will be based on an adjustable interest rate—a rate that can be adjusted upward or downward from time to time. Since it's impossible to know what future rate fluctuations will be, there's no way a borrower can accurately predict his or her mortgage costs over a long period of time. The dilemma is further compounded by the fact that different lenders use different formulas to vary the rate, thus making a comparison between lenders very difficult. The following worksheet is to help you ask the right questions in evaluating adjustable rate financing plans. The more you know about how the plans work, the more judicious your decision can be.

	Plan A	Plan B	Plan C
❏ What is the starting interest rate?	____	____	____
❏ How often can the rate be changed?	____	____	____
❏ How much can the rate be raised at any given interval?	____	____	____
❏ How much can the rate be raised over the life of the loan?	____	____	____
❏ How much can the rate be lowered at any given interval?	____	____	____
❏ How much can the rate be lowered over the life of the loan?	____	____	____
❏ By what outside index are the rate changes to be measured? (Consumer Price Index? Cost of funds? Prime rate?)	____	____	____
❏ Is there a prepayment penalty? If so, how much?	____	____	____
❏ If the rate is increased at any given interval, do you, the borrower, have the option of keeping the monthly payment the same (in which case the final maturity of the loan will be extended)?	____	____	____
❏ If your answer to the above question is yes, what limits, if any, are there to the option?	____	____	____

CONSUMER ALERT

Be Well Prepared for Loan Application Process

Exercise 7.9

In the late 1980s an excess of bad loans were made all across the country. (See chapter 11.) Since then, lenders have become stricter in the information they require from loan applicants. Because home loans involve many legal and technical matters, loan applicants must be ready to present a burdensome amount of documentation. It's wise to ask in advance for a list of all the items your lender might want. Then check off each item as you acquire it, and note the full list of items in a covering letter that you send to the lender along with your application. That will help you make sure you've supplied everything needed, which will speed up your application process.

Bank of America, for example, has asked home loan applicants to provide the following:

Your last two years' W-2 (wage and earnings) statements; your last month's current pay stubs; your most recent three months' bank statements (to verify funds for down payment); your most recent monthly mortgage statement *and* either the last full year-end mortgage statement or canceled checks for the last twelve months' mortgage payments (this is for those who already own a home); your federal income tax returns for the last two years; your most recent loan statements for all other debts, charge accounts, and credit cards.

There are additional requirements for those purchasing, for those refinancing, and for those who are self-employed. All told, plan to spend several hours digging through all your records before you even start filling out the application.

UPS & DOWNS   *The Economics of Everyday Life* ————————————

The Frenzies of Home Loan Interest Rates

Exercise 7.10

Before you read this segment, please read the Ups & Downs segments in chapters 12 and 13. They will provide a necessary introduction to interest rate movements in general.

The interest rate phenomenon in home loans can best be expressed as weird. Consider: With adjustable rate loans, the *starting* rate for a loan will be pegged to current *long*-term rates. But the up and down rate adjustments that are made periodically (usually every six months) are pegged to *short*-term rates (such as U.S. Treasury Bill rates or comparable measures). So you have a long-term (15 to 30 years) debt that is constantly being rearranged as short-term (3 to 12 months) interest rates move up and down. This protects the lender if interest rates trend upward and protects the borrower if rates fall.

With fixed interest loans there's an even more bizarre situation. Banks must keep a "spread" between the interest they earn from the loans they make and the interest they pay to their depositors. This spread provides money for the bank to operate and, hopefully, make a reasonable profit. When a bank makes a fixed rate home loan for thirty years, at, say, 8 percent, it is committed to earning only that 8 percent on that money for that time period. If, at that time, the bank is paying 5 percent (on average) to its depositors, it has a spread of 3 percent. But that payment to depositors is based on *short*-term trends, such as certificates of deposit for one or two years. A few years go by, and interest rates in general move up, so that the banks are paying 6 or 7 percent to their depositors. But they're still only earning 8 percent on the fixed rate loans they made years earlier. So they could be losing money on those particular loans. New loans will, of course, be made at higher rates, but it can be unhealthy for lenders to be making money on some loans and losing it on others—particularly if they loaned heavily while rates were low, and got caught in a competitive free-for-all for depositors when rates later turned higher. In this fixed rate scenario, as opposed to the adjustable rate one, borrowers are happier when interest rates go up (they're protected with their lower fixed rate), and lenders are happier when rates go down (they can pay less to their depositors and thus increase their spread).

The intervention of Ginnie Mae and her cousins (see the discussion in this chapter) as buyers of loans has helped to moderate the risks involved. But the ups and downs of home loan interest rates remain a puzzle for both borrowers and lenders.

?   WHAT IF . . . ?

How would you deal with these real-life possibilities?

1. You've applied for a home loan of $120,000. Your credit rating is fine, and your income status is secure. But because of a lower-than-expected appraisal, the bank is willing to lend you only $110,000. You definitely want to buy the house. How can you proceed to your desired end?

2. You've worked out a home-buying budget that has virtually no breathing room, considering all the costs of financing, furnishing, utilities, and other obligations that go with homeownership. Your home loan application is approved, but at a higher interest rate than you had expected. (Rates went up between the time you applied and the time the loan was paid out to you, and you didn't have a rate lock.) The higher interest rate will mean an extra $80 per month out-of-pocket. How will that impact on your life? What are your options?

3. Your home financing has been approved: you'll get the purchase money mortgage from a local bank, and the seller will take back a second mortgage of $25,000. However, at the last minute the seller tells you he'll carry your IOU for only one year. This matter hadn't been discussed before. You had assumed that he'd carry the IOU for a much longer, though unspecified, period. What problems does this pose? How can you resolve them?

NUMBER CRUNCHERS

Do the calculations to make decisions in these real-life possibilities.

1. See exercise number 1 in Number Crunchers in chapter 6. Using the mortgage tables in this chapter, take the calculations some steps further: Using the same housing prices and down payments, calculate the dollar amount of down payment and monthly payment using 7 percent and 12 percent fixed interest rates for a 30-year term. Of all the resulting possibilities, pick one at random, and calculate how much of the loan would be paid off after making payments on it for 5 years, 10 years, and 15 years.

2. You're shopping for a home loan of $100,000. Using current rates as a starting point, calculate what your monthly payments would be if your interest rate increased by one-half percentage point each year for 5 years. What if rates decreased by one-half percentage point each year for 5 years? Compare the results with the current rates on a fixed rate loan.

⚖️ *FOR BETTER OR FOR WORSE*

Things beyond our control often impact our personal and financial well-being, for better or for worse. Some are more predictable than others. How could you be affected if the following real-life phenomena happened? Could you have seen it coming? What steps could you have taken to minimize damage or maximize advantage? The better able you are to anticipate and recognize these forces, the better equipped you are to deal with them.

1. Believing that you have a good credit history, you apply for a home loan. But your credit report comes back with some information that causes your application to be rejected. You could lose the deal.

2. You've spent twenty hard hours of drudgery preparing all of the documents and applications for a home loan at Bank A. Then Bank B announces home loans—for which you would qualify—at an interest rate one percentage point less than Bank A.

3. At the closing of your home purchase you are told of about $2,500 in miscellaneous loan costs that you had not expected—at least, you couldn't recall being told about them.

Exercise 7.11

8

Housing Costs
and Regulations

A home is no home unless it contains food and fire for the mind as well as the body.
Margaret Fuller

The cost of maintaining a dwelling does not end with writing your monthly mortgage or rent check. Home or condo owners, in particular, feel a constant drain on their budget from such expenses as property taxes, property insurance, utilities, and maintenance. All these items must be properly anticipated if you are to keep your financial affairs on an even keel.

In addition to costs, your dwelling situation can be affected by local rules and regulations that must be complied with.

This chapter is designed to assist you in planning sensibly to meet your overall dwelling costs and to alert you to the legal rights and responsibilities that pertain to dwellings. You'll learn how to

- Choose the right type and amount of property insurance
- Take action to cut your property taxes if they are wrongfully too high
- Get control of your utility and maintenance costs
- Protect yourself and your property if neighbors or landlords violate housing rules and regulations

PROPERTY INSURANCE

Property insurance provides two forms of protection. First, it reimburses you for loss or damage to the building, the contents, and the furnishings. Second, it protects you in the event that harm comes to other people or to the property of other people. This latter form of protection is known as public liability insurance. As an owner or tenant of property, you can be responsible if others are harmed as a result of your negligence. The law does not require you to maintain public liability insurance on your house or apartment, as it does on automobiles in most states. But the law will require you to pay damages should a court find that you were responsible for injuries suffered by another. Lack of proper insurance either on the building or for public liability can prove financially catastrophic.

In general, homeowner's insurance will reimburse you in the amount needed to replace or repair lost or damaged property, based on its value at the time of loss. Some kinds of property, such as a house or jewelry, tend to increase in replacement cost. Other types of property, such as furniture and carpeting, tend to decrease in value. These changes in value are known as *appreciation* and *depreciation.* Your insurance should be adjusted periodically to reflect these changing values.

For those who rent, there is a special type of policy called the tenant's policy. It provides protection against loss or damage to furnishings and personal items as well as public liability protection.

The cost of your homeowner's or tenant's insurance will depend on a number of factors: the company you deal with, the risk rating of your property, and the amount of protection you seek.

The Company You Deal With

Exercise 8.1

As with all other forms of insurance, property insurance is competitive. Rates for similar coverage can differ from company to company. The cheapest protection is not necessarily the best. You must try to gauge the extent of service you'll get from the company, their response to claims, and the possibility of increased premiums when claims have been submitted.

The Risk Ratings of the Property

Each property insured will be rated by the insurance companies according to relative risk factors. These factors can include location of the building and proximity to fire stations and fire hydrants, construction of the building (for example, brick as opposed to wood frame), proximity to other buildings, and fire and crime statistics in the neighborhood in which the building is located. Check with your agent to determine what precautions you might

take to keep your property insurance premiums as low as possible. Such precautions might include installation of fire extinguishers and fire retardant materials, cleanup of attics and basements, installation of security devices such as smoke detectors and burglar alarms, and secure locking mechanisms.

The Amount of Coverage You Desire

If you have a mortgage on your house, the lender will require you to carry at least enough insurance to pay off your debt if the house is destroyed. You might not care to pay for any more protection than that minimum amount. Or, if you desire, you can carry much broader coverage. (Even flooding can be insured against under existing federal programs.)

THE TYPES OF POLICIES AND COVERAGE

Exercise 8.2

Homeowner's insurance comes in three primary forms: the basic form, or "Homeowners 1"; the broad form, or "Homeowners 2" (the tenant's form is similar to the Homeowners 2 and is known as Homeowners 4); and the comprehensive form known as "Homeowners 5." A special form, "Homeowners 3," combines the broad form (HO2) coverage on personal property with the comprehensive form (HO5) coverage on the dwelling itself.

The Basic Form (HO1)

With HO1, your premises are protected against the most common risks. These risks include:

- Fire
- Lightning
- Windstorm
- Hail
- Explosions
- Theft (except for certain items, among which are credit cards)
- Breakage of glass in the building
- Loss of, or damage suffered to, personal property that you removed from endangered premises (e.g., the building next door to you is on fire and you flee into the night clutching some private possessions that are later lost or damaged—they are covered under your basic form policy)

- Riots
- Aircraft
- Vehicles
- Smoke damage
- Vandalism, malicious mischief

The Broad Form (HO2)

The broad form (HO2) and the tenant's form (HO4) provide protection against additional risks at a nominal extra cost. These include:

- Falling objects
- Collapse of the building
- Damage to the building due to the weight of ice or snow
- Certain damage caused by escape of steam and water from a boiler, radiator, or similar device
- Certain accidents involving electrical equipment, such as an over-loaded circuit that blows out an appliance

The Comprehensive Form (HO5)

The comprehensive form is sometimes referred to as an *all risk* policy. But it will generally exclude certain risks from coverage, such as earthquakes, tidal waves, sewer backups and seepage, landslides, floods, war, and nuclear radiation. See each specific policy to determine what exceptions are listed. Even though flood may be excluded from coverage, the federal government has acted to make flood insurance more easily available to homeowners in flood-prone areas. Your agent can give you details on this coverage. The added cost of the comprehensive protection may not be worth it to many homeowners; examine your own circumstance to determine what kind of protection is best for the dollars available.

Protecting Other Property

Exercise 8.3

The typical homeowner's policy also provides extended coverage for other forms of property. For example, garages and storage sheds will customarily be covered for 10 percent of the full value of the main building. In other words, if the main building is covered for $80,000, the auxiliary buildings will be covered for a total of $8,000. Your personal property within the home, such as furniture, appliances, and bedding, may be covered for as much as 50 percent of the coverage on the house itself. Other types of personal property, including jewelry, chinaware, paintings, and furs, will be covered under your basic policy for loss due to fire but will have to be separately covered for theft or loss. (See the section "Valuables.")

If your home or apartment suffers damage and you are required to live elsewhere while the damage is repaired, the typical homeowner's and tenant's policies provide you with additional living expenses—usually 10

percent on the basic HO1 policy and 20 percent on the broad and comprehensive policies—with the percentages calculated on the total primary value. In addition, your trees, plants, and shrubs will be covered for up to 5 percent of the primary value in the event they are damaged.

Public Liability

Homeowner's policies also contain public liability protection. Commonly, the homeowner's policy provides up to $100,000 liability protection per occurrence, $1,000 in medical expenses payable to others, and 50 percent of your home's coverage in property damages. For example: A guest in your house slips on a banana peel that you have negligently left lying in the hallway. X-rays reveal that she has fractured her hip and has also broken her wristwatch in the fall. The homeowner's policy provides up to $1,000 in medical expenses and reimburses the injured party for the broken watch. The injured party then learns that she will be unable to work for a number of months and makes a claim against your homeowner's policy. The public liability provision would pay up to $100,000 in damages—loss of income— as a result of the accident.

If you live in an apartment or a condominium, the issue of public liability protection is a bit more complicated. You should maintain coverage to protect yourself for anything that may occur within *your* premises. The apartment building owner or the condominium owner's association should also maintain adequate coverage to protect all interested parties in the event of an injury in a *common area*, such as a parking lot, a hallway, or an elevator. You, as a tenant or condo owner, should make certain that the coverage on the common areas is adequate to protect you if someone is hurt in a common area and sues everyone in sight for as much as possible.

Much higher limits for public liability can be obtained at a fairly modest increase in premium, and a wise homeowner might do well to consider obtaining a much higher level of protection than the basic policy offers.

Valuables

Valuable personal property may *not* be adequately covered for theft or loss under your homeowner's or tenant's policies. Valuable personal property can include such items as jewelry, paintings, sculptures, china, silver, cameras, computers, collections (stamps, coins, medallions), golf clubs, furs, securities, cash, and credit cards. In order to be fully covered for loss of these items—whether at home or away—you may have to obtain a separate *personal floater*. The cost of this added insurance can be considerable. You should seek the assistance of your agent in determining exactly what personal property is covered under your homeowner's policy and under what circumstances you may wish additional protection for your valuables.

The Deductible

Exercise 8.4

The cost of your policy will vary in relation to the deductible you choose. The deductible is the amount you pay out of pocket for any losses before the insurance company becomes responsible. Some policies have a no-deductible clause, which means that the insurance company is responsible for the first dollar onward. A $50 deductible means that, in any given occurrence, you must pay the first $50 worth of expense before the insurance company becomes responsible. Deductibles can be as much as $250 or $500. In choosing a higher deductible, you are exposing yourself to more potential risk in return for a lower premium. The premium will not be lowered as much as the risk will be increased. For example, the difference in cost between a $50 deductible and a $250 deductible may be only $20 or $30, but you're exposing yourself to $200 more potential risk. However, the higher premium is an actual out-of-pocket cost that you can save, whereas the added risk is only a possible expense that you might never incur.

The Coinsurance Clause

This can be extremely important. The coinsurance clause states generally that, if you wish to receive full replacement value for any damage to the premises, you must insure the premises for at least 80 percent of its replacement cost. For example, a house has a current replacement cost (not counting the land and foundation) of $80,000. That means that at current going

prices, it would cost $80,000 to duplicate the house, in its depreciated condition, on the existing foundation. (The land and the foundation are not included in figuring costs for insurance coverage because theoretically they would not be destroyed.) But the owner had insured the building for only $56,000, which is $8,000 shy of the 80 percent level of $64,000. The owner has a fire in the house that results in an actual loss of $16,000. But because he has not insured up to the 80 percent coinsurance level, the company will pay him only $14,000 instead of the full $16,000. Why? Because the owner's coverage was only seven-eighths of what it should have been under the coinsurance clause ($56,000 is seven-eighths of $64,000). Thus, the owner will receive only seven-eighths of the actual damages ($14,000 is seven-eighths of $16,000). If the owner had insured the property for the full 80 percent coinsurance value, or $64,000, he would have recovered the full $16,000 on the loss. The difference in premium between the full 80 percent value and the lesser value would have been so relatively small that the owner could be accused of being woefully imprudent for not obtaining the balance of the 80 percent coverage.

Keeping Up with Change

Prudent homeowners or tenants will make a careful inventory of all furnishings, appliances, and personal property and evaluate current market or replacement costs of those items in order to determine whether they are adequately covered by a basic homeowner's policy. The owner or renter will also be aware of the effects of inflation in most areas of the country. Many policies offer clauses that automatically increase the amount of coverage in line with inflation, for as the replacement value of the house increases, so must the amount of coverage if the owner is to be adequately protected. Policies may also be available that will pay you the full amount needed to rebuild your home, no matter what the cost.

If a homeowner or tenant acquires new personal items, or disposes of old items that have been insured, the owner must notify the insurance company so that the new acquisitions can be properly covered and the old dispositions properly deleted. When the insurance company is notified, it will issue an endorsement amending the policy, which should be checked for accuracy and then attached to the policy.

Filing a Claim

Exercise 8.5

In the event you do suffer a loss or damage, notify your insurance agent immediately. The agent may require that you obtain estimates of the proper repair or replacement of damaged items. If a burglary or theft has occurred, it

Be Wise About Home-Improvement Costs

Adding major improvements to your home can increase the value of the home accordingly. But take care not to overdo it, or you won't be able to recapture the expense when you later sell. Two prime problems: improving the house so much that you price it out of the range of similar homes in the neighborhood; and improvements that are too personalized, which a prospective buyer might find frivolous or unnecessary. For example, new kitchen cabinets and bathroom fixtures are reasonably safe bets: you'll probably get back most of the cost of them when you sell. But building an observatory in your attic or installing a waterfall in your yard might not appeal to a buyer. Chances are you won't get your money back on such highly personalized items. Consider the items in Table 8-1.

TABLE 8-1   Payback Time

If you spend money remodeling or adding on to your home, how much of that money are you likely to get back when you later sell the home? Numbers can vary widely, depending on your location, the quality of the work, and when it is done, but here are some general guidelines that might influence you to go ahead, or not bother with, a specific project. Figures are national averages. Return is the percentage of the original cost that you're likely to get back on resale.

Item	Average Cost	Payback	Return
Attic bedroom	$22,840	$19,084	84%
Bathroom addition	11,645	10,593	91
Bathroom remodel	8,423	6,480	77
Major kitchen remodel	21,262	19,190	84
Minor kitchen remodel	8,057	8,030	94
Master suite addition	36,472	30,530	84
Refinish basement	16,665	8,499	51
Built-in media center	4,353	2,699	62
Hard-wired security system	1,303	756	58
Home office	8,706	5,423	67
Replace siding	5,458	3,983	73

Pools: Returns averaged 31% for vinyl-lined, 44% for concrete (gunite), and 45% for fiberglass.

Sources: Remodeling Magazine, Dec. 1996.

may be necessary to obtain copies of the police report. If someone is hurt on your property, you should also report this immediately to your agent, for a public liability claim may arise. Under the public liability provisions of your homeowner's policy, the insurance company is obliged to provide le-

gal defense for you against such claims as well as to pay any claims that are found to be valid. Delay in reporting to your agent could jeopardize your rights under your homeowner's policy.

PROPERTY TAXES

Property taxes (also called real estate taxes) provide the money that allows your city government to operate. A portion of the property taxes may also be allocated to the county and state within which your city is located to enable them to provide their respective services.

How are property taxes calculated? In order to meet the expenses of city services, the city must generate income from taxation. Representatives of the assessor's office review each property in the city periodically to determine the actual value of each parcel. When the current value of every property is known, the assessment rate is applied. For example, a given city may determine that residential property will be assessed at 20 percent of market value, while commercial property will be assessed at 25 percent and industrial property at 30 percent. (Business and industrial areas frequently contribute to a heavier share of tax dollars because they are using the property for income-producing purposes.) Thus, a house with a market value of $150,000 may be assessed at $30,000. In theory, all properties of the same type with equal market values are assessed equally.

They then determine the tax rate. Based on their budgetary needs, they may determine that the tax rate for a given year will be $100 for each $1,000 of assessed valuation. Thus, the house with the $150,000 current value, which has an assessment of $30,000 (20 percent of the current market value according to the formula) will pay taxes of $3,000 for the year.

The tax rate is adjusted annually to keep the city's income and expenses as close to equal as possible. Periodically all properties in the city, or a selection of properties in the city, may be reassessed to make sure they are in line with the prevailing market values.

Commonly, homeowners are billed for their property taxes in two installments six months apart. Tenants also indirectly pay a share of the tax because some of their rent is applied by the landlord to the tax bill on the property. If a property owner fails to pay property taxes, the city can sell the property at public auction to satisfy the unpaid taxes due.

Protesting Your Assessment

Exercise 8.6

Local laws allow owners to protest the assessment on their property and, if successful, reduce the assessment and thereby the taxes. Tenants can also take steps to have the assessment reduced in conjunction with the landlord, in the same way that individual property owners can.

STRATEGIES FOR SUCCESS

Energy Audit Can Save $$$$$

Your local utility company—gas, electric, water—may be willing to examine your home to see how you might be wasting energy. And wasted energy is wasted money. In addition to hints and tips that utilities publish from time to time, they may send representatives to your home to make an inspection that can result in money-saving suggestions. An energy audit can be particularly worthwhile if you are thinking of installing new major energy-using devices, such as water heater, furnace, air conditioner or refrigerator.

Although each local assessor's office attempts to value equal properties equally, errors can occur. Equal properties are those comparable in size, location, and date and quality of construction. Example: Your house and your next-door neighbor's house are identical. They were built at the same time by the same builder, and have the same size and room layout. They are virtual twins—with one exception: your house is assessed for $38,000 while your neighbor's house is assessed for only $30,000, with an annual tax bill roughly 20 percent lower than yours.

If an error exists concerning property you own or occupy, nobody other than you will take steps to correct that error. An improper assessment can mean hundreds of dollars lost each year, so it behooves any property owner to examine the local assessment rolls every few years to determine that the property is, in fact, being properly assessed.

The steps are relatively simple. Visit your local assessor's office and compare the assessments of the buildings in your immediate neighborhood. If you determine that your property is appraised too high, ask the assessor to explain how to file a protest. It's not necessary to have an attorney, but it might be wise if there is enough at stake. Regulations will differ from one community to the next, but it is common for there to be a cutoff date each year, after which assessments cannot be protested until the following year.

Exercise 8.7

Figure 8–1 illustrates a typical neighborhood. Assume that all houses were built at the same time and are equal in size and condition. Houses A and C are assessed at $20,000 each; house B is assessed at $25,000; houses D and E are each assessed at $30,000. Why the discrepancy? Since A, B, and C are indeed equal, it is likely that house B is overassessed by $5,000. House D might be rightfully assessed at $30,000 since it is a corner lot and in many communities a corner lot is considered more valuable than an interior lot. House E might be properly assessed at $30,000 if the street on which it fronts is considered to be a "better" street, such as a cul-de-sac, than the street on which the other houses front. But if you owned house B, D, or E, you'd be wise to make an inquiry of your local assessor.

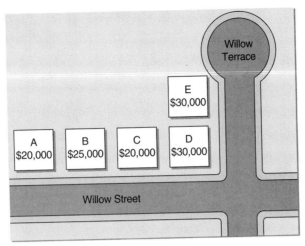

FIGURE 8–1   Property tax assessments

UTILITIES

The owner of a house makes arrangements with the local utility companies for them to provide water, gas, electricity, and telephone service. Utility bills, particularly for heating, can vary considerably throughout the seasons. Some utility companies offer budget payment plans in which the estimated annual cost is broken down into relatively even payments, allowing homeowners to even out their overall budgets.

The importance of energy conservation cannot be overstated. In addition to keeping your energy usage at a minimum—in line with your personal comfort needs—look into the tax credits and rebate plans offered by many states as well as the federal government for conservation improvements to your property. Explore these possibilities with your local utility companies.

MAINTENANCE AND REPAIRS

Human nature being what it is, we seldom get around to doing preventive maintenance on a house—such as seasonal lubrication and servicing of a furnace—until we hear the creaks and rattles warning that it is about to self-destruct. Unexpected maintenance costs can be a severe jolt to any budget.

To the homeowner, a periodic inspection is cheap insurance, alerting you to potential dangers and expenses. In addition to paying for ongoing maintenance costs, wise homeowners will set aside a reserve for replacements—a fund to take care of these costs without having to borrow, or dip into savings, or otherwise disrupt their normal budgets.

LAWS REGULATING HOUSING

A number of laws can affect the rights and obligations of both property owners and tenants. These laws differ from state to state and from city to city, so you should make inquiry in your own locality as to any laws that might affect you.

Zoning

Cities specify that certain areas may have only certain kinds of uses permitted in them. The city will be divided into zones according to the uses allowed in those zones. The broad categories in zoning regulations are residential, commercial, industrial, and agricultural. Within each category there may be subcategories. For example, within a residential category, there may be zones for just single-family housing, and zones in which multiple housing is permitted. Each zone may have regulations applicable to that zone. In a commercial zone, for example, there may be a requirement that so many off-street parking places are available for each thousand square feet of building space.

Generally, zoning regulations are like a pyramid: higher uses are permitted in any of the lower use zones, but lower use of zones may not be permitted in the zones above them. Figure 8–2 provides an illustration: In most cities, the highest use is for single-family homes, often designated as R (for

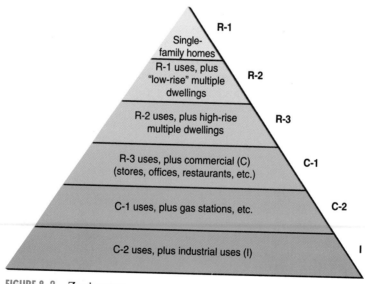

FIGURE 8–2   Zoning use

residential) -1. In areas zoned R-1, therefore, only single-family homes will be permitted. The next zone down may be designated R-2. These zones would permit R-1 uses (single-family homes) plus "low-rise" multiple dwellings. The next zone down might be called R-3, and it would permit all R-2 uses, plus high-rise multiple dwellings.

Zoning laws exist to maintain the quality of your neighborhood. For example: You wish to set up a beauty parlor in your home. You hang a sign on your front porch and accept clientele. If your home is in a zone that prevents businesses from being operated in the home, neighbors could have your business stopped because it is in violation of the zoning ordinances.

Residents of any municipality should make themselves aware of current zoning regulations and be on the alert for any change in the immediate vicinity that could affect the value of their residence. Zoning hearings are usually open to the public, and customarily appeals can be taken from unfavorable zoning rulings. If many people are affected by the possibility of a zoning ordinance change, they can group together and hire an attorney to represent all their joint interests.

Nuisances

One of your neighbors keeps a rooster that crows at dawn each morning; another plays a stereo at high volume every night; still another permits dangerous conditions to exist. These practices, and others like them, are known as nuisances. If you're located in an apartment house or a condominium, you may be able to get assistance from a sympathetic landlord or from the condominium owners' association. If you're a homeowner, you may have to resort to the local police or to your own attorney to get satisfaction. Nuisance laws exist in almost every city, but enforcing them can involve feats of diplomacy that the local magistrates may be incapable of carrying out to your satisfaction. If you can't resolve a nuisance problem with a neighbor by simple diplomacy, consider arbitration before getting involved with lawyers. Many communities offer free or low-priced arbitration services.

Eminent Domain

The law of eminent domain permits a government to acquire private property when the government can prove that the need exists for the public welfare. The process is generally known as condemnation, and it occurs where new highways and bridges are to be constructed, where urban renewal programs take place, and where other public uses are called for. Owners of property threatened by condemnation are entitled to fair payment for their property. Procedures vary as to how property owners are compensated.

There may be a hearing at which property owners present their claims for fair compensation. If the owners aren't satisfied with the offer, they may appeal, and if the appeal does not satisfy, the owners may take the matter into the courts. The aid of a lawyer and a competent real estate appraiser is advised in any condemnation situation.

The law of eminent domain can also affect your property indirectly, without actually taking any portion of it. For example, a new highway nearby may create noise and pollution problems for your house. None of your property has actually been taken, but the value of the property may suffer as a result. You may be entitled to some claim for damages as a result.

Anyone who is either buying or already owns any property should be aware of any possible eminent domain that could take place within proximity to your property. Knowledge of an impending condemnation might discourage you from buying certain property, and that knowledge can also permit you to take early action to protect your interests if a condemnation threatens currently owned property.

Rent Control and Condominium Conversion Regulations

If you live in a multiple-dwelling unit, rent control ordinances and condominium conversion regulations can have a very important effect on your rights. These laws will be discussed in more detail in the following chapter on renting.

PERSONAL ACTION WORKSHEET

Insurance Inventory

Whether you're a renter or an owner, it's important that your valuable personal possessions be adequately insured against damage or loss. Insurance coverage is advisable if the damage or loss would cause you financial distress. (Insuring items of sentimental value may be an unwise expense.) Too little or too much coverage can be costly. This checklist will help you determine the right amount of coverage. A color photo of each item can be very helpful if you ever have to file a claim.

Items	Current Protection	Replacement Cost	Cost to Insure Fully	Most Recent Appraisal
❏ Jewelry	_____	_____	_____	_____
❏ Collections	_____	_____	_____	_____
❏ Art	_____	_____	_____	_____
❏ Chinaware	_____	_____	_____	_____
❏ Silverware	_____	_____	_____	_____
❏ Cash, securities	_____	_____	_____	_____
❏ Musical instruments	_____	_____	_____	_____
❏ Electronic items (TV, stereo, VCR, computer)	_____	_____	_____	_____
❏ Sports equipment	_____	_____	_____	_____
❏ Furniture and furnishings	_____	_____	_____	_____

CONSUMER ALERT

Mortgage Insurance Can Be Confusing

There's one kind of insurance related to home ownership that really doesn't insure the property itself. Rather, it insures that your mortgage payments will be made in the event of the death or disability of the primary breadwinner in the family.

Since your mortgage debt is the largest you'll probably ever face, and since your payments represent a major obligation, it's wise to protect yourself against a catastrophe that could affect your ability to pay this debt.

Life insurance on your mortgage is generally of the "decreasing term" variety. The coverage decreases monthly as the amount of your debt decreases. Depending on your age, you might want to explore a level term or ordinary life policy instead of the decreasing term. Those might provide better long-term protection without greatly increasing your cost.

On the death of the breadwinner, proceeds of mortgage life insurance are commonly paid directly to the lender. This may not be best for you. It might be preferable to obtain a policy that would pay your named beneficiary (spouse, children) to do with as they please. Rather than have the mortgage paid off, they might prefer to continue making payments or to sell the house with the original mortgage intact. If the interest rate on the mortgage is lower than the current rate, it could prove costly later if the survivors needed to refinance the property at a higher interest rate.

Disability policies make your monthly payments for you if you are unable to work due to illness or accident. Many have a thirty- or sixty-day waiting period before payments commence. Compare the terms and costs of such policies, bearing in mind other sources of income that might be available to help you make your payments during a spell of disability. Your own insurance agent might be able to provide better coverage at lower cost than the lender can.

UPS & DOWNS   *The Economics of Everyday Life*

Why Utility Costs Fluctuate

As with food and travel prices, the seasons again are the main culprit for changing utility prices. You'll spend more on heating in the winter and more on cooling in the summer. Lawn watering boosts water bills in spring and summer; shorter days mean higher electric bills (for lighting) in fall and winter. Many of these fluctuations can be evened out: Most utility companies have budget plans that can offer you a level monthly payment throughout the year.

But other factors can also impact on your utility budget, and when they do you might have to increase your conservation vigil to keep costs down.

Commodity prices   You no doubt use gas or oil for heating, and your local electric company may burn oil to turn its generators. Worldwide fluctuations in the prices of these commodities will influence what you pay to warm your house, heat your water, or turn on your lights.

Mother Nature   Natural forces can play cruel tricks, such as shutting off the water supply. Recently, California suffered through a prolonged drought. Homeowners faced heavy penalties if their water usage exceeded certain levels. Farmers were also deprived of their full supply of water, which cut down the size of the crops, which in turn boosted food prices.

Competition   Telephone utilities didn't have any competition until the mid-1980s, when American Telephone and Telegraph (AT&T) was broken up into separate regional units, and a number of long-distance telephone companies emerged to challenge AT&T's historic monopoly. Today you have your choice of many long-distance carriers and local carriers. This change, together with the emergence of cellular phones, has transformed what once was a simple one-page telephone bill into a massive computer printout.

Regulation   With rare exceptions, suppliers of water, electricity, heating fuels, and telephone services are regulated by a state agency, the Public Utilities Commission (or a name similar to that). These agencies see to it that the utilities charge rates that are fair to consumers, but they still allow the utilities enough income to maintain and expand their facilities, and to attract investment capital. But mistakes can happen: nuclear power facilities were built across the nation in the 1970s that would supposedly reduce electricity costs. However, many of those expensive projects failed to meet their targets, and local consumers had to bear much of the excess costs.

? **WHAT IF . . . ?**

How would you deal with these real-life possibilities?

1. You would like to do some work out of your home. Examples might include dealing in baseball cards or other collectibles; setting up a beauty salon; becoming a mail order distributor; or providing services to the public, such as tax returns or piano lessons. Each of these activities might violate a local zoning ordinance or might otherwise upset neighbors. What can you/should you do in advance to minimize any problems?

2. In chatting with neighbors you learn that your property taxes are much higher than those of comparable dwellings in the immediate neighborhood. One neighbor suggests to you that if you try to get your taxes lowered, that effort could backfire and cause everyone else's taxes to go up. Where do you go from here?

3. You have some valuables that would be covered on your property insurance policy only if they were separately "scheduled." Your insurance agent tells you that the cost of doing so would be very high. What options do you have that would be cost-effective?

NUMBER CRUNCHERS

Do the calculations to make decisions in these real-life possibilities.

1. There are many ways to cut your utility costs, including better insulation, weather-stripping on doors and windows, and awnings and shades to reduce the need for air conditioning. Calculate the actual installed costs of any such devices that you think can be cost-effective. Estimate as closely as possible (with the help of your utility companies) what savings you can realize. What net benefits, if any, are there? How will the installation of any of these devices affect the value of your property when you want to sell it?

2. How much can you save on property insurance premiums if you increase your deductibles? How much financial risk does this expose you to? How much can you reduce your risk by reducing your deductibles?

3. Based on your existing property insurance policy (either as an owner or as a tenant), calculate how much you'd receive from your insurance company if you suffered specific damages: (a) Fire damages the building—reconstruction cost of the building is $30,000, and replacement cost of personal property is $10,000. (b) Smoke damages personal property—cleaning and replacement cost is $3,000. (c) A burglar breaks in and steals the TV set, VCR, computer, and golf clubs—replacement cost total $4,000. If you can't calculate the answers on your own, ask your insurance agent to help you.

FOR BETTER OR FOR WORSE

Things beyond our control often impact our personal and financial well-being, for better or for worse. Some are more predictable than others. How would you be affected if the following real-life phenomena happened? Could you have seen it coming? What steps could you have taken to minimize damage or maximize advantage? The better able you are to anticipate and recognize these forces, the better equipped you are to deal with them.

1. It's party time! Saturday night, and you're expecting thirty guests for a rousing birthday party. As the first guests arrive you remember that you forgot to renew your dwelling insurance policy the day before, the last day of the grace period.

2. A fire in your apartment building causes smoke damage to your furniture and all fabrics (clothes, linens, towels, drapes, etc.) They stink, and it will cost about $1,000 to clean and deodorize everything. You don't have tenant's insurance because you thought it cost too much.

3. A neighbor's home is burgled. A few days later you're visited by a home security company selling burglar alarms.

Renting

Many a man who pays rent all his life owns his own home. And many a family has successfully saved for a home, only to find itself at last with nothing but a house.

Bruce Barton

Tens of millions of Americans rent their dwellings. Many do so because they've not been able to accumulate enough money to purchase a house or condominium. Others do so because they prefer the freedom and flexibility that comes with renting. Renting entails many important legal and financial considerations. This chapter will make you aware of those considerations and will help you resolve common problems that come with renting. They include:

- What factors you should evaluate in deciding whether to rent or to buy
- How to understand the terms of a lease and how to negotiate a rental arrangement that's best for you
- How you may be able to obtain the right to buy the place you've been renting or want to rent
- What to do if your rights as a tenant are violated

If you are a renter, you are paying another person a fee for the privilege of living in his or her property. You might rent a person's house, or you might rent a multiple-unit dwelling, such as a duplex, a condominium complex, or an apartment house. Mobile home rentals are also not uncommon.

A renter occupies a dwelling in one of two ways: on a month-to-month basis or on a fixed-term basis. On a month-to-month basis, both the landlord and the tenant have the right to terminate the arrangement upon

giving 30 days' notice to the other party. Commonly, the landlord expects the tenant to comply with certain rules and regulations, which are often spelled out in a written agreement. On a fixed-term basis, the landlord and tenant agree in a written document that the tenant has the right to occupy the premises for a specific time, such as one year or two years. The agreement between the two parties is referred to as a lease.

PROS AND CONS OF RENTING

Exercise 9.1

Many people, particularly in larger cities, are dyed-in-the-wool renters. They simply prefer the apartment mode of living—being close to other people and free of the cares that often go with ownership. To them, rental is a way of life, and they don't think about buying a home.

Other people have no choice: They don't have the money to make a down payment on a home, and thus they must be renters. This group is further broken down into two categories: (1) those who prefer to spend their money on other things rather than accumulate it for a down payment, and thus will probably remain permanent renters, and (2) those who desire to become owners eventually and who structure their budget so as to accumulate the necessary down payment. As they struggle to accumulate those funds, they often wonder: Is it worth it to own a home, or should we just be content as renters?

Traditionally, homeownership has been considered a wise step financially. Over the long run, that probably remains true. But ownership is not the right choice for everybody.

To help you make the decision best suited to your needs, desires, and abilities, let's examine the pros and cons of renting, as illustrated in Figure 9–1.

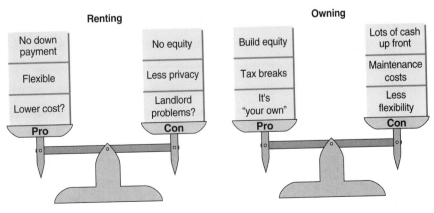

FIGURE 9–1   Renting versus owning

Flexibility

One of the primary advantages of renting—whether it's a house or an apartment—is flexibility. When a lease expires, the tenant is free to move on or renew. There are none of the time-consuming, expensive concerns of selling one home, buying another, and trying to dovetail the two transactions. The flexibility is even greater where furnished units are rented, for the chores of physically moving are considerably minimized. Renting is often preferred by people who have not yet settled into their chosen lifestyle or career and by those whose work or interests dictate frequent moves. The same is true for persons at or near retirement who might wish to be able to come and go as they please without the concerns of ownership.

No Money Tied Up

With few exceptions, ownership requires that a substantial sum of money be tied up in the property. When you buy a house or condominium, it's necessary to make a down payment. Moreover, as you make your monthly mortgage payments, a portion of which goes to reduce your mortgage debt, those additional sums are effectively tied up in the property. Money that's tied up in property is money that could otherwise be earning income for you if it were invested. Until you sell, borrow against, or refinance the property—all of which could be time consuming and costly—you cannot get at your money. In a rental, there's no need to tie up large sums of money beyond your security deposit, which usually is about two months' rent.

Income Tax Implications

Ownership provides certain income tax advantages that are not available to renters. Tax laws allow owners to take deductions for the interest they pay on their mortgage and for the property taxes they pay. This can mean a substantial saving in taxes. Furthermore, if you sell your home and realize a profit, that profit is subject to favorable tax laws. (See chapter 10 for a more detailed discussion.)

These tax advantages have often been the deciding factor for many people in purchasing a home rather than renting. But a closer look at the situation reveals that in many cases the advantages are not necessarily as attractive as they seem on the surface.

For example: The Alpers have saved $20,000 to use as a down payment for the purchase of a house. Considering the interest they pay on their mortgage, their property taxes, and their tax bracket, the ownership of the home results in an income tax saving of $2,000 a year. Had the Alpers *not* bought a home but had instead invested the $20,000 at 10 percent interest, they

would have earned $2,000 per year—before income tax considerations. In this particular case, careful arithmetic indicates that they may not be that much better off financially on a year-to-year basis as a result of buying instead of renting their dwelling and using their available funds for investment. It can be a very close call.

In deciding between owning and renting, this income tax factor should be calculated based on your own tax situation. The numbers differ from person to person, from deal to deal, and from year to year. The more costly the house and the higher the interest rate, the more favorable the tax advantage can be to an owner.

No Chance of Profit (or Risk of Loss)

Exercise 9.2

One of the attractions of ownership is the lure of profiting on a resale. Tenants have no such chance for profit, but they also face no risk of loss.

Indeed, the lure of profit often bears fruit. But profit is often the direct result of inflation, and although you may profit on the sale of your existing home, you'll soon realize that you have to live somewhere, and the cost of acquiring new housing will have risen in step with the price of your old housing. Thus, your profit can be easily absorbed by the simple change from one dwelling to another.

Profit can also be reduced by two other factors: real estate commissions and income taxes. In all likelihood, you will use a real estate agent to help you sell your house, and a commission of 6 or 7 percent of the selling price goes to the agent. Furthermore, if you sell your house at a profit, that profit might be subject to federal income taxes. (If you sell your house at a loss, that loss is not deductible.) See chapter 10 for further details.

No Protection Against Inflation

Neither owning nor renting can fully protect against inflation. For a month-to-month tenant, the rental can be increased on 30 days' notice. For a tenant on a lease, the rent can be increased upon renewal of the lease (subject to any rent control ordinances that may apply). Homeowners can expect increasing expenses for property taxes, property insurance, maintenance, repairs, and utilities. And if homeowners are making payments on variable rate mortgages, their monthly payments can be subject to increases as well. Homeowners with fixed interest rate mortgages have much greater protection against inflation because their payments for interest and principal will remain constant for as long as they own their property.

Overall, homeowners do have a better chance to protect themselves from inflation, because as prices rise over the years, so will the value of their homes. The only problem with this, as noted earlier, is that the prices of all

other homes will have risen comparably, so that any profit they realize on the sale may turn out to be illusory when they purchase new homes.

This particular advantage of homeownership is based on the assumption that housing values will continue to rise. But that phenomenon is by no means guaranteed. Housing markets are definitely subject to up and down fluctuations. If your timing is unfortunate enough to find you buying when the market is high and wanting to sell when the market is low, this inflation-proofing advantage of homeownership will not exist. Indeed, you might have been better off renting.

No Building Equity

"Why rent and collect worthless rent receipts when we can own and be building a hefty equity in our home?" Fact or myth? Although it's true that rent receipts have no tangible value, the other side of the question can be misleading. The average stay in a dwelling by a typical American family is from seven to ten years and, during those early years of the common thirty-year mortgage, the reduction of mortgage debt is very small indeed.

Equity is the difference between what your house is worth and what is owed on it. Part of each mortgage payment you make reduces your debt and, theoretically, when you later sell the property, you recapture that sum, plus any appreciation in the value of your house.

Chapter 7 discusses in more detail how interest is figured on mortgages. For the moment, note that during the first ten years of a 9 percent thirty-year mortgage, the reduction of debt on the mortgage is only about 10 percent of the total original mortgage.

For example, during the first ten years of a $150,000 mortgage that is set to run for thirty years at a 9 percent interest rate, you will have reduced your mortgage indebtedness from $150,000 to just $135,000 (see Table 7–5).

Added Expenses

If you're a tenant, the cost of certain repairs may be borne by the landlord, depending on the terms of the lease. If you are an owner, you'll usually have to bear most of these costs yourself. As a tenant, you're probably limited in the number of alterations and modifications you can make to the premises. As an owner, you are free to do as you please—paint your house or condominium walls purple and pink if you like—as long as you're aware of the implications of such modifications when it comes time to sell it. You run the risk of overpersonalizing your premises and scaring away would-be buyers. You also run the risk of overimproving the premises and thus pricing the dwelling out of the market for comparable units within that

neighborhood. But bearing those factors in mind, the freedom of modifying your dwelling is vastly greater in an ownership situation than with a rental.

TO BUY OR TO RENT: A CASE HISTORY

Let's examine a situation in which a family is debating buying versus renting. This example does not presume to answer the dilemma. It's merely intended to serve as a guide to help you know what arithmetic you should consider.

Exercise 9.3

The Browns have found a condominium, and they can either buy or rent it. The purchase price is $82,000; the monthly rental would be $900, which would include all utilities, maintenance, and association dues.

If they buy, they have $12,000 in cash to use as a down payment, and the property has an existing $70,000 mortgage with an annual interest rate of 12 percent. The mortgage can be assumed. Monthly payments on interest and principal total $720. Property taxes are $120 per month, property insurance is $40 per month, and utilities and maintenance total $100 per month. Thus, if they buy, their total monthly cash outlay would be $980.

The Browns estimate that, based on their current tax bracket, ownership will result in tax savings to them of $2,000 in the first year, or $166 per month.

On the other hand, if they decide to rent and they invest their $12,000 at 10 percent return, they will take in $1,200 during the first year (before income taxes), or $100 per month. After taxes, they estimate that the $100 per month would shrink to $76 per month. Thus as Table 9–1 shows, they are looking at a difference of $10 per month net savings if they buy instead of rent. This alone might convince them to buy, particularly if they felt that they'd have an opportunity to reap a profit upon a later sale.

TABLE 9–1   The Browns: Renting versus Owning

Monthly Costs			
As Owners		**As Renters**	
Mortgage	$720	Base rent (including utilities)	$900
Property tax	120	After-tax earning on invested $12,000	76
Property insurance	40		
Utilities and maintenance	100		
	980		
Tax savings	166		
Out-of-pocket cost	$814	Out-of-pocket cost	$824

But the Browns know their own circumstances very well: they suspect that within a year Mr. Brown's job might require them to move to a different city. They've also examined the local housing market and have found that prices are flat and seem likely to remain so for at least many months. Looking one year ahead, they realize that if they have to sell the condominium and find themselves without a buyer for just one month after they've been transferred, they will be out more than $900. That would more than wipe out the monthly savings they'd have realized during that year by being owners instead of renters.

The Browns, it appears, are almost in a "toss the coin" situation. Table 9–1 illustrates the arithmetic of the Brown's dilemma. Resolving the matter can depend on personal circumstances. How long might they stay in a given dwelling? How wisely will they invest their funds if they decide to rent instead of buy? Which way will the housing market turn? The case of the Browns is not intended to convince you to become a renter or a buyer, but merely to show you the arithmetic and the crystal ball gazing that you must do in order to reach a conclusion best suited to your own circumstances.

SHOPPING FOR RENTALS

Many of the same considerations apply when you are looking for a dwelling to rent or to buy. How close will it be to your place of work, to shopping, to schools, to entertainment? What is the condition of the building and of the neighborhood? How large are the premises and will they suit your foreseeable needs for the time you'll be living there?

Additional matters need to be considered if you are looking for an apartment. You should talk to other tenants in the building and try to determine the level of service and care provided by the landlord. Are reasonable requests by tenants taken care of promptly and courteously? Is the building well maintained, both aesthetically and mechanically? What has been the history of rent increases? Are there any local rent-control ordinances that apply to the building?

The Personal Action Worksheet at the end of this chapter will help you in your quest for an apartment.

Depending on your community, the classified ads in your local newspaper may be all you need to direct you to available apartments. In larger communities, you might find it desirable to seek the services of a rental agent. It's not uncommon for a rental agent to charge the tenant a fee for finding an apartment. Before you contract with a rental agent, determine what fees will be expected from you and get personal references from other individuals who have used that rental agent.

When you buy a house, you can reasonably expect that a real estate agent who is working for you will escort you from one house to another.

Exercise 9.4

STRATEGIES FOR SUCCESS

How to Compete for Rental Space

You want to rent an apartment, and it's your bad luck that there are more lookers than apartments on the market. The competition for a good apartment in your price range is tough. How can you win? Assume that any prudent landlord will want to check your credit and see references, particularly from your current landlord and from your employer. Get a copy of your credit history from your local credit bureau. Get copies of those references and have them in hand to give to the landlord when you apply. This will save the landlord time and trouble. Also, offer to give the landlord a cash deposit on the spot—maybe $50 or so—to take the apartment off the market while he or she checks you out. Make it refundable if he doesn't accept you, nonrefundable if you bow out. You're putting some money at risk, but if you're sure you want the unit, this strategy can help assure you of getting it.

But don't expect the same kind of service from a rental agent. In all likelihood, you will be given the address and instructions on how to view the apartment, and you'll be on your own.

Depending on the supply of apartments in your community, and on the demand for them, you might find it necessary to leave a deposit with the landlord immediately if you find a place you like. If the demand is high and the supply low, a landlord will rent to the first interested party who puts up the necessary deposit. On the other hand, if the demand is low, the landlord might be willing to "hold" a given apartment for you for a day or two, perhaps even longer. In such a case, it would be to your advantage to get that promise in writing from the landlord.

When you examine an apartment, determine whether the landlord expects you to rent on a month-to-month basis or to sign a lease. Examine the premises carefully and determine that everything is in proper working order (appliances, plumbing, electrical outlets). If you have children or pets, or expect to have them, make sure they will be acceptable to the landlord. And in addition to finding out what the monthly rental will be, find out what kind of deposits the landlord expects.

THE LEASE AND ITS KEY CLAUSES

Exercise 9.5

Renting a dwelling—be it a house, a mobile home, or an apartment—involves numerous rights and obligations between landlord and tenant. Those rights and obligations may be spelled out in a full-fledged contract called a lease. A lease is not of the same financial magnitude as the mort-

gage that corresponds to the purchase of a house, but it can entail many thousands of dollars, and you want to make sure you're getting what you bargained for.

Basically, the lease entitles you to occupy certain premises for a certain period of time at an agreed-on price. Here are some of the key clauses that could affect the nature and cost of your occupancy.

Expenses

The lease should set forth exactly who is responsible for what expenses including utilities and real estate taxes. If the tenant is responsible for utilities, will the tenant be separately metered so that the true utility costs can be exactly measured? If the tenant is paying based on a certain percentage of the total building occupancy and is not separately metered, will the tenant be getting a fair shake?

Repairs

Who will be responsible for *making* which repairs? And perhaps more important, who will be responsible for *paying* for the repairs that are made? The landlord may be responsible for seeing to it that repairs are made, but some repairs may be done at the tenant's expense, others at the landlord's. Generally, the landlord is responsible for repairing structural defects and for keeping the central heating unit in proper working order. The tenants may be responsible for attending to their own repairs on minor items within the premises, including but not limited to plumbing leaks and defective appliances. Examine the premises before you sign a lease to determine what possible repair bills you might be facing during your occupancy. If you determine that you would be more than normally vulnerable to repair costs, you might want to renegotiate the repair clause of your lease with the landlord before you sign.

Quiet Enjoyment

Quiet enjoyment is a legal term that assures you of the right to privacy and quiet in your occupancy of the premises. If the landlord fails to deliver quiet enjoyment—that is, fails to keep the neighbors from playing their stereo next to your bedroom wall at four o'clock in the morning—you will have the right either to withhold your rent payment or to get assistance in court in upholding your rights.

Extra Fees

Does your monthly rental include all the features of your occupancy, or will added costs be hidden in the small print on the back page of the lease, such as parking fees, use of recreational facilities, and assessments for improvements in the common areas? All rental costs and fees should be clearly understood prior to the signing of any lease.

Renewal Options

Will you have a right to renew your lease on the expiration of the original term? Not all leases contain this privilege, and it may be one worth bargaining for. Without a renewal option, the landlord can ask whatever the market will bear when the original lease term expires. If the tenant is not willing to pay what the landlord is asking, the landlord has the right to make the tenant move out. A renewal option is for the protection of the tenant: he or she has the right either to stay on at the agreed-on rental or to move out. It's reasonable to expect that the rental rate will be higher on a renewal than on the original term so that the landlord can be protected against rising costs. Even at a higher rent, however, the renewal option does offer the tenant flexibility and choice, things often worth paying for.

Some leases may contain an automatic renewal clause. When such a clause exists, the lease may automatically renew for another term unless the tenant gives written notice to the landlord that he or she does not wish to have the lease renewed. If you are involved in such a lease and you fail to give the proper notice, you could become responsible for lease payments for an additional term. For example, if the original term was for one year and the automatic renewal clause goes into effect, you could become responsible for an additional year's rent.

Sublease Privileges

You may be subleasing *from* another party, or you may wish to sublease *to* another party. If you are subleasing from the original tenant, you will be subject to the terms of his or her lease. Prior to subleasing from another party, you might want to determine whether in fact that party has the right to sublease to you and, if the landlord has given his consent, if such consent is called for in the original lease. If you sublease from another party and that party does not have the legal right to sublease to you, the landlord technically could evict you, and perhaps the main tenant as well, for violation of the lease.

On the other hand, if you wish to have the right to sublease to other parties while you are the main tenant, you must make certain that the lease

contains this privilege. In the sublease clause, the landlord may or may not reserve the right to approve of any sublessee, generally for reasons of creditworthiness. Unless the landlord consents, the fact that you subleased to another party will not relieve you of your obligation to pay the rent.

A sublease privilege is one that favors the tenant. It gives the tenant the flexibility of being able to move out before the lease has expired and to defray obligations by allowing another party to live in the apartment or house. If you do sublease to another party, you must make certain in advance, by way of a credit history and references, that the party is creditworthy and reliable.

Security Deposits

There are three possible types of security deposits you might be required to pay: deposits to ensure the payment of the rent, cleaning deposits, and damage deposits. The rental deposit is usually designated to cover the last month's rent of the lease. This gives the landlord some protection in the event you move out early. Moving out early does not necessarily relieve you of your remaining obligations under the lease. Technically, if you move out after eighteen months of a twenty-four-month lease, you'll be liable for the remaining six months. The landlord will apply the one month's deposit you have paid toward that six months' obligation and will be able to commence legal proceedings to collect the remaining five months' rent from you.

STRATEGIES FOR SUCCESS

Good P.R. with Landlord Can Pay Off

Relations between landlords and tenants are seldom all sweetness and light, but they can be more positive than negative if you, as a tenant, maintain good public relations with your landlord. You're not obliged to do so, but it can pay off for you. Paying your rent promptly leads to smooth relations and can win a good credit reference for you—which can be of value. If minor repairs or replacements are needed, do them yourself, which is usually a lot better than going through the aggravation of reporting minor problems and waiting for the landlord to correct them. It's appropriate for you to ask the landlord to reimburse you for for any out-of-pocket expenses the landlord would normally incur. And you can try to arrange for some payment for your labor. Landlords appreciate your handling small repairs, just as they appreciate prompt reports of leaks or any other problems that can escalate into expensive repairs. If you and your landlord understand each other's point of view, chances are you'll be able to negotiate a more favorable renewal.

If the premises need cleaning, he landlord can be expected to apply the cleaning deposit to that task, and the tenant might not receive any of the deposit back. If damage has occurred, the damage deposit will be applied to making the necessary repairs, but the tenant's obligation might not be limited to the amount of the deposit. If the damage exceeds the amount of the deposit, and the lease stipulates that damages aren't limited to that amount, the landlord can pursue the tenant for the excess needed to make the appropriate repairs.

For the fullest protection of the tenant, both parties should closely examine the premises before the tenant takes occupancy to determine the condition of the unit. For example, there may be a crack in a wall that would normally be covered by a piece of furniture or a wall hanging. If it's there when the tenant takes occupancy, the fact should be noted on the lease so that no one can claim that you caused the damage during your occupancy. The tenant and the landlord may trust each other implicitly, but the tenant has to remember that on moving out, there may be a different landlord who will not remember that the crack was there at the time the tenant moved in. Color photos of the premises can be particularly helpful in this regard.

Improvements

The tenant of an apartment or a house may wish to make certain improvements on the premises during the term of occupancy. Normally, if improvements are easily removable, such as curtains, they would remain the property of the tenant. Some improvements, however, may not be quite so portable. For example, a tenant may install built-in bookcases or a wet bar. Unless the tenant and the landlord have agreed otherwise in advance, improvements of this sort might be claimed by the landlord as part of the property. If any improvements are to be made in the premises, the landlord and the tenant should agree, *before* the improvements are made, who will have the benefit on termination of the lease.

Amending the Lease

Even though a lease is a binding legal contract, it can be amended in writing at any time by mutual agreement of the landlord and tenant. (The same holds true in a purchase contract for a house or condominium.) Any amendment should be signed by both parties. Any such changes could be inserted into a lease agreement even after the agreement has originally been signed and occupancy has been taken. Legal advice should be sought on the specific consequences of amendments.

Insurance

Landlords must insure themselves against damage to the building, such as fire damage. But you, as a tenant, will be responsible for insuring your own possessions. See chapter 8 for a discussion of tenant's insurance. If the building is extensively damaged by a fire or other catastrophe, you may not be able to occupy your apartment. In your tenant's insurance, determine how much payment you'll receive for temporary quarters until your building is again available to you.

MONTH-TO-MONTH TENANCY

Not all tenants have a written lease. Many people occupy dwellings on a month-to-month basis without the benefit of any written documents. This, in effect, is a one-month lease, which allows the landlord to alter the terms by giving one month's notice and allows the tenant to vacate by giving one month's notice. Laws may differ from state to state on precisely what the rights of the parties are on a month-to-month lease. Generally, a landlord wishing to raise rents or a tenant wishing to move out must give at least one month's notice from the start of any month of their respective intentions to do so. For example, if a tenant wishes to vacate on March 1, he or she should give proper notice to the landlord not later than the preceding February 1. If this is done, the rental obligation will cease after February, as will the right to occupy the apartment. If, however, notice isn't given until say, February 10, the tenant might be legally bound to pay the March rent.

COMBINATIONS OF LEASING AND BUYING

In some situations you might become a tenant and then an owner. You may have a lease with an option to buy or a lease with a first refusal to buy.

A Lease with an Option to Buy

A lease with an option to buy puts the parties in this status: tenants have the right to occupy the premises for the stated time and for the stated rent. At any time during their tenancy, they have the right to notify the owner of their intent to purchase the property at a previously agreed-on price. During the period of tenancy, the owner cannot sell the property to any other party unless the tenants agree to release their option to buy.

Here's an example. The Greens lease a house at $1,000 per month with an option to buy the house for $100,000. They may exercise their right to buy at

any time during their tenancy but at least thirty days before the end of the lease. If they wish to exercise their option, they give the owner the proper notice and enter into a sales agreement. If they fail to give the proper notice within the allotted time, their option will expire and they will no longer have the right to purchase at the agreed-on price.

By entering into a lease with an option to buy, the owner of the premises is taking the property off the market for at least the term of the lease. The owner has no assurance that the tenant will in fact buy the property and may be forgoing an opportunity to lease or sell the property to others at a better rental or purchase price. Thus, the owner can be expected to charge a price for giving a purchase option to the tenant. That price might be a higher than normal rent or purchase price, or a flat sum up front that would not be refundable if the option were not exercised, and that might be applied (in whole or in part) against the purchase price if the option is exercised.

A Lease with a Right of First Refusal

A lease with a right of first refusal to purchase is another alternative that should be considered. Under a lease with a right of first refusal to purchase, the owner will still be free to offer the property for sale to others during the term of the tenancy, subject, however, to the right of the tenant to meet any bona fide offer the owner may acquire. Here's how such an arrangement might work. The tenant and the owner agree on a $1,000 per month rental. During the period of the tenancy, the landlord has the right to offer the property for sale to anyone at all. A would-be buyer offers $105,000. The tenant then has the express right to meet that $105,000 offer within a period of, say, three days after receiving notification by the landlord of the offer. Or the tenant can pass on the offer, and either have to move out or become the tenant of the new owner.

In the case of a lease with a first refusal to purchase, the landlord is not taking the property off the market, as in a lease with an option to purchase. Thus, the landlord might be less inclined to charge a premium price for either the rental or the purchase.

RENT LAWS

Virtually every city has ordinances pertaining to health and safety measures in multiple-residence dwellings. These ordinances require landlords to maintain proper levels of sanitation, structural soundness, adequacy of plumbing and wiring, and precautions against fire. Such ordinances vary considerably from city to city. Tenants who think their rights have been violated with respect to these health and safety ordinances should notify the

landlord. If a violation of an ordinance is not corrected, the appropriate city offices should be notified. Rent-control laws and condominium-conversion laws have proliferated in recent years. These laws are designed to protect the interests of tenants, and you should become aware of any such laws that exist in your community.

Rent Control

Rent-control laws protect tenants by limiting the rental increases that a landlord can seek. The laws may also prohibit discriminatory leasing practices and may protect tenants against wrongful eviction. These laws can differ widely from city to city—with some cities having none at all—so you should determine what specific ordinances apply in your own case. Where rent-control laws do exist, they will generally spell out how tenants can seek relief from landlords who may have violated the law.

Condominium-conversion Laws

Leonard, the landlord, owns a four-unit apartment house, which he wants to sell for $300,000. But the economy is weak, and he has a hard time finding anyone who wishes to make the investment. Leonard then has a clever idea. Instead of looking for a single buyer for the whole building, why not convert the building into condominiums and sell each unit separately for $100,000 each? It may take some additional paperwork, but he will probably be able to dispose of the building faster and at a much better price: $400,000 instead of $300,000. This is an example of what is known as condominium conversion: apartments being converted into individual condominiums.

This can be bad for some tenants, particularly if they don't have the necessary down payment, and are thus forced to move. On the other hand, many tenants find it an attractive opportunity, enabling them to convert their non–tax-deductible rent into substantially tax-deductible mortgage payments.

Condominium-conversion laws were passed to protect the former type of tenants, those who found themselves dispossessed of their living quarters, often because of inconsiderate and greedy landlords.

Condominium-conversion ordinances typically require at least a majority approval of existing tenants before a landlord can convert the property into condominiums. The ordinance may also require approval of the city.

If you are a tenant, you may someday have to face the possibility of your apartment being converted into a condominium. If that time arrives, you should consider the advantages to becoming an owner and the advantages in remaining a tenant, even if it means having to move. The chapters

in this book on buying and financing a house can help you make a prudent decision.

TERMINATING A LEASE

As far in advance of your leaving as possible, read your lease carefully. Be certain that you know when the lease terminates. Watch out for any clause that would create an automatic renewal of the lease. Such a clause may read, "Unless either party gives notice to the other in writing of his intention to cancel this lease, the lease will automatically renew for another year upon [date]." This means that if you don't want the lease to renew automatically, you must give proper notice to the landlord in writing before a certain date. If you fail to do this, the landlord can technically hold you liable for another year's rent.

If you have given the landlord a security deposit, what does the lease state about getting it back? Many state laws stipulate when, and under what conditions, a landlord is to return a tenant's rental deposit. Know in advance what your rights are so that you won't have to forfeit any money.

If you're planning to move before your lease has expired, does your lease give you the right to sublet the apartment? If you do sublet, you should be certain that the subtenants are responsible. They should sign an agreement assuming all your obligations under the lease, including the obligation to repair at their own expense any damages they cause.

If you wish to move far in advance of the termination date and either you don't wish to or cannot sublet, you should discuss a settlement price with the landlord. You can, of course, simply move out, continue to pay your rent, and hope that the landlord will rerent your apartment quickly. Generally, the law puts some burden on the landlord to try to rerent as quickly as possible, but you can't always depend on the landlord to be diligent in this respect.

If you are renting any appliances or furniture or have any services under contract for an apartment or a rented house, be certain to examine the rental documents. For example, if you have leased the furniture or large appliances, you'll want to be certain that you can terminate those contracts concurrently with leaving the apartment.

If you are paying your own utilities, arrange well in advance to have all utility meters read as of your final day of occupancy. Ask the utility companies—telephone, electric, gas, water—to bill you for the final reading, and be sure that the meters are returned to the landlord's name following your departure.

If you suspect that there may be *any* question whatsoever regarding the condition in which you are leaving the house or apartment, settle it with the landlord *before* you leave. Go over the property with the landlord and be certain that he agrees that everything is as it should be. Then ask the landlord to sign a brief letter stating that everything is in the proper condition.

Renters are entitled to the same tax deductions for moving expenses as homeowners are, provided they meet the same distance and work tests. The cost of settling your lease obligation with your landlord if you move before the end of the lease may be included as one of the deductible expenses.

 PERSONAL ACTION WORKSHEET

A Guide for Renters

If you're comparing rental dwellings, this checklist will help you determine the respective advantages and disadvantages of various sites. The cheapest rent doesn't necessarily mean the best dwelling. If you choose one place and find you're unhappy with it, bear in mind the cost, energy, and aggravation involved in finding another place and making a move.

	Dwelling A	Dwelling B	Dwelling C
❏ Monthly rent	____	____	____
❏ Month-to-month, or lease? If lease, for how long?	____	____	____
❏ If lease, do you have options to renew? At what rental?	____	____	____
❏ Total amount of deposits required (security, cleaning, damage)	____	____	____
❏ Will deposits earn interest? At what rate?	____	____	____
❏ Estimated miles traveled per month to work, school, routine shopping	____	____	____
❏ Estimated travel cost per month	____	____	____
❏ Is there a resident manager to handle problems?	____	____	____
❏ Other tenants' opinions of building management	____	____	____
❏ General condition of building, grounds, your specific unit	____	____	____
❏ Are pets allowed?	____	____	____
❏ Is the building governed by any local rent-control ordinance? If so, what is the extent of your protection?	____	____	____
❏ Extra amenities available: pool, rec room, parking, laundry, storage area	____	____	____
❏ Security provisions: doorman, access to entryway, lighting?	____	____	____

CONSUMER ALERT ————————————————————————————————

Look Before You Lease

Renting an apartment (or house) on a month-to-month basis does not constitute a heavy commitment on your part. If things don't work out, you can leave on giving thirty days' notice in the proper fashion.

But signing a lease for a year or two can involve thousands of dollars, and if things don't work out, you could be caught in a costly hassle or have to endure considerable inconvenience. Take these precautions before you sign a lease:

- Determine whether there are objectionable noises from adjoining apartments. There might be little you can do to silence a tuba-playing neighbor once you've moved in. It might be a sign to look elsewhere.

- Check with other tenants in the building to learn how the landlord adjusts complaints, makes needed repairs, and otherwise fulfills the obligations specified in the lease.

- A rapidly growing phenomenon is the rental of condos. You rent a unit from an individual owner rather than a landlord who owns the whole building. In many cases, the owner of the unit has bought it as an investment and is renting it out until he or she can sell it at a profit. The owner may reside in another city and may not be concerned with the ongoing welfare of the tenants. In situations like this, overall management of the building is diluted, and there can be considerable difficulty in maintaining tenant satisfaction. A committee of absentee owners simply cannot maintain the same level of efficiency as can an on-premises landlord or management company. If you're faced with these possibilities, be forewarned accordingly.

- Learn the landlord's policies with respect to returning security deposits. If he or she is reputed to be slow, nit-picking, or argumentative, be prepared to exert your legal rights to ensure getting back whatever you're entitled to within the proper time limits set forth in your state's (or city's) laws.

UPS & DOWNS *The Economics of Everyday Life*

Why Rental Costs Go Up and Down

Being a tenant does not necessarily mean that your dwelling costs will forever spiral upward. If you're willing to take extra time in seeking a rental and if you're willing to make some compromises, you might find ways to lower your costs, or at least keep them reasonably stable. Consider the following:

Local laws   Different cities can have very different laws regarding rent control, property taxation, trash removal, police and fire protection, and so on. All of these elements can mean widely differing costs to landlords, who in turn pass those costs onto tenants. Main Street is the boundary between City A and City B. Comparable rental units on either side of Main Street may have widely different rental prices because City A and City B have widely different local laws.

New competition   Landlords of new apartment buildings often offer steep rental discounts to new tenants. This competitive pressure can cause landlords in comparable nearby buildings to drop their rents accordingly—at least until the competition subsides.

Furnishings   The more a rental unit is furnished, the higher the rent will be. If you have your own furnishings, particularly stove and refrigerator, you can keep your costs down. If you don't have furnishings and the landlord can provide them (at a somewhat higher rent), you might be better off making a deal with the landlord than buying or renting the furnishings from someone else. The landlord can get a nice tax break by buying and providing you with furnishings; take this into account in your negotiations with him.

Changing neighborhoods   As local conditions change, so do rental rates. Run-down areas have been renovated into trendy "where-it's-at" parts of town, and once-trendy places have become derelict. When pride of ownership becomes fashionable in a given area, you can expect rentals to rise. When you start seeing graffiti, rents will be stable or falling.

One-on-one negotiations   Simple negotiations that can affect the ups and downs of rental costs are as follows: (1) If a landlord is having vacancy problems, he or she will be much more flexible on the rental price for a tenant who has good character and credit references. (2) If a landlord wants you to sign a one-year lease and you're willing to commit to a two-year lease, you might well get a better price. (3) If you're willing to do your own repairs, the landlord might bless you, in addition to lowering your base rent. Those who don't ask don't get.

?

WHAT IF . . . ?

How would you deal with these real-life possibilities?

1. You have an opportunity to rent a delightful condominium. The owner is moving and is keeping the condo as an income property. But since it is a condo, and your landlord lives in a faraway city, you won't have the same relationship to other residents of the building that you would have in an apartment with local management. What are the pros and cons of such an arrangement? What can you do to protect yourself?

2. You find a terrific apartment, but no sooner have you moved in than you find out the landlord is an ogre. He's very unpleasant, slow to remedy problems, and of no help when it comes to resolving disputes among tenants. What would you do in such a case?

3. An apartment looks great to you, and you sign a lease and move in. Within a few days you realize there are problems that didn't appear during those few glowing minute when you first fell in love with the place. The traffic noises from the street are very annoying; there are musty odors; the water pressure is too low. All these problems are beyond the landlord's ability to fix. What would you do in such a case?

NUMBER CRUNCHERS

Do the calculations to make decisions in these real-life possibilities.

1. You're moving into a new apartment that has no stove or refrigerator. You don't own either of those appliances. Evaluate the numbers in each of these cases: (a) The landlord provides appliances of low quality, but adequate for your needs, for an extra $20 per month. (b) You can buy good-quality units for $1,000 and take them with you when you leave. (c) You can buy cheap units for $600 and worry when you move out about what you'll do with them. Which option will work best for you?

2. Moving into an apartment, you have a choice of a month-to-month tenancy starting at $800, with a high probability of frequent increases, or a one-year lease at $750 per month, followed by an option for a second year at $850 per month. You're not sure how long you'll be there. What do the numbers dictate to you?

3. You're leasing a house that you might want to buy at a later time. The owner offers you a lease with a right of first refusal to buy, with a monthly rental of $1,200. Or you can have a lease with an option to buy at a set price: the same monthly rental, but a $5,000 option fee that you lose if you don't buy and that applies to the price if you do buy. Evaluate your alternatives.

FOR BETTER OR FOR WORSE

Things beyond our control often impact our personal and financial well-being, for better or for worse. Some are more predictable than others. How could you be affected if the following real-life phenomena happened? Could you have seen it coming? What steps could you have taken to minimize damage or maximize advantage? The better able you are to anticipate and recognize these forces, the better equipped you are to deal with them.

1. You are renting, and your lease gives you a right of first refusal to meet any bona fide outside offer to buy the place. Soon after you've moved in, but before you've really had a chance to settle down, such an offer is presented and you have seven days to meet it, or you'll have to move out.

2. You move into an apartment knowing that rent-control laws prohibit your landlord from raising your rent more than 2 percent a year. Then the city does away with the rent-control laws.

3. You sublet your apartment to a friend of a friend. You don't know him, but your friend vouches for him. There's no written agreement. The subtenant trashes the place.

10

Selling Your Home

The super-salesman neither permits his subconscious mind to "broadcast" negative thoughts nor gives expression to them through words. For he understands that "like attracts like," and negative suggestions attract negative action and negative decisions from prospective buyers.

Napoleon Hill

Perhaps the only transaction more complicated than buying a home is selling a home. Indeed, many people find themselves doing both simultaneously. When selling a home—or even when vacating a leased dwelling—there are so many personal details to attend to that many of the important financial aspects of the matter are overlooked. This can be a costly error. This chapter will point out these important financial aspects and will prepare you to deal with them. They include:

- Setting the proper price and terms for the sale of your home
- Getting your money's worth from your real estate agent
- Investing the necessary time and money to bring the best possible offers from would-be buyers
- Taking advantage of tax laws that apply when you sell your home and when you move
- Getting out of a leased dwelling in the proper fashion

Exercise 10.1

Selling your home—be it a house, condominium, or cooperative—can be a leisurely activity or a hectic one. It's leisurely if you have all the time in the world; if you have not made a commitment to move to another dwelling until you've sold your existing one; if you're not under pressure to start a

new job in a different location. These situations are the exceptions rather than the rule. Most often, selling a home is hectic: You're already committed to a new dwelling, and you feel that you must sell your home by a certain date or risk having to make payments on two dwellings.

Time can be a costly pressure. Under the crush of a deadline, you are likely to accept a lower price than the house might otherwise bring. And you're liable to make other mistakes—financial or legal—that you could later regret. It's easy to say that you should allow yourself ample time to sell your house. But it's not always that easy, particularly when a job transfer occurs.

If a job transfer causes you to move, your first step should be toward your personnel office to find out what assistance your employer will offer you with respect to the sale of your home and your moving expenses. Many employers provide financial and legal assistance in such cases. But you might have to ask for it. If you are changing jobs to go with a new employer, determine what relocation assistance the new employer will offer.

WHAT'S YOUR HOME WORTH?

Your home is worth just what a willing buyer is prepared to pay for it. Not one penny more.

It's easy, however, to get caught in a trap of thinking your home is worth much more than it really is. Example: Your next-door neighbors recently put their house on the market, with an asking price of $150,000. Your house is identical to theirs, if not actually bigger and better. So if they're asking $150,000 for their house, then your house must be worth at least that much, if not more. Right? Wrong. That they're asking that much for their house doesn't mean they'll get it. In fact, their house might be worth only $120,000, or maybe even less. And yours might be worth no more than theirs in the final analysis.

Overpricing your house can be costly, because it can delay a sale of the house. And every month that goes by during which the house is not sold means mounting costs to you: your mortgage payment, your property insurance, your maintenance and upkeep. There will also be anxiety, security problems, concern over vandalism, and other dilemmas associated with being an absentee owner. Reread the discussion on the anxious seller in chapter 6.

Therefore, setting a realistic price for your home is the first and most important order of business. A realistic price is a factor of many things, some of which are not easy to calculate.

Factors to Consider

Exercise 10.2

The major factors to consider are the condition of the home itself, the condition of the neighborhood, how much "paper" you are willing to carry, how anxious you are to sell, whether or not your existing mortgage is assumable, and the availability of new financing at the time you are selling.

Condition of the House

Are you trying to sell what real estate people call a *move-in gem* or a *fixer-upper*? You must put yourself in the shoes of would-be buyers and see the house as they see it. Is it visually appealing? Is it structurally and mechanically sound? The more positive the answers to these questions, the higher the price you can ask and get.

Condition of the Neighborhood

Is the neighborhood in a state of improvement or decline? There's not much you can do about it if it's in a state of decline except to be ready to accept a lower price than you had otherwise hoped for. You have to anticipate that prudent buyers will recognize the trend of the general neighborhood and structure their offers to you accordingly. What about the immediate vicinity of your home? If your neighbors' houses are eyesores, that can have a negative effect on the value of your home. It might be worth a diplomatic chat with any such neighbors to urge them to correct the eyesores. It might even be worth your chipping in to help them do so in order to help you get a better price on your house.

How Much "Paper" Are You Willing to Carry?

If a potential buyer does not have as much cash down payment as you're asking, you might consider taking his IOU (in the form of a mortgage) in order to get your asking price. This will be discussed in more detail later in the chapter, but it must be considered as an element in setting your price in the first place.

How Anxious Are You to Sell?

In this respect, price and time work hand in hand. The more time you have, the higher the price you can afford to ask, with the knowledge that you can always lower the asking price as your ultimate deadline gets closer. When time is of the essence, you can't afford the luxury of overreaching on your price. The more critical the time factor, the closer to the actual market your pricing must be.

Is Your Existing Mortgage Assumable?

An assumable mortgage, particularly one whose interest rate is lower than the current market rate, can be one of the most attractive features of the deal you are offering. The assumability of any mortgage depends on the creditworthiness of the party who wishes to assume the mortgage. Furthermore, the lender may have reserved the right to alter the interest rate if the mortgage is assumed. You should find out what the terms and conditions would be to allow a buyer to assume your mortgage.

Is Financing Available?

It could be to your advantage to visit with local mortgage lenders to determine what kind of financing they would offer on the sale of your house. Not only can this help you set a realistic price, but it can also help facilitate a sale to a buyer who is seeking new financing.

Seeking Components

After taking into account all the factors just listed, perhaps your best guide to determining a proper price is to seek comparable sales in the past few months. Try to find houses similar to yours that have recently sold and determine the selling price. Your best source of information on this point will be local real estate brokers. Any information you can gather on your own from friends and neighbors will also be helpful. But be certain that you determine the actual *selling* price of any comparable properties, not the *asking* price. As noted earlier, there can be a big difference between the two.

Exercise 10.3

When you do seek comparables, make sure the houses you're comparing are truly comparable. They should be as similar as possible in size, configuration, age, condition, and amenities. Table 10–1 will help you evaluate comparables in your neighborhood.

TABLE 10–1   Comparable Housing Sales

	Your Home	House A	House B	House C
		Comparables		
Location (midblock, corner, cul-de-sac, etc.)				
Traffic (light, medium, heavy)				
Access to mass transit				
Access to freeways				
Access to shopping				
Lot size				
Square footage (house)				
Bedrooms, baths				
Year built				
Condition				
Extra amenities (pool, etc.)				
Asking price (original)				
Selling price				
Time on market				
Other pros, cons				

STRATEGIES FOR SUCCESS

Should You Refinance Before You Sell Your Home?

Dilemma: You plan to put your house on the market, with an asking price of $150,000. You owe only $60,000 on your home loan. Your loan can be assumed by a creditworthy buyer. Would it pay to refinance your home loan up to, say, $125,000, in order to make it easier for a would-be buyer to make a deal with you? Refinancing can cost a few thousand dollars. Can you recoup that money in your selling price? If your home doesn't sell very soon after you refinance, you'll have to be making payments on that much larger loan. Can you recoup those expenses in your selling price? Seek the advice of your real estate agent and lender. If the housing market is brisk, refinancing before you sell can help get a buyer into the fold, at relatively little risk to you. In a slow market, the reverse might be true. Know the costs before you proceed.

Condominium and Cooperative Restrictions

If you are selling a condominium or your interest in a cooperative building, you may be restricted in your ability to sell. Any such restrictions would be contained in the condominium or cooperative master agreement. You may, for example, be required to offer your unit back to the other owners at a fixed price, or at a price to be agreed upon, before you can offer it to the public at large. Examine the master agreement closely, with the help of a lawyer if necessary, to determine what restrictions, if any, you must comply with.

USING A REAL ESTATE AGENT

Exercise 10.4

Does it pay to use a real estate agent to sell your house, or should you try to sell it on your own and save the commission costs? Real estate commissions on the sale of a house average about 6 percent. On a $100,000 sale, the commission would be $6,000.

If time and money are no object to you as a seller, you might want to try, for a limited time, to sell it on your own. But at some point, except in rare cases, time and money will be of concern to you. If you've made arrangements to move and you haven't sold your old home before you take occupancy of the new one, you'll be faced with the double payment mentioned earlier. It takes only a few months of these double payments to equal what the real estate commission might have been.

If you try to sell your home on your own, give yourself a time limit: If you haven't received any acceptable offers within that time limit, it might be best to turn to real estate professionals for assistance.

What an Agent Can Do

What can a real estate agent do for you as a seller?

Market and Pricing

A good agent knows the condition of the market in your general neighbor-hood and can help you set a realistic price in accordance with the pricing criteria mentioned earlier.

Financing

A good agent is familiar with financing capabilities in your community at the time you are interested in selling. The agent, who has regular contact with mortgage lenders and knows what kind of down payments, interest rates, and other conditions currently apply, should also be able to assist a potential buyer in obtaining financing.

Advertising

Are you prepared to write—and pay for—effective advertising that will lure buyers to your home? Those are among the duties of the real estate agent, and you can test their effectiveness in creating good advertising by scouring the classified ads in search of advertising you find particularly appealing.

Showing Your Home

A real estate agent should be ready, willing, and able to show your home to prospective buyers at any time. You might not be able to do this because of your work commitments. Moreover, the agent should be able to separate casual lookers from serious buyers and save you time accordingly.

Sales Force

Not only is the individual agent working for you, but so are all the other members of the sales force of the firm. Thus, you multiply the number of potential sources of buyers.

Multiple Listing Service

Most real estate firms belong to a local multiple listing service, which pub-lishes a directory of all houses for sale through real estate agents in the com-munity. If your home is listed in the multiple listing directory, virtually every agent in town will be capable of acting as a salesperson for you. If a firm other than the one with whom you've contracted brings in a buyer, the

commission will be split between the firms, with your own agent getting a specified share of the commission.

Negotiating

As you read in chapter 6, both buyers and sellers who are working with real estate agents have skilled negotiators at their sides. You may be skilled at whatever you do, but not at the fine art of negotiating a price on the sale of a house. In this respect alone, a good agent can prove worthwhile.

Objectivity

It's only natural for homeowners to become emotionally involved in their homes. The decor, the furniture layout, the traffic patterns of your home— all these are your own creation and are important to you. But to a would-be buyer, it might all look like a hodgepodge. It's much easier for a real estate agent to take an unbiased view of the property and convince a buyer that everything can be altered to suit the buyer's own tastes and needs. You can't be your own best salesperson if you take offense at potential buyers turning up their noses at your own creations. The real estate agent can overcome this problem.

Finding a Good Agent

Exercise 10.5

As in seeking any other kind of professional help, it's important that you determine the reputation and integrity of real estate agents, as well as the firms they work for. Gather personal references from other people who have used the services of that individual or firm. How were they to deal with professionally? How would former clients rate their performance with respect to creativity and placement of advertising; their availability to show houses; their negotiating skills; their access to financial markets; their willingness to stick to their guns even if a particular property doesn't seem to attract potential buyers? You should also check with the local county Board of Realtors to learn whether the individual and the agency are in good standing. Check also with the state board of licensing that controls real estate brokers and sales agents to determine that their license requirements have been met and maintained.

As you interview potential real estate agents, you will discuss the price that they think they can obtain for your house. When you do, beware of a practice known as highballing. An agent, overanxious to get the listing, might lead you to believe that he or she can deliver a buyer at a much higher price than you might have expected. You could thus be lured into signing a long-term exclusive agreement with an agent whose actual performance might be far less than what you would have wanted. The real es-

tate industry has a code of ethics designed to protect the public, but, as in any industry, abuses occur. And once you've signed a listing contract with a real estate agency, you have little recourse if they don't live up to your expectations.

The Listing Contract

Normally, real estate agents will require you to sign an exclusive listing contract that will bind you to their firm for as long as the contract states. Six months is a normal minimum term in many communities. In addition to the length of time the agreement is to run, the contract will set forth your asking price. But there is no assurance whatsoever that the agent will be able to deliver a buyer willing to pay that price. Thus, the asking price stated in the listing contract is not binding on anyone. It's merely a target toward which the agent will be shooting.

In a standard listing contract, you, the seller, will be responsible for paying a commission to the agent if the agent brings in a buyer ready, willing, and able to pay your asking price. If such a buyer is brought in, and you have changed your mind and don't want to sell to that buyer, you may still be responsible for paying the commission to the agent. If a firm other than the one you're dealing with brings in the ultimate buyer, your own agent will still get a portion of the commission.

Negotiating the Commission

Generally, real estate agents state what commission they expect to receive, but it can be worth your while to negotiate for a lower commission. Nothing ventured, nothing gained. If it appears that the house will be easy to sell—because of its condition, location, asking price, or other factors—the agent might be willing to accept a lower commission. On the other hand, if it appears that the house will be difficult to sell, the agent might seek a higher than customary commission. Whatever commission is decided on, it will be due and payable upon the final closing of the transaction. If a listing contract expires without the agent having brought in a buyer, you are free to contract with any other agent or to renegotiate an extension of the contract with the original agent.

Preparing Your Home for Sale

If you want to sell your home as quickly as possible and at the best possible price, spend some money and energy putting the house in the best possible condition to attract buyers. Some of these expenses can be deducted

from any profit you realize, thus cutting your tax liability. Consider the following:

The Exterior

The exterior appearance of the house and grounds is vitally important. Many potential buyers will cruise around the area, and their first impression of the outside will stick in their minds. Even a house that is elegant inside can scare away buyers if the outside looks shabby. Keep your lawn, hedges, bushes, and other foliage properly trimmed. You might want to plant seasonal flowers to give the property a better appearance. Be sure your gutters and downspouts are all properly placed. A few gallons of paint to touch up exterior trim can be very important. Homeowners often neglect to notice signs of wear and tear because they have become accustomed to them. Ask some friends to give you their honest opinion of what might need improvement. Get rid of unsightly matter around the house. Winter and northern climates add a visual problem to any house. Be certain that snow is shoveled and that icicles are removed from overhangs. If winter days tend to be gray and dull in your area, consider some lighting that can improve the appearance of the exteriors, particularly in the late afternoon hours when many prospects are likely to call.

If there are any indications that you aren't keeping the outside of the house in good shape, a prospective buyer might suspect that there are problems lurking inside as well.

Step Inside

A would-be buyer entering your house should get the impression that it is bright and cherry, light and airy. To give a bright and cheerful impression during the daylight hours, raise the shades and open the blinds and curtains. If there is a room, such as a den or study, that you want to have appear particularly cozy, the reverse might be true. Try various combinations of natural and artificial light to achieve the best effect for each room. Keeping the windows clean will brighten the house and give a cared-for-impression.

The Kitchen

The kitchen might be the most important room to would-be buyers. Do all you can to make it sparkle. Stock a supply of kitchen deodorant: We often fail to notice odors in our kitchens because we're accustomed to them, but they could be displeasing to a prospect.

Touching Up

Any buyer examining a house will be constantly thinking. "How much will we have to spend to put the place in the shape we want it to be in?" Your

real estate agent can help you determine where touching up might improve the salability of the house. For example, some rooms could benefit from painting, particularly if they are now painted with a very strong color. Light, neutral colors please more buyers. Dirt smudges on the woodwork or torn window screens, which make a decidedly negative impression on buyers, are simple to correct.

Closets and Storage Space

Cluttered closets, basements, and attics discourage buyers. Before you begin showing your house, scour these areas thoroughly. Get rid of everything you don't need. Give whatever you can to charities—you may get a handsome income tax deduction by doing so—and throw away anything you can't give away. Otherwise, you'll end up paying to move it to your new location.

Mechanicals

Assume that any serious buyer will sooner or later check to see that everything in the house is in proper working order. To minimize troubles in this regard, make sure that everything works properly: electrical circuits, light switches, plugs, doorbells, plumbing, windows, furnace, air conditioning, and so on. Call a plumber to correct any rattles, knocks, or other annoying noises that ring through the house when water is running. Oil any creaking doors and loosen any stuck windows.

Design

Examine the major rooms in the house to see how minor changes of furniture or lighting might improve the room's appearance. You may be able to enhance the appearance of the house with throw pillows, scatter rugs, and other decorative pieces that you can acquire at reasonably low cost.

Leaks and Other Damage

A prospective buyer who sees signs of leaking—on the ceilings or around sinks, toilets, tubs, or showers—will immediately start tallying up many hundreds of dollars in repair bills to correct problems that are naturally assumed still to exist. If a leak has long since been repaired but evidence of it still shows on the surface, get it covered up. If the leak still exists, get it corrected. If nothing else, any sign of a leak gives a would-be buyer a better bargaining position.

What Financing Is Available?

The availability of financing is as important to the buyer as is the asking price.

If interest rates are high at the time you put your house on the market, you should be prepared to explore a wide range of creative financing possibilities, always with the advice of a good real estate agent and a lawyer. Chapter 7 explores some of these creative financing possibilities.

Is Your Mortgage Assumable?

As noted earlier, you should determine as quickly as possible whether your mortgage can be assumed and under what conditions. If your mortgage is not assumable, you should inquire of local lenders what types of financing plans are available to a creditworthy buyer. Take these steps before you start showing the house; let your real estate agent be your guide.

Will You Take Back "Paper"?

Whether by choice or necessity, you may find yourself having to take a buyer's promise to pay rather than cash. This will be in the form of a first or second mortgage, which should be drawn up by a lawyer. If it is necessary for you to carry the buyer's promise to pay, negotiate an interest rate close to the current going rate charged by conventional lenders. It is also advisable to keep the duration of such mortgages to a minimum. Try to get the buyer to accept a term of three years or less. At the end of that time, the buyer would be responsible for obtaining new financing independently. If a buyer insists on a longer repayment program, you should negotiate a higher interest rate as consideration for granting extra time.

All these negotiations will, of course, depend on your level of anxiety to sell. The more anxious you are to sell, the less room you'll have to negotiate the terms of any paper you may be taking back.

TAX IMPLICATIONS WHEN YOU SELL YOUR HOME

The Taxpayers Relief Act of 1997, while otherwise known as "mind-numbing complexity," (*The Wall Street Journal*) did make one aspect of taxation much easier to deal with. Unlike a confusing mess of possibilities prior to 1997, the new law states relatively simply that couples who sell their principal residence do not have to pay taxes on the first $500,000 worth of profit. For singles the tax-free profit is up to $250,000. In order to qualify for this tax break you must have lived in the home for at least two of the last five years. Sales of vacation homes are still subject to taxation. This law is effective for all home sales from May 7, 1997, onward.

STRATEGIES FOR SUCCESS

Good Timing for Your Move Can Save Money

If you're lucky enough to choose the time you want to move, you can save money in the process. Most moving takes place during the summer months—school's out, etc. That can mean a tougher (and more costly) time in getting movers to meet your schedule or in renting move-it-yourself vehicles. Moving in winter, especially in northern climates, poses extra hazards such as icy roads and snowstorms. If you have the luxury of choosing, spring and fall are the best times. What about taking the kids out of school? If they're young enough, it might not matter. In their teens, it could pose some problems. Discuss the situation with teachers at both the new and old schools. If you *can't* choose your own moving time, at least try to book the moving companies as far in advance as possible. That way you have more time to schedule other aspects of your move in the most economical way.

MOVING EXPENSES

Exercise 10.6

Moving involves many important considerations. Whether you hire a moving company or do it yourself will probably depend on the amount of household goods you'll be moving, the distance, and the time of year.

If your move is within the boundaries of your state, the moving company will not be controlled by the Interstate Commerce Commission. Customarily, such moves (intrastate) are charged on an hourly basis, plus time and materials for any packing that the mover does for you.

Generally, interstate moves of equal weight and equal distance will cost roughly the same with most moving companies. There may be important differences in the overall cost of the move based on the amount of packing and unpacking you wish the movers to do. These rates will vary from company to company. You may wish to pack your own nonbreakables and have the moving company pack the more fragile items, such as glassware, china, and lamps.

Representatives of moving companies can give you the estimates on the cost of your move, but bear in mind that these are only estimates and not firm bids. The actual cost can't be determined until the van is loaded and weighed prior to its departure. Moving companies are required to give you Interstate Commerce Commission information that spells out your rights. Be certain to read that document, for it informs you of the recourse you have if something goes wrong.

TAX DEDUCTION OF MOVING EXPENSES

Exercise 10.7

A major portion of your moving expenses (for which you are not reimbursed by your employer) may be tax-deductible. Because moving expenses can amount to a considerable sum of money, you should keep a careful record of all such expenses and take advantage of whatever the law allows. In order to deduct moving expenses, you must meet two tests: the distance test and the work test.

The Distance Test

As illustrated by Figure 10–1, measure the distance between your former home and your former place of work. Let's call the distance A and say it's ten miles. Now measure the distance between your former home and your new place of work. Let's call that distance B and say it's sixty miles. The law requires that the difference between distance B and distance A be at least fifty miles. If it is, you pass the distance test. Note that the distance does not refer to the location of your new *residence* but rather to the location of your new *place of work*.

The Work Test

During the twelve months immediately following your move, you must be employed full-time for at least thirty-nine weeks in order to pass the work test. If you are self-employed, you must be employed full-time for at least thirty-nine weeks during the first twelve months immediately following the

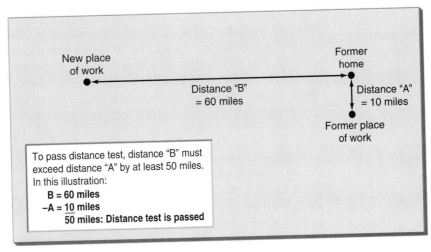

FIGURE 10–1   The distance test

move and you must also be employed full-time for at least seventy-eight weeks of the twenty-four months immediately following the move.

   If you meet both the distance test and work test, the following expenses of your move may be deductible, in whole or in part. Check current IRS regulations to determine the limits to these deductions: travel expenses, including meals and lodging while en route from your old residence to your new residence; the cost of moving your household goods; the cost of house-hunting trips; the cost of temporary quarters at your new location, if needed; and some of the costs involved in selling your former residence or settling your lease at your old location.

 PERSONAL ACTION WORKSHEET —————————————————————

A Guide for the Home Seller

This worksheet should help you *set* and *get* the best possible price for your home. It will cost money to complete some of the items, but the expense may return itself many times over in a better price and in a faster sale. You may need the assistance of your real estate agent. Some of the information can be found at your local tax assessor's or county recorder's office.

❏ What has been the actual selling price of three *comparable* homes in your area within the past few months? A _____ B _____ C _____

❏ How long were those homes on the market before they sold? A _____ B _____ C _____

❏ Based on these comparable sales, what do you realistically think your home should sell for? _____

❏ How will your home appear to a would-be buyer? _____

          Ask two friends, and your real estate agent, to give you an honest opinion of:

❏ The exterior (paint, trim, landscaping) 1 _____ 2 _____ 3 _____
❏ The entry (lighting, odors, a sense of clutter or of orderliness) 1 _____ 2 _____ 3 _____
❏ The kitchen (cleanliness, odors, does everything work the way it should?) 1 _____ 2 _____ 3 _____
❏ Closets, other storage areas (cluttered, or clean and spacious-looking) 1 _____ 2 _____ 3 _____
❏ Bathrooms (squeaky clean a *must*) 1 _____ 2 _____ 3 _____
❏ Other rooms (lighting, odors, traffic flow, condition of flooring and walls) 1 _____ 2 _____ 3 _____
❏ Mechanical elements, such as heater, appliances (Does everything work properly? Are there noises, odors, etc., that would be offensive?) 1 _____ 2 _____ 3 _____

          It's difficult to see your own home as others see it. Prospective buyers can be persnickety, and first impressions—such as the items listed here—can make the difference between "Thanks but no thanks," and "Let's talk about the price."

CONSUMER ALERT

Moving-day Headaches

Selling a home or leaving an apartment invariably involves one activity that many people regard with fear and loathing: moving day.

All major moving companies offer abundant literature on how to take the pain out of moving: how to do your own packing, how to complete a proper inventory of your goods, how to get the children out of your hair, and so on. Helpful though this literature may be, it may not prepare you for some of the common pitfalls of moving. These include:

- **The lowball estimate**   An overzealous sales representative from a moving company may give you an estimate on the cost of the move that is much lower than what you've received from other companies. This could be due to an honest error on the part of the salesperson; it could be due to your failure to disclose everything you had planned to move; or it could be an intentional ploy by the salesperson to win your business. Remember: An estimate is just an estimate. The total cost of the move won't be known until everything is packed and the van is weighed. Which leads us to:

- **"Bumping"**   The term *bumping* describes the practice whereby four burly 200-pound moving men sit in the back of the moving van while it's being weighed. And you pay for it. It may be a rare occurrence, but it can be costly. Interstate Commerce Commission regulations clearly state that you, the shipper, are entitled to be at the weighing of the truck. That can be a money-saving precaution to take.

- **Schedule demolition**   Despite the best intentions, the day of pick-up of your goods can be missed. And the day of delivery at your new destination can also be off-target. These missed dates can cause chaos, not to mention considerable cost, if you have to live in a motel for a few days waiting for the van to arrive. Moving companies generally can't guarantee pick-up and delivery dates unless you reserve exclusive use of a van. Your best protection against these scheduling problems is to anticipate that the worst will happen. Then if everything goes off smoothly, you'll be that much happier.

UPS & DOWNS   The Economics of Everyday Life ─────────────────

Why Housing Costs Go Up and Down—Part II (Continued from Chapter 6)

Trendiness   As a rule, newer homes with more modern decor and more up-to-date appliances can command higher prices than older homes that are otherwise equal in size, location, and quality of construction. As a seller, you're competing with houses that are newer than yours, all other things being equal. You may be able to ask a higher price for your home if you update it. But will the higher price offset the cost of the updating?

The "in" neighborhoods   Areas come and go in popularity, and prices for homes in those neighborhoods will fluctuate accordingly. There may be better buys in other parts of town, but if you feel compelled to be in the "in" area, you'll pay more to get in. And then you'll have to hope that it's still "in" when you want to sell.

Land-use changes   If there is a major change in how nearby land is used, the value of homes in that area can move up or down sharply. Heavier traffic patterns, construction of busy commercial uses, and spreading urban decay can blight home property values. Homeowners in such areas usually fight bitterly against any such impending changes. Development of parklands, reduction in traffic, and creative design controls in an area can be a boon to home values. Sellers should try to anticipate any such trends and time their sales accordingly. Local zoning laws limit some land-use changes, but zoning laws can always be changed, particularly if a developer holds out the promise of creating new property tax revenues for the community. Which brings us, directly, to:

Property taxes   Property taxes can have a major long-term effect on housing prices. Two examples can be found in the U.S. Northeast and in California. In the Northeast many older cities were faced with huge costs to keep their infrastructure (roads, bridges, public buildings, etc.) in repair. They had to boost property taxes to get the money to do that work. Higher property taxes clobbered the budgets of lots of families, many of whom sold out as quickly as they could (thereby putting more downward pressure on housing values) and moved to California, where they were willing to pay higher housing prices so that they could live without fear of rising property taxes. In 1978 California established a law that put a strict limit on property tax increases. State and local revenues increase as newcomers move in.

All these factors are interrelated. It's tough to second-guess them, but you have to try.

? WHAT IF . . . ?

How would you deal with these real-life possibilities?

1. In planning to sell your house, you interview a number of real estate agents. They range from passive to pushy, and the prices they think they can get for your house covers a wide range. They seem to be flexible on the length of time of the listing agreement, and you sense that the amount of the commission may be somewhat negotiable. What steps do you take to sort out of all the differences so that you can make the best choice?

2. Your house has been on the market for three months, and you've had no offers. The time is rapidly approaching when you have to move to your new place. The real estate agent suggests you lower your asking price by around 15 to 20 percent. What are your options?

3. You've received two offers on your house. One is on the very low side, but it's all cash. The other is what you've been hoping for, but the buyer will need time—probably six weeks—to get a firm commitment on getting financing. And there's no guarantee that he'll get the financing. During that time, the cash offer will have been withdrawn. How would you resolve this dilemma?

NUMBER CRUNCHERS

Do the calculations regarding these real-life possibilities.

1. You bought a new house before you sold the old house. Your monthly outgo (mortgage payments, property taxes, insurance, upkeep, etc.) is $1,800 on the new house and $1,100 on the old house. Until you sell the old house—for which you're asking $120,000—you're in a bind. The real estate agent tells you that if you drop your asking price on the old house to $100,000, it will sell quickly. If you hang in there at $120,000, you might get it eventually. You want to hold out for the best possible price, but that extra $1,000 a month outgo is starting to hurt. Evaluate how much and when you should drop the asking price.

2. Your real estate agent tells you that by putting some money into your house, you can command a higher price. Calculate what you can do and the cost thereof. How much higher a price will these improvements bring, and how quickly?

FOR BETTER OR FOR WORSE

Things beyond our control often impact our personal and financial well-being, for better or for worse. Some are more predictable than others. How would you be affected if the following real-life phenomena happened? Could you have seen it coming? What steps could you have taken to minimize damage or maximize advantage? The better able you are to anticipate and recognize these forces, the better equipped you are to deal with them.

1. You've sold your house and moved out, but the closing hasn't taken place yet. Before the closing there's a thunderstorm, and the new buyer tells you of some serious roof leaks that you had been totally unaware of.

2. You're going to sell your house to take a job in another city. The biggest employer in your current city announces layoffs of 30 percent of its work force.

3. You went to the Big City to make your fortune, but things didn't work out. You're close to broke. You reluctantly realize that your best tactic, at least until you can replenish your bank account, is to move back in with your parents. But they've just signed a contract to sell their home and will be moving into a small condo.

Financial Institutions

That's where the money is.

Notorious bank robber, Willie Sutton, on being asked why he robs banks.

Sutton's involvement with banks was a lot more clear-cut than yours will be. Dealing with banks and other financial institutions—savings associations, credit unions, and so on—can be complicated in these rapidly changing days. But the dealings can be worthwhile in terms of handling your money matters and making your money grow. This chapter is designed to acquaint you with how financial institutions work, what they can do for you, and what your rights are as a user of their services. You'll learn about such matters as

- Which institutions offer what services
- How checking accounts work, and the advantages and pitfalls in using them
- How to shop for the services you'll need
- What laws protect you with regard to financial matters, and how to pursue your rights if they are violated

YOUR CHOICES

Suppose you have some money and you have no immediate need or desire to spend it. What can you do with it? You have many choices. You can put it in your pocket, in the cookie jar, or under your mattress until you do need it. Or you can entrust that money to one of many financial institutions for a variety of purposes.

If you wanted to use that money to pay some of your debts, you could open a checking account at a financial institution. Then instead of having to deliver cash to each of your creditors, you could simply mail them a check to satisfy the debt. The check, in effect, allows the creditor to receive money from your checking account. You may wish to invest the money so that the total sum will assuredly increase until such time as you need it for other purposes. In such a case, you could establish a savings plan at a financial institution.

You might wish to speculate with the money in the hope that it might increase in the future. In this case you could establish an account with a stock brokerage firm—one type of financial institution. Or you might wish to put the money away for a very long time so as to provide an assured fund for yourself in later years or for your survivors upon your death. In such a case, you would contract for a life insurance policy with an insurance company, yet another type of financial institution.

On the other hand, suppose you need money—to buy a car or a house, to pay your taxes, to go on a vacation, or for any other purpose. If you couldn't borrow the money you needed from your friends or relatives, you would approach a financial institution for the appropriate type of loan.

THE MIDDLEMEN

Financial institutions play an important middleman role in the nation's economy and in your own personal financial situation.

At any given time, countless individuals (and businesses and governments) have more money on hand than they need for their immediate purposes. At the same time, countless others do not have the money they need for specific purposes.

Financial institutions act as middlemen by providing a safe place for those with excess money to keep it until they need it. At the same time, they supply services and loans to those who seek to borrow at a fair and reasonable cost.

Middlemen view this activity as a business. They must acquire their raw material (other people's money) at the lowest possible price (competition considered). And they must lend it out on the most prudent basis, taking into account the ability of the borrowers to repay the money at the agreed-on time. In order for middlemen to survive, they must make a profit. Thus, they must charge the borrowers more for the use of the money than they pay to the investors entrusting them with their money.

Some middlemen act not as a business but as a service to members of an association. The members band together to pool their excess money and provide for the needs of borrowers. Although it isn't important for the association to generate a profit, members must still generate enough income within the operation to pay for personnel and other overhead. This type of

financial situation is typified by credit unions, which commonly represent employees of a specific company or members of a particular trade union.

THE INSTITUTIONS

This chapter concentrates on institutions offering banking and lending services. Stock brokerage and insurance companies will be covered in chapters 14, 15, and 17.

Commercial Banks

Commercial banks are often referred to as full-service institutions. They offer a broad range of services, including checking accounts, savings accounts, trust facilities, and virtually all types of loans.

Commercial banks are generally limited to doing business within their state boundaries. They may be chartered by the state government or by the federal government to operate within a particular state. If a commercial bank is state-chartered, it will be controlled and regulated by the state banking commission. If a commercial bank is federally chartered, it will be controlled and regulated by the Comptroller of the Currency. (If a bank is federally chartered, it will have the word "national" in its name—such as First National Bank. Or it will have the initials N.A.—National Association—after its name.) Most major banks, and many smaller banks, are also members of the Federal Reserve system, which exerts additional controls and regulations on the nation's banking industry.

Exercise 11.1

Deposits in commercial banks are insured by the Federal Deposit Insurance Corporation (FDIC) (see Figure 11–1) for up to $100,000 per account in the event of the bank's failure. Congress can modify the amount of insurance and the number of accounts that can be covered by it; check the current limits. The FDIC is a federal agency that constantly scrutinizes the operations of all banks it insures for the protection of the depositors and the community. All federally insured banks pay an annual premium to the

FIGURE 11–1   Logo for Federal Deposit Insurance Company (FDIC)

FDIC, and the total is set aside as a reserve to be used to pay off the depositors, should a bank be liquidated. In addition to its own funds, the FDIC can call on the U.S. Treasury for additional money to back up its guarantee to depositors. The strength of the FDIC lies not just in its funds but also in its constant surveillance and its expertise in determining when banks are in trouble, intervening as swiftly as possible to prevent financial loss.

In addition to FDIC examination, banks may also be examined by state or federal authorities, depending on their charter. They are also examined by their own internal auditors and by outside independent auditors on orders from the bank's own board of directors. Examinations are generally by surprise and are very rigorous. All cash is counted. All loans are scrutinized in detail, including original credit information, current payment status, and prospects for ultimate full payment. If an excess of loans seem to be in jeopardy, the examiners will instruct the bank to take steps to correct the situation. The results of examinations are kept confidential between the examiners and the bank's officials. But examiners will follow up to determine whether the bank has taken necessary corrective steps to keep the operation in healthy condition.

Mutual Savings Banks

Mutual savings banks are state-chartered and are insured by the FDIC, which examines them as it does commercial banks. The major part of the business of mutual savings banks is savings plans and loans on real property—mortgages and home-improvement loans. Deregulation in the financial industry, however, has allowed mutual savings banks to extend their scope of business to include checking accounts and various types of consumer loans.

Savings and Loan Associations

Traditionally, savings and loan associations concentrated their business in savings plans and home loans, but the era of deregulation has given them powers to offer checking accounts and various consumer loans. Savings and loan associations are insured by the FDIC (see Figure 11–1).

In recent years, many savings associations have begun to call themselves banks, as permitted by law—thus the further blending in the public's eye of the various types of financial institutions.

Credit Unions

Because credit unions don't advertise the way commercial banks and savings and loan associations do, they're not as familiar to the public as those

other institutions. But credit unions are playing an increasingly important role in the U.S. financial system. They are associations of individuals who have a common bond—they work for the same employer, they belong to the same religious order, or they are members of the same union or trade association. Credit unions are not operated for profit; furthermore, they are tax-exempt. They are operated solely for the benefit of their membership, which is generally open to all individuals who meet their requirements.

Exercise 11.2

Credit unions offer checking accounts and accept savings accounts that may pay slightly higher interest than other institutions. This is possible because they do not have the profit motive, generally are located in modest quarters, and do not have to pay any federal income taxes. Credit unions in some areas make installment loans to their members of a rate slightly more favorable than that charged elsewhere.

Insurance on credit union accounts is available through the National Credit Union Administration (NCUA).

Consumer Finance or "Small Loan" Companies

These are private businesses, generally operating under state licensing, that make small loans available to creditworthy seekers. Consumer finance companies do not accept public deposits. They obtain their money by borrowing from larger institutions such as banks and insurance companies. A small number of these companies have branches throughout the entire country, but most are limited to individual states or cities in their sphere of operation.

Merchant Lenders and Credit Card Companies

Technically, these are not financial institutions in the same sense as banks and savings and loan associations are. But they do provide a financial service to many millions of Americans: making credit available virtually at the request of the customer. Generally, a merchant lender is a retail or service establishment that accepts a customer's IOU as payment for goods sold or services rendered. In other words, rather than pay cash, the customer can *charge it*.

In effect, the merchant lender is lending the money to the customer to enable the customer to buy the product. Many merchants do this strictly as a convenience for their customers and to be in line with services that their competitors offer.

Some companies—such as gasoline companies, hotels and motels, and airlines—issue charge cards to creditworthy applicants. Thee cards allow users to charge their purchases, thus creating a loan from the issuing company. The loan is repayable based on the terms contained in the original credit agreement.

Another form of quasi-financial institution is the credit card company: American Express, Diners Club, and Discover card are prime examples. They have made arrangements with many thousands of businesses across the nation and around the world to accept their credit cards in lieu of cash. When a customer makes a purchase on a credit card charge, the credit card company makes payment to the specific merchant and then seeks repayment of the amount borrowed by the customer. The credit card company is thus acting strictly as a middleman between the merchant and the customer. Most commercial banks also issue various forms of credit cards— VISA and MasterCard. When a purchase is made with a bank credit card, the banks pays the merchant and seeks repayment directly from the customer.

Insurance Companies

Insurance companies (life, health, property, and so on) act as financial middlemen in that they hold your money for you and invest it, waiting until such time as stated risks occur (death, illness, fire, and so on). They also offer some forms of investments, such as annuities. Their specific roles are explained in more detail in the respective chapters on insurance.

Financial Planners

A new type of financial "institution" has emerged in recent years: companies and individuals who perform financial planning services. Some are independent. Some are associated with insurance, brokerage, and accounting firms. Some perform services on a fee-only basis. Some earn commissions from products (insurance policies, mutual funds, etc.) they sell to their clients. Most are reputable; some are not.

The swift rise of financial planning as a profession has been accompanied by an equally swift rise in abuses. Throughout most of the nation, there are few laws governing or licensing financial planners. Virtually anyone can call himself or herself a financial planner, with or without credentials, education, or scruples. If a consumer gets involved with an unscrupulous so-called planner, there may not be any governmental agency with which to register a complaint. There may not be any recourse for lost money. There could be, in short, a disaster.

Exercise 11.3

Many major universities offer programs in financial planning. Two entities specialize in the field: The Institute of Certified Financial Planners (ICFP), based in Denver, offers a course leading to a Certified Financial Planner (CFP) designation, and American College in Bryn Mawr, Pennsylvania, offers a course leading to a Chartered Financial Consultant (ChFC) designation. These designations are not sanctioned by governmental licensing

STRATEGIES FOR SUCCESS

What You Should Know about a Financial Planner

Exercise 11.4

The strategy to use in choosing a financial planner should be similar to the methods you'd employ in choosing any professional in whom you must put a great deal of trust. As with a doctor or lawyer, you'd want to know the person's training, experience, and credentials. You'd want impeccable personal references from reliable sources. And you'd want to make sure that there is the right "chemistry" between you and the planner. Make certain you can distinguish personal rapport from a smart sales pitch. The two can easily be confused. If the planner earns a commission from selling, determine up front just what it is he or she does sell, so you'll know when you're being pitched. Be sure that the planner won't object if you seek second opinions on the recommendations he or she gives you. If the planner works on a fee basis, understand from the outset exactly how those fees will be charged.

agencies, rather they are in the form of a degree issued by the school. Another entity is the International Association for Financial Planning (IAFP), based in Atlanta.

Many who call themselves planners may be licensed or registered in a related field, such as insurance, real estate, stock brokerage, or accountancy. As noted, many have no governmental licensure or registration of any kind. If a planner works on a fee-only basis, you must determine what you get for that fee. If a planner earns a commission on products he or she sells you, you must determine how objective the planner really is: are you being sold something that's in your best interest or in the planner's best interest? In all cases, you must shop around, get personal references, compare services, and, when in the slightest doubt about the advice or sales pitch you've received, get a second opinion, preferably from someone who isn't selling anything.

SERVICES AVAILABLE AT FINANCIAL INSTITUTIONS

Exercise 11.5

The following financial services are those commonly found at larger commercial banks. They may also be available at smaller banks, savings and loan associations, mutual savings banks, and credit unions.

Checking and savings accounts	Special checks
Safe deposit facilities	Notarial services
Trust services	Electronic banking
Loans and credit cards	Collection services
Mortgages	Investment departments

Let's now take a closer look at what these services consist of. *Note:* Savings accounts (passbook accounts and certificates of deposit) are briefly noted here and are discussed in greater length in chapters 13 and 14. Installment, credit card, and business loans are dealt with in chapter 12, and mortgages are discussed fully in the chapters on housing, especially in "Financing a Home," chapter 7.

Checking Accounts

It would be both inconvenient and risky if we had to conduct all our financial transactions with cash. Checks, simply stated, act as a substitute for cash. Checks are more convenient, and the risk of loss is virtually eliminated.

The efficiency of our checking systems is founded on a combination of mutual trust and law. We have grown accustomed to accepting these money substitutes as having the value represented. In those rare cases when the documents prove invalid, there are laws that can punish those who have violated the law and the trust between the parties.

How Checking Accounts Work

Bob lives in Phoenix, Arizona, and works for the Ajax Supermarket. Each day, the supermarket gathers up all the money it has collected from its customers and deposits the money in its checking account at the Arizona National Bank. The store will then issue checks to its employees for their wages, checks to the landlord for the rent on the building, checks to suppliers for the food it obtains from them, and so on.

The checks order the bank to make payment to the holder of the check. That's the essence of the words "pay to the order of" that appears on all checks. The check—the order to pay—must be signed by a properly authorized representative of the store. The bank will have obtained copies of all the authorized signatures permitted on the checks and can compare those signatures with the signatures on the checks if they wish to determine the validity of the order to pay.

Bob's weekly paycheck, after all deductions have been taken out for income taxes, Social Security, and fringe benefits, looks like the one in Figure 11–2.

"Negotiating" a Check

Bob now holds a piece of paper that is worth $400 to him. The piece of paper is a legal document in which the Ajax Supermarket instructs the Arizona National Bank to pay to the order of Bob Rosefsky the sum of $400. The check is thus known as an order instrument. How can Bob then translate that piece of paper into real money? He can cash the check, he can

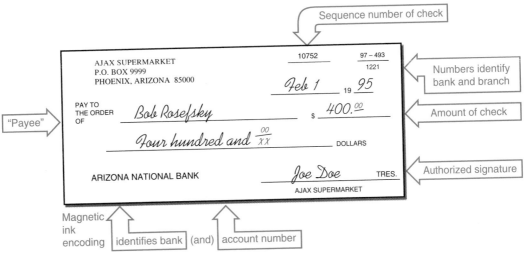

FIGURE 11–2   Sample check

deposit the check into his own account, or he can use the check to pay a debt or pay for a purchase.

Cashing the Check

Bob takes the check to a branch of the Arizona National Bank, identifies himself, and asks for cash in exchange for the check. Before the bank will give Bob the cash, it will want him to acknowledge that he has in fact received the money. The bank must do this to prove that it has fulfilled the order given it by the supermarket. Bob acknowledges that he receives the cash by signing his name on the back of the check in the area indicated. (See Fig. 11–4.) This is known as a blank endorsement. Bob receives his money; the bank has proof that it has properly fulfilled the order given it. As the check is processed internally, the supermarket's account with the bank will be reduced by $400 as a result of cashing the check.

Note this important precaution with respect to a blank endorsement: A blank endorsement converts the check from an *order* instrument into a *bearer* instrument. A check containing a blank endorsement can theoretically be cashed by anyone who is the bearer or holder of it. In other words, if Bob endorsed the check in blank when he received it, and it dropped out of his pocket on the way to the bank and was found by a dishonest person, that dishonest person could probably cash the check, and Bob would be out $400. A check should be endorsed in blank only at the time the money is received.

Depositing the Check

Bob can deposit the check to his own checking account at the Citizens Bank of Phoenix. To do so, he must properly endorse the check and fill out a deposit slip. He may endorse the check in blank, as if he were cashing it. Or, more prudently, he can put a restrictive endorsement on the check. A restrictive endorsement would read, "For deposit only to acct #007-085844," followed by his signature. A restrictive endorsement simply restricts what can be done with the check. In this particular case, it can only be deposited to Bob's specific account. If a restrictive endorsed check were lost, a finder would have a very difficult time doing anything with it. Restrictive endorsements should always be used on checks mailed to banks for deposit.

Figure 11–3 is a sample illustration of a deposit slip. Deposit slips are commonly preprinted with the name and address of the account holder. The person making the deposit writes the identifying number of the bank on which the check is drawn—in this case 97-493—and the amount of the check being deposited, $400. In this particular case, Bob is taking $50 in cash out of the check, as noted on the deposit slip, so the actual amount of the deposit is $350. When the deposit is processed, the receiving bank will encode its own identifying number as well as the identifying number of Bob's account, as shown in the illustration.

Clearing the Check

If Bob does deposit the check in his own bank, his bank technically doesn't know whether the check is any good. It has no way of knowing whether the Ajax Supermarket has money in its account at that time to honor the check.

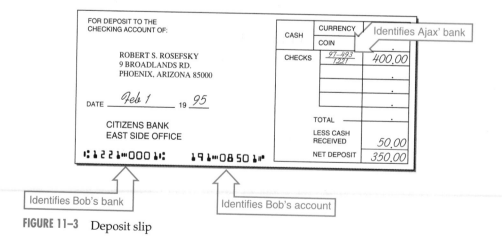

FIGURE 11–3   Deposit slip

It could thus say to Bob, "Technically, we can't permit you to take money out against this check until we're sure that it has *cleared*, that is, been honored by the bank on which it's drawn, Arizona National."

Bob's bank will actually send the check to the store's bank, where it will be processed. The Arizona National Bank does not notify Bob's bank that the check was good. Bob's bank will know that the check was good and was honored only if it does *not* get it back from the Arizona National Bank. If, in fact, the supermarket did not have enough money in its account to clear the check, the Arizona National Bank would return it to Bob's bank with a note that it was dishonored, or had *bounced*, in this case for lack of sufficient funds.

Because both banks are in the same city, it customarily takes only one or two days for the check to go from one bank to the other. Thus, Bob's bank can be reasonably sure that the check has cleared if it hasn't heard otherwise within two or three days—the time it would take for a check to go round-trip, if in fact, that was its fate. In common practice, Bob's bank knows that he has been depositing these checks from the Ajax Supermarket for many years and that there has never been a problem. Thus, they would probably allow him to draw against those funds without waiting for the check to be cleared by the originating bank.

While a check is in the clearing process—which can be many days if it was written on a bank in a distant part of the country—the funds are considered *uncollected* by the bank. Example: Bob receives a check for $1,000 from his cousin Bernie in Binghamton, New York. Bob deposits it to his account at the Citizens Bank of Phoenix. Bob's bank knows that it could take three or four days for the check to return to Bernie's bank in Binghamton. If the check is to bounce, it will take another three or four days before Bob's bank finds out about it. Or, if the check does not bounce, Bob's bank will still want to wait extra days to be assured that it hasn't in fact bounced. Bob's bank thus regards that $1,000 as uncollected funds for a period of six to eight days. But Bob thinks he has $1,000 in the bank, and he writes a check for $700 to a local used-car dealer as down payment on a car. The car dealer takes Bob's check into Bob's bank the next day, where it bounces. Bob has drawn a check against uncollected funds and the check is not honored. Not only does this cost Bob $20 for the bounced check fee, but it also causes him considerable embarrassment.

Federal law requires banks to clear deposits within a few days. To be on the safe side, particularly if you are depositing large checks or out-of-town checks, ask your bank how long the clearance time will be.

Using the Check to Pay Debts or for Purchases

Bob owes $400 to his friend Gary in Taos, New Mexico. He wants to use his paycheck to settle his debt to Gary. He thus puts a special endorsement on

BLANK	RESTRICTIVE	SPECIAL
ENDORSE HERE	ENDORSE HERE	ENDORSE HERE
Bob Rosefsky	*For deposit only*	*Pay only to*
	to acct. # 98765	*Gary Smith*
	Bob Rosefsky	*Bob Rosefsky*

FIGURE 11–4   Types of endorsement

the back of his check , which reads, "Pay to the order of Gary Smith," followed by his signature. A special endorsement gives only the named party the right to collect the amount of the check or to negotiate the check on to a subsequent holder. When Gary receives the check, he endorses it by signing his own name below Bob's signature, and the check eventually comes back to the original bank where, presumably, it will be honored.

Although Bob can pay off his debt in this fashion, it might be unwise for him to do so. It would be better for him to deposit the store's check into his own account and then draw his own check payable directly to Gary. He would ultimately receive back his canceled check and would thus have proof that Gary had received the payment and that the debt was paid. With a special endorsement, the store will get the check back, and Bob might have to seek the store's help in verifying that Gary received the money. Figure 11–4 shows samples of blank, restrictive, and special endorsements.

Following are some additional aspects of checking accounts.

Stopping Payment

The treasurer of the Ajax Supermarket learns that the computer has erroneously issued a check to one of the store's meat suppliers. The check is for $500 more than it should be, and the treasurer is concerned that the meat supplier will cash the check and will refuse to refund the excess $500 because there had been an ongoing dispute between them over a previous bill. The treasurer wants to stop the check before the meat supplier can cash it at his bank.

It's literally a race against time. The proper course for the treasurer is to go to his bank, Arizona National, and issue a stop-payment order. He must inform the bank in writing as to the number and amount of the check, the date it was issued, and to whom it was paid, and then sign the order. This done, the bank will then refuse to allow payment on the check when it is presented. But if the meat supplier gets to the bank first and is able to cash

the check, he will have the money in hand, and it will then be a hassle between the supplier and the store as to who is entitled to the money.

Once a proper stop-payment order has been filed with the bank, the bank might be responsible to the store if it makes payment on the check in error. Thus, once a stop-payment order has been signed, the bank alerts all its tellers and the appropriate bookkeeper on the Ajax account to refuse payment, should the check be presented. If a stop-order is conducted verbally and the proper documents haven't been signed, the bank might not be responsible if it does pay the check. Banks customarily charge for the processing of a stop-payment order.

Overdrafts

We previously noted the problems that can arise when a checking account customer writes checks against uncollected funds. The same costs and embarrassments can occur if you write checks when there simply isn't enough money in the account to cover the check. This is a case of being overdrawn. Customers who frequently overdraw their accounts jeopardize their credit standing with the bank. In some instances, a bank may pay a check even though it would overdraw the account. This may occur because the customer is in good standing, rarely has overdrawn, and is overdrawn by a relatively small amount. The bank isn't worried about getting its money, and, rather than put the customer to any inconvenience, the bank will allow the check to be paid.

In other cases, banks offer overdraft privileges to their customers. If a check overdraws an account, the bank automatically lends the customer at least enough money to cover the overdraft and deposits that loaned money into a customer's checking account. The loan must then be repaid at a specified rate of interest. This program can be convenient and eliminate embarrassment, but it can also be very costly. It may also act as too great a temptation for a customer who lacks the discipline to keep a checking account in proper balance.

Keeping Track of Your Account

The register, or stub, is where the checking account customer keeps a record of all deposits and checks. The register should be updated immediately with each transaction. One of the most frequent causes of overdrawn accounts and other errors is customer failure to enter deposits and checks. If you neglect to enter a check transaction in your register, you run the risk of forgetting that transaction and subsequently overdrawing. Registers come in several forms. Figure 11–5 shows some sample registers, indicating how transactions are noted in them.

a.

CHECK #	DATE	CHECK ISSUED TO (or description of deposit)	AMOUNT OF CHECK	AMOUNT OF DEPOSIT	BALANCE
					139.90
143	2/21	To Joe's Gas Sta For Gas	7.75		CHECK OR DEP. 7.75 / BAL. 132.15
Dep	2/27	To (Net Paycheck) For		200.00	CHECK OR DEP. 200.00 / BAL. 332.15
144	3/5	To Electric Co. For Feb. bill	28.10		CHECK OR DEP. 28.10 / BAL. 304.05
145	3/5	To Savings & Loan For March pmt.	242.00		CHECK OR DEP. 242.00 / BAL. 62.05

b.

CHECK # 144 DATE 3/5	
To Electric Co. Feb. bill	
BALANCE	332.15
CHECK	28.10
DEPOSIT	
NEW BAL.	304.05

CHECK # 145 DATE 3/5	
To Savings & Loan March pmt.	
BALANCE	304.05
CHECK	242.00
DEPOSIT	
NEW BAL.	62.05

FIGURE 11–5   (a) Sample checkbook register; (b) sample checkbook stubs

The Statement and Reconciliation

The bank sends a monthly statement to each of its checking account customers. This statement contains an itemized listing of all transactions made on the account and includes all checks written and cleared during the previous month, as well as all deposit slips. In this way, the customer has written verification of every transaction. The bank also makes a microfilm record of all items, which the customer can refer to if necessary.

The statement also contains instructions for determining that the balance shown by the bank matches the balance shown in the customer's account. This is known as *reconciling* the account. Figure 11–6 presents an example of a monthly account reconciliation.

	CHECKS NOT YET PAID		
	DATE	#	AMOUNT
1. Arrange canceled checks and deposit slips by number or date.	3/8	149	52.50
2. Check them off in your check book, verifying each amount as you proceed.	3/9	150	7.50
3. Add to your checkbook any deposits or other credits recorded on this statement that you have not already added.	3/10	151	10.00
4. Subtract from your checkbook any checks or other charges recorded on this statement that you have not already subtracted.			
5. List at right each check you have written that is not yet paid by bank (does not show on statement). Total them, and enter total on line 10.			
	TOTAL		70.00

	DEPOSITS NOT YET CREDITED	
	DATE	AMOUNT
6. List any deposits you have made that do not show on statement, and enter total on line 8.	3/10	100.00
	TOTAL	100.00

7. Ending balance as shown on statement.
8. Add total from line 6.
9. Subtotal
10. Subtract total from line 5.
11. This total should be the same as the balance in your checkbook.

$	182.00
+	100.00
	282.00
–	70.00
$	212.00

FIGURE 11–6   Sample reconciliation of checking account

Shopping for Checking Accounts

The distinction between checking accounts and savings accounts has been blurred in recent years. Formerly, checking accounts did not pay interest; only savings accounts did. Now we have checking accounts that pay interest, and savings accounts that allow check-writing privileges. The Personal Action Worksheet at the end of this chapter will help you to decide which plans offer you the lowest cost (or highest income). The important matters to consider in shopping for the best account are: the minimum required balance in order to earn interest and offset service charges, the number of checks you customarily write each month, and the overall convenience you can enjoy and beneficial relationships you can establish by dealing with a particular institution.

Savings Accounts

Savings accounts are available at commercial banks, mutual savings banks, savings and loan associations, and credit unions. Generally, they take one of three forms: passbook accounts, saving certificates of deposit (CDs), and money market accounts.

Unlike checking accounts, where money flows in and out constantly, savings accounts are relatively inactive. They're used as a device to accumulate money over a long period of time.

Financial institutions are willing to pay savings account customers for the use of their money. The payment is referred to as *interest*. In effect, customers are lending their money to the institution, and the institution is paying interest for the loan.

Passbook Accounts

The old standard type of savings account is the passbook account. A passbook account may be opened with any amount of money, and the customer may make deposits to, or withdrawals from, the account as desired. (Some institutions may limit the number of withdrawals permitted in a month or in a quarter, and if that number is exceeded, the institution may levy a service charge.) Passbook savings account customers will usually receive a small booklet, or *passbook*, in which each deposit and withdrawal is entered and in which the interest earned on the account is added to the customer's balance. (A variation of the passbook account is the statement account, in which a monthly or quarterly statement is mailed to the customer. The statement reflects all transactions in the account for the preceding period.)

Certificates of Deposit (CDs)

A certificate of deposit is a contractual agreement between customer and institution whereby the customer agrees to leave a certain sum of money with the bank for a fixed period of time—perhaps as short as seven days or as long as ten years. CDs generally pay a higher rate of interest to the customer than passbook accounts because the institution is assured that it will have the fixed sum of money available for lending for a known period of time. CD customers who withdraw funds before the agreed-on date suffer a penalty. Check current penalty regulations before you open a CD account.

Money Market Accounts

This type of account is, in a sense, like a super passbook account. Money market accounts pay a higher rate of interest than passbook accounts but usually require a fairly substantial initial deposit—perhaps $1,000 or more.

Many such accounts impose a service charge if there are too many deposits or withdrawals in a given period of time.

Competition is keen among institutions for savings accounts of all types. Careful shopping is essential if you are to obtain the best deal available at any given time. Because many consider savings accounts as a form of investment, they are treated more fully in chapter 14.

Safe Deposit Facilities

Safe deposit boxes provide the best security for valuable items and documents that cannot be replaced or duplicated. Financial institutions that rent safe deposit facilities make boxes of varying sizes available, generally on a yearly rental basis. The amount of the rent depends on the size of the box. The person or persons renting safe deposit facilities must sign a signature card at the time the box is rented, and they are given a key to the box. Then, only those persons who have signed the cards and who can present the key are permitted access to the box. It takes a combination of two keys—the one given the customer and the one held by the institution—to allow entry into a box. If the customer loses a key, the likelihood is that the institution will have to drill the door open, probably at the customer's expense. Naturally, access to the box is available only during normal banking hours.

Some institutions may offer safe deposit box facilities at a reduced charge for customers who utilize other services.

Trust Services

Trust departments are usually found in larger commercial banks. The basic function of a trust department is to act as a trusted custodian of money or property for customers who require such services.

One frequent use of trust services arises when an individual directs that, after his or her death, property go to survivors "in trust." The customer has thus established an agreement with the bank to act as trustee of the stated money and property. The trust department will then be responsible for investing the money prudently, for managing property (such as real estate), for selling any securities or properties it deems proper to sell, for assisting with the necessary tax returns and other accounting matters on behalf of the trust, and for distributing the proceeds in accordance with the wishes of the individual who established the trust. Charges are levied for trust services based on the total value of assets in the trust and the complexity of the instructions the trust department must follow. For further discussion of trusts, see chapter 19.

Special Checks

Traveler's checks provide a safe and convenient means of having funds available when you are traveling—in the United States, where personal checks may not be acceptable outside your own home community, and particularly in foreign countries, where neither personal checks nor American dollars may be acceptable as exchange. Traveler's checks can be purchased at most financial institutions in denominations of $10, $20, $50, and $100. The common charge is $1 per $100 in traveler's checks. If lost, traveler's checks can be replaced at offices of the issuing agencies, or by mail, as directed in the institutions included with each packet of traveler's checks. Keep a list of your traveler's check numbers to expedite replacement of lost or stolen checks.

Money orders are a form of check purchased at financial institutions (and from the U.S. Postal Service), usually for payment of bills or for any other personal needs. Money orders can be purchased in any denomination. They generally cost more than checks, and one must go to the institution in order to buy one; thus, they aren't nearly as convenient as a checking account.

If you're entering into an important transaction—such as the sale of your home—and you want to be absolutely certain that the check you receive from the other party is good, you may require that the party give you a cashier's check or certified check instead of a personal check. A cashier's check is drawn on the bank's own funds. A certified check is an individual's check, but the bank has certified (in effect, guaranteed) that the funds are indeed in the account and are set aside for payment of the certified check. If you are required to present a cashier's check or certified check, your bank can accommodate your request quickly and at little or no fee, depending on your status as a customer.

Notarial Services

We often have to sign documents requiring that our signature be notarized. This service is performed by a notary public, and most financial institutions have a notary public available to serve their customers. The purpose of notarization is to verify that the signature is indeed that of the person indicated. When a signature is to be notarized, the document must be signed in the presence of the notary, and the notary must be certain of the signer's identity. Many institutions do not charge for notarial services for their customers. Notarial services can also be obtained through law firms, governmental offices, and insurance agencies.

Electronic Banking

Exercise 11.6

Most institutions throughout the nation have installed electronic tellers. These automatic teller machines (ATMs) offer twenty-four-hour service on a variety of transactions: withdrawals, deposits, loan payments, and transfers from one account to another. Customers wishing to utilize these services are generally issued a plastic card with a secret code number assigned to it, thus preventing anyone except the authorized user from using the card. Be certain you know what fees your bank charges, if any, for use of its ATMs. If you use an ATM that is not your bank's, you can be charged additional fees.

Collection Services

Business and commercial accounts are more likely to make use of this little-known service. For example, a landlord who lives in a distant city may find it more convenient for tenants to make their payments to the local bank, which in turn deposits the payments into the landlord's account in that bank. The landlord might think that the rent gets paid more promptly if the payments are made to a local bank. Charges are made in accordance with the volume of services rendered.

Debit Cards

The newest popular product offered by banks is the debit card, which is some-what the reverse of a credit card. When a debit card is used by a customer to pay for a purchase, the amount of the purchase is immediately deducted from the user's checking account. In effect, it replaces writing a check. Debit cards look like credit cards, and merchants accept them as readily as credit cards. Indeed, some merchants will allow users to get extra cash, over and above the amount of the purchase. If the amount registered by a debit card exceeds the balance in the customer's account, a debt is created, which must be repaid plus interest. There might be a charge each time a debit card is used; and there's always a danger of forgetting to deduct the amount of a debit card use from your checking account. So care is called for when making use of this service.

Investment Departments

What banks don't lend out to the public or keep in reserve, they invest, usually in high-quality government and corporate bond issues. Many investors who seek such securities find it more convenient and less costly to acquire them through their bank investment department than through stock brokerage firms. Inquire at a local bank to see whether the investment department can provide service comparable to, or better than, local brokerage firms.

STRATEGIES FOR SUCCESS

It Pays to Have a Friend at Your Local Bank

Banking can be a very impersonal matter. More and more people are banking with automatic teller machines, telephone/computer hook-ups, and mail. Most of your deposits, withdrawals, and other ordinary banking needs can be handled in this manner. But it's a sound strategy to have a friend at the bank—preferably an officer—who knows you and who can lend a hand if you have any problems or questions. For instance, you might have a foul-up with a credit card statement or a checking account balance. Or you might need a loan in a hurry. A friend at the bank can help you in such circumstances. Prepare a financial statement to help expedite loan requests, and discuss your financial status with your banking friend once a year or so. And be ready: Someday your friend will be transferred to another branch of the bank. Have another friend waiting in the wings.

LAWS THAT GOVERN FINANCIAL INSTITUTIONS AND THEIR TRANSACTIONS

Financial institutions, and the transactions that emanate from them, are governed by a complex system of state and federal laws. As noted earlier, each institution is given its original license to operate either by the state in which it is located or by the federal government. The respective government then generally oversees and regulates the operation of the institution, including periodic audits and examinations to ascertain whether the institution is complying with governmental guidelines.

The State Laws

State regulations that institutions must comply with include laws of negotiable instruments (an important aspect of which is the concept of the "holder in due course"), laws of usury, and laws regarding secured transactions.

Negotiable Instruments

The negotiable instruments laws refer to instruments—such as checks and promissory notes (IOUs)—that are negotiated—sold, exchanged, and otherwise passed from hand to hand. Each state has its own laws of negotiable instruments, but they all tend to be similar. In essence, negotiable instruments laws determine what constitutes a valid negotiable instrument and what does not. A check is a good example of a negotiable instrument. It car-

ries an unconditional order to pay a fixed sum of money to the holder; it's dated; and the person who has drawn the check has signed it. If a check does not contain any of these elements—such as the signature of the drawer—it could be construed as being nonnegotiable. In short, it may be returned to the person who drew the check, and, thus, the intended transaction does not occur.

Another example would be a promissory note: You buy a TV set from a local appliance dealer, and, instead of paying cash for it, you sign a promissory note in which you agree to make payments over a specific period of time. The promissory note is payable directly to the dealer. The dealer, in turn, sells your promissory note to a local bank or finance company. You then end up making your payments to the bank. The bank has become a *holder* of your negotiable instrument *in the due course of business,* assuming that the instrument has been properly created and executed. If you had neglected to sign it, the TV dealer would not have been able to sell it to the bank. If the TV dealer had not properly endorsed it, the bank would not have bought it.

Assuming that all the paperwork was done properly, what would happen if you got the TV set home and found out that it didn't work? You'd want to refuse to make payments to the dealer, but the dealer would simply tell you that he had sold your IOU to the bank. Could you refuse to make payments to the bank? Federal Trade Commission regulations state that, in general, if you, a buyer, would have a valid claim or defense against the original dealer, you have the same claim or defense against a party that had subsequently bought your promissory note. In other words, if you could legally have refused to pay the dealer because the TV set was defective, you could just as legally refuse to pay the bank for the same reason. Before you sign any promissory notes be sure you understand contractual terms that could have a strong bearing on your obligation to pay.

Under these regulations, most consumer credit contracts must contain a notice stating that the holder of the contract or promissory note will be subject to the same claims and defenses that the buyer could have asserted against the seller.

Wary consumers should thus become aware of the protections the law allows and should promptly assert their rights if there is the least suspicion that these rights are being violated.

Usury Laws

Exercise 11.7

Each state has its own laws of usury. The usury laws dictate the maximum rate of interest that can be charged for various types of loans.

You should determine what the maximum interest rates allowable for various categories of loans are in your own state.

Lenders charging usurious rates of interest on any kind of financing may be subject to penalties. Borrowers in usurious transactions should determine what their rights are and take appropriate action.

In most states, the laws of usury apply to individuals only. Corporations do not have the same measure of protection when they borrow.

Secured Transaction Laws

You purchase an automobile and arrange for financing through your local bank. In the typical transaction, you sign documents that give the bank the right to take back your car if you fail to make the payments as promised. As a result of your signing these documents and the bank's recording in the appropriate government office, the bank has what is known as a *security interest* in your new automobile.

By recording the security agreements, the bank has put all other parties on notice that it has a first lien on that particular property. When you pay off the loan, the bank should release that security interest by completing and filing the appropriate papers.

Secured transaction laws are slightly different in each state. These laws describe how lenders can protect their security interest in properties and how they must release that security interest when the loans are eventually paid off. The law does not dictate when or if a borrower must put up security for a given loan or how much security should be put up. That's between the borrower and the lender. The law does, however, describe how each party is protected in such a transaction.

The Federal Laws

Federal laws with which institutions must comply include the Truth in Lending Law, the Truth in Savings Law, the Fair Credit Billing Law, the Fair Credit Reporting Act, the Equal Credit Opportunity Law, and the Fair Debt Collection Practices Act.

Truth in Lending Law

The main purpose of the Truth in Lending Law is to inform borrowers and consumers of the exact cost of credit so that they can compare costs offered by various credit sources.

The Truth in Lending Law applies to virtually all issuers of credit, including banks, savings and loan associations, credit unions, consumer finance companies, residential mortgage brokers, department stores, automobile dealers, furniture and appliance dealers, artisans (such as

electricians and plumbers), and professionals (such as doctors, dentists, and lawyers). If these parties, or any others issuing credit to the public, extend credit for personal, family, household, or agricultural uses, or for real estate transactions, they must comply with the Truth in Lending Law.

The main objective of the Truth in Lending Law is to establish a uniform means of quoting credit costs. The law dictates that any granter of credit must clearly set forth the *total finance charges* that the customer must pay, directly or indirectly, in order to obtain the desired credit. The finance charges can include any of the following costs: interest, loan fees, finder's fees, service charges, points (commonly, the added fees charged in a residential mortgage transaction), appraisal fees, premiums for credit life or health insurance, the cost of any investigation or credit reports.

In addition to stating the total dollar amount of finance charges, the credit granter must also express the cost in terms of a percentage. This is known as the *annual percentage rate* or *APR*. The APR formula requires all lenders and credit granters to quote credit costs using the same mathematics. APR, then, is the pure way of comparing credit costs between different lenders.

The Truth in Lending Law does not fix the interest rates that may be charged on credit. That's between the lender and the borrower within the limitations of state usury laws.

Figure 11–7 is a drastic simplification of a disclosure statement as required by the Truth in Lending Law. The real form can be very confusing, but this will give you a general sense of what a real disclosure statement attempts to do. Before you sign a real disclosure statement be certain that you understand every item listed on it.

If you have to put up your home as collateral for a loan, the Truth in Lending Law requires that the lender give you a three-day period in which you can cancel the transaction by sending proper notice to the lender. The purpose of this three-day cooling off period is to protect borrowers who may have second thoughts about a transaction, particularly if they have received a high-pressure sales pitch or misleading promises. If you do elect to cancel such a transaction and if proper notice is given to the lender, you are entitled to a return of any down payment you have given the lender or merchant.

The Truth in Lending Law also sets forth regulations regarding the use of credit cards, the liability for their unauthorized use, and the means by which credit may be advertised.

Truth in Savings Law

The Truth in Savings Law requires banks (all covered institutions that accept deposits) to quote the interest rates they pay on deposits in a uniform fashion. This will help customers shop for the best rates.

1. (A) Amount you are borrowing: $ _____
       Charges to be added to amount borrowed
       • Insurance costs (credit life, credit health, etc.) $ _____
       • Recording fees $ _____
       • Lien fees $ _____
       • Licensing, title, and registration fees $ _____
       • Loan fees (points, commitment fees, rate lock,
         appraisals, credit reports, notary, document
         preparation, etc.) $ _____

   (B) Total of extra charges $ _____

   Total amount financed (A + B) $ _____

2. Annual Percentage Rate: _____ %

3. Dollar amounts of finance charges:
       • Simple interest at _____% per year $ _____
       • And/or add-on or discounted interest $ _____
       • And/or flat charges $ _____
       • Other $ _____

   Total finance charges $ _____

4. Monthly payments: $_____ per month for _____ months. Note any balloon
   payments, if any, that are to be paid.

5. Prepayment privilege or charge: If the loan is paid in advance of the above
   schedule, what rebates will the borrower get, or what charges will the
   borrower have to pay?

6. Security: What collateral is being given for this loan? Describe:

7. List separately any charges that are to be paid separately by the borrower
   or are to be withheld from the loan proceeds and paid by the lender:
       $ _____ $ _____ etc.

FIGURE 11–7   Simplified Disclosure Statememt

The main feature of the law sets forth the Annual Percentage Yield (APY) as the standard method of quoting rates paid on deposits. The APY tells you, most simply put, how many dollars you'll earn if you deposit your money for one year. If you're depositing $1,000, and the APY is 5.3 percent, you'll earn $53 if you leave your money in the account for one year. This is meant to eliminate the confusion that arises when banks calculate interest in different ways (see chapter 14).

Other aspects of the law: Banks must pay interest on all funds in interest-bearing checking accounts; some banks had been excluding a portion of

each account from earning interest. Banks are restricted on how much interest they can dock you if your balance slips below a certain minimum amount; some banks had been overdoing that. In advertising their accounts banks may not call an account "free" or "no cost" if you are required to maintain a minimum balance to avoid fees; however, signs in bank lobbies do not fall under the rules for advertising, so consumer vigilance is still needed.

Fair Credit Billing Law

The Fair Credit Billing Law was designed to put an end to the frustration that credit customers experience when they receive a bill that contains an error and they cannot get the error properly corrected. It pertains to open-end credit—credit arising out of revolving charge accounts, checking overdraft plans, and credit card obligations. It does *not* apply to normal installment loans or purchases that are paid in accordance with a set schedule of installments.

The Fair Credit Billing Law covers only billing errors on your periodic statement. Billing errors are those that arise from the following: charges you did not make or charges made by a person not allowed to use your account; charges billed with the wrong descriptions, amount, or date; charges for property or services that you did not accept or that were not delivered as agreed; failures to credit your accounts for payments or for goods you have returned; mistakes in computing finance charges; billings for which you request an explanation or written proof of purchase; and failures to mail or deliver a billing statement to your current address, provided you gave at least ten days' notice of any change of address.

The Fair Credit Billing Law requires that open-end creditors give a notice summarizing the dispute settlement procedures to all customers who have active accounts. After the first notice, additional copies must be provided to customers every six months.

The dispute settlement procedures regarding a billing error, as outlined by the Federal Trade Commission, are as follows:

- **How you notify the creditor of a billing error**   If you think your bill is wrong, or if you need more information about an item on your bill, here's what you must do to preserve your rights under the law. On a sheet of paper separate from the bill, write the following: your name and account number; a description of the error and an explanation of why you think it's an error; a request for whatever added information you think you need, including a copy of the charge slip; the dollar amount of the suspected error; and any other information you think will help the creditor identify you or the reason for your complaint or inquiry.

Send your billing error notice to the address on the bill listed after the words: "Send inquiries to" or similar wording indicating the proper address.

Mail it as soon as you can but, in any case, early enough to reach the creditor within sixty days after the bill was mailed to you.

Do not simply notify the creditor by telephone. This will not necessarily protect your rights under the law.

- **What the creditor must do**   The creditor must acknowledge all such letters within thirty days, unless the creditor is able to correct your bill during the thirty-day period. Within ninety days after receiving your letter, the creditor must either correct the error or explain why the bill is correct. After explaining the bill, the creditor has no further obligation to you even if you still believe there is an error, except as provided in the fifth item of this list.

- **How you are protected from collection and bad credit reports**   After the creditor has been notified, neither the creditor not an attorney nor a collection agency may send you collection letters or take other collection action regarding the amount in dispute. But periodic *statements* may be sent to you and the disputed amount applied against your credit limit. You cannot be threatened with damage to your credit rating or sued for the amount in question, nor can the disputed amount be reported to a credit bureau or other creditors as being delinquent until the creditor has answered your inquiry. However, you remain obligated to pay whatever portion of your bill is not in dispute.

- **What happens if the dispute is settled?**   If it is determined that the creditor has made a mistake on your bill, you will not have to pay any finance charges on any disputed amount. If it turns out that the creditor has not made an error, you may have to pay finance charges on the amount in dispute, and you will have to make up any missed minimum or required payments on the disputed amount.

- **What happens if the dispute is not settled?**   If the creditor's explanation does not satisfy you and you notify the creditor in writing within ten days after you receive that explanation that you still refuse to pay the disputed amount, the creditor may report you to credit bureaus and other creditors and may pursue regular collection procedures. But the creditor must also report that you do not think you owe any money, and the creditor must let you know to whom such reports were made. Once the matter has been settled between you and the creditor, the creditor must report this to all those who were notified that you had been delinquent.

- **How the creditor can be penalized for not following the procedure**   If the creditor does not follow these rules, the creditor is not allowed to collect the first $50 of the disputed amount and finance charges, even if the bill turns out to be correct.

- **When can you withhold payment for faulty goods or services purchased with a credit card?** If you have a problem with property or services purchased with a credit card, you may have the right not to pay the remaining amount due on them if you first try, in good faith, to return the item or give the merchant a chance to correct the problem. There are two conditions on this right: (1) You must have bought the item or services in your home state or, if not within your home state, within 100 miles of your current mailing address; and (2) the purchase price must have been more than $50. However, these two conditions do not apply if the merchant's business is owned or operated by the creditor or if the creditor mailed you the advertisement for the property or services.

In brief, the Fair Credit Billing Law gives you the right of extensive protection against alleged errors in billing. But you must exercise your rights as they are stated in the law. If you fail to do so, you may have waived them.

Fair Credit Reporting Act

The Fair Credit Reporting Act is designed to give you access to any information that may be on file at local credit bureaus regarding your individual credit history. It also enables you to take steps to correct erroneous or outdated material that may be in your file.

It should be noted, contrary to what many people think, that credit reporting agencies are *not* governmental agencies. They are generally private firms, operating either on their own or as a cooperative of various merchants and lenders within the community. Their job is to accumulate appropriate credit information on individuals and make it available to their respective participating members. Easy access to credit information makes it more convenient for credit to be granted to creditworthy people. To this extent, the local credit bureau, as a clearing-house of information, serves a most valuable purpose. But there have been abuses within that industry, and the Fair Credit Reporting Act was designed to correct those abuses.

Exercise 11.8

Under the Fair Credit Reporting Act, you can, on presenting proper identification, learn the contents of your file at your local credit bureau. The identification requirements are for your own protection, to minimize the chance that a stranger may walk into a credit bureau, claim to be you, and view your credit file.

Regarding erroneous information, you can request the bureau to reinvestigate any items you question. If the information is found to be inaccurate or cannot be verified, it will be deleted. If the reinvestigation doesn't resolve the problem, you can write a brief statement explaining your position, and the statement will be included in all future credit reports. If an item is

deleted or a statement added, you can request that the bureau so notify anyone who has received regular credit reports on you during the last six months.

You may be able to get free copies of your credit file periodically. If you seek copies more frequently, you may have to pay a fee for the service.

Information in your credit file that is unfavorable to you may not be disclosed to creditors after seven years have elapsed—unless you have had a bankruptcy in your past. That information may remain in your file and be available to inquiries for up to fourteen years.

In late 1997 some additional consumer rights were added to the Fair Credit Reporting Law:

If you've ever wondered why you get unsolicited offers in the mail for credit cards or insurance plans, it may be because your local credit bureau has sold your name and relevant data to a credit card company or an insurance company. You can prevent this from happening by notifying your credit bureau accordingly. Notifying them by telephone will get your name off the lists for two years; notifying them in writing will get you off permanently. This is a highly advisable step to take. Not only will it remove unneeded temptations. It will also cut down on the chance that a scam operator will intercept a mailed solicitation and apply for a credit card in your name.

Also, credit bureaus must now also offer toll-free telephone lines so that you can talk to a real person about a possible credit bureau error, and any credit bureau mistakes must be corrected within 30 days. And other businesses (banks, merchants, finance companies, etc.) who supply information to credit bureaus are legally bound to clear up any misinformation on you that they have in their files. FTC enforcement powers were also expanded by the new law changes.

As with the other laws, the Fair Credit Reporting Act gives you rights, but it's up to you to exercise those rights.

Equal Credit Opportunity Law

The Equal Credit Opportunity Law is designed to prevent any discrimination on the basis of the gender or marital status of any person applying for credit. In the most general sense, this law was designed to correct abuses that often prevented creditworthy women from receiving credit for reasons relating specifically to their gender and marital situations. Highlights of the law include the following:

- Creditors must not discriminate against any applicant on the basis of gender or marital status in any phase of a credit transaction.
- Creditors must not make any statement to any applicant that would discourage a reasonable person from applying for credit because of gender or marital status.

- Creditors must open separate accounts for husbands and wives if requested and if both are creditworthy.
- Creditors must consider alimony and child-support payments as they would any other source of income in assessing creditworthiness if the applicant wishes to rely on those means of income.
- Creditors must allow applicants to open or maintain accounts in their birth-given name if they so desire.
- Creditors must give the reason why credit has been denied or terminated when asked by the applicant.

Fair Debt Collection Practices Act

The Fair Debt Collection Practices Act prohibits abusive, deceptive, and unfair debt-collection practices. The law covers personal, family, and household debts, including loans, charge accounts, and medical bills. Here, in brief, is how the law works:

- Debt collectors may contact you in person, by mail, telephone, or telegram, but not at unusual places or times, such as before 8 A.M. or after 9 P.M. Debt collectors may *not* contact you at work if your employer disapproves. Debt collectors may contact any other person for the purpose of trying to locate you but may not tell the other person anything other than that they are trying to contact you. If you have an attorney, they must contact only your attorney. The debt collector must not tell anybody else that you owe money; should not talk to any person more than once; should not use a postcard; and should not put anything on an envelope or in a letter to others that identifies the writer as a debt collector.
- Within five days after you are first contacted by debt collectors, they must send you *written notice* telling you the amount of money you owe, the name of the creditor, and what to do if you think you do not owe the money.
- If you think you do not owe the money, you must inform the debt collectors, in writing, within thirty days after you were first contacted. The debt collectors may then not contact you again except: (1) if they send you proof of the debt, such as a copy of the bill, in which case they can begin collection proceedings again, or (2) to notify you that certain specific action will be taken but only if, in fact, they usually do take such action. In short, you can stop the debt collectors from constantly harassing you if you properly notify them in writing to stop.
- A debt collector may not use false, deceptive, threatening, or abusive statements to induce you to pay and may not threaten to take any legal action that in fact cannot be legally taken.

PERSONAL ACTION WORKSHEET

Earnings and Costs of Checking Accounts

This is designed to help you compare the costs of various checking account plans—particular those that pay interest. As with so many other of our day-to-day concerns, the lower price is not always the best price.

	Plan A	Plan B	Plan C
❏ How much do you have to keep in the account in order to earn interest; in order to avoid charges for your checking account?	_____	_____	_____
❏ Are these minimums *averages* per month (or quarter) or fixed dollar minimums?	_____	_____	_____
❏ Can you keep the minimum balance in an account other than the checking account, such as a savings certificate?	_____	_____	_____
❏ What charges will you incur if your required minimum balance drops below the set level?			
Basic monthly charge?	_____	_____	_____
Charge per check written?	_____	_____	_____
❏ Based on your past history (if you've had a checking account previously), what type of average balance would you expect to keep in your account?	_____	_____	_____
How many checks would you write per month?			
❏ If you've not had a checking account before, estimate your average balance.	_____	_____	_____
❏ Based on these estimates, how much do you expect you'll earn (interest income less monthly charges) with this plan?	_____	_____	_____
❏ Business hours of institution?			
Open Saturdays?	_____	_____	_____
Automatic teller machine available?	_____	_____	_____
❏ Convenience in getting to and from the institution?	_____	_____	_____
❏ Personal feelings about the institution: helpfulness of staff, other services offered, etc.	_____	_____	_____

CONSUMER ALERT

A Flood of Plastic

Today some banks do nothing but offer credit cards. They don't have branch offices. They don't have checking accounts or savings accounts. They just offer credit cards. Actually, *offer* is not the correct word to describe what they do: "aggressively solicit customers" would be more like it.

Maybe you've received mail from some of them: "Congratulations! You have been *PRE-APPROVED*[1] for our new **TITANIUM** Card, which gives you an unlimited[2] line of credit, NO ANNUAL FEE,[3] a **LOW, LOW**[4] interest rate on your unpaid balance and $1 million worth of travel insurance.[5] All you have to do is tell us a little about yourself, and your *PRE-APPROVED* **TITANIUM** Credit Card will be on its way to you.[6]

The BIG PRINT GIVETH, the small print taketh away:

[1]Pre-approved? Does that mean you've been approved before you've been approved? No. It means that they got your name from some mailing list they bought.

[2]Unlimited? Yes, but subject to the limits we decide to put on once we've suckered you into sending us an application and have you salivating for this new credit card.

[3]No annual fee for the first week. Thereafter, an $89-a-year fee will be pro-rated and charged against your first month's bill.

[4]Low, low interest rate of 29.7% APR, which you'll have to admit is lower than 35.7%.

[5]Your life is covered, absolutely free, for a cool mill if you are killed while flying over the South Pole in a helicopter. See policy for other limitations and restrictions.

In a recent year, banks of all sorts sent out some 2.7 *billion* "pre-approved" credit card solicitations. That amounts to about seventeen offers to every American between the ages of 18 and 64, which translates into roughly $130,000 worth of available credit per household!

In addition to the danger of taking on more debt via plastic, many lenders now are increasing the interest rate on existing credit card debts when they learn that those borrowers have applied for extra credit. In other words, just by making an application for a loan or credit card you never accept, you risk having a higher rate of interest on your existing loans.

Stop and think: all these banks offering all these credit cards—they'd stop doing it if people didn't gobble up their offers. 'Nuf said.

UPS & DOWNS *The Economics of Everyday Life* ───────────────

Why the Health of Financial Institutions Changes

Prior to 1980, banks and S & Ls were limited as to how much interest they could pay on deposits. But the federal government was not limited as to how much interest it could pay to investors. When Uncle Sam went on a borrowing binge in the late 1970s to pay for various government programs, he offered higher interest rates to investors than could be obtained at local banks and S & Ls.

Not surprisingly, huge numbers of investors pulled their money out of local institutions to invest it with Uncle Sam. The banks and S & Ls cried, "Foul! The government limits the interest *we* can pay, then goes ahead and offers higher rates. We'll lose all our deposits and go bust! Unfair competition!"

Congress listened and cut out the interest rate controls to enable the local institutions to compete more freely. S & Ls were also given vastly broader lending powers: office buildings, hotels, shopping centers, oil rigs, you name it.

The S & Ls then found themselves in a very enviable position: they were able to attract deposits from the public because the federal government was insuring those deposits; and they were able to pay any rate of interest on those deposits they wanted to, because the limits had been taken off. Furthermore, they could now venture out into more exciting lending activities: "Why bother with dull, boring, safe single-family mortgages when we can lend our money to build skyscrapers in Peoria . . . or ritzy resort hotels in Fargo . . . or mega-maxi shopping malls (550 stores! 22,000 parking spots!) in Shinbone, Wyoming." So they made loans on projects like that.

All of this went hand in hand with the "greed" mentality of the 1980s. "I want *that* and I want it *now!*" "Debt is good because it lets us buy things!" "The economy will always grow, and we will always get richer."

Then—speaking of ups and downs—a funny thing happened. Nobody wanted to rent space in all the new shopping centers in all the Shinbones of America, and the high-flyers starting crashing to earth.

The debacle that resulted was unparalleled in our nation's history. As one of every three S & Ls folded, their insured depositors had to be protected. This cost hundreds of billions of dollars, most of which added to our national debt and annual budget deficit. In other words, the taxpayers paid the price of Congress's deregulation of the thrift industry.

Can it happen again? Commercial banks have been pleading their case to Congress, asking for broader powers that could include selling insurance, acting as stock brokers and being able to take an ownership (stockholder) position in nonbank corporations. This latter item has long been common in Japan, and has been blamed for the economic troubles Japan suffered throughout the 1990s. There's a potentially lethal conflict of interest between a *lender to* and an *owner of* a corporation. If Congress lets this happen, we could see the S & L catastrophe all over again.

?

WHAT IF . . . ?

Test yourself: How would you deal with these real-life possibilities?

1. A stranger telephones you, stating that she is a financial planner. She offers to give you an analysis of your financial situation at no cost. What opportunities and/or pitfalls might such a meeting present? What homework could you do before scheduling such a meeting?

2. Your request for a car loan at your bank has been refused. This amazes you, because you have always had an excellent credit rating. The loan officer says the loan request was denied because your credit history shows a delinquency on a debt to a local hospital. You've never had any dealings with that hospital. What might have gone wrong, and what can you do to correct the problem?

3. You've paid off your car loan promptly, and you have all the canceled checks to prove it. You're trading in the old car for a new one, and the dealer checks and finds that public records still show a loan against the old car. Showing him your canceled checks does not satisfy him. What has happened? How can you rectify the matter?

4. Your credit card bill shows a charge that you didn't make. What steps can you take to have the erroneous charge removed?

NUMBER CRUNCHERS

Do the calculations to make decisions in these real-life possibilities.

1. How much will it cost you per month for the following checking account plans, assuming that you write ten checks per month and make four deposits per month: (a) basic monthly service charge of $2, plus 10¢ for every check written; no charge for deposits made. (b) no monthly service charge; 20¢ per check and 10¢ per deposit. (c) no service charges at all if you keep a minimum of $500 in the account, and you will earn 3 percent interest per year on your average balance; if your balance falls below $500 in any month, there's a $3 charge, plus 15¢ per check and no charge for deposits. Which is the best account for you? How can you alter your checking account habits to improve your cost situation?

Exercise 11.9

2. You open a checking account with $100. After the following transactions, what is the balance in your account: (a) paycheck deposited—$444.85; (b) cash withdrawn—$50; (c) birthday gift check deposited—$100; (d) groceries—$32.90; (e) tax refund deposited—$379.58; (f) charge for new checkbook—$8.50; (g) paycheck deposited (net, after taking out $50 in cash)—$397.85; (h) rent (your share)—$420; (i) interest earned on balance in account—$1.41; (j) birthday gift check bounces; (k) charge for bounced check—$5.00.

FOR BETTER OR FOR WORSE

Things beyond our control often impact our personal and financial well-being, for better or for worse. Some are more predictable than others. How would you be affected if the following real-life phenomena happened? Could you have seen it coming? What steps could you have taken to minimize damage or maximize advantage? The better able you are to anticipate and recognize these forces, the better equipped you are to deal with them.

1. Your wayward brother-in-law finally pays you back the $4,000 he owes you. You deposit the check in your account and write out a number of checks against it for money that you owe. Then your brother-in-law's check bounces.

2. You sign a contract for home improvements, realizing that you have to give the contractor a second mortgage on the house as collateral for the loan. A week later you learn that the contractor has a very bad reputation.

3. You write a check for $500 as down payment on a used car. An hour later you change your mind but the seller of the car says "a deal is a deal." You phone your bank to stop payment on the check. The bank tells you over the phone that they will do so. But they don't, and the check is cashed by the seller.

12

Credit and Borrowing

There can be no freedom or beauty about a home life that depends on borrowing and debt.

Henrik Ibsen

Imagine what would happen to our economy if it weren't possible to borrow money. Everything would grind to a halt: People couldn't buy cars, houses, or appliances until they had accumulated enough cash to do so. Similarly, businesses and governments would be hard pressed to create new facilities, purchase needed equipment, and expand ongoing programs.

We live in a credit (borrowing) society. Making wise use of your ability to borrow can enhance your life. Abusing your credit can be very harmful. This chapter will explore the wise and unwise uses of credit and will guide you in the ways that credit techniques work. You'll learn:

- How to evaluate how much borrowing you can afford to do and under what circumstances
- Where to seek the credit you need and how best to ensure you'll get the money you need
- How to structure your borrowing to suit your ability to repay your loans
- How to avoid the dangers of credit abuse
- Where to look for help if you have credit problems

BUY NOW, PAY LATER

Most of us take the "Buy now, pay later" aspect of our economy for granted. But it was not always so.

It wasn't until about 1916, with the development of a phenomenon called the Morris Plan, that the individual working person could borrow from banks and other financial institutions. Prior to that, business, governments, and wealthy individuals were the predominant borrowers. Their loans were generally on a "demand" or "time" basis. A demand loan would be repayable in its entirety on the demand of the lender. A time loan would be repayable after the passage of the stated amount of time. If the borrower wished and the lender was willing, such loans could be renewed for an additional period of time, once the borrower had paid the interest due. It was generally felt that if plain working folk borrowed on such a basis, they would not be able to repay the lump sum at the agreed-on time.

Then a banker named Arthur Morris devised a plan that would enable the individual worker to borrow money that was needed for immediate purposes. Today, Mr. Morris's plan seems commonplace, but it was a revolutionary concept when it was originally devised.

The key to his idea—which came to be known as the Morris Plan—was that a loan could be repaid in monthly installments over a fixed period of time. The Morris Plan was the origin, and grandfather, of the installment loan, the time payment plan, the revolving charge account, the credit card loan, and all the other forms of borrowing that we are accustomed to.

Morris's reasoning was simple enough: although it might be difficult for the typical worker to repay one large lump sum, if individuals were prudent and well employed, they should be able to set aside a fixed amount each month to apply to the debt. This type of debt would command a higher rate of interest from the borrower, and the lender would have a constant inflow of money as payments were made each month on the loans, thus enabling the lender to keep putting the available money back to work on a constant basis.

From an initial institution in Virginia, the Morris Plan proved itself. Within a few years scores of Morris Plan institutions were in operation around the country.

Commercial banks soon saw the advantages and profits in making such loans, and merchants began to accept the installment IOUs of customers for many products. The buy now, pay later years were on their way.

The Morris Plan, and all that developed from it, proved successful on more than one level. By putting borrowing power into the hands of millions of American workers, more goods could be manufactured and sold. This, in turn, helped to create more jobs which, in turn, created more income for more people. This then enabled a much larger segment of the population to borrow and buy.

Today, there are very few adults in the United States who do not carry one of the descendants of the Morris Plan with them in their wallets or purses—the credit card. The credit card, in effect, allows holders to write personal installment loans—within limits—whenever and wherever they choose.

Understanding the workings of credit and borrowing is essential to all those who want to manage their personal and financial affairs wisely. Let's now take a closer look at their workings and how they can be put to proper and sensible use.

WHAT IS CREDIT?

Credit—the ability to borrow—is not a right. It's a privilege earned through careful planning and faithful performance. Good credit, properly used, can be a most valuable asset. Wise borrowers have studied their own financial situation with great care. They know the difference between needs and luxuries. They know within pennies their ability to repay. They know how to approach the lender, what to ask for and what to expect. They can resist the temptations that scream, "Buy me now!" and "Easy credit!"

They have carefully defined their *access to credit, credit needs*, and *credit capacity*. And they can keep each in proper perspective and balance. Let's take a closer look at these three important elements of credit.

Access to Credit

Access to credit refers to the amount of credit readily available to you through such means as charge accounts, credit cards, and installment loans. Access to credit, of course, is directly related to lender and merchant willingness to grant credit. That, in turn, depends on your past performance, income, other debts, work, and the purposes for which you wish to borrow.

Credit Needs

Credit needs refer to the various needs you may have that can be fulfilled through borrowing. Common needs for borrowing include purchasing an automobile; revolving charge accounts at department stores so that a large clothing purchase, for example, can be paid for over an extended period of time, thus making it easier on the monthly budget; home im-

provements; and personal emergencies. *Note:* We are referring to *needs*, not luxuries. Using credit to acquire luxuries, as opposed to using credit to fulfill needs, can be dangerous. If your available credit is used excessively to obtain luxuries, you can cut off your access to credit for the more important needs.

Credit Capacity

Capacity for credit refers to the amount of borrowing you can realistically handle, considering both your current and future income and expenses.

People often find that they have access to more credit than they realistically need. For example, Charlie and Charlotte estimate that they have access to roughly $15,000 worth of credit. Based on past experience, they are confident that their bank would lend them up to $5,000 without collateral, if necessary. The sum total of all their credit cards and charge accounts would allow them to go into additional debt of about $5,000. And a representative of a lending firm has told them that the equity in their house would allow them to borrow another $5,000—if, naturally, they were willing to give a second mortgage on the house. Their current credit *needs* are much more modest. Their automobile is paid off, and next year they'll need a new one. They estimate that they might need about $8,000 for this purpose. Over and above that, their credit needs don't exceed $1,000—to be used in their charge accounts to even out the monthly cost of clothing and home necessities.

Currently, then, their *capacity* for credit exceeds their credit *needs*. However, in a few years, Charlie and Charlotte's oldest child will be starting college, and they expect to have to borrow quite heavily to meet those costs. At that time, their credit *needs* may exceed their credit *capacity*. They should begin making plans to ensure that they'll be able to borrow what they need when they need it. They would be wise to visit a lending officer at their bank and review their *access* to credit, their *needs* for credit, and their credit *capacity* now and for the next three to five years. Such a periodic review is wise for anyone who wants to maintain good control over the wise use of credit.

Credit Sources

Installment loans for a variety of purposes are available at banks, savings and loan associations, credit unions, and consumer finance (small loan) companies. As a general rule, the cost of borrowing tends to be highest at the consumer finance companies. Interest rates at credit unions tend to be equal to, or slightly lower than, those at banks and savings and loan associations.

Exercise 12.1

Dealer financing is another common source of credit. When you purchase such items as automobiles, furniture, and appliances, the dealer may be able to arrange financing for you. The dealer may extend the loan to you directly or may place your loan with one of the financial institutions mentioned earlier. A dealer who places financing with another institution usually gets a fee for doing so. Before you accept a dealer financing arrangement, you should compare the cost of doing so with what you'd be charged if you dealt directly with a lender of your choice.

Charge accounts are frequently used as a source of credit. Department stores, for example, will approve open-end credit arrangements with credit-worthy customers. This will allow you to charge purchases at the store up to a certain limit. You'll be expected to pay at least a minimum amount each month toward your debt. If you don't pay your charge account debts in full each month, you'll be charged interest for the balance left owing. This interest charge is usually based on the average amount outstanding in your account during the prior month.

Credit cards have become one of the most popular sources of credit. The most common types of credit cards are those offered by banks: MasterCard and VISA. These cards are honored extensively throughout the United States and in foreign countries. These cards have also been offered through nonbanking entities, such as AT&T and affinity groups (airline frequent flyer plans, fraternal organizations, and the like). Dean Witter offers the Discover card. "Travel and entertainment" cards (American Express, Diners Club) are commonly used for business purposes at hotels and restaurants. Airlines and gasoline companies also issue charge cards for use in obtaining their specific products and services.

Applicants who are deemed creditworthy are granted a line of credit by the credit card company. That is, a maximum amount is established that these individuals can charge against the card. The card user is then expected to pay at least a certain monthly minimum and any debt unpaid will be charged interest.

The manner in which interest on credit card debts is calculated can be very complex. The best way to avoid the matter entirely is to pay your credit card debt in full each month so that no interest at all accrues against you. Most issuing institutions will also charge an annual fee for the use of the credit card. Interest costs on credit card usage tend to be higher than interest costs on a direct installment loan made at a bank.

Undisciplined use of credit cards and charge accounts can create serious financial problems. It's much easier to pay the minimum monthly amount than to pay off the entire month's charges. But this adds heavy interest costs to your debt, and those costs keep mounting over the months (and perhaps even years) that you take to pay off the debt. And the ease of using credit cards compounds the problem by adding new debts to your existing debt. If you pay off the full month's charges immediately, you

Beware Low-rate Credit Cards and High Loan-to-Value Home Loans

In the highly competitive world of selling credit cards, one common ploy is to offer a lower interest rate on your debt than what you now might be paying. "Pay off all your high interest debts with our low rate card. . . ." You don't have to look too far to read that this low rate is "introductory," and you therefore must assume that after the introductory period your rate will be kicked up to a higher level, and you'll be back where you started from. Or worse. Is it worth it? Proceed with caution.

Another come-on is the so-called high LTV mortgage, offered mainly by nonbank lenders. LTV stands for loan to value: If the value of your home is $100,000 and you have $70,000 in loans against it, your LTV is 70 percent. High LTV lenders—seeking to woo the millions of overanxious, overextended homeowners—offer loans of up to 125 percent of the value of their homes. As in the above example, a borrower could get an extra $55,000 on top of the current debt of $70,000 in a 125 percent LTV loan. This is DANGEROUS! Although you might lower the interest rate on some of your debt, you risk losing the house if you default on a high LTV mortgage. And if you sell before you've paid down the high LTV mortgage, you could end up still owing money after you no longer own the home. Or you might not be able to sell at all without paying off the loan.

should not incur any interest costs at all. But if you take the line of least resistance, paying only the minimum monthly amount, you'll sooner or later find yourself looking at a mountain of debt that can be very difficult indeed to pay off.

Credit Reporting

The promptness with which you pay your existing debts affects your ability to borrow in the future. Your performance is known as your credit history. Information that makes up your credit history is compiled by a credit bureau. Credit bureaus exist in every community for the purpose of gathering information on the credit performance of individuals in that community. See the discussion in chapter 11 on the Fair Credit Reporting Act, which controls what credit bureaus can and cannot do, and what your rights are with respect to your credit history.

Figure 12–1 illustrates a typical credit report in abbreviated form.

Date of report _____

Name and address of Credit Bureau _____

Name and address of company for whom the report has been created _____

Name and address of person whose credit is being reported _____

   Social Security # _____   Spouse's name _____

   Present employer _____   Since _____   Position _____

   Date employment verified _____   Monthly income _____

   Date of birth_____   Own or rent _____

   Former address _____   From _____ To _____

   Former employer _____   From _____ To _____

   Spouse's current employer _____ Since _____ Monthly income _____

Credit History

Business Reporting	Date Opened	Last Pmt.	Highest Credit	Present Status $ owed	Past Due	Times Past Due 30–59 days	60–90 days	90+ days
ABC Bank	06/17/98	01/17/99	$2,500	$1,970	-0-	1	-0-	-0-
XYZ Car Dealer	08/11/97	01/03/99	12,500	9,644	-0-	-0-	-0-	-0-
Credit Card	07/27/95	12/18/98	6,000	4,280	-0-	1	-0-	-0-

Public Record: Small Claims Court 11/16/97. Subject was sued for $300 by TV Repair shop. Subject claims repairs were incomplete. Case was dropped.

FIGURE 12–1   Credit History Report

Note: This is an abbreviated version of the typical report as created by the Associated Credit Bureaus, a national trade association of credit bureaus. It is meant to highlight only the most pertinent information relevant to this chapter.

HOW THE COST OF CREDIT IS FIGURED

Simple Interest

The fee you pay for the use of someone else's money is called <u>interest</u>. Interest rates are expressed as a percentage of the amount borrowed and for a given period of time. For example, if you borrowed $1,000 for one year and the interest rate was 10 percent a year, you would pay a fee of $100 (10 percent of $1,000) for the use of the money for a period of one year. If you were borrowing $1,000 and the interest rate was expressed as 1 percent per month, you would pay a fee of $10 per month (1 percent of $1,000 equals

$10), or a total over the year of $120 in interest. In these examples, you would have the use of the entire $1,000 for the full period, be it one year or one month. This calculation is what is commonly known as simple interest.

Loans calculated on a simple-interest basis are generally repayable in one lump sum at a specific time, such as 30, 60, 90, or 120 days from the date of the loan. Or the loan may be repayable on the demand of the lender. Businesses generally borrow on a simple-interest basis, and some individuals may also be able to borrow on that basis. (The expression *prime rate* refers to the simple-interest rate that banks charge their most creditworthy borrowers. Prime-rate loans, in theory, are the safest and lowest risk loans that lenders make. Thus, the prime rate is the lowest interest rate a lender will offer. Borrowers who do not have the financial strength and creditworthiness of prime-rate borrowers pay a higher rate of interest. As the prime rate moves up and down, as it tends to do regularly, other interest rates usually follow.)

Of more concern to the average individual is the mode of calculating interest on installment and open-end credit. Installment loans are those that are repayable in equal monthly installments; open-end credit refers to debts generated through charge accounts, credit card accounts, and checking account overdraft accounts. In an open-end account, you will be billed for a minimum monthly payment, based on the total amount of the current balance you owe.

Add-on Interest

Probably the most common way of calculating interest in an installment loan is the add-on method. Here's how it works. Say you want to borrow $1,000 for twelve months, and the rate is 6 percent add-on per year. Your rental fee for the use of the bank's money will be 6 percent of $1,000, or $60. The lender will then add the $60 on to the $1,000 worth of principal, making a total of $1,060.

That sum, $1,060, is divided by twelve, giving you twelve equal monthly payments of $88.33 each. Thus, with the add-on loan, you receive the $1,000 in cash and, over the course of one year, you will repay $1,060. It sounds like simple interest, but it is really quite different. In the simple-interest loan, you have the use of the full $1,000 for the full one year. Under the installment method, such as add-on, you have the use of the full $1,000 during only the first month of the loan, at the end of which you make your first payment. During the second month, therefore, you have the use of only 11/12 of the money and proportionately less each month until the final month, when you have the use of only 1/12 of the money. In effect, then, you are paying $60 rental, but you don't have the use of all the money all the time, as you would in the simple-interest loan. However, you do have the use of whatever it is you obtained with the money you borrowed—a car, an appliance, or whatever.

What if the loan is for more than one year? In the add-on method, the interest rate would be multiplied by the number of years. For example: if you are borrowing $1,000 for two years at a 6 percent per year add-on rate, your total interest obligation would be $120 over the full two-year period. (Six percent per year, or $60 per year, times two years equals $120.)

Discount Interest

Another way of figuring interest on installment loans is the discount method. A loan that nets the borrower $1,000 for twelve months at a 6 percent discount per year rate works like this. Working from a prefigured chart, the lender notes that 6 percent of $1,064 equals $63.84. Let's round that off to $64 for ease in figuring. A promissory note is signed for $1,064, and the lender *discounts,* or subtracts, the interest from that, leaving you with $1,000 in cash. The $1,064 is divided by twelve, giving you twelve equal monthly payments of $88.66. You receive $1,000. You repay $1,064. Comparing the discount with the add-on method, you can see that the discount results in a slightly higher cost to the borrower and a slightly higher return to the lender. In other words, in these examples, the 6 percent discount method costs the borrower $4 more a year than the 6 percent add-on method.

How Interest Costs Are Expressed: APR

If you were shopping for a loan, and one lender quoted you a 10 percent add-on rate, another quoted you a 10 percent discount rate, and still a third quoted you a 10 percent simple-interest rate, you'd be very confused. But, thanks to a federal law, the Truth in Lending Law, the confusion is removed. Under the Truth in Lending Law, lenders and granters of credit may *calculate* their interest rate and other finance charges any way they want (within the limitations of the state's usury laws). But no matter how those rates are calculated, they must be *expressed* in terms of annual percentage rate (APR). The Federal Trade Commission has prepared extensive tables by which any lender can convert add-on or discount rates to APR terms. Table 12–1 shows the conversion of add-on rates for common installment loans to APR, based on the FTC Tables.

For example, a 6 percent a year add-on rate for a 24-month loan is equal to an APR of 11.13. A 6 percent a year add-on rate for a 36-month loan is equal to an APR of 11.08.

Under the Truth in Lending Law, all lenders are required to quote their rates only in terms of APR, even though many of them may still calculate their rates on an add-on or discount basis.

TABLE 12–1   **Converting Add-on to APR**

Term (Months)	Add-on Rates (Percentages)			
	5½	6	6½	7
12	10.00% APR	10.90% APR	11.79% APR	12.68% APR
18	10.18	11.08	11.98	12.87
24	10.23	11.13	12.12	12.91
30	10.23	11.12	12.00	12.88
36	10.20	11.08	11.96	12.83
48	10.11	10.97	11.83	12.68
60	10.01	10.85	11.68	12.50

Open-end Credit

In the typical installment loan, the borrower receives a lump sum of money and pays it back in equal installments. In open-end credit, that's not necessarily the case. If, for example, you have a credit card account and you have not paid all your charges, you will be carrying an *open-end loan. Open-end* means that you can add to that debt by making additional charges or diminish it by making payments. Because the total balance you owe at any given time can fluctuate, the APR is normally calculated on the average balance owed throughout the monthly billing period.

The APR rate will be expressed on the billing statement each month as required by the Truth in Lending Law.

Figuring Your Installment Loan Costs

The APR gives us the means to compare true interest rates on various loan quotations. The actual dollar cost of any loan will be set forth in the disclosure statement provided you by the lender. See Figure 11–7 for a sample disclosure statement. Other financing costs can be included in the disclosure statement; so, for your best protection in comparing loan costs, you should have a complete tally of all the costs involved in any given quotation, expressed in dollar terms on the disclosure statement. Use that as your ultimate comparison.

Insuring Your Installment Loan

Many lenders suggest that you obtain credit insurance as a part of your installment loan transaction. There are two common types of credit insurance:

Exercise 12.2

life and health. If you obtain credit life insurance as a part of the transaction, the insurance will pay off any remaining balance on the loan if the borrower dies before the loan is paid off. The borrower's survivors need not, therefore, pay the remaining balance on the loan.

If you obtain health insurance on your loan, the insurance will make your payments if you become unable to work for an extended period of time because of illness or accident. Credit health insurance will differ regarding the initial waiting period involved before the insurance takes effect. For example, if a waiting period is fifteen days, you must be unable to work for fifteen days before the insurance takes effect. In such a case, if you're out of work for, say, twenty-five days, the insurance will protect you for the last ten days. Some credit health plans may protect you in case of partial disability.

Another form of credit insurance is unemployment insurance. It makes your payments for you if you lose your job for specific reasons.

If you wish to obtain any of these forms of insurance, you can pay the lender separately, or the cost of the insurance can be added to the amount you're borrowing, which would increase your interest cost and payments accordingly.

Paying Off an Installment Loan Ahead of Schedule

Loan officers frequently have to resolve a perplexing dispute that arises when customers wish to pay off their installment loans ahead of schedule. Here's a typical situation. Charlie had borrowed $5,000 for a thirty-six-month term. The interest cost for three years was $900, which, when added to the $5,000, gave Charlie a total debt of $5,900 and monthly payments of $164. Eighteen months have elapsed, and Charlie has accumulated some unexpected funds and wishes to use them to pay off his installment loan. Against the original debt of $5,900, Charlie has, during these first eighteen months, made payments totaling $2,952. That would reduce his debt to $2,948.

Charlie then figures that since he's halfway through the loan, he should pay half the interest he originally committed to, or $450. Subtracting the $450 from the $2,948, Charlie calculates that he owes the bank $2,498 to wipe the loan off the books. But the bank figures differently. They figure that Charlie is entitled to get back only 25.7 percent of the original $900, or $231. In other words, of the $900 Charlie was originally committed to pay, the bank is charging him 74.3 percent of that amount, or $669. In effect, then, $231 of his original interest commitment would be "rebated" to him. This would make his payoff figure $2,717. Charlie is enraged to learn that he owes the bank $219 more than he had expected to. What happened to that $219? The Rule of 78s happened.

The Rule of 78s

It was noted earlier that in the typical installment loan borrowers have the use of the full original amount borrowed only during the first month of the loan. Then, as borrowers make periodic payments, they have the use of progressively less and less of the original amount of the loan. That's the basis for the so-called Rule of 78s, which is used to determine how each month's payment is broken down into interest and principal.

In an installment loan, the borrower commits himself to pay a certain amount of interest over the term of the loan. If he pays off the full balance of the loan before the full term elapses, the borrower is entitled to get back a portion of his interest cost, plus a portion of any other rebatable charges such as insurance. But the borrower does not get back an amount directly proportional to the amount of time the loan has run. As in Charlie's case, if you pay off a thirty-six-month loan at the end of eighteen months, your interest rebate does not equal one-half of the original amount of interest, even though half of the loan has elapsed.

Here's an example of the Rule of 78s in action.

Exercise 12.3

On a twelve-month loan, a borrower has the use of all the money during the first month. She then makes her first payment. During the second month, she has the use of only 11/12 of the money. For the third month, it becomes 10/12. And so on until the last month, when she has the use of only 1/12 of the money.

Because the borrower has the use of more money in the earlier months, she has to pay proportionately more for it. Actually, the borrower has the use of twelve times more money in the first month than in the last month.

In the Rule of 78s, the sum of the number of months in a twelve-month loan equals 78 (1 + 2 + 3 + 4 . . . to 12 = 78). During the first month of a twelve-month loan, you're charged with 12/78 of the total interest. During the second month, you're charged with an additional 11/78 of the total interest. During the third month, you're charged with an additional 10/78 of the total interest. The last month, you'd be charged with 1/78. The total of the twelve fractions is 78/78, or 100 percent of the total interest.

If, therefore, you paid off the loan at the end of six months, you'd be charged for 57/78 of the total interest owed (12 + 11 + 10 + 9 + 8 + 7 = 57). Your rebate would be the remaining 21/78, or about 27 percent of the original interest charged to you. If the original interest has been $60, you'd thus be rebated about $16.

For loans of other than twelve months' duration, the key number becomes the sum total of the number of months.

For example, in a 24-month loan, the sum of the numbers 1 through 24 equals 300. During the first month of such a loan, you'd be charged for 24/300 of the total interest. During the second month, you'd be charged for 23/300 of the total of the interest. And so it would go throughout the term of the loan. Table 12–2 converts all these fractions into percentages to enable

TABLE 12–2   Rebate Schedule from the Rule of 78s (Showing Percentage of Finance Charge to Be Rebated). This Schedule Applies to All Interest Rates.

Number of Months Loan Has Run	Original Term of Loan (Months)				
	12	18	24	30	36
1	84.6	89.5	92.0	93.5	94.6
2	70.5	79.5	84.3	87.3	89.3
3	57.7	70.2	77.0	81.3	84.2
4	46.1	61.4	70.0	75.5	79.3
5	35.9	53.2	63.3	69.9	74.5
6	26.9	45.6	57.0	64.5	69.8
7	19.2	38.6	51.0	59.3	65.3
8	12.8	32.2	45.3	54.4	61.0
9	7.7	26.3	40.0	49.7	56.8
10	3.8	21.0	35.0	45.2	52.7
11	1.3	16.4	30.3	40.9	48.8
12	-0-	12.3	26.0	36.8	45.0
13		8.8	22.0	32.9	41.4
14		5.8	18.3	29.2	38.0
15		3.5	15.0	25.8	34.7
16		1.7	12.0	22.6	31.5
17		.58	9.3	19.6	28.5
18		-0-	7.0	16.8	25.7
19			5.0	14.2	23.0
20			3.3	11.8	20.4
21			2.0	9.7	18.0
22			1.0	7.7	15.8
23			.33	6.0	13.7
24			-0-	4.5	11.7
25				3.2	9.9
26				2.1	8.3
27				1.3	6.8
28				.65	5.4
29				.22	4.2
30				-0-	3.1
31					2.2
32					1.5
33					.90
34					.45
35					.15
36					-0-

Note: To calculate rebates for longer loan periods, halve the time frames. Example: To find the amount to be rebated after 24 months have elapsed on a 48-month loan, look for the number where the column "loan has run—12 months" meets the row "Original term of loan—24 months." That number (26 percent) is approximately the same as you'd find after 24 months have elapsed on a 48-month loan.

you to calculate the rebate on loans ranging from twelve to thirty-six months at six-month intervals.

For loans set to run for other terms than those shown in the table, your banker can give you a precise rebate breakdown. A good working knowledge of installment loans and how rebates are figured can be most important in determining when, how, and why you should consolidate loans, refinance them, or pay them off. Here's how you can figure the rebates on any loans included in the table.

1. Determine the total interest you have been charged for the loan.
2. Decide at what point you want to figure the rebate—say, after nine months of a twenty-four-month loan. Locate the factor on the rebate chart where the column "loan has run—9 months" meets the row "original term of loan—24 months." That factor is 40 percent, which is the percentage of your interest charge that you will get back or that will be credited to you if you pay off the loan after nine months.
3. Multiply your original interest cost by the rebate percentage to get the actual dollars to be rebated.
4. From your original total debt, subtract the amount of payments made so far. Then subtract the dollar amount of your rebate. The final total is your payoff figure.

Figuring Payoff

Here's an example using this formula. You had originally borrowed $2,000, repayable in thirty months. The interest cost was $250, making your total debt $2,250. Monthly payments are $75. You want to pay off the balance due after nine months. What will your rebate and your payoff amount be? (*Note:* The rebate schedule is the same for all interest rates.)

1. The percent of your total original interest that will be rebated to you is 49.7 percent. That's where the 30-month column (original term of loan) meets the 9-month row (number of months loan has run).
2. Your rebate is $124.95 (49.7 percent of $250).
3. Your payoff figure is $1,450.75. From the original total debt of $2,250, you subtract $675, representing the nine payments you made at $75 each. From that sum you further subtract the $124.25 that is your rebate. In other words, your payoff figure is your *original debt* less *payments made to date* less *rebate due you.*

Other rebatable charges, such as insurance premiums, are figured on the same basis. Thus, if you had a life insurance premium charge on the loan of $30, you would receive a rebate of that charge of $14.91 (49.7 percent of $30).

Does it make sense to pay off an installment loan early? In the preceding

example, the borrower presumably found himself with a windfall of $1,450. Even though his loan was only 30 percent paid off (9 months out of 30), more than half the total interest he was committed to pay had been used up. If he uses the $1,450 to pay off the loan, he'll save about $125, representing the remaining interest he's obliged to pay. If, instead, he invests that $1,450 at a 5 percent annual percentage yield (APY), it will earn roughly $150 over the next two years.

Refinancing an Installment Loan

Having the money to pay off an installment loan is a pleasant dilemma rarely faced. Much more frequent is the desire to refinance the loan to reduce the monthly payments. The Rule of 78s applies in this situation just as it would in an early payoff. Following the preceding example, an individual may wish to refinance the original $2,000 loan after nine of the thirty months have elapsed. As the formula indicates, he will have a balance owing of $1,450. Assume that he wishes to refinance that balance for a new thirty-six-month term at an 11.08 APR (6 percent add-on). He would have to obligate himself for an additional $261 in interest for that new loan. The $261 added to the $1,450 remaining payoff figure would give a new debt of $1,711 and monthly payments (interest and principal) of $47.53. He thus reduces his monthly payments by almost $30, but in so doing, incurs added interest expense and an ongoing debt for fifteen additional months. Refinancing a debt in such a manner should be done only after counseling with a loan officer. To extend the debt could create a bottleneck years down the road when other credit needs arise.

Increasing an Installment Loan

As with refinancing, individuals frequently want to borrow more money on their credit line. For example, in the preceding situation, assume that the borrower wants another $1,000. He does not wish to take out a separate new loan but wants to add the $1,000 to his existing installment loan to run for a period of thirty-six months. His payoff balance on the original loan is $1,450. To that the lender adds the $1,000 new money, plus interest. Assuming an 11.08 APR (6 percent add-on), the additional interest would be $441. This gives him a total debt of $2,891 with monthly payments of $80.30. For roughly $5 more than he is now paying each month, he has another $1,000 cash in hand. But, as with refinancing, he has stretched his payment schedule out fifteen months longer than the earlier payment period. As with refinancing, adding on to debt in this manner should be done only after counseling with a loan officer.

SHOPPING FOR LOANS

Interest Rates

A slight difference in the interest rate on an installment loan can have a considerable impact on the overall cost for the term of the loan. Table 12–3 illustrates the effect of varying interest rates on a sampling of different loans.

The Effect of Down Payment Size

To the extent that you borrow to buy anything, the cost of borrowing can add as much as 10 to 30 percent to the cost of the item. The less you borrow, the less interest you'll be paying, and the lower your monthly payment.

The question may arise as to whether you are better off financing the whole amount of a purchase and putting the available down payment dollars into savings where it can earn interest. Generally, when you're starting from scratch with an installment loan, before the Rule of 78s

TABLE 12–3   Comparing Interest Rates

APR (Percentage)	Add-on (Percentage)	Total Interest	Total to Be Repaid	Monthly Payments
On a Loan of $1,000 for 12 Months				
10.00	5.5	$ 55	$1,055	$ 87.92
10.90	6	60	1,060	88.33
11.79	6.5	65	1,065	88.75
12.68	7	70	1,070	89.33
On a Loan of $2,000 for 24 Months				
10.23	5.5	$220	$2,220	$ 92.50
11.13	6	240	2,240	93.33
12.12	6.5	260	2,260	94.16
12.91	7	280	2,280	95.00
On a Loan of $3,000 for 36 Months				
10.20	5.5	$495	$3,495	$ 97.08
11.08	6	540	3,540	98.33
11.96	6.5	585	3,585	99.58
12.83	7	630	3,630	100.83

comes into play, you probably wouldn't do as well going for the larger financing. Because a savings account pays less than what you must pay a lender for a loan, you'd probably be better off applying your available cash toward the purchase price and reducing the amount of the loan accordingly.

Table 12–4 illustrates the dollar effect of varying down payments on a specific loan.

How Long Should Your Loan Run?

The amount of time, or term, of an installment loan can affect overall costs considerably. The longer the term, the lower the monthly payments and the higher the interest costs. Do the lower payments make up for the higher interest costs? Table 12–5 illustrates the effect of different terms on loans of varying sizes.

Other basic guidelines are helpful in determining how long an installment loan should run. Generally speaking, the life of the loan should not exceed the expected life use of the product or service you're borrowing for. Also, when you borrow for a recurring need, the loan should be paid off before the need occurs again. Examples of recurring loans include those for taxes, vacations, and cars.

For example, say you borrow $600 on June 1 for a summer vacation. With a twelve-month loan, you'll be all paid up by the next summer. But with an eighteen-month loan, you'll be paying for this year's vacation until the end of next year. If you were to borrow again in June of next year for that year's vacation, you'd have a few hundred dollars of this year's loan still unpaid if you had taken the longer plan. If you then combined the remaining old bal-

TABLE 12–4 **Effect of Down Payment on Loan Costs on a $3,000 Purchase, at 11.08 Percent APR (6 Percent Add-on), for a 36-Month Loan**

Down Payment	Amount of Loan	Total Interest Cost	Total to Be Repaid	Monthly Payment
$ 0	$3,000	$540	$3,540	$98.33
300	2,700	484	3,184	88.44
500	2,500	450	2,950	81.94
800	2,200	396	2,596	72.11
1,000	2,000	360	2,360	65.55
1,200	1,800	326	2,126	59.05
1,500	1,500	270	1,770	49.16

TABLE 12–5   The Effect of Different Terms on Loan Costs

Amount Borrowed	Term of Loan (Months)	Total Interest Cost	Total to Be Repaid	Monthly Payment
$1,000	12	$ 60	$1,060	$ 88.33
1,000	18	90	1,090	60.55
1,000	24	120	1,120	46.67
1,000	30	150	1,150	38.33
1,000	36	180	1,180	32.77
2,000	12	240	2,240	93.33
2,000	18	300	2,300	76.67
2,000	24	360	2,360	65.55
2,000	30	420	2,420	57.62
2,000	36	480	2,480	51.67
3,000	12	360	3,360	140.00
3,000	18	540	3,540	98.33
3,000	24	630	3,630	86.42
3,000	30	720	3,720	77.50
3,000	36	900	3,900	65.00

ance and the new loan for yet another eighteen-month loan, you could still be paying for part of the year's vacation three years from now. This is an example of *pyramiding,* and it can be a dangerous practice.

Car loans should be geared to the time you expect to retain the car. If you trade every two years, for example, your loan should be paid off within that period. Running the loan longer than the life of the car makes the borrower prone to the risk of pyramiding.

Major household items, such as large appliances, might not need replacing for a decade or more. But they should not be financed for as long as they will last. These debts should be eliminated as quickly as your budget will allow in order to make room for other borrowing needs and to keep your interest expenses down. Most lenders won't exceed a few years for such loans anyway, but avoid the temptation of becoming involved in longer plans that might allow for lower monthly payments. The interest cost will be that much higher, and you could still be paying off a loan when you'd rather have that credit capacity available for some other purpose.

One-shot loans, such as those for special events (weddings, etc.), special trips, and other nonrecurring personal needs should also be paid up as

quickly as your budget will allow. The needs won't recur, but taking such a loan for too long a term can clutter up your future borrowing capacity and have you paying more interest than is wise.

Home improvements, particularly major additions such as patios, pool, and extra rooms, can get a bit tricky. These items can easily run into many thousands of dollars, and common installment financing plans run to five years, occasionally longer. For the most part, these improvements become a part of the house—you won't take them with you when you move. You may recapture all or most of the cost when you sell the house.

When these improvements are integral to the house, you might find it better to add the cost on to your mortgage if you can. Check with your mortgage lender to evaluate cost and feasibility. For example, a $4,000 home-improvement loan for five years could entail monthly payments of roughly $83. If you added that same amount to a mortgage that had twenty years left to run, the monthly payments would be about $35. If you expect to be selling the house within ten years or less, it could be better to add the home-improvement costs to your mortgage.

Home Equity Borrowing

With home equity financing, you give the lender a mortgage on your home as security for the loan. The attraction of this type of financing is that the interest on a loan secured by a mortgage can be tax-deductible, whereas interest on other types of consumer debt is not deductible. (Check the most recent tax regulations for current conditions.)

Exercise 12.4

Offsetting the advantage of tax deductions for the interest are the costs of acquiring home equity financing. Since a mortgage is involved, you should expect to pay for an appraisal, for title insurance, for recording fees, for document preparation, for points, and other related costs. (See chapter 7 for more details.) You should determine what these costs will be before you apply for the loan and compare them with the benefits of the tax deduction. You might find it cheaper in some cases to borrow directly rather than via the home equity route. Needless to say, if you don't own a home you can't use home equity financing.

There are two basic types of home equity financing: the home equity *loan*, and the home equity *line of credit*. With the loan, you apply to the lender for a specific amount, and if your application is approved you get that lump sum of money and repay it in accordance with a set formula. With the line of credit, you apply for the right to borrow up to a certain sum of money. As you need that money you take it from the lender, and you only pay interest on whatever amount you owe at any given time. Home equity financing might be available with either fixed or adjustable rates of interests. Costs will differ from lender to lender and from time to time.

DOS AND DON'TS WHEN YOU APPLY FOR A LOAN

The following list of dos and don'ts can help you communicate more effectively with your lender and help get your loan application processed more efficiently.

- **Do** all your shopping and homework beforehand. Whenever possible, know exactly what you're going to borrow for, how the money will be used, and what the total needs will be.

- **Do** make sure all your other credit accounts are up to date before you apply for credit. If necessary, check with each creditor and with your local credit bureau. A credit history showing late accounts may not kill your chances of getting a loan, but it can certainly cause delays and aggravation.

Exercise 12.5

- **Do** get an idea of the rates charged by various lenders. This can be done quickly, discreetly, and, if you wish, anonymously. Be certain that any quotes you receive are expressed in terms of APR (annual percentage rate), and determine what the total dollar charges are for interest and any other fees the lender may impose.

    You might be able to obtain a more attractive interest rate if you make a larger down payment or if you are a customer of the institution in other departments. Service and convenience must also be considered.

- **Do** prepare a list of all your other debts, including the name of each creditor, purpose of the loan, original amount borrowed, current amount owed, and monthly payment. This will make the loan officer's job much easier and your application simpler to process. Divulge all pertinent credit information, even if you think it might not look good. The lender will probably discover it anyway, and, if you haven't mentioned difficult accounts, the lender will wonder why.

- **Do** inquire in advance whether the lender has any specific requirements or taboos. Some lenders have strict requirements regarding a borrower's years on the job and period of residence in the community as well as the minimum down payment for specific purchases.

- **Do** be sure to tell the loan officer clearly and specifically just what the money is for. The more concise you are, the more the officer will be able to advise you if you appear to be going overboard on a certain debt.

- **Do** make sure that your requested time for loan repayment does not exceed the use period of whatever you're borrowing for. If you let the lender know you've considered this, it will demonstrate your prudence and could enhance your relationship with the lender.

- **Do** be prepared to discuss your budget in detail. The loan officer wants assurance that money will be available to pay off the loan, and if there is no room in your current budget for the repayment, your request may be declined—and perhaps wisely so. If you plan to trim other expenses to make room for this debt, or if you are anticipating a higher income in the future, discuss these factors with the loan officer.

- **Do** bring your spouse, if you have one. Granted, under the federal Equal Credit Opportunity Law it is no longer necessary for both spouses to sign credit agreements, but debt is still a family responsibility morally, if not legally—and both partners should have a full understanding of their involvements in each other's financial matters.

- **Do** seek the loan officer's specific advice on related financial matters. It's part of the job, and the officer may be able to discover and solve other money problems in ways you aren't aware of.

- **Don't** try to get a better interest rate by telling a loan officer that you can do better elsewhere. Chances are you'll be told to go ahead and do so. And if you can do better elsewhere, you might as well.

- **Don't** caution the loan officer not to check a certain credit reference. If there is a problem or a dispute with one of your creditors, clear it up in advance. If you raise suspicions, the loan officer will undoubtedly take steps to find out what it's all about.

- **Don't** be disturbed if the loan officer asks you to do your other banking business, such as your savings or checking account, with that institution. This is part of the job. Often, loan applicants are upset by such suggestions, and this can destroy an otherwise good relationship. A simple "I'll be happy to consider it" should suffice if you don't want to change at the moment.

- **Don't** fret if the loan officer starts "selling" life or health insurance for your loan. If, after you understand their program, you still don't want it, merely decline politely.

- **Don't** expect the loan officer to tell you whether your intentions regarding your borrowing are wise. If you aren't sure of the wisdom of your loan, maybe you shouldn't be asking for it.

- **Don't** be surprised, however, if the loan officer does question your wisdom. Loan officers are in the business of evaluating personal financial decisions, and their professional knowledge may help correct or amplify your thinking, or point out something you overlooked. Perhaps the officer can suggest alternatives, some of which may provide a better solution than the one you're seeking.

- **Don't** wait until the last minute to apply for a loan. Anticipate your needs far enough in advance to take care of all the details. If other matters hinge on whether you get the loan, keep the other parties informed of your progress. Careful and thoughtful planning in this regard can prevent serious problems.

- **Don't** demand an answer to your application within a certain time. You have a right to have your papers processed promptly, assuming that everything is in order. The lender will make every effort to do so. But delays, such as receiving an incomplete report from a credit bureau, can happen.

  Often, too, applications have to be considered by the loan committee. Loan officers aren't "passing the buck" when they refer applications to the loan committee. Requests might be for more than the loan officers have authority to approve, or they might just want to get other opinions on a puzzling point in the application. The committee can often be helpful simply by giving borrowers the benefit of all its best collective thinking.

  When you make your application, the officer should be able to give you a fairly good idea of how long it will take to process. Perhaps the officer can speed it up a bit for you if circumstances warrant. But a dead line or an "or else" will probably cause antagonism.

Exercise 12.6

- **Don't** balk if the loan officer asks you for a cosigner or collateral to support a given loan request. The officer is trying to help you get your loan, but lending policies require security. You might not want to comply, but rather than argue about it (which won't help matters), ask for an explanation.

  There is often room for compromise. A request for collateral or a cosigner doesn't necessarily mean your credit isn't good. There just might not be enough of it—because of your age, job tenure, and so on. Remember that the loan officer doesn't have to ask you for the extra security—she can turn you down flat. It doesn't hurt to inquire if the request for collateral or a cosigner can be altered so that the cosigner is obliged for only a part of the loan or the loan is only partly collateralized.

CREDIT ABUSES

Pyramiding

As noted earlier, pyramiding occurs when a loan for a recurring purpose has not been paid off by the time the purpose recurs. Let's look at a specific example.

Otto buys a new car and finances $10,000 for three years at an interest rate of 6 percent add-on (11.08 percent APR). His interest cost for the three years will be $1,800, which, added to the amount financed, gives him a total obligation of $11,800. This will require monthly payments of $328 (rounded off).

Two of the three years go by, and Otto falls in love with a brand-new car. He must have it. His credit is good—he has paid his $328 per month on

time without fail, and he has no qualms about financing $12,000 over and above his trade-in for the new purchase. But if he looked carefully at the arithmetic, he might develop some serious qualms.

Here's how it looks. After paying $328 a month for twenty-four months, he has paid in a total of $7,872, leaving $3,928 still owing on the original loan. If he refinances now, he'll be entitled to a rebate of some of the interest from the original loan—$210. (See Table 12–2: after 24 months of a 36-month loan, you get a rebate of 11.7 percent of the original interest charge; 11.7 percent of $1,800 is $210.60.) So Otto's payoff on the first loan is $3,718.

That amount is added to the new financing: $3,718 plus the $12,000 needed for the new car totals $15,718. Interest (same rate, same term) of $2,829 brings the total IOU to $18,547, which will mean monthly payments of $515! To satisfy his yen for the new car, Otto must increase his monthly payment by $187, and he's obliging himself to paying more than $2,800 in additional interest. He's still paying for part of the original car five and six years after he first bought it.

If he had waited to buy a new car until he had paid off the first loan— that is, the full three years—then he could finance a new $12,000 loan for about $395 per month.

As Otto's case illustrates, pyramiding can be costly, whether it originates innocently or as a result of lack of financial discipline. Otto took undue advantage of his access to credit, and exceeded both needs and capacity to borrow.

The pyramiding trap is equally dangerous, if not more so, as it affects credit cards and charge accounts. For example, Esther runs up $50 in gasoline bills for her car during a month. She charges them on a credit card. At the end of the month, the bill comes in and, rather than pay the full $50, she decides to send in only the minimum payment, say, $10.

The same thing happens the next month: $50 worth of gas bills and a $10 payment. And so on throughout the year. Unless Esther comes to her senses, she could still be paying for her January gas in December and even well into the following year.

The simple way to avoid pyramiding is to remember that an installment loan or an open-end credit debt should be paid off before the need to borrow for the same purpose occurs again.

Ballooning

Which is more appealing, a twelve-month loan for $1,000 with monthly payments of $88.33, or the same loan with monthly payments of only $60? The temptation is to take the loan with the smaller monthly payments, but obviously there's a catch—with the smaller monthly payments, there will be one very large payment at the end of the loan, for the loan is to run for only twelve months. In this particular case, after making payments for eleven months at $60 each, the borrower will still owe roughly $400 in the twelfth month. This is what's known as a balloon payment, and it can be dangerous. If the borrower can't make the large payment, it may be necessary to refinance and incur additional interest costs. Although the Truth in Lending Law requires lenders to disclose the annual percentage rate and the total costs involved in making the loan, there may not be adequate disclosure regarding the size of the monthly payments. Any borrower should know whether there are balloon payments at the end of the loan. Unless there are compelling circumstances for a balloon payment program, prudence dictates sticking to the repayment plan with equal monthly payments.

Oversecuring

If you were borrowing $1,000 to pay for your summer vacation, it would not seem wise to have to put up your car, your house, your bank account, and all your other assets as security for that loan. Reputable lenders would certainly not require such collateral. But some lenders may seek more security than is reasonable for certain loans. This security may include a general assignment of your wages and your personal property. If a borrower pledges those assets to obtain a loan, the lender can take action to recover them should the loan become delinquent. The borrower should determine exactly what collateral is being given to the lender, and if more is being required than seems necessary, the borrower would do well to shop around at other lending institutions.

Loan Sharks

Despite all the consumer-protection laws and publicized warnings, there will be loan sharks as long as there are people willing to pay exorbitant fees for borrowed funds. Loan sharks operate outside the limits of the law. Their interest rates are far above what the state usury laws allow, and their collection techniques can be brutal. If anyone becomes involved with a loan shark, he or she can expect to bear extremely severe consequences. Consult a banker or an attorney to seek out better ways to alleviate your debt problems.

Loan Consolidation

Exercise 12.7

The appeal is almost irresistible: "Why suffer with all those big monthly payments when you can consolidate all your debts into one loan with a much smaller monthly payment?"

If you have accumulated too much debt, loan consolidation seems a logical and convenient way out of the crisis. It's a line of least resistance too often taken by borrowers not aware of the potential pitfalls. Poorly planned, a consolidation loan can cause more troubles than the original loans did. Sound planning may provide more suitable alternatives. Using the following example of a loan consolidation and consulting the interest finders and rebate formulas in this chapter you can plan any consolidation and judge its value.

Charlie and Charlotte have the following loans:

- A car loan, whose original total amount was $3,540, including interest of $540. The loan has run for twenty-four months and has twelve months to go. Monthly payments are $98.33.
- A home-improvement loan that originally totaled $2,480, of which interest was $480. The loan has already run for thirty months and has eighteen months to run. The monthly payments are $51.67.
- A personal loan, originally totaling $1,090, of which interest was $90. Twelve months of the loan have already expired, with six months still to run. Monthly payments are $60.55.

Table 12–6 illustrates Charlie and Charlotte's debts and how much they would need to pay them all off.

Charlie and Charlotte need roughly $2,330 to pay off their existing debts. At an interest rate of 11.08 APR (6 percent add-on), they can obtain a loan of that amount for three years, which would entail an added $419 in interest, giving them a total new debt of $2,749. Their thirty-six monthly payments would be $76.30 each, compared with the $210.55 they're now paying.

It seems like an easy way out of what has become for them a serious jam.

TABLE 12–6   Loan Consolidation: Charlie and Charlotte's Debts

Loan	Current Balance	Monthly Payment	Months to Run	Payoff Figure Now
Car	$1,180	$ 98.33	$12	$1,117
Home Improvement	930	51.67	18	860
Personal	363	60.55	6	352
Total		$210.55		$2,330

But is it wise? Is it worth it? If they wait just six more months, the personal loan will be all paid off, reducing their monthly payments to $150. In twelve months, the car loan will be paid off, reducing their payments to $51.67. And in eighteen months, the home-improvement loan will be paid, eliminating their monthly payments altogether.

The consolidation loan will have cost them an additional $419 in interest and will require payments of $76.36 for thirty-six more months. During the next three years, Charlie and Charlotte will, in all likelihood, have new reasons to borrow. Rather than consolidating their loans, they might be better off if they simply tighten their belts and continue with their current debt load. It will be lightened considerably in just six months.

Careful communication with a lending officer is necessary to arrive at a sensible consolidation plan. If proper loan planning is done in the beginning, the need for a consolidation loan will never occur.

CURES FOR OVERINDEBTEDNESS

Charlie and Charlotte could be candidates for a severe case of overindebtedness. This problem, if not promptly treated, can seriously damage their credit history and can impair their ability to obtain credit for many months or possibly years. Eventually, it might force them to obtain credit through sources that specialize in higher-risk situations and that charge higher interest rates accordingly.

The first symptom of overindebtedness is late payments. Not only do late payments entail late charges, which can be as much as 5 percent of the amount of the payment (the law varies from state to state), but they can also result in a bad credit rating.

Borrowers who *anticipate* that they might be running into a delinquency problem should act *before* the actual delinquency occurs. Borrowers in such straits should visit *in person,* not by phone or by mail, with the creditors in question and explain the overall circumstances. It might be possible to arrange a different payment date that would be more convenient, or remake

the loan on favorable terms, or get a temporary reduction in payments. It might even be possible to have late charges waived if your reason for delinquency is acceptable to the creditor.

It's up to the borrower to keep the lender informed of the circumstances. If the lender doesn't know what the borrower's problems are, he could rightfully assume that the borrower is being willfully delinquent.

If the borrower is in default, the lender can commence whatever legal remedies have been reserved in the loan agreement. If collateral has been pledged for the loan, the lender can take steps to recover the collateral and sell it to pay off the loan. If a cosigner is involved in the loan, the lender can look to the cosigner for payment. In some instances, the lender may be able to attach, or garnishee, the borrower's wages.

Debt-counseling Services

Exercise 12.8

In many communities, lending institutions cooperate to create a debt-counseling service to assist people in financial trouble. In many communities, this is known as the Consumer Credit Counseling Agency. See your banker for more details on such services available in your community. The agency usually contacts your creditors and gets them to hold off on their collection procedures while you make an effort to reorganize your financial matters. You'll have to show good faith by making some regular periodic payments. If the counselors have been successful, those payments will be smaller than what your normal payments would have been.

If a reputable debt-counseling service is not available to you or not capable of helping you, the next step might be to consult an attorney, who can arrange for an Assignment for the Benefit of Creditors. This is similar to the services offered by debt counselors in that it tries to convince creditors to accept a smaller monthly payment until the full debt is paid off.

Bankruptcy

Exercise 12.9

The ultimate way out of overindebtedness is bankruptcy. If you reach this point, you should seek the aid of an attorney. Bankruptcy is a last resort for solving debt problems; it can remain on your credit history for as long as ten years.

Many lenders attempt to rehabilitate a bankrupt family or individual, particularly if the reasons for bankruptcy were beyond their control. But an ex-bankrupt can still find it difficult to obtain the kind of credit needed for his or her lifestyle. Indeed, bankruptcy often reduces the quality of people's lives dramatically for an extended period of time.

Bankruptcy laws are federal laws, though state laws may apply in determining the property that can be exempted from bankruptcy proceedings.

Credit Repair Clinics Can Be Costly Mistakes

You're up to your neck in debt, and the walls seem to be caving in. How can you get out of this jam? You see an ad that promises to help you get rid of your debts and restore your credit to A-1 condition. All these advertisers want is an up-front fee of $300, or $500, or however much they can get from you. They tell you to send them the amount of your monthly payments, and they'll parcel it out to your creditors, putting you back on a good footing with them all. You go along with them and within a month, your creditors are hounding you again. Didn't the credit repair clinic pay your creditors the money you gave them? You call them. The operator tells you that that number is no longer in service. Is your money gone for good? Probably. This is how some of these outfits operate. Be on guard for other, more subtle ways they can separate you from your money. You're most susceptible when you're having credit panic attacks.

There are two basic bankruptcy proceedings for individuals: Chapter 13, otherwise known as the wage-earner plan, and Chapter 7, often referred to as straight bankruptcy.

Chapter 13

Under Chapter 13, the debtor, under the supervision of a referee and the federal bankruptcy court, works out a plan for the repayment of outstanding debts. In effect, this wage-earner plan keeps creditors from getting at your wages and your property while giving you time to work out a timely payment of outstanding debts. (A similar plan for businesses is known as Chapter 11, in which owners of businesses attempt to reorganize their affairs to satisfy their debts while their creditors are kept at bay.)

A Chapter 13 proceeding generally carries less stigma than a Chapter 7 proceeding.

Chapter 7

In a Chapter 7 proceeding, your debts are discharged, or eliminated altogether. Under a Chapter 7 declaration, certain of the debtor's property can be exempted from creditors' claims. A debtor can choose whether to take the exemption allowed under federal law or exemptions that may be allowed under state laws. The Chapter 7 bankruptcy can be filed only once every six years. (A debtor can file a new Chapter 13 proceeding once he has completed payments based on a prior Chapter 13 proceeding.)

Sometimes personal catastrophe requires an individual to undergo bankruptcy proceedings. Sometimes, however, it is nothing more than the undisciplined use of credit that leaves an individual with little choice but to declare bankruptcy. The public at large has little sympathy for individuals who spend their way into bankruptcy. Know before you proceed that the specter of bankruptcy will haunt you for years to come.

DISCIPLINE

Making wise use of your ability to borrow can enhance your life. Imprudence can result in financial and emotional disaster. The lure of easy money—through charge accounts, credit cards, and other "cash-in-a-flash" enticements—can become addictive. Younger people, less experienced in the complexities of handling a budget, can easily be trapped in the credit bind. It's at the earliest stages of using credit that a firm sense of discipline must be self-imposed. Only you can determine the debt you're comfortably able to carry, considering your other financial needs and desires. But there is one unshakable rule that will apply to your use of credit: For every dollar you borrow (or charge) you will be adding ten to thirty cents a year to the cost of your credit purchase. It can be difficult enough to make ends meet without adding such a heavy burden.

PERSONAL ACTION WORKSHEET

Comparing Loan Costs

It *can* pay to shop around for the best interest rate available on loans—such as car loans, home-improvement loans, and any other personal or business borrowing needs. Loan sources include not only banks and savings associations but also credit unions, dealers, and some insurance companies. Employers, relatives, and friends might also be sources. Answering the questions in this checklist will aid you in comparing the pertinent terms of most common personal loans.

	Lender A	Lender B	Lender C
❑ Down payment required	_____	_____	_____
❑ Collateral required	_____	_____	_____
❑ Cosigner required (If so, when can cosigner be released from obligation?)	_____	_____	_____
❑ Annual percentage rate (APR)			
❑ Monthly payments	_____	_____	_____
❑ Total interest cost for life of loan	_____	_____	_____
❑ Late charges, if any	_____	_____	_____
❑ Will a better APR be offered if you maintain other accounts with the lender? (You may have to ask, but it can be worth it.)	_____	_____	_____
❑ Cost of credit life insurance	_____	_____	_____
❑ Cost of credit health insurance	_____	_____	_____
❑ If you pay off the loan early, are rebates of interest based on the Rule of 78s?	_____	_____	_____
❑ For credit cards and charge accounts, how is the APR calculated?	_____	_____	_____

Credit Traps Can Be Costly

Aside from ignoring the temptation to sign up for every credit card offering that comes in the mail, the cautious consumer should be on the alert for these abuses that can hit you with hidden costs.

The Myth of "E-Z" Credit   The ads look so appealing, particularly if you've had credit problems in the past: "EASY CREDIT . . . NO MONEY DOWN . . . PAST PROBLEMS FOR YOU ARE NO PROBLEMS FOR US . . . ." The reality is that if credit is that easy to get, it can be very hard to repay: high interest costs and harsh collection procedures if you don't repay on time. One couple fell for an E-Z credit offering from a furniture store. After two years of making their payments like clockwork to the store, they thought they'd have an excellent credit reference that they could use to borrow from the bank on better terms. But they found that the store did not, and would not, divulge their good payment record to the credit bureau. The store wanted to keep this couple—and others like them—as captive borrowers.

Bumping   Get in the habit of keeping the copies of your credit card charges. If a disreputable merchant sees you throw away the copy, he'll know that he has a good chance of "bumping" the amount of your charge—increasing the charge by changing the numbers on the charge slip that goes to the bank. It's easy to bump a 3 up to an 8, or a 1 up to a 4, thus turning a $30 charge into an $80 charge, or a $15 charge into a $45 charge. If you don't check your monthly statement closely—and lots of folks don't—you might never realize you've been stung.

Giving Your Credit Card Number to Strangers   Don't do it. Ever. For any reason. That goes double for people who call you on the phone to sell you something, or to tell you that you've won a free vacation, or anything of that sort. DON'T DO IT. EVER. FOR ANY REASON.

UPS & DOWNS   *The Economics of Everyday Life*

Why Your Consumer Interest Costs Go Up and Down

Aside from the general movements of interest rates (discussed in other chapters), the cost of consumer interest can fluctuate widely because of a number of factors.

Changes in calculations   This is particularly the case with credit cards, and it can be maddeningly complex. The lender may simply change the interest rate on the unpaid balance of your account, and it may be one change for balances owing from cash advances and another for balances owing from purchases. The lender may alter the formula for determining exactly what balance will be used for calculating that interest. The lender may change the grace period during which no interest is charged, or may alter the annual fee that you pay for the card, or any combination of these two methods.

Tax considerations   You might switch your consumer debt into home equity financing—as discussed in this chapter—and thereby gain tax deductibility for the interest you pay, which in turn can cut your overall cost. But, as noted earlier, it's essential that you calculate the costs involved in obtaining home equity financing versus the benefits you derive from the tax deductibility.

Charging habits   No one has ever seen a credit card jump out of a wallet or purse, lay itself down on the stamping machine, and ring up a sale. If you blame your credit cards for the debt burden you're carrying, you're aiming in the wrong direction. Look into the mirror and say to the person there: "Change your ways pronto!" As your charging habits change, so will your credit costs. Tighten up, and watch those costs come down. Lose your sense of spending discipline, and get ready for sleepless nights. Here are some simple techniques that can help you bring your charging habits in line with good sense:

- Pay off your balance in full each month. Easier said than done, you say? No. It *is* easy, if you don't charge more than you can afford to pay. Set an affordable charing limit for yourself each month. Write it bold and put it on the door of your fridge. Each time you charge, write it down on the tally and keep a running total. When you hit your monthly limit, put your credit card *into* the fridge and leave it there until next month.

- At all costs, avoid paying just the "minimum payment required this month." The monthly statement highlights that amount, and you're easily lured into paying just that much. Note well: If that's all you pay, and you never use the card again, it might take two to four years of those minimum payments to bring your balance to zero. And you'll be paying a huge amount of interest for taking the line of least resistance.

?

WHAT IF . . . ?

Test yourself: How would you deal with these real-life possibilities?

1. You go shopping on a Friday evening for a new stereo set. You fall in love with one that you absolutely must have right away. It'll set you back $600. (a) The store offers you a finance plan that will lock you into monthly payments at a high rate of interest, but you can go home with the new set. (b) You can use your credit card—it's the same high rate of interest, but there's more flexibility on the payments. And you can take the set home with you. However, charging $600 on your card will put you right up to the card's limit. Or, (c) for the best terms, you can go to your own bank or credit union. But you can't do that until Monday, which means you can't take the set home with you. And you're not sure that the bank will approve your loan request. What choice will you make? Why?

2. You've fallen two months behind in your debt payments, and it looks like you won't be able to make most of the payments for the third month. State the pros and cons of the following actions: (a) Confessing to your creditors that you're in deep trouble and don't see a way out. (B) Answering an ad from a company that promises to erase your credit problems. (c) Talking to a bank about a consolidation loan or any other solution it can offer. (d) Visiting a bankruptcy lawyer. (e) Asking someone close to you to lend you the money to bail you out.

NUMBER CRUNCHERS

Do the calculations to make decisions in these real-life possibilities.

1. Using the tables in this chapter, calculate the monthly payment on a $9,000 car purchase: (a) Down payment (or trade-in value of your old car): 15 percent; interest rate: 10.2 APR; term of loan: 36 months. (b) Down payment: 20 percent; interest rate: 12.91 APR; term of loan: 24 months.

2. Two years ago you borrowed $4,000 on a 36-month installment loan. The interest on the loan was $720, making your total IOU $4,720. Monthly payments, rounded off, have been $131. Now, after 24 months of making payments, you have come into a windfall of $2,000. You're thinking of using the money to pay off the balance due on your loan. Using the Rule of 78s, what will be your payoff figure? Instead of paying off the loan, what if you invested the $2,000 for one year at a 5 percent return? Which is the better option? By how many dollars?

3. What were the finance charges on your most recent credit card bill (or, if you don't have any, check someone else's)? What formula was used to calculate the charges? (rate of interest used and amount on which the interest was imposed)? Were the charges correct?

FOR BETTER OR FOR WORSE

Things beyond our control often impact our personal and financial well-being, for better or for worse. Some are more predictable than others. How could you be affected if the following real-life phenomena happened? Could you have seen it coming? What steps could you have taken to minimize damage or maximize advantage? The better able you are to anticipate and recognize these forces, the better equipped you are to deal with them.

1. Out of the blue you get what looks like a check in your mail, payable to you for $2,500. It's from a finance company, and the letter with it says that all you have to do is endorse the check and deposit in your bank account, and *abracadabra*, you've got a loan for $2,500.

2. You're told you'll need a co-signer for a car loan you've applied for. You ask a friend to do so, she agrees, and the bank agrees to accept her. At the last minute she changes her mind, and says she won't co-sign.

Exercise 12.10

3. You're deep in debt, and a so-called debt-counseling service offers to bail you out. You have to send them $300 to open the service with them. The next day their phone is disconnected and they've moved out of their offices.

13

Making Your Money Grow: An Overview

The expectations of life depend on diligence. The mechanic that would perfect his work must first sharpen his tools.

Confucius

If a man empties his purse into his head, no one can take it away from him. An investment in knowledge always pays the best interest.

Benjamin Franklin

The ads, the magazine covers, and the sale pitches shriek at you: "10 Hot Stocks That Will Double Before Sunset!" "5 Super Mutual Funds That Will Let You Retire at 40!" "Let *The Wall Street Psychic Newsletter* Turn Your Constant Worries into Instant and Permanent Wealth!"

What's a person to do?

A person with good common sense will ignore all of these get-rich-quick come-ons. They're after your money. That's how *they* get rich quick.

Putting your money to work wisely requires knowledge, and that takes study. It requires patience, and that takes saying no to the fast-buck lures. It requires vigilance, and that takes discipline. It requires knowing the difference between risk and safety, and that takes learning. And it requires working toward predetermined goals, as discussed in chapter 2, and that takes planning and prioritizing. If you think it's easy, you could be in trouble.

If you want a quick surge of excitement when you put your money to work, go to the casino or the track, knowing that you could walk away empty-handed. If you want to build long-term security and comfort for yourself and your family, give heed to this chapter, which will build a foundation by teaching you

- How to evaluate different types of investments
- How to measure the impact of taxes on your investments
- How to locate specific investment information and guidance

It will also give you the foundation for understanding more specific investment techniques discussed in subsequent chapters.

TODAY DOLLARS AND TOMORROW DOLLARS

An essential part of your financial program involves putting away dollars you don't need today so that they can be available to you in the future. There are many different ways you can go about accumulating Tomorrow Dollars. Some involve a high degree of risk; others involve relatively little risk. Some methods offer a comfortable measure of protection against inflation, whereas others provide little or no protection. Some ways may seem simple, others complicated; some require luck, others prudence.

The challenge is to find the right program, one that will enable you to accumulate the needed amount of Tomorrow Dollars safely, comfortably, and in such a manner as not to interfere with your ability to pursue today's needs and desires.

The importance of your future needs and desires will be a major factor in shaping which accumulation techniques you choose. In the opening of this book, we discussed the importance of establishing goals, and you were urged to set specific targets, subject to the inevitable changes that occur as we mature and as our needs and objectives change. Now let's examine the specific vehicles you can use to help reach your specific destinations.

Automatic Accumulation

In shaping our long-range accumulation program, we must remember that some Tomorrow Dollars are being created automatically as a result of other transactions we are making. For example, a homeowner makes monthly payments on a mortgage. A portion of those payments applies to interest on the debt, and a portion applies to debt reduction. Eventually, when the house is sold or refinanced, that portion of the payments that had been applied to the debt may be recaptured in cash. This recaptured money is commonly referred to as *equity*. It's a form of automatic accumulation.

Another form of automatic accumulation can occur with life insurance. Here a breadwinner is putting away Today Dollars to be used by the survivors after his or her death. In whole life insurance policies, the policy will also build values that allow the policy owner to either cash in the policy, or borrow against it, or convert the values into other forms of insurance. The insured is building these future values as an automatic part of paying the life insurance premium.

Deductions from our paycheck represent another form of accumulation of Tomorrow Dollars. Social Security taxes are automatically deducted from the paycheck of everyone covered by the system, and, in many cases, pension and profit-sharing plan contributions are also deducted. Thus, we are joining with our employers and our government to create a pool of Tomorrow Dollars.

Active Accumulation

Active accumulation of Tomorrow Dollars can take two broad forms. First, we can lend our dollars to another person or institution with the understanding that they will pay us a fixed amount of interest for the use of our money. This type of accumulating is referred to as fixed income investing; a savings account is perhaps the most familiar form of accumulating dollars within this category.

A savings account is, in effect, a loan to a financial institution, accompanied by an agreement stating that the institution will pay us "rent" for the use of our money—interest.

We may also make loans to governments and corporations. A U.S. savings bond (series EE bond) is an example of one of the many kinds of loans that we can make to the federal government. Loans made to cities and states are referred to as municipal bonds. Loans made to corporations are referred to as corporate bonds.

These forms of accumulating Tomorrow Dollars normally carry a high degree of assurance that we will get all our money back plus the agreed-on interest at the agreed-on time. We receive a contract from the debtor that promises to pay us what we are due, regardless of whether the debtor operates efficiently or profitably. If the debtor should fail, the interest and principal due us might be in jeopardy. Although there have been instances of corporations and municipalities defaulting on their debts, defaults by the federal government have never happened, nor have insured accounts in federally insured banks and savings institutions ever lost money as a result of the failure of the institution.

The other broad form of active accumulating of Tomorrow Dollars is to buy something we hope will generate income and also possibly increase in value while we own it. As owners, either in part or in whole, we have a stake in another entity—an equity.

We buy a portion of ownership in a company, hoping that the company will be profitable and that it will distribute a portion of its profits to its owners. We also hope that the value of our ownership interest will increase, allowing us to sell it at a profit in the future.

We may invest in real estate, hoping to operate that property so that it generates income and increases in value so we can reap a profit when we sell. Similarly, we may invest in our own business where, in addition to earnings and profits, we may also be able to pay ourselves a living. When we invest our money in owning a piece of another entity, there are many outside forces that can shape the destiny of our Tomorrow Dollars.

The distinctions between lending and buying are critical. When we lend, we have a binding legal contract that promises us the return of our money, plus interest. When we buy something, we are the owners, and we have to take our chances that we can get our money back at any time we wish. In addition, what our money will earn for us as owners is always questionable. Remember the distinctions when you make any plans regarding the accumulation of Tomorrow Dollars.

INVESTMENT CRITERIA

Safety: The Reward/Risk Rule

We'll now examine the main criteria you must evaluate when you embark on a program of accumulating Tomorrow Dollars. These criteria include safety (the reward/risk rule), liquidity, yield, pledge value, hedge value, and income tax implications.

STRATEGIES FOR SUCCESS

Investing Versus Speculating: All the Difference in the World

The words *investment* and *investing* are used commonly to describe putting your money to work. That's the generic sense. For purposes of this Strategy I want you to think of investing differently: as distinguished from *speculating*. Indeed, the single most valuable lesson you can learn from this course—or from a lifetime's worth of financial experience—is the critical difference between investing and speculating. It's a two-word vocabulary drill that can literally alter your life.

When you *invest*—in the sense we're using here—*you know with assurance* how many dollars you're going to have X or Y or Z years from now. You *know*. It's not a guessing game or a "hope so."

When you speculate, *you do not know, you cannot know, and no one can tell you* how many dollars you'll have X or Y or Z years from now. You might have a lot more than you'd expected. Or you might have a lot less. There is no way of knowing until that day arrives.

Investing means putting your money into *assured* plans: savings, money market instruments, and good quality bonds, and/or mutual funds that put their money into these types of securities. Speculating means the stock market, commodities, most real estate, and/or mutual funds that put their money into these types of securities.

To the extent that it is important to you to know how much money you'll have at any time, concentrate on investing. If it's not that important to you, speculate with your money. Know the difference before you write that check. Finding out later can be too late.

Exercise 13.1

The reward/risk rule is as simple and as powerful as the law of gravity: The bigger the reward you seek, the higher the risk you'll take. The more conservative individual may look at this a bit differently: The safer my money, the less return I'll have to be satisfied with. And yet a third, and perhaps more elemental viewpoint: In planning a program of savings and investments, much depends on whether you'd rather eat well or sleep well.

The various investment and speculation vehicles discussed in this chapter will be explained in greater detail in the following chapters.

Liquidity

Liquidity refers to how quickly and conveniently you can retrieve your money and at what cost.

For example, in a regular savings account, you can get all your money plus accrued interest immediately, simply by making the request in the proper fashion to the institution. With a certificate of deposit, or CD—in which you have placed your money with the institution for an agreed-on minimum amount of time—you might have to forfeit a portion of your interest and principal if you want to get your money out right away. But generally the certificate will pay you a higher rate of interest than the regular passbook savings account.

In other words, the passbook savings account is more liquid than the savings certificate, but at a price. The passbook account offers a lower rate of return in exchange for your ability to get your cash out more readily.

The need for liquidity varies from case to case. If you are confident that you won't need your money for an extended period of time, you can afford to give up liquidity in favor of higher return. On the other hand, if you think you'll need the money sooner, you should forgo the higher return for quicker access to your money. The amount of liquidity you need, or are willing to forgo, depends on the nature and timing of your own goals.

Yield

Generally, yield refers to how much money your savings or investments will earn for you. For example, if a savings account is paying 6 percent interest per year and you put $100 into the account, you will receive $6 interest for the year on that $100. Your yield may be expressed a "6 percent" or as "$6 per $100 per year." The term *yield* is often used interchangeably with *return* and *return on investment* (see chapter 11: "Truth in Savings Law").

In making any form of investment, you should determine not only what yield you can expect immediately but whether that yield will continue, for how long, and to what degree of fluctuation it might be subject.

If you put your money into long-term corporate, government, or munici-

pal bonds, you are assured of a constant yield for the amount of time you own the bonds, assuming that the debtor continues to pay the interest promised. The actual face value of the bond may fluctuate up and down during the time you own it, and you may sell the bond for more or less than what you originally paid for it. But the actual income you receive for the term of your ownership will remain constant. If you buy a government bond for $1,000 that promises to pay 8 percent a year, you will receive $80 for each year you own the bond, regardless of whether the market value of the bond increases or decreases.

Passbook savings accounts are subject to minor fluctuations in yield over the years.

If you buy a share of ownership in a company—stock—and that company distributes a portion of its profits to its owners—dividends—your yield, or return, is expressed as the amount of dividend dollars you receive. If you pay $100 for a stock and during the first year of your ownership the company pays you $5 in dividends, your yield can be expressed as 5 percent, or $5 per $100, per year, based on your purchase price.

Many companies have long histories of dividend payments, and many also increase their dividends from time to time. Even more companies have erratic dividend payment histories, and some companies pay none at all. If a company runs into hard times, dividend payments may suddenly halt. On the other hand, if a company suddenly has a surge in business, it might start to pay dividends unexpectedly. The stock market, then, offers a broad range of yield possibilities.

In choosing among various investments you will want to compare their yields relative to the amount you are investing. Bear in mind the likelihood of a yield continuing at a particular level. For example: $1,000 invested in a long-term government bond may pay you interest of $80 per year, and there is the highest degree of certainty that that yield will continue without interruption. At the same time, $1,000 invested in a given stock may pay you $90 in dividends. That would appear to be a better yield on your $1,000, but there's no way of knowing whether that dividend will continue, or be reduced, or be eliminated, or be increased. Then you must also consider the possibilities of gain or loss.

"Total Return"

It's important to keep a clear distinction between yield and "total return." For example, you buy stock for $100 and, during the first year of ownership, it pays a dividend of $5. But, at the end of the year, you sell the stock of $120. You have realized a gain of $20 on your investment, plus a dividend of $5, for a total overall increase in your fund of $25. Would this be considered a yield of 25 percent? Technically, no. It is indeed an overall gain of 25 percent, but it comes from two different sources: the dividend yield of 5 percent and the increase in value of 20 percent. Similarly, if you sold the

stock at year-end for $80, you still would have had a dividend yield of 5 percent, but you would have suffered a loss of $20, or 20 percent of your original investment.

Some forms of investment, such as mutual funds, announce their past performance in terms of "total return," which takes into account both the dividends and the gain/loss factor. This can represent an accurate picture of performance if, in fact, an investor bought and sold on the precise dates represented. But few fit that mold. Marketing strategies dictate that total return be trumpeted loudly for periods in which it would have been high; the number is muted, if not ignored, for periods when the total return would have been low, or negative.

In building toward a specific future goal, a relatively predictable yield can be far more useful than the relatively unknown total return. Prudent investors should structure their programs accordingly.

Pledge Value

From time to time, you have an unexpected need for money: to take advantage of a once-in-a-lifetime bargain, to pay pressing bills, to help out someone in need, to pay for expensive repairs. You may not have the cash on hand, and it thus becomes necessary for you to borrow the needed money. The quickest, and sometimes the cheapest, way to borrow money is to pledge your investments as collateral for such a loan. The pledge value of any investment is a measurement of what percent of the value of the investment you can borrow, how quickly you can get the money, and how much it will cost you.

Savings accounts—both passbook and certificate—have the highest level of pledge value among the common types of investments. Most depositors can usually borrow virtually all the money in their savings account at favorable rates, without any delay. This can be an excellent device for obtaining short-term funds in a hurry and may be preferable to actually invading the savings account or cashing in the certificate.

Because stocks are prone to fluctuation in value, they have a somewhat lower pledge value than savings accounts. The amount you can borrow from your banker against any given stockholdings will depend on the quality of the stock itself. You can also borrow from your broker on a margin account. In either case, of course, you have to surrender the certificate as collateral for the loan.

Good-quality real estate has a high pledge value but, because of the nature of the documentation required in borrowing against real estate, the process can be costly and time-consuming. This, in effect, detracts from real estate's otherwise good pledge value.

Hedge Value

Investors must be concerned about the ability of their investments to withstand the effects of inflation. The common expression is "hedging against inflation." This aspect of investing, then, may be called the hedge value of an investment.

This investment criterion is often discussed in terms of "the future value of money." In short: The spending power of your money erodes over the years as inflation nibbles away at it. Investment advisers might admonish you that because of this, you must invest larger amounts now than you might have thought necessary so that your *future* spending power can keep pace with your *current* spending power. Balance such precautions with the likelihood of your earning power increasing as well (thereby enabling you to create a bigger pool of future investment dollars), and that your future spending (such as in retirement) might be much more modest than it is now, thus not requiring as proportionately large a nest egg. The tightrope you have to walk is between maintaining a comfortable lifestyle now and providing adequately for your future. Too much investment for the future can crimp the present, and vice versa.

Many investors have theorized that the stock market should be a good hedge against inflation. The theory is that as prices rise, so should the profits of companies and, thus, so should the value of the stock of those companies. However, the paths of stock prices and inflation are not always parallel. Even if the stock market is a good hedge against inflation, that would be of no help to the individual investor who chooses stocks or mutual funds that do not follow the general trend of the stock market.

Savings accounts have long been accused of offering no protection against inflation because the principal amount invested doesn't grow except for periodic additions of interest to the account. There is actually some protection against inflation because interest rates paid on savings plans tend to rise in line with rising costs. By the same token, interest rates paid on savings plans may also decrease in the face of decreasing costs.

Real estate has long been considered a good hedge against inflation, but this depends on the nature of the property, the management of the property, and the trend in the community in which the property is located.

In short, no form of investment or speculation is a guaranteed hedge against inflation. But there is one very important caution to note regarding the psychology of inflation. Over the years, as inflationary trends have come and gone, thousands of small investors have let wily salespeople convince them that inflation was destroying their life savings. The salesperson offered a "better deal." But that better deal has frequently been a very risky, if not downright fraudulent, transaction in which the frightened investors have lost all or a portion of their life savings. Thus, the *fear* of inflation

caused them to lose much more money than they might have lost through inflation itself.

Tax Implications

Tax regulations are constantly changing. Investors must factor in the tax implications of the various types of investments available to them. Tax implications divide investments into three broad categories:

- **Taxable investments**   Taxable investments are investments in which, except as noted later, all your income will be taxed in the year in which it is earned.
- **Tax-deferred or tax-sheltered investments**   With tax-deferred or tax-sheltered investments, the payment of taxes on income earned can be delayed until some future time.
- **Tax-exempt investments**   All, or a substantial portion of, your income from tax-exempt investments is tax-free.

Taxable Investments

Interest earned on savings plans and corporate bonds is taxable at both the federal and state levels. Interest earned on U.S. Treasury securities is taxable on your federal return but not on your state return. Dividends received on stocks are taxable on both your federal and state returns. If you receive income from mutual funds in any of the above categories, that income is generally taxed in the same way as if you held the specific investments directly.

Congress often changes its mind about how investment income is taxed. The tax rate on capital gains (derived when you sell stocks or real estate at a profit) has gone up and down like a yo-yo over recent decades. You must determine the current (and likely future) tax status of any investment before you take the plunge.

Tax-Deferred and Tax-Sheltered Investments

U.S. savings bonds are probably the best-known form of tax-deferred investment. Another example of a tax-deferred investment is the Individual Retirement Account, or IRA, which allows workers to invest money each year for their retirement. The amount they invest in the plan each year may be a form of tax deduction, thus reducing their immediate tax obligation. Furthermore, the earnings on these funds are not taxed each year. However, when the money is withdrawn, the taxes on the withdrawn money must then be paid. The presumption is that when money is withdrawn on retirement, the individual investor will be in a much lower tax bracket than at the time the contributions were made. Thus, there can be a considerable tax

break. Moreover, all the money has been allowed to work without being subject to taxation, which can make a substantial difference in an overall nest egg over the long term. The Keogh plan, for self-employed individuals, is another example of a tax-deferred investment. IRA and Keogh plans, and their close cousin, the 401(k) plan, plus changes made to those plans by the 1997 Taxpayer Relief Act, will be discussed in more detail in chapter 18.

The most common form of tax-sheltered investment is real estate. Because buildings physically depreciate, tax laws allow real estate investors to deduct a *depreciation* factor from their income. This depreciation factor does not represent an actual loss in value on the building, but rather, a paper loss. Indeed, the buildings may be increasing in value even while the owners are deducting depreciation on their tax returns. The depreciation factor offsets income that the building may be earning, thus reducing the amount of taxable income the owner has to pay. When the building is sold, however, the tax payable by investors on any profit will be affected by the amount of depreciation they have deducted in earlier years. (Depreciation does not apply to one's residence.) This aspect of investing is discussed in more detail in chapter 16.

Tax-Exempt Investments

When local governments, such as cities and states, borrow money, investors do not have to pay federal income taxes on the interest they receive. These investments are known as municipal bonds, and the income the investor receives is referred to as tax-exempt.

There are some exceptions, however:

- As a result of some of the intricacies in the 1986 Tax Reform Act, some municipal bonds are now taxable. Investors should check on this before buying municipal bonds.
- If you invest in municipal bonds and sell the bonds at a profit, the profit itself is taxable, even though the interest you earned while you owned the bonds may not be.
- If you invest in municipal bonds issued by a government unit outside your state of residence, the interest earned will be subject to any state income taxes you have to pay. For example, if a California investor buys a municipal bond issued by the city of San Diego, the interest earned is exempt from both federal and California income taxes. But if that same investor buys a municipal bond issued by the city of Houston, the interest earned is exempt only from federal taxes. The investor has to pay California income taxes on that interest.
- The laws are always subject to change by Congress or by the Supreme Court.

Tax-exempt investments will be discussed in greater detail in chapter 14.

INVESTIGATION

"Investigate before you invest" is one of the essential maxims to remember when putting your money to work. An equally important statement all too frequently overlooked is "investigate before you un-invest." Do your homework before you place your funds in any kind of situation. But don't stop doing the homework after you've made the investment.

Knowing when to get out of a situation is as important as knowing when to get in. "But," many say, "I don't want to become a slave to my investments. I don't want to have to worry about it. I just want to be able to put it away and have it grow and deliver what I'm seeking without the worry or the constant checking."

All well and good—but such a course may result in a diminished nest egg compared to what it might have been. The decision is up to each individual; you don't have to become a fanatic. But investing can be likened to planting a grove of trees. For it to bear the most and the best possible fruit involves care, nurturing, and an awareness of all the steps you can take to improve your crop. In short, your ability to prosper will depend largely on your willingness to work.

Sources of Information

More literature is published every year on investments than on any other subject, with the possible exceptions of dieting and sex. It's impossible to keep up with the outpouring: hundreds of books, thousands of magazine and newspaper articles, tens of thousands of reports and analyses published by stock brokerage firms and investment advisory firms. Where is one to begin?

Books

Exercise 13.2

Books run the gamut from the "doom and gloom" variety to the "how to get rich overnight" type. The former tend to preach that the end of the world is rapidly approaching and that unorthodox investments are called for to cope with the calamity. The latter lure investors toward highly speculative types of portfolios. Between these two extremes are a number of worthwhile books published each year on basic money management and investment programs. Sample them at your local library or bookstore, and read one or two a year to give yourself some diversity of views and tactics. In general, the problem with books—including this one—is that a considerable amount of time elapses between the writing and the publication, and many of the ideas presented can be outdated before the book is in the stores.

Magazines

Exercise 13.3

Time, Newsweek, and *U.S. News & World Report,* all weeklies, contain good current information and informative columns on finance and investing. *Forbes* is published every other week and is directed to an audience of businesspeople and investors. It is most highly recommended as a source of specific information and general guidelines on a wide variety of investment techniques. *Financial World,* a weekly, contains in-depth articles on specific stock opportunities and much statistical information. *Fortune* (published every two weeks) and *Business Week* are both examples of excellent financial journalism, directed more to the businessperson than to the relatively inexperienced investor. If any of these periodicals prompt you to be interested in a specific investment situation, check with your stockbroker for more detailed information. Also worthwhile are *Money* and *Kiplinger's Personal Finance.*

Newspapers

Exercise 13.4

The Wall Street Journal, read daily and thoroughly, is the best of all possible tools to keep you alert, not only to specific investments but to the state of the economy as well. *Investor's Business Daily* is a relative newcomer, but is also an excellent source of financial data. *Barron's* is a weekly financial newspaper. The business pages of your local newspaper are a necessary supplement to these newspapers.

Seminars and Courses

Local community colleges, universities, and financial firms often conduct programs geared to the investor's needs. Such programs will normally be announced in the school catalogs and in newspaper articles or advertisements. Many seminars conducted by private firms and financial institutions are designed primarily to attract clientele or to sell specific investments to attendees.

Television

Exercise 13.5

Your television set can be the source of some very good, and some very bad, investment advice. The national Public Broadcasting System (PBS), Cable News Network (CNN) and CNBC offer a variety of worthwhile programs on money and investments. Some television channels offer stock market reports intermingled with advisories in which the host touts a particular form of investment disguised as an objective news presentation. Be certain that you understand the difference between an objective presentation and one that is designed to sell something.

STRATEGIES FOR SUCCESS

Investment Objectives Should Suit Your Age

A 25-year-old has more flexibility in investing than a 55- or 65-year-old. If younger people make mistakes, they have more time and more psychological resilience to recover than older people do. Thus, younger people can more easily afford to take risks than older people can. As investors get older, risk-taking should gradually decrease. For these reasons, you should define your investment objectives clearly in line with your age. All investment plans should start out with building a solid, risk-free foundation. During a person's twenties and thirties, a moderate amount of prudent risk can be taken to generate income and capital growth. In the forties and fifties, the objectives should tend more toward safeguarding income and preserving capital. By the time investors are in their sixties, preservation of capital, along with reliable income, should be the primary, if not exclusive, objective. That's a conservative approach. If you choose to differ, know the risks of doing so.

The third variety of investment information available on television can be more dangerous than beneficial. This is the "seminar" in which the host attempts to sell an expensive home study course, suggesting that you can learn all the secrets of successful investing in real estate, the stock market, commodities, you name it. This does not mean to say that you won't get some information for your many hundreds of dollars if you buy these courses. But if these were truly the secrets of success, then everybody who bought them would know them and they would no longer be secrets. It must be, therefore, that these pitchmen are making more money selling you the secrets than they could make by putting the secrets to use. Let the buyer beware.

The Internet

The Internet is the newest source of information on investing, but it is fraught with danger for the novice. Newspapers, books, and broadcast material have editors who screen material before it is distributed. Analysts for stock brokerage firms have their opinions scrutinized by someone in authority. But on the Internet, anyone can put out anything they want. There are no editors, no gatekeepers, no quality control systems to separate the worthwhile from the worthless. Even material from presumably credible sources can be altered by hackers, unbeknownst to you.

The overwhelming preponderance of investment material on the Internet

is designed to sell you something. If someone is trying to sell you something, they can't be objective. A great deal of investment material on the Internet smacks of potential fraud, misleading sales pitches and possibly illegal touting of various securities.

In due time the Internet might have more credibility as a source of investment information. But as of now, it would be prudent to use the Internet only as a source for verifiable statistical information. There can be decent material out there on the Web. But the dangers of being waylaid by sharp operators while on your way to the good stuff offset the benefit of cyber-researching.

Information Overload

There's an obvious hazard in the world of investment information: there's just too darn much of it. There are thousands of stocks, thousands of bonds, thousands of mutual funds, and all of them fluctuate second by second. Who can keep track of more than a few dozen at a time? There aren't enough hours in a day—or in a week or a month, if you've got a life to live—to do more than barely scratch the surface of all that's out there. And every brokerage firm and mutual fund company is clamoring to get their hands on your money, proclaiming that they have the best answers. They can't all be right, can they?

So what's a poor novice to do? Here are some tips from experience: Stay away from the "let me tell you about how I made a bundle" chit-chat. Turn a blind eye and a deaf ear to the sales pitches. Don't envy the boasters. Don't go riding on a band-wagon unless you know where it's going (and you never really can.) Don't send your money out to work for you unless you know where to go looking for it in case it doesn't come back when you expected it to. Know your goals and priorities (when, how much, what's most/least important) and stick to them.

Finally, learn well the basic concepts in this course. The knowledge you gain will then lead you to the resource materials most appropriate for you.

SOURCES OF INVESTABLE FUNDS

Exercise 13.6

All sources of investable funds must be accurately evaluated. You may have little control over the inactive investment activities you're now engaged in, such as building the equity in your home, your life insurance policies, your pension or profit-sharing programs, or your Social Security. But these funds can become actively investable at some future time, and you must determine how much will be available and when. Reasonable estimates, periodically revised, will be needed to help assure that you reach your goals. Check periodi-

cally with your employer and with your local Social Security Office to determine what you can reasonably expect from those respective sources.

Discretionary Income

The major source of active investment funds is your discretionary income—the difference between what you take home in earnings and what you currently spend for your needs. "But," say the majority, "I'm just living hand to mouth as it is. By the time everything is deducted from my paycheck and I keep up with rising costs and make some modest improvements in my lifestyle, there's barely a penny left to put away."

Or, as is also said: "There's too much month left at the end of the money." True enough, and in many cases there's little you can do about it. However, a close examination of your current living style, in comparison with your *desired future* living style, is in order. Investable funds can be created by cutting down on current expenditures or by increasing current income. Simply translated, this means additional work and/or belt-tightening. Whether you wish to do either depends on how closely your *existing* investment program meets your targeted goals. The alternative, of course, is to cut down on future goals. But that, perhaps, is the most dangerous course of all.

Consider that the most critical goal for most people is to have enough income to live in the desired style when work ceases and retirement begins. If, when that time rolls around, you don't have what you had hoped to have, *you don't get to do it over.* You're locked in. Again, it's up to each individual: How much, if anything, are you willing to sacrifice in your current lifestyle in order to assure a future lifestyle? When you can answer that question, you'll be able to determine what adjustments you want to make in your current discretionary income.

Inheritances and Gifts

Other sources of investable funds can include inheritances and gifts. This is a touchy area that must be handled delicately but nevertheless must be faced. A great many people will receive inheritances from parents and other family members; the amount may be token or considerable. It may occur soon, or it may not occur for many, many years. The amount ultimately received can have an important bearing on your overall plans. If you know or can determine what can be reasonably expected in the way of an inheritance, you may want to adjust your existing investment program or your current lifestyle accordingly.

WHO CAN HELP YOU?

Financial Planners

Help is available from a number of sources in structuring a long-range investment program. Financial planners, as noted in chapter 11, can provide assistance over a wide range of financial matters. Some may even have the expertise (and licensing) to help you in other areas, such as accounting and insurance. Learn in advance their reputation and credentials.

Mutual Fund "Families"

Many investors are finding good assistance in handling their money through "families" of mutual funds. Many of the larger mutual fund companies operate a number of different specific funds, each geared toward different investment objectives. They range from the rockbound conservative to the wildly speculative and all points in between. Mutual fund companies provide ample literature explaining what each of the various specific funds can provide. The attractive feature of the fund "families" is that it's easy for investors to switch all or part of their money from one fund to another quickly and at little cost.

You, the Investor

Nobody cares more about your financial well-being than you do, and you have to be able to sort out all the jargon, analyze all the proposals, evaluate all the opportunities, and make the final decisions. *You have to take responsibility for your own future,* and that requires obtaining the necessary information to know when the advisers are right or wrong.

In the chapters that follow, we'll examine the most common types of investments available: what they are, how they work, and their respective features regarding yield, liquidity, safety, hedge value, pledge value, taxation, and investigation.

There are no specific rights or wrongs in structuring an investment portfolio. Each must be tailored to the needs, both current and future, of particular individuals or families. And each must be structured with the thought that those needs can and probably will change over the years. Thus, although the discussions are presented from a relatively conservative viewpoint, there's ample room for disagreement.

PERSONAL ACTION WORKSHEET

Planning Your Future Income

Where will the money come from to allow you to meet your future goals? This exercise will help make you more aware of the potential sources of your Tomorrow Dollars. For the sake of this exercise assume that you plan to retire in 10 years (or that there is some other defined goal that you hope to accomplish at that time). Evaluate the following possible sources of money, and see how close you come to meeting your estimated needs. If there is a shortfall, how will you make up the difference?

	Lump Sum Available	Monthly Income, If Lump Sum Is Invested at 5 and 7 Percent Annual Interest
❏ Pension proceeds	————	————
❏ Profit-sharing plan	————	————
❏ Social Security	————	————
❏ Equity in your home (after setting aside enough to provide satisfactory living quarters)	————	————
❏ Cash or loan value in your life insurance policies	————	————
❏ Existing investment programs (savings, bonds, etc.)	————	————
❏ Existing speculative programs (stocks, metals, commodities, etc.)	————	————
❏ Inheritances realistically expected	————	————
❏ Discretionary income (excess of current income over current expenses that could be put to work to create a source of Tomorrow Dollars)	————	————
❏ Miscellaneous: collections, works of art, and so on, that could be sold	————	————

CONSUMER ALERT ——————————————————————————————————————

All the Economists in the World . . .

There's an old saying, "If you laid all of the economists in the world end-to-end, they still wouldn't reach a conclusion." Economists grouse about that. They think that their science (called *the dismal science* by some) is much maligned.

Exercise 13.7

In order to make wise decisions about putting money to work, the help of an economist would seem worthwhile. You can't afford your own private economist, but megabillion-dollar financial institutions can. Twice each year *The Wall Street Journal* does a survey of close to sixty of the nation's top economists to seek their opinions on important trends.

At the time of one such recent survey the interest rate on U.S. Treasury three-month bills was 4.15 percent; on thirty-year Treasury bonds it was 7.61 percent, the rate of inflation as measured by the Consumer Price Index (CPI) was 2.7 percent, and you could buy 98.5 Japanese yen for one U.S. dollar. The economists were asked to predict where each of these numbers would be one year in the future. Their estimates: three-month Treasury bills ranged from a low of 2.85 percent to 7 percent. The Treasury bond: low: 5.75 percent, high, 8.4 percent—22 of the economists predicted 7 percent or less; 14 predicted 8 percent or higher. For the CPI: low 2.0, high, 4.3. For Japanese yen per dollar the estimates ranged from 90 to 127.

If economists can't reach a conclusion, don't feel too bad if you are sometimes confused about all this.

UPS & DOWNS *The Economics of Everyday Life*

What Makes Interest Rates Go Up and Down?

The availability of money is to our economy—national and personal—as food is to our bodies. As the price of money (interest rates) fluctuates, so does the economy. Low interest rates encourage borrowing: we buy more cars, houses, computers, and so on, and that means more jobs for more people. That's a good thing. But as people have more money to spend, they tend to pay more for many items, and then inflation sets in. That's a bad thing.

High interest rates discourage borrowing, which can mean a slowdown in economic activity. That's a bad thing. But investors who earn interest much prefer higher levels, which gives them more money to spend, which can mean more jobs for more people. That's a good thing.

Yes, it's complex and confusing. No matter which way interest rates move, some people can benefit and some people can suffer. What, then, does cause these movements?

The Federal Reserve System   The Federal Reserve, our nation's central bank, dictates moves in short-term interest rates. It does so by manipulating the *discount rate*. That's the interest rate that regular banks are charged when they borrow from the Fed, which they often do. Those higher or lower borrowing costs are passed along to the bank's customers, and the rate change thus works its way through the nation's economy.

The banking industry   Banks can act on their own to move rates up or down. When they want to stimulate borrowing, they lower their rates. If borrowing demand is high, and banks sense they can make more profit they raise their rates. The *prime rate*, which is the rate banks charge their most creditworthy borrowers, is the key. As the prime rate moves up or down, all other rates soon follow, such as car loan rates, home loan rates, and the rates the banks pay on deposits.

Speculators   Those who bet in the futures markets (see chapter 16) on which way interest rates are headed can cause rates to fluctuate. Speculators play in the government bond market, hoping for profits if bond prices go up. Heavy buying or selling of bonds by speculators can influence the prices of those bonds. As the bond prices move up or down, the interest rates that can be earned on those bonds move down or up. (See the discussion in chapter 14 on how bond prices and interest rates move in opposite directions.)

International events   Global occurrences can influence interest rates. To keep U.S.-made goods competitively priced in other nations, the international value of the dollar must be at certain levels. Tweaking interest rates up and down can influence the value of the dollar accordingly.

No one can predict with certainty which way rates will move, or how far, or for how long. But it is an absolute certainty that interest rates will change, and knowledge is your best defense against uncertainty.

? WHAT IF . . . ?

Test yourself: How would you deal with these real-life possibilities?

1. Your employer offers a retirement/investment plan. The money that will be credited to your account can be put to work in a number of ways: (a) a fixed income plan that will pay interest at a guaranteed level for one year, after which the rate will be adjusted in keeping with current trends; (b) a mutual fund that invests in the stock market, seeking long-term growth (see chapter 15); or (c) stock in the company you work for. All earnings on the plan will be tax-deferred until the money is withdrawn. You have no other long-term investment program at the moment. The money that goes into this account can be divided up in any combination, and the combination can be changed once each year. Based on your own current circumstances, how would you allocate the money for the coming year? Why?

2. You have $1,000 to invest, and you have no specific plans as to how you'll use the money, now or later. But for safety's sake, you want to keep it in a savings plan. You can earn two percentage points more in a three-year plan than you can in a six-month plan. Considering your own needs for liquidity, which plan would you choose? Why?

3. You've received a windfall of $10,000. Based on your own needs and desires, how would you put that money to work, considering the ultimate purpose for which you'd spend the money—hedge value, pledge value, yield, and safety?

NUMBER CRUNCHERS

Do the calculations to make decisions in these real-life possibilities.

1. Your employer offers a retirement/investment plan. You can put up to 5 percent of your annual salary into the plan each year. For every dollar of your own that you put into the plan, the employer contributes 50 cents. The amount you put in on your own each year will not be subject to income taxes in that year. And all earnings from the plan will be tax-deferred. If you went for the maximum contribution, how much could you put in this year? What would be your employer's matching amount? How would that impact on your income taxes for the year? Do the same calculations based on putting in one-half the maximum.

Exercise 13.8

2. You have $10,000 to invest, and you're debating between taxable and tax-exempt securities. Right now you can earn, say, 7 percent on a one-year taxable savings certificate, or 5 percent on a 10-year tax exempt bond. (Assume they are equally safe.) What will be your actual earnings on each, after tax considerations, assuming the income from the savings certificate will be taxed at 15 percent? At 28 percent? What concerns, if any, do you have about the difference in term between the two?

3. What's the cheapest rate you can get on a subscription to *The Wall Street Journal*? *Money*? *Forbes*? Do they offer student discounts? How does the subscription rate compare with the newsstand price?

⚖️ *FOR BETTER OR FOR WORSE* ─────────────────────────────

Things beyond our control often impact our personal and financial well-being, for better or for worse. Some are more predictable than others. How would you be affected if the following real-life phenomena happened? Could you have seen it coming? What steps could you have taken to minimize damage or maximize advantage? The better able you are to anticipate and recognize these forces, the better equipped you are to deal with them.

1. A salesman convinces you to invest in gold, telling you that it's a perfect hedge against inflation: As prices go up, so does the value of gold. A year later, prices have gone up by 5 percent, but gold has gone down by 10 percent.

2. You subscribe to a magazine that promises to deliver money-making tips on the stock market. A few months later you are inundated by phone calls from stock brokers tempting you to buy all kinds of stocks you've never heard of.

3. You apply every penny you can against your mortgage. Objective: cut interest cost and build equity quicker. You're confident that if you ever need cash in a hurry, you can borrow it using the house as collateral. One day you need cash in a hurry. The bank tells you it will take four to six weeks and $3,400 in costs to process a second mortgage loan for you.

Making Your Money Grow: The Money Market

Certainly there are many things in life that money won't buy. But it's very funny. . . . Have you ever tried to buy them without *money?*

Ogden Nash

Not too many years ago, the average person had few safe choices for investing money. The most common methods were passbook savings accounts and government savings bonds. Today, however, the choices are many and varied. New techniques are constantly emerging. But you need *not* be perplexed by all the different offerings. You *can* distinguish clearly what each of them offers you. And you *can* choose which is best for you. That's the purpose of this chapter:

- To describe how different savings techniques work
- To help you evaluate the opportunities available to you in certificates, bonds, mutual funds, and other situations
- To acquaint you with certain tax-favored plans
- And, overall, to help you shape your own investment program, using these various devices

Chapter 13 described the two basic ways of making your money grow. One way is to lend it to others, in return for which you receive a fee known as interest. The other way is to buy something (such as stock or real estate) and hope that you can sell it later for more than you paid for it. During the time you own such an entity, you may also receive a share of the entity's profits if, in fact, it is profitable.

There is a critical distinction between the two basic techniques. With the former—lending—you have an agreement with the borrower (financial institution, corporation, government) that states that you are entitled to have all your invested money returned, either on demand or at some specified future time. The agreement also states the amount of interest you are to receive. That amount of interest either is fixed at a certain level or is subject to variation. If the interest rate is variable, there may or may not be limits as to how high or how low the rate may go. In summary, you are *assured* of getting all your money back (assuming that the borrower remains healthy) and of getting at least some interest.

When you *buy* something, you do *not* have assurances of getting all your money back or getting any return on your money during the period of ownership. If you are fortunate, your investment may increase many times in value. If you are unfortunate, your investment could wither and even disappear altogether. But there is no way of knowing for certain when you make the investment what the future will hold. This is the essence of *risk.*

A conservative investment philosophy dictates that you safeguard your future by using assured techniques. Once you have embarked on a well-disciplined plan to create such a foundation for your future security, you might then want to consider using the risk techniques. If you are fortunate, the risk techniques could later enhance your future; if you are unfortunate in your choice of risk investments, your future could suffer.

Let's now explore the various ways of lending your money so as to assure your future security. In the broad sense, the arena in which you find these opportunities is known as the money market.

WHAT IS THE MONEY MARKET?

The money market is not a place but a concept. In a general sense, when IOUs and money change hands, money market transactions have thus taken place. When you open a savings account or buy a savings bond, you have entered into a money market transaction: you have loaned your money to a bank or to the government and you have received their promise to repay you. (In a more technical sense, the money market refers to certain transactions involving short-term government and corporate bonds. See the later discussion on money market mutual funds for more detail.)

A wide selection of money market investments is available. Some plans are open-ended: there is no fixed time period, money can be deposited and taken out at will, and the rate of interest earned can fluctuate from day to day. Other plans have fixed interest rates and fixed maturities, which can range from as short as a few days to as long as thirty years and all the points in between. With these types of plans the investor might be limited in making additional deposits or withdrawals, and withdrawals prior to maturity could mean a penalty for the investor.

How Is Interest Figured?

As noted, interest is the fee a borrower pays in order to have the use of someone else's money. Interest is normally expressed as a percentage of the total amount borrowed, calculated on a yearly basis. In other words, if you make an investment of $1,000 at a 6 percent annual interest rate, you receive $60 in one year. If you were to remain with that investment for only half a year, you would receive $30 in interest. If you stayed with it for two years, you would receive $120. That's the simple part.

Aside from the rate of interest, two other aspects involved in calculating your true return can have a distinct effect on your overall investment: the compounding of interest and the crediting of interest to your account.

Compounding of Interest

The compounding of interest means that the interest you earn stays in your account and begins to earn interest itself. Following the preceding example, if you earned $60 in interest during the course of one year (on a $1,000 investment at a 6 percent annual rate) and you left that $60 in the account, you would then have $1,060 to work for you during the second year. During the second year, your $1,060 would earn $63.60. And so it would go for future years. You have an ever-increasing amount of money working for you because the interest is left in the account to compound.

In many types of accounts, interest is compounded more frequently than once a year. Quarterly compounding is very common, as is daily compounding. WIth quarterly compounding, the interest you earn during each quarter of the year is added to your original principal balance. Table 14–1 illustrates this method. During the first quarter of the year, with your $1,000 investment at 6 percent, you earn $15 (that is, one-fourth of $60). At the start of the second quarter, you have $1,015 working for you, which will earn $15.23. That $15.23 earned during the second quarter is added to the $1,015 of principal; thus, you have $1,030.23 at work for you during the third quarter. As Table 14–1 illustrates, more frequent compounding means a higher return to the investor.

Passbook savings accounts are the most common type of investment in which compounding takes place. But some investments do not offer com-

TABLE 14–1   **Comparisons of Compounding Methods—$1,000 at 6 Percent Annual Rate**

	Quarter	Quarterly Compounding	Annual Compounding
First year	1st	$1,000.00 earns $15.00	
	2nd	1,015.00 earns 15.23	
	3rd	1,030.23 earns 15.45	
	4th	1,045.68 earns 15.69	$1,000 earns $60
	Balance at work, end of first year	$1,061.37	$1,060
Second year	1st	$1,061.37 earns $15.92	
	2nd	1,077.29 earns 16.15	
	3rd	1,093.44 earns 16.40	
	4th	1,109.84 earns 16.64	$1,060 earns $63.60
	Balance at work, end of second year	$1,126.48	$1,123.60

pounding: corporate bonds, for example, will pay you interest twice a year by check directly from the company. If you don't reinvest that interest on your own, it will not be working for you.

Crediting of Interest to Your Account

Savings plans can differ with respect to the manner in which interest is actually credited to your account. Many institutions will credit you with interest from the day a deposit is made until the day the deposit is withdrawn. For example, if you made a deposit in such an institution on January 15 and withdrew the total balance on December 15, you would earn interest for the full eleven months the money was in the account. However, some institutions use different methods of crediting the interest to your account. For example, an institution might require that the money remain in your account for a full caldendar quarter in order to earn interest. Thus, if you made a deposit on January 15, you would not earn any interest until the beginning of the second quarter, April 1. Also, if you withdrew the money on December 15, you would forfeit interest for the entire fourth quarter of the year since you withdrew it before the end of the full calendar quarter. In such a case, even though your money was with the institution for a full eleven months, you would be earning interest for only six months—the second quarter and the third quarter.

Another method of crediting interest uses the low balance in any quarter as the amount on which interest is computed. For example, you start the first quarter of the year with $1,000 in your account. On January 15 you

TABLE 14–2 **How Does Your Money Grow? No. 1**

If You Invest $1,000 a Year at This Interest Rate	You'll Have This Much After This Number of Years			
	5 Years	10 Years	15 Years	20 Years
2 percent	$5,289	$11,044	$17,398	$24,414
4 percent	5,464	12,065	20,097	29,868
6 percent	5,980	13,970	24,570	38,990
8 percent	6,340	15,650	29,320	49,420
10 percent	6,710	17,530	34,960	63,000

Note: This table does not take into account income taxes on interest earned. Investments are presumed to be made at the start of each year.

Exercise 14.1

withdraw $600 to pay bills; on February 15 you put the money back into your account. During that first quarter of the year, you will be credited for interest on only $400, even though you had $1,000 in the account for the majority of the time. In a day-of-deposit to day-of-withdrawal account, the interest would be calculated on the balance in your account each given day of the quarter, and you wouldn't forfeit as much as you do in the low-balance type of calculation.

Determining the true yield on a money market investment requires more than just examining the rate of interest being paid. You must examine the frequency of compounding and crediting of interest to the account as well. The Truth in Savings Law (see chapter 11) restricts how banks may calculate and advertise such plans.

Tables 14–2 and 14–3 illustrate how your money will grow over various period of time at different rates of interest, compounded annually.

TABLE 14–3 **How Does Your Money Grow? No. 2**

If You Make a One-time Investment of $1,000 at This Interest Rate	You'll Have This Much After This Number of Years			
	5 Years	10 Years	15 Years	20 Years
2 percent	$1,104	$1,219	$1,346	$1,486
4 percent	1,217	1,482	1,803	2,193
6 percent	1,340	1,790	2,400	3,210
8 percent	1,470	2,160	3,170	4,660
10 percent	1,610	2,590	4,180	6,720

Example: To understand the power of compound interest, look at where the 20-year column crosses the 6 percent line: $1,000 will have grown to $3,210. In other words, your investment will have increased by $2,210 over 20 years, or an *average per year* of $110.50. That means, in effect, that you have had an *average* annual growth of 11.05 percent.

Note: This table does not take into account income taxes on interest earned.

TYPES OF MONEY MARKET INVESTMENTS

The variety of investment opportunities is staggering. As borrowers compete ever more aggressively for investors' dollars, new techniques and new twists on old techniques are emerging at a rapid pace. The selection of opportunities available to you today might be still broader and more varied than the selection that follows.

Passbook Savings Accounts

A passbook savings account is an open-end agreement between the customer and the financial institution. The customer can put in or take out as much money as desired at any given time. While the money is in the account, it will earn interest in accordance with the agreement between the institution and the investor. The institution may reserve the right to alter the interest rate being paid, on giving proper notice to its investors. The form of notice should be set forth in the rules of the passbook account. Some passbook accounts require a minimum balance—say, $100. If the balance falls below the minimum, the account stops earning interest *and* may be charged service fees.

Some institutions offer special types of passbook accounts that are a cross between a passbook and a time certificate. These accounts will have a fixed maturity, but the customer may be able to add or withdraw certain sums from the account periodically.

Financial institutions also offer money market accounts. These accounts generally require a fairly high minimum deposit—perhaps as much as a few thousand dollars—whereas passbook accounts have little or no minimum requirements. The money market accounts pay a higher rate of interest than passbook accounts, but they may limit the number of withdrawals you can make in a period without penalty. Federally insured institutions protect both types of accounts—as well as checking accounts—up to $100,000. Check with your institution for complete up-to-date details on how your account is insured.

- **Yield**   Passbook savings accounts have traditionally given the lowest yield of all money market instruments. To determine the true yield, it's important for the investor to be aware of the annual interest rate payable as well as the frequency of compounding and crediting of interest to the account.

- **Liquidity**   Passbook savings accounts and money market accounts are as liquid an investment as one can make short of storing the money in a cookie jar. You can withdraw your entire principal at any time. If interest is not credited daily to your account, you could sacrifice some interest if you withdrew funds prior to the end of the month or quarter.

- **Safety** Savings accounts insured by the federal government have the highest degree of safety.
- **Hedge value** The interest rate payable on passbook accounts and on money market accounts can rise as inflation boosts costs generally. That doesn't necessarily mean that they will rise. If an inflationary trend sets in, investors must pay careful attention to the possible earnings on their savings plans and move to those that offer the best return, all things considered.
- **Pledge value** Savings accounts have a very high degree of pledge value. You can normally borrow up to 90 percent or more of the total amount in your account at favorable rates by presenting your passbook to a loan officer and signing simple documents.
- **Tax implications** Interest earned on passbook accounts and money market accounts is fully taxable. Check the latest tax regulations.

Certificates of Deposit

Exercise 14.2

Certificates of deposit (or CDs) are fixed contracts for a specific amount of money to run for a specific length of time and to pay a fixed interest rate. A CD may be contracted for as short a period as seven days or for as long as ten years, perhaps even longer. The interest rate payable on any CD will depend on general interest rate conditions at the time the investment is made.

Once a fixed-interest CD investment is made, the interest rate agreed to will be in effect throughout the life of the CD, even though the general rates may change subsequently. For example, on Monday, you obtain a thirty-month CD from a local bank with an interest rate set at 6 percent per annum. You are guaranteed that 6 percent rate for the life of the CD. On Tuesday, the same bank announces that it will pay 5 percent on all thirty-month CDs. That change will not affect you. It will only affect people who obtain CDs from Tuesday onward until any other change in the interest rate is made. By the same token, if on Tuesday the bank should announce an increase in the CD rate, you will not be able to take advantage of the higher rate since you committed to a firm contract on Monday at the 6 percent rate.

Some institutions offer CDs with a variable rate of interest. This may entitle you to a higher rate of interest if rates go up during the life of your plan. If rates turn down, however, and the plan does not have a downward limit, it could mean that you will earn a lesser rate of interest than you started with.

As a general rule, the longer the life of the CD, the higher the rate of interest you'll earn. In other words, if a one-year CD was paying, say, 5 percent, a two-year CD might pay upwards of 6 percent, a three-year CD close to 7 percent, and so on. Bear in mind, however, that while the longer CDs

earn a higher rate of interest, you are tying up your money for that much longer and thus losing some flexibility in your overall financial structure.

Penalties

Since CDs are firm contracts for a set amount of time, you will be penalized if you withdraw money from your CD before the maturity date. Government regulations have changed from time to time with respect to the total penalty that can be charged.

Check with your own bank to determine the penalties currently in effect on early withdrawals.

Renewal

Commonly, when a CD reaches its maturity, the institution will renew it for another term at the interest rate then prevailing. For example, you have a six-month CD that was obtained at a 6 percent interest rate. Today the CD is maturing, and the current interest rate on such CDs is 5 percent. Unless you instruct the institution to the contrary, it will automatically renew your CD at the 5 percent rate. Some institutions, however, will not automatically renew CDs: they may instead place the funds in a passbook savings account, lacking your instructions to the contrary. In such a case, you would likely earn a much lower rate of interest than a renewed CD would have paid.

Here is a common problem that arises when investors fail to pay attention to the renewal provisions of their CDs. Your six-month CD will mature on May 15. At the end of a seven-day grace period—May 22—it will automatically renew for another six months. You have every intention of getting to the bank on or before May 22 to take the money out so that you can put it to some other use. But you get distracted and don't get around to doing this until May 23. By that time the CD has already renewed, and if you now want to take out the money, you will have to pay a penalty.

Choices

Exercise 14.3

Institutions offer a huge assortment of CDs. With a myriad of choices at hand, making the right decision becomes a complex matter.

The Certificate of Deposit Shopping List (Figure 14–1), used in conjunction with the Personal Action Worksheet at the end of this chapter, will help you locate the best deal for your money. As you shop, be certain you know the extent of insurance on your deposit. If it's anything less than the full Federal Deposit Insurance, you must determine exactly what protection, if any, you actually have.

Certificate of Deposit Shopping List

	Institution		
	A	B	C

☐ *Fixed or variable interest rate?*
There's no way of knowing which will be better for you over the long run. The fixed rate is a sure thing. The variable rate is a guessing game: it could do better for you than the fixed; it could do worse.

☐ *Frequency of compounding?*
Given two plans with identical *rates*, the one that compounds more frequently will give you a higher return.

☐ *Minimum deposit required?*
How much must you deposit in order to earn the desired rate of interest? Minimum will differ from place to place.

☐ *Size breaks?*
At many institutions, larger deposits will earn higher rates of interest. If you can come up with a larger sum of money, you might be able to get a higher return.

☐ *Add-on privileges?*
Will you be able to put additional sums of money into your certificate account? This might involve a blending of interest rates: combining the original rate with the new rate in effect at the time you make your additional deposit. Add-on privileges offer an extra measure of convenience, particularly for such accounts as IRAs.

☐ *Borrowing privileges?*
If you need the money before the certificate matures, you'll have to face a penalty for early withdrawal. It may be much cheaper for you to borrow against your certificate, rather than cashing it in. Compare borrowing costs with penalty costs.

☐ *Intangibles*
Difficult to judge, perhaps, but could be important. What other services might the bank offer you? Are you pleased with their manner, their way of doing business? Are they conveniently located and open at convenient hours? Are their personnel friendly, helpful?

FIGURE 14–1   Certificate of deposit shopping list

Investment Criteria

- **Yield**   You are certain to receive the yield you bargained for by virtue of your contract with the financial institution. Regardless of the interest rate offered, the Truth in Savings Law (see chapter 11) requires all banks to quote the annual percentage yield (APY). That's the best criterion for accurately comparing various offerings.

- **Liquidity**   The liquidity of CDs is somewhat impaired as a result of the penalty provisions for early withdrawal. It is possible, however, to

borrow against a CD rather than cashing it in if you have an immediate need for some of the money.

- **Safety**   As with passbook savings accounts, CDs at federally insured institutions are protected by the federal insurance programs up to $100,000 per account. Thus, CDs are considered to be at the highest level with respect to safety.
- **Hedge value**   None, with fixed rate CDs. Variable rate CDs can have attractive hedge value.
- **Pledge value**   As with passbook savings accounts, CDs can be used as collateral for borrowing. Many institutions will guarantee a fixed interest rate, should you wish to borrow against a CD. Such an interest rate might be 1 percent over what you're receiving on your CD. In other words, if you are receiving 6 percent interest and you wish to borrow against your CD, you would have to pay 7 percent a year for borrowing any of your funds. As noted, this could be a cheaper way of getting to your funds than cashing in the CD prematurely and suffering a heavy penalty.
- **Tax implications**   Interest income on CDs is fully taxable.

INVESTING IN THE BOND MARKET

What Are Bonds?

Just as you often borrow money—to buy a car, to fix up your home, to pay your bills, or to refinance existing older debts—business and governments likewise borrow money for similar needs. They may borrow for a long term, upward of forty years, or for a short term, a few years or even a few months. When they borrow for a long term, the IOU they issue is referred to as a bond. Short-term IOUs may be referred to as bills, notes, and, in the case of corporate short-term IOUs, commercial paper.

There are three major categories of bonds—corporate, federal government, and local government. And there are three ways an investor can get involved in bonds: directly, semidirectly, and indirectly.

You can buy bonds *directly* through a stockbroker and, in some cases, through the investment department of major banks. You can invest in bonds *semidirectly* through mutual funds that specialize in various bonds. The mutual funds pool the investments of many individuals and spread them out over a wide assortment of different issues. This is something the ordinary investor can't do individually.

Although you may not be aware of it, you *already* have *indirect* investments in the bond market. If you have a bank account, an insurance policy, or pension fund, it's very likely that some of your money is already invested in the bond market—and that in itself is a good reason for you to become familiar with the workings of bonds.

Corporate Bonds

Under the overall heading of corporate bonds are included the IOUs issued by railroads, public utilities (such as local electric and gas companies), and industrial firms (manufacturers, service companies such as airlines, retailing firms). Broadly speaking, there are two classifications of corporate bonds: straight and convertible. The straight bond is a simple long-term IOU of the issuing company in which the company agrees to pay the investor a fixed interest rate. The convertible bond carries with it the right of the holder to convert the bond into shares of that same company's common stock. Convertible bonds, or convertible debentures as they're sometimes called, are discussed in more detail later in this chapter.

Corporate bonds can usually be bought in denominations of $1,000, and the commission payable to a stockbroker is generally less than when buying stock. If you hold a bond until maturity, and it's redeemed directly by the issuer, there'll be no commission to pay.

How to Read Bond Quotations

Many major local newspapers carry bond quotations, as does *The Wall Street Journal* and *Investor's Business Daily. Barron's,* a financial newspaper issued weekly, also contains a full listing of traded corporate bonds.

In bond price quotations, the number quoted is the selling price of the bond expressed as a percentage of its face value. Thus, if a $1,000 bond is currently selling for $950, the quotation would appear as 95, which is 95 percent of its face value. Similarly, a bond selling for $985 would be quoted as 98½, which is 98.5 percent of its face value.

Exercise 14.4

An example: in 1978 the XYZ Company borrowed some money from public investors and issued bonds as IOUs. These bonds contained a promise to pay 6 percent interest per year for thirty years to everyone who bought the bonds, issued in $1,000 denominations. The bonds would thus mature in the year 2008, at which time the XYZ Company would pay all holders of the bonds $1,000 for each $1,000 bond. Over the years, investors traded the bonds back and forth among each other. Owing to market conditions, that bond today sells for $950. The quote in the newspaper would look like this, on a day when there was no fluctuation in its price:

Bond	Hi	Low	Last
XYZ 6s 08	95	95	95

This bond would be referred to as the XYZ Company 6s of 08. The 6s refers to the original interest rate that the company agreed to pay, or 6 percent; the 08 refers to the year of maturity, 2008; the three 95 figures refer to the high, low, and closing prices for the day. (Remember, we said that the price didn't fluctuate on this particular day.)

How Bond Yields Are Figured

Bonds have three different yields, and the difference must be clearly understood. The following description does not take into account brokerage commissions or income taxes payable on bond interest received.

COUPON YIELD   Referring back to the earlier example of the XYZ 6s of 08, we find that the 6 percent interest the company originally agreed to pay is known as the coupon yield. In other words, the company guarantees that it will pay $60 each year (usually in semiannual installments) to each holder of each $1,000 bond. The bond may fluctuate in price up and down, but the holder will continue to get $60 a year for each $1,000 bond held, regardless of the price of the bond.

CURRENT YIELD   We noted that the bond was quoted at $950 on a given day. If an investor purchased a $1,000 bond for $950 and received $60 per year in interest from the company, the actual current yield is 6.3 percent ($60 on $950, which is your actual investment). If, on the other hand, you had paid $1,050 for the bond, your *current yield* would be roughly 5.7 percent ($60 is 5.7 of $1,050, which is your actual investment).

YIELD TO MATURITY   The third concept of yield is called the yield to maturity, and it's a bit more difficult to understand. Say that you buy a $1,000 face value bond for $950, and you buy it exactly one year before its maturity date. It's paying 6 percent per year. When the bond matures one year after your purchase date, you get back the full face amount, or $1,000. That's $50 more than you paid for it, and that $50 is considered a capital gain. Also, you're going to get the $60 in interest during the year you hold the bond. Altogether you will receive $110 in one year for your $950 investment, or a *yield to maturity* of just over 11.6 percent ($110 is 11.6% of $950).

Exercise 14.5

If, however, you purchased the bond five years before maturity date, that $50 gain would be prorated over the remaining five years. Thus, you would be getting the $60 each year in interest plus an eventual extra $50 on redemption, which is equal to an extra $10 on average each year, assuming that you hold the bond until maturity. Your annual *average yield to maturity* would then be approximately $70 each year, or about 7.4 percent of your initial $950 investment.

How Bonds Fluctuate in Value: A Most Important Concept

If you buy a good-quality bond with a face value of $1,000, you will get your $1,000 back from the borrower—the government, the corporation— on the maturity date of the bond. But between the day you buy the bond and the maturity date, the market value of that bond *can and will* fluctuate. In other words, on any given day, the bond might be worth more or less than you paid for it. If you find yourself having to sell a bond before it reaches maturity, you might have to sell it at a loss. Or you could gain a profit. When people talk about the safety of bonds, they are referring to the *full*

value redemption at maturity date. In the intervening years, however, the safety factor is subject to two main influences: interest rate movements and the financial condition of the issuing entity.

As a general rule, the market value of a bond moves in the *opposite* direction of interest rate trends. (The market value of a bond is what you can get for it if you were to sell it at any given time.)

Why is this so? Let's look at another example of the XYZ Company. When XYZ borrowed the money in 1992, conditions were such that it had to pay an interest rate on those bonds of 6 percent or $60 per $1,000 per year. Let's say that you bought one such bond at that time. Nine years have elapsed, it's 2001, and conditions are such that if XYZ were to borrow now, the company would have to pay 8 percent interest per $1,000, or $80 per $1,000 per year. When you originally bought the XYZ bond, you intended to hold onto it for the full thirty years, earning interest as the years went along. But in 2001, you face a financial emergency and find it necessary to sell the bond. You come to me and say, "Bob, I have here a perfectly good $1,000 bond from the XYZ Company, paying 6 percent interest per year. I'd like to sell it to your for $1,000."

I reply, "Why should I pay you $1,000 for that bond when I can buy a brand-new bond from a company of comparable quality that will pay me 8 percent or $80 per year? If I can earn 8 percent on my money today, why should I settle for 6 percent, which is all I would earn if I bought your bond from you for $1,000."

I can see that you're dismayed. You had invested in this bond in good faith, being told that it was perfectly safe, and now you can't sell it for what you paid for it. I'm a good sport, though, so I make you an offer. "I'll buy your $1,000 bond from you for $750. I'll earn $60 a year, which means that on my investment of $750 I'll be earning 8 percent, which is what I can get in the open market by buying a brand-new bond today (8 percent of $750 equals $60)."

Now you are shocked. In order to sell your bond, you have to take a $250 beating. But now you understand the workings of bond values. It's not a cheap lesson, but it's a worthwhile one. If interest rates had moved *down* during the same period of time, you would have been able to sell your bond at a *profit.*

The reality is this: We never know in which direction interest rates will be moving, or how far, or for how long. Thus, there is always an element of risk in investing in bonds, whether you do so directly or indirectly.

The other factor that can affect the market value of a bond is the financial status of the issuing entity. If a company falls on bad times or if a local government runs into financial difficulties, the marketplace may evaluate the bonds of those entities as being worth less because of the problems. For example, the question might arise: Will the company be able to earn enough money to pay the interest it owes on its bonds? If the marketplace deems that payments of interest or principal are in jeopardy, then the value of those bonds will fall. It's a repeat of the reward/risk rule: investing in this

company is now riskier because of its impaired financial condition. Thus, the market value of its bond falls.

As bonds get to within a few years of maturity date, they are less susceptible to these various fluctuations.

Sinking Fund

When corporations borrow money, they often do something most individuals and families would be well advised to do. They set up what is called a sinking fund, out of which they will eventually pay off the bond. They put aside so much money each year toward the eventual redemption of that bond and actually use that money to pay off the investors, either at maturity or in advance of maturity if market conditions so dictate.

Call Privileges

A company has issued a bond paying 7 percent interest per year. After the passage of a number of years, the interest rates prevalent throughout the economy have dropped to 6 percent. The company sees an opportunity to refinance the existing IOUs and drop its interest rate from 7 percent to 6 percent, thus cutting its interest expense considerably. In order to take advantage of such opportunities, many bonds have written into them a call privilege, which means that the company has the right to call in the existing bonds and pay off the holders at an agreed-on price. Investors are then faced with the problem of having to reinvest the money at a lower interest rate than they had been earning.

A would-be investor in corporate bonds should determine what call privileges or protection exists. Because a bond is usually a relatively long-term investment, it would be to the investor's advantage to know that the company can't call the bond for at least five to ten years.

Corporate Bond Ratings

Thousands of corporate bonds are available to investors at any given time. How is one to determine the relative quality of so many bonds? Corporate bonds are rated according to quality by two companies: Standard & Poor's and Moody's. Both rating systems are very similar, taking into account the basic financial strength of the corporation and its ability to pay the interest on its debts. The highest rated bonds offer the lowest rate of interest and the lowest risk to investors. Following is a brief summary of the Standard & Poor's ratings:

Exercise 14.6

AAA	Highest grade obligations
AA	High-grade obligations
A	Upper-medium-grade obligations
BBB	Medium-grade obligations

BB	Lower-medium-grade obligations
B	Speculative obligations
CCC-CC	Outright speculations, with the lower rating denoting the more speculative
C	No interest is being paid
DDD-D	All such bonds are in default, with the rating indicating the relative salvage value

Generally, institutional investors—banks, insurance companies, pension funds and the like—will focus their bond investments in the AAA and AA ranges, and to a lesser degree in the A range. These are known as the *investment quality* ratings. Rarely, if ever, will they dip below A ratings. You might be guided according in your own choice of bonds, or of mutual funds that invest in bonds.

The ratings companies keep a watch on the financial status of all bond issuers, and if there is a change in the financial strength of a company, its rating will be changed accordingly. For more specific details on the ratings, refer to the monthly rating books published by the two companies, available at stock brokerage firms and at most local libraries.

Junk Bonds

Bonds had historically been considered a safe haven for investors' money. But hundreds, perhaps thousands of companies found the door to the bond market closed to them. They weren't able to raise funds by issuing IOUs because they weren't creditworthy enough.

In the mid-1980s, a concept emerged that enabled many of these companies to borrow money in the bond market, albeit at higher rates of interest than their more creditworthy peers. The higher rate of interest was due to the higher level of risk involved in lending money to less "proven" corporations.

For the most part these bonds were rated BBB or lower. Because of the low ratings they became known as *junk bonds,* even though many of the corporations issuing them were of reasonably good quality. The higher yields appealed to speculators, and a gambling-like atmosphere surrounded junk bonds for many years. Abuses were rampant, and many investors and brokerage firms were badly hurt. By the mid-1990s the tumult had subsided. But high-risk bonds still exist and can still pose problems for unsophisticated investors.

Investment Criteria

- **Yield**   With higher-rated companies you have a very high assurance of receiving the yield (interest payment) you have bargained for. With lower-rated companies the yield may be in doubt.

- **Liquidity**   The major bond exchanges (New York and American) maintain a market for buyers and sellers of bonds. But depending on the issue and the number of bonds being bought or sold, it could take from a few minutes to a few days to effect a transaction.

- **Safety**   The higher the rating of the bond and the closer it is to maturity, the safer your investment. As noted, bond prices fluctuate in value, moving in the opposite direction from interest rates.

- **Hedge value**   If a bond is bought at or near face value, there is little protection against inflation. As prices move upward—interest rates being among those prices—bonds are likely to decrease in value, as noted earlier. Thus, the hedge value might be considered negative. If, on the other hand, a bond is bought below face value and maturity is approaching, the bond price will move upward as maturity nears, thus offering a measure of protection against rising prices.

- **Pledge value**   The amount that one can borrow against bonds and the interest rate paid on such a loan depend on the quality of the bond as determined by the rating services. Generally, well-rated bonds provide ample opportunity for pledging at reasonably favorable interest rates. However, if a bond has decreased in value, the amount that can be borrowed against it will decrease proportionately.

- **Tax implications**   Interest earned on corporate bonds is taxable.

U.S. Government Bonds

The federal government is the biggest borrower of all. Federal IOUs range from the common savings bond for as low as $25 to the multimillion-dollar obligations issued frequently by the U.S. Treasury. The federal government even borrows from itself. For example, the Social Security Administration invests its own funds in U.S. Treasury IOUs. Federal government obligations are further broken down into three subcategories: U.S. Treasury borrowings, federal agency borrowings, and savings bonds.

U.S. Treasury Borrowings

The U.S. Treasury borrows frequently on a short-term, medium-term, and long-term basis. Short-term obligations are called Treasury bills, and their maturities range from three months to one year. Medium-term obligations are called Treasury notes, with maturities ranging from 2 to 10 years. Long-term issues are called Treasury bonds, with maturities ranging form 10 to 30 years. Any of these Treasury debts can be obtained at a nominal commission through a stockbroker or the investment department of a bank, or directly from the Federal Reserve Bank at no commission. The prices and yields (before commissions) of all U.S. Treasury obligations are listed daily in *The Wall Street Journal* in a column titled "Treasury Bonds, Notes, & Bills."

Exercise 14.7

Federal Agency Borrowings

A number of federal government agencies are frequent borrowers of large sums of money. The money they borrow is generally pumped back into the economy to subsidize such things as mortgage loans for home buyers and farm loans for the agricultural industry. Investments are available in a wide range of maturities. Short-term obligations, usually for a year or less, are commonly called *notes*. Medium-term obligations, which may run from one to five years, are commonly referred to as *debentures*. Long-term obligations that run from five to twenty-five years are referred to as *bonds*. Some of the more popularly traded federal agency obligations are issued by the Federal National Mortgage Association, the Federal Home Loan Bank, Banks for Cooperatives, Federal Land Banks, and Federal Intermediate Credit Banks.

The prices and current yields (before commissions) of Treasury obligations and agency obligations are quoted daily in *The Wall Street Journal* under the heading "Government Agency, and Similar Issues."

Savings Bonds

Savings bonds are the most commonly known and popular forms of bonds issued by the federal government. They are currently called EE and HH bonds. (Savings bonds sold prior to 1980 are E and H bonds.) EE bonds sold since November 1, 1982, offer a fluctuating rate of interest. This is designed to keep the bonds more competitive with savings programs offered by financial institutions.

Here's how the fluctuating-rate EE bonds work: If you buy and hold the bonds for at least five years, you will earn the fluctuating rate of interest or the guaranteed minimum, whichever is greater. The fluctuating rate is adjusted every six months, and it's based on 85 percent of the average yield on five-year U.S. Treasury securities. If that yield is 7 percent, the EE bonds will pay 5.95 percent for that six-month period.

Exercise 14.8

One particular advantage of E and EE bonds is that the interest you earn is not taxable on your federal income tax return until you cash the bonds in. The interest is also tax-exempt on state and local income tax returns. E and EE bonds continue to pay interest for forty years from their date of issue. Once they have reached forty years of age, they stop paying interest and should be cashed in. Taxes will be due on the accrued interest at that time.

HH bonds may be acquired in exchange for E or EE bonds. In thus exchanging your E and EE bonds, you can further defer taxation on the accumulated interest until the HH bonds are cashed. But interest earned on the HH bonds is taxable in the year you receive it. Check with the nearest Savings Bonds Division of the U.S. Treasury for full details on the current rates and terms of savings bonds.

Zero Coupon Bonds

As noted earlier, bonds typically pay interest twice a year, and the face amount is then paid to bondholders on the maturity date of the bonds. With zero coupon bonds, no interest is paid until maturity. The bonds are bought at one price and then redeemed in the future for a much higher price. In short, these bonds have a coupon yield of zero. The most commonly traded zero coupon bonds are derived from U.S. Treasury issues and have been nicknamed by various brokerage firms as CATS (Certificates of Accrual on Treasury Securities) and TIGRs (Treasury Investment Growth Receipts). Corporations also issue zero coupon bonds.

Zeros, as they are also called, have proved popular because they offer a guaranteed return for a set period of time, and there is no need to bother with reinvestment of your interest earnings. However, the IRS has ruled that although you are not receiving interest *in hand* each year, you must pay taxes on the accrued interest each year. Thus, zeros might not be advisable for personal accounts that are subject to taxation. But they could be appropriate for IRA and Keogh plans or for any other tax-deferred portfolio. Get full details from your stockbroker before you invest.

Inflation-Proof Bonds

Since 1997 the U.S. Treasury has been offering five- and ten-year bonds that have built-in "inflation-proofing." Here's how they work. You invest $1,000 in one of these bonds. During the first year the Consumer Price Index (CPI), which is the common measure of inflation, moves up by 4 percent. That means that a product that cost $1.00 a year ago will now cost $1.04. Your inflation-proof bond will automatically increase in value by 4 percent, from $1,000 to $1,040. Thus, the purchasing power of your money is protected. This adjustment will take place each year in keeping with the changes in the CPI. That's the good news.

The bad news is that the rate of interest you'll earn on such a bond will be a lot less than on a standard U.S. Treasury bond of similar duration. You can't have it both ways. What you gain in inflation protection you lose in current income. The best use of these bonds would be as a minority portion of your retirement portfolio to insulate you from the effects of long-term inflation. In the short term you can live with a 2 or 3 percent rise in the CPI, which has been its track record in recent years. But over a few decades, that constant edging upward of costs can clobber you if you've not taken some protective steps.

Some major mutual fund companies are now also offering similar inflation-proof funds. The same precautions apply, but with an added dose of care if the investments are of any lesser quality than that of the U.S. Treasury.

Investment Criteria

- **Yield**   On regular government, and zero bonds, you are certain to get the yield you are promised. The yield on EE bonds, as noted, fluctuates, with a minimum guarantee if you hold the bonds for five years. HH yield can be modified by the Treasury Department.

- **Liquidity**   There is an active market for government, agency, and zero issues, which allows you to cash in your holding prior to maturity at the going market price, subject to commissions. EE and HH bonds may not be cashed in until six months after date of purchase.

- **Safety**   Government issues are considered to be in the highest safety category. To the ultimate skeptic, it's safe to presume that before the government falls, everything else will have long since fallen.

- **Hedge value**   As with corporate bonds, an investor in *long-term* government issues has virtually no protection against inflation, assuming that interest rates go up as inflation increases, which is likely. The rate of income is fixed, and higher interest rates will mean lower market values for the bonds, as discussed earlier. Short-term investors are better able to guard against inflation. If inflation has boosted interest rates, short-term investors can move into higher-yielding issues as their older ones mature. The fluctuating-rate EE bonds do offer good protection against inflation.

- **Pledge value**   E, EE, and HH bonds cannot be pledged as security for a loan; thus, they have no pledge value. Other government issues can be pledged, usually at a very high percentage of their face values. Generally, government issues would have higher pledge value than corporate issues of comparable size and maturity.

- **Tax implications**   Government and agency bonds: federally taxable but exempt from state and local income taxes; E and EE bonds: tax-deferred for federal returns, tax-exempt on state and local income tax returns; H and HH: interest earned each year is federally taxable for that year; zeros: interest earned (even though not received by you) is taxable each year; tax-deferred if in IRA or Keogh accounts.

Municipal Bonds

States, cities, towns, water districts, school districts, sewer districts, highway authorities, and a variety of other local entities have periodic needs to borrow funds. The interest these bonds pay has been deemed exempt from federal income tax obligations. This, of course, benefits the local taxpayers. It makes the cost of building and maintaining schools, roads, sewers, or whatever, cheaper. If the bonds were not tax-exempt, they would have to be

issued at higher interest rates, resulting in higher interest costs, which would be passed along to taxpayers.

The two major types of municipal bonds are general obligation bonds and revenue bonds. The general obligation bonds are backed by the taxing authority of the locality. The revenue bonds are backed by the revenues produced by the entity, such as toll roads on a highway authority bond or water usage fees on a water revenue bond. As a rule, general obligation bonds have a higher level of quality than revenue bonds because the power to tax citizens is a more reliable source of income than the ability to raise revenues from toll roads, city-run hospitals, and the like, some of which can be risky.

The 1986 Tax Reform Act put limits on the purposes for which municipalities can issue tax-exempt bonds. Many had been using their tax-exempt borrowing status to attract investment funds and then turning the money over to private developers to build housing projects. Congress felt that this was a potential abuse of the tax-exempt borrowing privilege, and it created quotas on how much of that type of borrowing was tax-exempt. Municipalities will still continue to borrow for such purposes, but the interest they pay to investors may not be tax-exempt. In other words we have municipal bonds that are *tax-exempt* and a small number of municipal bonds that are *taxable*.

Tax Exemption

The most notable aspect of tax-exempt municipal bonds is that the interest they pay investors is exempt from the investors' federal income taxes. Interest earned is also exempt from state income taxes if the investor lives in the state in which the bond is issued. However, if you buy a municipal bond and later sell it at a profit, that profit is subject to full federal and state income taxes.

Exercise 14.9

In comparing a tax-exempt investment with a taxable investment, you must determine how many dollars are left in either case after paying any applicable taxes. Table 14–4 compares tax-exempt and taxable yields. Example: A taxpayer in the 28 percent tax bracket invests $1,000 in a tax-exempt security paying 7 percent, or $70 per year. If that same investor put $1,000 into a taxable security paying 9.7 percent a year, he would earn $97 before federal income taxes. If the $97 was taxed at the 28 percent rate, he'd owe a tax of roughly $27, reducing his *after-tax* yield to $70. In that case, a taxable yield of 9.7 percent would be the same as a tax-exempt yield of 7 percent. Numbers were rounded off, and state income taxes and commission costs are not included in the example.

Although tax exemption of municipal bonds is attractive, municipal bonds are not for everyone. Taxpayers in higher brackets can benefit considerably, but taxpayers in lower brackets might not be better off with municipal bonds than with taxable securities.

TABLE 14–4   **Comparing Tax-Exempt and Taxable Yields**

If You Are in This Tax Bracket:	A Tax-exempt Yield of				
	3%	4%	5%	6%	7%
	Will Net You the Same as a Taxable Yield of:				
15%	3.5%	4.7%	5.9%	6.9%	8.2%
28%	3.7	5.5	7.0	8.3	9.7
33%	4.5	6.0	7.5	8.8	10.4%

Municipal Bond Quotations

Quotations on the prices and yields of municipal bonds are not available in daily newspapers. An investor would have to contact a stockbroker for specific details on the prices and yields of any municipal bonds.

Municipal Bond Ratings

Municipal bonds are rated by the same two services that rate corporate bonds, Standard & Poor's and Moody's. As with the corporate bonds, these ratings services examine the financial status of the municipalities, and the ratings compare the relative qualities of the various issues. The formats in both ratings systems are similar. Following is a brief summary of the Standard & Poor's ratings.

AAA	Highest quality
AA	High grade
A	Good grade
BBB	Medium grade
BB	Speculative-grade
B	Low grade
D	Default

As with corporate bonds, if the financial condition of a municipality changes, so will its rating. Higher ratings mean a lower return to investors and a lower risk. Check with the rating services for more specific details.

Investment Criteria

- **Yield**   In higher-rated municipal bonds, you are assured of receiving the yield you bargained for. Lowest-rated bonds are subject to termination of interest payments and even possible loss of principal.
- **Liquidity**   Trading in municipal bonds is not as active as trading in stocks and corporate bonds. Thus, an investor wishing to sell municipal

bonds may have to wait many hours or days (or possibly even weeks in the case of smaller issues) until a willing buyer comes along. A seller anxious to get a quick trade may have to settle for a lower price.

- **Safety** As with corporate bonds, the higher the rating of a municipal bond, the higher the safety level. Municipal bonds, like corporate bonds, are subject to the same fluctuations and call privileges. Long-term investors in municipal bonds must be concerned about getting caught in a long-term downswing in the value of their holdings if interest rates move upward from the time they bought the bonds.

  Some private companies offer insurance on municipal bonds, which will cost you a small portion of your return. Note well, though, that this insurance is to guarantee you full payment on maturity. It will not protect you against the day-to-day market value fluctuations of the bond.

- **Hedge value** Municipal bonds offer rather indirect protection against inflation. Although the bond itself pays a fixed rate of income for as long as one holds it, the tax-exempt factor can be translated into some protection against inflation for the investor whose income is on the rise. As your income increases, you move into even higher tax brackets. The higher the tax bracket you're in, the greater the tax advantage the municipal bond affords you.

- **Pledge value** Holders of municipal bonds should be able to borrow against their holdings without much difficulty. The percentage of the total value they can borrow and the interest rate they'll have to pay depend on the quality of the issue, as well as its current price level. The higher the quality, the higher percentage of face value you may be able to borrow.

STRATEGIES FOR SUCCESS

Compare Yields Along with Maturities

One basic rule of money market investing is clear: all other things being equal, a security that promises a higher yield also carries a higher risk. But what if all other things are *not* equal? What if they are equal in quality (such as federally insured deposits or U.S. Treasury obligations), and the only difference is their maturity—that is, how long they have to run. That can also affect the yield. Generally, the *longer* the term, the *higher* the yield. But the longer term doesn't always produce enough improvement in yield to warrant tying up your money for those extra years. Here's a simple example at one point in time. A three-year obligation of the U.S. Treasury offered a yield of 5.9 percent. At the same time, a ten-year Treasury obligation offered a yield of 6.7 percent. Is it worth tying your money up for seven extra years to gain less than one extra percentage point in yield? Ask yourself before you take the plunge.

MISCELLANEOUS MONEY MARKET INVESTMENTS

Over the last decade, the ingenuity of the financial marketplace has been particularly bright with respect to the creation of new and unusual forms of fixed income investment. Some of the concepts outlined here have long been the domain of big-money investors. But as the competition for investment dollars has heightened, the concepts have been enlarged to allow the small investor access to these techniques. Over the years, some will capture the public attention, some will fail to, and new techniques will continually emerge.

Mutual Funds

The mutual fund concept has found great favor with the public at large. Mutual fund companies and stockbrokerage firms pool the investments of many small investors and put that money to work in a variety of ways.

The most common types of mutual funds invest in the stock market. These funds are discussed in more detail in chapter 15. But mutual funds in the money market have grown rapidly in popularity; these funds encompass corporate bonds, municipal bonds, U.S. government bonds, and money market instruments. Before examining each specific type of fund, let's examine some of the main distinctions among mutual funds in general.

- **Closed versus open**   The vast majority of mutual funds are open-ended. The managers of the fund are continually buying and selling securities at whatever pace they see fit. Thus, the composition of the overall fund is constantly changing. The ability to buy and sell allows the fund managers to adjust to changing market conditions. It also expands the possibility of the managers' making *wise* decisions *and unwise* decisions. Open-end funds are also often known as managed funds.

    There are also a small number of closed-end funds. These function in much the same way as the open-end funds with respect to buying and selling securities on a continuing basis. To invest in a closed-end fund, however, you buy shares in such funds on the stock market rather than dealing directly with the mutual fund company itself.

    Yet another type of pooled investment is the unit trust. Unlike investment funds, which are constantly buying and selling securities, the unit trust buys a group of securities and holds them until maturity. Thus, the income is more certain with a unit trust than it is with a managed fund, but the value of each share is susceptible to the ups and downs of the market—remember, interest rates and bond prices move in opposite directions.

- **Load versus no-load**   This refers to the commission price an investor pays to buy shares in a mutual fund. A load can be as much as 8 or 9

percent of the initial investment. In other words, in a typical 8½ load fund, 8½ percent of the investor's initial investment will go to pay the brokerage commission. On a $1,000 investment, $85 goes toward commissions and only $915 goes to work for the investor. A no-load fund implies that there is no commission to pay when acquiring the investment. But other charges may be incurred over the life of the investment with both load and no-load funds.

- **Maintenance and service charges** In addition to the loading commission, mutual funds will charge some kind of monthly or annual service fee. Commonly, the service fee is based on a percentage of the fund's assets. Some funds may also take a fee based on the earnings of the fund during the year. These fees may be deducted from the total fund assets or directly from each individual account. Either way, they are an added cost that can affect your yield.

  Some mutual funds charge a redemption fee when you cash in your shares. Before making your initial investment, you should determine any and all charges that may occur.

- **Fund objectives** With fixed income mutual funds, the most common objective is to generate maximum income for the investors. (With common stock mutual funds, the objectives fall into a broader spectrum ranging from income to speculative growth.) But there can be a distinct difference in the level of income and safety sought by various funds. How will a fund invest the money? Some funds will go for the highest quality investments available. This will mean the highest possible level of safety for investors but a lower level of income. It's necessary to determine the broad makeup of the portfolios of a number of funds before making an investment decision.

- **Minimum investment required** On average, the minimum initial investment required in fixed income mutual funds is $1,000. After the initial investment, investors may make additional investments in smaller amounts.

- **Extra privileges** Many mutual funds are a part of a family of other mutual funds. The owners of shares in such funds may therefore have the privilege of exchanging all, or a portion of, their shares for shares in another fund managed by the same investment advisory group. For example, you might switch from a corporate bond fund into a common stock fund or vice versa, at a minimal charge. Reinvestment privileges—whereby your earnings are automatically reinvested in additional shares of the fund—are commonplace, usually at no extra charge. Withdrawal privileges—taking out a fixed amount each month or each quarter—are also available, with some minimal restrictions as to the amount that can be withdrawn.

- **Investment criteria** The investment criteria of a given fixed income mutual fund are approximately the same with regard to yield, liquidity, safety, hedge values, and pledge values as for that specific type of

instrument in which the fund is investing. In other words, a mutual fund that concentrates exclusively on long-term corporate bonds has the same investment criteria as comparable individual corporate bonds. There is one important difference, however. The value of the investment criteria depends largely on the investor's own individual ability to interpret changes, trends, and concepts. Theoretically, professional money managers are better able to do this than individuals. It follows, theoretically, that an investor who is seeking high income may do well, but a professional money manager may be able to do better.

The mutual fund concept allows investors to spread the risk over many securities rather than place all their eggs in one basket. But a careful evaluation of the objectives, the management, and the overall risks involved is as necessary with a mutual fund as it is with a single investment and a specific issue. Investors are advised to read a number of prospectuses of various mutual fund offerings so as to distinguish among the various criteria noted in the previous discussion. Following is a summary of major types of fixed income mutual funds.

Corporate Bond Funds

These funds invest in a wide variety of corporate bonds: high-quality, low-quality, long-term, short-term. The range of possibilities is vast, and it is essential to examine the prospectuses to determine the level of risk and income an investor can expect.

Tax-Exempt Municipal Funds

These mutual funds invest predominantly in municipal bonds—those whose income payable to investors is exempt from federal income taxes. Some funds invest in bonds issued from a single state. Residents of those states who invest in such funds will receive their interest free of state and local income taxes. The range of quality and risk is not as wide as with corporate bonds, but a range does exist. As with municipal bonds, investors should be aware that not all the income will necessarily be exempt from federal income taxes. If, for example, a mutual fund buys a bond and sells it later for a profit, that portion of the profit that is distributed to shareholders will be considered taxable. Furthermore, interest income from a mutual bond fund can be taxable on the local level (state and city). As the prospectuses for these funds disclose, many funds do not invest 100 percent of their assets in tax-exempt municipals. They reserve the right to invest a small portion in other types of instruments that may be taxable. On the whole, however, the major portion of income on such funds would be tax-exempt. It's wise to check with your tax adviser to determine if tax-exempt mutual funds make sense in your situation.

Government Bond Mutual Funds

One of the fastest-growing segments of the mutual fund industry has been funds that invest in U.S. government securities, including bills, notes, bonds, federal agencies, and the government-backed mortgage pools. (See the discussion in chapter 16 on these mortgage pools.) As a rule, these government funds involve relatively high-quality securities, which means a relatively low rate of return to investors but a high level of safety and the peace of mind that goes with it. Investors must always be aware, however, that bond-market prices and interest rates move in opposite directions. Thus, even though these mutual funds are touted as being the ultimate in safety, the unavoidable risk of market fluctuation exists. The bonds in the fund are safe, but that means that they will pay 100 cents on the dollar *at maturity*. In the interim, there is always the risk of fluctuation that can send the value of an investment down suddenly if interest rates rise, and vice versa.

Money Market Mutual Funds

Exercise 14.10

Money market mutual funds have been very popular with investors. They give small investors access to higher rates of return that might not otherwise be available. And they provide a good "parking place" for investment dollars while investors wait for better opportunities to appear. Note one important distinction between money market *mutual funds* and money market *accounts* that are available at banks and savings institutions: Money market accounts are protected by the Federal Deposit Insurance programs. Money market mutual funds do not have that same protection. Otherwise, the accounts function in a similar way. It's best to compare the current rates of return of the funds versus the accounts before making an investment choice. Here are some of the main features of money market mutual funds:

- They are flexible. Investors can get out at any time without penalty.
- The return on these funds varies from day to day, as interest rates fluctuate. Thus, an investor will never know what the actual return will be in the long run. (With certificates of deposit, investors are assured a fixed rate for a fixed period of time.)
- Fees are reasonably low compared with other types of mutual funds.
- In virtually all money market mutual funds, the investor will be dealing with a salesperson or stockbroker. Sooner or later that investor should expect to receive a call from the salesperson or broker suggesting that the investor get out of the money market fund and into something else. An investor who isn't prepared for that sales pitch may agree to a switch that could prove profitable or unprofitable. In short, an investor may be wooed away from a highly secure position into a speculative one. This is not necessarily bad, but the investor should be aware of the potential before making the investment.

- Shares in money market mutual funds are not insured like bank accounts, but the bulk of money market fund investments are in highly secure instruments such as government issues and bank certificates.
- Many large brokerage firms will offer to tie in money market investments with checking accounts and credit card availabilities. In effect, the portion of your checking account balance that isn't needed for immediate use can be invested in the brokerage firm's money market fund, where it can earn a high rate of interest. Prospective investors should carefully examine the minimum deposits required for such services and the cost of these services.

Following are some other types of money market investments that may be available to individual investors directly or that may be included in a mutual fund portfolio.

Banker's Acceptances

Say a U.S. company sells a product to a Japanese company for $200,000. The Japanese company gives the U.S. company a written promise to pay for the goods on delivery, which is expected to be in six months. The U.S. company doesn't want to wait for its money, so it goes to a bank with the Japanese company's promise to pay. The bank examines the credentials of the Japanese company and agrees to buy its promise to pay from the U.S. company at a certain price. The bank has thus, in effect, "accepted" the Japanese promise to pay. The bank may then turn around and sell this IOU to investors. The instrument is known as a banker's acceptance. In effect, the investor is buying a foreign company's promise top pay. The investor is secured to the extent that a bank or other financial institution is willing to take the risk itself. Banker's acceptances tend to pay an attractive rate of interest for short-term investments.

Commercial Paper

When corporations borrow for a long term, as discussed, their promises to pay are called corporate bonds. Often, corporations borrow for a short period of time—such as a few months. Short-term corporate borrowings are referred to as commercial paper, and their quality tends to follow the quality of the corporation's bonds. As the bond is rated, so is the commercial paper commonly rated. Money market mutual funds frequently carry sizable amounts of commercial paper in their portfolios.

Floating-rate Bonds

As discussed previously, interest rates and the market value of bonds move in opposite directions. To recap briefly: If you invest in a bond that is paying, say, 8 percent interest a year, or $80 per $1,000 invested, and interest rates in general move upward, then the market value of your bond will shrink. This is because an investor in a higher interest rate environment can buy a brand-new bond yielding, say, 9 percent. So why should anyone pay you full face value for yours, which yields only 8 percent?

One type of investment gets around this problem: the floating-rate bond. If the interest rate on a given bond is permitted to move up and down, the principal value will not fluctuate. Example: using the same original 8 percent investment, if interest rate trends move upward to, say, 9 percent, and your bond is allowed to pay you the higher rate of return, your principal value will remain intact. By the same token, if interest rates move down, your principal will remain at the $1,000 face value level and you'll receive a lower yield. In other words, you can't have it both ways: in bond investments, you have to accept either a floating rate of interest or a floating market value.

Floating-rate bonds are available in both the taxable and tax-exempt categories. The most popular ones have been issued by banks.

Convertible Bonds

These issues (sometimes called convertible debentures) are corporate bonds that give the owner the right to convert the bonds into common stock of the issuing company. Here's an example: XYZ Corporation issues a convertible bond with a selling price of $1,000. The bond pays an interest rate of 10 percent—$100 per year. That rate is fixed for the life of the bond. Owners of the bonds have the right to convert their bonds into fifty shares of XYZ common stock, which is now selling for $20 per share and paying a $2 per share dividend. Thus, the income from fifty shares of the common stock is $100 per year, the same as the bond. At this point, the $1,000 bond and the fifty shares of common stock are equal in value. There would seem to be no point in converting from the bond to the stock. However, an investor may be hopeful that the dividend on the stock will increase, say, from $2 to $3 per share. If, in fact, that happens and the investor has converted from the bond to the stock, the yield will increase from $100 per year to $150 per year. The interest rate on the bond is fixed, but the dividend rate on the stock is not. Therefore, an investor who is willing to speculate on increased dividends might find convertible bonds profitable.

On the other hand, the bond is eventually going to be worth $1,000 at maturity. The investor knows that for sure. The stock could drop to a much

STRATEGIES FOR SUCCESS

A Formula for Safe Retirement Investing

How should your Individual Retirement Account, or 401(k) plan, or any other retirement money be invested? To the extent that you will be depending on this money for retirement living, it's not wise to take much risk with it. Take risks with money you don't need for retirement, but not with this important stash. It *must* be there at retirement time, and if you take risks it might *not* be there. Then what?

Consider this simple formula: Add your age plus forty. That's the percentage of your retirement money that should be risk-free. The rest can be put to moderate risk. So if you are thirty, your age plus forty equals seventy. Thus, 70% of your must-be-there retirement money should be risk-free. If you are fifty, 90 percent of your must-be-there retirement money should be risk-free. The older you are, the less risk you can afford to take, because there's less time and less resilience to recover from mistakes.

This is a very conservative formula. Take greater risk at your own risk. See Strategies for Success on page 353 for added views on this subject.

lower level than its conversion value. An investor who converts is taking a chance that the stock may decrease in value and result in a considerable loss and vice versa.

During the holding period, prior to a decision to convert, the bond and the stock will tend to move up and down on a fairly parallel course. Once investors have converted from the bonds to the stocks, they are stuck. They can't automatically convert back to the bonds again if their expectations don't work out.

PERSONAL ACTION WORKSHEET —————————————————

Comparing Returns, After Costs

The true return on any given investment can only be calculated after all costs have been taken into account. These costs include commissions (when both buying and selling), ongoing fees (such as those charged by mutual funds), and income taxes. To get a clear comparison of various types of money market investments, calculate the return, after costs, of the following securities. Use actual current returns now available. For the "Tax" column, use your own current tax rate. If you're not in a taxable situation, use the lowest current tax rate.

	Return Before Costs	Commissions to Buy	to Sell	Ongoing Fees	Tax	Total Costs	Return After Costs
❏ 12-month bank CD	____	____	____	____	____	____	____
❏ Bank money market account	____	____	____	____	____	____	____
❏ Broker money market fund	____	____	____	____	____	____	____
❏ Corporate bond mutual fund (low-risk, full-load)	____	____	____	____	____	____	____
❏ Government bond mutual fund (low-risk, full-load)	____	____	____	____	____	____	____

CONSUMER ALERT

What Is the Secret to Financial Success?

A friend asked me a fascinating question recently. "Is investing wisely the ultimate secret for financial success?"

My answer, and I hope you'll agree, was "No."

My questioner, thinking that he had hit upon a formula long sought by humankind, was puzzled by my answer.

I explained my brief but firm reply: Certainly investing wisely is something to strive for. But all the wise investing in the world won't help you a whit if you spend it all willy-nilly. And all the fat dividends and huge profits you can reap aren't worth a hoot if you are miserable day to day because of a dead-end job or marriage or social life.

Money can buy toys, but it can't buy self-esteem. Money can buy power, but it can't buy good health. Money can glamorize your exterior, but it can't uplift your interior. Money might provide the image of happiness, but not the spirit of happiness.

Everyone must find their own equilibrium, their own sense of balance between the material things they seek and the simpler pleasures of life. You should not feel beholden to anyone—it's your life to live as you choose it, subject to your responsibility to those who depend on you. But at the end of the day it's you who must say to yourself, "Way to go!"

Wise investing is only part of financial success. Wise spending, wise prioritizing, and wise risk management are the other prime elements of financial success. And financial success is only one part of overall personal success.

The friend who asked me the question was sixty-one. He hadn't learned yet. You may be a lot younger. I hope you learn a lot more a lot earlier than my friend.

UPS & DOWNS   *The Economics of Everyday Life*

How Stock Market Ups and Downs Affect Money Market Ups and Downs

You say you're *never* going to have anything to do with the stock market; you're just going to stick with safe and simple savings certificates and other money market types of investments discussed in this chapter. Be careful: You can never escape the ripple effects on the stock market. (See chapter 15.)

When the stock market moves sharply upward, for whatever valid or fanciful reason, it attracts money out of the money market like a super-magnet. Conservative money market investors see big gains being made in the stock market, and they abandon their lower yielding but *safe* accounts to take a plunge in the risky waters of the stock market. Greed, naiveté, lack of discipline—all are part of human nature. All of this money pouring into the stock market keeps the rally going, and that attracts still more money market investors. And so it goes until gravity reasserts itself and the stock market tumbles.

If such a stock market rally occurs when the nation's economy is strong and banks need depositors' money to lend to meet borrowers' demands, then banks will react to the outflow of deposits by increasing the interest rates they pay to depositors to lure them back.

If such a stock market rally occurs when the nation's economy is weak and banks aren't being hounded by would-be borrowers, then banks will let the interest rates they pay to their depositors drift—probably downward.

Why? Because lower rates will eventually stimulate borrowing, which will stimulate the economy, which will prod interest rates upward, which will create more profit opportunity for the banks. It's a cyclical thing.

Then there's always "the other hand." When the stock market tumbles—as it inevitably does after each rally—investors will flee Wall Street to the safe harbor of money market securities. If this happens at a time when the economy is strong and banks are competing for deposits, money market interest rates can go up. If it happens when the economy is weak and banks are not competing for deposits, money market interest rates will likely remain flattish.

The internal tie-ins between these markets are devilishly intricate. But it's worth the effort to understand them, so that you can make your own decisions more effectively.

?

WHAT IF . . . ?

Test yourself on the concerns of this chapter. How would you deal with these real-life possibilities?

1. You want to put away money for the following purposes: (a) college tuition for your children; (b) a super vacation traveling through Europe; (c) retirement. However little or however much you may really have to salt away, what percentage of it would you put into the money market for each of these three purposes? What types of plans would you favor for each?

2. An investment adviser suggests that she can put your money to work in a mutual fund specializing in high-yield corporate bonds and that the fund will give you a return five percentage points higher than what you could earn by investing in U.S. Treasury securities. What more should you ask of this adviser? What might be the pros and cons of making such an investment?

3. The company you work for is issuing bonds—borrowing money—from the public at large. You feel that it might make a good investment for you. The bonds are well rated, and the interest rate is two percentage points higher than what you're earning in your savings account. You plan to cash in the bonds in about five years. What would happen to your investment if interest rates five years from now had dropped from today's levels? What if they had risen? Why?

Do the calculations that are needed to help you make decisions in these real-life possibilities.

1. Grunt arithmetic, but worth the exercise: You invest $1,000 in a savings plan that pays 8 percent interest, compounding annually. You invest another $1,000 in a corporate bond that pays 8 percent interest per year, payable annually, with no compounding. You'll deposit the interest from the bond in a savings account paying 5 percent interest, compounding annually, but only if there is $500 or more in the account—otherwise it pays no interest. How would your money grow in either of these plans over five years? Ten years? (Forget income taxes for purposes of this exercise, but not in real life.)

2. A bond is quoted in the newspaper as follows: "ZYX 7s 04 Closing price 92." If you bought that bond at today's closing price, what would be your coupon yield? What would be your current yield? What would be your yield to maturity if you held the bond until maturity? (Assume that the maturity date of the bond is on the anniversary of the date you buy the bond.)

3. You're comparing two money market mutual funds. One has a load charge of 8½ percent plus annual fees totaling 3/4 percent of the value of your account. The other has a load charge of 4 percent, plus annual fees totaling 1½ percent of the value of your account. Assume you have $10,000 to invest and that both funds will grow by 7 percent per year. Where will you stand with each fund after one year? Three years? Five years?

FOR BETTER OR FOR WORSE

Things beyond our control often impact our personal and financial well-being, for better or for worse. Some are more predictable than others. How would you be affected if the following real-life phenomena happened? Could you have seen it coming? What steps could you have taken to minimize damage or maximize advantage? The better able you are to anticipate and recognize these forces, the better equipped you are to deal with them.

1. You want total complete safety for your retirement kitty, so you put it all into long-term government bonds. Five years later something urgent comes along, and you need to cash in those bonds. In the interim, interest rates have gone up, so if you cash in the bonds you'll have a loss of more than 20 percent.

2. You've invested a lot of money in a top-rated corporate bond, and you rest easy knowing that your income from it will be steady and reliable. One day you see that the value of the bond has fallen considerably. On checking, you find the rating on the bond had been dropped from AA to C.

3. You shop around for the highest yielding one-year CD. A year later you are happy to let the CD renew for another year, until you learn that the rate has fallen by two percentage points.

Making Your Money Grow: The Stock Market

If stockbrokers are so smart, where are all their customers' yachts?

Anonymous

This chapter continues our exploration of ways you can make your money grow—we hope. The stock market involves aspects of risk not found in money market investments. The nature of those risks is not always understood by would-be investors/speculators. If the risks aren't understood, serious damage can be done to your financial well-being. To help you understand and evaluate those risks, we'll examine:

- What makes the stock market tick
- How to understand the language and the numbers of the stock market
- What motivates various kinds of people to put their money to work in the stock market, the better to help you identify and understand your own motivations
- Which specific techniques you can use within the arena of the stock market
- How to evaluate the professional help available to you through stockbrokers

A PERSPECTIVE

From 1982 until late 1987, the stock market enjoyed one of the longest and most powerful run-ups in its history. For six years, nothing seemed to be able to dampen the enthusiasm of stock market players. Speculative fever ran amok, not just in the United States but in most of the other major stock exchanges around the world. Then, on October 19, 1987, the earth shook under Wall Street. The Dow Jones Industrial Average plummeted 508 points, its worst single day up to that point. It was the unthinkable, the incredible, the impossible, all rolled into one. In the space of just six and one-half hours, roughly one-half trillion dollars' worth of what could have been spendable wealth disappeared. That market crash, and its long-term after-effects, served as a grim, but real and healthy, reminder that speculation has its comeuppance.

To anyone who might think that that was a one-time-only phenomenon, another quake rocked Wall Street almost ten years to the day later. On October 26, 1997, the Dow Jones Industrial Average plummeted nearly 530 points. This wasn't as drastic a drop percentage-wise as the one in 1987 because the DJIA was much higher in 1997 than it had been 10 years earlier. But it could foreshadow even further turbulence for a gravity-defying stock market throughout the late 1900s. (Superstitious investors might want to be wary come October 2007.)

This chapter is a primer on how the stock market functions. It's not intended to predict the future. But there certainly is a new dimension in the stock market's future: As with earthquakes, until one *does* happen, you can always choose to believe that one might *never* occur. Once an earthquake *does* occur, it becomes etched in your brain permanently. From that moment on, you always know that it can occur *again*. Thus it is with the stock market: until a crash occurs, you can always pretend to believe that one might never occur. But once it has occurred, there's no denying that the "impossible" can happen again. Bear this in mind as you consider the basic functions of the stock market as outlined in the balance of this chapter.

STOCK OWNERSHIP AS A FORM OF INVESTING

In the previous chapter on money market investing, we explored the possibilities of creating future wealth by "lending" your money to another entity and receiving in turn a promise to pay a fee (interest) for the use of your money, plus the promise to return it at an agreed-on time. These promises are legally binding obligations of the debtor.

Stock ownership as a form of investment is quite different. With stock ownership, investors become part owners of a business enterprise and have no promise (legal or otherwise) that they will receive any fee for the use of their money or that anyone will be obliged to pay them any or all of their money back at any future time.

Lending versus Buying, Debt versus Equity

What's the difference between lending our money to a business (investing in a corporate bond) and buying a portion of ownership in the business (buying stock)? Businesses often need money to develop new products, expand their facilities, buy new equipment, modernize, and pay for other job-creating activities. Some of the money needed may come from the profits the business generates, but this isn't always enough. In order to acquire large sums of money relatively quickly, a business will either borrow from investors (issue corporate bonds) or will sell a portion of itself to investors (issue stock). The former route is frequently referred to as the debt market, and the latter as the equity market.

Regarding its debt, the company has a legal obligation to pay interest to the investors and to return the principal sum at the agreed-on time. With equity, or stock, the company has no such legal obligation. *If* profits are in fact generated, the company *may* distribute a portion of the profits to the stockholders. The company is under no obligation to buy the stock back from a stockholder. If stockholders want to sell their stock, they hope to find buyers willing to pay an attractive price.

The important priority to note in comparing debt with stock ownership is that debt service (interest) *must* be paid *before* profits are tallied. Profits are the dollars left over after the business has paid all its obligations, among which are the payments due on its debts.

The same holds true when a business is terminated, either voluntarily or otherwise. In such a procedure, commonly called a *liquidation,* everything the company owns is converted into cash. Out of that pool of cash, all the company's debts are paid, including any bonds that may be outstanding. What's left over is split up between the stockholders. In other words, creditors have priority over stockholders in liquidation as well as in the day-to-day operation of a business.

The profitability of any kind of business venture depends on a great many factors, including the management of the business, the nature of the competition, overall ups and downs in the nation's economy as well as in the particular industry, and the totally unpredictable quirks and whims of the investing public. It's this last element—the whims and quirks of the investing public—that makes the stock market an unending series of dilemmas. In the stock market, you are not just betting on how profitably the company can perform; you are also betting on how *other* people think the company might perform.

Primary versus Secondary Market

Distinction should be made between the primary, or new issues, market and the secondary market. The primary market is that aspect of stock

trading in which companies raise money from the investing public. Once the money has been raised and shares of ownership in the companies have been issued to the investors, the stock is traded in the secondary market. Only a tiny percentage of all stock transactions are primary market transactions; the vast majority are on the secondary market. New issues are called *initial pubic offerings,* or I.P.O.s. They are often extremely speculative.

The primary market serves a critically important purpose in the economy of the nation: it provides ready access for companies to raise money for expansion, research, and other worthwhile purposes. The secondary market is often looked on as little more than a gambling casino. There is, however, an important purpose for the secondary market: without the secondary market, the primary market could not exist. Businesses could not raise money by selling stock if investors did not know they could readily sell their stock at a fair price. Thus, despite the often speculative aspect of the secondary market, our economy would flounder without it.

Possibilities versus Probabilities

Virtually every transaction in the stock market, every purchase, and every sale of every share, is essentially a disagreement. Sellers want to get out because they don't think the stock offers them satisfactory income or potential any longer. Buyers want to get in because they think the stock *does* offer satisfactory income or profit potential. In other words, the two parties disagree about the potential of the stock.

The stock market offers a vast spectrum of possibilities. The challenge is to find that small cluster of possibilities that can help achieve your stated objectives.

In your own life, you have a spectrum of future needs and desires: some probable and some possible. It's *probable* that you're going to retire someday and will need adequate money to live on. It's *possible* that someday you might be in a position to enjoy a trip around the world. Goals that are probable or fixed or certain need appropriate techniques if they are to be achieved. Those techniques tend to fall into the fixed income investment spectrum. You can't afford to take chances that you will or will not achieve those fixed and necessary goals. You have to be certain, or at least as certain as you can be, that they will be reached.

Exercise 15.1

Other goals that are less certain may be appropriately sought by the *less certain* investment techniques, principally the stock market, *but not until after you have established a disciplined program that you feel confident will put you on the path to achieving your fixed goals.*

In other words, get a reasonable program under way that will take you to your fixed destinations. If you still have funds available to invest after you've put enough away toward those top priorities, you may want to consider the more speculative techniques to help you achieve lower priority goals—goals that if not achieved will not cause you real suffering.

For a more vivid comparison of the difference between fixed income investing and "ownership" investing, let's look at the following scale, which represents the likelihood of achieving stated objectives. The *objective:* to put away X dollars today and know that you will have Y dollars at some future date.

1	Almost totally certain
2	Fairly certain
3	Highly probable
4	Probable
5	Highly possible
6	Possible
7	Relatively uncertain
8	Totally uncertain

The better-quality ranges of the fixed income types of investment fall into the top half of the scale, from 1 to 4. The better-quality range of stock falls in the middle, from 3 to 6. The majority of investments in the stock market fall in the 4–7 range, and a considerable number are in the 6–8 range.

For the balance of this chapter, we'll examine in greater detail some of the inner workings of the stock market. In no way should any of the discussion be construed as recommendations to buy, sell, or hold any types of securities; the purpose is to help you determine whether the stock market offers the opportunities that will help you meet your goals, to understand how the mechanism works, and to motivate you to do further independent research to find those specific areas that will provide you with the returns you're seeking.

Cautions

As you read and discuss the material on the stock market, bear in mind the following cautions:

- Aided by sophisticated computers, millions of work hours are spent every day studying every movement, jiggle, and quiver of the stock market. Yet no one can predict with any degree of certainty what direction the market as a whole, or any individual stock, is liable to take even a minute or two from now.
- There have probably been more statistics compiled on the stock market, and more books written about it, than any other phenomenon on earth. Yet it continues to be one of the most confusing, mystifying, and frustrating subjects in our experience.

- The stock market touches our day-to-day lives in more ways than we can imagine, yet we are powerless to control it in even the slightest way. Even though you may never have had anything directly to do with the market and don't intend ever to have anything to do with it, it can still affect you. If the company that employs you is traded on the stock market, swings in the value of the stock can affect the future profitability of the company and possibly the future of your job. If your employer or boss is a stock market trader, his or her success or failure in the market on a day-to-day basis can affect his or her personality and attitude, which in turn can affect yours. If your pension fund or profit-sharing fund has money invested in the stock market, the investment expertise of those who manage those funds can have a profound bearing on your future.

- There is no person, no book, no system, no computer, that can assure you of making money in the stock market. The stock market can play an important function as an integral part of establishing your future security. But unless you approach it in the proper frame of mind, with the proper expertise, and with the proper degree of skepticism, its traps and pitfalls can play havoc with your aspirations.

How a Business Operates

A brief look at how a corporation functions will assist you in understanding the workings of the stock market.

A corporation is a legal entity in its own right. Each separate state has its own laws governing how a corporation may be created and run. Like a person, a corporation can own, buy, or sell property; it can be taxed; it can sue and be sued; and it can conduct business.

A corporation is owned by its stockholders. The stockholders determine what they wish their corporation to do. But it is cumbersome for the stockholders to meet and consult over every item of corporate business. Thus, the stockholders elect representatives who will act on their behalf in setting basic policy for the corporation. This group of representatives is referred to as the *directors*. The chairman of the board of directors controls the flow of the board's meetings, and as such can be the single-most powerful person in the corporation.

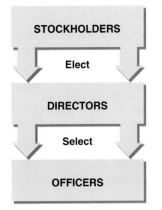

In turn, the directors select individuals to carry out the day-to-day operations of the business. These people are called the *officers* of the corporation. The chief officer of a corporation is usually called the president or chief executive officer (CEO). Answering directly to the president may be an array of vice presidents, each with their own areas of tasks, obligations, and responsibilities. Other officers of the corporation commonly include the treasurer, the secretary, and the comptroller, and each of these may have an additional hierarchy of assistants.

The stockholders generally meet once each year, at which time they are

informed of the progress and potential of the corporation. It's at the annual meeting that the stockholders elect the directors, who in turn select the officers. Stockholders who are unable to attend this annual meeting can send proxies, authorizations on which they indicate their selection of directors and their choices on issues on which they have been asked to vote.

It is the rule rather than the exception in most large corporations that the stockholders comply with the recommendations of the board of directors. In recent years the annual meetings of many major corporations have been enlivened by sharp discussions between ownership and management regarding corporate responsibility in the fields of discrimination, pollution, and political practices. As a result, many corporations have adopted policies in keeping with stockholders' wishes regarding these highly visible public issues.

HOW THE STOCK MARKETS OPERATE

An individual's share of ownership in a corporation is represented by the stock certificate, which stipulates how many shares the individual owns. The value of each share is determined by a number of factors: profitability of the company, future potential for the company, amount of dividends the company is paying, and, broadly, what the public at large thinks the stock is worth. Stockholders wishing to sell their stock must find buyers willing to pay the asking price. Investors wishing to buy stock must find willing sellers. In small local corporations, word of mouth may be all that's needed to find the respective buyer or seller. But with large corporations, particularly those with millions of shares outstanding, this would be impractical. If would-be investors in stocks did not feel confident that they could sell their shares quickly and efficiently, they would probably be discouraged from making investments in the first place.

Thus, throughout the nation and the world, exchanges long ago came into being to provide a ready marketplace for both buyers and and sellers. The most familiar is the New York Stock Exchange, located in lower Manhattan, in an area commonly referred to as Wall Street. Other major exchanges include the Nasdaq, the American Stock Exchange, and the Pacific Stock Exchange.

Exercise 15.2

The stock exchanges are basically a clearing house where buyers and sellers try to get the best buying or selling price. An investor who wishes to buy or sell stock places an order with a local stockbroker who works for a firm that owns a *seat* on an exchange. The order is relayed from the local broker's office to the firm's facilities on the floor of the exchange. In some cases, the brokerage firm may fill the order itself. In other cases, the order may be referred to a specialist on the floor of the exchange. Each individual stock traded on any given exchange is represented by a specialist, whose job it is to match buy and sell orders and to keep an orderly marketplace for the stock. In order to do so, specialists may be required actually to buy or sell stocks from their own account.

When the order is filled, word is relayed back to the local brokerage firm, which informs the customer of the results. Written confirmation of the transaction follows shortly thereafter.

The Prospectus

Exercise 15.3

Before a stock can be publicly traded on an exchange, it must comply with certain governmental regulations. If a stock is to be sold only to the residents of the specific state in which the company is located, the company must comply with local state regulations. If it is to be traded nationally, it must comply with requirements of the federal agency that oversees such matters, the Securities and Exchange Commission (SEC).

Federal regulations require that a company disclose a variety of facts relating to its operation, including the identity and experience of its management, its debts, its legal affairs, its overall financial status, and the potential risks an investor might face in investing in the company. All this information—usually spelled out at great length in cumbersome legal jargon—is contained in a document called the prospectus.

A prospectus is required when a company initially sells its stock, or when it issues subsequent securities, including stocks or bonds. Once the initial prospectus has been issued, a company need not issue subsequent ones unless it offers additional securities at a later date. Thus, while the prospectus is an important tool for the investor, if it is substantially out of date (as most are), its value is diminished. Yet it still serves as important background material and should not be ignored.

Corporations do issue annual reports for the stockholders and for the SEC that contain more up-to-date information than the prospectus. A would-be investor should examine the annual reports, and it would be wise to compare these reports with the original prospectus, if for no other reason than to determine how well the company has met its originally stated objectives.

Mutual funds also must issue a prospectus when they seek investment dollars from the public. The existence of a prospectus for either a mutual fund or a stock can mislead an investor into thinking that the government has somehow given its blessings to the validity and value of the given investment. Nothing could be farther from the truth. On the front cover of each prospectus is this often overlooked statement:

These securities have not been approved or disapproved by the Securities and Exchange Commission, nor has the Commission passed on the accuracy or adequacy of this prospectus. Any representation to the contrary is a criminal offense.

That statement means exactly what it says: The government does not in any way stand behind any of the statements made in the prospectus. If the prospectus is misleading or inaccurate, the corporation or mutual fund can be subject to criminal prosecution. The prudent investor will make wise use of the prospectus but will not be misled by it or by any sales pitch that implies governmental approval when none indeed exists.

Investors' Insurance

Exercise 15.4

The government does offer one measure of protection to investors, through the Security Investors Protection Corporation (SIPC).

When scores of banks folded as a result of the Great Depression in the 1930s, the government acted to create an insurance program that would prevent a recurrence of such a disaster. The Federal Deposit Insurance Corporation came into being to insure bank depositors against the institution's failure. But, until 1970, there was no comparable protection for investors who entrusted their funds to stock brokerage firms. A severe stock market collapse in 1969–1970 caused a number of brokerage firms to fail. Many more, on the brink of failure, were absorbed by larger and healthier firms. As a result of the near panic that ensued, the government, in conjunction with the securities industry, took steps to create the SIPC, which would insure investors' accounts for the value of any securities or funds held by their brokerage firm in the event of a failure of such a firm. Most major firms currently provide this protection to their customers, but some smaller firms do not. (*Note:* The insurance does *not* protect against the value of any stock going down.)

Keeping the Records

The shares of most major corporations are traded by the hundreds or thousands every business day. It's not uncommon for more than 500 million shares of stock to change hands in a single day on the New York Stock Exchange alone. This total volume is made up of many thousands of individual transactions, representing handfuls or major blocks of shares. Smaller corporations whose shares are seldom traded may hire clerical workers to do the bookwork involved in amending the list of stockholders. But most major corporations hire transfer agents to take care of this burdensome task. Transfer agents are usually affiliated with major banks.

When you buy or sell shares of a stock, the transfer agent is notified accordingly, and your name is either placed on, or removed from, the list of stockholders of that corporation. As dividends become payable, the transfer agent sees to it that the dividend is transmitted to you or to your account with the stockbroker.

When you buy stock, you have the choice of obtaining the certificate registered in your own name (or in the name of whatever parties you choose as

owners, such as husband and wife jointly) or of having the broker retain custody of the stock. In the latter case, the stock would be listed in <u>street name</u>—technically, it is in the broker's name and possession, but the broker is holding it for your account. Some investors prefer to have the certificate in their own hands, aware that they should make proper safekeeping arrangements for it. Other investors prefer the convenience of having it remain in the broker's custody, in which case the investor receives a monthly statement from the broker indicating the status of the account and detailing the securities being held in the investor's name.

Each buy and sell transaction is followed up by a written <u>confirmation</u> that indicates the date of the transaction, the price for which the security was bought or sold, the amount of the broker's commission and any appropriate taxes, and the net amount due to the broker or to the investor from the broker. These confirmation slips should be retained by the investor; they contain information helpful in determining future gains or losses on the stock. The confirmation slips also indicate the settlement date, which is the day by which payment must be made and the stock delivered.

Executing an Order

Once you have opened an account with a broker by signing the necessary papers, you can execute orders, that is, instruct your broker to buy or sell on your behalf. Most orders to buy and sell stock are handled by telephone. It's important, therefore, to make certain that your broker has followed your instructions explicitly, particularly concerning the number of shares you're selling or buying, the price at which you wish to buy or sell, and the specific type of order you're giving. These specifics should be repeated between you and the broker, and you should make immediate written note of them.

Orders to buy or sell stock can take many different forms. Here are the major types.

Market Orders

What is a <u>market order</u>? If you instruct your broker to buy or sell "at the market," the broker will then buy or sell your shares at whatever the going market price is, trying, of course, to get the best possible price, though it may not be exactly what you had in mind. For example, XYZ is currently selling at $50 per share, and you instruct your broker to buy 100 shares "at the market." At the moment your order reaches the floor, the best possible price for those shares may have risen to $51 per share. That's what you would end up paying. On the other hand, if you instruct your broker to sell 100 shares "at the market," the best possible price available when your order reaches the floor might be $49, and that's what you'll get. It could also work the other way around. You might be able to buy at a lower price than you had anticipated or sell at a higher price.

Limit Orders

A <u>limit order</u> sets a maximum or minimum price on the sale or purchase of shares. For example, you purchased 100 shares of XYZ at $50 per share. You have made up your mind that if it reaches $55 per share, you want to sell and take your profits. You can place a limit order at $55 per share, and that order will be executed only when the stock can be sold at $55 per share. If the stock never reaches that level, the limit order will never be executed. If you want to buy stock, a limit order can also be used. Say you wish to buy 100 shares of XYZ if the price drops to $45 per share. You place a limit order with your broker, and if and when XYZ hits $45 per share, your order will be executed. If the stock never does hit that price, your order won't be executed.

Time Orders

A <u>time order</u> can be attached to a limit order. It adds a time deadline to the limit order. A time order may be for a day, or for any number of days. One common type of time order is called a *good this week* (GTW) order. This order will remain in effect until the end of the calendar week. Example: You would like to buy 100 shares of XYZ for $45 per share, but only if XYZ hits $45 per share before the end of this week. You thus instruct your broker to enter a combined limit order and time order. If XYZ does hit $45 per share before the end of the week, your order will be executed. If not, then you will not have bought the stock. Another form of time order is called the *open order*, or *good till canceled* (GTC) order. It is a standing order to buy or sell at a fixed price until you, the investor, cancel the order or until it is executed at that price.

Fill or Kill Orders

A <u>fill or kill order</u> is an order to buy or sell at a fixed price immediately. Example: You wish to sell 100 shares of XYZ at $55 per share. With a fill or kill order, if your broker cannot execute immediately for al the shares you wish to buy or sell at that price, the order will be canceled.

WHO INVESTS IN THE STOCK MARKET, AND WHAT ARE THEY SEEKING?

The vast diversity of stock market investors can be broken down into three broad categories: by objective, by size, and by type.

Investors by Objective

What are investors seeking when they buy stocks? It could be any one, or a combination, of the following: short-term growth, long-term growth, income, and "no foggy idea." Let's look at each in turn.

Short-term Growth

This objective might be best described as "out to make a fast buck." If this is your objective, you might be as well served by your nearest racetrack or gambling casino as by the stock market. Humorist Will Rogers had some good advice for those who dive into the stock market looking for the fast buck: "It's easy to be successful in the stock market. You just buy stock, and when it goes up, you sell it. And if it don't go up, don't buy it."

Long-term Growth

This more prudent objective is more likely to reward the patient investor who has done the necessary homework. Investors whose objectives are long-term growth analyze industries and specific companies whose long-term future looks healthy and profitable and select investments accordingly. If such investors select wisely and luckily and are willing to wait long enough, they may well realize their objectives.

Income

Many investors get involved in the stock market with the primary objective of receiving income in the form of dividends. Although the dividends they earn may not be as rewarding as what they could have earned in money market investments, there is also the secondary hope that the stocks will increase in value over a period of time.

Investors whose objectives are balanced between growth and income are perhaps the ones who approach the market most intelligently. They are the investors who set targets for upside potential and downside potential. They might, for example, define their objective as a 15 percent annual return (after brokerage commissions) on investment—perhaps 7 percent might come through receipt of dividends and the other 8 percent through increase in the value of shares. Say that XYZ Company is selling at $50 per share and is paying $3.50 per share divided per year. That's equal to a 7 percent return in the form of dividends. If, during an investor's first year of ownership of XYZ, the price moves from $50 to $54 per share—an 8 percent increase during the year—the investor has realized his or her 15 percent objective. By the same token, the investor would also set a downside limit. If XYZ drops to $45 per share, the investor would get out at that price and thus be sheltered from any further losses. There re no strict rules of thumb as to what a desirable balance is. Many of your objectives in this area must relate to what can assuredly be attained with the same investable dollars in the money market.

"No Foggy Idea"

This well may represent the majority of stock market investors. In short, they haven't the foggiest idea what their objectives are. They're not sure

why they bought what they bought when they bought it. And they have no notion as to when or why they should sell. Their only hope for success in the market is good luck.

Investors by Size

Individual investors generally trade in small blocks of stock. Blocks of 100 shares are referred to as round lots; blocks of less than 100 shares are referred to as odd lots, which usually carry a slightly higher brokerage commission, called the *odd lot differential*.

The large investors, such as pension and profit-sharing funds, mutual funds, trust funds, large corporations, and insurance companies, often trade in very large blocks—many thousands of shares at a time. Large block trades can disrupt the normal flow of supply and demand of shares and can thus cause considerable fluctuations in the price of a given stock at the time such an order to buy or sell is placed.

Sharp fluctuation can also be caused by extremely sophisticated computer programs that investors use to tell them when to buy or sell shares of stock. This is known as *program trading*. It kicks in when certain criteria are met by a given stock and/or market conditions in general and/or a variety of specific technical indicators. Computers can react to these signals much more quickly than a human can, so a buy or sell order can easily catch mere mortals by surprise. There is no limit as to how much program trading can take place, and since this kind of electronically stimulated trading usually involves huge blocks of stock, it can have an extremely disruptive effect on the normal ebbs and flows of daily trading. All the more to muddle up anyone's attempts to analyze the stock market.

Investors by Type

The following are brief descriptions of eight broad categories of investors representing individuals or institutions. They are all in the market at the same time, all expressing a constant flow of opinions that may be in total accord or total discord with those of their colleagues. Let's take a closer look at the cast of characters.

Novices

Novices aren't really sure what they're doing. Their obvious motivation is to "make money," but they're not really certain how, or if, they will. If they have done any studying at all, it's probably been only superficial; probably they have become involved in the market because of the suggestion of someone else, and they're probably following the suggestion at its face value.

Insiders

There are three types of insiders: the way-insiders, the fringe-insiders, and the pretend-insiders. The way-insiders are people on intimate terms with the day-to-day operation of the corporation—officers, employees, directors or major stockholders. They are privy to information not yet available to the public that, when released to the public, can have a good or bad effect on the stock of the company. A way-insider may know, for example, that a potentially profitable deal is about to be completed or that a sharp loss is about to be announced. If the information is accurate and the announcement has the anticipated effect, the way-insider can reap a substantial profit, or avoid a sharp loss by selling out existing holdings.

Because of a business or personal relationship with a way-insider (such as being a stockbroker, lawyer, accountant, or supplier of the way-insider), the fringe-insider may have indirect and usually delayed access to the intimate information available to the way-insider. Perhaps the fringe-insider will get the information in time to benefit from it; perhaps not.

The pretend-insider is another step removed from the fringe-insider and is in the "friend of a friend" category. By the time the pretend-insider gets the information, the upswing or downswing may have long since occurred. Beware of pretend-insiders.

Trading on inside information is illegal. It's not supposed to happen, but it does, and the Securities and Exchange Commission admits that enforcement of their insider-information rules is extremely difficult. Even though certain insiders are required to report their buy and sell transactions, it is still very difficult to discover and prove wrongdoing. Illegal though it may be, and successful or unsuccessful though it may be, it does exert a distinct effect on specific stocks and, to a lesser extent, on the market as a whole.

Hunch Players

Often active seasoned veterans of the stock market, hunch players may be convinced that all the study in the world is for naught because the quirks and whims of fellow investors are imponderable and have a greater effect on the value of any given stock than the true value of the company itself. Hunch players listen avidly to tipsters. Much of their trading is based on gut reaction, a voice in the night, an omen.

Theory Traders

Theory traders base their transactions on specific theories that may be directly tied to something as tangible as governmental statistics or as intangible as international currency fluctuations. Theory traders can be very influential when their theories prove correct; however, they also have a way of

disappearing temporarily when their theories prove incorrect. Many theory traders are often found reading stock market advisory newsletters, generally the wellspring of their information and decisions. Because they paid a steep price for these advisory letters, they assume the information has to be correct—otherwise it wouldn't be so expensive.

Sentimentalists

This well-intentioned group of investors place their money in stocks of companies that they work for or that are located in their hometowns. Sentimentality or loyalty will be their primary reason for investing. Emotionally, it's like rooting for the home team, but rationally this can amount to nothing more than total speculation.

Technical Analysts

Technical analysts (sometimes called *chartists*) are serious students of the stock market. Technical analysts closely follow and chart short-, medium-, and long-term trends in individual stocks, in groups of stocks, and in the market movement as a whole. They have come up with a dazzling array of indicators that supposedly give signals to buy and sell. There are market peaks and market troughs; there are bellwether stocks that purportedly lead the way to one direction or another; high ratios and low ratios; moving averages; overbought and oversold indexes; and charts that plot every conceivable squiggle a given stock may be subject to.

But, in spite of all the information available, the problem is that the meticulously plotted signals of the analysts are often invalidated by the actions of other traders who pay no attention to these signals. Furthermore, the analysts don't necessarily agree with each other as to which signal means what, and often come up with conflicting conclusions.

Fundamentalists

Fundamentalists are serious investors who have done their homework and are willing to continue to do the necessary homework: Analyze profit-and-loss statements, dividend-payment records, the amount a company has earned on its invested capital, profit margins, the ratio of a company's assets to its liabilities and debts, and the trends in the company's overall performance over recent years, as well as the health and growth trends of the industry as it relates to the economy as a whole. Fundamentalists have learned how to evaluate the financial statements of the companies they are interested in, and how to seek out the basic value of each company. Fundamentalists are not necessarily frequent traders; they are willing to wait years for the value of a stock to prove itself in terms of price appreciation and dividend payments. They realize that market decisions are subject to

the actions of all the other types of investors but feel confident that their prudent and rational analysis of the facts at hand will survive the whims and flutters caused by other types of investors.

Fundamentalists know that there's no such thing as a sure thing in the stock market but they are willing to take the time necessary to find the best things available.

Fundamentalists shun advice from tipsters, don't rely on hunches, aren't seduced by sentimentality, and won't subscribe to any theories not borne out by accurate financial analysis of the specific companies of interest.

Prudent Investors

Prudent investors are the fundamentalists-plus. Plus what? Perhaps a bit of technical analyst, for many of the analytical devices can be helpful in the fundamentalist approach. Perhaps also a bit of the hunch player, for even the most prudent investor occasionally needs the guts that is second nature to the hunch player to survive unexpected turns for the worse. Prudent investors also have most of the following attributes.

- Prudent investors have a clear understanding of their current financial situation and overall investment objectives. They convey this understanding to their stockbroker and make a joint commitment with the broker to stick with the stated objectives. If prudent investors want the benefit of the broker's expertise, they must give the broker proper instructions. Without that basic understanding between investor and broker, both may be groping in the dark. Periodically, with a broker's aid, prudent investors review their objectives and determine whether they are still reasonable in view of the unpredictable nature of the stock market.

- Prudent investors clearly define their own roles. Are they investors or traders? Investors, broadly speaking, are putting their money to work and are willing to let it do the job over the needed span of time. Traders are working their money and must have the know-how to cope with weekly, daily, and hourly fluctuations and trends. Prudent investors can be a little bit of both, but to perform this balancing act, they must keep their more prudent investment funds and more speculative trading funds strictly segregated. When the two start to mingle, objectives can swiftly get derailed.

- Prudent investors do their homework. Investment decisions are ultimately the investor's, not the broker's. There are thousands of securities, no two alike, and no human being can keep track of the fine points of more than a few dozen at a time. A broker can give the investors research tools and an opinion, but investors must reach their own conclusions. And sound conclusions require work.

- Prudent investors avoid the quirk of human nature that drives people to want to recover losses as quickly as they have occurred. This can lead an investor out of one speculative situation into another.

- Prudent investors learn from past mistakes. Why did they buy or sell too soon or too late? Did they listen to a tip? Did they play a hunch? Did they panic? The ability to recognize one's own mistakes and benefit from them is a rare quality, one worth cultivating by the prudent investor who doesn't already possess it.

- When prudent investors invest in a stock, they determine, at that time, when they will be likely to sell. They set limits for themselves and stick to them. They have determined how great a loss they are willing to take in order to acquire a certain gain. They are well acquainted with that old maxim of the investment community: "Take your profits when you can, and cut your losses when you can."

- Prudent investors are well aware of the value of a good night's sleep. Or, for that matter, of a good day's work. Distractions and frustrations caused by involvement in the stock market can detract from one's productivity and pleasures.

- Prudent investors do not waste time or money chasing after systems that purport to "beat the market." There are none. And there aren't any books, brokers, newsletters, analysts, chartists, economists, or tipsters who know anything more about where the market is headed than you do. If there were, we'd have heard about them long ago.

STRATEGIES FOR SUCCESS

Put Your Money Where Your Knowledge Is

You want to take a fling in the stock market, but you don't know where to begin in choosing stocks. How about picking companies that specialize in an area of your own knowledge? Your field is chemistry—why not choose chemical company stocks? Your hobby is photography—consider photographic companies. You have a good background in Asian matters—maybe you should invest in a mutual fund that specializes in Asian companies. That's the basic idea: Put your money where your knowledge is. As somewhat of a specialist, you're better equipped to evaluate the potential of a company, or of a group of companies, that deal in a subject you're familiar with. It can make sense, can't it? At least you have a better chance of success than you might if you knew nothing at all about the company whose stock you chose to buy.

BASIC STOCK MARKET INFORMATION

The daily trading activity of all the major stock exchanges is contained in alphabetical order in fairly complete detail in *The Wall Street Journal* each day.

Price Quotations

Exercise 15.5

Many local daily newspapers also carry extensive listings, though many are abbreviated from the full listings used in *The Wall Street Journal*.

Figure 15–1 shows a sample New York Stock Exchange listing. Let's examine the details more closely. The listing is "AbtLab," which stands for Abbott Laboratories, a major manufacturer of various health-care products. (All companies traded on the exchange carry an abbreviation or trading symbol. Abbott's is ABT.)

- **52 Weeks High/Low**   This listing indicates that during the previous fifty-two weeks, Abbott Laboratories sold at a high of 68 ($68) per share and a low of 42.2 ($42.20) per share. The purpose of the high/low listings is to give you some idea as to the stock's recent trading history. This recent trading range may reflect the likely pattern of the next few months. But beyond that short-term outlook the past history offers no assurances as to the price of the stock over the longer haul.

- **Dividend (Div.)**   The <u>dividend</u> column indicates the rate of dividend paid based on the most recent quarterly dividend. It is not necessarily an indication of dividends that will be paid in the future. Abbott Laboratories paid a dividend in the prior year of 1.08, that is, $1.08 per share. An investor would have to dig more deeply to determine the likelihood of any company's continuing its indicated rate of dividend for the near future.

- **Yield % (Yld)**   This listing indicates the yield, in percentage terms, that you would receive if you bought the stock at its current price (64) and received the dividend of $1.08; $1.08 is roughly 1.7 percent of $64.

52 weeks		Stock	Div.	Yld. %	P.E. Ratio	Sales 100s	High	Low	Close	Net Chg.
High	Low									
68	42.2	AbtLab ABT	1.08	1.7	2.5	12209	65	63	64	+1

FIGURE 15–1   Sample newspaper listing of stock quotation

Dividends

Exercise 15.7

A <u>dividend</u> is that portion of a company's profit paid out to its owners, the stockholders. In some instances, a corporation may issue additional shares of stock as a form of dividend. This is known as a stock dividend, and the recipient is free to sell these shares or keep them.

The value of a dividend is usually referred to as the yield. The yield is the percentage return you're getting on your money, and it's figured very simply by dividing the stock's annual dividend by its price. If a stock is selling at $50 per share and it pays an annual dividend of $2 per share, its *apparent* yield is 4 percent (2 divided by 50 equals 0.04). We use the word *apparent* because the yield does not take into account the commission you'll have to pay when you buy or sell the stock. The commissions must be considered in order to come up with a more accurate yield figure.

Furthermore, if you don't hold the stock for a full annual cycle, you won't receive the apparent yield. For example, say the $50 stock paid its dividend quarterly on the first day of January, April, July, and October. It would pay 50 cents for each share four times a year, for a total of $2. If you bought the stock on January 2 and sold it during the subsequent December, you'd have received only three of the four dividend payments, or $1.50, even though you had held the stock for almost twelve full months. You would not have received the first dividend, payable on January 1, because you were not a stockholder "of record" on the date called for. In such a case, your yield would be only 3 percent, before the payment of both commissions.

Dividend payments are announced, or *declared*, by the board of directors of the company at its regular meetings. Here's how it works: At their February meeting, the board of directors of XYZ Company declares that it will pay a dividend on April 1 to stockholders "of record" as of March 5. If you are recorded on the books of the corporation as being a stockholder as of March 5, you'll be entitled to receive the April 1 dividend even though you sell your stock between March 5 and April 1. The time lag gives the company enough time to get an accurate list of all its stockholders so that checks can be prepared and other necessary bookwork done.

Ex-dividend Date

Continuing with the preceding example, what if you instructed your broker to buy XYZ stock on March 2? Would you be entitled to the dividend? Probably not. It usually takes four or five days from the time of an order until you are officially registered on the books of a corporation as an owner of the stock. Thus, the stock exchanges, in listing dividends payable on stocks, generally note that a stock is <u>ex-dividend</u> about four or five days prior to the *record* date. When a stock is quoted ex-dividend, it means that if you buy the stock at that time, you *won't* get the next dividend that has been declared by the company. XYZ might be quoted as ex-dividend on March 1—

five days before the record date. Anybody who buys the stock from March 1 onward will not receive the dividend payable in April.

Prudent investors, particularly those bargaining for a known return on invested capital, pay close attention to the history of dividend payments of any company they're thinking of investing in. These records can be found in the Moody's and Standard & Poor's guides or obtained directly from the broker. Some companies have long histories of regular dividends, many of which increase periodically as earnings increase. Companies that pay small dividends or no dividends, or that pay erratically, tend to fall into the speculative category of investment. The steady dividend payers constitute more conservative investments.

Unlike the movement of a stock's price, which is subject to countless and often indefinable pressures, the dividend payment rate is generally well rooted in the company's earnings and in its willingness to spread those earnings out among its stockholders. Earnings that are not distributed to stockholders are retained by the company (and are referred to as retained earnings) for investment within the company itself. Those retained earnings may be used as a cushion against troublesome economic times or to create new facilities, which in turn can create new jobs and new products, which can create additional earnings for stockholders.

Commissions

Exercise 15.8

Brokerage commissions are the fees you pay to brokerage firms for handling your transactions when you buy and sell stock. The commission you pay on any given transaction depends on the number of shares, the price of the shares, and possibly the total amount of business you do with a given broker in the course of a year. Full-service brokerage firms, which provide research and other facilities to their customers, charge higher commissions than discount brokers, who provide very little service other than the execution of orders. Table 15–1 illustrates a range of commissions charged by various types of brokerage firms.

TABLE 15–1 Sampling of Brokerage Commissions on Stock Transactions

	100 Shares @ $40	300 Shares @ $30
Discount broker A	$42	$ 62
Discount broker B	47	89
Full-service broker A	84	191
Full-service broker B	80	176
Full-service broker C	70	158

Abuses exist in all industries, and the securities industry is no exception. A common abuse, called churning, occurs when a broker convinces an investor to buy and sell securities much more often than is justifiable, generating large commissions for the broker, possibly to the detriment of the investor's account. Prudent investors have, in all likelihood, committed themselves to ride with their investments for a protracted period of time and do not succumb to churning.

Long and Short

When investors buy stock, hoping for an increase in value as well as receipt of dividends, they are buying long. This is the most common type of transaction, constituting the vast majority of all trades on the exchanges.

But what if an investor thinks a stock will go down in value? There is a technique called selling short that enables an investor to seek a profit as a stock declines in value.

Selling short is a sophisticated and risky transaction. Here's how it works. Let's say you think that XYZ, which is now selling at $10 per share, is due to slump in price. You want to bet that it will decline.

In effect, you borrow 100 shares from your broker and you sell them on the open market at the $10 price. You now have $1,000 cash in hand (before commissions), and you owe your broker 100 shares of XYZ.

If the stock then dipped to, say, $6 per share, you buy 100 shares at the going market price, for $600, and return the 100 shares to your broker. You took in $1,000, then paid out $600, so you're $400 ahead as a result—again, before commissions.

The broker usually obtains the "borrowed" stock from the brokerage firm's supply of customers' stock, which the firm is holding. You, as the short seller, must have cash or unmargined stock in your account before you can initiate a short sale. This is to assure the broker that you have available funds to repay the stock you've borrowed from him, and those funds are effectively tied up during the life of the transaction.

The element of risk involved in short selling can indeed be frightening. On a regular, or long, transaction, your ultimate loss is limited. If you bought XYZ long at $10 per share, and XYZ goes bankrupt, you can lose only the $10 per share. That's it. It can't go any lower than zero.

But if you sell a stock short at $10 per share, and it goes up instead of down, your loss can run on indefinitely. Say you bought 100 shares short at $10, and then the stock runs up to $50 per share. If you wanted to get out then, you'd have to shell out $5,000 to buy enough to pay back your broker the shares you owe him, for a net loss of $4,000. If you decide to wait, hoping for a drop, and it goes up another $10 to $60 per share, your loss is even greater. Such run-ups may be rare, but the risk is there.

One further problem with selling short: If you're holding stock in a long

position, you receive any dividends the stock pays. But if you're in a short position, you are obliged to pay the dividends to the broker since, technically, you owe him the stock. This can add to your losses or cut into your hoped-for gains.

Prudent investors would not be comfortable with short selling.

Buying on Margin

Buying on margin is a means of buying stock on credit. The rate of margin, or credit available, varies from time to time, depending on overall economic conditions throughout the nation and the condition of the stock market. The Federal Reserve Board sets the margin rate. If the margin rate is 40 percent, you can buy stock by putting up only 40 percent of the total purchase price. The remaining 60 percent you borrow from the broker, using the stock as collateral for the loan. Say that XYZ is selling at $30 per share, and you want to buy 100 shares. The margin rate at the time is 40 percent. You can thus buy $3,000 worth of XYZ by putting up $1,200 in cash and borrowing the remaining $1,800 from the broker. Let's say, further, that, at the time, the interest rate you'll pay your broker on the margin account is 10 percent, which means that, during the course of the year, you'll owe him $180 in interest on the $1,800 margin loan.

If XYZ goes to $35 per share at the end of one year and you sell, you have realized a profit of $500, less the $180 in interest, for a gain (before commissions) of $320. But you've invested only $1,200 of your own cash at the outset, so your return of $320 is equivalent to a yield of 26.7 percent for the year, not counting commissions or dividends. If you had invested the full $3,000 and realized a $500 gain, your rate of return would have been 16.7 percent before commissions. This is what's known as leverage. The gain on a sale and the rate of return on the dividends are magnified by the fact that you have less of your own money at work for you.

However, margin buying can be very dangerous, particularly if the stock declines in value. If you had purchased XYZ normally—that is, unmargined—for $30 per share, or $3,000, and it dipped to $25 per share, you'd have a loss of $500. But if you bought it on the margin account, your loss would be increased by the amount of interest you would have to pay on the loan. In our example, your total loss would come to $680.

If your loan with the broker exceeds the limit, that is, 60 percent of the market value of the stock, you will get what is known as a margin call. On the $3,000 transaction, the margin loan of $1,800 was permissible. But if the total value of the stock bought on margin falls to, say, $2,000, the amount of the broker's loan cannot exceed $1,200. If that should happen, the broker will call you to tell you to come up with $600 in extra cash, or additional collateral. If you fail to do so, the broker can sell your stock at a loss in order to recoup what you owe. As a result of these possibilities, trading on margin must be viewed as a highly speculative activity.

Stock Splits and Stock Dividends

Occasionally, a company issues a stock dividend to its stockholders. This may be instead of, or in addition to, a cash dividend. For example, if a company declares a 10 percent stock dividend, it will give all its stockholders one share of additional stock for each ten shares already owned. A 100 percent stock dividend means that stockholders will get one new share for every one already owned. In effect, this doubles the amount of shares of stock outstanding. Frequently, companies will continue to pay the same amount of dividend in dollars after a stock dividend. This has the effect of increasing the return to the investor, who has more shares of stock earning dividends.

Table 15–2 illustrates the before-and-after status of a 10 percent stock dividend. In this case, the effect of the stock dividend is to increase the value of the investment and the dividend income—assuming that the stock retains its pre-dividend market value.

A company splits its stock when it wishes to get more shares of stock out into the marketplace, and also perhaps to bring the price of the stock down into a more attractive range. For example, a two-for-one stock split means that you end up owning two shares of stock for every one you had owned originally. Generally, though, when a stock is split, its price is split accordingly, as is its dividend. If a stock was selling for $50 per share and was paying a $2 per year dividend, it would, after a two-for-one split, probably sell for $25 per share, and the dividend would be $1 per share. Thus, your actual net worth as an owner of that stock will not necessarily change as a result of the split.

Table 15–3 illustrates the effects of a 100 percent stock split.

A stock split is often taken as a favorable sign; investors are anxious to buy shares, and when the price has been effectively lowered, more investors will be able to get involved with the company. A buying surge often tends to boost the value of a stock. Thus, a stock split is viewed by traders as a sign of a possible upswing in a given stock. Often this is the case, but it is not necessarily so. Sometimes there are rumors of a stock split, but the split may never actually occur. This can cause wild gyrations in the value of a given stock.

TABLE 15–2   **10 Percent Stock Divided—Before and After**

	Before	After
You own	100 shares	110 shares
Current value per share	$ 50	$ 50
Current total value	5,000	5,500
Annual dividend per share	5	5
Total dividend income per year	500	550

TABLE 15–3   **100 Percent Stock Split — Before and After**

	Before	After
You own	100 shares	200 shares
Current price per share	$ 50	$ 25
Total value	5,000	5,000
Dividend per share	5	2.50
Total dividend income per year	500	500

Preferred Stocks

Preferred stock is a separate class of stock from common stock, which has been the type under discussion up to this point. If a company has bonds outstanding, the bondholders have to be paid before any dividends can be paid to any common stockholders. If a company also has preferred stock outstanding, the holders of the preferred stock also are entitled to preference over the common stockholders. This is the meaning of the term *preferred*. In other words, if a corporation has bonds *and* preferred stock *and* common stock outstanding, the bondholders are first paid the interest due them, then the preferred stockholders are paid their dividends, and then the common stockholders receive their dividends.

Preferred stock generally pays a higher rate of return on dividends than common stock, and preferred stock is less subject to fluctuation than common stock. For these reasons, preferred stocks tend to appeal more to conservative and relatively sophisticated investors.

In stock listings, preferreds are indicated by a "PF" following the name of the company.

Cumulative Preferred

Most preferred stocks are *cumulative*. This means that unpaid dividends will accumulate and that the preferred shareholders must be paid in full on all back unpaid dividends before common stockholders can be paid any of their dividends. For example, a company has preferred stock outstanding, on which it has set a fixed dividend rate of $3 per share. The dividend rate on its common stock has been $2 per share. The company runs into hard times and for three years pays no dividends. In the fourth year, it realizes a healthy profit. Before common stockholders can receive any dividends, the preferred shareholders must be paid $9 for each of their shares for the accumulated back dividends that had not been paid.

Convertible Preferred

Like convertible bonds, noted in chapter 14, convertible preferred stock may be converted into shares of the company's common stock at an agreed-on ratio. And, as with convertible bonds, the price of convertible preferred stock tends to fluctuate in tandem with the common stock, but the fluctuations are generally not as great as with the common stock. Thus, convertible preferreds are considered to offer attractive advantages: a relatively high rate of return on one's investment (from the dividends paid on the preferred stock); a chance to convert into the common stock if the common stock starts to rise rapidly; and a downside cushion of protection since the preferred stock will tend not to drop as rapidly or as deeply as the common stock might if prices begin to fall.

Convertibles are a sophisticated area of investing that require further study. Ample literature is available from most brokerage firms.

Warrants

On occasion, when a company is issuing bonds or new shares of stock, it may offer warrants to purchasers as an extra inducement to get them to invest. The warrant entitles them to purchase shares of common stock at a fixed price for a set period of time. In other words, if the common stock is selling at $20 per share at the time the bonds or new shares are issued, the warrant might entitle the holder to acquire a share of common stock at $25. The issuing company will fix the life of the warrant, which may be a few months or a number of years.

Warrants are totally speculative. Owners of warrants have no ownership in the corporation unless or until they exercise the warrants—that is, trade them in for the shares of stock to which they are entitled. Owners of warrants receive no dividends and have no voting rights in the company.

XYZ has issued warrants to buy its stock at $25 a share. You like XYZ, but you don't have $2,500 with which to buy 100 shares. You watch XYZ stock move to $27 a share, and you're confident that it will climb to $35 a share within the next twelve months. You buy 100 warrants at $2 per share for a total investment of $200. As the stock of XYZ climbs, so will the value of the warrants. Essentially, for every $1 increase in the value of the stock itself, the warrants will also increase by $1. Thus, if XYZ does reach a higher level, such as $35 a share, the value of the warrant may have increased from your $2 buying price to $8. You will have reaped a gain on the stock without having had to purchase the stock itself. The warrants did the job for you. However, there is an ultimate danger with warrants: they expire at a designated time. Once they expire, they are worthless. If the stock doesn't rise as you had hoped it would, neither will the warrant. The stock you can

keep owning forever. But the warrant becomes worthless at its expiration date. Trading in warrants is highly speculative. There are comparable opportunities in trading in stock options, which are explained in the next section.

Stock Option Trading

Trading in stock options is a sophisticated form of investing that can range from highly speculative to staunchly conservative. We will now examine the basic concepts of stock option trading, and readers who find the technique appealing will want to seek further information from stockbrokers about specific option-trading possibilities.

Placing a Bet

There are two main ways to gamble at the racetrack. First, you can buy a horse and enter it in races. If your horse wins, you receive the winner's purse. If the horse never wins, you can recoup some of your investment by selling it or using it for breeding purposes. In other words, even if your initial gamble never pays off (the horse never wins), the horse still has some residual value.

Second, you can place bets on other people's horses. The life of your bet will be approximately two minutes—the time it takes to run the race. If the horse you bet on wins, you win. If the horse you bet on loses, your betting ticket is instantly and permanently worthless. In short, there is no residual value on the bet.

The situation is very similar in the stock market: there are two basic ways you can gamble. First, you can buy stock and hope that it increases in value. If it does and you sell the stock, you have won. If the stock does not go up, there is still some residual value in the dividends you will receive and in the selling price you get for it at some later date.

Second, you can place a bet that the stock will increase in value. You can do this without actually having to buy the stock itself. You place your bet by buying what is known as an *option*. An option, in effect, is a bet on the stock. And like a bet on a horse, the option has a limited life, after which it will become worthless.

Option trading is to stock trading what horse betting is to horse owning. Let's take an oversimplified look at how it works.

Calls and Puts

The most common type of option trading is betting that a given stock will increase in value. Technically, this is known as a <u>call option</u>. It is also possible to bet that a stock will decrease in value. You can place such a bet by

buying what is known as a put option. For purposes of this discussion and for the sake of clarity, we'll restrict the material to call options.

Buying Call Options

Table 15–4 is a simplified sample of a call option quotation in the newspaper.

This quotation refers to call option trading in the stock of the XYZ Company. As the columns on the far left indicate, the actual price per share of XYZ common stock closed the preceding day at $41 on the New York Stock Exchange. The rest of the quote illustrates nine potential "bets" that can be placed on the future of XYZ's stock.

Look at the bottom line under Strike Price—the entry is 45. Let's assume that we are now in late November. You have a hunch that XYZ will rise from its current level of $41 per share to $45 per share by next January. You'd like to bet on your hunch. You can do so by buying the stock itself, but buying 100 shares will cost you $4,100.

Or, you can buy a call option. A call option gives you the right to buy the stock at a given price (known as the *strike price*) by a certain date, which is usually the third Friday of the month indicated. The price you pay for a call option is known as the *premium*. As Table 15–4 indicates, you can buy a call option that gives you the right to purchase XYZ at $45 per share any time between now and the third Friday of next January for $2 per share. Contracts are sold in 100-share lots, so a 100-share option contract would cost you $200.

Your objective here is not necessarily to buy the stock (although you do have that right). What you are really hoping for is to sell the call option contract at a profit. As the stock moves up (or down) the value of the call option moves accordingly.

If you bought 100 shares of the stock for $4,100 and it moved up to $4,500 by January, you'd have reaped a profit of $400 (before commissions). If you bought a 100-share call option contract for $200 and XYZ moved to $45 per share by, say, December, the value of the option would have increased by $4 per share, or $400 for 100 shares, to roughly $600, and you'd have a $400 profit (again before commissions) on a bet of only $200.

TABLE 15–4   Call Option Trading: Sample Quotation

Stock	NY Close	Strike Price	Jan. Premium	Apr. Premium	July Premium
XYZ	41	35	7	8	9
XYZ	41	40	3½	4½	5
XYZ	41	45	2	3	4

But note this critical difference: If you had bought the stock and the price did *not* rise, you would *still own* the stock *indefinitely*, and you'd still be entitled to any dividends the stock paid. However, with the option, if the bet doesn't work out, the option expires at the established date and you own nothing after that time.

Let's say you weren't quite as optimistic about XYZ going to $45 per share by January, but you thought it might reach that level before the following April. In that case, you could buy an option for a premium of $3 per share, or $300 for a 100-share contract. If you wanted to have until July to see whether the price moved up, a 100-share contract would cost $400. The longer the life of the option, the higher the price. This is because you have more time for the stock to reach the desired level. In effect, you're paying an added premium for the extra time.

Buying call options is highly speculative. Once you've bought an option, you receive no dividends on your invested money and the clock is running against you: The option becomes valueless at the expiration date. It's like the betting ticket on the horse that didn't finish in the money.

Selling Call Options

Who do racetrack bettors buy their bets *from*? They buy them from the racetrack owners, who have very carefully calculated that they will keep a portion of every bet for their own overhead and profit (not to mention taxes). For every dollar that is bet, the racetrack may pay back only about 80 cents in winnings to the bettors. Over the days and months and years, the track knows that it can't lose. That's why it's better to own a racetrack than to bet at one. The same philosophy holds true with call option trading: it's better to sell call options than to buy them.

From whom do option buyers buy their contracts? They buy them from option *sellers*—people who already own the given shares of stock and who are willing to sell them to buyers at a specific price.

Referring back to the quotations, let's assume that you had purchased 100 shares of XYZ some time ago for $35 per share. You've been happy with the stock and with the dividends it has paid, yet you'd be willing to part with the stock if it hit $45 per share. That would mean a $10 per share profit to you.

The option exchanges offer you intriguing possibilities. As the quotations indicate, you, as the owner of XYZ, can sell someone else the right to buy your 100 shares any time between now and next January, and you'll receive a $200 premium in exchange. Or you can sell an April contract for $300 and a July contract for $400. If you sell a call option and it is never exercised, you get to keep the whole premium. You also get to keep any dividends that are paid on the stock during the life of the option. That's like the racetrack keeping a portion of each bet for its own purposes. If the option is exercised, you must give up your stock at the strike price—$45 per share in

the current example. But you have expressed a willingness to do that—to take a $10 per share profit—as part of your overall investment philosophy. If the option is not exercised, you can sell yet another one and keep the premium. If the option is exercised and you give up the stock, you have the $4,500 to reinvest as you see fit. (None of these examples takes brokerage commissions into account.)

As this example indicates, selling call options can be a sound and secure way for owners of stocks to increase their return substantially without increasing their risk. As long as you are willing to let go of your stock at a fixed higher price than you paid for it, you literally have everything to gain and nothing to lose by selling call options on stocks you already own. If you plan to make new investments on stocks for the purpose of selling options against those stocks, you of course take on yourself the basic risk inherent in any stock investment: the potential fluctuations in value that could work for or against you. Since this discussion was intended as nothing more than a brief overview of option-trading possibilities, interested investors should seek further information on specific techniques from their stockbroker.

Rating the Stocks

Like bonds, stocks are ranked and rated by both Standard & Poor's and Moody's. The following excerpts from the Standard & Poor's explanation of their rating system not only is informational but also serves as a guide to the prudent investor in quest of the relative value of stocks within the broad selection available.

Earnings and dividends rankings for stocks: The relative "quality" of common stocks cannot be measured, as is the quality of bonds, in terms of the degree of protection for principal and dividends. Nevertheless, the investment process obviously involves the assessment of numerous factors—such as product and industry position, the multifaceted aspects of managerial capability, corporate financial policy and resources—that make some common stocks more highly esteemed than others.

Earnings and dividends performance is the end result of the interplay of these factors, and thus over the long run the record of this performance has a considerable bearing on relative quality. Growth and stability of earnings and dividends are therefore the key elements of Standard & Poor's common stock rankings, which are designed to capsulize the nature of this record in a single symbol. The rankings, however, do not pretend to reflect all other factors, tangible and intangible, that also bear on stock quality.

The Standard & Poor's rankings for common stocks are as follows:

A+	Highest
A	High
A−	Good
B+	Medium

B	Speculative
B−	Highly speculative
C	Marginal
D	In reorganization

Refer to the respective ratings themselves for more detail and information on this important aspect of evaluating one's investment alternatives.

Dividend Reinvestment Plans

Exercise 15.9

Dividends are usually paid to stockholders quarterly. If you own 100 shares of XYZ and it is paying a dividend of $5 per share, you will receive a total of $500 in dividends during the year, in quarterly checks of $125. That money is yours to spend or to reinvest. But many investors get lazy about reinvesting their dividend earnings and spend the money on nonessentials. This can erode the potential size of their nest egg.

Many companies offer an alternative to sending quarterly dividend checks. They offer automatic dividend reinvestment plans in which your dividend is used to purchase additional shares of stock in the company. If an investor wishes to acquire additional shares at no out-of-pocket cost the dividend reinvestment plan is an ideal way to proceed. There are some special advantages to the automatic dividend reinvestment plans, depending on the specific company. Brokerage commissions are very low or nonexistent. If your dividend check is not sufficient to buy a full share of stock, fractional shares can be purchased. And some companies even offer a discount on the purchase price as compared to the going market price.

Companies that offer automatic dividend reinvestment plans notify stockholders of the availability. To sign up, the investor merely fills out the form sent by the company. From that point on, dividends are reinvested automatically, and customers receive a quarterly statement of the account. The company retains the actual additional shares purchased, and the investor can cash them in at any time by notifying the company.

Here is how a dividend reinvestment plan can work. You own 100 shares of XYZ with a value of $50 per share and an annual dividend of $5 per share. Assume, for the sake of this illustration, that the price of the stock and the amount of the dividend do not vary over the years. As you can see (Table 15–5), in the first year, your 100 shares will earn $500 worth of dividends. Those dividends in turn will buy ten additional shares of stock, giving you a total of 110 shares going to work for you at the start of the second year. In the fourth year, you would have earned $665.50 in dividends on your original investment of $5,000. Your return has increased because you have more shares working for you earning dividends. The automatic dividend reinvestment plan does for your stockholding what compounding interest does for your money market investments.

TABLE 15–5 **Dividend Reinvestment Plan**

	100 Shares of XYZ, Value $50 per Share, Dividend $5			
Year	Shares Owned Start of Year	Dividend Earned	Buys This Many New Shares	This Many Total Shares by Year End
1	100	$500	10	110
2	110	550	11	121
3	121	605	12.1	133.1
4	133.1	665.50	13.31	146.41

Following is a brief list of some of the many hundreds of companies that have offered dividend reinvestment plans. Check with a stockbroker to determine the current status of available plans.

Allied Chemical	Exxon	PepsiCo
AT&T	General Electric	RCA
Bristol-Myers	General Motors	Sears
CBS, Inc.	Goodyear Tire	Texaco
DuPont (E.I.)	IBM	USX
Eastman Kodak	Mobil Corp.	Xerox

PRICE AND VALUE: WHAT CAN AFFECT THE WORTH OF A STOCK?

The distinction between *price* and *value* is as important in the stock market as in any other form of commerce. A patch of barren land in the middle of the desert may sell at a very low price, say, $10 an acre, because it seems to have no value. But if there is oil hiding under that patch of land, the *value* can be astronomically high, even though the price was very low.

On the other hand, that same barren patch may have absolutely no value—no oil or anything else hidden beneath it. But a fast-talking pitchman can sell the land to a gullible investor as the site of a future oil well. In that case, the price may be astronomically high in comparison with the value.

Whenever we spend money we try to make sure that we're getting good value for it; that value and price are compatible.

In the stock market, we have to maintain the same vigil, for the price and value of a stock can very easily take off in opposite directions. We might speculate on a stock with little intrinsic value, but, because of a speculative fever, the price of the stock may jump and reap a bonanza. Or we may invest in a stock with sturdy and dependable values only to find that a

reverse form of speculation has condemned the stock to a severe plunge, and our money with it.

Many factors can have a direct effect on the *value* of a given stock as well as on the *price*.

Value

The underlying value of a stock is related to the profitability of the company in selling its product and services to its customers. The essential factors involved are the expertise of management; the cost of its raw materials (which can be affected by weather conditions, labor costs, strikes, and delivery problems); its efficiency in producing its finished product from the raw materials (which can likewise be affected by the foregoing elements of labor, weather, and gremlins); and the efficiency with which it delivers the finished product to the market, at a price and in a package the public is willing to accept.

With a great many of our major companies now involved in global commerce, international factors must also be considered. These can include fluctuations in currencies between various nations, international politics, trade and tariff regulations, and the same unpredictability regarding weather and labor strife that we have in the United States, but compounded by distance and difficulty in communicating.

Price

Following are some of the important elements that, although they do not affect the underlying *value* of the company, can have a distinct bearing on the *price* of the stock.

- When a new issue of stock is being offered to the public, the salesmanship of the brokerage firm can have a bearing on the price of the stock. Persuasive salespersons can boost the price of new issues far beyond the true value of the stock. If a new stock is issued when the market is not receptive, even the best salesperson may not be able to prevent a sharp downturn in the value of the stock.
- The general health and outlook of the national economy can give a boost to the market as a whole, and sometimes to specific stocks, or it can have a depressing effect if the news is bad.
- Financial analysts periodically examine major listed companies to try to determine the true valuation of the company. Optimistic reports can have a positive effect on the price of a stock, and pessimistic ones can have a depressing effect. Minor errors or misstatements in these reports can also have a dramatic effect on the price of the stock.

- A large investor may be persuaded to make a substantial investment in a company. A major investment could inspire optimism in other investors. On the other hand, if a major investor pulls out of a situation, for whatever reason, this could result in pessimism. Either action can affect the price, at least for the short term.

- One of the great imponderables is competition. The threat of formidable competition can have a depressing effect on the stock of a given company; the fading of competition can have a buoyant effect.

- Merger mania can have a powerful effect on the prices of many stocks. XYZ, an electronics firm, announces that it plans to buy, or merge with, PDQ, a telecommunications firm. This signals that PDQ might be up for grabs—*in play* is the term Wall Streeters use—and that a bidding war may take place for PDQ, boosting its shares' prices. If investors think that such a merger would be good or bad for either XYZ or PDQ, the prices thereof can rise or fall sharply as a result. A not-infrequent side effect to the XYZ–PDQ merger is that investors might sense that other telecommunications firms will also become buyout targets, and the stock prices of those companies can be affected accordingly.

- The rumor mill is a potentially troublesome source of information (or misinformation) that can affect the price of a stock. Wall Street is a tight little community, and word gets around fast. The day-to-day ebb and flow of rumors is perhaps one of the most prevalent forces in shaping the daily fluctuations of the market.

MUTUAL FUNDS IN THE STOCK MARKET

Stock market mutual funds pool the dollars of many small investors and place them in a broad portfolio of various stocks. Thousands of mutual funds offer a wide variety of choices to the investor. The objective of *performance* funds is to create as rapid a growth pattern as possible. These funds tend to be more speculative, taking chances on stocks that fund management sees as having a quick short-term potential rise. *Growth* funds are geared more to long-term steady growth, with less emphasis on dividend income. *Income* funds are designed to generate maximum current dividend income. *Growth/income funds* attempt to achieve a balance between growth and income factors.

The primary task of the investor seeking mutual funds as a vehicle is to determine whether the fund's objectives are in line with his or her own: short-term growth, long-term growth, income, or a combination of these. These objectives are spelled out in the fund prospectus, which should be read before any investment decision is made.

See the discussion of mutual funds in chapter 14, in which some of their major features are described in detail.

Once a group of appropriate funds is selected, investors must review the factors that can shape their investment future: costs involved in buying into the fund, annual charges for management or maintenance, the history of the fund in meeting its stated objectives, and so on.

Sales costs (loading fees) vary considerably with stock mutual funds, from as much as 8½ percent of the investment to as little as zero (no load). Similarly, annual or monthly maintenance and management fees vary considerably. In many cases, load funds (those with a sales charge) may charge smaller annual fees than no-load funds do, and proponents of the load funds claim that this difference over the long pull offsets the initial commission factor. There is heated debate over which is better—load funds or no-load funds. Proponents of each side can find specific groups of funds over specific periods of time in which their viewpoint prevailed. There is no simple answer. Like the stock market itself, there's an element of speculation even in choosing one *type* of fund over another.

Mutual funds are quoted daily in *The Wall Street Journal* and *Investor's Business Daily,* as well as in many local daily newspapers, weekly in *Barron's,* and annually in *Forbes* magazine. *Forbes* devotes an entire issue (usually in August) to the mutual fund industry. It rates the funds based on their performance in general up and down markets, giving a perceptive analysis of how various funds have performed during periods of boom and adversity. Other good rating services are "Investment Companies," by A. Weisenberger and Morningstar.

The daily listings of mutual funds quote the net asset value (NAV), the offering price, and the net asset value change. The net asset value of a mutual fund is the actual value per share. It's arrived at by dividing the total assets of the fund by the total number of shares outstanding. If a fund has $10 million in total assets and 1 million shares outstanding, the net asset value per share will be $10.

The offering price is the price an investor would have to pay for shares in a particular fund. If the fund is a no-load fund, "N.L." may be indicated in the offering price. If the fund is a load fund, the offering price will be higher than the net asset value price, with the difference being the commission charges. For example, a fund may show a net asset value (NAV) of $12.68, and an offering price of $13.86. The investor pays $13.86 for each share, currently carrying an actual market value of $12.68. The difference of $1.18 represents the loading charge; $1.18 is 8½ percent of $13.86. But as a percentage of your money that's actually going to work for you, it is 1.18/12.68, or 9.3 percent.

Another fund shows a net asset value of $7.70 and an offering price of $8.28. The difference is the loading charge, which is equal to 7 percent of the dollars invested. A no-load fund will sell at the same price per share as the net asset value.

Mutual Fund Advertising

There have been abusive advertising and selling techniques in the mutual fund industry. In order to try to discourage inflated and misleading claims as to how a fund has performed, the Securities and Exchange Commission, in mid-1994, approved Truth in Advertising regulations for the mutual fund industry. Now, if a fund's performance ranking is being touted, the ad must also describe all the criteria on which the ranking was based (type of fund, number of funds in that category, and the time period of the rankings). Some funds had not counted their load charges when illustrating their performance, and some had waived certain fees or deferred certain expenses during a ranking period. Those practices could make the fund's performance look much stronger than it really was. Those practices are now prohibited. But the burden is still on the investor to discern the facts. And the most overpowering fact is this: Past performance of any mutual fund gives *absolutely no assurance as to how that fund will perform in the future.*

Mutual Fund Mistakes

Here are the most common mistakes made by mutual fund investors.

1. The investor does not know how much of the investment will go toward the selling commission. Given too high a commission, the prudent investor might prefer to shop for a comparably performing fund that has a lower commission or no commission at all.
2. The investor does not have a clear idea as to how the money will be invested. In short, the investor has not examined the mutual fund's objectives and does not know clearly whether the given fund is speculative or conservative.
3. The investor does not keep close account of the monthly statement. Unaware from month to month of how the investment is performing, the investor may not know when it would be a good time to sell the fund or to buy more of it.

Mutual Fund "Families"

As noted in the previous chapter, most major mutual fund companies operate a number of individual funds. These funds run the gamut from the conservative U.S. government securities type to the highly speculative types that invest in options, commodities, and risky stocks. The attractive feature of the fund families is that you can switch from one type of fund to another simply, quickly, and at very little cost. Thus, in shopping for a mutual fund,

you should shop for the families as well as for the specific funds within the families, and you should understand clearly the terms and conditions of switching funds before you make a commitment.

CHOOSING YOUR BROKER: A GUIDE THROUGH THE INVESTMENT JUNGLE

All these dilemmas are difficult enough for the advanced investor to cope with, let alone the novice. The right broker can be an invaluable aid in your evaluation of the various factors that face an investor. There is no assurance that the broker will know the truth or falsity of any given rumor or will be able to evaluate the long-term implications of a new competitor entering the market or an old one leaving it. And a broker can't spend as much time on your account as you might want. But a good broker, wisely chosen, can direct you to sources of information that can assist you in making a proper decision and can steer you away from unreliable sources.

Choose your broker carefully, remembering at all times that *you* must make the ultimate decisions based on the broker's recommendations and advice. A good broker can be a valuable ally in helping you meet your financial objectives, but only if you and the broker take the time to spell out those objectives clearly and only if the broker steadfastly assists you in meeting them.

Remember that a broker, with rare exception, earns a living by executing trades, getting a commission on each trade whether you are winning or losing. In other words, if your broker's going to eat, you've got to trade. If you invest a given sum of money in a given stock and instruct the broker to

STRATEGIES FOR SUCCESS

How to Resolve Problems with a Broker

The best way to solve a problem with a broker is to avoid getting into any difficulties at the outset. Every time you place an order you'll get a printed confirmation of the details. Be certain that the order has been placed precisely as you requested. If there are any mistakes on the confirmation, contact the broker immediately! If a broker seems to be uncooperative in resolving a dispute, go *in person* to explain the problem to the branch manager, and do so immediately! Send the details of your dispute in writing to the firm's Complaint Resolution Department (or office of similar name). If matters really get sticky, filing a written complaint with the National Association of Securities Dealers and/or the Securities and Exchange Commission and/or your state's office of securities regulation may be helpful. Most agreements with brokerage firms call for problem resolution by arbitration, if you haven't been able to nip the problem in the bud.

stash it away and forget about it for five or ten years and announce that that's all the market investing you plan to do, it's no wonder the broker doesn't regard you as a favored customer. Granted, the broker makes a commission on your initial investment, and if he or she is still around when you cash it in, the broker will make another commission on the sale. But meanwhile your money is sitting idle as far as your broker is concerned, with no further commissions in sight.

Naturally, brokers want their customers to do well. Each satisfied customer enhances the broker's professional image and is like a walking, talking billboard.

Many brokers do not keep close tabs on all their customers' various accounts and may neglect to advise them to buy or sell at an advantageous time. They may be too prone to listen to unfounded rumors and to pass them along to customers. They may not be making adequate use of research materials available through their firm and through other sources. They may be spending too much time hustling and too little time learning. On the other hand, a dedicated and conscientious broker can help you build and maintain an investment portfolio that can help you achieve short-term goals and long-term prosperity.

Consider these criteria in evaluating brokers: how closely their investment philosophy parallels yours; their reputation for integrity and hard work, which you can learn from other customers who have used their services; the amount and continuity of their schooling, scholarship, and research; their willingness to spend time helping you to set and achieve your goals; and, finally, chemistry—something that can't be described, shopped for, or cataloged. It's just got to be there and you'll know it when it is or isn't.

PERSONAL ACTION WORKSHEET

Playing the "Paper Game" with Mutual Funds

The "Paper Game" is a harmless—and free—way to acquaint yourself with the ups and downs, the trials and tribulations, of mutual funds. Play the Paper Game for six months or a year, and you'll have gained a good idea of whether it's the kind of place you want to send your money off to.

The rules of the Paper Game are very simple:

1. To simplify the Paper Game, we're just going to be concerned with the change in net asset value (NAV) of each fund. Select any five mutual funds whose shares are listed in your daily newspaper. Pick funds that you think have the best chance of appreciating in value (as opposed to generating income.) Make believe you buy 100 shares at today's price. We'll call this Group A.

2. Write the names of twenty-five other growth-type mutual funds on separate slips of paper. Pick five at random, and make believe you buy 100 shares of each at today's price. We'll call this Group B.

3. Use the tally sheet below to keep track of your purchases. You may sell Group A mutual funds whenever you like, but you must then pick a replacement. You can also sell Group B funds whenever you like, but must replace it by picking another one of the slips at random.

4. At the end of the designated time—you choose, six or twelve months—tally how you have done. Compare your Group A results with your Group B results. What has this exercise taught you about putting real money into mutual funds?

	Purchase Price and date*	Selling Price and date*	Gain or Loss in $	Gain or Loss Annual %**
Group A Funds				
1.				
2.				
3.				
4.				
5.				
Group B Funds				
1.				
2.				
3.				
4.				
5.				

*List the price paid or received for 100 shares less all commissions, redemption fees, etc. **List the annualized percentage gain or loss: If your investment was, say $1,000 and you realized a gain of $100 in twelve months, your annualized gain would be 10 percent. If you realized a $100 gain in six months your annualized gain would be 20 percent, and so on.

Choose Your Mutual Funds Wisely

For many years I had a phone-in show on the ABC network station in Los Angeles. One of the most frequent questions I had from listeners boiled down to this: "Should I invest in mutual funds?" I would usually answer— not meaning to be a wiseguy, but to make an important point: "That's like saying, 'I'm hungry. I want to go to the market to buy some food.' What kind of food will you buy? Filet mignon or Twinkies? Caviar or Pop-Tarts?"

I never ceased to be amazed that so many people were so unaware of the incredibly vast array of choices to be made among mutual funds, from the raging speculations to the conservative dull-but-you'll-sleep-well variety. And beyond that, I was just as amazed when people told me they had bought mutual funds because of an advertisement or a sales pitch that boasted of a high rate of return, without giving the faintest attention to whether their choice matched their personal objectives.

And then there were those poor folks who had bought the wrong fund and had seen their nest egg waste away, and all they could say was, "But the salesman told me that it should go up, not down." Ah, the word *should*. Of course it *should* go up. But it didn't.

These days billions of dollars are flowing into mutual funds for 401(k) plans and IRA plans and all sorts of other retirement and investment programs, and the marketing people with the mutual fund companies are targeting these investors with all the power at their disposal. It's easy to sell mutual funds when the stock market is booming, as it has been through most of the 1990s. People begin to think they are mutual fund geniuses, when in fact they're just lucky to be in a rising market. When the law of gravity reasserts itself, which it will do with regularity, a lot of the fortunes that have been made during the 1990s' bull market will fast disappear. And what will you have learned from the experience?

The criteria for making wise mutual fund choices have been discussed in this and the preceding chapter. Add to those criteria some numbers regarding specific mutual fund costs:

Most mutual funds charge customers annual 12b-1 fees, which can amount to about .25 percent of your balance in the fund. 12b-1 fees cover the funds' costs of marketing their product (that's right—you're helping to pay for the advertising that they use to lure you in as a customer) and at .25 percent that means that $2.50 of every $1,000 you have invested goes toward these fees.

In addition to the 12b-1 fees there are other management fees charged against your account—over and above any sales commissions you pay when you invest, and any redemption fees you pay when you cash in your chips. The total average mutual fund expenses, including 12b-1 fees, are about 1.27 percent a year for mutual funds that invest mainly in stock, and about .97 percent for bond funds, according to Lipper Analytical Services, a major mutual fund tracking company.

Say you invested $10,000 with a load charge (sales commission) of 6 percent. That means that only $9,400 of your money is working for you, the other $600 (6 percent of $10,000) going as sales commission. If your $9,400 grew by 8 percent in a year—or $752—you'd have a total in the fund of $10,152 (the initial $9,400 plus the $752 growth). If the fund then took away 1.27 percent of your total of $10,152, or about $129, you'd be left with $10,023. Remember that your original investment was $10,000. Your *net earnings* in the above year came to $23. That's a return of just one one-fourth of one percent for the year on your original investment.

Take it from there and crunch those numbers with all your might before you take the plunge. No, I'm not against mutual funds. But neither am I selling anything.

UPS & DOWNS   *The Economics of Everyday Life*

What Makes Stock Prices Go Up and Down?

Most of the other Ups & Downs segments in this book describe matters of relatively reasonable predictability: weather conditions will impact on food prices, wars can frighten oil prices, and so on. But the stock market can defy any crystal ball. Here are some examples of stock market behavior in recent years.

Bad news   The nation's economy is in a tailspin, which, you would think, would send the stock market into retreat. To stimulate the economy the government lowers interest rates. This is supposed to encourage borrowing by business and by individuals, all of whom will go out and buy things and thus put an end to recession. Lower interest rates scare investors out of low-yielding but safe securities and into what seems to be a more promising stock market. The huge inflow of investment dollars causes a spurt in the stock market. So much for bad news.

Good news   The economy is booming. Employment is up. This should bode well for the stock market: more workers means more people can buy more things, which should give companies a shot at better profits. But the stock market sees it differently. As industry demands more workers, workers will bargain for higher wages. Higher wages means lower profits, and in anticipation thereof the stock market takes a tumble. So much for good news.

"Discounting" of expected news   Some events and trends can be anticipated with reasonable accuracy: car sales, unemployment, changes in tax laws, Federal Reserve policies on interest rates, and so on. The stock market doesn't usually wait for the events to happen. It will react *in anticipation* of the events, up or down, days or even weeks before the event. When the event does occur, the market has already factored it into the price of stock. This is referred to as the market having *discounted* the news in advance. The trick is to figure out when that discounting will occur. No one really ever knows.

Profit taking   After every rally there is a fallback. There's never any way of knowing when a mass profit-taking selloff will occur. It's usually a mob psychology function, and, if you can figure out mob psychology, you'll make more money at that than you ever will in the stock market.

Frenzy   There are buying frenzies and there are selling frenzies. Both are motivated by the absolute loss of common sense. Call it temporary insanity. You get a hot tip on a stock. For one brilliant moment in time, you actually believe that you're the only person on earth with this knowledge. Then, when you and the millions like you who share the information buy or sell on the tip, you are part of a frenzy. It's sheer madness. But in a way this is what makes the stock market more interesting than root canal surgery.

? WHAT IF . . . ? ————————————————————

Test yourself: How would you deal with these real-life possibilities?

1. The stock market is going through a protracted downturn. Nothing seems to be able to stabilize it. You hear rumors that your company's pension fund is heavily invested in the stock market and that it is suffering considerable losses. What steps can you take to learn the facts? What steps *will* you take to learn the facts? If you find that the rumors are true and that your future pension benefits might be in jeopardy, what, if anything, can you do about it?

2. Reverse of the above: The stock market is going up with a vengeance, and your pension fund is making a handsome profit. What, if anything, can you do to share in that good fortune here and now, rather than waiting until retirement? If you can't do anything on your own, with whom can you ally to get something done?

3. A mutual fund sales pitch indicates that the fund has had an annual average total return of 17 percent for the last three years. That's double what you've been earning in your current mutual fund. What further information should you get about this fund before you make an investment decision?

4. You become privy to information about a company which, when made public, will sharply influence the price of that company's stock. Or at least, so you believe. What options do you have? What option(s) will you choose?

NUMBER CRUNCHERS

Do the calculations to help you make decisions in these real-life possibilities.

1. You buy 100 shares of XYZ at $40 per share. XYZ pays an annual dividend of $2. The company offers an automatic dividend reinvestment plan. Assume that the dividend will remain constant over the next five years and that the stock will increase in value by 5 percent each year. How much will your XYZ investment be worth after five years if you partake of the dividend reinvestment plan? How much will your XYZ investment be worth after five years if you spend all the dividends as you receive them? (For purposes of this exercise, don't worry about commissions or taxes.)

2. You embark on a long-term plan to accumulate stock in National Pripichik and Gumball (NP&G). Your initial investment is $4,000, which buys 200 shares. Every year for the next five years you will spend another $1,000 buying NP&G. The prices you pay per share each year are $18 in the first year; $16 the second year; $19 the third year; $21 the fourth year; $20 the fifth year. How many shares (including fractional amounts) of NP&G will you own after five years, and what will they be worth? (Forget dividends and commissions for purposes of this exercise.)

3. You have $10,000 to invest. Half goes into a savings plan that will pay 6 percent interest per year, compounding annually. The other half goes into 100 shares of a stock that pays no dividends. How much will the stock have to appreciate each year, on average, in both dollars and percent, to equal what you'll have in the savings plan after five years? (Forget commissions and taxes for this exercise.)

FOR BETTER OR FOR WORSE

Things beyond our control often impact our personal and financial well-being, for better or for worse. Some are more predictable than others. How would you be affected if the following real-life phenomena happened? Could you have seen it coming? What steps could you have taken to minimize damage or maximize advantage? The better able you are to anticipate and recognize these forces, the better equipped you are to deal with them.

1. You shop around for a mutual fund that invests in stocks, seeking one with the best winning track record possible. A year later the stock market has gone south by 8 percent, but your fund has dropped 24 percent.

2. The government creates very attractive tax breaks for companies that do a lot of genetic engineering research and development. The market reacts most positively, and you jump in yourself. A year later the government revokes the tax breaks and gives them instead to the home-building industry.

3. All of the stock market commentators and pundits are predicting a huge rise in the Dow Jones Industrial Average over the next year. You take a big plunge, as does your pension plan. The next day war breaks out in the Middle East and the oil supply to the United States is severely threatened.

Making Your Money Grow: Real Estate and Other Opportunities

Character and personal force are the only investments that are worth anything.

Walt Whitman

Beyond the money market and the stock market, there is a whole galaxy of opportunities for making your money grow—or shrink. Some can be relatively simple, and even fun—such as collecting coins, stamps, sports cards, and autographs. Others are much more complex—real estate, commodities, or investing in precious metals or gems. Many of these "opportunities" are aggressively sold by smooth-talking pitchmen. The naive investor who does not do the necessary homework can end up in trouble. The serious investor who studies hard and realistically evaluates all risks can be successful. After reading this chapter, you should be able to

- Distinguish between the various types of real estate investments
- Understand the time and expertise needed to manage real estate investments properly
- Recognize the pros and cons of speculating in such areas as commodities, precious metals, and gems
- Evaluate the true risks and tax implications in any of these methods of making your money grow

MYTHS AND FACTS ABOUT REAL ESTATE INVESTING

Property values sometimes increase at a rapid rate throughout much of the country, and as those values increase, the mystique about investing in real estate grows, too. Fostered by myriad get-rich-quick books and seminars, and by the proud boastings of investors who claim to have "made a killing" in real estate, the mystique takes on dangerous proportions for the uninformed would-be real estate investor. Let's first examine some of the myths and some of the facts about investing in real estate.

Myth: Real estate is easy; anybody can make money at it.

Facts: Successful real estate investing always has and always will require a considerable amount of expertise. As in any kind of investment, there will always be a handful of lucky ones who make it look easy to others. But those are the exception. Real estate is a fast track: experts profit at the expense of novices. The experts know when to buy, when to sell, how to finance, and how to manage property properly. And even the experts can make mistakes. Expertise in real estate investing can take years to achieve. It requires the ability to deal efficiently and profitably with tenants, tax assessors, lenders, insurance agents, contractors, lawyers, appraisers, and other prospective buyers and sellers. The novice real estate investor, lured by the myth of fast and easy money, is apt to make serious mistakes and incur serious losses.

Myth: Real estate offers an assured return on your investment.

Facts: Real estate investing is very much like the stock market in that there is no assurance of profit: A tenant defaults, seriously decreasing your income. Your furnace or central air-conditioning unit self-destructs, leaving you with a multithousand-dollar repair bill. The taxes on real estate double in a short period of time. A visitor to your building trips on a piece of broken flooring material and sues you for five times the amount of your public liability insurance. The neighborhood in which your building is located begins to deteriorate seriously. An unexpected rerouting of traffic makes your building far less attractive to good-quality tenants.

Events such as these can greatly reduce your expected return. Any would-be investor in real estate must approach any project with a keen awareness of the potential unknowns.

Myth: Property values always go up.

Facts: Real estate is cyclical. There are up periods, there are flat or down periods, and it's impossible to predict the cycles in any community at any given time. Real estate is also subject to the "greater fool" theory. That theory states that if you buy something at whatever price, eventually a greater fool than yourself will come along and buy it from you at an even higher price. This theory fails when property values have gone too high too quickly and the community runs out of greater fools. Then you're stuck.

Always be aware that in any time of investment, winners always boast, but losers are never heard from. This contributes to the myth of profitability in real

estate. Winners not only boast; they exaggerate. Losers keep their mouth shut. Thus, you'll hear an excessive amount of good news and a sore lack of bad news from people who have tried their hand in real estate.

Myth: You don't need any money to invest in real estate. You can buy property with "no money down."

Facts: Perhaps more money has been made selling books and seminars on this subject than will ever be made in real estate itself. The simple facts are: sure, you can buy real estate with no money down, if you can find a seller who is willing to part with property for no down payment. Or, you can try to find a lender who is willing to lend you 100 percent of the purchase price. In either case, you're liable to be paying a higher price than the property is worth or a higher interest rate than would be called for in a normal deal. And once the hefty monthly payments begin, you could really be behind the eight ball. The novice real estate investor who tries these techniques is on very risky ground.

The Good Points

Despite these pitfalls, real estate can provide an attractive investment to individuals willing to do the homework and put forth the energy to maintain their investments. If the local marketplace is properly researched, if the premises and legal documents are properly scrutinized, and if the required amount of time is devoted to the project, real estate can be very productive over the long run. One of the most attractive aspects of some real estate investment is the tax deduction allowed for the physical depreciation of the building. This factor can not only render the income from the real estate investment free of income taxes but can also shelter some of the investor's other income from taxes. This will be discussed in more detail in the section on income-producing real estate.

A World of Opportunities

There are four major categories of real estate investments, plus one category that allows you to invest as part of a group. The categories are as follows:

- **Income-producing real estate**   You purchase a building with the intent of renting it out to tenants, thereby realizing income. You may also realize a profit when you sell the building.
- **Vacant-land investing**   You buy unimproved land with the intent of either developing it, renting it out, or selling it at some future date at a profit.
- **Turnover investing**   You buy a property with the intention of reselling it as soon as possible at a profit. Income is a secondary consideration.

- **Mortgage investing**   You lend other people money, with the loan being secured by real estate. You don't actually acquire an ownership interest in the property at the time you make the investment, but you might if the borrower defaults. Thus, it's essential that you know the values that apply to the underlying real estate that is collateral for the loan you've made.
- **Group ventures**   You pool your money with that of other investors in any or all of the preceding categories. Group ventures can include real estate investment trusts, syndications, and partnerships.

The whole world is made up of real estate, and opportunity exists in every country in which the free enterprise system is at work. Common sense, however, dictates that the closer to home you invest, the more knowledge and control you have with respect to your investment. Let us now examine the basic categories of real estate investment.

INCOME-PRODUCING REAL ESTATE

The primary objective in investing in income-producing real estate is to earn income on your investment and, to the extent possible, obtain tax sheltering of that income through the depreciation deduction. But, as noted earlier, many factors can affect the flow of income. Here are some of the main factors that must be considered.*

Factors Affecting Income-producing Property Investments

Quality and Type of Tenants

Consider the problems involved in an apartment complex that rents primarily to young, single people. An owner can expect a relatively high rate of turnover. With each turnover comes the chance of a vacancy and the possible need to refurbish the apartment. On the other hand, an apartment complex catering to older persons might have a low rate of turnover. Applying the reward/risk rule, which relates as much to real estate as it does to any other form of investment, the properties with the highest chance of turnover and higher refurbishing costs should carry a higher rent than the more stable properties.

In commercial properties, a broad spectrum of possible tenants can occupy any given space. Consider, for example, uses that are possible in a small neighborhood shopping center—a popular type of moderate real es-

---

*If you expect to be a tenant running your own business—as discussed in detail in chapter 21—much of the following material will also be important for you.

tate investment for small- to medium-sized investors. A given space might be occupied by a business such as an insurance agency. It will have relatively little traffic and will need no special plumbing, electrical, or drainage installations. The same property might be occupied by a coffee shop, which could have a high level of traffic that can contribute to the more rapid deterioration of the premises; in addition, such installations need specialized plumbing, electrical, and drainage connections. Moreover, these uses can generate smoke and grease and are possible fire hazards that could increase the insurance rates for both the building and the adjoining tenants.

The creditworthiness of tenants should not be overlooked. When entering into a lease, landlords should check with the local credit bureau to determine a tenant's creditworthiness. A sloppy credit history suggests a number of possible actions that landlords should consider: They might want to decline renting to such a tenant altogether; they might feel that the credit problems justify asking a higher rent; they might seek a cosigner to ensure payment of the rent; and they might request a substantial rental deposit from the tenant.

A tenant who is tardy with rent can cause more than one problem. In addition to the headaches and aggravation landlords must endure in collecting overdue rent, landlords might have to dip into their own funds to meet *their* monthly payments as they fall due.

Nature and Quality of the Building

The potential risks and rewards for the landlord are directly related to the quality, location, and nature of the building itself. As in buying a house (chapter 6), the investor in income-producing real estate must pay attention to all the mechanical and structural details of the building. It is wise to hire a construction specialist to make a detailed inspection and provide a report on the building. A building with hidden defects can cause serious problems for the unsuspecting landlord; a building in good physical condition will keep risk at a minimum and cut down problems of maintenance, repairs, and replacements. Many investors in real estate are content to take the seller's or realtor's word concerning the condition of the building. More prudent investors discover, with professional assistance, whether the building measures up to their standards.

Location is important to the investor, who must determine whether traffic patterns or changes in adjoining neighborhoods can have an effect on the investment. An attractive gas station, motel, shopping center, or restaurant on a heavily trafficked thoroughfare might seem most appealing. But if a new highway diverts all the traffic away from the street, the result can be disastrous. A neighborhood shopping center might seem to offer attractive possibilities; but when a bigger and better shopping center is constructed a few blocks away, the unaware investor may regret ever having signed the down payment check.

Prudent investors check with the local zoning board to determine what uses are permitted in areas near their property. They check with the traffic and highway agencies to determine what possible changes in traffic routings are anticipated. And they check with other real estate firms to learn what new developments are pending within the trading area of the property they're buying.

The nature of the building must also be considered. Many buildings are limited by their size, shape, and type of construction as to the uses to which they can be put. Food franchise buildings often fall into this category; they might prove unadaptable to other uses. On the other hand, some buildings are easily converted to suit different purposes. The more limited the use of a given building, the more difficult it may be to find tenants.

Property Taxes

Prudent investors also check with the local tax assessor to determine the current and probable future trends with respect to property taxes. If property taxes are likely to be moving upward sharply in the years ahead, prudent investors will want to know if they can still meet their financial projections. Can they expect their tenants to absorb a share of increased property taxes? How will the long-term trend in property taxes affect their ability to sell the building profitably in the future?

Utility Costs

All other things being equal, it's better for the landlord if the tenants pay their own utility and fuel costs—water, electricity, gas, heating oil. That can take a lot of financial pressure off the landlord, particularly in areas of climatic extremes, where heating or air-conditioning costs can demolish the most carefully planned budget. If a building, either residential or commer-

cial, is not already separately metered for such utilities, the prudent investor will think twice about making the investment. If a landlord does pay the utility costs, he or she can require tenants to pay a pro rata share of any such costs beyond a certain agreed-on base amount. Lacking such protection, the landlord is at the mercy of broken thermostats, leaky faucets and toilets, and other costly energy wastes.

Management of the Property

Perhaps the biggest shock to the novice real estate investor is how much time and aggravation it takes to manage the property. When you call your doctor in the middle of the night with a mysterious pain, you may be told to take two aspirins and call back in the morning. When a tenant calls you in the middle of the night to complain of a leaking toilet, you can't just tell him to throw two aspirins into it and call you back in the morning. Management takes time, patience, skill, diplomacy, expertise, and a sense of humor. If you're not a good handyman yourself, you have to find people in the trades on whom you can depend: plumbers, electricians, painters, carpenters, and so on. When you have a vacancy, you must be prepared to refurbish it to get it up to standard, and you must show it to prospective tenants, many of whom will not show up at the agreed-on appointment time.

If the property generates enough income, it might be advisable to hire a professional manager who can deal with all these matters. A good management firm will cost you between 5 and 8 percent of your rental income. A good management firm can be the landlord's best ally; a shoddy management firm can be the landlord's worst enemy. Get personal recommendations before you hire a management firm. If the management firm is also acting as rental agent, be certain that it will screen prospective tenants to your strict standards. Otherwise, the management firm could rent the premises to tenants unacceptable to you in order to generate a rental commission in a hurry.

Financing

The mechanics of financing income property are generally the same as financing one's own home. The investor (unless paying all cash) gives a down payment to the seller of the property and either assumes an existing mortgage or obtains a mortgage loan from outside sources.

The prudent investor seeks a good return on invested capital (the cash down payment) and to that end attempts to structure the mortgage so that there is adequate cash flow to meet objectives. If there are interest rate escalation clauses, the owner must be prepared to adjust rents accordingly if he or she wants to maintain a constant rate of cash flow.

The real estate investor may also need large sums of money at indeterminate dates for major renovations and repairs. The investor should negotiate with the lender to obtain such funds by adding them on to the existing mortgage at the best possible terms.

When lenders are considering mortgage loan applications on income property, they examine not only the owner's credit but also the caliber of tenants. The owner's ability to pay the mortgage is directly related to the ability of the tenants to make their rental payments. The better the tenants, the more favorable terms the borrower can negotiate with the lender. Better quality tenants, as noted earlier, may be able to bargain for a lower rent from the landlord. The landlord can make up this difference by seeking the most favorable terms on the mortgage payments.

The Lease

At the heart of any real estate investment is the lease: the agreement between the investor/owner and the tenant/user. Whether the property is commercial, residential, or a combination, the specific terms of the lease have an important bearing on the investor's success. Residential leases tend to be shorter and simpler, usually running for a period of not more than one or two years. Commercial leases are more complex. In either case, the prudent investor sees to it that an attorney prepares a lease best suited to the investor's interests.

Following are some of the more important terms that should be evaluated, particularly in commercial leases.

LENGTH OF THE LEASE In commercial leases tenants want to know that they have the right to use the property for as long as the business is profitable. If it ceases to be profitable, a tenant will probably want to leave.

A preferred situation for a commercial tenant would be to have a medium-term lease—say, three to five years—with options to renew at an agreed-on rent. This option offers the tenant both flexibility and fixed overhead. But this might not be to the landlord's advantage. By giving a tenant the privilege of renewing, the landlord is effectively taking the property off the market for the length of the original term and possibly the period of renewal.

Where renewal clauses exist, the tenant must give notice of intention to renew prior to the expiration of the lease. Technically, the landlord does not know until notice is given whether the space will be vacated. The landlord can make inquiry, but tenants are legally not obliged to express their intentions to renew or depart until the time stated in the lease agreement. Where there are no renewal privileges, the landlord knows exactly when to expect the premises to be vacated and can begin seeking new tenants, certain of when they can take occupancy. Or the landlord can renegotiate the lease with the existing tenant and hope that conditions permit an equal or better rent on the renewal term.

The landlord should bear in mind that because a tenant has a right of renewal at an agreed-on rent, this does *not* guarantee that the tenant *will* pay that rent. The renewal date may roll around, and the tenant may want to continue in the space, but at a reduced rental. This can cause a predicament for the landlord, who now has a relatively short period of time in which to try to find a better tenant for the premises. Working out such problems often comes down to nothing more than plain old hard-nosed bargaining. If there's a surplus of tenants looking for space, the landlord is in a better position, and vice versa. There's no way of knowing what these conditions will be like years in advance, so the parties just have to be prepared to cope with situations as they arise.

Another factor to consider, particularly in a commercial building, is that a long-term lease with a good-quality tenant can translate into a lower interest rate on the financing.

THE RENTAL RATE   In most cases, market conditions and the tenant's creditworthiness will determine the probable amount of rent a given tenant will pay. In residential rentals, the rent is quoted as a flat rate: "Apt. 106 rents for $875 per month." In commercial rentals, the rent is often expressed in terms of square feet. A space of 1,000 square feet that rents for $1,000 per month, or $12,000 per year, will be quoted as "$12 per square foot per year" or, in some cases, "$1 per square foot per month."

Commercial rentals are also referred to as "gross" or "net." In a gross lease, the landlord is responsible for virtually all operating costs on the property, including real estate taxes, utilities, maintenance, cleaning, and generally servicing the premises. The tenant in a gross lease pays a higher rent, in return for those services. In a net lease, the tenant is responsible for those expenses.

The landlord who wants a minimum of involvement in the management of the building will prefer a net lease. Some tenants may prefer a net lease because they can more directly control the operating expenses in the building. Whether a lease is gross or net, the building must still be properly maintained. A landlord, even with the most perfect net lease, must still see to it that the tenant performs all the proper management, maintenance, and repairs required under the lease.

Rental payments may be fixed for the term of the lease, or they may escalate in line with rising prices or simply by agreement between the parties. In addition to the basic flat rent, commercial leases often have percentage clauses.

A percentage clause states that the tenant must pay additional rent to the landlord in an amount equal to an agreed-on percentage of the volume of business the tenant does. For example: The tenant may be required to pay 6 percent of all gross income in excess of, say, $100,000 per year. In such a case, if the tenant's business does not gross over $100,000 in a year, the percentage clause does not go into effect. But if the tenant generates

$150,000 of volume, the percentage lease requires the tenant to pay 6 percent of $50,000 or $3,000 in additional rent for that year. The existence and terms of a percentage clause are a matter of negotiation between the parties. If a landlord feels that a tenant's business prospects are good, the landlord may prefer a lower base rent with a percentage clause. A more conservative landlord may simply prefer a higher base rent and no percentage clause. A percentage lease allows the landlord the right to look at the books and records of the tenant so that the correct amount of the payment can be determined.

USE OF THE PROPERTY   The lease stipulates the purposes for which the premises can be used.

In addition, particularly in a shopping center, the tenant may request a *noncompetition* clause. This would prevent the landlord from allowing other spaces in the center to be rented to competitors. The landlord has to evaluate such a request in light of current market conditions, eagerness to rent the space, and the rent the tenant is willing to pay.

REPAIRS AND RESTORATIONS   The lease should stipulate who is responsible for every kind of repair. Customarily, the tenants are responsible for making minor interior repairs, and the landlord is responsible for structural repairs and matters affecting mechanical equipment, such as the heating plant and the air-conditioning unit. Of course, the parties can agree to any combination of who does what and who pays for what.

A restoration clause is also subject to negotiation between the parties. This clause can require tenants to restore the premises to their original condition at the time they first took occupancy. If tenants have made renova-

tions within the premises, they will have to see to it, at their own expense, that the property is brought back to its original condition unless the landlord later agrees otherwise. If a restoration clause is agreed on between the parties, it is necessary to obtain a careful description of the premises at the time of the start of occupancy (including color photographs as an added precaution.)

DEFAULT   What if tenants don't live up to the agreement? They may damage the property and not repair it. Or the tenant may leave in the middle of a lease and try to escape making further payments. As a measure of protection against default, a prudent investor insists on a rental deposit and a breakage and damage deposit from a tenant. The rental deposit, usually designated as the last month's rent on the lease, ensures that the landlord will have at least some cash in hand should the tenant skip. The breakage and damage deposit protects the landlord to some extent in the event the tenant neglects to make repairs. But it should be clearly understood that the amounts of the rental deposit and the breakage and damage deposit are not the limit of the tenant's obligation. The tenant should still be obliged to make whatever payments are due over and above the amount of the deposits.

"Compounding" Your Income

In fixed income investments, your earned interest can be automatically reinvested in your account and go to work for you. This is known as compounding interest. The same ends can be accomplished in the stock market through either a dividend reinvestment plan or a mutual fund that pumps your earnings back into additional shares of the fund. But can you compound your earnings in a real estate investment? Yes, prudent real estate investors realize that a portion of their income should be reinvested back into the property, by way of refurbishing and modernization. The net effect of this *should* be to generate higher income from tenants of the property.

It's not as simple or as automatic as the compounded interest on your savings account, and it requires some expertise to know which dollars can generate additional rent. The investor may prefer to take all income out and invest it in some other fashion, or spend it. But the investor should examine the possibilities of reinvesting the money in the property before making an ultimate decision.

For example, a tenant might agree to an increase of $20 per month if the landlord repaints the premises. The paint job might cost $1,000, but the landlord will be getting an additional $240 per year for the balance of the lease period. That's a 24 percent return on the $1,000 investment—an attractive situation, indeed. The prudent investor is continually on the alert for ways to increase and compound income by plowing profits back into the property.

Real Estate Investing and Taxes

Before we proceed to analyze how a real estate investment works, it's necessary to understand one of the basic principles of income tax law. Suppose that your taxable income in a given year was $35,000. All that income came from work. (Taxable income is what's left after all your deductions and exemptions have been subtracted from your gross income.) You are married and filing a joint return. You are in the 28 percent tax bracket. If you could come up with another deduction of, say, $1,000, that would reduce your taxable income from $35,000 to $34,000. At a 28 percent tax rate, that means that you would reduce your tax bill by $280. The $1,000 deduction reduces the amount of tax you have to pay to Uncle Sam by $280. This is an example, in very oversimplified fashion, of a tax shelter. It's a deduction generated from some outside source that allows you to reduce the tax you would have to pay on the income you earned from work.

For many investors, ample opportunity to reduce taxes by this means is available in real estate. *If your adjusted gross income is under $100,000, you can still use deductions from real estate investments to offset as much as $25,000 per year worth of income from work.* (If your adjusted gross income is between $100,000 and $150,000, you can still achieve a partial deduction. The concept of adjusted gross income is explained further in chapter 20, on income taxes.)

Let's now study an example of how such a deal can work.

The Depreciation Deduction

You own and actively manage a small apartment house. Your purchase price was $150,000. You made a down payment of $10,000 and obtained a mortgage of $140,000, payable over twenty years at a fixed interest rate of 13 percent. Your monthly payments on that mortgage will be $1,640. See Table 16–1.

Your operating figures are set forth in Table 16–2: your annual income is $26,400. Your annual expenses are $25,680. This leaves you with a net income, after expenses, of $720. You invested $10,000 of your own cash, so you are receiving a return of 7.2 percent on your invested money. That's a decent return, but you could earn as much by putting your money into bonds and not have all the hassle of managing a building. So where's the attraction? It comes from the depreciation deduction.

Tax laws permit investors to show a loss on their income tax forms to reflect the supposed physical deterioration of their property. Obviously, this

TABLE 16–1 **Purchase of Real Estate Investment**

Purchase price	$150,000
Down payment	10,000
Mortgage	$140,000

13% fixed rate for 20-year term = monthly payments of $1,640

TABLE 16–2   **Operating Income and Expenses**

	Per Month	Per Year
Rental income	$2,200	$26,400
Expenses		
Interest	$1,600	
Taxes (approx.)	100	
Insurance	100	
Maintenance	200	
Misc.	140	
	$2,140	$25,680
Net income	$60	$720

loss is not a real out-of-pocket loss, particularly if the building is appreciating in value. An investor who owns an income-producing residential property can claim those losses over a period of 27½ years. An investor in commercial property can claim the losses over a 39-year period.

Exercise 16.1

The tax law states that only the building portion of a property, not the land portion, is depreciable. For purposes of the depreciation deduction, you must separate out the cost basis of the building itself. As Table 16–3 indicates, the value of your building is $110,000. That's the depreciable portion of the total investment. Dividing 27½ years into $110,000, we get a $4,000 per year depreciation deduction.

Here's how the arithmetic works: You are entitled to an annual depreciation deduction of $4,000. Assume you're in the 28 percent tax bracket on your federal income tax return. The depreciation deduction of $4,000 erases the tax liability on the $720 you earned from the building. Assuming you've been actively involved in managing the building and otherwise qualify, the rest of the depreciation deduction will erase the tax liability on $3,280 worth of your income from other sources, such as work. A total of $3,280 worth of income that is not taxed currently means a tax savings for the year of $918. (That is, 28 percent of $3,280 is $918.)

So your actual income, as Table 16–4 indicates, amounts to $1,638, which represents a return of 16.38 percent on your cash investment of $10,000. In addition to that, you will be building equity in the property as you pay

TABLE 16–3   **Depreciation Breakdown**

Land (not depreciable)	$ 40,000
Building (depreciable)	110,000

Depreciation period of 27½ years

$110,000 ÷ 227½ = $4,000 depreciation per year

TABLE 16–4   Return on $10,000 Cash Investment

Operating profit	$720
Taxes saved in current year on nonbuilding income as a result of depreciation deduction	918
	$1,638

down the loan each month and as the value of the property (hopefully) increases over the years.*

Now the Bad News

You paid $150,000 for the building. Say that you own the building for ten years and you take depreciation of $4,000 for each of those years, for a total of $40,000 in depreciation deductions. At the end of ten years, you have the opportunity to sell the property for $250,000. Naturally, you'll have to pay a tax on your profit.

What is the extent of your profit? You paid $150,000 and received $250,000 for an apparent profit of $100,000. But you'll have to pay income taxes on more than $100,000. Because you claimed $40,000 in depreciation deductions while you owned the building, the tax law requires that your cost basis be reduced by that amount. In other words, in calculating your profit on the building, you must calculate your cost (for tax purposes) as the original price you paid for the building *minus* any depreciation deductions you had claimed. The original price was $150,000 and you claimed deductions of $40,000. Thus, your cost basis for tax purposes would be $110,000. The gain that is subject to income taxes is, then, the difference between your selling price and your cost basis, $250,000 minus $110,000; or $140,000. In other words, some of the tax advantages you enjoyed while you owned the building are taken away at the time you sell the building. Again, it is necessary to make a careful analysis of tax laws in effect at the time of sale to structure the best terms and the best time for a sale.

INVESTING IN VACANT LAND

Investing in vacant land can be one of the most extreme forms of speculation. We do hear of "killings" made in land by investors; and we hear statements, such as the one Will Rogers made, "You ought to buy land, cuz they ain't gonna print no more of it." But success in vacant land investment, for

---

*Tax laws affecting real estate investments (and all other types of investments) change frequently. The tax implications in the preceding example may be different by the time you make an investment in real estate. It's absolutely essential that you check current tax laws and get professional assistance in analyzing how the laws affect any investment you plan to make.

the most part, remains the province of the skilled professional, who has the expertise, the capital, and the selling skills needed to turn a profit most of the time. *Note:* We said *most of the time.* Even the skilled professional will have setbacks.

Other forms of investment pay some income to investors—interest on fixed income investments, dividends on stocks, rentals on income properties. But vacant land requires investors to be constantly *paying out* money: real estate taxes, liability insurance and security. Investors in vacant land have also put their capital beyond reach until the land is actually sold. It is difficult and costly to borrow against vacant land.

Factors Affecting Vacant-Land Investments

Whether you are buying land for future building purposes or in hope of profit on a fast turnover, you should take into account the following factors:

"Known" Land

There's a much better chance for success if you're dealing with known land—that is, land in a community with which you're familiar and on which you can get estimates from real estate professionals on probable future value. Known land also implies that you are certain of the availability of utilities, sewers, roadways, and other necessary facilities.

"Unknown" Land

Uncounted millions of dollars are lost every year by people who sign contracts and checks to buy parcels of unknown land—generally, land in distant places that is being sold as part of a development program for the creation of a "new city," a resort, or a retirement village. Although there are legitimate developments in all parts of the country, the abuses, intentional or otherwise, that have arisen have been all too frequent.

Anyone considering investing in vacant land for future personal use, particularly if it's unknown land, must observe the following cautions.

SEE THE LAND   View the land and walk it from corner to corner before you sign any documents. The majority of people who have been bilked on such deals haven't done this.

CONSULT AN ATTORNEY *BEFORE* YOU SIGN ANYTHING   The attorney can determine whether the land you saw is the land you'll actually be buying. He will also scrutinize the other documents involved and help you ascertain exactly what you can expect for the money you're paying.

READ THE PROPERTY REPORT   If a developer is selling land on an interstate basis—to buyers in many states—federal law requires that a Property Report be provided. It must contain information prescribed by the In-

Exercise 16.2

terstate Land Sales Act, a federal law. If a developer fails to provide the Property Report within the prescribed time limits, the buyer may be entitled to revoke the contract and obtain a refund.

Appraisal

Get professional help in order to determine the true value of vacant land. The seller's asking price and the true current market value may be far apart, and you don't want to pay more than you should. A professional appraiser can assist you in learning the true current market value. The appraiser will take into account recent comparable sales of similar property, existing and future potential traffic patterns in and around the land, future population trends and the stability of the tax base.

Tests

Whether you're planning to build on the land or hoping to sell it to someone else who will, certain physical tests will have to be done. These tests are the soil test and the percolation test. You should know the results of these tests before you buy any vacant property.

The soil test determines the bearing capacity of the soil. In other words, how much of a building load can the soil withstand? Percolation tests determine the drainage capacity of the land—how much rainfall and moisture the land can absorb without turning into a swamp or a sea of mud.

Surveys

The boundary survey and the topographical survey assure a would-be buyer/builder of the true boundaries of the property and of the precise slopes that may exist on the property. If there is, for example, too much slope to the property, a prospective builder might be faced with expensive earth-moving costs, and those costs could affect the price a buyer is willing to pay for the property.

Dollars and Cents

If a parcel of vacant land doubles in price within the short space of five years, an investor might only break even. Here's the arithmetic. Assume that an investor pays $10,000 cash for vacant land, forgoing a return on the money of, say $600 per year by simply investing the money in insured savings. In addition, the investor may have the following typical expenses: property taxes, $500; insurance (mainly for public liability, to avoid lawsuits if anyone is hurt while crossing the property), $200; signs, advertising, and security, $200. Total annual expenses (including lost interest) are thus $1,500, or a total over five years of $7,500.

Assume that five years later the investor is able to sell the property for $20,000. If the investor has used a real estate agent to find a buyer—which is likely—the commission to the real estate agent will be 10 percent of the selling price, or $2,000. In addition, there will probably be expenses related to the sale, particularly legal fees and recording costs, which can easily total $500. The total expenses then are $10,000—$1,500 per year for five years, or $7,500, plus $2,500 at the time of sale. The selling price of $20,000 thus results in a net of $10,000. Over a five-year span, the property has doubled in value, and the investor has broken even.

This example is intended to provide you with the kind of "what if" arithmetic you face before making a decision. The time to evaluate this risk is before making any commitment to invest in vacant land. Once the commitment is made, you can't get out of it as you could selling stock or cashing in a savings certificate. You're stuck with it until a buyer comes along, and if that buyer isn't willing to meet your price, you may have to take whatever is offered. And the longer you hold on, the more it costs.

"TURNOVER" INVESTING

Probably somewhat more speculative than higher quality income property investing, and probably less speculative than vacant land investing, is the purchase of existing homes for subsequent resale: "Turnover" investing. It's a tricky business, requiring expertise, hard work, and patience. But many small investors have found handsome profits in such endeavors.

Many opportunities are attractive to investors with talents for making repairs. Such talents allow you to make accurate estimates of what renovations might be needed, how much they'll cost, and how much they can boost the potential selling price. A few hundred dollars wisely spent on paint, paneling, or flooring can increase the potential selling price by a thousand dollars or more.

The procedure involves seeking out houses that have good underlying basic value but can be bought for less than the normal market price, usually because the owners are anxious to get out.

The success of any venture depends on the investor's ability to buy wisely and to finance wisely.

Buying Right

Buying right requires careful evaluation of the neighborhood as well as of the physical structure itself. A rundown house in an area of better homes can command a handsome price if it's spruced up and put on a par with its surroundings. Another rundown house might offer little or no profit potential regardless of how much you do because the neighborhood isn't that

desirable. Remember that your buyers are looking for location as well as a house, and the selling price is affected accordingly.

There are three major ways you can seek attractive situations. You can scout around for people who are hard pressed to sell, because of either time or money pressures. Word of mouth and simply driving around looking for "For Sale" signs are ways of discovering such opportunities. Advertising is another way. The seller may place a classified ad with a tip-off that indicates a good buy; or you, as the investor, can advertise in the "Homes Wanted" or similar classifications of the want ad pages.

A second source: real estate agents in your area. Make it known to a number of them that you're in the market for such houses, and ask them to contact you if they spot any. Often, agents might be reluctant to take a listing on rundown houses from the seller, but if they know they have a possible buyer, they could put you into a number of opportunities.

A third source: banks and savings and loan institutions that have delinquent property loans. This deserves particular attention because you might have a source of automatic financing when you later sell to another party.

Financing Right

If you've bought right, and if you've refurbished correctly, your chances of finding a willing buyer will be greatly enhanced if you can offer the property fully financed. This means that a creditworthy buyer can step right into a mortgage for which you have made prior arrangements. In order to make such arrangements, it will be necessary to develop a relationship with a lender who will be willing to cooperate with you in such transactions. As part of the negotiations involved in setting up such relationships, you may have to guarantee all or part of any loan that is arranged for your buyer. Although this can improve your potential profitability in the sale of the house, it does put you on the hook for an extended period; you should be careful that the buyer makes an adequate down payment and that his or her credit history justifies your assuming that risk. As noted earlier, mortgage lenders in the community may have an inventory of used homes that they'd be willing to sell at attractive prices to investors willing to fix them up and offer them for resale. In such cases, they may be willing to make advance commitments for long-term financing to creditworthy buyers.

The Profit Margin

Perhaps the biggest challenge in this kind of investment is building a big enough profit margin into the deal to cover all the initial expenses, as well as continuing expenses, and yet not price the property out of the market. Investors must be aware that once renovations are completed and the prop-

erty is on the market, time can start working against them. Every month that goes by in which the house remains unsold means added costs—interest, taxes, insurance, advertising, and so on. As these costs mount, investors, for lack of buyers, may drop the price. As the expenses rise and the asking price drops, investors may succumb to feelings of panic. That's the worst danger. Carefully estimate the difference between what you will pay for the property, the renovations, and the continuing expenses, and what you'll receive in the sale.

A well-structured deal offers the opportunity for substantial profit if a buyer is found in the early months, but, as time goes by, profitability rapidly erodes. Anyone investing in homes for resale purposes must give careful consideration to this risk.

INVESTING IN MORTGAGES

Mortgages are not actually real estate investments, but many people think of them as such. These investments fall more into the fixed income category: You're buying someone else's IOU with a piece of real estate as security. But because you could end up owning the real estate if the borrower defaults on the payments it should be considered a real estate investment.

Prudent investors must scrutinize the value of property just as they must scrutinize the creditworthiness of a borrower. They must exercise the same precautions that a bank would in making a mortgage loan: appraising the property, determining the credit status of the borrower, and getting adequate protection regarding title and property insurance. An attorney is needed to prepare all the required documents, and the cost of the legal service must be taken into account. It's not unusual in private mortgage investing for the costs of legal matters and related documentation to be passed along to the borrower. In addition, the private mortgage lender might be able to impose extra fees or points in much the same way institutional lenders do.

Before you become an investor in mortgages, it would be valuable to meet existing mortgage brokers in your community and determine what the current going prices and interest rates are. You might even, as a would-be investor in mortgages, prefer to deal through such brokers before you set out on your own. The mortgage brokers will place your money for you in mortgages and will take a fee for their service. Most communities have many mortgage brokers who are always looking for funds they can invest, content to take a service fee for their efforts. You can find them listed in the Yellow Pages.

If you do choose to use a mortgage broker, make sure that the broker is reputable. If you turn your money over to a disreputable individual, you might never see it, or the person, again.

"Taking Back" a Mortgage

If you sell property and agree to accept the buyer's IOU in full or partial payment, this is known as "taking back" a mortgage. The buyer becomes obligated to you to make the payments called for in the mortgage agreement. Many people who sell their homes or business properties don't have immediate use for the full proceeds and might prefer to let the money stay in the property as a form of investment.

Initiating a New Mortgage

This involves making a new mortgage loan to people who are buying someone else's property. The interest rate, costs, and added fees that you, as an investor, can generate are subject to negotiation between the parties. Some important cautions are in order if the deal is to be structured to your best advantage.

First, you must determine why the people are not able to obtain conventional financing through a normal lending institution. If it's because the borrowers' credit status is weak, you might be asking for trouble. In such a case, you might be able to command a higher interest rate (subject to state usury laws) because you are taking on a higher than normal risk. Or the property buyers may simply not have enough down payment to meet the requirements of the institution, even though the credit status is perfectly acceptable. This is a lesser risk but one that you should evaluate nonetheless.

Second, protect yourself in setting the number of years the loan will run. Banks measure their mortgage loans in decades, but it's not wise for an individual to tie up money for that long. You can establish a payment program that is based on a thirty-year payout, for example, but you should reserve the right to have the full amount payable in a much shorter time, say five years. This is subject to negotiation between the parties. The borrowers might not like the prospect of having to refinance the loan at the end of five years, but they may be willing to go along with it if there's no better deal elsewhere.

Your documents should state that the buyers cannot sell the property without your express permission. You would not want the property to be sold to a person whose credit status is unacceptable. You might permit the property owners to do so if they remain liable for the debt in case the new buyer defaults.

In establishing the interest rate on a new mortgage or a taken-back mortgage, you might also want to consider what many institutional lenders are doing: putting in clauses that permit them to alter the interest rate when and if interest rates in general change.

Buying Mortgages at "Discount"

Some years ago, Murphy bought Johnson's house, and Johnson took back a mortgage from Murphy at a 10 percent interest rate. Today Murphy still owes Johnson $40,000 on that mortgage, and payments are to run for another ten years. Johnson needs money now. He can't wait ten years to collect what is owed him. Johnson approaches you to sell you Murphy's IOU. You know that Murphy is very creditworthy and that the value of the property is more than ample to cover your investment. But comparable investments are available today that will give you a yield of 14 percent. So why would you buy Murphy's IOU, which pays only 10 percent?

You might offer to buy Murphy's IOU at a *discount;* that is, for less than the face value. Depending on how anxious Johnson is to get cash, he might be willing to sell you the $40,000 IOU for, say, $30,000. If such a deal is made, you will receive 10 percent on the amount of capital you have at work, and you will also, over the ten-year period, receive $10,000 over and above what you invested. The attractiveness of this kind of investing depends on the original interest rate on the mortgage, the amount of discount you can negotiate, and the true yield that results from the combination of the interest rate and the discount.

Mortgage Pools

Instead of just investing in a single mortgage, you can also pool your money with that of other investors in an assortment of numerous mortgages. The most popular program for this type of investing is offered through the Government National Mortgage Association (GNMA, or "Ginnie Mae"), an agency of the U.S. government. Ginnie Mae buys mortgages from lenders (banks, etc.), packages a few dozen into a pool, and then offers certificates to investors. Each certificate represents a share of ownership in a specific pool of mortgages; the minimum purchase price for a new certificate is $25,000. Ginnie Mae certificates are guaranteed by the U.S. government, which has made them very attractive to investors.

As a Ginnie Mae investor, you receive monthly checks, just as if you owned a single mortgage. The problem of return of principal, as discussed below, also exists with Ginnie Mae investments: if you don't reinvest each monthly payment as you receive it, it ceases to work for you. However, there are many mutual funds that invest in Ginnie Mae certificates. Shares in these funds can be obtained for as little as $1,000, and they do offer automatic reinvestment of your monthly income.

Other government-related programs offer similar forms of mortgage

pool investing: the Federal Home Loan Mortgage Corporation ("Freddie Mac") offers participation certificates (PCs) and collateralized mortgage obligations (CMOs), and the Federal National Mortgage Association ("Fannie Mae") offers mortgage-backed securities (MBSs). Get full details on these plans from stockbrokers. And be certain to shop around, since prices and terms can differ from place to place.

Pitfalls: Return of Principal and Early Payoffs

There's one catch to investing in mortgages. Each monthly payment you receive contains some interest and some of your own investment that you're getting back. (Review the section on mortgage financing in chapter 7 to refresh your recollection of how this aspect of mortgages works.) Since you're receiving a small part of your investment back each month, that means that you have less and less of your original investment working for you as the months go by. Unless you take steps each month to reinvest your principal, your ultimate return won't be as much as you might have thought it would be.

For example, you invest $10,000 in a mortgage paying 12 percent interest for ten years. You will receive monthly payments of $143.50. Over the full ten years, those payments will total $17,220. You will have received, therefore, $7,220 more than you had invested. Divide that figure by 10 (for 10 years), and you come up with an average annual return of $722, which is equal to a 7.22 percent return on your original investment of $10,000. What happened to the 12 percent return that you were expecting? Each month, as you received the checks from the borrower, your original $10,000 investment dwindled because you were getting some of it back. In short, the whole $10,000 wasn't working for you all the time. In order to have kept it working for you, you would have had to reinvest the principal portion of each monthly payment as you received it. In all likelihood, the only way you could invest such small monthly sums safely would be in a passbook savings account, where your return would be far lower than 12 percent.

Another problem can arise when mortgages are paid off by the borrowers earlier than anticipated. Many investors in mortgage pools got soaked in 1993 because of this. Interest rates on home loans had reached a twenty-year low in 1993—under 7 percent for thirty-year fixed-rate loans. This prompted millions of homeowners to refinance their existing loans, which carried rates of 8 percent, 9 percent, 10 percent, and higher. This was a bonanza for the homeowners, but it was a bomb for those who had invested in the higher-yielding mortgage pools. Instead of having their investments run for ten to fifteen years at high rates, the investors were paid off early and then had to reinvest their money at much lower rates. They may have received all of their principal, but their in-

come was cut substantially. This happens every time home loan interest rates take a dramatic plunge.

GROUP INVESTING

Small investors can pool their money with that of other small investors in real estate to take advantage of the depreciation laws discussed earlier.

Syndication and Limited Partnerships

Usually a promoter will embark on a project such as an apartment complex or a shopping center. Shares will be parceled out in denominations of $5,000, $10,000, and so on, to investors who wish to become involved. The promoter will take a fee for efforts in organizing the syndicate and may also share in the profits of the project. These syndicates are usually structured so that the promoters reserve all control of the money and the property, and the investors have no say in the matter.

Real estate syndications often take the form of a limited partnership in which individual investors are known as limited partners and the promoters are known as general partners. Syndications and limited partnerships are not without risks. Often, unwary or gullible investors believe grossly exaggerated profit potentials on such deals, only to find that such rewards never materialize. The prudent investor in a syndication will take every precaution, including viewing and appraising the property, making certain that all legal documents are in order, and determining the reputation and reliability of the organizers.

Real Estate Investment Trusts (REITs)

Exercise 16.3

These are investment programs set up under the federal tax laws to allow small investors access to the real estate investment market. A REIT is like a mutual fund. It will pool the money of small investors to acquire a variety of real estate investments and, as long as it adheres to tax regulations, it can pass its profits, income, and depreciation deductions along to individual investors. REITs tend to be much larger and more broadly based than syndicates. Since REIT shares are sold on stock exchanges, not only is the value of REITs affected by the income and profitability of the real estate interests they own, but they are also subject to the whims of the stock market. Because of this, REITs lose much of their element of certainty for prudent investors.

Potential investors should carefully examine the prospectus of a REIT to determine the nature and type of investments it is making and what the potential returns are.

Private Partnerships

Because so many real estate investments require a large down payment, an individual might seek partners in a particular venture.

But there can be problems. All the individuals involved must be firmly committed to the same long-term objectives. For example, investment partners must determine how much of the income will be pumped back into the property for refurbishing. They must determine who will be responsible for managerial duties, bookkeeping, tenant problems, and all other matters relating to the investment.

If one partner wants to sell out, will she be required to offer the share to the other partners first and, if so, on what terms? What kind of vote will it take to determine whether the property should be sold or refinanced?

The natural human tendency is not to worry about such matters until they arise. This can be foolhardy, for nothing can stand between friends and business associates more harmfully than disagreement over money. All possible items of dispute, including these noted here, should be reduced to a binding contract among the parties at the inception of the deal. A contract can't eliminate disputes, but it can minimize them.*

INVESTING IN SMALL BUSINESSES

Many people come across opportunities to invest in local businesses, becoming involved either as silent partners, active partners, or proprietors. An existing business may be seeking fresh capital for expansion or renovation or for the purchase of equipment. The owner may prefer to seek private financing rather than bank financing. The owner may prefer to offer a share of the profits to an investor rather than having to pay interest on a loan. Or an owner may wish to sell for a variety of reasons: retirement, illness, or simply a desire to move on to something else. On the other hand, the owner may be trying to get out from under a bad situation.

In any case, a would-be investor in a going business must do extensive and detailed investigation and will need the assistance of a lawyer and an accountant. Here is a brief checklist of matters the prudent investor must examine with the aid of those professional assistants.

- **Use of funds**   If the business is seeking funds for expansion, renovation, or new equipment, how specifically will the funds be put to use?

---

*The previous discussion offers only rudimentary guidelines on real estate investing. If you contemplate becoming seriously involved in real estate investing, it would be advisable for you to take the courses and exams given in your state leading up to the licensing of salespeople and brokers. Check with your local county Board of Realtors to determine how these courses of instructions can be obtained.

What are the prospects of the new capital being able to generate added profits?

- **Reason business is being sold**   If a business is being sold, you must determine the reasons for the sale. Is it a genuine case of retirement, illness, dissatisfaction with an associate, or lack of a successor? Or is there some problem that might not be visible on the surface?

- **Goodwill**   If you will be replacing the existing owner, either totally or partially, in the day-to-day operation of the business, you'll want to determine how much of the business's success (or lack thereof) is due to the owner's presence.

- **The lease**   Your attorney should review the lease on the premises to determine how well protected you are. How long does the lease run, and what kind of renewal options do you have? What provisions are there for increases in the rent or utilities, property taxes, and maintenance? To what extent will you be responsible for repairs? Will there be any percentage clauses requiring you to pay a portion of your gross business volume to the landlord as additional rent?

Working for Yourself

Chapter 21, "Working for Yourself," was created to help you evaluate the pros and cons, the dollars and cents, of going into business on your own, either by investing in an existing entity or starting one from scratch. Whether you are looking for self-employment or just for an investment opportunity, chapter 21 will help you do the analysis and arithmetic needed (with the help of the appropriate professionals) to make sound decisions.

GAMBLING IN COMMODITIES

Like vacant land and new business ventures, the commodities market represents a form of pure speculation. It's one of the most volatile, unpredictable, and high-pressure gambles yet devised. Next to a commodities exchange, a Las Vegas casino seems tame.

A commodity transaction is a bet on how much a given item will be worth at some date in the future. All of the items on which the bets can be placed (see Table 16–5) fluctuate wildly in value, moment to moment and day to day.

There's an old saying, "If you want to make a small fortune in the commodities market, start with a big fortune." That's not a joke. Horror stories abound from investors—some sophisticated, but most naive—who have been lured into the commodities market with the hopes of fast profits. Part of the extremely speculative nature of the commodities market involves the

TABLE 16–5   **Commodities and Exchanges**

Commodities	Exchanges
Grains and oilseeds (corn, oats, soybeans, wheat, etc.)	Chicago Board of Trade
Livestock and meat (cattle, hogs, pork bellies, etc.)	Chicago Mercantile Exchange
Food and fiber (cocoa, coffee, sugar)	Coffee, Sugar & Cocoa Exchange
Metals (copper, gold, silver, platinum, paladium)	New York Commodity Exchange, New York Mercantile Exchange, Chicago Board of Trade
Petroleum products (crude oil, heating oil, gasoline)	New York Mercantile Exchange
Foreign currencies (British pound, Canadian dollar, Japanese yen, German mark, U.S. Treasury Bonds and notes	Chicago Mercantile Exchange
Stock market indexes (Standard & Poor's 500 Index, New York Stock Exchange Index)	Chicago Mercantile Exchange, New York Futures Exchange

fact that your "bet" has a time limit to it. If you make a bet on a given commodity, there's a time limit on that bet. In effect, if your horse hasn't finished in the money within the set period of time, you lose your bet altogether. In the stock market, you can own a stock as long as you like, waiting for it to hit whatever target price you have in mind. You can live with the stock for years and years as it goes through its ups and downs. But, with commodities, when the expiration date arrives, your betting ticket becomes worthless.

Your bet can be won or lost because of many exotic and unpredictable influences, including weather conditions, crop blights, national and international politics, major shifts in the world's economy, minor shifts in the economy of any given nation, consumer boycotts, wars and insurrections, and even subtle shifts in popular opinion.

Exercise 16.4

Table 16–5 lists a small sampling of some of the items that can be bet on in the commodities market, as well as the exchange where the betting can be done. Any student interested in learning more about speculating in the commodities market can obtain abundant material through a stockbroker or through individual exchanges.

Commodity Funds

If the commodities market intrigues you, but the high level of risk frightens you, you might find commodity funds more to your liking. Commodity

funds pool small investors' money and bet it on a diversified selection of commodities. In effect, commodity funds act like mutual funds, but technically they are a form of limited partnership.

Commodity funds can be somewhat less risky than direct speculations in commodities because of the diversification that is not available to individuals speculating on their own. Furthermore, at least it is hoped, professional management of the fund should be capable of making better decisions than an individual can.

Commodity fund investors should be wary of the costs they can incur by investing in the fund. It's not unusual for total costs, including management fees, brokerage commissions, and incentive fees, to total as much as 20 to 30 percent per year. That means that the investor won't make any money at all until after the fund has earned enough to cover those fees.

The prospectus of any commodity fund should be read thoroughly before an investment decision is made. In examining the prospectus, you should determine the extent of diversification of the fund's assets, the experience of the portfolio manager, and your ability to get your money out when you want it.

FOREIGN EXCHANGE AND DEPOSITS

Foreign Investing

In addition to speculating on various foreign currencies in the commodities market (see Table 16–5), there are many other ways that people can invest and/or speculate in the economic facets of other nations.

Bank Accounts

U.S. investors often open bank accounts in other nations, particularly Canada and Mexico. They may be lured by attractive interest rates, or they may be planning to spend time in those other nations and want the convenience of having accounts there. The latter reason makes more sense. If you're simply hoping to earn a higher rate of interest abroad than you can at home, then you must take into account a number of factors that can be unpredictable: the future exchange rate of the U.S. dollar versus the other currency; the tax laws of the other nation; and the ever-present possibility of the other currency's being devalued. In order to open a bank account in the currency of another nation, you have to convert your dollars to, for example, pesos. Then, when you want to retrieve the money to spend it back at home, you have to convert it from pesos back to dollars. These exchanges will cost you something, which could offset much of the seemingly attractive rate of interest you had hoped to earn. Tax laws in the other nation might require that a portion of your earnings be withheld to pay taxes in

STRATEGIES FOR SUCCESS

Beware of Unregulated Businesses

Stock markets and banks are strictly regulated by the government. If something goes wrong, you *might* have an ally in the state or federal government who can help you unravel the problem. But in many other areas of investment opportunity, governmental regulation ranges from slim to none. Simply stated, this means that if something goes wrong, you're on your own. You may have no recourse to any official agency. Generally speaking, franchising, distributorships, investments in precious metals, and limited partnerships are subject to relatively little governmental regulation. Even where regulation does exist, the road to recovery can be long and tortuous. Before you send away your money, know who's out there to help you get it back if things go wrong.

that nation. With respect to the possibility of devaluation, your investment can be immediately diminished in value if the other nation unilaterally declares that its currency is worth less per dollar today than it was yesterday. Another overriding concern: Your bank deposits in the United States enjoy the protection of the Federal Deposit Insurance programs. Would you enjoy the same protection if you invested in the banks of other nations?

Stock and Mutual Funds

Exercise 16.5

A small number of stocks in foreign companies can be bought and sold on United States stock exchanges using the device called American depository receipts (ADRs). In effect, a major U.S. bank buys a supply of shares of those particular companies and holds them in an escrow account for the benefit of American investors who purchase the ADRs. As an owner of the ADRs, you're subject to the same market fluctuations as you would be if you owned the stock directly.

Most major U.S. mutual fund companies offer a variety of funds specializing in foreign regions or specific nations. By investing in these funds, you get the benefit of supposedly expert analysis and advice in choosing particular stocks.

PRECIOUS METALS

Gold, silver, and platinum are extremely risky speculations. This was made clear at the start of the 1980s, and matters aren't likely to change for the rest of the century. Witness: In the early months of 1980, gold

soared to more than $825 an ounce from the previous year's level of about $250 an ounce. At the same time, silver reached $50 an ounce from its level a year earlier of about $10 an ounce. In early 1982, gold had plummeted to less than $330 an ounce—a loss of more than 60 percent to those who had bought it at its peak. And there were many who had done so. The silver debacle was much swifter. One wealthy Texas family, the Hunts, had virtually cornered the silver market in early 1980, borrowing heavily to do so. When their ability to repay those debts came into doubt, the price of silver plunged by 80 percent within just a few months. Many small investors were wiped out.

Would-be investors in precious metals should remember the reasons why gold and other metals became tarnished: Widespread abuses and fraudulent dealings scared many people away from buying metals. Metal prices no longer seemed to respond to the signals that had set price moves just a few years earlier, signals such as world crises, inflationary trends, and interest rate movements. Many of the so-called gold bugs—commentators and analysts who touted the metals—began to lose their loyal followers because of bad advice. The speculative fever could return at any time, and when it does, many more innocents will get burned.

If you must speculate in precious metals, it is imperative that you deal only with firms whose reputations are totally reliable. Particularly avoid dealing with strangers over the telephone or through the mail. Whomever you deal with, use the following standards of measurement to be certain that you're getting what you bargained for.

Gold and silver are weighed in troy ounces. There are 31 grams to a troy ounce, and there are 480 grains to a troy ounce. It can be dangerous to confuse grains and grams and ounces.

What is referred to as pure gold is known as 24-karat gold. Anything less than 24-karat gold means that gold is mixed with another metal. Thus, 18-karat gold is $^{18}/_{24}$ (or 75 percent) real pure gold and 25 percent other metal; 12-karat gold is 1/2 pure gold and ½ other metal. Similarly, what is referred to as sterling silver is not pure silver but, rather, roughly 92.5 percent silver and the rest other metal.

The commonly quoted prices for these metals do not refer to a single ounce but to a much larger quantity. The price is known as the spot price; gold is quoted in 100 troy-ounce lots and silver in 5,000 troy-ounce lots. You would, then, expect to pay a higher price per ounce for quantities under the spot level.

Where to Speculate

- **Commodity exchanges**   You can bet on the future value of precious metals on a number of commodity exchanges. Gold is traded on the

New York Commodity Exchange. Platinum is traded on the New York Mercantile Exchange. Silver is traded on the New York Commodity Exchange and the Chicago Board of Trade. Most major stock brokerage firms can place these bets for you.

- **Mining companies** Rather than buy the metals themselves, you can buy stock in the companies that mine them. Again, stock brokerage firms can handle the transactions for you. Mining stocks can be every bit as speculative as the metals themselves, but many do pay dividends, so your money is earning something for you as long as you own the stock.

- **Coins** Many nations, including the United States, have minted gold coins over the years. Some of them are older and, if in good condition, may have collector value over and above the gold value itself. To determine the true value of any such investment seek the assistance of a reputable coin dealer. All coins are subject to counterfeiting.

- **Jewelry** All gold jewelry manufactured in the United States is by law required to have the correct karat content stamped on the piece. But this law is not rigidly enforced. The best protection is to deal with reputable jewelers. Speculating in gold by way of jewelry purchases is probably the least feasible in terms of making money, for you will pay the dealer's markup plus the cost of any artistry that has gone into making the piece. It's unlikely that you'd be able to recapture those costs unless the value of gold triples or quadruples within a fairly short period of time.

One final caution: Trading in gold and silver—except on the commodity exchanges—is virtually unregulated. That means you'll have no governmental agency to turn to for help if you find you've been bilked.

STRATEGIC METALS

Strategic metals, in the broad sense, include cobalt, manganese, iridium, molybdenum, and chromium, among others. These metals are considered important to our national defense and industrial production, but we must import them from other countries in large quantities. Advances in technology could render some currently strategic metals not so strategic in the future; conversely, other currently insignificant metals and chemicals could become very important in the future.

As with the precious metals, the strategic metals are often touted as easy paths to getting rich quick by the same kinds of promoters who push gold and silver. As with gold and silver, the strategic metals investments are highly speculative.

GEMSTONES

The most popular form of gemstone speculation has been in diamonds. But speculation in colored gemstones (rubies, emeralds, and sapphires, primarily) has also been popular.

Gemstones are as unique as snowflakes. They vary not only in size and color, but also in basic quality, from priceless to pure junk. If you buy any gemstone sight unseen, you could be getting the junk. To buy any gemstone without first having it appraised by an independent certified gemologist is extremely hazardous.

Whether it's your intent to speculate in gemstones or to acquire them as jewelry pieces, you should be aware of the characteristics that contribute to their value or lack thereof. Diamonds are considered to be the most easily appraised of all gemstones. Colored gemstones are more difficult to appraise accurately because of the wider range of colors and chemical compositions in them. But, even with diamonds, experts can vary by as much as 10 to 20 percent in their estimates of value.

Diamonds are evaluated in accordance with the four "Cs." Colored gemstones use similar formulas. The four Cs are color, cut, clarity, and carat weight.

Exercise 16.6

- **Color**   Diamonds can range in color from the highly regarded "pure blue-white" to murky yellows. The better the color, the higher the value. Gemologists can grade the color of a diamond by use of a spectroscope. Even slight differences in the color grade can make a substantial difference in the value of a given stone.

- **Cut**   Raw diamonds (in the rough) will be cut into various sizes and shapes. The more highly valued cuts are those that permit the maximum brilliance of light to refract through the stone. The depth of the stone and the faceting contribute to brilliance or lack of it. The shape of the finished stone can also bear on its value. Gemologists can measure the precision of the cut of any diamond and grade it numerically.

- **Clarity**   When a diamond is looked at under a magnifying glass or microscope, impurities appear. (Some may even be visible to the naked eye.) The highest-clarity diamonds are those with the fewest flaws. Clarity is also rated numerically by gemologists.

- **Carat weight**   There's a lot of confusion between *karat* and *carat*. *Karat*, as noted earlier in the discussion on gold, measures the percentage of pure gold in a given item. *Carat* is an actual unit of weight. Thus, a diamond might weigh—on an actual scale—one carat, or two carats, and so on. A carat is divided into 100 points. Thus, a 25-point diamond is equal to one-quarter of a carat. Of two diamonds equal in color, cut, and clarity, the heavier one (carat weight) is the more valuable. But a one-carat stone of high quality in terms of color, cut, and clarity could be worth

vastly more than a three-carat stone whose cut, color, or clarity is poor. Also, a single stone is worth more than an aggregate of smaller stones of equal quality and total weight. Thus, a single one-carat stone will be worth more than four 25-point stones of equal quality.

COLLECTIBLES

The possibilities are limitless: from old comic books to Chinese jade, from antique buttons to hubcaps, and everything in between. Whether prudent investment or wild speculation, the field of collectibles offers a measure of personal satisfaction in the hobby aspects of the endeavor. Thus, it is difficult to evaluate the financial considerations of collecting. If you get enough pleasure out of accumulating beer cans, movie posters, or original Picasso oil paintings, then perhaps the money doesn't matter.

But whether your objectives in collecting are personal, financial, or any combination of these, you need to observe some basic precautions lest you be separated from too much money needlessly.

- Coins and stamps are the most established forms of collectibles. Abundant information has been published on both, and the novice should take advantage of that literature. Both before buying and before selling, the latest price lists should be consulted. If major transactions are contemplated, an outside appraisal can be inexpensive insurance to protect a large investment.

- Many forms of collectibles cannot be readily converted into cash. The more exotic the items, the fewer potential buyers there may be. Finding a buyer for a collection may require considerable time and expense—such as advertising in specialized publications that deal with those types of items.

- Art collectors may have to turn to dealers to convert their collectibles into cash. A dealer is likely to pay only half the item's retail value, and that could mean a loss to the collector. On the other hand, some dealers are willing to take an item on consignment and take a commission on a sale. The commission may range from 10 to 25 percent. If the dealer is not successful in selling it, you take it back.

- Many collectibles go through fads. They may be hot one year, cold the next. If you get involved in a fad collectible that is on the wane, you could end up a big loser, but if you're lucky enough to get in on the rise, you could be a big winner.

- All collectibles require some level of expertise. Much of that expertise can be acquired by studying; much of it only by trial and error. Before embarking on a program of collectibles, therefore, do whatever studying you can and then proceed with caution until you are confident of when and what to buy, and when and what to sell.

TELEVISION "INVESTMENT OPPORTUNITIES"

Hardly a day goes by in which the average television viewer, flipping through the channels, doesn't find yet another get-rich quick scheme being offered on the tube in the form of a seminar, a lecture, a classroom full of "eager students," or some other such sales gimmick. Popular subjects for these spiels have been real estate, the stock market, mail-order distributorships, and a variety of cleverly disguised pyramid schemes. If anyone makes money from these so-called investments, it's the cable TV operator and the promoter—not the person who spends many hundreds of dollars for the "learn-at-home self-study kit." Valid information may be contained in those kits, whether it's on audiocassette or in printed form. But putting the information to use is never as easy as the TV pitchman makes you think it is. Nor are the "students" in the TV seminar classroom as honest or as eager as they seem to be. They are probably hired actors performing a role for a day's pay rather than satisfied investors who have already gotten rich from the product. These self-promoting television programs prey on the naive and gullible individual trying to to find a new career or investment opportunity. They should be approached with the utmost caution. And note well: The money-back guarantees that are generally offered are worthless if, in fact, the company does not honor those guarantees. That has been the case all too often, leaving customers out many hundreds of dollars, with no recourse to anyone to get their money back.

PRIVATE LENDING

While not generally thought of as such, lending money to individuals or businesses is a form of investment. Whether they approach you or you approach them, the same precautions are in order: Establish terms (interest rate, repayment date) that will be fair and reasonable. Check the credit of the borrower to determine the level of risk you are undertaking. If you think that the borrower's signature alone on the promissory note does not adequately protect you, seek either collateral or a cosigner for the loan. Be certain that you know the borrower's financial status: What other debts does the borrower have? What kind of income sources does he or she have? And, all things considered, from what sources will the borrower be able to make repayment on the loan? Have a promissory note properly drawn up by a lawyer, setting forth all the appropriate terms, including your rights should the borrower default on the payments. Have the borrower (and cosigner, if any) sign the note.

In short, take all the same precautions a bank would take when making a loan. If you find yourself faced with the prospect of making a private loan, a chat with your banker could be helpful to make sure you protect yourself adequately. In addition to having the banker show you the specifics of the

loan procedure, it might be wise to inquire whether the banker would be willing to make the loan himself or to buy the loan from you should you later wish to sell the borrower's IOU. A banker who balks at either prospect probably sees some flaw in the loan that you might want to know about. Are you willing to take a risk that the bank would not?

KNOWLEDGE

Whether you're investing in the money market, the stock market, the real estate market, any of these assorted miscellaneous investments/speculations, or any new activities that may come along, the best investment of all is your own investment in knowledge. The world of money is changing at an increasingly rapid pace: taxes, interest rates, governmental regulations, the emergence of new techniques, are all in a state of flux. Your own individual circumstances are also changing. You can't afford to ignore this outpouring of new information. If you want to make your money grow, you must fertilize it. And knowledge is the best fertilizer.

PERSONAL ACTION WORKSHEET —————————————

Income Property Evaluator

Before undertaking an investment in income property, make a careful analysis of both the cash flow and the condition of the property. The following analysis sheet will help you get started. Further analysis as to the specific investment advantages should be done with the help of your accountant and real estate agent.

	Prop. A	Prop. B	Prop. C
❏ What is the general condition of the building, including foundation, walls, roof, landscaping?	_____	_____	_____
❏ What is the specific condition of "working" aspects, including plumbing, heating, air conditioning, electrical system, elevators, appliances?	_____	_____	_____
❏ What is the current rental income (all sources)?	_____	_____	_____
❏ Are there any controls on raising rents?	_____	_____	_____
❏ What is the potential rental income within 12, 24, and 36 months?	_____	_____	_____
❏ What are the current operating expenses?	_____	_____	_____
❏ Do leases provide that tenants absorb any portion of operating expenses?	_____	_____	_____
❏ What are the potential total operating expenses within 12, 24, and 36 months? (Allow for likely increases in property taxes, insurance, maintenance, etc.)	_____	_____	_____
❏ What is the general condition of the immediate neighborhood, and what are the future trends?	_____	_____	_____
❏ Are nearby traffic patterns likely to remain stable, or might they be changed?	_____	_____	_____
❏ Can the existing mortgage be assumed by the buyer? At what interest rate?	_____	_____	_____
❏ What is the cost of interest for new financing, if needed?	_____	_____	_____

❏   What type of secondary financing will be needed?

_____   _____   _____

❏   Will the seller make secondary financing available? At what interest rate? Terms?

_____   _____   _____

❏   What is the estimated management time and money needed to run the property efficiently (in hours and dollars per week)?

_____   _____   _____

If You're So Rich, How Come You're Not Smart?

Pardon the reversal on the old saying. It used to be that if you were smart you should also be rich. Nowadays, there's growing evidence that just because you are rich doesn't necessarily mean you're smart, too. If you have all the money in the world to hire the best talent and pay for the best research, how far wrong can you go, particularly if the players are the Rockefellers in the United States and the Mitsubishi people from Japan? And if players like that can goof horrendously, what's the poor novice investor to do? Here's what happened to these heavy hitters:

Mitsubishi bought an 80 percent interest in Rockefeller Center for about $1.4 billion, of which $1.3 billion was a mortgage owed to the sellers, Rockefeller Center Properties, Inc. But despite having such major-league tenants as General Electric, NBC, Simon & Schuster, and Radio City Music Hall, there wasn't enough rental income to make the mortgage payments. Attempts to renegotiate the mortgage failed, so Mitsubishi threw the property into bankruptcy, which could take years to unravel.

But don't pity the poor Rockefellers. They had the good sense to lay off their bet with a Real Estate Investment Trust (REIT), which took in money from some 40,000 small investors to cover the Rockefeller exposure. Shares in the REIT plummeted from $20 to $5. How far wrong can you go with names like Rockefeller and Mitsubishi? Ask the REIT 40,000.

But that sad deal pales by comparison with the experience of Dr. Sasaki, a Japanese investor who saw his net worth go from $4.7 billion to *minus* $2.4 billion in just a few years. *The Wall Street Journal* dubbed Dr. Sasaki the *poorest person in the world.* Here is what happened to the good doctor:

In the 1980s speculation was rampant in real estate in Japan, due largely to the government opening up the lending spigots full blast at the banks. Dr. Sasaki took advantage of the cheap and easy borrowing and accumulated ninety buildings! With all that money chasing a finite amount of property (the classical definition of inflation), property values soared out of sight.

Then in 1990 the erstwhile clueless Japanese government began to worry about the high property values. If borrowers couldn't pay their loans, the defaults could bring down the entire economy. So, to curb the speculation, the government forced the banks to raise interest rates on existing loans and curtail new lending. Guess what? The real estate market crashed, and Dr. Sasaki ended up owing $2.4 billion more than the buildings were worth. Don't you hate it when that happens?

Could U.S. lenders do the same thing? Not only could they. They did! It was called the Savings and Loan debacle. And yes, it could happen again.

UPS & DOWNS   *The Economics of Everyday Life*

Why Collectibles Go Up and Down in Value

Collecting things can be fun. If you can have fun and make money too, all the better. With this kind of attitude imbedded in the minds of many people, a collectible "industry" has emerged, making things for people who want to have fun and make money. The fun part is easy; the money part can be quite tricky. Originally, collectibles meant stamps and coins. While governments printed and minted millions of each, there was a known limit to the number created, and each had the legitimacy of a government behind it. And governments are nonprofit entities.

When private companies make *collectibles*, there is concern as to how their profit-making motives will impact on the future value of the items they make. Those items include huge numbers of plates, dolls, figurines, souvenirs, toys, sports cards, lithographs, and comic books. The following techniques can be used to manipulate values.

Fad   Clever marketers will spot fads and be ready for them with a supply of collectibles to sell. Olympic pins were all the rage at the Atlanta games in 1996. Sports memorabilia come and go with the popularity and incomes of our athletic heroes. (On a morbid note, when Magic Johnson announced that he was HIV-positive, a run began on his memorabilia and prices went sky-high.) When the fads fade—and they always do—so do the prices.

Questionable advertising   Collectibles are worth more if they are made in limited number—and still more if each one is numbered—and still more if each one is signed by the artist—and still more if the mold or engraving plate is destroyed after the limited number is made, which assures that no more can ever be made. Many ads may say that they are *limited editions*, but that can mean anything: "limited to how many we can make in the next twelve months" or "limited to the number of orders we get." A true limited edition must state a specific number. Legitimate manufacturers will stick to that number, and the long-term value of the object will be reflected accordingly.

Secondary market   One way to artificially boost the price of *new* collectible items is to manipulate public opinion as to the value of *older* items in the series. Say that each year a company makes a porcelain doll of that year's Oscar-winning director. They are marketed as *collectibles*, with hints that they will increase in value each year. The 1993 doll was issued at $100, and later models went up by $25 each year. When the newest model is announced, collectors salivate when they hear that the market value of the 1993 model is now $500! But it can all be a sham. To manipulate the secondary market (the price of the older dolls), a few ads can be placed in catalogs that collectors read, offering to buy the 1993 doll for $500. Word travels fast. When you call to sell them yours, you'll be told they've already bought all they can afford. Sorry. Similar gossip can also be spread at collectible shows and on the Internet. The new models sell out, and the game begins anew the next year.

? WHAT IF . . . ?

Test yourself: How would you deal with these real-life possibilities?

1. There's yet another crisis in the Middle East. A shooting war seems likely. You get a phone call from a stranger pitching gold: "The price will go through the roof because of international uncertainties." He may be right. Evaluate the pros and cons of dealing with this person.

2. You are on the Building Committee of your synagogue or church. Money is being pledged by members to build a day school. It's expected that it will take two to three years for the money to come in, and another year after it's all in before construction is ready to proceed. In the meantime the money has to be invested. Other members of your committee include a commodity broker and a mortgage broker. They both offer plans to invest the money through their own channels. In each case they will relinquish their normal commissions if the investments flow through them. You are asked for your thoughts on those modes of investing. What would you say?

3. On a visit to Mexico you learn that Mexican banks are paying five percentage points more to savers than are banks back home. You're intrigued, and you consider shifting most of your savings there to boost your earnings. If millions of Mexican citizens are doing it, why shouldn't you? What further information do you need in order to make a sound decision?

 NUMBER CRUNCHERS

Do the calculations to make decisions in these real-life possibilities.

1. Some friends are urging you to chip in with them to buy a vacant parcel of land on the outskirts of your city. They feel there's a good chance to make a tidy profit as the city grows in that direction. A one-fourth interest would cost you $10,000. Total annual expenses on the property are $2,200 (including property taxes and insurance). When the property is sold, assume that you'll have to pay a real estate commission of 10 percent of the selling price and that income taxes on any profit will be 15 percent of the profit. If the property is sold after three years, how much will it have to sell for so that you can reap an average annual net return of 10 percent on your $10,000 investment?

2. You're thinking of investing in real estate. You look at a residential property priced at $175,000 and find that 35 percent of that price represents the land value. A commercial property is priced at $240,000, and 68 percent of that price represents the land value. Based on the depreciation periods noted in this chapter, how much of an annual

depreciation deduction would you be entitled to on each of these buildings, if you paid the asking price?

3. You invest $500 a year for five years in stamp collecting. That money could have earned 6 percent per year, compounding annually, in a savings plan. At the end of five years, how much would the stamps have to be worth to be equal to what you would have had in the savings plan (not counting income taxes)?

FOR BETTER OR FOR WORSE

Things beyond our control often impact our personal and financial well-being, for better or for worse. Some are more predictable than others. How could you be affected if the following real-life phenomena happened? Could you have seen it coming? What steps could you have taken to minimize damage or maximize advantage? The better able you are to anticipate and recognize these forces, the better equipped you are to deal with them.

1. You invest in a small apartment building. Even though the rental income in the first year will be offset by your expenses, the expected 10 percent annual increases in rent will produce a nice profit for you. Shortly thereafter, the city passes a rent control ordinance limiting rent increases to 2 percent a year.

2. A broker convinces you to bet a lot of money on the future value of the British pound. If the pound is strong against the dollar, you're a big winner, and the British government looks certain to succeed economically. Along comes a three-month dock strike against British shippers. The British economy is crippled, and the pound plunges against the dollar.

3. A late-night TV infomercial is selling a course on how to get rich in real estate by buying property with no money down. For $499 you can buy the course, with a money-back guarantee within thirty days if you're not satisfied. After twenty-nine days you're not satisfied, and you call the company to ask for your money back. You're told that you didn't use the right technique to buy the properties, and that you should "try it this way for another month and see if it doesn't work out for you."

17

Life, Health, and Income Insurance

This is a world of action, and not for moping and groaning in.
Charles Dickens

Part Five is titled "Protecting What You Work For." In order to do that, you must take steps to minimize the risks that everyone faces in day-to-day life: loss of life, serious medical problems, and loss of income. All the best financial planning in the world can come to naught if you do not take these steps to protect yourself.

This chapter isn't going to try to sell you any insurance; rather, it's designed to enable you to

- Understand how life, health, and income insurance policies work
- Distinguish among different types of policies, their benefits, and their costs
- Gain a working knowledge of the language and jargon of insurance policies so that you can communicate clearly with sales personnel
- Determine how much of what type of insurance you actually need as part of your overall protection plan
- Be aware, and take advantage, of insurance programs available through various governmental agencies

COPING WITH RISK

Life is full of surprises—risks—that we don't always anticipate or prepare for. Some of these risks we accept willingly: driving a car, taking on a new job, investing or betting our money. Others may be strictly a matter of fate: illness, natural disaster, an employer going bankrupt.

In earlier chapters, we examined automobile insurance and home-owner's (and tenant's) insurance. Those types of insurance reimburse us for damages suffered to our cars and our dwellings and also reimburse people who suffer losses arising from automobile accidents that involve us and accidents to others on our property. We may never suffer losses in connection with our cars or our homes, but we still need the insurance to protect us against the *possibility* of such losses.

Likewise with health and income insurance: We may never be ill, and we may never suffer loss of income from extended illness, accident, or other unforeseen cause. But we still need insurance to protect us against the *unforeseen*.

Life insurance is designed to provide money to the survivors of an insured person when that person dies. Death is certain to occur, but we never know when. If the breadwinner of a young and growing family dies prematurely, life insurance will, in effect, reimburse the survivors for lost earnings, thus enabling them to continue to live in relative comfort and security. If an insured person dies at or after the normal life-expectancy age, the proceeds of the insurance may be needed to pay estate taxes, to provide support for a surviving spouse, to allow the insured's business to continue, or simply to add to the wealth of the survivors. Let's take a look at insurance in general as a device to protect us against loss. Then we'll examine the basic mechanics of life insurance.

Insurance Is Protection Against Risk

That is what insurance is all about. Example: On an average day, 1,000 skiers will run a slope and one will end up in the hospital. The cost of hospitalization may be $5,000. You never know whether that injured skier will be you or one of the 999 others. If it is you, your injuries will cost you $5,000. But if each skier chipped in $5 to cover the cost of that day's accident—whomever it might happen to—you have eliminated your risk at a very insignificant cost. For the price of $5, you may have saved yourself $5,000. You may run the slope 1,000 times and never be hurt, but experience indicates that that's not likely.

If all the skiers don't chip into a kitty to protect themselves, some enterprising person may make the arrangements for them: point out the risks each skier faces, arrange to collect and hold all the money in safekeeping, and pay the proceeds to the injured parties as injuries occur. For this

service, the entrepreneur is entitled to a fee; thus, instead of charging $5 per skier, the charge may be $5.10 or $5.20. In so doing, the entrepreneur is acting as a one-person insurance company.

That, in a nutshell, is how the insurance industry operates. The insurance company determines the probability of loss in many given situations, such as a house burning down, an automobile crashing, a person dying before the normal life expectancy, and so on. The company further determines how much money it must collect from each individual to insure protection for all the individuals, should the stated loss occur. (These calculations are known as the actuarial phase of insurance.) That money, or premiums, paid by the insured is invested prudently, so that the fund, or reserve, can grow until it comes time to pay benefits to people who have suffered losses.

When one enters into an agreement with an insurance company the parties sign a contract that sets forth all the specific rights, duties, and obligations of the parties. This contract is called an insurance policy. Its details are discussed later.

WHY LIFE INSURANCE?

Victor is forty years old with a wife and two teenage children. He's in good health and makes about $45,000 per year with good prospects for improvement. He wants his children to have a good college education, but meeting his mortgage payments hasn't allowed him to put much money aside for college. Even though Victor's life expectancy is about an additional thirty-five years, he's very much aware that he could die tomorrow. Contemplating this possibility, Victor thinks, "If I died suddenly, where would the money come from to keep my family reasonably comfortable and provide for the college educations? I'd need an immediate nest egg of about $300,000. If they invested that wisely, the income and some of the principal could take care of their needs for quite a long time. But right now I'd have trouble raising the price of a new suit, let alone $300,000."

Instant Solution?

How can Victor resolve this dilemma? He might be lucky enough to beat multimillion-to-one odds and win a lottery. Or he could stash money in a savings plan; at the rate of $300 per month, he'd meet his goal in just under twenty-five years. These aren't very satisfactory solutions.

To solve his problem, Victor needs an *immediate* and *guaranteed* way to create protection for his family. That is the main purpose of life insurance.

Life insurance can be created instantly (or, more correctly, in the few weeks it takes to process an application). Rather than take chances on a lottery ticket or wait decades for a savings fund to build up, Victor can immediately create the level of protection he wants through life insurance.

STRATEGIES FOR SUCCESS

Insure Before It's Too Late

The single most important lesson in this chapter, and perhaps even in the whole book, is that *you never know when you might become uninsurable!* Whether for life, health, disability income, or long-term care insurance, you can become uninsurable as a result of unexpected medical problems. A slightly less worst-case scenario is that a medical condition might cause you to have to pay a lot more for the coverage you want, compared with if you were in good health. Further, the older you are, the more costly the insurance can be. When it comes to insurance, playing the waiting game can definitely be a losing proposition.

The protection is guaranteed as long as the premiums on the policy are paid. Victor may also consider the desirability of life insurance for his wife and children. If his wife works and if the family also depends on her income, she should consider insuring her life so as to replace the income that would be lost in the event of her premature death. Insurance on the life of a nonworking spouse can pay the costs of treating a terminal illness or paying for child care now provided by the nonworking spouse. If the spouse's estate is subject to estate taxes, life insurance can be used to pay those taxes in lieu of having to sell other assets to pay the tax. The *primary* objective of a family's life insurance portfolio should be the replacement of income in the event of a breadwinner's death.

On learning how the dilemmas can be solved, Victor (and you) are likely to ask, "Can I afford to do it?" But a more appropriate question might be, "Can I afford *not* to do it?" The material that follows will give you guidelines that will be useful in establishing any life insurance program suitable for your own needs.

THE BASIC ELEMENTS OF LIFE INSURANCE

A life insurance policy is a contract between an individual and a life insurance company. The individual agrees to pay premiums, in return for which the company guarantees to pay a certain amount to the beneficiaries named in the contract at the death of the insured party. But life insurance policies are as different as snowflakes. There are more than 1,800 life insurance companies in the United States, and all of them offer many different types of policies. Furthermore, the mathematics of life insurance differ widely, depending on the age of the insured at the time the policy is purchased, the amount and type of coverage, and the specific terms of the contract. The most visible common thread in all life insurance contracts is that the

younger you are when you initiate a contract, the lower your costs will be. Let us now examine some of the major diversities in life insurance.

Kinds of Companies: Stock and Mutual

There are basically two different kinds of life insurance companies: stock companies and mutual companies. Stock companies are owned by stockholders, in much the same fashion as stockholders own such companies as General Motors and AT&T. If the company is run profitably, the stockholders will receive dividends on their stock in much the same way as stockholders of industrial companies.

Mutual companies are owned by their policyholders. In a mutual company, when the premium income exceeds the expenses (benefits paid and other expenses) by a certain amount, the policyholders/owners will receive back a portion of the excess. These sums are also referred to as dividends, but they are technically not the same thing as dividends received on common stock.

Par and Nonpar Policies

The kinds of policies issued by mutual companies, for which dividends are paid to policyholders, are referred to as participating policies—the policyholders participate in a distribution of excess income over expenses.

Stock companies generally do not pay such dividends to their policyholders. These policies are referred to as nonparticipating policies. In some instances, however, stock companies do issue participating policies.

Participating and nonparticipating policies are commonly referred to as par and nonpar.

The difference between stock and mutual companies may be better understood by referring back to the earlier example of the skiers. The skiers who banded together on their own to chip in $5 for each day formed a kind of mutual company. The skiers who declined to do this on their own but entrusted the matter to an outsider took part in a stock company.

Premiums on par policies will customarily be higher than premiums on nonpar policies, all other things being equal. But the owner of a par policy has the hope of receiving dividends each year that may be used to offset the cost of the policy. The dividends on a par policyholder could reduce the out-of-pocket cost of insurance to less than that of an equal nonpar policy. For example, two policies of equal face value, one par and one nonpar, have annual premiums of $300 and $250. If the par policy pays a dividend of $60 per year, then the par policy will end up being less expensive than the nonpar policy. But insurance companies cannot give any guarantee of what dividends will be paid in any given year. It will depend on their actual experience of premium dollars received and expense and benefit dollars paid out.

How Is Life Insurance Acquired?

Life insurance is generally acquired in one of three ways: group plans, private plans, and credit plans.

Group Plans

Group life insurance is designed for groups of people in similar circumstances. Your employer, for example, may provide a plan for all employees. Group insurance may also be issued to members of social organizations, professional organizations, and unions. The insured individuals may not be required to take physical examinations to prove the state of their health. The group insurance policy will cover all eligible persons, and each will receive a copy of the master policy, or an outline of it. In some cases, the employer or union may pay the premiums for all the individuals; in other cases, such as professional associations, individuals make their own payments.

When an individual ceases to be a member of the group, his or her insurance may terminate. But, in many cases, it's possible for the individual to continue the coverage by paying the necessary premiums personally.

Because administration costs on a group policy can be much lower than those on individual policies, the premium cost to those in a group plan is generally lower than what it would be in a private plan.

Private Plans

Private insurance is contracted for directly between the individual and the insurance company. Depending on the issuing company and the amount of insurance involved, a physical examination of the insured may be required.

Credit Plans

When you borrow money, the lender may offer you life insurance that will pay off any balance on the loan should you die. This is available in mortgage loans and in installment loans, such as for an automobile or home improvements. The amount of the insurance decreases as the balance on the loan decreases. (This is known as decreasing term insurance.) In short-term installment loans, the insured will generally pay the full premium in one lump sum at the inception of the loan. In long-term loans, the amount of the insurance premium is frequently added to the amount of the loan and is included in the payments.

Types of Life Insurance

Life insurance policies are generally either permanent or temporary. Permanent insurance is designed to run permanently: that is, for the life of the

insured individual. This type of insurance is known as ordinary, straight or whole life insurance.

Temporary insurance is designed to run for a specific period of time, such as one year, five years, or ten years. This is known as term insurance. At the end of the term, the insurance ceases. With renewable-term policies, the insured can renew for an additional term, but at a higher premium cost. Term policies may also be convertible to ordinary policies.

Universal life insurance offers a variety of flexible features: Within limits, the face amount of the policy and the amount of annual premium can be adjusted by the owner of the policy.

Another type of life insurance contract is the annuity, in which the insured is guaranteed a fixed monthly payment, which will begin at a specified time and will last for the agreed-on length of time. Let's take a closer look at these various types of life insurance.

Permanent Insurance

Permanent insurance is a lifetime contract. You agree to pay a fixed premium, and the insurance company agrees to deliver a stated sum of money at your death or, in certain cases, at some earlier time. If the money is to become payable prior to death, the insured may elect to receive it in a lump sum or in periodic installments, plus interest. The company can also hold the money (paying interest on it) for as long as the insured lives and then pay it to the beneficiaries. The rate of interest payable on money held for the insured or survivors will be set forth in the contract.

A permanent policy builds up *cash values*, also referred to as conversion values or nonforfeiture values. These values permit the insured to terminate the policy and obtain either cash or some other form of insurance at some later time. These values are discussed in more detail later.

Examples of permanent insurance include:

- You agree to pay the stated premiums for, say, twenty years. At the end of that period, the policy will be *paid up*—the full face value will be payable on death, and you don't have to pay any more premiums. This policy would be referred to as a Limited Pay Plan or, in this case, Twenty-pay Life: Twenty years of payments pays it up in full.

- You agree to pay the stated premiums for the remainder of your life. At your death, the full face value will be payable. This policy would be referred to as a Whole Life Policy.

- You agree to make certain premium payments, and the full face value is then paid at a stated age, say, 65. If you don't elect to take the cash, you can exercise other options such as receiving installment payments or having the company hold it for you for later payment to you or your beneficiaries. Such a policy may be referred to as *endowment at age 65*.

The amount of the premiums for these various policies varies considerably. For example, in the Twenty-pay Life policy, the insurance company has only 20 years in which to accumulate the money needed to pay the benefits, even though the life expectancy of the individual may be much longer. So the company must charge a higher premium than it would for Whole Life, for it has fewer years in which to accumulate the needed funds.

In the endowment policy, the full face value becomes payable at a specific age. Again, the company has fewer years in which to accumulate the needed money than it would on a Whole Life policy, so it must charge more accordingly.

Term Insurance

Term insurance is "pure" insurance. You obtain a fixed amount of protection at a fixed annual price for a fixed amount of time. For example, a 25-year-old might obtain a term policy for $25,000 for five years at an annual premium of $100 per year. In most term policies policyholders can renew for an additional term but at a higher annual premium, since they are older. Thus, the 25-year-old, on reaching age 30, might find that his $25,000 worth of protection will now cost $120 per year. To renew for another five-year term at age 35, the annual premium might go to $150 per year. As the insured gets older still, the cost will increase at greater rates on each renewal.

With rare exceptions, term insurance policies do not build up any of the cash or conversion values found in permanent policies.

Many term insurance policies contain a right to convert to a permanent insurance policy at stated times. Depending on the company and the amount of insurance, the insured may or may not have to take a physical examination, either on initiating or renewing the term policy or on converting it to a permanent policy.

Because term insurance does not have any cash value buildup as a rule, it is the least expensive for initial out-of-pocket premium expenses. But as term insurance is renewed at ever-increasing ages—and thereby at increasing rates—the ultimate out-of-pocket expenses can exceed those of permanent life insurance.

As indicated earlier, another, and still cheaper, form of term insurance is decreasing term insurance, which accompanies mortgage loans and installment loans. Such insurance is cheaper because the amount of actual insurance decreases each year as the balance on the loan decreases.

Universal Life Insurance

Universal life insurance is a variation of whole life insurance. In general, the universal policy allows the owner to make periodic adjustments in the amount of coverage and the amount of premium to be paid. Universal life mixes investment features with insurance features. When interest rates are

high, universal policies can be very attractive because your premium dollars are invested at higher rates of return, and those returns are, in large part, credited to you. When interest rates are lower, the universal policies are not as attractive. For the relatively unsophisticated individual, the complexities and variabilities of universal life may render it not the best product for your needs.

Annuities

An annuity provides income for an individual who purchases such a contract. This individual is called the *annuitant.* The buyer of an annuity contract pays money to the insurance company either in one lump sum or in periodic payments over a number of months or years. The insurance company then agrees to pay back to the contract holder a sum of money each month for an agreed-on amount of time.

That sum of money may be fixed in the contract (a fixed-dollar annuity) or may vary (a variable annuity), but there is a guaranteed minimum. With a fixed-dollar annuity, the funds are invested conservatively—predominantly in government and corporate bonds as well as mortgages.

With a variable annuity, a substantial portion of the money may be invested in the stock market. The theory is that the stock market can provide protection against inflation. If the theory works, the annuitant may get more back than might have been received under a fixed-dollar annuity.

Here's a brief description of the common types of payment programs available with annuities.

- **Straight life annuity**   Once you have made your payments, you will begin to receive the agreed-on monthly sum at the agreed-on date. The payments last for as long as you live. Whenever an annuitant dies the payments cease. If the annuitant lives far beyond the normal life expectancy, she will continue to receive the monthly payments as long as she lives. The company, in effect, is taking the risk that the annuitant will live no longer than the life expectancy.
- **Annuity with installments certain**   This provides monthly payments for a fixed period of time—perhaps ten or twenty years. If annuitant dies before the time has elapsed, the named beneficiary receive the payments until the term finally ends.
- **Refund annuities**   If an annuitant dies before receiving b money paid in, the beneficiary will get back the balance may be in installments or in one lump sum.
- **Joint and survivor annuity**   This type can cover two a husband and a wife. When one dies, the other co the payments until the agreed-on fund or the leng exhausted.
- **Single premium annuity**   Rather than make an annuity, you can make a single lump-sur

accumulate until your payout plan begins. As with cash values on straight-life insurance, the earnings on annuities accumulate on a tax-deferred basis. That is, no income taxes are payable on those earnings until the earnings are withdrawn. Because of this the single premium annuity is often regarded as a form of investment rather than as a form of insurance. Indeed, it is heavily marketed as such.

Single premium annuities may offer a fixed or a variable rate of return. The single premium annuity will also have a penalty provision: you forfeit some of your original investment if you withdraw any of it during the earlier years of the contract. (If the rate of interest being paid on the annuity drops below a certain level, you might be able to withdraw your money without penalty. This is known as the bailout provision.)

The Parties to an Insurance Policy

As many as five parties can be involved in an insurance policy contract: the insured, the owner, the beneficiary, the contingent beneficiary, and the company. The roles of each of these parties are important to understanding life insurance. Let's take a closer look at each.

The Insured

This is the person whose life is insured by the policy. It is on the death of the insured that the proceeds are paid. The insured may also be the owner of the policy, but it is possible for the insured and the owner to be different parties.

A fairly new product is the second-to-die policy, in which two people—usually husband and wife—are insured in the same policy. In these policies, the death benefits are paid only when the second of the two insured parties dies. Because two parties are insured, the company has a longer time span before it has to pay death benefits. Thus, the cost to the insured parties can be much less for a given face amount than if only one party were insured.

The Owner

The owner is the most important person in the policy, for it is the owner who has the power to exercise various options including naming and changing the beneficiary, making loans against the policy or cashing in the policy.

Consider Harold and Esther. Harold applies for a life insurance policy on himself and retains ownership in his own name. He names Esther as the beneficiary. In this case, Harold is both the insured and the owner. Harold can later transfer ownership to Esther.

Here are other examples of the owner and the insured not being the same party. Lillian is a valuable employee, so her boss pays for a policy on

Lillian's life payable to the company. This is to protect the company in the event of Lillian's death—it would alleviate, for example the expense of getting along temporarily without Lillian's services. This is known as *key employee* insurance. The company is the owner of the policy, and Lillian is the insured.

Jim needs a loan from his bank. The bank may offer Jim a life insurance policy, with the proceeds payable to the bank in the event of Jim's death. As discussed in chapter 12, this is known as credit life insurance. In such a case, the bank is the owner of the policy and Jim is the insured.

The owner has exclusive powers regarding a life insurance policy. The owner can assign the policy to a creditor. For example, Jim, instead of buying a new credit life policy, assigns an existing policy to the bank to protect the bank in the event of his death. Should Jim default on the loan, the bank can take whatever cash values exist in the policy. (An assignment is valid only if the insurance company has been properly notified and has accepted the assignment.)

The owner can change the beneficiary of the policy, provided that that right has been reserved in the original policy.

The owner can transfer ownership to another party, and this might be wise in certain instances of estate planning.

The owner can exercise the conversion provisions in the policy.

The owner can dictate the manner in which the face amount will be payable to the beneficiary, where a choice exists.

Only the owner can make these changes, and they must be done in accord with the insurance contract. The insured cannot exercise these powers unless the insured is also the owner. If Harold conveys a life insurance policy on his own life to Esther as the owner, then it is Esther, and Esther only, who can exercise the rights granted in the policy. As long as Harold retains ownership, only he can exercise those rights.

The Beneficiary

The beneficiary is the one who receives the payments to be made on the death of the insured. The choice of the beneficiary is up to the owner of the policy, who, as noted earlier, may be the same party as the insured. The beneficiary may be one or more persons, a charity, a business concern, or the estate of the insured.

The Contingent Beneficiary

There is always the possibility that the originally named beneficiary will die before the insured. The owner of the policy can name a contingent beneficiary, who will take the place of the original beneficiary if that person dies before the insured. If no contingent beneficiaries are named, the policy will set forth how the proceeds will be distributed.

The Company

The company is, of course, the insurance company with whom you are entering into the contract. You, as the insurance buyer, will deal with a representative of the company—either an agent connected directly with the company or an independent agent who may represent a number of various companies. The agent is the party to whom the insured should turn when any question arises.

The Life Insurance Contract and Its Clauses

A life insurance policy is a legally binding contract once it has been properly signed by the owner and the company. The policy sets forth all the rights, duties, and obligations of the parties. The only way the contract can be amended is by written agreement between the parties. Changes to a life insurance policy—or any other kind of insurance policy—are called endorsements or riders.

The Application

The application is the questionnaire the applicant for insurance must fill in to have the policy issued. The application contains pertinent information about the individual applying for insurance, including medical data. If the application contains false or misleading information, the policy may later be voided if the insurance company does learn the truth. For example, an individual applying for life insurance may have recently had a severe heart attack but states that he is in perfectly good health. If the policy is issued, he has entered into the agreement on false premises, and the policy may be voided if the company learns of the circumstances within the stated time limit.

Insurance companies go to considerable lengths to avoid being defrauded. Physical examinations are conducted, and neighbors may be interviewed to learn an individual's personal habits. All doctors the applicant has seen in the past few years may be questioned.

The Medical Information Bureau assists the insurance industry in minimizing fraudulent applications. When people apply for life, health, or disability insurance, they sign a statement giving the insurance company permission to relay all health information to the Medical Information Bureau (MIB) and seek out any information that may exist there relative to the individual's health.

Of all applications for life insurance in the United States, only 3 percent are declined. Eighty-five percent have policies issued at the standard risk levels, and 4 percent of the applications have policies issued at extra risk levels. Where there is an obvious health problem but one not so great that the company will refuse coverage, the policy may be issued, but at a higher premium.

Face Amount, or Face Value

The face amount is the amount of money due the beneficiary on the death of the insured. It is set forth on the policy, and it is what we usually refer to when we talk about the amount of an insurance policy. For example, if we say a "$10,000 life insurance policy," we're talking about the face value of the policy.

It is possible that the beneficiary could receive more or less than the original face value. The beneficiary may receive more than face value if a double indemnity clause was activated in the policy. The beneficiary may also receive more than the face value if the owner had applied dividends that had been received toward the purchase of additional insurance.

If the owner has borrowed against the policy and has not paid off these loans the beneficiary will receive the face value minus any unpaid loans (and accrued interest owing on those loans).

Double Indemnity, or Accidental Death Benefit

A double indemnity clause, which is available at an additional premium, provides for the payment of double the face amount in the event of accidental death, as opposed to natural death.

Incontestable Clause

The insurance company has a set time, usually two years, during which it may contest any suspected false information in the application. During that period, a company can void the policy if improper statements were made. But once the two years have elapsed, the company can no longer contest any statements.

Guaranteed Insurability

Some policies will, for an additional premium, guarantee you the right to increase the face value regardless of your health. The cost of obtaining this guarantee should be carefully evaluated.

Premium and Mode of Payments

The policy contract will spell out how much the premiums are on the policy and how they can be made. The policyholder may elect to pay premiums annually, semiannually, quarterly, or monthly. Monthly or quarterly payment plans might cost slightly more due to increased bookkeeping.

Lapse, Grace Period, and Reinstatement

The company will pay the face value to the beneficiary as long as the policy remains in force. The term *in force* means that the owners have paid their

premiums on time. If a policyholder does not pay on time, the policy can lapse. When a policy lapses, it is terminated. There is no more insurance.

It can be most imprudent to let a policy lapse. Money paid in up to the date of lapse will be forfeited, and if you wish to obtain life insurance at a later time, it will cost more because of increased age. In some cases physical problems may prevent you from being able to get the insurance at all.

The insurance industry has structured the typical life insurance policy so that a lapse does not occur that easily or that automatically.

If a premium is not paid by the stated due date, policyholders will have a grace period of usually thirty-one days, during which they can still make payment and continue the policy in force without any penalty.

If payment still has not been made by the end of the grace period, many permanent policies have an automatic cash loan provision. If cash values have already begun to build up in the policy and there is enough to cover the payment of one premium, the company automatically borrows against those values and uses the proceeds to pay the premium, thus continuing the policy in force for another period.

Even after a lapse has occurred, policyholders have a limited time within which to reinstate the policy. They may have to take a new physical examination or sign a statement about health conditions. If the company is satisfied about the state of the insured's health and all back premiums and any interest owing thereon are paid, the policy can be reinstated.

Waiver of Premium

This is available at a slight additional cost on most life insurance policies. It provides that if the insured is totally disabled, the need to make premium payments will be waived. It's like a miniature income disability policy built into the life insurance policy. Note that the definition of *totally disabled* differs from policy to policy. It might, for example, be defined as "unable to work in a job for which you were trained" or "unable to work at all." The difference can be important.

Conversion Values

Conversion (or nonforfeiture) values become available to policyholders under permanent life insurance policies. The values build up as you pay premiums over the years, but the rate of buildup varies from policy to policy. In shopping for life insurance, you should carefully compare the rate of growth and relative size of these values. Policy A may have a lower premium than policy B for the same face value. Thus, policy A may seem to be the better value. But policy B may have higher conversion values, which could be of considerable importance years later. Thus, what you get for your premium dollar isn't just the face value of the policy. These values must be considered most carefully.

Here's how conversion values work. If you cease paying your premiums by choice or otherwise, these conversion values will allow you to convert your policy into a number of alternative plans.

CASHING IN   You can cash in the policy. You then receive the amount of cash set forth in the cash value table, and the policy terminates.

BORROWING   You can borrow against the policy up to the amount in the loan value table, at a rate of interest set forth in the policy. It might be a very attractive rate compared with what one would have to pay at a bank.

Borrowing is simple: notify the company of your wishes and receive a check shortly thereafter. Repayment is up to you: you need not repay the principal at all; but you must pay interest annually. If you do not repay the principal, the face value will be diminished by the amount of the outstanding loan at the time of the insured's death. For example, if the face value on a given policy was $10,000 and the owner borrowed $1,000 against it and then died before repaying the loan, the beneficiary would receive only $9,000.

From time to time, it might pay to borrow against your life insurance values. For example, if you can borrow against your policy at 8 percent, and you can invest at, say, 10 percent, the 2 percent differential is profit. If you invest conservatively, you will still be protecting your family, since the investment itself would be available to them in the event of your death. However, if you speculate, you are jeopardizing the well-being of your survivors.

If you borrow against your life insurance policy for consumer debt purposes (to buy a car, to pay off debts, etc.), the interest you pay on the debt will not be tax-deductible. If you borrow for business purposes, or for investment, the interest might be deductible in full. Check with your tax advisor for most current regulations.

CONVERTING TO EXTENDED TERM INSURANCE   You can convert your existing program to extended term insurance. With such insurance, you will be covered for the same original face value of the policy, but only for a *limited period of time* rather than for the rest of your life.

CONVERTING TO PAID-UP INSURANCE   You can convert to paid-up insurance. If you cease paying premiums, you can still be covered for a *portion* of the face value for as long as the original policy would have protected you.

AUTOMATIC PREMIUM LOAN   This provision, as noted earlier, will allow the company to borrow against your loan values automatically in order to make premium payments you have neglected to make.

Conversion Tables

Each policy contains a table of conversion, or nonforfeiture, values. Table 17–1 is an abbreviated sample. Values are based on the age of the insured at the time the policy is taken out. Values will vary from company to company and from one type of policy to another.

TABLE 17–1   **Conversion Values, Sample Policy, $10,000 Face Value**

End of Policy Year	Cash or Loan Value	Paid-up Insurance	Extended Term Insurance
5	$1,590	$1,410	14 yr. 48 days
10	1,340	2,900	20 yr. 310 days
15	2,100	4,130	22 yr. 288 days
20	2,890	5,180	22 yr. 303 days

Here's how the tables work. The face amount of the insurance policy is $10,000, and the age of the insured at the time the policy was taken out was 25. At the end of the tenth policy year the policyholder will have $1,340 worth of cash/loan values. That means he or she can stop making payments, cash in the policy, terminating the insurance altogether, and have $1,340 cash in hand. Or the policyholder can borrow that much against the policy and continue the policy in force by paying the annual premiums.

If the policyholder converts to paid-up insurance, at the end of the tenth policy year he or she will have a permanent policy with a face value of $2,900. There are no more premiums to pay, and protection is guaranteed for life for $2,900 in face value. Or at the end of ten years, this individual could convert to extended term, in which case he or she would be covered for the full face amount ($10,000) for 20 years and 310 days. At the end of that time, the coverage would cease altogether. Table 18–4 (chapter 18) illustrates how values can build up over longer periods.

In order to do any of the conversions, the insurance company must be notified. It would be advisable to discuss such a move with your insurance agent before you actually proceed.

Dividend Options

If you own a dividend-paying policy, you'll have choices as to how those dividends are paid. You can get a check to do with as you please; you can apply the dividends toward the next premium due on the policy; you may let the dividend "ride" with the company, where it will earn interest; or you can use the dividends to purchase additional life paid-up insurance. This last option increases your protection at no out-of-pocket cost to you.

An annual statement from the company will indicate what dividends are payable and will instruct you how to choose the way dividends will be applied. If you have any questions, discuss the matter with your agent.

Settlement Options

Settlement options may include paying the entire face amount in one lump sum to the beneficiaries; paying periodic payments, including interest, to

the beneficiaries; paying interest only to the named beneficiary, with a lump sum payable to a subsequent beneficiary on the death of the primary beneficiary. As a rule, the owner of the policy can choose the settlement option. In some cases, a beneficiary might also be able to select an option. Each policy will spell out exactly what options are available and how to go about choosing them and changing them.

BUYING LIFE INSURANCE: WHO NEEDS IT, AND HOW MUCH?

When we're hungry, we go to the market and buy the food we need; we don't have to wait for someone to tell us that our stomachs need refilling. Not so with life insurance; the need is not as clear-cut. Indeed, contemplating the need for life insurance reminds us of our own mortality, and it's no surprise that human nature would short-circuit such thoughts.

Sound personal financial planning demands that life insurance be carefully investigated. Not everyone needs life insurance, but everyone should at least examine how life insurance can function with respect to their long-term needs and objectives.

Who needs life insurance? In short, if you want to protect or enhance the well-being of anyone who is dependent on you, and your existing assets aren't adequate to provide that protection, life insurance can get the job done quickly and assuredly.

Premature Death

Exercise 17.1

If a young breadwinner dies unexpectedly, how will his or her family survive? For example: You have two children, ages 10 and 12. You want to be sure that there is enough money for your spouse and children to live comfortably, and for college for the children. Term insurance designed to run for fifteen or twenty years can provide the protection that's needed.

Or you might prefer permanent insurance, which will cost more at the outset but is likely to cost less many years down the road. A combination of the two might work best for you. Remember: Your family is unique. What's right for other families might not be right for yours. Evaluate the financial exposure your family has in the event of the premature death of a breadwinner, and act accordingly.

Normal Life Expectancy

Once the children are grown and most major obligations have been taken care of, the need for life insurance diminishes. Many families, though, continue their life insurance in order to provide an inheritance for the survivors.

Tax and Business Purposes

Chapter 19 will help you determine whether your heirs are facing the prospect of federal estate taxes on your death. If they are, life insurance can be used to pay that tax. Lacking the needed cash, survivors might be faced with having to sell other assets—house, investments—in order to pay the tax. Having to sell off those other assets could provide a hardship for survivors. Life insurance eliminates the need to sell off other assets.

Similarly, business interests can be protected by life insurance. If you are the sole proprietor in a small business, your death could cause the business to have to terminate. If, however, there is life insurance payable to the business, those proceeds, which are not taxable to the recipient, could be used to keep the business running, or they could buy time to allow for an orderly liquidation of the business. Either way, your survivors can be protected by that immediate infusion of cash into the business.

How Much Insurance Is Needed?

The first task is to determine who is going to be protected by the insurance and to what extent. For example, do you want to ensure that the children will have at least half of their college tuition guaranteed in the event of your premature death? 75 percent? 100 percent? Are they on their own after that? Or do you want them to have a nest egg to help get them started in their chosen careers? These are individual questions that only you can answer.

Now comes the time for some thoughtful arithmetic. You must determine, as accurately as possible, the following:

- What might be the possible extent of "final" expenses, which can include uninsured costs of a terminal illness, burial or cremation expenses, estate taxes, and money to help survivors get through the early difficult time of adjustment. (If you're amply protected against terminal illness costs through your health insurance you may exclude them from your life insurance planning.)

- How much existing debt—mortgages, personal loans, and so on—might the survivors have to pay? If you don't want the family to sell assets to pay off the debt, you can cover such contingencies through life insurance.

- How much per year will the survivors need to maintain themselves in a suitable style of living? Consideration must be given to the possibilities of the spouse remarrying, of a previously nonworking spouse going to work and the child-care expenses that might entail, of children going to work, and of other potential sources of income that might materialize. Elimination of the deceased's own cost of living—food, clothing, recreation, and so on—must also be evaluated.

- What extraordinary expenses will the survivors face, and what part of those expenses do you want to ensure them of being able to meet? Such expenses might include education, weddings, a stake to go into business on their own, and so on.
- For how many years would you want the survivors to continue their particular lifestyle on a worry-free basis?
- What benefits will be provided by Social Security? A visit with your nearest Social Security office can provide this information.
- Inventory all assets at current market value, potential future value, liquidity and their earning potential. Determine when assets could, or should, be converted to cash to meet family needs, and which non-earning assets might be converted to earning assets.
- What other sources of income might there be in the future, such as inheritances or scholarships? You can't count on these sources, but you should be aware of the possibility.
- Evaluate current life insurance policies. Determine what the proceeds could earn annually if they were conservatively invested (see Tables 14–2 and 14–3) and how long the proceeds would last if the principal were invaded by a certain amount each year (see Table 18–5, chapter 18). Evaluate all your other assets in the same manner. This information may not be easy to compile, and you may want the impartial help of an accountant or your insurance agent. This information is essential to forming an intelligent plan.

A Case History

Exercise 17.2

When you've surveyed your data, the gaps can be measured and the alternatives for filling those gaps can come into focus.

Let's examine a fairly simple case. This exercise illustrates the type of analysis you should make to estimate your own life insurance needs.

Phillip is married, has a 12-year-old child, and earns $3,000 a month after taxes. His wife does not work but is capable of doing so should the need arise.

Phillip's current financial status is as follows:

- He owns his home, which has a current market value of $150,000. He owes $60,000 on a mortgage with monthly payments of $620.
- He has $5,000 in a savings plan.
- He has $10,000 in the profit-sharing plan at work. This could be payable immediately to his survivors in the event of his death.
- He owns two cars, both used, with a current total value of $8,000.
- He has a life insurance policy, with a face value of $45,000.

Phillip has estimated what his family's financial status would be if he were to die suddenly. His existing health and burial insurance would take

care of all his final expenses. His assets are not high enough to make him liable for estate taxes. His wife and child would need approximately $1,720 a month for living expenses (mortgage payment, $620; other living expenses, $800, taxes and miscellaneous, $300).

If he died now, Phillip would not want his wife to sell the house. She could, however, make use of the savings account, the profit-sharing plan, and the life insurance proceeds, all of which would total $60,000.

Phillip and his insurance agent, using Table 18–5 in this book, calculate very conservatively that if the $60,000 were invested at 7 percent per year, before income tax considerations, it would generate earnings of $360 per month. If Phillip's widow were to embark on a ten-year program of dipping into principal, the $60,000 could generate an income of $696 per month, as indicated in Table 17–2. A fifteen-year dipping plan would give her an income of $538 per month. In order to provide enough for his wife and child to be comfortable, Phillip needs an additional $100,000 in life insurance. That amount, if invested in accordance with the program in Table 18–5, would provide an additional $1,160 per month, for a ten-year period, at the end of which time the sum would be depleted. But the total of the $696 from the existing $60,000 nest egg, plus the $1,160 per month from the new insurance to be acquired, will provide Phillip's survivors with a grand total of $1,856 per month.

After ten years, when the entire nest egg is gone, the child will have completed college. The house will have increased in value considerably, and the mortgage on the house will have decreased considerably. Phillip's wife will be left with a substantial equity in the home, which she can sell to create a sizable nest egg for her living expenses.

These calculations do not include earnings of Phillip's widow and child from work. And it does not take into account estimated Social Security benefits of $1,110 per month until the child reaches the age of 16. Furthermore, Phillip's widow can resume receiving Social Security benefits when she reaches the age of 60. All this income can be banked to create an even greater security blanket. Phillip's wife might choose to return to work herself and embark on a fifteen-year dipping plan, which would give her an income of $1,434 per month. That, plus her earnings from work, might be a more satisfactory program for her.

Phillip's situation is a *relatively* uncomplicated one. If he were concerned about such matters as paying estate taxes, creating a substantial college

TABLE 17–2   Income Sources

	Interest Only[a]	10-Year Payout	15-Year Payout
From existing $60,000	$360	$ 696	$ 538
From extra $100,000	585	1,160	896
Total income available	$945	$1,856	$1,434

[a]Principal amount always remains intact.

tuition fund, protecting a business interest, or any other matter beyond the ordinary, his need for insurance would be much greater. Now, having solved the puzzle of how much insurance he needs, Phillip must tackle the far more perplexing matter of what kind of insurance to buy.

What to Buy

Exercise 17.3

Buying life insurance is a lot like buying a car. You can choose a subcompact with no frills, or you can go lavish and splurge on a fancy sedan with all the trimmings. The sticker price isn't always the determining factor in what you buy. If you need a car just to hop back and forth to the office or the shopping center, the subcompact might make the most sense. But if you're a traveling salesman and expect to be driving thousands of miles every week, it may well be worth the added price to buy the luxury car so that the physical comfort of the automobile reduces the wear and tear on your body. There's no easy answer.

Life insurance is just as complicated. You, or Phillip, could go for the stripped-down term policy or for a "loaded" Whole Life policy. Both have pluses, both have minuses.

The cost of life insurance has long been the subject of debate between advocates of term life and advocates of whole life. SInce whole life insurance builds up conversion values within the policies, those who favor such policies feel that the real cost of the insurance should take into account what those values are in future years. This is generally referred to as the "cost adjusted" method. Whole life insurance costs more than term life at the inception of the policy, but years later, for example, if a policyholder cashes in a whole life policy, the total cost of premiums, offset by the cash-in value, could be much less than the out-of-pocket cost of a term policy of equal face value. Term advocates prefer to measure cost strictly on an out-of-pocket basis.

The debate will rage on, and it would take a huge book to list all the possible costs of all the possible combinations of policies. It's a jungle out there for price shoppers. As a rough guideline, the following tables illustrate the range of costs you might find for various types of policies. The prices are from surveys conducted in recent years and represent the better values among those companies and policies surveyed. Note well that all prices are subject to change.

Exercise 17.4

Table 17–3 illustrates price ranges for various types of term policies for non-smokers age 35 and 45. Term policies are for $250,000 face value. Annual renewable policies will increase in cost each year. Ten- and 20-year level term policies have a fixed cost for the first 10 and 20 years, respectively, and after that premiums will increase considerably. (There are also term policies available with 5 years and 15 years of level payments. An agent can quickly provide you with costs for those plans.)

TABLE 17–3   **Costs of Term Policies, $250,000 Face Value**

Age	Gender	Annual Renewable First Year	10-Year Level Premium Per Year, 1st 10 Years	20-Year Level Premium Per Year, 1st 20 Years
35	Male	$195–$238	$210–$230	$273–$350
35	Female	188–248	185–210	265–330
45	Male	260–348	360–430	535–675
45	Female	250–275	285–343	398–505

Source: Consumer's Digest, Sept./Oct. 1996.

Table 17–4 illustrates both low and high ranges of whole life policies with face values of $100,000. Policies in the higher ranges might have higher conversion values. Neither dividends nor conversion values are taken into account in these examples. See Strategies for Success on page 521, which compares rates for smokers.

If you have questions about the stability of any life insurance company, refer to *Best's Insurance Reports* and *Best's Recommended Life Insurance Companies*, both of which are available in most libraries. Your state's insurance department can help too.

The Insurance Agent

Exercise 17.5

There is no such thing as a typical insurance agent. An agent's training might range from minimal to the rigorous demands of the courses leading to the CLU (Chartered Life Underwriter) designation. His or her experience might encompass weeks or decades. His or her income level can range from paltry to six figures. And personality, sales techniques, and sense of ethics can run the full human spectrum.

Many agents will seek you out. If you can find the right agent, you've made a valuable catch. But how do you know what to look for? Before we get into a shopping list, let's take a quick look at some of the dilemmas in the industry.

TABLE 17–4   **Costs of Whole Life Policies, $100,000 Face Value**

Age	Gender	Low Range	High Range
35	Male	$ 634–$1,052	$1,280–$1,300
35	Female	634–897	1,069–1,098
45	Male	1,178–1,514	2,425–4,504
45	Female	1,140–1,178	2,055–2,070

Source: Consumer's Reports, August 1993.

- **Dilemma No. 1** Insurance agents make their living by selling insurance policies. Proper counseling may be of equal or greater value to you than the policy itself, but agents don't make a penny unless they make a sale. Needless to say, good counseling can produce a good sale, but it might not.

  Agents, therefore, take a calculated risk on how much time they can spend with any given prospect in counseling sessions. This can result in counseling and selling efforts becoming intermingled, to the point where you might not be able to tell them apart.

  If an agent is not willing to take the time needed to understand your goals, you might not be getting the service you need. And agents might not take the time if they are not confident that there will be a sale as a result. This dilemma is perhaps best resolved by frank communications at the outset: "Agent, this is what I have to learn from you before I will even consider doing business with you. If you're willing to teach me what I think I have to know, I may well be a customer, but there's no guarantee. If you're willing to proceed on those terms, fine. If not, perhaps it would be best if we didn't waste each other's time."

- **Dilemma No. 2** With rare exceptions, richer people have better access to more sophisticated insurance counseling than poorer people. This, for better or worse, is the way of our world.

  It might take an agent the same time to sell a $10,000 policy to a working family as it would to sell a $100,000 policy to an executive. The rewards to the agent are drastically different. Moreover, the agent who is going for the big sale will probably be better equipped to handle the more sophisticated problems wealthy prospects will have. People with lower incomes also need sound advice, but it may be more difficult for them to get it.

  The more you learn about life insurance, the better able you will be to take advantage of any advice given, and the better you understand the more sophisticated advice that could be of greater value.

- **Dilemma No. 3** Each of us has so many dollars to spend. Some of those dollars will be spent on our current needs, and some will cover future needs and desires. Many institutions would like to take care of our future dollars for us—insurance companies, mutual funds, banks, savings institutions, stockbrokers. They all make their living by putting our future dollars to use until we need them, and the competition is keen to get access to these dollars.

  Each of these giant industries has become envious of the others. Some segments of the life insurance industry have reacted, for example, by putting mutual funds in the same attaché case as their insurance policies. The funds might be good; so might the policies. Mixing them together too much may not be.

  With all these financial industries competing with each other for our future dollars, it's essential that we keep a clear distinction between insuring and investing. Each has its separate set of purposes

and goal-fulfillment abilities. Insurance offers certainty; some forms of investment offer a measure of certainty, whereas others offer little more than possibility.

Evaluating the Agent

Keeping these dilemmas firmly in mind, what then do you look for in an insurance agent?

As in choosing all professional advisors, you must have trust in their ability, confidence in their training, and knowledge of their integrity. You don't usually get these on a hunch or a first impression, although it's not impossible. Personal familiarity, recommendations from others, and reputation in the community are indicators. The individual who comes on with a hard sell after the first "How do you do?" may have the same program to offer you as the agent who holds fire until after the proper rapport has been established. The choice is up to you.

What are the agent's credentials, background, training, and prior experience? Does the agent represent only one company or, as is the case with independent agents, a number of different companies? These are important factors to determine and evaluate. It is, of course, possible for a novice who is eager to get established to serve you just as well as an old pro. But the perennial job hopper is liable to leave you with some loose ends hanging.

THE CLU   Chartered Life Underwriters (CLUs) are insurance agents who have been through rigorous courses of instruction. Only a small percentage of agents are CLUs. The time and educational requirements may scare off many from pursuing the credential. These educational requirements include courses on economics, taxes, estate planning, corporate law, contract law, pensions and profit-sharing plans, accounting, and the technical aspects of life insurance.

Each course requires about sixty hours of classroom work, as well as abundant outside homework. On completing the courses, each agent must pass a four-hour written exam in each of five subject areas.

A CLU doesn't have any product or secret policies to offer you that other agents don't have, but a CLU does possess the education that might enable her to make the best determination of your needs and find the best policies to satisfy those needs. (Certainly, there are many fine agents without the CLU designation who can serve your needs most adequately.)

In dealing with a CLU, you are working with an individual who has invested hundreds of hours becoming more expert in the insurance field. That fact alone might induce many insurance shoppers to lean toward doing business with a CLU.

Remember that any insurance agent, CLU or not, can make a living only by selling policies. The amount of time an agent can give to counseling a client is limited. But the *quality* of counseling is important, perhaps more so than the amount of time given it. And that might well be where the CLU has another edge.

Exercise 17.6

IT'S YOUR CHOICE The difference between *choosing* an agent and *being chosen by* an agent can be very important. The selection process is up to you. Remember that you are not buying a simple product that you'll use today and be done with tomorrow. You're striving to build a structure that will shelter you and your dependents for many years. If it's built right, it will last, it will perform, and it will have been worth the time and the money involved.

INSURANCE WHEN THE RISK MIGHT NOT OCCUR

There is a very important difference between life insurance and the other common forms of personal insurance. With life insurance, as long as the policy remains in force, the company must pay the benefits to the beneficiary at a fixed date: the death of the insured. There is no question that the loss being insured against—the death of the insured—will occur. The insurance company is able to make a reasonably accurate estimate as to when that date will probably be, and it knows precisely how much it must then pay.

With the other common forms of personal insurance—health, income, property, and public liability—the risk that is being insured against may not occur. If it does, it might occur tomorrow or ten years from now. When it does occur, the company may have to pay a token amount to the insured, or a moderate or substantial sum. There may be a dispute as to whether or not anything should be paid.

With life insurance, you know for certain that a fixed sum of money will be available to you or your beneficiaries. With the other forms of insurance, the money you pay out may never be seen again. Human nature may lead us to think—dangerously so—that serious illness will come to others but never to us. We would thus never be out of pocket as a result of such occurrences, and therefore we should keep our costs for such insurance to a minimum.

In many respects, the losses that can be suffered as a result of risks relating to health, income, property, and public liability can be far more devastating than the death of a breadwinner who leaves no life insurance. Vague and unpredictable though these risks may be, it would be careless not to acquire protection against financial disaster.

The basic mechanics are generally the same for life insurance and the other forms of personal insurance. A contract (policy) is entered into between the insured party and the insurance company. The contract sets forth all the rights and obligations of the parties.

But the claim procedures with these other forms of personal insurance can be much more complicated than with life insurance. When an insured individual dies, the company is notified of the death and makes the payment. But in the other forms of insurance, there may be many questions about the status of the insured or of the injured parties, and the extent of damages suffered may be subject to question.

STRATEGIES FOR SUCCESS

Don't Smoke, Don't Age, Be a Female

Smokers pay through the nose for life insurance. And smoking can also mean much higher premiums for health, disability income, and long-term-care insurance. Look at the difference in costs for a smoker and a nonsmoker from a mass-market term-life insurance company. For $100,000 worth of term coverage, here are the annual costs for nonsmokers and smokers, male and female, at varying ages. Costs are just for that one year and will differ from company to company.

Age	Nonsmoking Male	Smoking Male	Nonsmoking Female	Smoking Female
30	$150	$ 200	$150	$ 200
40	155	270	151	210
50	205	445	165	345
55	275	730	215	495
60	480	1,180	295	795
65	625	1,644	505	1,245

These numbers speak incredibly well for themselves. Not only do they show the added cost of smoking—and the added cost of waiting to buy life insurance, if you haven't become uninsurable in the meantime—they also give you some clear ideas about the longevity of smokers versus nonsmokers.

Presenting a claim for payment with these types of personal insurance may require filling out extensive forms. The information you submit is subject to investigation by the insurance company to determine the validity of the claims.

Although the vast majority of all claims are paid in accordance with the company's obligations, the insured must see to it that the full measure of the claim is clearly stated and paid for.

HEALTH INSURANCE

In order to know where we're headed it can often be helpful to know where we're coming from. Follow along, then, for a perspective on this important subject.

Of every dollar spent in the United States each year, roughly fourteen cents goes into health care in all its many forms, including the cost of health insurance itself.

Prior to the 1990s, despite rapidly rising health care costs, the whole proposition was relatively easy to understand and deal with, if for no other reason than that we had gotten used to a decades-old system. Roughly 85 percent of

the nation's population was covered by health insurance policies, either through a group policy at work or a privately purchased policy, most or all of the time. (A person between jobs, for example, might have been temporarily not covered, though that need not be the case today, as will be discussed later.)

Almost all health insurance policies had a number of common characteristics:

1. You could see the doctors of your choice. This was the one feature the U.S. citizens seemed to care most about.

2. You had to pay a *deductible* before the insurance would kick in on your behalf. The deductible is a set amount per person and/or per family per year, such as $250, $500, $1,000 or more. Those who had private policies could choose the deductible they wanted. Those covered by group policies usually had no choice; the employer would pick one deductible that everyone was subject to.

3. After you had paid the deductible amount—out of your own pocket—the policy would then pay a set percentage of all your covered medical expenses. Commonly, policies would pay 80 percent of those expenses and you'd be responsible for paying the difference.

4. All policies had limits as to what they would pay for and how much. These limits would vary from policy to policy, but in general they would include how much a policy would pay for a hospital room, a specific surgical procedure, a visit to a doctor's office, and so on. There would also be limits on the total amount a policy would pay during the course of one year and over a lifetime.

5. For the most part, most people were familiar enough with their policies to be able to get along with them. Yes, there were inequities and abuses and overcharges and underpayment of claims from time to time. Yet the system functioned, and as the old saying goes, "If it ain't broke, don't fix it."

But then it broke.

We Needed a Fix

Forces in the economy took hold of the health care industry, and it's been chaotic ever since. Review chapter 1 to familiarize yourself with how forces beyond our control can affect our economic well-being. The health care industry is a perfect example.

The first fracture came in 1988. People had been complaining long and loud about rapidly rising health care costs, but the 1988 incident began to prompt many people to do something about all these complaints. That incident was a change in the income tax laws that took a lot of money away from a lot of people. The law was enacted in 1986, to take effect in 1987. So the first time most people were impacted by the law was when they filled out their 1987 tax returns in 1988.

Here is how the tax law changes took away a lot of money from a lot of people: Prior to the income tax law change, if people spent money on health care for which they were *not* reimbursed by insurance, they could get a fat income tax deduction as a result. It wasn't so bad having to pay for medical costs out of pocket as long as you could get a tax deduction for them. But the tax law change took away that deduction for most people.

For example, prior to 1987, if a family had an adjusted gross income of $30,000 and unreimbursed medical expenses of $2,000, they would be entitled to a tax deduction of $1,400. The deduction was allowed for the amount that unreimbursed medical costs exceeded—on a rough average—2 percent of adjusted gross income (2% of $30,000 is $600). The deduction is for the difference between the $2,000 expenses and the $600 limitation, or $1,400.

From 1987 onward, the deduction was allowed for unreimbursed medical expenses in excess of 7.5 percent of adjusted gross income. The same family, therefore, would have no deduction at all during a year in which their adjusted gross income was $30,000 and their unreimbursed medical expenses were $2,000. Seven and a half percent of $30,000 is $2,250. Their expenses were less than $2,250. Therefore, no deduction was allowed. Ouch!

Medical costs were rising rapidly, and taking away the deduction rubbed salt into the uninsured wounds. The media got on the case. The politicians got on the case. Health care costs had become the demon spirit of our land.

The second fracture came in 1992 with the election of a Democrat to the White House—the first such since 1980, when health care concerns were far secondary to skyrocketing gasoline costs and hostages in Iran and nuclear weapons in the USSR.

The Republican economic philosophy has always been *"Hands off:* the private sector can take care of the economy better than the government can." The Democratic philosophy has always been *"Hands on,* particularly if the economy seems to be going haywire." Then governmental intervention can be more effective in solving the problem than the private sector can, the argument goes.

In 1993, the Clinton administration began a project to overhaul the entire health care system in America. *Entire.*

A Case of Overkill

After almost two years of meetings a plan was finally presented to the media and the public. It was gargantuan in scope and mind-boggling in complexity. Perhaps the single most negative aspect of it was that it seemed to threaten that Americans might have to give up one of their most cherished freedoms: the right to choose their own doctors. The media did an about face: "Yes, we felt that the health care dilemma was an awful one, but this overhaul plan is overkill."

The public and the politicians agreed, and the overhaul proposal died swiftly in Congress. But while all of this was going on, there was one

segment of the economy that was actually doing something about it all: the health care industry. They said, in a nutshell, "If we don't get our act together, and soon, we're going to end up being regulated by the government. The government will tell us how much we can charge and how much treatment we can offer and how much we'll get reimbursed from certain insurance programs. Better we regulate ourselves than let the government do it for us."

The Dawn of Managed Care

Thus began the era of *managed care.* We're just a few years into this new era, and the dust of confusion may not settle for many more years. So this portion of this chapter is, of necessity, a work in progress, a transitional essay on one critical aspect of personal finance going through enormous change.

The essence of managed care is that instead of each doctor/hospital/ lab/out-patient surgical center/running its own facilities and personnel, groups of these health care deliverers have banded together to form organizations with the hope that one central management for the organization can be more cost-efficient than a whole lot of individual management arrangements. Think of the cost-savings that can be achieved by combining twenty doctors' offices into one: lower administrative costs, lower paperwork costs, lower rent, lower personnel costs, lower purchasing costs, and so on.

Further, all specialty work can be referred within the organization rather than losing it to outsiders. And by having central management instead of each doctor having to worry about payrolls and computer programs and form-filling-out-by-the-ton, life will become more pleasant, and the doctors can concentrate on doing what they're trained to do best: doctoring.

Costs to consumers will come down. To some extent, the freedom of choice of doctors can be retained (life, after all, is a series of compromises) and the government will leave the industry relatively alone.

All well and good. Is it working? Sort of. When massive change comes to any entity, particularly one as gigantic as the health care industry, there are going to be glitches and bad publicity, consumer complaints and lawsuits, and the continuing nightmare of possible governmental intervention. Then energies have to be directed toward putting out the fires and reassuring the public, and that can cost a lot of money.

A lot of hospitals and older doctors have seen their incomes plummet, particularly as the government cuts back on reimbursements from treating governmentally insured patients on Medicare. At the same time, a lot of hospitals are cutting costs by merging, and a lot of younger doctors are entering the profession with an eye toward living a more ordered life, even though at a lower income level than their older colleagues.

The core of all this is that you as a health care consumer (and we all are, or will be, whether we like it or not) must be ready to change as the industry changes. And the changes are already momentous. Before the 1990s,

about 70 percent of all health care payments were made by regular insurance plans, either private or group, and the balance was through managed care facilities. Today those numbers are reversed: 70 percent of health care is through managed care facilities, and the balance is through regular insurance. One educated guess: By 2010, if current trends continue, close to 90 percent of all health care will be through managed care facilities.

The vast majority of workers covered by group plans are having to pay for an increasing portion of their health care coverage—whether through regular insurance plans or managed care plans. In 1986, about 40% of workers with single coverage were paying for part of their coverage. A decade later, 85% were. How much have those workers been chipping in over the same time frame? Worker contributions have increased from about $360 per year in 1986 to almost $500 per year a decade later (that's before deductibles, co-payments and the like). And here again the trend is upward, even though the inflation of medical costs has somewhat stabilized.

So What Do We Do Now?

One unavoidable conclusion to all of this is that individual choice of doctors has been severely curtailed. Yet we seem to be getting along all right. We gripe at different things for different reasons. But our life expectancy rates and our general health conditions seem to be surviving the changes without harm. We are adapting, but we must be vigilant, protective of our rights, and, above all, well informed. With that in mind, let us survey the health care industry in these changing times, with an eye toward helping you get the best medical care that circumstances will allow.

If You Don't Have Choice . . .

. . . Don't give up hope. Many people who have health plans at work are more or less stuck with whatever the company has decided to provide for them. Some workers fear leaving their jobs because they might lose their health coverage. That should no longer be of concern. The Health Insurance Portability Act of 1997 allows workers to change jobs without putting their coverage in jeopardy. This will be discussed in more detail later in the chapter.

Many employers offer Cafeteria Plans as a part of their overall fringe benefits program. These plans allow you—as in a real cafeteria—to pick and choose from a number of benefits available. Such a plan might enable you to improve your health insurance coverage. This might involve giving up some other benefit, but you've certainly nothing to lose by researching the plan in full. Flexible Spending Accounts are another form of benefits that can allow you to set aside some of your earnings on a tax-free basis to use toward unreimbursed medical expenses. This, too, should be explored. (See chapter 2 for more details on Cafeteria and Flexible Spending Plans.)

It costs employers between $3,000 and $5,000 per employee per year for typical health plans. Employers want to keep good workers, and a good health plan is a way of doing so, despite the healthy price tag. Most workers shopping for private coverage on their own would likely find that it would cost a lot more because of the savings involved in insuring a group as opposed to an individual. But not all employers are diligent in researching health plans for their workers. If stimulated to do so by a group of workers, or by a union, or by an aggressive health plan salesperson, a new and better program could emerge, to the benefit of all concerned. So if you don't like your current plan, don't give up hope. A job change or a concerted effort to get your employer to improve the existing plan are clear possibilities.

Some people might have a choice of health plans one day, and not have a choice the next day. How can this happen? Some unforeseen medical problem can crop up that can render them uninsurable, not just for health coverage, but for life, disability income, and long-term-care insurance as well. See the Strategy for Success on page 499.

If You Do Have a Choice . . .

. . . You have a lot of homework to do. Here are the general guidelines of the types of plans available, and checklists to help you determine the relative value of each. First, let's look at the spectrum of possibilities. That spectrum ranges from complete freedom of choice to very limited freedom of choice. The former is what's known as *fee for service.* You choose your own doctor, hospital, clinic, or any other facility. You get the service you seek, and your health insurance policy pays the fee, subject to limitations in the policy and deductibles, as described earlier.

Limited freedom of choice is characteristic of managed care. *Health maintenance organizations* (HMOs) are the strictest example. You join an HMO for a set annual fee. You are assigned a *gatekeeper*—a family doctor who will act as your first contact. Whatever specialists may be needed will be assigned to you by this primary care doctor, and those specialists will be affiliated with the HMO. The HMO will also have its own lab and other related facilities, and may have its own hospital. In most cases, all of your care takes place at the HMO facility. In short, you pretty much do what the HMO tells you to do, and your annual fee covers all, or most all, of your expenses. If you're not happy with your HMO gatekeeper or specialists, you can request different ones. Circumstances will dictate whether you can get a change. As a general rule, HMOs cost less, perhaps a lot less, than comparable fee for service care through an insurance policy.

In between these two ends of the spectrum, there are a number of shades of grey. Most common is the *preferred provider organization* (PPO). In a PPO, numerous doctors and care facilities have signed a contract to care for covered individuals at fixed rates, which are usually discounted from normal rates. For example, if your health plan at work offers you PPO services, you

can choose your own doctors—primary and specialists—from among the PPO's list of members. The same goes for hospitals, labs, and other facilities. You see the doctors at their own offices. So your freedom of choice can be much broader than with an HMO. Your plan will pay agreed fees to the PPO, which may be all or part of the set PPO fee. If the plan doesn't pay it all, you make up the difference. You can also choose non-PPO providers, but you'll have to pay more out of pocket for that privilege.

Two other similar facilities are independent physicians associations (IPAs) and point-of-service (POS) plans. Both of these allow you some broader choice than the HMO, but likely at extra cost to you. IPAs are made up of doctors who maintain their own private practice but are linked into a broad network of specialists. You can choose your own primary care doctor from among those participating in the IPA, and then that doctor will refer you to specialists—perhaps a choice of specialists—as the need arises. POS plans allow you to see out-of-network providers for an extra fee, not unlike the PPOs.

Go Figure

Confusing? Without a doubt. To make matters more so, not all of these plans will cover or pay for the same services. For example: some plans will cover you only in your home city or state, with you having to pay extra if you need medical attention when you're away from home. Some will only prescribe certain drugs for certain conditions—presumably from a pharmaceutical company that offers them a fat discount if the plan gives them an exclusive on a specific drug. Plans can also differ widely on coverage for emergency room visits, mental health services, rehabilitation services, and more. The fact that a lot of facilities that used to be nonprofit are now for-profit muddies the water even more.

It is appropriate to say a few words about nonprofit versus for-profit, since that is a critical element in the emergence and ultimate success or failure of managed care. Many nonprofit medical facilities—such as community hospitals—are heavily subsidized by taxpayers. Critics of nonprofit institutions allege that they are not efficiently run. They lose money as a result, and the ripple effect is a compromise in the quality of service they can render. Those who favor the for-profit concept maintain that free enterprise can run any business—hospitals among them—more efficiently than nonprofits. They can even turn a profit, and if some of that profit is plowed back into the institution, the quality of service can improve. That's a big if. Critics of for-profit institutions say that they are interested only in making money and in rewarding the stockholders (many of whom might be doctors affiliated with the facility), and that service to patients is of secondary concern. Indeed, for-profit hospitals have been accused of fraud, mismanagement, and more, all in the interest of lining the pockets of investors.

Remember: This is all in a state of flux. There might even be significant differences in the health care scene between the time this book was printed

and the time you read this chapter. Private enterprise continues to play an increasing role in the health care industry by way of mergers, acquisitions, and technological developments (lasers, scanners, etc.). Fifty state legislatures have bills before them that would create more regulations of various players in the industry. Biotech and pharmaceutical companies are hard at work developing new treatments and medications that can revolutionize overnight how health care is delivered. And there will always be the shadow of the federal government lurking over the industry, waiting to pounce if abuses seem to become too frequent, or the quality of the nation's health seems to be deteriorating.

HEALTH CARE CHECKLISTS

Insurance

If you already have a health insurance policy (as opposed to a managed care plan), the most important thing you must do is to see if it is up-to-date with today's actual costs. If your policy is more than two or three years old, you might be shocked to learn that the benefits promised in the policy are far less than today's real-world costs. That includes all aspects of coverage under the policy: physicians, surgeons, hospitalization (how much will they pay for what types of rooms and for how many days, intensive care, emergency room service), prescriptions, and so on. Your policy may have an inflation rider that would boost coverage based on the actual rise in costs. Don't assume that that's the case. Determine exactly what your coverage is. If you deem it necessary to increase your coverage, discuss that with your agent.

Now comes the homework to see if your health insurance plan is as healthy as you need it to be. Needless to say, the extent of coverage you have—or need—will affect the cost of your policy.

Hospital Coverage

_____   Does your insurance policy cover the hospital you're likely to use if the need arises? Not all policies provide coverage for all hospitals.

_____   Must you be an in-patient to be covered? What coverage is there for out-patient care?

_____   Are you covered for anything that puts you into the hospital? Are any conditions excluded from hospital coverage?

_____   When does the hospital coverage kick in—on the very first day, or is there a waiting period of, say, six or seven days?

_____   What limitations are there, if any, for miscellaneous services such as x-rays, scans, radiation treatment, lab tests, nursing care, anesthesia, oxygen, traction gear, plasma and other blood supplies, ambulance costs, drugs, medications?

Surgical Insurance

_____   Are the surgical schedules in your policy in line with today's actual surgical costs? Most surgical procedures are limited as to how much they will pay you for the main surgeon, assistant surgeons, anesthesia, surgical nurses, operating room fees, and the like.

_____   Is your coverage limited to surgery done in the hospital, or are you also protected for procedures done in the doctor's office or in ambulatory-care facilities?

_____   Is your schedule of surgical benefits tied to your room rate? In other words, if your policy pays more for your hospital room, will they also pay proportionately higher surgical fees?

Physician Insurance

_____   How much will the policy pay for visits to the doctor's office, and does that represent a satisfactory portion of what the doctor actually charges today? Is there a limit as to how many visits the policy will pay for, per person and/or per illness?

_____   What limits are there as to the practitioners who are covered? For example, are you covered for visits to chiropracters, osteopaths, podiatrists?

Miscellaneous Insurance Items

_____   What are the deductibles in your policy—per person, per family, per year, per illness? Once the deductible is met, how much above that amount will the insurance company pay?

_____   What are the policy limits—the total amount the policy will pay per person, per family, per illness, per year, per lifetime?

_____   Do you need maternity benefits, and if so, are they included in the policy, and with what limitations? If you don't need maternity benefits and they are in your policy, you are paying for coverage you can do without. (Better make sure before you cancel it, though.)

_____   To what extent are your dependents covered? When will coverage cease for dependents, especially children?

_____   If you are shopping for a new policy and you have any preexisting conditions, will those conditions be excluded from coverage, and if so, for how long? Will any current health conditions cause you to be excluded from protection altogether, or can you have the desired coverage if you pay a higher premium? (This is called a *rated risk*.)

_____ What are the policy's terms regarding renewability, cancellation, lapse (because of nonpayment of premium), and reinstatement (if a lapse occurs)?

_____ Overall, what kind of service can you expect from the insurance agent and the insurance company that issues the policy? Get referrals from others, and discuss the matter with your family doctor.

Managed Care

The selling of managed care plans—to those who have the luxury of being able to choose—is an aggressive marketing phenomenon not unlike the selling of cars and trucks, soda pop, and beer. The commercials and ads for HMOs are more sedate, but the come-on is no less feverish: "We want your money, and we'll give you the best value for your money!" Some initial precautions are in order:

Don't mistake the sizzle for the steak. Advertising for managed care plans may tout such things as "satisfied patient surveys" and "most for the money" analyses. Patient satisfaction and lowest cost do not necessarily translate into *best patient care.* That's a much harder thing to gauge, but it's what you really must be most concerned about. It's easy to "satisfy" a big percentage of an HMO's patients, particularly those who aren't really sick. Give them TLC, keep their appointments punctually, point out "how much this would have cost you elsewhere," and you can have them purring like a kitten. But have they been given the right treatment? The patients don't necessarily know. But they are "satisfied," and will say so if asked in a Patient Satisfaction Survey. Not all such surveys would be so devious, but the possibility exists. The better course would be to do your own survey of a given HMO. Talk to people who are members. Ask them tough, straightforward questions about their experiences. On any given day you can find dozens of them in the HMO's waiting room. Be discreet, but assertive. It's your health you're worrying about.

More specific questions to answer regarding HMOs:

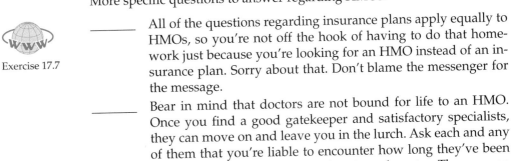

Exercise 17.7

_____ All of the questions regarding insurance plans apply equally to HMOs, so you're not off the hook of having to do that homework just because you're looking for an HMO instead of an insurance plan. Sorry about that. Don't blame the messenger for the message.

_____ Bear in mind that doctors are not bound for life to an HMO. Once you find a good gatekeeper and satisfactory specialists, they can move on and leave you in the lurch. Ask each and any of them that you're liable to encounter how long they've been with the HMO and how long they intend to stay. There are no

guarantees, of course, but you'll get some signals that can be of value. In an older and more established HMO you're less likely to find a lot of turnover—the doctors are presumably happy there. Newer ones that have not settled in for the long run might be more susceptible to turnover. But remember, too, that private-practice doctors can also retire, move, quit, die, or become otherwise unavailable. The more you're concerned about this particular issue, the more likely you are to be happier with a PPO instead of an HMO, even though it might cost you more.

———— If you already have *any* conditions, take *any* medications or need *any* specific treatments, find out if the HMO will cover you in full, in part, or not at all.

———— Find out how large a roster of primary care doctors and specialists the HMO carries. Are there enough to suit the needs of the clientele and the community? Find out how long a wait there is to see various specialists—cardiologists, OB-gyns, orthopedists, pediatricians, allergists, ophthalmologists, and so on. Inquire particularly about any you think you or your family might be needing.

———— Locate the HMO's treatment facilities. Is there a facility within easy reach of you, or will you have to travel long distances?

———— Spending an hour or so in its waiting room will tell you a lot about the efficiency of normal service at an HMO.

———— Learn what coverage limitations there are, if any, on emergency room care, prescriptions, mental illness, reproductive problems, maternity matters, and treatment needed when you are out of the HMO's jurisdiction. Do not take any of these matters lightly.

———— Find out what you have to do if you want to switch doctors, either primary care or specialist. Is it quick and easy? Or a pain in the neck? Ask the HMO administrators for their versions, then ask some of the friends you'll be making in the waiting room.

———— Find out when, and at what cost, you can see doctors outside the HMO or PPO system. You should know whether you have to get permission first, and if so under what circumstances.

———— Check on the HMO's facilities. As in any business, neatness counts. If a building, or any of its facilities, are unkempt or poorly maintained, that's a sign that someone isn't managing something as well as possible. That could extend to patient care.

Other Forms of Health Care Protection

Some relatively minor sources of health care protection can be available to you. You should know the extent of coverage from all of the following:

_____ Workers' Compensation insurance pays benefits if you are injured or become ill as a result of your work. Benefits can include medical expenses, income reimbursement, and rehabilitations costs. The amount of benefits is fixed by each state.

_____ Medical coverage in your homeowner's and automobile insurance policies can provide some protection to reimburse you or guests when injury occurs in your home or car. The amount of this insurance can be negotiated with your insurance agent.

_____ If harm comes to you through the fault of another, such as in an accident in a car, home or business, the party at fault may be liable for all or part of your medical expenses, as well as lost wages and mental anguish. This is the legal route, which you may have qualms about taking if the circumstances arise. Do as your conscience dictates, but bear in mind that the other party would probably expect reimbursement from you if the situation were reversed.

_____ Governmental assistance can help defray some costs arising from poor health. At the federal level, Social Security can provide benefits in some cases of death and disability. These benefits are paid to surviving spouses and/or children. Supplemental Security Income (SSI) is another aspect of the Social Security program designed to help lower-income people. It provides benefits for disability and blindness for qualifying children and people over 65. At the state or local level Medicaid can pay for a wider range of medical costs for qualifying lower income people.

_____ Medicare is a rather large program and so will be covered in greater detail in the following section.

Medicare

Exercise 17.8

Medicare is a health insurance program administered by the Social Security Administration designed to protect citizens sixty-five years of age and over. The costs of and the benefits provided by Medicare are amended from time to time, and anyone currently eligible for Medicare, or soon to become eligible, should check with the local Social Security office to determine what current costs and benefits are.

There are two aspects of Medicare: hospital insurance (the basic plan), and medical insurance (the supplementary plan). These are referred to as Part A and Part B, respectively.

Persons eligible for Medicare must pay an initial deductible amount with Part A, and a monthly premium in order to be protected by the medical insurance coverage, Part B. Part A, after the deductible has been paid, covers the bulk of the cost of hospital services and extended-care facilities, including rooms, meals, nursing, and certain drugs and supplies. Part B is designed to defray the cost of doctors' services, as well as related medical expenses for such things as x-rays, various equipment, and laboratory fees. Medicare will cover a major percentage of these various expenses, but the insured may be responsible for a certain percentage as well. Part A, the hospitalization insurance, is also limited to a specific number of days.

Exercise 17.9

Many older citizens have the mistaken belief that Medicare is the ultimate protection for them against health-care expenses in their later years. Although Medicare does cover a substantial portion of normal medical expenses, many people may still be burdened by the cost of nursing care and other costs not covered by the program. A number of supplemental programs are available through major insurance companies, and any existing or prospective Medicare recipients should explore the advisability of obtaining some supplemental protection.

Before 1992, buying supplemental Medicare insurance—or Medigap coverage, as it's often called—involved tracking through a jungle of confusing and often misleading policies issued by hundreds of companies. In 1992 Congress passed a Medigap law that standardizes all such policies into one of ten formats. The types of policies range from A to J, with A being the stripped-down version offering minimal supplemental protection, and J being the top of the line, offering a much broader range of protection. Although this may make it easier to sort out the levels of coverage available, you still must compare costs carefully. Not all A policies cost alike, and the same goes for B through J. Careful shopping is still required to get the best value for your money.

INCOME INSURANCE

How long could you get by without any income? One week? One month? Six months? A year? What other sources could you call on for funds to live on? Your savings account? Your investments? The equity in your home? Friends or relatives or institutions who might lend you money?

Income can be lost in one of four ways: quitting your job, being fired, being laid off temporarily, or being laid up as a result of disabilities. With the possible exception of quitting your job, all these occurrences are totally unpredictable.

Loss of work because of disability can mean more than simply lost income. With the disability may come added expenses of rehabilitation, recuperation, medicine and drugs, nursing, and other miscellaneous medical costs. There can also be intangible costs: the depression that the laid-up breadwinner may suffer, the extra demands imposed on other members of the family, the natural worry over what prospects the future holds.

Existing Programs

A number of existing programs give a moderate degree of protection against lost income. But for many people these programs will not be enough, and they will want to examine the opportunities offered by private disability income insurance policies. Before we delve into the specifics of that kind of personal insurance, let's briefly examine some of the other on-going programs that may already be protecting your income.

Sick-pay Plans

Some employers have a set policy on how much sick pay they will provide. Others may play it by ear when an employee is unable to work. You must learn what your employer's program is regarding sick pay, for this is the core of your basic income-protection plan. A private plan, should you acquire one, must be built on the foundation of your employer's sick-pay program.

Worker's Compensation

Workers' Compensation offers a measure of disability income to workers who are injured on the job or who contract a job-related illness. But you could be disabled from causes not related to your work, in which case Workers' Compensation would be of no help to you. Determine what Workers' Compensation benefits for disability income would be, because this, along with the sick-pay plan, is important in structuring any private plan.

Social Security

Exercise 17.10

If you become totally disabled—that is, "unable to engage in any substantial gainful activity," according to the Social Security laws—you may be eligible for monthly benefits under the Social Security system. You can obtain more specific details from your local Social Security office.

Unemployment Insurance

Unemployment insurance offers a measure of income if you are laid off from work. Your state unemployment office can assist you in learning what benefits are payable and for how long. You will be expected to look for work if you are receiving unemployment benefits, and you may waive your rights to the benefits if you do not comply with state regulations.

Waiver of Premium Clauses

Waiver of premium provisions in your life and health insurance policies can protect you, at least to the extent of those obligations. If you are disabled

and unable to work, the premiums for those policies would be automatically paid for you. This is only a minimal level of protection, but it would at least assure that those important payments were being met.

Credit Health Insurance

With credit health insurance, if you are disabled and unable to work, loan payments will be made for you during the period of disability. The same protection may be available with your home mortgage. The cost of such insurance, and the benefits payable, will vary from lender to lender.

Evaluating Your Needs for Disability Income Insurance

Exercise 17.11

In order to determine how much disability income insurance you may need, you must evaluate the foregoing sources of protection as well as other personal sources of available income. These latter sources would include the ability of other family members to work; the size of your personal savings and how much you'd be willing to dip into them and for how long; other assets that may be converted into cash such as the equity in your house, the cash values in your life insurance, vested rights in profit-sharing and pension funds that you may be able to get access to; part-time or temporary work that you yourself could do; and loans or gifts from family, friends, and associates.

Once you have made a reasonable determination of outside sources of supplementary income, you can begin to examine the benefits available from private disability income policies.

Private Disability Income Policies and How They Work

Like life and health insurance, disability income insurance is available in a vast variety of sizes and shapes. You may obtain a policy on your own or on a group basis.

Depending on your age, your occupation, and your income, you may be required to take a physical examination for a policy to be approved. The cost of the policy will also vary, depending on your age, income, and occupation.

The Waiting Period

One of the most important factors in shaping a disability income policy is the waiting period—the amount of time you have to be disabled before the insurance will begin to pay benefits. It's possible to obtain a policy that will begin payment of benefits on the very first day of disability due to accident. Or you might obtain a policy with a waiting period of 15, 30, 60, or 90 days,

or even longer. Waiting periods may differ for accidental disability and for disability caused by illness (usually a seven-day minimum wait). Obviously, the shorter the waiting period, the higher the premium, for the company will become obliged to pay you that much sooner. This is why it's so important to know what your sick-pay plan is at work. If your sick-pay plan will cover you fully or substantially for, say, thirty days, there's not much point in paying for a disability plan with a very short waiting period. Once your sick-pay benefits have been exhausted, you might want to look to other ready sources of income before you begin the disability plan. If your sick-pay plan will last thirty days and other readily available sources can provide for another thirty days' worth of income, it might make sense to have a plan that begins after sixty days from the date of the disability.

Total and Partial Disability

Disability income policies pay you a flat fixed monthly amount if you are totally disabled. Should you be partially disabled, the company will pay you a portion, usually half, of the full total disability benefit. The definition of total disability is very important. If, in order to receive total disability benefits, you must be totally unable to perform *any kind* of work, it may be more difficult to obtain such benefits. Many people who become disabled are unable to perform their normal job but can perform other jobs or work on a limited basis.

If the definition of total disability states that you are not able to perform *your own specific tasks*, you might be more readily able to obtain total disability benefits. In this case, it would not matter that you could perform other duties. The important distinction is whether you can perform your own normal duties in order to be considered totally disabled.

You should also determine whether the policy requires you to be either bedridden, homebound, or under the care of a physician in order to maintain continuing benefits, whether total or partial. As with all insurance, the more liberal the benefits, the higher the premiums. You're probably getting more protection; therefore, you're paying extra dollars for the desired security.

How Much Protection?

Once the disability payments begin, how long will they continue? One year? Five years? Ten years? Lifetime? Policies differ widely in this respect, as do the costs of the policies. There may also be maximum limitations on how much the policy will pay you over a lifetime. Many income disability policies cease paying benefits or curtail benefits once you have reached age 65, even though you may still be working. Naturally, when you do cease work, it can be expected that the disability income policy will also cease, since it's designed to protect you against lost income from work.

Benefits that you receive from a disability income policy are not subject to income taxes. Thus, it's not necessary for you to try to obtain a monthly benefit that's equal to your actual income.

Some disability income policies offer extra benefits in the event of a loss of a limb or limbs or loss of eyesight. Some also offer death benefits.

Exercise 17.12

All things considered, a sound program of disability income protection is similar to a sound program of medical expense protection. You may prefer to take your own chances on short-term minor disabilities and use the available money to insure amply against major long-term crippling disabilities. As with other forms of personal insurance, the right agent will help you evaluate your needs and illustrate your alternatives for protecting yourself against the probable losses.

Long-Term-Care Insurance

As with matters of retirement and estate planning, this subject might be of greater interest to your parents or others close to retirement age. But remember that the financial well-being of anyone who might become dependent on you is very much your concern as well.

Long-term-care insurance used to be referred to as nursing home insurance. But the coverage available has expanded considerably, and now includes at-home custodial care for those who do not need a nursing home, but do need help in their own homes in order to get along comfortably.

Nursing home care can cost between $40,000 and $70,000 per year—that's for moderate facilities, nothing luxurious. At-home custodial care can cost about $120 per day for one eight-hour shift. That translates to $600 for a five-day week, or more than $30,000 for a full year. You can conservatively expect those costs to increase by about 5 percent per year. In other words, in less than twenty years the costs will have about doubled. Any of those expenses can eat up even a big nest egg in a hurry. Medicare pays for very little, if any, of it.

Long-term-care policies are the cheapest to buy the younger you are. By buying while younger, you avoid the risk of becoming uninsurable because of unforeseen medical problems. It takes some number crunching with a few different policies to come up with the best plan. Here are the main details you will want to evaluate:

Waiting Period

When will the policy begin to pay? From the very first day, or will you have to wait perhaps 30, 60, 90 days, or even longer? The choice is up to you. The shorter the waiting period, the higher the cost. But the difference in cost between no waiting period and a moderate one is relatively small. You might have more peace of mind, therefore, with the shorter waiting period. How much of the possible cost of nursing home or in-home care do you think you can handle on your own without needing insurance help? Therein lies the answer to the waiting period question.

Policy Limits

Policies will typically pay $50 to $100 per day for nursing home facilities, and the amount of at-home care will be pegged to the daily nursing home benefit. Or you can just obtain the nursing home coverage without the at-home benefits.

Inflation Protection

You can opt for no inflation protection, which will be the lowest-cost plan. Or you can choose between a simple and a compounding inflation protection. Example: A policy may offer a simple 5 percent inflation protection, which means that if you start off with a $100 per day room benefit, in the second year that benefit will rise to $105 per day, then $110 per day in the third year, $115 in the fourth year, and so on. In a 5 percent compounding plan, your second year will also be $105, but after that the protection compounds. In the third year your benefit will increase by 5 percent of $105, to $110.25; in the fourth year it will increase by 5 percent of $110.25, to $115.51 and so on. These differences may seem small in the early years—and indeed, they are—but farther down the road it can make a very big difference. After twenty years, the 5 percent simple plan will provide you with a daily room benefit of about $195, whereas the 5 percent compounding plan will provide you with a daily room benefit of about $252. Thus, a person who starts a plan at, say, age 50, will have much more substantial benefits by age 70, when such coverage is more likely to be needed. The at-home benefit should increase at the same rate as the daily nursing home benefit.

The added cost of the simple and compounding plans (the latter being the highest) may prove worth it later on. Having no inflation protection at all affords you the lowest-cost coverage, but you'll have to make up a bigger difference later on if you need the services covered by the policy.

Return of Premium

Some plans offer to refund all or part of what you've paid in to the policy if you never have any claims. This seems attractive on the surface, but you have to pay extra for the privilege. And the amount you have to pay, if otherwise invested conservatively, can grow to an even bigger amount than what you will have paid the insurance company. So crunch those numbers most seriously before you accept this provision.

Discounts

Some policies will offer discounts if both spouses sign up for policies at the same time. And some charitable organizations may make even bigger discounts possible if you join and/or make a contribution to them.

Health Condition

The better your health, the better chance you stand of getting a "preferred" rating, which means a lower cost for the policy. Normal health conditions, even some with slight medical problems, will result in a "standard" rating, and a higher cost accordingly. You don't necessarily have to take a physical for one of these policies, but the companies do scrutinize your medical history very carefully, and problems can easily result in a higher rating or a rejection.

Most major companies that offer these policies have abundant literature that explains all the provisions. Study carefully before you make a choice.

Medical Savings Accounts (MSAs)

This began as an experiment in 1997, to run to 2001. If successful, they will be continued. If not, they will be canceled, but anyone enrolling during this four-year trial period will be able to continue the plan even if the concept is canceled after 2001.

MSAs are designed for self-employed persons and for companies with two to fifty employees. To be eligible you first obtain a high-deductible health insurance plan—that being a deductible between $1,500 and $2,250 per year for singles, and $3,000 to $4,500 for families. Then you can separately invest a large sum of money tax-free, provided that the invested money is only used to pay for medical expenses (or retirement expenses once the investor reaches age 59½). How much can you invest for tax-free earnings? Singles can invest up to 65 percent of their deductible amount, and families can invest up to 75 percent of their deductible amount. In other words, a family with a policy that has a $4,000 deductible can invest up to $3,000 per year in an MSA. If the money is not needed for medical expenses, it can accumulate tax-free until retirement and then be spent at that time.

For younger persons, MSAs offer a most attractive way to build up a long-term retirement fund with an excellent tax shelter. For older persons— say, closing in on age 60—the benefits are not as appealing. The true benefits do take a long time to come to fruition. If you are putting away the money each year to earn tax-free, and you have to take it out each year to pay for medical costs, your tax-free earnings are minimized accordingly. The longer you can let the tax-free earnings stay in the MSA, the bigger the bonanza over the long term.

Health Insurance Portability

The Health Insurance Portability Law of 1997 gives workers the right to continued health care coverage while on the job, between jobs, or when

they move to a new job. The law applies to individuals and to businesses with fifty or fewer employees. Here are the basics, with examples as set forth by the U.S. Department of Health and Human Services:

- Small businesses are guaranteed access to health insurance. No insurer can exclude an employee or a family member of an employee from coverage based on health status. Example: The owners of Good Food Cafe have been deterred from buying health insurance for their twenty-five employees. Insurance companies wanted to exclude from any policy one worker, Bill Smith, because he had been diagnosed with cancer. Under the law, all of the employees of the cafe can obtain coverage.

- Once an insurer sells a health policy to a group or individual, they must renew coverage regardless of the health status of any member of a group. Example: Mary Jones, one of Good Food Cafe's employees, develops a heart condition. Under the law, the insurance company must renew the Cafe's policy without dropping Mary or the Cafe from coverage.

- If an individual has previously had health insurance coverage at work, and the job is terminated, or the person moves to another job that does not offer health insurance, that person is guaranteed access to coverage in the individual market without regard to health status, and renewal will be guaranteed. In the alternative, states may develop their own programs to assure that comparable coverage is available to such people. Example: Mary Jones leaves her job at Good Food Cafe to take a new job at Zenith Tool Co., which does not offer health coverage. Under the law, Mary will be able to buy private insurance even if she is in poor health. *Note: The law does not stipulate the cost of such private insurance.* Indeed, it could be quite expensive in Mary's case. But it will be available.

- Coverage cannot be denied for preexisting medical conditions for more than twelve months. Example: Mary Jones's new policy at Zenith can exclude coverage of her heart condition for a maximum of twelve months. And this exclusion may be reduced in relation to the time she was covered for the condition at the Good Food Cafe.

These provisions of the law were quite new at the time this book went to press, so it would be wise to check for more up-to-date regulations and amendments that may have taken place in the interim.

PERSONAL ACTION WORKSHEET

Life Insurance Policy Comparisons

Shopping for life insurance can be very confusing. Companies differ. Specific policies differ. Salespeople differ. Decisions are often made on the basis of the personality of the salesperson or on the "name-brand" reputation of the company. These aren't necessarily improper decisions, but close attention must, of course, be paid to the actual coverage you're obtaining and its cost. The following comparison chart will help you keep a close eye on the numbers themselves.

	Policy A	Policy B	Policy C
❏ Annual premium for a $10,000 straight life policy at your current age	___	___	___
❏ Participating or nonparticipating	___	___	___
❏ If participating, what would have been the dividend paid during the past year?	___	___	___
❏ If participating, what is the company's estimate of dividend for the coming year?	___	___	___
❏ If dividends are left to accumulate with the company, what interest rate will they earn?	___	___	___
❏ Total premium cost over the next 10 years (excluding dividends, since their actual amount won't be known until each year occurs)	___	___	___
❏ At the end of 10 years, what will be your: cash/loan value?	___	___	___
paid-up conversion value?	___	___	___
extended term conversion value?	___	___	___
❏ Total premium cost over next 20 years	___	___	___
❏ At the end of 20 years, what will be your: cash/loan value?	___	___	___
paid-up conversion value?	___	___	___
extended term conversion value?	___	___	___
❏ At what interest rate can you borrow against the policy?	___	___	___

CONSUMER ALERT

An Experiment with Mail-Order Insurance

Health insurance and disability insurance are heavily marketed through the mail, via ads in newspapers and on television. As an experiment, I responded to a number of mail-order insurance offerings. My survey was not scientific, but the results were convincing. You might want to try a survey of your own before you commit yourself to buying health or disability insurance through the mail.

Inquiry No. 1 Eight weeks after sending in the coupon, I had still received no reply. Had I really been in need of the insurance, or had I suffered any malady that could have given rise to a claim, I would have been out of luck.

Inquiry No. 2 I received a policy by return mail, and the bills for it started flowing in. It was a disability income policy, and I compared it in detail with other plans from local agents. The local agents' plans all offered far broader coverage for about the same cost.

Inquiry No. 3 I never received a policy from the company, but I did receive bills urging me to pay the premium before my "valuable coverage" (whatever that may have been) lapsed and left me unprotected.

Inquiry No. 4 In response to the coupon, an agent called on me without an appointment. He was personable and tried to be helpful but would not talk about any of the limitations on the policy unless I asked him directly. He seemed surprised that I knew to ask such questions, and, in some cases, he wasn't sure of the answers. He had no literature to leave with me and said there was absolutely no way for me to see a sample policy unless I signed up with him. Then, he said, I would have ten days to cancel if I wanted to. His main concern was to sign me up on the spot. Can't blame him for trying.

Even with a cancellation privilege, insurance is not a product to be bought sight unseen. All too often, one doesn't exert the effort to cancel an inadequate policy, and the risk is then that you think you're protected when in fact you may be drastically underprotected.

Why Life Insurance Costs Can Vary

Two individuals of the same age are buying the same amount of life insurance. Their costs can vary widely, yet the ultimate payoff for each will be the same. One year later each buys additional policies for the same amount. The one who paid more last year might pay less than the other this year, and vice versa. Why do these costs go up and down?

Smoking versus nonsmoking Life insurance (as well as other forms of insurance) will cost considerably more for a smoker than for a nonsmoker. The life insurance industry, having recognized the higher risk of paying off sooner to the smoker, has boosted the rates accordingly. See the Strategies for Success on page 521.

Male versus female Women have longer life expectancies than men. Accordingly, their life insurance costs less.

Underwriting risks In addition to smoking, some insurance applicants may pose higher risks than others. Known health conditions and participation in hazardous activities are two risk areas that may cause an insurer to charge a higher premium or to reject an application outright.

Type of policy As noted in this chapter, different types of life insurance—term, whole, endowment, and so on—carry different cost factors, as well as different conversion values.

Actuarial changes Periodically, the life insurance industry will alter its assumptions as to life expectancy. These are known as mortality tables. As life expectancy increases over the years, insurers have longer to invest the insureds' money. This means that insureds don't have to pay as much to get given benefits as they would have under a previous shorter life-expectancy assumption. These tables are done for the general population, not for individuals. A change in mortality tables will not affect existing policies.

Dividend performance Participating, or par, policies will pay a sum to policyholders based on the company's performance in taking in money, investing it wisely, and paying it back out in the form of claims. Better performance can mean higher dividends, which can translate into lower out-of-pocket costs for the policy. And vice versa.

Overall company performance Some insurance companies operate more efficiently than others. Some of the savings they thus realize may be passed on to policyholders in the form of lower premiums. Some companies provide a broader base of service to the public—more offices, more informational literature, more training for agents and staff, and so on. This may result in higher costs to policyholders, who might deem it worth the few extra dollars. Some companies may invest imprudently, thus risking everything for themselves and their insureds.

? WHAT IF . . . ?

Test yourself: How would you deal with these real-life possibilities?

1. You have a whole life par policy for $50,000. Your annual premium cost is $500. You've been paying on the policy for five years. Your annual dividend is now projected to be $40. Up to now you've been lazy, letting the annual dividends stay with the company, which is paying you 4 percent interest on the accumulated amount. But now you want to change things. You can either let the dividend apply against your annual premium, thereby reducing your out-of-pocket cost each year, or you can use the dividend to purchase paid-up additions to the policy each year. This year your dividend will buy you $120 worth of paid-up life insurance, and the amount should grow each year. Which will you choose. Why?

2. The only doctor you've ever known is the old family doctor whom your parents have had you see since you were a kid. He's getting on in years now, and you're on your own. You want to get set up with practitioners your own age. You have a choice between (a) a standard insurance plan that allows you to choose any doctor or any hospital you want; (b) an insurance plan that is tied in with a PPO or (c) an HMO. What homework would you do to make your choice, and which choice will you make?

3. Your company has long had a very liberal sick-pay policy. Now it is shifting to a very rigid plan: five paid sick days per year, period. What can/would you do to protect yourself?

NUMBER CRUNCHERS

Do the calculations to make decisions in these real-life possibilities.

1. Uncle Moe and Uncle Joe each have a $10,000 life insurance policy with double indemnity provisions. You are the beneficiary of both policies. At the time of Uncle Moe's death at the hands of a hit-and-run driver, he had borrowed $4,000 against the cash value of his policy. Uncle Joe had been more prudent, using his annual dividend to buy extra paid-up insurance, which totaled $3,000 at the time of his death from natural causes. How much will you collect from each uncle's insurance policy?

2. You are covered by a $50,000 life insurance policy that happens to have the same conversion values as the one illustrated in Table 17–1. After the policy has been in force for twenty years, how much can you borrow against the policy? How much can you cash it in for? How much paid-up insurance can you convert to? What extended term insurance can you convert to?

3. Your company's sick-pay policy will provide full pay for ten sick days per year, then half pay for ten sick days per year, and that's all. You're evaluating three different disability policies, each of which will pay you $1,000 a month for up to five years in the event of total disability. If need be, you can dip into your savings for $1,000 a month for up to six months to keep you afloat, but you'd rather not touch that nest egg. The policies will cost respectively, $520 per year with a 60-day waiting period, $392 with a 90-day waiting period, and $347 with 180 days. Evaluate your options and pick one.

FOR BETTER OR FOR WORSE

Things beyond our control often impact our personal and financial well-being, for better or for worse. Some are more predictable than others. How would you be affected if the following real-life phenomena happened? Could you have seen it coming? What steps could you have taken to minimize damage or maximize advantage? The better able you are to anticipate and recognize these forces, the better equipped you are to deal with them.

1. Your good health depends on a common prescription drug, which costs $100 per month. You join an HMO and learn, after you've paid, that they don't prescribe that particular medication, but a similar one. The similar one doesn't do the job for you.

2. Your widowed mother has a stroke and can no longer care for herself, but she refuses to go to a nursing home. She needs someone with her for at least twelve hours a day for her to be comfortable. Her total assets are $25,000, and she gets $900 a month from Social Security. She has no long-term-care insurance.

3. You are planning to get a major life insurance policy to protect your family. You develop a very severe cough, which you suspect might be due to your smoking.

Exercise 17.13

Exercise 17.14

Financial Planning for Later Years

Hell begins on the day when God grants us a clear vision of all that we might have achieved, of all the gifts that we have wasted, of all that we might have done that we did not do.

Gian Carlo Menotti

Inside every person there's an echo of years earlier, when the younger self did something very right—or very wrong—that had a very distinct effect on the older self. "If only I hadn't let that fast-talking salesman con me into that bum deal with my whole life's savings." "If only I had started to salt away money for retirement when I was 30, instead of now, when I'm 60." "If only I had paid attention to my pension benefits before I quit that job in a huff." So it goes.

Your years of financial maturity may seem far off, but the planning you do now, and the actions you take now, can have a most decisive effect on your security, or lack of it, when that time does come. This chapter is intended to motivate you to think of the eventuality of that day and to ignite an awareness of

- Your housing needs as your family begins to diminish
- Your sources of income when work ceases
- Your legal rights under your pension plan
- Your capabilities of combatting inflation
- How to take best advantage of the Individual Retirement Account, 401(k), and other tax-sheltered retirement plans

IF NOT FOR YOU, THEN FOR YOUR PARENTS

"Wait a minute," you might be saying now. "This retirement stuff is not for me. I'm decades away from those concerns, so why don't I just skip this chapter?" Not so fast. You may be right about how little these matters apply to your present-day concerns. But your parents, or other people close to you, might be very much involved in these "later years" issues. And your knowledge can be helpful to them. Look at it this way: Wouldn't it be worth it to you if you could help your parents structure their later years so as to reduce the chances of their becoming financially dependent on you? If you answered yes, this chapter is very important to you.

REACHING FINANCIAL MATURITY

Exercise 18.1

There comes a time—and it's different for everyone—when we reach a plateau that we'll call financial maturity. This time, particularly for families, generally is when children have grown up and moved out on their own. It's a period when we look at our personal and financial affairs from a new perspective. Many of our needs have changed, and many previously vague goals now come into focus.

As we reach financial maturity our needs and attitudes are in a state of change regarding housing, investing, insurance, use of leisure time, and the ultimate direction of our working career. Many of the financial decisions we make in our twenties and thirties can have a profound bearing on our ability to fulfill goals during the mature years. Thus, thinking about and making plans for the years of financial maturity should begin at the earliest possible time.

The most dangerous course is to ignore the future totally. We live in an age of instant gratification, constantly urged and teased into buying things for the here and now. If we succumb to such urges excessively, we can end up ruining tomorrow for the sake of today. Tomorrow *will* come, and we must be ready for it.

Let's take a close look at some of the major elements of financial planning for the later years in order to get a broad view of the alternatives. We can present only possibilities and probabilities; specific solutions will be strictly up to each individual and family.

Housing

"This is the old homestead. This is where we raised our family. This is where we feel comfortable. It's almost all paid for—why should we move?"

Or, "Without the children, we don't need this house to rattle around in any longer. Do we sell or do we stay, and what are the ramifications of either choice? If we sell, do we find another place in our community, or do we move to a new community? Do we find another house? A condominium? An apartment?"

Our housing requirements are often drastically altered with the onset of financial maturity, and our personal feelings may easily stand between us and many thousands of dollars that could help provide added security and comfort in the years beyond.

The dilemma is simple enough: retaining the old "family homestead," with its comforts and its memories, or exchanging it for another home that may be more practical and economical.

Many homeowning couples in their fifties and sixties have substantial equity in their homes. In addition to what they have paid in on their mortgage debt, the value of the property itself will probably have increased considerably. But as long as that equity is tied up in the house, it's not working for you—except to provide a roof over your head. You may be perfectly content with that roof. However, by selling or refinancing the house, you could get a large sum of money with which to buy other pleasures.

Moreover, one of the main financial advantages in homeownership—the deductibility of mortgage interest and real estate taxes—may be of far less value to you after you have retired than they were in earlier years.

Let's examine the case of the Johnson family to see what alternatives face them. Mr. and Mrs. Johnson are in their mid-fifties. The large family home they purchased fifteen years ago is far too big for just the two of them now that their children have moved out. They've started to think seriously about retirement—planned for ten years hence—and they realize that their home represents their single biggest asset as well as their single largest monthly expense. Should they keep the house or sell it? And if they sell it, should they rent or buy another?

Their house originally cost them $75,000: they paid $15,000 as a down payment and obtained a thirty-year mortgage for $60,000 at 8 percent interest, with monthly payments of $440. Today, with fifteen years yet to pay on their mortgage, they still owe roughly $48,000.

If they sold their house today, they could get $150,000 after brokerage commissions. Thus, if they were to sell it and pay off their existing mortgage, they

would have a $102,000 tax-free cash-in-hand nest egg to do with as they please. In addition to their mortgage payment of $440, they have real estate taxes averaging $120 per month, property insurance costs of $40 per month, utility costs averaging $120 per month, and maintenance expenses averaging $80 per month. Their total outlay for shelter, is therefore, $800 per month.

Staying As Is

Let's assume that the Johnsons are willing to spend $800 per month for their basic shelter. They realize that inflation will boost their property taxes, insurance, utilities, and maintenance costs. But because they have a fixed-rate mortgage, the monthly mortgage payment will not be affected by inflation. Table 18–1 illustrates the approximate effect of inflation on their future monthly housing costs, assuming that inflation will double these costs in fifteen years. If the Johnsons remain in the house, then ten years from now, when Mr. Johnson plans to retire, their outlay will have crept up to $970. Anticipating that his wages will continue to increase between now and retirement, he has no worries about being able to handle that increased monthly housing outlay. Fifteen years from now, the mortgage will be paid off, and, as Table 18–1 indicates, their monthly outlay will drop to about $720.

Staying put seems to be the simplest course for the Johnsons, but is staying put the *best* course for them? What are their other choices?

Becoming Renters

If they sold the house now, they could rent either an apartment or another house. Instead of spending the $800 per month on the mortgage and housing expenses, they could apply it toward their rental. By selling, they'd also have $102,000 in cash to spend or invest. If they invest the $102,000 they could use some of the income from that investment toward their rental.

If, for example, they invested the $102,000 in a plan that yielded 6 percent after taxes, that would generate $510 per month income for them. That, added to their current monthly housing outlay of $800, would allow them to spend $1,310 per month on rent. And they would always have their

TABLE 18–1 **Monthly Housing Outlay—Existing Home**

	Now	In 10 Years	In 15 Years
Mortgage	$440	$440	$ 0
Property taxes	120	200	240
Insurance	40	70	80
Utilities	120	160	240
Maintenance	80	100	160
Total	$800	$970	$720

$102,000 nest egg intact to do with as they pleased in the future.

If the rental increased on their apartment, and if the yield on the $102,000 investment also increased proportionately, they could maintain a fairly level standard of housing over the long term. Otherwise they would have to adjust accordingly.

Buying Another Dwelling

Another alternative would be to buy another dwelling—house, townhouse, or condominium—with the proceeds of the sale of their existing home. Let's say that the Johnsons find a smaller dwelling with a $100,000 price tag. They put $40,000 of their total $102,000 nest egg toward a down payment on the new house, and sign up for a $60,000 mortgage for fifteen years at 9 percent. The new monthly mortgage payments would be $609. Let's assume that the other costs would be lower in their new dwelling because it's a more modest property: $100 for property taxes, $30 for insurance, $60 for utilities, and $60 for maintenance. This brings the grand monthly total outlay to $859—$59 more than they have currently been paying. Table 18–2 illustrates what their current outlay in a new smaller house would be for the present, and for ten and fifteen years hence.

Remember that the Johnsons have $62,000 left over from the sale of their previous house. Assume that they put that to work in an investment that will earn them 6 percent after taxes, or roughly $310 per month. They can apply that income toward their housing expense and still leave the $62,000 nest egg intact for future use. Table 18–3 shows the net housing cost for the Johnsons in their new home, assuming that they apply the income from their investment toward these costs.

Currently, their net housing costs would be $549 per month. That's $251 per month less than what they now have budgeted for housing. They could, if they wish, begin an additional investment program with that $251 per month and create an even larger nest egg for their retirement years.

TABLE 18–2   **Monthly Housing Outlay—New, Smaller House**

	Now	In 10 Years	In 15 Years
Mortgage	$609	$ 609	$ 0
Property taxes	100	160	200
Insurance	30	50	60
Utilities	60	100	120
Maintenance	60	100	120
Total	$859	$1,019	$500

Note: Projections are based on an approximate annual inflation rate of 6 percent for property taxes, insurance, utilities, and maintenance costs.

TABLE 18–3   **Net Housing Costs—New, Smaller House**

	Now	In 10 Years	In 15 Years
Base costs (from Table 18–2)	$859	$1,019	$500
Income from $62,000 investment	310	310	310
Net housing cost, after applying investment income	$549	$ 709	190

What About Refinancing?

If the Johnsons decided to stay put for the time being, would it make sense for them to refinance their existing mortgage? Unless the current interest rates are *equal to or less than* the original 8 percent interest rate on their existing mortgage, refinancing at this time would be of relatively little benefit. Assume they were to refinance their existing $48,000 mortgage for a new period of 30 years at 12 percent interest each year. Their monthly mortgage payments would actually *increase* by $54 per month, to $493 per month. Obviously, there's no advantage to such a move. Careful calculations, including all costs involved, will be necessary to determine the value of refinancing at any particular time.

Profit Potential

The Johnsons face yet another perplexity to reach a decision: What profit potential might they be giving up if they sell their existing house? The house has doubled in value in the past fifteen years. Will it double again in the next fifteen years? If they sell now and become renters, would they then be giving up a veritable small fortune? On the other hand, if they sell now, and buy another house, what is the profit potential on that other house? Could it be more or less than the potential on the existing house?

If the Johnsons are risk-takers, they might prefer to hold onto their existing house and take their chances on the future housing market. If they are more conservative, they might prefer to sell now and have a greater sense of security for the years to come.

There is no rule of thumb as to which choice is best for any given family. But there are choices to be made, and those choices should be evaluated clearly, with professional help, wherever uncertainty emerges.

Investing

Our investment attitudes and tactics are likely to undergo a considerable change as we reach financial maturity. Until now, we've been concerned with *generating* capital to meet the heavy expenses of housing, educating the children, and other family needs. Now, with those needs substantially accomplished, we turn to the philosophy of *preservation* of capital. While we

were younger, we could afford to make mistakes and still recoup. Now we may be at an age when a financial loss is more alarming: we may have neither the time nor the ability to recoup.

The advantages of fixed income investing, as opposed to more speculative forms, become clearer. Although many are just reaching their peak earning years at this stage, the wisdom of taking risks is diminishing. We simply have less time to recover from a loss. Anticipating that time when work may cease, we begin to realize the importance of preserving our capital so that there will be adequate funds available. This does not imply that all attempts to generate capital more speculatively should be abandoned. But the risk factor must be examined more closely and should be considered with much more respect than it may have been a decade or two earlier.

A portfolio of fixed income investments to preserve capital can take many shapes. Perhaps the line of least resistance is to take whatever lump sum you may have accumulated and just put it into long-term high-yield bonds and leave it there. This minimizes the need to have your nose buried in *The Wall Street Journal* constantly looking for better opportunities. If you're locked into a given situation, you may regret it later if better opportunities do present themselves. On the other hand, nothing better may come along, and you'll be content to ride it out with your locked-in situation.

The prudent investor in the mature years must be aware of the value of liquidity and flexibility. To obtain liquidity and flexibility in the fixed income portfolio, consider the advantages of building a portfolio based on *staggered maturities*.

Staggered Maturities

Instead of investing a lump sum for one long period, you break up the lump sum into perhaps three or four or five nearly equal segments and invest them for different maturities. For example, you have a $10,000 lump sum that you want to put into fixed income securities. Consider breaking it into four equal parts of $2,500 each and investing each of the four segments for a different maturity: one segment for one year, one for two years, one for three years, and one for four years. Within each time span, you can take advantage of the highest yield security available. Then as each segment matures, starting in one year, you can reinvest that money into whatever is best at that time, considering safety and yield.

With a portfolio like this, you'd have one-quarter of your total nest egg roll over every year. In some years you might have to take a lesser yield than you had previously been earning on that segment because of a drop in interest rates. In other years, you might be able to obtain a better return. With a program of staggered maturities (not exceeding a five- or six-year maximum), you're going to have a higher degree of control and liquidity with your nest egg, which could bring you a greater sense of satisfaction and financial return.

Overall, as noted in chapter 14, the fixed income portfolio allows you to predict with reasonable certainty how much money you will have available at any given future point. By sticking to fixed-income investments with shorter maturities, you can avoid the problem of being caught in a long-term downtrend of prices on such fixed-income securities as bonds. If you need to tap your next egg, you will have minimized any worry that the value will have shrunk because of fluctuations in those securities.

Insurance

Financial maturity brings accompanying changes in our insurance program. We may have had a life insurance program designed to protect our family in the event of the premature death of the breadwinner. Now the family is on its own, and we may have far better uses for those dollars.

Life insurance programs begun when you are in your twenties and thirties can have a most important effect on financial status in your fifties and sixties. If, when you're young, you sacrifice a bit of current pleasures for the sake of greater security in the future, you can create a life insurance program that will serve you well in the later years. In chapter 17, we examined some of the alternatives facing young people in choosing various kinds of life insurance programs. Let's now look at the effect of one particular choice decades later.

When Joe was age 30, he bought a straight life insurance policy with a face value of $50,000. His annual premium for this protection was $653. From the very first day the policy was issued, Joe and his family had the peace of mind of knowing that $50,000 would be payable to his family in the event of Joe's death. Joe has lived a full and healthy life, and today, twenty years later, he looks at the conversion values in his life insurance program.

Table 18–4 illustrates Joe's policy. (See chapter 17 regarding how these values work.) When Joe is age 50 and the policy is twenty years old, Joe's life insurance needs are quite different than when he bought the policy. His

TABLE 18–4   Joe's Life Insurance

		Conversion Values		
At Age	Total Premiums Paid to Date	Cash/Loan Value	Paid-up Insurance	Extended Term
50	$13,060	$14,450	$28,550	19 years, 103 days
65	22,855	27,550	39,950	14 years, 160 days

Note: Policies will differ with respect to these values.

children are grown now, and there is little need for immediate cash to take care of his family in the event of his death.

At age 50, Joe will have paid premiums totaling $13,060. The policy now has a cash surrender value of $14,450. In other words, Joe can cash in the policy and receive back *more* than what he paid in. If he invests the $14,450 at 6 percent per year, he will have a return of $867 per year, leaving his $14,450 nest egg intact. The net results: For the past twenty years he has guaranteed his family a substantial lump sum of money—$50,000—in the event of his premature death. Now, instead of being out of pocket $653 for premiums each year, he can have an added income of $867 per year, plus a cash nest egg of $14,450. If he cashes in the policy, the $50,000 coverage will terminate.

Joe may also elect to borrow the $14,450 from the company, to do with as he sees fit, while paying interest on the loan at the rate stated in the policy. If he chooses this alternative, the policy will remain in force, except that in the event of Joe's death, the proceeds payable will be the face value of the policy minus any loans outstanding against the policy.

Joe's other alternatives are to convert the policy to a paid-up or an extended-term status. If he chooses the paid-up method, he can cease paying the annual $653 premium and will have a life insurance policy with a face value of $28,550, paid up for the rest of his life. He doesn't have to pay any more premiums, and, on his death, his survivors will receive that sum. If he converts to extended-term insurance, he will be able to stop paying premiums and still be insured for the full $50,000 face value for a period of 19 years plus 103 days, until he's almost 70.

What if Joe continues to pay on the policy and keep it in force until he reaches age 65? He will have paid in a total of $22,855 in premiums, and he will have a cash value of $27,550. The other conversion values for that age are indicated in Table 18–4.

Another option open to Joe at this time would be to convert the paid-up values in his policies to second-to-die coverage. To do this, he would add his wife to a new joint policy so that both of their lives would be covered. The proceeds would be payable on the death of the second of the two insured parties. Assuming that both Joe and his wife are in good health, converting the paid-up values in the old policy to a second-to-die policy could give them a much higher face value, which could benefit their children or pay off any other debts, including estate taxes.

The important thing is that the 30-year-old Joe did in fact create the program that the 50-year-old Joe or the 65-year-old Joe can now either continue or convert to suit current needs. *The young man created a liquid and flexible package that can benefit the older man.*

Health insurance is also important. Anyone covered by a group medical plan should, at the earliest possible time, investigate what health insurance alternatives are available at retirement, particularly if you plan to retire before reaching Medicare eligibility at age 65. Does your health insurance cov-

erage continue after you retire? If so, at what cost, if any? If not, what kind of supplemental coverage is available to you and at what cost? Long-term-care insurance should also be explored. (This subject is discussed in greater detail in chapter 17.) Careful examination should also be made of eligibility for Medicare, what coverage it provides, and at what cost. Will you want supplemental coverage in addition to what Medicare provide you? The sooner you look into these matters, the better off you'll be.

Activities and Idleness

Our personal activities and pleasures may undergo substantial alteration when we reach financial maturity. Much of our free time in the younger years may have been devoted to family affairs or community activities. We may also find that friends are shifting from old patterns into new ones, and there may be a desire to pursue various interests with those friends.

Very serious problems can arise if you don't develop outside interests that will provide satisfaction and self-fulfillment in later years. In spite of all the money one may have accumulated, the loneliness, boredom, and help-lessness that can attack retirees are overpowering.

To Work or to Retire

As financial maturity begins, we start to think about how long we wish to continue working in our current jobs, whether we wish to take on some new work, or whether we wish to enjoy a leisurely retirement. Our choices, and how we move toward them, can have a critical influence on the quality of our later years.

If you intend to continue working, either voluntarily or out of necessity, what kind of employment might be available to someone with your skills, desires, experience, and needs? If gradual retirement is in your future, when will you begin to taper off, and how quickly? Will you want to try something that you'd always wished you could do?

The earlier you start shaping those thoughts into something tangible, the better. If you anticipate a work activity that will take some investment on your part, the earlier you start setting aside the necessary funds, the better you'll be able to accomplish your desires. If no investment will be needed, you'll have all that much more time to establish extra reserve funds to see you through, should the business venture not work out.

Some Particular Thoughts for the Older Single Person

The single person reaching financial maturity has some different considerations from those of the married person. Single people who do not have dependents obviously have little need for life insurance and can allocate those dollars elsewhere. To the extent that single people want to leave an inheri-

tance, life insurance does provide a good vehicle for that purpose, as it does for married people.

Many single people may have life insurance policies acquired many years ago. When the original need for insurance has diminished, single people should examine the conversion privileges in the policies, as noted earlier in the case of Joe.

If disability strikes, the single person who is alone can be at a disadvantage—long-term convalescence can be costly and time-consuming. Housekeeping, shopping, nursing care, and the like must be considered, and the costs can run high. It's essential for single persons to maintain comprehensive insurance programs or other alternatives that will protect them in the event of long-term disability.

A single person facing a long-term disability may need a lawyer's help. If you are unable to act on your own behalf, someone trusted should be allowed to step into your shoes and take care of important matters for you. These matters could be as simple as writing or endorsing checks, or as complex as selling a home. The Power of Attorney can be a valuable tool for the single person, particularly in the event of an extended disability.

A Power of Attorney need not be given to a lawyer; it can be granted to anyone you choose. But a lawyer should definitely draw up the documents. A Power can be limited to specifically stated acts or can be general in scope. A general Power of Attorney is very broad and should be entered into only in the most compelling circumstances. Your lawyer can give you more details.

Concerns About Health Care

Preretirement financial planning includes keeping a close eye on health insurance, particularly if a couple's main health plan is based on one spouse's job, with the other spouse being covered as a dependent. To what extent will the dependent spouse be covered when the working spouse retires? Presumably, the retiring spouse will be covered by Medicare and/or a continuation of the employer's group plan. But the dependent spouse might not yet be eligible for Medicare, and the employer's plan might not cover spouses of retirees. If neither kind of coverage is available to the dependent spouse, can that spouse obtain the needed health insurance privately? Would preexisting conditions limit the protection available to such a person? Discuss this with a good agent so that any problems can be minimized while the dependent spouse is still insurable.

FINANCIAL ARRANGEMENTS FOR THE LATER YEARS

Exercise 18.2

How much money will you have to live on when your work tapers off and/or ceases altogether?

Before we take a closer look at planning a retirement budget, we must discuss one very common concern: "Whatever we have to live on, it won't be enough because inflation will eat away at it."

The Specter of Inflation

Inflation can be a specter, particularly if the ability to work has diminished or disappeared. But it can be coped with.

On reaching the later years, many individuals reduce their living expenses and thus blunt the effects of inflation. Moving to smaller quarters, moderating clothing needs and having only one car can sharply reduce financial needs. Many families will have paid off their home mortgages and many will terminate or convert existing life insurance programs, and no longer have those costs.

Beyond what families do unconsciously to meet their diminished needs, they might also take some conscious steps to cut spending. A review of any budget can reveal minor excesses that can be reduced without materially affecting lifestyle.

The effects of inflation can also be blunted on the income side. Social Security payments are scheduled to increase in line with Consumer Price Index fluctuations, and many pensions have escalation clauses tied to rising prices. Furthermore, as costs move upward, so inevitably do yields on fixed income investments, and those higher yields can offset the inflationary bite.

STRATEGIES FOR SUCCESS

Don't Leave Safe Harbors Foolishly

Investing for retirement requires an emphasis on safety: putting a major portion of your money into the safe harbors of federally insured savings plans, government bonds, and high-quality corporate bonds. But even with the best of planning, interest rates might fall, or inflation might rise. Either phenomenon can erode your supply of spendable dollars. When either occurs, Snake Oil Sam is not far behind, offering mystical plans to beat the low interest rates or the high inflation. Don't leave your safe harbors at the beckoning of Snake Oil Sam. He can lead you into risky waters where you can suffer grievous losses. If you stay in the safe harbor, interest rates will eventually go back up, and inflation will go back down, and things will stabilize. More importantly, in the safe harbor your money *will be there when you need it*. With Sam, it *may be gone forever*. Keep your expectations reasonable, and learn to live comfortably on lower yields. Then higher yields, when they come, will be a bonus for you.

Shaping the Budget

Two primary sources of sustenance must be considered in detail: income and principal. Income is money received from all sources such as Social Security, pensions, investments, and work. Principal is accumulated money working for you that may be dipped into for living purposes as the need arises. The prudent course is to attempt to live off income and keep principal in reserve until needed. A careful review of your investment program is necessary. How much principal do you have? How well is it protected? Can you count on the projected income from principal? If not, how can you restructure your investments to offer a more assured income flow?

Income Sources

The younger you are, the more difficult it will be to get specific figures on what retirement income will be available to you. But at least ten or fifteen years before you anticipate retirement, you should begin to estimate what might be expected. As the date approaches, you should check with regularity—at least every second year, tapering down to every year—in order to focus more clearly on the actual income figures. One very sad mistake is to conjure up in your own mind what these income sources may be—those who guess too high can be sharply disappointed. The proper way is to check with the specific sources and get their best estimates as to the actual dollars that will become available, and when.

Income from Social Security

Exercise 18.3

Social Security payments are increased periodically as the Consumer Price Index increases. A visit to your local Social Security office can be helpful; the closer you get to actual retirement, the more closely the Social Security Administration can estimate your income.

Income from Pensions and Profit-Sharing Plans

Visit with your employer's pension or profit-sharing plan administrator to determine what money you may have coming from those sources. What options do you have with those funds? Will you be paid a fixed monthly amount and, if so, for how long? Will you be able to obtain a lump-sum payment, what will it be, and when can you get it? Will payments continue beyond the death of the working spouse and be available to the surviving spouse and, if so, for how long? The Pension Reform Law of 1974 makes many provisions for the benefit of pensions-to-be. That law is discussed later in this chapter; included in the discussion is a rundown of the Individual Retirement Act 401(k) plans and other tax-sheltered retirement plans.

Income from Investments

As retirement nears and the ability to earn income from work diminishes, you'll seek more assurance that a fixed amount will be available to meet your needs. This means, most simply put, that you have to take less and less risk when you put your money to work. Putting your money at risk means that you have less assurance, perhaps none at all, as to how much income or principal you'll have during those years when you must depend upon an assured amount. The stock market may have been fine for you as a capital-building vehicle when you were a few decades younger. But verging on retirement, you can't afford all the risks that go with the stock market. Develop a sound program of fixed-income investments—high rated bonds and savings plans—with perhaps some high quality stocks that pay a good level of assured dividends. Risk means potential loss, at a time you can least afford it.

Income from Working

Many people continue to work long after they are eligible to retire. They may go into business for themselves or take a full- or part-time job out of either choice or necessity. But the younger you are, the more difficult it is to predict how much post-retirement income you might earn from working, or for how long it might continue. With the earning potential from work so unpredictable, it would be prudent not to rely on any such income for your basic well-being. It might be best to consider any such income as "icing on the cake" to provide for extra comforts and leisure activities during retirement.

Owing to peculiarities in the income tax laws and Social Security regulations, it is possible for some people to end up with more spendable income—after taxes—once they have retired as compared with before retirement. For example, when Flora was age 64, she had a total income from her job of $30,000 per year. After all taxes and voluntary pension contributions were taken into account, she was left with a net spendable income of $24,000. The following year, she retired. Just to keep busy, she took a part-time job, from which she earned $10,000 during her first year of retirement. She received an additional $8,000 for that year from a pension plan and $10,000 from Social Security. The Social Security income was not taxable. Considering all taxes on her sources of income, Flora ended up with a net spendable income of $25,000 during her first year of retirement, even though her actual income from work was a fraction of what it had been during her working years. In other words, she had more spendable money after retirement than she did while she was working.

Post-retirement income from work can also be affected by Social Security regulations, which can reduce your benefits if you earn more than a set amount during a given year from work. Anyone planning to work after starting to receive Social Security benefits must determine what effect the

earnings will have on benefits. There are three ways that Social Security laws can reduce your postretirement income.

1.   If you earn income from work, that income will be subject to the same Social Security taxes you've been paying all through your working years.

2.   Once you start receiving Social Security benefits, up to 85 percent of what you receive can be subject to income taxes if your overall income exceeds a certain level. That overall income includes earnings from work and from investments. So working can push your Social Security benefits into a taxable level.

3.   If you are receiving Social Security benefits, those benefits are reduced by income you receive from work. The latest regulations on this matter are that Social Security recipients under age 70 will forfeit one dollar's worth of benefits for every three dollars they earn at work over a certain threshold. That threshold for 1999 is $15,500. In other words, if Robin Retiree earned $16,500 from work in 1999, Robin's Social Security benefits will be reduced for the year by $333. (Earnings from investments do not count in this matter.) The threshold is scheduled to rise in the following years to $17,000 for the year 2000, $25,000 for 2001, and $30,000 for 2002. From age 70 to onward these forfeits no longer apply.

All of these Social Security regulations are subject to change at any time, so you must check the current ones as they pertain to you.

The Principal Sources

The principal sources of future spendable dollars may be easier to estimate than income sources, particularly if an investment portfolio is in fixed income situations. The potential principal sources are the following.

Equity in Your Home

As noted earlier, many people refinance or sell their homes to get access to the dollars they've been paying on their mortgage. This equity can represent a substantial portion of anyone's ultimate nest egg and should be estimated as carefully and as far in advance as possible.

One technique for tapping the equity in a home is known as a reverse mortgage. Instead of borrowing a lump sum and then making monthly payments to the lender, the lender sends you a monthly payment, and the debt (plus interest) builds up over the years. The accumulated debt must be paid off when the homeowners move, sell, or die. Very few lenders offer such plans; they are complicated and need careful study. The American Association of Retired Persons (AARP) offers literature on the subject. Another

equity-tapping technique is a sale-leaseback, which is usually done between parents (the homeowners) and their children. The parents, in effect, sell the house to the children, who in turn give a lifetime lease back to the parents. The parents thus get cash up front. The children get monthly rent plus some possible income tax breaks. The advice of a lawyer and an accountant should be sought before embarking on these techniques.

Life Insurance Values

Individuals with conversion values in their life insurance policies should determine precisely what those values currently are and what they will be in future years. Personal circumstances will dictate whether to continue the protection of the life insurance in full, convert it to one of the other forms of life insurance, or retrieve the cash that's available.

Pension and Profit-Sharing Funds

If lump-sum distributions are available instead of monthly payments, these should be counted in your overall sources of principal. See the discussion later in this chapter on lump-sum pension and profit-sharing distributions.

Business Interests

If you have an interest in a business, either wholly or partially, how might that be converted into investable funds, and at what time? How can you best sell out your business or professional practice and on what terms?

Anyone in these circumstances must recognize when a business or professional practice is at peak potential and reach a decision as to how much energy should be devoted to the business compared to other pursuits. A common problem arises when a business owner begins to feel a diminution in energy regarding operation of the business. As energy diminishes, so can profitability and, in turn, the opportunity to reap the best possible price on a sale of the business. The sad end result can be that the business falls far short of being able to provide for the needs of the owner at the time of retirement because the ability to sell it has been so negatively affected.

Prudent planning dictates that when business owners or professionals recognize the peak potential, they should immediately begin a phaseout plan. This generally would involve selling the business to a younger successor, turning over the reins to a family member, or putting the enterprise on the market.

Existing Investment Portfolio

This includes all money you now have invested. Some of it currently may not be offering any return—you are hoping for a gain in value to realize

your ultimate rewards. As retirement approaches, you may deem it wiser to convert such nonearning assets into earning ones, so you can specifically gauge how much will be available to you in the future.

Potential Inheritances

Realistically, try to estimate inheritances from family members in the fore-seeable future. Will the funds be in cash, securities, property, or some other form? Will they be earning assets or nonearning assets, and what would be involved in converting them into situations best suited to your personal needs? For example, you might inherit a parcel of income-producing real estate. Although this could generate an attractive measure of income, you might not want to continue ownership of the building. It might be a great distance away from where you live or you may simply not have the desire or expertise to deal with income-producing real estate. What are the prospects of selling the building? What taxes would have to be paid on such a sale? How much income could the net proceeds generate? These considerations apply to any inherited assets.

Nest-Egg Dipping: How Much and for How Long?

Most of us face this ultimate dilemma in the later years: to have enough money available to live within a desired framework for an *indeterminate* time, always having enough money to take care of virtually any contingency. Life expectancy and health factors are unknowns, but the amount of money available should be known. If, after work has ceased, you can live comfortably on income alone, your later years should be relatively worry-free. The dilemma is compounded in those many situations where principal has to be invaded, minimally or substantially, to provide for necessities and contingencies.

In many cases, it's necessary for a lifestyle to be trimmed in order to conserve enough principal to guarantee future comforts and necessities. Temptations to dip into principal should be examined carefully. When your principal is reduced, so is your earning power.

Let's say that you have a nest egg soundly invested, and you want to dip into it to increase your monthly spending money. How much, and for how long, can you dip into the next egg before you deplete it? As Table 18–5 shows, starting with a lump-sum nest egg of $30,000, you could withdraw $269 per month for fifteen years. At the end of fifteen years, you would have depleted the nest egg. Or you could withdraw $179 per month indefi-nitely and always have the original nest egg intact. (In this latter case, you are withdrawing only the interest earned by your investment.) Table 18–5 is based on an interest rate of 7 percent per year, compounded quarterly, be-fore income tax considerations.

TABLE 18–5   **Dipping into Your Nest Egg**

Starting with a lump sum of . . .	you can withdraw this much each month, for the stated number of years, reducing the lump sum to zero . . .				or you can withdraw this much each month and always have the original nest egg intact
	10 Years	15 Years	20 Years	25 Years	
$ 10,000	$ 116	$ 89	$ 77	$ 70	$ 59
15,000	174	134	116	106	88
20,000	232	179	155	141	118
25,000	290	224	193	176	142
30,000	348	269	232	212	179
40,000	464	359	310	282	237
50,000	580	448	386	352	285
60,000	696	538	464	424	360
80,000	928	718	620	564	467
$100,000	1,160	896	772	704	585

TAX AND PENSION LAWS: HOW THEY AFFECT THE RIGHTS OF WORKERS AND RETIREES

The Effect on Retirement Age

Exercise 18.4

The Tax Reform Act of 1986, in conjunction with Social Security regulations, affects the time at which retirees will be entitled to full benefits from their pension plans. The law states that employees must be at least 65 years of age before they can receive 100 percent of their pension benefits. If they want to retire earlier, the formula for the payout must be the same as that used by the Social Security Administration. For example: Social Security regulations say that workers are entitled to 80 percent of full benefits if they retire at age 62. Thus, if employees wanted to retire at age 62, they would be entitled to only 80 percent of what otherwise would be forthcoming from the employer's pension plan at age 65. So, as with Social Security, early retirees get a lesser pension amount, though they start getting it at an earlier time.

The law also sets forth a gradual increase in the minimum retirement age, again in line with the Social Security formula. For individuals born Dec. 31, 1937, or earlier, the retirement age at which you are entitled to full benefits is 65. If you were born Jan. 1, 1938 or after, and before January 1, 1945, the retirement age is 66. And if you were born after December 31, 1944, the retirement age is 67. Check current Social Security regulations to determine how this will affect you.

The Pension Reform Law (ERISA)

In September 1974, Congress passed the Employee Retirement Income Security Act of 1974, more commonly known as the Pension Reform Law, or ERISA. The purpose of the law was to correct abuses that occurred in the administration of pension funds that resulted in pensioners being deprived of money that was due them.

The administration of the law is under the jurisdiction of two governmental agencies: the Internal Revenue Service and the U.S. Department of Labor. The following discussion is intended to acquaint you with the overall concepts. Persons accumulating pension benefits subject to ERISA should determine from their employer exactly what their benefits will be and what their rights are under the law.

The law is aimed at those pension funds that are "qualified" under the Internal Revenue Service regulations. Qualified pension funds, generally, are those that allow the employer tax deductions for the cost of contributions, and that permit the employees receiving the benefits not to have to report those contributions as income until the money in the fund is later withdrawn. About 60 million Americans are covered by this law.

Exercise 18.5

The Law does *not* require any company to start a pension plan. But if a company does begin one, it must meet the requirements of the law. Furthermore, the law does *not* stipulate how much money an employer should pay in pension benefits for employees, nor how much, if any, an employee should contribute. But the law does establish that once promises are made regarding pension contributions, those promises must be kept.

If your employer does not have a pension or profit-sharing plan, you should still be aware of the benefits available under the law. You may change jobs and go to a company that does have a pension plan, or people close to you may be affected by the law, and your awareness of its benefits can be helpful to them.

The Pension Reform Law attempts to correct abuses in these main areas: vesting, funding, folding, reporting, and managing.

Vesting

Vesting refers to that time when your benefits are *locked up* or guaranteed as a result of the time you've spent on the job. The law is designed to eliminate the problem of when you are entitled to how much money. To understand what this means, let's follow the basic steps involved in obtaining pension benefits from a company.

First, you must become *eligible* to participate in the plan. The law states that any employee who is at least 25 years old with at least one year on the payroll must be taken into the pension plan if the company has one.

Once you become eligible, the company *credits* a certain sum to your pension or profit-sharing account each year until you either leave the company or retire.

The next step in receiving the benefits is *vesting,* or locking up whatever benefits have been set aside in your name.

The law gives an employer two choices with regard to vesting programs for employees who are covered by the employer's pension plan.

GRADUAL VESTING   The first choice is a gradual schedule, which requires that workers who are eligible for the plan be 20 percent vested after three years, then an additional 20 percent vested per year after the third year, which would get them 100 percent vested after seven years. Table 18–6 illustrates this plan, assuming that the employer is contributing $500 per year to the eligible employees' pension fund.

Example: The employee must be 20 percent vested after three years of eligibility in the plan. At the end of three years, the employer has put $1,500 into this employee's plan. Being 20 percent vested means that 20 percent of the $1,500 that has been contributed to the plan, or $300, is now *vested* for that employee. In other words, at some future time, the employee will be entitled to receive at least that $300 unconditionally. If that employee quits after three years of service, nothing further will be contributed to his or her plan. If the employee remains on the job, vesting will grow year by year in accordance with the table.

ALL-AT-ONCE VESTING   The second vesting choice is an *all-at-once* vesting. After five years of eligible service, an employee is 100 percent vested in whatever money has been contributed to the plan. If that employee quits the job after 4 years 11 months and 29 days, he or she will not become vested at all.

Employers may choose more rapid vesting schedules if they wish. Union pension plans can have ten-year vesting schedules.

These vesting choices do not mean that you're entitled to a full pension once you've achieved full vesting. You may have to wait until you actually retire before any of the funds are available. In certain cases, an employer may be willing to pay the vested funds to an employee in the event of an

TABLE 18–6   Gradual Vesting

Year	Total Amount Contributed	Percent Vested	Dollars Vested
1	$ 500	—	—
2	1,000	—	—
3	1,500	20	$ 300
4	2,000	40	800
5	2,500	60	1,500
6	3,000	80	2,400
7	3,500	100	3,500

earlier termination. This must be determined directly with each employer in any specific individual case.

Note also that these vesting requirements refer to the *employer's* contribution to the pension fund. If you are making your own contribution, either directly or through payroll deduction, you are fully and immediately vested regarding those contributions.

An employer's plan must state which vesting alternative is being used. The employer must keep records of every employee's service and vesting. Each employee is entitled to *a yearly statement* from an employer concerning vesting and accrued benefit status.

Funding

Funding refers to putting enough money into the pension fund to meet the future promises to pay the benefits.

Say that XYZ Company has ten employees in its pension plan. By reasonable estimates, the ten employees will receive pension benefits of $50,000 each over their lifetimes after retirement. Let's assume that all ten employees retire on the same day and that they all request a lump-sum distribution of their benefits. On this mass retirement day, therefore, the XYZ pension fund should theoretically have at least $500,000 in it.

But what if the XYZ pension fund has only $200,000 in it? Why might this be so? Perhaps through some bookkeeping shenanigans or perhaps due to a simple shortfall in the amount it was contributing, the company has missed the mark considerably. What, then, happens to the ten employees? They split up the $200,000 into lumps of $20,000 each and sit there in amazement wondering what happened to them.

The Pension Reform Law attempts to correct this possible abuse. It imposes very stringent requirements on managers of all pension funds to put away the amount that they, according to reasonable expectations, will need to meet the targeted promises.

Despite the rigid requirements of the Pension Reform Law, a company may still violate the law and not properly fund enough money to meet its obligations. You may not discover this until the time for your retirement, at which point, of course, it's too late.

Folding

A company for whom you've worked could fold after you've started receiving your pension benefits, thus putting those benefits in jeopardy.

Exercise 18.6

The Pension Reform Law has created an insurance program that will guarantee retirees at least a *portion* of their benefits if their company folds. The law established the Pension Benefit Guarantee Corporation (PBGC) to administer this program.

This insurance program is intended to provide for benefits that are *vested*. The benefits you're entitled to under PBGC are related to your

earnings with the company and your age. If your plan was terminated in 1997, the maximum monthly amount you could get from PBGC would have been $2,761 if you were age 65; $2,181 if you were 62; $1,795 if you were 60, and $1,243 if you were 55. Note again: these are the maximum amounts you can get per month, based on what your benefits with the terminated plan would have been. The amounts are adjusted for inflation every year.

In effect, the PBGC is like a safety net under the overall pension programs throughout the United States. But don't rely on it to the exclusion of any other safety nets you might provide on your own through individual initiative and planning.

Reporting

The law has created these benefits and protections, but how is the average individual supposed to learn about them and keep up to date with them?

The law has seen to that, too. Every eligible participant in a plan must be given a description of the plan, plus a periodic summary of the plan "written in a manner calculated to be understood by the average plan participant." This summary must explain in detail the participant's rights and obligations under the plan. In addition, the company must maintain open access to the latest annual report on the plan, and related documents must be available for examination by participating employees.

The written explanation shouldn't be treated lightly. You should study the booklet when you get it and ask questions if you don't understand. Sound financial planning requires that you know the exact status of your pension rights at all times.

Managing

The law sets stringent guidelines for the management of pension funds. It sets forth fiduciary duties, the punishment for their breach, prohibited transactions, and steps to avoid conflicts of interest between the respective parties. In short, the investment philosophy of pension funds should be conservative enough to comply with this requirement of the law.

Employees have a stake in how their pension money is invested, although they may not have a very strong voice in those decisions. If you think that your company's pension plan is taking too many risks in its investment philosophy, you and your co-workers can voice your opinion to management accordingly. If you belong to a union, your union might be able to do this for you. A pension plan investment manager who makes serious errors may be punished under the law. But that will not satisfy you if, as a recipient of that pension plan, you're getting less than you had been entitled to. The time to voice your concerns is before the mistakes are made, not afterward.

DO-IT-YOURSELF PENSIONS: IRAS, KEOGHS, 401(k)

There is no one—no company, no government, no union—who can take as good care of your future as you can. The sooner you begin taking care of your own financial future, the better off you'll be. Pension and profit-sharing plans may hold the promise of future security. But you might leave the company; the company might fold; the plan might suffer losses as a result of unwise investment strategies. As for Social Security, it is unwise for people born in the 1960s or later to rely on Social Security as more than a token portion of their overall retirement income.

Do-it-yourself retirement planning is enhanced by a variety of plans that offer attractive advantages to those who participate. These plans are the Individual Retirement Account (IRA) and the 401(k) plans for employed individuals, and the Keogh plan for self-employed individuals.

Individual Retirement Accounts (IRAs)

Along with the 401(k) the IRA is the most common do-it-yourself plan. In order to be eligible for a standard IRA, you must have income from work. Income from investments or pensions does not qualify. If you have less than

---

STRATEGIES FOR SUCCESS

Will You Outlive Your Money? You Had Better Hope Not!

Studies and surveys galore address one extremely vital subject: Are Americans saving enough to provide themselves with a decent retirement? The consensus answer is a resounding NO!

A recent book by Peter Peterson, *Will America Grow Up Before It Grows Old?*, hits the nail on the head with its frightening scenario of what lies ahead if we don't take better care of our financial future. The author reviews all the surveys and reaches this chilling conclusion: Only thirty percent of all U.S. families are saving specifically for their retirement, with the other 70 percent choosing instead to rely on Social Security, pensions, and good luck. Of those who do save, the median amount stashed away is only $1,000. (That is not a misprint.) Further, one-half of all adults aged 55 and over have nest eggs of less than $10,000. Again, that is not a misprint. Too little. Too late.

If you are in your twenties or thirties as you read this—just at the starting point of establishing your financial independence—the message is loud and clear: DON'T WAIT ANY LONGER to build a nest egg over and above what you might get from Social Security, your pension and your good luck. Even if you have to forgo some of the bells and whistles today, you must begin to position yourself for security and comfort tomorrow.

$2,000 income from work in a given year, the amount you can put into an IRA investment is equal to the amount of income you had from work. In other words, if you earned $1,500 from work in a given year, you would be eligible to invest as much as $1,500 that year in an IRA. If your income from work is more than $2,000 in a given year, then the most you can put into an IRA for that year is $2,000. If each spouse in a family has more than $2,000 income for work in a given year, then the couple can invest up to $4,000 each year in their IRAs. You can put in less than these amounts if you wish. Or you can put in nothing in a given year if you wish. There's no minimum requirement, only a maximum limitation.

Effective for tax years 1998 and onward, if you have a nonworking spouse who does not participate in an IRS-qualified pension plan and the couple's adjusted gross income is not more than $160,000 for the year, that nonworking spouse can put up to $2,000 into an IRA, even if the working spouse does participate in a plan.

Something Old, Something New

The Taxpayer Relief Act of 1997 created new forms of IRAs, which will be discussed after the features of the standard IRA concept have been described. The 1997 law, described by *The Wall Street Journal* as "mind-numbing complexity," will require more study and planning than had previously been the case. But if fully taken advantage of, these new elements of the IRA law can be most beneficial.

Tax Deferral of the Standard IRA

There are two major income tax advantages to the standard IRA. The first advantage is that the earnings in your plan are tax-deferred. You don't pay income taxes on your IRA earnings until you cash in your plan. That means that every dollar your IRA earns goes back to work for you. None of it goes to pay taxes. This tax-deferred feature applies to *all* IRA accounts.

Tax Deductibility of the Standard IRA

The second major advantage to the standard IRA plan is limited to certain individuals. The advantage is that the amount you invest in an IRA each year is tax-deductible to you. Say, for example, you are a married taxpayer filing a joint return, and your income is $30,000. That would put you in the 28 percent tax bracket. If you invest $2,000 in an IRA, that reduces the amount of your income that is subject to income taxes by $2,000. In other words you'll be taxed on $28,000 instead of $30,000. In the 28 percent bracket, that means an immediate cash-in-hand tax saving to you of $560 for that year. The attractiveness of this advantage is clear enough.

If you are *not* covered by a retirement or profit-sharing plan at work, you can claim the deduction for your IRA investment each year. But if you are

covered by such a plan at work, your right to claim the annual deduction is determined by how much you and your spouse earn.

Table 18–7 illustrates how this works. For tax year 1998, for example, a couple filing a joint return has an adjusted gross income (AGI) of between $50,000 and $60,000. (See chapter 20 for a definition of adjusted gross income.) If the AGI is $50,000 or less, the couple can claim a tax deduction equal to 100 percent of their standard IRA investment. So, if they had invested a total of $1,500 in their standard IRA, their tax deduction would be $1,500. For every $1,000 in AGI over $50,000, the size of the deduction is reduced by 10 percent. So, if they had an AGI of $51,000, the deductible amount on a $1,500 IRA investment would be 90 percent of $1,500, or $1,350. If they had an AGI of $55,000, the deductible amount on a $1,500 IRA investment would be 50 percent of $1,500, or $750. And so on, until they had an AGI of $60,000, when there would be no deduction.

As you can see in Table 18–7, the phase-out level of the deduction is scheduled to increase every year until 2007.

Penalty for Early Withdrawal from Standard IRAs

In general, if you withdraw money from a standard IRA before you reach the age of 59½, you must pay a penalty to the IRS of 10 percent of the amount withdrawn. You must also pay income taxes on the amount withdrawn for the year in which you made the withdrawal. (You might also have to pay a penalty to the bank or mutual fund where your money was invested if it has penalty provisions for early withdrawals in the contract.) The law also requires you to begin withdrawing from your IRA no later than age 70½.

TABLE 18–7   **Standard IRA Deducation Limits**

Tax Year	Joint Return AGI	Single Return AGI
1998	$50,000–$60,000	$30,000–40,000
1999	51,000–61,000	31,000–41,000
2000	52,000–62,000	32,000–42,000
2001	53,000–63,000	33,000–43,000
2002	54,000–64,000	34,000–44,000
2003	60,000–70,000	40,000–50,000
2004	65,000–75,000	45,000–55,000
2005	70,000–80,000	50,000–60,000
2006	75,000–85,000	50,000–60,000
2007 and beyond	80,000–100,000*	50,000–60,000

*For every $2,000 increment between $80,000 and $100,000, the amount of the deduction is reduced by 10 percent.

Avoiding the Penalties on Early Withdrawals from Standard IRAs

If you take out standard IRA money before you reach 59½, you can avoid the penalty by arranging for your bank or mutual fund to pay out the money to you in equal, periodic installments over your lifetime. (Some standard IRA withdrawals may also be penalty-free if they are made after death or disability of the IRA owner has occurred, or for certain deductible medical expenses.)

The 1997 Taxpayer Relief Act has added a number of important new provisions to allow penalty-free withdrawals from standard IRAS:

There is no penalty to the IRS if withdrawals are used for the benefit of children, grandchildren, spouse, or yourself for the purpose of higher education expenses or first-time homebuyer expenses. The penalty-free withdrawal is unlimited for educational expenses, but there is a lifetime limit of $10,000 for homebuyer expenses. Note that your bank or mutual fund may have penalties of their own for early withdrawals. Those are not affected by the federal law. And note also that on any withdrawals from standard IRAs for whatever purpose, income taxes must be paid on the withdrawn amount for the year in which the withdrawal is made.

The New IRAs

Effective starting tax year 1998, there are new IRAs that are distinctly different from the standard IRA that has just been discussed.

First, and most intriguing, is the Roth IRA, named after the senator who first introduced the concept. It's also been referred to as the "Plus IRA," and the "American Dream IRA." Which name will stick only time will tell. For now we'll stick with the Roth designation. It's essentially the opposite of the standard IRA. Here's how it works: The maximum you can invest each year is $2,000 per person. (If your adjusted gross income is between $150,000 and $160,000 for couples, or between $95,000 and $110,000 for singles, the amount you can invest each year is phased out in a fashion similar to that of the standard IRA, as earlier described and illustrated in Table 18–7.)

Unlike the standard IRA, the Roth IRAs are *not* tax deductible. You get no tax deduction at all for the amount you invest. However, *all* of your earnings are tax-free. The earnings while the plans are in effect are tax-free, *and* when you withdraw the money it is tax-free—Tax-free, not tax-deferred. Tax-free means no taxes ever. Tax-deferred, as is the case with the standard IRA, means that income taxes will come due at some future time, such as when you withdraw the money from the plan. Furthermore, there is no 10 percent penalty to the IRS for a withdrawal before age 59½. (Again note that your bank or mutual fund may impose an early withdrawal penalty that is not affected by this new federal law.)

So, what's the catch? In order to enjoy these tax-free earnings and penalty-free withdrawal ability, you must not make a withdrawal until five years have passed since you first invested in the plan, *and* the withdrawal

must be used to buy a first home for yourself or a family member (child, grandchild), *or* you are in a long-term unemployment situation, *or* upon your disability or death, *or* you are over the age of 59½. In summary, you have to let the money ride in the plan for at least five years, and then to get the full tax-free benefits you must meet any one of the four requirements. If you don't meet the requirements at the time you withdraw, *and* you are under age 59½, the 10 percent penalty kicks in and income taxes are due on the withdrawn amount.

Exercise 18.7

The Roth IRA should be very attractive if you can afford to put the money away for the minimum five years before you can get it back later completely tax-free. What about having a standard IRA versus a Roth IRA? If you can afford it, you can have both. And the more money you can shelter from taxes —either deferred or exempt—the better off you'll be down the road, *provided* you invest the money prudently. A fully taxable prudent investment can end up better than a wildly speculative tax-free investment that falls apart on you. Remember the old reward/risk ratio: The bigger game you're going after, the higher the risk you're taking. Choosing between the two is a very iffy proposition, since you don't know what tax rates will be in the future. The standard IRA gives you tax breaks now; many folks would rather have them in hand than wait a decade or two or three for the breaks. In any case, the wisdom of Solomon may guide you best: divide whatever IRA money you can invest in half and have a go at both.

Bear in mind the description of the 1997 Taxpayer Relief Act of 1997 by *The Wall Street Journal: Mind-numbing complexity*. Many facets of this new law might undergo modifications and interpretations until well into the twenty-first century. As with all other major financial steps that you take with tax ramifications (and they all do) you should check the most current regulations to make certain you're getting the benefits you expect.

Converting Standard IRAs to Roth IRAs

Here's a bit of that mind-numbing complexity we referred to. If you have money in a standard IRA, you can convert it to a Roth IRA if your adjusted gross income is under $100,000. You have to pay income taxes on the amount you withdraw from the standard IRA, but that tax can be spread over four years if you do the conversion before January 1, 1999. The 10 percent IRS penalty does not apply to a withdrawal that's made for conversion purposes.

Does it pay to convert? Not even an accountant can tell you for sure. You're converting money that will some day be taxable (the standard IRA) into money that will come back to you completely tax-free (the Roth IRA). The key to a decision: Will the taxes you have to pay on the withdrawal now be higher or lower than the taxes you'd have to pay when you cashed in your standard IRA? If you think your tax rate will be higher at withdrawal time, the Roth IRA may be your best bet. If you think you're better off taking the tax breaks now and having to pay the taxes on withdrawal at

a relatively low rate, then the standard IRA might be better. Or going half-and-half might give you the best results.

The Education IRA

This is a spin-off of the new Roth IRA in that your investments are not tax-deductible, but the money earns tax free and can be withdrawn tax free. Here are the conditions:

The account must be for the benefit of someone under the age of 18, and the maximum that can be put into the account each year is $500. (If your "modified" adjusted gross income exceeds $160,000 for couples, or $110,000 for singles, the Education IRA is not available.)

The account must have a bank as custodian or trustee, which basically means that you must set up the account through a bank. If need be, you can change the beneficiary to another family member with no income-tax consequences.

In order for the withdrawals to be tax-exempt, the proceeds must be used to pay post-secondary (after high school) education expenses of the designated child. These expenses can include room, board, and tuition. If in any given year the withdrawals exceed the education expenses, then income taxes and the 10 percent IRS penalty must be paid on that excess. Any family member (parent, grandparent, aunt, uncle) who qualifies under the income limits can set up an Education IRA for a child. Education IRAs are separate and apart from your own personal standard IRAs or Roth IRAs.

401(k) Plans

Only employees of companies that offer the plans can participate in 401(k) plans. In a 401(k) plan, a certain portion of your wages will be placed in an investment program offered by the employer. Those wages will not be taxable to you until you later withdraw the funds. The earnings will also be tax-deferred. You generally have a choice of investment programs. Common choices include a guaranteed income plan, similar to a savings program; a mutual fund type of plan that invests in a variety of stocks; and a plan that invests in the stock of your company. It's generally possible to mix and match among the different plans, and you can usually change your mix at certain intervals. It's also common for your company to chip in a certain amount of its money for your benefit. For example, for every dollar you put in of your own, the company might put in another 25 cents or 50 cents. The amount you can put into a 401(k) plan was about $8,000 per year in the late 1990s, with increases allowed each year for inflation. Your employer can contribute over and above that amount to your account, subject to the limits of the law.

The withdrawal restrictions for a 401(k) plan are similar to, but slightly more liberal than, those for IRA plans. It might also be possible to get your

funds out at an early age in the event of death, disability, or financial hardship. Withdrawals from 401(k) plans are controlled both by the employers' plan and by tax regulations.

A 401(k) plan can be advantageous, particularly if the employer is contributing money on your behalf over and above what you are putting in. Similar plans are available to employees of schools, tax-exempt organizations, and governments.

SEP Plans

A relatively uncommon form of do-it-yourself retirement program is the Simplified Employee Pension (SEP). This concept was designed for small companies that did not want the trouble of all the paperwork involved in a major pension or profit-sharing plan. A SEP operates similarly to a standard IRA. The employer can make contributions to the IRAs that the workers maintain on their own. And the workers can also make their own contributions. If your employer does not have a pension plan, she might be intrigued with the idea of setting up a SEP. It can work to the benefit of both employer and employees.

Keogh Plans

Keogh plans are available to self-employed individuals. The maximum amount of an annual Keogh investment is $30,000, or 25 percent of income from work, whichever is less. The 25 percent is calculated on the amount left after the Keogh investment has been made. Example: a self-employed person earns $60,000 in a year. Her maximum Keogh investment will be $12,000. Why? Her 25 percent limit is based on $48,000 (the $60,000 income less the $12,000 Keogh investment): 25 percent of $48,000 is $12,000. Another self-employed individual earns $200,000 in a year. The maximum Keogh investment allowable is $30,000 for that year. Keogh investments are tax-deductible to the participant. If self-employed individuals have employees, they must make contributions on behalf of certain of those employees. Earnings on Keogh plans are tax-deferred. Withdrawals from Keogh plans are similar to those of IRAs: There's a penalty for withdrawals made before age $59\frac{1}{2}$, and a withdrawal program must begin by age $70\frac{1}{2}$. Keogh plans do have further complexities involving the types of plans that can be set up and how much can be contributed to each one. It's advisable for individuals contemplating a Keogh plan to get professional assistance from their own tax adviser or from the institution in which they're opening the plan.

Setting Up Your Plans

IRAS, Keoghs, and SEPs can be set up relatively simply at banks, savings institutions, stock brokerage firms, mutual fund companies, and insurance

companies. The Keogh plan will require more paperwork than the IRA. An IRA or Keogh participant should shop around to determine what types of plans are available. Stock brokerage firms offer IRA and Keogh plans that can be self-directed by the participants. That is, you can instruct the broker how your money is to be put to work. But be aware that if undue risk is taken, it can have a hazardous effect on your retirement nest egg.

Relocating Your Plans

You do not have to keep your IRA or Keogh investments with the same institution forever. The law allows you to move these accounts from one place to another periodically without penalty.

If you do wish to relocate your IRA or Keogh investment, be aware that it can take the bank or brokerage firm weeks to complete the paperwork. Thus, plan in advance to give notice to them so that the paperwork will be ready in time. Also, if you do relocate your funds, keep copies of every document connected with the transfer. If the Internal Revenue Service ever asks what happened to your IRA money, you can prove that you simply transferred it to a different institution rather than withdrawing it to spend it, in which case the IRS would expect you to pay taxes on it, and possible penalties.

How to Invest Your IRA, 401(k) and Keogh Money

There are no hard and fast rules. There is abundant counsel given in this book to assist you. Let's recap the most important points.

1. As noted earlier in this chapter, all the tax breaks in the world are for naught if the investments themselves aren't prudent. A fully taxable but wise investment can work better for you than a speculative venture that is tax-sheltered. The bigger reward you're going for, the bigger risk you're taking. If you risk the money, you chance losing it.

2. Retirement money is money you can't afford to take undue risk with. You don't want to discover at retirement time that you don't have enough to retire on in comfort. You can't go back twenty or thirty years—you don't get a do-over.

3. It's never too early to start stashing money away for your later years. They will be here sooner than you think.

4. If you wander off blindly into "mutual fund land" you're liable to get lost, and so is your money. There are thousands of mutual funds from which to choose, and they range from extremely speculative to very conservative. If the stock market has been hot—as was the case for most of the 1990s—that doesn't mean the same trends will continue. The law of gravity has a way of asserting itself every so often. People who generally say they're going to put their retirement

money into "mutual funds" are speaking too broadly. You must narrow your search. You must find funds whose objectives and investment philosophy match your own. And if you don't yet have any objectives or investment philosophy, you'd better get some real soon.

5. The Age + 40 Rule noted earlier can be of some help. To quickly review it: For that portion of your retirement money that MUST be there, come what may, when you need it, it should be invested in safe securities, such as well-rated bonds and insured savings plans, in a proportion equal to your age plus 40. In other words, if you are 30 years old, 70 percent of your must-be-there retirement funds should be invested safely. The other 30 percent can be put to some speculation. This is admittedly a very conservative course to take. Vary from it as you will, and at your own risk.

PENSIONS AND TAXES

When you receive your pension, all, or a portion of it, could be subject to income taxes. The portion your employer contributed on your behalf is likely to be taxable. Some money that you contributed may have already been taxed in the year in which you earned it and thus won't be taxable when you receive it in your pension check. It would be nice to think that tax matters became easier upon retirement, but taxation of pensions is regrettably complex and must be planned for accordingly.

Lump-sum Payout versus Monthly Payments

You may have the choice of receiving pension or profit-sharing benefits in either a lump sum or a long-term program of monthly payments.

If you are given such a choice, some very careful arithmetic is required—perhaps with the help of an accountant—to determine what is best. How you handle such a decision can mean the difference of many thousands of dollars in your pocket or the tax collector's.

The lum-sum payout means exactly that: you get all you're entitled to in one check. The monthly payout plans can take a variety of forms: You might choose one fixed amount per month for as long as you live, with payments ceasing at your death; or you might choose a plan that provides you with a smaller amount per month but with continuing benefits payable to your survivors after your death.

The first choice that has to be made is between the lump-sum payout and the monthly plan. Each choice will differ, but here is the type of arithmetic you can do to help determine the best choice. Let's assume that you are given a choice between a $50,000 lump-sum payout (after taxes) or $400 per month until your death, after which payments cease. If you choose the lump-sum payment, and if you invested the $50,000 at an 8 percent annual

rate of return, you would receive an income of $333 per month (before income taxes.) And you would always have the $50,000 nest egg available to you. On the other hand, if you choose the $400 per month (again, before income taxes), you will indeed be receiving a slightly higher monthly income, but there is nothing at all left after your death; and while you're still alive, there is no nest egg into which you can dip, should the need arise. Based on this example, which is reasonably typical of the choices people have, you might find that if you are ready, willing, and able to handle your own investment of this money, you could do better over the long run by taking the lump-sum instead of the monthly payout. Get professional assistance before you make your choice.

Minimizing the Tax Bite

If you do choose the lump sum payout, there are two devices that can minimize or delay the income taxes payable on that lump sum, the IRA rollover and forward averaging.

The IRA Rollover

With the IRA rollover, if you receive a lump-sum payout from a pension or profit-sharing plan, you can, within sixty days of receipt of the money, reinvest that money in an account designated as your IRA rollover account. By so doing, you postpone the payment of income taxes on the lump sum until such future time as you withdraw the money to spend for your own purposes. By putting the money into an IRA rollover account, the investment will earn interest on a tax-deferred basis until such a time as you withdraw it. The IRA rollover account is generally preferable for those people who do *not* need the funds for current spending purposes.

Forward Averaging

This device is generally preferable for people who *do* need the money to spend currently. By using the forward averaging formula, you pay your income taxes on the lump sum you received in the year in which you receive it but at a much lower rate than normal income taxes. Forward averaging reduces your tax by calculating the tax as if you had received the lump-sum payout over a five-year span. You must meet current IRS eligibility formulas in order to claim the forward averaging device.

ONE FINAL CAUTION

The laws referred to in this chapter can be of great assistance to people who are covered by pension and profit-sharing plans at work. But roughly half

the U.S. work force is not covered by any kind of pension or profit-sharing plan. These workers must depend on their own discipline to put away money for the future. They are on their own, and as noted earlier, if they are in the younger generations, they should not expect much from Social Security. They should take advantage of the IRA and 401(k) concepts as much as possible, as well as any other new do-it-yourself programs that may be created by Congress. For those who are not covered by an employer or union pension plan, it's worth repeating the admonition stated earlier in this chapter. *No one can take better care of you than you can yourself. And if you don't take care of yourself, no one else will do it for you.*

PERSONAL ACTION WORKSHEET

Estimating Retirement Costs

Even though retirement may be a long way off for you, this exercise can help you envision changes in your financial situation once your working career has ceased. Assume you'll be retiring within the next few years. Estimate the changes in your income and expenses once that occurs. This will help you shape a workable budget for your retirement—something that most people don't do until it's too late.

	Now	Then
❏ After-tax income from work	_____	_____
❏ After-tax income from investments	_____	_____
❏ Social Security income	_____	_____
❏ Pension, profit-sharing, IRA, 401(k) or Keogh income (assume lump sum is invested at 7 percent annual income, and you're taking out only the income)	_____	_____
❏ Lump sum from any of the above, on hand for whenever you need it	_____	_____
❏ Housing expenses, assuming you stay where you are	_____	_____
❏ Housing expenses, assuming you move to smaller quarters	_____	_____
❏ Extra income resulting from net gain on sale of home, after setting aside any down payment needed for purchase of new home	_____	_____
❏ Transportation expenses (consider particularly that the "going-to-work" car may no longer be needed or will be used much less)	_____	_____
❏ Clothing expenses	_____	_____
❏ Food, both at home and out, considering work lunches	_____	_____
❏ Entertainment	_____	_____
❏ Insurance premiums (life, health, disability; retirement and Medicare often change one's insurance program considerably)	_____	_____

CONSUMER ALERT

Excerpts from a Survey of Recent Retirees

"When I was 30, my employer told me that my pension plan would provide $511 per month at age 65. That, plus my Social Security, seemed enough to meet all my needs and allow my wife and me to have a leisurely and comfortable life at retirement. I left it at that and didn't make any other plans. We spent what we earned and lived well.

"Then came the blow. I was made to retire at age 62, at a $405 per month pension benefit. And times have changed! Not only am I getting more than $100 less than I expected, but the money I am getting doesn't go very far at all. If I had my life to live over again, I'd have anticipated this possibility and would have salted away some of my earnings in an investment program."

• • •

"I retired from my dental practice ten years ago, at age 62. We had no children and, quite honestly, I never became involved in any hobbies or activities. Now I'm paying the price. . . . The worst part of retirement is too much time on your hands. Retirees should have hobbies or sports interests consistent with their health. The worst habit is getting bored and turning to the bottle."

• • •

"Think young and resolve to be independent as long as you're able. Neither your children nor any organization owes you anything. If you think you've reached the age where now someone will take care of you, you're sadly mistaken. If you haven't long ago accepted the fact that only you are responsible for your future, then you're in for a rude awakening."

• • •

"Don't expect to be missed for long by former business associates, and don't visit them unless invited. You should be realistic and accept the loss of clout gracefully."

• • •

"The best advice is for a couple to get as mentally close together as when they were first married, and to remember that they cannot enjoy leisure without doing some work, nor can they enjoy pleasure without having some pain."

UPS & DOWNS *The Economics of Everyday Life*

Why Living Costs Go Up and Down During Retirement

For most folks, retirement means living on a fixed income from pensions, Social Security, and investments. If costs go up, expenses have to go down accordingly; or work has to be resumed (which is often not possible); or principal must be tapped (which is often not desirable).

Basic inflationary trends Inflation will still have its impact, but less so for retirees than for those raising families. Retirees will have less money to spend, but there will be fewer things that they will have to be buying.

Automobiles During the working years, a couple might have needed two cars, and those cars might have been fancier and traded in more often in order to maintain a certain image. On retirement, one car will often be adequate, and it can be a more basic model and kept for more years. The annual difference in auto insurance for just one car instead of two can mean a big savings, not to mention the end of commuting.

Clothing The working wardrobe (and the dry-cleaning and laundering thereof) may have imposed quite a cost burden. (Again, the cost of maintaining an image enters the picture.) The retiree can get by with lower cost and less formal clothing, which doesn't have to be replaced with every change in fashion trends.

Taxes Those 65 and older get some breaks on their income taxes. At the same time, what they paid in for Social Security over the years provides them with continuing increases in monthly allotments as the cost of living goes up.

Senior citizen discounts These are available in movie theaters, airline fares, restaurant specials, hotels and motels, insurance plans, barber and beauty salons—the list goes on and on. Many stores offer senior discounts on certain days of the week. And senior organizations such as AARP offer a wide variety of cost-saving plans.

Activities These are the years to enjoy all that's been put off during the working years: the books that have remained unread, the hobbies that weren't given a fair chance, the videos that were put on the shelf to be viewed "later." "Later" is now, and there's much to enjoy that doesn't involve spending money. Attitudes change: A social life that used to be tumultuous (and costly) may now become *serene* (and inexpensive).

Housing As noted in the text, there are many alternatives that can reduce the cost of housing—from refinancing a mortgage to moving into smaller quarters. In addition, the lower-cost quarters bring with them lower-cost operating expenses (utilities, maintenance, etc.).

For some, reducing expenses may be a necessity; for others, it may be by choice. Either way, it can be painless and, in the long run, satisfying.

? **WHAT IF . . . ?** _____

Test yourself: How would you deal with these real-life possibilities?

1. Your parents (or your spouse's parents) are thinking about moving to a retirement community. Would you be interested in buying their home? How important is it to you that they be close by (say, within an hour's drive)? Are they being realistic about the price they think they can get for their house? Will they have enough to live comfortably in their new home? Is there a chance that they might become financially dependent on you, and if so, are you prepared to help them? If you have siblings, will they be happy with the proposed changes, or will there likely be a lot of family static over the issue? Evaluate all of these matters as they would apply to your own personal situation.

2. An unexpected disability forces you to take a long leave of absence from work. It could be as long as twelve months. As the days go by, you begin to get glimmers of what it might be like to be retired. How do you think such an event might influence you to prepare for your eventual real retirement?

3. You have a choice between a job that offers no pension plan and one that does. The job without a pension will give you 10 percent more take-home pay than the other job, which would stash away that 10 percent toward the pension. Which would you prefer? Why? Would you feel differently if you were ten yers older? Why?

NUMBER CRUNCHERS

Do the calculations to make decisions in these real-life possibilities.

1. Using the examples of the Johnsons in this chapter, and other tables throughout the book, calculate the following: A retiring couple plans to stay in their home for the duration. There's a $70,000 balance left on their mortgage. Monthly payments are $1,660, and the interest rate is 11 percent. If they continue making their current payments, the mortgage will be all paid off in about six years. They can refinance today at 8 percent, for 15, 20, 25, or 30 years. What will their numbers look like with each choice, including not refinancing and just continuing on with their current payments?

2. Your pension plan at work offers the gradual vesting illustrated in Table 18–6. Calculate how much money would be guaranteed to you eventually in the following cases: (a) You and the company each put $1,000 per year into the plan for four years. (b) The company puts in $2,000 a year for five years. (c) You put in $1,500, and the company puts in $500 for seven years.

3. Using Tables 14–2, 14–3, and 18–5, calculate the following: (a) Investing $2,000 per year at 8 percent, how many years would you have to do this to build up a big enough nest egg to allow you to withdraw roughly $900 per month for 15 years? (b) You have $20,000 to invest for the long term. If you stash it away for 20 years at 6 percent, what monthly income can you withdraw starting in 20 years without ever dipping into your nest egg?

FOR BETTER OR FOR WORSE

Things beyond our control often impact our personal and financial well-being, for better or for worse. Some are more predictable than others. How could you be affected if the following real-life phenomena happened? Could you have seen it coming? What steps could you have taken to minimize damage or maximize advantage? The better able you are to anticipate and recognize these forces, the better equipped you are to deal with them.

1. You have invested all of your 401(k) money in the stock of the company you work for. You know the company, and you're loyal. The boss dies suddenly and the stock plunges when it's announced that the boss's lame-brained son will succeed his dad.

2. The government announces that, as a result of a national survey, almost 15 percent of all pension recipients are not getting all the money they should be getting.

3. You know that you have only one more year on the job until your pension rights are fully vested, but you can't stand the job. Then your boss tells you you're being transferred to the worst post in the company for the next year, like it or not.

Exercise 18.8

Estate Planning

A son can bear with equanimity the loss of his father. But the loss of his inheritance may drive him to despair.

Machiavelli

No one ever sat on his deathbed wishing he had spent more time at the office.

Anonymous

One of the most important—and most overlooked—aspects of personal financial concern is estate planning. It's important because it goes right to the heart of your financial structure, both while you are living and after your death. And it's overlooked because people don't like to think about their own mortality, let alone make plans regarding it.

When people do investigate planning for their own purposes, they are often mystified and put off by the strange language and concepts that prevail in the field.

This chapter will examine the jargon and the tools used in the field of estate planning, as well as the many considerations that must be taken into account in establishing a sound and sensible estate plan. After reading this chapter you should know

- What a *will* is, and how it works
- Who are the various parties involved in an overall estate planning program, and what are their roles
- Specific things you can accomplish, and problems you can avoid, with a properly prepared estate plan

IF NOT FOR YOURSELF, THEN FOR YOUR PARENTS

Exercise 19.1

You said it about retirement at the start of chapter 18, and you're saying it again now about estate planning: "This stuff is not for me. I'm decades away from those concerns, so why don't I just skip this chapter?" Hold on. As with planning for retirement, estate planning is best started early—not intensely, but at least gently. Moreover, the knowledge you can gain about estate planning now can be of help to your parents or others close to you. And, as in chapter 18, look at it from this somewhat selfish, but realistic, perspective. If you stand to inherit something from your parents, or others, and they have not done the proper estate planning, wouldn't it be worth it to you to diplomatically guide them toward taking the right steps to assure that their wishes are met? If you answered yes, the importance of this chapter to you increases accordingly.

UNEXPECTED PROBLEMS

Barlow was 37 years old, in good health, and financially self-sufficient. All was well with him. Well, almost all.

Barlow's widowed mother lived with him. She was in failing health, but happy that she could live out her remaining days in comfort, close to her son and three beloved grandchildren. But this arrangement deeply troubled Barlow's wife. The wife was extremely bitter about having her mother-in-law live with them. She thought it was an intrusion on her privacy and a negative influence on the children and, perhaps most important, that the money Barlow had to spend on his mother's care was money that could have been spent by the wife for her own benefit. Barlow and his wife frequently fought over this issue. The wife had often expressed her preference for sending her mother-in-law to the county home for the aged to be done with the whole problem.

Every Saturday morning, Barlow played three sets of tennis with his friend Murray. Murray was very overweight, and Barlow constantly chided him that their Saturday morning exercise was the only thing keeping Murray from an early grave. On one Saturday, with Barlow leading three games to one in the second set, Murray raced to the baseline to return a high lob. In midstep, he suddenly clutched at his chest, emitted a loud moan, and fell to the ground. He was declared dead on arrival at the emergency room, a victim of cardiac arrest.

It was weeks before Barlow recovered from the shock of Murray's death. But one of the first things he did when order returned to his life was to ask his lawyer one simple question: "Do I need a will?"

"Not necessarily," the lawyer responded.

"But I thought everyone should have a will," Barlow said, perplexed.

"If someone dies without a will," the lawyer responded, "the state in which he lives will determine how his wealth and property are to be distributed. This is what's known as the law of intestacy."

"What would happen to my wealth and property if *I* died without a will?" Barlow asked.

"Under the laws of our state—and each state has its own separate laws on this matter—your wife and children would split whatever there was. Your mother would get nothing," the lawyer noted.

Barlow felt a cold chill go through his body. Under these circumstances, he felt certain that his wife would immediately deliver his mother to the county home for the aged and that his wife would likely embark on a spending spree that could quickly erode the funds he had set aside for his children's college education.

Barlow expressed these fears to his lawyer who, in turn, suggested that Barlow quickly embark on an estate plan.

"Let's begin," said Barlow. "I had thought that such matters were best left to the later years. But I have learned now, the hard way, that it's time to do what's right."

This chapter is intended to acquaint you with the rudiments of estate planning. *It is not by any means a guide to preparing one's own estate plan.* But with the understanding that can be obtained by reading this material, you will be capable of discussing your own estate planning matters with a lawyer who is properly qualified to tend to those matters.

A Minor Device to Aid in Your Reading

One of the most commonly used devices in estate planning is the last will and testament, commonly called a will. To minimize the confusion between a will in this sense and the other uses of the word ("I will follow my lawyer's advice"), *will,* the legal document, is typeset as follows in this chapter: WILL.

WHAT IS AN ESTATE?

While a person is living, his or her estate is all that the person owns, less all that person's debts. On the death of the person, the estate becomes a legal entity in its own right. When John Doe ceases to exist, the "estate of John Doe" comes into existence. This estate becomes the legal machinery that pays the estate taxes, distributes the property and money, and carries out all other legal wishes of the deceased.

If the deceased has executed the proper legal documents, most commonly a WILL, the activities of the estate will be carried out by the executor, a person or an institution named by the decedent to carry out these functions. If the person has died without a WILL, the state in which he or she resided at the time of death will name an administrator, who will be responsible for carrying out the laws of intestacy of that state as they apply to the individual's estate.

WHAT IS ESTATE PLANNING?

Estate planning, simply put, is the development of a program that will ensure that any individual's last wishes are carried out regarding the estate.

We have two primary choices in distributing our estate. The first choice is to take steps on our own to ensure that our wishes are *clearly stated,* that they will be *carried out,* and that they will receive the *full protection of the courts.*

There are many devices to establish the desired program. The most common is the preparation of a WILL. Other devices include life insurance, gifts, trusts, and simply spending it all, leaving nothing behind.

The second choice is to do nothing, in which case the laws of the state of residency at the time of death will determine the distribution of any estate.

Each state has its own laws concerning this, known as laws of intestacy. All state laws are somewhat similar, yet different. You must determine what your state's laws of intestacy are and how they might affect you. Table 19–1 illustrates how the laws of intestacy can vary from state to state.

TABLE 19–1   Who Gets What If You Die Without a WILL (Intestate)?

	If You Are Survived by Spouse and Children, but No Parents:	If You Are Survived by Spouse and Parents, but No Children
State A	Spouse gets ½; children get ½	Spouse gets all; parents get nothing
State B	Spouse get ⅓; children get ⅔	Spouse gets ½; parents get ½
State C	Spouse gets first $50,000, plus ½ of any balance; children get residue	Spouse gets first $50,000, plus ½ of any balance; parents get residue
Your state	?	?

Note: Further differences exist under differing survival conditions. For example, no spouse survives; only parents survive, etc.

THE RIGHTS INVOLVED IN ESTATE PLANNING

Rooted deeply in our legal tradition are the rights of individuals to determine what will happen to their accumulated wealth upon death. Over the years, certain limitations have been placed on the overall freedom to distribute our accumulated wealth as we wish. For example, the federal government and some state governments have a right to tax our wealth. When an estate is required to pay taxes, these taxes are known as estate taxes. The federal government levies estate taxes on a very small percentage of estates. Furthermore, many states levy estate taxes.

In some states, those who *inherit* may become liable to pay taxes to the state. These are known as inheritance taxes.

Our wishes may be limited because they are contrary to public policy. For example, a court may not carry out the wishes of a deceased person who leaves money to an individual on the condition that the individual marry or divorce a certain person, or change religions, or do other things that society at large would deem improper or immoral.

Another limitation exists regarding surviving spouses. Laws differ from state to state but, generally, a surviving spouse has a right to at least a minimum portion of the deceased spouse's estate. If, for example, the laws of a state proclaim that a surviving spouse is entitled to one-third of the deceased spouse's estate, and the deceased spouse has expressed in his WILL that his widow will receive only 25 percent of the estate, the surviving widow has a "right of election against the WILL." In effect, she can disclaim that portion of the WILL that gives her only 25 percent, and, if everything else has been done in proper legal fashion, the widow will then be entitled to the minimum allowed by the state, or one-third.

The overriding limitation on our freedom to distribute our wealth as we wish is that we must do so in accordance with the law. If we want the full protection of the courts, we have to play the game by the established rules.

The most obvious purpose of an estate plan is to determine who will get our money and property after our death. But there are other important purposes. In addition to distributing property, the legal documents of the estate plan can establish who will be responsible for carrying out the wishes of the deceased. If the individual has not named a party to do so, the courts will appoint one.

The proper use of an estate plan can minimize taxes; it can recommend guardians of orphaned children or other individuals previously under the guardianship of the deceased; and it can set forth specific instructions, such as funeral and burial procedures.

The deceased individuals will of course never know the difference, but an estate plan enables them to live with a greater degree of peace of mind knowing that these wishes will be carried out.

THE LANGUAGE OF ESTATE PLANNING

The language of estate planning contains many strange words and phrases. Lawyers bandy these strange words about, not knowing whether their clients understand the meanings. To understand estate planning and to prepare yourself to work with your lawyer on your plan, it's necessary that you grasp the meanings of the most common bits of jargon. Following is a brief glossary of the language of estate planning. (Certain words have a separate feminine form, indicated by the suffix *-trix*. The use of these separate forms for women is declining.)

- A testator, or testatrix, is a person who makes out a WILL. When you ask your attorney to prepare your WILL for you, you are regarded as the testator.

- A decedent is a person who has died. The testator eventually becomes the decedent.

- A beneficiary is one who receives an inheritance in the estate of a decedent. For example, your WILL may say, "I leave my summer cottage to my sister Melba." Melba is thus a beneficiary of a portion of your estate, namely, your summer cottage. But what if Melba should die before you? in your WILL, or in other estate documents, you can name a contingent beneficiary.

- A contingent beneficiary is one who takes the place of a named beneficiary who has already died. For example, "My summer cottage shall go to my sister Melba, and if she dies before I do, it shall go to my other sister, Lucy." In this case, Melba is your beneficiary and Lucy becomes your contingent beneficiary in the event that Melba dies before you do. Had you not named a contingent beneficiary, the summer cottage might have passed through Melba's estate, to whomever she may have named to receive whatever she owned.

- A bequest is the specific property or money given to a beneficiary. In the preceding example, the bequest consists of the summer cottage.

- A life estate is a form of bequest with some strings attached. To create a life estate, the WILL might read: "My summer cottage shall go to my sister Melba for as long as she lives, and on her death it shall go to the Boy Scouts of America, local chapter 123." In other words, Melba has the use of the cottage for her life, but she has no right to pass it on to anyone else on her death, at which time it will go to the local Boy Scout chapter. You have given her a life estate in the summer cottage, and you have further directed who shall get it after her death.

- An executor, or executrix, is a person or an institution named in a WILL to handle the affairs of the estate. Generally, executors will be granted broad powers to allow them to carry out the directions of the WILL. For example, executors commonly will be given the power to buy and sell

properties and securities and to do whatever else may be needed to carry out the wishes of the deceased as closely as possible. Executors may be entitled to receive a fee for their duties, but it is possible to arrange for an executor to serve without a fee. The testator may require that the executor post a bond. This is a form of insurance that will protect the estate from financial harm at the hands of the executor.

The duties of the executor can be considerable. In addition to following the specific wishes of the decedent, the executor may also have responsibilities of a more personal nature to the family members. In all likelihood, the executor will need the assistance of a lawyer and an accountant in fulfilling all the needs of the estate, which can include the payment of estate taxes and income taxes when the estate has earned income on investments or properties prior to the disbursement of the funds to the ultimate beneficiaries. If an executor is unable or unwilling to fulfill his or her duties, the court will generally appoint a successor executor.

- If an individual dies without a WILL, the court will appoint a person or an institution to handle the affairs of the estate. This person is called the administrator. Duties are similar to those of an executor, and the question of fees and bonds will probably be determined by the court.

- Probate is a court proceeding in which the validity of a WILL is established. The term *probate* comes from a Latin word meaning "to prove" or "to examine and find good." If the WILL is properly drawn and executed and no one challenges its terms, the court will direct that the terms of the WILL be carried out. If a challenge arises that can't be settled by the parties, the WILL is thus "contested," and additional court proceedings might be needed.

The laws of probate differ from state to state. Generally, the attorney for the estate, acting in conjunction with the executor, will request that the appropriate court commence the probate proceedings. All potential heirs will have been notified and will be given the opportunity to accept or challenge the WILL as written. Would-be heirs who wish to challenge an otherwise valid WILL will have to do so at their own expense, which can be considerable.

A challenge to a WILL, or a contest, can be a most bitter and costly struggle. Even the most carefully planned and painstakingly drawn estate plan cannot guarantee that an outside party will not challenge it. But the chances of an outside party succeeding in such a challenge will be drastically reduced by virtue of the professional expertise that has gone into creating the plan.

Probate procedures are constructed so that frivolous claims or challenges will be quickly dismissed. In order for a challenge to be successful, the challenging party must have fairly clear and convincing proof that all or part of a WILL was invalid or that the WILL being probated was not in fact the last WILL of the decedent.

THE WILL

Exercise 19.2

A WILL is the most common form of device utilized in the formation of an estate plan. A simple WILL, which is adequate for most individuals, can be prepared quickly and inexpensively.

What Goes into a WILL—the Basic Clauses

Exercise 19.3

In a sense, a WILL is a form of contract: it is a legally binding document that sets forth certain rights and responsibilities of the parties and cannot be changed without the consent of the person who drew up the WILL. If the testator has had a WILL prepared in full compliance with the laws of his or her state, then, on his or her death, the executor has the responsibility for carrying out the wishes stated in the WILL, and the courts of the state are responsible for seeing to it that the rights of the survivors are given the full protection of the law.

The major clauses of a WILL that set forth primary responsibilities and rights are as follows.

The Introductory Clause

This generally is the opening clause of a WILL, and should clearly and unmistakably state, "This is my last WILL and testament," or, "My WILL is as follows." It is essential that this clause establish that you are creating the WILL and that the document is in fact your WILL. If both you and the document are not clearly identified as to who and what they are, it's conceivable that another party might claim that this is not your actual WILL. For example, you might intend to create a WILL by writing a personal letter to your spouse, children, or attorney. You do not clearly identify the letter as being your purported WILL. In the letter, you disinherit one of your children. After your death, the letter is introduced as being your actual WILL. The disinherited child, who would stand to gain considerably if there were no WILL (and the property passed through the law of intestacy, which assures each child a certain percentage of the estate), attacks the letter, claiming that it is not in fact the true WILL of the deceased. The court will probably uphold the disinherited child, thus invalidating the purported WILL and requiring that the property pass through intestacy.

Revocation of Prior WILLS

An individual creating a WILL who has previously made another WILL should clearly revoke the entire prior WILL by stating so clearly in the new WILL. If the testator does not do this, it's possible that the prior WILL, or at least portions of it, might be included in the probate with his new WILL. If

there are two WILLS, the later one will generally control, except to the extent that the specific provisions of the two WILLS are consistent with each other. But even this can cause unnecessary complications, which can be avoided by clear revocation of the former WILL.

For example, a testator prepares a WILL in which he leaves $10,000 to each of his grandchildren. At the time he drew the WILL, he had two grandchildren. Many years later, he draws another WILL but does not revoke the earlier WILL. The new WILL contains the same clause giving $10,000 to each of his grandchildren. But now he has eight grandchildren, which means a total bequest to them all of $80,000. This is a very substantial portion of his estate. The question arises as to whether only the original two grandchildren were entitled to the $10,000 bequest or whether all eight are entitled to it. If all eight are entitled to it, other heirs might receive much less. The actual wording of the old WILL and the new WILL, with the court's interpretation of the clauses, will determine who gets what. The example illustrates how confusion can result where there are two WILLS that may convey the same intentions but each with a substantially different effect on the overall estate.

Debts and Final Expenses

Before your survivors can receive their share of your estate, the remaining debts, funeral expenses, and taxes must be paid. Commonly, a testator includes a clause in his WILL instructing the executor to make all these appropriate payments. But even if there is no such clause, the executor is still required to make them.

Each state law sets forth the *priority* of who gets what and in what order. If your state laws require that a "widow's allowance" be paid, that generally is the item of first priority. This is not the widow's ultimate share of the estate but is usually a minimum allowance to enable her to get by for at least a short time. After the widow's allowance, the priorities generally run as follows: funeral expenses; expenses of a final illness; estate and other taxes due to the United States; state taxes; taxes of other political subdivisions within the state, such as cities and counties; then other debts owed by the decedent.

Creditors of the estate must generally file a claim against the estate if they wish to be paid. The executor may determine, or the testator may have instructed the executor accordingly, that certain claims are not valid. A testator cannot invalidate legitimate claims against his or her estate by simply stating in the WILL that those claims are not valid.

If, after all debts, taxes, funeral costs, and final illness expenses are paid, there is enough left to make payments to the survivors, such payments are then made in accordance with the *bequest clauses*. If, however, these expenses consume all the estate, then the survivors receive nothing. In such a case, the estate is considered to be insolvent.

Bequest Clauses

These clauses determine which survivors get how much. Broadly speaking, there are four ways in which property can be left to the survivors: through joint ownership with right of survivorship; through a specific bequest; through a general bequest; and through the residual. (Sometimes the word *legacy* is used in place of *bequest*.)

If property is owned in joint names—such as a home or a savings account—the property will pass to the survivor of the two joint owners. The WILL need not necessarily specify such matters, but it would be wise to note these items in the WILL to avoid misunderstanding.

A specific bequest will refer to a particular item or security. For example, a testator may bequeath to a child "my stamp collection, which is located in safe deposit box 1234 at the Fifth National Bank." The collection will pass to the survivor on the death of the testator, assuming that the testator still owns it at the time of death. If he no longer owns it, then obviously it cannot pass, and the gift will dissolve. The heir will receive nothing in its place unless the testator has specifically instructed the substitution of other items of value, or money, should he no longer own the collection. In addition, if the subject of a specific bequest is not free and clear—it has been pledged, for example, as collateral for a loan—the heir will receive that property subject to the debt against it and will be responsible for paying off the debt unless the testator has instructed that he is to receive it free and clear. For example, the stamp collection may have been pledged as collateral for a loan. The collection is worth $10,000, and the balance on the loan is $2,000. If the testator has not stated that the heir is to receive it free and clear, the heir can be responsible for paying the $2,000 owed. If the testator has instructed that the heir should receive it free and clear, however, the $2,000 debt will be paid out of other estate resources.

General bequests are those payable out of the general assets of the estate. Commonly, general bequests will be in the form of cash, such as "I bequeath to my housekeeper, Marsha Margolis, the sum of $3,000."

After all property has passed through either joint ownership specific bequests, or general bequests, everything that's left is called the residual. Commonly, this will represent the bulk of many estates. A typical residual clause might read as follows: "All the rest, remainder, and residual of my estate I hereby bequeath to my wife and children, to be divided equally among them." There may be further detailed instructions concerning the manner and timing of such distributions, including the possibility of trusts that would parcel out the payments over a specific period of time.

In planning a WILL, it's essential that the testator and attorney discuss all these various provisions for distribution. As individual circumstances change over the years, these clauses should be reviewed to determine that the bequests are still what the testator wishes; and if the subjects of specific bequests are no longer owned by the testator, provisions should be made for the proper substitution.

Other elements of who gets what—and who doesn't—may include clauses of disinheritance; clauses that set forth a preference among various heirs; gifts to charities; and clauses that release individuals from debts owed to the decedent.

Survivorship Clauses

Though rare, it can happen that a husband and wife are killed in a common disaster, such as an automobile accident or an airplane crash. Each of their WILLS should have been created with this possibility in mind, particularly if there are minor children. The couple will want to state their preference as to who will be the guardians of the children in the event of such a disaster. If estate taxes are of concern to the couple, a survivorship clause should also set forth the sequence of the deaths (who is to have been presumed to have died first) in such a way as to minimize the effect of estate taxes.

Appointment Clauses

In this clause, the testator appoints the person or institution who will be the executor of the estate. Where circumstances dictate, a testator may also name an attorney for the estate to act in conjunction with the executor.

If other individuals—such as minor children or elderly parents—are dependent on the testator, the testator should also recommend the guardian for such individuals. The guardian will have the duties and responsibilities, and fee if any, that are specified in this appointment clause.

It's common for one spouse to name the other spouse as executor. The testator wants to know that some one who is deeply concerned with the welfare of the survivors will be in charge of carrying out the duties of the executor. It should be noted, however, that the duties of the executor can be demanding; the more complicated the estate, the more exacting the duties. A surviving spouse may not be equipped to handle many of the duties; thus, many prudent individuals will name an institution, such as a trust department of a bank, as a coexecutor. The institution is fully staffed and capable of carrying out the specific legal and accounting responsibilities of the executorship. Such a move can minimize the burden on the surviving spouse, and adds an element of permanence to the whole matter. Evaluate fee schedules when considering naming a coexecutor.

The Execution

The final clauses of a WILL are very important. They are called the testimonium clause and the attestation clause. In the testimonium clause testators

express that they are signing this document as their true last WILL and testament, as of the specific date on which the document is being executed. In the attestation clause the witnesses to the WILL agree that they have witnessed the signing of the WILL in each other's presence and in the presence of the testator on the specific date.

The combination of these two clauses serves as proof that the document is the last WILL and testament of the testator, that the document has been properly signed, and that the witnesses can verify all of this.

The execution of a WILL is a ritual that must follow the letter of the law. Each state's law determines how many witnesses should attest to the signing of the WILL by the testator. It is imprudent for any individual who may receive a share of the estate—either as a family member or as a recipient of a bequest—to act as a witness to the signing of the WILL.

In addition to the signing and witnessing of the WILL, the attorney may have the testator and each witness sign or initial each separate page of the WILL. This may help serve as added proof that the WILL that is finally presented for probate is the true and complete WILL of the testator

Until the WILL is signed and witnessed, it is not valid. Any attempt to shortcut the execution procedure might open the doors to a contest of the WILL if it can be proven that the WILL was not properly signed or witnessed by the appropriate parties.

Changing a WILL

A WILL can be legally changed in one of two ways: it can be totally revoked by a brand-new WILL, in which case the brand-new WILL should expressly state that the former WILL is totally revoked. Or minor changes can be effected by means of a brief document called a codicil.

A WILL *cannot* be legally amended by crossing out or adding words, by removing or adding pages, or by making erasures. A codicil should be drawn up by an attorney and should be executed and witnessed in the same fashion as the original WILL itself. The codicil should then be attached to the WILL. If a WILL is amended in any way other than the creation of a new WILL or the creation of a properly executed codicil, it's all that much easier for anyone to succeed in contesting the WILL. Furthermore, a court might not admit to probate a WILL that has been changed by hand. Such improper changes could conceivably invalidate the entire WILL and could render the estate subject to the laws of intestacy. In short, testators should not destroy all that they have created in the estate plan by making changes unless they are made in the proper, legally prescribed fashion.

Once a will has been drawn and executed, it's common for the attorney to keep the original in a safe or a fireproof file. You should keep a copy or two for your own reference, and if you've named a bank or other institution as executor or coexecutor, the proper people there should also receive a copy for their files.

When Should a WILL Be Amended?

You should review your WILL and overall estate plan at least every three years. Depending on any changes in your circumstances, revisions may or may not be called for. These are the common circumstances that dictate the need to amend a WILL or any other portion of an estate plan:

- If the individual has moved to a different state, the WILL should be reviewed. Remember that the law of WILLS and estate distribution are state laws, and there can be differences from one state to another. You should have your plan reviewed by an attorney in your new state of residence.
- Changes in family circumstances might dictate the need to alter a WILL. A divorce may have occurred. Children may have grown up and moved out on their own. If one child has been particularly affluent and another has suffered economically, you might want to make provision to assist the less fortunate child. You may wish to add or delete charitable contributions, to amend your funeral and burial instructions, to add or delete specific bequests that you have made to individuals—there are myriad possibilities.
- If there have been substantial changes in your assets and liabilities, a review of your WILL might indicate that changes are in order. If you have either acquired greater wealth or suffered financial reversals since the original drawing of the WILL, this may dictate different modes of distribution to your heirs.
- If heirs named in your WILL have died before you, you might want to review the effect that would have on the distribution of your estate.
- If an executor or guardian named in the WILL has died or has become incapable of acting in the desired capacity, or if you simply no longer wish to have that person representing your interests, an amendment to your WILL would be in order.

STRATEGIES FOR SUCCESS

Beware of "Do-it-yourself" Estate Planning Shortcuts

You want to save some money on legal fees, so you buy a book on how to write your own WILL . . . or you copy your cousin Elmer's WILL for your own because you and he tend to think alike . . . or you just buy some blank WILL forms at the local stationary store and fill in the blanks. These moves could be a *big* mistake. Estate planning is complex. Shortcuts can mean that the wrong people can be cut short if you make a mistake in the do-it-yourself process. The proper estate plan, created by properly trained people, can help assure that the courts of your state will see to it that your wishes are carried out. If your do-it-yourself attempt isn't legally proper, chaos could result.

- If tax laws change regarding estates, a review of your WILL would most certainly be in order. The 1976, 1981, and 1997 federal estate tax law changes had a sweeping effect on millions of estate plans already in existence. Virtually all estate plans and WILLS prepared prior to the effective date of these tax laws should be reviewed by an attorney.

It's impossible to know when further changes may come about in the laws, and often court decisions cast slightly new and different interpretations on existing laws. Any of these decisions could affect your own estate, and your attorney should advise you accordingly to make the appropriate changes.

Uncommon WILLS

Occasionally, a court will receive for probate a WILL that has been prepared by the testator in his own handwriting. It may or may not have the appropriate number of witnesses. A WILL that's prepared in the handwriting of the testator is called a holographic WILL. Some states permit the probate of holographic WILLS under certain circumstances, but such WILLS are definitely not substitutes for WILLS prepared under proper legal guidelines. The courts recognize that individuals may be in dire circumstances and unable to acquire the proper legal counsel to prepare a totally valid WILL. Thus, allowances are made for the occasional probate of a holographic WILL.

In more extreme cases, a WILL may be spoken by the dying individual to another party or parties. Such a spoken WILL is referred to as a noncupative WILL. It's allowed only by some states, and then only under strictly defined conditions.

Neither a holographic WILL nor a noncupative WILL should be relied on as a substitute for a properly prepared WILL. A court may find such a WILL invalid and could throw the entire estate into intestacy. Where at all possible, proper legal assistance should be used in creating a WILL.

OTHER DEVICES FOR PASSING ON ACCUMULATED WEALTH

In addition to the common WILL, there are other means whereby you can pass wealth to heirs and other generations.

Trusts

Exercise 19.4

A trust is a "strings-attached" way of passing money or property to another party. For example, you have $50,000 that you would like eventually to pass to your son, who is now 25 years old. But you're concerned that he might run through the money. You thus decide that until he reaches age 40, he should be entitled only to the income that the $50,000 will generate through

investments. When he reaches 40, he can have the entire amount. In order to accomplish this, you create a trust.

To be sure that your wishes are carried out without further concern on your part, you make an arrangement with your bank to administer the trust. The bank then becomes the *trustee.* You deposit the $50,000 with the bank, which then agrees to invest it and pay out the income to your son until he reaches age 40, at which time he will be paid the full principal amount.

That's an oversimplified view of the creation and function of a trust, but it's intended to make the point that passing money by trust is not an outright transfer. There are, as noted, strings attached. The trust agreement can stipulate just how much the beneficiary (in this case, your son) will get at what time and under what circumstances.

In the foregoing example, both parties involved in the trust are still living. This would be called an *inter vivos* trust, or a trust between the living.

A trust can also be established in your WILL to take effect at your death. Instead of property passing outright to the beneficiary of your WILL, it may go in trust. For example, you might leave $50,000 in your WILL in trust for your son until he reaches the age of 40, with the full amount payable to him on that date. Where a trust is established in one's WILL to take effect on death, it's referred to as a testamentary trust.

A trust can be revocable or irrevocable. A revocable trust is one that can be revoked or canceled. An irrevocable trust may not be canceled; it is permanent.

Under certain circumstances, trust arrangements may be desirable in place of a WILL or may be used in conjunction with a WILL. There is no fixed rule—it all depends on individual circumstances.

The law of trusts is complicated. A great deal can be accomplished with trusts, both in the control of property and in the minimization of estate taxes. An attempt at a do-it-yourself trust might be even more foolhardy than a do-it-yourself WILL because of the added complexities of the trust laws.

The trustee is the person or firm that has the duty of carrying out the directions of the trust. The trust document, which is a form of contract, spells out the trustee's powers and responsibilities. Many people prefer to use a financial institution as a trustee instead of an individual. Bank trust departments are operated by professionals, and there is assurance of permanence. Such permanence has obvious advantages if a trust is designed to continue for many years. As with naming executors in a WILL, an individual might prefer to name both a corporate trustee (such as a bank) and a person close to the family as cotrustees.

Gifts

Making gifts of money or property is another form of estate planning. Gifts have long been popular with more wealthy individuals as a means of cutting down on their potential estate tax liability. By making gifts prior to death, money or property may escape taxation, wholly or partly. The over-

STRATEGIES FOR SUCCESS

Be Aware of Life Insurance Settlement Options

The common thinking is that when someone who has life insurance dies, the insurance company pays a lump sum of money to the beneficiary of the life insurance policy. That generally is the case, but it need not be. The owner of a life insurance policy has a number of options—called settlement options—that can call for a different form of distribution of the life insurance money. Know what these options are and use them where appropriate. For example: a husband might think that his beneficiaries (wife and/or children) are not capable of handling the large sum of money that the insurance proceeds would be. So he might choose a settlement option in which the insurance company would pay the money out over a period of time, including some interest, rather than one lump sum. Do you know what options your policies offer?

all desirability or feasibility of making gifts a part of an estate plan should be discussed in detail with professional advisors.

Insurance

For many families, life insurance is the main way of passing wealth from one generation to the next. Indeed, in families of moderate means, life insurance may be the only estate planning necessary. But it would be unwise to rely on life insurance policies as a substitute for estate planning. Even the most modest estates should be reviewed with professionals to determine what will occur on the death of each individual. Insurance can pass money from one generation to another, but planning is needed to assure that the parties who need the money most, or who are most entitled to it, will get what the testator wishes. For example, a man may have little estate other than life insurance, and if his children are named as beneficiaries, his widow may not receive what she needs for her own survival. If the children aren't willing or able to help her, she could be in dire straits. On the other hand, the widow could be the sole beneficiary of the insurance policies, and the children could thus be deprived of funds their father wished them to have. These matters should be discussed with a life insurance agent, in conjunction with an attorney and accountant.

Joint Names

Putting property in joint names, such as husband and wife, often seems a simple way to ensure that the surviving spouse will receive everything on the other spouse's death. This may be true, but it can subject the estate to taxes that could have been avoided, and it may prevent the money from

ultimately going where you had wished it to go. For families of more modest means, a joint-names program might suffice. It's not safe to make any assumptions about the ultimate distribution of an estate in which everything is owned jointly—the advice of a competent attorney is still essential.

HOW TO PROCEED

At the beginning of this chapter, you were introduced to Barlow and his problems. Barlow followed his lawyer's advice and created an estate plan to pass his accumulated wealth and property to those he wished to have it. In addition to the distribution of wealth, Barlow also provided that his mother should remain in his home until it became no longer medically feasible for her to do so. He also established a trust program by which his wife and children would receive their inheritance over a period of years rather than in one lump sum. This arrangement, Barlow felt, would protect the interests of all concerned. Having thus created his estate plan, Barlow achieved a peace of mind that had eluded him for some time.

As Barlow's situation indicates, there are purposes for estate planning other than the distribution of accumulated wealth and property. An estate plan can be utilized to provide care for others, to manage money, to ensure a continued lifestyle for survivors, and to minimize taxation.

If you go about it the wrong way, you may fail to achieve what you want your estate plan to accomplish. Let's take a closer look.

The Wrong Way

Nelson was a wealthy widower with two daughters, Jessica and Rhonda. Jessica had taken over the family business and was dutiful, loyal, and devoted to her father. Rhonda, on the other hand, had had a bitter argument with her father many years before and had run off to Paris. She had been there ever since, earning her living as a jazz guitarist. Nelson had long ago vowed that Rhonda would "never get a penny from me."

One reason for Nelson's wealth was that he carefully watched every penny he spent. Thus it was that, when he was ready to create an estate plan, he shunned the expense of a lawyer. Rather, he went to a local stationery store where, for $2, he bought a blank WILL form and proceeded to fill it out himself, leaving his entire estate to Jessica. The blank WILL indicated that there were to be two witnesses to Nelson's signature. But since Nelson didn't want anyone other than Jessica to know of this WILL, he had only Jessica sign as a witness.

When Nelson died, Rhonda was shocked to learn that she had been disinherited by her father. She asked her lawyer to look into the matter, and, after doing so, the lawyer recommended that Rhonda contest the WILL. If

the WILL could be proved invalid, Nelson's estate would be divided equally between Jessica and Rhonda. The lawyer pointed out that there had been only one witness, whereas the state law requires two witnesses. Furthermore, the only witness, Jessica, was the heir to the entire estate, and that threw a further cloud over the validity of the WILL.

Under such circumstances, Rhonda had an excellent chance of having the WILL invalidated, thereby upsetting Nelson's intent to disinherit her. By saving a small sum on legal fees, Nelson allowed half his wealth to go where he had not intended it to go.

The Right Way

There is really only one proper way in which a desired estate plan should be implemented: with the aid of a capable lawyer. Any attempts—repeat, *any attempts*—at do-it-yourself estate planning can be fraught with danger. Last wishes may not be carried out as expressed; taxes may have to be paid when they could have been avoided; and survivors could be left in a variety of predicaments that could have been avoided.

Citizens of the United States have a very precious right: to pass a substantial portion of their acquired wealth to the survivors of their choice. These rights are protected by our courts. For the fullest protection, however, individuals must express their wishes in full accordance with the law.

Each state has its own laws regarding how property passes from a deceased person to survivors. In our highly mobile society, individuals move from state to state and may own property in states other than the one in which they live. Thus, it's possible to be affected by the estate laws of more than one state.

Furthermore, federal laws on estate taxation can have a bearing on the estate of any individual, regardless of which state he or she lives in.

Thus, a lawyer specializing in estate matters, is *the best* qualified party to tend to estate planning. The lawyer may see fit to call in other professionals—bankers, insurance agents, accountants—as the need arises.

The first necessary step in creating an estate plan is a visit with the chosen lawyer. During this initial meeting, you should disclose all your assets, liabilities, and, most important, your estate-planning objectives. The lawyer will then be able to determine what estate-planning documents might be best suited to achieving your stated objectives.

WHAT SHOULD YOUR ESTATE PLAN ACCOMPLISH?

Keep four main objectives in mind when creating or amending any estate plan.

- To establish the proper liquidity and distribution of assets
- To establish a program of sound management of assets

- To provide for the assured continuation of a family's lifestyle in the event of death, disability, or retirement
- To minimize taxation

Three aspects of taxation must be taken into account: the federal gift and estate taxes that would come out of the estate assets; the taxes the heirs may have to pay on inherited property; and the income taxes the estate may have to pay, if it has had earnings before the distribution to the heirs. Let's now take a closer look at each objective.

Distribution and Liquidity

Distribution of assets and the liquidity of those assets go hand in hand. Distribution refers to who gets what. Regardless of the size of your estate, you want to be certain that it will be distributed in the manner you've specified. Liquidity refers to the ability to put cash on the table as quickly as possible and with as little expense as possible. The more liquid one's assets, the easier it will be for everybody to get whatever it is they are to have. The most important reasons for having liquidity are to be able to provide for the immediate needs of one's survivors—spouse, children, and so on—and to be able to pay any estate taxes when they are due.

Mike's case illustrates the dangers in failing to make adequate provision for proper distribution and liquidity in one's estate.

Mike was a good provider, or so he had thought. Twenty years ago, when he was 40, Mike made some major changes in his life. He gave up his job as a plumber, and with a partner, Willy, he opened up a wholesale plumbing supply firm. His only child, Maryanne, was soon to be married, so Mike and his wife, Sybil, decided to sell their home and buy an apartment house. They would live in one of the apartments. Mike also bought a large tract of vacant land fifteen miles outside the city. He was confident that the city would grow in that direction, and that in ten to fifteen years, this land would be extremely valuable as a site for a shopping center and new housing.

All these things accomplished, Mike visited a lawyer to have a WILL prepared. He left the land to Sybil; the apartment house to Maryanne; and his interest in the plumbing supply business to be divided equally between Sybil and Maryanne.

Twenty years later, this is the status of Mike's estate.

- Mike and Willy worked hard at their business, and it prospered. Mike, with an easy and outgoing personality, was the "Mr. Outside" of the business. He took care of the sales, the customer relations, and the goodwill for the venture. Willy, on the other hand, was the "Mr. Inside." He took care of the books, the inventory, and the detail work. Mike was proud that he could draw a salary of $50,000 a year and that his share of the business was now worth $200,000.

- The apartment house also proved to be a good investment. Today, after all expenses, it was generating $20,000 a year income and, if Mike wanted to sell it, he could reap $200,000 after all selling costs. He and his wife continued to live in the same apartment.

- The vacant land didn't fare as well as Mike had hoped, but his potential profit was still substantial. Mike felt that the land could now be sold in various parcels to net him $300,000.

- Mike had no other assets of any consequence. All available income from the business and the apartment house was reinvested back into those entities, and Mike felt that this growing wealth precluded the need for any life insurance.

- Daughter Maryanne's financial situation was constantly in chaos. Mike had given her some financial help, but nothing seemed to change her wasteful, spendthrift ways. Many years ago, Mike had given up. He would no longer help her, and Maryanne felt very bitter and angry toward her parents because of this.

- Mike was a wealthy man—at least on paper. His net worth exceeded $700,000. But in the twenty years since he had drawn his original WILL, he had never taken the time to reexamine it or change it in any way.

A Costly Failure to Plan

In spite of Mike's apparent wealth, after he died his distribution of assets and lack of liquidity resulted in terrible turmoil. The problems Sybil faced were as follows:

- An appraisal of the plumbing supply business verified that, at the time of Mike's death, his interest was indeed worth $200,000. But no buyer could be found. Willy had become very difficult to deal with, and, without Mike's talents, the profitability of the business quickly declined. The income that Mike had been bringing home quickly shriveled to a fraction of what it had been. And that was the money Sybil needed to live on.

- The apartment house had been willed to Maryanne, and she took the opportunity to get her revenge against her parents. She sold the property as quickly as she could and pocketed the profits. Sybil's rent-free days were over.

- In desperation, Sybil looked to the vacant land as her source of salvation. But in her grief and anxiety, she was easily taken advantage of by a buyer. Given enough time and clear-headedness, she could have sold the land for a gain of $200,000. But Sybil found herself accepting half that amount. And, after paying the capital-gains taxes on the profit from the sale of the land, her nest egg was reduced even further.

Alternatives?

Mike's greatest error was his failure to review and update his estate plan. Had he done so periodically, he could have corrected the problems: total lack of liquidity and a distribution plan that gave the wrong things to the wrong people.

What else could Mike have done? He could have worked out an arrangement with Willy whereby Willy would buy out Mike's interest on Mike's death. This could have been accomplished through a *key-person life insurance*. It would work like this: Each partner would have his life insured for an agreed-on amount—say, $200,000 in Mike's case. In the event of either partner's death, the life insurance proceeds would be paid to that partner's survivors, and the other partner would then gain the dead partner's interest in the business. In Mike's case, Willy would have ended up with total control of the business, and Sybil would have ended up with $200,000 cash.

By giving the apartment house to Sybil instead of Maryanne, Mike could have assured Sybil of the continuing rental income, as well as a place to live rent-free.

It would have cost Mike relatively little to implement these or other alternatives. He, of course, is not around to feel the brunt of his planning errors. But his wife will have to live with them for the rest of her life.

Establishing a Program of Sound Management for Estate Assets

The bulk of Marsha's estate consisted of life insurance and stocks. By the time she reached her mid-forties, she had accumulated a large enough estate to provide for her family in a most comfortable style, including education for the children and total peace of mind for her husband, Ned, in the event she should die suddenly, as she unfortunately did.

Her plan had been carefully prepared, but she had made one major miscalculation. Marsha had always handled the bills and other financial decisions. Between Ned's grief and his lack of familiarity with money matters, the estate was wiped out within a few short years.

Marsha had at one time thought that because there was a sizable sum involved, she should arrange to have it flow through some form of managed program whereby the money would be allocated to the family as needed. But because of her faith in Ned and because of the cost involved in a managed program, she didn't do so.

Proper management of assets in an estate is a factor all too often overlooked. Tales are legion of widows and children who have squandered money, been bilked, or were ill-advised.

A thoughtful person planning an estate must be aware of the need for sound management of assets for as long as the survivors will have need of those assets. Management can be accomplished in a number of ways. Assets can flow through a trust whereby income is paid to the survivors, who can

have a right to tap the principal as and if the need arises for specific purposes. Insurance policies can be arranged so that the money is paid out over an extended period rather than in one lump sum. Similar extended withdrawal plans can be set up with annuities, mutual funds, and pension and profit-sharing plans. Whether a management program is set up formally, as through a life insurance company or a trust, or whether it's established by common consent among the parties, there is still no substitute for a basic knowledge on the part of family members about the nature of the assets of the estate, an awareness of what can jeopardize those assets, and a cool head to keep things on an even keel, particularly during the difficult early months following the death of the breadwinner.

As with all other elements of estate planning, the matter of management should be reviewed from time to time and amended as needed.

Assurance of Continued Lifestyle

Oliver worked out a fine estate plan, taking into account all the foregoing questions of distribution and management of assets. But his mistake came in viewing the estate plan as something that commenced at the time of death. His primary concern—the concern of many—was to provide ample funds so that his family members could continue to live in their accustomed manner after his death.

But he erred in failing to provide for that same lifestyle while he was still living. When Oliver first fell ill, his business associates continued to pay him full salary for a number of months, even though he was contributing nothing to the business. All his medical expenses were paid by a very comprehensive health insurance program. But after several months, his associates came to him and said they'd have to reduce his salary since the business was hurting from his continued sick-pay benefits and the loss of his energies.

Oliver could understand this and consented to it, feeling that he would soon be on the road to full recovery and at full earnings. But it didn't work out that way. A few months later, his associates told him sadly that they would have to cut his salary down to a minimum level and, a few months after that, it was terminated completely. Even though his medical expenses continued to be paid, there was no income, and Oliver had to start dipping into his reserves.

His illness lingered, and when he died three years later, the bulk of his estate had been used up. His heirs received virtually nothing. Oliver's case illustrates a most tangible problem that has very intangible solutions: an otherwise adequate estate demolished by unforeseen events. In Oliver's specific case, a solid program of life and disability insurance could have provided ample protection and allowed him to leave his estate almost intact. Those are insurable risks, but other occurrences are less insurable. A portfolio of investments can suddenly turn sour. The need to support

elderly or disabled family members can drain one's assets suddenly and sharply.

Prudent individuals insure against all foreseeable risks, within reason, without becoming "insurance-poor." And they will further structure their portfolio of investments and business relationships to at least minimize the chaos that could result from unforeseen catastrophes.

Perhaps most important is to communicate with family members about the size of the estate and what they can expect from it. They should be prepared for the contingencies they will face, realizing that the more knowledgeable they are, the better they will be able to cope on their own.

Minimizing Taxes

Carl had no worries about estate taxes. Two years ago, when he had his WILL prepared, his lawyer told him that his estate was not large enough to incur any estate taxes. At that time, Carl's total wealth was approximately $350,000; his house was worth $180,000; his investments, $120,000; his vested rights in a pension fund, $30,000; and his personal property, $20,000. Carl signed his WILL, content that all his wealth would go to his wife and children and that none would go to the government.

But a lot can happen in a short period of time. Carl's wife ran off with Roger, a film critic from Los Angeles, and Carl sued for divorce. His wife didn't contest the divorce—she was content to let Carl keep everything, including the three children. Moreover, and unbeknownst to Carl, his great-aunt Trudy had fallen critically ill and had included Carl in her WILL.

On January 2, 1999 Carl awakened groggily—he had suffered through the previous day with a massive hangover due to overindulgence on New Year's Eve. Now that headache was gone, but his mailbox contained the makings of another one. There were two letters. One was from his lawyer, informing him that the divorce proceedings had become final. The other was from a lawyer in Vermont telling him that his Aunt Trudy had died and that Carl was now the proud owner of one-third of Aunt Trudy's Vermont dairy farm, with his interest worth approximately $400,000. Carl telephoned his lawyer to discuss the inheritance. "Congratulations!" said the lawyer. "The value of the inheritance boosts your total worth to $750,000. However, the divorce means that you can no longer take advantage of the important estate tax-savings device known as the marital deduction. In other words," the lawyer cautioned, "If you were to die today, your estate would owe federal estate taxes of about $30,000."

Carl was dumbfounded. "How can that be?" he gasped. "When I went to bed last night, I could have died in my sleep and not owed Uncle Sam anything."

Carl's lawyer then proceeded to explain to him how estate taxes work.

HOW ESTATE TAXES WORK

Exercise 19.5

Very few estates will be subjected to estate taxes. But as Carl's case illustrates, an obligation to pay those taxes can arise unexpectedly. Or, more usually, the obligation to pay taxes can arise gradually as one's worth increases over the years as a result of inflation (such as in the value of one's house), appreciation in the value of one's investment portfolio, the addition of life insurance and pension benefits to one's net worth, and so on. If you are in your twenties or thirties today, your estate may seem too small to cause you concern about estate taxes. But as you reach your forties, fifties, and sixties your total wealth is likely to increase by many times its current value, thus exposing you to estate taxation.

Sound financial planning dictates that continued attention be paid to one's potential estate tax liability. With proper advance planning, the costly bite of estate taxes can be minimized.

Three Kinds of Taxes

Three possible kinds of taxes can arise when a person dies. They are:

Exercise 19.6

- **Estate taxes**   When a person dies, his or her "estate" becomes a legal entity. If the estate is large enough, the federal government will levy a tax on the value of the estate. The tax is to be paid out of the assets of the estate, generally before anything is distributed to the survivors. It often happens that an estate will have to sell investments or other property in order to pay the federal estate taxes. The federal estate tax is the biggest of all possible taxes arising at one's death.

  Tax laws allow a very big exemption for estate taxes. Through tax year 1997 the first $600,000 of a person's estate (after allowable deductions) was not subject to estate taxes. The Taxpayer Relief Act of 1997 increases the amount of this exemption, as Table 19–2 illustrates.

TABLE 19–2   **Amount of Estate Exempt from Federal Tax under Taxpayer Relief Act of 1997**

Year of Death	Exemption	Year of Death	Exemption
1998	$625,000	2003	$700,000
1999	650,000	2004	850,000
2000	675,000	2005	950,000
2001	675,000	2006	1,000,000
2002	700,000		

Example: If a person dies in the year 2002, the first $700,000 of the estate (after allowable deductions) is tax-free. Everything over $700,000 is taxable at rates that start at about 20 percent of the taxable amount, up to 50 to 55 percent of the taxable amount.

The most important deduction that can reduce estate-tax liability is the marital deduction, which is what one spouse can leave to the surviving spouse. The amount of the marital deduction is unlimited. Thus, if one spouse leaves his or her entire estate to the surviving spouse, there will be no estate taxes on the estate of the first spouse to die. However, the entire estate of that first spouse will then become part of the estate of the second spouse. And unless the second spouse remarries, there will be no marital deduction on the second spouse's estate. That is where the estate tax trap can catch the unprepared.

Exercise 19.7

There are other ways to cut down or eliminate the federal estate tax. They include reducing one's estate by making annual gifts while living to selected beneficiaries, life insurance trusts, and private annuities. All of these steps involve legal complexities and should be undertaken only with professional counsel.

Further, if you expect an inheritance from someone whose estate might be subject to the federal estate tax, it could behoove you to explore with that other person how the estate tax bite could be minimized so that the government doesn't get any more than it's legally entitled to.

Exercise 19.8

- **Inheritance taxes**   Some states levy an inheritance tax. This tax is paid by those who receive inheritances. The basic difference between estate taxes and inheritance taxes is that estate taxes are paid out of the assets of the estate *before* anything is distributed to the heirs. Inheritance taxes are paid by the heirs *after* the estate has been distributed.

- **Income taxes**   Many months, if not years, can elapse before an estate is distributed to all the heirs. During that time, the assets of the estate may be invested and receive income. In such cases, the income is subject to income taxes. A separate return must be filed for income earned by an estate. An inheritance that you receive is not subject to income taxes. If, say, you receive $10,000 from Uncle Willy's estate, the $10,000 is not considered taxable income to you. If you invest that $10,000 and earn $1,000 a year in interest, however, then the $1,000 income is subject to income taxes on your own personal return. If you receive property as an inheritance and you later sell that property at a profit, the profit is subject to income taxation.

It's Never Too Early

Although estate planning is commonly thought of as an activity for older people, you are never too young to consider the importance and benefits of estate planning. Thought should be given to estate planning when an individual marries and as children are born. Then, as the family grows, further review should be given to a plan at least every few years. As the family changes, so does the need for reviewing the plan. In addition to the financial benefits that can result from sound estate planning, the peace of mind that can be achieved cannot be denied.

PERSONAL ACTION WORKSHEET

Distribution of Your Estate

Estate planning, properly done, should involve an attorney with expertise in the field. The assistance of an accountant and a life insurance agent can also be worthwhile.

Even though federal estate taxes affect only a very small percentage of the population, there are still many important matters that must be resolved: Who will get what? How liquid are your assets? What provisions have you made to take care of the immediate and long-term needs of your survivors?

The following checklist is designed to motivate you to commence a proper program of estate planning. It is based on the assumption that you will die tomorrow. You should acquaint yourself with your state's law of intestacy to learn what would happen if you died without a WILL or other satisfactory distribution arrangements (trusts, for example).

Your Assets	Value	Who Would Get What?
❏ Your home	_____	_____
❏ Your personal possessions	_____	_____
❏ Proceeds of pension or profit-sharing plans	_____	_____
❏ Proceeds of life insurance policies	_____	_____
❏ Any debts owed you	_____	_____
❏ Your investment portfolio, specifically:	_____	_____
Stocks	_____	_____
Bonds	_____	_____
Savings accounts	_____	_____
Real estate	_____	_____
Collections	_____	_____
Other	_____	_____
❏ Any business interests you may have	_____	_____

Proceed with Caution on "Living Trusts"

A relatively new device for estate planning has grown in popularity in recent years. It's known as the "living trust" and, for certain families, it can provide a number of advantages. In oversimplified terms, it requires that you transfer your assets now, while you are living, into a trust arrangement. The trust, not you individually, will thus become the technical legal owner of your assets. Since those assets are no longer technically a part of your estate but rather are owned by the trust, they can pass to your designated heirs without having to go through the often costly and time-consuming probate proceedings.

But there can be serious problems. First, living trusts are not for everybody. The initial cost of creating the trust, plus the expense of maintaining it, make it more beneficial for larger or more complicated estates. Second, con artists pitch living trusts to unwitting victims. They use scare tactics. They make misleading claims as to what the living trusts can do. They falsely assert that they have the blessings of such respected groups as the American Association of Retired Persons. They charge more than legitimate local lawyers charge. And in the worst of cases, they build language into the documents that entitles them to horrendous fees upon the death of the person creating the trust.

A living trust should be compared with all other possible alternative methods of estate planning, and you should get the advice of a trusted and objective attorney who is a specialist in estate planning. If you have any doubts about the wisdom of one method over another, seek a second opinion without delay.

UPS & DOWNS   *The Economics of Everyday Life* ───────────

How the Liquidity of an Estate Can Go Up and Down

Very few people have to worry about having cash on hand (liquidity) to pay estate taxes. But everyone should be concerned as to how liquid their estates are so as to provide quick and easy access to cash to take care of the immediate needs of survivors. If an estate lacks liquidity, the survivors might have to sell assets at far less than they might be worth in order to generate cash. Or, they might have to borrow heavily, which can erode the value of the estate. The time of death is unpredictable, but the immediate cash needs of survivors can be very predictable. Prudence dictates being aware of these ups and downs of estate liquidity:

Equity in the home   This is often the largest single asset a family has, but converting it to cash can be costly and time-consuming. The house can be sold, but in a weak housing market that could take many months. You can borrow against the existing equity, but that can be costly and can take many weeks. If there is already a second mortgage against the property, it will be quite difficult to borrow further—third mortgages are considered risky, and lenders will charge high fees for the arrangements, both in up-front costs and in the rate of interest.

Pension funds   The ability to get fast cash from a vested pension depends on the terms of the overall pension arrangement, which you should learn about in advance. When can a lump-sum payout be made in the event of the pensioner's death? How much will it be? What are the long-term payout options available to the survivors? What taxes (estate and/or income) will be payable, thereby reducing the amount of cash available?

Investments   If the estate is heavily invested in long-term bonds, the immediate cash-in value of those bonds may be much lower (or higher) than the face value of the bonds. It depends largely on current interest rate levels, compared with what they were when the bonds were purchased. (See chapter 14 for a full discussion.) If the bonds are worth less than face value (because interest rates have gone up over the years), you might have to wait many years before you can sell the bonds for the price that was paid for them. With stocks, though they are liquid, an urgent need to sell might result in losses.

Family business or professional practice   If the deceased operated solo, his or her death might slash the value, and the liquidity, of the business immediately. Any business or practice should take into account the unexpected death of any principal. "Key person" life insurance can be an excellent way to provide instant liquidity. (See the discussion of this insurance earlier in this chapter.)

Windfalls   Inheritances, gifts, insurance proceeds, even lottery winnings can make a big difference in an estate's liquidity. But any windfall has its own built-in "cashability," or lack thereof. The more expected a windfall is, the better you can measure how liquid it might be when you receive it.

?

WHAT IF . . . ?

Test yourself: How would you deal with these real-life possibilities?

1. Who would receive what if you died intestate unexpectedly? Check your state laws to learn the distribution formula. Who would get what if your spouse died intestate unexpectedly? Who would get what if either or both of your parents died intestate unexpectedly? If these intestate distributions don't seem right to you, what can you do to change the outcome?

2. Think of a number of married couples close to you—friends, relatives, and yourself if you're married. If both spouses of those couples were killed simultaneously, what arrangements are in place for the care of their children or any other dependents they might have? Who would handle their affairs? If the results of such unlikely tragedies don't seem right to you, who could each of these couples name now, in a WILL, to become legal guardians in the event of simultaneous deaths?

3. A relative of yours dies. You had expected an inheritance from her of $5,000 to $10,000. You learn that you are not mentioned in the WILL. You also learn that the WILL was improperly drawn. If you contest the WILL, you can have it declared invalid, and a lot of money will be distributed differently from the way the WILL specifies. You still wouldn't get a penny from the WILL, but other heirs might pay you to not contest the WILL. What would you do? What if the stakes were $25,000? $100,000? (Keep in mind that your legal fees will be about 35 percent of anything you collect.)

NUMBER CRUNCHERS

Do the calculations to make decisions in these real-life possibilities.

1. You have the following assets: (a) equity in your house worth $60,000; (b) vested interest in a pension plan worth $80,000; (c) life insurance with a face value of $100,000, (d) other investments worth $50,000. Assume that all these assets are increasing in value, after taxes, by 6 percent per year, compounding annually. (Aren't you lucky!) Assume also that the tax-exempt amount of an estate remains at $600,000. How long will it be before your estate hits a taxable level? Assume that no marital deduction is available to you.

2. Using the same assumptions in #1, assume that Congress today lowered the taxable threshold to $400,000. How long will it be before your estate hits a taxable level? In such a case, how much of your estate will be exposed to the estate tax 15 years from now? That is, by how much will your estate exceed $400,000 15 years from now?

3. Sharpen your awareness of estate distribution: At John's death, he owned his house jointly with his wife; value $130,000, mortgage $40,000. His other assets were worth $100,000, including an antique car worth $25,000, which he left to his son Tom. In his WILL he left $5,000 to "each grandchild." When he drew the WILL he had two grandchildren, but when died he had four. The remainder he left in equal shares to his wife and Tom. All things considered, what will Tom and the widow each get?

FOR BETTER OR FOR WORSE

Things beyond our control often impact our personal and financial well-being, for better or for worse. Some are more predictable than others. How would you be affected if the following real-life phenomena happened? Could you have seen it coming? What steps could you have taken to minimize damage or maximize advantage? The better able you are to anticipate and recognize these forces, the better equipped you are to deal with them.

1.   Your father has a sizable estate, but has never drawn a WILL. He and your mother have been estranged for years—they hate each other—but they never divorced. If your dad dies without a WILL, your mother (under the laws of your state) would get half the estate. Dad wouldn't want her to have a penny. You point this out to your dad, and he agrees to have a WILL drawn. The next day he dies of a heart attack.

2.   Above facts again, except that Dad does have a WILL prepared, leaving everything to his children and nothing to his wife. After his death the wife contests the WILL claiming that it was entered into fraudulently.

3.   A man and a woman are about to be married, the second marriage for both of them. She has a lot of wealth, but poor health. He has the opposite: a lot of health but no wealth. They both have grown children from their first marriages, all of whom are happy for their parents' remarriages. You are one of her children. Everyone has been getting along beautifully, until just before the wedding, when your sister flips out and accuses the stepfather-to-be of marrying Mom for her money.

Income Taxes

*If we can prevent the government from wasting the labor of people under the
pretense of caring for them, they will be happy.*

Thomas Jefferson

You can't get away from income taxes. Virtually every facet of your financial affairs is affected in one way or another by the federal income tax: when
you borrow, when you invest, when you set up a recordkeeping program,
when you plan for your retirement, and when you do your just plain day-
to-day budgeting.

To complicate matters, not only will your own finances change from year
to year, but tax laws are also in a continual state of flux. Sweeping over-
hauls of the tax code take place once or twice a decade. And as the tax code
changes, the IRS issues new regulations and the courts issue new interpretations. You might have to alter your financial plans if you want to take advantage of what the law allows, or escape any disadvantages that the law
may impose.

This chapter is not intended to be a step-by-step guide to filing your tax
return. That information is available in a variety of commercial publications. Rather, this chapter is designed to

- Give you a basic understanding of how the income tax laws work

- Illustrate the strategies and decisions you should consider to keep
  your taxes at a minimum

- Acquaint you with audit procedures and how to deal with them

BE PREPARED

Exercise 20.1

As you read this chapter, you should have at hand the most current copies of the latest 1040 form and the schedules that accompany it. These forms are included in the instruction package the Internal Revenue Service (IRS) mails to all taxpayers each January. They are also available year-round at local IRS offices and during the first few months of each year at most banks, libraries, and post offices.

Examples of tax issues and illustrations of the tax forms are included in this chapter to give you a general understanding of the laws and the forms. For the year in which you are studying this chapter, or doing your return, you must determine the current laws and how they apply to the current forms.

You should complete the Personal Action Worksheet at the end of this chapter *before* you read this chapter.

This chapter discusses federal income taxes. Some states and cities also levy income taxes. State and city tax formats generally follow the federal format, so this chapter will also be helpful to you in understanding your local income tax situation.

THE IMPORTANCE OF KNOWING ABOUT INCOME TAXES

The following stories illustrate what can happen to people who are *unaware* of income tax provisions.

- Ralph and Marcia hired a babysitter to take care of their children while they were at work. Like many people, they hated to do the work connected with filing their tax return. So they went to a low-cost tax preparation service. You get what you pay for: The cheap service neglected to ask Ralph and Marcia if they had child-care expenses. And Ralph and Marcia didn't know enough to mention them. Had they known the facts, they could have cut their tax bill by over $1,000 by claiming the child-care expenses as a credit against their tax!

- Jessica moved from Detroit to Los Angeles to take a better job. When it came time for her to file her tax return, she overlooked the opportunity to claim most of her moving expenses as a deduction from her income. This could have cut her tax bill by many hundreds of dollars—and it would have taken only a few minutes to enter the necessary information on the form.

- Karl was a machinist. His boss required Karl to provide his own tools and work clothes for the job. The boss didn't reimburse Karl for these expenses, but Karl didn't mind the expense. Nor did he pay attention to the tax laws, which allowed him a deduction for part of the unreimbursed cost of the tools and work clothes.

- Brent was a traveling salesman. He returned from the road every Friday afternoon and spent hours sitting at his dining room table doing paperwork associated with his job. Another salesman had once told him that if he did work at home, he could claim a deduction on his tax return for the expense of having an office in his home. Brent thus figured that the use of his dining room table for a few hours each week was worth $2,400 a year in deductible expense, which resulted in a tax savings of over $800. But Brent was dismayed when an auditor for the Internal Revenue Service disallowed it as an *improper deduction,* for it did not meet the guidelines for claiming office-at-home expenses. Brent had to pay up accordingly, *plus* interest and penalty.

- Joel received an inheritance of $2,000. Wanting everything about this windfall to be perfectly legal, Joel included it as income on his return. By doing so, he increased his taxes by $600. But, he figured, he was still better off by $1,400, and the IRS couldn't claim he was hiding income. The IRS gladly accepted the extra $600 from Joel. But if Joel had done his homework, he would have learned that inheritances are *nontaxable income.* He should *not* have reported it, and he should *not* have paid the tax. If he later realized his mistake, he could have filed an *amended return* and gotten back the overpayment.

The Pervasiveness of Taxes in Our Lives

These examples illustrate just a few of the hundreds of common situations involving income taxes. As the examples show, many people pay more than they must. Or they may court costly problems by *not* paying the taxes they do owe. With hundreds, perhaps thousands, of dollars at stake in your own tax return, it's essential that you learn all the possible ways to keep your taxes at the legal minimum. To an extent, a professional tax preparer can help you, but preparers spend only a few hours a year with you. They may not think to ask, and you may not remember, all the transactions you conducted during the year that could have tax consequences.

Your knowledge of the tax laws will help you to be a better recordkeeper and a better manager of your financial affairs. The preparer can only work with the information you provide him. It's up to you to know which transactions have tax implications and to collect the necessary documentation that will enable you to support whatever claims you make on your return.

The income tax structure also requires that you make a number of important choices, such as which form to file, which filing status to choose, whether to itemize your deductions, and so on. Making the wrong choice could mean paying higher taxes than necessary or running into a hassle with the IRS. If you make a choice that favors the government, you *cannot* assume that they'll correct the matter for you. For example, if you choose *not* to itemize your deductions, when in fact doing so would lower your

taxes, the IRS will *not* come back to you with the suggestion that you itemize. They'll gladly accept the extra taxes you've paid.

Let's examine the basic workings of the income taxes and how you can make the correct decisions to minimize your taxes legally.

THE BASIC CONCEPT OF INCOME TAXES

Of all the income you receive in a year, only *some* of it is subject to income taxes. There are many ways that the total amount of your income can be *reduced* to find the taxable portion. And once that taxable portion is determined, there are ways to minimize the taxes you owe on that income.

Your assignment, should you choose to accept it, is to find all the ways you can legally reduce your taxable income and the taxes thereon. You might think that this is an impossible mission. It isn't, if you're willing to do some homework, for which you can be amply rewarded.

Following, in brief, are the steps you'll take. We'll examine each one in more detail later.

1. Tally all your income that is subject to taxes. (Do not include income that is not subject to taxes, such as inheritances or life insurance proceeds that you might have received.)
2. Reduce that total by the proper legal methods—adjustments, deductions, and exemptions.
3. Then, figure the lowest possible tax by choosing the right filing status and claiming all proper credits.

Let's look at an oversimplified example of how the income taxes are calculated in accordance with these three steps. Table 20–1 illustrates the case of Glenda and Mac.

Exercise 20.2

TABLE 20–1   Glenda and Mac's Income Taxes

1. Income subject to taxation:		$38,000
2. Less: Adjustments	$ 3,000	
Deductions	5,000	
Exemptions	10,200	
Total "subtractions"		18,200
Income on which taxes must be paid:		19,800
3. Tax on $19,800	2,974	
Child-care credit	−330	
Net tax due	$ 2,674	
Withheld during year	3,100	
Refund due Glenda and Mac	$426	

Step 1:

Glenda and Mac had a total of $40,000 in income for the year. Of that, $2,000 was tax-exempt income from an investment and $38,000 was income from work and other taxable sources. This, their total income that is subject to taxation was $38,000.

Step 2:

Calculate all the legal subtractions. Glenda and Mac had $3,000 in adjustments as a result of their eligible individual IRA account investments. Their deductions total $5,000 for the year. In that particular year, each exemption was worth $2,550; Glenda and Mac have two children, so they were entitled to a total of four exemptions, or $10,200. Their subtractions totaled $18,200. That left them with $19,800 of income on which taxes must be paid.

Step 3:

Their proper filing status is as a married couple filing jointly. The tax on $19,800 for the year in question for that filing status was $2,974. Further, Glenda and Mac had paid for child care in order to hold jobs. That expense entitled them to a credit of $330, subtracted from the tax due. That left them with a net tax due of $2,674. During the year, Glenda and Mac had had a total of $3,100 withheld from their pay for federal income taxes. That's $426 more than they ended up owing, so they were entitled to a refund of $426.

We'll now take a closer look at how these specific steps are taken on the tax forms themselves. Bear in mind that the tax laws and forms can change from year to year; thus, this discussion must be general in nature.

If you have not yet completed the Personal Action Worksheet at the end of this chapter, do so now. It's designed to help you to understand how your own personal taxes are to be calculated.

STRATEGIES FOR SUCCESS

Best Bet: Do Your Own Income Taxes

If not every year, then at least every other year, you should do your own income taxes. Because income taxes play such a role in our financial matters, you serve yourself best by being knowledgeable about how income taxes work. And the best way to get that knowledge is to prepare your own returns. Doing so will keep you more aware not only of current tax regulations but also of changes that are slated to occur in the tax laws. By anticipating changes, you can make better decisions regarding such matters as investing and borrowing. If you *don't* do your own taxes at least once every few years, you could make costly *wrong* financial decisions.

Who Must File?

Your first step is to determine whether you are legally required to file an income tax return for the past year.

Depending on your *age* and *marital status,* there are different levels of gross income at which you will be required to file a return. You may not owe any taxes; indeed, you might be entitled to a refund. But you must file a return if you fall within the legal requirements. Determine what the minimum income requirements are for the current tax year. (If you've completed the Personal Action Worksheet at the end of this chapter, you will have obtained this information as well as other specific data that are likely to change from year to year.)

There are a few other circumstances under which you might be required to file a return:

- If you are claimed as a dependent on someone else's tax return, such as your parents', you may be required to file your own tax return if you had a certain amount of *unearned* income during the year. (Unearned income is income from investments as opposed to earned income, which is income from work.)
- Even if your income for the year falls below the minimum levels, you'll have to file a return if you owe certain taxes other than income taxes, such as taxes on a distribution from an IRA account, or Social Security taxes on tips that you didn't report to your employer.
- You will have to file a tax return if you have net earnings from self-employment that exceed a fixed amount. Self-employed persons must also pay self-employment tax on the self-employment income. This is comparable to the Social Security tax that employees have withheld from their wages.

There are some circumstances in which you may not be *required* to file a tax return, but *should* file one. These circumstances include the following:

- You may not have earned enough income to be required to pay taxes, but you did have income taxes withheld from your pay. If you file a tax return, you can get a refund of the taxes that were withheld. If you don't file a return, even though you're not required to, you won't get a refund.
- If you are entitled to the "earned income credit," you must file a return to receive the money that is due you.

Check specific IRS instructions for the current year to determine today's exact filing requirements.

Which Form Should You Use?

Individuals can use one of three forms to file their returns: the 1040EZ, the 1040A, or the 1040. The 1040EZ is the simplest to use, but it can only be

used if you are single or married filing jointly and do not claim dependents; are not 65 or older or blind; did not receive any advance earned income credit payments; and had taxable income of less than $50,000 (not more than $400 of which can be from interest income). The 1040A, often called the short form, is available to every filing status but cannot be used if your income is $50,000 or more or if you want to itemize your deductions.

To take full advantage of all the tax-cutting devices available—itemizing deductions, all possible credits—you should use the 1040 form, often called the long form. For the balance of this chapter, we'll be referring to the long-form provisions.

Choosing Your Filing Status

The first important choice you have to make regards your filing status. The segment on the form looks like this:

Filing Status
1 _____ Single
2 _____ Married filing joint return
3 _____ Married filing separate return
4 _____ Head of household
5 _____ Qualifying widow(er) with dependent child

There are five possible choices. Many taxpayers can qualify for more than one status, but choosing the wrong one can result in higher taxes.

Married Taxpayers

Married taxpayers can file separate returns, or they can file a joint return. With few exceptions, it will be to their benefit to file a joint return. If you have doubts as to whether it's better to file jointly or separately, calculate the tax both ways, and choose whichever is the lower tax.

If you were legally married on the last day of the year, you are considered to have been married for the whole year. If your spouse died at any time during the year, you also are considered to have been married for the whole year.

If married persons do file separately, they must do the same with respect to their deductions. Both must either itemize their deductions or use the standard deductions. This is a disadvantage to filing separately.

(There is a possible exception to this general rule if you live with your dependent child apart from your spouse. In order to qualify for this unusual status, you must also meet *all* four tests set forth in the IRS instructions.)

Unmarried Taxpayers

Unmarried taxpayers choose from the other three filing statuses: single, head of household, and qualifying widow(er) with dependent child. Of these three choices, the single status will pay the highest tax, followed by the head of household and the qualifying widow(er). In one recent year, for example, an individual with a taxable income of $27,000 would have paid the following taxes, depending on his or her status.

Single	$4,447
Head of household	4,054
Qualifying widow(er)	4,054

As you can see, choosing the correct legal status can make a considerable difference in the amount of taxes you'll have to pay.

Head of Household

In order to qualify, you have to be unmarried on the last day of the year and you must have paid more than half the costs of keeping up a home that was the principal home for the *whole* year for any relatives whom you can claim as a dependent (see the later discussion on who qualifies as a dependent.) Note that these family members must actually have lived with you.

You can also qualify if unmarried children or grandchildren lived with you, even though they may not technically be your dependents. You can also qualify if your mother or father were your dependents, even though they did not actually live with you.

Qualifying Widows and Widowers

People who qualify for this status pay at the same tax rate as married couples who file a joint return. If your spouse died in a preceding year, you can file as a qualifying widow or widower if you were entitled to file a joint return with your spouse for the year in which he or she died, *and* you did not remarry before the end of the current tax year. You must *also* have a child, stepchild, or foster child who qualifies as your dependent for the year, and you must have paid more than half the costs of keeping up your home, which had to be the principal home of that child for the whole year.

Your Exemptions and Dependents

As was noted earlier, for every exemption you can legally claim, you are allowed to reduce your income that is subject to taxation.

For tax year 1997, each personal exemption was $2,650. After that, it's scheduled to be adjusted for inflation. (High-bracket taxpayers may lose the

benefit of all or part of the personal exemptions if their income exceeds certain thresholds established from year to year.) Check current regulations for the year in which you are filing.

The section of the 1040 form looks something like this:

Exemptions

☐ Yourself
☐ Spouse

Total boxes checked ☐

Dependents

Name	Relationship	No. of Months lived in your home	If age 1 or older, dependent's Social Security number	Total other dependents ☐
____	____	____	____	
____	____	____	____	
____	____	____	____	
____	____	____	____	

Add numbers entered in boxes above ☐

Obviously, the more exemptions you can legally claim, the lower your taxes will be.

You are entitled to claim one exemption for yourself and one exemption for your spouse. You can claim an exemption for a spouse even if the spouse died during the year. You may claim additional exemptions for every person who is your legal dependent.

Dependents are not limited to children. Other persons may qualify as dependents if all necessary tests are met.

In order to qualify as a dependent, a person must meet *all* of the following five tests:

- The support test
- The gross income test
- The member of household or relationship test
- The citizenship test
- The joint return test

The requirements, in brief are as follows.

- **Support test**   You must provide more than half of the dependent's total support during the calendar year.
- **Gross income test**   Generally, you may not claim a person as a dependent if that person had gross income during the year in excess of the amount of the personal exemption. The gross income test can be

ignored if the person you claim as a dependent is your child and is either under age 19 or is under age 24 and is a full-time student, in accordance with IRS definitions.

- **Member of household or relationship test** A person who lives with you for the entire year and is a member of the household can qualify as a dependent, even though that person is not related to you.

  Certain relatives can qualify as dependents even if they do not live with you, provided they meet all the other tests. These relatives can include children and grandchildren, parents and grandparents, brothers, sisters, stepfamily, and in-laws.

- **Citizenship test** To qualify as a dependent, the person must be a U.S. citizen or a resident of Canada or Mexico for some part of the calendar year in which your tax year begins.

- **Joint return test** If the person you wish to claim as a dependent has filed a joint return on his or her own with a spouse, you cannot claim that person as a dependent.

The tax regulations are very specific about what constitutes support of a dependent. Some expenses qualify, whereas others do not. Check current regulations to be certain that you are proper in claiming your dependents. Note also that you cannot claim a partial dependent.

Declaring Your Income

This is the area in which you must declare all your income that is legally taxable and you must, as noted earlier, take care *not* to report any income that is *not* taxable.

The income section of the 1040 form looks something like this:

Income		
	Wages, salaries, tips, etc.	———
Attach	Interest income	———
Copy B of your	Dividends	———
Forms W-2 here.	Alimony received	———
	Business income (or loss)	———
	Capital gain (or loss)	———
	Pensions, annuities, rents, royalties, partnerships, etc.	———
	Miscellaneous income	———
	Total income	———

The sample income section of Form 1040 does *not* contain all the possible income items. It has been abbreviated to include the more common types of income only. Check current regulations and forms to determine the full extent of reportable income.

Taxable Income

Let's take a more detailed look at each of these items of taxable income.

WAGES, SALARIES, TIPS, ETC.   For most taxpayers, this is the major source of taxable income. Early in the year, employees receive copies of W-2 forms from their employer, which summarize the total income earned during the previous year and how much was withheld to pay income taxes, Social Security taxes, state income taxes, and any other withholdings required or voluntary. The amount of total income on your W-2 form should be inserted on this line, and a copy of the W-2 should be attached to this part of your form when you mail it in.

INTEREST INCOME   On this line, you place the total of all taxable interest you've earned during the year. The current form will dictate whether you are required to itemize on a separate schedule. Taxable interest includes any interest earned on accounts with banks, savings and loans, and credit unions; also interest earned on mortgages, trust deeds, promissory notes, corporate bonds, and U.S. government bonds (except for Series E and EE savings bonds). With Series E or EE bonds, you have the option of declaring the interest earned in a given year and paying taxes on it during that year or of deferring the taxation until you later cash the bonds.

If you own municipal bonds, or mutual funds that invest in municipal bonds, the interest you earn on those investments may be exempt from federal income taxes. If you own municipal bonds that are issued by a local government unit in your state, the interest may also be exempt from state income taxes. However, if you sell municipal bonds or funds at a profit, that profit is fully taxable. Interest earned on U.S. obligations is exempt from state income taxes.

Some types of interest earned are not taxable in the year in which you earned it but will be taxable in some future year. This is known as tax-deferred income. It includes interest earned from annuity plans, IRA and 401(k) plans, Keogh plans, and other pension and profit-sharing programs.

The effects of tax-deferred earnings can be very attractive, since all your earnings remain in your account to work for you. A simple example: Say, you have an account of $1,000 earning 10 percent per year, or $100. In a normally taxable situation, a taxpayer in the 28 percent bracket would have to pay $28 in taxes out of the $100 earned. That would leave $1,072 in the account after one year.

In a tax-deferred account, however, the entire $100 would be added to the $1,000, which would leave $1,100 in the account after one year. Table 20–2 traces a taxable and a tax-deferred account.

TABLE 20–2 **$1,000 Earning 10% per Year**

	Taxable Account	Tax-deferred Account
After		
1 year	$1,072	$1,100
2 years	1,149	1,210
3 years	1,232	1,331
4 years	1,321	1,464
5 years	1,416	1,610

DIVIDENDS This includes dividends you receive on common stocks, mutual fund shares, and dividends that have been reinvested in shares of common stock or a mutual fund. If the dividends you've received exceeds a certain limit, the form will indicate that you are to itemize all dividend income on a separate schedule.

Any party that pays you more than $10 per year in interest or dividends must prepare a form 1099, which indicates the amount paid to you. Copies of this form are sent to you and to the IRS. Thus, the IRS has a record that you received that money; should you fail to report it on your tax return, expect to be questioned by the IRS.

ALIMONY RECEIVED This is considered fully taxable income. However, child-support money received is not taxable income. See current regulations for definitions of taxable alimony.

Separately Scheduled Income

If you receive certain other types of income, you will be required to complete additional schedules. These types of income include:

BUSINESS INCOME OR LOSS—SCHEDULE C If you ran your own business, part-time or full-time, as a sole proprietor, you must complete Schedule C and show the income or loss from that business. (If you operated the business as a partnership or a corporation, you'll have to file the appropriate partnership or corporate income forms.)

CAPITAL GAINS AND LOSSES—SCHEDULE D Congress has probably changed the regulations on capital gains and losses more often than any other aspect of the entire tax law.

The concept applies to the sale of *capital assets,* which, in general terms, are investments such as stocks, bonds, and real estate. If you sell such items at a profit, you have realized a capital gain. If you sell such items at a loss, you have realized a capital loss. If you hold capital assets for less than the designated holding period, it is a short-term capital gain or loss. If you hold the capital asset for longer than the designated holding period, it is a long-term capital gain or loss.

Both the tax rate on capital gains and the holding period (to distinguish between long- and short-term gains) have bounced around frequently over the last ten or twenty years, making it difficult for investors to anticipate the tax implications of their strategies. Prior to 1987 the maximum tax rate on long-term capital gains was 20 percent. From 1987 to 1990 it was as high as 33 percent. From 1991 to 1997 it was 28 percent. And in 1998 it went back down to 20 percent as a result of the Taxpayer Relief Act of 1997. The holding period has been as short as six months. From 1998 onward the holding period to qualify for the long-term tax rate will be eighteen months. For capital assets purchased after the year 2000, the long-term capital gains rate will be 18 percent if the assets are held for at least five years.

The capital gains tax issue has always been a political football. It is always subject to change, and that must be taken into account in building any kind of investment portfolio.

List capital gains and losses separately on Schedule D. Note, too, that your state may have different requirements on capital gains taxes. This may require more recordkeeping on your part.

If you have net investment *losses,* either short term or long term, you can subtract all or part of these losses from your otherwise taxable income. The maximum amount you can subtract has been $3,000 each year. Example: In 1998 you had investment gains of $2,000 and investment losses of $7,000, for a net loss during the year of $5,000. On your 1998 federal tax return, you can reduce your otherwise taxable income by $3,000 as a result of this loss provision. Assuming that in 1999 you have no investment transactions at all, you can, for that year, subtract the remaining $2,000 worth of 1998 losses from your 1999 income. Check to see what regulations are in effect at the time you file any annual return.

PENSIONS, ANNUITIES, RENTS, ROYALTIES, PARTNERSHIPS— SCHEDULE E   This schedule covers a number of possible income or loss areas, as designated in the heading.

MISCELLANEOUS TAXABLE INCOME

- Fees for services you perform, such as serving as a member of a jury, an election precinct official, a notary public, an executor or administrator of an estate, to name a few, are all miscellaneous taxable income.

- Property you receive through barter. If you receive services or property in exchange for your services, you must include as income the fair market value of the services or property on the date you received it.

- Gambling winnings are taxable income. However, you can deduct gambling losses during the year up to the extent of your winnings. Winnings from lotteries and raffles are considered gambling winnings. If you win property other than cash, the fair market value of that property must be counted as taxable income.

- Prizes and awards received from drawings, television or radio programs, beauty contests, and the like are taxable. So are awards and bonuses you receive from your employer for your good work or your suggestions. Prizes in the form of property must be included in taxable income at their fair market value.
- Unemployment insurance benefits might be taxable income. See the instructions in Form 1040 for the formula that determines how much of your unemployment insurance benefits are taxable.

This discussion includes just a sampling of the most common types of taxable income. Refer to the 1040 instructions to determine whether you have any other form of taxable income.

Nontaxable Income

Nontaxable income should not be reported on your 1040 form. Following is a sampling of the more common types of nontaxable income. Check the 1040 instructions for more specific details.

- **Interest income** *Some* types of interest income may be nontaxable, including interest received on tax-exempt bonds.
- **Accident and health insurance proceeds** Payments you receive from the following are exempt from tax: Workers' Compensation; Federal Employees Compensation Act; damages received for injury or illness; benefits from an accident or health insurance policy for which you paid the premiums; disability benefits for loss of income; compensation for loss of a function of your body; and reimbursement for medical care.
- **Gifts and inheritances** These are not considered income. But if the cash or property you received as a gift or inheritance generates income for you, the income generated is taxable.
- **Life insurance proceeds** Proceeds paid to beneficiaries are generally not taxable. Possible exceptions: If someone else turned an insurance policy on their life over to you and you paid a price for the transfer of that policy, proceeds payable to you as beneficiary may be taxable to you.
- **Social Security benefits** Not generally taxable, unless your income from all sources exceeds levels set by law.
- **Scholarships, fellowships, and grants** Generally, money received in this form is not taxable if you are a candidate for a degree.
- **Prizes and awards** These may be tax-free if the prize was awarded in recognition of your accomplishments in religious, charitable, scientific, educational, artistic, literary, or civic fields. You must also have been selected as a possible recipient without any volunteering on your part. And you must not be required to perform future services as a condition of receiving the prize. Athletic awards are not tax-exempt.

Total Income

In completing this portion of your 1040 form, you add up all the items that are considered taxable income. From this total income figure, we now begin the subtractions, the first being for *adjustments to income*.

Adjustments to Income

Items included in the adjustments category are often referred to as deductions, but technically they are not deductions. You are entitled to claim these adjustment items even if you do not itemize your deductions.

The most common types of adjustments will appear on your 1040 form in the following manner:

Adjustments to Income
Payments to IRA plans   _____
Payments to Keogh plans   _____
Alimony paid   _____
Total adjustments   _____

Payments to IRA Plans

You might be able to claim an adjustment for money you invest in an IRA plan. (Chapter 18 explains who can qualify for this deduction.)

Payments to Keogh Plans

If you have income from self-employment, you're eligible to take part in a Keogh plan, which can entitle you to an adjustment. (See chapter 18 for details.)

Alimony Paid

Alimony *received* is taxable income. On the other hand, alimony *paid* is an adjustment that can reduce your total income.

Adjusted Gross Income

At this point, total your adjustments and subtract them from total income. The result is the adjusted gross income.

The adjusted gross income is important: the amounts you can claim for some of the itemized deductions are keyed to your adjusted gross income. These formulas will be explained with respect to each deduction to which they apply.

Deductions: To Itemize or Not to Itemize?

Certain types of expenses are deductible from your income. These expenses include those for medical purposes, charitable contributions, taxes you've paid, interest you've paid, casualty or theft losses you've suffered, and other expenses related to your ability to generate income. Some deductions have limits.

Even if you haven't actually incurred such expenses, the law allows you to claim a certain fixed amount of such deductions anyway. This is known as the standard deduction.

The amount of the standard deduction depends on your filing status. Table 20–3 indicates the standard deduction for different filing statuses for 1997. These amounts are subject to change each year due to inflation and/or act of Congress.

Here's an example: Let's assume that during 1997 a married couple did not actually incur one penny's expense for any of the deductible items: they had no medical expenses, had no home loan interest, paid no state income taxes, and made no charitable contributions. Even though they had not incurred *any* deductible expenses, they were entitled to claim a $6,900 standard deduction for that year, which would reduce their taxable income accordingly.

Your Choice

If you have, in fact, spent *more* on deductible items than the standard deduction allows, you are entitled to claim *all* those expenses as deductions. But you must itemize each of them, and you must have proper evidence that you did incur such expenses.

The choice is yours: You can take the easy route and claim the standard deduction, in which case you won't have to keep records of all the particular expenses, and completing your tax form will be that much simpler. Or you can keep all the proper records to prove what you paid for such items. If your true

TABLE 20–3 Standard Deduction

Filing Status	1997
Married, filing jointly	$6,900
Married, filing separately	3,450
Head of household	6,050
Single	4,150

deductible expenses exceed the standard deduction amount, it will pay you to itemize. Many taxpayers take the shortcut of the standard deduction when in fact, if they had itemized, they could have saved a lot of money.

How do you decide whether you should itemize? If you are a homeowner, it's very likely that you will have deductible expenses in excess of the standard deduction amount. For most homeowners, the interest on their mortgage and their real estate taxes, both of which are a deductible, will be close to, if not more than, the standard deduction amount.

If you're not a homeowner, you'll have to determine whether your deductible expenses exceed the standard deduction. The following will familiarize you with the types of expenses that are deductible.

To itemize your deductions complete Schedule A of the 1040 form. An abbreviated example of Schedule A is shown here; the actual form is subject to change from year to year. Check current regulations to be certain you are claiming all proper deductions in the proper form.

Schedule A—Itemized Deductions

Medical and Dental Expenses	Casualty or Theft Losses
(Follow formula on current version of Schedule A to arrive at proper deductions.)	(Follow instructions on current version of Schedule A. Complete and attach Form 4684 to your return.)
TOTAL MEDICAL _____	TOTAL CASUALTY OR THEFT LOSSES _____
Taxes	
State and local income _____	
Real estate _____	**Miscellaneous Deductions**
Personal property _____	Union dues _____
Other (itemize) _____	Other (itemize) _____
_____ _____	_____ _____
_____ _____	_____ _____
TOTAL TAXES _____	_____ _____
Interest Expense	
Home mortgage _____	TOTAL MISCELLANEOUS
Other (itemize) _____	DEDUCTIONS _____
_____ _____	
_____ _____	**Summary of Itemized Deductions:**
_____ _____	Total medical _____
TOTAL INTEREST _____	Total taxes _____
Contributions	Total interest _____
Cash contributions _____	Total casualty _____
Other than cash _____	Total miscellaneous _____
TOTAL CONTRIBUTIONS _____	TOTAL DEDUCTIONS _____

Deductible Expenses

Expenses not specifically listed on Schedule A are included under "Miscellaneous Deductions." All deductions are subject to change by law.

MEDICAL AND DENTAL EXPENSES You can claim a deduction for your nonreimbursed medical expenses only to the extent those expenses exceed 7½ percent of your adjusted gross income. In other words, if your adjusted gross income was $40,000, you can claim a deduction for nonreimbursed medical expenses in excess of $3,000.

TAXES You can claim a deduction for any local (state, city) income taxes, real estate taxes, and personal property taxes. Taxes that are *not* deductible include sales taxes, utility taxes, federal income taxes, fines and penalties, and taxes on tobacco and alcohol products.

INTEREST EXPENSES Individuals must keep track of five different types of interest that they pay, and each type is subject to its own rules regarding deductibility.

- **Consumer interest** This includes such items as credit-card debt, charge account debt, car loans, and personal loans. You cannot deduct any of your consumer interest.
- **Home loan interest** See chapter 7 for what is deductible.
- **Investment interest** Interest paid on loans relating to investments is deductible within limitations relative to the amount of investment income you receive.
- **Business interest** If you borrow money for legitimate business purposes, the interest on such loans is deductible.
- **Student loans** Interest can be deductible in accordance with the Taxpayers Relief Act of 1997.

CONTRIBUTIONS You can deduct charitable contributions made to properly qualified charitable organizations. Contributions may be cash or property. If you give property, the deduction would be the fair market value of such property. In order to justify charitable deductions, you must have proper documentation and appraisals. If you are actively involved in a charitable organization, you cannot deduct the value of your time contributed to the organization, but you can deduct out-of-pocket expenses you incur on behalf of the charity.

CASUALTY OR THEFT LOSSES If you suffer a sudden and unexpected loss or casualty, you can deduct the value of the loss if the amount of each separate casualty or theft loss is more than $100, *and* the total amount of *all* losses during the year is more than 10 percent of your adjusted gross income for that year. For example, say your adjusted gross income is $25,000, and you suffer a casualty loss of $2,000. You *cannot* claim that loss as a deduction because it is *less* than 10 percent of your adjusted gross income. But if you had a loss of $3,000 you could claim a deduction. How

much? First, you must subtract the $100 just noted; then, you must subtract the 10 percent of your adjusted gross income: $3,000 less $100 less $2,500 equals a deduction of $400.

Deductible casualty losses may result from many causes, including fire, hurricanes, tornadoes, floods, storms, sonic booms, and vandalism.

Nondeductible casualties include car accidents when your own negligence caused the accident; breakage of household items, such as china and glassware, under normal conditions of use; damage done by a family pet; damage caused by termites, moths, plant disease; and damage caused by progressive deterioration of your property.

Theft losses include those arising from burglary, robbery, larceny, and embezzlement. If, however, you simply misplace or lose money or property, that is not a deductible theft loss.

MISCELLANEOUS DEDUCTIONS   The Tax Reform Act of 1986 imposed a formula for calculating these miscellaneous deductions: the 2 percent rule. The rule states that qualifying expenses can be deducted only to the extent that they exceed 2 percent of your adjusted gross income for the year. Example: Your adjusted gross income is $30,000. Two percent of $30,000 is $600. You tally up, say, $1,000 worth of miscellaneous deductions. But on your tax return, you can only claim $400 worth, the extent to which you exceed the 2 percent level, which, in your case, is $600. If your adjusted gross income for the year is $40,000, 2 percent of that amount is $800. In such a case, you can claim miscellaneous deductions only to the extent that those expenses exceed $800.

Here are the major miscellaneous expenses that might be claimed as deductions—subject to the 2 percent rule:

- Fees for investment advice and management
- Fees for administration of trusts
- Legal expenses relating to the collection of income
- Subscriptions to publications on investing
- Rental costs for safety deposit boxes, to the extent the box is used to store investment-related items
- Cost of tax advice and preparation of returns
- Appraisal costs relating to a casualty loss or a charitable contribution
- Unreimbursed employee business expense
- Continuing education expenses
- Business use of your residence
- Literature relating to your job or profession
- Dues to unions or business related associations
- Work uniforms and tools
- Certain costs related to seeking a new job

(If you are self-employed, many of these expenses might be business-related expenses, which may be fully deductible on Schedule C.)

Total all your deductible expenses. If the total exceeds the current standard deduction, you should include that total of itemized deductions on your return. If the itemized deductions do not exceed the standard deduction, then you should claim the standard deduction.

What Is not Deductible

If you claim deductions that aren't legal, the IRS will disallow them, which means that you will have to pay back taxes plus possible interest and penalties. Following is a brief list of some nondeductible items that are often erroneously claimed as deductions.

- Commuting to and from work
- Life insurance premiums
- Property insurance premiums on your home
- Hobby expenses
- Social Security taxes
- Attorney fees (except for producing and collecting income)
- Home-related expenses, such as allowances for children, clothing, utility expenses, school tuition
- Home repair and maintenance expenses
- Losses you might suffer on the sale of your house or personal effects

Computing Your Taxes

Exercise 20.3

We've now reached the point where the actual tax can be calculated. Table 20–4 illustrates what the tax tables in the IRS instruction look like. For those whose taxable income exceeds the limits in the tax tables, there are tax rate schedules to calculate their taxes.

TABLE 20–4   Sample of Tax Tables (In a Recent Year)

If Your Taxable Income is . . .		And You Are . . .			
At Least	But Less Than	Single	Married Filing Jointly[a]	Married Filing Separately	Head of Household
		Your Tax is:—			
30,000	30,050	5,762	4,504	6,197	4,858
30,050	30,100	5,776	4,511	6,211	4,872
30,100	30,150	5,790	4,519	6,225	4,900

[a]A qualifying widow(er) would also use this column.

Example: You subtract from your *total income* all of your *adjustments, deductions,* and *exemptions.* What's left is your *taxable income.* If, in the year illustrated in Table 20–4, your taxable income was $30,027, and you were married and filing a joint return, your tax would have been $4,504. If your taxable income was $30,121, and you were single, your tax would have been $5,790. And so on. Are the taxes different in the current year than in the year illustrated in Table 20–4? By how much?

After calculating the tax due, you then subtract the amount of any *credits* to which you may be entitled. For example: if the married couple in the prior paragraph was entitled to a child-care credit of $300, their tax would be reduced from $4,504 to $4,204.

New types of credits were introduced in the Taxpayer Relief Act of 1997, to take effect in tax year 1998 and onward.

For tax year 1998 taxpayers with children will be entitled to a credit of $400 per child under the age of 17. For 1999 and beyond that credit will be $500 per child under 17. (The child must be 17 at the end of the calendar year to qualify.) The credit is not available to high-income taxpayers: it phases out for couples with incomes of $110,000, and for individuals with incomes of $75,000. The credits are in addition to the personal exemptions.

The so-called Hope credit is available for higher education tuition and fee expenses at colleges, community colleges, and post-secondary (after high school) vocational schools. During the first two years of a student's post-secondary education the credit is $1,500 per student per year. For following years the credit is $1,000 per student per year. Taxpayers may claim the credit for up to two years for each student. (See the following paragraph on the Lifetime Learning credit for further details.) After 2000 the amounts of the credits will be indexed for inflation. There are some technical limits to these credits, such as that the student must be carrying at least one-half of the normal course load. Also, credits may not be fully available in years when the taxpayer takes money out of an Education IRA (see chapter 18) and uses that withdrawal to reduce his or her taxes under the Education IRA rules. This credit phases out for taxpayers with modified adjusted gross incomes of $80,000 to $100,000 for couples, and $50,000 to $60,000 for individuals.

The Lifetime Learning Credit is somewhat of a piggy-back onto the Hope credit. It's available for post-secondary education and for courses that create or improve job skills. It applies to courses that begin after June 30, 1998. The maximum credit is $1,000 per taxpayer per year for 1998 through 2002, and $2,000 per taxpayer per year for 2003 and beyond. Phase-outs for higher income taxpayers are the same as for the Hope credit. The Lifetime Learning credit cannot be taken in the same year that the Hope credit is taken or that deductions for the Education IRA are taken.

The Lifetime Learning credit is available for the third and fourth year of college as well as for graduate school and for adults preparing for new careers.

Note the difference in tax due at the various breakpoints: a single person

with taxable income of $30,049 will owe a tax of $5,762, while a single person with a taxable income of $30,051 will owe a tax of $5,776. In other words, with just two dollars more in taxable income an extra $14 in taxes will be owed! On the other hand, the single person with a taxable income of $30,001 pays not a penny more in taxes than the single person with a taxable income $48 higher, or $30,049. This is all the more reason to pay attention to detail in your recordkeeping and tax preparation.

Other Taxes and Payments

Follow IRS instructions on the 1040 form to determine whether you owe any taxes over and above the income taxes. If you had self-employment income during the year, you may owe additional self-employment taxes. If you had more than one employer during the year, more than necessary Social Security taxes may have been paid on your behalf, and you can claim a refund for the excess. The amount of tax withheld from your pay, and the amount of any estimated tax payments you've made on your own, are then either payable by you or refundable to you. This net amount is entered in the section titled "Refund or Balance Due." The return should then be signed and dated by you and by your spouse, if you are filing jointly, and by the paid preparer, if you used one. Mail the return, and a check for any balance owing, to the IRS in accordance with current instructions.

Estimated Taxes

If you have earnings from which there has been nothing withheld for taxes, you may have to pay what is known as the Estimated Tax. This is payable quarterly, in conjunction with filing Form 1040ES. Check current regulations to determine who must pay this tax, and what the penalties are for failing to do so.

Alternative Minimum Tax

The Alternative Minimum Tax (AMT) is designed to make certain that high-income-tax-bracket earners pay at least a minimum amount of tax. Less than one-half of 1 percent of all taxpayers will have to deal with this thorny problem.

TAX-CUTTING STRATEGIES

If you don't claim all the exemptions, adjustments, deductions, and credits to which you are entitled, the Internal Revenue Service won't do it for you. It's your job to keep proper track of all those items and incorporate them into your tax return.

Similarly, you can check out other tax-cutting strategies. The government

will not hand them to you. Following are examples of some of these basic strategies.

Tax-Exempt or Tax-Deferred Income

To the extent feasible, take advantage of opportunities to earn tax-exempt or tax-deferred income in your investment program and at work.

Tax-Exempt Income

You can earn tax-exempt income by investing in municipal bonds or in mutual funds that specialize in municipal bonds. (See chapter 14 for a further discussion of these techniques.)

Tax-Deferred Income

Tax-deferred investment income may be available through tax-deferred annuities. In such plans, the earnings on your invested money are not taxed until you withdraw the money.

Some of your income from work may also be on a tax-deferred basis, such as with pension and profit-sharing plans. Your employer may contribute money each year to a pension or profit-sharing plan on your behalf. In effect, he's paying you a form of future income: you won't have the use of the money until some future time, but, in the meantime, you don't have to pay income taxes on it. In addition to pension and profit-sharing plans, some employees might establish a tax-deferred compensation plan that would delay payment for work done until some future year. The object of this is to delay the payment of taxes into a future year when the taxpayer will be in a lower tax bracket, such as during retirement.

One popular device that allows you to earn tax-deferred income is the 401(k) plan. If your employer offers this plan, a portion of your income may be invested instead of being paid to you. That income, and its earnings, will be tax-deferred, as are any contributions your employer makes to the plan. Individual Retirement Accounts (IRAs) and Keogh plans can also be ideal ways to defer taxes. (See chapter 18 for a detailed discussion of these plans.) To the extent you are eligible, you should take advantage of these plans.

U.S. Savings Bonds Series EE also offer the opportunity to earn tax-deferred income. With these bonds you can delay paying taxes on interest earned until you cash in the bonds.

Tax Withholding and the W-4 Form

Suppose someone advised you to embark on an investment plan of $90 per month, and you were guaranteed to earn no interest at all. At the end of the

year, you would get back the $1,080 that you had paid in and not a penny more. You'd think such advice was rather absurd, wouldn't you?

The fact is that tens of millions of people do just that.

Of the more than 100 million individual tax returns filed annually, more than 80 percent get a refund from the government. The average refund check is more than $1,000. The reason these taxpayers get a refund check is that they have had more withheld by the employer than was necessary. The government holds these excess payments for the full year and then returns them to the taxpayers in the form of a refund check, once the taxpayers have filed their returns for the year.

Employers are required to withhold from workers' pay only enough to meet each worker's tax obligations for the year. Employers estimate the amount they must withhold based on information the employee provides on a W-4 form. Each employee completes a W-4 form when starting work with an employer. The W-4 form sets forth the number of allowances the employee is claiming. The *more* allowances an employee claims, the *less* is withheld from his or her pay.

What qualifies as an allowance? Most commonly, each exemption you claim on your tax return is equal to one allowance, and if you itemize your deductions, you are entitled to claim additional allowances.

W-4 forms contain a worksheet that will assist you in calculating the correct number of allowances. If you have been having too much withheld from your pay, a proper adjustment in your W-4 form can fatten your weekly paycheck. Then, rather than sending excess money to the government where it earns no interest all year long, you'll have that money to invest or spend as you see fit.

Year-end Strategies

As each year draws to a close, you should estimate your probable tax liability for the year compared to what it might be next year. The reason for doing this is to determine whether it would make sense to shift income or deductions from one year to another in order to cut your tax bill. The strategy behind such moves is to claim deductions in years in which you'd be more highly taxed, and to receive income in years when you'd be taxed less.

For example, if your tax rate or income is going to be lower next year (as is sometimes the case), it could make sense to delay year-end income from December of the current year into January of the next year. A drop in income from one year to the next can occur in many ways: a pay cut is in the offing; a spouse who was working may stop working; or you may have had an exceptionally high income this year due to bonuses, commissions, or capital gains, which are not likely to be repeated next year. Reason? It will be taxed at a lower rate next year, and you'll save money accordingly. It can also make sense to accelerate deductions. This means making deductible expenses this year that you'd otherwise make next year. A deduction is worth

more to you in a higher tax year than it is in a lower tax year. Shifting incomes or deductions need span only a few weeks—from late December into early January.

Examples of shifting income include year-end bonuses that can be declared or paid in early January instead of late December; payment for fees or services; sales that result in capital gains. Examples of deductions that can be shifted from one year to the next at year-end include charitable contributions; payment of state income taxes and local property taxes; interest expenses; medical and dental expenses.

Vice versa

On the other hand, it may happen that tax rates are scheduled to go *up* next year, or that your *income* is likely to *increase* substantially next year. In either of those cases, reverse strategies may be worthwhile. In other words, you might want to accelerate income (take it this year instead of next year) and delay paying deductible expenses.

Income Shifting

A family with children can cut their income taxes by making gifts of income-producing assets to the children. The tax saving is based on the assumption that children do not earn as much as their parents and are thus taxed in lower brackets or are not taxed at all.

In a given year, the first $500 of investment income received by each child is free of income tax. The second $500 of investment income received by each child is taxed at the child's tax rate, not the parents' tax rate. If a child is *under* 14 years of age, any investment income over $1,000 received by each child in a given year is taxed at the parents' tax rate (if the parents' tax rate is higher than the child's tax rate). If a child is 14 or over, investment income in excess of $1,000 a year continues to be taxed at the child's tax rate.

Here's an example of how this strategy works: You have a savings account of $6,000 earning 8 percent, or $480, per year. If you make a gift of that account to your child, the $480 of income (assuming it's the only income the child has) will escape federal income taxes. If the account were to remain in your name, you'd have to pay income taxes on the earnings each year of roughly $75 to $150.

Tax Shelters

At any given time, tax advantages may become available in a variety of investments and speculative schemes. It's up to the prudent investor and sensible taxpayer to examine any such opportunities thoroughly; to exercise

caution with respect to the enthusiasm of the salesperson; and to proceed with the knowledge that today's tax break could be eliminated tomorrow. If you do claim deductions or credits arising out of a tax shelter scheme, you increase your chances of being audited by the IRS. We'll examine that phenomenon more closely in the remainder of this chapter.

FILING YOUR RETURN

What happens if you are not able to file your return by the due date, or if you discover that a return that you did file was incorrect? The law does allow you an opportunity to get an extension on your filing date, and it also allows you to correct a return already filed if the need arises.

Filing Extensions

Taxpayers can get an automatic four-month extension for filing of their individual returns by filing a form 4868 with the Internal Revenue Service. This form must be filed by April 15 with the IRS center in your area. The extension of the time to file your return is *not* an extension of the time to pay the taxes. Your taxes must be fully paid at the time you file the extension form. You can incur a penalty if you've not paid your taxes by the time you file for the extension. Interest charges on late payments may also be imposed.

If you need more time beyond the automatic four-month extension, you may be able to get an additional extension by sending a letter to the Internal Revenue Service stating your reasons or by filing form 2688.

Amending Your Return

Once you've filed your return you can amend it later if you determine that you owe the government or that they owe you a refund.

The form to use to amend your return is a 1040X. Follow the 1040X instructions carefully, and attach any forms or schedules that are needed to explain the changes.

The law allows you ample time to file an amended return. You have three years from the date you filed your original return, or two years from the time you paid your tax, whichever is later, to file the amendment.

WHAT HAPPENS TO YOUR RETURN? EXAMINATIONS AND AUDITS

For about 95 percent of all individual taxpayers, the year's concerns end with the filing of the return and the payment of any taxes due. But for the

other 5 percent, the struggle is not over: about half of them will hear from the Internal Revenue Service with respect to arithmetic errors made on their return, and the other half will be subjected to some form of examination or audit.

Where errors in arithmetic are involved, the taxpayers will hear relatively quickly. But it may be two years, three years, or even longer before some audits are announced and resolved. The Internal Revenue Service generally has three years from the date you filed your return to assess additional taxes. If you have failed to report a substantial item of income, the IRS has six years from the filing of your return to claim back taxes. If someone has filed a return with false or fraudulent information intending to evade taxes, or if someone has failed to file a return at all, there is no time limit as to when the IRS can pursue its claim. But taxpayers are not totally at the mercy of the IRS. The law sets forth clear-cut rights for all taxpayers to appeal and protest decisions that go against them. Let's examine what happens once your return is filed.

The Initial Screenings

All returns are checked to determine that the arithmetic is correct and that any checks attached thereto have been properly completed and signed. If a mistake in arithmetic is discovered, the IRS recalculates the amount of tax due and sends you either a refund for the amount overpaid or a bill for the amount you owe them. If other corrections are needed (for example, you forgot to sign your return), you will be notified accordingly.

A further screening will be conducted to determine whether there are errors in the return with respect to deductions, exemptions, and the like. These are some of the most common areas in which errors are found:

- You have claimed deductions for medical expenses without taking into account the stated limitations in the law.
- You have claimed a partial exemption.
- Your reported income does not match the W-2 form your employer has provided, or the 1099 forms that have been provided by various brokers, dealers, and financial institutions. The IRS will cross-check the information it receives on 1099 forms with the information that you report. If you have failed to report any of that income, assume that the IRS knows about it.

If the IRS finds any such errors, you will be notified by mail of the correction. If you disagree with their findings, you can ask for a meeting with an IRS representative, or you can submit whatever information is necessary to support your claim. Matters such as these may be resolved fairly quickly after the filing of your return. But that does not mean you're off the hook with respect to a more detailed audit.

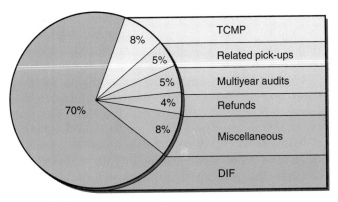

FIGURE 20–1 Reasons for audit selection

Audits

In recent years, the IRS has been auditing about 1 percent of all individual returns filed. Although this may suggest that your chances of being audited in a given year are only 1 in 100, bear in mind that that chance occurs every year, and sooner or later the law of averages might catch up with you.

Out of roughly 100 million returns filed each year, how does the IRS select the 1 million returns for actual auditing? Figure 20–1 illustrates the approximate breakdown of reasons the IRS used to choose returns for auditing.

Exercise 20.4

Discriminate Income Function (DIF)

About 70 percent of the returns chosen for audit are selected by the Discriminate Income Function, or DIF. Computers examine your total income, your adjusted gross income, your deductions, your adjustments and your credits. Based on past statistical evidence, agents can determine which returns have the greatest potential for recovering additional taxes through an audit.

The majority of DIF audits are conducted via correspondence. You may, for example, receive a letter requesting that you send photostats of checks, receipts, or other evidence to support your specific claims. If you can provide such evidence, the audit may be ended quickly. If you are unable to provide the evidence, an additional tax will be payable, or you may be requested to appear at the local IRS office. In some cases, the audit can be at your place of business or home, particularly if the records involved are extensive or if the matter is complex.

Taxpayer Compliance Measurement Program (TCMP)

About 8 percent of all returns chosen for audit are selected via the Taxpayer Compliance Measurement Program (TCMP). This is a random selection by

the IRS and is a much more comprehensive and thorough review of your overall situation. A TCMP audit can be very detailed and time-consuming, even if you have nothing at all to hide. The purposes of the TCMP program are to police the voluntary-compliance aspects of the law and to unearth more statistical data to support the DIF program.

Related Pick-ups

About 5 percent of those returns chosen for auditing are based on "related pick-ups." If, for instance, your business partner was chosen for audit, you might also be chosen; the questionable deductions claimed by the one partner might be suspect with regard to the other partner. In addition, if you have not reported all the income that your W-2 and 1099 forms show you actually received, this could be cause for an audit under this category.

Multiyear Audits

About 5 percent of those returns selected for audit are chosen because more than one return is in question. For example, if you had reported deductions from a real estate investment in your 1996 return, you might be audited for your 1995 and 1994 returns as well.

Refunds

About 4 percent of all taxpayers who claim refunds on their returns are audited for no other reason than to verify the facts that would allow a refund.

Miscellaneous

These audits can be searching for verification of capital gains transactions, appraisals of charitable contributions, appraisals of casualty losses, and so forth. The IRS also exchanges tax information with state taxing authorities, and a mismatch of information between your state and federal returns may also prompt an audit in this category.

Audit Red Flags

Aside from the aforementioned ways in which returns are chosen for audit, the following are generally regarded as common *red flags* that will prompt an IRS audit of your return.

- Excessive deductions claimed for travel and entertainment expenses
- Improper deductions claimed for the expense of maintaining an office in your home
- Losses arising out of what the IRS determines to be a "hobby," even though you determine such activity to be an ongoing business

Audit Strategies: Yours

Subconsciously or otherwise, the government has instilled a fear of the audit procedure in all of us. In so doing, they may hope to encourage taxpayers to be as honest and forthright as possible in preparing their returns, so as to avoid a possible audit. Whatever the reason for our fear of audits, the fact is that most audits really do not have to be feared, particularly if your return is honest and you have the documentation necessary to back up your claims.

Bear in mind that in an office audit you are dealing with another human being. Very likely, you will be treated in much the same way that you treat the auditing agent. If you are surly, don't be surprised if you are met with surliness. If you are pleasant, cooperative, and polite, chances are better that you'll be met with those same traits. If you arrive with your documents in well-organized fashion, you're going to make the agent's job that much easier, which in turn could make your examination that much easier.

If a reasonably small amount of money is involved, you may feel comfortable in handling the audit proceedings on your own. If, however, a substantial amount of money might be involved, consider hiring an accountant or tax attorney to assist you. If you have had a tax preparer do your return initially, that person would be the likely candidate to assist you with the audit.

An audit proceeding is a legal entanglement. Your legal rights and the government's legal rights are in apparent opposition. As in any legal entanglement, you must determine what your likely overall costs will be in terms of money, time, and aggravation. If you feel that your case is weak, it might be better to resolve the matter quickly, pay the tax due (or a lesser negotiated amount if you're able to do so), and save yourself time and aggravation. On the other hand, if you feel that your case is strong and there is enough money involved, you might deem it worthwhile to fight the matter all the way. The IRS looks at the matter in much the same way: the agent's time and energy must be evaluated in line with the hoped-for amount of back taxes that can be recovered. Thus, negotiations are always a possibility.

Audit Strategies: Theirs

An auditing agent of the IRS is expected to produce tax revenues as efficiently as possible. The IRS denies that there is any "quota" as to how much a given agent should produce; but a good agent should justify his or her work by producing as much revenue as possible in the most cost-efficient way. It might be assumed that a good agent, considering a contested amount of, say, $500, might be willing to accept perhaps $350 on the spot rather than to go for the whole $500 over a protracted period of protests and appeals. In short, negotiations are possible, and your success in them will be in direct proportion to the strength of your case.

Be assured that an efficient agent will probe to determine just what your strengths and weaknesses may be. Following, for example, are some of the interrogation guidelines that an agent might use.

- With respect to claims for charitable deductions, the agent will attempt to determine whether the payments were made to properly qualified organizations. If property was contributed, the agent will seek to verify the true fair market value of the property at the time it was given.
- With respect to claimed deductions for interest payments, the agent will ascertain whether the interest payments were made on a valid, existing debt that you, the taxpayer, owed. This may necessitate your providing copies of all the documents relating to the loan agreement.
- With respect to claims for medical deductions, the agent will seek to determine whether any insurance reimbursement has been made to you or is expected by you, and will also probe to be certain that amounts you've claimed as child-care expenses aren't also claimed as medical expenses.
- If a deduction is claimed for a casualty or theft loss, the agent will attempt to determine that a theft or casualty loss has actually occurred and that your loss was the direct result of such an occurrence. The agent will also determine whether insurance proceeds have been received by you or are expected by you.
- If you claim a deduction for educational purposes, it will be the agent's job to determine if your expenses were incurred primarily for the purpose of maintaining or improving skills, or for meeting requirements for retaining your job status. This may necessitate evidence from your employer.
- If you've claimed alimony expenses as an adjustment to your income, the agent may request a copy of the underlying divorce documents for inspection.

These are just a random sampling of the *preliminary* probes you should expect the agent to make. If you are armed with all the necessary documentation at the initial meeting, you might be able to bring the audit to a swift conclusion. If you can't document your claims immediately, the agent will give you a reasonable time to collect the necessary documents and will schedule a future meeting at which the matter should be resolved.

Resolving an Audit: You Agree

If you and the agent agree on the findings at your initial meeting—which could take less than an hour—ask the agent to tell you how much in additional taxes you owe. You will then be asked to sign an agreement, and shortly thereafter you will receive a written report plus a bill for whatever

taxes you may owe, plus any interest or penalties that have been agreed on. Note that if you sign the agreement, you waive your rights to appeal in the future. If paying the back taxes in one lump sum will cause a hardship for you, you can ask the agent to put the payments on an installment plan. You have to ask for this, for it's unlikely that they'll volunteer it.

Resolving an Audit: You Disagree

If you are unable to settle the matter in the IRS office audit, you should immediately ask for a written copy of your legal rights under such circumstances. Where disagreement occurs, you can ask for an immediate meeting with a supervisor, with the hope that such a meeting may result in a more favorable compromise.

If you don't reach an agreement with the supervisor, the agent will then send you a report explaining the additional tax liability. You then have the right to request a conference at the district level to see if the matter can be resolved. If a settlement still isn't reached at the conference, you'll then receive a Notice of Deficiency, which is commonly referred to as a "90-day-letter." In this letter, the government notifies you that you will be assessed the additional tax owed ninety days from the date the letter was mailed.

If you still believe that your case is valid, you have ninety days in which to choose one of three courses to further your appeal.

- You can file a petition with the tax court.
- You can pay the tax that the government claims is due and file a refund claim for it. If the refund claim is turned down, you can then sue for your refund in either a federal district court or the court of claims.
- If the amount of the tax is $5,000 or less, you can proceed in the Small Claims Division of the tax court.

The first two choices would be more suitable for claims involving substantial sums of money; and you'd likely need professional representation. In the Small Claims Division procedures are relatively informal and, in many instances, you can plead your own case.

The IRS has been taking a liberal attitude about making compromises with taxpayers who owe overdue amounts. In one recent year the IRS received about 50,000 offers of compromise from delinquent taxpayers. (up from 10,000 two years earlier) and it accepted 18,000 of the 50,000 offers. The total amount the IRS accepted as compromise was $209 million; the original amounts owed totaled $1.38 billion! That's less than 20 cents on the dollar.

As with all tax matters, rules and regulations are subject to change from time to time. If you find yourself involved in a tax dispute, make certain that you know your rights as they currently exist.

STRATEGIES FOR SUCCESS

Bugged by Auditor? Ask for a New One

Most income tax auditing takes place by mail. There's only a remote chance that you will be called upon to deal face to face with an IRS auditor. If you are, and if there is enough money at stake, you might well want to have professional help accompany you. Tension can be high, and personalities can clash when auditor meets taxpayer. Many taxpayers may feel intimidated, "stressed out" by the mere fact of an audit. This can impair your ability to present your own position. If you do feel uncomfortable with the auditor assigned to your case, you *can* ask to have that auditor replaced by another one. Talk to the local IRS supervisor and present your request. There's no guarantee that you'll like the new one either, but at least there is an opportunity to cut the tension. It can work in your favor. But you have to ask for it.

Your Best Protection

There is nothing that can insulate you better from the rigors of a tax audit than an accurate return accompanied by all proper documentation for all claims made. If you have those in hand, an audit should be nothing more than a minor inconvenience. If you lack either a correct return or the proper documentation, an audit can become a major source of stress—not only might you have to pay back taxes, plus possible interest and penalties; the proceedings can also interfere with your day-do-day life. It may seem tempting to put some extra money in your pocket by evading taxes. But the consequences of doing so can ultimately be costly.

PERSONAL ACTION WORKSHEET ─────────────────────

Updating Tax Information

You should complete this checklist *before* you read Chapter 20. The information you will gather in completing the checklist will help you to complete the current year's tax returns accurately and quickly.

The information you need to complete this checklist is available in the most recent IRS instructions for the 1040 form as well as in the most recent IRS Publication 17, "Your Federal Income Tax."

Fill in the blanks as they apply to the current tax year:

- **Who Must File a Return?** You must file a return: if you are single, under 65, and had a gross income of $_____ for the year; if you are single, 65 or over, and had a gross income of $_____ for the year; if you are married, both spouses under 65, and had a combined gross income for the year of $_____ ; if you are married, one spouse 65 or older, and had a gross income of $_____ ; if you are self-employed (part-time or full-time); if you had net earnings from self-employment of $_____ or more.

- **Exemptions** The value of each exemption for the current year is $_____ . Generally, if you wish to claim someone as a dependent, that person's gross income for the year may not exceed $_____ . (See exceptions for children and full-time students.)

- **Standard deduction** For married persons filing jointly, and for qualifying widow(er)s: $_____ ; for singles, or heads of household: $_____ ; for married persons filing separately: $_____ .

- **Expenses** Estimate your own actual expenses subject to the tax law limitations in effect for the year: medical and dental expenses that are not reimbursed by insurance, by your employer, or otherwise $_____ ; taxes paid for which deductions are allowable $_____ ; interest paid, including home mortgage, and other debts for which interest is deductible $_____ ; charitable contributions $_____ ; casualty or theft losses not reimbursed by insurance or otherwise $_____ ; other deductions $_____ .

See the text and IRS instructions for specific details. If the total of proper itemized deductions exceeds the standard deduction for your filing status, you should itemize your deductions.

CONSUMER ALERT

Some Tax "Helpers" Can Harm You

Exercise 20.5

Every year without fail—usually between Super Bowl Day and Groundhog Day—the landscape in every town becomes littered with Income Tax preparation signs and newsstands are overloaded with books offering do-it-yourself guidelines for completing your tax returns.

Care should be taken in choosing either a tax preparer or a book. With respect to the preparers, beware of high-sounding promises that they can "guarantee" you lower taxes. The most any preparer can guarantee you is an accurate return, based on the information you provide. Preparers can't create deductions where none legally exist. They must follow the same rules that you must.

Compare prices carefully. Some advertise very low prices, but those might be only for the simplest forms, and extras can add up quickly. Determine, before you commit yourself, what the *total* price will be for the service.

Fly-by-night preparers have been a problem, both for the public and for the IRS. Some have filed false or erroneous returns, leaving the taxpayer to answer to the IRS. Others have pocketed their customer's tax payment or refund checks and disappeared into the night.

Tax preparation services can be helpful, but you must use care in selecting one. How long has it been in business? What personal recommendations can you get from satisfied customers? Don't overlook the regular full-time accountants who don't advertise. They may be no more expensive than the seasonal services, and they're available to assist you all year.

As for the books, some of them are nothing more than reprints of official IRS books that you can obtain at little or no cost from the nearest IRS office. Worthwhile books include J.K. Lasser's *Your Income Tax* and the H. & R. Block annual tax guide. The Lasser book is very comprehensive; the Block book offers an easy step-by-step guide to completing the returns.

Preparers and books aside, though, nobody can help you better than yourself: your ongoing knowledge of and attention to the income tax laws is your best assurance of keeping your taxes as low as possible.

Why Income Taxes Go Up and Down

Many, if not most, taxpayers face a rollercoaster of changes every few years. Tax laws change. Your eligibility for deductions changes. (For example, you become a homeowner instead of a renter.) Your number of exemptions changes. (You have a new child.) Your filing status changes. (You get married or divorced.) Your income changes. (You get a raise or your spouse gets fired.) All of these events can mean higher or lower taxes from one year to the next. But there are more substantial aspects of public and governmental policy that strongly influence how we are taxed.

Taxation as a business incentive Tax breaks given to certain industries can stimulate desired activity. Oil drilling, real estate development, and high-tech research have all benefited from tax breaks when the nation needed the end results: petroleum, housing, space exploration, and so on. When those tax breaks are in place, the companies and their employees benefit, but at the expense of other taxpayers. Sooner or later those favored industries lose their breaks and others get them.

Taxation as a social policy California passed a steep tax on tobacco products. The revenues were used for nonsmoking advertising. The advertising was so successful that more people quit smoking than had been anticipated. This resulted in such a sharp drop in income from the tobacco tax that the education program had to be curtailed.

Taxation in reaction to international events How much was defense spending cut as a result of the collapse of the former Soviet Union? How much of those spending cuts were used to reduce the burden on U.S. taxpayers? Or was the money saved from defense cuts (at the expense of defense workers) used to boost some other sector of economic activity (education, health care, welfare, research) to the benefit of those who worked in those fields? In short, some people's taxes can go up and down, while other people's job opportunities ride on the other side of the seesaw.

Taxation in response to special interest groups It has long been argued whether cutting capital gains tax rates benefits the rich at the expense of the poor. Some argue that lowering capital gains tax rates pushes the tax burden onto those who have no investments. Others say that cutting the tax rates frees investment dollars for economic growth, increasing the wealth of everyone. Both sides lobby Congress ferociously for their respective causes, resulting in changes to the capital gains tax rates over the years.

Taxation as a political football As with the capital gains issue, the political parties profoundly stress that their tax proposals are better for the public than those of the other party. And taxation can thus go up and down with the fortunes of the respective parties.

Taxation in response to economic trends   When the economy slows down, as in a recession, tax revenues fall—fewer people working means less income taxes being paid. If government spending is not reduced accordingly, then taxes must be increased on the remaining workers to pay the cost of government programs. The alternative is for the government to borrow more, which will put a heavier tax burden on taxpayers years down the road. As the economy grows, so do tax revenues. That increased revenue can be used either to lower taxes or to increase government spending.

?   *WHAT IF . . . ?*

Test yourself: How would you deal with these real-life possibilities?

1. You add up all your expenses for the past year that are deductible on your tax return. You find that your itemized deductions are $50 more than your standard deduction. To claim the itemized deductions you must file form 1040, instead of one of the simpler forms. Would you itemize? If so, why? If not, why not? What if the itemized deductions were $100 more than the standard deduction? $300?

2. Your spouse, whose earnings are about the same as yours, will not be working for at least one-half of next year. What year-end tax-planning strategies can you utilize this year that would affect your income taxes? Reverse the situation: your spouse has worked only half of this year but next year will work full time. What strategies can benefit you taxwise?

3. Last year the amount that was withheld from your pay for income taxes was $4,200. Your tax bill was actually $3,100, making your refund $1,100. What are the advantages and disadvantages of this situation? What can you do to modify the arrangement?

NUMBER CRUNCHERS

Exercise 20.6

Do the calculations to make decisions in these real-life possibilities.

1. Using the *current-year tax tables,* calculate the taxes due in the following cases: (a) a single person with total income of $24,500, adjustments to income of $1,300, standard deduction, one personal exemption; (b) a married couple filing jointly with total income of $56,700, adjustments to income of $3,300, itemized deductions of $9,350, five personal exemptions; (c) a head of household with total income of $37,900, adjustments to income of $680, standard deduction, two personal exemptions.

2. Based on current law, calculate how much deduction can be taken in the following cases: (a) for medical expenses, when the taxpayer had an adjusted gross income of $32,000 and unreimbursed medical expenses of $4,100; (b) for "miscellaneous deductions," when the taxpayer had an adjusted gross income of $46,500 and had spent $660 on continuing education expenses, $427 on work uniforms and tools, $175 on union dues, and $634 on his homeowner's insurance.

3. With $10,000 to invest you can earn 6 percent on a high-quality tax-exempt bond that has twenty years to run, or 7.5 percent on a federally insured savings plan for three years at your local bank. If your income is taxed at 15 percent, which of these plans will give you a better return? What if your income is taxed at 28 percent? What else should you consider before making your choice?

FOR BETTER OR FOR WORSE

Things beyond our control often impact our personal and financial well-being, for better or for worse. Some are more predictable than others. How could you be affected if the following real-life phenomena happened? Could you have seen it coming? What steps could you have taken to minimize damage or maximize advantage? The better able you are to anticipate and recognize these forces, the better equipped you are to deal with them.

1. You do some freelance work, for which you're paid $1,000. The person who hired you neglects to send you a 1099 form by the required time. So you don't report the income on your return. Months later, the employer tardily sends you the 1099 showing the $1,000 you were paid the previous year.

2. During the year you win $5,000 at the race track. You know that you can offset gambling winnings with gambling losses for tax purposes. So next trip to the track you go about picking up losing tickets after every race to substantiate $5,000 in losses. A stranger in a suit observes you and asks what you're doing. You've heard that the IRS has agents posted at all the tracks, so you don't say a word and walk away with your pocket full of losing tickets.

3. You know that your brother plays fast and loose with his income taxes, evading anything he thinks he can get away with. So far, he's been lucky. You've always been 100 percent honest with all of your tax matters. He invites you to go into a business deal with him. It looks too good to be true, mainly because it involves some tax dodge. But he assures you that if the IRS comes after you for any taxes, he'll pay them on your behalf.

Exercise 20.7

Working for Yourself

If you wish in this world to advance, your merits you're bound to enhance. You must stir it and stump it and blow your own trumpet, or trust me, you haven't a chance.

W.S. Gilbert

A man's reach should exceed his grasp, or what's a heaven for?

Robert Browning

Almost everyone has said, at one time or another, "Take this job and shove it! I'd be better off working for myself."

Many people go off on their own and, after hard work and persistence (and often a dose of good fortune), achieve satisfaction in their own business or professional practice. That satisfaction can be a mix of financial success and psychological fulfillment. Many others dive into the deep end, poorly prepared and undercapitalized, and sooner than later face failure. Still others vex and perplex themselves for years, wondering, "Could I? Should I?"—never coming to a conclusion; never scratching the itch to become their own boss.

And then there are those who have already taken the plunge in their own business, but they are unsettled and disturbed that it's not working out the way they had hoped.

This chapter will present:

- The basic considerations that any would-be entrepreneur must take to heart, not just in the planning stages but on an ongoing basis

- The pros and cons of self-employment: the risks that must be faced in order to reap the benefits of independence and financial gain

- Sources of important information on planning and executing a new business venture

This material is only a starting point. The lessons herein may stimulate some to take the chance of a lifetime and embark on the perilous journey of self-employment. And it may prove so precautionary that others will be deterred from doing so, and they might well be grateful for having been forewarned. In any case, you will have at least become familiar with essential elements that make our free-market economy run: entrepreneurism, risk-taking, and the role of capital.

WHEN IS A GOOD TIME TO START A NEW VENTURE?

Many factors will flash "red light" or "green light" with respect to getting started. These same factors may also indicate to a floundering business just why it is floundering.

Personal Factors

Do a lot of self-evaluation and homework before you even think of becoming a successful entrepreneur. Consider the following:

Inflated Expectations

The prospect of being your own boss is exhilarating. Indeed, common sense can fly out the window when one anticipates the joys of self-employment: no more boss to face every day (other than when you look in the mirror); no more timeclock to punch (though you may miss the regular paycheck that is activated by that timeclock); more income than you ever dreamed possible (though those dreams can turn into nightmares); and, above all, freedom! (except when you're beholden to your customers, creditors, landlord, suppliers, and governmental regulators).

In short, when the harsh light of reality shines on your expectations, they may not look as attractive as you had thought. Expectations have a way of getting inflated, sometimes inordinately so, and that can interfere with the process of making sound judgments. Expectations can also be further inflated by well-meaning friends and relatives who, wishing you well, get on the bandwagon without knowing the risks and pitfalls you may be facing. They might tell you what you *want* to hear, not what you *should* hear.

Evaluate your expectations honestly and frankly. You don't get a green light for self-employment until those expectations are reasonable and attainable.

What Do You Really Want to Be When You Grow Up?

Is your ambition based on a solid foundation, or on something that may be frivolous and, therefore, dangerous? Are you aiming for a self-employed career that was born out of an impractical, youthful fantasy? Are you striving to be on your own just to prove a point to someone else, rather than genuinely attempting to reach the greatest potential that your skills and aptitude will allow? Are you honestly seeking a life of self-employment for its own sake, or are you just running away from a bad situation at work, or a troubled home life, hoping that working for yourself will cure those problems? This is the time for serious soul-searching, and the light stays red until you've done it—then let it simmer for a few months and do it again. Vocational aptitude tests might also be in order to help you determine if your ambitions and your capabilities are well-suited to each other.

What Are You Giving Up?

Life is a series of compromises. Leaving a regular job to go on your own entails a lot of trade-offs. You must evaluate giving up a regular paycheck for a questionable inflow of money. You must evaluate giving up the security of fringe benefits—pension, health plan, etc.—for the uncertainty of do-it-yourself protection. You must evaluate giving up a somewhat-predictable ladder of advancement for a totally unpredictable future. This is more than just a whimsical matter. It requires hard and serious number crunching, and the light stays red until you've done it.

Credit

Unless your credit history is squeaky clean you are asking for heartache as an entrepreneur. Landlords, suppliers, lenders, investors, and advertising media will likely shun you unless you have a good track record in the bill-paying department. Until your credit history sparkles: red light.

What's Your Fallback?

It's cruel to make you consider what your situation will be if your business venture fails, but it would be more cruel to let you go off on your own without making sure that you've asked, *and answered,* all the necessary "what-if?" questions. These include:

- "What if I run out of money before I've reached a plateau of success?"
- "What if my venture fails and I find I can't go back to my old job, or get another good job?"
- "What if—despite the money I might be making—I find out that I don't really like working for myself?"

- "What if everything in my new business is going along nicely, but the demands of work are interfering with my family life?"
- "What if my partner, with whom I thought I had an incredible bond, and without whom I thought the business couldn't succeed, turns out to be a totally unreliable and incompetent jerk?"

Energy Sources

The regular job was a nine-to-fiver, plus some overtime now and then. Self-employment must be a labor of love, and there can't be any such thing as "work hours." At least until you're well established and can afford an easier regimen, you might be on call around the clock. Those might not necessarily be hours in the office or shop. They might be hours in the middle of the night when you lie awake worrying whether that big job will come through, or whether the bank will lend you what you need to buy new equipment, or whether the landlord will give you an extra week to pay the rent, or whether you'll get paid by the sharpy you think may have conned you last week.

Working for yourself requires energies that you may never have had to tap before. How deep are your sources? How much energy can you devote to your work without interfering with your other personal interests? It's tough to know the answers to these questions until you're actually in the fray, but no green light until you've pondered this tricky issue.

The Business Plan: Don't Leave Your Regular Job Without It

It is *mandatory* to have a *Business Plan* before you venture out on your own. A Business Plan, most simply stated, is a serious and carefully drawn roadmap of where you want to get to. It is goals, priorities, and hard numbers that will tell you what it will take to get to your destination. Any lender or investor from whom you seek financial support will insist on seeing your Business Plan. (If one doesn't, be suspect. He might not be discerning enough to help you see the possible dangers in your venture, which could just hasten the onset of serious problems.)

Your banker or the Small Business Administration can give you specific material that will help you create your own business plan.

The Small Business Administration (SBA)

Exercise 21.1

The SBA is a federal agency with offices in most cities. It exists to help small businesses get up and running, and stay running. It can help you get loans. It has abundant data on many types of businesses. It provides counseling services. In short, it is invaluable to the would-be entrepreneur, and you can't get a green light until you've visited your nearest office and taken advantage of all it has to offer. Banks, libraries, and bookstores also have information relevant to your particular needs.

To answer the overriding question at the start of this chapter: Once you get green lights flashing simultaneously on all of the preceding items—plus those that follow—*then* is a good time to start a new venture.

Economic Factors

As ready as you may feel—and be—on a personal level, there are forces at work in the economy that may dictate whether it's wise to proceed.

Growth or Recession?

Don't try to swim up a waterfall. If the nation, or your region, is suffering through a recession, that does not bode well for new business ventures. On the other hand, if times are good there is reason to feel encouraged about a new venture. The tides of the economy ebb and flow, so *anticipatory* timing is critical. Base your decisions on what you think the state of the economy will be when you're ready to launch your venture, which may be months, or even a year or two, from today. Yes, accurate crystal balls are hard to come by, but if you're a good student of the economic trends (see chapter 1), you should be able to sense opportunities as they ebb and flow.

Specific Industry Trends

Be aware of any particular trends in the field of your endeavor that could impact on your business venture. While the national or regional economy may be moving in one direction, specific industries may have different forces at work. For example: housing (and all its related components, such as furniture, appliances, lumber, decor, and so on) may be in a boom or bust cycle out of sync with the rest of the economy. The same can hold true in automotive, electronics, leisure and recreation, health care, financial services, aviation, and many other industries. And these trends may vary from locale to locale, which in turn can be of importance to you.

Some business ventures are subject to fads and technological change, and you must take care to avoid traps that can arise as a result. Franchising has its share of fads. At one time it was fast foods, and for every successful McDonald's and KFC there were countless Beauty Burgers and Chicken Pickin's that failed. Then there was the frozen yogurt hoopla and the quick-lube shop phenomena that left the highways littered with more failures.

In the fast-track world of technology, will video rental stores be rendered obsolete if video-on demand through your telephone becomes a reality, as some are predicting? Will the automotive industry be revolutionized by the advent of electric engines? Will books be replaced by digitized readable

discs, and bookstores thus merged into electronic/music outlets? The future gets here quicker than we think, and any investments that depend on continuity can be distorted by rapid changes in technology.

To the extent that your venture may be impacted by technological change, you must anticipate how you can avoid being hurt by change, and how you can profitably anticipate change.

Easy Money?

Another trend that can't be avoided is the ever-changing cost of money: interest rates. To the extent that you may be a borrower—either directly from lenders or indirectly, as in having your suppliers extend credit to you—the cost of money can have a major impact on your financial well-being. The easy availability of money—regardless of the cost—can also be a consideration. There are times when lenders tighten their purse strings and make borrowing difficult. Businesses that need to borrow during tight money times can easily find themselves in a most uncomfortable bind. One step to avoid the problem is to arrange for an open line of credit that you can draw against whenever you need to. For small business venturers who own their own homes, a home-equity line of credit can be an ideal way to get protection against tight money times.

Changing Neighborhoods

If your venture requires a specific kind of location, you must evaluate the possibilities of change in the various locations. Timing plays a key role in choosing a location. If you can get into a good location that's on the upswing, and you can lock in a good long-term rental rate, you have the best of both worlds. On the other hand, if a location seems cheap, be wary of the possibility that it may be a decaying area, and moving in might turn out to be a fiasco.

Some other factors to consider:

- If you depend on traffic (foot or vehicular), are any changes in traffic patterns likely to take place in the foreseeable future?
- If you're in a shopping mall and depend on a "magnet" enterprise (such as a major department store or food store), determine if the magnet is likely to remain in place. Your fortunes may be tied to the magnet, and if the magnet shuts down, you may have to do the same. On the other hand, if a weak magnet is about to be replaced by a strong one, that may offer you a very attractive opportunity.
- If your success depends on having clientele with particular demographics (age, income levels, etc.), you want to find a location that will have a stable population representing those demographics.
- You must consider competition as a factor of location. Some kinds of businesses can thrive while in the midst of competitors (a fast-food

stand in the food court of a shopping mall, for example), while others will do better being far away from competitors (a video rental store, for example). It's extremely difficult to control who might move in across the street from you, but in a shopping mall you might be able to get some exclusivity to prevent competitors from being too close.

- Nonretail businesses, such as offices, repair shops, and manufacturing and service facilities, might not be quite as sensitive to changing conditions in a location, but they cannot be overlooked. All businesses must consider the current and future situation regarding parking, loading access, customer access, noise and other pollution, security, and overall appearance of a given area.

While You Wait . . .

As you're carefully watching and waiting for all of these various personal and economic factors to fall into place at approximately the same time, you'll also have to do your homework on the following issues.

TAKING THE LEAP

Choices, choices—and you thought this was going to be easy. As part of your overall planning you must decide on the *legal status* and *start-up form* of your venture. They are two distinctly different matters, and the decisions you make can be critical to your success. Let's examine each.

STRATEGIES FOR SUCCESS

Try It on for Size

Before you embark on any self-employment venture, give it a test run. Do it before you quit your current job, so that you haven't given up anything if the test run tells you that you don't really like the business you thought you'd be so happy with. If you've always wanted to be a travel agent / landscaper / interior decorator / restaurateur / retailer / sales rep / disc jockey / financial planner / whatever. . . . Get a part-time job doing that work for someone else—weekends, perhaps, or evenings. Or do it on your vacation. Or maybe you can get a leave of absence from your current job for a month or so; try on your new career during that time. Get the feel of the rhythms and the stresses of the business. Get a sense of how the work flows, from the initial paperwork down to depositing the payment check when the job is completed. Do it for nothing if you can't get paid for it; the time alone that you invest can bring huge returns in terms of learning experience.

The Legal Status of Your Venture

There are a number of ways you can establish yourself in a business entity. You must discuss the specific legal ramifications of each option with your attorney to determine how the law applies to you, and how it affects your rights. By way of overview, these are the main options, starting with the simplest and working our way up to the most complicated.

Temping

Being a temp, or in a newer format, a leased employee, is perhaps the simplest way to be relatively on your own. A temp may work at a number of different places over the course of time; a leased employee may stay on one job for a lengthy period. In either case you may still be considered an employee in the strict sense of the word. The temp agency or the employee-leasing company pays you and takes the necessary deductions from your check. Temps are less likely to have such benefits as health insurance or a pension plan; leased employees might be better able to negotiate those fringes. Workers' Compensation should be in place to protect you if your are hurt in the line of work. You must also inquire as to what unemployment benefits might exist.

It's essential that you determine the reputation of any placement agency. If the agency fails to pay promptly or to send the payroll deductions to the government, you could be in for some major headaches. Temping might be a good bridge between full employment and full self-employment for many would-be entrepreneurs who want to make their big move one small step at a time.

Independent Contractor

Independent contractors are people who provide services to an individual or business on a direct one-on-one basis. The users pay the contractors directly, and the contractors are responsible for their own payroll taxes, Workers' Compensation, fringe benefits, and public liability insurance.

Many corporations use independent contractors for a wide variety of services: engineering, accounting, sales, marketing consultancy, and so on. For the user corporations there are many advantages, most notably not having to pay for fringe benefits or Social Security taxes, not having to deduct withholding taxes, and not having to provide pensions, Workers' Compensation, or unemployment insurance. Not having to administer all of these matters can save user corporations large sums of money.

For the independent contractors there is a sense of freedom and a chance to move ahead in accordance with one's own potentials, as opposed to being limited by a corporate hierarchy.

It would appear to be a win–win situation, but it's not that simple. The

Internal Revenue Service has something to say about who qualifies as an independent contractor for tax purposes. In the IRS view true independent contractors are those who provide services for a variety of clients, who set their own work schedules, and who use their own tools of trade. The IRS takes a tough position on allowing users to avoid paying withholding taxes by claiming that some workers are independent contractors. If a claimed independent contractor does not meet *all* of the IRS standards, the IRS will disallow the user's claims. That can put the independent contractors back into employee status, whether they like it or not.

It's therefore incumbent on you to determine if your claim to be an independent contractor will jibe with IRS requirements. If not, you're not as free as you'd want to be.

As an independent contractor you'll have to pay your income taxes on a quarterly basis—see IRS form 1040ES and the equivalent state form. You'll report your income from work on Schedule C of the 1040. As a self-employed person, you'll be eligible for the attractive retirement benefits of Keogh, or HR-10, plans.

Sole Proprietorship

For manufacturers and retailers the simplest form of doing business is as a sole proprietor.

You may choose to do business just in your own name or under a business name. The latter will require you to meet local legal requirements for doing business under an assumed name, known more commonly as "getting a D.B.A." (doing business as . . .). This usually requires advertising your assumed name in a local newspaper and paying the proper fees. Get details from your local city clerk's office. Any other local business license fees will also have to be paid.

As a sole proprietor you are personally liable for any harm you cause to anyone in the course of doing business. Depending on the amount of risk you're willing to take, you might want to acquire an insurance policy to protect you. The same conditions hold true for independent contractors.

Sole proprietors are required to pay their income taxes on the quarterly estimated basis (IRS from 1040ES), and they report their income on Schedule C. Many start-up businesses lose money in the first years of operation—indeed, on a broad average it takes about 28 months for new ventures to *break even*. The IRS also keeps an eye on this, and if a business reports losses consistently over a period of a few years, they may take the position that the enterprise is not really a business, but a hobby. And as a hobby, the losses would not be deductible. This could be devastating to the new venture.

Here's an example: You claim to be in the business of buying and selling baseball cards. You claim deductions for expenses incurred in visiting sports shows, entertaining potential "customers" who you take to dinner often, plus telephone, office and equipment costs. These costs are never as

much as what you earn from selling cards, so you report a loss year after year on your income tax return. Very likely the I.R.S. will deem your activity to be a hobby, not a business. In addition to disallowing your deductions, you'd have to pay back taxes, interest and possible penalties for previous years in which the same conditions prevailed.

The I.R.S. has used a "3 out of 5" rule to generally distinguish between a business and a hobby. If you can show a profit in three years out of five, you have a better chance of being regarded as a business than as a hobby. In recent years court decisions have begun to nibble away at the "3 out of 5" rule, giving taxpayers a little more room. But there's no assurance how you'll be treated if you're audited on this subject.

The best precautions are to make sure you have all the trappings of a business: a written and updated Business Plan; copies of any advertising, public relations and any other efforts you've undertaken to show that you're an ongoing business; a well-detailed diary showing how much time you've put into the business; copies of all business licenses, DBA certificates and any other legal documents that validate your claim as an ongoing business. And by all means keep a separate bank account, along with copies of all business-related checks you've written (wages, rent, utilities, advertising, etc.).

Exercise 21.3

Self-employed persons are eligible for a particularly attractive type of do-it-yourself pension program called a Keogh, or HR-10, plan. This allows you to put a considerable amount—roughly 25 percent—of your self-employment income into a retirement plan. The amount that you put away each year is tax deductible, and the earnings are tax-deferred. This is similar to IRA plans (see chapter 18), except that a much larger amount can be put into a Keogh plan than an IRA each year.

Sole proprietors and independent contractors should discuss all tax implications with their appropriate advisors.

Partnerships

This is as much a matter of chemistry as it is of law. If you're launching your self-employment with one or more other people, you should have an agreement setting forth all of your rights and obligations, including: Who is contributing what to the venture (labor, ideas, money, property) and what is it to be worth? Who will be entitled to take out how much (money, property) at what times and under what circumstances? Who is to perform what services? Who is entitled to what if the partnership is terminated? Negotiating these issues will tell you a lot about the chemistry between you, for better or for worse. If these matters are not reduced to writing, you are in for painful arguments when questions of money arise. You can buy fill-in-the-blank partnership forms, but the better way to structure your agreement is through a lawyer.

Partnerships are required to file tax returns, but they are for informational purposes only. Partnerships file Form 1065, and individuals report

their own partnership income or loss on Schedule K of the 1040. Partners are individually liable for harm to others and are subject to the same tax implications as those for sole proprietors.

Corporations

Forming a corporation can be a complex and costly matter, and the benefits of doing so might not offset the costs until your business is grossing around $200,000 to $300,000 a year.

A corporation is a legal entity in its own right. It can sue and be sued. It pays taxes. It must comply with many difficult laws and regulations. Corporations are creatures of the laws of your state. But in many ways a corporation may also be subject to federal laws; if you have a corporate pension plan, for example, you will have to file voluminous forms with the U.S. Department of Labor, plus additional tax forms with the IRS.

There are two primary reasons why businesses incorporate. The first regards personal liability. If, say, a customer is harmed by some act of the corporation, it is the corporation, and not the individuals behind it, that bears the brunt of liability. In other words, the corporation gets sued and not you. If the corporation does not have any "worth," then a suing party can collect little or nothing.

However, it is well established that individuals can't hide from personal liability behind a corporate veil. A court can "pierce the corporate veil" and hold individuals liable for acts of the corporation. This can also hold true for debts that the corporation owes: individuals will not necessarily escape liability for their corporation's debts if a court finds impropriety in the facts of the case. So, the limitations on liability that are offered by incorporating are certainly not guaranteed.

The other main reason for incorporating is to benefit from the liberal pension programs that a corporation can offer its officers and employees. These benefits can exceed what the generous Keogh plans allow, which in turn exceed what employees can get under their IRA and 401(k) plans. But take fair warning: the paperwork and the legal regulations are a nightmare, and compliance can be costly. You should not entertain forming a corporation for pension purposes unless you're certain that the corporate benefits clearly exceed the Keogh benefits you could otherwise have.

Whether you set up a regular corporation or a Sub-Chapter S Corporation, which is designed for a smaller number of persons, you will need ongoing legal and accounting assistance. Know in advance what these costs will be before you take the plunge.

THE START-UP FORM OF YOUR VENTURE

You can get underway either by starting from scratch or by buying an existing entity. Let's look at some of the complexities you'll have to deal with in evaluating your start-up choices.

Leases

Unless you're going to work at home or float around to various customers' places of business, you're going to need premises—office, store, workshop, whatever. You can rent a place or buy a place. For purposes of this discussion, let's eliminate buying as an option; until your business is on solid footing it can be unwise to tie up capital in premises.

If you're starting from scratch, either on your own or in a franchise, you'll enter into a lease from scratch. If you're taking over an existing entity, you'll take over an existing lease, assuming that the existing lease gives you that right. If it doesn't, you'll have to negotiate that matter with the landlord.

The best lease from the tenant's standpoint is one that gives you short commitments with a lot of renewal options. A one-year lease with four one-year renewal options can be preferable to a five-year lease, even if the rental cost on the options is higher than with the straight five-year plan. Why? Because the options give you *flexibility*. You're just starting out, and flexibility—to be able to move, to close down, to possibly expand—is one of the most valuable assets the budding entrepreneur can have.

Evaluate lease costs from two standpoints: *gross* and *net*. In a gross lease the landlord provides all services: utilities, janitor, maintenance, and repairs. In a net lease, the tenant is responsible for all of those costs. Your base rent will be much higher with a gross lease, but that covers all the services. If you have a choice, and you're confident that you can control your own occupancy costs efficiently, the net lease might be the better choice.

Many commercial leases have percentage clauses. These require the tenant to pay a certain percentage of their income as rent, in addition to the base rent. A percentage clause might say that the tenant is to pay 2 percent of revenues in excess of $100,000 per year. That means that for every dollar of revenue (total income) over $100,000, the tenant will have to pay an extra two cents in rent. So if the business has $150,000 in revenue in a year, the tenant will owe an extra $1,000 in rent ($50,000 is the excess over the base amount, and 2 percent of $50,000 is $1,000).

If a landlord is flexible, any of these terms can be negotiated. And it might pay you to negotiate. Table 21–1 is a comparison of two sample percentage clauses, one calling for 2 percent of revenue in excess of $100,000, and the other calling for 3 percent of revenue in excess of $200,000.

Which is better? In low revenue years, which will presumably be the case at the outset, the 3 percent plan gives you more breathing room. In high revenue years, which will presumably come later, the 3 percent costs more. But for the new entrepreneur, it might be more important to have the extra margin that the 3 percent plan gives early on; if you're that successful later, the 3 percent plan won't hurt you.

If a landlord is willing to build out the premises for you and add the cost thereof to your lease, that can help you conserve capital you may need for other purposes. Indeed, this can be an attractive incentive: in effect, the

TABLE 21–1 **Comparing Percentage Clauses**

Annual Revenue	Extra annual rent based on	
	2% over $100,000	3% over $200,000
$200,000	$ 2,000	–0–
300,000	4,000	$ 3,000
400,000	6,000	6,000
500,000	8,000	9,000
600,000	10,000	12,000
700,000	12,000	15,000

landlord is helping finance the start of your business. And the landlord can get some attractive tax breaks in the process.

When you do negotiate a lease—and remember that all leases are negotiable—get as many options as you can: options to renew, options to enlarge or decrease the size of the premises, and an option to sublease all or part thereof. Options may cost you some extra money, but they provide that all-important flexibility that you need in starting out.

Review the section on income-producing real estate in chapter 16 for more details on seeking a location for your business. As a tenant you'll have many of the same concerns as the landlord regarding building condition, location, lease terms, and so on.

Purchase Contracts

If you are buying an existing business you will enter into a purchase contract with the seller. Before you do, scrutinize all of the seller's income and expense records and be sure that they are all correct. It might be wise to compare those records with the business's tax returns for the past two to three years. A professional audit can also be helpful.

You will need to determine the wisdom of having the seller remain involved with the business after you take over. Will the seller's continuing presence help you or hinder you with respect to retaining the confidence of customers, suppliers, lenders, and regulators? Determine, too, if you want a noncompete clause in your contract. This would prohibit the seller from starting a competing business within an agreed time and place. Any agreements relating to the seller staying on or noncompeting must be in writing.

Terms of payment are critically important. Just as your landlord can help finance your start-up by adding the cost of improvements to your rent, so too can the seller help you by agreeing to a small down payment and stretching out the balance due over a long period of time. Points to negoti-

ate are the rate of interest you pay on the balance due and any share of profits you agree to pay in return for the stretched-out payment schedule.

You should have a lawyer represent you in any such dealings, particularly for a franchise contract.

Franchise Contracts

Exercise 21.4

You must be *extremely* careful to ascertain the difference between the hype that the franchise salesperson presents and the realities that the franchise contract sets forth. See the earlier discussion on "Inflated Expectations": that problem is often caused by the sales pitch for franchises.

Franchise contracts are complex and unyielding. It would be sheer folly to enter into a franchise agreement without having a lawyer assist you. Franchise contracts will dictate exactly how you must run your business and how much you must pay the franchisor. These contracts can run for up to 20 years, and you may not be able to bow out, or move your location, without heavy penalty. Even your right to sell your interest may be restricted by the franchisor's right to approve any successor. There may be little in a franchise contract that your lawyer can actually negotiate for you, but at least your lawyer can make you aware of all the implications more clearly than the small print in the contract will.

While proven franchises can offer good hope for success, you must surrender a lot of freedom to the franchisor, and you may have to work harder than the salesperson indicated to achieve satisfaction.

Keeping these legal issues in the back of your mind, let's now look at the basic start-up forms, beginning with the one with the fewest unknowns and proceeding to the one with the most unknowns. Only you know how much unknown you want to face as you enter self-employment. It will indeed be a time of uncertainties. Everyone must seek his or her own comfort level. I hope this material can guide you accordingly.

Buying an Existing Franchise Operation

You have the track record of the franchise company and the track record of the local operator available to you. If you scrutinize those carefully—preferably with the help of an accountant—you can reduce unknowns to the lowest possible level. This doesn't mean that there aren't risks entailed. There are, but the risks will be more clearly defined. This arrangement might be more costly than the others, but your chances of getting the income you seek and the return on your investment are based more on experience than on guesstimates. Do additional research in trade magazines in the franchise industry and at the Small Business Administration.

Buying an Existing Business (Nonfranchise)

If the business has a long history and well-kept books, this start-up might have very close to the same low number of unknowns as the previous form. The difference would be that the back-up from the franchise company would continue if you were buying into an existing franchise operation, whereas when you buy an independent business there is no such back-up. (The back-up can consist of advertising support, consulting capabilities, and the continuing association with a known "brand name.")

The shorter the history of an existing business, and the less clear its books, the more unknowns you have to conjure with. Given a choice between a long-established and well-documented business and a fairly new entity, those seeking a lesser risk level might prefer the former. In either case you must determine the reason that the business is being sold, and verify that there are no demons hiding in the woodwork who will pop out to harass you.

Buying an existing independent business allows you more freedom and flexibility than you'd have with the franchise. But to many a newcomer, freedom to expand and change means moving into unknown areas. The trade-offs must be carefully evaluated.

Starting from Scratch with a Franchise

You know up front what the franchisor will provide for you, and what the franchisor will expect from you. But there are still a lot of unknowns in the franchise formula. If you're a victim of inflated expectations after hearing the franchise sales pitch, the biggest unknown of all might be, "Why in the devil am I not making the kind of money they said I would make, and why am I having to work so hard to make what I am making?"

Your best protection, *before* you take the plunge, is to interview as many other franchisees of the same company as you can. Don't rely just on the referrals that the franchisor gives you; they're not likely to give you names of any franchisees who will badmouth the company. Seek out all the franchisees within reach, *including* those who have given up the franchise. If possible, examine their books; better still, have your accountant do so. Ask them about their experiences with the franchisor, including the ease or difficulty of communicating with responsible parties; the quickness and fairness with which they deal with problems and disputes; and the promptness with which they respond to calls for assistance. Follow these same steps if you're buying an existing franchise operation.

Before you get in bed with *any* franchisor, whether existing or new, check out their credit standing and overall financial strength. If the company is publicly traded on a stock exchange you can research them through the Standard and Poor's publications at your library. Stockbrokers, bankers,

and Better Business Bureaus can also provide information. If a franchisor is not publicly traded, it would be highly advisable to have your accountant and/or banker check them out for you. The franchise industry has had its share of winners, and perhaps more than its share of losers. Buyer beware.

Starting from Scratch Independently

Here almost everything is unknown. And almost everything is possible.

This is the arena for those whose adrenalin pumps fastest at the thought of striving for fullest potential.

It's also the arena wherein one faces the highest risks, and wherein one might find the greatest rewards.

Before you take the plunge, talk to as many people as you can who have done anything remotely like what you're planning on doing. Evaluate their experiences carefully, taking into account their backgrounds, personalities, education, and skills. Reflect discerningly on the failures and successes of others: some might have failed because they went about it all wrong, and others might have succeeded because of a lot of dumb luck.

Take full advantage of what the SBA can do for you. Scour your local library for any books and articles that may be of value: reference librarians can be amazingly helpful. And seek the counsel of your F.A.I.L.-Safe Team of advisors, which will be discussed later.

Some Special Considerations for Professionals

There has been no intention in this chapter to slight the concerns of professionals: lawyers, doctors, dentists, accountants, engineers, architects, financial planners, insurance specialists, therapists, and all others with advanced learning in their chosen careers.

In many respects these professionals have the same interests as the retailers, wholesalers, distributors, manufacturers, artisans, and personal service providers who seek independence. All must look for locations, negotiate leases, prepare Business Plans, develop ways to market their skills, and learn how to work with or manage others.

In other respects the professionals may have certain advantages over the others, arising from the skills and licenses they have obtained as a result of their higher education. Those attributes—the skills and licenses—may be more portable, and thus more valuable, than those of the nonprofessionals. That, in turn, might allow the professional greater liberty in choosing associations. Indeed, they may be wooed by existing groups to join in an already successful practice. The professional might be able to negotiate a considerable amount of independence, while at the same time enjoying the benefits of the practice's clientele and credentials.

Many new professionals are eager to start off on their own. Before they do, they should evaluate the benefits of first associating themselves with a compatible established group. An early association with an existing practice can enable professionals to develop clientele without taking on undue financial risks of overhead. It can help the professional learn the customs, traditions, politics, and taboos of the community and of the local professional society while sheltered under a wing of "the establishment." It can help assure a flow of dependable income during a time when heavy educational debts must be repaid. And it can provide a trial-and-error period during which each individual professional can determine whether a group practice or a solo practice is the better way to go. Perhaps a better time for a professional to go off alone would be after an experiment as just outlined.

WHERE WILL THE MONEY COME FROM?

Probably the most common reason start-up businesses fail—despite all other excuses and rationalizations—is a shortage of capital. This can take a number of forms:

- There wasn't enough there to begin with, either in hand or available from pledged sources. The most visible flaws in planning are that income did not materialize as hoped, or expenses exceeded what was expected.
- There was enough there to begin with, but it was improperly allocated. This involves overspending on some things at the expense of others. For example: too much was spent on rent, and there wasn't enough left to properly advertise. So no customers ever showed up. Or, the restaurateur took out too much in salary, which didn't leave enough to pay the provisioners the cash they wanted, so there was no food to serve to the customers.
- There was enough to begin with, and it was properly spent, but when the business reached a point that it needed a major new capital infusion there was none available at an affordable price because advance plans had not been made for such a contingency.
- The right amount of money was planned, but too much of it was borrowed. When interest rates went up or when lenders declined to renew the loans there was big trouble.

These are not just problems of start-up businesses. They can plague any venture at any time. Planning for capital needs, for the present and for the future, is most important for any entrepreneur. Your Business Plan must deal with this issue. You can get help in projecting your needs from your banker and your accountant. The SBA may have services available to give you further aid. At the outset, this process may seem an overpowering challenge, but as you gain experience it becomes more manageable. You should explore all these possible sources of capital.

Personal Savings

The farther in advance you can plan, the bigger nest egg you can build as the initial stake for your venture. It's best to have a separate fund for your business, rather than tapping into general funds that might otherwise be used for family rainy days, education, or retirement. If you do tap into those other funds, you should make provision to replace them, so that you can be ready to meet those expenses when the time comes.

Family and Friends

They can be of help in a number of ways:

- They might give you money out of the goodness of their hearts.
- They might lend you money, possibly on more favorable terms than you'd get from a bank.
- They might invest in your enterprise, taking their chances that you'll generate profits for them, but willing to risk a failure.
- They might co-sign or provide collateral for you to enable you to borrow more expeditiously from a bank.
- They might network for you, helping you find other possible investors or lenders.

If you do involve friends or family as financial partners in your enterprise, remember these immutable rules:

1. Friends and family who provide financial support usually think that they have the right to give you advice. Take it in the right spirit, being aware of their own agendas in giving you the advice. Be wary that some may be resentful if you don't follow their advice.
2. Nothing can come between friends or relatives more swiftly or more harshly than a dispute over money. Any dealings that you do have with friends or relatives should be handled in the most businesslike way. Put it all into writing so as to minimize misunderstandings.

Lenders

At the earliest possible time start building up a rapport and a line of credit with a local bank. Better still, do it with two local banks in case one changes policy against you. Seek out a lender who will give you guidance on developing a plan for your capital needs. Novice entrepreneurs often find bank borrowing difficult without the help of a co-signer or without some collateral. Don't be offended if you're asked to provide either. In due time, given good payment performance, those supports will no longer be needed. Be most cautious about borrowing from nonbanking sources: interest rates and

repayment terms can be harsh. And watch out for the advance fee loan scheme, which often entraps small business operators who are having a hard time finding money. You're promised a loan if you pay a big fee in advance, and then scammers disappear with your money.

"Built In" Credit

As noted earlier, some of your capital needs can be built into other aspects of your venture.

- The landlord can add the cost of certain improvements to your rent, thereby relieving you of the need to finance those items separately.
- Suppliers of equipment and inventory can provide you with payment terms that can reduce your need for some outside capital.
- If you are buying an existing business, favorable terms from the seller can help you conserve your capital.
- Banks, as well as companies known as *factors,* will lend you money with your accounts receivable as collateral. Banks can also finance your inventory acquisitions.

These arrangements will come at a price. But don't turn down any possibility without weighing it seriously.

Governmental Sources

Exercise 21.5

The Small Business Administration can arrange to guarantee loans from banks. An adjunct of the SBA, the Small Business Innovation Research program (SBIR), helps fund technological start-ups, particularly if the product is one in which the government might have an interest.

Many state governments have programs to help new ventures, particularly those that are technologically oriented or minority-owned. Of special interest are ventures that will provide jobs in the community. Your local banker can help you locate these sources.

Other Investors

Aside from friends and family, there may be local individuals who seek business opportunities, and they even advertise the fact in the local want-ads under "Money to Invest" or "Money to Loan." These local versions of "venture capitalists" have big-time counterparts who deal in million-dollar deals. If you're in that class, a local banker or stockbroker can help you find the names of likely prospects.

Many corporations would rather invest in a start-up business that's cre-

ating something useful to the corporation than set up a whole new division within their ranks. Whatever product or service you're developing, you might want to explore this route. If you do, though, be alert to the age-old warning against putting all your eggs in one basket.

Tax Breaks

Self-employed persons are entitled to a number of tax breaks (and also subject to one harsh tax cost) that can make a difference to your bottom line. On the good side, self-employed persons can put a lot of their earnings into tax-sheltered retirement plans that are much more generous than IRAs or 401(k)s. Self-employeds can claim a deduction (technically an adjustment) for a major portion of their health insurance costs. This amount is scheduled to increase considerably in the years to come. For the years 1998 through 2002, 45 percent of health insurance premiums can be deducted, for 2003 it is 50 percent, for 2004 it's 60 percent, for 2005 it's 70 percent, and for 2006 and beyond it's 80 percent. If you buy business equipment you can take a deduction for up to $17,000 worth for tax year 1997, and that amount increases to $25,000 by 2003. (The normal situation regarding business equipment is that you must spread the deduction out over a number of years; self-employeds can take it all in one helpful chunk.) You can also take a deduction for that portion of your home you use for business purposes; formerly tight regulations in this area have become more liberal in recent years.

On the bad side, self-employeds must pay self-employment tax in lieu of Social Security taxes, and you must pay an amount that almost equals what you and your employer paid combined when you were an employee. Half of this self-employment tax can be claimed as an adjustment, thus easing the blow.

All of these tax matters should be taken into account in figuring your total income and expenses for your first year of business, and then reviewed each following year.

Debt vs. Equity?

As you raise capital, you will face a question that plagues all businesses: Should you borrow or give up shares of your business in exchange for money? There is no easy answer, but there are some guidelines.

Debt and interest must be paid; that's a cost of doing business. All profits are yours to keep, but if the debt can't be repaid, or if interest costs get too high for you, there could be serious problems. Defaulting on debt can mean the loss of the business: The creditor who has wisely gotten the proper collateral can foreclose and take everything to settle the debt.

Equity—money that's been invested in your business—does *not* have to be repaid. The investors have put their money at risk by investing it with you, and they share your fortunes accordingly. You don't have to pay interest on the equity money, but you would be expected to distribute a fair share of profits to the investors in proportion to their ownership shares, and the investors might require that they have a say in how the business is run. In short, you no longer have total control, and you have to divvy up the profits. A proper investment arrangement requires written agreements, in which you can protect yourself by maintaining ultimate control—a 51 percent ownership interest, whether you're operating as a partnership, a corporation, or any other arrangement by mutual consent. But even if you retain a majority interest, that won't deter the investors from putting demands on you to help protect the money they've entrusted to you.

It's certainly possible to have a blend of debt and equity. And there are some people you might prefer to have as lenders and others as investors; this is a matter of chemistry and personality. You can also shift the balance between debt and equity from time to time. You can have an agreement with lenders in which they might agree to accept a share of ownership in exchange for the debt. You can have an agreement with investors that they will sell their share of ownership back to you on certain terms (and you might have to borrow money to accomplish this). All things are possible, provided you don't get yourself too locked in with too much debt or too much equity. Keep flexible. That's the healthy way.

STRATEGIES FOR SUCCESS

Pay Yourself Last

You're not going into business for yourself just for fun or as an experiment in living. Yes, those might be some of your reasons, but deep down, you can't deny that you want to make money at it. Well and good. You're entitled to. But the rate at which you take money out of your enterprise can bode well or poorly for your long-term success. The temptation is clear to want to pay yourself a regular salary, whether you take it out of earnings or dip into your capital funds. And you want to continue living in the style to which you've been accustomed. But beware: it's likely that something will have to give, at least in the early start-up period. By paying yourself first you may be depriving the enterprise of badly needed capital. Unless you're willing to endure some personal sacrifice, you may starve the enterprise prematurely. Consider paying yourself last—after all other expenses have been met. In doing so you'll see a much more honest picture of the business's potential; and you'll be motivated to work that much harder to meet your own goals.

NIT-PICKED TO DEATH BY REGULATIONS?

Regulations are the bane of many a small business's existence. When you're someone else's employee, some hidden office full of paper-pushers takes care of complying with all the regulations. When you're your own boss, you've got to do it yourself, or else pay for others to do it for you.

The cost of regulatory compliance, and the cost of *failing* to comply, are matters that cannot be overlooked by any entrepreneur. Many of these regulations have been referred to in chapter 2, in the context of your rights as an employee. Review those workplace regulations with the tables turned: you as an employer have to deal with them, like it or not, in correct and timely fashion. It's not a pretty picture, and those are just the *workplace* regulations.

In summary, here are the major areas of regulatory chokehold. When you're an employee you look upon these as rules meant to protect you. As an employer you'll likely look upon them as rules meant to destroy you. It's interesting how the perspective changes.

Employment Regulations

The going gets tough as soon as you have one single employee. If you can hire your needed help as independent contractors or temps (see the discussion earlier in this chapter) you might be able to save yourself a lot of administrative costs. Here's a rundown of the federal, state, and local paperwork you may have to wrestle with regarding employment.

Tax Matters

- W-2 and W-4 forms for employees (and 1099s for independent contractors)
- 1040ES (quarterly estimated returns for yourself)
- Payroll deduction bookkeeping and remittance to proper governmental agencies
- IRS bookkeeping and compliance regarding any pension program you provide for yourself or for your employees

IRS Publication 334, *Tax Guide for Small Business,* can help you deal with these forms and regulations.

Employee Well-being

- Health and safety provisions, including the Occupational Health and Safety Act (OSHA), the Family Leave Act (if you have more than 50 employees), the Americans with Disabilities Act, and workers' compensation

- Unemployment insurance
- Right to work laws: Federal Fair Labor Standards Act, Age Discrimination Act, Fair Employment Practices Law, age and hour laws, plant closing laws, union and labor relations laws
- Health insurance plans, and the cost of providing same, could become a paperwork and financial nightmare

Financial Regulations

Credit Matters

If you don't extend credit to customers, you might sail easily through these waters. But if you do extend credit you may have a raft of concerns. (See the section, "Laws That Govern Financial Institutions and Their Transactions" in chapter 11.) Although the main thrust of these regulations are geared toward banks, they apply to a wide array of small businesses that take customers' IOUs in payment, particularly if the business is charging interest or taking a security interest in the buyer's property. Unless there's some compelling reasons to the contrary, it would seem more efficient for the small business to allow customers to pay by credit card, which can allow a bypass of these regulatory requirements.

Retirement Plans

There is no law that requires an employer to provide pension plans. But if you do offer a pension plan you must comply with governmental regulations, and they can be awesome. Pension plans require compliance with regulations of the Employees Retirement Income Security Act (ERISA) and the Pension Benefit Guarantee Corporation (PBGC). Regular reports have to be made to the IRS and the U.S. Department of Labor.

A much simpler way to proceed, at least until your business is a proven success, is to offer employees a Simplified Employee Pension, or SEP, plan. (See chapter 18 for details.)

Miscellaneous Regulations

On a state and local level, you must comply with regulations regarding:

- Doing business under an assumed name (it's likely that a bank won't open an account for you under your assumed name unless you've complied with local laws on the subject)
- Licensing of your business, if any is required
- Zoning requirements (this might also apply to you if you're doing business in your home)

- Building and safety codes
- Taxes that your business may be subject to
- Sign and advertising restrictions as set by local ordinance
- Pollution controls (federal as well as state and local)

You can't ignore regulations. And they never diminish. Set your mind to those realities at the outset, and you might find them easier to tolerate.

WHERE TO GET HELP: THE F.A.I.L.-SAFE TEAM AND THE M & Ms

Working for yourself is not a day at the beach. But there are people who can help make it more pleasant and productive; indeed, wise use of these helpers can spell the difference between success and failure in your venture.

The F.A.I.L.-Safe Team

This team is composed of professional advisors: Financial, Accounting, Insurance, and Legal. Some may cost a lot of money. Some cost none. But the issue of cost should not deter you from seeking counsel. Without the right counsel the cost consequences could be far worse.

Financial

A cooperative and knowledgeable banker and a friend at the nearest SBA office can be invaluable allies. They can help you determine your credit needs and your credit capacity (see chapter 12). They can help you develop a Business Plan. They can help you project your overall capital needs. And, if all the circumstances are right, they can arrange loans for you. The advice is generally free. The loans cost money.

Accounting

Services can cover bookkeeping, tax preparation, auditing, and documentation (helping you put together your financial statements, profit and loss statements, and Business Plan). An accountant can also evaluate the financial status of anyone with whom you might be doing important business, such as a franchisor, a potential major customer, or a would-be partner.

Insurance

You'll need a knowledgeable agent to help you with a variety of business insurance needs: rental interruption, public liability, casualty coverage for premises and contents, malpractice (if applicable to your work), and appropriate health and disability protection. A good life insurance agent should

be consulted with respect to "key person" insurance, which pays off on the death of a person who is essential to the business. It can be wise coverage, particularly if you've invested a lot of your net worth in your business. The insurance proceeds can be used to continue the business or provide for the family of the deceased entrepreneur. As with the banker, the advice is free, the policies cost money.

Legal

Most of the general legal issues you'll encounter have already been discussed: leases, contracts, regulations. You may also benefit from a lawyer's skills in negotiating employment arrangements and contracts for services; for protecting your "intellectual rights" (patents, copyrights, trademarks, etc.); and for being on the alert as to how your rights are being violated so that prompt action can be taken. Not all lawyers are familiar with the business world, however. It's an area of specialized skills, and you'd be wise to seek out one properly equipped to handle your specific needs. Your local Bar Association Referral Service can help you.

The M & Ms

You may be the world's best at what you do, and you have every confidence that working for yourself will be a roaring success. But you may not know enough about marketing and management to fill a thimble, and without those skills you might never find and keep a paying audience.

Marketing and management consultants can play a critical role in your venture. The marketing people can help you design, package, advertise, price, and deliver your goods and services in the most cost-effective way. The management people can help you structure your own operation and can help you best understand the operational structures of the businesses you're trying to sell to.

Seek and You'll Find

In looking for help in these areas, seek referrals from friends and family. Ask past and current customers/clients for reviews of their experiences with any of your prospective helpers. Before you hire any, interview them and get a sense of the chemistry that will be generated between you. And don't be embarrassed to ask any or all of them if they would accept a share of ownership in your venture in lieu of cash payment. Some might, and it might be worthwhile for you to pursue that course.

It's Your Move

No, you're not ready yet to go off on your own. But once you've absorbed all of the information and guidelines in this chapter you're well prepared to start doing the right specific homework that can turn your dream into a reality. Do all that homework as if your life depended on it—in a sense, it does, so take your time. Despite the anxiety to get on with your new career, the worst threat to your success is jumping in before you're *totally prepared*—in terms of capital, skills, energy, and emotions. Be patient. You've waited this long; another few weeks or months for study and preparation can't hurt you. Do it right the first time. If you don't, you may never have the will to try it again.

PERSONAL ACTION WORKSHEET —————————————————

Set Goals. If You Can't Achieve Them, Let Go.

Do try your best at your new venture. Give it your all. But be ready to let go gracefully if it's not working out. Set realistic goals and strive to achieve them: "Based on my anticipated expenses, I must raise, and/or earn, X dollars within Y months. If I can, I'm on my way. But if I fall short within that time frame, it's time to bow out and say proudly, 'At least I gave it my best shot.'" Don't prolong agony needlessly. The pain of staying in may be worse than the pain of getting out.

Here are some blanks for you to fill in, to help you *start* shaping cash-flow goals. One set is for pre-starting expenses; the other is for ongoing expenses. Basic expenses are much more predictable than income. Match the totals with your estimated available capital from all sources, including income. Do best-case and worst-case projections for both income and expenses and design your time frame targets accordingly.

Pre-starting Expenses

Legal fees	$_____
Accounting	_____
Deposit for rent	_____
Stationary, supplies	_____
Down payments for equipment	_____
Licenses	_____
Permits	_____
Consultants	_____
Advertising	_____
Research	_____
Initial inventory	_____
Fixtures, furniture	_____
Decor	_____
Other	_____
Transition costs	_____
All personal expenses—food, housing, insurance, etc.—incurred from when you give up your paying job until you can derive a comparable income from your new venture	
TOTALS	_____

Ongoing Expenses

Legal fees	$_____
Accounting	_____
Rent	_____
Stationary, supplies	_____
Equipment payments	_____
Wages to others	_____
Payroll taxes	_____
Consultants	_____
Advertising	_____
Utilities	_____
Telephone, fax	_____
Property insurance	_____
Liability insurance	_____
Personal insurance	_____
Transportation	_____
Postage, delivery	_____
Payments on debt	_____
Maintenance, repairs	_____
Ongoing inventory	_____
Security	_____
Other	_____
	_____

CONSUMER ALERT

Snake Oil Sam Strikes Again

Small businesses are terribly susceptible to the wiles of Snake Oil Sam and his army of con artists. That's because of the high level of anxiety that often accompanies self-employment. Here's a brief sampling of some of the more common schemes.

- **Telemarketing**   You receive a call from a so-called office supply distributor offering fantastic deals. You pay, but the goods are never delivered or they are of shoddy quality. And when you try to get restitution, their phone number is no longer in service. Beware, also, of phony investments sold by phone—very slick.

- **Phony invoices**   A favorite is for "renewal" of nonexistent telephone directory advertising. A tight system of cross-checking orders with bills is essential to avoid such scams.

- **Advance fee loan schemes**   See chapter 4.

- **Business investment offerings**   These are rampant in a variety of magazines and tabloid newspapers. If the business ventures being offered were so profitable, why would they be offering you the opportunity? It must be that they will make more money by selling you their "secrets of success" than you will make by trying to put those secrets to work. Simple and compelling logic; be guided accordingly.

- **Bankruptcy scams**   These really hurt. A customer who owes you a lot of money threatens to declare bankruptcy unless you accept, say, 25 cents on the dollar in full payment. Some will actually manipulate the bankruptcy laws to turn a profit and leave you holding the bag. Beware of customers who beg to have a high credit balance and those who show only a post office box for an address and have just an answering machine to take their phone calls.

- **Phony insurance swindles**   Small employers, fearful of the cost of providing health insurance for employees, fall prey to too-good-to-be-true offers of group health plans from con artists. Premiums are paid and the scammers split with the money.

Be extremely cautious when dealing with strangers. Check with the Better Business Bureau for more help on how to protect yourself.

UPS & DOWNS   *The Economics of Everyday Life*

Why Do the Fortunes of Small Businesses Go Up and Down?

The fortunes of all small businesses are tied to the ups and downs of many other entities and forces. Aside from the general status of the economy (national and regional), here are some of the specific influences that will increase or decrease your bank account and your peace of mind.

- Your suppliers may raise or lower the prices they charge you. If the former, you can shop for new suppliers. If the latter, be careful that the level of service doesn't drop along with the price.
- Your competition may increase or decrease. If the former, you have to work harder and/or lower your prices to stay afloat. If the latter, don't let yourself get complacent. Don't compromise on your quality or integrity.
- Your capital sources may tighten or expand. If the former, be ready with a fall-back position that will allow you access to funds as you need them. If the latter, determine if now is a good time to acquire more capital, either from lenders or investors, and how can you best put such capital to productive use. It's sometimes wise to get extra capital when the getting is good and invest it safely until you need it for business purposes.
- Your personal energies may ebb and flow, and the dynamics of the business will ebb and flow accordingly. If you're exhausted and in a low funk it may be that you've spread yourself too thin. It may pay to hire someone to help you; the cost of doing so can be justified if it gets your energy back up, which will get your cash flow back up. If you're on a high, on a roll, enjoy it. But be careful of the workaholic syndrome. Make sure you allow yourself enough time to enjoy spending the money you're earning.

? WHAT IF . . . ?

Test yourself: How would you deal with these real-life possibilities?

1. You are about to embark on your life's dream: opening a shop to make and sell farnolas. You seek advice from various friends. The first is very enthusiastic; he owns a small shopping center with a vacancy in it that you could rent. The second is thrilled for you; she sells the raw materials from which farnolas are made. The third is exuberant; he owns an advertising agency. What are the pluses and minuses of what your friends can offer you?

2. Still another friend knows a famous farnola designer. It's suggested that you and the designer team up and become partners in the venture. The idea has merit, but the designer is a total stranger. What specifically must you learn about the designer in order to make a sound judgment?

3. Your banker agrees to lend you the $25,000 you need to start your venture, but you must provide a satisfactory co-signer or collateral. Who can you call on to help? For real now, not pretend.

NUMBER CRUNCHERS

Do the calculations to make decisions in these real-life possibilities.

1. Your business has earned $70,000 in the year, after all expenses except interest.
   (a) Suppose you had borrowed $100,000 to start the business, paying an interest rate of 8 percent per year. How would this affect your bottom line?
   (b) Suppose that instead of borrowing, friend Pat had invested $100,000, for which you promised to pay 10 percent of your earnings. How would this affect your bottom line?
   (c) Suppose that you had borrowed $50,000 at 8 percent interest, and Pat had invested $50,000, to earn 5 percent of your earnings. How would this affect your bottom line?
   Compare all three scenarios. Calculate others that may be closer to your own real situation.

2. The landlord of the space you want to rent offers you either (a) a 10-year lease at $1,800 a month with no renewals; or (b) a five-year lease at $2,000 a month with an option to renew for five more years at $2,200 a month; or (c) a one-year lease, followed by nine one-year renewal options, the rental to be 20 percent of your gross sales, not to exceed $30,000 in a year. Your business plan estimates that your gross sales will be $125,000 in the first year and $150,000 in the second year. Compare and evaluate the deals.

FOR BETTER OR FOR WORSE

Things beyond our control often impact our personal and financial well-being, for better or for worse. Some are more predictable than others. How would you be affected if the following real-life phenomena happened? Could you have seen it coming? What steps could you have taken to minimize damage or maximize advantage? The better able you are to anticipate and recognize these forces, the better equipped you are to deal with them.

1. To become your own boss you buy Kline's Clothing Store, a small local shop that has had a successful track record for decades. Once you've taken over, the customers stay away in droves. One of them explains to you that customer loyalty was due to Mr. Kline and his sons' delightful personality. And you're not Mr. Kline, nor will you ever be.

2. You do the selling and your partner handles the books. You don't know numbers, and she can't sell worth a darn. It's a good mix, until one day you discover that your partner has embezzled $50,000 from the business.

3. You run a mom-and-pop restaurant in a suburban area outside a big city. The city annexes the suburb, and you must spend an unavailable $25,000 to bring the restaurant up to the city's safety and health code standards.

Glossary

Numbers in parentheses indicate chapter reference. Words are defined in the context in which they are used in the text. Italicized words within the definitions are separately defined within the glossary.

Acquisition fees (7)   Expenses that a borrower will have to pay in obtaining a home financing loan. Generally payable to the lender, these expenses can include legal fees, appraisal fees, and *"points."*

Add-on interest (12)   One method of calculating *interest* costs in an *installment loan*. Example: If one borrows $1,000 for one year at 10 percent add-on interest, the interest cost—$100—is "added on" to the amount borrowed, making the total debt $1,100. Dividing $1,100 by 12 results in monthly payments of $91.67.

Adjustments (6)   In a real-estate transaction, the prorating between buyer and seller of any prepaid expenses (such as property taxes) that the seller has incurred prior to the *closing*.

Adjustments to income (20)   In the calculation of one's income taxes, a main category of expenses that can be used to reduce the amount of income subject to taxation.

Administrator (19)   A court-appointed person responsible for handling the *estate* of a person who died without a *will*.

Advance fee loan scheme (4)   A scam in which a would-be borrower of money is convinced to pay a large fee in advance in order to secure a loan. The loan never materializes and the money paid in advance is lost.

Age Discrimination in Employment Act (2)   A federal law that protects workers between the ages of 40 and 65 with respect to hiring and firing problems because of their age.

Amended tax return (20)   A tax return that may be filed after the original return was filed to correct errors in the original return.

Annual Percentage Rate (APR) (12)   The interest rate that the federal government requires be disclosed to borrowers in most installment loan transactions. The APR is designed to offer an accurate comparison of interest costs on different loan offerings.

Annual Percentage Yield (APY) (11)   Determines the amount of money you will earn in one year if you invest your money at the stated percentage. Example: An APY of 6 percent means that an investment of $1,000 will earn $60 in one year. Under the 1993 Truth in Savings law, all banks and other covered institutions must use this standard method of quoting rates they pay.

Annuity (17)   A type of investment with an insurance company that guarantees the investor a fixed monthly income for a specific period of time.

Assessment (8)   A percentage of the market value of a parcel of real estate, used to establish the property taxes on that parcel.

Assets (2)   The total value of everything you own, plus everything owed to you.

Assumable mortgage (7)   A *mortgage* that allows future creditworthy buyers of the property to take over responsibility of paying the existing loan.

Attestation clause (19)   A clause in a *will* in which the witnesses to the will confirm that they have performed their duties in accordance with the law.

Audit (20)   The procedure in which the Internal Revenue Service examines in detail one's income tax return.

Bait and switch (4)   An illegal selling scheme in which a seller offers a product at an unreasonably low price (the "bait"). A would-be buyer, lured by the bait, is then "switched" to a higher-priced item.

Balloon clause (7)   A provision in a loan agreement (mortgage or installment) that allows the lender to demand full payment of the loan at a set time.

Banker's acceptance (14)   A form of investment that arises when a bank holds a foreign company's promissory note (IOU) and sells portions of that note to investors.

Bankruptcy proceedings (12)   Federal court proceedings in which the debts of individuals or companies can be wiped out or in which the court may instruct creditors to hold off in their attempts to collect debts due them from the bankrupt person or company.

Beneficiary (17, 19)   One designated to receive an inheritance from the *estate* of a *decedent*; also, one who receives the proceeds of a *life insurance* policy on the death of the insured person.

Benefits (17)   Money received from an insurance company when the insured party suffers a loss covered by the insurance policy.

Bequest (19)   The specific property or money given to a *beneficiary* from the *estate* of a *decedent*.

Blue-chip stock (15)   *Stock* of a company considered to have high investment quality: relatively stable prices and strong dividend payment history.

Bond (14)   A long-term debt instrument.

Bumping (3)   If you are denied a seat on an

airplane, and you had had a confirmed reservation, the airline is "bumping" you and must pay you a certain penalty fee.

Buying down (7)   A type of "creative" home financing plan whereby the seller pays part of the interest charges for the buyer for a specified period of time.

Cafeteria plans (2, 17)   A fringe-benefit program that allows employees to select from a variety of benefits that most closely suits their individual needs.

Call option (15)   A contract that gives the owner the right to buy 100 shares of a given common *stock* at a predetermined price (the "strike price") at any time until a fixed future date.

Call privilege (14)   The right of a *corporation* or other issuer of debt to pay off the holders of the debt at an agreed-on price prior to the scheduled maturity of the debt.

Cashier's check (11)   A check drawn on a bank's own account.

Cash management account (11)   A type of account offered by stock brokerage firms that provides a combination of checking, investing, and borrowing capabilities for its customers.

Caveat emptor (4)   A Latin phrase that means "let the buyer beware." This is especially important for consumers to remember if they think they're getting something that is too good to be true.

Certificate of deposit (CD) (11, 14)   A contractual investment with a financial institution wherein the investor agrees to deposit a fixed sum of money for a fixed amount of time in return for a guaranteed interest rate.

Certified check (11)   An individual (or business) check that has been guaranteed by the bank on which it is drawn; that is, the funds are guaranteed to be available when the check is presented for payment.

Churning (15)   An improper practice wherein a stockbroker creates excessive trading in a customer's account to generate commissions.

Civil Rights Act (2)   See *Fair Employment Practices Law.*

Closed-end lease (5)   In car leasing, this arrangement sets a predetermined amount at

which you can buy your leased car at the end of the lease, subject to various costs and charges you may have to pay.

Closing (6) In a real estate transaction, the event at which the transfer of *deeds,* money, and promises-to-pay takes place.

Codicil (19) A document that, when properly executed, amends a *will.*

Coinsurance clause (8) A provision in most property insurance policies stating that the insured party will receive full replacement value for losses only if the premises are insured for a stated percentage (usually 80 percent) of full value.

Collision insurance (5) Coverage for the insured's auto for damages resulting from a collision with another vehicle or object.

Commercial paper (14) An instrument of short-term debt issued by a *corporation.*

Commodities (16) A variety of products (such as cattle, wheat, precious metals) whose future values are subject to fluctuation. Commodity markets offer the opportunity to speculate in those future values. (Also known as futures trading.)

Compounding of interest (14) Occurs when the *interest* you earn stays in your account and begins to earn interest itself.

Comprehensive insurance (5) Coverage for the insured's auto for damages resulting from other than collision, such as fire and theft.

Condominium (6) An owned dwelling unit that is part of a multi-unit structure.

Condominium conversion (9) The act of modifying the form of ownership of a multiple-unit building from single ownership of the entire structure to individual ownership of each specific unit within the entire structure.

Contingent beneficiary (17) One who takes the place of an original *beneficiary* (in a *will* or *insurance policy*), should the original beneficiary die before the *testator* or the insured.

Cooperative (6) A type of housing arrangement wherein each resident owns a percentage of the total building and has an agreement with all the owners for the right to use a specific unit in the building for his or her own dwelling.

Corporate bond (14) A long-term debt instrument issued by a *corporation.* Some bonds may contain a *call privilege.* Some bonds are convertible; that is, the owner has the right to convert the bond into *stock* of the same company, upon stated terms and conditions.

Corporation (14) A legal entity created under state law for the purpose of conducting a stated business. A corporation is owned by its stockholders, who in turn elect a board of directors to set the ongoing policies of the corporation. The directors, in turn, select officers to run the day-to-day affairs of the corporation.

Cosigner (12) One who jointly signs a credit agreement with the principal borrower. The cosigner must pay the debt if the borrower fails to do so.

Creative financing (7) A general term describing home financing arrangements that are privately negotiated between seller and buyer, with or without the participation of outside lenders or investors.

Credit bureau (12) A nongovernmental organization that collects and distributes credit information. Merchants and lenders use this information to make decisions on granting credit to those who apply.

Credit capacity (12) The amount of borrowing a consumer can realistically handle, considering his current and future income and expenses.

Credit health insurance (12) A form of health insurance that will pay loan payments if an insured borrower is disabled due to health or accident.

Credit history (12) The record of one's credit activity, as maintained by the local *credit bureau.*

Credit life insurance (12) A form of life insurance that will pay off any balance due on an installment loan should the borrower die before the loan is otherwise paid.

Credit Repair Clinic (4) The term used to describe a shady operation that offers to help debtors get out of trouble. They can create even worse problems by keeping the money the debtor gives them to parcel out to legitimate creditors.

Credit union (11) A type of financial institution that is owned by individuals who have a common bond, such as the employees of a company or governmental agency.

Debt counseling service (12) An agency that assists creditors who are having financial troubles.

Decedent (19) One who has died.

Decreasing term insurance (17) A type of life insurance; the amount of coverage decreases from year to year.

Deductible (5, 8) With respect to insurance, the amount that an insured must first pay out of pocket before the insurance company becomes liable; for example, if one suffers a casualty valued at $200 and has a $50 deductible for such occurrences, the insured will be responsible for the first $50, and the insurance company will then reimburse $150.

Deductions (20) Regarding income taxes, a category of expenses that are subtracted from adjusted gross income to lower the amount of income subject to taxation. Taxpayers may claim *itemized deductions* or *standard deductions*.

Deed (6) A document by which title to real estate passes from the seller to the buyer.

Deficit (1) The status of a budget (one's financial condition) when more money has been spent than has been taken in.

Disability income insurance (17) Insurance that provides some income to a worker who becomes unable to work due to injury or health problems.

Discretionary income (2, 13) Extra money available once one's basic needs have been paid for.

Discriminate income function (DIF) (20) A computerized procedure used by the IRS to select tax returns for *audit*. The computer compares various elements of a given return (income, deductions, etc.) and further compares those ratios to average levels for such claims.

Dividend (15) That portion of a company's profit that the directors vote to pay out to stockholders. Usually paid quarterly.

Double indemnity (17) A life insurance policy provision that will pay *beneficiaries* double the *face value* of the policy in the event of the accidental death of the insured.

Dow Jones Industrial Average (15) The most commonly referred to index of stock prices and their movements. It reflects the prices of 30 major industrial stocks.

Down payment (12) That portion of the purchase price (of a house, a car, etc.) paid by the buyer in cash at the time of purchase.

Earnest money (6) A token payment of cash to bind a preliminary agreement between the buyer and seller of a house (or other item).

Easement (6) The right given to someone to use your land for a specific purpose (to cross over the property, to construct utility lines, etc.).

Education IRA (18) A new form of Individual Retirement Account made possible by the Taxpayer Relief Act of 1997. It allows attractive tax breaks for those who are saving money for higher education.

Eminent domain (8) A legal concept that permits a local government to acquire, or condemn, private property when a proven public need for the property exists. For example: to widen a highway, build a school. Owners of the private property must be adequately paid for their property.

Employee Retirement Income Security Act (ERISA) (18) A federal law that protects the right of employees with respect to pension and profit-sharing plans. Also known as the Pension Reform Law of 1974.

Endorsement (11) Writing one's signature on the back of a check (or other negotiable instrument), thereby acknowledging receipt of the cash or credit indicated on the check. Endorsements may be in blank (signature only), restrictive (limiting how the check may be further negotiated), or special (such as when the funds are to be paid or credited to a third party).

Equal Credit Opportunity Law (11) A federal law designed to prevent discrimination regarding sex or marital status of individuals applying for credit.

Equity (9) The difference between what your house (or other property) is currently worth, and what you owe on it.

Escrow (7, 9)   (1) A third party who acts as an intermediary in a real estate transaction, seeing to it that the instructions of the parties are complied with. (2) Money paid monthly to a mortgage lender to pay property insurance premiums and property taxes as they fall due. Also referred to as a reserve account.

Estate (19)   The legal entity that comes into being upon the death of a person; that is, upon John's death, the estate of John comes into being. Also refers to the net worth of the decedent; that is, John's estate is worth $100,000.

Estate taxes (19)   A federal or state tax on the *estate* of a *decedent*.

Exclusion (10)   An amount of income that is free of income taxes. For example: if the seller of a home is over the age of 55, he or she may be able to exclude from taxable income up to $125,000 worth of profit on the sale of the home.

Ex-dividend date (15)   A date that determines whether a buyer of *stock* is entitled to a recently declared *dividend*. One who buys before the ex-dividend date receives the dividend. One who buys after the ex-dividend date does not receive the dividend.

Executor/Executrix (19)   The person or institution designated by a *testator* to carry out the settlement of the testator's *estate*.

Exemptions (20)   With regard to income taxes, the number of persons dependent on the taxpayer, including the taxpayer him/herself. For each proper exemption the taxpayer is allowed to reduce his income subject to taxes by a fixed amount.

Face amount (face value) (17)   The amount of money that a *life insurance* policy will pay to the beneficiary on the death of the insured person.

Fair Credit Billing Law (11)   A federal law that protects the rights of persons who receive erroneous bills from creditors.

Fair Credit Reporting Law (11)   A federal law that gives individuals the right to view their *credit history* and the right to take steps to have errors corrected.

Fair Debt Collection Practices Law (11)   A federal law that protects debtors from unfair, deceptive, and abusive debt collection practices.

Fair Employment Practices Law (2)   A federal law designed to prevent job discrimination because of an individual's race, sex, religion, or national origin. Also known as the Civil Rights Act of 1964.

Federal Deposit Insurance Corporation (FDIC) (11, 14)   The federal agency that insures accounts in commercial banks and mutual savings banks against the failure of the institutions.

Federal Fair Labor Standards Law (2)   A federal law that protects certain minors with respect to jobs that could be hazardous or detrimental to their well-being.

Federal Occupational Safety and Health Act (OSHA) (2)   A federal law that sets health and safety standards for working environments.

Filing extension (20)   Available to taxpayers who file the proper form, an added time to file their tax return.

Filing status (20)   One of five categories chosen by taxpayers as a part of completing their returns; the choice of category, which is broadly based on taxpayer's marital situation, affects the amount of tax payable.

Fill or kill order (15)   An order given to a stockbroker to buy or sell stocks at a specific price, with the understanding that if the order can't be filled immediately at the given price, then the order will terminate.

Financing contingency clause (6)   A provision in a contract for the purchase of real estate that allows buyers to be released from their obligations if they are not able to obtain financing at a certain rate of interest by an agreed-on date.

Fiscal policy (1)   The policy that determines how a government will raise money, and for what purposes it will spend it.

Flexible spending plans (2, 17)   A fringe benefit program that allows employees to set aside part of their earnings on a tax-sheltered basis, provided that the money set aside is used for certain designated purposes, such as dependent care or unreimbursed medical expenses.

Floating rate bond (14)   A *bond* in which the interest rate payable to holders fluctuates up and

down, usually within set limits and/or in accordance with some outside index.

Foreclosure (7)   The procedure by which a lender can obtain title to property that has been pledged as security for a loan when the borrower has defaulted on that loan.

Foreign exchange (16)   Generally, the currency of other nations. The future values of the currencies of major nations can be bought and sold at commodity exchanges.

Form 1040 (1040A) (20)   The basic forms used to file one's federal income taxes. Taxpayers who wish to claim certain *adjustments, tax credits,* and *itemized deductions* use the 1040 (long form). Taxpayers who do not wish to claim these items use the 1040A (short form).

401(k) plans (2, 18)   A retirement savings plan set up by employers, in which employees can invest a portion of their wages on a tax-sheltered basis. Employers might also contribute to these plans for the benefit of their employees.

Fringe benefit (2)   A form of payment to a worker, other than current money. Examples include insurance protection, pension plans, and profit-sharing plans.

Funding (18)   The placing of money in a pension plan by an employer. Proper funding requires that enough money be placed in the fund to meet future promises to pay benefits to covered employees.

Garnishment (2)   A legal procedure by which a creditor can get access to a debtor's wages to satisfy a debt due the creditor.

General obligation bond (14)   A type of *municipal bond* backed by the taxing authority of the municipality.

Generic products (3)   Grocery, pharmaceutical, and other items with "plain" or nonbrand labels.

Glamour stock (15)   *Stock* of a company that the investment community perceives as "hot," as a "winner." Compared to blue-chip stocks, glamour stocks are relatively less stable in their prices and dividend payment records.

Graduated payment plan (7)   A home financing plan that permits the borrower to make lower than usual payments in the first few years, with payments then increasing in the later years.

Gross lease (16)   A commercial lease that requires the landlord to pay for virtually all expenses relating to the property.

Group insurance (2)   One of many kinds of insurance plans (usually life and health) offered to members of a group, such as company employees or members of a fraternal organization. Because many individuals are covered under a single master policy, the cost to each insured is less than the same insurance would be if purchased individually.

Group venture (16)   The pooling of money among several investors to purchase real estate (or other investments).

Health insurance portability (17)   This federal law gives employees the right to retain health insurance when they change jobs.

Health maintenance organization (HMO) (17)   A prepaid medical care facility.

Hedge value (13)   Generally, the ability of an investment to withstand the effects of inflation.

Heir (19)   One who receives an interest in the *estate* of a *decedent*.

Highball (5)   A selling technique whereby the salesperson attempts to convince you that your property (trade-in car, house) is worth much more than you thought it was, to lure you into doing business with him.

Holographic will (19)   A *will* prepared in the handwriting of the *testator*; not always valid.

Homeowner's insurance (8)   A form of *insurance policy* that will reimburse the owner of a home for losses suffered due to fire, theft, and other causes. Risks covered and cost of policy depend on the type of policy: generally, basic form (the least coverage and cost), broad form (middle range), and comprehensive (highest coverage and cost). (See also *Tenant's insurance*.)

Hospital insurance (17)   A form of *insurance policy* that will reimburse the insured for costs of being hospitalized, including room, board, and other specified services.

Income-producing property (16)   Generally, real estate that is produced as an investment, and from which rental income and depreciation deductions flow to the investor.

Rollover (10,14)   Regarding the sale of a home, a technique that allows the postponement of taxes otherwise due on a profit from such sale; also, a form of *IRA plan* that allows postponement of taxes payable on the lump-sum payout of a pension or profit-sharing plan.

Roth IRA (18)   A new form of Individual Retirement Account made possible by the Taxpayer Relief Act of 1997. Unlike the standard IRA, which allows tax breaks when money is invested but incurs taxes on later withdrawal, the Roth IRA gives no tax break at the time of investment, but allows the money to be withdrawn free of taxes.

Round lot (15)   A block of 100 shares of stock, or a block divisible by 100.

Rule of 78s (12)   The most common method of calculating the rebate of prepaid interest charges on an installment loan when the loan is paid off before its scheduled maturity.

Schedules A and B (20)   Federal income tax forms, used in conjunction with the *1040 form* for declaring itemized deductions (A) and income from interest and dividends (B).

Securities and Exchange Commission (SEC) (15)   A federal regulatory agency that oversees the trading of stocks.

Securities Investors Protection Corporation (SIPC) (15)   A federal agency that insures certain aspects of investors' accounts with brokerage firms in the event of the firm's failure.

Security (12)   A tangible asset that a borrower pledges to a lender in order to obtain a loan. If the borrower defaults, the security may be sold by the lender to satisfy the debt.

Settlement options (17)   Various ways that the proceeds of a life insurance policy can be paid out.

Shared appreciation mortgage (7)   A form of mortgage wherein the lender charges the buyer a favorable interest rate in exchange for a share in future profits from the sale of the property.

Shared housing (6)   Two or more individuals or families combine their financial resources to purchase a dwelling for themselves.

Short selling (15)   A speculative technique that,

when successful, allows an investor to profit from the drop in value of shares of stock.

Simple interest (12)   One means of calculating loan costs, usually in a loan payable in one lump sum as opposed to installments. The interest cost is expressed as a percentage of the amount borrowed, usually on an annual basis. Example: 10 percent annual simple interest on a $1,000 loan would be $100 for a one-year loan, $50 for a six-month loan, $25 for a three-month loan.

Sinking fund (14)   A reserve account set up by a corporation; money is put into the account each year to be used to pay off a debt of the corporation when it falls due.

Sleeping second (7)   A creative financing tool involving a second mortgage that will be owed by the buyer to the seller but on which no payments will be required for an agreed-on time.

Standard deduction (20)   For taxpayers who choose not to itemize their deductions, this is a fixed amount that can be used to reduce the amount of income subject to taxation. The deduction may be taken whether or not the taxpayer actually incurred such expenses.

Stock (15)   Form of ownership of a fractional part of a corporation. One owns "shares of stock." Unless otherwise specified, stock is considered "common." Some corporations also issue another class of stock known as "preferred." Owners of preferred shares have a higher claim to company dividends (and assets in the event of liquidation) than owners of common shares.

Stock investment program (2)   A fringe benefit in which employees are offered the opportunity to buy shares of stock in the company at a lower price than they could on the open market.

Stop-payment order (11)   Written instructions to a bank, given by the maker of a check, ordering the bank not to pay a specific check that the maker had issued.

Strike price (15)   The price at which you can buy the underlying stock in a *call option* contract.

Surgical insurance (17)   A form of health insurance that reimburses the insured for surgical and related expenses.

Surplus (1) The status of a budget (one's financial condition) when more money has been taken in than has been spent. (See also *Deficit*.)

"Take back a mortgage" (16) Expression that applies to a situation in which the seller of property accepts the buyer's IOU instead of cash. The IOU is secured by a *mortgage* on the property. (Also referred to as "take back paper.")

Takeover operation (5) A sales technique involving a succession of salespersons, one taking over after the other, at ever increasing pressure; designed to wear down your resistance, especially with automobile sales.

Tax credit (20) An amount that may be deducted from your computed federal income tax. Every dollar's worth of credit reduces your tax by one dollar. A number of new credits were made possible by the Taxpayer Relief Act of 1997, specifically for families with small children and for certain educational expenses.

Tax-deferred investments (13) Investments whose earnings are not subject to taxation during the year earned but will be subject to taxation in some later year. (See also *Individual retirement account (IRA), Keough plan*.)

Tax-exempt investments (13) Investments whose earnings are not subject to taxation at any time. (See also *Municipal bond*.)

Tax rate (8) With respect to real property taxes, the factor used to determine the amount payable; usually expressed in terms of dollars per $1,000 worth of *assessment* value. For example, a tax rate of $20 per $1,000, applied to property assessed at $40,000, will result in an annual property tax of $800.

Tax tables (20) With respect to federal income taxes, the format from which most taxpayers can determine their taxes due.

Taxable income (20) In the calculation of taxes payable, the income on which the tax is figured after having taken into account all proper *deductions, exemptions*, and *adjustments*.

Taxable investments (13) Investments whose earnings are subject to taxation in the year in which earned.

Taxable transfer (19) With respect to federal estate and gift taxes, the amount on which the tax is figured after having taken into account all proper deductions.

Taxpayer Compliance Measurement Program (TCMP) (20) A random selection by the Internal Revenue Service of tax returns to be audited.

Tenant's insurance (8) A form of property insurance for those who rent their dwellings. (See also *Homeowner's insurance*.)

Term insurance (17) Also known as temporary insurance; a form of life insurance wherein the premium cost increases as the age of the insured increases. Policies run for a set number of years, and premiums are increased on renewal of policies. (See also *Permanent insurance*.)

Testator/testatrix (19) A person who makes a *will*.

Testimonium clause (19) A clause in a *will* in which the *testator* states that he or she is signing the document as his or her true last will and testament.

Time order (15) An order to a stockbroker to buy or sell stock subject to a time deadline; usually attached to a *limit order*.

Time sharing (3) An arrangement whereby one buys the right to use a specific dwelling unit (such as at a resort) for one or more specific weeks each year for many years.

Title insurance (6) Insurance that will reimburse the insured for losses suffered (within stated limits) should a claim be made against the title of property owned by the insured.

Townhouse (6) (Also known as rowhouse.) A form of dwelling unit adjoined on both sides by similar units.

Trade Policy (1) Government policy setting forth which nations will be favored or disfavored in international commercial dealings. Trade policy can be used to protect home-based industries from foreign competition, and it can stimulate other forms of competition to benefit home-based companies.

Treasury Bill (14) A short-term (less than one year) federal government debt instrument, minimum denomination $10,000.

Treasury Bond (14) A long-term (up to 30 years, or more) federal government debt instrument.

Treasury Note (14)   A medium-term (one to seven years) federal government debt instrument.

Trust (19)   An arrangement, often in complex legal fashion, whereby one person or institution (the trustee) has custody of someone else's (the trustor's) money or property, for ultimate distribution to a named third party (the beneficiary). An *inter vivos* trust is one that comes into being while the trustor is alive. A testamentary trust is one that comes into being upon the death of the trustor.

Truth in Lending law (11)   A federal law which, among other things, requires covered lenders to provide a uniform interest rate quotation to borrowers. (See also *Annual Percentage Rate*.)

"Turnover investing" (16)   With reference to real estate investing: a program of buying property with the intent of reselling it at a profit as soon as possible.

Unemployment insurance (2, 17)   A state-administered insurance program, paid for by employers, that provides financial benefits to employees who are laid off.

Uninsured motorist insurance (5)   A form of coverage in automobile insurance policies that protects the insured if he or she is injured in an accident with an uninsured driver.

Unit pricing (3)   The pricing of food and other grocery products expressed in units of measurement (ounces, pounds, etc.); that is, the price per ounce.

Usury laws (11)   State laws dictating the maximum rate of interest that can be charged for various types of loans.

Vanity rackets (4)   Various schemes, sometimes fraudulent, in which the promoter offers to "publish" your book or song, etc., for a fee, no matter what the quality of the work.

Variable rate mortgage (7)   A home financing arrangement in which the interest rate payable by the borrower may fluctuate up or down.

Vesting (18)   The concept that pertains to one's pension benefits becoming irrevocably due; vesting occurs according to a preset schedule.

Waiver of premium (17)   A clause in an insurance contract (usually life, health, or disability plans) stating that if the insured becomes disabled, the need to pay the premiums on the policy will be waived during the period of disability.

Warrant (15)   Sometimes part of a *stock* offering, it allows the holder to purchase shares of the company's stock at a set price for a limited period of time.

W-4 form (20)   A federal tax form in which a worker claims a number of allowances, which in turn determine the amount of tax withheld from the worker's pay.

Will (19)   A document that, when properly drawn and executed, assures the protection of the state court over the distribution of the individual's (*testator's*) *estate*, in accordance with his or her wishes as expressed in the document.

Workers' Compensation (2, 17)   A state-administered health and disability program, paid for by employers, which provides certain benefits to workers who suffer job-related injuries or illnesses.

Wraparound mortgage (7)   A creative home financing plan, in which a buyer makes a single monthly payment to the seller and the seller in turn makes two or more payments to actual mortgage holders. The *wraparound*, in effect, is a form of consolidation of two or more mortgage debts.

Yield (13)   Generally expressed as a percentage, the earnings received from an investment; for example, a return of $5 in one year on an investment of $100 equals a yield of 5 percent.

Zone (8)   A specified area within a community that can only be used for specific purposes, such as residential and commercial.

Index

A

Accessory shopping. *See*
Clothing and accessories
Accidental death benefits, 508
Accidents
automobile, 164–165
insurance, 630
liability and, 532
Accounting services, start-up
business, 679
Acquisition costs, in home
financing, 205–206
Active accumulation,
investment, 352–353
Activities
in later years, 556
retirement and, 582
Actuarial charges, life insurance
costs and, 543
Adjustable rate mortgage,
202–204
annual cap, 203–204
base rate, 203
index, 203
initial rate, 202
lifetime cap, 203
margin, 203
negative amortization, 204
vs. fixed rate, 204–205
Adjusted gross income, 631–632
Administrator, will, 592
Advertising
loss-leader, 120–121
real estate agents and, 269
shopping and, 80
Age, life insurance costs and, 521
Age Discrimination in
Employment Act (1967),
51, 678

Age of dwelling, home
purchasing and, 182–183
Air fares, 96–98
Airlines. *See also* Vacation and
travel
air fares and, 96–98
frequent flyer miles, 97
travel rights and, 104
wholesalers and, 98
Alimony, income taxes and, 628,
631
All-at-once vesting, 566–567
Alternative Minimum Tax, 638
American Association of Retired
Persons (AARP), 561
American depository receipts
(ADRs), 482
American Society of Travel
Agents, 95
American Stock Exchange, 413
Americans with Disabilities Act,
52, 677
Annual cap, in adjustable rate
mortgage, 203–204
Annual percentage rate (APR),
324–325
Annuities, 502, 504–505
income taxes and, 629
with installments fixed, 504
joint, 504
refund, 504
single premium, 504–505
straight life, 504
survivor, 504
Anxious sellers, home
purchasing and, 180–181
Appliance shopping, 92–93
budget for, 61–62
Application, for life insurance,
507

Appointment clauses, Will, 596
Appraisal, land investments and,
470
Appreciation, property, 225
Aptitudes, career and, 36
Architectural factors, home
purchase and, 173–174
design, 173
layout and size, 174
physical condition and, 174
Art collections, 486
Asia, 27
Aspirations, work and career
and, 34–35
Assessment, property, 232–234
Assets in financial statements, 71
Assumable mortgage, 199–200,
266, 274
Assumption clauses, in home
financing, 207
Athletic clubs, 109
Attestation clause, Will, 596–597
Attitudes, work and career and,
34–35
Audits, tax
best protection against, 649
capital gains and, 645
casualty losses and, 645
charitable contributions and,
645
discriminate income function
and, 644
initial screenings, 643
interrogation guidelines, 647
multiyear, 645
reasons for, 644
red flags and, 645
refunds and, 645
related pickups and, 645
requesting different auditor, 649

resolving, 647–648
strategies, 646–647
taxpayer compliance
    measurement program,
    644–645
time limitations and, 643
Automatic accumulation,
    investment, 351
Automatic teller machines,
    300
Automobile clubs, 165
Automobile insurance, 161–165
    accident procedures and,
        164–165
    automobile clubs and, 165
    bodily injury liability, 161
    collision insurance, 163
    comprehensive insurance, 163
    costs of, 164
    costs per mile and, 149
    medical coverage in, 532
    medical payments, 162
    property damage liability,
        161–162
    uninsured drivers, 163
    uninsured motorists, 162–163
Automobiles
    buying, 149–157. *See also*
        Dealerships, automobile
    best time to buy, 157
    dealer games, 152–156
    flair and, 150
    haggling room and, 156–157
    needs vs. desires, 149–150
    new vs. used, 151
    old car and, 156
    optional extras, 150–151
    price quotes, 153
    shopping criteria, 151–152
    size and, 150
    car pooling, 165
    car rental, 166–167
    cost per mile and, 147–149
        calculating, 147–148
        driving habits and, 149
        equipment and, 148
        insurance and, 149
        knowledge and, 149
        maintenance and, 148
    expenses in retirement, 582
    financing, 157–159
        interest rates, 158
        leasing, 158–159
        rebate incentives, 158

insurance, 161–165. *See also*
    Insurance, automobile
shopping comparison
    checklist, 167
warranties, 159–160

B

Bait and switch tactics, 120–121
Balloon clauses, in home
    financing, 207
Balloon loans, 339
Bank accounts, foreign, 481–482
Banker's acceptances, 398
Bank for Cooperatives, 388
Bankruptcy, 342–343
    chapter 7 proceedings, 343–344
    chapter 13 proceedings, 343
    scams, 683
Banks. *See* Financial institutions
Bargaining, home purchasing
    and, 181
Bargains, shopping and, 85
Barron's, 426
Barter, income taxes and, 629
Base rate, in adjustable rate
    mortgage, 20
Basic cost, in automobile leases,
    158
Bedding shopping, 90–91
Beneficiary
    defined, 591
    life insurance, 506
Bequests
    clauses, 595
    defined, 591
Best's Insurance Reports, 517
*Best's Recommended Life Insurance
    Companies*, 517
Bets, stock market, 436
Better Business Bureau, 139–140,
    671
Birth rate, work force and, 37
Blank endorsement, check, 290
Blue chip stocks, 427
Bodily injury car insurance, 161
Boiler room operations, 132–133
Bonds, 381–393
    convertible, 399–400
    corporate bonds, 382–387
        bond ratings, 385–386
        call privileges, 385
        investment criteria, 386–387
        junk bonds, 386

reading bond quotations,
    382
sinking funds, 385
value fluctuations, 383–385
yields, 383
floating-rate, 399
municipal bonds, 390–393
    investment criteria, 392–393
    municipal bond quotations,
        392
    municipal bond ratings, 392
    tax exemption, 391–392
U.S. government bonds,
    387–390
    federal agency borrowings,
        388
    inflation-proof bonds, 389
    investment criteria, 390
    savings bonds, 388
    Treasury borrowings, 387
    zero coupon bonds, 389
vs. stocks, 409
yield and, 354–355
Books, investment, 360
Borrowing. *See* Credit and
    borrowing; Financing
Boundary survey, land
    investments and, 470
Brand labels, 81–82
Brand name frauds, home
    improvement, 131
Broadcast services, fraudulent
    practices and, 139
Brokers, stock, 446–447
    problems with, 446
Building issues, real estate
    investment and, 459
"Built-in" credit, 674
Bulk-buying, 83
Bumping
    airline, 104
    credit, 346
    moving and, 278
Business cycles, 38–39
Business issues
    folding, pension benefits and,
        567–568
    income taxes, 628
    investment offerings, 683
    in later years, 562
    life insurance, 513
    start-up. *See* Business start-ups
    tax audits, 645
    tax incentives, 652

Business plans, 659
Business start-ups. *See also* Self-
    employment
accounting services, 679
debt *vs.* equity and, 675–676
financial advisors, 679
fluctuations in fortunes of, 684
franchises
    contracts, 669
    decision process, 670–671
    purchases, 669
insurance, 679–680
leases and, 667–668
legal advice, 680
management consultants,
    680
marketing consultants, 680
nonfranchise businesses
    decision process, 671
    purchase, 670
    professional help, 671–672
    purchase contracts and,
        668–669
raising capital, 672–675
    built in credit, 674
    family and friends, 673
    government sources, 674
    lenders, 673–674
    other investors, 674–675
    personal savings, 673
regulations and, 677–679
    credit matters, 678
    employee well-being,
        677–678
    retirement plans, 678
    tax matters, 677
schemes and, 683
tax breaks and, 675
worksheet for, 682
Buying down, in home
    financing, 217
Buying long, stocks, 431
Buying on margin, stocks, 432

C

Cafeteria plans, health
    insurance, 42
Call options, stock, 436–438
    buying, 437–438
    sample quotation, 437
    selling, 438–439
Call privileges, bond, 385

Capital, 28
    raising, 661, 672–675. *See also*
        Business start-up
    shortage, 672
Capital gains, income taxes and,
    628–629
Capital investment, 4, 23
Caps, in adjustable rate
    mortgage, 203–204
Career changes, 45–47. *See also*
    Workplace/employment
    issues
    flow patterns in, 46
Carpeting, shopping for, 91–92
Car pooling, 165
Cars. *See* Automobiles
Cashier's check, 299
Cash values, permanent life
    insurance and, 502, 510
Casualty losses, income tax and,
    634–635
Cellular phones fraud, 126–127
Certificates of Accrual on
    Treasury Securities, 389
Certificates of deposit (CDs),
    297, 378–381
    choices, 379
    investment criteria, 380–381
    penalties, 379
    renewal, 379
    shopping list, 380
Certified checks, 299
Chain letters, 123
Chapter seven proceedings,
    343–344
Chapter thirteen proceedings,
    343
Charge accounts, 320
    interest costs and, 347
Charitable contributions
    budget, 65
    income tax and, 634
Chartered Life Underwriters
    (CLUs), 519
Chartists, stock, 421
Checking accounts, 289–297
    blank endorsement, 290
    cashing check, 290
    checkbook register sample,
        295
    clearing checks, 291–292
    depositing a check, 291
    deposit slip sample, 291
    earnings and costs of, 311

    negotiating a check, 289–290
    operating principles, 289
    overdrafts, 294
    paying debts or purchases,
        292–293
    record keeping, 294
    restrictive endorsement, 291
    sample check, 290
    shopping for, 296
    statement and reconciliation,
        295–296
    stopping payment, 293–294
    types of endorsements, 293
Chicago Board of Trade, 484
Children
    clothing purchases for, 88
    home furnishing purchases
        for, 88
Children expenses, planning for
    future, 67
Churning abuse, by stock
    brokers, 431
Citizenship test, for dependent
    exemptions, 626
Claim filing, insurance, 230–231
Clearing process, checks, 291–292
Closed-end funds, 394
Closing, home purchase, 191–192
    adjustments and, 192
    closing date, 190–191
    recording, 192
Clothing and accessory
    shopping, 85–88
    budget, 62
    for children, 88
    cleanability and durability, 87
    counterfeits, 87
    ego and impulse and, 86
    money savers, 87–88
    rummaging, 88
    seconds and, 87
    simplicity and, 86–87
    store policies and, 88
    timing and, 87
Clothing expenses, retirement
    and, 582
Codicils, Will, 597
Coins
    counterfeit, 136
    investment in, 484, 486
Coinsurance clause, 229–230
Collateral, loan, 339
Collateralized mortgage
    obligations (CMOs), 476

Collectibles, 486
    value fluctuations and, 492
Collection services, 300
College education, cost of, 36
Collision insurance, automobile,
    163
Commercial banks, 284–285
Commercial paper, 398
Commissions
    brokerage, 430–431
    real estate agents, 271
Commodities funds, 480–481
Commodities market, 479–481
    commodities funds, 480–481
    exchanges and, 480
Communications, budget, 61
Competition, rental prices and,
    261
Compounding income, in fixed
    income investments, 465
Comprehensive automobile
    insurance, 163. See also
    Insurance, automobiles
Computers, for recreation, 107
Condominiums, 176–177
    conversion laws, 257–258
    sales restrictions, 268
    vacation rentals, 102
Confirmation, stock market
    transactions and, 416
Consolidation, loan, 340–341
Consumer Credit Counseling
    Agency, 342
Consumer finance companies, 286
Consumer Price Index, 389
Consumer Reports Buying Guide,
    93
Contingent beneficiary
    defined, 591
    life insurance, 506
Contract, for home purchase,
    186–191
    closing date, 190–191
    deed, 189–190
    default and recourse, 191
    easements, 187–188
    liens, 188–189
    payment, 190
    property description, 187
    restrictive covenants, 189
    seller's obligations, 191
    status of parties, 186–187
    title, 187–189
    title insurance and, 189

Contracts, frauds and, 130
Convenience food shopping,
    83–84
Conversion tables, life insurance,
    510–511
Conversion values
    life insurance, 509–510
    permanent life insurance and,
        502
Convertible bonds, 399–400
Cooperative apartments,
    176–177
    sales restrictions, 268
Corporate bonds, 382–387. See
    also Bond funds
Corporations
    forming, 666
    stock market workings and,
        412–413
Cosigner, loan, 337, 342
Cost per mile, automobile,
    147–149
Counseling programs, employer
    sponsored, 43
Counterfeit versions, of designer
    items, 87
Coupons
    in food markets, 114
    manufacturer, 84
Coupon yield, bonds, 383
Courier services, fraudulent
    activity and, 127
Courses, investment, 361
Covenants, restrictive, 189
Credentials, frauds and, 130–131
Credit and borrowing, 93,
    316–349. See also
    Financing
    access to credit, 318
    add-on-interest, 323–324
    annual percentage rate,
        324–325
    comparing interest rates, 331
    consumer interest costs, 347
    credit abuses, 337–341
        ballooning, 339
        loan consolidation, 340–341
        loan sharks and, 340
        oversecuring, 339
        pyramiding, 337–339
    credit capacity, 319
    credit needs, 318–319
    credit reporting, 321
    credit sources, 319–321

credit traps, 346
    discipline and, 344
    discount interest, 324
    financial statements and, 72,
        73
    installment loans
        costs, 325
        figuring payoff, 329–330
        increasing, 330
        insuring, 325–326
        paying off, 326
        refinancing, 330
        rule of 78s, 327–329
    against life insurance, 510
    loan applications, 335–337
    loan cost comparison, 345
    meeting future goals and,
        68–69
    Morris plan and, 317–318
    overindebtedness cures,
        341–344
        bankruptcy, 342–344
        chapter 7 proceedings,
            343–344
        chapter 13 proceedings, 343
        credit repair clinics, 343
        debt-counseling services,
            342
    shopping for loans, 331–334
        down payment size and,
            331–332
        home equity borrowing, 334
        length of loan, 332–334
    simple interest, 322–323
    small business regulations, 678
    spending habits and, 76
    starting business and. See
        Capital
Credit bureaus, 321
Credit cards, 320
    companies, 287
    giving numbers to strangers,
        346
    low-rate, 321
    soliciting customers for, 312
Credit checks, tenant, 459
Credit costs, budget, 63
Credit health insurance, 326, 535
Credit history, 321
    report, 322
    self-employment and, 658
Credit plans, life insurance, 326,
    502
Credit repair frauds, 137

Credit unions, 285–286
Cruises, 100–101
Current yield, bonds, 383

D

Day care, 43
Dealer financing, 320
Dealerships, automobile
  bugged closing rooms, 155
  highball quotes, 154–155
  sales practices, 152–156
  schemes, 155–156
  "takeover" operation, 155
Debit cards, 300
Debt, start-up businesses and,
  675–676
Debt-counseling services, 342
Deductibles, insurance, 229, 529
Deed, property title and, 189–190
Default, in home purchase, 191
Default clauses, lease, 465
Deficits, 5
Deflation, 5
Dental expenses, income tax
  and, 634
Dependent coverage, health
  insurance, 529
Dependents, income tax, 624–626
Depreciation, property, 225
Depreciation deduction, 466–468
  breakdown of, 467
  operating income and
    expenses, 467
  profit tax when sold, 468
  purchase price and, 466
  return and, 468
Depreciation factor, investment,
  359
Descendent, defined, 591
Diamond speculation, 485–486
Disability
  in later years, 557
  parents, planning for future,
    67
Disability income insurance
  evaluating needs, 535
  extra benefits in, 537
  income taxes and, 536
  limitations on, 536
  mail order, 542
  private policies, 535–536
  total or partial disability, 536
  waiting period and, 535–536

Disclosure statements, 305
Discounting news, stock market,
  451
Discounts
  buying mortgage at, 475
  long-term-care insurance, 538
Discretionary income, investing,
  364
Discriminate Income Function,
  tax audits and, 644
Discrimination in employment,
  50
Distance test, moving, 276
Distribution of assets, estate
  planning and, 604–606
Dividend options, life insurance,
  511
Dividends
  income taxes and, 628
  life insurance costs and, 543
  payments, 355
  stock, 424, 429–430, 433
    apparent yield and, 429
    declaration of, 429
    ex-dividend date, 429–430
    reinvestment plans, 440–441
Do-it-yourself tours and
  vacations, 100
Double indemnity clause, life
  insurance, 508
"Double whammy" frauds, 137
Dow Jones Industrial Averages,
  426–427
Down payments
  in home financing, 210–212,
    266
  loan shopping and, 331–332
Downsizing, 38–39
Driving habits, 149
Due on sale clause, in home
  financing, 207

E

Early payoffs, mortgage, 476–477
Easements, 187–188
Eastern Europe, 27
Economic growth, 5
Economic trends, 38–40
  starting business and, 660–662
  taxation and, 653
Economies, forces in, 3
Education
  budget, 62

career and, 35–36
  employer sponsored, 43
  planning for future, 66
  programs, 42
Education Individual Retirement
  Accounts, 574
Ego, shopping and, 86
Electronic banking, 300
Electronic equipment,
  recreational, 106–109
Eminent domain laws, 236–237
Employee Retirement Income
  Security Act (1974). See
  Pension Reform Law
  (ERISA)
Employer benefits
  cafeteria plans, 42
  education, 42, 43
  family-freindly benefits, 42
  flexible spending accounts, 42
  health insurance plans, 41
  housing-related perks, 43
  investment programs, 41
  life insurance, 41–42
  pension plans, 40–41
  personal benefits, 43
  profit-sharing plans, 41
  stock options, 43
Employment contracts, 53–54
Employment policies, 53–54
Employment regulations, small
  business, 677–678
Energy audits, 233
Entertainment budget, 62
Envelope addressing schemes,
  124
Equal Credit Opportunity Law,
  309–310
The Equal Employment
  Opportunity
  Commission, 51
Equity
  defined, 351
  renting dwelling and, 247
  start-up businesses and,
    675–676
Escrow accounts
  in home financing, 206
  in home purchase, 190–191
Estate planning
  definitions of, 589
  distribution worksheet, 611
  estate taxes, 609–610
  financial statements and, 73

gifts, 600–601
goals of, 603–608
    distribution and liquidity, 604–606
    lifestyle continuance, 607–608
    minimizing taxes, 608
    sound management, 606–607
insurance, 601
joint names and, 601–602
language of, 591–592
liquidity fluctuations, 613
living trusts, 612
proceeding with, 602–603
rights and, 590
trusts, 599–600
unexpected problems and, 587–588
Wills, 593–599. *See also* Wills
Estate taxes, 590
Estimated taxes, 638
Exchanges
    bonds. *See* Bonds
    commodity, 480
    precious metals, 483–484
    stocks. *See* Stock market
Executor (Executrix), defined, 591–592
Exemptions, income tax, 624–426
Expectations, spending habits and, 76

F

Face amount, life insurance, 508
Failure fees, in food markets, 114
Fair Credit Billing Law, 306–308
Fair Credit Reporting Act, 308–309
Fair Debt Collection Practices Act, 310
Fair Employment Practices Law, 51, 678
Family, raising business capital and, 673
Family and Medical Leave Act, 52, 677
Fannie Mae. *See* Federal National Mortgage Association
Fax machines, 108
Federal agency borrowings, 388

Federal Aviation Administration, 104
Federal Consumer Credit Protection Act (1968), 53
Federal Deposit Insurance Corporation
    commercial banks and, 284–285
    mutual savings banks and, 285
Federal Fair Labor Standards Act, 50, 678
Federal Home Loan Bank, 388
Federal Home Loan Mortgage Corporation, 209, 476
Federal Housing Administration (FHA) loans, 208–209
Federal Intermediate Credit Banks, 388
Federal Land Banks, 388
Federal National Mortgage Association, 209, 388, 476
Federal Reserve Bank, 387
Federal Reserve System, 368
Federal Trade Commission, 138–139
Fees, in rental lease, 252
Fellowships, income taxes and, 630
Filing, income tax, 623–624. *See also* Income taxes
Filing requirements, income tax, 622
Fill orders, stock, 417
Financial contingency clause, in home purchase, 190
Financial factors, home purchase and, 172
Financial institutions, 282–315
    changing health of, 313
    commercial banks, 284–285
    consumer finance companies, 286
    credit card companies, 287
    credit unions, 285–286
    federal laws and, 303–308
        Equal Credit Opportunity Law, 309–310
        Fair Credit Billing Law, 306–308
        Fair Credit Reporting Act, 308–309
        Fair Debt Collection Practices Act, 310

Truth in Lending Law, 303–304
Truth in Savings Law, 304–306
financial planners, 287–288
fraudulent practices and, 140
insurance companies, 287
merchant lenders, 286
mutual savings banks, 285
role of middlemen, 283–284
services
    certificates of deposit, 297
    checking accounts, 289–297
    collection services, 300
    debit cards, 300
    electronic banking, 300
    investment departments, 300
    money market accounts, 297–298
    notarial services, 299
    passbook accounts, 297
    safe deposit facilities, 298
    special checks, 299
    trust services, 298
state laws and, 301–303
    negotiable instruments laws, 301–302
    secured transaction laws, 303
    usury laws, 302–303
Financial planners, 287–288, 365
Financial planning, later years
    activities and, 556
    budgeting and, 559
    business interests and, 562
    existing investment portfolio and, 562–563
    health care concerns, 557
    home equity and, 561–562
    housing and, 548–552. *See also* Housing, in later years
    income from pensions/profit-sharing, 559
    income sources and, 559–563
    inflation and, 558
    insurance and, 554–556
    investing and, 552–554
    investment income and, 560
    life insurance values and, 562
    nest-egg dipping, 563–564
    potential inheritances and, 563
    retirement and, 556
    single people and, 556–557

Financial planning, later years
    (Continued)
  social security and, 559
  tax and pension laws, 564–579.
      See also Pension and
      retirement plans
  working and, 560–561
Financial regulations, small
    businesses, 678
Financial rewards, work and
    career and, 40
Financial services, start-up
    business, 679
Financial statements, 69–73
  elements of
    assets, 71
    liabilities, 71
    net worth, 71
    sample, 70
  uses of
    borrowing and, 73
    credit and, 72
    estate planning and, 73
    life insurance and, 73
    long-range budgeting and,
        73
    protecting against loss, 72
Financial success, secret to, 402
Financing
  automobile, 157–159
  home purchases, 179, 190,
      198–222
    acquisition costs, 205–206
    adjustable rate loans,
        202–204
    applying for, 214–215
    assumption clauses, 207
    balloon clauses, 207
    buying down, 217
    conventional loans, 210
    creative financing, 215–216
    determining costs, 184
    down payments and,
        210–212
    due on sale clause, 207
    escrow or reserve accounts,
        206–207
    Fannie Mae loans, 209
    Federal Housing
        Administration loans,
        208–209
    financing comparisons, 219
    first steps, 199–201
    fixed rate loans, 201–202

fixed rate vs. adjustable,
    204–205
Freddie Mac loans, 209
Ginnie Mae loans, 209
insurance costs, 206
interest rates and, 201–202,
    210
jumbo loans, 210
land contracts, 216
lender services, 212–114
loan affordability table, 200
loan application process,
    220
mortgage length and, 212,
    214
rate lock, 216
Real Estate Settlements
    Procedures Act and, 210
repayment clauses, 207
shared appreciation loans,
    217
shopping for financing,
    208–214
the sleeping second, 216–217
tax considerations, 217
timing and, 218
Veteran's Administration
    loans, 208–209
home sales and, 267, 274
income property, 461–462
real estate agents and, 269
First mortgage, 199
Fiscal policy, example of, 15–16
Fixed income investing, 352
  vs. ownership investing, 409,
      410–411
Fixed rate mortgages, 201–202
  vs. adjustable rate, 204–205
Fix-it chores, 174
Flexibility advantages, of renting
    dwelling, 245
Flexible spending accounts, 42
Flextime, 42
Floating-rate bonds, 399
Food and beverage budget, 60
Food prices, 114
Forces, in economic entities, 3
Forecasting, 23–24
Foreclosures, 200–201
  buying, 181
Foreign investing
  bank accounts, 481–482
  commodity funds, 481–482
  stock and mutual funds, 482

Foreign money, vacationing and,
    103
Forward averaging, 578
401(k) plan, 41, 359, 574–575
  investment rules, 576–577
  relocating, 576
  setting up, 575–576
Franchises
  buying, 669
  contracts, 669
  decision process and, 670–671
Frauds and swindles
  advance loan schemes, 136
  alternative opinions and, 138
  bait and switch, 120–121
  best defense against, 140–141
  coins and gems, 136
  credit repair clinics, 137
  double whammy scam, 137
  ebb and flow of, 143
  filing complaints, 138–140
    Better Business Bureaus,
        139–140
    Federal Trade Commission,
        138–139
    financial institutions, 140
    local newspapers and
        broadcast services, 139
    Postal Service, 139
    small claims court, 140
    State and local government
        agencies, 139
  fraud avoidance techniques,
      141
  health insurance scams, 137
  home frauds, 126–127
    cellular phones and,
        126–127
    courier services and, 127
    "900" scams, 126
    scholarship scams, 127
  home improvements, 128–131
    avoiding, 131
    furnace swindle, 128–129
    model home swindle, 129
    "squirrels" swindle, 128
    warning signals, 129–131
  investment schemes, 132–134
    boiler room operations,
        132–133
    media and, 134
    ponzis and pyramids,
        133–134
  land frauds, 135

mail-order, 121–125
    get-rich quick schemes, 123
    quackery, 124–125
    vanity rackets, 122–123
    work-at-home schemes, 124
saying no, 142
street fraud, 125–126
    phony goods, 125–126
    pigeon drop, 125
time sharing, 135
vacation ripoffs, 135–136
Freddie Mac. *See* Federal Home
    Loan Mortgage
    Corporation
Frenzy, stock market, 451
Frequent flyer miles, 97
Friends, raising business capital
    and, 673
Full warranty deed, 189
Fundamentalists approach, stock
    investment, 421
Furnace repair frauds, 128–129
Furnishings, rental prices and,
    261
Furniture costs, home
    purchasing and, 185
Furniture purchases, 89–90

G

Gain and loss, investment,
    355–356
Gambling winnings, income
    taxes and, 629
Garnishment of wages, 53
Gasoline prices, 169
Gems, junk, 136
Gemstone speculation, 485–486
    carat weight, 485–486
    clarity and, 485
    color and, 485
    cut and, 485
Gender
    life insurance costs and, 521,
        543
    work force and, 37–38
General obligation bonds, 391
Generic labels, 81–82
Geographical factors, home
    purchase and, 172–173
Geographical shifts, workforce,
    39
Get-rich-quick schemes, 123

Gifts
    estate planning and, 600–601
    income taxes and, 630
    investing and, 364
Ginnie Mae. *See* Government
    National Mortgage
    Association
Glamour stocks, 428
Global marketplace, 27
Goal setting and budgeting
    annual budget four-person
        family, 60
    current/ongoing expenses
        charity and religious
            expenses, 65
        clothing and linens, 62
        cost of credit, 63
        current/ongoing expenses,
            58–65
        education, 62
        entertainment, 62
        family concerns and, 56–58
        food and beverage, 60
        health care, 62–63
        income taxes, 65
        luxuries, 64
        master plan and, 54–56
        need to update, 58
        personal business, 64
        personal expenses, 64
        rainy day funds, 63
        risk management and, 58
        risk protection, 62
        shelter, 60–62
        transportation, 63
        travel and recreation, 63
        worksheet for, 59
    financial statements and. *See*
        Financial statements
    future goals
        big rainy day fund, 67
        children expenses, 67
        education, 66
        elderly or disabled care, 67
        housing, 66
        one-shot expenses, 67
        retirement, 66
        stake in yourself, 67
        worksheet for, 65
    satisfying yourself not others,
        75
    sources for accomplishing
        borrowing, 68–69
        enforced savings, 69

equities, 68
    inheritances, gifts, and
        windfalls, 69
    savings/investment, 68
    work income, 68
spending habits and, 73–74,
    76
Gold. *See* Metals, precious
Gold-painted lead fraud, 136
Government bond mutual funds,
    397
Government bonds, interest
    income and, 627
Government National Mortgage
    Association, 209, 475
Government policy and
    regulations, 4, 20–21, 28
Government sources, of business
    capital, 674
Grace period, life insurance, 509
Gradual vesting, 566
Grants, income taxes and, 630
Groceries and toiletry shopping,
    80–85
    brand *vs.* generic labels, 81–82
    bulk buying, 83
    convenience foods, 83–84
    coupons and specials, 84
    money saving tips, 84–85
    pharmaceuticals and
        prescriptions, 82–83
    unit pricing, 80–81
Gross income test, for dependent
    exemptions, 625–626
Gross leases, 667
    commercial, 463
Group life insurance, 501
Growth periods, 38
Growth stocks, 428
Guaranteed insurability, 508
Guarantees, money-back, 129
Guidebooks, travel, 95

H

H. & R. Block annual tax guide,
    651
Handicraft kit schemes, 124
Health and safety regulations,
    workplace, 52
Health care
    budget, 62–63
    concerns in later years, 557

Health insurance
  accident liability and, 532
  alternative insurance
    coverage, 532
  cafeteria plans, 525
  checklists
    hospital coverage, 528
    managed care, 530–531
    miscellaneous insurance
      items, 529–530
    physician insurance, 529
    surgical insurance, 529
  choices, 526–527
  Clinton administration and,
    523–524
  deductibles, 529
  dependent coverage, 529
  flexible spending accounts,
    525
  Health Insurance Portability
    Act of 1997, 525
  health maintenance
    organizations and, 526
  historical perspective on,
    521–522
  income taxes and, 630
  income tax law of 1986 and,
    522
  independent physicians
    associations, 527
  long-term-care insurance, 539
  mail order, 542
  managed care, 524–525
  maternity benefits, 52
  Medicare and, 532–533
  plans, 41
  point-of-service plans, 527
  portability of, 539–540
  preexisting conditions and, 529
  preferred provider
    organizations, 526–527
  private enterprise and, 528
  profit *vs.* nonprofit
    institutions, 527
  rated risk and, 529
  scams, 137
  self-employed, 675
  Worker's Compensation
    insurance and, 532
Health Insurance Portability
  Law (1997), 539–540
Health maintenance
  organizations (HMOs),
  530–531

Health spas, 109
Hedge value
  certificates of deposit and,
    381
  corporate bonds and, 387
  investment, 357
  municipal bonds and, 393
  passbook savings accounts
    and, 378
  U.S. Treasury borrowings, 390
High definition television, 109
HMO. *See* Health maintenance
  organizations
Hobbies, 109, 110
Holidays, 42
Holographic Will, 599
Home entertainment
  health spas/athletic clubs,
    109
  nature appreciation, 111
  night on the town, 110
  personal enrichment, 109
  professional sports, 110
  sports activities, 109, 110
Home equity
  estate liquidity and, 613
  financing, 334
  in later years, 561–562
  loan swindles, 137
Home-exchange programs, 102
Home frauds, 126–127
Home furnishing shopping
  appliances, 92
  bedding, 90–91
  carpeting and other flooring,
    91–92
  changing tastes and, 89
  children and, 88
  considerations in, 88–89
  furniture, 89–90
  home entertaining and, 89
  information sources, 93
  payment and financing, 93
  renting *vs.* buying, 91
  service and warranties, 92–93
Home improvement
  costs, 231
  frauds, 128–131
Homeowners and tenant
  insurance, 225–232
  basic form (HO1), 226
  broad form (HO2), 227
  change and, 230
  coinsurance clause, 229–230

  competitive nature of, 225
  comprehensive form (HO5),
    227
  coverage amount, 226
  coverage desires, 226
  deductibles and, 229
  filing a claim, 230–232
  medical coverage in, 532
  other property protection,
    227–228
  public liability, 228–229
  risk ratings and, 225–226
  types of policies and coverage,
    226–232
  valuables, 229
Home ownership, 175. *See also*
  Home purchasing
Home precautions, vacationing
  and, 103–104
Home purchasing. *See also*
  Housing costs
  architectural factors, 173–174
  closing, 191–192
  financial factors, 172
  financing. *See* Financing, home
  fix-it chores and, 174
  fluctuations in costs, 195
  geographical factors, 172–173
  guidelines, 193
  in later years, 551–552
  leisure activity considerations,
    174
  personal factors, 174–175
  price determination, 178–186
    age of dwelling and,
      182–183
    anxious sellers and, 180–181
    bargaining, 181
    comparable values, 182
    financing and, 179, 184
    foreclosures, 181
    furnishing costs and, 185
    knowing needs, 182
    knowing your price range,
      179
    property taxes and, 185
    real estate agents and,
      179–180
    resale potential and,
      185–186
    timing and, 180
    utility costs and, 184–185
    warranties and, 183–184
  privacy considerations, 174

Model home frauds, 129
Monetary policy, example of, 16–17
Money, future value of, 23–24
Money market accounts, 297–298
Money market investments
  banker's acceptances, 398
  bond market, 381–393
  certificates of deposit, 378–381
  characteristics of, 373–374
  commercial paper, 398
  comparing returns, after costs, 401
  convertible bonds, 399–400
  floating-rate bonds, 399
  interest and, 374–376
  mutual funds, 394–398
  passbook savings accounts, 376–378
  stock market effect on, 403
Money orders, 299
Month-for-month tenancy, 255
Monthly payments, retirement funds, 577–578
Moody's
  bond ratings, 385–386
  municipal bond ratings, 392
  published stock listings, 426
Morris plan, 317–318
Mortgage-backed securities (MBSs), 476
Mortgage insurance, 239
Mortgage pools, 475–476
Mortgages
  assumable, 266, 274
  debt reduction rates, 183
  home financing and, 199–201. *See also* Financing, home purchases
  investment in, 473–477
    at discounts, 475
    early payoffs, 476–477
    initiating, 474–475
    mortgage brokers and, 473
    mortgage pools, 475–476
    return of principal, 476
    taking back a mortgage, 474
  length and costs of, 212–213
  monthly mortgage payment finder, 211
  payment budget, 60
  reduction schedule, 213
  reverse, 561

Moving, 274–276
  pitfalls in, 278
  tax deductions for, 276–277
    distance test, 276
    work test, 276–277
Multiple listing services, 269270
Multiple unit housing, 178
Multiyear audits. *See* Audits, tax
Municipal bonds, 390–393, 391. *See also* Bond market
Mutual companies, life insurance and, 500
Mutual funds, 394–398
  corporate bond funds, 396
  extra privileges, 395
  foreign, 482
  fund objectives, 395
  government bond mutual funds, 397
  investment criteria, 395–396
  load *vs.* no-load, 394–395
  maintenance charges, 395
  minimum investment required, 395
  money market mutual funds, 397–398
  open *vs.* closed end funds, 394
  service charges, 395
  stock market, 443–446
    advertising, 445
    choosing, 449–450
    families of, 334–336, 365
    growth/income funds, 443
    mistakes, 445
    net asset value and, 444
    offering price, 444
    performance funds, 443
  tax-exempt mutual funds, 396
Mutual savings banks, 285

N

Nasdaq, 413
National Credit Union Administration, 286
National Labor Relations Act of 1935, 52–53
National Labor Relations Board (NLRB), 53
Natural resources, 4, 25
Nature
  appreciation of, 111
  investing in, 4, 25

Near-home vacations, 98
Negotiable instruments law, 301–302
Neighborhoods
  home sales and, 266
  housing costs and, 279
  rental prices and, 261
Nest-egg dipping, in later years, 563–564
Net leases, 667
  commercial, 463
Net worth in financial statements, 71
News, stock market reaction to, 451
Newspapers
  fraudulent practices and, 139
  investment-related, 361
New York Commodity Exchange, 484
New York Mercantile Exchange, 484
New York Stock Exchange, 413
  Common Stock Index, 427
"900" number telephone scams, 126
No-fault laws, automobile, 164
No-load fund, 395
Noncompetition clauses, lease, 464
Noncupative Will, 599
Nonparticipating policies, life insurance, 500
Nontaxable income. *See* Income taxes
Normal life expectancy, life insurance and, 512
North America, 27
Notarial services, bank, 299
Notice of Deficiency, 648
Nuisance laws, 236

O

Occupational Safety and Health Act (OSHA), 52, 677
Occupations. *See also* Workplace/employment issues fastest growing, 44
Odd lot differential, 419
Official Airline Guide, 94
Open-end funds, 394
Open-end loans, 325

Optional equipment, automobile, 148
Option to buy, in rental lease, 255–256
Option trading, stocks, 436
Orders, stock market, 416–417
  fill or kill order, 417
  limit orders, 417
  market orders, 416
  time orders, 417
Overdrafts, checking, 294
Overindebtedness, 341–344. *See also* Credit and borrowing
Oversecured loans, 339

P

Pacific Stock Exchange, 413
Package tours, 99
Paid-up insurance, converting to, 510
Participating policies, life insurance, 500
Participation certificates (PCs), mortgage, 476
Partnerships
  forming, 665–666
  income taxes and, 629
Passbook savings accounts, 297, 376–378
  yield and, 355
Paychecks, 48
Pension and retirement plans
  estate liquidity and, 613
  401(k) plans, 574–575
  income taxes and, 629
  individual retirement accounts (IRAs), 569–574
  interest income and, 627
  investment rules, 576–577
  Keough plans, 575
  in later years, 559–560
  meeting future goals and, 69
  Pension Reform Law (ERISA), 565–568
  plans, 40–41
  relocating your plans, 576
  self-employed and, 663–666, 675
  setting up, 575–576
  Simplified Employee Pension (SEP) plans, 575
  small business regulations, 678

taxes and, 577–578
  forward averaging, 578
  IRA rollover, 578
  lump-sum payouts *vs.* monthly payouts, 577–578
Pension Benefit Guarantee Corporation (PBGC), 467–568, 678
Pension Reform Law (ERISA), 50, 565–568, 678
  folding and, 567–568
  funding and, 567
  managing and, 568
  purpose of, 565
  reporting and, 568
  vesting and, 565–567
    all-at-once vesting, 566–567
    gradual vesting, 566
Percentage clause, lease, 463–464
  in commercial leases, 667–668
Percolation tests, land investments and, 470
Permanent life insurance, 501–503
Personal business, budget, 64
Personal enrichment activities, 109
Personal expenses, budget, 64
Personal experience, work and career and, 37
Personal Finance magazine, 93
Personal savings, raising business capital and, 673
Pharmaceutical shopping, 82–83
Phony goods swindles, 125–126
Physician insurance, 529. *See also* Health insurance
Pigeon drop scheme, 125
Plant closing laws, 51, 678
Pledge value
  certificates of deposit and, 381
  corporate bonds and, 387
  investment, 356–357
  municipal bonds and, 393
  passbook savings accounts and, 378
  U.S. Treasury borrowings, 390
Pocket money, vacationing and, 103
Points, in home financing, 205
Political changes, affecting work environment, 40
Political parties, taxation and, 652

Ponzi scheme, 133
Portfolio maturities, in later years, 553–554
Postretirement income. *See* Financial planning, later years
Power of Attorney, 557
PPO. *See* Preferred provider organizations
Precious metals investment. *See* Metals, precious
Preexisting conditions, health insurance and, 529
Preferred provider organizations (PPOs), 531
Preferred stocks, 434–435
  convertible, 435
  cumulative, 434
Premature death, life insurance and, 512
Premium, call options and, 437
Premium load, automatic, 510
Premium return, long-term-care insurance, 538
Premium waiver, life insurance, 509
Prepayment clauses, in home financing, 207
Prescription purchasing, 82–83
Price, stock, 442–443
Price-earnings ratio, stock, 425
Price listings, stock market, 424–426
  dividend, 424
  52 weeks high/low, 424
  footnotes, 425–426
  high/low/close, 425
  net change, 425
  price-earning ratio, 425
  sales 100s, 425
  yield, 424
Price quotes, automobile, 153
Price range, in home purchasing, 179
Primary market, stocks, 409–410
Prime-rate loans, 323
Privacy, home purchasing and, 174
Private lending, 487–488
Private life insurance, 501
Private partnerships, real estate, 478
Prizes and awards, income taxes and, 630

Probate, defined, 592
Product delivery, 28
Productivity, conditions
    effecting, 20
Profit and loss risks, rental
    dwelling and, 246
Profit-sharing plans, 41
    in later years, 559–560
    meeting future goals and, 69
Profit-taking selloffs, stocks, 451
Program trading, 419
Property damage car insurance,
    161–162
Property description, in home
    purchase contract, 187
Property insurance. *See also*
    Homeowners and tenant
    insurance
    budget for, 61
Property location, real estate
    investment and, 459
Property management, 461–465.
    See also Leasing, property;
    Real estate investment
Property reports, land
    investments and, 460
Property structure, real estate
    investment and, 459
Property taxes, 232–234
    budget, 60
    home purchasing and, 185
    housing costs and, 279
    income tax and, 634
    real estate investment and, 460
Prospectus, stock, 414–415
Prudent investors, stock market,
    422–423
Public liability insurance, 228-229
Purchase contracts, buying new
    business and, 668–669
Purchase money mortgage, 199
Purchase option, in automobile
    leases, 158–159
Put options, 437
Pyramiding, loan, 337–339
Pyramid schemes, 133–134

Q

Quackery schemes, 124–125
Quiet enjoyment clause, in rental
    lease, 251
Quit claim deed, 189

R

Rainy day fund, 63, 67
Rated risk, health insurance and,
    529
Rate lock, in home financing,
    216
Real estate agents, 179–180
    advertising and, 269
    commission negotiation and,
        271
    financing and, 269
    finding, 270
    listing contract, 271
    market and pricing and, 269
    multiple listing service and,
        269–270
    negotiating with, 270
    objectivity of, 270
    sales force and, 269
    showing home and, 269
Real estate investing, 455–478
    compounding income, 465
    group investing, 477–478
        limited partnerships and,
            477
        private partnerships, 478
        real estate investment
            trusts, 477
        syndication and, 477
    income producing
        building and, 459–460
        property taxes and, 460
        tenants and, 458–459
        utility costs and, 460–461
    income property evaluator,
        489–490
    mortgage investing, 473–477.
        See also Mortgage
        investment
    myths and facts about,
        456–458
    property management
        financing and, 461–462
        lease and, 462–465. *See also*
            Lease, property
    taxes and, 466–468. *See also*
        Taxes, real estate
        investing
    turnover investing, 471–47
    vacant land, 468–471. *See also*
        Vacant land investment
Real estate investment trusts
    (REITs), 477

Real Estate Settlements
    Procedures Act (RESPA),
    210
Real estate taxes, 232–234
    income tax and, 634
Real income, worksheet on, 74
Rebates
    automobile purchasing and,
        158
    in food markets, 114
Recession, 5
Recession periods, 38
Reconciliation, checkbook,
    295–296
Recreation
    budget for, 63
    expenses
        disposable income and,
            93–94
        for home recreation, 106–111
        for vacation and travel,
            94–106
    facilities, employer sponsored,
        43
Red flags, tax audits, 645–646
References, job search and, 44
Refinancing, home sales and,
    217, 268
    in later years, 552
Refund annuities, 504
Refunds, tax audits and, 645
Regulatory policy, example of,
    17–18
Reinstatement, life insurance, 509
Related pickups, tax audits and,
    645
Relationship test, for dependent
    exemptions, 626
Religious expenses, budget, 65
Renewal options, in rental lease,
    2252
Renewals, certificates of deposit
    and, 379
Renovation, budget, 61
Rent-control laws, 257
Renting
    automobile, 166–167
    dwelling, 243–263
        budget for, 60
        case history, 248–249
        comparison checklist, 259
        competition for, 250
        lease. *See* Leases, tenant
            rental

Renting *(Continued)*
  month-to-month tenancy, 255
  options to buy, 255–256
  precautions, 260
  price fluctuations, 261
  price negotiating, 261
  pros and cons of, 244–248
    equity, 247
    expenses, 247–248
    flexibility, 245
    income tax implications, 245–246
    inflation protection, 246–247
    money, 245
    profit and loss, 246
  rent laws, 256–258
    condominium-conversion laws, 257–258
    rent control, 257
  right of first refusal options, 256
  shopping for, 249–250
  terminating lease, 258–259
  in later years, 550–551
  vs. buying, 91
Rent laws, 256–258
Repairs
  budget, 61
  home, costs of, 234–235
  in rental lease, 251, 464
Resale potential, home
    purchasing and, 185–186
Research and development, 4
Resorts, 99
Restoration clauses, lease, 464–465
Restrictive endorsement, check, 291
Resume, job search and, 44
Retirement. *See also* Financial
    planning, later years
  estimating costs, 580
  excerpts from recent retirees, 581
  in later years, 556
  living costs during, 582
  planning for future, 66
Retirement investing. *See*
    Pension and retirement
    plans
Return of principal, mortgage, 476

Revenue bonds, 391
Reverse mortgages, 561
Reward/risk rule, investing, 353–354
Right of assignment, in home
    purchase contract, 187
Right of first refusal, in rental
    lease, 256
Right to work laws, 50, 678
Risk protection, budget, 62
Risk rating, property, 225–226
Roth Individual Retirement
    Accounts, 572–573
  converting to, 573–574
Royalties, income taxes and, 629
Rule of 78s, 327–330

S

Safe deposit facilities, 298
Safety
  certificates of deposit and, 381
  corporate bonds and, 386
  municipal bonds and, 393
  passbook savings accounts
    and, 378
  U.S. Treasury borrowings, 390
Sale-leaseback, home, 562
Savings, meeting future goals
    and, 68
Savings accounts, 297–298, 352
  certificates of deposit, 297
  money market accounts, 297–298
  passbook accounts, 297
Savings bonds, 352, 388
Savings frauds, 130
Scholarships, income taxes and, 630
Scholarship scams, 127
Seasonal bargains, vacation, 98
Secondary market, stocks, 409–410
Second hand clothes shopping, 87
Second mortgage, 200
Secured transaction laws, 303
Securities and Exchange
    Commission, 414, 445
Security deposits, in rental lease, 253–254
Security Investors Protection
    Corporation, 415

Self-employment. *See also*
    Business start-ups
  business plans and, 659
  cost of money and, 661
  credit history and, 658
  economic factors and, 660–662
  energy sources and, 659
  evaluating expectations, 657
  evaluating motives for, 658
  evaluating tradeoffs, 658
  fallback options, 658–659
  growth or recession and, 660
  industry trends and, 660–661
  location and, 661–662
  Small Business Administration
    and, 659
  test runs, 662
  types of
    corporations, 666
    independent contractor, 663–664
    partnerships, 665–666
    sole proprietorship, 664–665
    temping, 663
Self-employment tax, 675
Self-indulgence, spending habits
    and, 76
Seller's obligations, in home
    purchase, 191
Selling short, stocks, 431–432
Seminars, investment, 361
Senior citizens
  discounts, 582
  financial planning and. *See*
    Financial planning, later
    years
Sentimentalists, stock
    investment, 421–422
Service charges, mutual funds
    and, 395
Service contracts, buying
    appliances and, 92
Services, income taxes and, 629
Service station frauds, 168
Settlement options, life
    insurance, 511–512
Shared appreciation loans, in
    home financing, 217
Shares. *See also* Stock market
  stock, 413
Shelter budget, 60–62
Shopping
  bad habits, 80
  consumer alert, 113

credit considerations, 93
good habits
    clothing and accessories,
        85–88
    groceries and toiletries, 80–85
    major home furnishings,
        88–93
    information sources, 93
Short-term growth, stock
    objectives, 418
Sick leave, 42
Sick-pay plans, 534
Silver. *See* Metals, precious
Simplicity, shopping and, 86–87
Simplified Employee Pension
    (SEP) plans, 575
Single person, in later years,
    556–557
Single premium annuity,
    504–505
Sinking fund, bond, 385
"Sleeping second" mortgage,
    216–217
Slotting allowances, in food
    markets, 114
Small Business Administration,
    659–660, 674
Small business investments,
    478–479
Small claims court, fraudulent
    practices and, 140
Small loan companies, 286
Smoking, life insurance costs
    and, 521, 543
Snack foods, shopping and,
    84–85
Social costs, 28
Social policy, taxation as, 652
Social Security
    death and disability and, 532
    disability and, 534
    income from, 559, 560–561
    income taxes and, 630
    meeting future goals and, 69
    retirement age and, 564
Soil test, land investments and,
    470
Sole proprietorship, business,
    664–665
Special endorsement, checks,
    292–293
Specials, shopping, 84
Speculators, interest rates and,
    368

Spending habits, 73–74, 76. *See
    also* Expenses
Splits, stocks, 433–434
Sports
    professional, 110
    recreational, 109, 110
"Squirrels" scheme, 128
Stamps, 486
Standard deductions. *See* Income
    taxes
Standard & Poor's
    bond ratings, 385–386
    municipal bond ratings, 392
    published stock listings, 426
    Stock Price Index, 427
    stock ratings, 439–440
State government agencies,
    fraudulent practices and,
    139
Stock certificates, 413
Stock companies, life insurance
    and, 500
Stock exchanges. *See also* Stock
    market
    role of, 413
Stock funds, foreign, 482
Stockholders, role in
    corporations, 412–413
Stock investment, 417–423
    by objective
        income objectives, 418
        long-term growth
            objectives, 418
        no specific objectives,
            418–419
        short-term growth
            objectives, 418
    by size, 419
    by type
        fundamentalists, 421–422
        hunch players, 420
        insiders, 420
        novices, 419
        prudent investors, 422–423
        sentimentalists, 421
        technical analysts, 421
        theory traders, 420–421
Stock market, 407–453
    bonds *vs.* stock investments,
        409
    brokers, 446–447
    buying long and selling short,
        431–432
    buying on margin, 432

cautions, 411–412
classification of stocks,
    427–428
    blue chip stocks, 427
    glamour stocks, 427–428
    growth stocks, 428
    income stocks, 428
    by industry grouping,
        428
    by objective, 428
    by personality, 427–428
commissions, 430–431
corporation functions and,
    412–413
dividend reinvestment plans,
    440–441
dividends, 429–430, 433. *See
    also* Dividends, stock
Dow Jones Industrial
    Averages, 426–427
effect on money market, 403
as form of investing, 408
indicators, 426
investors. *See also* Investors,
    stock
    by objective, 417–419
    by size, 419
    by type, 419–423
mutual funds, 443–446,
    449–450. *See also* Mutual
    funds, stock market
operations of, 413–417
    investors' insurance, 415
    order execution, 416–417
    prospectus, 414–415
    record keeping, 415–416
option trading, 436–439
paper game and, 448
perspectives on, 408
possibilities *vs.* probabilities,
    410–411
preferred stocks, 434–435
price and value, 441–443
price fluctuations and, 451
price quotations, 424–426. *See
    also* Price listings, stock
    market
primary *vs.* secondary market,
    409–410
rating stocks, 439–440
Standard & Poor's stock
    index, 427
stock splits, 433–434
warrants, 435–436

Stock options, employer sponsored, 43
Stop-payment orders, check, 293–294
Store policies, 88
Straight life annuity, 504
Strategic metal investment, 484
Street fraud, 125–126
Street name listing, stocks, 416
Strike price, call options and, 437
Student loans, income tax and, 634
Subleasing dwelling, 252–253
Support test, for dependent exemptions, 625
Surgical insurance, 529. *See also* Health insurance
Surpluses, 5
Survivor annuity, 504
Survivorship clauses, Will, 596
Syndications, real estate, 477

T

Taft-Hartley Act, 52
"Taking back," mortgage, 474
Tax deductibility, IRAs
    Roth IRAs, 572
    standard, 570–571
Tax deferral, IRAs
    Roth IRAs, 572
    standard, 570
Tax-deffered income. *See* Income taxes
Taxes
    automobile leases and, 159
    corporate, 666
    corporate bonds and, 387
    estate
        kinds of, 609–610
        minimizing, 608
    home financing and, 217
    home sales and, 274
    income. *See* Income taxes
    independent contractors and, 664
    interest costs and, 347
    investments and, 358–360
        taxable investments, 358
        tax-deferred investments, 358–359
        tax-exempt investments, 359

tax-sheltered investments, 358–359
    life insurance and, 513
    partnerships and, 665–666
    passbook savings accounts and, 378
    real estate investment and, 466–468. *See also* Depreciation deduction
    property taxes, 460
    retirement and, 564, 582
    self-employment and, 675
    shelters, 641–642
    small businesses and, 677
    sole proprietorships and, 664–665
    U.S. Treasury borrowings, 390
    withholding, 639–640
Tax-exempt bonds, 391
Tax-exempt income, 639. *See also* Income taxes
Tax-exempt municipal funds, 396
Tax Guide for Small Businesses, 677
Taxpayer Compliance Measurement Program, 644–645
Taxpayer Relief Act (1997), 274, 359, 637
    Individual Retirement Accounts and, 570, 572
Tax Reform Act (1986), 359
    retirement age and, 564
Technical analysts, stock, 421
Technology, 4
    advancement and, 21
    food prices and, 114
Telecommuting, 42
Telemarketing scams, 683
Television
    investment opportunities on, 487
    investment-related, 361–362
    large-screen, 108–109
Temping, 663
Tenant insurance. *See* Homeowners and tenant insurance
Tenant issues, real estate investment and, 458–459
1040A form, 622–623
1040 ES form, 48
1040 EZ form, 622–623
1040 form, 618, 622–623. *See also* Income taxes

1099 form, 628
Term insurance, 502–503
    converting to, 510
    costs of, 517
    decreasing, 501
Term length, loans, 332–334
Testator (Testatrix), defined, 591
Testimonium clause, Will, 596–597
Theft losses, income tax and, 634–635
Theory traders, stocks, 420–421
Time orders, stock, 417
Time sharing, vacation, 105
    frauds, 135
Timing
    in home financing, 218
    in home purchasing, 180
    in shopping, 87
Title, property, 187–189
Title insurance, 189
Toiletry shopping. *See* Grocery and toiletry shopping
Topographical survey, land investments and, 470
Trade policy, example of, 18–19
Transfer agents, stock record keeping and, 415
Transportation. *See* Air fares; Automobiles budget, 63
Travel. *See* Vacation and travel budget, 63
Travel agents, 94
Traveler's checks, 103, 299
Travel scams, 102
Treasury bills, 387
Treasury bonds, 387
Treasury Investment Growth Receipts, 389
Treasury notes, 387
Trip insurance, 101
Trust deed, 175
Trusts, 599–600
Trust services, 298
Truth in Lending Law, 53, 303–304
Truth in Savings Law, 304–306
Turnover investing, 471–473. *See also* Real estate investing
    buying right, 471–472
    financing right, 472
    profit margin and, 472–473

Turnover rate, real estate
investment and, 458
Two-income families, 38

U

Unanticipated costs, in
automobile leases, 159
Uncollected funds, checks, 292
Under $25 a Day travel guides, 95
Underdeveloped countries, 22
Underwriting risks, life
insurance costs and, 543
Unemployment, 5
insurance, 49–50, 326, 534, 630,
678
Uninsured motorists, 163
protection, 162
Union matters, 52–53
Unit pricing, 80–81
Unit trust, 394
Universal life insurance, 502,
503–504
Unregulated businesses,
investment in, 482
U.S. government bonds, 387–390.
See also Bond funds
U.S. Postal Service, fraudulent
activity and, 121–125, 139
U.S. Treasury borrowings, 387
Used cars
alternative sources of, 151
vs. new car purchases, 151
warranties, 160
Usury laws, 302–303
Utilities
budget for, 61
costs of, 234
fluctuations in, 240
home purchasing and,
184–185
real estate investment and,
460–461

V

Vacant land investment, 468–471
familiarity with land and, 469
unfamiliarity with land and,
469–471
appraisal, 470
attorney consultation, 469
financial considerations,
470–=471

property reports, 469–470
surveys, 470
tests, 470
viewing land, 469
Vacation and travel, 42, 94–106
air fares and, 96–98
air travel rights, 104
buying vacation
accommodations, 104–105
condo rentals, 102
cruises, 100–101
do-it-yourself tours/vacations,
100
foreign money and, 103
frauds, 135–136
frequent flyer miles, 97
home-exchange programs, 102
information resources, 95–96
near-home vacations, 98
package tours and resorts,
99–100
pocket money and, 103
precautions before leaving,
103–104
seasonal bargains, 98
time sharing, 105
travel agents and, 94–95
travel scams, 102
trip insurance, 101
vacation planner worksheet,
112
wholesalers (consolidators)
and, 98
Vacation home, purchasing,
104–105
Valuables, insurance for, 229
Vanity rackets, 122–123
Vesting
benefits, 567
Pension Reform Law and,
565–567
plans, 40–41
Veteran's Administration (VA)
loans, 208–209
Video cameras, 107
Video cassette recorders, 106–107

W

Wage and hour laws, 51
Waiting period
disability insurance, 535–536
long-term-care insurance, 537

Waiver of premium clauses,
534–535
Wall Street, 413
Wall Street Journal, 22
federal agency borrowing
yields, 388
U.S. treasury yields, 387
Warranties
appliances and, 92
automobile, 159–160
home, 183–184
Warrants, investment, 435–436
Weekend getaways, 98
Western Europe, 27
W-2 form, 48, 627
W-4 form, 48, 639–640
Whole Life Insurance, costs of,
517
Wholesalers, international travel,
98
Wills
basic clauses of, 593–597
appointment clauses, 596
attestation clause, 596–597
bequest clauses, 595–596
debts and final expenses,
594
introductory clause, 593
revocation of prior wills,
593–594
survivorship clauses, 596
testimonium clause,
596–597
changing of, 597–599
do-it-yourself, 598
holographic, 599
noncupative, 599
uncommon, 599
Windfalls
estate liquidity and, 613
meeting future goals and, 69
Worker's Compensation, 49, 532,
534, 677
Workplace/employment issues.
See also Employer benefits
Age Discrimination in
Employment Act (1967),
51, 678
Americans with Disabilities
Act, 52, 167
aptitudes and employment,
36
attitudes and aspirations,
34–35

Workplace/employment issues
(*Continued*)
business cycles and, 38–39
changing careers, 45–47
changing composition of, 37–38
choosing job, 33–34
discrimination, 50
economic trends, 38–40
education, 35–36
Employee Retirement Income
Security Act. *See* Pension
Reform Law (ERISA)
employment policies and
contracts, 53–54
Fair Employment Practices
Law, 51, 678
Family and Medical Leave
Act, 52, 677
Federal Fair Labor Standards
Act, 50, 678
financial rewards and, 40
geographical shifts and, 39
health and safety regulations, 52

income protection/regulation,
47–50
job location, 43–44
job retraining and, 40
job searching, 44–45
in later years, 560–561
leaving, 43
paychecks, 48
personal experience and
employment, 37
plant closing laws, 51
political changes and, 39–40
power, 3
right to work, 50
success in, 54
unemployment insurance. *See*
Unemployment insurance
union matters, 52–53
wage and hour laws, 51
worker's compensation, 49.
See Worker's
compensation
Work test, moving, 276–277

Y

Year-end strategies, tax, 640–641
Yield
certificates of deposit and, 380
compared with maturities, 393
corporate bonds and, 386
investment, 354–355
municipal bonds and, 392
passbook savings accounts
and, 377
stock, 424
U.S. Treasury borrowings, 390
Yield to maturity, bonds, 383
Your Income Tax, 651

Z

Zero coupon bonds, 389
Zoning
laws, 235–236
real estate investment and, 460
requirements, business, 678